THE CAMBRIDGE HISTORY OF
NINETEENTH-CENTURY MUSIC

This comprehensive overview of music in the nineteenth century draws on the most recent scholarship in the field. It avoids mere repertory surveys, focusing instead on issues which illuminate the subject in novel and interesting ways. The book is divided into two parts (1800–1850 and 1850–1900), each of which approaches the major repertory of the period by way of essays investigating the intellectual and socio-political history of the time. The music itself is discussed in five central chapters within each part, amplified by essays on topics such as popular culture, nationalism, genius, and the emergent concept of an avant-garde. The book concludes with an examination of musical styles and languages around the turn of the century. The addition of a detailed chronology and extensive glossaries makes this the most informed reference book on nineteenth-century music currently available.

JIM SAMSON has been a Professor of Music at the Universities of Exeter and Bristol and is now Professor of Music at Royal Holloway, University of London. He has published several books on Chopin including *The Cambridge Companion to Chopin* (1992), as well as books on Szymanowski, late Romantic music, and music of the early twentieth century.

The Cambridge History of Music comprises a new group of reference works concerned with significant strands of musical scholarship. The individual volumes are self-contained and include histories of music examined by century as well as the history of opera, music theory and American music. Each volume is written by a team of experts under a specialist editor and represents the latest musicological research.

Published titles

The Cambridge History of American Music
Edited by David Nicholls

The Cambridge History of Western Music Theory
Edited by Thomas Christensen

The Cambridge History of Nineteenth-Century Music
Edited by Jim Samson

THE CAMBRIDGE
HISTORY OF
NINETEENTH-CENTURY
MUSIC

*

EDITED BY
JIM SAMSON

CAMBRIDGE
UNIVERSITY PRESS

PUBLISHED BY THE PRESS SYNDICATE OF THE UNIVERSITY OF CAMBRIDGE
The Pitt Building, Trumpington Street, Cambridge, United Kingdom

CAMBRIDGE UNIVERSITY PRESS
The Edinburgh Building, Cambridge CB2 2RU, UK
40 West 20th Street, New York, NY 10011-4211, USA
10 Stamford Road, Oakleigh, VIC 3166, Australia
Ruiz de Alarcón 13, 28014 Madrid, Spain
Dock House, The Waterfront, Cape Town 8001, South Africa

http://www.cambridge.org

First published 2001

Printed in the United Kingdom at the University Press, Cambridge

Typeface Renard Beta 9.5/13pt   *System* QuarkXPress™   [SE]

A catalogue record for this book is available from the British Library

Library of Congress Cataloguing in Publication data

The Cambridge history of nineteenth-century music / edited by Jim Samson.
p.   cm. – (The Cambridge history of music)
Includes bibliographical references and index.
ISBN 0 521 59017 5
1. Music – 19th century – History and criticism.   I. Samson, Jim.   II. Series.
ML196.C36   2001
780'.9'034–dc21   00-067469

ISBN 0 521 59017 5 hardback

Contents

PART TWO 1850–1900

Notes on contributors

ANDREW BOWIE is Professor of German at Royal Holloway, University of London. He is the author of *Aesthetics and Subjectivity: from Kant to Nietzsche* (1990; rev. edn 2000), *Schelling and Modern European Philosophy* (1993) and *From Romanticism to Critical Theory: The Philosophy of German Literary Theory* (1997). He has also made editions and translations of Schelling, *On the History of Modern Philosophy* (1994), Manfred Frank, *The Subject and the Text* (1997) and Schleiermacher, *'Hermeneutics and Criticism' and Other Texts* (1998). He is at present writing a book on *Music, Meaning and Modernity*.

JOHN BUTT is author or editor of four books for Cambridge University Press, including *The Cambridge Companion to Bach* (1997) and *Music Education and the Art of Performance in the German Baroque* (1994). His latest monograph, *Playing with History: The Historical Approach to Musical Performance* will be published by Cambridge University Press in 2002. He is also active as a performer, having released more than ten discs on organ and harpsichord for *Harmonia Mundi France*. Having been an Associate Professor at the University of California at Berkeley and a Lecturer at Cambridge, he took up the Gardiner Chair of Music at the University of Glasgow in 2001.

DEREK CAREW is Lecturer in Music at Cardiff University. His principal interests are keyboard music, the long nineteenth century, analysis, and music in its social and cultural setting. He has contributed to the *Mozart Compendium* (1990) and *The Cambridge Companion to Chopin* (1992), and is currently preparing a book on piano music in the late eighteenth and early nineteenth centuries.

JONATHAN DUNSBY has been the Professor of Music at the University of Reading since 1985. A prize-winner in international piano competitions, he became founding editor of the journal *Music Analysis*, and has written extensively on the history and theory of nineteenth- and twentieth-century music.

KATHARINE ELLIS is Lecturer in Music at Royal Holloway, University of London. She is the author of *Music Criticism in Nineteenth-Century France: 'La revue et gazette musicale de Paris', 1834–1880* (1995) and articles on Berlioz, the French Palestrina revival, and the careers and reception of women performers. She is currently preparing a book on early music in nineteenth-century France.

JAMES HEPOKOSKI teaches at Yale University and is the co-editor of the journal *19th Century Music*. In collaboration with Warren Darcy he has completed a book on Classical musical structure, *Elements of Sonata Theory: Norms, Types, and Deformations in the Late-Eighteenth-Century Sonata*, forthcoming from Oxford University Press.

THOMAS GREY is Associate Professor of Music at Stanford University. He is author of *Wagner's Musical Prose: Texts and Contexts* (1995) and contributing editor of *Richard Wagner: 'Der fliegende Holländer'* (2000) and the *Cambridge Companion to Wagner* (forthcoming). Recent articles and chapters on opera and other topics in nineteenth-century music have appeared in *The Arts Entwined: Music and Painting in the Nineteenth Century* (2000), *Music and German National Identity* (2000), and *The Mendelssohn Companion* (2001).

SARAH HIBBERD is a Research Fellow at Royal Holloway, University of London. She has been an editor for the *New Grove* and has published articles on opera and theatre in early nineteenth-century Paris. She is currently working on historical representation on the Parisian stage in the 1830s.

JOHN IRVING is Senior Lecturer in Music at the University of Bristol. His publications include *Mozart's Piano Sonatas: Contexts, Sources, Style* (1997), *Mozart: the 'Haydn' Quartets* (1998), the Musica Britannica edition of Tomkins's Consort Music (1991) and the CEKM edition of the Anders von Dueben Organ Tablature (2000).

K. M. KNITTEL recently joined the music history faculty at the University of Texas at Austin. In addition to her work on Beethoven, she has published on Mahler and is currently completing a book, *Seeing Mahler, Hearing Mahler: Mahler and Antisemitism in fin-de-siècle Vienna*.

MAX PADDISON is Professor of Music at the University of Durham. He studied musicology at the University of Exeter and philosophy and sociology at the Johann Wolfgang von Goethe University, Frankfurt am Main. His research specialisms are in the aesthetics and sociology of music, music of the *fin de siècle*, and popular music, with a focus on Adorno. His publications include *Adorno's Aesthetics of Music* (1993) and *Adorno, Modernism and Mass Culture: Essays on Critical Theory and Music* (1996).

ROGER PARKER teaches at Cambridge University. He was founding co-editor of the *Cambridge Opera Journal* and is general editor (with Gabriele Dotto) of the Donizetti Critical Edition. *Leonora's Last Act*, a book of essays on Verdi, came out with Princeton University Press in 1997.

ANTHONY POPLE has been a Professor of Music at the Universities of Lancaster and Southampton and is now Professor of Music at the University of Nottingham. He was editor of *Music Analysis* from 1995 to 1999. He is the author of books on Berg, Messiaen, Scriabin and Stravinsky, and is currently writing a book which studies types of tonality in music from the turn of the nineteenth and twentieth centuries.

JOHN RINK is Professor of Music at Royal Holloway, University of London. He works in the fields of performance studies, nineteenth-century studies, and theory and analysis. His books include *Musical Performance* (2002) *Chopin: The Piano Concertos* (1997) and *The Practice of Performance: Studies in Musical Interpretation* (1995).

JULIAN RUSHTON is West Riding Professor of Music at the University of Leeds. His books include three on Berlioz (1983, 1994, 2001), *Classical Music: A Concise History* (1986), and Cambridge Opera Handbooks on *Don Giovanni* (1991) and *Idomeneo* (1993). He is General Editor of Cambridge Music Handbooks, Chairman of Musica Britannica, and was President of the Royal Musical Association from 1994 to 1999.

JIM SAMSON has been a Professor of Music at the Universities of Exeter and Bristol and is now Professor of Music at Royal Holloway, University of London. He has published widely on the music of Chopin and on analytical and aesthetic topics in nineteenth- and twentieth-century music. His current projects include a book on Liszt's *Transcendental Studies*.

DEREK B. SCOTT is Professor of Music at the University of Salford, Greater Manchester. He is the author of *The Singing Bourgeois* (1989; rev. edn 2000) and editor of *Music, Culture, and Society* (2000). His articles have appeared in the *Musical Quarterly*, the *Journal of the Royal Musical Association* and other scholarly journals.

JOHN WILLIAMSON is Reader in Music at the University of Liverpool. His publications include *The Music of Hans Pfitzner* (1992), *Richard Strauss: 'Also sprach Zarathustra'* (1993), and essays on Mahler and his contemporaries. He is currently writing a book on d'Albert's *Tiefland* and editing *The Cambridge Companion to Bruckner*.

SUSAN YOUENS is Professor of Music at the University of Notre Dame. She is the author of *Retracing a Winter Journey: Schubert's Winterreise* (1991); *Schubert – Die schöne Müllerin* (1992); *Hugo Wolf: The Vocal Music* (1992); *Schubert's Poets and the Making of Lieder* (1996); *Schubert, Müller, and Die schöne Müllerin* (1997); and *Hugo Wolf and his Mörike Songs* (2000).

Editor's preface

Single-author histories of nineteenth-century music are probably no longer tenable in light of today's specialised knowledge. The last credible contender may well turn out to be the challenging study by Carl Dahlhaus, frequently cited in our volume. Yet existing multi-authored histories present their own problems. Putting it baldly, they tend either to define their subject-matter too narrowly in terms of genres and styles, or to sacrifice thematic penetration to geography. Of course it is easy to criticise. However you approach a task like this, you will be wrong. But we hope to be wrong in the right sort of way. In general our approach is thematic, or topical. We try to offer explanations rather than assemble information, and that usually means focusing selectively on key areas that seem to illuminate our subjects rather than presenting straightforward repertory surveys. How, anyway, can such surveys be anything other than partial and arbitrary? More to the point, what do they really say about music history? So we are moderately (though not completely) relaxed about our coverage of repertory. Lacunae will not be hard to find for those who seek. But then what is the framework of certainties that allows them to be identified as lacunae in the first place?

To evaluate just how topics might be selected is the task of our first chapter, which reflects generally on historiography and on the competing claims made on us as historians of music within the Western tradition. In the process two very broad issues are raised, and they in turn feed into the structure of the book as a whole. One is the relationship between the components of music's 'double history', compositional and contextual: between, in other words, works and practices. Our hope is that aesthetic values are properly respected in this volume, but that they are at the same time integrated within broader social and intellectual contexts. That is easily said. In practice it amounts to a perilous balancing act between the demands of the text – 'the music itself' – and the claims of its context. The second issue concerns periodisation. And here (for reasons that will be argued out in the first chapter) we feel that a history of nineteenth-century music has some obligation to bring into focus the caesura separating the two halves of the century, since this is obscured by conventional periodisation. (Paradoxically a history of eighteenth-century music should arguably do the reverse, i.e. highlight continuities between late Baroque and Classical periods.) Hence, at some risk of overstating the case, we have divided our volume into two parts, with parallel structures in each part. This layout bears some of the marks of a structural history, except that we make no easy assumptions about the 'spirit of the age', nor about the interconnectedness of its constitutive activities, events and products. Nor do we deny the explanatory power of chronology.

Very broadly, the tendency within each part is to proceed from context to music, though it need hardly be said that this separation of function is anything but watertight; contextual chapters occasionally discuss notes, and repertory chapters frequently invoke context. Thus there are two accounts of music and intellectual history: chapter 2, which looks at the changing status of music within German Idealist and Romantic aesthetics, and in particular at its liberation from an integral association with language; and chapter 12, which extends this to debate understandings of the 'autonomy character' of music in the later nineteenth century, embracing Schopenhauer reception, the influential position established by Hanslick, and the watershed between Idealism and Positivism. Likewise there are two social-historical commentaries: chapter 3, which examines the several professions of music associated with the emergence of a middle-class musical culture; and chapter 13, which documents the consolidation of the practices and institutions associated with that culture during the second half of the century. The repertory itself is then examined in central blocks within each part – chapters 4–8 and 14–18 respectively. But it should be emphasised that even in these chapters none of the authors is involved in mere survey; each of them, without exception, takes an angle on their repertory, elaborating positions which at times overlap with, and even occasionally contradict, the positions adopted by other authors.

These chapters provide central information on the 'great music' of the period, a focus which is entirely defensible, not least because this was an age which thought of itself in precisely these terms. At the same time we remain alive to the ideological dimension of that perception, and we foreground it explicitly in chapter 10, which addresses the nineteenth-century preoccupation with genius, while at the same time relativising that concept by discussing the development of what would later be called the culture industry. We are mindful, after all, that most of the music enjoyed in the nineteenth century was by no means 'great', and that point is usefully developed in chapters 9 and 19, which examine music in the marketplace, including what might loosely be called the 'popular music' of the time. Chapter 11, in contrast, turns to the debates of the 1850s: debates about the new, about absolute music, and about music and the poetic. These debates, centred on Weimar, were of major importance. Not only did they set the compass reading for a great deal of later nineteenth-century thinking about music; they fed directly into compositional praxes. Then, as the new century loomed, they made room for insistent questions concerning the musical expression of a prevailing nationalist ideology. Our penultimate chapter addresses these questions, but it closes by arguing that the differences promoted by nations and nationalism were ultimately subordinate to those generated by the major shifts in musical syntax that took place around the turn of the century. These shifts are addressed in our final chapter.

Our hope is that this constellation of contrasted approaches will light up the history of nineteenth-century music in novel and interesting ways. At the same time, we are aware of our obligation to provide a source of basic and necessary information – to allow the Cambridge History to serve as a major work of reference. Hence the balancing act referred to earlier. We hope that the central chapters on repertory can pass muster in this respect. But given the general thrust of the volume, it has seemed to us important to provide unusually full and ambitious reference material, comprising a chronology (offering a kind of skeletal 'narrative' history of music), a select list of institutions (publishing houses, conservatories, opera companies, music societies, and the like), and a personalia (including composers, performers, patrons and publishers). In contrast, we have been more sparing with bibliographical information. In general, the bibliographies for individual chapters record the major sources used in the preparation of the chapter, though in most cases they extend beyond that role to provide a modest indication of useful further reading.

I am grateful to the British Academy for financial assistance in the preparation of this book.

· PART ONE 1800–1850 ·

The musical work and nineteenth-century history

JIM SAMSON

Compositional and contextual histories

Even the formula 'compositional and contextual', suggestive of a dual perspective – a 'double root'[1] – may not fully embrace the materials and methods of a music history, whose very subject-matter must be open to debate. Texts, sounds, activities: all are primary data – objects, facts and events that are variously foregrounded, ordered and interpreted to generate our narratives. One obvious starting-point would be to place musical works centre stage, prioritising the cultural forms in which art music has most often been presented in the West. But that signals an analytical enquiry. If we want to write history we need to fill the spaces between works, to find strategies for connecting them. Two such strategies, conversely related, are prominent in histories of nineteenth-century music. One is intertextuality. We join up the works through similarity, as we might note the resemblances between visual stills. This quickly brings us to composers, to suggestions of influence or mutuality, and eventually to stylistic genealogies. The explanatory focus shifts – one may justly say 'reverts', for this is the mode of the past, of the nineteenth century itself – from the work to its creator. The present volume is well served by this approach, and there are strong arguments for privileging it, given the historicism of the age. Yet, paradoxically, intertextuality risks undermining 'work character'. If I choose to focus on the work, after all, I presumably value that quality of uniqueness that marks it off as more than the instantiation of a type. I celebrate its individuality, its embodiment of a singular idea.

This invites my second strategy. We might term it individuation, and its concern is to trace the historical process by which the particular (the special) emerges from the general (the generic). This too was privileged in the nineteenth century, an age of individualism no less than historicism. Indeed Harold Bloom suggests that the two are locked together in symbiosis – the weight of the past and the quest for a voice, dependency and originality.[2] His proposal

---

1 The notion of a 'double root', social and stylistic, was developed for art history especially by Heinrich Wölfflin; see his *Principles of Art History*, trans. M. D. Hottinger (New York, 1950; original edn 1917).
2 Harold Bloom, *The Anxiety of Influence: A Theory of Poetry* (Oxford, 1973).

unites two of the big themes of nineteenth-century art histories. At the same time it unites the artwork and its author. For Bloom's 'anxiety of influence' really describes a kind of collective authorial *mentalité*, shaped by certain aspects of Enlightenment thought, and as such it is an implicit celebration of authorship (indeed the celebration becomes explicit in his later writings).[3] Again the focus shifts inexorably from the work to its composer. Music history becomes the story of certain highly valued composers, whose genius and originality made possible our present-day canon of masterpieces. The work becomes part of an output or *oeuvre*. It finds its place within a larger narrative, one that characteristically develops from the composer's earliest formative stages to his full creative maturity and, often, his final flowering (the organicist metaphor is unmistakable). It is characteristic or exceptional – early, middle-period or late. It becomes a fragment of biography, since it is deemed to express particular thoughts and emotions in response to a shared culture, and to exemplify a unique style in relation to a more general style system.

To identify the work with its composer may seem a minimal rationalisation. But actually the work may exemplify other things – its performance, for instance. Even the most basic ontology recognises that the written score underdetermines a musical work, which can only be fully realised in performance. During the eighteenth century the space between notational and acoustic forms widened considerably. That century strengthened the autonomous character of the work by loosening the threads binding it to genre and social function. But it also 'created' the virtuoso, an international figure in whom the activity of performance gained (or regained) its own measure of autonomy.[4] In the nineteenth century the separation between 'text' and 'act' increased.[5] On the one hand the score was thought to embody a kind of intentional knowledge – an 'idea' that originated with the composer, so that the performer's responsibility was to unlock the mysteries, to make available the idea, to interpret. On the other hand the virtuoso performer could act as a magnet drawing the listener away from the qualities of the work towards the qualities of the performance. This of course rehearsed an ancient argument about vocal music – that virtuosity threatens meaning. But in the nineteenth century the terms of the argument were transformed by an ascendant individualism. Great performers, no less than great composers, could stake their claim to the high ground of a liberal ideology. They could transform the work, and even redeem it.

A musical work, then, may exemplify its composer and its performer. It may

---

3 Harold Bloom, *The Western Canon: The Books and School of the Ages* (London, 1995).
4 See Sylvette Milliot, 'Le virtuose international: un création du 18e siècle', *Dix-huitième siècle*, 25 (1993), pp. 55–64. 5 My terms here pay tribute to Richard Taruskin; see *Text and Act* (Oxford, 1995).

further exemplify its tradition, as also its style, medium or genre. These categories make their own claims on the historian, and it will be worth considering each of them briefly as components of the chronicle. Tradition is perhaps the most implicative, though it is also the most elusive. The construction of traditions is usually linked to larger issues of cultural politics, and in particular to the politics of national identity. The 'invention' of a German tradition in the nineteenth century (converted to 'Austro-German' in the twentieth) is certainly the paradigmatic instance. But the case for a tradition might also be made on geographical (as distinct from national) grounds, as in discussions of a putative northern identity that subsumes the individual identities of the Scandinavian and Baltic nations in the late nineteenth century. Whatever the rationale, the tradition to which a work might be said to belong is invariably culturally and politically contingent. Yet for all its contingency the act of transmission – the process of 'handing over' (Latin: *tradere*) – still depends on the persuasive qualities of individual works. Cultural and political establishments may make their claims on these works, manipulating them to their own ends. But they do so mainly because the music is thought to be well worth claiming. However we locate its ideological roots, then, a tradition is usually closely identified with a corpus of significant works that have certain shared characteristics. In other words, it is described at least partly through commonalities of style.

When Guido Adler formulated his influential scheme for academic musicology, he presented musical styles – their growth and development – as central to the historical, as distinct from the systematic, branch of the discipline.[6] Adler's periodisation of stylistic history will be discussed presently, but we may note here that it privileges only one of several hierarchical levels on which the concept of style may function. That concept is defined by processes of selection and negation, but also by processes of standardisation. Leonard B. Meyer focuses on one side of this coin, observing that it is the selection of some elements rather than others from an existing stock of handed-down, 'pre-formed' materials that constitutes a style.[7] But a style also establishes its own normative markers, and it confirms these by temporarily falsifying them – by deviating from the norms. Thus style in music may be understood in relation to a dialectic between universal and particular, collective and unique, schema and deviation. The difficulty for the historian is that this process is almost endlessly recursive, taking us from something larger than a tradition (the Classical style) to something smaller than a work (the contrasted middle section). As an

6 Guido Adler, 'Umfang, Methode und Ziel der Musikwissenschaft', *Vierteljahrsschrift für Musikwissenschaft*, 1 (1885), pp. 5–20.

7 Leonard B. Meyer, *Style and Music: Theory, History, Ideology* (Philadelphia, 1989).

historical tool, then, it is valuable in that it allows for a discussion of normative elements that help us to place the musical work, yet limited in that its range of application is so wide as to seem permissive. It is arguably at its most useful when it functions in tandem with other categories such as medium or genre.

Both medium and genre have commonly been used as principal categories for organising and presenting music histories. This elevated status has been assigned them partly for categorical convenience, but also because they possess a degree of internal consistency that can override stylistic differences, providing a narrative thread that connects composers from very different musical worlds. Even more crucially, both concepts can provide us with useful strategies for linking music to its immediate social context. To take an example: a history of the string quartet medium in the nineteenth century would trace a stylistic journey that can be adequately explained only in relation to a social journey. Like the orchestra before it, the quartet crossed from private to public arenas, and that shift made its own demands on musical materials. Or consider the rise of the piano. Not only did the instrument generate a new repertory, where style and medium are locked together by an idiomatic imperative. It also transformed the social history of music; the instrument itself became a social agent. And here we return to performance. There is a case to be made – indeed I shall make it later in this chapter – for an 'alternative history' of nineteenth-century music, one that centres on practices rather than composers, works and institutions, that builds the instrument and the performer – the act of performance – centrally into the historical study of a repertory.

Like media, genres are rooted in social functions, and their classifications to some degree codify those functions musically – even in the nineteenth century, as the generic histories embedded in this volume will demonstrate. Yet it has been argued (by Adorno and Dahlhaus among others) that the potency of genre as a classificatory mechanism declined during the Romantic era, a consequence of the rise of aesthetic autonomy and of a swerve towards the musical work.[8] Self-contained works, in other words, resisted the closure and finality of meaning conventionally offered by a genre title. It may be nearer the mark to speak of transformation than decline. Increasingly genres took on a crucial role as orientating factors in communication, allowing conventional expectations to be manipulated in various ways. This rhetorical role was by no means new to the nineteenth century, but it came into its own, with its potential for irony fully realised, during that period. Moreover the 'rhetoric of genre' had repercussions on musical form, notably through the deployment of generic

---

8 Theodor W. Adorno, *Aesthetic Theory*, ed. Gretel Adorno and Rolf Tiedemann, trans. Christian Lenhardt (London, 1983), pp. 285–9; and Carl Dahlhaus, 'New Music and the Problem of Musical Genre', in *Schoenberg and the New Music*, trans. Derrick Puffett and Alfred Clayton (Cambridge, 1987), pp. 32–44.

fragments as 'topics'.[9] The ordering of such topics by way of underlying plots had some potential to replace, or at least to complement, the structuring devices of a Classical repertory, and some commentators have found it helpful to describe this process through the metaphor of narrative.[10] Again a social dimension is inescapable here, since the topics (especially when drawn from popular culture) carry with them some memory of an original social function. Adorno referred to the 'clatter of dishes' accompanying Mozart.[11]

It will be worth retracing our steps. We began with a working assumption that a history of music is primarily a history of musical works. However, in order to discuss works in historical terms it was necessary to make concepts of them, and that meant grouping them into classes. As we did this our approach began to shift from the compositional towards the contextual, from a consideration of the objects themselves towards a consideration of the uses to which they are put and the responses they engender. Thus, performance is already a category of reception history. So too is tradition, which, as we are reminded by Foucault, is contained within, rather than prior to, the discourses about it.[12] And as soon as we begin to work with categories such as style, medium and genre we become aware that they can only be partially explained as aggregates of musical works. They take us inexorably into the social domain. We might indeed have begun there – not with a history of music, but with a history of 'musical life' (a much-used if mysterious term), of music as lived experience. We might have begun, in short, with context. Our subject-matter, then, would range widely across the many and varied practices involved in making music, promoting music, listening to music, and thinking about music. It would embrace performance, teaching and manufacturing sites, together with their several related professions; taste-creating (and one might say tradition-carrying) institutions such as journals and publishing houses; ideas about the nature and purpose of music; and – most important – responses by listeners from particular social and cultural communities.

On the face of it that represents a very different history. And even if the two histories shade into one another (as my discussion of work-based categories

9 See the chapter 'The Function of Genre', in Heather Dubrow, *Genre* (London, 1982). Jeffrey Kallberg has developed this idea in several papers, including 'Understanding Genre: A Reinterpretation of the Early Piano Nocturne', *Atti del XIV Congresso della Società Internazionale di Musicologia* (Bologna, 1987), pp. 775–9.

10 See, for example, Anthony Newcomb, 'Once More Between Absolute Music and Programme Music', *19th Century Music*, 7 (1984), pp. 233–50, and 'Schumann and Late Eighteenth-Century Narrative Strategies', *19th Century Music*, 11 (1987), pp. 164–74. Also my discussion of narrative in *Chopin: The Four Ballades* (Cambridge, 1992), pp. 81–7, and Jean-Jacques Nattiez, 'Can One Speak of Narrativity in Music?'; *Journal of the Royal Musical Association*, 115/2 (1990), pp. 240–57.

11 In Theodor W. Adorno, *In Search of Wagner*, trans. R. Livingstone (London, 1981), p. 48. Strictly speaking, he cites Wagner's reference to this in Mozart.

12 See Michel Foucault, *The Archaeology of Knowledge*, trans. A. M. Sheridan Smith (London, 1972; original edn 1969).

suggests) they have two quite separate starting-points; they ask different questions of the past. In a word, the one focuses on works that have survived (and
therefore on questions of aesthetic value), the other on practices that need to be
reconstructed (and therefore on questions of social and ideological function).
The stories can be told separately, and frequently are. Even in this book several
chapters address contexts almost exclusively, while others are primarily concerned with repertory. But it is perhaps more usual to find them intertwining
informally, or alternatively – as in many English-language histories – to see the
music projected against a backdrop of 'general' history. In such cases it is not
always easy to see just how text and context are supposed to interrelate. Indeed
to locate the interface between the compositional and the contextual – crudely,
between the notes and the world outside the notes – is probably the greatest
single challenge facing any music historian. We may at least make a start by
identifying three distinct levels on which social content can be made available
to the music historian, three levels of mediation that are all addressed in different ways by this volume. These levels, corresponding more-or-less to categories
familiar to semiology, are the social cause of a work, the social trace imprinted
on its materials, and the social production of its meanings.

   The first, the province of a social history of music, explains the work with
reference to the conditions of its production. A traditional Marxist historian
might want to argue that these conditions are the primary and exclusive cause
of the work,[13] but it goes without saying that we can recognise the explanatory
value of functional contexts without committing to any single ideological position. Put simply, this approach investigates the external motivation for a work,
and the environmental and circumstantial factors that may have shaped it. To
return to my earlier example of the string quartet in the nineteenth century.
Behind those transformations of style lay a whole array of historical causes.
Socio-political contexts take pride of place, as aristocratic societies gave way to
a bourgeois-liberal ascendancy that increasingly shaped and directed the
formal musical culture of Europe. That has an obvious bearing on practical contexts. From an intimate drawing-room genre (promoting instrumental characterisation and thematic-motivic exchange), the quartet became a public genre,
positioned on the platform, with obvious implications for both the manner of
writing new quartets and the manner of playing old ones. Intellectual contexts
are also invoked, especially by the subscription series devoted to chamber
repertories, 'classical' and 'modern', which were common by the mid-century.
These, after all, reflected the historicism and aestheticism of an age in which

---

13 We might consider here, for example, George Knepler, *Musikgeschichte des XIX. Jahrhunderts* (Berlin,
1961), though there is much more to Knepler's history than this formulation of its ideological starting-
point suggests.

cultural roots and cultural ambition were established through canon formation and an avant-garde. We could go on to discuss pedagogy, public taste, and many other factors making up the complex ecology within which composers and performers made decisions about the shape and character of individual string quartets.

The second level (social trace) is a good deal more elusive, concerned less with immediate shaping influences than with a deeper level of causality. This is really the terrain of a sociology of musical materials, and it is naturally subject to the interpretative licence of particular positions in critical theory. The core assumption is that changes in the nature of musical materials – in what is often called 'musical language' – do not occur in a vacuum, unrelated to the broader sweep of political, social and intellectual histories. Rather these changes, appropriately interpreted, can actually function as a mode of cognition, a way of understanding the world, since they encode its history at very deep levels. Music in this sense is a cipher; it possesses what Adorno described as a 'riddle character'.[14] To take a simple example: we might view the development of the nineteenth-century orchestra as an analogue to the rise of industrialism, with all the attendant connotations of a division of labour, dehumanisation of resources, and so forth, without suggesting for a moment that composers promoted, or were aware of, any such link. More radically, we might propose that the long, overarching 'project of autonomy' within European art music (manifest in the rise of instrumental music and of a subsequent and consequent aesthetic of absolute music) was mapped on to musical materials themselves through the rise and development of harmonic tonality. And that, incidentally, would make heavy interpretative demands of the post-tonal music developed in the early twentieth century.

The tendency of enquiries into these first two levels (social cause and social trace) is to congeal the musical work into a stable configuration. The third level (social production of meanings) proposes rather an unstable work, one that recedes or 'vanishes' before our eyes as it encounters the different preconceptions of particular cultural communities.[15] This is really the province of reception histories. Long before the term 'reception' came into general use in art histories, musicologists attempted to generalise about people's awareness of, and attitudes towards, particular repertories, and even to uncover the ideology informing their responses. The afterlives of works, in short, have long been integral to the study of music history, and perhaps especially for the nineteenth

14 See the discussion in Max Paddison, 'The Language-Character of Music: Some Motifs in Adorno', in R. Klein and C.-S. Mahnkopf (eds.), *Mit den Ohren denken: Adornos Philosophie der Musik* (Frankfurt am Main, 1998), pp. 71–91.

15 Stanley Fish refers to a 'vanishing text' in *Is There a Text in this Class? The Authority of Interpretative Communities* (Cambridge, Mass., 1980).

century, which cultivated Palestrina and Bach alongside Mozart and Beethoven. But dedicated reception histories have allowed us to observe more closely just how a work can thread its way through many different social and cultural formations, attaching itself to them in different ways, adapting its own appearance and in the process changing theirs. Of course such histories may choose to focus on certain unchanging themes (as in Eggebrecht's study of Beethoven),[16] implicitly reinforcing a characteristic identity for the music. But more often (as in Lissa's study of Chopin),[17] they demonstrate that the music is heard 'with a different ear' by particular cultural communities, indicating in the process just how susceptible it can be to appropriation, and how easily its identity can slip away from us.

Then and now

The history of nineteenth-century music, then, is a history of works, composers and performers; of traditions, media and styles; of institutions, ideas and responses. Importantly, it is also a history of mediation between these several categories, and above all between text and context, between music and the world around it. As I intimated earlier, this can also involve the mediation of aesthetic value and social function. If our principal concern is with musical works, we will tend to value their atemporal quality, their presence and greatness (qualities that may be easier to recognise than to demonstrate), their capacity to endure what is often called the 'test of time'.[18] Thus there is a sense in which the major repertory chapters of this book present a kind of syllabus of masterworks. This position will be mediated, however, by our knowledge that a powerful ideological element participated in the formation of this syllabus, which is not to deny the presence and greatness. If, on the other hand, our interest lies primarily in musical life, we will focus initially on the role that music plays in people's lives, on the nature and immediacy of its functions rather than on its quality *qua* music. The mediating factor here will be our realisation that social responses to art are in considerable measure shaped, and may even be controlled, by the character and quality of the cultural artefacts themselves. Moreover, as Simon Frith has argued,[19] it is by no means easy to do justice to the full range of social and psychological functions performed by music, beyond the most obvious ones.

16 H. H. Eggebrecht, *Zur Geschichte Beethoven-Rezeption: Beethoven 1970* (Wiesbaden, 1972).

17 Z. Lissa, 'The Musical Reception of Chopin's Works', in D. Żebrowski (ed.), *Studies in Chopin*, trans. E. Tarska, H. Oszczygieł and L. Wiewiórkowski (Warsaw, 1973), pp. 7–29.

18 See A. Savile, *The Test of Time* (Oxford, 1982).

19 Simon Frith, 'Towards an Aesthetic of Popular Music', in Richard Leppert and Susan McClary (eds.), *Music and Society: The Politics of Composition, Performance and Reception* (Cambridge, 1987), pp. 133–50.

In other words, there are no absolutes in this antinomy (if it is an antinomy) between value and function, as a glance at music in our own time will confirm. A superficial view would contrast the contingency and functionalism of today's popular music with the relative autonomy of classical music and an avant-garde. But a second's thought is enough to remind us that the classical concert, no less than the popular music event, has its ceremonies and rituals, and that these speak eloquently of social identifiers and validating social functions. Moreover, even the genres and materials of the classical repertory are themselves 'grounded' in very particular socio-political contexts. Likewise, it would be entirely misleading to suggest that the aesthetic ambition associated with the Romantic and modernist art work is unknown in popular music circles (though it does perhaps remain rather more clearly subordinated to the commodity status of the record-as-artefact within the culture industry). Indeed a case could be made for reversing conventional approaches to these repertories, if only as a potentially illuminating sleight-of-hand of historical method – a corrective to pedigreed habits of thought. In other words, we might learn something by examining popular music (and for that matter much of the non-Western repertory examined by ethnomusicologists) as 'works', capable of making their own statement in the world and of yielding some of their secrets to analytical probing. Conversely we might regard art music primarily as a 'practice', its shared materials revealing the social world of which it is a part.

All that said, the broad sweep of music history in the West does seem to take us from functional contexts towards that 'project of autonomy' mentioned earlier. And within this trajectory the nineteenth century again occupies a privileged position. It was in the late eighteenth century that music slowly disengaged itself from existing social institutions and began to create its own institutions, its own share in what Peter Bürger called the 'institution of art'.[20] The rapid growth of public concerts in the early nineteenth century was the most obvious marker of that shift (a 'cultural explosion' is how William Weber described it),[21] but, as chapter 3 will indicate, this was just one dimension of a more widespread professionalisation of musical life, embracing the conservatory, the music shop and the manufacturer's *salle*, as well as the benefit concert and the subscription series. This is not to suggest that a patronal culture disappeared from view. But even where court institutions persisted (as in the German states) they were increasingly transformed into public institutions, and were therefore subject more and more to market forces – to the rule of the box office. Moreover the project of autonomy also found expression and support in the world of ideas, initially through the rise of the aesthetic

20 Peter Bürger, *Theory of the Avant-Garde*, trans. M. Shaw (Manchester, 1984; original edn 1974).
21 William Weber, *Music and the Middle Class* (London, 1975).

described in the next chapter, and later through an exponential growth in music criticism – a direct and immediate response to the replacement of functional by aesthetic judgements. At root, it resulted in two related developments: a growing composer-centredness and an increasing focus on the musical work.

In a bold generalisation about changing historical phases in the theory of art, Carl Dahlhaus allowed the nineteenth century to embrace these two developments.[22] The first, centred on the biographies of individual composers, was especially relevant to the first half of the century (though it reached some way backwards), and it gradually replaced earlier approaches predicated on social functions and on the affections. The second, based on the structure of self-contained works, came into its own in the second half of the century, and extended into twentieth-century structuralist thought, before yielding to more recent hermeneutical approaches. However rough-and-ready, this analysis throws into relief a central problem of historiography. Just how do we square the perceptions of the present-day subject, coloured as they are by the mode of thought of the present, with the self-perceptions of historical subjects, shaped by a very different mode of thought? Consider the early nineteenth century, the starting-point for our history. The collision of these two perspectives – of then and now – penetrates through to the relative importance of vocal and instrumental music, of opera and symphony, of Rossini and Beethoven.[23] Thus, we should not assume that our present-day view of Beethoven as the central figure of early nineteenth-century music would have been shared by his contemporaries, or that a so-called 'tradition' of German sonata-symphonic music would have been given greater privilege than Italian opera. To the historical subject Rossini was arguably the towering figure.

More generally, the present-day subject inclines to a reductionist view of the past, allowing an analytical quest for common principles to subordinate constitutive diversity (of music and of musical life) to an identity principle. We may present the position polemically. In today's world, we might argue, the early nineteenth-century musical work will be viewed as a unified statement, and then drawn into a notionally unified style system. That style system will in turn be explained through a series of causes and effects, including the influence and rejection of earlier stylistic periods (Baroque, Classical), as well as the growth and development of competing national traditions. Coeval developments in the non-musical world will also be embraced, and in the process will them-

22 Carl Dahlhaus, *Foundations of Music History*, trans. J. B. Robinson (Cambridge, 1983; original edn 1967), pp. 21–3.
23 See Dahlhaus's remarks in his Introduction to *Nineteenth-Century Music*, trans. J. B. Robinson (Berkeley and Los Angeles, 1989). Dahlhaus's discussion is picked up again in chapters 4 and 9 of this volume.

selves be reduced to manageable dimensions. Thus, for the early nineteenth century notable political events such as revolutions will be given due explanatory value, and so too will socio-historical categories such as the middle class, key political ideologies such as liberalism and nationalism, and broad cultural and intellectual currents such as Romanticism. This reductionist analysis is not 'wrong'. But arguably it tells us as much about now as then. Specifically it tells us about what the past might mean to our world, and for that reason it carries with it a kind of authenticity – the authenticity of an active present. We read our history backwards from the standpoint of canonised music and an avant-garde.

The alternative would be to try to read it forwards from the very different perspective of the (early nineteenth-century) historical subject. The difficulty here is that this perspective is never really fully recoverable, however much we may investigate contemporary theoretical, critical and autobiographical writing. And even if it could be recovered, it is hard to avoid viewing it through the prism of subsequent events and ideas. All the same, through an exercise of historical imagination (as much as an archaeological quest) we can make an attempt to recapture the 'present' of the historical subject, restoring to it something of the complexity, diversity and contradiction that attends any subject position; indeed we must make the attempt if we are to avoid collapsing history into analysis. Essentially our aim is reconstruction rather than construction, and for that reason our evidence is by no means exclusively confined to the extant record. That enables me to refine my opening remarks on history as a dialogue. In reality it is a dialogue between these two perspectives – between an active present and a recovered past. Moreover, our dialogue with the past with the historical subject – is like any other dialogue; a knowledge of where our respondent comes from influences the kinds of questions we ask. And as in any other dialogue we understand what motivates the answers partly from the answers themselves. Through a kind of feedback process we learn to ask productive rather than unproductive questions of the past.

I will return to the rise of the piano and its repertory for a brief case study. The present-day subject is likely to view this topic from a work-centred perspective, encouraged by the presentation of a select handful of major works in the familiar format of the piano recital. The recital has been (until relatively recently) a surprisingly stable and resilient institution. We can date it from the 1840s (Liszt's 'musical soliloquies' or 'monologues'), but it was only later in the century that it became recognisably similar to today's occasions, replacing casual programming (in which transcriptions and improvisations featured heavily) with carefully structured, implicitly educative litanies to the great composers. The recital, in other words, came to represent a major forum for canon formation, manipulating an innocent repertory (centred on Bach, Scarlatti and the so-called 'Viennese Classics') to ideological ends through a massive investment in the musical work, and in its greatness. It became, in short, one of the principal ceremonies of the musical work, and struggles to retain that status today. During the 'age of the recital', we can locate the practice of pianism within a complex network of social and cultural agencies, grounded by the institution (the recital), focused on an object, albeit an ideal aesthetic object (the musical work), and cemented by an ethos (its adequate interpretation). I say 'age of the recital', incidentally, because there is every reason to argue that we have now moved into a post-recital era, where music is predominately and increasingly transmitted and received in electronically mediated forms.

None of this would have been familiar to our historical subject, who would have viewed contemporary repertory from the perspective of a pre-recital pianistic practice, one not yet centred on the musical work and on its interpretative forms. Pianism in the early nineteenth century was grounded by different institutions (principally the benefit concert, the salon and the conservatory; but we might include – more loosely – the 'tour' and the 'season'); it was supported by different agents (notably the piano manufacturer and the music publisher); it was focused on an event (the performance) rather than an object and concept (the work and its interpretation); and it was held together by a different ethos, which I would describe as a balance between the mercantile and the aesthetic values of a developing instrument. Liszt put it succinctly, describing his own efforts to '[steer] a course between the Ideal and the Real, without allowing myself to be overly seduced by the former, nor ever to be crushed by the latter'.[24] Interpretation played a subsidiary role within this pre-recital practice – a component of its product rather than the product itself. A performance, after all, may exemplify or promote many things other than a musical work (a technique, an instrument, a genre, an institution, a direct communicative act). It was in the age of the recital that these functions, including the last, were subordinated to the claims of the musical work.

It was above all through this pre-recital pianism that instrumental music cut its teeth in the marketplace, taking the first steps towards something akin to the culture industry of modern parlance. Indeed it is arguable that concert life in the early nineteenth century approached the condition of today's 'mass culture' more closely than later in the century, when cultural forms solidified and high culture drew popular and elite publics into a new kind of synthesis. Through the piano a functional link was created between the vested interests of

---

24 In a letter to Lambert Massart. See Franz Liszt, *An Artist's Journey*, trans. and annotated by Charles Suttoni (Chicago, 1989), p. 88.

the celebrity touring virtuoso and those of the amateur in the home. The one depended on the other, albeit indirectly, through the ever expanding market for pianos, for published music, and of course for music instruction. The touring virtuoso drove this market, and the training of virtuosos accordingly became a highly specialised activity, carving a space for keyboard technique outside the general field of musical training. Hence the 'swarm' of pianists in the 1820s and 1830s, all of them performing their own music, for composition and performance were intimately fused within this post-Classical concert life. Pianism was a popular – even a populist – art, an art of conformity, in which the favoured genres (variations, fantasies, independent rondos, concertos) had something of a formulaic character, moulded to the requirements of a new taste public (see the discussion in chapter 3). Individuality was also an active ingredient, but it was usually translatable as novelty, and interpreted – at least by the more high-minded critics – as a kind of excess, which incidentally raises questions of taste that I am unable to explore here.

Our dialogue, then, would allow a voice to the historical subject, as well as to the present-day subject. When we find 'structures' in canonised piano music of the early nineteenth century – unifying threads, wholes – we are not creating fictions. Composers themselves were concerned about such things, especially in cyclic works such as sonatas. Yet this organicist quest belongs essentially to the mode of thought of the later nineteenth and the twentieth centuries. It draws out of the music qualities that have only subsequently gained an overriding importance for our culture. In this sense we engage in an assimilationist history, reducing a genre- and performance-orientated culture to a canon of notionally unified masterworks. Of course all history is assimilationist to a degree; it draws many threads into few figures, and those figures are shaped by the needs of today. But we can at least temper this rationalising tendency by cultivating some sense of how the repertory was understood in its own time. My brief characterisation of public pianism in the early nineteenth century already suggests that this was not yet a work-orientated culture: the borderlines separating categories such as composition, transcription and improvisation were by no means clearly demarcated; the formulaic demands of conventional genres were in competition with work character; and the programming practices of the time undermined any perception of works as unified wholes (the movements of concertos were frequently separated out, and they would often be performed as solos or with whatever forces were available).

It was really only in the second half of the century that this orientation changed decisively. And that change – a shift in priority from practices to works – extended well beyond the orbit of pianism. We could equally have traced it through the proliferation of subscription series (orchestral and chamber), for example. Or through the consolidation of repertory opera. Or through journals and publishing houses. Or for that matter through developments in music theory and pedagogy. It may be worth rounding off this section by expanding just a little on the theory and pedagogy. It is a complex subject of course – there were divergent theoretical traditions, notably in Paris, Berlin and Vienna – but in very broad terms the early nineteenth century witnessed a gradual institutionalisation of music education, a transition from craft instruction to the classroom, associated above all with the rise of the conservatories. The intensive debates over teaching methods at the Paris Conservatory, culminating in the conference of 1802, were symptomatic, and they were driven as much by pragmatism as by their ostensible ideology of progress; the real need was to devise teaching methods which might cope efficiently with large numbers of potential teachers and performers. Catel's harmony treatise, triumphant in 1802, took its stand on pragmatism, and following Catel the counterpart of the instrumental tutor became a new kind of dedicated theory textbook. By the 1840s and 1850s, especially in Austro-German circles, a key stage had been reached through the dissemination of influential books on harmony by Simon Sechter (to oversimplify drastically, Sechter's work systematised a general tendency to replace Fux and thoroughbass with Rameauvian harmonic theories), and on *Formenlehre* by A. B. Marx (see chapters 7 and 15).[25] In Marx, pragmatism and idealism joined forces. A generic or aesthetic sense of form began to give way to a structural or dialectical sense of form in the general training of musicians, and in that lay the foundations of modern analytic thought.

25 Simon Sechter, *Die Grundsätze der musikalischen Komposition*, 3 vols. (Leipzig, 1853-4); A. B. Marx, *Die Lehre von der musikalischen Komposition, praktisch-theoretisch*, 4 vols. (Leipzig, 1838-47). Prior to Sechter, the two indispensable treatises for teaching purposes were Kirnberger's *Die Kunst des reinen Satzes* (1771-9), where the four-part chorale texture is an harmonic starting-point for contrapuntal activation, and Albrechtsberger's *Anweisung zur Composition* (both in its original 1790 version, where the harmonically reinterpreted species formed the core of counterpoint instruction, and in the later Seyfried compilation of *c.* 1825, which prefaced the manual with harmonic theory of rather different orientation). By and large theory teaching at the conservatories in the early nineteenth century drew on these and other eighteenth-century sources in a fairly flexible way. It embraced thoroughbass, modified species counterpoint and chordal progression – or at least validation of chordal progression – by *Grundbass*, as practised in Kirnberger (though Kirnberger's *Grundbass* is not synonymous with Rameau's *basse-fondamentale*). This describes Chopin's musical education, as also Mendelssohn's (see chapter 8). The training of Liszt and Berlioz was of a different order altogether, and that may account in considerable measure for later differences of style and aesthetic.
It should be noted that following Sechter's treatise harmonic theory again turned away somewhat 'from pedagogical efficacy' towards speculative modelling (Leslie David Blasius, 'The Mechanics of Sensation and the Construction of the Romantic Musical Experience', in Ian Bent (ed.), *Music Theory in the Age of Romanticism* [Cambridge, 1996], p. 22). Blasius cites Fétis's scale-based theory of tonality and Hauptmann's appropriation of Hegel's dialectics as indicative. More crucially, these theorists effected a fundamental departure from tradition through their investment in history rather than nature; as Blasuis puts it, both declared their work to be a 'radical break with the eighteenth-century specification of an acoustic basis for harmony' (Blasuis, p. 22). For an account of nineteenth-century theoretical traditions, see chapter 25 of Thomas Christensen ed., *The Cambridge History of Western Music Theory* (Cambridge, 2002).

This represented a decisive shift in thinking, and one that resonated in intellectual history. The core of the matter is that order and beauty were increasingly located in the musical work rather than in what were thought to be generalised properties of music. A pedagogy that fetishised the great work began to take shape, in other words, at just the time that the institutions of music-making were consolidating an Ars Classica – a core repertory of masterworks. One result of this – a very particular dimension of 'then and now' – was a dialectic or interference between history and aesthetics which remains with us even today. How, we may ask, are we to do historical justice to canonised works, given that these are still a vital, living part of our present? The greater our aesthetic appreciation of the work, the more it is drawn into our 'now', and the harder it is to consign it to 'then' – to give it the status of a past event. In this sense the past constantly invades the present in music history (much more than in political or intellectual histories, for example), so that notions of historical 'becoming' are inevitably compromised by the atemporal 'being' represented by individual works. This interference between history and aesthetics has not of course remained constant. It really only became a significant issue at all in the late eighteenth century; it grew increasingly marked in the nineteenth century (Mozart as part of a nineteenth-century present); and it has reached a culminating point, arguably resulting in a major reformulation, in the new kinds of objectification of musical works made possible by today's technology.

The structures of history

At almost every stage, a history of music engages in rationalisations. In trying to make sense of the past we tidy it up. I have tried to show that even decisions about the basic components of the chronicle involve rationalisations of this kind; likewise the levels of mediation between them. Whether we begin with works or practices, we need to make concepts of them before we can sift, order and structure the chronicle to create our narrative. Moreover these rationalisations already include an element of emplotment. If I tell the story according to intertextuality I construct a plot based on genealogies, and that usually draws into play the construction of traditions. If I tell it according to a process of individuation I present a narrative of evolving styles and emergent genius. If I shift the angle and look at musical practices, I plot a drama of instruments and institutions, often motivated by developments in the socio-political world and in the climate of ideas. Underlying many of these plots are two major rationalisations of history, based respectively on geography and temporality. The first of them invokes the notion of centres and peripheries, mainstreams and tributaries. It is a history based essentially on geographical difference, on north and south, east and west, nation and region. It includes understandings of an 'other', and of a music at the edge. Such ideas, which carry covert (and often overt) value judgements, permeate several chapters in our history and they are addressed specifically in our penultimate chapter.

The second major rationalisation, the periodisation of history, will be discussed here. Of course it is easy to dismiss periodisation as a kind of reductionism – or even as a mere strategy of presentation. Yet many historians have found it natural to assume that there are elements of relative stability that define an historical period, overriding elements of change. There may even be some mediation here of the constructions of 'now' and the experiences of 'then'. Our individual perceptions of temporality do, after all, involve retentions connected to particular 'now-moments', allowing closures and completions to punctuate the temporal continuum. Thus, even at the most immediate hour-by-hour level, we constantly translate experienced life into constructed history. The real question is how far this inflates to larger levels – our own biography, for instance (the school years), the recent past (the nineties; the sixties), and a more remote past (the age of revolutions). In all these cases we tend to combine classificatory convenience (a well-defined unit) and interpretative coherence (a strongly characterised unit). However, some so-called 'structuralist' historians go further.[26] They liken a period to a structure or a system, in that it will change fundamentally only when there have been functional changes to the nature of its components or to their interaction. Even where such changes are cumulative rather than abrupt, at some stage (it is argued) they coalesce into a new, relatively stable, configuration.

At the heart of this approach lies an essentialist reading of history. The periodisation is applied once a period-defining theme has been identified. And paradoxically the identification of that theme usually implies an evolutionary process, where the story unfolds as an organic development from creation to dissolution, and where the supposed climax of this development is represented as a kind of ideal, a 'point of perfection'. This ideal in turn allows us to generate an essence that is presumed to characterise the period as a whole. In many accounts of nineteenth-century music that essence is taken to be Romanticism, and although this is usually understood primarily in relation to cultural history, it may also embrace philosophy, socio-political history and, more widely, the 'spirit' of the era. For this reason historians of nineteenth-century music history have frequently used the term Romanticism as their principal point of reference. However there has been considerable variation in the periodisations that have resulted, as well as a certain fluidity in the understanding of the term

---

26 I am thinking here especially of the 'Annales' group of social historians, notably Ferdinand Braudel.

itself. It will be of some interest, then, first to scrutinise these periodisations in relation to a general background of socio-political history as well as to the comparable structures established by literary and art historians, and then to reflect on possible 'meanings' of Romanticism.[27]

It has been common for social and political historians to refer to a 'long nineteenth century', inaugurated in 1789, sub-divided in 1848, and brought to a close in 1914. These are the explosive political dates that have been taken to punctuate, and at the same time to formalise, major changes in the underlying social history of Europe. And although the momentum for change developed prior to the political events and continued after them, the dates have acquired potent symbolic values. To put it synoptically, we have, respectively, the demise of aristocratic society, the consolidation of middle-class power, and the victory of bourgeois nationalism over dynastic government. It is rather striking that – until recently – historians of literature and the visual arts have followed this socio-political periodisation rather more closely than musicologists. They preserve, in other words, a sense of two 'halves' of a long nineteenth century, each distinctively profiled. Thus literary Romanticism is usually traced back to late eighteenth-century polemical and creative writings by the Schlegel brothers and their circle in Germany. And although it is usually accepted that Romantic features continued to exert an influence after the mid-century, the period label gives way at that point to 'Realism' and 'Symbolism', movements associated initially with French writers. Historians of the visual arts have conventionally adopted a broadly similar chronology, identifying early Romantics such as Géricault and Delacroix in France, Turner in England, and Caspar David Friedrich in Germany, and again arguing for a dispersal of the original Romantic impetus following the mid-century.

In music, on the other hand, the Romantic movement has often been located somewhat later, beginning in the post-Beethoven era (c.1830) and carrying right through to the early twentieth century. Significantly, contemporary perceptions were rather different. Thus Hoffmann identified Romantic tendencies in the music of the late eighteenth century, paralleling rather than succeeding comparable tendencies in literature, and this conformed to a general usage of the term from around 1800. And several years later Goethe confirmed this usage by describing an antithesis of Classical and Romantic art, characterising it in terms of 'objective' and 'subjective' tendencies respectively.[28] In such early

---

27 See my entry 'Romanticism', in Stanley Sadie and John Tyrrell (eds.), *The New Grove Dictionary of Music and Musicians*, 2nd edn (London, 2001), vol. 21, pp. 596–603, for a fuller exposition of this discussion of the periodisation and 'meaning' of Romanticism.

28 Goethe's well-known comments on a polarity between Romantic and Classical are scattered through the *Conversations of Goethe with Eckerman*, trans. J. Oxenford, ed. J. K. Moorhead (London and Toronto, 1930); see especially, pp. 305, 335, 356–7 and 366.

nineteenth-century polemics Romanticism was clearly identified as a 'move-ment' concurrent with Classicism (Goethe as Classical; Schiller as Romantic) rather than a 'period' succeeding it. The idea that Mozart as well as Beethoven might be regarded as a Romantic composer remained current right through to around the mid-century, at which point a change in the understanding of Romanticism seems to have occurred, allowing it to emerge as a definable period term in something like our modern sense. 'Romantic' music in this sense was defined increasingly through its separation from a Classical golden age, though the position of Beethoven remained purposefully ambivalent within this periodisation.

An early suggestion that there might be a division between 'Classical' and 'Romantic' periods is found in Karl August Kahlert, who (in 1848) described Mozart as 'the most truly classical of all composers' and Beethoven as 'a roman-tic composer', whose 'tremendous hold over the minds of his contemporaries' enabled 'music's romanticism [to] ma[k]e its presence felt'.[29] But it was later in the century, when music history was subjected to the quasi-scientific study of styles, notably by Guido Adler, that a cleaner separation of Classical and Romantic periods was proposed. For Adler the Romantic movement crystal-lised (or achieved full maturity, to adopt his own organic model) in the *post*-Beethoven generation of Chopin, Schumann, Berlioz and Liszt. Beethoven and Schubert were viewed as 'transitional' within his scheme, but were linked essentially to so-called Viennese Classicism. From this perspective (positioned at the end of the nineteenth century), the composers of the *Neue Deutsche Schule*, together with several leading composers from the late nineteenth-century nationalist schools, were classified not as 'Romantics' but as 'Moderns' or even in some cases as 'Realists', and that view remained largely intact until the upheavals of the early years of the twentieth century cast new light on their achievements. Later historians tended to draw the Romantic period right through to the first decade of the twentieth century, at which point it may be understood to give way to modernism.

There are, however, two significant variants of this model. The first (asso-ciated above all with Friedrich Blume) identifies a single Classic–Romantic era reaching back into the eighteenth century and extending well into the twenti-eth.[30] To some extent this view seeks to recover something of the early nine-teenth-century sense of the term as a movement or tendency running concurrently with Classicism. The second is now rather widely accepted.

29 C. A. T. Kahlert, 'Ueber den Begriff der klassischen und romantischen Musik', *Allgemeine musikalische Zeitung*, 50/18 (1848), pp. 289–95.

30 F. Blume, *Classic and Romantic Music*, trans. M. D. Herter Norton (London, 1972; original style-period article in *MGG*, 1949).

Several historians (Carl Dahlhaus and Peter Rummenhöller among them)[31] have, like their colleagues in literature and the visual arts, located the end point for musical Romanticism around the middle of the century, and in some cases have coined the term 'neo-romanticism' as an appropriate description of its second half. I have already suggested that many of the structures of modern musical life and thought began to take shape around the mid-century – that it was a point of qualitative change in the journey from our historical subject to our present-day subject. And some such sense of a mid-century caesura also emerged from that analysis of Dahlhaus mentioned earlier. There are other, rather more obvious markers. A generation of composers departed or stopped composing around the mid-century (Chopin, Schumann, Mendelssohn); a very different generation came to maturity (Brahms, Bruckner, Franck); both Liszt and Wagner took off in radically new directions; the separation of art and entertainment was formalised in music drama and operetta; nationalist programmes were launched around the edges of Europe.

This periodisation naturally invites comparison with the periodisation of political history, where the mid-century caesura was of course the 1848 revolutions. The impact of the revolutions (strictly speaking, of their failure) changed the course of European societies. Above all there was a separation of liberal and radical thought, as the propertied bourgeoisie of France and Central Europe turned its back on revolution, secured its position against the lower orders, and consolidated its new social and political status by investing heavily in formal culture. The revolutions effectively brought to a close the 'age of revolutions', to adopt Eric Hobsbawm's phrase, a period of turbulence in the underlying social order of France and Central Europe. They also brought to an end the utopian phase of liberalism in political ideology, to which the majority of leading writers, artists and composers subscribed heavily. Indeed an entire generation of artists stepped directly into the political arena in those pre-1848 years, helping to shape what came to be known as the 'revolution of the intellectuals'. The failure of the revolutions accordingly marked the moment when those idealist myths were shattered, when artists and intellectuals withdrew from politics to art, from engagement to detachment. Wagner's biography around the mid-century speaks for the larger tendency.

It is in this sense that we can justly claim that the age of Romanticism ended in 1848. Indeed it is reasonable to regard Romanticism as the counterpart within imaginative culture to the rise of political liberalism in the late eighteenth and early nineteenth centuries (given radical expression in the idea as

31 C. Dahlhaus, *Between Romanticism and Modernism: Four Studies in the Music of the Later Nineteenth Century*, trans. Mary Whittall (Berkeley and Los Angeles, 1980; original edn 1974); Peter Rummenhöller, *Romantik in der Musik: Analysen, Portraits, Reflexionen* (Munich, 1989).

well as the practice of revolution) as also to the parallel investment in subjectivity within philosophical systems, notably those of Kant and his successors within German Idealist thought, Fichte and Schelling. Above all Romanticism shared with these developments in political and intellectual histories the invention or reinvention of the individual as a potent enabling force. This focus on the individual – on the self – takes us close to one of two 'essential' meanings of Romanticism. The Romantic artist, privileged by his genius, would reveal the world in expressing himself, since the world (according to the influential position established by Kant) was grounded in the self. Hence the growing importance of expression as a source of aesthetic value, overriding the claims of formal propriety and convention. Music in particular was viewed as a medium of expression above all else, and crucially its power of expression was at the same time a form of cognition, albeit one precariously poised between sensory perception and intellectual understanding, between *sensus* and *ratio*.

There is, however, a second 'essential' meaning of Romanticism, and it generates considerable tension with the first. We might describe it as an investment in the self-contained, closed work of art. The theorists of Romanticism, from Fichte to Schelling to Coleridge, were clear about the unifying power of genius. Through the force of the creative imagination those characteristics that had already been attributed to art in general within philosophical aesthetics of the late eighteenth century – its capacity to arouse the strongest emotions, and its value as a mode of intuitive knowledge of the world – were now particularised, referring to the individual creator and the individual (original and 'great') work of art. What this tended to encourage – and we should remember that it was a discourse developed only by a self-consciously progressive intelligentsia – was a view of musical works in particular as monads, 'containing' their own meaning rather than exemplifying a genre, articulating a style or confirming an institution. To put it rather simply, it encouraged a shift from function and genre to the work itself. Moreover this investment in the work, itself a product of the growing autonomy of the aesthetic, resulted in a significant change of focus in the relation between art and the world, as *mimesis* (imitation) made way for what has been termed an 'ideology of organicism'. Through the creation of closed, organically unified works, art was presumed to project an idealised image of what the world is, or more pertinently, of what it might become. And absolute music, free of any obvious representational capacity, was especially well placed to bear the burden of this meaning.

It is this second meaning of Romanticism that bears on the question of a 'work concept' in the nineteenth century. It is principally due to Lydia Goehr's book, *The Imaginary Museum of Musical Works*, that the term 'work concept' has become such a live one in Anglo–American scholarship, though Goehr's rationalisation of music history builds to some extent on the work of German scholars in the 1970s.[32] Her central claim is that 'given certain changes in the late eighteenth century, persons who thought, spoke about, or produced music were able for the first time to comprehend and treat the activity of producing music as one primarily involving the composition and performance of works. The work concept at this point found its regulative role.' We may note the periodisation here, which is premised rather differently from conventional periodisations of Romanticism. Goehr views the period around 1800 as a kind of watershed; that was the point at which the work concept took on what she calls a 'regulative' rather than a 'constitutive' role, a distinction borrowed from Kant. Her proposal, taken in conjunction with the writings of Walter Wiora and Carl Dahlhaus, can rather easily tempt us to view the entire post-1800 era (at least until relatively recently) as an 'era of the work concept', predicated on the priority of instrumental music. It has the effect of strengthening any sense we may have of the hegemony of an Austro-German sonata-symphonic tradition. The centre of gravity is presumed to shift from Italy to Germany in the nineteenth century, and the symphony is assigned the status of a musical ideal.

This is clearly a thesis that no history of nineteenth-century music can afford to ignore. However there have been vociferous objections to it, notably from Reinhard Strohm, who regards the work concept as a product of Renaissance humanism, already alive and well in the vocal music of that earlier era.[33] Instrumental music, far from transcending the condition of vocal music, was in reality 'catching up' with it. Strohm's argument is persuasive. But even if persuaded, we may concede that a qualitative change in the understanding of the musical work accompanied the ascendancy of instrumental music. To grasp this, we need to return for a moment to that second level of social mediation (social trace) discussed earlier. In these terms, we might view the rise of instrumental music (culminating in the Classical symphony) in relation to a larger historical process of progressive rationality, by means of which notational and compositional systems gradually acquired the capacity to generate a time-dependent musical narrative.[34] It was the perceived competence of the musical work to stand alone, to become a world in and to itself, that eventually privileged narrative forms of instrumental music. And, as we note in the next chapter, this competence gave to music – to 'absolute music' – a special potency

32 Lydia Goehr, *The Imaginary Museum of Musical Works: An Essay in the Philosophy of Music* (Oxford, 1992).
33 Reinhard Strohm, 'Looking Back at Ourselves: The Problem with the Musical Work-Concept', in M. Talbot (ed.), *The Musical Work: Reality or Invention?* (Liverpool, 2000), pp. 128–52.
34 The most sustained application of concepts of progressive rationalisation to music is in Max Weber's classic text, *The Rational and Social Foundations of Music*, trans. and ed. D. Martindale, J. Riedel and G. Neuwirth (Illinois, 1958; original edn 1921). Weber's ideas were later adapted by Adorno, notably in *Aesthetic Theory*. For a discussion, see Max Paddison, *Adorno's Aesthetics of Music* (Cambridge, 1993), pp. 135–48.

for the Romantics, paving the way for a powerful nineteenth-century idea, the pre-eminence of music among the arts. The musical work – monadic, unified, closed off from the world – became the perfect symbol of aesthetic autonomy. Indeed autonomy was in a sense its very content, replacing reference and image, and promoting that ineffable, unknowable quality, which gave music privileged access to a plane beyond the real (variously characterised as the transcendental, the inexpressible or the infinite).

It is partly this unprecedented aesthetic ambition that distinguishes Goehr's work concept, or alternatively that might mark a kind of gear-change in Strohm's. Yet it is by no means obvious that the change in thinking can be neatly periodised in the way that Goehr suggests. In terms of compositional history, the forging of narrative forms of instrumental music – where beginnings, middles and ends are structured through tonal argument and thematic development – was a very gradual process. If we were to adopt for a moment the premises of an evolutionary, essentialist history, we might suggest that the tools were assembled in the early Renaissance (structural harmony, thematic working, metric invariance), and that the entire process reached its *point de la perfection* with the arrival of the so-called 'Classical style', pre-dating Goehr's watershed of 1800 by around half a century. In terms of reception history, the chronology looks rather different. The appropriation of those narrative forms by an Idealist aesthetics (the priority of absolute music) probably does indeed date from around the turn of the century. That is the second 'meaning' of Romanticism I outlined earlier. But the wider institutionalisation of a work-orientated musical culture came rather later, post-dating Goehr's watershed – and again by about half a century. There are no clean breaks in history, but if we are looking for any single moment in which the musical work emerged triumphant over genre, performance and social function it would be around the middle of the nineteenth century.

Prior to that, and despite an emergent modernism in the discourses of philosophers and artists, musical life as a whole can be more reasonably characterised through practices than through works. The concept of a practice (with its own setting, history, tradition, values and ideals) can be a useful working tool for music historians, not least because practices are by no means synonymous with institutions, and it is the institutions of music-making that have tended to dominate social histories of music.[35] Unlike an institution, which will often be structured in terms of power and status, a practice has an ethos; it promotes virtues as well as skills; it encourages the exercise of personal authenticity, to which indeed the interests of the institution may be at times inimical. It may be

---

35 My understanding of the functioning of a practice owes a good deal to Alasdair MacIntyre, *After Virtue* (London, 1981).

helpful then to allow our account of early nineteenth-century music to embrace the perspective of the practice as well as that of the work or the institution. This perspective would of course acknowledge multiple, often overlapping, practices, each with its institutions, its sub-practices (the several professions outlined in our third chapter, for instance), its enabling agencies, its repertory. Moreover, to reconstruct these practices would be to remind ourselves that music history is not a uni-linear development, where everything marches in step – as some discussions of a work concept might suggest. At the very least, we would need to invoke Braudel's splendidly arcane principle of the 'non-contemporaneity of the contemporaneous' if we were convincingly to draw into a single narrative, say, the French salon, the English subscription concert, the German choral association, and the Italian opera company.

A history of practices might well make better sense of the empirical diversity of early nineteenth-century music-making than the familiar 'grand narratives', based on style systems and notional traditions, of more conventional histories. In truth, the overlapping and interactive, yet at the same time recognisably separate, practices of late eighteenth- and early nineteenth-century music have been ill served by a general tendency to reduce them to two competing paradigms, where a notionally unified period style, labelled 'Classical', is duly followed by a plethora of more individual styles generically described as 'Romantic'. This is an inadequate interpretation on several counts. It certainly does little justice to early nineteenth-century popular (almost mass-cultural) forms such as Rossinian opera and post-Classical pianism, neither of which can easily be accommodated within such a straightforward paradigm shift. Far from describing a progress towards Romantic individualism and subjectivity, these forms actually tolerated a much greater degree of stylistic uniformity than anything we find in so-called Viennese Classical music. Each of them, in short, was first and foremost an art of conformity. Nor should this surprise us greatly, given the tendency of any mercantile culture (including today's popular music) not only to embrace standardisation, but also, to borrow Adorno's formulation, to standardise its apparent individuality. At the very least, these examples are enough to indicate that for some practices there is a space between what are usually termed Classical and Romantic periods.

In any case it goes without saying that the boundaries of practices are blurred. We can identify threads linking the practice of early nineteenth-century pianism to the aristocratic culture that preceded it as well as to the no less elitist middle-class culture that followed it in the second half of century. Likewise we can connect that same pianistic practice to contemporary practices associated with violin virtuosity and the opera house. These latter connections might even encourage us to venture some bolder, more reductive rationalisations of music history. We might, for instance, take the operatic voice, the violin, and the piano as respective starting-points for an 'alternative history' that locks together contextual and compositional readings of the tonal tradition. Each of these instruments generated a range of practices sufficiently broadly-based to dominate music's social history at particular times, and in particular places. At the same time each of them generated vast repertorial cycles, and these in their turn profoundly changed the stylistic history of music through performance-led compositional innovation. They did so in a kind of sequence, with the piano last in line, retracing many of the well-worn paths of the operatic voice and the violin. Like its predecessors, the piano established its own institutions, treatises and taste-publics, and like them it built its own armoury of idiomatic devices, partly in response to the demands of those publics. Moreover, it arrived at many such devices by borrowing unashamedly, and then transforming, those of the voice and the violin.

It would be foolhardy to pursue this approach any further in the present chapter, where the intention is to be suggestive rather than prescriptive. But it might be noted that one effect of focusing on practices in the early nineteenth century would be a shift in the balance between composition and performance in music history. Whether in the opera house or on the concert platform, the relation between text and performance in the early nineteenth century retained much of the fluidity we usually and properly associate with eighteenth-century traditions. Thus for Rossini, Paganini or Liszt the text remained in a sense in search of 'completion' by the performer. There is a focus on medium, on a sensuous or brilliant surface persuasively communicated by the performer rather than a form of knowledge embedded (concealed) in sound structures by the composer. It was the work of a later generation, and above all through Beethoven reception, to highlight the work-as-text, where the notational form is presumed to embody a kind of intentional knowledge – an 'idea' that originates with the composer and is then made available to the listener. In other words it was around the mid-century that a work orientation definitively replaced a performance orientation. From that point onwards, the work concept swept all before it; such is the power of institutions. Through subscription series and recitals dedicated to a 'Classical' repertory, through the canonising efforts of journals and publishers, and through the academy, the diversity of early nineteenth-century practices was reduced to a monolithic Classical culture. In the process, incidentally, alternative voices were presumed to have adopted an oppositional, counter-cultural stance, and 'popular culture' was born.

The picture drawn by this chapter is not a clear-cut one. Nevertheless certain themes emerge, and certain antidotes to conventional readings of history are proposed. In the first place it is suggested that a history of works can only become history at all when the works are contextualised within practices. This is really a methodological point, and it is by no means confined to histories of nineteenth-century music. At the same time it is recognised that works and practices remain separate objects of enquiry and that their interrelation is multi-levelled. Secondly, it is proposed that a work-orientated perspective on music history is above all a product of our present musical culture, and that it can act as a distorting lens when we seek to recover the musical culture of the first half of the nineteenth century. To achieve the best 'seeing' for that period (to adopt the language of astronomy), we will need to do justice to practices as well as to works. Finally, and this complicates the second point, it is argued that a work-orientated culture was already in formation during the early nineteenth century. What has been described as a project of autonomy in European music is in reality more-or-less synonymous with a shift in priority from practices to works. That shift was anything but uniform across different centres and different forms of music-making. Quite apart from multiple local variations, it was registered differently and at different times on the levels of compositional praxis, intellectual discourse and public reception. But by the middle of the nineteenth century, it had to all intents and purposes been fully accomplished.

Bibliography

Adler, G., 'Umfang, Methode und Ziel der Musikwissenschaft'. *Vierteljahrsschrift für Musikwissenschaft*, 1 (1885), pp. 5–20

Adorno, T. W., *Aesthetic Theory*, ed. Gretel Adorno and Rolf Tiedemann, trans. Christian Lenhardt. London, 1983

In Search of Wagner, trans. R. Livingstone. London, 1981

Bent, I. (ed.), *Music Theory in the Age of Romanticism*. Cambridge, 1996

Bloom, H., *The Anxiety of Influence: A Theory of Poetry*. Oxford, 1973

The Western Canon: The Books and School of the Ages. London, 1995

Blume, F., *Classic and Romantic Music*, trans. M. D. Herter Norton. London, 1972; original style-period article in *MGG*, 1949

Bürger, P., *Theory of the Avant-Garde*, trans. M. Shaw. Manchester, 1984; original edn 1974

Christensen, T. (ed.), *The Cambridge History of Music Theory*. Cambridge, 2002

Dahlhaus, C., *Between Romanticism and Modernism: Four Studies in the Music of the Later Nineteenth Century*, trans. M. Whittall. Berkeley and Los Angeles, 1980; original edn 1974

Foundations of Music History, trans. J. B. Robinson. Cambridge, 1983; original edn 1967

Schoenberg and the New Music, trans. D. Puffett and A. Clayton. Cambridge, 1987

Nineteenth-Century Music, trans. J. B. Robinson. Berkeley and Los Angeles, 1989

Dubrow, H., *Genre*. London, 1982

Eggebrecht, H. H., *Zur Geschichte Beethoven-Rezeption: Beethoven 1970*. Wiesbaden, 1972

Fish, S., *Is There a Text in this Class? The Authority of Interpretative Communities*. Cambridge, Mass., 1980

Foucault, M., *The Archaeology of Knowledge*, trans. A. M. Sheridan Smith. London, 1972; original edn 1969

Frith, S., 'Towards an Aesthetic of Popular Music'. In R. Leppert and S. McClary (eds.), *Music and Society: The Politics of Composition, Performance and Reception*. Cambridge, 1987, pp. 133–50

Goehr, L., *The Imaginary Museum of Musical Works: An Essay in the Philosophy of Music*. Oxford, 1992

Goethe, J. W. von, *Conversations of Goethe with Eckerman*, trans. J. Oxenford, ed. J. K. Moorhead. London and Toronto, 1930

Hobsbawm, E. and Ranger, T. (eds.), *The Invention of Tradition*. Cambridge, 1983

Kallberg, J., 'Understanding Genre: A Reinterpretation of the Early Piano Nocturne'. In *Atti del XIV Congresso della Società Internazionale di Musicologia*. Bologna, 1987, pp. 775–9

Knepler, G., *Musikgeschichte des XIX. Jahrhunderts*. Berlin, 1961

Lissa, Z., 'The Musical Reception of Chopin's Works'. In D. Żebrowski (ed.), *Studies in Chopin*, trans. E. Tarska, H. Oszczygieł and L. Wiewiórkowski. Warsaw, 1973, pp. 7–29

Liszt, F., *An Artist's Journey*, trans. and annotated by Charles Suttoni. Chicago, 1989

MacIntyre, A., *After Virtue*. London, 1981

Marx, A. B., *Die Lehre von der musikalischen Komposition, praktisch-theoretisch*. 4 vols., Leipzig, 1838–47

Meyer, L. B., *Style and Music: Theory, History, Ideology*. Philadelphia, 1989

Milliot, S., 'Le virtuose international: un création du 18ᵉ siècle'. *Dix-huitième siècle*, 25 (1993), pp. 55–64

Nattiez, J.-J., 'Can One Speak of Narrativity in Music?' *Journal of the Royal Musical Association*, 115/2 (1990), pp. 240–57

Newcomb, A., 'Once More Between Absolute Music and Programme Music'. *19th Century Music*, 7 (1984), pp. 233–50
  'Schumann and Late Eighteenth-Century Narrative Strategies'. *19th Century Music*, 11 (1987), pp. 164–74

Paddison, M., *Adorno's Aesthetics of Music*. Cambridge, 1993
  'The Language-Character of Music: Some Motifs in Adorno'. In R. Klein and C.-S. Mahnkopf (eds.), *Mit den Ohren denken: Adornos Philosophie der Musik*. Frankfurt am Main, 1998, pp. 71–91

Rummenhöller, P., *Romantik in der Musik: Analysen, Portraits, Reflexionen*. Munich, 1989

Samson, J., *Chopin: The Four Ballades*. Cambridge, 1992

Savile, A., *The Test of Time*. Oxford, 1982

Sechter, S., *Die Grundsätze der musikalischen Komposition*. 3 vols., Leipzig, 1853–4

Seidel, W., *Werk und Werkbegriff in der Musikgeschichte*. Darmstadt, 1987

Talbot, M. (ed.), *The Musical Work: Reality or Invention?* Liverpool, 2000

Taruskin, R., *Text and Act*. Oxford, 1995

Weber, M., *The Rational and Social Foundations of Music*, trans. and ed. D. Martindale, J. Riedel and G. Neuwirth. Illinois, 1958; original edn 1921

Weber, W., *Music and the Middle Class*. London, 1975

Wiora, W., *Das musikalische Kunstwerk*. Tutzing, 1983

Wölfflin, W., *Principles of Art History*, trans. M. D. Hottinger. New York, 1950; original edn 1917

2

Music and the rise of aesthetics

ANDREW BOWIE

Music, rhetoric and representation

The development of the new subject of aesthetics from the middle of the eighteenth century onwards and the changes in the status of music associated with the rise of 'Romanticism' form a constellation which has profoundly affected many aspects of modern thought. Perhaps the most striking illustration of this constellation is the quite widespread acceptance, between the later part of the eighteenth and the middle of the nineteenth centuries in Europe, of the Romantic idea that music might be able to say more about philosophy than philosophy can say about music. Just how strange such an idea would have been during much of the eighteenth century can be gauged by the fact that in his *Critique of Judgement* of 1790 Immanuel Kant, who was in other respects decisive for the development of Romanticism, still saw music as a lowly art form, the effects of which were analogous to a person in society taking out a perfumed handkerchief whose smell could not be avoided. The wider significance of the changes in the status of music derives from their connection both to major transformations in conceptions of language in the later eighteenth and early nineteenth centuries, and to the new accounts of the mind in the philosophy of the same period. These issues do not fit straightforwardly into the nineteenth century, and it is only possible to understand them if one recognises that the conceptions which determine the aesthetics of at least the first half of the nineteenth century are a product of the later part of the eighteenth century. 'Nineteenth-century' music aesthetics should in this sense be said to emerge around the 1780s and to be already established by the later 1790s.

The crucial innovation in conceptions of language during the second half of the eighteenth century has been characterised by the philosopher Charles Taylor as a move from regarding language exclusively as the symbolic means of representing pre-existing ideas and of representing already constituted objects in the world, to regarding it as 'constitutive' or 'expressive' of what becomes intelligible to us. In this latter view language reveals aspects of the world and ourselves which could not even be assumed already to exist before their articulation in language. In consequence, forms of articulation which are not understood as linguistic if language is conceived of solely in representational terms can come to be considered as linguistic if they disclose otherwise inaccessible aspects of the world. This is most obviously the case in the realm of human feelings, which are – in certain respects at least – only manifest to the person who has them and which are therefore often thought of as being resistant to adequate articulation in the words used by everyone else.

Music was, of course, not regarded as divorced from feelings prior to the later part of the eighteenth century. Indeed, the majority of eighteenth-century theorists thought of music precisely as a means of representing feelings. The major difference between their theories and the subsequent theories relates to the notion of representation and to the conceptions of language associated with it. Ideas about the relationship of music to a verbal text from earlier parts of the eighteenth century presuppose a very straightforward notion of representation. In 1704 Le Cerf de la Viéville had demanded, for example, that music 'apply such proportionate tones to the words that the verse is indistinguishable from and lives again in the music',[1] and thinkers like Abbé Dubos claimed that music imitated the sounds nature makes to express feelings. A recurrent feature of views of music and language during the first two-thirds of the eighteenth century lies, as John Neubauer has shown,[2] in the way they connect the theory of the affects to the theory of rhetoric, rather than, as in the previous two centuries, to mathematically orientated Pythagorean theories. The connection of affect theory to rhetoric, which is first made explicit by Johann Mattheson, presupposes a transparent relationship between language and music, with the former as the dominant partner. Neubauer suggests that 'Rhetorical theories tend to focus on the pragmatic question of how to affect an audience, but they tacitly or expressly upheld the representational, imitative function of the arts' (*Emancipation*, pp. 60–1), and Mattheson talks, for example, of how an *Adagio* indicates distress, a *Lamento* lamentation, a *Lento* relief, an *Andante* hope, an *Affetuoso* love, an *Allegro* comfort, a *Presto* eagerness, etc.' (Strunk, p. 699). For eighteenth-century representational theories there is always a verbal equivalent of what music says, the apparently non-representational aspect of music being catered for by an underlying representational or mimetic conception of language.

Music and the sources of Romantic aesthetics

The move away from conceptions based on the connection of rhetorical theory to music is associated with a whole series of factors, from the new musical prac-

1 In O. Strunk (ed.), *Source Readings in Music History*, rev. edn L. Treitler (New York, 1998), p. 681.
2 See J. Neubauer, *The Emancipation of Music from Language: Departure from Mimesis in Eighteenth-Century Aesthetics* (New Haven and London, 1986).

tice of Haydn, Mozart and others, in which 'pure' or 'absolute' instrumental music begins to take priority over music with words, to new theories of language, to Kant's philosophical revolution, and the related rise of aesthetic theory. Late eighteenth- and early nineteenth-century conceptions of music are often understood in terms of the idea of musical 'autonomy', the establishment of the independence of music both from representational (and thus rhetorical), and from subordinate social functions. Michel-Paul-Guy de Chabanon already argues in 1785, for example, that music is 'in its essence . . . not an imitative art' (in Strunk, p. 979) and that it 'pleases independently of all imitation' (p. 972). However, in the wake of the empiricism of Locke and Hume, Chabanon limits the significance of music to the pleasing sensations it brings about. It is only when this limitation is dropped that the real effects of the new conceptions become apparent and the idea that music can affect philosophy becomes an issue. These transformations also become likely because of changes in music itself, which reveal a new power that tended to be masked in earlier music by its liturgical or subordinate social functions. Why is it, then, that in a very short space of time more and more people rejected the assumption of a transparent relationship of the musical sign to human feelings and moved to a version of the position adumbrated in J. N. Forkel's assertion in 1778 that music 'begins . . . where other languages can no longer reach',[3] and in Wilhelm Heinse's remark in 1776-7 that 'Instrumental music . . . expresses such a particular spiritual life in man that it is untranslatable for every other language'?[4]

Neubauer rightly regards Kant's notion of an 'aesthetic idea' in the *Critique of Judgement* – 'that representation of the imagination which gives much to think about, but without any determinate thought, i.e. *concept* being able to be adequate to it, which consequently no language can completely attain and make comprehensible'[5] – as a major factor in the genesis of the new conceptions which culminate in Romantic views of music. However, this genesis is highly complex; the emergence of the notion of 'aesthetic idea', for example, in fact relates to a particular understanding of rhetoric. Philosophical concern with the 'Wahrscheinliche', both with what appears as true and with the 'truth of appearances', which was already present in Aristotle's attention to rhetoric as the non-truth-determinate complement of 'analytic' and 'dialectic', informs Alexander Baumgarten's new concept of aesthetics, a term he first introduces into philosophy in 1735, and which he elaborates in his *Aesthetica*, part one published in 1750, part two in 1758. Baumgarten aims to revalue the 'Wahrscheinliche' on the basis of the individual's pleasure in particular perceptions that had been

3 J. N. Forkel, *Musikalisch-kritische Bibliothek* (Gotha, 1778), p. 66.
4 J. J. W. Heinse, *Hildegard von Hohenthal* (Berlin, 1795–6), III, p. 83.
5 I. Kant, *Kritik der Urteilskraft* (Frankfurt, 1977), pp. B 193, A 190.

obscured by the Enlightenment concentration on 'clear and distinct' scientific ideas. He thereby already helps pave the way for the elevation of non-verbal instrumental music to the status of the highest art.

The following contrast reveals just how radical the shift in the thinking of this period is. Leibniz had summed up a central aspect of many Enlightenment views of music in his remark that music was 'the unconscious counting of a mind which is unaware of its own numeracy'. Friedrich Schlegel, the most significant thinker in early German Romanticism, some of whose work was known both to Schubert and to Schumann, suggests in 1798, on the other hand, that 'One has tried for so long to apply mathematics to music and painting; now try it the other way round'.[6] How he arrives at this revolutionary assertion will become clear in a moment. The assumption underlying the Enlightenment philosophy of Leibniz and Spinoza had been that the mathematically based laws of nature constituted the inherent structure of reality, which was one of the reasons why Pythagorean views had dominated musical thinking. The advance of empiricism, which saw no grounds for accepting that there was an inbuilt structure of reality, because all we can know of that structure depends on what is given to us through our own senses, was part of what led to the musical views of the earlier eighteenth century. Doubts about the capacity of empiricism to account for the cognitive and inventive capacities of the human subject are what lead in the directions now to be explored.

Two issues crystallise what is at stake in the new agenda of nineteenth-century music aesthetics. The first is the growing rejection of the divine origin of language; the second is Kant's view of the active role of the – subjective – mind in the genesis even of objective scientific judgements. In both cases the assumption that thought simply 're-presents' what is already there in the world can no longer be accepted. J. G. Herder already argues that language is one expressive manifestation of our nature, rather than a means of imitating a ready-made world, in his *Essay on the Origin of Language* of 1772. Thinkers of the late eighteenth century, like Herder, J.-J. Rousseau, J. G. Hamann (who, though, defended the idea of the divine origin against Herder), and of the early nineteenth century, like Wilhelm von Humboldt, and F. D. E. Schleiermacher, regard the Enlightenment ideal of a 'general philosophical language' (Hamann) as an illusion. Such a language was, they argued, anyway undesirable, because it would diminish the multiplicity of ways in which particular natural languages articulate the world. The way 'man-made' languages divide up the world cannot, in any case, be *shown* to correspond to how the world is divided up independently of those languages, because this would involve the

---

6 F. Schlegel, *Kritische Schriften und Fragmente* I–VI (Paderborn, 1988), V, p. 41.

vicious circularity of showing within a man-made language how this is the case. For Kant the 'synthesising' activity of the mind is required for what is given to us from the world to become intelligible in judgements, which link together the material of perception. Consequently, thought cannot be seen as merely imitating pre-existing objects, and our awareness of an intelligible world cannot be said to derive solely from the impressions we passively receive from the world. Once it is also demonstrated, as it is most clearly by Schleiermacher from the early 1800s onwards, that thought itself relies on language to be determinate, these two positions become linked.[7]

The positions are, furthermore, often connected to music, which comes to be regarded in terms of its capacity for 'saying' what nothing else can, because verbal language has lost the privilege accorded to it by the assumption of its divine origin or by the assumptions of Enlightenment rationalism. Verbal language can therefore be understood as just one of the means by which the inner and outer world is articulated, rather than as the pre-existing 'logos' which is the ground of all other forms of articulation. The main initiators of the rejection of language's divine origin, like Rousseau and Herder, also linked the origin of language to song, but they did not develop the consequences of these ideas in any detail. It is the early German Romantics' linking of the question of language to issues in Kant's philosophy that helps give rise to the most perceptive new approaches to music.

Consider the following remarks about the origin of philosophy in Greece, which might seem to be from Friedrich Nietzsche's Schopenhauer-derived *Birth of Tragedy from the Spirit of Music* of 1872. The author claims that the people of the Orphic period encountered the first 'inkling of the infinite', not with 'joyous astonishment, but with wild horror'; later, dances to Artemis at Ephesus are carried out by people who were

> full of the living idea of an incomprehensible infinity. If this idea is the beginning and end of all philosophy; and if the first inkling of it expresses itself in Bacchic dances and songs, in inspirational customs and festivals, in allegorical images and poems; then orgies and mysteries were the first beginnings of Hellenic philosophy; and it was not a happy idea to begin philosophy's history with Thales, and to make it suddenly appear as if out of nothing.
>
> (Schlegel, Kritische Schriften, II, p. 10)

This is not Nietzsche, then, but Friedrich Schlegel, writing in 1798 in his *History of Greek and Roman Literature* as one of the first in modern Western thought to turn the origin of philosophy from water into wine. Schlegel's contribution to music aesthetics has often been neglected in favour of the work of

7 See F. Schleiermacher, *'Hermeneutics and Criticism' and Other Texts*, ed. and trans. Andrew Bowie (Cambridge, 1998).

more familiar figures, like Nietzsche and Schopenhauer. However, despite his frequent inconsistencies and his lack of detailed specialist knowledge of music,[8] Schlegel was actually the first to map out many radically new structures of thought, some of which are silently appropriated by subsequent thinkers.

How important Schlegel thought music could be is evident in the following:

> beauty (harmony) is the essence of music, the highest of all arts. It is the most *general* [art]. Every art has musical principles and when it is completed it becomes itself music. This is even true of philosophy and thus also, of course, of literature (*Poesie*), perhaps also of life. Love is music – it is something higher than art.[9]

Some of what Schlegel means by this spectacular hyperbole will emerge in a moment. Schlegel's remarkable prescience is best illustrated by the fact that in 1799 he was already characterising in unusually precise terms a vital aspect of the transformation of music that was beginning to be undertaken at the same time by Beethoven: 'One has tried the way of harmony and of melody; now rhythm is left to form music completely anew; the way of a rhythm where melody and harmony only *formed* and amplified the rhythm' (Schlegel, *Kritische Schriften*, V, p. 86). Furthermore, Schlegel was perhaps the first to establish the notion of a 'musical idea' against affect theories of music, and in doing so he hinted at the technique of developing variation:

> those who have a sense for the wonderful affinities of all arts and sciences will at least not look at the matter from the flat viewpoint of so-called naturalness, according to which music is only supposed to be the language of feeling, they will in fact not find it *per se* impossible that there is a certain tendency of all pure instrumental music towards philosophy. Must pure instrumental music not create a text for itself? and is the theme in it not as developed, confirmed, varied and contrasted as the object of meditation in a sequence of philosophical ideas?
> (Schlegel, *Kritische Schriften*, II, p. 155)

This passage also exemplifies the characteristic Romantic refusal to give ultimate precedence to any form of articulation over any other. Ideas like Schlegel's about the new centrality of music were by this time quite widespread. Wackenroder and Tieck, Schlegel's friends and the authors of *Fantasies on Art* of 1799, echoed his remarks when they claimed that 'Without music the earth is like a desolate, as yet incomplete house that lacks its inhabitants. For this reason the earliest Greek and biblical history, indeed the history of every nation, begins with music.'[10] Later in his discussion of the origin of philosophy

---

8   In his lectures of 1804–5 he claims contemporary music is in a desolate state because composers are ignoring its basis in mathematics, for example.

9   F. Schlegel, *Literarische Notizen 1797–1807*, ed. Hans Eichner (Frankfurt, Berlin, Vienna, 1980), p. 151.

10   W. H. Wackenroder and L. Tieck, *Phantasien über die Kunst* (Stuttgart, 1973), p. 102.

in relation to music, Schlegel made the following striking assertion about how the initial chaos of human self-consciousness came to be ordered into something durably intelligible: 'rhythm in this childhood of the human race is the only means of fixing thoughts and disseminating them' (*Kritische Schriften*, II, p. 16). Rhythm, then, is the means by which 'incomprehensible infinity' becomes determinate, so that the 'logos' is inseparable from the foundation of music.

How, though, do Schlegel's assertions connect to the technical concerns of Kant's theory of knowledge, to which they were in part a response?[11] Schlegel's connection to Kant becomes apparent if one looks at why he regards rhythm as so important to the genesis of intelligible thought. As we saw, Kant describes cognition in terms of the 'spontaneous' – in the sense of that which is not caused by something else – synthesising of the data we receive from the world by the categories and concepts of the human mind. What concerned many of his successors, though, was the status of this self-caused 'activity' of thought. Because the activity was not subject to the law of causality in the manner of the objects in the world of appearing nature, which 'condition' and thus limit each other, the German Idealist philosopher J. G. Fichte conceived of the activity as an unlimited, 'infinite' 'drive'. Schlegel claims in the wake of Fichte that: 'The idea is what is present in the self-conscious being, and the drive is the ground of what is present in the self-conscious being'; 'the drive' is consequently 'there before the idea' (*Kritische Schriften*, V, p. 165). This already suggests what leads Schopenhauer (via Fichte's and Schelling's versions of such ideas) to the conviction that music is the best way of representing 'the will', because music supposedly gives access to the conceptually unrepresentable motivating ground of the world of 'representation', the world of conscious ideas and knowledge. Like Fichte, Schlegel thinks the drive has to be limited if it is not to be dissipated into 'incomprehensible infinity'. This is why thoughts are not determinate before they become so through the limiting differentiation of rhythm, which links together moments that are given an identity by their relations to other moments. Rhythm is in this respect, of course, common both to music and to language.

The question Schlegel addresses is therefore what makes the appearance of 'language' possible, and this is indissolubly linked to the kind of intelligibility associated with music. Music relies both on patterns of identity in difference that do not need to be semantically determinate and – crucially for ideas in aesthetics – on the *pleasure* associated with the establishing of these patterns. How, though, is one to *explain* 'music' as the basis of intelligibility, if wordless music comes, as it also does at the end of the eighteenth century, to be seen as

---

11 See A. Bowie, *Aesthetics and Subjectivity: From Kant to Nietzsche* (Manchester, 1993), and *From Romanticism to Critical Theory: The Philosophy of German Literary Theory* (London, 1997).

the means of 'saying' the unsayable? If what would explain intelligibility cannot itself be explained, because intelligibility depends on it, any claim to explanation is necessarily circular, depending on what is already presupposed as rendering things intelligible to begin with. The realisation that one therefore cannot ultimately ground such explanations is one of the main sources of Romantic 'irony'. Irony in this sense undermines claims to truth at the same time as allowing for the fact that language compels us to make such claims. The link of irony to the new conceptions of music and the other arts in the early nineteenth century will be made most systematically by K. W. F. Solger (1780–1819) (see below).

By accepting what is behind the idea that rhythm is the condition of possibility of the world's intelligibility, thinkers in this period are led to questions about Kant's account of how the propositions of mathematics, which form the basis of quantifiable scientific knowledge, are possible. The point of Schlegel's inversion of the priority between maths and music is, therefore, that if maths is based on the ability to differentiate and identify, one must ask how this ability itself came about. Given the idea of the primacy of rhythm in the initial ordering of thought, Schlegel's provocative suggestions about mathematics, music and rhythm cease to be implausible.

As many people pointed out at the time, Kant himself gave no account of the genesis of the structures of human thought. The place to begin developing such an account was widely seen to be Kant's notion of 'schematism', the 'talent' required to prevent a regress of rules for the application of rules of judgement, which relies, as Kant put it, on a 'hidden art in the depths of the human soul'. The schema is meant to overcome the divide between the empirical and the a priori, the receptive and the spontaneous aspects of our relations to the world, by enabling the mind to apprehend what are empirically different things, such as a bonsai and a giant redwood, as in some way the same. Schematism is therefore also the basis of the ability to understand and create metaphors. Furthermore, Kant sees schemata as the grounds of identity in temporal difference that allow the object world to become explicable at all. Kant terms schemata in this latter respect 'nothing but determinations of time a priori according to rules'.[12] We need these determinations in order to be able to apprehend things in terms of the categories of, for example, causality, which relies on temporal succession; reality, which relies on presence at a specific time; necessity, which relies on presence at all times, etc. The vital point is, then, that the schemata of time are also necessary (but, as we shall see in a moment, not sufficient) for hearing music as music, beginning simply with the

---

12 I. Kant, *Kritik der reinen Vernunft* (Frankfurt, 1968), pp. B 184, A 145.

experience of a rhythm *as* a rhythm, rather than as random noises, and moving from pulse, to metre, to more differentiated musical forms.

For these 'schematic' forms of apprehension to be able to function one also, though, requires the continuity of the conscious subject between differing moments, and this adds a vital dimension to the issue. This requirement led the Romantics to the idea of a sense of self that they termed 'feeling', which, as Schlegel's friend Novalis puts it, 'cannot feel itself'. 'Feeling' connects the differing moments of the self without itself being knowable in the manner of the objects of the appearing world which it renders knowable. Novalis consequently asks: 'Can I look for a schema for myself, if I am that which schematises?'[13] The task becomes to understand the most fundamental aspect of the self which is required for the world to be rationally intelligible, and this is the basis of the most interesting theories of music at this time. Once this move towards understanding the self is made, the philosophical role of aesthetics becomes inescapable, and aesthetics becomes increasingly concerned with the new conceptions of music.

Music in German Idealist philosophy: 'feeling' and 'mediation' (1)

It should already be clear that, despite many still current assumptions about 'Romanticism', the music aesthetics of the actual founders of Romanticism has almost nothing to do with the aesthetics of feeling characteristic of eighteenth-century affect theories.[14] Schlegel does claim that *'Feeling* is the really aesthetic capacity and so is suspended in the middle between drive and sensation' (*Kritische Schriften*, V, p. 61). What he means by 'feeling', though, has to do with what we have just begun to investigate, not with affect theories of music. The concept of feeling is vital to Romantic aesthetics, and the reasons why must once again first be sought in Kant. The decisive aspect of Kant's aesthetics is, as Anthony Cascardi suggests, its attention to 'the specific element in subjectivity that is "incapable of becoming an element of cognition"',[15] because any attempt to render it in verbal language obscures that element's immediate individual significance by reducing it to a general concept. What is being referred to here is the fundamental qualitative dimension of individual experience manifest in pleasure and pain (a vital source of Schopenhauer's view of the will is also apparent here). Pleasure and pain are not known in the manner we classify

13 Novalis, *Band 2. Das philosophisch-theoretische Werk*, ed. Hans-Joachim Mähl (Munich and Vienna, 1978), p. 162.

14 See C. Dahlhaus, *Die Idee der absoluten Musik* (Munich and Kassel, 1978).

15 A. J. Cascardi, *Consequences of Enlightenment* (Cambridge, 1999), p. 17.

external objects that are accessible in receptive 'sensation'. Neither are they expressible in terms of ethics, which is based on the conscious direction of our will – in Schlegel's terms, on the 'drive' – and which relies upon being binding on more than one individual. Aesthetics is therefore concerned with ways of being which cannot be fully characterised in the terms used for knowledge of things or for ethics. There is, as such, 'no class of "things beautiful" that it is the task of aesthetic reflection to delimit' (Cascardi, Consequences of Enlightenment, p. 101), because there can be no binding rules for inferring whether something is beautiful or not. Beauty is therefore connected to the human freedom to judge without the restriction of rules.

The result for the Romantics is a link between non-inferential aesthetic judgements based on the aspect of the subject that is not reducible to concepts and the subject's related, non-inferential, immediate awareness that its existence transcends what it can know of itself. These two aspects of the subject become linked by the concept of 'feeling', and music is often regarded as the primary means of understanding feeling in this particular sense, as in this passage from Schlegel's lectures on philosophy of 1804–5:

> Now if feeling is the root of all consciousness, then the direction of language [towards cognition] has the essential deficit that it does not grasp and comprehend feeling deeply enough, only touches its surface . . . However large the riches language offers us for our purpose, however much it can be developed and perfected as a means of representation and communication, this essential imperfection must be overcome in another manner, and communication and representation must be added to; and this happens through *music* which is, though, here to be regarded less as a representational art than as philosophical language, and really lies higher than mere art. Every effort to find a general philosophical language had to remain unsuccessful because one did not touch on the fundamental mistake of philosophical experiments with language. – Feeling and wishing often go far beyond thinking; *music* as *inspiration*, as the language of feeling, which excites consciousness in its well-spring, is the only universal language.[16]

Ideas like this, which are also developed by Novalis and Schleiermacher, help form the basis of the Romantic notion of 'literature', *Poesie*, the form of verbal language, which, like music, cannot be represented or replaced by something else: 'The higher language as well should be music; here literature is the link which connects music and language' (Schlegel, *Philosophische Vorlesungen*, II, p. 58).

The essential division in nineteenth-century music aesthetics results from differing attitudes to the non-inferential 'immediacy' of 'feeling' in relation to

---

16 F. Schlegel, *Philosophische Vorlesungen*, II (Munich, Paderborn and Vienna, 1964), p. 57.

the aesthetic, as well as from the conceptions of the self associated with the aesthetic. Many of the thinkers who regard immediacy as essential to our self-understanding give a substantial role to music, whereas those, like Hegel, who regard it as a non-conceptual residue which philosophy will eventually eliminate by conceptually 'mediating' it, see music as relatively unimportant.

An influential attempt to systematise some of the ideas explored so far, which has significant effects on subsequent thinkers, like E. T. A. Hoffmann, and both Hegel and Schopenhauer, is present in the early work of F. W. J. Schelling,[17] who is located somewhere between the Romantic thinking explored above (and in the next section), and the German Idealist thinking of Hegel outlined below. In his *System of Transcendental Idealism* of 1800, written while he was in contact with Schlegel and Novalis, Schelling gives art the culminating role, because it reveals the limits of philosophy. Although he does not specifically give music a leading role, his claim that art combines 'unconscious productivity', the natural 'drive' that gives rise to our conscious ideas in ways we cannot finally explain, with the 'conscious productivity' involved in the artist working according to the rules of art, can easily be assimilated to theories which reject representationalist conceptions of language in the name of music as that which articulates what concepts cannot. In Schelling's *System* art shows what philosophy cannot finally say, namely how necessity and freedom can be understood as ultimately unified aspects of the same world. The work of art is in one respect an object in the world like any other: it is subject to causal laws and is therefore conceptually identifiable, for example as a series of pitches of specifiable frequency and duration. At the same time, *qua* work of art, it is never finally determinable, because its significance cannot be exhausted by any classifying conceptual description.

In his *Philosophy of Art* (the first work to bear this title) of 1802–3, Schelling gives philosophy and art equal status as different means of understanding 'the Absolute', thus moving away somewhat from the more Romantic conception of the 1800 *System*. The basic idea of his thought at this time, which is characteristic of German Idealism, is that, in order to avoid questionable divisions between mind and the object world, the 'ideal' and the 'real', any such differences can only be seen as relative, depending upon a preponderance of one or other side of the difference in the constitution of a particular aspect of the world. Philosophy's task is to show the relativity of all such differences, which are aspects of what is ultimately identical with itself, the 'Absolute', or 'absolute identity'. Art and philosophy therefore offer different ways of 'constructing' the same 'absolute identity', so that 'beauty is the indifference of freedom and

---

17 See A. Bowie, *Schelling and Modern European Philosophy* (London, 1993).

necessity seen in something real', namely the art work *qua* material object that is not reducible to concepts, whereas truth is the same 'indifference' expressed in an 'ideal' system of thought which explicates the relationship between freedom and necessity.[18]

Schelling offers revealing insights into the question of music, language and rhythm on the basis of these metaphysical ideas. His apparently extravagant claim that 'music is nothing but the archetypal [*urbildlich*] rhythm of nature and of the universe itself' (*Sämmtliche Werke*, I/5, p. 369) begins to make sense when, reminding one of Schlegel's view of rhythm as that which limits 'incomprehensible infinity', he claims that 'The secret of all life is the synthesis of the absolute with limitation' (p. 393). In this context he uses Kant's notion of 'schematism' for the 'intuition of the particular through the universal' (p. 407), and claims that schematism is the basis of language because it enables identities to be established from a chaos of differences. Language itself, as Hamann had already argued against Kant's separation of pure and empirical concepts in 1784, is precisely dependent upon a synthesis of universal 'ideal' meaning in thought with particular 'real' material in the form of the external spoken or written signifiers of a particular natural language. Schelling therefore sees *all* intelligible reality as a 'primary speaking', because it is both knowable via 'ideal' conceptual discrimination and empirically manifested as 'real' matter. Music's status as the form of art most dependent upon time means it is 'the living which has entered death – the word *spoken* into finitude – which still becomes audible as sound' (p. 484). This is because, like all sound, music ceases to be, even as it becomes manifest.

In Schelling's account of the ascending continuum of the arts, which he sets out in terms of the relative roles of the ideal and the real, the infinite and the finite, within each art, music comes first, being the 'most closed of all arts' because it only articulates the movements of things and does not determine the things conceptually (p. 504). Music's essential relation to time – elsewhere Schelling says 'time is itself nothing but the *totality appearing in opposition to the particular life of things*' (*Sämmtliche Werke*, I/6, p. 220) – is based on the fact that music's form is 'succession'. This connects music to self-consciousness, which makes possible the unity between successive moments of time, and music's essence is rhythm, the 'imprinting of unity into multiplicity' (*Sämmtliche Werke*, I/5, p. 492), 'the transformation of a succession which is in itself meaningless into a significant one' (p. 493). Schelling's idea further illuminates the connection of the new perception of music to theories of knowledge: in the *Critique of Judgement* Kant had linked the aesthetic aspect of judgement to

18 F. W. J. Schelling's *Sämmtliche Werke*, ed. K. F. A. Schelling, I Abtheilung, vols. I–x, II, Abtheilung Bde. 1–4 (Stuttgart, 1856–61), I/5, p. 383.

judgement in general: 'Admittedly we do not feel any noticeable pleasure any more in the graspability of nature and in its unity of division into genera and species . . . in its time there must have been some, and only because the most common experience would not be possible without it has it gradually merged with mere cognition and is no longer particularly noticed' (Kant, *Kritik der Urteilskraft*, B p. XL, A p. XXXVIII). As it was for Schlegel, rhythm for Schelling is the most fundamental form of such 'unity of division' and its significance derives from the pleasure of making identity out of difference. Schelling terms rhythm 'the music in music' (*Sämmtliche Werke*, I/5, p. 494), because the structure of identity in difference is repeated both in melody's unifying different pitches into intelligible forms and in the unification in harmony of different pitches, from the overtones in a single note to the notes in a chord.

Schelling's later ideas, which are less reliant on the idea of an ultimately harmonious philosophical conception of the Absolute than the *Philosophy of Art*, help to initiate conceptions which are fundamental both to many aspects of modern thought and to some important modern art. He asserts in 1809–10, linking music to Dionysus, that 'because sound and note only seem to arise in that battle between spirituality and corporeality, music [*Tonkunst*] alone can be the image of . . . primeval nature and its movement'.[19] The 'battle' in question results from the production of sound by the oscillation in space of a resisting material body that is set in motion by something opposed to it. This gives rise to an alternation between 'something' and 'nothing', which are thereby made determinate in relation to each other. In its most general form, Schelling's idea of a dynamic relationship between something and nothing, in which things in the world become determinate by being related to things beyond themselves, rather than remaining inertly enclosed within themselves like unplayed strings, can be read as a metaphor for Hegel's whole way of constructing his philosophical system, which he developed via his assimilation and criticism of Schelling's earlier philosophy. The idea of a primeval conflict from which a differentiated world painfully emerges is also the basis of Schopenhauer's main work, *Die Welt als Wille und Vorstellung* (1818), in which music is seen in analogous terms to Schelling's.

How, then, do the radical differences with regard to music and philosophy of the main post-Kantian thinkers come about? Nearly all the significant post-Kantian thinkers share the conviction, resulting both from the historical changes taking place in the wake of the French Revolution and from the dissolution of traditional truths by the modern sciences, that philosophy must be able to come to terms in new ways with change and temporality. The music of

19 F. W. J. von Schelling, *Die Weltalter*, ed. Manfred Schröter (Munich, 1946), p. 43.

the same period, particularly that of Beethoven, also evidently reflects changes in temporality. How, though, is one to respond to these changes? In philosophy there is a paradigmatic division between German Idealist thinkers like Hegel (and, at times, Schelling), who wish to sustain the Platonic idea that philosophy can still get beyond finitude via a new kind of dynamic, but systematically complete thinking, and Romantic thinkers, like Schlegel and Schleiermacher, who consider such completion as at best a necessary orientating goal, and as one which may not ever be attainable. Both Idealist and Romantic positions rely on the sense that human existence is characterised by a constitutive, motivating sense of lack, but their conceptions of how that lack is to be understood diverge, and this is the source of their conflicting understandings of music. Music's relationship to this sense of lack, which Schlegel termed 'longing', results from its temporal structure, in which each note in a piece only derives its significance from the other notes, depending for its identity upon what it is not and only really attaining this identity when the music comes to an end. The question therefore becomes how what is articulated by music relates to other forms of articulation, from art to science, which also function in terms of 'negative' relations between elements that mutually define each other.

Hegel's *Science of Logic* of 1816 aims to integrate all the ways in which thought grasps the world into an interlinked dynamic system. In the *Logic* Hegel gives a characterisation of the structure of his thought as a whole in terms of music's relation to chemical 'elective affinities': 'the single note has its sense only in the . . . connection with another note and with the sequence of other notes . . . The single note is the tonic of a system but just as much again a member in the system of every other tonic.'[20] Linking music even more emphatically to the whole of his thought, he claims in his *Aesthetics* (which he gives as lectures in the early 1820s) that dissonance:

> constitutes the real depth of notes [*Tönen*] in that it also progresses to essential oppositions and is not afraid of their severity and disunity. For the true concept is admittedly unity in itself but this subjectivity negates itself as ideal transparent unity into its opposite, into objectivity, indeed it is as the simply ideal itself only a one-sidedness and particularity . . . and only truly subjectivity when it goes into this opposition and overcomes and dissolves it . . . Only this movement, as the return of identity to itself, is the Truth.[21]

These passages illustrate how Hegel's philosophy proposes to overcome the split between the finite and the infinite, and at the same time they provide a model which has echoes in the music of the time, particularly in the work of Beethoven (whom Hegel, perhaps surprisingly, does not mention in the

20 G. W. F. Hegel, *Wissenschaft der Logik I*, Werke 5 (Frankfurt, 1969), p. 421.
21 G. W. F. Hegel, *Ästhetik*, II (Berlin and Weimar, 1965), p. 297.

Aesthetics). The aim of philosophy for Hegel is the demonstration of the unity of concept and object. However, the development of knowledge seems to point to the opposite, to a sceptical separation between thought and the world, because theories constantly turn out to be false in the light of subsequent theories. Were this situation to be understood as entailing scepticism, philosophy would have failed to unite the finite with the infinite, and knowledge would be like an endlessly unresolved series of dissonances without a tonal basis.

The musical analogy itself already points to Hegel's attempted counter to scepticism: unresolved dissonances can only be apprehended as such within an overall tonal order which makes one aware of them *as* dissonances. If the very 'dissonance' – the 'non-identity' – between thought and its object which gives rise to new theories can itself be regarded as the motor of the development of truth, what appears as negative and as a loss of unity can, when seen from the perspective of the whole process, be seen as positive and as productive of a higher unity. The structure of the 'identity of identity and difference', via which Hegel constructs his system, is present even in the most simple musical material: the major triad, he claims, expresses the 'concept of harmony in its simplest form, indeed [it expresses] the very nature of the concept. For we have a totality of different notes before us which shows this difference just as much as undisturbed unity' (*Ästhetik*, p. 296). The same structure is repeated in more complex forms throughout his work. In the terms of the passage on dissonance cited above, the famous C♯ in the opening bars of the *Eroica* Symphony could, for example, be understood as 'subjectivity', in the form of the self-contained unity of the tonality of E flat, 'negating itself' into what is opposed to itself in order to articulate its own content more fully. The symphonic movement finally resolves this tension by revealing its goal some 400 bars later when the C♯ recurs in the context which retrospectively gives its initial occurrence its real significance. In consequence, rather than having remained 'one-sidedly' within itself, the home key with which the movement eventually concludes has become more significant via its relations to what temporarily 'dissolved' it. Seen from the end of the movement, the 'negativity' of the famous dissonance thus becomes a way of expressing unity at a higher level. However, such an account leaves open a vital question. Does the truth of the music therefore simply consist in what philosophy can tell us about it, in the manner just outlined, or do philosophical concepts miss something essential about what music communicates?

An answer to this question in Hegel's terms depends upon music's place in relation both to the other arts and to philosophy and the sciences. At the most general level Hegel is insistent that in the modern period, because art is 'limited to a distinct content', it no longer 'fulfils our highest need . . . The *science* of art is thus in our time much more necessary than at times in which art for itself as art provided complete satisfaction' (*Ästhetik*, I, p. 21). Art's connection to particular aspects of the empirical world means that its significance will always be limited in ways that scientific theories, for example, which abstract from the unique particularity of the object in order to attain more general truths, are not. The highest truths are those of philosophy, which transcend even the kind of particularity involved in scientific laws by showing how such particular laws constitute an interlinked system in the manner of the notes in a piece of music. The philosophical system is therefore not dependent upon the contingent material instantiation of the laws themselves. In this respect music has a hybrid status. Its abstract structure would seem to bring it close to philosophy because it is not tied to 'a distinct content'; at the same time, its content is not determinate because it does not represent an aspect of the world that is open to the process of progressive conceptual articulation which culminates in philosophy.

Hegel places music above architecture, sculpture and painting, but below literature, in the hierarchy of the arts. His conception is based on the ways in which *Geist*, 'mind' or 'spirit', is manifested in the different arts. Architecture is the lowest form of art because it is ruled by the material of a building, which is subject to the physical laws of gravity. The principle of painting is 'subjective inwardness', which frees it further from dependence on matter. However, the fact of painting's material manifestation and its dependence on space means that painting does not fully realise this principle. Music, as that which completely abolishes space and consists of 'sound', a 'material which . . . itself already disappears once again in its coming to be and its existence' (*Ästhetik*, II, p. 260), is for Hegel a more complete instantiation of the principle of subjective inwardness. This is, however, also the reason for music's limited status. At this point we come back to the issue of 'feeling' and to the crux of music aesthetics in the first half of the nineteenth century. For Hegel literature is the highest form of art because, rather than depending, as music does, upon 'our completely empty I, the self without further content' (p. 260), it combines subjective inwardness with 'the specificity and the particularity of external existence' (p. 328), such as the conflicts in a drama (which is the highest form of art for Hegel). Music, then, is subordinated to literature because it relies on narcissistically 'hearing oneself' in 'feeling' (*Empfindung*) (p. 308), instead of engaging with the objective world of society and history. However, literature is itself subordinated in turn to religion and philosophy because they are less reliant on representing particular aspects of the empirical world, of the kind that restrict the more universal significance of *Geist*'s appearance in literature.

In one sense Hegel's position is, then, straightforwardly Platonist: philosophy is the highest form of *Geist* because it articulates the timeless structures that constitute the truth of the transient appearing world by revealing the merely relative status of anything material and anything particular. Unlike the formalism Hegel sees in music, which derives from its non-representational aspect and its lack of determinate conceptual content, philosophy's formalism is the result of having *overcome* all specific 'finite' appearing contents and incorporated them into itself by showing how they are relative to other specific contents. Above all, of course, philosophy overcomes the particularity of 'feeling', which, as subjective inwardness, is merely an unmediated part of the infinite totality that can be mediated by philosophy. Music is, then, the realm of intransitive feeling which 'returns to itself' (p. 308) by being expressed in transient sound rather than relating transitively to 'external existence' or being rendered durable as part of the truth of philosophy. The implications of this issue have turned out to be germane to thinking about music ever since.

Hegel's formalist view is, for example, developed in Hanslick's *On the Beautiful in Music* of 1854, which intends to refute the 'unscientific aesthetics of sentiment/feeling'.[22] Hanslick's rejection of feeling as unscientific is often used to underpin the insistence of much twentieth-century musicology on musical analysis, which takes the aspect of music that can be subordinated to concepts and which can be thought of independently of actual – transient – performances as the source of the only true apprehensions of music. In such views the use of metaphor, for example, to characterise what is important in the score of a piece of music or in a performance of music should only be the prelude to the cashing in of the metaphor by a more scientific 'literal' analysis. Admittedly, neither Hegel nor Hanslick believes that music can always be translated into conceptuality, but they do not think this means that music is therefore the source of insights which transcend what concepts can express.

Music in German Romantic philosophy: 'feeling' and 'mediation' (2)

The idea that music can transcend conceptuality obviously makes considerable metaphysical demands on music. However, Hegel's position with regard to music itself relies on the success of his metaphysical project of overcoming 'immediacy'. At the most grandiose level this means that Hegel must account for the world's intelligibility by showing that the nature of our understanding is exhausted by what concepts can say about it. As we saw, Kant's aesthetics was based precisely on an unmediated ground in experience – the qualitative difference between pleasure and unpleasure – which could not be dissolved

22 E. Hanslick, *Vom Musikalisch-Schönen. Teil 1: Historisch-kritische Ausgabe*, ed. Dietmar Strauss (Mainz, 1990), p. 21.

into concepts, and this ground is vital both to Romantic philosophy and to Schopenhauer. The most extensive version of the implications of such conceptions for music is given by Friedrich Schleiermacher, who was for a time friends with both Schlegel and Schelling, and whom Hegel attacked for his insistence on the central role of 'feeling' in philosophy.[23] Schleiermacher's *Aesthetics*, based on lectures given in Berlin from 1819 onwards, distils some of the most durable Romantic ideas about music.

Schleiermacher's essential philosophical concern is the nature of human understanding, and he is best known for his work on hermeneutics, the 'art of interpretation', in which he seeks to do justice both to the structural constraints imposed on individuals by language and to the fact that meaning in real communication always involves an aspect which is inseparable from the individuality of the language-user.[24] This means that interpretation, while relying on rules, cannot be reduced to the application of rules, and this forms the crucial link in Schleiermacher between art and language, both of which involve the freedom to transcend rule-bound relations to the world. Schleiermacher refuses to make absolute divisions between different kinds of articulation, because the production and the understanding of a scientific treatise, of a lyric poem and of a piece of autonomous music, for example, all involve both cognitive and affective activity, albeit in very differing degrees. Furthermore, he asserts, taking up a key aspect of the rhetorical tradition, language itself 'as a totality of tones is a musical system. The musical element also has an effect in every utterance, and as this effectiveness has a different basis from that of the significant, they can come into conflict with each other' (*'Hermeneutics and Criticism'*, p. 238). Because he believes it is impossible to draw a definitive line between what our minds contribute and what the world contributes to our experience, Schleiermacher is able to claim that there is a constitutive, active aspect to all forms of thought, while at the same time avoiding wholesale idealism. In consequence, 'All people are artists';[25] even apparently passive cognitive relations to the world involve a degree of active individual apprehension, and even the receptive relationship to a work of art requires active attention if the work is to be apprehended aesthetically.

The central terms in Schleiermacher's *Aesthetics* are 'feeling', which he also terms 'immediate self-consciousness', and 'free productivity'. The first two of these are required to account for the transition between the receptive ways in which we are determined by the world, for example in being subject to the constraints of the objective world, and the spontaneous ways in which we can

23 See Bowie, 'Introduction' to Schleiermacher, *'Hermeneutics and Criticism'*.
24 See Schleiermacher, *'Hermeneutics and Criticism'*.
25 F. Schleiermacher, *Entwurf eines Systems der Sittenlehre* (Berlin, 1835), pp. 254–5.

respond even to such constraints with 'free productivity', for example in artistic production. Receptivity and spontaneity cannot finally be separated, as otherwise the continuity of my conscious experience as *my* experience would disintegrate in the move from passive to active, or vice versa. For Schleiermacher, the only relative separation of the cognitive and the aesthetic means that art is 'free production of the same functions which also occur in the bound activity of humankind'.[26] Free production depends precisely upon 'immediate self-consciousness', and the movements of immediate self-consciousness are seen as the core of music. Immediate self-consciousness cannot, as its name indicates, be 'mediated' or objectified; as Novalis had put it, 'feeling cannot feel itself'. It therefore expresses the irreducibility of each individual's relationship to the world, which they can never make fully transparent, even to themselves.[27] Each mediated moment of our experience which we can objectify by reflecting on it in relation to other moments depends on the fact that there must always have already been a 'complete [hence immediate] taking up of the whole of existence in a moment' (Schleiermacher, *Vorlesungen über die Ästhetik*, p. 122) which is never within our control, but which is essential to the intelligibility of our individual being. Without it experience would disintegrate.[28] Such consciousness is not just passive receptivity, but is productive in ways which concepts cannot express. Concepts rely on the aspects of experience which are common to all people, and therefore cannot articulate my individual way of being. This requires a kind of expression which, although it relies on the same material as is used by everybody else, transcends what can be common to all people by organising this material, be it notes, words, or whatever, in individual ways.

Schleiermacher links these ideas to music as follows: 'just as the infinity of combination of articulated sounds belongs to human thought being able to appear in language, so the manifold of measured [*gemessen*] sounds represents the whole manifold of movements of self-consciousness, to the extent that they are not ideas, but real states of life' (*Vorlesungen über die Ästhetik*, p. 394). This means music is closely related both to other forms of expression which do not have a semantically determinate verbal equivalent, such as gesture and mime, and to 'living' metaphors which resist literalisation. Even though music relies on mathematical proportions, that is not what makes something music: this

---

26 F. Schleiermacher, *Vorlesungen über die Ästhetik* (Berlin, 1842), p. 375.

27 The notion therefore plays a similar role to Martin Heidegger's later idea of 'being in the world', as the never finally objectifiable ground of our existence which cannot be understood in terms of the subject's relation to a separate world of objects. See A. Bowie, 'Adorno, Heidegger and the Meaning of Music', *Thesis 11*, 56 (1999), pp. 1–23.

28 The idea that there must be a non-perceptual, non-propositional form of self-knowledge of this kind is increasingly widely accepted in the contemporary philosophy of mind.

depends on its relation to the 'mobility' of human awareness; otherwise, by terming a 'sequence of mathematical formulae' a musical 'key', for example, one confuses 'the physiological with the artistic' (p. 391). At the same time, music differs from direct natural expressions of feeling by the fact that free production involves elements of conscious reflection, of the kind which are present in 'bound' cognition, which help transform the initial unreflective impulse that gives rise to the need for expression into an intelligible articulation. Music and verbal language differ because music does not express determinate thoughts, but their difference is relativised in lyric poetry, which, like music, is not 'communication and presentation of something known, but rather of a moved inner state' (p. 381).

In one sense this brings Schleiermacher close to Hegel's idea of music as mere narcissistic 'hearing oneself'. However, the point of 'feeling' is not that it is simply internal and is to be incorporated into philosophy by the demonstration that its truth lies in its becoming conceptually accessible. Instead, because it is always already inextricably involved in a world which affects it, feeling requires its own irreducible forms of articulation, which range from forms, like music, that articulate more internal movements, to forms, like mime and drama, that involve a more external aspect. Schleiermacher sums up his view of music as follows: 'The connection of artistic productivity with the movements of self-consciousness, which are so immediately connected with activity in the movements of life, is . . . unmistakably the main issue in musical production' (p. 393), so that the more the mobility of life appears in the combination of the notes, 'the more the idea of music is attained' (p. 395). Some aspects of Schleiermacher's concrete views on particular kinds of music are just a product of their era, and some of his assertions about the limitations of autonomous music might be questioned on account of their role in now largely obsolete debates on music's role in religious observance. However, his account of the need for transitions between differing verbal and non-verbal modes of apprehending and articulating the world and his account of the irreducibility of self-consciousness required to account for the significance of the aesthetic have turned out to be much more durable than their limited reception might have suggested.

Music, theology and the will

Hegel's subordination of music to the 'concept' relies on the idea that the progress of philosophy and science is bought at the price of hollowing out the significance of art (and traditional religion) for the modern world. Schleiermacher's attention to 'feeling' reclaims ways of articulating the aspects of ourselves and the world, such as music, which are both irreducibly individual and can gain a universal significance that philosophy or science cannot explain. What, though, of the theories at this time which give music the kind of status suggested, for example, in the writings of E. T. A. Hoffmann and Schopenhauer? In his famous 1810 review of Beethoven's Fifth Symphony Hoffmann claims, employing Schlegel's key term, that 'Beethoven's music . . . awakes that infinite longing which is the essence of Romanticism'.[29] Moreover, on hearing the symphony one 'leaves behind all feelings that can be determined by concepts in order to devote oneself to the unsayable' (*Schriften*, p. 23). Writing about Beethoven's Opus 70 piano trios in 1813 (both reviews, though, also contain acute analyses of the music), he suggests that 'in the midst of this unlocked realm of spirits the delighted soul listens to the unknown language and understands all the most secret intimations by which it is seized' (p. 121). In the essay 'Old and New Church Music' of 1814, however, Hoffmann presents the conception of music as the means of access to a realm beyond the sensuous, not, as he did in the Beethoven pieces, in terms of wordless instrumental music that is free of the compulsion to relate to what words may say, but instead in terms of the church music tradition deriving from Palestrina, which, of course, relies on the setting of liturgical texts.

The blunt inconsistency between these positions could only be overcome by making a necessary link between what is 'said' by wordless music and the content of liturgy. This illustrates the problem for theories which wish to give propositional metaphysical content to music by stating in what music's transcendence of concepts consists, rather than, as the early Romantics do at their best, using music to show how concepts themselves involve elements which are inseparable from music, and thus suggesting limitations in philosophical and scientific ways of grasping the world. The question of music's relationship to metaphysics and religion evidently has much to do at this time with debates concerning the relationship between music and Protestant theology, which is seeking to sustain itself at an intellectual level adequate to a world more and more determined by the secular modern sciences. These debates are, though, part of an even more significant issue.

What is at stake here really becomes apparent when, in the 1880s, Nietzsche claims that 'The *dangerousness of the Christian ideal* lies in its value feelings, in that which can do without conceptual expression: my fight against *latent Christianity* (e.g. in music, in socialism)'.[30] The later Nietzsche's antagonism towards forms of consolation, such as certain kinds of music, which he thinks

29 E. T. A. Hoffmann, *Schriften zur Musik: Singspiele* (Berlin and Weimar, 1988), p. 25.

30 F. Nietzsche, *Sämtliche Werke*, ed. Giorgio Colli and Mazzino Montinari (Munich, Berlin and New York, 1980), XII, p. 453.

encourage the illusion that life could be metaphysically justified, is clearly directed against views like Hoffmann's. Novalis had characterised philosophy as 'homesickness' and claimed that music allowed us temporarily to feel at home, thus suggesting that music can do what philosophy cannot, namely reconcile us for a time at an affective level with our transience and finitude. The question suggested by Nietzsche is, then, how far and in what ways such ideas are necessarily connected to theology.

At the end of the essay on church music, Hoffmann asserts:

> May the time of the fulfilment of our hope no longer be far off, may a pious life in peace and joyfulness begin and may music move its seraph's wings freely and powerfully, in order once again to begin the flight to the beyond which is its home and from which consolation and well-being shine down into the troubled breast of man!   (*Schriften*, p. 247)

In *Human, All Too Human* (1878), written after he had said farewell to the Romantic- and Schopenhauer-inspired ideas of *The Birth of Tragedy*, Nietzsche comments that 'the highest effects of art can easily produce a resonance of the metaphysical string which has long been silent, indeed has broken' (Nietzsche, *Sämtliche Werke*, II, p. 145), referring as an example to part of the last movement of Beethoven's Ninth. The essential tension manifest in the contrast between Nietzsche and Hoffmann lies in the fact that, despite his fondness for metaphysical (and theological) hyperbole, Hoffmann does also articulate a powerful sense of utopian promise, a promise which many other thinkers and musicians in the modern period will argue is kept alive by music, *despite* the processes of secularisation. Music is regarded by such theorists as being resistant to modern rationalisation, which increasingly grants significance only to what can be quantified and explained in rule-bound terms. This is because music's distance from representational functions, of the kind which dominate much use of language, gives it the potential to articulate a sense of freedom from the existing orders of things. This idea of the utopian promise of music would later play a role in the work of Wagner, as well as of twentieth-century theorists like T. W. Adorno and Ernst Bloch.[31]

At much the same time that Hoffmann wrote his essay on church music, two other figures, K. F. W. Solger and Schopenhauer, also made their views on music public in Berlin. Both gave a central role to music's relation to finitude, but Solger did so from a theologically informed perspective, whereas Schopenhauer did so not least in opposition to the ideas of German Idealism upon which Solger partially relied. Solger's fundamental conviction is that art is the means of presenting the timeless, universal 'idea' of things, but that art

---

31 For an account of this issue, see L. Goehr, *The Quest for Voice: Music, Politics and the Limits of Philosophy* (Oxford, 1998).

necessarily also relies upon the negativity inherent in the transience of all particular things. This means art has an ambiguous status that Solger characterises by the term 'irony', which he adopts from Schlegel. Art is constituted, Solger maintains, by the destruction of the very timeless 'idea' which gives aesthetic status to the transient material of the work. In line with a basic thought of German Idealism, the particulars of the empirical world are inherently 'negative' – limited – because their existence as whatever they are at a particular moment is dependent on time and on their relations to other particulars. The contrast between the universal idea, which makes an artefact into art by revealing a truth not manifest in the chaotic diversity of the empirical world, and the contingent particulars that are required to make up a work of art, such as the actual pitches and the durations of the vibrations in music, makes the limitations of the particular manifest. In doing so this contrast also gives temporary access to a universality beyond the limitations of the particulars by making them significant as part of a whole whose meaning transcends them. However, at the same time, the universality of the idea is sacrificed by its having to appear via the material of the work. This is the source both of the notion that irony – the coexistence of the positive and the negative – and art are inseparable, and of the link Solger, like Hoffmann, makes to Schlegel's notion of 'longing', the combination of our feeling of the unlimited capacity of thought with the feeling of limitation experienced in relation to the transient appearing world and our own transience.

Solger's conception becomes easier to grasp when he discusses music, and here the metaphysical abstractions turn out to be related to a subsequent concrete development in nineteenth-century music. In the philosophical dialogue, *Erwin*, of 1815 the question arises as to how the essence of time, which is both universal and irreducibly particular – all moments of time are different and yet are also part of the same time – can be presented: 'the effect of music consists in the fact that in the sensation of every present moment a whole eternity emerges in our mind . . . Music . . . therefore really achieves what is not achievable for the usual activity of the understanding. But it also does not achieve it for real objects, but only in the universal empty form of time.'[32] In order to achieve a real unification of the finite and the infinite music must therefore link itself to other forms of art. Wagner will try to realise such a conception in his idea of the dramatic *Gesamtkunstwerk*. Solger thinks it is realised in the 'complete musical church service, in the singing of holy hymns before paintings of divine actions' (*Erwin*, p. 292) in inspiring architectural surroundings. Only in religion, then, can the irony constitutive of art be dissolved, but the consequence is that art 'seems to have to destroy itself once again' (p. 293).

---

32 K. W. F. Solger, *Erwin: Vier Gespräche über das Schöne und die Kunst* (Munich, 1971), pp. 287–8.

What, though, if it is religion which in fact destroys itself, as the essential developments of nineteenth-century thought from Feuerbach and Marx to Nietzsche suggest? In the realm of music aesthetics it is Schopenhauer who is generally regarded as the main representative of anti-idealist and atheistic conceptions of art in the early part of the century. However, it is too often forgotten that Schopenhauer's work had virtually no effect in the first half of the century, becoming significant only in the wake of Wagner's reading of the *Die Welt als Wille und Vorstellung* in 1854, of the decline of Idealist and Romantic thinking in the face of the successes of materialistically conceived natural science, and of the ideas of Darwin on the 'survival of the fittest'. For this reason I shall confine myself here to a few observations (see chapter 12 for Schopenhauer's importance for the later part of the century). It is worth noting in any case that little of what Schopenhauer says about art and music is original. Although he was famously rude about many of his philosophical contemporaries, most of his key ideas are adaptations of the ideas of post-Kantian thinking we have already examined, and the elevated role he attributes to music is, as we have seen, quite widespread in Romantic thought.[33] The main difference from his contemporaries lies in his thoroughgoing pessimism (and misanthropy), which, of course, fitted better into the post-1848 climate of disillusion with the hopes for human progress that had emerged with the French Revolution.

Despite the venom which he directs at Fichte, Schelling and Hegel, Schopenhauer's conception of art is in one essential respect actually identical with the ideas of the overtly Christian, Idealist- and Romantic-orientated Solger (who develops his positions at exactly the same time as Schopenhauer). Art is concerned, Schopenhauer claims, with 'what is not subject to any change and thus is known for all time with the same truth, in a word, with *the ideas*'.[34] The role of music in his main philosophical work is suggested in its title: the changing world of '*Vorstellung*', 'representation', in the sense of 'appearance', is not the true world. The true world is the world as 'will', which cannot itself appear, therefore cannot be represented, and is intuitively present in feeling – hence its connection to music. The metaphysical structure of this conception is much the same as we saw in Schlegel's Fichte-derived account of the 'drive' which is 'the ground of what is present in the self-conscious being'. Because it is not concerned with the world of causally linked objects, music 'does not talk of things, but rather of nothing but well-being and woe, which are the sole realities for the *will*' (*Sämtliche Werke*, V, p. 507). The parts of the body are objectifications of this fundamental ontological principle, so that, for example, 'teeth, gullet and intestine are objectified hunger' (*Sämtliche Werke*, I, p. 168). The will 'in itself . . . is an endless striving' (I, p. 240), and its particular objectifications

---

33 On this see Bowie, *Aesthetics and Subjectivity*, chapter 8.
34 A. Schopenhauer, *Sämtliche Werke*, I (Frankfurt am Main, 1966), p. 265.

necessarily come into conflict with each other. Instead, then, of reason transcending its basis in the drives that constitute the motivating ground of reality, as it does in Idealist and Romantic philosophy, reason is revealed – and this idea will be vital for Nietzsche – as a mere masking of this inherently agonistic ground. This is the source of Schopenhauer's pessimism, and of his schizoid combination of a Platonist conception of art – epitomised by his concentration on the mathematical basis of music and on the idea of music as an escape from the endless lack which is present in the sensuous world – with a Hobbesian conception of the human and natural world.

Schopenhauer's view of music is summed up in the dictum that 'One could . . . just as well call the world embodied music as embodied will' (I, p. 366): the essential conflictual nature of reality is manifest in tonal music's creation and resolution of tension. The complete philosophical explication of music would therefore give one 'the true philosophy' (I, p. 369). Such an explanation is, though, not possible because it would entail representation of the will in terms of the appearing world of objects. On the one hand, then, music *qua* aesthetic experience temporarily redeems one from the fundamental lack in which life consists; on the other hand, music does this while expressing precisely what makes life a torment. The point is *not*, then, that we experience the emotions which music articulates – that would merely be a further form of subjection to the will – but that music should turn them into Platonic, will-less forms. The result of these arguments is to give music an absolutely autonomous aesthetic status which divorces it from any role in disclosing new aspects of the world: the truth of music is always the same truth, because it is the non-conceptual expression of the way the world ultimately is. Whereas the Romantic connection of feeling and music could allow for an infinite, fluid diversity of individual ways of being in the world, Schopenhauer's conception of music ends up being a monolithic comment on the futility of individual existence.

The distance between Hegel and Schopenhauer is, then, in one important sense actually not as great as it might seem: both give a definite answer to the 'question' of music, one by transcending it in philosophical concepts, the other by defining it in terms of the metaphysics of the will, the intuitively known basis of existence. The choice between Hegel's tendency to conjure away the ability of music to say what nothing else can, and Schopenhauer's homogenisation of the significance of music has, from the widespread exclusive concentration on music analysis and on the objectifiable acoustic and other properties of music, to the frequent mystifications of music as something wholly divorced from the social and historical world, dominated too much thinking about music in the modern era. The strength of the best early Romantic music aesthetics lies in its hermeneutic exploration of the link between the non-representational aspect of music and the realisation that language itself cannot be adequately understood in representational terms. This is the source not just of insights into music, but also of insights into how music can suggest the limits of philosophy.[35] The resources in the early Romantic tradition both for avoiding the subordination of music to the natural sciences and for resisting the use of music in crude opposition to any form of rationality are far from exhausted.

Bibliography

Bowie, A., 'Adorno, Heidegger and the Meaning of Music'. *Thesis 11*, 56 (1999), pp. 1–23
    Aesthetics and Subjectivity: From Kant to Nietzsche. Manchester, 1993
    From Romanticism to Critical Theory: The Philosophy of German Literary Theory. London, 1997
    Schelling and Modern European Philosophy. London, 1993
Cascardi, A. J., *Consequences of Enlightenment*. Cambridge, 1999
Dahlhaus, C., *Die Idee der absoluten Musik*. Munich and Kassel, 1978
Goehr, L., *The Quest for Voice: Music, Politics and the Limits of Philosophy*. Oxford, 1998
Hanslick, E., *Vom Musikalisch-Schönen. Teil 1: Historisch-kritische Ausgabe*, ed. D. Strauss. Mainz, 1990
Hegel, G. W. F., *Ästhetik*. 2 vols., Berlin and Weimar, 1965
    Wissenschaft der Logik I, Werke 5. Frankfurt, 1969
Heinse, J. J. W., *Hildegard von Hohenthal*. 3 vols., Berlin, 1795–6
Hoffmann, E. T. A., *Schriften zur Musik: Singspiele*. Berlin and Weimar, 1988
Forkel, J. N., *Musikalisch-kritische Bibliothek*. Gotha, 1778
Kant, I., *Kritik der reinen Vernunft*. Frankfurt, 1968
    Kritik der Urteilskraft. Frankfurt, 1977
Neubauer, J., *The Emancipation of Music from Language: Departure from Mimesis in Eighteenth-Century Aesthetics*. New Haven and London, 1986
Nietzsche, F., *Sämtliche Werke*, ed. G. Colli and M. Montinari. Munich, Berlin and New York, 1980
Novalis, *Band 2. Das philosophisch-theoretische Werk*, ed. H.-J. Mähl. Munich and Vienna, 1978
Schelling, F. W. J., *Die Weltalter*, ed. M. Schröter. Munich, 1946
    Sämmtliche Werke, ed. K. F. A. Schelling, I Abtheilung, vols. I–X, II Abtheilung Bde. 1–4. Stuttgart, 1856–61
Schlegel, F., *Kritische Schriften und Fragmente I–VI*. Paderborn, 1988
    Literarische Notizen 1797–1807, ed. H. Eichner. Frankfurt, Berlin and Vienna, 1980
    Philosophische Vorlesungen, II. Munich, Paderborn and Vienna, 1964
Schleiermacher, F., *'Hermeneutics and Criticism' and Other Texts*, ed. and trans. A. Bowie. Cambridge, 1998
    Entwurf eines Systems der Sittenlehre. Berlin, 1835
    Vorlesungen über die Ästhetik. Berlin, 1842
Schopenhauer, A., *Sämtliche Werke*. Frankfurt am Main, 1966
Solger, K. W. F., *Erwin: Vier Gespräche über das Schöne und die Kunst*. Munich, 1971
Strunk, O. (ed.), Treitler, L. (rev. edn), *Source Readings in Music History*. New York, 1998
Wackenroder, W. H. and Tieck, L., *Phantasien über die Kunst*. Stuttgart, 1973

---

35 See Goehr, *The Quest for Voice* – which, though, does not take account of Schlegel, Schelling and the other early Romantics – and Bowie, 'Adorno, Heidegger'.

3

The profession of music

JOHN RINK

This chapter explores a rich seam within music's economic and social history during the first half of the nineteenth century. Successive political and economic developments and demographic responses to them impacted heavily on musical culture, causing an exponential increase in the number of public concerts as well as rapid expansion in the worlds of music publishing, music journalism, music teaching, and instrument manufacture and sales. New musical professions sprang up as a largely urban music-consuming public voracious in appetite but variably refined in taste exerted growing financial power. Established professions either evolved in reaction to intense market pressures or disappeared entirely.

Certain obstacles make it difficult to chart the profession of music – or, more accurately, the professions of music – from 1800 to 1850. One is the sheer diversity of professional activities, which prohibits detailed investigation and watertight conclusions across the board. Another is the diversity of centres in which they were practised, ranging from capital cities to provincial locations in any number of different countries. A third is the diversity of consumers at the time – above all, the 'middle class', a socially disparate group with complex hierarchies of status and taste that defy concise summary. My approach is therefore highly selective, offering case-study illustrations drawn from a broad spectrum of professions, geographic locations and consumers, rather than a comprehensive coverage doomed from the start. Although eclectic, my strategy at least reflects the lack of cohesion within the profession of music itself during this period.

The chapter has two parts. The first paves the way for a survey of the principal professions by defining such contexts as the music profession before 1800, political and demographic developments early in the century (including the consolidation of the middle class and the establishment of key centres of activity), and the structure of concert life. The second part presents a catalogue of professions, including composers, solo instrumentalists, singers, conductors, orchestral and chamber musicians, church musicians, instrument makers, publishers, music journalists, teachers and scholars. The role of the amateur will also be addressed.

PART I CONTEXTS

The music profession before 1800

The lives of most professional musicians in the eighteenth century did not correspond to modern norms. Many earned income from non-musical pursuits, especially in the provinces; hence Cyril Ehrlich's distinction between music professionals – those 'essentially dependent upon the practice of music for their livelihood' – and semi-professionals who found it even harder to earn a steady income from music. Ehrlich notes that the late eighteenth-century music profession 'embraced extremes of fame and obscurity, genius and mediocrity, mobility and quiescence'[1] – as remains characteristic of the profession today.

Many of the musical professions that flourished in the nineteenth century had their origins in the Classical era, particularly in the most sophisticated centres of musical culture, London and Vienna. As the home of the Industrial Revolution, late eighteenth-century Britain offered the fruits of sustained economic growth to its 2,000 or so professional musicians, as well as those in associated occupations (including copyists and paper-rulers). Musicians benefited in particular from 'a slow, cumulative expansion in employment opportunities, ranging from fairly stable jobs in theatres and subscription concerts to a few days at a provincial festival, occasional professional "stiffening" of amateur groups' and participation in ad hoc bands. Dominated by foreigners (whose training and skills were generally superior), the profession in late eighteenth-century London embraced Jewish families and women, to whom most other occupations were closed. But the risks of poverty were severe, despite the (limited) protection of the Society of Musicians, established in 1738 'for the Support of Decayed Musicians or their Families', and the New Musical Fund, founded in 1786, to which semi-professionals from the provinces could subscribe (Ehrlich, *Music*, pp. 1–29 *passim*). Another eighteenth-century institution – the Concert of Ancient Music, founded in London in 1776, with royal patronage conferred in 1785 – restricted its subscription concerts to the highest social echelons. An important presence for many years, its influence on London's musical life would wane as the market evolved and its specialist repertory became part of the canon.

1 C. Ehrlich, *The Music Profession in Britain since the Eighteenth Century: A Social History* (Oxford, 1985), pp. 2, 44, 49.

In the 1790s, Vienna experienced a similar increase in the number of independent musicians whose primary source of income was teaching. Public concerts grew more frequent, and additional performing opportunities arose in the salons of upper middle-class merchants, bankers and civil servants. But as yet the latter patrons played a relatively small role within Vienna's high musical culture, which was monopolised by an aristocracy espousing new 'values of musical seriousness and learnedness' and supporting the freelance activities of only a few select musicians (Beethoven included).[2] The 'star system' that emerged would dominate European musical life in general for years to come, although the aristocratic patronage behind it would gradually be eclipsed by that of middle-class consumers.

Political and demographic developments

It is beyond the scope of this chapter to summarise fifty years of political history in all the countries that feature in it, ranging from the United States to Russia. But one event – the storming of the Bastille on 14 July 1789 – had especially far-reaching repercussions throughout the period. Among other things, it led to the reign of Napoleon in France, the Napoleonic Wars and the collapse of the Holy Roman Empire, events which precipitated not only a radical realignment of the social hierarchy, especially in France, but also successive population displacements towards Europe's key urban centres. Economic migration encouraged similar gravitation to capital cities, with a significant impact on social structures and culture in general. Musical life flourished in particular from 1815 to 1848, a period of relative political stability and economic growth throughout most of Europe and America. A steady rise in the standard of living benefited the rapidly expanding middle class, which acquired unprecedented financial clout as well as increased leisure time to pursue the vast range of entertainments on offer in the major cities.

That there was no one socially and aesthetically homogeneous 'middle class' must be stressed. William Weber has identified two principal strata within the sprawling middle-class populations of London, Paris and Vienna, one of which included 'shopkeepers, clerks and lower-level professionals', while a wealthier group constituted a 'second elite' often overlapping in taste and cultural aspiration with an aristocracy that continued for some time to hold considerable sway over musical life. Although the shift in cultural activity from court to city was dramatic, royal patronage still provided income to performers appearing at palaces from Brighton to St Petersburg, and it also helped to draw crowds in

---

2 T. DeNora, *Beethoven and the Construction of Genius: Musical Politics in Vienna, 1792–1803* (Berkeley and Los Angeles, 1995), pp. 18, 58.

London and elsewhere. But the most important patrons in the first half of the century came from the middle class, which comprised numerous 'taste-publics' with distinct cultural orientations ranging from low to high, and occupying varying positions on the social ladder.[3]

Vienna's musical culture, for instance, grew less tied to its aristocracy and more dependent on 'a rapidly growing class of officials, products of the academic reforms of the later eighteenth century, who became the carriers of a [quite separate] bourgeois culture . . . And it was mostly this relatively small minority that favoured what is usually referred to as art music.'[4] Of course, music was consumed by other social groups as well, and in such disparate venues as theatres, restaurants, ballrooms and churches. But the domination of aristocratic and bureaucratic members of the taste-defining stratum played a significant role in ensuring Vienna's status as 'leading musical city in Europe' for the first two decades of the century, after which the combined forces of conservatism and trivialisation hastened its descent from pre-eminence, as the waltz 'became not only big business but to all intents and purposes the popular identification mark of a city passionately dedicated to maintaining the status quo' (Wiesmann, pp. 88, 104).

Its leading position was seized by Paris in the 1820s and 1830s, while London's own cultural importance grew ever more considerable as its population expanded from about 1 million in 1800 to 2.5 million in 1851, by which time 'it was the financial and commercial capital of an immeasurably rich world empire'.[5] Ehrlich estimates that in 1840, approximately 7,000 musicians were working in Britain among a total population of 27 million (*Music*, p. 51), and many of these were based in London, which offered its 'destitute majority' the informal musical pleasures to be found on the streets and in taverns, and its wealthier citizens a host of musical entertainments ranging 'from tawdry mediocrity, vigorously marketed, to the highest quality, appealing only to a limited audience' (Sachs, p. 201). But the typical concert price of half a guinea in *c.* 1800 'was beyond the reach of most people, who were lucky to have an income of £50 a year', and even the middle class, with an income of £150 or more, found concert-going expensive.[6] London's Italian Opera attracted an especially elite audience in the short social season, as did the Concert of Ancient Music and the Philharmonic Society (founded in 1813). In

---

3 W. Weber, *Music and the Middle Class: The Social Structure of Concert Life in London, Paris and Vienna* (London, 1975), pp. 7, 8, 10, 11. See chapter 9 for fuller discussion of this social-historical background.

4 S. Wiesmann, 'Vienna: Bastion of Conservatism', in A. Ringer (ed.), *The Early Romantic Era* (London and Basingstoke, 1990), p. 85.

5 J. Sachs, 'London: The Professionalization of Music', in Ringer (ed.), *The Early Romantic Era*, p. 201.

6 Ibid., p. 202. Weber (*Music*, p. 23) claims that less prosperous families in Vienna, London and Paris generally spent about 1 per cent of their income on entertainment, while more prosperous ones spent roughly 2 per cent.

contrast, a 'broad spectrum of humanity ranging from the educated to prostitutes and thieves' frequented the patent theatres at Drury Lane and Covent Garden (Sachs, pp. 202, 203). Reserved seats were an important innovation in 1830s London, fostering greater social discrimination while enabling promoters to charge higher prices.

By then Paris had established itself as 'capital of the nineteenth century' (Walter Benjamin). A mecca for composers and performers alike, Paris catered to a wide variety of musical tastes, offering such diverse entertainments as satirical comedies at boulevard theatres, featuring songs accompanied by a few players; melodrama and pantomime, which 'often employed elaborate and original musical accompaniments'; and opera at 'the most distinguished venues'. At the grandest theatre of all – the Opéra – cheap seats at 2 francs could in principle be afforded by the lower middle class, but it remained almost as exclusive as the Théâtre-Italien by virtue of restrictive booking practices. The remarkable administrator Louis Véron fought against lowering ticket prices to avoid attracting (as he put it) 'the lower classes'.[7]

Opera in Italy conformed to a similar social pecking order throughout a vast network of opera houses which contrasted with the centralised cultural infrastructures of other European countries. John Rosselli observes that for many years the 'layout of the theatre auditorium itself was a means of displaying the [social] hierarchy's upper sections', whereas the new opera houses built in Italy in the 1840s were designed for a 'more popular audience than the old royal or aristocratic theatres – though "popular" still meant artisans, shopkeepers, commercial travellers and clerical workers rather than labourers or peasants'.[8] Even if limited in scope, this popularisation reflects a Europe-wide expansion of audiences from the 1830s onwards, to the point that in London the aristocratic Concert of Ancient Music ceased to exist in 1848, while in 1841 the Philharmonic Society began selling tickets to the general public. The middle class's hold on concert life grew ever tighter at this time.

The structure of concert life

Three main types of concert flourished during the first half of the century: those run by institutions, that is, established organisations of (mostly) professional performers, generally on a subscription basis; concerts for the benefit of individual promoters; and concerts given by amateur musical organisations. Together these served various purposes: 'economic gain, professional recognition, charity fund-raising, celebration of events, product publicity, and indeed

---

7 R. Locke, 'Paris: Centre of Intellectual Ferment', in Ringer (ed.), *The Early Romantic Era*, pp. 43, 46.
8 J. Rosselli, 'Italy: The Centrality of Opera', in Ringer (ed.), *The Early Romantic Era*, pp. 177, 195.

simple entertainment'. Sponsorship was equally diverse: 'individual musicians, formal and informal groups of performers, cultural societies, music magazines, charity organisations, theatres, and music publishers', as well as 'government agencies, pension organisations, and even a few fledgling concert managers' (Weber, pp. 17–18). Concerts tended to be either 'popular' in orientation, with the spotlight on instrumental and vocal virtuosity and so-called salon music, or 'classical', featuring the increasingly canonic symphonies, overtures and chamber music of composers like Haydn, Mozart and Beethoven. Other concerts promoted 'ancient' (mainly Baroque) repertory, and these, along with classical concerts, occupied the 'high art' or 'serious music' end of a spectrum which in fact was dominated by popular musical events. Alongside this teeming concert life was the world of opera, not to mention domestic music-making, which, as we shall see in Part II, played a central role in the profession-alisation of music throughout the period.

Institutional concerts

The numerous musical institutions of London and Paris mounted subscription concerts which on the whole attracted high-brow audiences. One of the most important, the Philharmonic Society in London, assembled the first profes-sional orchestra in Europe, offering remuneration to players from 1815 in response to the competition of a rival band. Although for many years it had sufficient resources to engage the finest musicians, declining audiences in the 1840s led to wage cuts, redundancies and the decision to stop commissioning new pieces.[9] The eight concerts performed each season followed a similar pattern focused on the works of Haydn, Mozart and Beethoven as well as 'new-comers' like Mendelssohn. The Concert of Ancient Music remained wedded to Handel until the bitter end, although it embraced Classical repertory after 1826 partly in recognition of the growing canon. As for Paris, its Société des Concerts du Conservatoire – founded in 1828 by François-Antoine Habeneck, a keen champion of Haydn, Mozart and Beethoven as well as Cherubini – rapidly became 'the most modern of all concert organisations in Europe', with 'strictly professional management and performing practices [that] made its orchestra the best anywhere' (Weber, p. 69). But the Concerts du Conservatoire was only one of the series of subscription concerts launched in Paris during the 1820s and 1830s which provided permanent or freelance employment for orchestral players. Others included L'Athénée musicale (1829–32) and Fétis's Concerts historiques (1832–3).

---

9 Sachs, 'London', pp. 211, 229. According to Weber (*Music*, p. 65), subscriptions reached a low of 310 in 1842, with a normal level of 650.

The role of institutions in the concert life of other European cities was also significant – a mark, no doubt, of economic success as well as cultural sophistication. For example, Berlin's Singakademie (founded in 1791) presented four subscription concerts each year featuring new works as well as the first nineteenth-century performances of Bach's Passions and B minor Mass. The numerous concert societies founded in early nineteenth-century Warsaw – including the Resursa Muzyczna, the Resursa Kupiecka and its offshoot the Nowa Resursa – contributed to a small but lively musical culture which flourished particularly between 1815 and 1830.[10]

Benefit concerts

Concerts became genuinely public only after about 1800, when benefit concerts began to proliferate. Although some operated on a subscription basis, most benefits were one-off events promoted not by institutions but by individual organisers for their own financial gain and that of the other participants. Their eclectic programmes – typically several hours long – consisted of instrumental and vocal solos interspersed with ensemble pieces, and they needed to appeal to as wide an audience as possible in order to cover the considerable costs of hiring, heating and lighting a hall; paying copyists, performers and attendants; and preparing posters and press advertisements, along with other expenses. All of this served to dictate the prevailing repertory, which generally had to be unchallenging and entertaining, even titillating, and was not really meant to last. In London, the popularity of benefit concerts peaked in the 1830s, with up to seventy in the brief social season, while the 1840s saw their decline in the face of increased repertorial and professional specialisation. Innovations around this time included Liszt's 'recitals' in 1840, which encouraged greater coherence in concert programmes, and Moscheles's 'historical concerts', at which 'the harpsichord reappeared after long obscurity and "ancient" was at last united with "modern"' (Sachs, pp. 219, 226). In their heyday, benefit concerts took place in both the major cities and the provinces, often involving touring virtuosos in collaboration with local musicians. One sponsored in Truro in 1818 by 'Mrs White', a singer, featured a 'greater number of performers than has been usual upon similar occasions, and a judicious, *yet short*, selection, [to] insure satisfaction to the company'.[11] Concerts promoted by individuals but on a more modest scale than full-blown benefits occurred

10 W. Smialek, *Ignacy Feliks Dobrzyński and Musical Life in Nineteenth-Century Poland* (Lewiston, N.Y., 1991), pp. 13–15.
11 *West Briton*, 11 April 1818, quoted in R. McGrady, *Music and Musicians in Early Nineteenth-Century Cornwall: The World of Joseph Emidy – Slave, Violinist and Composer* (Exeter, 1991), p. 75.

with frequency, typically in a smaller hall and without the participation of a full orchestra. Such an event was called a *soirée* or *matinée musicale*, or, in Germany, *musikalische Akademie*.

Salons and parties

Salons took place up and down the social ladder throughout Europe, but the most prestigious were held at the homes of upper middle-class families, many of them Jewish. Hosted by the lady of the house, they often featured extended musical performances amounting to formal concerts in which new solo or ensemble works – possibly of the lightweight nature denoted by the problematic term 'salon music', but more frequently of real compositional substance – could be unveiled in relative privacy before a supportive yet discerning audience. Older repertory was also performed, including such large-scale pieces as oratorios by Handel and operas by Mozart. Celebrated virtuosos appeared at the most glittering salons, sometimes 'out of friendship for the host'[12] or, at least in Paris, in preference to truly public concert engagements. Performers derived material advantages from salon appearances, for instance by gaining pupils or by indebting their hosts to attendance at their own annual benefit concerts. However, more immediate financial rewards could be obtained by performing at private parties, which, paying up to 25 guineas in London, were highly lucrative, especially for 'favoured performers' who made the 'rounds of the mansions, playing at as many as three parties a night'.[13]

Opera

Although English and German opera had its place in the first half of the nineteenth century, the operatic scene was entirely dominated by France and Italy (see chapter 4 for fuller discussion). Paris was the unrivalled centre, boasting numerous opera houses of distinction and a musical culture in which opera's influence was universally felt. From the artistic vision and marketing instincts of Véron emerged the long, brilliant and carefully rehearsed productions of French grand opera, which greatly expanded the dramatic and musical role of the chorus and generally offered no fewer than five major vocal parts. According to Locke (pp. 53, 54), 'the obvious emphasis on display, on conspicuous consumption, on the coordination of high individual achievement into a greater enterprise – or at least a more impressive "product" – clearly marks French

---

12 C.-H. Mahling, 'Berlin: "Music in the Air"', in Ringer (ed.), *The Early Romantic Era*, p. 128.
13 Sachs, 'London', p. 219. A more typical fee around 1830 was 3 guineas for a dinner party performance, while soloists at private concerts earned 5 guineas (Ehrlich, *Music*, p. 41).

grand opera as a prime cultural expression of the entrepreneurial and professional classes that profited so much from the July Monarchy'. In Italy, where
opera was more widely dispersed, the proliferation of theatres and seasons from
the 1820s onwards led to an 'unrelenting' rhythm of productions and, eventually, a vast industry of impresarios, singers and agents (Rosselli, pp. 176, 177).
Italian singers were avidly sought after throughout Europe, receiving some of
the highest fees of any musicians for their appearances on the operatic stage, in
benefit concerts and in other performances like those at provincial festivals.

Festivals

Many festivals were held in the first half of the nineteenth century in associa-
tion with societies to commemorate such composers as Handel, Mozart and
Beethoven. In Vienna, for instance, annual festivals celebrating Handel's and
Haydn's oratorios took place from 1812 onwards, when the Gesellschaft der
Musikfreunde was founded as part of a mission to educate the middle classes.
These public events – held in Vienna's largest hall and designed to 'offset the
prevailing fashion for vocal and instrumental virtuosity' – were 'large-scale cultural manifestations in which the educated bourgeoisie that formed the
nucleus of the state bureaucracy took special pride' (Wiesmann, p. 97).
Festivals throughout Europe typically engaged a distinguished guest conductor, while those in the provinces tended in addition to import leading singers
and professional players from the cities. Oratorios dominated, but other repertory also featured. For instance, a festival in Truro in September 1806 included
three sacred concerts, a performance of Handel's *Messiah* (in Mozart's version)
and several 'Grand Miscellaneous Concerts' including 'Symphonies, Songs,
Solos, and Concertos, by most of the principal performers; and some of the
most favorite Glees'.[14]

Promenades and 'cheap' concerts

The concerts described thus far primarily appealed to the wealthier members of
the middle class, but plenty of opportunities existed for the lower middle-class
public to partake of music, especially after 1830. What Weber calls 'low-status'
concerts were held in cafés, restaurants, taverns, parks, dance halls, cultural
societies and churches, including ones given by amateur orchestras (some
under professional management) and amateur choral societies (Weber, pp. 85,
86). In Paris, orchestral entertainment was provided year-round at the

---

14 *Royal Cornwall Gazette*, quoted in McGrady, *Music and Musicians*, p. 51.

Concerts Valentino (1837–41) and Philippe Musard's promenade concerts or 'balls', which members of the lower middle class and even the working class could attend, thanks to cheap, plentiful tickets. In London, the public gardens of Vauxhall, Cremorne and the Eagle Tavern offered broad, socially mixed audiences a host of musical entertainments including military bands, concerts (often of dance music), operas and concerto performances. The Promenade Concerts à la Musard began in London in 1838 as 'off-season, low-brow events serving popular music – quadrilles, waltzes, opera pot-pourris etc. – with food and drink to an audience seated at tables' (Sachs, p. 226). Louis Jullien was instrumental in extending London's concert life to the lower middle classes: his Concerts d'Hiver, held from 1841 to 1859 at various theatres, succeeded in capturing the 'one-shilling public', as did his *concerts monstres* at the Royal Zoological Gardens in 1845 (Ehrlich, *Music*, p. 60). In Vienna, Strauss and Lanner were universally revered for their waltzes, while in Berlin, private (or 'salon') orchestras played to wide audiences in concert halls, restaurants and open-air venues, charging as little as 2.5 Groschen as against 1 Thaler for high-brow Kapelle concerts (Mahling, p. 134). The standard of musicianship was excellent, as indeed in Jullien's Concerts d'Hiver.

PART II THE PROFESSIONS

The nature of professional life

Ehrlich warns against applying 'modern stereotypes of "professionalism", in the sense of an institutionalized pride of calling and allegiance to idealized codes of practice', to the lives of musicians around 1800. At that time there were no 'generally acknowledged forms of training, technical accomplishment, promotion, and hierarchy, for music was long to remain a profession singularly lacking firm career lines of accreditation and advancement' (Ehrlich, *Music*, p. 31). Of course, the growing availability of conservatory training during the first half of the century would significantly hasten music's professionalisation, as would the proliferation of tutors, journals and other publications which secured greater prominence and cultural distinction for the profession. These will all be discussed in due course, but first it is important to note the substantial risks faced by professional musicians in an increasingly competitive marketplace, which conferred new freedoms but also caused greater vulnerability. Musicians were forced into mercenary behaviour, not least because their income was 'highly seasonal and subject to fluctuations in the economy, changes in fashion, and political events'. Illness and loss of technique were constant threats, and there was little or no assistance from unions and professional associations, nor the degree of legal protection available today. Nevertheless, composers, performers and teachers alike could 'cross frontiers of wealth and class' closed to other occupations, with the possibility of 'more permanent social elevation' (Ehrlich, *Music*, pp. 18, 31, 32). For those who made it to the top, the social and financial rewards were considerable.

Composers

Until late in the period, composers tended to earn their living from a range of professional activities – especially performance and teaching – rather than composition alone. Gradually, however, the profession of composer took on a more individual identity, both for aesthetic reasons and in response to changes in performing practices. From the late 1830s onwards, most performers stopped writing their own music (which had traditionally been expected of keyboard and string soloists among others), and instead turned their attention to the 'interpretation' of works in the emerging canon. At the same time, composition moved on to a higher aesthetic plane largely through the influence of Beethoven, whose unrivalled genius and artistic legacy set a standard to which generations of composers would aspire.

At the other end of the spectrum, however, were the innumerable pieces churned out for popular consumption, whether in the 'low-status' concerts described above, in private homes or elsewhere. There was little concern for posterity in producing such music: the profit motive held sway, with an inevitable effect on quality and quantity. It would be wrong to suggest that 'serious' composers had no interest in financial gain (some were shrewd businessmen, even sharp operators), but compositional ethics assumed greater importance in guiding their creative activity, as did a heightened sense of their place in history. A culture of ephemerality gave way to one of permanence, attaching particular value to 'works' while denying the ongoing creative role of performance in defining musical content. 'Works' were meant to last longer than the one season for which much virtuoso repertory earlier in the century was intended. 'Works' were artistic statements, not mere commodities.

Of course, such lofty ideals were by no means universally shared, nor were most compositions from the period admitted to the canon. This was partly due to the speed with which some music was produced. For instance, a composer in Italy

> might contract in June . . . to write an opera for the forthcoming Carnival season, compose an intervening opera for the autumn season, receive Act 1 of

the libretto for the Carnival opera (if it was on time) in early November, compose the last act in the second half of December as rehearsals went on, and accompany the first performance from the keyboard on 26 December – all this in three different towns, widely separated, with much correspondence and horse-drawn travel in between, not to mention delays and mishaps...

(Rosselli, pp. 176–7)

Conditions were better in Paris, where excellent resources (including singers, orchestral players and designers) and the prospect of lucrative performance royalties and publication fees for both complete scores and excerpts seduced composers of all abilities into writing operas. After the Restoration, French composers also devoted themselves in earnest to sacred music but generally not to the principal orchestral genres, although Berlioz is an obvious exception. In France as elsewhere, very few professional composers were women, and (according to Katharine Ellis) these tended to concentrate on salon pieces, romances and other 'lesser' genres rather than 'conform to the virtuoso-composer paradigm' deemed suitable only for men. One example was Loïsa Puget, who wrote 'over three hundred romances, many of which she sang herself; for the piano, her counterpart was Joséphine Martin, who composed a host of salon pieces that were always warmly welcomed in the press'.[15]

For decades the only composers in Britain of international stature were foreign, and that prompted the founding of the Society of British Musicians in 1834 for 'the advancement of native talent in composition and performance'. It attracted some 250 members by 1836 but remained active only until 1865. William Sterndale Bennett, an early graduate of the Royal Academy of Music, was the most distinguished composer to emerge from England during the period, although his creativity was largely confined to a short phase in his youth, when he produced several major orchestral works each year. He devoted the bulk of his career to teaching, performing and administration, becoming Principal of the Royal Academy of Music in 1866.

Renowned composers presided over other leading European conservatories, for instance Cherubini in Paris and Mendelssohn in Leipzig. Józef Elsner served as rector of two educational institutions in Warsaw, in addition to his leading role in Warsaw's musical life more generally. Schumann dedicated himself not only to teaching but also to criticism and journalism, as of course did Berlioz, who also held a post as assistant librarian at the Paris Conservatoire. Others channelled their energies into such disparate activities as conducting, music publishing and instrument manufacture, alongside their work as composers.

15 K. Ellis, 'Female Pianists and Their Male Critics in Nineteenth-Century Paris', *Journal of the American Musicological Society*, 50 (1997), pp. 357–8.

Solo instrumentalists

Virtuoso pianists and singers monopolised Europe's concert platforms during this period, although solo violinists – especially Paganini – also reigned supreme. The first half of the century witnessed an inexorable rise in keyboard virtuosity, which was facilitated by developments in piano design and driven by an insatiable demand on the part of audiences. A distinct compositional style evolved at this time in the music of composer-pianists; known as the *stile brillante*, it thrived on an opposition between bravura display and lyrical thematicism (often operatic in inspiration), normally manifested in a highly sectional construction leading to the peak of virtuosity towards the end. The brilliant style prevailed not only in the innumerable opera fantasies, concertos, rondos and sets of variations produced by composer-pianists (who played mostly their own music, as indicated above), but also in the improvisations that typically ended their concert programmes. Improvising on themes given by members of the public was one way of manipulating audience reaction; another was planting 'claqueurs' in halls. There was a financial imperative to do so, given the cut-throat competition above all in Paris, the capital of virtuoso pianism throughout the 1820s and 1830s.

Earlier in the century Vienna had dominated the piano 'scene', with such leading performers as Beethoven, Ries, Hummel and Moscheles. By 1830 or so, however, it had lost the edge to Paris, to which keyboard virtuosos flocked each year 'like swarms of locusts' (Heine). The leading lights included Dussek, Steibelt, Hummel, Kalkbrenner, Herz, Pixis, Liszt, Thalberg and Chopin, of whom the last three were particularly prominent. Nevertheless, these three 'differed so strikingly in their attitudes towards public acclaim and the concert stage that a sketch of their Parisian careers amounts almost to a panorama of the options and limitations that the city presented to the serious instrumentalist' (Locke, p. 66). While Chopin earned his living by composing and teaching, having shunned a virtuoso career after a series of disillusioning concerts in Paris from 1832 to 1835, Liszt and Thalberg engaged in a public rivalry made all the more intense by the latter's assimilation into aristocratic circles as against Liszt's struggle for acceptance. Both enjoyed huge successes in the concert hall, however. Ellis notes that a typical review of Thalberg's or Liszt's playing dwells on 'the element of conquest', a common trope indicating a 'quasi-sexual possession of the audience' and the 'issues of control' implicit in male-dominated pianism more generally ('Female', pp. 356, 357). But female pianists also made a place for themselves, especially during a 'reign of the women' (*Le Ménestrel*) in mid-1840s Paris which saw the development of specialisms in chamber music, Classical (pre-Beethovenian) sonatas and concertos, and early music. Women played an important role in canon formation with their interpretations of music by other composers (usually men); often 'unintrusive' in nature, such interpretations 'ensured that the works themselves remained the focus of attention' rather than the playing in its own right ('Female', pp. 359, 379, 384). One result of the new emphasis on interpretation and the development of the canon was the virtual disappearance of public improvisation after about 1840; another was a heightened sensitivity on the part of musicians and critics alike to stylistic 'appropriateness' in performance.

London too succumbed to the cult of virtuosity during its heyday. Soloists with the Philharmonic Society in the 1820s and 1830s included the pianists Liszt, Mendelssohn, Hummel, Moscheles and Maria Szymanowska, as well as the violinist De Bériot. Such musicians typically played their own solo concertos, a genre initially banned by the Society in favour of less virtuoso repertory. For many years the remuneration for these performances was low: in 1823, for instance, the Philharmonic Society offered Moscheles 10 guineas, but observed that 'no other resident piano player has hitherto received any remuneration for his performance'.[16] It was not until Paganini that instrumentalists started receiving the high sums routinely paid to leading singers. Paganini's successes in London were undeniably brilliant. He charged 'double the usual prices' and gave an 'unprecedented number of concerts' (twenty-seven in 1831) in the 3,300-seat opera house, transforming 'concert life in London, as everywhere, by raising the expectations of audiences' (Sachs, p. 219). His fifteen concerts at the King's Theatre in 1831 apparently brought in £9,000 (of which the manager Laporte 'allegedly took £4,142, out of which he was supposed to pay the orchestra'), while he received a colossal fee of £500 for a performance in Dublin (Ehrlich, *Music*, p. 46). There were also 'purely commercial spin-offs' in London and elsewhere, including Vienna, where dishes, clothing and hairstyles were named after Paganini, 'whose portrait also appeared on medals, jewellery boxes and walking-sticks' (Wiesmann, p. 97). For most violin and piano virtuosos, however, professional life was fraught with difficulty, and the bulk earned at least part of their living by teaching and other activities.

Other leading solo instruments included clarinet, horn and bassoon. Spohr collaborated with the clarinettist Simon Hermstedt, for whom he composed four clarinet concertos (the first requiring seven new keys on his instrument), and both Weber and Mendelssohn wrote works for Heinrich Baermann, a celebrated clarinet player who toured widely from 1808 to 1832. Frédéric Duvernoy joined the Opéra orchestra in 1796 and became its solo horn in 1799, in which capacity his playing was often prominently billed; he later served as first horn in

---

16 Philharmonic Society Archive Directors' Meetings, 23 March 1823, quoted in Ehrlich, *Music*, p. 46.

the imperial chapel until the 1830 Revolution. As for bassoonists, noted players included Georg Friedrich Brandt, for whom Weber composed a concerto and rondo, and the Belgian Friedrich Baumann, whom Jullien imported to Britain.

Singers

As noted above, Italian singers – among others, Angelica Catalani, Giulia Grisi, Luigi Lablache, Giuditta Pasta and Giovanna Battista Rubini – were in great demand during the first half of the century, and the best commanded enormous fees. Singers at the Italian opera in London sometimes earned in excess of £5,000 per annum,[17] in addition to income from concerts, private functions and festivals. Those in the English opera at Covent Garden, Drury Lane and smaller theatres – for instance, Elizabeth Billington, John Braham and Nancy Storace – received salaries close to those of their Italian counterparts but gave more performances each season (Sachs, p. 205). According to Ehrlich, the noted mezzo-soprano Maria Malibran was paid £2,000 for fifteen appearances at the Drury Lane Theatre in 1833, but two years later received approximately £3,463 for nineteen nights plus seven extra performances. Such fees, if accurate,[18] seem astronomical when compared to average incomes and the fees earned by instrumentalists. Italy itself literally paid the price of its singers' celebrity, with the rising costs of opera from the late 1820s attributable to increases in their fees (which accounted for about half of total production costs). Salary cuts occurred, however, at the time of the 1848 Revolution, although not without protest (Rosselli, pp. 181, 193).

Just as the timbre of pianos, violins and other instruments developed during the period partly in order to fill the larger concert halls needed for more sizeable audiences, the vocal types used in Italian opera experienced something of an evolution. Although lyric tenors appeared on stage well into the 1820s even as the castrato's importance declined, new prominence was given to the prima donna, generally a soprano. The *tenore di forza* (dramatic tenor) had come into fashion by the 1830s (one of them, the French tenor Gilbert-Louis Duprez, could sing a high C in chest voice 'to devastating effect'), while basses such as Lablache and Filippo Galli were given more rapid, florid parts (Rosselli, pp. 188, 189). Rosselli notes that the rise of repertory opera from the mid-1840s meant that 'singers were expected to have a repertory they could sing at short notice. In many theatres this probably meant performances of deteriorating quality: a day's rehearsal or none, with the prompter kept busy' (p. 195).

17 Catalani allegedly received £5,250 for a seven-month season in 1808, performing twice a week (Ehrlich, *Music*, p. 45).

18 Ehrlich (*Music*, p. 41) comments that 'reliable information on musicians' fees was, like the "trade" price of pianos, customarily obscured by coy reticence'. Exaggeration also occurred, for obvious reasons.

Quality was also threatened by the excessive ornamentation that singers lavished on their arias until late in the period – and not just those from contemporary Italian operas. Unlike pianists and violinists, singers generally did not compose their own works, instead exerting their creative individuality by means of improvised (or quasi-improvised) embellishments. Those executed with skill and discretion earned high praise from discriminating listeners, while singers pandering to bravura-mad audiences were accused of bad taste and even artistic 'abuse'.[19] Clive Brown observes that 'by the 1830s and 1840s a widespread prejudice was developing against the addition of ornaments where the composer had not indicated them', although arias like 'Una voce poco fa' from Rossini's *Il barbiere di Siviglia* continued to be embellished until well into the twentieth century (Brown, pp. 419, 423). A host of performance tutors (for instance, Manuel García's *Traité complet de l'art du chant* of 1840) appeared during the period to instruct singers of varying abilities on ornamentation, as well as rubato, vibrato and other techniques.

The singing profession embraced not only the leading Italians but also such stars as Pauline Viardot-García and Jenny Lind, the latter of whom caused a sensation in Europe and America, where she was vigorously marketed as the 'Swedish Nightingale' by P. T. Barnum in extensive tours from 1850. The pyramid supporting this pinnacle included less distinguished soloists as well as paid singers in opera choruses and church choirs. From early in the period, French operas – for instance, Spontini's *Fernand Cortez* (1809; revised 1817) – featured larger and dramatically more important choruses (as noted earlier), but so too did Italian and German operas, including Beethoven's *Fidelio* and Weber's *Der Freischütz*. In London, the Concert of Ancient Music had a professional choir of up to fifty singers, in which boys from the choirs of Westminster Abbey and the Chapel Royal initially sang the soprano parts (later to be replaced by women). According to Sachs, however, boys from St Paul's Cathedral 'spent most of their time singing in fashionable concerts' during the first decade or so of the century (Sachs, pp. 208, 209). In 1809, Zelter founded a male chorus (Liedertafel) in Berlin, the twenty to twenty-five amateur members of which belonged to the Singakademie and worked in the sciences, arts and upper echelons of the civil service. Like the many other choral societies burgeoning throughout Europe at the time, this group provided valuable custom to the teaching profession.

Brief comment is warranted on those who ran the 'opera industry' in general. Opera managers throughout Europe faced both commercial pressures and constant government interference, yet certain individuals succeeded in

---

19 See Anton Reicha's comments in C. Brown, *Classical and Romantic Performing Practice 1750–1900* (Oxford, 1999), pp. 418, 420.

reversing an opera house's ill fortunes or taking it to new heights. The most brilliant was Véron at the Opéra in Paris, while from 1828 Pierre Laporte established administrative order and ended a legacy of bankruptcy at the King's Theatre in London. His tenure was nevertheless controversial. Laporte's first music director, Nicolas Bochsa, precipitated a mass resignation of the orchestra in 1829 by attempting to restrict players' outside engagements (for instance, at the Philharmonic Society), while Laporte himself tried to limit the concert performances of his Italian opera singers to the concert hall of the King's Theatre. As for opera in Italy, Rosselli notes that most impresarios at the time were 'bazaar traders in outlook' concerned 'at best with quality and punctuality of execution – singers were "goods" and opera was a "product"' (Rosselli, p. 182).

Conductors

The conducting profession experienced more fundamental change during the period than those of any other performing musicians, not least because rapidly expanding orchestras required greater directorial control. Until well into the century, most orchestras were conducted either from the keyboard or, with increasing frequency, by the principal violinist, who kept time with his bow by playing, gesturing or tapping a stand. Following on from eighteenth-century practice, some conductors used rolls of paper to maintain the ensemble (for instance, Spohr in 1809), but gradually baton conducting became more widespread, especially in Germany, with early efforts on the part of Spontini (conducting the Berlin opera) and Weber (in Dresden). Moscheles and Mendelssohn had a positive impact on orchestral standards in 1830s London partly by using a baton (a 'white stick' in the latter's case), as well as by more rigorous rehearsal techniques.

Conducting in London had long been amateurish in the sense of both standards and, in some cases, remuneration. At the Philharmonic Society, for instance, conductors, as 'gentlemen', received no payment for many years, and the musical results were often wanting. Spohr complained that its orchestra in 1820 was much too large and spread out to achieve a proper ensemble, and after a Philharmonic concert in 1844, the *Musical World* observed that a pianist playing Chopin's first concerto was 'fettered by the discordant beatings of no less than three different individuals, viz. – Sir George Smart, who wielded the baton – Mr Loder, the leader of the evening – and Mr T. Cooke, *not* the leader of the evening. These gentlemen were all beating different times.'[20]

20 Quoted in Ehrlich, *Music*, p. 38.

Ehrlich notes, however, that this concert occurred late in Smart's distinguished (if technically deficient) career, during which he conducted some 1,500
concerts and taught hundreds of students, including professionals. Smart was
commercially astute and amassed great wealth: for instance, his three-year contract at Covent Garden, signed in 1826, guaranteed a minimum annual income
of £1,000, and between 1832 and 1861 he earned commissions from piano
manufacturers totalling over £1,000 (*Music*, pp. 40, 42). He also served as director of many music festivals, among them the 1836 Liverpool Festival, where he
conducted the English première of Mendelssohn's *St Paul*, while at a
Westminster Abbey Festival in 1834 he was reported to have used a baton,
rather than conduct from the piano or organ (his normal practice). This may
reflect the influence of the German opera companies that visited London in the
early 1830s, which helped to raise standards, as indeed did the conducting of
Michael Costa, who served as *maestro al piano* at the King's Theatre from 1830
but later wielded an authoritative baton over the Italian Opera and the
Philharmonic Society, where he was appointed permanent conductor in 1846.
Costa did more than any other person to 'professionalise' conducting in
London.

For many years the standard of conducting in Paris was much higher than in
London. Not only did such eminent musicians as Méhul and Cherubini carefully coach the Conservatoire orchestra in rehearsal, but for each of the later
Concerts du Conservatoire, Habeneck – a skilled violinist who usually conducted with his bow and from the first violin part – held at least two rehearsals
at which attendance was obligatory. He achieved an unprecedented level of
professionalism in the Opéra orchestra, which he led from 1817 and eventually
conducted as *premier chef*, and at the Société des Concerts du Conservatoire,
where he ran the orchestra democratically, with profits equally divided
between members except for his own double share. Although occasionally criticised for his technique and his vigorous championing of German masterpieces,
Habeneck exerted great influence over Paris's musical life and earned the admiration of Wagner, among others, for his conducting of Beethoven's Ninth
Symphony, the individual movements of which he rehearsed for three years
before its 1831 Paris première (Locke, p. 72).

Orchestral and chamber musicians

Habeneck's democratic policy was by no means universally followed in the
orchestras of Paris. Although musicians at the Opéra benefited from an annual
salary and a 'pension for life when too old to sing or play',[21] pay levels varied

---

21 George Smart in 1802, quoted in Ehrlich, *Music*, p. 39.

considerably according to instrument and status, with the leader paid 3,000 francs per annum, a rank-and-file violinist 1,000 francs and a bass-drum player 600 francs (as against a top singer's 16,000 francs).[22] Such disparities occurred in London's orchestras as well. At the Philharmonic Society, Spohr and Christoph Gottfried Kiesewetter received 250 guineas as leaders in the 1820 and 1821 seasons respectively, while front-desk string players in 1821 were paid about £52 for ten rehearsals and eight concerts, principal woodwinds £27 and brass players £20. London's opera orchestras generally paid better, while leading instrumentalists such as the celebrated bass player Domenico Dragonetti earned up to £1,000 a year (about 10 per cent of what fashionable lawyers and doctors could make), although £500 per annum was more typical for leading instrumentalists (Ehrlich, *Music*, p. 49; Sachs, p. 214). Not only did most early nineteenth-century instrumentalists rank 'scarcely above an ordinary artizan',[23] but their lives were parlous for all the reasons stated earlier. This meant that 'elderly musicians who had no financial resources kept performing long after they had passed their prime in order to avoid the poor house' (Sachs, p. 214), with an obvious effect on orchestral standards.

As noted above, the quality of London's orchestras also suffered as a result of limited rehearsal time, especially for the ad hoc ensembles performing at benefit concerts. Nevertheless, the finest performances were reputedly on a par with those in Paris, where the quality of training and the expertise of such conductors as Habeneck defined an orchestral standard which no other city could consistently match. From 1840, however, Berlin's concert life dramatically picked up with the advent of high-quality private orchestras vigorously competing for middle-class audiences, and London gradually benefited from better conductors and growing specialisation among instrumentalists, which, according to Ehrlich, 'reflected both economic and musical change', in that 'only a large market could provide sufficient employment for a specialist', and 'only highly skilled specialists could perform the increasingly difficult music placed before them' (*Music*, pp. 47–8). The former point is borne out by comparing orchestral life in the provinces, where standards inevitably were lower[24] and professional reinforcement was often required from peripatetic leaders as well as instrumentalists imported from the large cities.

---

22 J.-M. Nectoux, 'Trois orchestres parisiens en 1830', in P. Bloom (ed.), *Music in Paris in the Eighteen-thirties* (Stuyvesant, N. Y., 1987), pp. 474, 493–4.

23 'The learned Dr Maurice', quoted in Ehrlich, *Music*, p. 50.

24 For instance, in 1827 an orchestra in Truro was criticised for its out-of-tune playing, and its leader dismissed as a 'country-dance scraper elevated to a situation wholly foreign to his powers' (*Royal Cornwall Gazette*, 13 October 1827, and *West Briton*, 9 November 1827, quoted in McGrady, *Music and Musicians*, p. 141).

London and Paris boasted sizeable populations of orchestral players, whereas more remote centres like Warsaw had small forces adequate for opera but less amenable to large-scale concerts. This may be one reason why few performances of Beethoven's symphonies can be documented in Warsaw between 1815 and 1830,[25] and the need to make do with the available instrumentalists may explain the solitary bass trombone part in Chopin's F minor Piano Concerto and various orchestral works by his colleague Ignacy Feliks Dobryziński. In contrast, London's horde of permanent and freelance players serviced large ensembles like the Philharmonic, which soon after its inception had almost fifty strings; double flutes, oboes, clarinets and bassoons; four horns, two trumpets, three trombones and timpani; and additional wind or percussion as needed (Sachs, p. 211). Composers in Paris had at their disposal the colouristic and dynamic forces of its rapidly expanding orchestras, and Berlioz's scores and *Grand traité d'instrumentation et d'orchestration modernes* of 1843 amply testify to orchestral standards and innovations in the French capital.

Paris was also home to an important professional chamber music series launched in 1814 by Pierre Baillot, who during the next sixteen years presided as first violin over some 150 chamber concerts, introducing his audiences to works by Haydn, Mozart, Boccherini, Cherubini, Onslow and Mendelssohn. Baillot's Beethoven performances were less well received by his musically conservative, high-brow subscribers, but Beethoven featured in the numerous chamber concert series that followed in Baillot's wake, one of which (promoted by the Bohrer brothers) premièred Beethoven's last six quartets as a set in 1830.[26] Many years earlier, in 1809, Beethoven's 'Rasumovsky' Quartets had been professionally unveiled in the public quartet evenings founded by Ignaz Schuppanzigh in Vienna a decade before Baillot's series commenced in Paris. In London, chamber music was traditionally performed between orchestral pieces at the Philharmonic, and groups of professional string players initiated two series of chamber music concerts in 1835.

The fact that a 'surprisingly large' number of women – for instance, Wilhelmine Szarvády and Louise Mattmann – found 'professional space' as chamber musicians in Paris from 1840 onwards may be attributable to a generalised association between femininity and chamber music in the minds of

---

25 Smialek, *Dobrzyński*, p. 21; according to Smialek (p. 20), Warsaw had 213 professional musicians in 1829.

26 J.-M. Fauquet, 'Les Sociétés de musique de chambre', in *La Musique en France à l'époque romantique* (Paris, 1991), pp. 172–3.

both performers and the public (Ellis, 'Female', pp. 378, 384). But women presided over another domain in which chamber music thrived: the private home. Ellis describes piano playing as 'that most appropriate female domestic accomplishment' ('Female', p. 355), although amateurs of both sexes devoured solo and four-hand arrangements of a vast amount of repertory, including operatic overtures and arias, symphonies, and string quartets and quintets, as well as simplified versions of the virtuoso piano works heard in the concert hall (often styled 'reminiscences' and 'souvenirs'). Similar arrangements for small instrumental ensembles were also produced by the dozen, as were songs for one or two voices with piano, guitar or harp accompaniment. All of this reflected music's central place in the middle-class home and 'a mode of life in which education and conviviality each served as the goal of the other'.[27] The result was a steadily increasing demand for instruments, published scores and lessons with noted teachers, all of which paid the wages of many a music professional.

Church musicians

Employment for professional musicians could be found in city churches such as Westminster Abbey and St Paul's Cathedral in London and the Chapelle Royale in Paris (which in 1810 had a choir of thirty-four and an orchestra of fifty, expanding to 115 in total by 1830), but provincial churches offered 'one of the few opportunities for a musician, particularly in a rural community, to earn part of his livelihood from his art' (McGrady, p. 90). Most provincial church musicians supplemented their meagre salaries from a range of occupations including tuning, repairing and trading instruments, teaching privately or in schools, promoting concerts, publishing music, composing for the local theatre, and even serving as postmasters. According to Ehrlich, organists in Norwich received up to £25 per annum in 1780, augmenting their income by teaching students 'up to fifteen miles out of town – a day's ride' (*Music*, pp. 21, 22). In 1816, the Town Clerk's Office at Helston advertised for an organist at £40 per annum with additional teaching work (McGrady, p. 111), while St Austell Parish Church annually devoted £20 to choral singing from 1814 onwards – and it 'very much improved' as a result.[28] Like many provincial churches at the time, St Austell installed a barrel organ – a typical 'compromise between financial and musical considerations' – at a cost of some £150 in the 1820s, and its choir began to perform

---

27 C. Dahlhaus, *Nineteenth-Century Music*, trans. J. B. Robinson (Berkeley and Los Angeles, 1989), p. 42.
28 Canon Hammond, parish historian, quoted in McGrady, *Music and Musicians*, p. 105.

in concerts of sacred music which belonged to Britain's rapidly expanding amateur choral tradition (McGrady, p. 105).

Instrument makers

Reference has been made to improvements in instrument design during the period as well as innovations in the make-up of orchestras. Instrument manufacture gained greater commercial momentum, especially the fiercely competitive piano industry. Piano manufacturing was well established in England and Austria by the late eighteenth century, but instruments were expensive: square pianos at £20 or more were too costly for most people, while in 1790s Vienna, 'only members of the old aristocracy, the second aristocracy, and the rich bankers would have been able to purchase a piano with financial ease' (DeNora, p. 48). By 1850, pianos were still 'luxury goods': a Broadwood or Stodart square piano cost 60–70 guineas, and uprights cost 50–100 guineas, 'roughly equal to the annual income of a clerk or school teacher'.[29] But every respectable middle-class home in Europe's major cities had to have an instrument, which dominated domestic life to the point that 'in families the piano has extinguished conversation and the love of books'.[30] Broadwood in London produced no fewer than 1,000 square pianos per annum during the first half of the century, and by 1850 'the total world output was probably about 50,000 pianos a year, nearly half of them made in England, which shared a generally acknowledged leadership of the industry with France, though many musicians still preferred the simpler Viennese instruments. Neither German nor American production was yet significant' (Ehrlich, *Piano*, pp. 9, 10).

Other London piano firms included Chappell, Cramer and Clementi, the last of which benefited from the vigorous marketing of the entrepreneurial composer himself, who toured extensively to promote the company's merchandise (both instruments and editions). John Field also acted on Clementi's behalf as far away as St Petersburg, where the firms of Diederichs, Schreder, Becker and Lichtenthal competed with Broadwood, Erard and other Western European makers.[31] Some companies paid commissions to prominent composer-pianists like Chopin, who received a cut of 10 per cent from the sale of six Pleyel instru-

29 C. Ehrlich, *The Piano: A History* (Oxford, 1990), pp. 9–10.

30 *Connoisseur* (January 1846), p. 7, quoted in Weber, *Music*, p. 17.

31 A. Swartz, 'Chopin as Modernist in Nineteenth-Century Russia', in J. Rink and J. Samson (eds.), *Chopin Studies 2* (Cambridge, 1994), pp. 37, 38.

ments to friends and associates,[32] while Liszt promoted Erard pianos from a tender age.

It was Sébastien Erard who patented the double-escapement action in 1821, perhaps the most important technological innovation during the period. Others included larger hammers and different hammer coverings, cross-stringing, thicker or overspun strings, wooden and iron bracing to reinforce the frame, increases in compass, refinements in damping mechanisms and modifications to the action (down-striking, 'Anglo-German' etc.). All of these had a major impact on sonority and/or playability, and some helped lower prices and thus increase sales. Accessories for the piano and other instruments also appeared on the market, not least the metronome, invented in 1812 by Dietrich Nikolaus Winkel but patented in 1815 by Johann Nepomuk Mälzel, who published a pamphlet on its use three years later. The chiroplast, patented in 1814 by Johann Bernhard Logier, was a horizontal frame fitted over the keyboard on which the hands moved laterally, in principle freeing the arm of tension and developing finger independence. It was publicised throughout Europe and America and appeared in an improved version devised by the celebrated Friedrich Kalkbrenner, who lined his pockets not only by requiring his assistants and students to use it, but also from his *Méthode pour apprendre le piano-forte à l'aide du guide-mains* (1831). In addition, there were various gadgets to enhance finger development, some causing real physical damage.

London also specialised in the manufacture of harps and wind instruments, while violins ('factory fiddles') were mass-produced in France and Germany, in response to the need for less expensive instruments following the upsurge in conservatory training after 1795. Individual craftsmen producing the finest violins included Jean-Baptiste Vuillaume in Paris, who also commissioned bows from leading makers and dealt in old instruments. As for innovations, the chin rest (invented by Spohr *c*. 1820) gave the left hand greater freedom, and new body designs ranged from François Chanot's guitar-shaped instrument (1817) to Félix Savart's trapezoidal violin (also 1817), not to mention pear-shaped and triangular models and trumpet and folding violins. But the most significant innovation dated from several decades earlier: the 'perfected' Tourte bow, which increased the violin's viability as a solo instrument and allowed violinists to compete with the nineteenth century's larger orchestras, while also serving as the 'virtual blueprint for all subsequent bow makers' after 1800.[33]

---

32 J.-J. Eigeldinger, 'Chopin and Pleyel', *Early Music*, vol. 29 (2001); see above, p. 72, regarding Smart's commissions from Broadwood, Chappell and Erard.

33 R. Stowell, *Violin Technique and Performance Practice in the Late Eighteenth and Early Nineteenth Centuries* (Cambridge, 1985), pp. 23, 27, 31.

Publishers

Music publishing flourished throughout Europe during the period, especially in London, Paris and Leipzig but also more remote centres like
Warsaw, St Petersburg and Moscow.[34] The printing workshop established
by Elsner in Warsaw in 1803 at first produced scores by Polish composers
only, and the national dances, variation sets and rondos of Elsner, Kurpiński,
Stefani, Nowakowski and Dobrzyński dominated the production of the
other Warsaw firms founded before 1830. But piano arrangements of the
operas by Rossini, Weber, Auber and Boïeldieu then in production at
Warsaw's theatres were also published, as well as piano pieces by Hummel,
Field and Ries. Moreover, Warsaw's music shops sold imported editions of
Haydn, Mozart and Beethoven. In Russia, the fledgeling music-publishing
industry specialised in almanacs with music supplements and 'musical
albums' containing romances, 'Russian songs' and, for piano, dances and
variations on popular folksongs, opera and romance melodies, most by
native composers. Other albums favoured the music of Western composers;
in one, Beethoven's Rondo in C major appeared as 'Une soirée d'été au bord
de la Newa'.[35]

Publishers throughout Europe used fanciful titles like this to maximise sales
appeal, sometimes to the irritation of such composers as Chopin, whose
Nocturnes Op. 9 were marketed as 'Les Murmures de la Seine' in Wessel's
London edition of 1833. Unscrupulous publishers in Britain and elsewhere
made their living by producing unauthorised complete editions or pirated
single works, and certain composers, Chopin among them, bent over backwards to achieve maximum copyright protection by publishing their music
more or less simultaneously in several different countries. Despite such efforts,
publishers 'frequently sued one another over illegal reprints, not only of valuable compositions but also in cases where only trivial pieces were at stake'.[36]
Chopin for one typically sold his works to publishers for a lump sum and
received no royalties; for instance, Breitkopf & Härtel paid 1,000 francs for his
Etudes Op. 25 in 1837, with a copyright domain of Germany and all countries
except France and Britain.

A combination of 'free enterprise, aggressive marketing and cost-cutting
production methods' had turned London into a major centre for music publishing by the 1830s (Sachs, p. 229), with such firms as Chappell, Novello,

---

34 See chapter 9 for a discussion of printing methods.
35 G. Seaman, 'Moscow and St Petersburg', in Ringer (ed.), *The Early Romantic Era*, p. 254.
36 K. Grabowski, 'The Original French Editions of Fryderyk Chopin's Music', *Chopin Studies*, 4 (1994),
Annex, p. 10.

Boosey, Cramer and Clementi active during the first part of the century. Publishers also operated in Liverpool, Manchester, Dublin and Edinburgh, some specialising in piracies of London editions. In Restoration Paris, music publishing took off with an increase in amateur music-making, and for decades the *romance* found a 'comfortable niche in commercial musical life', whether published singly (sometimes with elaborate title-pages) or in albums (Locke, p. 57). Opera vocal scores (in the so-called 'Parisian format' from 1840 onwards) appeared in bulk, as did arrangements of operatic airs and other newly composed piano music; these were the primary source of at least one publishing house's profits, although eighteenth- and earlier nineteenth-century music also appeared in its catalogues.[37] Leipzig specialised in editions of older repertory as well as contemporary works. As early as 1798, Breitkopf & Härtel published complete editions of Mozart, Haydn, Clementi, Dussek and others, as well as editions of Bach's motets (1802–3), chorale preludes (1803–5) and *Das Wohltemperirte Klavier* (1819). Hoffmeister and Kühnel's Bureau de Musique, established in 1800 and later taken over by Carl Friedrich Peters in 1814, released the first complete edition of Bach's works for keyboard and organ, an edition of Mozart's quartets and quintets, and Forkel's pioneering Bach biography.[38] Such initiatives, at a time when the canon was only taking shape, were by no means without financial risk.

Partly for that reason, publishers in Leipzig and elsewhere printed their scores in small quantities of 25 to 100, producing later impressions as necessary when supplies were exhausted; this also gave them the opportunity to correct errors and introduce altogether new readings (with or without authorial approval). According to James Deaville,[39] Liszt's *Apparitions*, published by Friedrich Hofmeister in 1835 at a cost of 12 Groschen, was initially printed in a batch of 100 and thereafter in batches of 50. But Hofmeister produced the *Grand Galop* in much larger quantities, with a total of 6,000 copies between 1838 and 1850, in print runs from 50 to 300 scores. Deaville notes that issues of marketability, not aesthetics, drove the early dissemination of Liszt's music, and furthermore that the largest sales were for works beyond the technical grasp of most buyers.

Publishers also profited from the innumerable performance treatises

---

37 K. Ellis, *Music Criticism in Nineteenth-Century France* (Cambridge, 1995), p. 142; the publisher in question was Maurice Schlesinger.

38 S. Döhring, 'Dresden and Leipzig: Two Bourgeois Centres', in Ringer (ed.), *The Early Romantic Era*, pp. 154–5.

39 'Publishing Paraphrases and Creating Collectors: Friedrich Hofmeister, Franz Liszt and the Technology of Popularity', paper delivered at International Conference on Nineteenth-Century Music, Royal Holloway, University of London, 29 June to 2 July 2000.

flooding on to the market for amateurs and lesser professionals and for use in teaching (both privately and in conservatories). Capitalising on their celebrity, almost all the leading performers wrote such methods and for nearly every instrument, including voice. Piano tutors included Hummel's *Ausführliche theoretisch-practische Anweisung zum Pianoforte-Spiele* (Vienna, 1828), Kalkbrenner's *Méthode pour apprendre le pianoforte* (Paris, 1830), and Fétis and Moscheles's *Méthode de méthodes de piano* (Paris, 1837), all of which were also published in London in English translation. Violin treatises (to name but a few) were released in Vienna by Spohr (*Violinschule*, 1832) and in Paris by Baillot (*L'Art du violon*, 1834) and Habeneck (*Méthode théorique et pratique de violon* . . ., c. 1840), while in Mainz Carl Guhr brought out a Paganini spin-off (*Ueber Paganinis Kunst die Violine zu spielen*, 1829). Guides to keyboard improvisation also appeared, among them Czerny's *Systematische Anleitung zum Fantasieren auf dem Pianoforte* (Vienna, 1829). The notated improvisations offered by Czerny as model cadenzas, fantasies, potpourris and capriccios are probably a pale reflection of the virtuoso *tours de force* heard in Europe's concert halls.

Music journalists

The early nineteenth century witnessed a virtual explosion in music journalism, both in specialist publications and in the general press. As with music publishing in general, the main centres were London, Paris and Leipzig, but countries from America to Russia joined in with such journals as *The Euterpeiad* (Boston, 1820) and *Literaturnoe pribavlenie k Nuvelisty* (St Petersburg, 1840). In London, newspaper coverage of musical events was patchy for many years; the most important contributions came late in the period from J. W. Davison, appointed music critic to *The Times* in 1846. By then Davison had made his mark as editor of *The Musical World* (1836), which, like its French and German models, featured historical articles, foreign reports, and reviews of performances and new compositions. It was one of several prominent music journals to follow the pioneering *Quarterly Musical Magazine and Review* (1818), which rapidly became London's 'leading musical voice' (Sachs, p. 213). Others included the *Harmonicon* (1823) and *The Musical Times and Singing Class Circular* (1842/1844). In the *Athenaeum*, the music reviews of Henry Chorley consistently attacked low standards in composition and in performance, as did Davison's contributions to *The Musical World*.

The fight against triviality and ephemerality – especially the virtuoso cult

– was an avowed aim of Robert Schumann's *Neue Zeitschrift für Musik* (*NZfM*), founded in Leipzig in 1834. Like its most important predecessor, Breitkopf & Härtel's *Allgemeine musikalische Zeitung* (*AmZ*; 1798), the *NZfM* was comprehensive in scope and intellectual in tone, intended for professional musicians and musically educated readers rather than the amateur music-lovers to whom journals like Leipzig's *Signale für musikalische Welt* (1843) appealed. Both the *AmZ* and the *NZfM* set the highest standards in music journalism, the former in particular serving as a model for specialist publications in Germany and elsewhere, with a panel of some 130 collaborators in its first decade alone.

Professional music journalism also flourished in Paris. The dilettantish writing of Julien-Louis Geoffroy early in the century gave way to the more informed contributions of Castil-Blaze, who wrote musical *feuilletons* for the *Journal des débats* from 1820 to 1832, reviewing concerts, competitions, instrumental tutors, treatises, new compositions and editions of early music. According to Ellis, Castil-Blaze, who above all was 'concerned with the realities of the business of composition and performance', produced music criticism 'so professional and practical as to be isolationist' (*Music*, pp. 27, 30, 32). Another important professional was François-Joseph Fétis, whose *Revue musicale* (1827) had a largely didactic mission. In 1835 it merged with Maurice Schlesinger's *Gazette musicale* (1834), and the hybrid *Revue et Gazette musicale* initially concentrated on 'the appreciation of Beethoven, the use of the *conte fantastique* as a vehicle for aesthetic discussion, and the war against the piano music industry', pursuing an alliance between music and literature which reversed the idea promoted by Castil-Blaze and Fétis that 'professional criticism was the surest means of introducing musical ideas to the public' (Ellis, *Music*, pp. 50, 143).

Editors and contributors to the *Gazette* before 1850 include Adolphe Adam, Berlioz, Henri Blanchard, Maurice Bourges, Castil-Blaze, Liszt, Ludwig Rellstab, François Stoepel and Wagner. It appeared weekly at an annual rate of 30 francs to Paris subscribers in 1834–44, and 24 francs from 1845 onwards. As of 1836, both the *Gazette* and Heugel's *Le Ménestrel* (another 'publishing-house journal' offering musical samples to its readers) averaged 600 copies each per issue (versus 10,008 per day for the *Journal des débats*), while in 1846, *La France musicale* – 'by far the most popular music journal' – printed 1,662 copies of its February issue, as against 875 copies of the *Gazette*, 765 of *Le Monde Musical* and 500 of *Le Ménestrel*. These figures (which are approximate) 'do not necessarily reflect the number of readers', as the public could peruse such journals in *cabinets de lecture* (Ellis, *Music*, pp. 1, 45, 243, 266).

The role of Europe's musical press in defining the canon and in shaping individual musicians' careers cannot be overstated. By indoctrinating different middle-class 'taste-publics', journals of every ideological and aesthetic hue left an indelible mark on aesthetic predilections and patterns of consumption. The fact that many suffered from blatant commercial bias and the personal prejudices of editors and writers only made their influence more potent (or pernicious). Success came most readily to composers and performers who were allied to powerful, vociferous champions, whether individual reviewers or a publishing house with its own journal. In this respect and others, professional life required political cunning as well as economic acumen.

Teachers and scholars

The professionalisation of music benefited enormously from the rapid spread of conservatory training throughout Europe following the Paris Conservatoire's establishment in 1795. Musicians had traditionally been trained as apprentices or in the family, church or court, and although Naples and Venice had conservatories dating from the late sixteenth century, they had declined by 1800. The Paris Conservatoire emerged from Sarrette's Ecole de Musique de la Garde Nationale, founded in the wake of the Revolution to provide military music for public festivals. It engaged the most prominent musicians on its teaching staff, which eventually would feature Gossec, Méhul, Boïeldieu, Cherubini, Le Sueur, Baillot, Duvernoy and others mentioned earlier. Although for many years instrumental tuition was limited to flute, oboe, clarinet, bassoon, horn, violin, cello and piano, detailed curricula were devised for 'all branches of the art of music'[40] and textbooks were commissioned from such specialists as Adam, Baillot, Le Sueur and Reicha for the purposes of systematic training. Furthermore, rigorous examinations and competitions ensured that students – some 400 in number by 1806 – achieved the highest standards. All these innovations utterly transformed musical training in France and indeed Europe in general, with new conservatories founded in Prague (1811), Vienna (1817), London (1823), Milan (1824), Brussels (1832), Leipzig (1843), Munich (1846) and elsewhere.

Whereas the Paris Conservatoire had sufficient resources to offer students free tuition, London's Royal Academy of Music initially charged 10 guineas for talented 'foundation students' and 20 guineas for others. It suffered successive

---

40 Quoted in J. Ritterman, 'On Teaching Performance', in J. Rink (ed.), *Musical Performance* (Cambridge, forthcoming).

funding crises during its first four decades, and as early as 1824 tuition fees climbed to a colossal £40 and teachers lost three months' pay. Wages were 'well below prevailing market rates': by the 1840s, most teachers earned only 3s. 6d. per hour, though some were paid 5 shillings. But 'nobody received a regular stipend', and '"sub-professors", barely trained pupil-teachers who received no payment, were widely employed' (Ehrlich, *Music*, p. 81). Although standards inevitably fell below those in Paris, the Royal Academy nevertheless managed to improve music-making in London. Later in the century, Leipzig's Conservatory offered teaching of unrivalled quality. Founded by Mendelssohn in 1843, the Conservatory engaged a glittering constellation of teachers including Moscheles, David, Schumann, Gade and Joachim, all of whom were expected to maintain an active professional career. Students received specialist tuition on their instruments as well as general training in thoroughbass, ensemble performance, and keyboard and singing skills, and courses in composition, music history, aesthetics, score-reading and conducting were also available.

Private teaching provided a living to innumerable musicians during the period, at all levels of the profession. By 1851, England and Wales had some 2,800 male and 2,300 female music teachers attending to vast numbers of students (Ehrlich, *Music*, p. 53). In Britain as elsewhere, young women tended to study the piano, harp and flute as well as singing, while young men gravitated to the piano, strings, winds and percussion. Wealthier families tried to engage the most prestigious performers, whose successful benefit concerts generated considerable interest and income, and who could ease access to the profession through their contacts. Although he accepted few pupils, Liszt, for instance, gave Valérie Boissier a series of lessons in 1832 at his house, supposedly two hours per week but in fact rather more. Chopin's lessons 'were even more in demand than those of Liszt or Kalkbrenner', and they cost 20 gold francs (30 at the pupil's home) for forty-five minutes to an hour.[41] At the opposite end of the spectrum were provincial teachers who for three lessons per fortnight might earn an annual fee of 8 guineas plus an enrolment fee of 1 guinea – a 'not inconsiderable sum, though a successful teacher would need quite a large group of pupils to provide a comfortable living'.[42] Scrounging for students and hours spent travelling between lessons were the fate of countless music teachers – then as now.

41 J.-J. Eigeldinger, *Chopin: Pianist and Teacher as Seen by His Pupils*, trans. N. Shohet with K. Osostowicz and R. Howat, ed. R. Howat (Cambridge, 1986), pp. 6–7.
42 McGrady, *Music and Musicians*, p. 39, with reference to a piano and singing teacher in Cornwall in 1813.

Alongside the development of conservatory training was the introduction of music to school curricula, for instance at the Scottish experimental school established by Robert Owen in 1816 for the children of mill workers. The first music textbooks intended for school use were published in the 1830s, among them John Turner's *Manual of Vocal Instruction* (1833) and Sarah Anna Glover's *Scheme to Render Psalmody Congregational* (1836), but John Hullah's *Manual* of 1841 was more influential. The singing movements of Hullah and Joseph Mainzer aimed to teach some 50,000 working-class children to read music, while Lowell Mason's goal of universal musical literacy in America resulted in the Boston Academy of Music in 1832, which initially provided free instruction to approximately 1,500 children.[43] These socially important initiatives built upon the solid professional base that music had developed by then.

Instrumental and vocal lessons were given in many schools on a freelance basis. Ehrlich notes that in 1802 R. J. S. Stevens earned approximately £600 at one school teaching keyboard and voice on three eleven-hour days. But most public schools in the nineteenth century 'did not employ musicians on their staff', and at Oxford in the 1820s 'hardly a college had a piano' (Ehrlich, *Music*, pp. 34, 43, 72). Oxford produced seven music graduates from 1800 to 1830, and music degrees were also conferred at Cambridge and Dublin and by the Archbishop of Canterbury. For men of breeding, however, such qualifications were thought demeaning. It was not until the second half of the century that music in British universities came into its own as a subject, a phenomenon paralleled in France, where the energetic research of Choron, Villoteau, Fétis, de La Fage and others was conducted on an amateur, not professional, basis. In contrast, the well-developed system of universities and research institutions in Germany had introduced music into the curriculum long before 1800, with such distinguished scholars as Forkel at Göttingen, Türk at Halle and A. B. Marx in Berlin during the late eighteenth and early nineteenth centuries. Forkel's *Allgemeine Geschichte der Musik* (1788) and *Allegemeine Litteratur der Musik* (1792) were important contributions to the emerging discipline of musicology ('musikalische Wissenschaft'), as were the general histories of Burney and Hawkins and the numerous historical studies that ensued. But as a profession, musicology had yet to take off, and it would become established throughout Europe and America only with the broad institutional support that it began to receive after 1850.

---

43 K. Bumpass, 'The USA: A Quest for Improvement', in Ringer (ed.), *The Early Romantic Era*, p. 272.

Bibliography

Brown, C., *Classical and Romantic Performing Practice 1750–1900*. Oxford, 1999

Colette, M.-N., J.-M. Fauquet, A. de Place, A. Randier and N. Wild, *La Musique à Paris en 1830–1831*. Paris, 1983

Corder, F., *A History of the Royal Academy of Music from 1822 to 1922*. London, 1922

Dahlhaus, C., *Nineteenth-Century Music*, trans. J. B. Robinson. Berkeley and Los Angeles, 1989

DeNora, T., *Beethoven and the Construction of Genius: Musical Politics in Vienna, 1792–1803*. Berkeley and Los Angeles, 1995

Devriès, A. and F. Lesure, *Dictionnaire des éditeurs de musique français*, 2 vols. Geneva, 1979

Ehrlich, C., *The Music Profession in Britain since the Eighteenth Century: A Social History*. Oxford, 1985

The Piano: A History. Oxford, 1990

Eigeldinger, J.-J., 'Chopin and Pleyel'. *Early Music*, 29 (2001)

Chopin: Pianist and Teacher as Seen by His Pupils, trans. N. Shohet with K. Osostowicz and R. Howat, ed. R. Howat. Cambridge, 1986

Ellis, K., 'Female Pianists and Their Male Critics in Nineteenth-Century Paris'. *Journal of the American Musicological Society*, 50 (1997), pp. 353–85

Music Criticism in Nineteenth-Century France. Cambridge, 1995

Fauquet, J.-M., 'Les Sociétés de musique de chambre'. In *La Musique en France à l'époque romantique*. Paris, 1991, pp. 167–97

Foster, M. B., *History of the Philharmonic Society of London, 1813–1912*. London, 1912

Grabowski, K., 'The Original French Editions of Fryderyk Chopin's Music'. *Chopin Studies*, 4 (1994), Annex, pp. 1–42

Kaden, C. and V. Kalisch (eds.), *Professionalismus in der Musik: Arbeitstagung . . . Bad Köstritz vom 22. bis 25. August 1996*. Essen, 1999

McGrady, R., *Music and Musicians in Early Nineteenth-Century Cornwall: The World of Joseph Emidy – Slave, Violinist and Composer*. Exeter, 1991

Nectoux, J.-M., 'Trois orchestres parisiens en 1830'. In P. Bloom (ed.), *Music in Paris in the Eighteen-thirties*. Stuyvesant, N.Y., 1987, pp. 471–505

Ringer, A. (ed.), *The Early Romantic Era*. London and Basingstoke, 1990

Ritterman, J., 'On Teaching Performance'. In J. Rink (ed.), *Musical Performance*. Cambridge, forthcoming

'Piano Music and the Public Concert'. In J. Samson (ed.), *The Cambridge Companion to Chopin*. Cambridge, 1992, pp. 11–31

Salaman, C. K., 'On Music as a Profession in England'. *Proceedings of the [Royal] Musical Association*, 6 (1880), pp. 107–24

Smialek, W., *Ignacy Feliks Dobrzyński and Musical Life in Nineteenth-Century Poland*. Lewiston, N.Y., 1991

Stowell, R., *Violin Technique and Performance Practice in the Late Eighteenth and Early Nineteenth Centuries*. Cambridge, 1985

Swartz, A., 'Chopin as Modernist in Nineteenth-Century Russia'. In J. Rink and J. Samson (eds.), *Chopin Studies 2*. Cambridge, 1994, pp. 35–49

Thomson, H. B., *The Choice of a Profession: A Concise Account and Comparative Review of the English Professions*. London, 1857

Weber, W., *Music and the Middle Class: The Social Structure of Concert Life in London, Paris and Vienna*. London, 1975

4

The opera industry

ROGER PARKER

Introduction

Even with endorsement from a figure as eminent as the great Italian politician Cavour, who called opera 'a great industry with ramifications all over the world',[1] the title of this chapter accepts a number of prejudices. Why should opera of this period be thought an 'industry' when, say, orchestral music or secular choral music is not? All these types of public entertainment were fostered by institutions in which were embedded power relations and social hierarchics; all had systems of production limited by economic circumstance; all depended on the agency of performers, and so forth. But opera, and perhaps particularly opera of this period, seems historiographically more deeply marked by its means of production than other musical genres; the mechanics of how operas come into being are thus more difficult to disentangle from the 'works themselves'. What is more, this circumstance is often used as a means of devaluing the repertory, questioning its seriousness of purpose as 'art'. To repeat the question, why is this?

The simplest explanation lies in a marked shift in opera's aesthetic status. The very idea of 'opera' underwent an important transformation during the eighteenth century, evolving from a sub-species of spoken theatre into what was essentially a musical genre. And even though elements of the earlier definition remained in force in some areas during the early decades of the nineteenth century (perhaps particularly in the otherwise very different cases of Italian opera seria and French opéra comique), the period covered by this chapter saw a gradual consolidation of this new status, with music regarded more and more as the dominant element, and with the position of the librettist as a literary/dramatic figure experiencing sharp decline. In 1750 Metastasio had been thought a prince among poets, composers vied with each other to do justice to

---

1 For an amplification of the argument here and elsewhere, see the present author's entry on 'Opera, The 19th century', in Stanley Sadie and John Tyrell (eds.), *The New Grove Dictionary of Music and Musicians*, 2nd edn (London, 2001), vol. 18, pp. 434–44. Cavour's statement is quoted in John Rosselli, 'Opera Production, 1780–1880', in Lorenzo Bianconi and Giorgio Pestelli (eds.), *Opera Production and its Resources* (Chicago, 1998), p. 81.

his works; by 1850 the average librettist was deemed the meanest of scribblers, far inferior as an artistic figure to the composer, unworthy even of the name 'poet', derided by every hack journalist.

However, as its position as a musical genre became more fixed, opera gradually lost aesthetic prestige, particularly in comparison with 'pure' instrumental music. The reasons for this are complex, but in part have to do with changing aesthetic views: opera as a theatrical event seemed more reliant on performance than other musical genres, and hence was seen as somehow lacking in 'essence'. Later nineteenth-century attempts to give the genre new prestige – by notions of the *Gesamtkunstwerk*, by publishing libretti as independent literary works, or by developing the idea of *Literaturoper* (in which the composer uses a pre-existing and independent literary text) – were in some ways an attempt to dignify anew the non-musical aspects, an attempt to reclaim for opera some the ground it had lost in the aesthetic universe during the early nineteenth century. We can see some sporadic beginnings of this process of reclamation in the first half of the century, but ideas of 'operatic reform', which have so driven retellings of operatic history, are mostly absent. It is partly for these reasons that the early nineteenth-century repertory became increasingly unfashionable during the first decades of the twentieth century; indeed, hardly any works from 1800 to 1850 were regularly performed.[2] Although the last fifty years have seen a partial reversal of that neglect (at least so far as Italian music is concerned), some of the old prejudice may still remain.

Of course, this decline in status was only part of the story, and a part perhaps more important to theorists and historians than to the mass of consumers. Throughout the period, opera in its most elevated forms remained at the centre of power and prestige so far as audiences and the ruling classes were concerned. Because of this, opera composers could earn comparatively large sums (though rarely as much as star singers); as a 'repertory' formed and as copyright laws began to deliver income from revivals, several of them amassed considerable fortunes. More than this, the sheer bulk of operatic production inexorably expanded. Towards the end of the eighteenth century, regular operatic performances could be seen through much of Europe, even as far afield as Russia. Fifty years later, though, the genre had become a well-nigh global phenomenon, perhaps the earliest example of 'world music'. Apart from certain pockets of resistance, this expansion was primarily of Italian opera, first in a huge wave of Rossini-fever (there was, to give one startling example, a Rossini vogue in Chile in the 1830s), and then of his followers, in particular Verdi. By 1850 the most

---

2 There were some exceptions, notably *Fidelio*, *Der Freischütz* and Wagner's so-called 'Romantic' operas in German-speaking lands, and a few hardy Italian works – *Barbiere*, *Norma* and *Lucia di Lammermoor* in particular.

popular Italian operas were being performed in many a far-flung outpost of North, Central and South America, and had also spread to Australia, India and South Africa. In the more remote regions, opera was often brought in by means of intrepid touring companies, bravely making use of an expanding system of rail transportation. But the expansion was just as pronounced within Europe, where the number of theatres dedicated to fixed seasons of operatic performance showed a marked increase.

The period also saw a vast expansion in the dissemination of opera. While printed vocal scores and (in France) orchestral scores gradually became a prime physical means of making available to performers the complete musical text of an opera, a far larger market emerged around the published operatic transcription. Particularly in Italy and France, a successful opera at mid-century would give rise to a bewildering variety of arrangements: for voice and piano, piano solo, piano duet, for various instruments and piano, for other (sometimes unlikely) combinations; and in more 'creative' genres such as fantasias or 'reminiscences'. This corpus of material demonstrates that operatic music was a major part of the repertory of private salons, indeed of anywhere where the piano and other instruments were played by amateurs. Nineteenth-century concerts were also much more likely to involve operatic excerpts, arrangements or 'reminiscences' than their counterparts today. Nor should we ignore the constant diffusion of operatic texts and subjects in less grand venues: in the marionette theatres of Italy, the burlesques of England, the magic lantern shows of Germany, and the barrel organs of all these places. There is even evidence that operatic melodies sometimes drifted into the channels of oral transmission, to re-emerge as 'folk material' collected by ethnographers in the twentieth century. Opera, as publicly performed in urban theatres, can rarely be termed 'popular' entertainment in anything like a modern sense; but during this period it certainly became a phenomenon much broader than its theatrical diffusion might suggest.

The opera explosion is nowhere more evident than in discourse about the topic. The early nineteenth century saw a huge rise in periodical publication, and of these a large number either included extensive reference to or were entirely dedicated to operatic activity. Distinguished titles such as the *Allgemeine musikalische Zeitung* (Leipzig), the *Gazzetta musicale di Milano* and the *Revue et Gazette musicale de Paris* were accompanied by a mass of less ambitious publications. The centre of this activity, at least in terms of sheer bulk, was Paris, in which an important première at mid-century would stimulate as many as twenty or thirty separate reviews, many of them lengthy. Much of the 'criticism' thus produced was of course directed towards performances and performers, and was written to routine formulas. However, many of the century's most acute critics plied their trade in periodicals: E. T. A. Hoffmann, Schumann, Berlioz, Castil-Blaze and many, many others.

How best can we make sense of this sprawling, trans-national activity? The present survey, which is organised around chronological divisions that have strong political resonance, needs some explanation. The connections between operatic history and such obvious political watersheds as 1814–15 and the collapse of the Napoleonic empire, or the revolutions of 1830–31 and 1848–9, are not as obvious as is sometimes suggested, even though opera was in most countries under some loose form of government control. With the exception of the 1848 revolutions, which were eventually understood to have done lasting economic damage to the opera 'industry', these historical events punctuated the steady production and consumption of operatic pleasure in what were often no more than superficial ways. What is more, the persistent association of certain operatic composers with insurrection and social unrest (Verdi is the obvious case) has far more to do with later nineteenth-century imaginings – in particular nostalgia for a lost time of action – than with contemporary evidence. Although it was inevitable that the opera house, as an important (sometimes virtually the only) meeting-place for the urban bourgeoisie, occasionally became caught up in the century's great bourgeois revolutions, it was far more often a place where the ruling classes could rely on stability and an opportunity to display power. We might also recall that, as the century progressed and revolutionary movements embraced an ever-wider socio-economic spectrum, an increasingly large element of the revolutionary population was excluded from all but the humblest of operatic representations. This is not, of course, to deny that opera in the early nineteenth century was in many areas inescapably bound up with the idea of nation and national representation; merely that political 'events' and operatic 'events' are very different, their relationship often complex and subterranean.

It happens, though, that these 'watershed' years also coincide with important moments in operatic history, even if the conjunction may sometimes be no more than fortuitous. Although the end of the Napoleonic era marked no profound changes in the nature of operatic institutions, the years around 1814–15 did see the establishment of Gioachino Rossini as the most influential opera composer, first in Italy, and in the following few years virtually throughout Europe. And the end of Rossini's career, at least as creator of opera, came on the eve of 1830, just at the time when a highly influential strand of French grand opera was emerging, and when both Bellini and Donizetti were establishing an identifiable 'post-Rossinian' style in Italian opera. The years around 1850 are also, as it happens, a convenient moment at which to halt an operatic journey.

Two of the three most important composers in the latter half of the century, Verdi and Wagner, both reached an important stylistic boundary in their careers at roughly that moment; and the third, Meyerbeer, completed *Le prophète*, a long-awaited sequel to his most famous opera *Les Huguenots*, on the eve of 1850.

Whatever the disadvantages of dividing operatic history by means of 'watershed' years, it seems safer than relying, as music history has for so long, on terms drawn from intellectual or cultural history. Possibly connected to the decline in opera's literary status, its relationship to such broader currents remains a source of lively debate and not infrequent puzzlement. Key cultural terms such as 'Classicism', 'Romanticism' or 'Realism' seem often to manifest themselves in opera at periods removed from their appearance in the other arts, or in strangely unemphatic contexts. To give just one example, the literary polemics over Romanticism in Italy *c.* 1816–18, or in France *c.* 1830, although they focused on drama, largely ignored opera, partly because the genre had already (and without great resistance) escaped those restrictions of time and place that 'Classicists' saw as crucial to spoken drama, and partly because one imagines its mode of discourse was too extraordinary to be co-opted into the debate on either side. Of course, opera in many countries then partook freely of the new, 'Romantic' dramas as literary sources; but it was often able do so without radical readjustments to its outer nature, 'Romantic' and 'Classical' subjects frequently existing side by side in an otherwise unchanged formal and stylistic language. This is not to say that such broad cultural currents did not affect opera profoundly: as we shall see, the new subjectivities that emerged with 'Romanticism' certainly played powerfully across opera's expressive world; but the conjunctions are typically not as immediate as the sharing of certain literary texts might at first suggest.

One last point. Although, as mentioned above, early nineteenth-century Italian opera, in particular the works of Rossini, Bellini, Donizetti and early Verdi, has experienced a revival over the last fifty years, other repertories once hugely popular, notably the Singspiel tradition, opéra comique and – with one or two exceptions – grand opera, have been almost totally eclipsed. While it is impossible (and would anyway be undesirable) entirely to ignore the vagaries of our present repertory, it is also worth taking seriously, and trying to explain aesthetically, works that were once at the centre and have since moved to the side. The temptation to indulge in what Michael André Bernstein has called 'backshadowing'[3] is perhaps nowhere more powerful than in writing operatic history: once-famous works that have long lain unperformed have suffered that fate for many reasons;

---

3 Michael André Bernstein, *Foregone Conclusions: Against Apocalyptic History* (Berkeley and Los Angeles, 1994).

the temptation to justify our present operatic universe by automatically assuming that they are in some way aesthetically inferior should mostly be resisted.

Imperial opera (1800–1814)

Carl Dahlhaus started his still-influential history of nineteenth-century music in 1814, and from a strictly operatic point of view this decision has much to recommend it.[4] Operatic activity between 1800 and 1814 – whether creative or institutional, and in whatever country – retained many aspects of eighteenth-century practice, a point that would seem to find confirmation in the almost complete absence of works from these years in our present-day repertory (Beethoven's *Fidelio* is the only significant exception). Looking at this period, then, has unusual challenges for the historian; as mentioned in the introduction, we should be careful not to favour uncritically those works that seem most surely to predict a time when 'our' opera begins.

One aspect that *did* experience change, however, was the economic basis on which operatic establishments ran. Although traces of what might loosely be called 'court' opera in the seventeenth- and eighteenth-century sense (the theatre controlled and financed by a ruling aristocratic house) occasionally survived into the early nineteenth century (most often in Germany and Austria), by far the most common financial basis for a nineteenth-century opera house was within a 'mixed' economy, a system occasionally seen in previous decades. The key figure, of increasing power during the first half of the century, was the impresario (already much in evidence in the later eighteenth century), who arranged seasons, hired singers and composers, usually receiving some kind of subsidy from the theatre's owners (who might or might not constitute the local government) but also speculating at his own financial risk. If opera was an 'industry', then its chief entrepreneurial energy came from these men of business.[5] The presence of this gradual but fundamental economic shift, from a system based around aristocratic privilege to a system strongly reliant on public support, needs to be borne in mind as we consider the operatic production of this period, if only because its existence can easily be forgotten when contemplating the very obvious national differences between the main operatic centres then in play.

It is, though, according to those still-pronounced national styles that imperial opera is best addressed; and as my section title suggests, the story most obvi-

---

4 Carl Dahlhaus, *Nineteenth-Century Music*, trans. J. B. Robinson (Berkeley and Los Angeles, 1989).

5 The key text in understanding opera's changing economy in the nineteenth century, albeit from an exclusively Italian perspective, is John Rosselli's *The Opera Industry in Italy from Cimarosa to Verdi: The Role of the Impresario* (Cambridge, 1984). A broader treatment of the same issue is to be found in Rosselli's 'Opera Production, 1780–1880', pp. 81–164.

ously begins in France, the motor of political change in mainland Europe during the century's first decade. The revolutionary turmoil of the 1790s had stimulated operatic activity in a way that later revolutions would not, at least overtly. This 'politicisation' of the genre partly reflected the theatrical nature of the revolution itself, in particular the fact that so-called *faits historiques* – vast open-air allegorical stagings of revolutionary deeds – were a primary means of state propaganda. Equally important, though, was a radical gesture made by the Constituent Assembly in January 1791: after decades of strict control over theatrical privilege, they proclaimed that any genre of opera could be performed in any type of theatre. In the wake of this liberalisation, the 1790s saw a mass of overtly propagandistic operas in a proliferation of genres, from opéra comique to vaudeville and pantomime. Republican tales in which the heroic deeds of the Revolution were allegorised crowded on to the Parisian stages, often in the form of so-called 'rescue' operas, in which beleaguered heroes and heroines were miraculously saved from mortal danger in the final moments of the plot.

However, the first decade of the nineteenth century, the years of the Consulate (1799–1804) and then the Empire (1804–1814/15), saw a marked retrenchment from the Constituent Assembly's liberal position, and in 1807 Napoleon restored many of the old theatrical privileges, so putting into place a system that continued more-or-less intact until 1864, and was a defining aspect of the French operatic scene. Operatic genres were again, as in the eighteenth century, defined not only by various dramatic differences, but also by the physical spaces in which they were permitted to be performed: opéra comique (which used spoken dialogue, and in which music was not expected to carry the burden of drama in the manner of tragedy) took place at the theatre of the same name; foreign works (mostly Italian, whether comic or serious, and by virtue of their provenance not liable to dramatic restrictions) were at the Théâtre-Italien; and tragedy (the highest form, in which works were judged against a line of august precedents from the previous century) was at the Opéra.

In spite of a fiercely chauvinistic attitude to the arts, French operatic audiences in the first years of the nineteenth century, although they acknowledged the visual splendour of indigenous forms, often thought them unable to compete with Italian models in the crucial matter of vocal melody. The continuing vogue at the Opéra for Gluck – deemed by the French an honorary Italian – in the first decade was an important reminder of the Italian melodic arts: if French-language opera was to be made 'exportable', it would have to come to terms with the dominant Italian tradition, which had as its great showcase the Théâtre-Italien. Cimarosa and Paisiello were among the earliest staples here, soon to be followed by the French premières of Mozart's mature comedies, and operas by Paër and Mayr. In terms of audience taste, these Italian works – some of them now distinctly old-fashioned – presented a powerful challenge to the native repertory.

However, three notable composers of French-language opera can give an idea of the variety on offer. The oldest is the Italian-born Luigi Cherubini (1760–1842), who had made a considerable reputation in the 1790s with generically hybrid works such as *Lodoïska* (1791) and *Médée* (1797), both performed at the Théâtre-Feydeau (which merged with the Opéra-Comique in 1801). But Cherubini's greatest popular success was with *Les deux journées* (1800), a comédie lyrique in three acts: the first production managed more than 200 performances, and the opera was still being revived in the 1840s, becoming popular also in Germany, where it elicited praise from such luminaries as Beethoven and Goethe. Although set in the seventeenth century, the plot was clearly meant to resonate with the revolutionary tastes of the audience: the characters, for instance, are strongly defined by abstract virtues. It tells of a Savoyard water-carrier who hides a parliamentarian and his wife from Cardinal Mazarin. In common with many such 'rescue' operas, the parliamentarian is finally pardoned, and the opera ends by reminding everyone that 'le premier charme de la vie c'est de servir l'humanité'. In many ways *Les deux journées* is a typical opéra comique of the period. It makes full and dramatic use of its various modes of operatic discourse, from spoken dialogue to so-called *mélodrame* (words spoken over musical accompaniment), to recitative, aria and then ensemble. But there is a marked imbalance between these last two: the opera's only arias are its first two numbers after the overture (out of a total of fifteen numbers), and both of them are simple, strophic, 'characteristic' pieces – a narrative ballad and a prayer – which then recur at key moments in the plot. The rest of the work is made up of choruses and ensembles, the most ambitious of the latter being multi-tempo and multi-key, not unlike a Mozartian comic opera finale.

Etienne-Nicolas Méhul (1763–1817) had also made his name in the 1790s, as both an opera composer and contributor to revolutionary *faits*. Befriended by none other than Napoleon, Méhul's most successful works with the public during the Empire were opéras comiques that derived some of their style from Italians such as Paisiello. But Méhul was also a committed innovator, and modern scholars have been more interested in his Ossian cult opera *Uthal* (1806), which, together with near-contemporary works such as Jean-François Le Sueur's *Ossian* (1804) and H. M. Berton's *La romance* (1804), tapped into a vein of proto-Romanticism that was to prove prophetic. This was not simply a case of subject-matter: *Uthal* omitted violins from the orchestra in an attempt to give a darker, more 'Romantic' flavour (the comparison, frequently made, with Berlioz is interesting, and we might recall that Berlioz wrote admiringly of Méhul in *Les soirées d'orchestra*). *Uthal* was not particularly popular at the time, and it is significant to the French context that the public's indifference was due at least in part to the work's generic instability: performed at the Opéra-Comique, but termed simply 'opéra', it could easily have been put on at the Opéra had it been furnished with a ballet and recitatives rather than spoken dialogue. Even more outlandish was Méhul's *Joseph* (1807), a *drame melée de chants* also performed at the Opéra-Comique. Here the biblical theme is matched by occasional forays into the 'learned' style and by a kind of solemn diatonicism reminiscent of *The Magic Flute*. Although again not popular at first, *Joseph* won important official recognition, and was much performed through the nineteenth century as an oratorio.

In the surge of innovation that took place in opéra comique during 1790, the great tradition of tragédie lyrique at the Opéra, which had produced the works of Lully and Rameau, seemed somehow less exciting. In the more ordered world of the Empire, however, the tragic tradition began to reassert creative vitality. The key figure was Gaspare Spontini (1774–1851), an Italian who arrived in Paris in 1802. At first considered a foreign interloper, his risc was striking, albeit assisted by the patronage of Empress Josephine. Spontini started by writing opéras comiques inspired by Italian models, but his most influential work was *La vestale* (1807), a tragédie lyrique premièred at the Opéra, and the only serious opera from this period to gain an international reputation and remain in the repertory for several decades. Set in Ancient Rome, *La vestale* centres on a conventional story of love vs. duty, the vestal virgin of the title being condemned to death for neglecting her sacred duties. The opera looks both backwards and forwards. Aspects of eighteenth-century opera seria certainly remain, not least in an extravagantly sudden happy ending in which the protagonist is pardoned; and some of the formal recitative and simple arias are reminiscent of Gluck. On the other hand, Spontini's large-scale control of dramatic tension powerfully adumbrates operatic developments of the following decades. This is particularly evident in Act II, in which the sonic progression – from the protagonist's solo aria to a love duet and then terzetto with chorus – comes to a climax in the highly effective sentence of death, which is then capped by a grandiose choral finale.

The other two main centres of operatic activity during this period – Italy and the German-speaking lands – must be dealt with more briefly. Italian opera in the eighteenth century continued to be decisively influenced by French dramaturgical models, but in strictly musical terms remained largely impervious to foreign influence. However, the years of revolution and Napoleonic domination in Italy

(1796–1814), although they saw none of the tumultuous institutional changes that had occurred in France, did finally encourage Italian composers to take heed of French operatic models, especially developments in opéra comique. In this respect no one was more important than Johann Simon Mayr (1763–1845), an Italianised Bavarian whose career centred in Bergamo, and who was also a famous teacher (of Donizetti among others) and church musician. Several of Mayr's most important operas were taken from subjects previously treated by Cherubini, and showed a new orchestral and harmonic adventurousness, both of which may also have come from his understanding of and sympathy with German and Austrian instrumental music (at that time very rarely performed in Italy). Although we know too little about Mayr's entire corpus, and are yet more ignorant of his contemporaries, it is clear that he was also innovative in formal matters, most notably in making the multi-movement 'number' a norm in solo arias, so departing from the single-movement practice of much of the eighteenth century.[6] This was a crucial development, in that it allowed even the 'normative discourse' of Italian opera (that is, solo song) to be one in which stage action, or at least stage events, could be reflected by changes in a continuous musical argument. The internal divisions of these multi-movement numbers were, however, anything but stable, although there was a tendency (occasionally found in the late eighteenth century) to finish with a fast movement, now often called the 'cabaletta'.

The grandiose, tragic side of imperial French opera did not make as much impact, except possibly in Naples, where some of the most ambitious French and French-influenced works were staged. The most influential of these was probably Mayr's *Medea in Corinto* (1813), which was successful enough to be taken up by such famous singers as Giuditta Pasta in the 1820s. Mayr was specifically commissioned to write in the French manner, which meant employing orchestrally accompanied recitatives (rather than the continuo-accompanied variety still normal in Italian opera seria), and this 'surface' gesture towards French style was seconded by an enrichment of the ensemble scenes, which powerfully anticipate the grandest moments of Italian opera in the following decades. However, perhaps a more thoroughgoing assimilation of the French manner came about in the Italians' adoption of 'romantic' or 'sentimental' subject-matter, often in a 'mixed' style that blended comic and serious elements in the manner of opéra comique. Ferdinando Paër (1771–1839) was influential here, in particular with *Leonora* (1804) and *Agnese di Fitz-Henry* (1809), a so-called opera semiseria in which a father is driven mad by his daughter's marriage to an unsuitable young man. Again, though, Mayr was the dom-

---

6 See in particular Scott L. Balthazar, 'Mayr and the Development of the Two-Movement Aria', in Francesco Bellotto (ed.), *Giovanni Simone Mayr: l'opera teatrale e la musica sacra* (Bergamo, 1997), pp. 229–51.

inant figure in this genre, most notably in his *La rosa bianca e la rosa rossa* (1813), a *melodramma eroico* set during the War of the Roses, whose ending is plainly modelled on the 'rescue' plots that had been so popular in France.

As mentioned earlier, 'court' opera survived well into the nineteenth century in various German states and principalities; but it did so mostly in the form of imported Italian or (more rarely) French offerings. Indeed, German-language opera, which had throughout the eighteenth century maintained only a fragile hold on German-speaking audiences, continued to struggle during the first decades of the nineteenth, and this in spite of a number of notable individual works. The Singspiel tradition, of light works with spoken dialogue, deriving both from English ballad opera and from opéra comique, continued to be the order of the day, in particular the sub-genres of 'exotic opera' (in the manner of Mozart's *Die Entführung aus dem Serail*) and 'magic opera' (in the manner of his *The Magic Flute*). Peter von Winter (1754–1825), based in Munich after 1800, and Adalbert Gyrowetz (1763–1850), a Bohemian composer who knew Mozart and Haydn, and after travels in Italy became fixed in Vienna, are perhaps the two best-known composers. But none of their works managed to compete with the French and Italian serious operas that adorned prestigious court events.

There did, however, emerge one substantial work by an even more substantial composer: Ludwig van Beethoven's *Fidelio* (first performed in Vienna, as *Leonore*, in 1805, and then revised in 1806 and 1814). In spite of the work's musical originality, its dramaturgical origins in post-revolutionary French opera are obvious: Beethoven studied Spontini's *La vestale* and – more noticeably on the musical surface – Cherubini's *Les deux journées* in preparation for writing his only opera; and the 'rescue' element in the plot is plainly derived from the latter. But the influence of Mozart, in particular the way in which Sarastro in *The Magic Flute* is a progenitor of Don Fernando, is also strong. Unlike any of these models, however, is the oratorio-like manner of much of the score, notably the final scene, which adopts the hymn to liberty so well known from opéras comiques such as *Les deux journées* but on an enormously grand, and, for Beethoven, suitably symphonic scale. Even more unprecedented are the opera's blatant stylistic breaks: the manner in which the domestic drama of the opening numbers entirely disappears as the plot thickens; or the radically new musical atmosphere of the final scene. It is perhaps in this sense, of projecting extreme dramatic/musical discontinuities, that *Fidelio* most powerfully relates to the French Revolution, that central discontinuity which made all Europe think again about the progress of history.[7]

7 For more along these lines, see Paul Robinson, '*Fidelio* and the French Revolution', *Cambridge Opera Journal*, 3/1 (1991), pp. 23–48.

Rossini fever (1814–1830)

From Ludwig van Beethoven to Gioachino Rossini (1792–1868). One is reminded again of Dahlhaus's history of nineteenth-century music, with its now-famous discussion of 'the twin styles': can one write an account of music history that sees these two composers in dialectical opposition, that can solve what he calls the 'riddle . . . of their contemporaneity'?[8] In operatic terms, there may simply be no riddle. The world in which Beethoven conceived *Fidelio* (first performed in 1805) was very different from that in which Rossini dominated the stages of Europe; both composers might plausibly be seen as 'of their time', and both shared a common operatic legacy, albeit one differently inflected by national traditions.

The defeat of Napoleon, and the Congress of Vienna that followed it, ushered in a period commonly called the 'Restoration', one conventionally seen as a misguided (or at least unsuccessful) attempt to reinstate the late eighteenth-century political status quo. Was anything *operatic* restored in the Restoration? was there any sense of turning back the clock? There might at first glance seem an obvious corollary between operatic and political history. On the one hand, the unambiguous political message of Beethoven's opera marries with his violent, unmediated juxtaposition of an 'old-fashioned' comic language and a new music of libertarian commitment; on the other, Rossini's notorious lack of political radicalism marries with his willingness to reuse comic music in serious plots and vice versa, a practice that would have been unthinkable for the 'committed' Beethoven. But again we should be wary of painting too simple a picture of opera's reaction to the changing times. The opéra comique tradition from which Beethoven drew so much of his inspiration continued across the political divide with no great stylistic or ideological change; and to equate Rossini's self-borrowing with some kind of deep cynicism is a risky decontextualisation of a complex artistic and aesthetic attitude.

There is, though, no doubt that, both for us and for audiences of the time, the Restoration period is inescapably characterised by the achievement of Rossini. After opening his career with farces and lighter comic operas, his breakthrough into national and then international prominence came in 1813 with a comic opera, *L'italiana in Algeri*, and a serious one, *Tancredi*. Most of his early activity was in the northern part of Italy, but in 1815 he moved to Naples, and for that centre produced a sequence of great serious operas including *Otello* (1816), *Ermione* (1819), *La donna del lago* (1819) and *Maometto II* (1820). Comic works also continued to appear, notably *Il barbiere di Siviglia* (1816) and *La Cenerentola*

---

8 Dahlhaus, *Nineteenth-Century Music*, p. 58; see also pp. 8–15.

(1817). In terms of reception, though, there was a crucial difference between the comic and serious works. The serious operas were at first popular, and were certainly influential on the next generation; what is more, they have been partially rehabilitated during the late twentieth century. But the vogue for several of the comic works, in particular *Barbiere*, was altogether of a different order: they have remained in the world's opera houses ever since their first performances.

The *Barbiere* phenomenon leads us to the first of two vital contexts, without which Rossini's extraordinary success would not have been possible. The first concerns the gradual formation during this period of an 'operatic repertory', a body of works that were revived countless times in countless different venues. Repertory operas were of course not unknown in previous centuries: in France the works of Lully and Rameau had achieved something like that position in the eighteenth century, as did those of Gluck and Mozart in the imperial period. But the true 'repertory works' before 1800 consisted of libretti rather than music: several of Metastasio's dramas were endlessly restaged, in numerous musical settings. The crucial change occurred in the second and third decades of the nineteenth century in Italy (the centre previously most resistant to repertory formation), and began, as mentioned, with Rossini's comic operas, whose permanent position around the globe was equalled by a favoured few works by Bellini, Donizetti and Verdi. By the 1840s the term 'repertory opera' was in common use in Italy and rapidly spread elsewhere (for further discussion of this issue, see chapter 13); the political disruptions of 1848–9, which put many theatres into such financial difficulties that they were obliged to rely increasingly on revivals of past works, and the international successes of Meyerbeer and Verdi's middle-period operas, solidified the process.

The second contextual issue surrounding Rossini concerns operatic forms. As we have already seen, the rigid alternation of recitative (involving dialogue, stage action) and single-movement aria (involving monologue, reflection) had already been challenged in the later decades of the eighteenth century; and the first decades of the nineteenth saw the decisive emergence of the multi-movement 'number' as a basic formal unit. This unit tended (perhaps as in all formal matters) to be most predictable in Italy, but it nevertheless formed the backbone of much opera elsewhere (a partial exception was German opera, which favoured the strophic romance and tended to use multi-movement forms only to demonstrate a character's 'Italianate' – read 'Other' – qualities). The 'number' contained within it both 'static' and 'kinetic' movements, thus allowing for a variety of emotional representations (and a variety of vocal manners), as well as the injection of stage action to precipitate new moods. During the early decades (longer in comic opera), continuo-accompanied recitative or spoken dialogue alternated with these 'numbers'; but this gradually became orchestrally accompanied, and thus absorbed stylistically into the 'number'.

It was certainly one of the keys to Rossini's success, and possibly a main reason why he dominated the evolving repertory of the 1820s, that – at least on the formal level of the 'number' – he was less adventurous than Italian predecessors such as Mayr. Indeed, at the hands of Rossini a formal discourse emerged that would remain highly influential through the next several decades. The normative structure was the solo aria, called 'cavatina' if it marked the first appearance of a character, and typically made up of an introductory scena and recitative followed by three 'movements': a lyrical first movement, usually slow in tempo, often called 'cantabile'; a connecting passage stimulated by some stage event and called the 'tempo di mezzo'; and a concluding cabaletta, usually faster than the first movement and usually requiring agility on the part of the singer. The grand duet was identically structured, though with an opening block before the cantabile, commonly employing patterned exchanges between the characters. Large-scale internal finales followed the pattern of the grand duet; the slow movement in ensembles was often called the 'largo concertato', and the final movement a 'stretta'. (A brilliant example of the latter, one that already gestures ironically to the generic norm, occurs in the Act I finale of *Il barbiere*, with the *largo concertato* 'Fredda ed immobile' and the stretta 'Mi par d'esser con la testa'.)

We should always bear in mind that the above was *normative* discourse. The reality of the Rossinian surface can often be radically different, especially in the ensemble movements of the later Italian operas, where he was increasingly likely to experiment. Sometimes, as in Act II of *Semiramide* (1823), he would expand the range of the number by constructing large spans by means of an 'additive' technique, a sequence of single-movement numbers responding more immediately to the particularities of the dramatic situation. More radical still is the final act of *Otello*, which is a bold attempt to transpose the 'Romantic' subject matter of Shakespearean drama on to the Italian stage, in the process all but ignoring the fixed forms in favour of brief atmospheric numbers, sudden juxtapositions and injections of local colour. More often, though, Rossini would retain the broad structure of the multi-movement 'number' but expand it from within: the famous 'terzettone' from Act I of *Maometto II* is a remarkable example, in which a simple terzetto is overtaken by dramatic events, to spin off into a chorus and the solo prayer before recovering its formal presence to close with a cabaletta.

In spite of these well-nigh constant manipulations, however, the presence of fixed forms aided communication in two important ways: first, it assured the principal performers a space in which to claim audience identification; second, it assured a level of audience expectation that could be harnessed to dramatic effect. On a smaller level, the same could be said of 'trademark' devices such as the famous Rossini crescendo (in which a fixed period of – say – eight or sixteen bars is repeated again and again, each time with increased orchestration and an increased dynamic level): the fact that everyone knew at the start how a crescendo would develop enhanced pleasure rather than dampened it. The 'crescendo' was endlessly imitated by others, but the Rossini style has other elements that few subsequent composers could match. Perhaps the most important of these was a calculated use of disruption: even the simplest of Rossini's melodies is liable to sudden harmonic and rhythmic displacements that give an infectious energy to the Rossinian surface. However, in spite of this characteristic restlessness, there was one aesthetic constant: Rossini's continued belief in vocality as the supreme expressive means. This can sometimes be misunderstood. Rossini's melodies are, famously, festooned with elaborate vocal decoration, a trait that can seem to us mechanical and even superficial. But for Rossini and his adoring public, this florid writing *was* expression; the endless gruppetti, trills and roulades were not *ornaments*, not additions to a basic expressive melody that lies underneath, but rather the very means by which beautiful melody could communicate its special message from performer to audience.

Most of Italy quickly came under the sway of Rossini: a prolific contemporary, Giovanni Pacini (1796–1867), ruefully remarked that to imitate the Rossini style was in the end the only way to earn a living. However, as Rossini's fame spread to other countries, it is hardly surprising that his ascendancy was more fiercely contested, at least in those regions with strong operatic traditions of their own. France is a good case in point. It is arguable that the most important event in French operatic history during the early part of this period was the triumphant Parisian success of *Barbiere* in 1819, which brought in its wake a prolonged bout of Rossini 'fever'; but that event also inaugurated a long period in which the French cognoscenti, both critics and composers, struggled hard to protect their national identity in the face of this energetic foreign interloper.

If there remained something definably French against which to measure the Rossinian incursion, it probably sprang most powerfully from national developments in spoken drama, in particular from the emergence of a powerful new strand of *mélodrame*, a theatrical genre born in the late eighteenth century. Aspects of this style, which flourished in boulevard theatres far less elevated than those in which opera took place, were present in opéra comique as far back as the 1790s: a liking for tableau effects, close attention to – almost an idealisation of – non-verbal gesture, stock-in-trade characters who carried with them obvious moral messages. In some ways *mélodrame* might even be seen to have grown out of opéra comique.[9] But during the Restoration these techniques began to take on a new edge in their operatic context, one that was associated with 'Romanticism' and that provided one of the few effective ways of challenging Rossini. The most long-lived and successful example of the trend was *La dame blanche* by François-Adrien Boïeldieu (1775–1834), first performed at the Opéra-Comique in 1825 and by 1862 reaching its 1,000th performance at that theatre. With a libretto by Eugène Scribe, and a plot taken from Walter Scott, replete with haunted castles and a gloomy Scottish local colour, the opera was much admired by later composers (notably Wagner) who would overtly parade themselves as 'Romantic'. The main musical difference from Rossini, however, lies in the opera's avoidance of large-scale arias or grand choral movements. There is admittedly some occasional 'Italian' virtuosity; but more often brief ensembles and simple strophic numbers prevail, the latter often in so-called *couplets* form, with a 'refrain' at the end of each verse (an example is Jenny's famous ballade 'Ici voyez ce beau domaine', which ends with the refrain 'La Dame blanche vous regarde, la Dame blanche vous entend!').

Initially it seemed as though life at the Paris Opéra was relatively little affected by the Restoration. Works such as Spontini's *Olympie* (1819) merely continued the older, Empire traditions, and until about 1825 much of the repertory – a still-resilient Gluck and the earlier Spontini works – remained unchanged. There was an often-stated (and, as often, passionately contested) view that the 'real' operatic action was happening at the Théâtre-Italien, where Rossini's defenders had set out their stall, and where the composer himself was appointed Director in 1824, a year after he had settled permanently in Paris. Eventually the Opéra gave way and opened its doors to Rossini. His first outing was with *Le siège de Corinthe* (1826), an enormously successful French-language adaptation of *Maometto II*. Comparison of the two operas shows how Rossini skilfully adapted his style to suit French taste, in particular by reducing the amount of vocal decoration, and by purging the most overtly comical elements of his musical language. *Moïse* (1827) and *Le Comte Ory* (1828), two more adaptations from earlier Italian works, were equally popular, and paved the way for Rossini's first and only opera conceived especially for the Opéra, *Guillaume Tell* (1829). But by this time a new operatic genre was emerging at France's first theatre. It was a style that *Tell*, Rossini's last opera, did much to define; but its story is best left until the next section.

Superficially, the German-speaking lands might seem to have undergone the same trauma of foreign invasion as had France. Performances of *Tancredi* in

9 See Gabrielle Hyslop, 'Pixérécourt and the French Melodrama Debate: Instructing Boulevard Theatre Audiences', in James Redmond (ed.), *Melodrama* (Cambridge, 1992), pp. 61–85.

Vienna in 1816 opened the floodgates of a considerable Italian opera boom, albeit one that at first existed side by side with Singspiele and other traditional forms. But indigenous opera took a new turn as the various debates about literary Romanticism spread to music in a more thoroughgoing manner than they had in Italy or even France. Famously, the composer and critic E. T. A. Hoffmann (1776–1822) declared in an 1810 review of Beethoven's Fifth Symphony that 'the instrumental compositions of [Haydn, Mozart and Beethoven] breathe the same Romantic spirit',[10] and fairly soon after that works such as Louis Spohr's *Faust* (1816) and Hoffmann's own *Undine* (1816) showed the evident influence of literary Romanticism in setting mysterious supernatural characters within a 'rustic' context defined by folksong-like arias and choruses.

But the key figure of the period was undoubtedly Carl Maria von Weber (1786–1826), whose *Der Freischütz* (1821) was hugely influential not only on later German opera but on parallel developments in France. The latter influence was reciprocal, in that *Freischütz* plainly owes as much to opéra comique as to the Singspiele of the previous twenty years in Germany and Austria (its spoken dialogue, short numbers and use of local colour could all derive from either tradition). This is worth remembering, if only because *Freischütz* has sometimes been too easily pigeon-holed as a 'national' opera: its invention of an uncomplicated, folklike village ambience against which to set the sinister underworld is precisely that – an invention; only later was it appropriated as genuine 'folk music'.

The opera, though, is also significant in at least two further respects. First is the manner in which orchestral thought interacts with a system of recurring musical ideas, most notably in the supernatural music; this comes to a climax in the famous 'Wolf's Glen' scene, which features a distinctive orchestral combination of diminished chords, low clarinet sonorities, tremolo strings and pizzicato bass. This tendency to assign an individual colour to an opera by means of what we might call 'orchestral thought' will be an increasingly important means of operatic articulation in subsequent decades, especially in Germany. The second significant feature follows on from this, involving as it does Weber's attempts to make his opera unified in a more thoroughgoing manner. The composer laid out his ideas on this topic in a review of *Undine*, written some four years before the first performance of *Der Freischütz*:

> In no other art form is [a succession of irregular flashes of brilliance, individually attractive but leaving no lasting impression as a whole] so frequently encountered as in opera. Of course when I speak of opera I am speaking of the

10 Quoted from David Charlton (ed.), *E. T. A. Hoffmann's Musical Writings* (Cambridge, 1989), p. 237.

German ideal, namely a self-sufficient work of art in which every feature and
contribution by the related arts are moulded together in a certain way and dis-
solve, to form a new world.[11]

Needless to say, the idea that staging and other non-musical aspects of operatic
production might be closely co-ordinated had existed well before Weber: some
German-speaking theatres were already in the late eighteenth century giving
considerable attention to the total effect of theatrical performance. By the
1820s, Weber in Dresden put into operation a system in which all staging elements of an opera were self-consciously to be united, taking particular pains
with soloists' (and even the chorus's) histrionic abilities. This again was a tendency that spread rapidly in Germany during the next few decades.

Weber's next work, *Euryanthe* (1823), was a logical extension of this striving
for a 'unified' opera, as it attempted finally to escape the confines of opéra
comique and Singspiel by employing more complex musical forms within a
through-composed format, thus avoiding the fact that spoken dialogue interrupted the sense of musical continuity. In part this merely meant borrowing
from yet another French operatic genre, that of the old tragédie lyrique, and
indeed the use of the chorus can in places recall Spontini or even Gluck. But
again, Weber's harmonic and orchestral daring make the opera, in spite of its
highly convoluted libretto, an important document on the road to what is
sometimes called 'Romantic opera'.

Cross-currents (1830–1850)

In the previous two sections, it was relatively easy to organise our discussion
around various national schools. This approach now becomes more problematic, but will, *faute de mieux*, be retained. It is of course a commonplace that
the national distinctions so important to eighteenth-century opera gradually
began to erode during the nineteenth century, eventually to give way to an
'international' style; but significant differences remain between the mainstream traditions even to the century's end, and not merely those tied to the
prosodic patterns of the various languages. What is more, this process of 'inter-
nationalisation' did not always move in a direct line. One could argue, for
example, that the pull of French dramaturgical practice, together with the
unprecedented prestige and magnificence of French grand opera and the cosmopolitan leanings of post-Restoration Paris, made the 1830s and early 1840s
a significant moment of rapprochement between the major European traditions, at least within the most elevated genres. With Italian composers such as

11 Review dated January 1817, quoted in John Warrack (ed.), *Carl Maria von Weber: Writings on Music*
(Cambridge, 1981), p. 201.

Bellini and Donizetti looking towards Paris and Parisian style, and with the young Wagner deeply influenced by grand opera, one could suggest that Paris had fashioned around itself a 'European' style. But it was not to last; the three most influential composers of the 1850s and 1860s – Meyerbeer, Verdi and Wagner – all to some extent reinscribed a sense of national difference.

There are some further general trends that merit discussion. One of the most striking is a marked change in vocal type that occurred over much of Europe (albeit with regional variations) in the years around 1830. By that date, the castrati, already in steep decline during the later eighteenth century, had all but disappeared from the operatic stage, their heroic roles first taken by the *musico* (a cross-dressed soprano or contralto) and then by the 'romantic' tenor. This drop in the tessitura of heroes continued through the nineteenth century. In the 1820s and 1830s, for example, tenors freely used a 'mixed voice' to produce graceful high notes, but by the 1840s this had all but disappeared (at least in Italy and Germany; it coexisted with the earlier style for far longer in France), giving way to a concentration on the more baritonal, heavier tenor range. And the rise of this 'heroic tenor' roughly coincided with the emergence of the dramatic baritone as his central antagonist, or even – though rarely up to 1850 – as the principal character. All voice types gradually sacrificed flexibility for sheer power: the ornamental vocal writing that had been the province of all up to about 1820 became by mid-century the exclusive domain of female singers.

These changes are of course related to other developments in operatic practice. On a practical level, the need for greater vocal power, for example, clearly went hand in hand with the expansion of the orchestra, and of theatres generally. A more complex equation could be drawn between the shift away from soprano voices in heroic roles, and also the rise of the tenor and baritone, and an increasing desire for a degree of operatic 'realism': opera came closer to the communicative codes of spoken drama if the singing voices of characters were differentiated in a manner similar to their differentiation in a stage play. This new interest in 'realism' was undoubtedly fuelled and encouraged by technology: gas lighting appeared in theatres around 1820. As well as being (a little) safer than previous, naked-flame expedients, gas also allowed for greater sophistication of stage illusion, as did enlarged back-stage spaces and more complex machinery.

Another equally important, and pan-European, development, was a 'dialogising' process, the gathering sense in which opera from about 1830 began to present musical dialogue as the central aspect of its communicative project. This in one sense also brought opera closer to the 'realism' of spoken drama, and meant that the duet (or, more precisely, the duologue) began to replace the aria as opera's 'normative' discourse. However, partly because the solo was so

central to the genre's dissemination outside the theatre (in concerts and private
venues both humble and elevated), the aria – or at worst the chunk of monologue – continued in firm currency in almost all types of opera through to the
end of this period (indeed to the end of the century), typically remaining an
unproblematic aspect of the dramaturgy, not requiring special plot preparation
to justify its presence.

However, the combined effects of 'dialogising' and increased continuity,
together with a falling away of predictable formal patterns, left room for
(perhaps necessitated) other levels of musical communication within opera.
Probably the most important of these was by motivic means. As we have seen,
reminiscence motifs began to be used during the first half of the nineteenth
century in most national styles, perhaps most commonly in German opera,
least often in Italian – a point surely reflecting the 'symphonic' aspirations of
German composers. Just as significant, though: opera simply got noisier.
Although the string sections of orchestras did not get much larger during the
nineteenth century, the orchestral 'centre of gravity' gradually slipped, with
lower tessituras used for certain woodwind instruments (flutes and bassoons),
a strengthening of the lower brass, and the gradual addition of further wind
instruments of various kinds. These changes were of course related to developments elsewhere: in the demands made of operatic orchestras within an
increasingly continuous operatic fabric; in theatre architecture and in the sheer
size of venues; in changes in singing style; and in more general organological
developments.

Amidst the huge diversity of operatic plots in the early nineteenth century,
it is difficult to trace firm lines of development. On the most basic level,
however, the domination of French dramaturgical models seen at the end of
the eighteenth century was in large part maintained. As we have seen, when sea
changes occurred in French spoken theatre – such as the advent of *mélodrame* –
then opera followed, and did so regardless of the various inflections brought
on by national differences. But certain large shifts in cultural attitude nevertheless left their mark. For example, opera plots are surely implicated in the
now familiar idea that the nineteenth century saw an important turn away
from what the sociologist Richard Sennett has famously called the idea of
'public man': an increasing tendency for ever more stressed and crowded
urban dwellers to seek coherence not within the 'public' world of politics and
public display, which had so often betrayed them and was obviously beyond
their control, but rather within the 'private' world of the family and of personal relationships.[12]

12 Richard Sennett, *The Fall of Public Man* (New York, 1977).

This notion of public vs. private immediately calls attention to what is probably an inevitable starting-point for this period: the international style par excellence which was grand opera, that most influential of French opera types, whose impact is hard to overestimate in the latter half of the century. Definition of the term is sometimes very broad, but it is probably best to restrict it to those large-scale serious operas (usually in five acts, with integral ballet and much use of grand choral effects) and historical subjects from the Middle Ages or the Early Modern period, created for the Académie Royale de Musique, otherwise known as the Opéra. This could plausibly be thought to include the tragédie lyrique of the first decade (Spontini in particular), but the genre is generally agreed to find its first long-lasting example in *La muette de Portici* (1828), music by Daniel-François-Esprit Auber (1782–1871) to a libretto by Scribe. *La muette* was followed the next year by another enormous success, Rossini's *Guillaume Tell*. In the 1830s and 1840s a relatively small number of similar works joined these two to dominate the repertory. Three of them were written by the German composer Giacomo Meyerbeer (1791–1864), whose production virtually defines the genre: *Robert le diable* (1831), *Les Huguenots* (1836) and *Le prophète* (1849). The success of these works was matched only by Halévy's *La juive* (1835) and Gaetano Donizetti's *La favorite* (1840). By 1850 the genre had changed in some basic ways: it occupies, then, a span of about two decades, indeed a major way in which the period 1830 to 1850 hangs together is precisely through the presence of this particular genre.

What were its chief characteristics? It is perhaps simplest to see a 'classic' grand opera as one defining itself through the presentation of difference, through the sheer variety it offered audiences. First, there was what we might call an historical level. One of the central features of the genre was its use of stage spectacle, a presentation of public life in all its grandeur, most notably in ensemble scenes that were vastly enlarged versions of the Italian *concertato finale*. Then, as a foil to this element, and often in open conflict with it, came the domestic sphere, the world of private emotion: this sphere was often played out in long confrontational duets formed along Italian models and involving intense personal expression. The third important element, and perhaps the main one that differentiated grand opera from the more elaborate Italian serious operas, was decoration and ornament. The most obvious manifestation of this was the presence of an elaborate ballet embedded somewhere within the plot, but it also appeared in highly ornamental, 'characteristic' arias, and in the depiction of 'couleur locale', a sense of precise geographical ambience musically depicted by orchestral colour and piquant harmonies.

The list of its most successful composers immediately reveals that this was above all an international genre, with Italian and French modes particularly important in the stylistic mix. Indeed, the closer one looks, the more levels of variety one can see: comparison is hard to avoid with what is often depicted as *the* characteristic artistic genre of the nineteenth century, the great historical novel. There was resistance to the new style, of course, not least from those who felt the entire business was simply too grandiose, in particular that the audience's delight in scenic spectacle ruthlessly overpowered all other aspects. The poet Heinrich Heine opined that 'nothing exceeds the luxury of the grand opera, which is now become a paradise of the hard of hearing';[13] Wagner put it more succinctly when he talked about 'effects without causes'.

Necessary though such broad definitions might be, the grand opera of this period was of course inflected powerfully by individual preferences among its most prominent composers. It is, for example, certainly true that the two earliest successes, *La muette de Portici* and *Guillaume Tell*, betray significant similarities, in particular their use of 'couleur locale' and of 'the people' as a new dynamic force – one quite different from the generic choruses of previous decades. But the two works also have notable individual traits. *La muette* ends with a remarkable scenic spectacle in which the heroine flings herself into the lava of an erupting Vesuvius, and the simplicity of the music at this climactic moment (nothing more than a sequence of mechanically repeated scales) underlines the fact that the visual element is meant to carry all before it. Rossini's *Tell*, on the other hand, never relinquishes musical elaboration to this extent. As we might expect, Rossini is more reliant than Auber on Italian formal models, in particular in his use of multi-movement grand ensemble. And this opera's final moment of visual splendour (the revelation of a magnificent Alpine landscape) is accompanied by music that aspires to translate the sublime scenic effect into sound, its grand musical gestures seeming to slow down the very passing of time as man contemplates nature.

The key, perhaps the defining compositional personality, though, was Meyerbeer, who gained extraordinary international acclaim during his later life and for a few decades afterwards, then to fall into a black hole of neglect and critical hostility from which he has barely emerged since. The international quality of grand opera would seem summed up in Meyerbeer's career: German born, and with a solid Germanic training; a prolonged sojourn in Italy, where inevitably he became a follower of Rossini – although his last opera in Italy, *Il crociato in Egitto* (1824), already shows some significant emancipations from

---

13 Heinrich Heine, 'Über die französische Bühne', quoted in Jürgen Maehder, 'Historienmalerei und Grand Opéra: zur Raumvorstellung in der Bildern Géricaults und Delacroix und auf der Bühne der Académie royale de Musique', in Sieghart Döhring and Arnold Jacobshagen (eds.), *Meyerbeer und das europäische Musiktheater* (Laaber, 1998), p. 258.

Rossinian style, notably in its tendency to more complex orchestration; then the move to Paris. Meyerbeer's first French opera, *Robert le diable*, which was initially planned as early as 1827 but did not see its first performance until 1831, enjoyed an international success that rivalled even Rossini, being seen in ten countries during its first five years. Perhaps the central work, however, was *Les Huguenots* (1836), in which the essential traits of grand opera – its grandiosity and cosmopolitan variety – are magnificently displayed within a plot that takes as its backdrop the struggles in sixteenth-century France between Protestants and Catholics. But within the kaleidoscope of 'characteristic' scenes such a plot offers, the carefully wrought orchestral effects and the massive choral numbers, it is well to remember that Meyerbeer was also a great master of dramatic pacing. In a scene such as that in Act IV, in which Catholic conspirators meet to have their daggers blest before attacking the Protestants, the subsequent love duet between Raoul (Protestant) and Valentine (Catholic) gains much of its effect from the fact that Raoul, hearing the massacre taking place outside, becomes desperate to join in the defence of his religion.

If grand opera was so influential, why is it that, almost alone among the major operatic types discussed in this section, it has so thoroughly fallen from our repertory? Why in this case is there such a disjunction between 'their' taste and 'ours'? The appalling expense of marshalling the forces required to perform grand operas is of course significant, as is the fact that the voices which dominated the genre are now difficult to find; but these can hardly be determining factors (they have, after all, rarely discouraged revivals of later Wagner or Verdi). We might of course retreat into arguments about 'musical value', but it is probably more interesting to concentrate again on the sheer variety that characterises the genre, a trait so suited to the times in which it flourished, but so much less in tune with the newly nationalist, and newly racist, atmosphere of the later nineteenth and twentieth centuries. When 'cosmopolitanism' became a threat rather than something to be proud of, it is easy to see how Meyerbeer, especially the *idea* of Meyerbeer, would become distasteful. It is, though, harder to see why that reputation has remained so stubbornly into our own times.[14]

We must pass more rapidly over the 'other' side of indigenous French operatic creation, that centring around the opéra comique, even though among the public at large it was at the time at least as popular. Indeed, the 1830s were a

---

14 In the earlier twentieth century this criticism would sometimes be couched in overtly anti-Semitic terms. For example, Dyneley Hussey, *Verdi* (London, 1940), p. 30, describes Meyerbeer's move from Italy to Paris: 'With that flair for what a given public wants, so often displayed by artists of Jewish descent, he changed his style . . .'. But even in modern reference works such as the *New Grove Dictionary of Opera*, where one would expect the entry on Meyerbeer to be something of a case for the defence, the summing-up of the 'Operatic Style and Influence' lists more on the negative side than it does on the positive.

high-watermark in the international success of the genre, with the injection of a new, more Italian-influenced manner making the product more exportable than it had been previously. Auber, already discussed as one of the pioneers of grand opera, was again a leading figure, with numerous opéras comiques and opéras ballets to his name. In hugely successful works such as *Fra Diavolo* (1830) and *Le domino noir* (1837), we find that some arias have gained in (Italian) expansiveness, but there remains a preponderance of ensembles and simple, *couplets*-style solos, the whole bound together with a rhythmic energy to rival that of Rossini. Indeed, fuelled with the work of other prominent composers, such as Adolphe-Charles Adam (1803–1856) with *Le postillon de Longjumeau* (1836), Joseph-Ferdinand Hérold (1791–1833) with *Zampa* (1831), and Donizetti with *La fille du régiment* (1840), the genre managed to vie with Rossini even as it assumed many of his formal trademarks. Nor should we underestimate the influence of opéra comique in the second half of the century. On the one hand the genre was crucial in the development of Offenbach and the operetta; but it had an equally important effect (at least equivalent to that of grand opera) on composers of serious opera as disparate as Verdi and Bizet.

The operatic career of Hector Berlioz (1803–69) is, as ever with this composer, difficult to fit into the usual categories. A self-confessed admirer of Gluck and Spontini, Berlioz was in his copious and highly entertaining operatic criticism often dismissive of modern manifestations of both grand opera and opéra comique, not to mention the works of the new Italian school. Even so, it is possible to see much of his music during this period as that of an opera composer manqué. In spite of his strenuous activities at the Opéra in reviving other composer's works, notably with an arrangement of *Der Freischütz* (1841), his only original work for the theatre was *Benvenuto Cellini* (1838), which fared badly with the public in spite of its innovative orchestration and rhythmic energy. After the failure of his 'légende dramatique' *La Damnation de Faust* at the Opéra-Comique in 1846, a disillusioned Berlioz toured far and wide as a conductor; the unexpected and highly original climax to his operatic career would occur only in the 1850s and 1860s.

The first signs of a significant post-Rossinian voice in Italian opera emerged just before 1830, with the appearance of Vincenzo Bellini (1801–35). Bellini's earliest operas had shown the (inevitable) influence of Rossini, but both *Il pirata* (1827) and, in particular, *La straniera* (1829) were immediately recognised as a new departure, one often signalled by contemporary critics as 'Romantic'. This appellation had less to do with details of the operas' plots (although both were somewhat influenced by a fashion for the 'gothic') than with Bellini's highly individual writing for the solo voice, in which single words and phrases were communicated to the listener in a far more direct manner than Rossini would have thought aesthetically pleasing. Though Bellini for the most part kept to the standard multi-movement forms codified by Rossini, he largely avoided Rossinian vocal decoration, instead concentrating on an intense vocal declamation, with long melodies evolving often without obvious phrase repetition and with frequent expressive rests and non-periodic phrase rhythms. Bellini's operas in the early 1830s – *Norma* (1831) and, in particular *Beatrice di Tenda* (1833) – step back a little from these extremes, but even when his writing is 'ornamental', as for example in the famous aria 'Casta diva' from Act I of *Norma*, the ornamentation is always of motivic significance.

Gaetano Donizetti (1797–1848) was a little slower to emerge from the Rossinian background. After a decade of writing both comic and serious operas, his 'maturity' is sometimes declared to arrive with *Anna Bolena* (1830), an opera that certainly brought him new national and (eventually) international prestige: in formal terms the opera shows considerable freedom from the Rossinian norms, in particular by investing emotional significance in moments of heightened recitative. If thought of strictly in terms of Bellinian radicalism (the intense vocal declamation of *La straniera*), however, *Anna* is still rather old fashioned, with a continued use of Rossinian ornamentation in the vocal line. A more important Donizettian landmark was reached in the series of overtly 'Romantic' operas that he wrote in the early and mid-1830s, which included such works as *Parisina* (1833), *Maria Stuarda* and *Lucia di Lammermoor* (both 1835) and *Roberto Devereux* (1837). Another of these 'Romantic' operas, *Lucrezia Borgia* (1833), is particularly interesting in that the play on which it is based was by that arch-Romantic French dramatist Victor Hugo. Although the librettist Felice Romani attempted to deflect criticism of this audacious subject in a preface to the printed text, all the major reviewers saw as a root cause of the opera's failure Hugo's pernicious influence: Donizetti was accused of betraying the true nature of Italian opera, by not allowing the characters to express themselves at sufficient length in florid song. Behind this was all too clearly the fear of foreign contamination – a conviction that the loose morals and 'prosaic' habits of the French were in some way deeply connected, and could infect a vocal 'purity' that was seen as classically Italian.

Bellini's last opera, *I puritani* (1835), was first performed at the Théâtre-Italien in Paris, a further sign of the French capital becoming a mecca for European opera composers with 'international' aspirations. Donizetti in his final creative years (from 1838 until 1844) went further, dividing his time between Paris and Vienna, and producing a string of innovative works in a startling array of genres, from full-scale grand opera, to opéra comique, to both serious and comic Italian opera. Three of the most remarkable of these works were written for Vienna. *Maria di Rohan* (1843) is powerfully influenced by *mélodrame*, to the extent of radically condensing Italian fixed forms and focusing attention on moments of intense theatrical tension in which the music was little more than 'atmospheric', and of juxtaposing the passing of musical and dramatic time in a manner unprecedented in opera of any previous period; *Linda di Chamounix* (1842) engages with the tradition of opera semiseria, in which liberal injections of local colour engage with a plot that wavers between the tragic, the sentimental and the downright comic; and *Don Pasquale* (1843) is a 'classic' example of opera buffa, one in which Rossinian stylistic traits are coloured by a sentimental vein of light melancholy that was a Donizettian trademark. The sheer variety of these last works displays how stylistically 'international' and eclectic Italian opera had now become.

In some ways the early operas of Giuseppe Verdi (1813–1901) show a retrenchment from the last works of Bellini and Donizetti. His first great success, *Nabucco* (1842), with its massed choral effects and clear-cut forms, is closer to Rossini than to either of the two later composers, both in its treatment of the chorus and in its clear-cut divisions between recitative and aria. But from the start there was a rhythmic energy, melodic power and gift for theatrical effect that carried all before it. By the time of *Ernani* (1844), Verdi became the most popular and often-performed Italian opera composer, a position he has held ever since. *Ernani*, much more 'domestic' than the oratorio-like *Nabucco*, betrays the influence of Hugolian 'Romanticism' in its plot (it is based on a Hugo play) but, rather than follow the formal experiments of Donizetti, Verdi preferred to express the passion of the situations by maintaining a tight control on formal numbers, building maximum tension through the harnessing of ornamental features within a rigidly defined periodicity. After *Ernani*, Verdi produced a series of operas up to 1850, each of which seems consciously to break new ground. Although they are all serious, the variety of dramatic type is enormous: the 'oratorio' style of *Nabucco* was continued in *Attila* (1846), *Jérusalem* (1847, his first opera written for Paris, and a remake of the earlier *I Lombardi* of 1843) and *La battaglia di Legnano* (1849); a Romantic interest in the supernatural together with a bold attempt to realise unconventional main characters is found in *Macbeth* (1847); traces of the semiserio genre, with more than a bow to the example of Donizetti in *Linda di Chamounix*, are folded into a tragic plot in *Luisa Miller* (1849).

Verdi moved to Paris in 1847, to remain there for most of the next two years; it was a crucial step, in that all the operas after that time betray the vivid impression of Parisian operatic style. This shows itself in a gathering interest in French-style arias, in particular the *couplets* type, and by an increased refinement and complexity of orchestral writing. Much of this doubtless came from exposure to Meyerbeer and other grand opera composers; but there is evidence that Verdi was also attending more humble theatrical events. In *Stiffelio* (1850), for example, the final scene owes an obvious debt to the techniques of *mélodrame*: intense personal confrontation is mimed or merely declaimed over a spare but atmospheric orchestral background. This was a style that Verdi would use to even greater effect in the operas of the early 1850s, in particular *Rigoletto* and *La traviata*.

It is worth stressing this continuing openness to foreign influence, as Verdi has traditionally been portrayed as above all a nationalist composer, the creator of 'patriotic' choruses such as 'Va pensiero' in *Nabucco* that are supposed to have crystallised the Italian people's sense of national identity, encouraging them to eject the 'foreigners' who controlled much of the peninsula and proclaiming themselves a nation. This is an attractive story; but, at least until the 1850s, it is supported by very little evidence. True, operatic performances were occasionally the site of public demonstrations during the immediate run up to the 1848 revolutions (small wonder when the opera house was the principal venue in which the bourgeoisie could congregate in large numbers), but Verdi's music was no more often involved than that of other composers. His reputation as 'bard of the Italian *Risorgimento*' was real enough, but it was for the most part constructed in the latter half of the nineteenth century, when a young, newly consolidated Italy urgently required such cultural monuments in order to create a sense of national identity.

As it happens, though, the period between 1830 and 1850 did see the decisive establishment of a number of 'national operatic traditions', in particular those in Russia, Poland and various parts of the Habsburg empire, notably Hungary. All of these areas had seen vernacular opera during the eighteenth century, but the formation of a 'national opera' was, as in Italy and Germany, intimately bound up with the process of cultural nation-building. In some cases one can identify key works that managed, more by dint of multiple performance and/or association with political events than by their occasional use of 'authentic' folk materials, to collect around them a potent miscellany of musical and dramatic/literary motifs that could function as symbols of an emerging nation. The process here is important, and is often misunderstood: rather than *appropriating* an already existing fund of 'national' musical material, these operas typically tended to *construct* that material – becoming (as Verdi would in Italy) 'national' through the cumulative acts of national reception they underwent.

A good case in point, and the earliest of these 'national' operas, is by the Russian Mikhail Ivanovich Glinka (1804–57). His *A Life for the Czar* (1836), which describes itself rather grandly as a 'patriotic heroic-tragic opera', is in many ways a 'rescue' opera in the style of Cherubini's *Les deux journées*, and also shows more than a hint of Rossinian influence, doubtless deriving from Glinka's Italian sojourn in the 1830s. Centring around the seventeenth-century figure of Ivan Susanin, a peasant fighting again the Polish invasion, the score makes one or two gestures towards folk material, but most of its 'Russianness' derives from the distinctly urban tradition of salon music. The newness in Glinka's work, however, comes through the manner in which this material, which had been used often enough in earlier works as 'local colour', inhabits the core of the drama, in particular during climactic moments of the action. The novelty and importance of *A Life for the Czar* was very quickly appreciated, and the opera is to this day regarded as a watershed in the development of Russian music. Glinka's second opera, *Ruslan and Lyudmila* (1842), has never been as successful with the public, although it was much imitated by later Russian composers, in particular those who developed its fairy-tale and orientalist themes.

In other Eastern European countries we can see similar developments during the same period, although none would match the eventual international dissemination of the Russian repertory. Hungary established a national theatre in Pest in 1837, an institution directed for many years by Ferenc Erkel (1810–93), who was the central figure in nineteenth-century Hungarian opera, and whose *Hunyadi László* (1844) is liberally laced with Hungarian idioms such as the *Verbunkos* (a style of dance music with alternations of slow and fast sections and various characteristic rhythms), later to be made internationally famous by Liszt. Equally, though, the opera shows the influence of Donizetti and Bellini, whose operas remained a staple of the Hungarian repertory. In Poland the best-known figure is Stanisław Moniuszko (1819–72), in particular for his opera *Halka* (1848, concert performance; staged 1854). The work also shows the influence of an earlier generation of Italian opera composers (i.e. Rossini rather than Verdi) while also owing a debt to French grand opera. There are again 'national' episodes but, unlike Glinka, these tend to get overpowered by the 'emotional' ones: in other words they drift into being merely local colour – always the danger in this kind of opera, as it had been for *Freischütz* some thirty years earlier.

Finally we come to Germany, and inevitably to Richard Wagner (1813–83), who was to dominate German opera in the latter stages of the nineteenth century in a manner equalled only by Verdi in Italy. One of Wagner's central achievements was to launch, by means of both literary and operatic texts, the most thoroughgoing challenge to the declining aesthetic prestige that opera had experienced in the early nineteenth century. Most of this story involves his operas post-1850, and will be dealt with in chapter 14, but Wagner's early works have often been caught up in the story, often seen through the lens of the later ones. One still-repeated cliché, for example, is that his first three operas, *Die Feen* (1833), *Das Liebesverbot* (1835) and *Rienzi* (1842), reflect a fascination, in turn, with German, then Italian, then French opera. Certainly *Die Feen*'s supernatural subject can be related to current trends in German opera (it has substantially the same plot as Hofmann's *Undine*), and the musical forms owe much to Weber and Marschner; and it is also true that *Rienzi* was planned as a Meyerbeerian vehicle with which to storm the Paris Opéra (it failed to find a performance there, and was eventually produced, with great success, in Dresden). But *Das Liebesverbot* has little that can be laid at the door of Italian opera, whether of Bellini or, still less, Rossini, again relying on a mixture of French and German models. The likely reason behind disseminating this idea of an early tour through the main European operatic styles (a tale encouraged by the composer himself) was to place Wagner as a synthesis of these styles, quite possibly as a rival to Meyerbeer, whose early training, as we have seen, did indeed involve exposure to German, Italian and then French opera.

The success of *Rienzi* did, however, allow Wagner to complete *Der fliegende Holländer* (1843), a self-styled 'Romantic Opera' also premièred in Dresden. This opera, with its story of a ghostly seafarer condemned to sail the seas perpetually until the love of a woman can redeem him, clearly anticipates one of the principal themes of Wagner's post-1850s operas. What is more, the work (particularly in its single-act version) strives for an unusual consistency of tone and atmosphere, and a blurring of the distinction between recitative and aria, that had previously been rare in German opera. On the other hand, one should be sceptical about claims (again originating with Wagner himself) that the entire musical fabric of the piece is born from Senta's balled 'Johohoe! Johohohoe!', which was apparently the first piece to be sketched musically: the musical ideas in this extraordinary number certain recur from time to time, but much of the rest of the opera is occupied with motivically discrete, stock situations deriving from contemporary German and French opera. Wagner's next work, *Tannhäuser* (1845), was certainly another large advance, with a vastly expanded canvas (it was called a 'Grand Romantic Opera'), an increased tendency to blur recitative and aria, and with the orchestral accompaniment becoming an unprecedentedly important musical strand. Yet again there are obvious elements relating to earlier German opera, particularly perhaps in the old-German local colour and its attendant choral episodes; and again the language of French grand opera is gestured towards in the grand ensemble scenes. One of the most significant passages, though, is the Act III narrative in which Tannhäuser describes his pilgrimage to Rome. Here, in a remarkable prefiguring of Wagner's post-1850s style, the orchestral contribution is of the greatest importance, bringing at it does a web of motivic connections to enrich the through-composed progress of the hero's narration.

From *Les deux journées* and *La vestale* to *Tannhäuser* and *Stiffelio*: in the space of half a century opera had changed in numerous important ways. But there were also important continuities. In spite of a brief period in the later 1830s and 1840s, when 'Parisian' opera had laid some claim to be regarded as an 'international' style, the sense of discrete national traditions still holds, indeed might even be said to have intensified in the early works of Verdi and Wagner. It would be left to the remainder of the century to negotiate that difficult path between the increasingly strident demands for 'national' expression and the inevitable, technology-driven sense in which opera communicated across cultures and shared influences. By 1850 this future was perhaps difficult to see: Verdi was nearing the height of his global fame, and although Meyerbeer had begun to make his mark internationally, in particular with *Robert le diable*, Wagner had barely started to emerge from his local successes. As we shall see, though, the future was emphatically on Wagner's side.

Bibliography

Abbate, C., 'Erik's Dream and Tannhäuser's Journey'. In A. Groos and R. Parker (eds.), *Reading Opera*. Princeton, 1988, pp. 129–67

Adamo, M. R. and Lippmann, F. (eds.), *Vincenzo Bellini*. Turin, 1981

Ashbrook, W., *Donizetti and his Operas*. Cambridge, 1982

Balthazar, S. L., 'Mayr and the Development of the Two-Movement Aria'. In F. Bellotto (ed.), *Giovanni Simone Mayr: l'opera teatrale e la musica sacra*. Bergamo, 1997, pp. 229–51

Becker H. and Becker G. (eds.), *Giacomo Meyerbeer: His Life as Seen through His Letters*. Portland, Oreg., 1989

Bloom, P. (ed.), *Music in Paris in the Eighteen-Thirties*. Stuyvesant, N.Y., 1987

Budden, J., *The Operas of Verdi*. 3 vols., London, 1973, 1978, 1981

Charlton, D. (ed.), *E. T. A. Hoffmann's Musical Writings*. Cambridge, 1989

Cohen, H. R. (ed.), *The Original Staging Manuals for Twelve Parisian Operatic Premieres*. Stuyvesant, N.Y., 1991

Dahlhaus, C., *Richard Wagner's Music Dramas*. Cambridge, 1979
    Nineteenth-Century Music, trans. J. B. Robinson. Berkeley and Los Angeles, 1989

Dean, W., in the *New Oxford History of Music*, VIII. Oxford, 1982 (essays on German, French and Italian opera)

Döhring, S. and Henze-Döhring, S., *Oper und Musikdrama im 19. Jahrhundert*. Laaber, 1997

Fulcher, J., *The Nation's Image: French Grand Opera as Politics and Politicized Art*. Cambridge, 1987

Gerhard, A., *The Urbanization of Opera*. Chicago, 1998

Gossett, P., *Anna Bolena and the Artistic Maturity of Gaetano Donizetti*. Oxford, 1985

Gossett, P. *et al.*, *The New Grove Masters of Italian Opera*. London, 1983 (chapters on Rossini, Bellini, Donizetti, Verdi and Puccini)

Holoman, D. K., *Berlioz*. London, 1989

Hyslop, G., 'Pixérécourt and the French Melodrama Debate: Instructing Boulevard Theatre Audiences'. In J. Redmond (ed.), *Melodrama*. Cambridge, 1992, pp. 61–85

Kimbell, D., *Italian Opera*. Cambridge, 1991

Millington, B., *Wagner*. London, 1984; 2nd edn 1992

Mongrédien, J., *French Music from the Enlightenment to Romanticism, 1789–1830*. Portland, Oreg., 1996

Osborne, R., *Rossini*. London, 1986

Pendle, K., *Eugène Scribe and French Opera of the Nineteenth Century*. Ann Arbor, 1979

Robinson, P., '*Fidelio* and the French Revolution'. *Cambridge Opera Journal*, 3 (1991), pp. 23–48

Rosselli, J., *The Opera Industry in Italy from Cimarosa to Verdi: The Role of the Impresario*. Cambridge, 1984

  Singers of Italian Opera: The History of a Profession. Cambridge, 1992

  'Opera Production, 1780–1880'. In L. Bianconi and G. Pestelli (eds.), *Opera Production and its Resources*. Chicago, 1998, pp. 81–164

  The Life of Bellini. Cambridge, 1996

Warrack, J., *Carl Maria von Weber*. London, 1968; 2nd edn 1976

Warrack, J. (ed.), *Carl Maria von Weber: Writings on Music*. Cambridge, 1981

5

The construction of Beethoven

K. M. KNITTEL

Beethoven vs. 'Beethoven'

On 28 May 1810, a young woman wrote to the German poet Johann Wolfgang von Goethe describing her new acquaintance, Ludwig van Beethoven:

> When I saw him of whom I shall now speak to you, I forgot the whole world . . . It is Beethoven of whom I now wish to tell you . . . but I am not mistaken when I say – what no one, perhaps, now understands and believes – he stalks far ahead of the culture of mankind. Shall we ever overtake him? – I doubt it, but grant that he may live until the mighty and exalted enigma lying in his soul is fully developed, may reach its loftiest goal, then surely he will place the key to his heavenly knowledge in our hands so that we may be advanced another step towards true happiness.
>
> . . . I may confess I believe in a divine magic which is the essence of intellectual life. This magic Beethoven practises in his art. Everything that he can tell you about is pure magic, every posture is the organization of a higher existence, and therefore Beethoven feels himself to be the founder of a new sensuous basis in the intellectual life . . . Who could replace this mind for us? From whom could we expect so much? All human activities toss around him like mechanism, he alone begets independently in himself the unsuspected, uncreated. What to him is intercourse with the world – to him who is at his sacred daily task before sunrise and who after sunset scarcely looks about him, who forgets sustenance for his body and who is carried in a trice, by the stream of his enthusiasm, past the shores of work-a-day things?[1]

The picture of Beethoven drawn here – the isolated, eccentric genius committed to his art and its importance to the point of forgetting to eat – is immediately recognisable. When the young woman writes that Beethoven reported to her 'I have not a single friend; I must live alone', we can feel the pain of Beethoven's loneliness and deafness. When she reports that he told her 'music . . . is the mediator between the life of the mind and the senses', the words resonate with our experience of his music. The strength of Beethoven's personality

---

1 Cited in O. G. Sonneck, *Beethoven: Impressions by His Contemporaries* (New York, 1967), pp. 79–80.

combined with the 'magic' of his art ensure that even a mere mortal – the author – can forget 'the whole world'.

Towards the end of the same letter, the young woman tells Goethe of Beethoven's intense desire to meet him, and with her help, the two did meet during the summer of 1812. Writing soon after this long-awaited event, Beethoven described it to her in a letter. He reports that on one of their walks together in the countryside at Teplitz (a spa in Bohemia), he, Beethoven, had refused to cede the road to the approaching Austrian imperial family. While Goethe had stood aside with head bowed, Beethoven had strode on, forcing members of the ruling family – including the empress and her son the Archduke Rudolph (Beethoven's patron and composition student) – to make room for him. In recounting these events, Beethoven emphasises his own 'nobility' based on his talent, implying that Goethe clings to the older idea of the 'natural' superiority of the aristocracy. This 'Teplitz incident' (as it is now called) has come to exemplify our image of the independent, strong-willed Beethoven.

As someone who had met Beethoven personally, Bettina Brentano von Arnim's (1785–1859) vivid descriptions offered here are highly valued, even if, as one commentator has noted, 'her writings are altogether too hyper-romantic for present taste'.[2] In 1835, she published her correspondence with Goethe under the title *Goethes Briefwechsel mit einem Kinde* (Goethe's Correspondence with a Child – which included the above letter), and four years later published the three letters that she had received from Beethoven. Still alive when Alexander Wheelock Thayer – the great Beethoven biographer – was interviewing Beethoven's friends and acquaintances during the years 1849–51, Bettina, who continued to support musicians and artists into her old age, easily captivated everyone with her charm and beauty.

Bettina's Beethoven seems so real – so familiar – that it comes as a shock to find out that hardly a single word that she published can be trusted. Of the three letters (1810, 1811 and 1812) that she claimed to have received from Beethoven, only the one of 1811 exists in Beethoven's hand, suggesting that she was the author of the other two. The Teplitz incident, so *characteristic* of Beethoven, is thus almost certainly a fabrication. Even her exchange of letters with Goethe is unreliable: before publication, she significantly rewrote not only her side of the correspondence, but Goethe's as well.

Despite the dubious nature of Bettina's descriptions, however, authors continue to rely on her works as primary sources. In his Beethoven monograph, William Kinderman downplays the question of reliability by stating that 'it is not necessary to have full confidence in the details of Bettina Brentano's report

2 *Ibid.*, p. 75.

in order to evaluate the general import of her testimony'. He cites the words that 'Beethoven' supposedly spoke to her as evidence that the poet Friedrich Schiller's ideas regarding 'a merging of the rational and sensuous in the work of art' (from his 'On Naive and Sentimental Poetry' written in 1795–6) were taking root in the culture and thought of the time.[3] Yet not only are 'Beethoven's' words almost certainly fabricated, they most likely date from the 1830s – and not from 1810 as Kinderman suggests.

Kinderman's unreflective use of Bettina's letters helps to illustrate what Carl Dahlhaus means when he writes 'The Beethoven myth . . . is separated from empirical biography by a chasm that represents something more than a simple opposition of truth and falsehood'.[4] The problem is not that authors are unaware that a Beethoven myth exists – and Bettina's 'Beethoven' represents but one piece of a much larger collage – but rather that the myth itself is so compelling: Beethoven, the fiery genius, perhaps the greatest musical mind ever known, loses his *hearing*, the one sense a musician cannot do without; yet somehow he perseveres, making his accomplishments that much greater for having originated in a life so filled with pain and sadness. We find Beethoven's ability to overcome his circumstances reassuring – for, ultimately, are we not simply suckers for a happy ending?

Even if the Beethoven myth contains a kernel of truth, however – he did, after all, continue to compose despite his deafness – it nevertheless reduces him to a cipher: within the myth, Beethoven is not a human being, but rather a symbol of a larger aesthetic doctrine or concern. The myth ignores anything – biographical facts, musical works, real suffering – that cannot reify the happy ending. Thus, it includes only a few biographical details (such as his deafness, frequent illnesses and love of solitude) and instead emphasises primarily anecdotes, including many like 'the Teplitz incident' that cannot be shown to be true, but which nevertheless seem to illustrate something 'real'. Musically, the myth restricts Beethoven's *oeuvre* to a mere handful of pieces that are valued for their ability to illustrate his strength – Dahlhaus lists '*Fidelio* and the music to *Egmont*; the Third, Fifth, and Ninth Symphonies; and the *Pathétique* and *Appassionata* sonatas' – ignoring those pieces that are too 'happy' or that do not foreground conflict. This limited collection of pieces, facts and anecdotes is then overlaid with a Romantic plot of struggle and transcendence, suggesting not just a reading of Beethoven's life, but a reason and a way to value his works as well.

As Dahlhaus points out, 'we seldom think of how much we lost as the Beethoven tradition took root'. He gives as an example Beethoven's early

3 William Kinderman, *Beethoven* (Berkeley and Los Angeles, 1995), p. 147.
4 Carl Dahlhaus, *Nineteenth-Century Music*, trans. J. B. Robinson (Berkeley and Los Angeles, 1989), p. 76.

works in the divertimento tradition which 'vanished virtually without a trace from the late-nineteenth-century repertoire and sank into oblivion'.[5] The way we interpret Beethoven controls not just which genres are valued (symphonies, string quartets), but even how we perceive Beethoven's own works: by valuing the strong or 'heroic' works for example, we automatically place 'non-heroic' works into the shadows. Beethoven's influence transcends chronology – we often see Haydn and Mozart solely as precursors to Beethoven, and the generations following Beethoven suffer in comparison to him, both during their own lifetimes and in our present histories. Only by understanding and acknowledging that the Beethoven myth controls the way we think about music in general can we open the way for alternative histories.

That said, however, one cannot dismiss as negligible the claims that the Beethoven myth has had *as history*: composers and writers in the nineteenth century were reacting to or against not Beethoven, the real historical person, but 'Beethoven' the myth. In order to evaluate Beethoven's impact on the history of nineteenth-century music, it is necessary to understand the Beethoven myth not in order to replace it with history 'as it really was', but because for thinkers in the nineteenth century, Beethoven and the myth were one and the same. It is thus necessary to acknowledge the importance of the myth even while aspiring to move beyond it.

In his influential *Tropics of Discourse*, Hayden White writes that 'no historical event is *intrinsically tragic*', but 'can only be conceived as such from a particular point of view'. What historians do, according to White, is to make 'stories out of mere chronicles' by a process he calls 'emplotment':

> no given set of casually recorded historical events can in itself constitute a story . . . The events are *made* into a story by the suppression or subordination of certain of them and the highlighting of others, by characterization, motific [sic] repetition, variation of tone and point of view, alternative descriptive strategies, and the like – in short, all of the techniques that we would normally expect to find in the emplotment of a novel or play.[6]

In histories of Beethoven, the overpowering desire to read Beethoven's life as a narrative of struggle and transcendence has had two major effects. First, those events, sources and witnesses that support this Romantic plot have been highlighted, while other conflicting views have been suppressed, generating a limited vision of Beethoven's life – the Beethoven myth. The second, subsequent effect is the belief that those narratives grew out of the material rather than being generated by a preconceived notion of the 'happy ending'. While our interest in the Romantic plot may have many motivations – not least our

5 *Ibid.*, p. 77.
6 Hayden White, *Tropics of Discourse: Essays in Cultural Criticism* (Baltimore and London, 1978), p. 84.

own fear of deafness – it is hardly the only plot that one can construct from Beethoven's life. In fact, as I have argued elsewhere, immediately after his death the tragic plot was predominant because critics could not come to terms with Beethoven's final compositions; only when Wagner asserted that deafness helped rather than hurt Beethoven's compositional power did the Romantic plot become ascendant.[7]

White stresses that narrativity is not a neutral form but rather 'entails onto-logical and epistemic choices with distinct ideological and even specifically political implications'.[8] It is these choices that I wish to reveal in the histories of Beethoven. To do so, it is first necessary to identify the specifically Beethovenian themes of the Romantic plot. The five I offer below are in no way meant to represent an exhaustive analysis of the Beethoven myth,[9] but instead will allow us to isolate moments when an author seems motivated primarily by the larger narrative of struggle and transcendence. The first three can be found very clearly in the full text of Bettina's letter to Goethe:

1. Beethoven's superiority, and his conviction of his own superiority (as Bettina writes: 'he stalks far ahead of the culture of mankind'; and later in the letter 'Beethoven' says: 'God is nearer to me than to other artists; I associate with him without fear'). The Teplitz story also clearly emphasises this tenet.
2. The transcendent nature of his music, and its ability to enact transcendence ('he will place the key . . . in our hands'; 'Everything he can tell you about is pure magic, every posture is the organisation of a higher existence').
3. Beethoven's independence, isolation, introspection ('what to him is inter-course with the world?').

Two other important themes found in the Beethoven myth are:

4. Beethoven's music as expression of his own feelings of pain or suffering (or even the equation of Beethoven with his music), and the necessity of that sacrifice and suffering for his creativity.
5. Beethoven's strength of both character and music.

While neither four nor five is emphasised in Bettina's letter, they can easily be found in other writings: for example an obituary written by the editor of the *Allgemeine musikalische Zeitung*, Friedrich Rochlitz:

---

7 K. M. Knittel, 'Wagner, Deafness, and the Reception of Beethoven's Late Style', *Journal of the American Musicological Society*, 51 (1998), pp. 49–82.

8 Hayden White, *Content of the Form: Narrative Discourse and Historical Representation* (Baltimore and London, 1987), pp. ix and xi.

9 My five themes are derived from the thirteen constants of Hans Heinrich Eggebrecht (*Zur Geschichte Beethoven-Rezeption*, Spektrum der Musik, 2nd enlarged edn [Laaber, 1994; original edn 1972], p. 56) and the six 'personalities' identified by Arnold Schmitz (*Das romantische Beethovenbild* [Berlin and Bonn, 1927], pp. 1–14).

On 26 March, at sunset, B[eethoven]'s great, extremely strong spirit fought its way free of its mortal frame, which in many respects surrounded him as a burden, but which he victoriously overcame with the energy of his entire being and, at the end, through quiet resignation.

Not just Beethoven's spirit, but his music, too, embodies strength (no. 5): Rochlitz calls the works 'bold, powerful, and energetic', and Beethoven himself 'is the foremost inventor of his contemporaries'. Beethoven wrote what he had to write, risking 'being scarcely understood by even a few people', and his strength in the face of pitiable circumstances gave birth to his art (no. 4):

> He was separate from [other people], and since the time his unfortunate fate had befallen him almost totally, he created his own world, wonderfully made up of musical notes that were only thought and not heard. He gave his world life and made it complete . . . That is the meaning of manfully running the course of this earthly pilgrimage staked out by a higher power.[10]

The remainder of this chapter will explore how history has lost sight of Beethoven, the person, in favour of 'Beethoven', the myth and the subsequent musical-historical effects of that choice. Rather than examining Beethoven's biography in detail, I will instead highlight several key issues where the selection and suppression of evidence is most striking. The next section will focus on how descriptions of Beethoven's early promise and arrival in Vienna, his piano technique and his composition lessons with Haydn have led to assumptions about his personality. The third section will consider the ways in which Beethoven's music was received and classified in the context of his deafness and the historical significance of equating his music with his personality. The overall goal is not only to re-examine the evidence in order to suggest alternative readings or possibilities, but also to illuminate how and why the nineteenth century inherited a single, simplistic reading of Beethoven's life. Therefore, the final section will scrutinise the nineteenth century's fascination with certain themes: in particular, how and why Beethoven was transformed into the strong, masculine hero of German nationalism. It is the legacy of this final image that has perhaps the most lasting impact, not just on music history but on history in general.

Beethoven 1770–1802: pianist-composer

Beethoven was born in Bonn – one of the electoral courts of the Holy Roman Empire – in 1770, probably on 16 December (his baptismal certificate, dated 17

10 Friedrich Johann Rochlitz, 'Nekrolog', *Allgemeine musikalische Zeitung* (hereafter *AmZ*), 29 (28 March 1827), cols. 227–8; quote is col. 227; trans. in Wayne M. Senner, Robin Wallace and William Meredith (eds.), *The Critical Reception of Beethoven's Compositions by His German Contemporaries* (Lincoln, Nebr., and London, 1999), I, pp. 99–100.

December 1770, is the only record that exists). His grandfather (1712–73), after whom he was named, was the Kapellmeister at Bonn, and his father, Johann, a tenor there. One of the earliest descriptions of Beethoven that we have was written by his teacher Christian Gottlob Neefe. Neefe had arrived in Bonn in 1779 and had been appointed court organist in 1781; he probably took over Beethoven's education from Johann in 1780 or 1781. Neefe was convinced of Beethoven's talent, even leaving him in charge (as assistant organist) for a time when Beethoven was only eleven years old. In addition to arranging for the publication of Beethoven's earliest compositions, Neefe published the following in *Cramers Magazin der Musik* on 2 March 1783:

> Louis van Beethoven, son of the tenor singer mentioned, a boy of eleven years and of most promising talent. He plays the clavier very skilfully and with power, reads at sight very well, and – to put it in a nutshell – he plays chiefly 'The Well-Tempered Clavichord' of Sebastian Bach, which Herr Neefe put into his hands. Whoever knows this collection of preludes and fugues in all the keys – which might almost be called the *non plus ultra* of our art – will know what this means. So far as his duties permitted, Herr Neefe has also given him instruction in thorough-bass. He is now training him in composition and for his encouragement has had nine variations for the pianoforte, written by him on a march [by Ernst Christoph Dressler] engraved at Mannheim. This youthful genius is deserving of help to enable him to travel. He would surely become a second Wolfgang Amadeus Mozart were he to continue as he has begun.
>
> (Sonneck, p. 10)

While this notice has been read as evidence of Beethoven's obvious early genius – Thayer, for example, praises Neefe's 'insight' and the 'striking' nature of his praise of his pupil – it reveals more about Neefe himself. Neefe is careful to itemise his contributions to Beethoven's education, and Solomon suggests that Neefe 'hoped to be associated with the discovery of a second Mozart'. Mozart, by far the most famous child prodigy, was in 1783 a recognisable benchmark of quality and early promise: the comment cannot yet refer to the mature Mozart's Viennese career. Beethoven, while clearly worthy of patronage, in 1783 is 'a prodigy and promising talent, but also as a talent not yet proved'. One schoolmate recalled a different Beethoven, one who showed no sign of 'that spark of genius which glowed so brilliantly in him afterwards'.[11]

The elector sent Beethoven to Vienna in late 1792, probably assuming he would spend a short time there studying composition and then return to his court position in Bonn. As is well known, Beethoven never did return to his native city. According to the myth, Beethoven's success in Vienna was

---

11 *Thayer's Life of Beethoven*, rev. and ed. Elliot Forbes (Princeton, 1967) (hereafter Thayer–Forbes), pp. 66, 58, and Maynard Solomon, *Beethoven*, 2nd rev. edn (New York, 1998), p. 34; Tia DeNora, *Beethoven and the Construction of Genius: Musical Politics in Vienna, 1792–1803* (Berkeley and Los Angeles, 1995), p. 85.

unmediated and absolute: Beethoven takes the city by storm, convincing every-one of his talent and genius; in return, he receives offers of financial and social support. Tia DeNora, on the other hand, has recently emphasised the many factors that were necessary – in addition to Beethoven's very real talent – for him to gain a foothold in Viennese society. Given Vienna's notoriously rigid social hierarchy, by assuming that Beethoven was able easily to overcome its obstacles we underrate his ability to find and exploit the proper connections in order to navigate its labyrinth. DeNora emphasises that given the familial rela-tionships between aristocrats in Bonn and those in Vienna, 'Beethoven's well-connected position was an important resource for his entry into and acceptance by the upper echelons of Viennese musical life'. Connections to aristocratic families allowed Beethoven opportunities to perform (and thus become known as a pianist) and provided commissions for compositions and dedicatees for those compositions. DeNora points out that while 'these advantages (such as approval from important people, commissions, and the like) simultaneously functioned as indications of his talent, his promise, and his previous success . . . there were numerous other musicians who, under different circumstances, could have also ended up celebrities'.[12]

Beethoven could thus have hardly arrived in Vienna under more auspicious circumstances. However, while the traditional story assumes early composi-tional success, Beethoven first received recognition as a pianist. The forums available to him for performance were private rather than public: Vienna, at that time, had no real venue for regular public concerts, unlike both Paris and London. Most public concerts took place during the period from the last days of Advent until Lent (when operas were forbidden, thus leaving a gap in public entertainment), and virtuosi could rent the theatres and organise concerts at their own expense. The concert programmes were fairly standard, opening and closing with symphonies, with vocal and instrumental works thrown in between (though it was rare to hear chamber works under these circum-stances). Most of Mozart's piano concertos, for example, were written as vehi-cles for these public concerts.[13]

Private concerts were thus more frequent and required little or no financial commitment on the part of the performer. The aristocracy competed openly

12 DeNora, *Beethoven and the Construction of Genius*, pp. 60–1 and 69; on Vienna's social hierarchy, see her chapters 2 and 3, and Johann Pezzl, 'Sketch of Vienna', trans. in H. C. Robbins Landon, *Mozart and Vienna* (New York, 1981), pp. 53–191. Beethoven's first visit to Vienna, in 1787, lasted only two weeks. He had scarcely arrived before word of his mother's final illness necessitated his return to Bonn.

13 On Viennese concert life, see John A. Rice, 'Vienna under Joseph II and Leopold II', in Neal Zaslaw (ed.), *The Classical Era: From the 1740s to the End of the 18th Century* (Englewood Cliffs, 1989), pp. 126–65; Volkmar Braunbehrens, 'Aristocratic and Bourgeois Salons', in his *Mozart in Vienna, 1781–1791*, trans. Timothy Bell (New York, 1989), pp. 142–72; Mary Sue Morrow, *Concert Life in Haydn's Vienna: Aspects of a Developing Musical and Social Institution*, Sociology of Music 7 (Stuyvesant, N.Y., 1989), esp. chapters 1 and 2.

with the emperor to see who could afford to spend the most money on resident musicians or private concertising. Patronage was thus a way to prove both affluence and sophistication, and many aristocrats held regular musical gatherings in their salons. Baron Gottfried van Swieten (1733–1803), for example, had been an important supporter of Mozart, and the weekly concerts in his home focused on his love of the polyphony of Bach and Handel. Beethoven soon became a regular participant at these concerts, and van Swieten in turn received the dedication of Beethoven's First Symphony. Another important patron, Prince Franz Joseph Maximilian von Lobkowitz (1772–1816), maintained an orchestra from 1796 which Beethoven was allowed to use – his early symphonies (most famously the Third, Op. 55, nicknamed the *Eroica*) were premièred in Lobkowitz's palace.

Beethoven's early performances in Vienna soon established him as one of the greatest pianists of his age. Just what he sounded like or exactly how he differed from other pianists is difficult to determine, however, since his performance career was cut short by his encroaching deafness, and his performances – both public and private – declined drastically after 1800. Eyewitness accounts of Beethoven's skill do exist, but even those who heard Beethoven in his prime did not necessarily write down their impressions until many years after the events that they depict. Other witnesses may have heard Beethoven play only after the onset of his deafness. One of the earliest was published in Bossler's *Correspondenz* by Carl Ludwig Junker in 1791. Junker was the chaplain at Kirchberg and heard Beethoven when he was travelling with the elector's court to Mergentheim. Junker's account is valuable in that he published it only months after his experience, and a number of issues arise in Junker's letter which return again and again in descriptions of Beethoven at the keyboard. The first is the preference for improvisation over simply performance: 'what was infinitely preferable to me, I heard him extemporize in private; yes, I was even invited to propose a theme for him to vary'. Second, the greatness of Beethoven as a virtuoso, according to Junker, comes 'from his almost inexhaustible wealth of ideas, the altogether characteristic style of expression in his playing, and the great execution which he displays'. Junker compares Beethoven to Abbé Georg Joseph Vogler, another important virtuoso of the time, and finds Beethoven's playing superior because Beethoven 'has greater clearness and weight of idea, and more expression – in short, he is more for the heart – equally great, therefore, as an *adagio* or *allegro* player'. It is Beethoven's ability to express himself that Junker finds appealing, while Vogler has only 'astonishing execution'. Junker also points out that Beethoven's style of playing 'is so different from that usually adopted', and he draws the conclusion that Beethoven has been isolated from fashionable playing styles to a certain extent and 'by a path of his own discovery he has attained that height of excellence whereon he now stands' (Sonneck, p. 13).

The privileging of improvisation over performance, the emphasis on the compositional aspect of improvisation ('wealth of ideas'), the coexistence of execution and expression, and the implication that Beethoven's style at the keyboard was somehow different are all important themes that run through early descriptions of Beethoven's technique. The first three, however, are not unique to descriptions of Beethoven. Improvisation was an important skill for any performer, all the more if the performer was able in an improvisation to indicate his creative ability as a composer. Beethoven, in an early letter written from Vienna, writes that he is afraid that other pianists, after hearing his improvisations, would try to copy down 'peculiarities of [his] style and palm them off with pride as their own'. Additionally, the value of feeling alongside execution was another common indicator of pianistic skill. Mozart, after his piano duel with Muzio Clementi in late 1781, wrote to his father calling his rival 'an excellent cembalo-player, but that is all. He has great facility with his right hand. His star passages are thirds. Apart from this, he has not a farthing's worth of taste or feeling; he is a mere *mechanicus*.'[14] While these 'differences' in Beethoven's style have been claimed as absolute, they nevertheless reflect the aesthetic climate of the period. For our purposes, then, the issue of primary importance is the difference that Junker attributes to Beethoven's 'style of treating his instrument'.

Junker says no more about exactly what he found different about Beethoven's playing, and there has been much speculation among scholars and biographers about the nature of that difference. Junker's language, however, should put us on the alert. it sounds suspiciously like the mythical themes of isolation and superiority. Beethoven is made to seem all the more superior if that level of quality is achieved without help from anyone and is based solely on his own innate talent. Even if there truly were few opportunities for Beethoven to hear other virtuosi in the relative backwater of Bonn, that isolation is nonetheless turned into a means to place Beethoven above other pianists. Franz Wegeler (a friend from Bonn and co-author of the biographical *Beethoven-Notizen* of 1838) also emphasises Beethoven's superiority when reporting Beethoven's encounter with the Abbé Sterkel (probably also in 1791, but written about thirty years later): 'Because he had not yet heard any great or celebrated pianists, Beethoven knew nothing of the finer nuances of handling the instrument; his playing was rough and hard'. On hearing Sterkel, whose style was described as 'somewhat ladylike', 'Beethoven stood beside him

14 Beethoven's letter cited in Solomon, *Beethoven*, p. 78; Mozart letter no. 441, 16 Jan. 1782, in Emily Anderson (ed.), *The Letters of Mozart and His Family*, 3rd rev. edn (New York, 1985), p. 793.

concentrating intensely'. On being asked to perform himself, he first resisted, but then 'played everything in precisely the same pleasant manner with which Sterkel had impressed him'.[15] Here Beethoven, though unacquainted with this way of playing, nevertheless is immediately able to imitate it, showing his talent to be superior to Sterkel's.

Some writers may have conflated Beethoven's playing and personality – especially if they were writing many years later. Franz Glöggl had heard Beethoven play in 1812 and reports that 'after Beethoven's fantasia half of the pianoforte strings were broken' (Thayer–Forbes, p. 541). Another writer, Edward Schultz, preserved his impressions of Vienna in an article in the *Harmonicon* in 1824: 'I should mention though, that when he plays on the pianoforte, it is generally at the expense of some twenty or thirty strings, he strikes the keys with so much force' (Sonneck, p. 151). Both Glöggl and Schultz may have been seeking to liven up their accounts with some seemingly realistic details by making Beethoven's manner of playing match the common view of his personality. After all, Glöggl had only been a boy when Beethoven visited and he misremembers other details in his account. He also reports that Beethoven broke some porcelain dishes in his hurry to rejoin the dinner guests, a detail which recalls Bettina's assertion that Beethoven was unable to deal with mundane things – 'what to him is intercourse with the world?' Similarly, Schultz's account lacks the characteristic obstacles recounted by others from this period, when Beethoven usually had to be tricked into performing. It is even possible that these writers never heard Beethoven at all.

Other commentators, however, paint a different picture. Carl Czerny, one of Beethoven's piano pupils, seems to be careful to distinguish between the manner in which the sound was produced and the nature of the sound itself. Czerny reports that Beethoven's playing 'was masterfully quiet, noble and beautiful, without the slightest grimace (only bent forward low, as his deafness grew upon him)', but then states that 'as his playing, like his compositions, was far ahead of his time, the pianofortes of the period (until 1810), still extremely weak and imperfect, could not endure his gigantic style of performance' (Thayer–Forbes, pp. 368–9). Two other eyewitnesses – who, like Czerny, wrote down their experiences much later – make the same comments regarding Beethoven's still and calm manner of playing. Countess Giulietta Guicciardi (another piano student and the dedicatee of the 'Moonlight' Sonata, Op. 27, No. 2) wrote that Beethoven 'made a point of playing without effort' even as she reports that 'he was prone to excitement' in other aspects of his life

---

15 Franz Wegeler and Ferdinand Ries, *Beethoven Remembered: The Biographical Notes of Franz Wegeler and Ferdinand Ries*, trans. Frederick Noonan (Arlington, Va., 1987), p. 23; original German edition *Biographische Notizen über Ludwig van Beethoven* (Coblenz, 1838).

(Sonneck, p. 33). The painter Willibrord Joseph Mähler reported to Thayer that he had heard Beethoven play in 1803 and said that 'Beethoven played with his hands so very still; wonderful as his execution was, there was no tossing of them to and fro, up and down; they seemed to glide right and left over the keys, the fingers alone doing the work' (Thayer–Forbes, p. 337). Thus, even if Beethoven's manner of playing was very calm, he might have been able to produce a big tone from any of the pianos he played on; therefore, while some authors seem to keep these two aspects of his style separate, others may have simply relied on assumptions about Beethoven's tempestuous personality to add authority to their accounts.

More revealing in terms of Beethoven's stylistic differences, perhaps, are the many comparisons to other pianists of the day. In 1799 Beethoven competed with the pianist Joseph Wölffl at the home of Baron Raimund Wetzlar von Plankenstern. Piano duels were very common forms of entertainment during this period: DeNora likens them to 'sporting events' in which competing pianists were expected to showcase a variety of different skills, including improvisation, playing at sight and sheer virtuosity.[16] After the Beethoven–Wölffl duel, a correspondent for the *AmZ* reported that although a winner could not be chosen, the majority seemed to favour Wölffl: Beethoven's style was 'extremely brilliant but has less delicacy and occasionally he is guilty of indistinctness'. The *AmZ* describes Wölffl as 'sound in musical learning and dignified in his compositions, [he] plays passages which seem impossible with an ease, precision and clearness which cause amazement (of course he is helped here by the large structure of his hands) and that his interpretation is always, especially in Adagios, so pleasing and insinuating that one can not only admire it but also enjoy'. The *AmZ* also contrasts Wölffl's 'amiable bearing' to 'the somewhat haughty pose of Beethoven' (Thayer–Forbes, p. 205).

By 1832, however, when Ignaz von Seyfried wrote down his memories of the same duel, his language has become ornate and the aesthetic categories more distinct. Seyfried claimed that Beethoven's playing 'tore along like a wildly foaming cataract, and the conjurer constrained his instrument to an utterance so forceful that the stoutest structure was scarcely able to withstand it'. He contrasts this to Wölffl's Mozartian manner which was 'always equable; never superficial but always clear and thus more accessible to the multitude'. Thus, Seyfried sets up an opposition between Wölffl's accessibility and 'well-ordered ideas' to Beethoven himself who 'did not deny his tendency toward the mysterious and gloomy' (Thayer–Forbes, pp. 206–7).

For the *AmZ* and perhaps more obviously for Seyfried, the categories that are

---

16 DeNora, *Beethoven and the Construction of Genius*, p. 150.

being used for comparison set up an opposition of the two artists in more than simply piano technique. Immanuel Kant uses similar language in an early essay titled 'Observations on the Feeling of the Beautiful and Sublime' where he distinguishes between the feelings aroused by the sublime and the beautiful – the sublime 'moves' while the beautiful 'charms'. He further claims that 'The sublime must always be great; the beautiful can also be small. The sublime must be simple; the beautiful can be adorned and ornamented.' These categories become explicitly gendered in his Section Three, where he states that 'The fair [female] sex has just as much understanding as the male, but it is a beautiful understanding, whereas ours [the male] should be a deep understanding, an expression that signifies identity with the sublime'.[17] The categories in both the *AmZ* and in Seyfried may thus reflect a gendering of the performers, where Beethoven's style was perceived to be more masculine; in terms of the Beethoven myth, the themes of both strength and superiority are embodied in such a gender dichotomy.

Such gendered categories become even more explicit in Czerny's comparison of Beethoven to Hummel which uses similarly distinct language for each performer. What Czerny calls Hummel's 'purling, brilliant style', that was 'well calculated to suit the manner of the time, was much more comprehensible and pleasing to the public'. On the other hand, as if to emphasise Beethoven's superiority (and strength), Czerny notes that 'nobody equalled [Beethoven] in the rapidity of his scales, double trills, skips, etc. – not even Hummel' (Thayer–Forbes, pp. 368–9). In his memoirs he recalled that 'Whereas Beethoven's playing excelled in its extraordinary strength, character, and unprecedented bravura and fluency, Hummel's performance [was] the model of the highest purity and clarity, the most ingratiating elegance and delicacy'.[18] Again, the categories seem to reflect a gendering of each performer: Hummel is the feminine player, wanting only to please, while Beethoven is independent and seems to go his own way.

Themes of superiority, isolation and strength that are pronounced in descriptions of Beethoven at the piano have also come to permeate the story of Beethoven's relationship and composition lessons with Haydn. The outlines are familiar from all the biographies: Beethoven goes to Vienna to 'receive Mozart's spirit from Haydn's hands', as his Bonn patron Count Ferdinand Ernst von Waldstein (1762–1823) wrote in Beethoven's autograph book as the young composer set out for Vienna. Beethoven quickly realises that Haydn is jealous of his abilities and is trying to hold him back. Ferdinand Ries (co-author

---

17 Immanuel Kant, *Observations on the Feeling of the Beautiful and Sublime*, trans. John T. Goldthwait (Berkeley and Los Angeles, 1991), pp. 47, 48 and 78. Kant's essay dates from 1764.

18 Cited in William S. Newman, *Beethoven on Beethoven: Playing His Piano Music His Way* (New York and London, 1988), p. 79.

of the *Beethoven-Notizen*) claims that Haydn advises against publishing Op. 1, No. 3, and this proves that Haydn is out to get Beethoven, because everyone acknowledges (now) that No. 3 is the best of the three Op. 1 piano trios. In any event, the relationship is strained. Beethoven claims he is learning nothing – he is forced to seek help with his counterpoint exercises from Johann Schenk and Johann Georg Albrechtsberger – and Haydn refuses to take Beethoven with him to London in 1794, thus leaving Beethoven all alone. Their subsequent encounters before Haydn's death in 1809 show the continued tension in their relationship and Haydn's antipathy towards the younger man.

Recent re-evaluations of this biographical episode, however, offer different interpretations. James Webster has shown that 'no direct word or action of Haydn's or Beethoven's, and few reliable contemporary observers document any falling out or feeling of artistic incompatibility between the two. The tradition to this effect depends chiefly on anecdotal accounts, of which almost all originated after Beethoven's death, and many seem marked by special pleading.' There is no indication, other than Ries – writing many years later – that Haydn disliked or was unsure of Op. 1, No. 3, let alone advised against publishing it. Likewise, there is no confirmation that Haydn ever planned to take Beethoven to London in the first place. The only direct evidence that we have of Beethoven's lessons with Haydn are a number of written counterpoint exercises. These are, as everyone from Gustav Nottebohm onward has pointed out, full of errors, some introduced by Haydn attempting to correct Beethoven's mistakes. While these may seem conclusive on their surface, they can only serve as the barest trace of what must have happened in lessons. As Solomon makes clear, what the two men discussed – musically or otherwise – cannot be recovered, and it is impossible to know just how and in what manner Beethoven may have benefited from Haydn's instruction.[19]

DeNora argues that Haydn himself – like Neefe in 1783 – had much to gain from being known as Beethoven's teacher, just as Beethoven had much to gain from the older man's connections at court and greater experience. There is no reason, according to DeNora, to see the relationship as anything but mutually beneficial and that 'collaborating or playing along with the "Haydn's hands" story, as this story became increasingly public, could be useful to both musicians even if the private reality of their relationship was more complex'.[20] Haydn himself was in the process of redefining his career after the death of his long-time patron, Prince Paul Anton Esterhazy, perhaps making his desire to

19 James Webster, 'The Falling-out Between Haydn and Beethoven: The Evidence of the Sources', in Lewis Lockwood and Phyllis Benjamin (eds.), *Beethoven Essays: Studies in Honor of Elliot Forbes* (Cambridge, Mass., 1984), pp. 3–45; Ries's account is found in Wegeler–Ries, *Beethoven Remembered*, p. 74. See also Solomon, *Beethoven*, pp. 93–4.   20 DeNora, *Beethoven and the Construction of Genius*, p. 110.

be associated with this rising star stronger; the focus of attention, therefore, on but a single player in the drama obscures the complexity of the events and reactions involved and results from a desire to see Beethoven in a particular kind of light.

It is important to realise that the issue is not whether Beethoven resented Haydn, or whether Haydn was exasperated by Beethoven – or even the extent to which these feelings can be exposed – but rather that historians have read the evidence in a way that benefits their version of Beethoven's music and his personality. Rather than reading Waldstein's and other similar statements as prophecy, DeNora instead characterises them as 'publicizing' events, ways in which both Beethoven and Haydn could define or redefine their positions within a competitive musical world. The 'Haydn's hands' story thus provided a 'pretext' rather than a prediction, and, like the comparison to Mozart that Neefe invokes, reading Waldstein's words as prophetic obscures other possible meanings of the story. While narrations of Beethoven's early life can be shown to emphasise strength, isolation and superiority, it is only with the onset of his deafness that themes of suffering and transcendence become necessary in order to sustain the Romantic plot of Beethoven's life.

Beethoven 1802–1827: composer

'Think of a flower' – 'Rose'. 'Think of a colour' – 'Red'. 'Name a composer' – 'Beethoven'.[21]

To Martin Cooper's list, one could add 'Name one thing about Beethoven' – 'He was deaf'. There is no mystery in our fascination with a deaf composer: to write music and be unable to hear it oneself seems the saddest fate imaginable. Beethoven's deafness underlies the entire Beethoven myth, turning his not-so-ordinary life into a journey of struggle and transcendence. Had he been able to hear, he probably would have become a great composer; his deafness made him the greatest composer.

It seems likely that a severe illness, perhaps during the summer of 1797 (or 1796 at the earliest) may have given rise to the onset of deafness, but no one has been able to agree on a cause.[22] In 1801 Beethoven admits for the first time in a letter to his Bonn friend, Dr Franz Gerhard Wegeler, that over the past three years his hearing had 'become weaker and weaker'. He details his attempts to find medical help, and then writes:

---

21 Martin Cooper, *Beethoven: The Last Decade, 1817–1827*, rev. edn (Oxford and New York, 1985), p. v.
22 Edward Larkin, 'Appendix A: Beethoven's Medical History', in Cooper, *Beethoven: The Last Decade*, pp. 439–66; Hans Bankl and Hans Jesserer, *Die Krankheiten Ludwig van Beethoven: Pathographie seines Lebens und Pathologie seiner Leiden* (Vienna, 1987).

I must confess that I lead a miserable life. For almost two years I have ceased to attend any social functions, just because I find it impossible to say to people: I am deaf. If I had any other profession I might be able to cope with my infirmity; but in my profession it is a terrible handicap . . . In order to give you some idea of this strange deafness, let me tell you that in the theater I have to place myself quite close to the orchestra in order to understand what the actor is saying, and that at a distance I cannot hear the high notes of instruments or voices. As for the spoken voice, it is surprising that some people have never noticed my deafness; but since I have always been liable to fits of absentmindedness, they attribute my hardness of hearing to that. Sometimes, too, I can scarcely hear a person who speaks softly; I can hear sounds, it is true, but cannot make out the words. But if anyone shouts, I can't bear it. Heaven alone knows what is to become of me.   (Solomon, pp. 146–7)

On 1 July, he wrote to another close friend, Karl Amenda, that 'You will realize what a sad life I must now lead, seeing that I am cut off from everything that is dear and precious to me' (p. 148). Beethoven did not immediately become deaf: rather, he experienced a slow, uneven decline in his ability to hear that continued until the end of his life. He began to use the 'Conversations Books' – in which visitors would write down what they wished to say, and Beethoven would answer verbally – in 1818, suggesting that from this point he could no longer carry on a conversation. Even after 1818, however, there are contradictory reports concerning just how much Beethoven was able to hear. It has recently been suggested that Beethoven retained at least some hearing ability until the end of his life.[23] Nonetheless, the onset of deafness undoubtedly had several profound effects. First, Beethoven could no longer continue as a virtuoso performer, and he turned instead towards composition to support himself. Second, his natural inclination to withdraw became more pronounced, and his pattern of maintaining only a few close friendships to the exclusion of everyone else would continue for the rest of his life. Finally, Beethoven may have briefly contemplated suicide. The Heiligenstadt Testament, dated 6–10 October 1802, is a bizarre and moving document apparently begun as a last will and testament. It was discovered among Beethoven's papers after his death and made public for the first time in the *AmZ*.[24]

While Beethoven's deafness itself is an indisputable fact, his 'heroism' in the face of his malady is often exaggerated at the expense of understanding the real suffering he endured. The many witnesses who document Beethoven's increasing reluctance to play for an audience may have been unaware of his problem.

23 George Thomas Ealy, 'Of Ear Trumpets and a Resonance Plate: Early Hearing Aids and Beethoven's Hearing Perception', *19th Century Music*, 17 (1994), pp. 262–73.
24 The text of the Heiligenstadt Testament is provided by Thayer-Forbes (pp. 304–5); Solomon discusses its psychological implications in *Beethoven*, pp. 145–62; the text was published for the first time in the *AmZ*, 29 (17 October 1827), cols. 705–10.

Countess Guicciardi reportedly told Otto Jahn that 'at the least sound [while he was playing] he would rise and go away'. Frau von Bernhard, a pupil of Beethoven in her youth, told Ludwig Nohl that she had seen 'the Countess Thun, the mother of Princess Lichnowsky, lying on her knees before him (who was seated on the sofa) and begging him to play something – and Beethoven would not do it'. Wegeler reports that Beethoven's reluctance to perform 'was frequently a source of considerable dissension between Beethoven and the best of his friends and patrons'.[25] These anecdotes are often included with the Teplitz incident as proof that he refused to think himself a servant and indeed felt himself to be equal to the aristocrats if not better. They have thus consistently defied logical explanation: however unlikely that the young musician would jeopardise his new-found position for political ideals, however understandable Beethoven's discomfort, this is the 'Beethoven' who scorned social convention, convinced as he was of his own strength and superiority.

Beethoven's discovery of his deafness is all the more poignant because he was perched on the pinnacle of real freedom and success. On 2 April 1800, he had put on a huge public concert (*Akademie*) for his own benefit at the Bergtheater. The programme for the concert gives a sense of the scope not only of public concerts in the early nineteenth century, but also of Beethoven's growing corpus of compositions:

> To-day, Wednesday, April 2nd, 1800, Herr *Ludwig van Beethoven* will have the honour to give a grand concert for his benefit in the Royal Imperial Court Theatre beside the Burg. The pieces which will performed are the following:
>
> 1. A grand symphony by the late Kapellmeister Mozart.
> 2. An aria from 'The Creation' by the Princely Kapellmeister Herr Haydn sung by Mlle. Saal.
> 3. A grand Concerto for the pianoforte, played and composed by Herr *Ludwig van Beethoven* [most likely Piano Concerto No. 1, Op. 15].
> 4. A septet [Op. 20], most humbly and obediently dedicated to Her Majesty the Empress, and composed by Herr *Ludwig van Beethoven* for four stringed and three wind-instruments, played by Herren Schuppanzigh, Schreiber, Schindlecker, Bär, Nickel, Matauschek and Dietzel.
> 5. A Duet from Haydn's 'Creation', sung by Herr and Mlle. Saal.
> 6. Herr *Ludwig van Beethoven* will improvise on the pianoforte.
> 7. A new grand symphony with complete orchestra, composed by Herr *Ludwig van Beethoven* [Symphony No. 1, Op. 21]. (Thayer-Forbes, p. 255).

The concert was reviewed in the *AmZ*, and it was called 'truly the most interesting concert in a long time'. Beethoven 'played a new concerto of his own composition, much of which was written with a great deal of taste and feeling. After

---

25 Sonneck, *Impressions*, pp. 33 and 21; Wegeler-Ries, *Beethoven Remembered*, pp. 24–5.

this he improvised in a masterly fashion, and at the end one of his symphonies was performed in which there is considerable art, novelty and a wealth of ideas.' The *AmZ* did complain that the winds were used too much (presumably in the symphony) and that the orchestra did not play well or follow the soloist (Thayer-Forbes, pp. 255–6).

The very next spring he experienced his second major public success, his ballet *The Creatures of Prometheus*, which was given twenty-three performances over the next two years. Perhaps to capitalise on this success, Beethoven reused the theme from the finale several times: it appeared as one of the Twelve Contredanses (WoO14 no. 7), became a theme for a set of piano variations (Op. 35), and formed the finale of the Third Symphony (Op. 55). In addition to Beethoven's burgeoning public successes and fame, he had begun to receive from Prince Lichnowsky 600 florins a year, a sum which allowed him a certain degree of independence. Beethoven's success with his aristocratic patrons is exemplified by the Annuity Contract, signed in 1809, by three aristocrats: Archduke Rudolph, Prince Lobkowitz and Prince Ferdinand Kinsky. They agreed to pay him a total of 4,000 florins a year for life, provided that he did not leave Vienna or the Habsburg hereditary lands.[26] This agreement was in response to an invitation from King Jérôme of Westphalia, Napoleon's brother, for Beethoven to become his Kapellmeister at a considerable salary. Beethoven was quite tempted to take the position, not least because his lifelong dream had been to be a Kapellmeister like his grandfather and namesake before him. Beethoven subsequently declined the offer and remained in Vienna.

By the time Beethoven began his Fourth Piano Concerto in early 1804, his performing career was unavoidably over: in 1808, he did première the concerto (Op. 58), and performed a few more times, including the première of his 'Archduke' Trio, Op. 97, in 1814, but witnesses suggest that only the barest traces of his former power remained. His final public performance was accompanying his song, 'Adelaide', on 25 January 1815, with the singer Franz Wild. In his later years, visitors and friends report occasionally being able either to coax or trick him into playing the piano for them, and it is reported that when alone and undisturbed, he was fond of playing the Andante from his Op. 28 Piano Sonata.[27] Hearing Beethoven play, however, had become a privilege and a rarity to be cherished by those who experienced it.

26 Text of annuity contract is in Thayer-Forbes, pp. 456–7; regarding the complicated monetary systems in Vienna, see the explanation and bibliography in Senner, *Critical Reception*, I, pp. xv–xviii. For details of the annuity contract, see Solomon, *Beethoven*, pp. 193–4; Thayer-Forbes, pp. 522–5, 552–3, and 611; and Barry Cooper (ed.), *The Beethoven Compendium: A Guide to Beethoven's Life and Music* (London, 1991), pp. 68–70 and 110–23.

27 See Thayer-Forbes, pp. 577–8; *Beethoven: The Man and the Artist, as Revealed in His Own Words*, ed. Friedrich Kerst and trans. Henry Edward Krehbiel (New York, 1964; original edn 1905), p. 46.

The idea that Beethoven's works could be divided into three groups or styles began during his lifetime – the first attempt dates from 1818 – and it has come to be one of the most enduring ideas in Beethoven literature. Writers continue to utilise the concept of Beethoven's 'three styles' despite the fact that many critics realise that it is 'as misleading as it is useful'.[28] The music that he wrote in the years following the Heiligenstadt Testament has been called the 'middle period' or 'heroic' style, and it is almost impossible not to make the connection, as Solomon does, between Beethoven's own life and his 'Eroica Symphony, a portrait of the artist as hero, stricken by deafness, withdrawn from mankind, conquering his impulses to suicide, struggling against fate, hoping to find "but one day of pure joy"'. Solomon goes so far as to suggest that 'his deafness was the painful chrysalis within which his "heroic" style came to maturity' (pp. 158 and 162).

In the years leading up to the Heiligenstadt crisis – his so-called 'early' or 'first' period of works – Beethoven was still considered primarily a performer. Many early compositions involve the piano, since Beethoven could use his performing reputation to attract both publishers and purchasers. The Op. 1 Trios (mentioned above in relation to his studies with Haydn) were published in 1795, dedicated to Prince Karl Lichnowsky (1756–1814), and were the first works to bear an opus number (those not so designated bear an WoO number – *Werke ohne Opuszahl*, Works without Opus Number). He had published a small number of works while still in Bonn (some variations for piano, small piano pieces, and songs), and several sets of variations appeared without opus numbers during the years 1793–4. Over the next several years, Beethoven published a steady stream of pieces, including the Op. 2 Piano Sonatas (dedicated to Haydn) as well as the Sonatas Op. 7, the String Trio Op. 3, several more sets of variations, and the song 'Adelaide' (Op. 46, on a text by Friedrich von Matthisson). All in all, twenty of Beethoven's thirty-two piano sonatas and three of the five piano concertos (Opp. 15, 19 and 37) were composed before 1802.

The six String Quartets of Op. 18 (dedicated to Prince Lobkowitz) are an exception and represent Beethoven's first foray into the genre, probably begun around 1798 and completed in 1800. The grouping of six separate pieces under a single opus number was common, especially with string quartets: Haydn's Op. 20 and 33 and Mozart's 'Haydn' quartets are notable examples. Joseph Kerman believes it implausible that Beethoven studied quartet composition with the 'lesser Viennese' composer Emanuel Aloys Förster (as often claimed),[29] and Thayer too emphasises that Beethoven's comment (to Karl

28 Charles Rosen, *The Classical Style: Haydn, Mozart, Beethoven*, expanded edn (New York and London, 1997), p. 389; see also K. M. Knittel, 'Imitation, Individuality, Illness: Behind Beethoven's Three Styles', *Beethoven Forum*, 4 (1995), pp. 17–36.
29 Joseph Kerman, *The Beethoven Quartets* (New York, 1967), pp. 10–12.

Amenda) that he had 'just learned how to write quartets properly' does not prove he had studied with Förster. However, according to Förster's son, Beethoven spent many evenings with the elder composer, performing quartets and discussing musical composition. Beethoven particularly admired Förster's ability to teach counterpoint and convinced him to publish a book, *Anleitung zum Generalbass* (Instructions for Basso Continuo, brought out in 1805 by Breitkopf and Härtel) (Thayer–Forbes, pp. 261–4). The desire to believe not only in Beethoven's superiority but also in his independence clearly underlies scholars' desire to dismiss any possible influence of Förster.

Additionally, the exalted position that the quartet genre now holds – Kinderman calls Op. 18 Beethoven's 'biggest single compositional project of [his] first decade at Vienna' – may make writers particularly loath to admit that Beethoven was influenced by anyone or anything while writing Op. 18. Special note is usually made of Beethoven's delay in attempting a string quartet and of turning instead to the string trio (Opp. 3 and 9) as a way of 'avoiding' the genre. Kerman claims that Beethoven's 'care and industry and worry and high seriousness in writing the six Op. 18 Quartets . . . is evidenced by his sketchbooks', of which two complete books chronicle the composition of nos. 3, 1, 2, and 5.[30] Perhaps, however, Beethoven's 'hesitation' (if it can be called that) is more an indication of performance practice than fear of being compared to Mozart or Haydn: after all, aristocrats – Prince Lichnowsky and Count Andreas Razumovsky (1752–1836), for example – often participated in the performances of string quartets, and were thus in a position to offer more comprehensive criticism.

Even in regard to the earliest works, the Beethoven myth clearly privileges not just certain genres, but also certain types of pieces, especially those which hint at unhappiness and struggle. For example, C minor has been called 'Beethoven's key', said to be the key in which he expressed his 'pathétique' or most personal sentiments. Those early works now considered to be his most important utilise this key: the Op. 13 *Pathétique* Piano Sonata, the aforementioned Op. 1, No. 3, the Third Piano Concerto Op. 37, the String Quartet Op. 18, No. 4, and the Violin Sonata Op. 30, No. 2. In addition to the adherence to C minor, these works also often break some convention of form or style. The first movement of Op. 13, for example, opens with a dramatic slow introduction that, contrary to normal expectations, returns several times in the first movement – at the beginning of the development and the beginning of the coda. Perhaps this gesture originated in one of Beethoven's improvisations; nevertheless, the privileging of Op. 13's irresistible combination of pathos and independence objectifies the compulsion to see Beethoven's life mirrored in his music.

---

30 Kinderman, *Beethoven*, p. 53; Cooper (ed.), *The Beethoven Compendium*, pp. 232–3; and Kerman, *Quartets*, p. 9.

As already noted, Dahlhaus and others have pointed out that the Beethoven myth, and to a large degree his posthumous reputation as a composer, relies mainly on works written during the so-called 'heroic' period. One of the reasons for this lies in the idea that Beethoven, in these works, is attempting to 'break the bonds of Classicism' or to somehow expand beyond the strictures imposed by the style of Mozart and Haydn. The exposition of the first movement of the Third Symphony, for example, is 155 bars long, nearly as long as an entire movement of a Mozart or Haydn symphony. Additionally, the development section is nearly twice as long as that and the coda not only becomes a section in its own right but seems to encompass the same procedures as the development section – centring on the breaking down of themes, dramatic juxtaposition of ideas and resolution of conflict. Probably the most famous moment of the first movement is the insertion of a 'new theme' into the development section: the E minor theme at bar 284 that appears out of nowhere and creates a sense of displacement and confusion. Needless to say, commentators have been quite perplexed by this seemingly bold disregard of sonata form.[31]

Where the Third seems expansive and boundless (it lasts approximately fifty-five minutes if all the repeats are taken), the Fifth, another touchstone of Beethoven's style, is an essay in brevity and condensation. Its key of C minor may have started the idea that this was 'Beethoven's key', or at least perpetuated the idea that that key encompasses Beethoven's most meaningful and personal music. Schindler, in his biography, claimed that Beethoven provided the 'key' to the symphony when he indicated the beginning of the Fifth and said, 'Thus Fate knocks at the door!'[32] While this anecdote is one of Schindler's known fabrications, it has nevertheless had a profound influence on all who have subsequently heard or performed the symphony. Gustav Mahler, when preparing to conduct the work for the opening concert of the Vienna Philharmonic's season in 1899, agonised over exactly how to best render these 'knocks of Destiny', admitting that he never had felt clear as to what exactly Beethoven had intended.[33]

E. T. A. Hoffmann, in his famous 1810 review of the Fifth Symphony published in the *AmZ*, calls the symphony 'one of [Beethoven's] most important works'. Hoffmann identifies many characteristics that continue to fascinate critics: the use of thematic and motivic connections throughout the composition, the linking of the movements to one another 'in a fantastic way', the 'great

31 See Scott Burnham, *Beethoven Hero* (Princeton, 1995), pp. 3–28.

32 Anton Felix Schindler, *Beethoven as I Knew Him*, ed. D. W. MacArdle, trans. C. S. Jolly (Mineola, N.Y., 1996), p. 147.

33 Henry-Louis de La Grange, *Gustav Mahler. Vienna: The Years of Challenge (1897–1904)* (Oxford and New York, 1995), p. 202.

ingenuity and extreme care' exhibited by Beethoven's compositions, the unity of feeling that pervades the movement and its ability to 'tear the listener irresistibly away into the wonderful spiritual realm of the infinite'. For Hoffmann, Beethoven's music 'induces terror, fright, horror and pain and awakens that endless longing which is the essence of Romanticism'. Like the sublime in Kant's essay whose 'feeling is sometimes accompanied with a certain dread', Beethoven's Fifth Symphony opens 'the realm of the colossal and the immeasurable'.[34]

Other compositions of the period that have received disproportionate emphasis also exhibit the 'breaking the bonds' aesthetic: for example, the 'Waldstein' Piano Sonata, Op. 53, which utilises the mediant key instead of the more common dominant for the second theme in the exposition (in C major: E major instead of G major); the Op. 59 'Razumovsky' String Quartets which in scope strive towards 'symphonic' proportions; and Beethoven's only opera, *Fidelio*, which involves the literal breaking of bonds as a wife struggles to free her unfairly imprisoned husband from his jailer. These pieces speak to us because they seem to stem so obviously from Beethoven's own struggles. Works in minor keys, such as the 'Appassionata' Sonata, Op. 57 (F minor) or the *Coriolan* Overture (C minor) also manifest the idea of struggle in the form of pathos.

The 'heroic' works, writes Scott Burnham, give the listener 'a high level of almost visceral engagement', and the musical techniques used to achieve this – thematic instability, metric ambiguity, tonal shifts, rhythmic drive – have come to epitomise what we consider to be Beethoven's 'style'. Yet many of Beethoven's works exhibit distinctly non-heroic tendencies: the Sixth Symphony, for example, employs none of these techniques, and in fact seems consciously to subvert them. Where the Fifth pushes relentlessly forward on all levels (rhythmic, metric, motivic), the Sixth seems to revel in stasis. Its harmonic rhythm is much slower (even passages in the development are often over a pedal point, which stabilises the tonality), motifs are repeated at the same pitch level rather than in sequence (again stabilising the harmonic language), dynamic and registral shifts are minimised, melodies are symmetrical, and potentially climactic moments – the recapitulation, for example – are downplayed (by continually emphasising the first subject in the development of the first movement, for example). Whereas according to Burnham the Fifth presents 'no safe . . . future', the Sixth projects exactly the opposite. This is amply illustrated by comparing the opening fermatas: while in the Fifth, the listener

34 E. T. A. Hoffmann, '[Review of the Fifth Symphony]', in Elliot Forbes (ed.), *Beethoven: Symphony No. 5 in C Minor*, Norton Critical Score (New York and London, 1971), pp. 150–63.

is presented with hardly any information (key, melody, rhythm, metre are all ambiguous at the moment of the first fermata), in the Sixth, the fermata arrives on the half-cadence of the first phrase, and the listener has a firm sense of harmony, rhythm, melody and metre.[35] Other non-heroic works include the 'Harp' String Quartet Op. 74, the Tenth Violin Sonata Op. 96, the Piano Sonatas Opp. 28 and 90, and the song cycle Op. 98, titled *An die ferne Geliebte*.

Unfortunately, the non-heroic stance of these works has insured that many have been unfairly ignored as somehow 'un-Beethovenian'. Charles Rosen suggests that many of these works represent 'Romantic' experiments abandoned by Beethoven and then later picked up by the early Romantics. Other writers look for 'hidden' aspects of these pieces that may point to more heroic categories: Kinderman, for example, believes that the Op. 96 Violin Sonata is 'an intimate work, rich in lyricism and subtle in its motivic relationships'.[36] Motivic relationships, of course, are one of the aspects of the heroic style that were considered innovative even by Beethoven's contemporaries, and thus the 'discovery' of subtle relationships implies not only the genius of the discoverer but the 'hidden' genius of Beethoven himself.

The year 1814 was probably the highpoint of Beethoven's career in terms of patronage and public acclaim; however, it was a year preceded by a terrible personal crisis and followed by a period of reduced productivity. Found after Beethoven's death was the letter to the 'Immortal Beloved', in which Beethoven expressed his deep love for an unnamed – and for many years unidentified – woman. It now seems likely that the addressee was Antonie Brentano, sister-in-law to Bettina, who probably met Beethoven in 1810 while she was in Vienna taking care of her father's estate after his death. Unfortunately, Antonie was married with several children and the relationship had probably reached a crisis point during the summer of 1812 when the letter was written. Beethoven went into a profound depression following the Brentanos's departure from Vienna in late 1812, and for the next four years composed only a few major pieces, including the song cycle, *An die ferne Geliebte* (To the Distant Beloved), written in all likelihood for Antonie. A diary (*Tagebuch*) that Beethoven kept from 1812 until 1818 chronicles his despair during these bleak years.[37]

It is all the more ironic, then, that the height of Beethoven's public acclaim would coincide with the depths of his worst depression. The years 1812–14 were notable for a heightened state of patriotic feeling as Vienna watched

35 Contrast Burnham, *Beethoven Hero*, pp. 29–65 (quotes are pp. 45 and 38) with David Wyn Jones, *Beethoven: Pastoral Symphony* (Cambridge, 1995), pp. 54–80; on the pastoral in music see pp. 14–16.

36 Rosen, *Classical Style*, pp. 379, 400–4; Kinderman, *Beethoven*, p. 162.

37 Solomon (*Beethoven*, pp. 207–46) is credited with solving the mystery; he also translates the Tagebuch in *Beethoven Essays* (Cambridge, Mass., 1988), pp. 233–95.

Napoleon's decline. Beethoven wrote *Wellingtons Sieg* (Wellington's Victory) to celebrate the battle of Vittoria on 21 June 1813, and it was performed during the December concerts to great acclaim. In May of 1814 his opera *Fidelio* was revived (in its third and much revised version) and its theme of rescue now took on new meaning in the wake of the wars. Beginning in September 1814 the Congress of Vienna was in session, and the European heads of state convened in order to reassemble – to the extent that it was possible – pre-Napoleonic Europe. Beethoven wrote a series of patriotic and commemorative works for the festivities, and was introduced to many heads of state by Razumovsky and Archduke Rudolph – an indication that aristocratic patronage was still important for Beethoven. Historians now cringe at Beethoven's works from this period, which seem to be bombastic pot-boilers intent on audience response; that these compositions also represent Beethoven's biggest popular successes should be instructive as to how the Beethoven myth controls which works can be considered 'Beethovenian'.

The works that Beethoven completed following the Congress of Vienna include often called his 'late-' or 'third'-period works. I have remarked elsewhere that although many of these pieces are now considered by connoisseurs to be his greatest, they were initially met with uncomprehending reviews. Many blamed Beethoven's deafness for what was taken as impossible music, while others even suggested that Beethoven was losing his mind. In hindsight, it is difficult to know whether critics were reacting to real musical difficulties or simply to the knowledge that Beethoven was deaf. By 1816, it was probably fairly widely known, at least in the musical communities, that Beethoven was no longer able to hear: that year, the *AmZ* had lamented 'One can not help but feel sorry for this great artist, as he loses his hearing more and more', and visitors to Beethoven during his last years often commented that his hearing was worse (or better) than they had been led to expect.[38]

The compositions from this period are the Ninth Symphony, the *Missa Solemnis*, five piano sonatas (Opp. 101, 106 the 'Hammerklavier', 109, 110, 111) plus some shorter piano works, the two cello sonatas Op. 102, and the last string quartets, Opp. 127, 132, 130, 131 and 135. The *Grosse Fuge* (Great Fugue) originated as the finale of Op. 130, but was replaced with a newly written finale at the insistence of the publisher and the fugue published separately as Op. 133 several months before Beethoven's death. Many of these works, perhaps because of Beethoven's deafness, focus on homogeneous instrumental textures, and almost all experiment with the pacing of the multi-movement form. Especially in the last quartets, Beethoven expands the number of movements and plays with the placement of emphasis. For example, Op. 132 has five

38 *AmZ*, 18 (February 1816), col. 121; Sonneck, *Impressions*, pp. 100, 150, 194, 210.

movements, rather than the more typical four, and the emotional highpoint is the middle – the 'Heiliger Dankgesang', or 'Holy song of thanksgiving to the Godhead from a Convalescent, in the Lydian Mode', written in April 1825 after a serious illness – rather than the more conventional first or last movement. Likewise, Op. 131 with its seven movements positions the only real sonata form movement at the very end, and by 'weakening' the earlier six in a variety of ways (some are very short and none can stand alone) insures that the trajectory continues until the end of the piece.

Beethoven's last work perhaps best exemplifies the havoc that can be wrought by the Beethoven myth. The String Quartet in F major, Op. 135, has caused critics no end of agony because it seems to back away from the formal and generic experiments of Beethoven's later years. Not only is it extremely conventional in numbers and forms of movements, but it also follows Op. 131 which even Beethoven himself supposedly considered his greatest work (Thayer–Forbes, p. 982). The cheerful mood of Op. 135 seems to fly in the face of what we know of Beethoven's final months: alone, deaf, ill much of the time, plagued by money problems and difficulties with his nephew Karl – cheerful is not the way we would describe the period which brought Op. 135 into existence. But by insisting that 'Beethovenian' music must somehow reflect 'Beethovenian' personality, we fail to see Beethoven or his music: in November 1826, pitiable, maybe – but even at that point dreaming of writing a new symphony, of taking a trip to London, even of returning to his native Bonn.

Discussions of Beethoven's style, 1810–1852

In his *Beethoven Hero*, Burnham asks why it is that Beethoven, and not Haydn, 'became the canonic composer, the embodiment of music'. As James Webster has so convincingly shown, many of the traits that we now point to as quintessentially Beethovenian – the 'through-composed' symphony, motivic unity between movements, destabilised openings, rhetorical music – were present and even originated in the music of Haydn.[39] Why then, does Beethoven get all the credit? Why is Beethoven considered the greatest of all composers?

Even during his own lifetime, Beethoven was rarely compared to any composers other than Haydn and Mozart, and almost always in that order. Critics identified Haydn as the originator, Mozart as the explorer, and Beethoven as the master of instrumental music. Beethoven was universally seen as having absorbed and then superseded the music of his predecessors. And almost as universally, critics view Beethoven's music as a product of deeper feelings –

39 Burnham, *Beethoven Hero*, p. 64; James Webster, *Haydn's 'Farewell' Symphony and the Idea of Classical Style* (Cambridge, 1991).

stemming from his unique circumstances – and this became the factor that distinguished his from other music. An obituary, written by Dr Wilhelm Christian Müller, draws a direct line between Mozart's cheerful personality and his cheerful music, drawing the same line between Beethoven's loneliness and his 'brooding fantasy':

> [Beethoven] remained shy and taciturn because he exchanged few ideas with people, observed and pondered more than he spoke, and abandoned himself to the feelings and brooding fantasy awakened by music and later by poets. Mozart, on the other hand, was already introduced to the world as a seven-year-old boy, which explains his versatile, affable, communicative, friendly nature, his early skill in composition, and his universal, highly structured, and pleasing; cosmopolitan music. On the contrary, Beethoven did not think about writing down his creations for others or himself. He improvised at an early age on the pianoforte, and later even more on the violin, so that in his loneliness he forgot all of the necessities of life and often had to be fetched to the table by his threatening mother.[40]

E. T. A. Hoffmann draws the same conclusions, claiming that Haydn and Mozart may 'breathe the same romantic spirit . . . [but] the character of their compositions . . . is noticeably different'. The sources for those differences lie in the composers' personalities. Haydn's disposition is 'cheerful, childlike' and this 'can be found everywhere' in his compositions. Hoffmann asserts that here 'there is no suffering, no pain, but only the sweet, melancholy longing'. However, while Mozart 'leads us into the inner depth of the realm of the spirits', only Beethoven's music can 'open the realm of the colossal and the immeasurable for us'. Beethoven's music is different because 'deep within Beethoven's heart dwells the romanticism of his music', and this he reveals to us 'with great ingenuity and extreme care in his works'.[41]

Some critics remained unconvinced: Ernst Ludwig Gerber wrote that Beethoven's works clearly surpass Haydn's, but comments that 'it is a pity that, in a great number of his art works, his genius is inclined towards seriousness and melancholy'. In most cases, however, it was precisely the depth – or difference – of feeling in Beethoven's works that interested critics the most. Johann Aloys Schlosser, whose short and inconsistent biography of Beethoven was published in 1828, claims that while Mozart's music 'charms more in performance by means of perfection', Beethoven's music 'towers through greater design'. All in all, says Schlosser, Beethoven displays 'more passion, while Mozart, on the other hand, [displays] more an abundance of inner satisfaction'. C. T. Seiffert links the quality and value of Beethoven's compositions to the fact

---

40 Dr W. C. Müller, 'Etwas über Ludwig van Beethoven', trans. in Senner, *Critical Reception*, I, p. 102.
41 Hoffmann, in Forbes (ed.), *Symphony No. 5 in C Minor*, pp. 152–3.

that he 'in no way indulges the often very small demands of his contemporaries'. Unlike Mozart, who despite a desire to write 'deeply moving' compositions, nevertheless 'wrote light, playable works, as the public desired'. For
Beethoven, 'art stands too high for him to subordinate it to fashionable taste,
and fortunately, he was mostly in a position that this was allowed to him'.[42]

The desire not only to see Haydn, Mozart and Beethoven as a triumvirate but
also to plot musical progress through their works cannot and should not be
separated from the emergence of German nationalism. Gottfried Herder had
laid the foundations for this when he emphasised the importance of a German
national literature: while he himself never specifically invoked nationalism, he
nonetheless insisted on the importance of a 'communal bond woven by a
common language'.[43] The idea that the Germans as a people were bound by cultural, not territorial, boundaries became the dominant image during the nineteenth century. The continued references to these three German composers
helped to underscore the truth of that claim of cultural unity. Beethoven
appealed to the nationalists because he represented unarguable greatness, a
superiority that could be easily mapped on to Germany itself. It was important
for that image to be a strong and powerful one, and this may account for the
gendered language that attaches itself to Beethoven and his music. While it
does not justify the emphasis on masculinity, it does explain its perpetuation.
The equality of the classes proposed by the French Revolution made it all the
more important to distinguish between male and female, in particular in the
realm of music which was considered to be the woman's sphere. A powerful,
masculine composer thus presented not only a nationalistic symbol for the
Germans, but a strong image to counter music's supposed effeminacy. That the
distinctness of Beethoven's playing and personality came to be expressed in
terms of gender therefore reveals more about the classifiers than it does about
Beethoven himself.

Often, that gendering is quite subtle. Carl Czerny's description (in a supplement to his *Pianoforte-Schule*) of Beethoven's works relies on carefully selected
adjectives to emphasise Beethoven's masculinity: 'the general character of his
works is serious, strong, noble, extremely full of feeling, in addition often
humorous and wilful, sometimes even Baroque, but always brilliant, and even
though occasionally dismal, certainly never sweetly elegant, or whiningly
sentimental'. Even the performer of Beethoven's music must not simply be a

---

42 E. L. Gerber, 'van Beethoven (Ludwig)', *Neues historisch-biographisches Lexicon der Tonkunstler,
1812–1814*, ed. O. Wessely (Graz, 1966), I, col. 316; J. A. Schlosser, *Beethoven: The First Biography*, ed. B.
Cooper, trans. R. G. Pauly (Portland, Oreg., 1996), p. 148, translations have been emended; C. T. Seiffert,
'Charakteristik der Beethoven'schen Sonaten und Symphonien' *AmZ*, 45 (7 June 1843), col. 419. (My translation.)

43 H. S. Reiss, *The Political Thought of the German Romantics, 1793–1815* (Oxford, 1955), p. 3.

'good, well-trained pianist' but also must have spiritual as well as physical strength – Beethoven's music is not for children, even *Wunderkinder*. Not until they have thoroughly studied the works of Clementi, Mozart, Dussek, Cramer and Hummel and have 'begun to develop understanding and feeling' should they be allowed to begin studying Beethoven's works.[44]

Not only Czerny but many, many writers emphasise that Beethoven's works are not for everyone. Hoffmann wrote in 1810 that 'the thoroughly Romantic nature of [Beethoven's] instrumental music may be the reason that it seldom receives the acclaim of the multitude'. Hoffmann goes on to state that even those who do not 'appreciate the profundity of Beethoven' nevertheless do not 'deny him an active imagination'. In a later revision of the same essay, Hoffmann's language is stronger: 'the musical rabble is oppressed by Beethoven's powerful genius; it seeks in vain to oppose it'. While Haydn 'is more suitable for the majority' and Mozart 'claims the superhuman' and 'dwells in the inner spirit', Beethoven's music 'induces terror, fright, horror and pain and awakens that endless longing which is the essence of Romanticism'. Beethoven's genius is 'serious and solemn'; his music is not 'mere entertainment for an idle hour'.[45]

According to many authors, Beethoven's music, unlike the more accessible (read: feminine) composers, could only be fully understood with serious effort. Writing about the Wölffl piano duel, Seyfried had called Beethoven's improvisations 'the mystical Sanscrit language whose hieroglyphs can be read only by the initiated'. Schlosser asserts that even educated people do not always fully comprehend Beethoven, perhaps because they are 'too dependent on conventional forms'. In order to 'penetrate Beethoven's spirit which is freer and more original', the 'study of the score is absolutely necessary'. Czerny believes that if one wants to learn Beethoven's solo piano sonatas, it is 'most advantageous . . . to study them in the same order that they appeared during the course of his life. That way, one can follow the development of his genius and learn to recognise and differentiate the three periods of his works'. Hoffmann writes that 'only a very deep penetration into the inner structure of Beethoven's music [will] reveal the extent of the master's self-possession'.[46]

The reward for such study is the revelation of the inner unity of Beethoven's works. Although Hoffmann certainly did not invent the interest in organicism,

44 Carl Czerny, *Die Kunst des Vortrags, Supplement (oder 4ter Theil) zur grossen Pianoforte-Schule, Op. 500* (Vienna, [1844?]), pp. 50 and 33.

45 Hoffmann, in Forbes (ed.), *Symphony No. 5 in C Minor*, pp. 152–3 and 'Beethoven's Instrumental Music (1813)', in Oliver Strunk (ed.), *Source Readings in Music History: The Romantic Era* (New York and London, 1965), pp. 37, 39–40.

46 Thayer–Forbes, p. 207; Schlosser, *The First Biography*, pp. 152–3; Czerny, *Op. 500*, p. 34; and Hoffmann, in Forbes (ed.), *Symphony No. 5 in C Minor*, p. 153.

his notice of it in the review of the Fifth Symphony is one of the most famous
early examples: 'it is particularly the intimate relationship of the individual
themes to one another which produces the unity that firmly maintains a single
feeling in the listener's heart'. While Hoffmann notes that this unity is present
in the music of Mozart and Haydn, Beethoven's is 'a more profound relationship . . . communicated from the heart to the heart'. Seiffert claims that this
unity is a characteristic of Beethoven's music in general:

> It is of the highest interest to observe in his compositions how gradually, next
> to the solidity and the substance of the purely musical idea, the inner spiritual
> unity – the self-contained progression of thought – continually comes to the
> fore. In one regard he is particularly unsurpassable, in the invention of motifs.
> So pithy, so characteristic are these that within bars we are transported to that
> frame of mind necessary to grasp the whole.
>
> Thus, like Minerva from Jupiter's head, [so] most of his artworks, according
> to their main idea, sprang resolutely and completely to him from his own.

Wilhelm von Lenz, discussing a claim by François-Joseph Fétis that
Beethoven's compositions are characterised by the 'spontaneity of the
episodes', suggests that even in such instances Beethoven never loses sight of
the unity of the whole. 'When the effect of the surprise begins to weaken,
Beethoven knows to reassert the unity of his plan and make it clear that in the
whole of his composition the variety is dependent upon the unity'. Czerny
makes a similar observation when he writes that:

> Every one of his tone-pieces expresses a special, consistently tightly held mood
> or view, which remains true to itself to the smallest shades. The melody, the
> musical thought predominates over all: all passages and moving figures are
> always means and never purpose; and if one also (especially in the early works)
> finds many places where the so-called brilliant performance style takes utter-
> ance, so should these never be the main point. Whoever only wants to produce
> therein his dexterity, would fail the spiritual and aesthetic purpose and prove
> that he does not understand the work.[47]

Underlying all these comments is the idea that Beethoven's works contain
nothing superfluous: every bit is meaningful to the whole. As a metaphor for
the German nation, this image works very well. Germany at the time did not
exist as an autonomous state, but rather a loose collection of smaller kingdoms.
The unity – in language, culture and customs – of these small states, however,

47 Hoffmann, in Forbes (ed.), *Symphony No. 5 in C Minor*, p. 163; Seiffert 'Charakteristik', col. 420;
Wilhelm von Lenz, *Beethoven et ses Trois Styles: Analyses des sonates de piano suivies d'un essai d'un catalogue cri-
tique, chronologique, et anecdotique de l'oeuvre de Beethoven* (Paris, 1855; rept. 1980), p. 54; François-Joseph
Fétis, 'Beethoven, Louis van', *Biographie universelle des musiciens*, ed. François-Joseph Fétis (Brussels, 1837),
II, pp. 100–12; and Czerny, *Op. 500*, p. 33.

could be discerned if only one looked closely enough. Like the unity of Beethoven's works, the unity of Germany was not obvious on the surface, ensuring that only those who are truly serious and worthy could find this inner meaning. The flip side of this, of course, is the dark side of German nationalism: the desire to expunge any part of the whole that does not fit. In Beethoven's music – and perhaps, it was hoped, soon in Germany itself – nothing is superficial, nothing is there that does not belong or serve a purpose.

Franz Brendel, in his 1852 history of music, specifically links Beethoven's musical accomplishments to national advancement. Brendel identifies Beethoven's major 'deed' as a 'turn back towards the spirit', a move inward away from the outer world. As Italian music declines, Brendel sees in Beethoven the opportunity for Germany to come to the fore:

> Germany could in *Beethoven take a new, higher, upward turn*, and now unfold the subjectivity of the entire wealth of its contents. Germany's art takes in Beethoven the turn back towards the spirit, and with it at the same time towards the fatherland in a narrower sense . . . This indicates the great upward turning which our tone-art in modern times has taken. An infinity of spirit has opened up and a sweeping horizon is revealed.[48]

Beethoven (along with Bach) is the 'highest indication of a special German territory or arena'. Brendel explicitly equates Beethoven's music with the advancement of the national cause as well as establishing musical achievement as a particularly German endeavour. No longer do the Italians control the musical scene (Brendel seems to suggest that the universality of Italian opera is being surpassed by German instrumental music), music now functions as both symbol and proof of Germany's existence. What here is but a small part of Brendel's argument will become in Richard Wagner's language the issue of primary importance: Beethoven and music are the sole property of the German people.

Beethoven, mostly through the Beethoven myth, became a vehicle of German nationalism, a powerful symbol that quickly eclipsed the real, historical Beethoven in prominence and importance. The impact of this, as Sanna Pederson has shown, was the gendering of the composers in the generation following Beethoven (Schumann, Schubert, Mendelssohn) as feminine, and the elevation of the symphony to a similarly high pedestal.[49] Beethoven's presence was certainly felt elsewhere – specifically England, France, Russia, and America which all had Beethoven cults to varying degrees – and he continues even now

---

48 Franz Brendel, *Geschichte der Musik in Italien, Deutschland und Frankreich von den ersten Christlichen Zeiten bis auf die Gegenwart* (Leipzig, 1852), p. 27, emphasis original.

49 Sanna Pederson, 'A. B. Marx, Berlin Concert Life, and German National Identity', *19th Century Music*, 18 (1994), pp. 87–107, and her 'On the Task of the Music Historian: The Myth of the Symphony After Beethoven', *repercussions*, 2 (1993), pp. 5–30.

to function as a universal symbol of creativity and genius and to dominate concert programmes worldwide. It was, however, German consciousness that most specifically had to carry the burden of Beethoven: to try and live up to, but of course never surpass, his example.

Ludwig van Beethoven died on 26 March 1827, at about a quarter to six in the evening. Even as he lay dying, he could not escape the mythic proportions that his own life had taken on: outside, like a cosmic joke, a storm raged, and it is said that with his last breath he raised a clenched fist as if to heroically challenge death itself. This image of the heroic Beethoven protects us from the real tragedy of Beethoven's death – not just that he died, but that he died with no family to comfort him and only a few friends, many of whom (like Anton Schindler) cared more about their own positions in history. Every event in Beethoven's life, from the earliest accounts of Neefe to the recollections of those who visited him on his deathbed have been interpreted to emphasise not Beethoven the man, but Beethoven the myth. To begin to question those interpretations is not to lessen Beethoven's greatness nor to imply that he was not influential in the nineteenth century; it is merely to ask why we remain so enamoured of one particular – peculiar, simplistic – image of the composer which obscures all others.

Bibliography

Albrecht, T. (ed.), *Letters to Beethoven and Other Correspondence*. 3 vols., Lincoln, Nebr., and London, 1996
Anderson, E. (ed. and trans.), *The Letters of Mozart and His Family*. New York, 3rd rev. edn 1985
Anderson, E. (ed.), *The Letters of Beethoven*. London, 1961
Braunbehrens, B., *Mozart in Vienna, 1781–1791*, trans. T. Bell. New York, 1989
Brendel, F., *Geschichte der Musik in Italien, Deutschland und Frankreich von den ersten Christlichen Zeiten bis auf die Gegenwart*. Leipzig, 1852
Burnham, S., *Beethoven Hero*. Princeton, 1995
Burnham, S. and M. P. Steinberg, *Beethoven and his World*. Princeton, 2000
Charlton, D. (ed.), *E. T. A. Hoffmann's Musical Writings*. Cambridge, 1989
Comini, A., *The Changing Image of Beethoven: A Study in Mythmaking*. New York, 1987
Cooper, B. (ed.), *The Beethoven Compendium: A Guide to Beethoven's Life and Music*. London, 1991
Cooper, M., *Beethoven: The Last Decade, 1817–1827*. Rev. edn. Oxford and New York, 1985
Czerny, C., *Die Kunst des Vortrags, Supplement (oder 4ter Theil) zur grossen Pianoforte-Schule, Op. 500*. Vienna, [1844?]
Dahlhaus, C., *Nineteenth-Century Music*, trans. J. B. Robinson. Berkeley and Los Angeles, 1989
    Ludwig van Beethoven: Approaches to His Music, trans. M. Whittall. Oxford, 1991
Dennis, D. B., *Beethoven in German Politics, 1870–1989*. New Haven and London, 1995
DeNora, T., *Beethoven and the Construction of Genius: Musical Politics in Vienna, 1792–1803*. Berkeley and Los Angeles, 1995

Ealy, G. T., 'Of Ear Trumpets and a Resonance Plate: Early Hearing Aids and Beethoven's Hearing Perception'. *19th Century Music*, 17 (1994), pp. 262–73

Eggebrecht, H. H., *Zur Geschichte Beethoven-Rezeption*. Spektrum der Musik, 2nd enlarged edn. Laaber, 1994

Fétis, F.-J., 'Beethoven, Louis van'. In *Biographie universelle des musiciens*, ed. F.-J. Fétis. 8 vols., Brussels, 1837, II, pp. 100–12

Forbes, E. (ed.), *Thayer's Life of Beethoven*. Rev. edn, Princeton, 1967

Beethoven: Symphony no. 5 in C minor. Norton Critical Score, New York and London, 1971

Gerber, E. L., *Neues historisch-biographisches Lexicon der Tonkunstler, 1812–1814*, ed. O. Wessely. 3 vols., Graz, 1966

Hoffmann, E. T. A., 'Beethoven's Instrumental Music [1813]'. In O. Strunk (ed.), *Source Readings in Music History: The Romantic Era*. New York and London, 1965, pp. 35–41

Jones, D. W., *Beethoven: Pastoral Symphony*. Cambridge, 1995

Kant, I., *Observations on the Feeling of the Beautiful and Sublime*, trans. J. T. Goldthwait. Berkeley and Los Angeles, 1991

Kerst, F. (ed.), *Beethoven: The Man and the Artist as Revealed in His Own Words*. Dover reprint, trans. H. E. Krehbiel. New York, 1964; original edn 1905

Kinderman, W., *Beethoven*. Berkeley and Los Angeles, 1995

Knittel, K. M., 'Imitation, Individuality, Illness: Behind Beethoven's Three Styles'. *Beethoven Forum*, 4 (1995), pp. 17–36

'Wagner, Deafness, and the Reception of Beethoven's Late Style'. *Journal of the American Musicological Society*, 51 (1998), pp. 49–82

La Grange, H.-L. de, *Gustav Mahler. Vienna: The Years of Challenge (1897–1904)*. Rev. edn, Oxford and New York, 1995

Lenz, W. von, *Beethoven et ses Trois Styles: Analyses des sonates de piano suivies d'un essai d'un catalogue critique, chronologique, et anecdotique de l'oeuvre de Beethoven*. Da Capo reprint 1980; Paris, 1855

Morrow, M. S., *Concert Life in Haydn's Vienna: Aspects of a Developing Musical and Social Institution*. Sociology of Music 7. Stuyvesant, N.Y., 1989

German Music Criticism in the Late Eighteenth Century: Aesthetic Issues in Instrumental Music. Cambridge, 1997

Newman, W. S., *Beethoven on Beethoven: Playing His Piano Music His Way*. New York and London, 1988

Pederson, S., 'On the Task of the Music Historian: The Myth of the Symphony After Beethoven'. *repercussions*, 2 (1993), pp. 5–30

'A. B. Marx, Berlin Concert Life, and German National Identity'. *19th Century Music*, 18 (1994), pp. 87–107

Pezzl, J., 'Sketch of Vienna'. In H. C. Robbins Landon, *Mozart and Vienna*. New York, 1981, pp. 53–191

Rochlitz, F., 'Nekrolog'. *Allgemeine musikalische Zeitung*, 29 (1827), cols. 227–8

Rosen, C., *The Classical Style: Haydn, Mozart, Beethoven*. Expanded edn, New York and London, 1997

Schindler, A. F., *Beethoven as I Knew Him*, ed. D. W. MacArdle, trans. C. S. Jolly. Dover reprint, Mineola, N.Y., 1996

Schlosser, J. A., *Beethoven: The First Biography*, ed. B. Cooper, trans. R. G. Pauly. Portland, Oreg., 1996

Schmitz, A., *Das romantische Beethovenbild*. Berlin and Bonn, 1927

Schmitz, W. and Steinsdorff, S. von (eds.), *Bettine von Arnim Werke und Briefe*. 4 vols., Frankfurt am Main, 1992

Schulze, H., *The Course of German Nationalism: From Frederick the Great to Bismarck, 1763–1867*, trans. S. Hanbury-Tenison. Cambridge, 1994

Seiffert, C. T., 'Charakteristik der Beethoven'schen Sonaten und Symphonien'. *Allgemeine musikalische Zeitung*, 45 (1843), cols. 417–20, 433–8, 449–52, 465–9

Senner, W. M., Wallace, R. and Meredith, W. (eds.), *The Critical Reception of Beethoven's Compositions by His German Contemporaries*. 4 vols., Lincoln, Nebr., and London, 1999–.

Sipe, T., *Beethoven: Eroica Symphony*. Cambridge, 1998

Sisman, E., *Mozart: The 'Jupiter' Symphony*. Cambridge, 1993

Solomon, M., *Beethoven Essays*. Cambridge, Mass., 1988.

   Beethoven. 2nd rev. edn, New York, 1998

Sonneck, O. G., *Beethoven: Impressions by His Contemporaries*. Dover reprint, New York, 1967

Stanley, G. (ed.), *The Cambridge Companion to Beethoven*. Cambridge, 2000

Wallace, R., *Beethoven's Critics: Aesthetic Dilemmas and Resolutions During the Composer's Lifetime*. Cambridge, 1986

Webster, J., 'The Falling-out Between Haydn and Beethoven: The Evidence of the Sources'. In L. Lockwood and P. Benjamin (eds.), *Beethoven Essays: Studies in Honor of Elliot Forbes*. Cambridge, Mass., 1984, pp. 3–45

   Haydn's 'Farewell' Symphony and the Idea of the Classical Style: Through-Composition and Cyclic Integration in His Instrumental Music. Cambridge, 1991

Wegeler, F. and Ries F., *Beethoven Remembered: The Biographical Notes of Franz Wegeler and Ferdinand Ries*, trans. F. Noonan. Arlington, Va. 1987

White, H., *Tropics of Discourse: Essays in Cultural Criticism*. Baltimore and London, 1978

   The Content of the Form: Narrative Discourse and Historical Representation. Baltimore and London, 1987

Zaslaw, N. (ed.), *The Classical Era: From the 1740s to the End of the 18th Century*. Englewood Cliffs, 1989

6

Music and the poetic

JULIAN RUSHTON

A traditional assumption of historiography that musical trends followed those of the other arts after a lapse of time is hard to sustain with the burgeoning of Romanticism, a movement which among other things embraced the emerging category of the 'poetic'. Pointers to Romanticism in literature of the 1770s isolate phenomena within a predominantly Classicistic culture; Goethe could write an *Iphigenia auf Tauris* as well as *Faust*. An early and important identification of the musically Romantic by the composer, jurist and man of letters E. T. A. Hoffmann (1776–1822) extended the definition back to include the instrumental music of Haydn and Mozart. The 'poetic' in music reflects a tendency to artistic synthesis outside the self-evidently synthetic field of theatre music: permeation of an artistic form by the values of another, or indeed by ideas normally considered beyond the realm of art, is traceable in song and in certain genres of instrumental music, but there is no need to assume that it alone constitutes the phenomenon of Romanticism, and its development is continuous with eighteenth-century opera, song and programme music.

Writing about Beethoven's Fifth Symphony in 1810, Hoffmann argued that purely instrumental music, without programme or literary allusion, is quintessentially Romantic; he resisted pointing to developments in French opera, even before the Revolution, as precursors of Weber's operas or, indeed, his own.

> When music is spoken of as an independent art the term can properly apply only to instrumental music, which scorns all aid, all admixture of other arts – and gives pure expression to its own peculiar artistic nature. It is the most Romantic of all arts – one might almost say the only one that is *purely* Romantic. . . . Music reveals to man an unknown realm, a world quite separate from the outer sensual world surrounding him, a world in which he leaves behind all feelings circumscribed by intellect in order to embrace the inexpressible.[1]

Hoffmann must be assumed to mean, not inexpressible, but inexpressible other than through music; he was not condemning music to expressive impotence. Although Hoffmann's view of musical purity had notable offspring, his

---

1 E. T. A. Hoffmann, *AMZ*, 12 (4 and 11 July 1810), cols. 630–42, 652–9; translated in David Charlton (ed.), *E. T. A. Hoffmann's Musical Writings* (Cambridge, 1989), pp. 234–51, at p. 236.

ideal was not universally subscribed. It became usual, to some extent in Germany and particularly in France, to view Beethoven as a giant, whose achievements could not be matched in their sublime grandeur, but also as a light, revealing new perspectives that a new generation, while sensing itself unable to equal him, could at least explore independently. Berlioz offered the following paradox inherent in what he called the new genre of 'expressive instrumental music':

> Instrumental music used only to be intended to please the ear or engage the intellect . . . but in Beethoven and Weber, poetic thought is ubiquitous and cannot be overlooked . . . This music needs no words to make its expression specific; it develops a language which is generally imprecise, and which as a result has all the greater impact upon *listeners endowed with imagination* . . . the composer is no longer constrained by the limitations of the voice and produces melodies which are more active and varied, phrases that are more original, even bizarre, without being afraid that they might be unplayable . . . From this stem the astonishing effects, the strange feelings, the ineffable sensations, which the symphonies, quartets, overtures and sonatas of Weber and Beethoven produce in us, quite unlike those stimulated in the theatre. There we are in the presence of human emotions; here a new world is displayed, and we are raised towards a higher ideal region, sensing that the sublime life dreamed of by poets is becoming real . . .[2]

Berlioz credits music with expressive autonomy, and attributes power to what, in his preface to *Roméo et Juliette*, he called its 'indefiniteness'.[3] The new generation stood at a crossroads. In one direction, Beethoven illuminated the possibility of self-referential musical expression, in which genres such as the untitled symphony will be interpreted by the listener in ways that are personal and in most cases incommunicable. Such music may be poetic by metaphor, but it aspires to complete independence as the model to other arts as they approached abstraction. Paradoxically, this path, often considered musically more traditional, represents a novel element within culture, as expressed by Carl Dahlhaus:

> Originally, in the nineteenth century, vocal music was in equal measure part of the literary and the musical culture of the educated classes, the 'carrier strata' for culture; and these classes only gradually, under the influence of Beethoven's symphonies and string quartets, accustomed themselves to the notion that music by itself, without an explanatory and justifying text, might exercise an educational and cultural function comparable to literature.[4]

---

2 Hector Berlioz, in *Le Correspondant*, 22 October 1830; see *Critique musicale 1823–1863*, ed. H. Robert Cohen and Yves Gérard (Paris, I: 1823–34, 1996), pp. 63–8.

3 Berlioz, *Roméo et Juliette*, ed. D. Kern Holoman, New Berlioz Edition 18 (Kassel, 1990), II, p. 383.

4 Carl Dahlhaus, *Nineteenth-Century Music*, trans J. B. Robinson (Berkeley and Los Angeles, 1989), p. 6.

In the other direction, Beethoven (particularly by the Ninth Symphony) illuminated a road which itself divided as new genres were tried, cast aside and
revived by a later generation. This is not only a question of blending music and
words, which continued in opera and received significant new emphasis in
song; it is also an interest in associating music with narrative, poetry, and visual
imagery, leading to new genres such as the piano cycle, the programme overture and symphony, and the symphonic poem.

In the realm of the musically poetic, poetry is not confined to verbal communication organised in verses, significant though that is for vocal music of all
kinds. Poetry is conceived more widely, as the direction of imaginative experience beyond the perceptible limits of the (musical) communication itself. A
piece of instrumental music with a 'programme' or an explicit extra-musical
association conveyed by a title may direct the imagination through music to a
visual, dramatic or poetic experience which the musical notes cannot literally
be said to contain. This may be so even when word-setting is involved. Many
composers throughout the nineteenth century wrote music free of text or programme. But much of the peculiarity of nineteenth-century art music results
from the inter-penetration, co-ordination or synthesis of the arts. Within the
ambit of instrumental and domestic music, the period is typified by genres
whose titles are at the very least evocative, such as the Nocturne; by exploitation of different dance types such as the Polonaise and waltz, and by pieces with
evocative titles. Other works aspire to narrate, whether a well-known story or
one specially concocted. Compared to these instrumental developments, vocal
music in the early nineteenth century may appear to show less discontinuity
from the eighteenth century than instrumental music. Opera continued to
flourish, solo song developed. But if one had to select a genre, and a composer
within that genre, to epitomise what was new in music of the first thirty years
of the century, it should surely be song, and Franz Schubert (1797–1828).

Sacred vocal music

In vocal music, the sung words provide a specific context for interpretation of
the musical choices made by the composer, and this must necessarily apply in
all kinds of vocal music, not just the overtly poetic. The early nineteenth
century continued the distinctive traditions of church music. In Russia, this
was the area of art music least dominated by Western composers; dispensing
with instruments, the Russian Orthodox Church permitted the evolution of
magnificent unaccompanied polyphony by the Ukrainian D. S. Bortnyansky
(1751–1825, appointed to the imperial chapel in St Petersburg in 1796). The
language of his liturgical settings, anthems and 'sacred concertos' is founded in

eighteenth-century tonality, permitting a clean intonation often missing in unaccompanied vocal music of greater harmonic complexity (see also chapter 8). In England, the cathedral and collegiate tradition carried a unique strand of musical tradition into the twentieth century; but even in the output of the most original composer, S. S. Wesley, its practice exemplified a widespread tendency, also apparent in Mendelssohn and the revival of Bach and Handel, to confirm its own roots by looking back beyond the immediately preceding generations to earlier periods. In such traditions sensitivity to text must be understood in terms of the broad response appropriate to the liturgical context, and the resonant acoustic; liturgical propriety largely excluded Protestant traditions in Germany and England from the development of the musically poetic.

The same cannot be said of Catholic music, where a tendency to dramatise by an affective response to the text brought church music closer to the theatre. J. F. Le Sueur (1760–1837) set out his ideas in a pamphlet of 1787, the year he was dismissed by the clergy of Notre Dame, Paris; appointed by Napoleon to the Royal chapel at the Tuileries, which was not beholden to a bishop, he freely developed his ideal of associating drama with liturgy at major church festivals.[5] His pupil Hector Berlioz (1803–69) developed a more complex musical language than his teacher's, but his *Grande messe des morts* (1837) and *Te Deum* (1849) are the greatest monuments both to Le Sueur and to the traditions of ceremonial music developed under the Revolution and Empire.[6] These works are entirely independent of the parallel Austro-German tradition of liturgical text-setting, exemplified by Haydn, Beethoven, Cherubini, Weber, Schubert and Bruckner, in which the liturgical form embraced a more poetic response to the text.

The text 'Sanctus, Sanctus, Sanctus, Dominus Deus Sabaoth', overtly an act of glorification and so treated by Bach (B minor Mass) and the Viennese tradition, became in the nineteenth century a place to evoke the mystery of the godhead. Beethoven in his *Missa Solemnis* (Op. 123, completed in 1823) takes the archaic as a metaphor for the numinous. Concentrated imitative counterpoint in a slow tempo is coloured by an orchestra without flutes, oboes and violins; moreover, within the Mass this is 'the only movement to begin without a clear sense of harmonic direction'.[7] Trombone cadences, like a liturgical response, restore classic periodicity, but the music eventually drifts into a prolonged minor ninth with tremolo, inescapably like the passage in the

5 Jean Mongrédien, *Jean-François le Sueur, contribution à l'étude d'un demi-siècle de musique française (1780–1830)* (Bern, 1980), II, p. 912.

6 Hugh Macdonald, 'Berlioz's *Messe solennelle*', *19th Century Music*, 16 (1993), pp. 267–85; Edward T. Cone, 'Berlioz's Divine Comedy: *The Grande Messe des morts*', *19th Century Music*, 4 (1980), pp. 3–16, reprinted in *Music: A View from Delft* (Chicago, 1989), pp. 139–57.

7 William Drabkin, *Beethoven: Missa Solemnis* (Cambridge, 1991), p. 73.

finale of the Ninth Symphony (composed shortly afterwards) where Schiller's text proclaims that God dwells above the stars ('Über Sternen müss er wohnen', bars 647–54). For the subsequent 'Pleni sunt coeli', Beethoven invokes a brilliant modern style (violin scales, *forte* dynamic, orchestral tutti), banishing mystery in the face of divine glory. Schubert, in his two late Masses, drew directly upon harmonic resources to evoke the numinous. In the Mass in A flat (D.678, 1822) he presents a threefold enharmonic progression, also punctuated by trombones (which retained an ecclesiastical and supernatural association). The triad acquires an augmented fifth, and the bass rises a semitone in turn. With two sequential repetitions, this passage traverses virtually the whole of tonal space. A more lyrical 'Pleni sunt coeli' disperses the clouds. Berlioz, on the other hand (*Grande messe des morts*), runs the 'Sanctus' and 'Pleni' clauses together in a ritualistically conceived movement for high solo tenor with choral responses; he too employs enharmonic modulations, less systematic than Schubert's, which equally suggest the numinous. The orchestration is characteristically economical; four solo violins and a flute, underpinned by string tremolo and, at the repeat, *pianissimo* strokes of the cymbals and bass drum, like the last resonance of a distant bell. In sacred music, nineteenth-century composers applied new resources to achieve effects whose essential rhetoric is not new at all; one might make a similar point about the continuity of operatic rhetoric, just as there is a considerable measure of continuity in operatic forms. However, the same certainly cannot be said of the nineteenth-century response to lyric poetry.

Song

The emergence of song as high art is among the most remarkable cultural phenomena of the early nineteenth century. Nevertheless, late eighteenth-century music possessed, and sometimes combined, nearly all the elements of early nineteenth-century art song; the catalysts which make the songs of Schubert and his contemporaries and immediate successors appear virtually a new genre are Romantic lyric poetry, an interest in popular culture including folksong, and a developed style of accompaniment for the pianoforte, closely reflecting the mechanical reliability, increased range, and enhanced dynamic and expressive potential of the instrument itself. The piano proved an ideal domestic possession, handsome to the eye and attractive to the ear as well as useful for providing a variety of types of accompaniment: a continuum, chordal or flowing, abstract or representative (for instance of water), above which the voice can stand out in relief; independent lyricism as well as doubling the lyricism of the voice; dynamic and textural contrast which played a part in evocation of all kinds of ambience and could even suggest temporal distance by the use of polyphony or an organ-like resonance.

The stimulation to deeper exploration of the possibilities available to a voice and (usually) piano accompaniment ran parallel with the publication of collections of 'folk' poetry, both genuine and manufactured, for a public happy to read it in periodicals as well as in books (musical settings were also published in periodicals). At the same time, and particularly in English and German, new lyrical and narrative verse proved highly stimulating to musicians. The cultivation of folksong in the later eighteenth century, and writing music in a folk idiom (like Robert Burns), can be associated with the practice of writing verses to existing tunes which continued to flourish, for example in Thomas Moore's *Irish Melodies* (see chapter 9). With both Moore and Burns, however, it was the poetry in translation, rather than the word–music combination, which affected Romantics such as Berlioz and Schumann. Beethoven composed numerous accompaniments to British folk melodies for the Edinburgh publisher George Thomson, who also commissioned work from Haydn, Pleyel and Weber, but there is little sign of such work affecting their original compositions; on the other hand, Haydn's finest contribution to song, his English 'canzonets', some in a folklike idiom, some almost operatic, and all with independent piano accompaniment, affected the development of German and English song.

German song; ballads; Schubert and Loewe

The cultivation of folklore affected original poetry, such as the lyrics included in Goethe's dramas *Egmont* and *Faust* and especially his novel *Wilhelm Meisters Lehrjahre* (1795–6). The *Egmont* songs received definitive settings from Beethoven; the Faust lyrics, in German or translated into Russian or French, inspired diverse musical responses; and the songs of Mignon and the Harper (from *Wilhelm Meister*) were set again and again, from Beethoven to Wolf. The cult of exotic tints in poetry, both Celtic (Walter Scott) and oriental (Goethe, *West-östlicher Divan*, published 1819) naturally attracted song composers and encouraged the application of musical analogues. But much of the finest lyric verse, for instance that of Joseph von Eichendorff (1788–1857), depended upon alienation of the poetic sensibility from the modern world; the world of nature (including the German forest) became idealised as a poetic domain.

Much eighteenth-century song, perhaps naturally in an age which prided itself upon rationalism, is little more than rhythmic notation of the poem, with the simplest harmonic under-pinning. For much of his life, Goethe himself preferred such settings, which left no doubt that poetry was the leading art; it is, however, an exaggeration to say that he also insisted that strophic poetry should be set to unchanging music. Nor is strophic setting an inferior form of song, although strophic settings work best for simpler poems, or for ritualistic use, as in hymnody. It is not easy to produce a single musical stanza appropriate to all the stanzas of a poem; the music may easily be perceived as matching only the lowest common denominator of the poetic stanzas, their syllable-count, rather than their narrative or affective content. Goethe's three-stanza narrative 'Heidenröslein' was set by Schubert (D.257) to a charming folkloric melody, with a neutral accompaniment which allows the singer ample scope for variation, or indeed innuendo (the tale of a boy violently plucking a rose is evidently a metaphor). But Mozart's justly famous Goethe setting, 'Das Veilchen' (K.476), is the ancestor of the dramatic Lied, and employs the operatic technique of recitative to complete the narrative, like Schubert in 'Erlkönig' (D.328, 1815).

Schubert composed the paradigmatic through-composed song as early as 1814, 'Gretchen am Spinnrade' (Gretchen at the Spinning Wheel) from Goethe's *Faust* (D.118). An unbroken piano continuum, responding to harmonic shifts which move almost casually to remote regions in following the singer's train of thought, supports a vocal line which is neither simply a declamation of the poem, nor simply a lyrical melody. The apparently objective accompaniment, representing the spinning-wheel (which is hardly evoked in Loewe's setting of the same poem, and not at all in Berlioz's), symbolically embodies Gretchen's restless feelings (at this stage in Goethe's drama, Faust has seduced, but not yet deserted, her). At the thought of his kiss, she drops her work and the accompaniment falls still, then slowly the wheel begins to turn again: even a kiss cannot long suspend time. The last stage of the song goes beyond the confines of the poetic form, by repeating part of the first stanza, a musical intervention Goethe would probably have deplored, as he certainly deplored Schubert's 'Erlkönig'.

Although a ballad, 'Erlkönig' is not a long poem. Following the lead of Johann Rudolf Zumsteeg (1760–1802), several composers enjoyed the opportunity of writing substantial dramatic or narrative pieces for voice and piano. For Schubert, the long ballad was a recurring preoccupation, and his early, complicated setting of Schiller's lengthy 'Der Taucher' (D.77, 1813–14) represents an extreme point in the form. Carl Loewe (1796–1869), who propagated his own songs by singing them, showed a predilection (which was not exclusive) for ballads, some with their origins in German or Scottish folklore, but turned into modern verses by Herder or Goethe. Clear enunciation of the text is paramount, and much of the text is set syllabically, and even intoned on a single pitch, a procedure supportable by the listener when the recitation takes place over a musically characterised accompaniment. Such a technique is best as an introduction, as in 'Die verfallene Mühle' (The Ruined Mill: poem by J. N. Vogl):

> Es reitet schweigend und allein
> Der alte Graf zum Wald hinein:
> Er reitet über Stein und Dorn,
> Zur Seiten schlendert Schwert und Horn.[8]

The reciting-tone, the third of the major key, is used for the first and third lines of verse apart from upbeats, and for most of the second; the fourth line describes a larger circle of pitches to illustrate the accoutrements of nobility, but homes in on the principal pitch. The regular accompaniment embodies a swaying rather than galloping movement, as of a horse moving carefully, but also as a metaphor of the inexorable ageing of the count.

The legend that Loewe set Goethe's 'Erlkönig' (Elf King) in response to Schubert's version, because the latter was insufficiently dramatic, is implausible. Loewe's version, and his parallel setting of Herder's 'Herr Oluf' in which a bridegroom is destroyed by the elf king's daughter, are indeed dramatic, but so is Schubert's; in 'Erlkönig' the composers employ quite similar techniques for differentiating the speeches of the four voices (the narrator, the father, the son, the elf king).[9] Only Schubert, however, provides the frenzied gallop of a near-unplayable accompaniment, and his wide modulation generates a sense of panic which, in Loewe's version, has to be contributed largely by the singer. The comparison could be turned the other way: Loewe offers perhaps the greater scope for the singer; and in live performance, a sharper focus on poetry and declamation at the expense of instrumental virtuosity is self-evidently a valid priority.

The less exacerbated 'Flower ballads' by Franz von Schober offered Schubert a different opportunity to control a long poem musically. 'Viola' (D.786, 1823) describes the premature flowering of a violet, which dies when wintry conditions return before the true spring. Abrupt key-changes divide up the narrative, but also arouse terror, as in the brutal interruption of the dominant of D flat at bar 265 (stanza 16) when Spring (the groom) sees that Viola is missing. Tonal structures derive from the diminished seventh (A♭, B, D and F) rather than the circle of fifths, and the final modulation, by a tritone (D minor to A flat), complements, rather than resolves, an earlier move from B to F. Even in medium-length narratives where the situation changes radically, Schubert is

---

8 Translation of the text: The old Count is riding, / silent and alone, into the woods; / he rides over stones and thorns, / his sword and horn swinging at his side.

9 Edward T. Cone, 'Some Thoughts on *Erlkönig*', in *The Composer's Voice* (Berkeley and Los Angeles, 1974), pp. 1–19.

happy to dispense with tonal unity: the Goethe setting 'Ganymed' (D.544, 1817) begins in A flat and ends in F. The restoration of the original tonic in 'Viola', therefore, is not perfunctory, and plays its part in suggesting a metaphorical interpretation of the text which mere words may only imply.

Song cycles: Schubert and Schumann

Substantial narratives, literal or metaphorical, may also be embodied in a song cycle. Part of the attraction of this genre is the absence of any conformity, in its finest examples, to their ostensible model. In Beethoven's *An die ferne Geliebte* (To the Distant Beloved, Op. 98, 1816), six songs, each quite simple in form, are bound together by discreet piano variation within their strophes, and by instrumental connections which modulate from one song to the next; in addition, the last song returns decisively to the melody of the first. This structural radicalism is ignored by Schubert in his two magnificent, and much longer, cycles to texts by Wilhelm Müller, whose folkloric poetry has been unnecessarily maligned. The cycles consist of discrete songs in a variety of forms, from the simplest strophic settings such as the opening of *Die schöne Müllerin* (The Fair Maid of the Mill, D.795, 1823), through the subtle ternary and through-composed forms more frequent in *Winterreise* (Winter Journey, D.911, 1827).[10] The textural archetype of 'Gretchen am Spinnrade' expands throughout *Die schöne Müllerin* where the millstream becomes a character and eventually a narrative persona (in the final song, when the young miller drowns himself). The varied movement of water is a natural source of accompanimental figuration. *Winterreise* explores more harrowing feelings; the lover's rejection comes before the cycle begins, and in a model which affects many later cycles, the narrative trajectory is of secondary importance to the evocation of mood: anger, hope, nostalgia, despair. There is no equivalent to the stream, but evocations of the natural world – wind, ice, a solitary crow – become metaphors of the singer's mental state.

'Der Lindenbaum' (*Winterreise* No. 5) is exemplary. The poem has six four-line stanzas; Schubert sets the first two together, in a sixteen-bar melody of such limpid beauty that it acquired an independent life as a 'folksong'. The entire poem could have been used up by two repetitions, but only with a serious discord between text and music. The first two stanzas are about the remote, happy past; the singer used to find peace by the linden tree at the city gate. Stanzas 3 and 4 are about the immediate, bitter past: as he leaves the town where his lover has rejected him, repose by the tree offers another kind of peace

---

10   Susan Youens, *Schubert: Die schöne Müllerin* (Cambridge, 1992); *Retracing a Winter's Journey: Schubert's 'Winterreise'* (Ithaca, N.Y., 1991).

(death by exposure in the depth of winter). The wind is represented in the introduction, as a pleasant breeze; in the interlude before stanza 3 it becomes chilly, and although stanzas 3–4 repeat the melody of stanzas 1–2, stanza 3 is in the minor, with stanza 4 back in the major for the tree's seductive offer of peace. So far the song has kept within the confines of the strophic variation, but stanza 5 is presented in a short passage of shuddering intensity: disintegrative in its declamatory style of text-setting, and its emphasis on the bass C♮ (whereas the song is in E), but integrative in that the voice is accompanied by piano material (the chill wind) that has previously been heard only as an introduction and interlude. The wind acts directly on the singer, blowing his hat off: but as he remembers the scene, he did not turn to collect it, and nor did he submit to the lure of the tree. Finally, in stanza 6, looking back, he admits: 'there I might have found peace'. Schubert sets this to the original melody, rounding off the musical form and underlining the singer's distance from that past paradise. Schubert has to repeat stanza 6 to fill out the whole melody, the claims of musical form overriding the form of the poetry.

A third song-cycle by Schubert, his so-called 'Swan Song', *Schwanengesang*, was created by its posthumous publication and has been recognised by criticism and performance. Nevertheless, it was not thus designed by the composer, although a short cycle has been discerned in the six Heine settings. More recently, other groupings, potential cycles, have been detected within his output of over 600 songs, but most of them stand alone rather than as part of any poetically meaningful set or collection.[11] The distinction of cycle and collection is intriguingly blurred by Robert Schumann (1810–56). Only one of the sets of songs he composed in a prodigious outpouring during the year 1840 is governed by a narrative line. In *Frauenliebe und Leben* (Op. 42, poems by Chamisso) a young woman is courted by an older man, marries him, and has his child; then he dies. The sequence of emotions, ranging from a sense of unworthiness through gratitude, ecstasy, and the chill of bereavement, may appear – despite or perhaps because of the quality of Schumann's response – to validate a pattern of female dependency which many today find distasteful.[12] Since the signifiers in song are both verbal and musical, and since the articulation of poetry provides leads for musical interpretation, a rich vein of musicology has been devoted to reinterpretation of this repertory; however, suggestive though new readings often are, it should be remembered that they belong to critical traditions more recent than those of the nineteenth century.

---

11 Richard Kramer, *Distant Cycles: Schubert and the Conceiving of Song* (Chicago, 1994).

12 John Daverio, *Robert Schumann: Herald of a 'New Poetic Age'* (New York, 1997), p. 213; Ruth Solie, 'Whose Life? The Gendered Self in Schumann's Frauenliebe Songs', in Steven Scher (ed.), *Music and Text: Critical Inquiries* (Cambridge, 1992), pp. 219–40.

Schumann's concept of cycle ('Liederkreis') otherwise resists any explicit narrative. In 1840, he produced some 130 songs mainly drawn from the most distinguished living lyric poets, and grouped most of them for publication. *Myrthen* (Op. 25) has no cyclic pretension, being a collection of poems by Burns, Byron and Moore in translation, and Goethe, Heinrich Heine (1797–1856) and Friedrich Rückert (1788–1866) in their original German. Two cycles, however, derive from Heine alone, *Liederkreis* (Op. 24) and *Dichterliebe* (Op. 48), and two from Eichendorff, twelve songs Op. 37 and *Liederkreis* Op. 39. But poetic uniformity need not imply any 'plot'. Op. 39 begins with songs of alienation and love ('In der Fremde', 'Dein Bildnis wunderselig'), before a dialogue with the mythical witch Lorelei, set to a rolling motif which distances the frightening outcome (unlike the 'Erlkönig' settings, which seem all too real). 'Auf eine Burg' shows Schumann's power to suggest another age through musical style, without a trace of pastiche; a solemn tempo and spare contrapuntal texture suffice. The level of dissonance, from which resolution seems always one step removed from where it would be in textbook counterpoint, underlies the crux of the poem, which is that the bride, seen far below in the castle yard, is weeping; the song ends unresolved, on the dominant. As a piece of understatement, the subtle blend of imagery and feeling achieved by combining word and tone is more deeply imbued with poetic Romanticism than the more passionate, sentimental or self-pitying utterances which usually get branded 'Romantic'.

'Auf eine Burg' also exemplifies a characteristic procedure, which is to complete the vocal part without reaching a cadence. At the same time it avoids another, in which the piano takes on the role of completion, adding something untranslatable to the sense of the song as a whole. This procedure acquires especial poignancy in two of the cycles. In *Frauenliebe und Leben* the piano coda reverts to the music of the first song, as if the singer in her distress (or the composer, in his, or the listeners, in ours) finds comfort in the past. In *Dichterliebe*, some songs run smoothly into the next, as when the second song closes an unresolved harmony from the first, but most are potentially independent ('Ich grolle nicht' is often performed separately). But independence is qualified at the end. With pained fury, the singer shuts his songs into a coffin and plans to drown them along with his sorrows. The song ends with a fifteen-bar piano coda which is mainly a reprise of the coda to an earlier song, 'Am leuchtenden Sommermorgen' (No. 12); it is thus fatally subversive in relation to the admirable defiance of the final song, for it restores the earlier mood of perplexed introspection.

Schumann set 'Am leuchtenden Sommermorgen' in a three-part 'bar' form (A A' B), despite its being a two-stanza poem; 'B' is the piano coda. The opening augmented sixth is followed by dominant and tonic, so that the song *begins* with a formula of closure:

> Am leuchtenden Sommermorgen
> Geh' ich im Garten herum.
> Es flüstern und sprechen die Blumen,
> Ich aber wandle stumm.
>
> Es flüstern und sprechen die Blumen,
> Und schau'n mitleidig mich an:
> Sei unser Schwester nicht böse,
> Du trauriger, blasser Mann.[13]

The persistent accompaniment might be interpreted as representing the summer morning; or, in Eric Sams's words, as 'wind-stirred movement of tall flowers nodding'.[14] Such interpretations, however, mainly serve to confirm the imprecision of musical analogues. The outline structure of each stanza is simple. Each line of verse is a two-bar phrase; the third text-line incorporates a flattened mediant (D♭) and an aberrant local cadence in C flat or B natural: 'Schumann is thinking of flowers in colour' (Sams, p. 119). For the second stanza the poet repeats the third line of the first, necessarily to the music of the first line, by which process the oddity of whispering flowers is normalised. For the last two lines (reported speech of the flowers) Schumann reserves a new harmonic field from a deceptive resolution (G major where E flat is expected, bar 17). The bass stands still for over two bars before the swift return, through the original augmented sixth, to the home dominant.

The voice stops, but does not cadence; the coda prolongs dominant harmony until the last two bars. This is the delicate, floating material Schumann recalls, transposed, after the last song. Schumann has often been accused of failing to respond to Heine's irony. Irony is a rhetorical element nearly impossible to transfer to any other medium, and arguably all Schumann needed to do was set the words appropriately, and audibly, for it to come across. In practice, however, song not only assimilates, but consumes a poem; irony might require musical distortion, as (somewhat crudely) in Berlioz's *Symphonie fantastique* (see below); Schumann argued that while a composer should reach for the truth of a poem, he should present it beautifully dressed.[15] But Schumann was not without his own subtle sense of irony. The implied consolation at the end of the cycle coincides nicely with the unwinding of tension from the point of view of

---

13 Translation of the text: In the gleaming summer morning, / I walk around the garden. / The flowers are whispering, speaking: / but I walk in silence. / The flowers are whispering, speaking, / and looking at me with compassion: / Do not be angry with our sister, / you sad, pale man!

14 Eric Sams, *The Songs of Robert Schumann* (London, 1969; 2nd edn 1975), p. 119.

15 Daverio, *Robert Schumann*, p. 211.

musically autonomous analysis, but the juxtaposition of the last poetic, and the last musical utterance qualifies any sense of consolation as ambivalent.[16]

Schubert's and Schumann's achievements in song are far from isolated, and although they reach heights, and plumb depths, seldom perceived in their contemporaries, the central terrain is fully occupied with masterly works by, to name only a few, Loewe, Emilie Zumsteeg (1796–1857), Fanny Henselt née Mendelssohn (1805–47), Felix Mendelssohn (1809–47), Robert Franz (1815–92) and Clara Schumann née Wieck (1819–96). Collections of Mendelssohn and Schumann songs were published with works by Fanny and Clara alongside their (respectively) brother (Opp. 8 and 9) and husband (Op. 37), without any stylistic or qualitative incongruity.

French song

French song in the early nineteenth century may be interpreted as a genre trying to escape its own origins. The standard romance was simple, tuneful, with supporting accompaniment, and almost invariably strophic. The accretion of such features as harmonic adventure, quasi-dramatic declamation, strophic variation, or an expressively modified final verse, led Noske to the pleonasm 'the Romantic Romance'.[17] The most prolific composers of French song belong to later in the century, but for Berlioz, whose earliest published works are romances (*c.* 1822–3), song-form was a vital stylistic foundation.[18] His bold melodic idiom helped to move French song forward, even when controlled by the mainly strophic forms in settings of translations from Goethe by Gérard de Nerval (*Huit scènes de Faust*, with orchestra, published 1829) and from Thomas Moore by Thomas Gounet (*Neuf mélodies irlandaises*, published 1830). In the latter title, itself a translation from Moore, Berlioz assisted the French language in choosing the word 'mélodie' for the genre equivalent to the German 'lied'.[19] The solo songs in these two collections (which also include choruses) revel in a rhythmic suppleness quite at variance with the expectations of the Romance; yet the accompaniments remain generally simple, and the songs are either strophic or, in one case, declamatory ('Elegie en prose'). The exception, ironically entitled 'Romance', is the translation of 'Gretchen am Spinnrade' ('D'une amoureuse flamme'), especially as the spinning motif is not used as a continuum; instead the setting is sectionalised, and the complex (orchestral) accompaniment is coloured by a new voice of Romantic melancholy, the cor anglais.

16 Sams, *The Songs of Robert Schumann*, pp. 123–4.
17 Frits Noske, *French Song from Berlioz to Duparc* (New York, 1970), pp. 12–22.
18 Julian Rushton, *The Musical Language of Berlioz* (Cambridge, 1983), pp. 144–80.
19 Noske, *French Song*, pp. 22–5.

It was only in 1840, setting original French poetry, that Berlioz realised the mélodie fully in *Les nuits d'été*, six songs to poems by Théophile Gautier (1811–72), through-composed but more lyrical than declamatory and thus unrelated to genres like opera and cantata. These songs were later orchestrated, and are sometimes claimed as the first orchestral song cycle.[20] Berlioz's achievement, even in the original versions with piano, was to integrate poem, voice and instruments into a homogeneous texture. Berlioz gave the third of *Les nuits d'été* (*Sur les lagunes*) the subtitle 'Lamento', but the poet, and Fauré in his much later setting, used the title 'Chanson du pêcheur'. Berlioz has the opening phrase of the voice part grow out of the sighing motif which haunts the entire song; the vocal phrase is extended to four bars by agogic elongation of the crucial word, 'morte', and in the second phrase the surprising duration of 'Je' moves the attention from the death of the beloved to a quasi-authorial voice; the line ends with a simple local modulation and the delicate intrusion of a stylised sob on the last syllable of 'pleurerai'. The song is laid out in a broadly ternary design, with each of the three sections ending in the refrain: 'Ah! Sans amour s'en aller sur la mer', in which the instruments pursue the voice, more echo than canon, from top to bottom; the song ends by realising the implication of this refrain and frustrating normal harmonic expectations, for the last chord is still the dominant.

Berlioz was by nature a dramatic composer, who learned the conventional forms when competing for the annual Prix de Rome, for which he wrote a cantata in each of the years 1827 to 1830. Where Mendelssohn, in approaching such a mixed genre, chose fine poetry (Goethe) for his masterpiece in *Die erste Walpurgisnacht* (Op. 60, 1832), Berlioz had to make do with whatever poetry the Fine Arts section of the Institut de France could provide. These cantatas raise acutely the question of the relationship between a poor text and fine music. Their musical strengths may be said to derive both from the conventional gestures of dramatic music, derived in turn from French opera since Gluck, and from Berlioz's response to the dramatic elements in the subject. His cantata of 1829, *Cléopâtre*, has the Queen of Egypt reflect upon her defeat after the death of Mark Antony, her inability to seduce Octavius Caesar, her fear of death, and the still worse prospect of being displayed in triumph in Rome; finally she dies through the bite of the asp. The naturalistic broken phrases of the dying queen, in the text destined by the examiners for an aria, are evidence for Berlioz's commitment to dramatic truth. The 'meditation', in which Cleopatra dreads the fury of her ancestors whose country she has failed to defend, commands most attention, not for the measured declamation of the

20 Peter Bloom, 'In the Shadows of *Les Nuits d'été*', and Julian Rushton, '*Les Nuits d'été*: Cycle or Collection?' in Bloom (ed.), *Berlioz Studies* (Cambridge, 1992), pp. 81–135.

text, but for the developing sense of the musically poetic which emerges from a unique adventure in harmony, rhythm and texture. But the inessential nature of the word–music relation was demonstrated when Berlioz used the same music for a 'Chorus of shades' in his 'mélologue' *Le retour à la vie* (1831, a sequel to the *Symphonie fantastique*). The speaker, or 'Lélio', introduces the music (text in square brackets is mine): 'What is the strange faculty which substitutes imagination for reality? What is this ideal orchestra which seems to sing within me? Sombre instrumentation [trombones, low clarinets, horns and bassoons, lower strings], broad and sinister harmony [replete with enharmonic change and unexpected progressions], a lugubrious melody [poised above an ostinato rhythm short–long, contrary to the long–short usual in the period], the choir in unison and octaves like a huge voice giving vent to a menacing lament. . .'. The music bears out this description fully, but the oddity of the poetry–music relationship here lies in an association, already made explicit by the speaker, with the ghost scene in *Hamlet*; whereas in *Cléopâtre*, at the head of the same music, Berlioz added an epigraph from *Romeo and Juliet*. From this it appears that the essential qualities of 'poetic' music are not subject- or even word-specific.

Poetic instrumental music

Music's inarticulate nature undermines most attempts to establish links between it and other semantic systems, and Romantic instrumental music is resistant to interpretation unless some kind of clue is offered; for that reason, perhaps, in the first half of the nineteenth century it became more intimately connected with extra-musical ideas. Yet an absence of specificity is a vital part of the Romantic project which finds poetry in unmediated sound. Mendelssohn's eight books of *Lieder ohne Worte* (Songs Without Words) include few with titles other than 'Gondollied' (barcarolle). Both the generic and the specific titles suggest a vocal model, bearing out Charles Rosen's description of the archetypal Romantic piece as a lyrical melody over an accompaniment whose undifferentiated motion suggests Baroque rather than Classical ancestry, like Gounod's 'Ave Maria', sung over Bach's C major prelude.[21] 'Song without words' becomes a genre, embracing music under various titles, like Schumann's pieces for an instrument and piano (Romances, Fantasy pieces, and fairytales, Märchenbilder). Numerous symphonic, chamber or sonata slow movements as far ahead as Mahler's Fifth Symphony (the 'Adagietto') could also be called songs without words. The

---

21 Charles Rosen, *The Classical Style: Haydn, Mozart, Beethoven* (London, 1971), p. 453; see also Edward T. Cone, *Musical Form and Musical Performance* (New York, 1968), pp. 78–87; Leonard G. Ratner, *Romantic Music: Sound and Syntax* (New York, 1992).

listener experiences a song in an unknown language; either music has thrown off the yoke of poetry, while retaining the musical forms to which poetry gave rise, or the penetration of music by poetry has reached a point where, saturated by poetic essence, music would be hampered by the precision of verbal imagery.

The short piano piece more generally is another Romantic archetype. Precedents include the 'eclogues' of Václav Jan Tomášek (1807), Beethoven's Bagatelles, and Schubert's *Moments musicals* (D.780, published 1828). The sixth *Moment musical*, originally published in 1824 under the title 'Lament of the minstrel', invites hermeneutic investigation.[22] Larger forms were affected by cultivation of the same less formal, improvisational musical impulses as found an outlet in short forms. Invasion of the sonata by improvisational elements associated with the fantasia is an outgrowth of eighteenth-century practice, but Schubert stretched this model near to breaking-point in the slow movement of his late A major sonata (D.959, 1828); the melancholy lyricism of the outer sections surrounds music in such tonal, motivic and rhythmic flux as to be barely coherent.[23] Beethoven's achievement in sonata composition not surprisingly inhibited the generation born after 1800, which either avoided such forms or qualified them with its own preoccupations, often in such a way as to suggest extra-musical meaning. Mendelssohn's A minor string quartet (Op. 13, 1827) is indebted to Beethoven (notably Op. 95 in its slow movement), but it is framed by a song (offered without the words) in A major, which distances it from the Classical model. Schumann similarly introduced his F sharp minor piano sonata (Op. 11, 1836) with a song which also forms the basis of the slow movement. Both these composers moved away from such equivocations towards a more austere division between post-Classical and Romantic forms. The penetration of symphonic music by song was taken in another direction by Berlioz (see below).

Use of dance measures

Leonard G. Ratner divided eighteenth-century dance music into 'social', 'theatrical' and 'speculative'.[24] The first category is unrelated to the topic of this chapter, and theatrical dance, including mime, develops from the most original ballet music of the previous century (Gluck, *Don Juan*; Beethoven, *Die Geschöpfe des Prometheus*) to such works as *Giselle* (Paris Opéra, 1841: scenario by Théophile Gautier, music by Adolphe Adam). The close association of

22 Edward T. Cone, 'Schubert's Promissory Note', *19th Century Music*, 5 (1982), pp. 233–41.
23 Hugh Macdonald, 'Schubert's Volcanic Temper', *The Musical Times*, 99 (1978), pp. 949–52.
24 Leonard G. Ratner, *Classic Music: Expression, Form, and Style* (New York, 1980), p. 17.

musical signification with the stage is exemplified by the role of Fenella in Auber's *La muette de Portici* (Paris Opéra, 1829; a predecessor is Weber's *Silvana*, 1810). The music assigned to the mute is the most expressive and formally unconventional, extending the idiom in the dimensions of rhythm, pitch-relation, and rapid mood-change. Such integration of music with, in the wide sense, the poetic requires a musical style which is the antithesis of the symphonic self-sufficiency identified by Hoffmann: yet the influence of such music on Wagner, among others, places it at the heart of the Romantic project.

Ratner's speculative category typically involves the employment of dance in symphonic music and opera. In eighteenth-century music dance may suggest specific social meanings; in the nineteenth century hermeneutic investigation may be directed more by a programme, as when Berlioz (1803–69) introduces elaborated character-pieces, a waltz and a march, into his *Symphonie fantastique* (1830). Interest in dance-types may be intended to add local colour. The presence of a fandango as the main material of the first movement in Schumann's Second Piano Sonata is difficult to interpret; but the merest programmatic hint suffices to release the listener from any obligation other than to enjoy and be moved in, for instance, Mendelssohn's Fourth ('Italian') Symphony and Berlioz's *Harold en Italie*, which both contain pilgrims' marches. The Mendelssohn ends by turning the saltarello into a topic for symphonic discourse, and the third movement of the Berlioz is a serenade (song without words) framed by dance-like music imitating the local bagpipe, the pifferari. Local colour may also lie behind the cultivation of dance-types originating in Eastern Europe; the Polacca, or Polonaise, already internationalised in eighteenth-century instrumental music, reappears as a finale in Beethoven (Triple Concerto Op. 56) and Field (Third Piano Concerto, H.32), and for an aria in Weber's *Der Freischütz*, ostensibly the most Germanic of operas (1821: 'Kommt ein schlanker Bursch gegangen').

With Fryderyk Chopin (1810–49), however, the poetry behind Polish dance rhythms is no longer merely colouristic, but signifies the national sentiment of an exile. Where the waltz in Chopin's hands is public, virtuosic, the mazurka is intimate, seeming to embody thoughts, perhaps of love, perhaps of frailty, too deep, or too precise, for the too-articulate medium of words. The mazurka became a genre, and not only by quantity (Chopin produced over sixty) but because within the constraints of its typical rhythmic patterns he was stimulated to his most daring projections of thematic invention, harmony and tonality, and to a degree of stylisation in which the dance origins of the music are virtually lost. This is scarcely less true of the polonaises, although by association with the fantasia a polonaise rhythm is exploited in a work whose elaboration approaches the symphonic, the remarkable *Polonaise-Fantaisie* (Op. 61, 1846).[25]

Piano cycles

From Chopin's twenty-four Preludes in all the keys (Op. 28, 1839), as from Schumann's piano cycles, there emerges a sense, defying analysis, of a whole greater than the sum of its fascinatingly diverse original parts. Some of these preludes (which precede nothing) are cryptic, like Beethoven's Bagatelles; for instance the peculiarly sombre E major and quicksilver C sharp minor. Some conform to dance types, some might be studies exiled from the magnificent sets Opp. 10 and 25. The D flat major Prelude, its reception contorted by the acquired title 'raindrop', is a nocturne, affiliated to one of the most characteristic new genres of the early nineteenth century. The nocturne was developed from earlier pianistic idioms which crystallised in the work of the Irish composer John Field (1782–1837), who worked principally in Russia. The archetype, a languid melody, richly ornamented, over a widely spaced arpeggiated left hand, suggests the general model proposed by Rosen (see above), and is well illustrated by Field's Fifth Nocturne.[26] The genre imposes no conditions upon tempo (usually fairly slow), nor upon metre, and can coalesce with other genres; one of Field's is a polonaise (No. 9). Chopin is if anything more stylised; the archetype is clear in his first published nocturne, Op. 9, No. 1 (1831) and many more. But for him the genre becomes more erotic than playful, and may evoke a broken heart, as in the sombre tread of Op. 37, No. 1 in G minor (1838); while Op. 32, No. 1, in B major (1837), for most of its length the perfect embodiment of the archetype, changes course drastically when its well-prepared final cadence is interrupted (bar 62) by an alien harmony, a distant drum-beat, a fragment of recitative, and an Adagio cadence in B minor: a broken dream.

Chopin and Schumann each wrote three piano sonatas, to which may be added Schumann's sonata-scale cycle of 'fantasy pieces', *Faschingsschwank aus Wien* (Op. 26, 1840). But Schumann also found original means of co-ordinating cycles of piano music without the need to doff his hat to sonata forms or tonal unity. In his criticism he exhibited some generic uncertainty when discussing Schubert, accepting a publisher's suggestion that the highly integrated G major sonata (D.894) was a fantasy, and a set of Impromptus (D.935) a sonata, which if so titled would be unique among Schubert's output in its key-scheme and sequence of

25 Adrian Thomas, 'Beyond the Dance', in Jim Samson (ed.), *The Cambridge Companion to Chopin* (Cambridge, 1992), pp. 145–59.

26 David Rowland, 'The Nocturne: Development of a New Style', in Samson (ed.), *The Cambridge Companion to Chopin*, pp. 32–49; Field, *Nocturnes*, ed. Robin Langley, Musica Britannica 71 (London, 1998).

musical types.[27] Schumann's earliest publications co-ordinated musical moods
in traditional non-sonata forms: variations, sets of dances (*Papillons*, Op. 2, 1831)
and character-pieces (*Davidsbündlertänze*, Op. 6, 1837). But in *Papillons*, the disruption and decay in the coda demand programmatic understanding, and receive
it by reference to Jean-Paul Richter's novel *Flegeljahre*; Daverio suggests that
Schumann viewed his works as 'literary products'.[28] *Carnaval* (subtitled 'Scènes
mignonnes', Op. 9, 1837) adds an intertextual layer to the cycle of short pieces by
quoting *Papillons*, and Schumann evokes or imitates the styles of Chopin (with
uncanny accuracy), Paganini, and with typical introversion himself, naming the
two sides of his musical personality 'Florestan' and 'Eusebius'. That *Carnaval*
never degenerates into mannered fragments, but is a true cycle, is the result of
intense preoccupation in nearly every piece with motifs derived from letters,
mainly ASCH (As can appear as A♭, or, separating the letters, A and E♭; H is B♮).
The challenge to harmonic ingenuity, the rhythmic variety assisted by using
dance measures only occasionally, and the unpredictable forms, give this set
exceptional charm, its kaleidoscopic patterns precariously but convincingly co-
ordinated. *Kreisleriana* (Op. 16, 1838) is not a whit less original. Its eight more
substantial pieces are potentially self-contained and contain none of the clues
scattered throughout *Carnaval*; the persona of E. T. A. Hoffmann's eccentric
Kapellmeister Kreisler is no more a 'programme' than Schumann implied when
he called his first symphony 'Spring'. Perhaps we hear the master's violin in the
opening figuration, or the middle section of the first number where a rich
polyphony is made although only one note is struck at a time, and in the gigue-
like finale which, like the end of *Papillons*, fades into nothingness.

Intertextuality in this type of composition is not the casual borrowing of
material in order to make better use of it, such as occurs in the eighteenth
century (among many examples, the overture to Mozart's *Die Zauberflöte* takes
its fugal subject from Clementi); it is a deliberate allusion, intended to affect
interpretation of the new work by reference to the old. No. 8 of *Dichterliebe* has
a piano coda, unrelated to the rest, which refers to the opening of *Kreisleriana*;
the magnificent, sonata-scale Fantasie in C (Op. 17, 1839) cites the principal
motif of Beethoven's *An die ferne Geliebte*, which returns as a principal motif in
Schumann's Second Symphony (1846), an event which may be related to his
biography, and particularly his relations with his wife.[29] While Schumann's

27 Robert Schumann, *Gesammelte Schriften über Musik und Musiker*, 5th edn (Leipzig, 1914), I, pp. 124, 371; Schumann, *On Music and Musicians* (London, 1947), pp. 112, 118.
28 Eric Frederick Jensen, 'Explicating Jean Paul: Robert Schumann's Program for *Papillons*, Op. 2', *19th Century Music*, 22 (1998), pp. 127–43; Daverio, *Robert Schumann*, p. 89.
29 Nicholas Marston, *Schumann: Fantasie, Op. 17* (Cambridge, 1992); Charles Rosen, *The Romantic Generation* (London, 1996), pp. 100–12; Anthony Newcomb, 'Once More Between Absolute and Program Music: Schumann's Second Symphony', *19th Century Music*, 7 (1984), pp. 233–50.

aspirations to meet Beethoven on his own soil, in the chamber, symphonic and choral music composed after 1840, have had a disputed critical reception, his piano cycles remain magnificently original, and have few real successors; in part this is due to their curious kind of self-referentialism, in which the composer allows his personality and life to direct his invention. To an extent this policy was continued in Liszt's great collections, but his *Années de pèlerinage*, while more than travelogues, do turn attention outward from the contemplating composer to the scene contemplated, a step already taken by Berlioz between his first two symphonies.

Instrumental narrative: ballade, symphony and overture

In his piano Ballades, Chopin offered no programme, no specific reference to any story; yet the title clearly implies a narrative, as does the compound metre, which reflects the metre of poetic ballads. Only the Second Ballade may be related to a specific poem; the others, more extended in their musical forms which to an extent intersect with the sonata, have no programme. Their narrative quality emerges from the handling of thematic order and the transformation of material: in the Third Ballade, the peaceful themes return in reverse order, the second subjected to a stormy and texturally elaborated reprise, and the first to an apotheosis.[30]

The narrative metaphor affected symphonic composition, in the avoidance or stretching of traditional forms and a growing desire for continuity, and explicit thematic connections, between movements. In the 1820s to 1840s the symphony that most inspired emulation was perhaps Beethoven's Sixth, the 'Pastoral'. Its five-movement form, taken over by Berlioz (*Symphonie fantastique*), ended with the last three movements playing continuously, and thematic transformation in the passage from the storm to thanksgiving for deliverance in the finale. The continuity model affected Mendelssohn, who asked for the movements to be played without interruption (Scottish Symphony) or composed links between them (Violin Concerto). But the example of the 'Pastoral' was more widely disseminated by music with implied or explicit extra-musical associations. An equally potent model was the overture. Beethoven's finest overtures were not originally intended for concert use but became divorced from their original theatrical context. An epitome of each tragedy is presented in the overtures *Egmont* and *Coriolan*, the former ending with the 'symphony of victory' which Goethe planned for the end of his play, the latter with thematic

---

30 J. Samson, *Chopin: The Four Ballades* (Cambridge, 1992).

transformation (disintegration) as a metaphor for the hero's death. Beethoven also provided the model for a choral symphony, variously followed by Berlioz (the 'dramatic symphony' *Roméo et Juliette*, 1839), Mendelssohn (Symphony No. 2, *Lobgesang* [Hymn of Praise], 1840), and Liszt (*Eine Faust-Sinfonie*, 1857). In the resultant ferment of genre, the least controversial type is the picturesque, of which the paradigmatic examples are Mendelssohn's overtures (*Meeresstille*, 1828, *Die schöne Melusine*, 1833), his fourth ('Italian') Symphony (1833), and pieces of Scottish inspiration, the Piano Fantasia Op. 28 (1833), the Third Symphony (1842), and the *Hebrides* Overture (1830–2).[31] Such pieces establish an unequivocal context to which the composer's invention may be related, and which to varying degrees affects our hearing of the music. From the composer's point of view, it facilitates escape from thematic routines. Thus *The Hebrides* transforms a theme from a smooth to a choppy character in a way abstract 'development' would not normally accommodate; its marine inspiration may not be an issue for the listener whose experience is different from Mendelssohn's, but it provides a framework for understanding so radical a piece of textural manipulation. The incorporation of hymnody, and the 'Dresden Amen', may be explained by Mendelssohn's title 'Reformation' (Symphony No. 5), but the listener will not be concerned with Luther or religious wars. The Swedish composer Berwald (1796–1868) entitled his symphonies 'capricieuse', 'sérieuse' and 'singulière', the last perhaps disarming criticism of its unconventional and refreshing merger of slow movement and scherzo; whereas Berlioz's similar designation 'fantastique' was accompanied by an autobiographical programme. All these works extend, while still in some degree conforming to, expectations equally appropriate to untitled works identified by genre: symphony, overture, etc. Berlioz, however, crossed over into the area of narrative, which in music without words is evidently problematic.

Symphonic music represented an ideal of Romantic expression even when, or perhaps especially when, no poetic or representation intention was proclaimed by its composer (see above, Hoffmann). A substantial strand of interpretative opinion, stimulated, somewhat paradoxically, by both Hanslick and Wagner, condemned instrumental music with subject-matter, Hanslick favouring its exclusion, and Wagner favouring its open adoption as musical drama.[32] A more recent strand of hermeneutic investigation uses terms no

31 R. Larry Todd, *Mendelssohn: The Hebrides and Other Overtures* (Cambridge, 1993); 'Mendelssohn's Ossianic Manner', in Jon W. Finson and R. Larry Todd (eds.), *Mendelssohn and Schumann: Essays on Their Music and its Context* (Durham, NC, 1984), pp. 137–60.

32 Eduard Hanslick, *Vom Musikalisch-Schönen* (Leipzig, 1854); Richard Wagner, *inter alia*, 'Über Franz Liszt's symphonische Dichtungen' (1857); 'Über die Anwendung der Musik auf das Drama' (1879), *Gesammelte Schriften und Dichtungen* (Leipzig, 1907–11); V, pp. 182–98; X, pp. 176–93.

longer exclusively music-analytical, on the kind of non-programmatic repertory for which the symphonies of Brahms may be considered representative;
such interpretations may take the form of implied or ideal narratives, and are
sometimes socio-political, with a particular leaning towards the politics of
nationalism, imperialism and difference.[33] Again, however, such preoccupations belong to the late twentieth century. In the period between the death of
Beethoven and about 1860, the symphony without a programme might have
been considered moribund, and the present (and thus the future) could have
been perceived to belong to music that was explicitly poetic. Although numerous composers contributed to this trend, Berlioz has left perhaps the largest
footprints in this particular geological stratum.

Berlioz was perceived by the poet and critic Gautier as one of a trinity of
French Romanticism, with Victor Hugo and Eugène Delacroix, but this is
more an indication of his perceived stature as a major outsider than to any artistic affinity. Berlioz is too readily associated with the use of an explicit programme, because *Symphonie fantastique* is by far his best-known work. In fact,
Berlioz wrote mainly vocal music. His period of intense, though not exclusive,
exploration of instrumental forms is quite short. Having previously produced
two overtures, one for the opera *Les francs-juges* (1826), the other a concert
piece, *Waverley* (c. 1827), Berlioz in 1830 composed *Symphonie fantastique* and
an overture after Shakespeare, later titled *Fantaisie dramatique, La tempête*. In
1831, he added two concert overtures, *Le roi Lear* and *Rob Roy*; and in 1834,
Harold en Italie, symphony in four movements with solo viola. The seven-move-
ment *Roméo et Juliette* has four long instrumental movements; *Symphonie funèbre
et triomphale* (1840) is a ceremonial composition originally for wind band in
three movements. There is only one later overture independent of a dramatic
work, *Le corsaire* (1844, revised 1851).

Very little of Berlioz's instrumental music is without extra-musical reference, but it usually falls well short of a narrative programme. The changing
associations of musical ideas, however, should not be used to assert that the
extra-musical information is entirely extraneous. The overture *Rob Roy* was
withdrawn by the composer and some of its material cannibalised for *Harold en
Italie*. Such transformations are commonplace in Berlioz's vocal and instrumental music, and are known from the work of many other composers.[34] The
desire to write expressive music did not compel him to regard musical ideas as
inalienable from their original inspiration. Berlioz took a pre-existing melody,

33 For example Newcomb, 'Once More Between Absolute and Program Music'; Susan McClary,
'Constructions of Subjectivity', in Philip Brett, Elizabeth Wood and Gary C. Thomas (eds.), *Queering the
Pitch: The New Gay and Lesbian Musicology* (New York and London, 1994), pp. 205–33.

34 Hugh Macdonald, 'Berlioz's Self-borrowings', *Proceedings of the Royal Musical Association*, 92 (1965–6),
pp. 27–44.

the 'Dies irae' plainchant, into the finale of *Symphonie fantastique* because it would signify something specific to his audience as the subject of parody. Later, setting the 'Dies irae' in his *Grande messe des morts*, he constructed a 'plainchant' of his own because using the traditional melody would have created an undesirable intertextual complication between two works. The intertextual connection of *Rob Roy* and *Harold* is of another order; any semantic confusion results from the accidental survival of the earlier score, and from the modern practice of reviving everything we can find by composers we admire.

In the work he called *Episode de la vie d'un artiste: Symphonie fantastique en cinq parties*, Berlioz made considerable use of earlier material, but its integrity need not be questioned for that reason. Much of its material, and nearly all its actual *composition*, belongs only to the symphonic conception, although there is speculation that some ideas may have been conceived for unrealised works on *Faust* or *Romeo and Juliet*. The theme of the slow movement was taken from the 'Gratias agimus' of an early Mass (1824-5), and the principal theme of the entire symphony, the 'idée fixe' which signifies the artist's vision of the beloved woman, was employed in the cantata *Herminie* (1828); its handling in the successive movements became a model for meaningful thematic transformations in later programme music. Berlioz recognised the immaturity of these works and decided to put their ideas to better use. The association of the beloved with the idée fixe is a connotation assigned only by the programme, which, contrary to what is frequently stated, was never withdrawn by Berlioz.[35] Berlioz argued that the programme provided a reason for the sequence of movements, analogous to spoken dialogue in opera, an argument implicitly accepted by Leonard B. Meyer.[36] The programme also explains why the 'Dies irae' is used. But the essence of the communication, for instance of the 'flux of passions', a phrase Berlioz derived from Chateaubriand, is contained in the arrangement of the musical notes, which include not only harmonic and contrapuntal inventions, for example the constant reinterpretations of the idée fixe through metre and harmony, but also instrumental colour and the spatial disposition of forces, in which the symphonic genre intersects with the theatre.[37]

This imaginative synthesis of music, programme and imagery could not easily be repeated, but *Roméo et Juliette* develops the concept by incorporating the programme into the performance, as a prologue in choral recitative. Not

35 Nicholas Temperley, 'The *Symphonie fantastique* and its Program', *The Musical Quarterly*, 57 (1971), pp. 593-608.

36 Leonard B. Meyer, *Emotion and Meaning in Music* (Chicago, 1956), pp. 271-2.

37 Wolfgang Dömling, 'Die Symphonie fantastique und Berlioz' Auffassung von Programmusik', *Die Musikforschung*, 28 (1975), pp. 260-83; 'En songeant au temps ... à l'espace', *Archiv für Musikwissenschaft*, 33 (1976), pp. 241-60; Jeffrey Langford, 'The "Dramatic Symphonies" of Berlioz as an Outgrowth of the French Operatic Tradition', *The Musical Quarterly*, 69 (1983), pp. 85-103.

only does this provide sufficient indication of the plot for the listener to share the poetic and dramatic inspiration of the instrumental movements, but it goes so far as to mention Shakespeare, without whose poetry we should not understand young love the way we do; and, in the original version of 1839, Emile Deschamps's prologue ends by addressing the audience in four Alexandrines:

> Tels sont d'abord, tels sont les tableaux et les scènes
> Que devant vous, cherchant des routes incertaines,
> L'orchestre va tenter de traduire en accords.
> Puisse votre intérêt soutenir nos efforts![38]

Something of a hostage to fortune, these lines were withdrawn when Berlioz revised his score, but, however stiffly, they convey the excitement of the enterprise, and challenge the audience's willingness to participate. Berlioz later proposed that the sixth movement should normally be omitted, because most audiences would not know Shakespeare's drama with Garrick's dénouement: the music clearly matches the frantic energy of Romeo breaking into the tomb, the awful stillness within the tomb, Romeo's 'aria' for tenor-register instruments, and Juliet's awakening and their temporary reunion, based on themes transformed from the earlier love scene. Yet to isolate the moments when Romeo takes poison and Juliet stabs herself runs the risk of interpretative literalism. What is most vital in this music it its tremendous emotional charge, achieved by musical daring: the avoidance of closure, manic fragmentation, and the lasts chromatic whisper from the oboe. While the brilliant ball scene, the prolonged rapture of the love scene, the mercurial Queen Mab scherzo, and Juliet's funeral procession are musically more satisfying, the tomb scene, a stumbling-block for critical reception in 1839 and through much of the twentieth century, seems finally to have achieved critical, and public, acceptability.[39]

Berlioz's search for poetic essence led him, in *Roméo et Juliette*, to further generic mixture, for the finale is pure opera. With *La damnation de Faust*, which has no symphonic component, he incorporated his lyrics of 1829 (see above) within a design which appeals to an ideal mental theatre, making no concessions to normal performing conventions; not surprisingly he had trouble finding the right generic designation, eventually rejecting the matter-of-fact 'opéra de concert' for the vaguer 'légende dramatique'. In the course of composing *La damnation*, Berlioz took the significant step of writing much of his own text. Although the design remains dependent on Goethe for many details, he produced a *Faust* as French as Marlowe's was English. The haunting poetry

---

38 Translation: These, therefore, are the first group of images and scenes / Which, seeking uncharted ways, / The orchestra before you will try to translate into sound. / May your attention support our attempt!
39 Julian Rushton, *Berlioz: Roméo et Juliette* (Cambridge, 1994), pp. 70–8.

of Faust's four solos, which reflect his alienation, his suicidal despair, his self-deluding hope of finding true love, and his defiant self-identification with nature, ranks among the finest characterisations of the philosopher, precisely because so much of it is applicable to Berlioz himself; in that respect, Faust's damnation is Berlioz's own, and a sequel to *Symphonie fantastique*.

In common with most composers of *Faust* material, Berlioz confined himself to Part I of Goethe's tragedy. He and Liszt dedicated their Faust compositions to each other, but they have little in common. Liszt's *Eine Faust-Sinfonie*, like Beethoven's Ninth, introduces voices only at the end, and his three orchestral movements are neither operatic nor stages in a narrative, but character-studies of Faust, Gretchen and Mephistopheles. The scherzo which characterises the last owes something to the ironic distortions of the finale to *Symphonie fantastique*, but Liszt hit on the inspired strategy of representing devilry, as the spirit of denial, by parodying the grandiose aspirations of Faust's music, and representing the purity of Gretchen by the absence of parody.

Each of the symphonies of Berlioz and Liszt was an isolated formal experiment; but their other orchestral works form part of a larger pattern. Programmatic concert overtures were stimulated by opera, for which composers, building on a perceived Gluck–Mozart tradition, increasingly used overtures to summarise the dramatic action, and secondly because the design of public concerts required short orchestral pieces to make up a programme, and opera overtures were a popular and stimulating way of fulfilling that requirement. From programming overtures by Beethoven, Cherubini and Weber to the programmatic concert overture was but a step, taken by the teenage Mendelssohn (*A Midsummer Night's Dream*, 1826) before Berlioz. Overtures continued to migrate from the theatre to the concert hall (Schumann's magnificent Byronic *Manfred*, 1848–9), while other works of equivalent length were newly composed (Wagner, *Eine Faust-Ouvertüre*, 1840, revised up to 1855). Shakespeare remained a favoured source of subject-matter, and in 1858, Liszt composed a *Hamlet* overture portraying the hero. Subsequently, with the addition of an 'Ophelia' interlude, it was included in the category of symphonic poems. This generic concept, in which we legitimately include related categories such as the 'Fantasy-overture' preferred by Tchaikovsky, was at first associated with 'progressive' or 'avant-garde' music (see chapters 11 and 13). But the new genre, developed specifically to favour the musically poetic, was part of a complex response to the symphonic achievement of Beethoven on the one hand, and rejection of the values of opera (particularly Rossinian opera) on the other.

The poetic values of opera were recognised and re-created in other venues when Liszt transcended the merely virtuosic operatic paraphrase by his imaginative fantasias on themes from Bellini, Berlioz, Meyerbeer and Verdi. But the social and economic barriers erected between an operatic career and the 'advanced' composer, which skewed Berlioz's ambition away from its most natural outlet, and the theatrical apparatus of opera which was difficult to reconcile with the musicality of Schubert, Mendelssohn, Schumann or Liszt, may have contributed positively to the development of each of these composers by compelling them to find strategies for articulating dramatic and poetic values in other, often novel musical forms. For this development, major poets deserve a share of the credit. Liszt concluded his *Faust* symphony by setting the last four lines of Part II of Goethe's tragedy:

> Alles Vergängliche ist nur ein Gleichnis,
> Das Unzulängliche hier wird's Ereignis;
> Das Unbeschreibliche hier wird es getan.
> Das Ewig-Weibliche zieht uns hinan.

These celebrated, but virtually untranslatable, lines have been eloquently set by other composers (Schumann, *Szenen aus Goethes Faust*; Mahler, Eighth Symphony). But the words themselves suggest a poetry which aspires to the condition of Romantic music: intelligible through sound rather than the intellect, just as a painting might be appreciated for its pictorial (formal and colouristic) values, rather than for allegory, instruction or representational exactness. As far as music itself is concerned, the roads which led from Beethoven ultimately converged in agreement that what music conveys, even in its most poetic, narrative or dramatic modes, is the otherwise indescribable.

Bibliography

Berlioz, H., *Critique musicale 1823–1863*, ed. H. Robert Cohen and Yves Gérard. Paris, I: 1823–34, 1996

Bloom, P. A. (ed.), *Berlioz Studies*. Cambridge, 1992

Bonds, M. E., *After Beethoven: Imperatives in the Symphony*. Cambridge, Mass., 1996

Charlton, D. (ed.), *E. T. A. Hoffmann's Musical Writings*. Cambridge, 1989

Cone, E. T., *Musical Form and Musical Performance*. New York, 1968
   The Composer's Voice. Berkeley and Los Angeles, 1974
   'Schubert's Promissory Note'. *19th Century Music*, 5 (1982), pp. 233–41
   Music: A View from Delft. Chicago, 1989

Dahlhaus, C., *Nineteenth-Century Music*, trans. J. B. Robinson. Berkeley and Los Angeles, 1989

Daverio, J., *Robert Schumann: Herald of a 'New Poetic Age'*. New York, 1997

Dömling, W., 'Die Symphonie fantastique und Berlioz' Auffassung von Programmusik'. *Die Musikforschung*, 28 (1975), pp. 260–83
   'En songeant au temps . . . à l'espace'. *Archiv für Musikwissenschaft*, 33 (1976), pp. 241–60

Drabkin, W., *Beethoven: Missa Solemnis*. Cambridge, 1991

Elvers, R. (ed.), *Felix Mendelssohn, a Life in Letters*, trans. C. Tomlinson. London, 1984

Finson, J. W. and Todd, R. L. (eds.), *Mendelssohn and Schumann: Essays on Their Music and its Context*. Durham, NC, 1984

Hanslick, E., *Vom Musikalisch-Schönen*. Leipzig, 1854

Jensen, E. F., 'Explicating Jean Paul: Robert Schumann's Program for *Papillons*, Op. 2'. *19th Century Music*, 22 (1998), pp. 127–43

Kramer, R., *Distant Cycles: Schubert and the Conceiving of Song*. Chicago, 1994

Langford, J., 'The "Dramatic Symphonies" of Berlioz as an Outgrowth of the French Operatic Tradition'. *The Musical Quarterly*, 69 (1983), pp. 85–103

Macdonald, H., 'Berlioz's Self-borrowings'. *Proceedings of the Royal Musical Association*, 92 (1965–6), pp. 27–44

'Schubert's Volcanic Temper'. *The Musical Times*, 99 (1978), pp. 949–52

'Berlioz's *Messe solennelle*'. *19th Century Music*, 16 (1993), pp. 267–85

Marston, N., *Schumann: Fantasie, Op. 17*. Cambridge, 1992

McClary, S., 'Constructions of Subjectivity'. In Philip Brett, Elizabeth Wood and Gary C. Thomas (eds.), *Queering the Pitch: The New Gay and Lesbian Musicology*. New York and London, 1994, pp. 205–33

Meyer, L. B., *Emotion and Meaning in Music*. Chicago, 1956

Style and Music: Theory, History, and Ideology. Philadelphia, 1989

Mongrédien, J., *Jean-François le Sueur, contribution à l'étude d'un demi-siècle de musique française (1780–1830)*. 2 vols., Bern, 1980

Newcomb, A., 'Once More Between Absolute and Program Music: Schumann's Second Symphony'. *19th Century Music*, 7 (1984), pp. 233–50

Noske, F., *French Song from Berlioz to Duparc*. New York, 1970

Ratner, L. G. *Classic Music: Expression, Form, and Style*. New York, 1980

Romantic Music: Sound and Syntax. New York, 1992

Rosen, C., *The Classical Style: Haydn, Mozart, Beethoven*. London, 1971; rev. 1976, new edn 1997

The Romantic Generation. London, 1996

Rushton, J., *The Musical Language of Berlioz*. Cambridge, 1983

Berlioz: Roméo et Juliette. Cambridge, 1994

The Music of Berlioz. Oxford, 2001

Sams, E., *The Songs of Robert Schumann*. London, 1969; 2nd edn. London, 1975

Samson, J., *The Music of Chopin*. London, 1985

Chopin: The Four Ballades. Cambridge, 1992

Samson, J. (ed.), *The Cambridge Companion to Chopin*. Cambridge, 1992

Schumann, R., *Gesammelte Schriften über Musik und Musiker*. 5th edn, Leipzig, 1914; selected translations, Schumann, *On Music and Musicians*. London, 1947

Solie, R., 'Whose Life? The Gendered Self in Schumann's Frauenliebe Songs'. In Steven Scher (ed.), *Music and Text: Critical Inquiries*. Cambridge, 1992, pp. 219–40

Temperley, N., 'The *Symphonie fantastique* and its Program'. *The Musical Quarterly*, 57 (1971), pp. 593–608

Todd, R. L., *Mendelssohn: The Hebrides and Other Overtures*. Cambridge, 1993

Wagner, R., 'Über Franz Liszt's symphonische Dichtungen' (1857); 'Über die Anwendung der Musik auf das Drama' (1879). *Gesammelte Schriften und Dichtungen*. Leipzig, 1907–11, V, pp. 182–98; X, pp. 176–93

Youens, S., *Retracing a Winter's Journey: Schubert's 'Winterreise'*. Ithaca, N.Y., 1991

Schubert: Die schöne Müllerin. Cambridge, 1992

· 7 ·

The invention of tradition

JOHN IRVING

An imagined past

Whenever I was in Berlin, I would seldom miss Möser's quartet-evenings. For me, such artistic presentations were always the most intelligible forum for appreciating instrumental music, in which one heard four reasonable people conversing, as it were, believed their discourse to be profitable and became acquainted with the individuality of the instruments. *Goethes Briefe* Band IV: *Briefe der Jahre 1821–1832*'. Textkritisch durchgesehen und mit Anmerkungen versehen von Karl Robert Mandelkow (Hamburg, 1967), no. 1443.[1]

Goethe's letter to Carl Friedrich Zelter (9 November 1829) is sometimes cited as an idealisation of the Classical string quartet, in which this genre is treated as a musical embodiment of civilised Enlightenment conversation between intellectual peers, the 'thread' of the conversation passing effortlessly through the entire musical ensemble. In other respects Goethe's comment sheds light upon the relationship between early Romantic instrumental music – specifically chamber music in this context – and its immediate Classical past. The evocation of an ideal mode of Enlightenment conversation suggests a nostalgia for a past, even if that past were nothing but an imagined construction (that is, one of many such possible pasts), in relation to which the early Romantic present might be situated. Although he mentions no specific event, either public or private, nor even a specific repertory, it is clear enough that what Goethe had in mind was one of a series of quartet performances organised in Berlin by Karl Möser, at first informally, as an outgrowth of a tradition of chamber and orchestral concerts he had initiated in 1812, and continued on a more permanent footing from the mid-1820s. Möser's quartet concerts rapidly became an established feature of Berlin musical life in the early nine-

---

1 Wär[e] ich in Berlin, so würde ich die Möserischen Quartettabende selten versäumen. Dieser Art Exhibitionen waren mir von jeher von der Instrumentalmusik das Verständlichste, man hört vier vernünftige Leute sich untereinander unterhalten, glaubt ihren Diskursen etwas abzugewinnen und die Eigentümlichkeit der Instrumente kennenzulernen.

teenth century, noted for their concentration on the works of 'the classics'.[2] The *Allgemeine musikalische Zeitung* for 1832 claimed that in Möser's concerts 'the great symphonies of the three heroes of German music [Haydn, Mozart and Beethoven] alternate with more recent compositions in the symphonic genre'. According to a later report in the *Berliner musikalische Zeitung* (1846), Möser's concerts 'did the most to pave the way for the symphonies of the German masters [again, Haydn, Mozart and Beethoven] in Berlin and win understanding for them'.[3] Symphonies by the 'three heroes of German music' were regularly performed in Berlin, either in Möser's series, or else in one of the numerous competing concert series that characterised Berlin's lively musical life in the 1820s, 1830s and 1840s, encompassing solo, orchestral, choral and chamber presentations. For instance, symphonies by Haydn and Mozart were given in a winter subscription series at the Berliner Residenz-theater in 1821–2; Beethoven's orchestral works were regularly performed, with the 'Pastoral', *Eroica* and 'Battle' symphonies particular favourites. It has been calculated that in 1848 no fewer than fifty-three performances of Beethoven's symphonies occurred in Berlin, compared to thirty-six by Haydn and twenty by Mozart.[4] Surviving programmes, diary entries, reviews and reports from such concerts display both a tendency towards generic eclecti-cism (mixing arias, instrumental solos, concertos and symphonies in a contin-uation of established concert traditions) and, above all, a strong preference for the works of Haydn, Mozart and Beethoven.[5] The abiding impression is that of an emerging core repertory consisting of solo, chamber and symphonic music by the three great composers of the 'Viennese Classical tradition', a tra-dition that grew up in parallel with the developing social phenomenon of European concert life in the first decades of the nineteenth century. This phe-nomenon, in turn, played a major role in the civic aspirations of certain key geographical centres such as Berlin, Vienna and Leipzig. In each of these centres, the instrumental genres of the sonata, the various chamber music groupings (trio, quartet, quintet, octet and so forth) and, above all, the sym-phony, gradually acquired an unassailable cultural status.

Within Viennese concert life, Beethoven's symphonies were especially ven-erated (principally his Third, Fifth and Sixth). Indeed, their intellectual

---

2 So described in a review of one of Möser's concerts printed in the *Allgemeine musikalische Zeitung* (1832), cols. 331–2; quoted in C.-H. Mahling, 'Berlin: Music in the Air', in A. Ringer (ed.), *The Early Romantic Era* (London and Basingstoke, 1990), p. 118.

3 Quoted in Mahling, 'Berlin', p. 17. See also S. Pederson, 'A. B. Marx, Berlin Concert Life and National Identity', *19th Century Music*, 18 (1994), pp. 87–107.

4 Mahling, 'Berlin', p. 136.

5 So strong was this tendency that one commentator, writing in the *Allgemeine musikalische Zeitung* in 1831, complained that 'We get nothing but frequent repetitions of the quartets of Haydn, Mozart and Beethoven, although they are of course fine works at any time [and] of the last-named composer's magnifi-cent symphonies' (quoted in Mahling, 'Berlin', p. 136).

demands may have been partially responsible for the creation of an oft-performed, 'central' orchestral repertory, since familiarity with and comprehension of these difficult works could only really come about though repeated performances. No less prominent in the public domain was Beethoven's chamber music. The Op. 59 'Rasumovsky' string quartets were actively promulgated by the Schuppanzigh quartet, and it was perhaps the prospect of reliable professional performances that encouraged Beethoven to invest these works with their quasi-symphonic character, orchestral breadth of scale and sonority, and expanded technical demands, all challenges to the identity of this formerly 'domestic' genre that were taken up by the early Romantic generation, especially Schubert, whose late quartets and other chamber works were also included in Schuppanzigh's chamber music concerts in the 1820s.

The works of the 'Viennese Classics' were likewise central to concert repertory in Leipzig. Leipzig had enjoyed a rich tradition of public or semi-public concerts, stretching well back into the eighteenth century and including the Collegium Musicum associated with the university. From 1781 this environment was dominated by the series of professional concerts emanating from the newly founded Gewandhaus, including performances of Beethoven's First Symphony in 1801, the *Eroica* in 1807 and the Fifth in 1809. Most famously under Mendelssohn's direction from the 1820s, the Gewandhaus concerts established a tradition of so-called 'historical' concerts in which modern orchestral music, such as Schubert's Ninth Symphony, premièred by Mendelssohn in 1839, Schumann's First and Fourth symphonies, premièred in 1841, and his own Third ('Scottish') Symphony, given in 1842, were performed side by side with works by Bach, Handel, Haydn, Mozart and Beethoven. Thus presented, modern symphonic works would be heard within the context of established masterpieces (such as Beethoven's 'Choral' Symphony, a particular favourite of Mendelssohn's, often produced by him in the Gewandhaus). While emphasising stylistic change, such concerts implied, as in Vienna, tacit acceptance of a framework in which a pre-formed canon, enshrining the authority of the past, was accorded due deference by modern composers who largely adopted the established genres and structures in their own work.[6]

Partly by means of such developing traditions of concert programming, the works of the 'Viennese Classical tradition' came to acquire a canonic status, within which the central position was occupied by the instrumental music of Haydn, Mozart and Beethoven. Their instrumental compositions were represented as timeless exemplars, touchstones of taste around which were grouped

6 Beethoven's solo and duo sonatas were also central to the Gewandhaus concerts. On 26 April 1846, Mendelssohn presented a concert jointly with the singer, Jenny Lind, each half of which opened with, respectively, the Violin Sonata, Op. 30, No. 3 in G and the 'Moonlight' Sonata, Op. 27, No. 2.

compositions by aspiring modern composers within similar genres. We may see this trend, perhaps, as part of a broader project to invent a 'Viennese Classical style', one of whose parallel purposes was to validate the notion of an early Romantic school whose modernist aesthetic was to be seen in opposition to a perceived classical stability, but which was nevertheless grounded in the concept of a continuing tradition. The construction of this tradition, out of which the more recent productions of, for instance, Schumann, Mendelssohn or Liszt might be regarded as a natural outgrowth, is confirmed to some degree by contemporary attempts to hallow the memories of Haydn and Mozart through collected editions of their works, through reviews of such publications, in the biographical sphere and also in contemporary pedagogy.

Especially significant within the biographical accounts of Griesinger and Carpani in the case of Haydn,[7] and of Niemetschek and Nissen in the case of Mozart,[8] was the portrayal of their subjects as personifying 'genius', appropriating for historical ends a modern aesthetic stance habitually used to characterise early Romantic artistic aspirations. Incidentally, such writers produced an image of past, unimpeachable greatness, as embodied in the works of these composers. Against such an image, early Romantic composers of the generation of Mendelssohn and Schumann could believe themselves to be, and portray themselves as, rightful heirs and successors, their own music emerging from the revered Viennese Classics in a natural progression. At times, this historical positioning was overtly sanctioned by the composers themselves, most often in relation to Beethoven. According to Lobe's 1855 account of a conversation with Mendelssohn about the overture to *A Midsummer Night's Dream*[9] Mendelssohn makes a comparison between his overture and that of Beethoven's *Fidelio*, noting that in *A Midsummer Night's Dream* he had not 'broken new ground' as such but had utilised the same maxims as had Beethoven, meaning that although Mendelssohn's particular musical ideas were original, their means of presentation were not (he employed tonal harmonies, recognised periodic phrasing, sonata form and so on). He locates his achievement within a validating tradition: '[Beethoven] painted the content of his piece in tone-pictures. I tried to do the same thing.'

Theoretical writings played a highly important part in the establishment of the 'Viennese Classical style' wherein these composers acquired iconic status, representatives of a glorious past to be admired and emulated. For example, the

7 G. A. Griesinger, 'Biographische Notizen über Joseph Haydn', serialised in *Allgemeine musikalische Zeitung*, 11 (1809), pp. 641, 657, 673, 689, 705, 721, 737, 776; G. Carpani, *Le Haydine ovvero Lettere su la vita e le opere del celebre maestro Giuseppe Haydn* (Milan, 1812).

8 F. X. Niemetschek, *Leben des k.k. Kapellmeisters Wolfgang Gottlieb Mozart nach Originalquellen beschrieben* (Prague, 1798); G. N. Nissen, *Biographie W. A. Mozart nach Originalbriefen* (Leipzig, 1828).

9 See R. L. Todd (ed.), *Mendelssohn and His World* (Princeton, 1991), p. 194.

puzzling chromaticism of the opening of Mozart's 'Dissonance' Quartet, K.465 prompted vigorous discussion in periodical musical literature of the late 1820s and early 1830s. Precisely because Mozart had attained canonic status, an unfamiliar aspect of his work (namely, the remarkable chromaticism of just the first page of this piece) was felt worthy of extended critical comment. Indeed, it *needed* explication to the wider audience to which that canon was addressed (and which was served by contemporary journals).[10] Such a conception is noticeable too in early nineteenth-century textbooks of the *Formenlehre* type. Joseph-Jérome Momigny included an extended discussion of the first movement of Mozart's D minor quartet, K.421 in his *Cours complet d'harmonie et de composition* (Paris, 1806).[11] Momigny's appropriation of this movement was intended as a detailed demonstration of phrase divisions, cadence structure and harmonic grammar, though his underlying purpose was to convey the expressive qualities of Mozart's music (thus representing Mozart's achievement in contemporary terms), to which end he imported a text of his own selection, aligned beneath the principal melodic part throughout the movement, in order to give voice to the narrative quality that he perceived in the work of the genius Mozart. Subsequently, Adolphe Bernhard Marx's seminal *Die Lehre von der musikalische Komposition* (1838–47) devoted considerable attention to the instrumental music of Beethoven in his demonstration of sonata form and its technical processes. Increasingly, the main focus of attention in such traditions of pedagogy (to which should be added the work of Czerny and Reicha) is instrumental music of the 'Viennese Classics'; collectively, these theoretical writings reinforced the pre-eminence of that repertory (in relation to which modern instrumental compositions were to be understood).[12]

---

10 See, for instance, Fétis in *La Revue musicale* series 1, vol. 5 (July, 1829), pp. 601–6, Perne in vol. 6 (August 1829), pp. 25–34; and Fétis's response in series 2, vol. 8 (July 1830), pp. 321–8; Gottfried Weber in *Cäcilia*, 14 (1832), pp. 1–49; and the summary in *The Harmonicon*, 10 (1832), pp. 243–6. The debate is surveyed in J. A. Vertrees, 'Mozart's String Quartet K.465: The History of a Controversy', *Current Musicology*, 17 (1974), pp. 96–114, and J. Irving, *Mozart: The 'Haydn' Quartets* (Cambridge, 1998), pp. 76–8.

11 Vol. I, pp. 307–82; vol. II, pp. 387–403; vol. III, pp. 109–56 (comprising an extended musical example).

12 Marx's tripartite division of sonata form is discussed further below. It is anticipated in the writing of Czerny, whose views reached definitive form in the *School of Practical Composition* (London, 1848), originally published in French in 1834. Possibly Marx was influenced further by Czerny's German translations of the theories of form advanced in Antoine Reicha's *Traité de haute composition musicale* (Paris, 1826), published in Vienna in 1834. Reicha had famously characterised the sonata form as the 'grande coupe binaire', stressing its historical derivation from the binary pattern. Nevertheless, within his scheme, thematic functions were assigned a far greater prominence than had typically obtained in the late eighteenth century, and this began to highlight a tension between a bipartite tonal conception and a tripartite thematic conception, within which thematic development is crucial. Such was the perceived importance of the element of thematic development following the exposition of the main themes that it began to acquire an independent status within the structure of a movement as a whole – a development section sandwiched between the initial thematic presentations and their reprise towards the movement's close. Within Reicha's 'grande coupe binaire', there lurked a three-stage pattern of exposition, development and recapitulation, a pattern that was to become the norm for nineteenth-century understandings of sonata form, in whatever genre. Reicha

Early nineteenth-century critical accounts of the type inspired by E. T. A. Hoffmann's article, 'Beethoven's Instrumental Music' (1813),[13] refine the contemporary conception of the 'Viennese Classics' somewhat by privileging instrumental, rather than vocal repertories. The notion of 'absolute music', in which, freed from the associations or dictates of a text, music might speak 'purely', entirely within the terms of its own metaphorical 'language' (that is, its internal structural interrelations), became powerfully symbolic of the highest achievements of 'Viennese Classicism'. Allied to an emergent neo-Platonic aesthetic in the late eighteenth century, according to which, in opposition to the former Aristotelian, rule-based approach to art philosophy, genius became a privileged term pointing the way beyond mere reason to a world of feeling, Beethoven's instrumental music (sonatas, chamber music, symphonies) came to set the standard for early Romantic composers. This state, in turn, had its origin in the instrumental output of Haydn and Mozart, who, in Hoffmann's figuring of recent musical history, had pointed the way towards what Beethoven ultimately achieved independently of a text:

> Mozart and Haydn, the creators of our present instrumental music, were the first to show us the art in its full glory; the man who then looked on it with all his love and penetrated its innermost being is – Beethoven! The instrumental compositions of these three masters breathe a similar Romantic spirit . . . In Haydn's writing there prevails the expression of a serene and childlike personality . . . Mozart leads us into the heart of the spirit realm . . . Beethoven's instrumental music opens up to us also the realm of the monstrous and the immeasurable.[14]

The three great Classical composers are portrayed here as individual manifestations of a single 'striving'. While their succession is temporal, the striving (for expression of 'the Romantic spirit') is timeless. A related project of early Romanticism in music is its sense of 'writing for posterity': different not just stylistically from 'Classical' music, but also in that its claims were intentionally projected forwards in time, not content to serve the immediate pleasures of a

---

classified the development's various functions under several headings: the development of melodic ideas already heard in the exposition; their fragmentation; their presentation in new environments; their novel combination with other material; and the revealing thereby of unexpected facets of those familiar melodic ideas (*Traité de Haute Composition Musical*, II, p. 240). 'Development' here is exclusively to do with thematic manipulation, also broadly true of Marx's discussion. For a comprehensive account, see B. Shamgar, 'The Retransition in the Piano Sonatas of Haydn, Mozart and Beethoven', Ph.D. diss., University of New York (1978).

13 Hoffmann's essay appeared, unascribed, in the *Zeitung für die elegante Welt* in December 1813, drawing upon material contained in reviews he had published earlier (and anonymously) in the *Allgemeine musikalishe Zeitung* (Leipzig) in July 1810 and March 1813. For the original German text, see 'Beethoven's Instrumental-Musik', in C. G. von Massen (ed.), *E. T. A. Hoffmann: Sämtliche Werke*, vol. I (Munich and Leipzig, 1908), pp. 55–8, 60–1 and 62–4.

14 This translation from O. Strunk (ed.), *Source Readings in Music History*, rev. edn, VI, *The Nineteenth Century*, ed. R. A. Solie (New York and London, 1998), p. 152.

patron, but speaking instead to humanity at large, in no particular time or place. While such an attitude is discernible already in chamber works such as Haydn's Op. 71 and Op. 74 string quartets, or his later piano trios, written expressly for public performance (and therefore 'anonymous' with respect to particular time and place of performance), the flight from patronal functionality in instrumental music is seen most clearly in the work of Beethoven, who famously described his later quartets as being for the ears and sensibilities of later generations.[15] The instrumental works of Chopin, Mendelssohn, Schumann, Liszt and others aspired to a similar status, speaking to an audience remote from the orbit of composition itself. Vitally important in this regard was dissemination in print. From the composer's viewpoint, publication in its various forms potentially brought contemporary recognition on a broad scale. Its relationship to an evolving contemporary concert life was symbiotic. So far as the early Romantics were concerned, printed works became more saleable if their composer was a virtuoso performer on the public stage (though this generalisation did not hold good for long in the case of Chopin). For instance, a complete edition of Kalkbrenner was envisaged by Probst, its marketability supported to no small extent by the composer's immensely successful international career on the concert platform during the 1820s and early 1830s. Publication likewise opened a composer's work up to critical attention. The appearance of Chopin's variations for piano and orchestra on Mozart's *Là ci darem la mano* (1827; publ. Vienna, 1830) was famously welcomed by Schumann ('hats off, gentleman – a genius') in the Leipzig *Allgemeine musikalische Zeitung* in 1831.[16] While reviews of music and performers are a valuable source of information on early reception of the 'Romantic' style, their contemporary significance as agents in the formation of traditions should not be overlooked.

In this respect, the location of Schubert's instrumental music within the early nineteenth-century tradition becomes problematic precisely because of its absence from print. One possible reason for this surprising fact is that Schubert was, by comparison with virtuosi such as Kalkbrenner, a reclusive personality, conspicuously lacking a career as a performer as a means to popularise his own music and enhance its saleability. At about the same time as Probst was publishing Kalkbrenner's piano works, he was rejecting Schubert's. Remarkably, only three of Schubert's chamber works (the String Quartet in A minor, D.804, the Rondo in B minor for violin and piano, D.895 and the Piano Trio in E flat, D.929) and three of his piano sonatas (in A minor,

---

15 Beethoven's ambivalence towards his patrons is explored in chapter 5.

16 Schumann's writings were central to his career, and, incidentally, to the emergence of a Romantic aesthetic; see L. Plantinga, *Schumann as Critic* (New Haven and London, 1967).

D.845, in D, D.850, and in G, D.894) were published in his lifetime. Not that his chamber output was wholly unknown, of course: professional performances of Schubert's quartets and trios in Vienna are well documented (the first performance of the A minor Quartet, D.804 was given by the Schuppanzigh quartet on 14 March 1824, for instance). But while such performances – very few of which could truly be called 'public' – certainly gained him a foothold as an instrumental composer, his contemporary reputation was almost entirely based on his lieder and copious quantities of relatively ephemeral piano works such as the sets of waltzes, *ländler*, deutsche and ecossaises, D.145, 365, 734, 779, 781, 782, 783 and 969. A brief overview of first publication dates for some of his most famous piano and chamber music demonstrates significant delays in achieving published status, partly explaining the relatively slow conferring of 'canonic' status, while simultaneously raising the important question of whose 'tradition' Schubert's works belonged to, that of his contemporaries or that constructed by the competing agendas of later generations:[17]

title	composed	published
Sonata in A minor, D.537	1817	1852
Sonata in A minor, D.784	1823	1839
Four Impromptus, D.935	1827	1839
Sonata in C minor, D.558	1828	1839
Sonata in A major, D.559	1828	1839
Sonata in B flat major, D.960	1828	1839
String Trio, D.581	1817	1897
'Trout' Quintct, D.67	1819	1829
'Quartettsatz', D.703	1820	1870
'Arpeggione' Sonata, D.821	1824	1871
Octet, D.803	1824	1889
String Quartet in G, D.887	1826	1851

Taken together, these various strands point to an attempt to situate early Romantic instrumental music firmly within a traditional framework that strongly implicated the 'Viennese Classics', a canon whose invention in contemporary concert life indirectly contributed to the artistic validation of the New. Precisely when, where and by whom this enabling canon was invented is impossible to pin down, though an early trace of it may perhaps be gleaned in Count Waldstein's alleged exhortation to his protégé, Beethoven, to 'receive the spirit of Mozart at the hands of Haydn'.[18] This may be construed as an

17 In this regard, see also O. Biba, 'Schubert's Position in Viennese Musical Life', *19th Century Music*, 3 (1979), p. 106. 18 See E. Forbes (ed.), *Thayer's Life of Beethoven* (Princeton, 1967), I, p. 115.

attempt to position the young genius in relation to the Classical 'canon' which could, apparently, be represented in terms of just those two composers. Moreover, the remark is constructed in such as way as to imply a mystical network of transmission, by which the 'spirit' of Mozart now inhabited his older contemporary, whose historical role in this connection was to pass on the sacred flame of 'genius' to the standard-bearer of the future, Beethoven. Thus imagined, the tradition to which Schubert, Mendelssohn, Schumann and their contemporaries were heirs was given a life, a strength and therefore a challenge that could not be denied. The technical specifics of this scenario remain to be surveyed.

Envisioning a present

Current critical thinking on Romanticism tends to stress its contiguity with earlier stylistic trends, in contrast to earlier critical traditions which propose a 'profound shift . . . Intellectually [Romanticism] marked a violent reaction to the Enlightenment.'[19] Aidan Day's recent study of Romanticism[20] has addressed this important duality:

> It is possible to see the Enlightenment solely in terms of an exaltation of reason. Looked at this way . . . the Romantics . . . might be seen as reacting against Enlightenment rationalism in their emphasis on the importance of feeling . . . But it would be unfair to the Enlightenment to see it solely as a cold exaltation of critical intelligence . . .   (p.65)
> To characterise Romanticism as the revolutionary movement overturning Neoclassicism in general is to oversimplify what was happening in the late Enlightenment culture in Europe in the later eighteenth century . . .   (p.76)

According to this redrawing of the boundaries, Romanticism admits an 'emphasis on feeling, not to the exclusion of but *as well as* on reason . . . The poems of [Wordsworth's] *Lyrical Ballads* [for the second edition (1800) of which Wordsworth wrote the famous phrase 'all good poetry is the spontaneous overflow of powerful feelings', that has been taken as a 'manifesto' of Romanticism] did not mark "the beginning of a new age". They were essentially compositions of the late Enlightenment' (Day, *Romanticism*, p. 76).

Seen in this light, the instrumental music of the early nineteenth century exhibits continuity with the recent Enlightenment past while simultaneously reaching out on new paths, a context within which, for instance, the chamber music of Schumann might usefully be understood. Holding to the established Classical genres, works such as his Piano Quartet, Op. 47, the string quartets,

---

19 M. Drabble (ed.), *The Oxford Companion to English Literature*, 5th edn (Oxford, 1985), s.v, 'Romanticism'.   20 A. Day, *Romanticism* (London and New York, 1996).

Op. 41, the trios, Opp. 63, 80 and 110, the 'Phantasiestück' Trio, Op. 88, and the violin sonatas, Opp. 105 and 121 were addressed, like his journalistic endeavours, to musical *Liebhaber* who could appreciate not only the masterly technique in the handling of material and structure, but also the expressive idiom in which these were cast. In the opening Allegro of the Piano Quintet, Op. 44, for instance, such a *Liebhaber* might admire the skill with which the connecting passage leading out of the presentation of the main theme seems to evolve from the same intervallic patterns (though contrasted in gesture); likewise, the gradual coalescing of the secondary theme out of the cadential pedal-point material from bar 51. But such technical fabrication sits securely within the *expressive character* of the musical discourse: the overall impression here is of a vigorous, effervescent piece, tempered periodically by moments of repose. By contrast, the older viewpoint dismissed by Day has traditionally been engaged in relation to Schumann's solo piano works. From this standpoint, the privileged features of this repertory include: colouristic harmonic chromaticism; overt programmaticism (extending to the evocation of a masked ball attended by fictional and real characters such as Chopin and Paganini in *Carnaval*, Op. 9);[21] and virtuosity as *topos* – as at the beginning of 'Traumeswirren' from the *Fantasiestücke*, Op. 12 or the opening 'Äusserst bewegt', from *Kreisleriana*, Op. 16. Especially significant is the foregrounding of particular expressive gestures such as the exploitation of a dissonant ninth at the beginning of the 'Romanze' from *Faschingsschwank aus Wien*, Op. 26, or the *Affekt*-laden intervals in the opening melody of 'Warum?' from *Fantasiestücke*; the separation of registers later in the same piece; interruption of slow by quick tempos in 'Fabel' from the same set – and so on. All this appears comparatively radical at first sight, perhaps ('a violent reaction to the Enlightenment'). But while such fingerprints may be characterised as 'progressive' ingredients, it is interesting to note that they cohabit with 'old-fashioned' form-schemes such as sonata and ternary, that, as it were, embody an earlier Classical tradition. Important fingerprints of the Baroque era survive in this repertory: the opening of Schumann's *Arabesque*, Op. 18, is manufactured from a string of sequences, a Baroque device that survived contextual transplantation in several later traditions of tonal music; formally, it is an extension of the ternary principle, consisting of a series of contrasting episodes separating restatements of the opening idea; and within the first minute of 'Sehr rasch', No. 7 from *Kreisleriana*, we have references to two more 'Baroque' fingerprints: a 'circle-of-fifths' progression, and fugato texture (which epitomises the abiding fascination of the early Romantics with the music of J. S. Bach), though within a

---

21 See chapter 6.

'modern' context that privileges gesture and virtuosity. So, to view the early Romantic tradition as an explosive, dramatic avant-garde that swept away the objective Classical perspective in its pursuit of the subjective 'Beyond' would be premature diagnosis, relying on a one-dimensional interpretation of instrumental music from the early decades of the nineteenth century. In fact, a truly self-conscious avant-garde project only emerged in the years immediately following the mid-century (see chapter 11). The remainder of this chapter will explore the connection of the instrumental work of the early Romantic generation to the 'Classical' past.

In the early string quartets and symphonies of Schubert, the musical language operates along strongly 'Classical' lines, departing only rarely from a conventional symmetry, as, for instance in the opening paragraph of the B flat quartet, D.112 (1814), whose irregular scansion is gradually dissolved by means of foreshortened motivic repetitions (bars 30ff.) and utterly negated in the dramatic, quasi-orchestral passage that follows from bar 45. In the Presto finale of the D major quartet, D.94 (1813) Schubert approaches the character of, say, Mozart's K.428, while the first movement of D.87 in E flat (1813) demonstrates a sure handling of conflicting rhythmic profiles in a polythematic movement that suggests the young composer was familiar with Mozart's techniques as exemplified in, for instance, the opening Allegro of the 'Dissonance' Quartet, K.465. Among the early six symphonies the best known are the Fourth ('Tragic') in C minor, D.417 (a work that effects a convincing approximation of the later eighteenth-century vogue for works in the 'Sturm und Drang' idiom, as seen, for instance, in its slow introduction, and in the urgent rhythmic and intervallic patterning allied to irregular phrasing that characterises the opening passage of the ensuing Allegro), the Fifth in B flat, D.485, and the Sixth, D.589, each probably composed not as 'concert' symphonies in the public sense, but for the more 'domestic' setting of a Viennese amateur orchestra in which Schubert himself played viola. While the Fifth evokes the idiom of Mozart in its phrasing and proportioning (incorporating, too, a subdominant recapitulation in its first movement – a trick found in Mozart's Piano Sonata, K.545), the sixth skilfully assimilates an Italianate tone (Rossini especially), its melodies by turn light and lyrical, its rhythms elastic and its wind colouring brilliant – qualities perhaps not unexpected of a pupil of Salieri.

In contrast, Schubert's later symphonic efforts belong to an altogether different world. In the 'Unfinished' Symphony, D.759, and in the 'Great' C major, D.944, his earlier fluency is sacrificed to a more studied emulation of his revered Beethoven. The briefest comparison of the sonata-form first movements of the sixth and ninth symphonies reveals a profound shift in attitude towards greater depth of thematic and rhythmic integration. Following a brief rehearsal in 1828, the orchestra of the Wiener Musikverein declared the work 'too difficult' and replaced it in performance with the more appealing Sixth. 'Too difficult' might refer to the symphony's technical demands, although it is conceivable also that the directorate felt that the 'Great' lacked popular accessibility: following its tightly argued network of motifs allied to a sophisticated tonal evolution on a grand scale requires a considerably greater degree of effort from the listener than does the relatively compact and conventional Sixth.[22] In his later symphonies, Schubert typically lends thematic coherence to the changing surface of a movement or an extended passage within a movement by concentrating on a single underlying motif whose intervallic or rhythmic properties are fragmented, developed or transformed in some way. Two examples of 'fragmented' continuity occur in the first movement of Schubert's 'Unfinished' Symphony in B minor, D.759. The extension of the exposition's 'second subject' is founded upon a modulating dialogue between upper and lower strings in which a fragment of the theme (its third and fourth bars) is relentlessly pursued as a means of exploring keys closely related to G major, indirectly confirming the credentials of this tonal-structural counterpole to the tonic, B minor. In the development, Schubert returns to the mysterious unison opening of the symphony, which here goes through a remarkable transformation. Its material consists of two elements, bars 1–2 and 3–4 of the theme, respectively, which appear in canon, inversion and thematic fragmentation, eventually achieving a climax of shattering intensity (bars 123–76). Each stage of this evolution is punctuated by a dramatic shift in the orchestral texture whose overt variety is a striking counterpoint to the motivic unity, throwing both elements into sharp relief and challenging conventional understanding of their respective roles.

One way of imagining the relation of an emergent early Romantic musical syntax to its Classical ancestry is in terms of an assumed process of 'normalisation' of previously 'extraneous' elements. Elements such as texture and register, formerly peripheral to musical discourse, become centred in the works of Schubert, Mendelssohn and Schumann. At the beginnings of Haydn's C major String Quartet, Op. 33, No. 3 ('The Bird'), the Allegro of Mozart's 'Dissonance' Quartet, K.465, and his C major String Quintet, K.515, similar patterns of repeated quavers are established at the outset as chordal accompaniments to themes that exploit a particular registral feature, but in each case the contribution of such characteristics is always subsidiary to the main business of the musical argument, which is grounded in thematic and tonal process. That cannot be said of the opening of, say, Mendelssohn's Octet, Op. 20, in which the

22 The 'Great C major' was eventually performed by Mendelssohn in Leipzig in 1839, at the instigation of Robert Schumann.

textural and registral elements are absolutely and indissolubly the focus of events, lending the movement its peculiar ethos.[23] A similar point might be made of the opening of his D major String Quartet, Op. 44, No. 1, or, in respect of differing textural and registral profiles, of the openings of Schubert's string quartets in D minor, D.810 ('Death and the Maiden'), G major, D.887, and the C minor 'Quartettsatz', D.703; likewise the finales of Schumann's Piano Quintet, Op. 44, and his Piano Quartet, Op. 47 (the latter invoking a fugal idiom).

Occasionally within what was regarded by the early Romantics as 'the Viennese Classical style', the foregrounding of expressive events is already con-figured in such a way that these momentarily break out of their conventional 'frame of reference'. In the Adagio ma non troppo of Mozart's String Quintet in G minor, K.516 (1787), there is a moment within the B flat minor episode beginning at bar 18, in which a background 'accompaniment' figure in the viola 2 suddenly steps forward to assume centre stage (bar 19). The reversal of textu-ral roles here is not in itself the issue (interplay within the instrumental polyph-ony of chamber music is a normal characteristic of the genre). What is unusual is Mozart's stretching of the etiquette of Classical musical language, within which the conventional hierarchy of foreground and background elements dic-tates also the respective functions of particular shapes: a 'throbbing' figure such as that in operation here is normally 'background', not 'foreground'. Its function within the phraseology is likewise refocused: while its two soloistic appearances balance dominant and tonic statements, its 'searching' quality (three ascending steps, left hanging in the air at the end) suggest rather more than conventional 'filling'. The viola suddenly usurps the position of 'narrator'. While the 'foregrounding' lasts only a moment (and the figure in question remains – in context – subsidiary) it unquestionably assumes an expressive force that exceeds the bounds of convention. A similar expressive weight, now assuming far greater prominence within its environment, is to be observed in the C sharp minor Andante sostenuto of Schubert's Piano Sonata in B flat, D.960. The dotted 'accompaniment' pattern, spread over several octaves' range, is, in functional terms, a background element to the rather fragile theme traced at the top of the right-hand chordal texture. While the harmonic pro-gressions unfold the Andante's tonal panorama, the 'accompaniment' pattern is effectively an ostinato, undeniably contributing a large part of this move-ment's luminous expressive character. Its form is straightforward ternary (in the reprise, Schubert slightly develops the 'accompaniment' pattern).

---

23 A possible ancestor of Mendelssohn's opening is that of Haydn's 'Sunrise' Quartet, Op. 76, No. 5 in B flat. Here too, the characteristic disposition of register and texture is secondary to the process of thematic and tonal extension and development.

However, this is dramatised to an extraordinary degree: almost everything hangs on an appreciation of the extreme contrast of character between the 'plaint' of the opening section and its grandiose successor. In all of this the 'accompaniment' pattern is paramount, by virtue of its absence from the middle of the movement as much as its dominance of the framing sections. A similar illustration of Schubert's foregrounding of 'accompaniment' as rhythmic ostinato is to be seen in the Adagio of the String Quintet, D.956, whose ostensible 'melody' likewise occupies a rather tenuous position in a whole that is dominated by a steady tread of harmonies and a dotted rhythm. The expressive character assumed by this particular ostinato is once again the bearer of much of this movement's structural definition, being absent from the turbulent middle section, and afterwards reprised in varied guise (the ascending cello ripples).

Such redefining of the relation of thematic substance to its setting is especially acute in the early Romantic symphony. In contrast to the tightly controlled symmetry typically exhibited by the Classical symphony (not only within and between individual phrases, but as a whole in which statement and development of material achieve a satisfying balance), the early Romantic symphony placed far greater emphasis on lyrical theme, colourful harmony and a desire to unify the individual movements in a cyclic way. Though frequently retaining the outward forms of individual movements (sonata, scherzo or minuet, ternary, variation or rondo) and their number (four, sometimes with a separate slow introduction), symphonic composers of the generation after Beethoven transformed the internal relations somewhat. Contrast between themes becomes more extreme, serving to dramatise the movement. This is illustrated in the first movements of Schubert's 'Unfinished' and 'Great' C major Symphonies, in both of which the element of transition from one thematic-tonal network to another is almost non-existent (in each case, the transition lasts only a bar or two, the 'second subject' confronting, rather than complementing its predecessor).[24]

A related tendency in symphonists of the post-Beethoven generation is the pursuit of unusual, even remote key-relationships, resulting in a more overtly sectional approach to continuity than had obtained in the work of their Classical predecessors. Whereas the principal focus within the first movement of, say, Beethoven's *Eroica* Symphony is undoubtedly the central development – into which, admittedly, a 'sectional' episode in E minor intrudes – this is less

24 In contrast, the sonata-form first movements of Schubert's earlier symphonies follow the 'Classical' pattern of a relatively extended transition between 'first' and 'second' subjects. That in the fifth, in B flat, incorporates a typically 'Classical' shift to the secondary dominant degree, C, itself prepared by chromatic augmented-sixth harmonies.

true of the symphonic sonata forms of Schubert, Mendelssohn and Schumann. In their work, the thematic processes to be observed in the *Eroica* are replaced by techniques such as sectionalisation (in Schubert's 'Great' C major especially), thematic repetition, transposition or reharmonisation, isolation of a rhythmic feature or an exploitation of orchestral colour contrasts. These strategies were dictated in large part by the fact that the lyrical themes so beloved of the early Romantic generation were less suitable for the kind of fragmentation and synthesis than were Beethoven's more motivically inspired examples. As an illustration of this, we may take the first movement of Mendelssohn's 'Italian' Symphony. Its opening theme plays only a subsidiary role in the development section, which is largely engaged in contrapuntal manipulation of a brand-new theme first sounded at bar 202. The main theme does not appear until bar 245, from which point its leading phrase is announced by the wind in novel harmonic settings. At bar 266 a chromatic variant of this leading phrase is introduced, but is treated to a single sequential repetition before the development reverts once again the new theme (from bar 274). From this point, even the new theme is reprised in whole phrases. The only 'development' as such of the main theme occurs from bars 296–7, where it is resited as a part of a plagal cadential preparation, leading back from v/F sharp minor, to the tonic, A for the curiously understated recapitulation (bar 346). Interestingly, Mendelssohn does develop his opening theme, but within the exposition, not the development section. The forward propulsion of bars 1–51 depends crucially upon Mendelssohn's practice of fragmenting the 'suffix' of the theme (that is, bars 9–10). Adapted to a slightly different rhythm, the descending steps of bars 9–10 account for the following phrase (bars 11–18) through repetition, transposition and extension. From the upbeat to bar 24, Mendelssohn reconfigures the opening portion of his theme, situating it now as the leading element in a dialogue between wind and strings.[25] Largely, though, the narrative flow of this movement hangs on lyricism and on decorous contrast rather than penetrating motivic engagement. While Mendelssohn's technique of handling his material is beyond reproach, one is left with the feeling that content and form achieve a more equitable balance in the remaining movements, in particular the minuet–trio and tarantella finale, in each of which the composer's gift for evoking an atmosphere is allowed to speak for itself, independently of the need to conform to a set of structural expectations. The same might be said of the 'Scottish' Symphony (No. 3 in A minor), memorable for its quicksilver scherzo, rather than for the intensity of its developmental practices.

So, while thematic process is evidently an important feature within

25 Interestingly, a similar process of 'suffix fragmentation' is observable at the analogous point in the main first-movement Allegro of Beethoven's Seventh Symphony, another A major, $\frac{6}{8}$ movement.

Mendelssohn's symphonic language, and one which assisted his aspiration to be placed in a Beethovenian tradition, the more memorable characteristic of that language is its contextual placement of the technical within the gestural. The early Romantic tradition of foregrounding gesture is suggestive too of a redefinition of priorities in musical expression, suggesting a musical realisation of those contemporary philosophical strivings towards subjectivity articulated by the Schlegels, Wackenroder, Tieck and Hoffmann. Here, it is not conventional structures, but a surface allure that lifts out of the frame, speaking directly to the listener. Two illustrations of this tendency will be pursued a little further here: virtuosity and chromaticism.

The early Romantics' grandest forum for the exhibition of virtuosity was the solo concerto (most often for piano or violin, less frequently for cello or for wind instruments such as the clarinet). If one of music's functions in the political turbulence of the 1830s and 1840s was to provide private solace, then another was to fulfil the public, socio-psychological need for 'herocs', both on the operatic stage and on the concert platform. The virtuoso concerto rose superbly to that challenge. In these works the traditional forms (sonata; aria; ternary; variations; rondos) became backcloths against which the soloist could indulge in unabashed showmanship. Here, solo–tutti interaction is profoundly altered compared to the closely integrated, quasi-chamber music textures of Mozart's Viennese concertos, for instance, in which the character and use of material placed soloist and orchestra in an intimate relationship. In the piano concertos of Liszt and Alkan, and in the violin concertos of Paganini, the soloist assumed instead the status of a principal character in a drama – a role sustained by unremitting recourse to virtuosity of sometimes breathtaking proportions. In such virtuoso concertos the soloist is strikingly foregrounded against the orchestra, so much so that, at times (in the two Chopin piano concertos, for instance) the function of the orchestra is reduced to near-passivity.[26] Such a radical generic shift was clearly a response to changing public tastes: within burgeoning early nineteenth-century European concert life, the concerto became more and more a vehicle for the display of showmanship, a 'competition' between rival composer-virtuosi, acted out before an adoring public. During the Classic era, virtuosity had always been aimed at popular, rather than 'academic' taste. It sat uncomfortably with the latter owing to the adoption of naturalness and simplicity of utterance as touchstones of refinement in the aesthetic writings of Batteux and Rousseau (disseminated in Central Europe through the German translations of Hiller, Marpurg and Schultz). It was

---

26 The Irish pianist John Field sometimes performed his concertos in solo recitals, simply omitting the connecting orchestral tissue in which the solo piano was not involved. This was by no means an unusual practice; Chopin played his own concertos as 'solos'.

substantially less problematic for the Romantics, however, whose embrace of the Sublime discriminated positively in favour of the superhuman-seeming exertions of Liszt, Alkan and Paganini. Their Mephistophelian ability to encompass seemingly insurmountable technical feats at phenomenal speed was physically and temporally analogous to the contemplation of some startling natural phenomenon, characterised by the Romantic philosophers as the adoration of the Beyond (Kant's 'mathematical' Sublime).

In the realm of the concerto the intricate network of motivic correspondences that had characterised the later Classical concerto was now replaced by (or overlaid with) a succession of exciting idiomatic gestures grounded in technical difficulty, including extreme register shifts; string crossings; digital dexterity; rapid transitions between contrasting figurations; tonguings; bowing patterns (demanding expert muscular control and therefore uncomfortably beyond the ability of most amateurs); and, in the case of piano concertos, sheer power, augmenting in step with the contributions of piano manufacturers. Through such gestures, the soloist exercised dominance over the accompanying orchestra, and henceforth the actual thematic substance of a concerto existed as a counterpoint to the powerful – and occasionally overriding – element of display.

Weber's concertos prefigure trends that were to become typical of developments in the genre following Beethoven. In his two piano concertos, in C, Op. 11 (1810), and in E flat, Op. 32 (1812), virtuosity takes centre stage. Much of the 'argument' in the outer movements of the C major concerto eschews anything approaching motivic development in favour of extensive scalic and arpeggiaic passages based around simple harmonic progressions (which, denuded of their scintillating surface, would appear quite banal). Weber's impetuous and exciting solo textures are enhanced by occasional colouristic orchestration and, especially in the E flat concerto's Allegro maestoso, by the persistent march idiom. This movement is notable also for its sheer variety of figuration – one of the factors that distinguishes 'concerto' virtuosity from that of, say, the étude (in which typically a single figuration is pursued throughout). The soloist has to manage an impressive array of pianistic devices. In its first entry the piano part exploits extremes of register in rapid arpeggiated contrary-motion patterns; later on come flowing left-hand accompaniments to the major thematic presentations above; extended semiquaver passages in octaves between the hands; rows of double thirds; rapid chromatic scales; double trills; arpeggiated flourishes. In its scale and in its frequently thick-textured patterning, this concerto is a worthy successor to Beethoven's 'Emperor' Concerto on which it is overtly modelled (it even mirrors the overall key-scheme of Beethoven's piece, with a slow movement in B major).

Virtuosity's achievement within the concerto genre was to establish a tradition of embodying changing moods in the play of figurations that flitted across the music's surface.[27] While no overtly narrative 'programme' was normally intended by such a strategy, the careful articulation of virtuoso textures could allude to familiar dance topics such as the polonaise, other national characteristics, or stock operatic gestures, which provided by induction the desired sequence of *Affekts*. Among the most conspicuously successful illustrations of the early Romantic concerto of this type are those for piano by Chopin, Schumann and Mendelssohn, and for violin by Mendelssohn and Schumann. In none of these works does the sophistication of the sparkling figuration obscure the sense of structural clarity within each movement, even when, as in the case of Mendelssohn, considerable liberties are taken with the form, eliminating the customary orchestral exposition before the soloist's entry in the First Piano Concerto, resituating the cadenza in the middle of the first movement of the Violin Concerto or running ostensibly separate movements into each other by means of subtle modulating links – a strategy perhaps derived from Beethoven's 'Emperor' Concerto.

Imposition of overarching continuity in concerto movements is perhaps to be considered as an attempt to raise the 'respectability' of a genre in danger of too much showmanship to the level enjoyed by the symphony. One technique by which this was achieved was monothematicism, such as dominates the first movement of Schumann's A minor Piano Concerto, Op. 54, a work which began life in 1841 as a free-standing fantasy for piano and orchestra, and to which the remaining two movements – connected by a linking passage retrospectively referring to the opening theme of the first movement – were added in 1845. The main theme, first sounded by the winds at bar 4 and immediately answered by the soloist, returns in various guises during the course of the movement and although there is of course contrasting material, this theme dominates much of the exposition, including the second-subject group (in which it is recast as a strident clarinet fanfare accompanied by triplet cascades from the piano). The development section, beginning with a dreamy, nocturne-like reformulation of the main theme, is almost wholly bound-up with further sequential explorations of its potential.

Arguably, the co-ordination of virtuosity and musical coherence is less satisfying in the concertos of Hummel, Field, Weber, Kalkbrenner, Moscheles, Alkan, Liszt and Paganini, in whose work the overwhelming figurative assault

27 An achievement reflected also in the contemporary fashion for single-movement *Konzertstücke* for piano and orchestra, incorporating considerable diversity of emotional effect, tempo and even mensuration – including passionate and lyrical episodes – into an otherwise sonata-based structure. There are well-known examples by Weber (Op. 79), Mendelssohn (Op. 22, Op. 29) and Schumann (Op. 92, Op. 134).

at times threatens coherence. That, though, is the price to be paid for the gain in expressivity offered by such works as Alkan's Piano Concerto, Op. 39, or the two examples by Liszt, which portray a kaleidoscopic range of moods through their dazzling passage-work. This new tradition of composing concertos in order to exploit a superior instrumental technique was one which soon gained detractors in the theoretical establishment. Indeed, the plethora of 'formalist' writings that emerged in the generation after Beethoven's death (for instance, by Czerny and A. B. Marx) might be interpreted in part as an attempt to reclaim the 'moral high ground' for formalism in the face of virtuosity's remarkable success, personified above all by Alkan, Liszt and Paganini.

Rather as in the case of virtuosity, 'traditional' usage of chromaticism had functioned 'ornamentally', in this case as an exotic and temporary departure from a diatonic norm. Overt chromaticism tended to be *sui generis*, as for instance in Mozart's gigue, K.574, or else 'covered' by a peripheral genre such as the capriccio or fantasia; the extraordinary opening of Mozart's C minor Fantasia, K.475, is complemented in the associated sonata, K.457, by a much more diatonic gesture, more suited to that 'mainstream' genre. Such appropriation of chromaticism for rhetorical effect is heightened in works by the early Romantics. Its expressive possibilities were significantly enhanced by Chopin. In the central episode of his E major Etude, Op. 10, No. 3 is a highly charged chromatic outburst, founded on rapidly shifting diminished-seventh chords, that supplants the gently diatonic profile so strongly as to acquire the status of an opposing pole of attraction (itself subsumed in the reprise, which takes on an almost redemptive quality as a result). In this instance, chromaticism is rather more than 'local colour'; it becomes instead an essential determinant of the étude's structure. Other works by Chopin in which chromatic writing is raised to the level of structural function are not difficult to find (the F minor Fantaisie, Op. 49, and the Polonaise-fantaisie, Op. 61, are prominent examples, along with the C minor Polonaise, Op. 40, No. 2, in which the A flat section explores several remote regions by means of enharmonic shifts). 'Structural' chromaticism is a feature of Schumann's work also, in the finale of the Sonata, Op. 14, or the first-movement development of the A major String Quartet, Op. 41, No. 3, for instance. Typically, though, chromaticism in Schumann is employed for the purpose of subtle 'local' expressivity, as an enhancement of an otherwise diatonic harmonic environment. Examples include the *Toccata*, Op. 7, the first number of *Kinderscenen*, Op. 15, the 'Intermezzo' from *Faschingsschwank aus Wien*, Op. 26, No. 4, and the F sharp *Romanze*, Op. 28, No. 2, where chromaticism highlights the shift to a contrapuntal texture in its closing paragraph. None of these works represents a radical departure from convention. While they offer new expressive possibilities through chromaticism, they do not challenge the supremacy of the diatonically dependent forms and formulae of the preceding generations.

Liszt, on the other hand, does. One thinks immediately of his 'Faust' Symphony, whose opening theme outlines successive augmented triads, opening up a harmonic world in which the traditional (and comforting) pull of the tonic triad loses much of its authority. Liszt's piano music is also memorable for its chromatic harmony, not only in masterpieces such as the Sonata in B minor, 'Valée d'Obermann', or the 'Dante' Sonata, but equally in an underrated work such as 'Funérailles', from the *Harmonies poétiques et réligieuses*. Here, chromaticism is an indispensable element. Much of its mock-sepulchral *Affekt* derives from contrapuntally conceived rhetorical gestures, such as the searching, restless fragments of the *introduzione*, the low-lying *pesante* theme at bars 23ff. and its continuation, in which the chromatic pull becomes ever stronger until from bar 52 the distinction between triadic and 'non-harmonic' tones (passing-notes, suspensions, appoggiaturas) virtually dissolves. At bar 56 ('lagrimoso') Liszt reverts to a characteristic mode of utterance that epitomises his harmonic style: a delicate melody suffused with expressive patterns such as the opening $c^1-f^1-f\flat^1-e\flat^1$ is supported harmonically by chromatic chords whose resolutions are subtly 'out of phase' with the pulse (bars 71ff. provide an especially fine illustration of this practice).[28] In this piece diatonic harmony is the 'alternative' region to a chromatic norm – a distinctly modern approach to tonal structure, and one possibly intended to convey in a programmatic way the 'liberation' of the soul from the material body. Its only extended diatonic passage is that framed by the left-hand triplets (bars 109–55), traversing D flat, A, F and D majors, during the course of which, the supporting triplets shift from diatonic to chromatic patterns.

The duality suggested by Liszt's opposition of diatonic and chromatic realms was prefigured in the opposition of major and minor modes so frequently encountered in Schubert (for instance, at the beginning and first-subject recapitulation in the first movement of the G major String Quartet, D.887). Although it points the way to new realms of feeling (discussed presently), this colouristic 'fingerprint' is nevertheless situated firmly within a feeling for the past. Schubert's instrumental music – whether for chamber forces, piano solo or orchestra – demonstrates a thorough assimilation of the high Classical style, most especially as encountered in the work of Mozart. Sometimes this influence reveals itself mainly in thematic terms, as in the Menuetto of the 1815 String Quartet in G minor, D.173, or else structurally, as

28 In fact, Liszt does not wholly cut his ties to the past here. The chromatic melody at bar 56 of 'Funérailles' still relies on periodicity as a means of continuity (the 'lagrimoso' opening gesture is immediately repeated in a slightly varied phrase of the same, two-bar, length, for instance).

in the sonata allegros of the early series of quartets (D.18, 32, 36, 46, 68, 74, 87, 94, 112 and 353). While the earliest quartets (1811–13) display a more than occasional monothematic tendency, D.112 and 353 explore a broader panorama. Common to all these works (to which may be added the three 'sonatinas' – Diabelli's title: they are properly sonatas – for violin and piano, D.384, 385 and 408 (1816) and the string trios, D.471 and 581 of 1816–17) is a carefully crafted balance of form and content in which the individual ideas and textures have but limited pretensions. This accommodation of Schubert's lyrical gift to the comparatively 'literal', *Gebrauchmusik* kind of Classicism – in which the significance of a movement is contained wholly within the materialist-formalist domain, unconcerned with the revelation of any deeper 'spiritual' (or even extra-musical) quality – is one from which his later works (the 'Death and the Maiden' Quartet, D.810 (1824), or the B flat Piano Sonata, D.960 (1828), for instance) were to depart radically.

This is apparent not only in the extra-musical associations of D.810's slow movement (quoting Schubert's 'Der Tod und das Mädchen', and thereby departing the realm of 'pure' chamber music for the grim poetic connotations of the earlier song-setting). The dramatic power of this quartet's opening Allegro breaches that barrier too. It acquires a voice whose expressive power is arguably rivalled only by the late quartets of Beethoven in the chamber music literature of this time. Its *raison d'être* depends at least as much upon the portrayal of contrast, principally between passages of explosive rhythmic agitation counterpointed against moments of uneasy calm as upon any conventional, even doctrinal claims of the sonata form in which it is actually cast. The separation of two 'worlds' of expression in this movement is a recurring feature of Schubert's later instrumental work. It appears too in the first movement of the B flat Sonata, D.960 – a far more introverted piece than 'Death and the Maiden' and yet no less dramatic in its way. Within the development section (again, the movement is in sonata form, but such conventions contribute little to the effect here) Schubert introduces a bleak new theme (bars 180ff.[29]) in D minor, which in its wide interval spread, accompaniment pattern and remote key seems to represent an opposite pole of expression, confronting the warmth of the opening theme. Yet, soon after establishing this environment Schubert amazingly announces within it the familiar main theme (as a 'false recapitulation'), adapted to its harmonic contours and luminous high register. It is a moment of particular intensity in the unfolding of the structure (notice how it is not timed to coincide with the recapitulation itself). It is as if by delicate shuffling of a kaleidoscope, our constructed definitions of the 'remote' and the 'familiar' are

29 That is, counting all of Schubert's first-time bar at the end of the exposition as bar 125a, and the second-time bar as 125b.

shown to be not substantive inherent qualities but simply different ways of viewing. After this, there could be no return for Schubert to the (retrospectively imagined) 'conventional sonata form' of the textbooks. Instead, the sonata (whether for solo piano or string quartet) had become a means to attaining an expressive purpose: a purpose perhaps extra-musical in its claims, perhaps, for the composer, an interior journey.

Such self-absorption, while emblematic in one respect of a powerful *topos* in Romanticism, is, at one and the same time, symptomatic of a growing self-confidence in the linguistic and expressive self-sufficiency of one's musical art. It is especially noticeable in Schubert's piano and chamber music in which self-quotation features prominently. Examples include the 'Wanderer' Fantasy, D.760 (1822), whose Adagio variations are based on the song, 'Der Wanderer', D.489, of October 1816; the 'Trout' Quintet, D.667 (1819), whose variations are based on the 1817 song, 'Die Forelle', D.550; the A minor String Quartet, D.804, whose Menuetto refers to the Schiller setting, 'Schöne Welt, wo bist du?' D.677 of 1819 (its slow movement is likewise based on a self-quotation, from the famous *Rosamunde entr'acte* music of 1823); and the D minor Quartet ('Der Tod und das Mädchen'), D.810, whose slow movement is a set of variations on the song, D.531 of 1817. These and other networks of correpondance within Schubert's instrumental works are an important dimension of their identity and meaning, a so-called 'intertextual' dimension that has been much investigated in recent literary criticism. By intertextuality is meant ways in which particular musical compositions (or, indeed genres in general) may be regarded as 'texts' that derive their meaning not solely from principles of internal organisation but by association with other 'texts' to which they – consciously or otherwise – refer.

Intertextuality is, of course, about more than just direct quotation. It addresses a variety of compositional strategies, giving a particular work a level of meaning in relation to other works, and transcending, therefore, the 'formalist' agenda that has characterised successive generations of musicological writing since at least the time of Fétis. One such strategy is apparent in Schubert's A minor String Quartet, D.804, which marks an important advance in his instrumental style. Its two-bar introduction, *pianissimo*, featuring a memorable dotted-minim-four-semiquaver pattern at the bottom of the texture, is a technique borrowed directly from the lied repertory, creating an immediate association with Schubert's creative mood-setting accompaniments. A very similar case is the slow movement of the E flat Piano Trio, D.929, which also begins with a two-bar lied-like accompanimental introduction (this time featuring a plagal chord-progression and repetitive dotted rhythm) and prefiguring a tragic (or mock-tragic) mood reminiscent of songs such as 'Gute Nacht' and 'Der Wegweiser' from *Winterreise* before the entry of the cello's plaintive melody. Towards the end of that melody there occurs a repeated octave descent creating a hiatus not predicated upon any of the preceding material. While it is perfectly possible to regard this, from a formalist standpoint, as a tonally determined postponement of the forthcoming tonic cadence by the dominant pitch, an intertextual interpretation highlights the generic cross-referencing to the lieder repertory, hypothesising a device borrowed from song-writing to emphasise a particular poetic image in the text (or else to portray an echo). The threefold reappearance of this melody in the middle of the rondo finale of the E flat Trio (the second time in counterpoint to the material of an earlier episode) suggests that generic cross-referencing is not restricted to slow movements and is, indeed, a possible way of creating affinities of topic between movements of instrumental works. The positioning of the final quotation of the slow movement theme as a peroration to the whole work points to a tension between the demands of 'metaphorical' expressive values (hinting that the essence of the Trio is that which stands outside the notated text) and the Classical dictates of tonal completion inherited from eighteenth-century theories of form. Viewed within the early Romantic 'tradition' as a whole, this represents at best a temporary accommodation of the poetic and the Classic-formalist agendas that perhaps helps to define one element of Schubert's transitional status. In such movements Schubert seems to be reaching out towards an expression of something beyond the notes themselves, perhaps suggestive of that quality encoded by contemporary philosophers of the early Romantic age such as Hegel and literary figures such as E. T. A. Hoffmann as *Geist* (Spirit). Schubert's later chamber music points to a genre whose meaning lies in an allusive play of images lying outside the purely musical structure, escaping – despite the survival of Classical formal procedures – from the relatively 'literal' mode of speech found in his early string quartets. In one sense, the opening of, for instance, the A minor quartet is a *Lied ohne Worte*, in which Schubert finds his mature voice.

Intertextuality also embraces formal protocol in Schubert's later chamber music. The first-movement development sections of the E flat Piano Trio, D.929 and the String Quintet in C, D.956, share very similar episodic structures, characterised by the refrain-like recurrence of overtly thematic passages taken from the closing part of their respective expositions. Each refrain serves to segment a substantial area of musical space and to mark out a protracted tonal course leading eventually back to the tonic. The resulting opposition of relatively uniform and balanced paragraphs is suggestive of a succession of mood-pictures – a strategy perhaps derived from a combination of strophic and through-composed lieder plans. In this respect, Schubert's policy is rather

different from such 'integrated' motivically inspired processes of fragmentation and transformation that were among Beethoven's normal developmental
credentials.

And yet Beethoven steadily became central to Schubert's instrumental art.
In 1818 he dedicated the eight variations on 'Reposez-vous, bon chevalier',
D.624, fulsomely to Beethoven ('by his admirer and worshipper, Franz
Schubert'). The Octet, D.803 (1824), was a deliberate response to Beethoven's
Septet, Op. 20, closely resembling Beethoven's piece in its divertimento idiom,
form and instrumentation (Schubert adds a second violin, otherwise the
ensemble is identical). The trio of the fifth movement contains a strong thematic reminiscence of the opening of Beethoven's *ländler*-like menuetto (even
the texture is similar) and this movement, indeed the Octet as a whole, makes
sense not simply in its own terms, but especially in relation to Beethoven's
model – which, indeed, provides an essential framework of meaning for
Schubert's piece.[30] Such cross-referencing between different works is also a
species of intertextuality (which posits that works gain identity in relation to
other works), but in the case of the Octet the intertextuality operates at more
than one level, for the theme of the variation movement is another vocal self-
quotation from the love duet 'Gelagert unter'm hellen Dach der Bäume' from
Schubert's early opera, *Die Freunde von Salamanka* (1815).

For the generation after Beethoven, the challenge of his music loomed especially large. The prevailing critical attitude to his legacy was one of profound
reverence, primarily for his instrumental music whose meaning and significance rested upon purely constructional foundations, independent of a text.
Enshrined in the theory of Czerny and Marx among others, and in E. T. A.
Hoffmann's influential essay, 'Beethoven's Instrumental Music' (mentioned
above), attempts to rationalise Beethoven's greatness – as revealed above all in
series of sonatas, string quartets and symphonies – focused on the inherently
'organic' qualities of his music. Above all, such theoretical responses to
Beethoven claimed to systematise interrelationships of form and content
according to an organic model and grew, in part, out of recent philosophical
currents (discussed in detail in chapter 5). In Marx's case, those theoretical pre-
sumptions stemmed from his respect for the Hegelian notion of 'progress' in
the arts, in which the production of artworks represented a striving towards
the attainment of the *Geist* ('World Spirit'): not only insofar as musical language evolved towards new states (for example, the emancipation of purely
instrumental music as a mode of expression), but in terms too of the internal

---

30 The trio theme, for instance, may be read as a 'challenge' to Beethoven's, retaining the dotted anacrusis pattern and falling step, but highlighting other intervallic and rhythmic features in the continuation: the
'influence' here is as much about denial as acceptance of the model's parameters.

workings of that language. For Marx, the representation of those workings in theory rested upon the identification of motifs (*Ideen, Sätze*) and developmental procedures for giving these outward form. According to this theoretical standpoint, a musical idea had value not simply *in itself* but in its *potential to become*. Musical continuity acquired value not for its surface variety but for its latent and enabling unity. Motifs were reconfigured theoretically as building-blocks and the individual piece or movement became the means through which the *idea* symbolised by its musical motifs was revealed; at one and the same time, the composer revealed himself through the individual artwork which served as a vehicle for his self-expression. (The analogy with Hegel's notion of the revelation of the *Geist* is obvious here.)

Marx's *Die Lehre von der musikalische Komposition* is at one and the same time a justification of Beethoven's music and of organicism as critical tool. For Marx and his generation, Beethoven's achievement is revealed to be great insofar as its constructive principles rest upon the working-out of the potential of motifs. Sometimes this process of *Ausarbeitung* was difficult. Beethoven's sketches demonstrated that, at times, the refinement of ideas as well as their subsequent elaboration was a struggle. This, however, was part of the attraction for the emerging historical consciousness of the early Romantic generation. Beethoven's struggle with his intractable material was evidence that greatness in artistic production was not lightly achieved. To fashion a musical structure which grew from its material in an organic way – each musical 'cell' or 'germ' giving rise through purely constructive manipulations such as repetition, sequence, inversion, adaptation to new environments (principally contrapuntal ones) – this was Beethoven's great contribution, and it was the dream of his successors (as they imagined themselves) to emulate it.

Where tonal function had once exercised unchallenged dominance, thematic organisation now staked a powerful claim to the long-range control of musical structure. Attempts to extend its influence beyond the limits of a single movement are significant within the chamber music of Mendelssohn and Schumann which increasingly demonstrates 'cyclic' principles of organisation possibly suggested by the late quartets of Beethoven (especially the C sharp minor, Op. 131 whose 'sectional', rather than 'movement', layout is reinforced by subtle motivic interconnections – principally the transformation in the final section of the opening fugue subject). Resonances of Beethoven's later quartets are encountered in the early string quartets of Mendelssohn, in E flat, Op. 12 (1829), and A minor, Op. 13 (1827), in both of which the separate movements are related by subtle thematic interconnections. Op. 12's slow introduction borrows thematically from the opening of Beethoven's 'Harp' Quartet, Op. 74, and, subsequently, in the main theme of the Allegro non tardante, from the first movement of Beethoven's Op. 127. But the debt to Beethoven does not stop with mere quotation. In every respect, the bar-to-bar manipulation of material is Classical in its procedures. Both main themes are extended beyond their initial statement by varied repetition of the whole (the latter by injection of contrapuntal dialogue) before continuing with sequential treatment of just a portion; the transition between the two prepares for the dominant key by chromatically enhanced modulation to the sharp side (in this case, as far as v/G minor); the exposition offers repeated distinctive cadential gestures before closing, as expected, in the new key of B flat (in this case, reprising the main theme). Formally, however, the movement is a hybrid, combining sonata procedures with a semblance of rondo. Immediately after the close in the dominant (separated from what follows by a double-bar *without* the repeat-marks), Mendelssohn returns to the main theme in the tonic, diverting cadentially to v/F minor, at which point he introduces a new theme, 'episodic' in function, but whose treatment is entirely in keeping with a Classical 'development' section. Thereafter, the secondary and main themes are reprised (again within the context of development), straightforward restatement in the tonic being withheld until bar 177, after which, for all that the secondary theme is brought back within the tonic frame expected of Classical sonata practice, the 'new' theme once again intrudes as an episode in v/F minor (bar 245), a strategy that configures the subsequent reappearance of the main theme at bar 259 within a rondo context. Such creative reinterpretation of movement-structure suggests the Beethoven of the late quartets, to which the subsequent movements also pay homage (the second movement offers a 'Canzonetta' in place of a scherzo; the Andante espressivo attempts the 'Ausdruckvoll' idiom; while the finale is segmented into paragraphs of contrasting tempos (into which the 'Op. 127' theme and the episodic theme from the first movement are sprinkled towards the end). Other chamber works which rely to some extent on this 'cyclic' procedure include Schubert's E flat Piano Trio, D.929, whose finale incorporates a reference to the slow movement's main theme; Mendelssohn's Octet, Op. 20 (in which the finale and scherzo are interrelated), and his Piano Sonata, Op. 106; Schumann's Piano Quintet, Op. 44, which combines the main finale theme with that of the first movement towards the end as an impressive peroration to the work as a whole; and most impressively, his Fourth Symphony, Op. 120 in D minor (1841; revised 1851).

While the D minor represents the summit of Schumann's cyclic achievement in the symphonic genre, he had previously attempted to relate different symphonic movements by relatively loose thematic associations. Thus in the First ('Spring') Symphony in B flat, Op. 38, the brass theme of the slow introduction is an obvious forebear of the succeeding Allegro's main theme.

Thematic correspondences are also found between the slow movement and scherzo (played without a break). Similar procedures are encountered in the C major Symphony, Op. 61, in which, once again, a prominent brass entry in the slow introduction is taken up later, serving as the basis for much of the main Allegro's material and recurring in the finale (which also harks back to a theme in the slow movement). But it is in the Fourth Symphony that Schumann truly attempts to integrate an entire symphony by thematic cross-reference, so that structural repetitions and transformations of motifs extend beyond the confines of a single movement to provide an overarching unity. Its slow introduction sows the seeds of the Lebhaft's two main themes (in reverse order, that of the opening (A) relating to bars 147ff.; that at bar 22 (B) to the main theme), while the prominent dotted figure from bars 121ff. anticipates the main theme of the finale (C). Further reminiscences of the introduction break into the Romanze from bar 12, presenting theme A in a variety of guises, including an ornamented violin solo. In the scherzo and trio further references to A are offered: the opening crotchet figure perhaps derived by inversion; the lilting trio's quavers harking back to the Romanze's solo violin triplet variant. The slow introduction to the finale begins by counterpointing B with the dotted figure, C introduced in the first-movement development; the ensuing Lebhaft combining these two themes at first, though theme C soon dominates (especially in the development). As a sustained piece of musical argumentation this work is remarkably successful, the more so, perhaps, in view of its unusual approach to structure in the outer movements. Both begin as if they were sonata forms (the 'exposition' is, in each case, marked for a repeat), but in neither case is there a true 'recapitulation'. In the first movement, there is no attempt to bring back the main theme (B) in the conventional way. Perhaps Schumann felt that a thematic recapitulation would prove ineffective in a movement so saturated by this theme, and so conceived instead of the novel idea of replacing the conventional 'Classical' manner of resolving tonal tensions at this point in a sonata form with the introduction of a new theme (bar 147), exploding the hitherto 'monothematic' mode. In the finale, neither B nor C are reprised, the recapitulation beginning from the second subject (bar 129), now over a dominant pedal.

Similar integrative techniques are evident in the work of the Swedish composer, Franz Berwald (1796–1868), whose four symphonies, dating from the 1840s, interlock different movements in interesting and original ways. In the *Sérieuse* in G minor (1842) the third-placed scherzo is followed by an extended reprise of material from the slow movement; more radical is the *Singulière* (1845), in which the scherzo is wholly embedded within the slow movement. While the unusual external designs are an important signal of originality, they should not blind us to other attractions of Berwald's symphonic output. He was as capable as any of his Central European contemporaries of monothematic control over large-scale dimensions, as demonstrated by the opening movement of the *Capricieuse* (1842), while the impressive opening paragraph of the *Singulière* is suggestive of 'organic' growth, not purely for its intervallic and rhythmic constancy, but equally for its purposeful harmonic evolution.

Such works pose important questions regarding generic identity. The 'Classic' symphony had consisted of, usually, four movements, each of which was a self-contained whole, pursuing its own argument separately from the others. Overarching thematic unity was a secondary concern (indeed, a novelty in Beethoven's Fifth and Ninth symphonies). By enmeshing the entire multi-movement structure, the composer fractured its traditionally enclosing boundaries; so revolutionary was the concept of integration that Schumann originally (1841) entitled the D minor Symphony a 'symphonic fantasy'.

Organic integration in the symphonic sphere was paralleled in the realm of the solo sonata. To a great extent, the history of genre in early nineteenth-century instrumental music is bound up with the survival of the sonata. Beethoven's late piano sonatas had departed, sometimes radically, from Classical conceptions of sonata and sonata form. Traditionally, the 'weight' of a sonata had resided in the first Allegro. Beethoven's work redefined this priority to varying extents. In one model, the relative significance of each movement is revised. The A major Sonata, Op. 101, begins with a gently ambling movement that is immediately overshadowed by the ensuing march (possibly a model for the march section in the second movement of Schumann's *Fantasie*, Op. 17 – see below), while the plaintive 'Adagio, ma non troppo, con affetto' gives way without a break into the fugal finale. In the E major Sonata, Op. 109, sonata form becomes insufficient to bear the expressive load of a genre so fundamentally transformed. Here we are confronted by two sonata-form movements of radically opposing character (the first alternating tenderness and passion, the second exuding desperation) which ultimately negate each other and require a different kind of continuation, provided by the serene variations that become the heart of the work. (More economical, perhaps, in this reinvention of the sonata genre, is the C minor, Op. 111, in which an uneasy balance is struck between sonata form and variations in just two movements.) A second model is the dissolution of boundaries between movements formerly provided by tonal closure so that the whole sonata becomes a series of sections. To some extent this is already true of the relatively compact Op. 101 and it is true in a different way in Op. 110 in which the declamatory slow movement leads into and is then reprised within the fugal finale.

Beethoven's late sonatas raise serious issues regarding generic identity.

Separate movements are at times replaced by interlocked and interrelated sections in the manner of a fantasia, a procedure which has resonances, for instance, in 'cyclic' works such as Schubert's 'Wanderer' Fantasy, D.760, Schumann's *Fantasie*, Op. 17, and Liszt's Sonata in B minor. Schubert's 'Wanderer' Fantasy is, in effect, a four-section sonata-form movement in which the first Allegro section is the 'exposition'; section two – the slow movement – is an episodic 'development' in C sharp minor/E major (quoting Schubert's 1816 song, 'Der Wanderer', on which a set of variations is built); section three – the scherzo and trio – marks the 'recapitulation' (though in A flat, not C); and the fugato finale is a culminating 'coda', ultimately reinforcing the true tonic, C. Deliberate cross-references between different sections help to cement this huge work. For instance, the fugato theme is clearly derived from the opening of the work (whose rhythm is just as clearly indebted to the original song); the scherzo adapts this same theme to triple-time, while the trio takes up the Allegro's lilting 'second subject'. Schubert's piece was to cast a powerful shadow on the emerging Romantic tradition; its generic impact continues, in a broader sense, the intertextuality that inhabits his own chamber music and which was discussed previously.

Schumann's *Fantasie*, Op. 17, takes up the concept of thematic transformation inherent in Schubert's piece, though not in an obviously audible way. While its three movements are thematically cross-referential, the 'motto' theme of the work, to which Schumann refers in a letter to Clara Wieck of 9 June 1839, is ambiguous. While the first movement of Schumann's *Fantasie* is motivically rather closely-knit, its content is not generated in a chronological sequence from specific material sounded at the beginning. If anything is the 'motto' it is surely the concluding allusion to Beethoven's *An die ferne Geliebte* at bars 295ff. (an allusion perhaps intended to symbolise Schumann's enforced estrangement from Clara during 1836 and 1837, when this movement was composed). Intervallically, this motif draws together the various threads explored earlier in the movement (it is also the first strong appearance of the tonic, C major), and the movement as a whole may be interpreted as a structure whose progress emanates not so much from *Ausführung* as *Entdeckung*, the hidden source to which previous themes relate (for instance, at bars 14, 28, 41, 45, 49, 156) emerging in full focus only at the end of the movement. If so, this suggests a 'private' world of expression, the labyrinth of motivic interweavings representing Schumann's striving towards that thematic source.

The internal workings of its first movement have often been understood in terms of sonata form.[31] At first sight, this seems reasonable, since there is an element of large-scale reprise (bars 225–309 relate closely to bars 29–102). Yet

---

31 For an extended discussion, see N. Marston, *Schumann: Fantasie, op. 17* (Cambridge, 1992), chapter 4.

it is inherently problematic. There is no reprise of the opening; indeed, the 'first subject' is itself hardly apparent at the beginning – along with the 'true' tonic, C major, it only emerges strongly towards the end; the 'second subject' (bar 41) is in the 'wrong key' of D minor; the reprise omits some bars of the exposition and transposes others down by a tone (subverting the dominant–tonic polarity normal in sonata form); the development section is difficult to locate, and unless it is to be regarded as an unusually brief episode (bars 82–97) it must incorporate the C minor episode marked 'Im Legendenton', parts of which make a reappearance towards the end of the movement (again, a strange practice in sonata form); alternatively, 'Im Legendenton' might be an episode within the recapitulation (but that would also be an unusual practice); and so on. The casting of this movement in sonata form actually problematises far more than it resolves, and the movement is perhaps best understood not within the sonata 'mould', but rather *against* it, as a large-scale structure that does not depend on the tonal drama established by the powerful sonata 'tradition', but constructs an alternative 'narrative' mode in which three large sections (bars 1–128, 129–224, 225–309) each make their individual contributions (and are themselves identifiable as multi-sectioned), the overarching 'whole' – if such a reference point be required – being underscored by latent thematic cross-currents pointing towards an ultimate melodic and harmonic resolution in the quotation from *An die ferne Geliebte* entering at bar 295.

Liszt's Sonata in B minor (1853) likewise betrays the influence of Schubert's 'Wanderer' Fantasy (which Liszt arranged for piano and orchestra), but more overtly. It conflates 'sonata genre' and 'sonata form' in a single movement which operates structurally in terms of 'exposition', 'development' and 'recapitulation', simultaneously embracing the changing tempos and expressive characteristics of 'first allegro', 'slow movement', 'scherzo' and 'finale'. Its coherence also rests strongly upon the subsequent transformation of material sounded at the outset. One example of this is the extended fugato at bars 460–508, transforming and developing material originally sounded at bars 8–17; another is the lyrical reformulation at bars 153–62 of what originally appears as a 'sinister' motto, sometimes associated programmatically with Mephistopheles (bars 14ff.).[32] Various conflicting attempts have been made to describe the fusion of form and genre, none of them wholly convincing.[33]

32 K. Hamilton, *Liszt: Sonata in B Minor* (Cambridge, 1996), p. 29.

33 W. S. Newman, *The Sonata Since Beethoven* (New York, 1972), p. 373; R. M. Longyear, 'Liszt's B minor Sonata: Precedents for a Structural Analysis', *The Music Review*, 34 (1973), pp. 198–209; S. Winklhofer, *Liszt's Sonata in B Minor: A Study of Autograph Scores and Documents* (Ann Arbor, 1980), p. 115. Unlike Newman and Longyear, Winklhofer regards the whole piece as being a single sonata-form movement rather than a conflation of different movements. A detailed review of the several analytic positions is attempted in Hamilton, *Liszt: Sonata*.

Newman regards the 'exposition' of Liszt's sonata as outlining an abridged sonata-form 'movement' (sonata form without development) covering bars 1–330; the 'development' is then in two parts, a 'slow movement' (bars 331–459) and 'scherzo' (bars 460–525); the 'recapitulation' and 'coda' (bars 525–681, 682–760) equate to the 'finale' in Newman's scheme. By contrast, Longyear sees only three, not four, 'movements'. The 'exposition' (incorporating also an 'introduction' of seven bars) lasts only up to bar 178. The ensuing 'development' extends to bar 459 and comprises the rest of the 'first movement' (to bar 330) and the 'slow movement' (bars 331–459). Longyear's 'recapitulation' lasts from bar 460 to bar 649 and the 'coda' from bar 650 to bar 760; together, these form the 'finale'.

As with Schumann's *Fantasie*, the sonata-form model is not unproblematic. For instance, Longyear equates the 'recapitulation' with the beginning of Liszt's extended fugato (bars 460–508), and while this is undoubtedly an important juncture in the unfolding texture of the work, bars 533–53 subsequently offer an exact reprise of a substantial part of the 'exposition' (bars 32–52) – a seemingly obvious aural clue that is surely more than a 'false reprise'? In Newman's interpretation, the fugato is the lion's share of the 'scherzo' (the second part of his 'development'). Functionally and tonally, the fugato seems to belong to a 'development section' (it contrapuntally 'develops' two themes originally sounded at bars 8–17), and in this respect Newman's reading seems the clearer of the two (though neither is wholly 'true'). While obviously conceived against the backdrop of the Classical sonata as filtered by Schubert's 'Wanderer', Liszt's own Sonata applies it ambiguously, revealing its presence more as fleeting shadow than focused image.

The enduring power of sonata structure for the early Romantics is apparent also in a work such as Liszt's F minor 'Transcendental' study which progressed through three stages of evolution. Liszt's first version originated in 1826 as the *Etude en douze exercises*; in 1837 it was reworked in *Douze grandes études*; finally, it reached its 'definitive' form (if such a state can be imagined for Liszt's 'extempore' virtuoso manner, replete as it often is with revisions, *ossias*, cuts and so forth) in 1851 with the *Douze études d'exécution transcendante* (for ten of which programmatic titles were invented). Though not perhaps the most spectacular study from the virtuoso standpoint, the F minor nevertheless encompasses a range of effects (including rapid 'cross-handed' chords; 'mordent' patterns spread across several octaves; arpeggiated 'cushions' of sound supporting expansive themes; dramatic shifts of register) that requires an expert control of figurative neatness and physical stamina that few besides Liszt himself could accomplish at first. (As always in these pieces, it is not the technical difficulty of the individual elements that is so formidable, but their particular juxtapositions.) Altogether, it makes an exciting effect. But this piece is far more than a mere vehicle for finger-crunching. The 1837 revision of the *Etude en douze exercises* attempted to raise their level of respectability somewhat by recasting some of them in sonata form, a strategy that is far from beneficial due to an over-reliance on literal schemes of tonal recapitulation. The version of 1851 weakens this reliance, in the process creating music of irresistible affective drive supported, rather than impeded, by an imaginative form suggested by the material itself.

The F minor study retains a vestige of sonata form in at least two respects. First, its material is apportioned between two main areas: a 'first-subject group', consisting of two main elements (bar 3, bar 13) and a contrasting 'second subject' of more lyrical character (bar 54). Secondly, it contains clear recapitulation of earlier material towards the end. The key structures of conventional sonata form are not present, however. The 'first-subject' material is fragmentary in nature, its scalic motion seasoned by prominent chromatic semitones. The 'second subject' is approached via a chromatic transition rich in ambiguous diminished-seventh chords, and when it arrives (postponed by a restatement of bar 13's pattern at bar 42) it is in E flat minor (rather than the expected relative major, A flat). Its continuation refers freely to the material of bar 3 before a full recapitulation of the 'first subject' at bar 90. Within the recapitulation are two important departures from conventional practice. Thematically, the succession of 'first-subject' figures is dramatically interrupted by the return of the 'second subject' at bar 100 (an interruption resolved only at bar 136 with the continuation of 'first-subject' material). Related to the thematic departure is a tonal one, for the 'second subject' occurs not in the tonic minor but initially in the raised mediant minor (A minor) and thereafter in D flat major, so that the eventual arrival of the tonic key simultaneously with the postponed 'first-subject' idea is all the more convincing a dénouement.[34]

In addition to such large-scale pieces as those just discussed, the early Romantics cultivated a variety of less ambitious genres, historically associated with the salon, rather than the concert hall. In the realm of solo piano music, for instance, this period saw the rise of such titles as the impromptu, ballade, scherzo, barcarolle, romanze, novellette, étude and berceuse, along with a range of imported dance topics such as the waltz, mazurka and polonaise. Dance pieces occur widely within this repertory, both as single pieces and as part of longer sets of character pieces, sometimes, as in Schumann's *Carnaval*,

---

34 Excessive tonic perorations were arguably a problematic feature of the 1837 versions of these studies, as also of other large-scale works, such as the 1850 revision of 'Valée d'Obermann' whose sonata structure as it appears in the *Années de pèlerinage* removes the first-subject recapitulation altogether, allowing the tonic major reprise of the secondary theme group to crown the work more economically.

with overt programmatic intent. On one level, these genres simply replaced such free-standing Classical genres as the fantasia, variation-set and capriccio. However, they also usurped to a considerable degree the central place within the solo repertory formerly occupied in the output of Haydn, Mozart and Beethoven by the sonata. (Although both Chopin and Schumann wrote piano sonatas these are hardly so central to their output for that instrument.) In the case of Chopin, one thinks primarily of concert-pieces such as the ballades, polonaises and scherzos, while in the case of Schumann the most representative solo pieces are extended sets such as *Davidsbündlertänze* or *Carnaval*.

While each of these new genres brought along its individual characteristics (obviously rhythmic in the case of the polonaise and mazurka; less easily defined in the case of almost all the others listed above) these too continued to operate within a (greatly expanded) tonal dialectic inherited from the Classical era. This tonal dialectic remained strongly bound to the sonata principle, even within works such as the Chopin ballades whose structures can most usefully be understood against a residual feeling for sonata form, in which two principal thematic groups and key-areas are first opposed and then synthesised in a dramatic peroration. Chopin's procedures in each of the ballades transform the sonata functions in interesting new ways. As Jim Samson has remarked,[35] the traditional expectations of the sonata form are subverted by Chopin, so that, for instance, in the Third Ballade the opening theme affirms the tonic, not the dominant, at its close; the second theme stresses the submediant; the central section (analogous to a sonata 'development') is tonally stable, not restless; the true 'development' occurs during the reprise; and the ballade ends not with a dramatic reconciliation of the two principal themes, but with a reprise of yet a third one. Tonally, too, the ballades operate against a network of expectations inherited from the Classical era – principally the polarity of two keys: tonic and dominant – but creating their own generic space by virtue of deviations from that norm. In Chopin's G minor Ballade, Op. 23, for instance, the two-key polarity remains: its principal keys are G minor and E flat major (not the expected relative major, B flat). There is also an extensive reprise, in which, however, the original order of themes is reversed, along with the tonal sequence in 'mirror' fashion, so that at bar 166 the second theme recurs in E flat, followed at bar 194 by the first theme in the tonic, G minor (though this key emerges firmly only in the subsequent coda (bars 208ff.) which also harks back to the Neapolitan harmonies of the introduction. A different course is followed in the second ballade, Op. 38, in which a sonata-inspired two-key scheme controls alternate sections. Once again, these are not tonic and domi-

35 J. Samson, *Chopin: The Four Ballades* (Cambridge, 1992), pp. 76–81.

nant, but third-related, F major and A minor. In this case the work culminates not in the original tonic, but in the opposing key, A minor (in which the first theme is briefly reprised). More generally, 'Each ballade transforms the sonata-form archetype in such a way that the resolution of tonal tension is delayed until the latest possible moment, usually after the thematic reprise . . . The bravura closing sections function then as a catharsis, releasing in a torrent of virtuosity all the tension which has been steadily mounting through the piece.'[36] Within such an interpretative strategy virtuosity has, in part, taken the place of tonality in achieving the dramatic dénouement. It is a strategy suggestive of a 'narrative' quality within the music. For example, towards the close of the G minor Ballade, the reprise of the second theme is radically altered from a calm to an impassioned statement, while that of the first theme is destabilised. In such an environment, texture functions importantly as a structural sign.

Common to all these key piano works is a sense of generic fusion between sonata and fantasia, underlying which is a new conception of the relationship of thematic succession and tonal closure in pieces of relatively large scale. In a general sense, this underpins the approach to form in much of the music discussed in this chapter. While sectionalisation could be perceived as structural weakness (by adherents of the theories of Reicha, Czerny and Marx, for instance), novel techniques for organising the forward musical 'flow' provided ample expressive compensation. Undoubtedly within such fusions of the old and new, the specific identity of genre is dissolved somewhat, though the ancestral 'Classical' ethos (especially sonata practice) was not destroyed as an organising force within the early Romantic tradition: rather, it provided fresh linguistic possibilities to an emerging generation.

Bibliography

Biba, O., 'Schubert's Position in Viennese Musical Life'. *19th Century Music*, 3 (1979), pp. 106–13

Carpani, G., *Le Haydine ovvero Lettere su la vita e le opere del celebre maestro Giuseppe Haydn.* Milan, 1812

Czerny, C., *School of Practical Composition.* London, 1848; original edn 1834

Dahlhaus, C., *Ludwig van Beethoven: Approaches to His Music*, trans. M. Whittall. Oxford, 1991

Daverio, J., *Robert Schumann: Herald of a 'New Poetic Age'.* Oxford, 1997

Day, A., *Romanticism.* London and New York, 1996

De Nora, T., *Beethoven and the Construction of Genius: Musical Politics in Vienna, 1792–1803.* Berkeley and Los Angeles, 1995

Drabble, M. (ed.), *The Oxford Companion to English Literature.* 5th edn, Oxford, 1985

Forbes, E. (ed.), *Thayer's Life of Beethoven.* 2 vols., Princeton, 1967

36 *Ibid.*, p. 81.

Griesinger, G. A., 'Biographische Notizen über Joseph Haydn', serialised in *Allgemeine musikalische Zeitung*, 11 (1809)

Hamilton, K., *Liszt: Sonata in B Minor*. Cambridge, 1996

Irving, J., *Mozart: The 'Haydn' Quartets*. Cambridge, 1998

Longyear, R. M., 'Liszt's B minor Sonata: Precedents for a Structural Analysis'. *The Music Review*, 34 (1973), pp. 198–209

Mahling, C.-H., 'Berlin: Music in the Air'. In A. Ringer (ed.), *The Early Romantic Era* . London and Basingstoke, 1990, pp. 109–40

Marston, N., *Schumann: Fantasie, op. 17*. Cambridge, 1992

Newman, W. S., *The Sonata Since Beethoven*. New York, 1972

Niemetschek, F. X., *Leben des k.k. Kapellmeisters Wolfgang Gottlieb Mozart nach Originalquellen beschrieben*. Prague, 1798

Nissen, G. N., *Biographie W. A. Mozart nach Originalbriefen*. Leipzig, 1828

Pederson, S., 'A. B. Marx, Berlin Concert Life and National Identity'. *19th Century Music*, 18 (1994), pp. 87–107

Plantinga, L., *Schumann as Critic*. New Haven and London, 1967

Reed, J., *Schubert*. Oxford, 1997

Reicha, A., *Traité de haute composition musicale*. Paris, 1826

Rosen, C., *The Romantic Generation*. London, 1995
      Sonata Forms. New York, 1980

Samson, J., *Chopin: The Four Ballades*. Cambridge, 1992
      The Music of Chopin. Oxford, 1985

Shamgar, B., '*The Retransition in the Piano Sonatas of Haydn, Mozart and Bethoven*'. Ph.D. diss., University of New York (1978)

Strunk, O. (ed.), *Source Readings in Music History*, rev. edn VI, *The Nineteenth Century*, ed. R. A. Solie. New York and London, 1998

Todd, R. L. (ed.), *Mendelssohn and His World*. Princeton, 1991

Vertrees, J. A., 'Mozart's String Quartet K.465: The History of a Controversy'. *Current Musicology*, 17 (1974), pp. 96–114

Winklhofer, S., *Liszt's Sonata in B Minor: A Study of Autograph Scores and Documents*. Ann Arbor, 1980

8

Choral music

JOHN BUTT

The decline of traditional choral foundations

Johann Nikolaus Forkel paints a grim picture of the state of German choral foundations in 1801. Now that music is dominated by the untutored tastes of the 'Liebhaber' its necessity as a serious fundamental of education and worship is eroded:

> but so much comes out of the fact that it is mainly the lack of knowledge in musical things, that brings about musical disaster, that has led so many men, and still leads them, to desire an ever greater reduction of music in churches and schools, and will finally take things so far that it will either completely rob the church of its most powerful means of devotion or at least bring it so low that no enlightened Christian can any longer hold it for a means of devotion.[1]

What seems particularly ironic about Forkel's statement is his sense that a modern Christian should be 'enlightened' (later he notes that the Enlightenment has brought many improvements to religion, if not yet to religious music). It was, after all, the Enlightenment that had swept away the last vestiges of music as a fundamental of education. The scholastic notion of music theory as the basis of mathematics and cosmic order survived into the early eighteenth century, and some of this traditional prestige reflected on music's more practical, rhetorical function as an adornment of liturgy and a medium of scriptural interpretation. The Enlightenment brought both a demystification of the powers of music and a turn away from the general hegemony of religion *per se*. If music was no longer central to the academic core of education, if the educational establishments were less intimately connected with the church and if the churches no longer recognised any special spiritual power in music, the decline that Forkel observes seems hardly surprising.

Yet in many other respects Forkel's views are typical of Enlightenment attitudes at the outset of the nineteenth century: Kantors should choose music with a simplicity of style – not the simplicity coming from a lack of the

---

1 J. N. Forkel, *Allgemeine Geschichte der Musik*, II (Leipzig, 1801), pp. 22–3.

necessary knowledge of art, but 'that noble simplicity that is only the fruit of the highest culture'. The type of music that most appeals to the common man is the chorus; arias are simply too personal to be of general use and recitatives are unappealing and unedifying. If one is using compositions that are already part of the church library, it is the choruses that should be selected (Forkel, pp. 66–8). The advice of the Leipzig Kantor, Johann Adam Hiller, is similarly biased towards choral singing: recitatives should be avoided and a chorus, aria and chorale should be woven together to make a cantata based on the sermon (1792).[2]

The importance of communal singing is also evident in Forkel's description of fugue as something that creates a community of equal citizens who all work independently but harmoniously towards the common good. It was precisely this aspect of choral performance that continued to be handed down in the supremely accessible oratorios of Handel and that would eventually contribute to the Romantic reception of Bach as a model of sacred choral music. What Forkel could not be fully aware of – since he was part of it – was the sea-change in both society and its attitude to music in the decades straddling the turn of the nineteenth century. As traditional choral institutions declined, the amateur chorus rose to be one of the most potent musical institutions in Europe and America. It ultimately contributed to the survival of some of the older foundations and secured the performance of both older repertories and new compositions. If church choirs came to be re-established in nineteenth-century Germany they were, more often than not, based more on the model of the choral society than on the education system devised by Luther and Melanchton.[3]

The situation in Italy paralleled that in Germany in many respects at the turn of the nineteenth century. Italy had one historical advantage in the establishment, since the seventeenth century, of the first conservatoires to make practical music the central part of their curriculum. Many of these institutions declined during the latter years of the eighteenth century, but the system was revitalised, following the newer French model, during the Napoleonic occupation. Complaints about the increasingly light style of church music accord with the German criticisms, and, as religion declined as a central aspect of educated society, most capable composers found far more profit in operatic production. On the other hand, many concerned with the direction or performance of opera also served the church (the prohibition of female voices in church music had been relaxed in many parts of Italy), so standards could not have declined below a certain level of professionalism. But church music was basically a second-class musical activity and the compositional production generally undistinguished.

2 J. A. Hiller, *Kurze und erleichterte Anweisung zum Singen* (Leipzig, 1792), Foreword.
3 C. Dahlhaus, *Nineteenth-Century Music*, trans. J. B. Robinson (Berkeley and Los Angeles, 1989), p. 180.

England's traditional cathedral and collegiate foundations, if ultimately the best-preserved traditional choral institutions in Europe, underwent their period of greatest neglect at the turn of the century. The reasons for this lay partly in the laxity of the clergy in general and in particular their apathy towards the conducting of services. Reports abound concerning the behaviour of cathedral choirs, showing little musical discipline or decorum. William Gatens also senses an attitude he describes as 'neo-puritanism': traditional Puritan antipathy to music in worship is expanded into a general distaste for music in general and 'the tone of religious seriousness might be claimed to have blurred and expanded the rationalist intellectual verdict on music into an emotive moral conviction'.[4] This again shows parallels with the situation in Protestant Germany, where the anti-liturgical impulses of seventeenth-century Pietism blended with the rationalist distrust of music during the Enlightenment era.

The most striking collapse of traditional choral foundations was, of course, in France, where the ecclesiastical establishment was so often seen as part of the *ancien régime* during the Revolution years. Napoleon's re-establishment in 1801 of the Chapelle Royale (initially under Paisiello and later under Berlioz's teacher, Le Sueur) was the first of many musical restorations that characterise French cultural and social history during the nineteenth century. The sumptuousness of the massed forces at his own coronation in 1804 capitalised on the tradition for enormous musical pageants that the Revolution had set in train, an ironic use of choral democracy for an event that many must have seen as a political step backwards.

Towards a new choral culture

Turning now to the establishment of new choral institutions, it is important to recognise some continuity with the traditional foundations. A tradition of massed choirs in concert performance began with the oratorio productions of Handel of the 1730s, in which the composer combined several of the cathedral and royal choirs of London to create a bulk of sound that must have been relatively new for its time (although massed choirs had long been used for coronations and other important national events). In other words, the concept of the large chorus was born out of a duplication of the traditional resources rather than a wholesale change in personnel. The Handelian oratorio also provided a forum for religious music outside the context of the liturgy, one that allowed a substantial cross-over with theatrical music – in other words, with the mainstream of European music. Moreover, the founding of the Three Choirs

4 W. J. Gatens, *Victorian Cathedral Music in Theory and Practice* (Cambridge, 1986), p. 22.

Festival in *c.* 1715 initiated the concept of massed cathedral choirs within the context of an annual festival, an institution that was to become one of the powerhouses of nineteenth-century musical culture. The London 'centenary' of Handel's birth in 1784 provided something of a watershed for massed choral performance, an event that involved forces on a scale and of a type that Handel could not possibly have envisioned. The commemoration was repeated for another seven years during which time the number of performers doubled, from over 500 to over 1,000.[5] Hiller's Berlin Messiah performance of 1786 proved a parallel landmark in Germany, one that was swiftly followed by the foundation of countless choral societies and glee-clubs. Carl Fasch founded the seminal Berlin Singakademie in 1791 (it was taken over by Carl Friedrich Zelter on Fasch's death in 1800). Zelter, from the start, was interested in promoting the music of J. S. Bach, beginning with the motets which appeared in print in 1803. The rehearsal of other Bach works (including several movements from the *St Matthew Passion*), by a smaller group of experienced singers from within the academy soon followed.[6]

Anton Friedrich Thibaut founded a Singverein in Heidelberg in 1811, and, just as Zelter's society was to be the centre of the Bach revival, this became the impetus for the Protestant Palestrina revival. Of all the various choral societies of the time, this was perhaps the most private, elite and quasi-religious, singing in Thibaut's own house, often in darkness, and allowing select visitors to hear the society only four times a year.[7] Zelter also founded another type of singing society in 1809, the Berlin Liedertafel which was an elite all-male glee-club that required its members to be poets, composers or singers, but which engendered – in the characterful opinion of Carl Dahlhaus – a shallow, sanctimonious simplicity of musical style that degenerated into kitsch.[8] The Liedertafel music was given much of its ideology by Hans Georg Nägeli (a pupil of the educational reformer, Pestalozzi) in Switzerland. It was an ethos that stressed the sense of fellowship and essential democracy afforded by the communal pursuit of good music (Dahlhaus, p. 47).

Cecelia Hopkins Porter has examined the spread of festivals and the associated amateur choral culture in the Lower Rhine. Düsseldorf was the first city in the area to develop a municipalised musical culture: a Musikakademie founded in 1800, a Musikverein in 1818, together with a number of male singing groups. Organisations devoted to oratorio performance arose in Elberfeld (1811), Cologne (1812) and Aachen (1818) and many more institu-

5 N. Temperley, *Haydn: The Creation* (Cambridge, 1991), p. 4.

6 M. Geck, *Die Wiederentdeckung der Matthäuspassion im 19. Jahrhundert*, Studien zur Musikgeschichte des 19 Jahrhunderts (Regensburg, 1967), pp. 12–15.

7 J. Garratt, 'Palestrina and the German Romantic Imagination: Interpreting Historicism in Nineteenth-Century Music', Ph.D. diss., University of Wales Cardiff (1999), pp. 109–10, 120.

8 Dahlhaus, *Nineteenth-Century Music*, p. 48.

tions arose over the next few decades. The festivals that began in 1818 circulated between these Rhineland cities and were administered by the city governments (which also generously covered the losses after ticket sales). Each year the cities pooled their forces along the lines of the Three Choirs Festival or the Handelian oratorio productions in England; they could thus produce music on a scale that a single city could never achieve alone.

Hopkins Porter shows how the number of performers at the Lower Rhine Festivals steadily grew after 1818 (209 initially and 789 by 1847). Over this period the chorus also grew from being of equal dimensions with the orchestra to four times its number. The range of composers for the oratorio performances is surprisingly wide, with the 'classics' of Beethoven, Handel and Mozart always the strongest presence. Various contemporary composers also enjoyed shorter periods of favour: initially Weber and Friedrich Schneider, moving on to Ferdinand Ries and Cherubini, followed by Mendelssohn and Schumann; earlier composers came more to fore in the latest period (1840–67): Schubert, Gluck and J. S. Bach.[9]

The other interesting trend throughout this period is the move from a largely amateur music culture (often mixed with a few professionals) towards a more professionalised institution. By the 1850s Viennese orchestras, for instance, were almost entirely professionalised.[10] The organisers of the Lower Rhine Festivals represented the governmental and mercantile backbone of their cities and were thus of more influence than they would have been as merely vocational music administrators. After 1848 most organisations were controlled more by professional musicians. One extremely interesting observation by Hopkins Porter is that music critics tended to favour the performances of amateur soloists in the earlier performances at the Lower Rhine Festivals but from the 1840s onwards there was a dramatic increase in professional soloists and critical censure of those who were still dilettantes (Hopkins Porter, pp. 216–20).

Similar developments in massed amateur choral singing occurred elsewhere. The Tonkünstler-Societät of Vienna was founded in 1771 as a charity for the families of deceased musicians, producing oratorios during the penitential seasons. This provided a substantial chorus of about sixty men and boys for Haydn's late oratorios.[11] 1812 saw the founding of the mixed-voice Gesellschaft der Musikfreunde in Vienna and the following year the Philharmonic Society was founded in London. Despite the catastrophic decline in the ecclesiastical choral foundations, England maintained the

9 C. Hopkins Porter, 'The New Public and the Reordering of the Musical Establishment: The Lower Rhine Music Festivals, 1818–67', *19th Century Music*, 3 (1979–80), pp. 211–24.
10 L. Botstein, 'Listening through Reading: Musical Literacy and the Concert Audience', *19th Century Music*, 16 (1992–3), p. 134. 11 Temperley, *Haydn*, pp. 2, 36 and 111.

impetus of the oratorio tradition into the nineteenth century. Operatic institutions such as Drury Lane and Covent Garden continued to provide oratorio performances with amateur choral societies, and choral festivals spread to provincial capitals such as Birmingham and Leeds. Beethoven's Ninth Symphony was commissioned by the Philharmonic Society (albeit that Beethoven made the first move); but it probably did not expect the choral finale at the outset, and the archaic system of musical direction was not equal to the task of the first English performances.[12] However, the attempt at least suggests that London had ambitions to participate in the European musical scene, even if much of the talent still had to be imported. The French system of amateur choral societies (Orphéons) began in the 1830s and massed choral performance spread to Switzerland, Belgium and The Netherlands (Hopkins Porter, p. 212). In America, William Billings's Musical Society of Stoughton was originally founded for sacred music in 1786, but it soon evolved into a more secular institution. The Handel and Haydn Society of Boston was the first American group founded specifically for oratorio performance (1815).

It is almost a commonplace to suggest that these amateur choral movements had their roots in the French Revolution. But it must be remembered that massed choral performance in England and Germany was already significant before the 1790s (indeed Billings's efforts might be more appropriately associated with the American Revolution). Certainly, the concept of massed amateur singing took on a political significance in France that it had never had before and this undoubtedly had an impact on neighbouring countries. Amateur choruses were often associated with democratic or nationalist sentiments that preserved some memory of the French Revolution: many amateur choruses, especially men's, were prohibited in Austria during the Restoration era, 1814–48.[13]

The desire for massed choral forces is evident in the early days of the Revolution: for the first anniversary of the Revolution in July 1790 a – presumably metaphorical – request was made in the *Chronique de Paris* for a hymn to the God of liberty involving refrains to be sung by a choir of 24 million people.[14] Maximilien Robespierre, on being elected president of the National Convention on 4 June 1794, took a particular interest in the festival of the Supreme Being which was to take place only four days later. Following the deist stance of Rousseau he treasured the sense of moral worth generated by the congregation of the people and decreed that the 'Hymne à la Divinité' be sung by everyone rather than just the experienced singers. Gossec, 'lieutenant maître de

12 N. Cook, *Beethoven: Symphony No. 9* (Cambridge, 1993), pp. 7, 40–7.
13 Dahlhaus, *Nineteenth-Century Music*, p. 47.
14 A. Coy, *Die Musik der französischen Revolution*, Musikwissenschaftliche Schriften 13 (Munich and Salzburg, 1978), p. 54.

musique' in the national guard and director of music for the national festivals, had immediately to compose a simpler piece than the one he had prepared, in which a refrain, sung by all, alternated with verses sung by the choir in four-part harmony to the same melody. The organisation for the rehearsal of the piece – in such a short time – by the entire Paris population, must count as one of the most remarkable events in performance history, one that could not have failed to have repercussions elsewhere. On the other hand, this event marks the highpoint of the integration of music within the political and revolutionary process in France: never again would music be used on such a scale as the medium for 'both political and mass-psychological tendencies' (Coy, pp. 76–7, 92–7), although this potential remained latent in all subsequent choral movements throughout Europe and America. Moreover, this event came at the climax of the Reign of Terror, to which Robespierre himself was to fall victim only a few weeks later; the memories associated with the performance could surely not have been unremittingly positive.

Social developments and their relation to choral practice

While the French Revolution, for a time, secured the partnership of state and music, and also of revolutionary ideology and the event-based notion of music as an expression of the people's will, it was also complicit in affording music a degree of autonomy and isolation from the political process. The institutionalisation of music by the state under the auspices of the national guard and the Festivals led to the founding of the National Institute of Music in 1793, which ultimately freed music from its subordination to the military sphere. Like the Italian academies and German schools it also fulfilled a philanthropic function in offering free instruction to the talented children of the poor. While the notion of a vocational conservatoire was already evident in Italy and even in Germany, the French establishment, which became the Paris Conservatoire in 1795, was far more influential in shaping music education in the century to come. The isolated study of music not only allowed a separation of music from its immediate function; it separated it from the broader education of which it had hitherto been a part (especially in Germany). With the emphasis on specialisation and the focused study of specific techniques of performance and composition, a division of labour became that much stronger in musical practice.

The growth of amateur choral performance can be seen as running alongside – and directly counter to – this tendency. As long as there were still composers willing to cater for the limitations of the medium (together with a suitable canonical repertory of classic oratorios), principles of utopian community, democracy and even moderate republicanism could flourish within the choral society and festival, almost in the face of the growing division of labour. As William Weber has suggested, music festivals may well have 'lent the bourgeoisie a social dignity – a public image industrialists needed more and more as workers began protesting the sweatshop and extortion at the company store'.[15]

Leon Botstein, following Jürgen Habermas, has tried to account for the emergence of the late eighteenth-century concept of a public sphere. It was a consequence of developing literacy, growth in urban life together with a market economy and the improvement of print technology. The Industrial Revolution itself thus facilitated not only the greater consumption and commercialisation of music but also the growth of musical institutions. The legitimisation of collective opinion (together with freedom of expression and exchange of ideas) coincided with the emergence of the public concert. The arena of productive, active public involvement in ideas flourished in the early nineteenth century but, according to Habermas, gradually became debased into a passive consumer society as the century progressed.[16] In musical culture the amateur sphere became both less skilled and more passive in the wake of increasing professionalisation in all fields; thus the division of labour institutionalised by the conservatoire system ultimately enervated the amateur field.

In some sense then, the new choral movements, distinct as they were from the old ecclesiastical foundations, preserved something of the pre-industrial notion of music as integrated into a wider context of belief and social practice. Any autonomy music may have had in the culture of festivals and choral societies was hardly absolute. On the other hand, the new choral institutions established music as a leisure activity (Weber, p. 184), something separated from the day's work.

One bias inherited from the past was the continued emphasis on vocal performance in music education. The cultivation of singing, especially for participation in choral performance, was the first priority of the newly founded Vienna Conservatoire in 1813, for instance. Botstein argues that the intensity of vocal training, with its necessary pitch security, gave the educated public a greater competence in music than the more passive pitch recognition afforded by the piano-based amateur culture of the later nineteenth century. While this might not entirely follow – in that the keyboard had lain behind most advanced compositional practice in the seventeenth and eighteenth centuries, and was, after all, essential for figured-bass theory – the aural training concomitant with regular massed vocal performance would certainly have encouraged an active, rather than a passive, musical culture.

Such continuities between older and new forms of choral institution are

15 W. Weber, 'The Muddle of the Middle Classes', *19th Century Music*, 3 (1979–80), p. 185.
16 Botstein, 'Listening through Reading', p. 132.

mirrored by social continuities. It is all very well to affirm that the concept of public opinion and the new amateur choral movements represent the rise of the middle classes but, as William Weber has shown, the concepts of both the middle class and their 'rise' are by no means clear-cut. The very notion of the articulate public involved nobles almost as much as commoners initially, and only the most wealthy of the middle class actually 'rose' in the nineteenth century to become what is sometimes termed a 'second aristocracy' (Weber, pp. 176–9). Nobles were often involved in the running of concert societies: they were, for instance, essential in the production of Handel's oratorios from their inception until well into the nineteenth century.[17] As Dahlhaus has suggested, the bourgeois institutions of the early nineteenth century form an historical link between the culture of the nobility and modern mass culture; the system both antedated and outlived its period of greatest influence, that restoration era during which Biedermeier tastes sought the union of technical simplicity in music with high cultural breeding (Dahlhaus, p. 173).

Whatever the variety of their backgrounds or the extent of their democratic pretensions, most of the people involved in amateur music societies could be categorised as 'upper class'. Moreover, many still saw professional musicians as being at the top of the servant class rather than social equals (Dahlhaus, p. 42). Thus there is some irony in the notion that precisely the least specialised performance institution throughout the nineteenth century – the amateur chorus – was that which considered itself most socially superior, its utopian ideals notwithstanding.

Revolution, restoration and continuity

In all, it is relatively easy to associate the new choral movements with the various forms of social and political revolution strewn throughout the nineteenth century. And it is equally easy to write a music history of the nineteenth century that concentrates mainly on the revolutionary composers and institutions. Certainly, the loudest philosophical voices of that age and beyond have emphasised the aesthetic of originality and individuality. Thus it is always tempting to relegate everything else to the irrelevant categories of the reactionary or the merely stable.

One obvious alternative approach is to suggest that the revolutionary spirit of the nineteenth century is balanced by a spirit of restoration or historicist revival. After all, even the French Revolution itself sought precedents in Classical politics and many nineteenth-century musical figures looked both to

17 Weber, 'The Muddle of the Middle Classes', pp. 182, 185. See also Dahlhaus, *Nineteenth-Century Music*, p. 162.

the distant and the more recent past for inspiration or discipline. This approach is certainly worth pursuing, although it carries with it dangers equal to those inherent in the purely revolutionary approach. First, it is all too easy to see each revolutionary swing as neatly countered by a reactionary one so that the era is treated as if it were a well-oiled machine rather than a messy heterophony of diverse human individuals, cultures and institutions. Secondly, as Carl Dahlhaus has warned, efforts at restoration cannot be taken at face value since any attempt at restoration will always contain traces of the original break in tradition, however strong the efforts to make that tradition appear 'natural'. Restoration is caught between Schiller's dialectic of the naive and the sentimental as nineteenth-century attempts at recovering the Palestrina idiom fail to avoid an element of longing and historical distance, and sixteenth-century modality unwittingly sounds as an 'other' within the context of Romantic tonality, rather than a universal norm (Dahlhaus, pp. 28–9). All this is true enough, but it does not necessarily invalidate the attempts at restoration; indeed, by showing that they cannot escape the environment and attitudes of the present Dahlhaus seems almost tacitly to justify them within the aesthetic of the new. However antiquarian the intentions of the restorers they cannot avoid sounding in some sense up-to-date, new or even exotic.

Here there is not room to undertake a comprehensive study of historicism in music in the early nineteenth century, but several points made by Walter Wiora are worth taking: first, while commentators in the visual and spatial arts were tending towards the view that all epochs should be viewed equally positively, this was still far less pronounced in music criticism and practice; secondly, the greatest interest in full-blown historicism was to be found in the field of church music and its associated genres. [18] This was obviously partly because the use of earlier styles was already an established feature of church music but also because church traditions had only recently been ruptured and were thus obvious candidates for restoration.

It is perhaps no coincidence that the first country to promote concerts of historical music was England, a country whose revolution and restoration preceded those in the rest of Europe by more than a century. Societies such as the Academy of Ancient Music (1710) and the Concert of Antient Music (1776) were characterised by a conservative stance and an antipathy towards modern music, even if they were not so consciously historicist as the nineteenth-century movements associated with the likes of Thibaut and Zelter. [19] France,

18 W. Wiora, 'Grenzen und Stadien des Historismus in der Musik', in W. Wiora (ed.), *Die Ausbreitung des Historismus über die Musik*, Studien zur Musikgeschichte des 19 Jahrhunderts 14 (Regensburg, 1969), pp. 299–327, esp. pp. 314, 316.

19 M. Lichtenfeld, 'Zur Geschichte, Idee und Ästhetik des historischen Konzerts', in W. Wiora (ed.), *Die Ausbreitung*, pp. 41–53, esp. pp. 43–4.

which had experienced the most pronounced demolition of older institutions, was another obvious environment for the restoration of earlier music. Indeed, Katherine Ellis has shown that many of the seeds of the historical performance practice movement – cultivating not only the music of the past, but also its manner of performance – were sown in France. As early as 1804 Geoffroy was stressing the maintenance of earlier performance traditions as essential to the future success of early music.[20] Alexandre Choron was influential both in the publication and performance of older music. His *Institution royale de musique classique et religieuse* (1817) had the multiple aims of restoring both the best music of the past and the traditional liturgical use of music. His historical concerts of vocal music from the age of Josquin to Handel began in 1822 and lasted until the July Revolution of 1830. A wider range of historical music was undertaken by Fétis during the 1830s, first in Paris and later in Brussels; his concerts, lasting several hours, embraced music of the sixteenth and seventeenth centuries and at least made the claim to use original instruments and sources (although this was later disputed). Joseph-Napoléon, Prince of Moscow, promoted, published and often conducted choral music of the same period during the 1840s.[21] All these undertakings show in their antipathy to 'modern' trivial and operatic music a purifying and moralising tendency. Yet since all the historical music patently comes from pre-revolutionary Europe, it had originally been part of the very society which the revolutions themselves sought to purify. Now it was the trivial populist music of the age that reeked of moral corruption.

It is important to highlight how radically these conceptions of historicist revival differ from the seemingly similar early music movement of the twentieth century. One striking example is Zelter's practice in reviving Bach's choral works in the context of the Berlin Singakademie. He used Bach's original performance materials whenever they were available to him, copying out his own parts only as a way of completing and doubling the original material. This was hardly the equivalent of using facsimile editions in the twentieth century: Zelter was quite content to annotate the original parts with dynamics and other performance markings in a manner that would be grounds for a charge of criminal vandalism a century later. In all, then, Zelter's work on Bach – an historical revival if ever there was one – differs from that of the twentieth century in that he considered Bach's music to be literally – even in the physical sense – his property. In other words, he did not have a deep sense of distance from

20 K. Ellis, *Music Criticism in Nineteenth-Century France: 'La Revue et Gazette Musicale de Paris', 1834–80* (Cambridge, 1995), p. 13.

21 *Ibid.*, p. 56; Lichtenfeld, 'Zur Geschichte, Idee und Ästhetik', pp. 45–6; J. Bowen, 'The Conductor and the Score: The Relationship between Interpreter and Text in the Generation of Mendelssohn, Berlioz and Wagner', Ph.D. diss., Stanford University (1993), I, pp. 11, 265–7.

Bach; the music may have fallen into disuse but it was still very much part of a tradition that was still essential to his historical being.

Dahlhaus's view that restoration can never cover its breaks in continuity implies that tradition has a seamlessness, or at least a continuity, that is somehow more authentic than naked restoration. Yet as this study is already suggesting, one form of continuity can come with a radical break in some other regard. The very respectability of continuity can be used to disguise a departure. Moreover, the idea of tradition as an authentic articulation of nineteenth-century history underplays the concept of revolution, the violent breaks with tradition that are so characteristic of the era. In sum then, neither tradition nor restoration guarantee continuity; nor is there any reason why they should be expected to do so. A conscious sense of tradition may conceal breaks and departures, just as restoration carries with it an inevitable sense of alterity or longing for the truly absent; moreover, revolution itself may carry with it hidden continuities of tradition and utopian notions of restoring an idealised historical past.

The issue of continuity is particularly complex. Continuities are not so conspicuous as revolution or restoration to the historian; they may have been unnoticed by the subjects of the age itself; or institutions and attitudes may have been perceived as continuous when, in fact, they obscured many changes or ruptures. Just as restoration can never be entirely free of the attitudes of the modern age, the most consistent of continuities will never be immune from the changes surrounding it. The Anglican choral tradition in the first half of the nineteenth century maintained many continuities of performance forces and liturgical style. Moreover, the composers were writing music to fit within the spiritual and liturgical context and could hardly subscribe to the tenets of Romantic revolutionary genius. Originality was neither sanctioned nor proscribed and composers could mix elements from a number of ages or styles or sometimes follow in the footsteps of a particular composer: Handel was obviously still an influence, and Thomas Attwood had a conscious affinity with his teacher Mozart, as had S. S. Wesley with Mendelssohn. William Gatens makes a perceptive connection between Victorian church music and the Biedermeier movement in Germany: both are conservative, middle class, ordered and somewhat homely. While both can err towards 'kitsch', they preserve nonetheless something of the Classical ethos of order, poise and flexible, formalised gestures – a genealogy that leads back to Mozart rather than to Beethoven (Gatens, p. 53). It may also be significant that Dahlhaus sees the Biedermeier spirit as inhering more in institutions than in the intellectual history of the age; the 'Romantic' constellation of ideas parted company with the non-Romantic system of institutions (Dahlhaus, pp. 171–2).

The Biedermeier analogy already shows that Victorian church music cannot represent a seamless continuity with previous centuries, however consistent the institutional framework: the very middle-class ethos of the Biedermeier period was inconceivable much before the latter half of the eighteenth century. There are several other discontinuities besides: Anglican music now had the backdrop of the non-conformist denominations, that which Gatens terms 'neo-puritanism', and the Evangelical and Tractarian opposition. In the wider musical world, there was the growth in concert culture and an association of religious sentiment and public piety within the context of the oratorio. Moreover, there was the unprecedented industrialisation of Britain, a form of modernity unparalleled elsewhere, along with the growth of a gargantuan empire and the rise of sceptical scientific positivism that would challenge the very basis of religion. In this light, the continuity of the choral foundations would have taken on a particularly reactionary and stubborn character. Only with the positive sense of renewal and restoration later in the century – in other words, a certain break in the continuity – would the sense of tradition again seem vital and relevant to the age. Continuity clearly could not work unaided.

There were several older institutions which were especially celebrated during the early nineteenth century, precious relics that seemed to keep alive something from the past. The Thomaskirche and school in Leipzig not only had a reputation for excellence since the time of J. F. Doles and J. A. Hiller; it also benefited increasingly from its connection with J. S. Bach. Even more widely admired was the choir of the Sistine Chapel in Rome, associated as it was with the continuous performance of Palestrina and thus representing the longest extant performing tradition of a specific composer's repertory. In this way it could represent the concepts of the historical, the Classical model, the individual genius and the living tradition all in the one institution.

Allegri's *Miserere*, a piece that was still treasured in the repertory of many Catholic churches, was traditionally performed there during Holy Week. E. T. A. Hoffmann is particularly perceptive in suggesting that its fame might have derived more from the manner of performance in the Sistine Chapel than from its actual musical quality. This might relate to Mendelssohn's remarks about the performances of the Sistine choir in a letter from 1830. First, he claims to detect little of the special performance tradition for which the choir is so famous; instead he notices the 'little decorations and trills like those that were popular at the beginning of the last century'.[22] This is perhaps one of the most striking and ironic examples of how history and tradition can be so easily misread and confused. When Mendelssohn was expecting a 'special manner of

22 Garratt, 'Palestrina', pp. 70–1, 137; see also Bowen, 'The Conductor', p. 133.

performing' he was, according to the beliefs of the age, doubtlessly listening for something especially pure and inspiring in its asceticism. The little ornaments he heard he believed to be Baroque accretions, the persisting corruptions of an intervening age. In fact, the weight of historical evidence now suggests rather that Palestrina's own performances might well have been quite lavishly ornamented and that what Mendelssohn actually heard may have been the survival – doubtless in an altered form – of an 'original' historical practice.[23] Mendelssohn's further observations of inaccurate singing and various cuts in the music also point out the distance between his own aesthetic (highly trained and long-rehearsed choirs singing masterworks accurately and faithfully) and an enduring pre-aesthetic cavalier attitude towards performance.

Only one other 'ancient' institution rivalled the Sistine Chapel for its legendary choir, and this was that of the Petersburg court chapel, directed by Dmitry Bortniansky – the 'Russian Palestrina' – during the first quarter of the nineteenth century. Here, not only historical depth contributed to the myth but also the horizontal distance of Russia and the exoticism of its Orthodox liturgy. The most colourful impression of Bortniansky's choral concertos is offered by Berlioz who heard them *in situ*: he wonders at the vivid expression, extremes of dynamic and attack and freedom of part-writing. Like the Sistine Chapel choir, it seems that the choir performed with a subtlety of expression that went beyond what could be notated, and, partly owing to its remoteness, used expressive devices that were unusual in the more uniform performance of Western Europe.[24]

The role of the composer and the special case of Mendelssohn

The various forms of continuity that most choral institutions, both ancient and modern, display are matched by continuities in compositional attitude and training. Many composers, especially in Catholic Europe, were brought up to cultivate the strict contrapuntal textures of Fux's *Gradus ad Parnassum*. This tradition kept alive compositional principles – seen as eternal and impersonal – from Renaissance polyphony. In the nineteenth century they could still form the stylistic basis for pieces in a specific church style but they were also often regarded as the abstract basis of all compositional practice. This latter view of Renaissance style dates from precisely the era marking the end of its hegemony

23 G. Dixon, 'The Performance of Palestrina: Some Questions, but Fewer Answers', *Early Music*, 22 (1994), pp. 667–75.

24 M. Kuzma, 'Bortniansky à la Bortniansky: An Examination of the Sources of Dmitry Bortniansky's Choral Concertos', *Journal of Musicology*, 14 (1996), pp. 207–8.

as the principal compositional idiom – i.e. the time of Monteverdi's insistence that the *seconda prattica* had its roots in the *prima prattica*. Moreover, as a myth that bound a culture together over several centuries, it survived well into the twentieth century. But in the nineteenth century it must have taken on a particular resonance amid the growing interest in historicism and the restoration of ancient models. The Fuxian tradition persisted side-by-side with the Palestrina revival as a tradition and practice that was already in place.[25] Thus many composers had access to an idealised past through two subtly differing routes: the 'passive' conditioning of the Fuxian tradition and the 'active' restoration of a portion of the historical repertory.

Mendelssohn is perhaps the most interesting figure to examine as a 'case study' at this point. He was a major figure in the new German choral institutions, through them he was an active restorer of a specific repertory of the past (Bach's choral works), and, as a composer, his upbringing and compositional stance show remarkable continuities with the past. First, he had a direct family connection with the Bach family through his great-aunt, Sarah Levy, and his teacher, Carl Friedrich Zelter. The latter had been a pupil of Johann Philipp Kirnberger, a student of Bach, who had produced the most comprehensive summary of his master's teaching.[26] Mendelssohn's surviving exercises with Zelter (*c.* 1819–21) reveal a typically Bachian progression from figured-bass exercises, chorales of increasing complexity, invertible counterpoint, through to canon and fugue (Todd, pp. 95–9). There is a sense in which his upbringing may have foreshortened his sense of distance from Bach. In other words, Mendelssohn's service to Bach may have seemed like a momentous effort of rediscovery to many of his contemporaries (including, perhaps, Schumann, who lamented his much less luxurious background and education), but perhaps to Mendelssohn it was more the continuation of a relatively recent tradition, one of which he was inextricably a part. As Susanna Grossmann-Vendrey has suggested, Mendelssohn often saw history as a means of fleshing out what he considered a living tradition.[27]

Dahlhaus portrays Mendelssohn as an archetypal 'Classical' composer, not in the sense of one who lived in the 'Classical' era but one who retained a strong concept of genre.[28] The moral compulsion towards generic differentiation was as strong in the early nineteenth century as the more revolutionary, 'high

25 Garratt, 'Palestrina', pp. 254–7.

26 R. L. Todd, *Mendelssohn's Musical Education: A Study and Edition of his Exercises in Composition* (Cambridge, 1983), pp. 2–3. See also Geck, *Die Wiederentdeckung der Matthäuspassion*, p. 18.

27 S. Grossmann-Vendrey, 'Mendelssohn und die Vergangenheit', in W. Wiora (ed.), *Die Ausbreitung*, pp. 73–84.

28 C. Dahlhaus, 'Mendelssohn und die musikalischen Gattungstraditionen', in C. Dahlhaus (ed.), *Das Problem Mendelssohn*, Studien zur Musikgeschichte des 19 Jahrhunderts 41 (Regensburg, 1974), pp. 55–60.

Romantic' tendencies of Berlioz and Liszt. Dahlhaus notes the interest of conservative contemporary theorists in defining musical genres and naming
'Classical' composers in each. What he could well have added is the fact that
such theorists reoccupy a view of music that can be traced back to the early
seventeenth century. The idea of generic categories is hardly 'Classical' in itself
since it is an extension of the dual practice of the Monteverdi period. What is
new, however, is the proclamation of specific classic composers in each genre:
according to Thibaut these were Palestrina for church style, Handel for oratorio and Mozart for opera. For such a well-trained composer as Mendelssohn
this meant that it was perfectly acceptable to adopt different historical styles
depending on the genre at hand. As Dahlhaus suggests, Mendelssohn's closeness to Handel in his oratorios is not a matter so much of stylistic affinity but
rather a respect for the generic tradition of the oratorio itself. Moreover, his
consciousness of the norms of the oratorio was stronger than it was for non-
texted genres because his Classicism was essentially engendered by his wider
literary education. Generic differentiation was greater in the vocal genres and –
especially significant for the oratorio and its institutional basis – this would
have been of particular importance for the educated public of the early nineteenth century.

Martin Geck has examined the most representative work in the oratorio
genre before the 'discovery' of the *St Matthew Passion* and Mendelssohn's own
oratorios. Friedrich Schneider's *Das Weltgericht*, first performed in 1820, was
the dominant oratorio in Germany for nearly twenty years.[29] Johann August
Apel's text provides a dense mass of 'pseudo-religious speculation' that the first
reviewers considered entirely incomprehensible. Geck suggests that this might
have been a positive advantage to the public of the time, believing themselves
to be participating in the great ideas of the age, the religious-Romantic hunger
for myth that is clearly evident in the fascination with Faust. But it was the
music that made this such an irresistible work: for however dark and murky the
text may have been, the music was entirely cliché-ridden and platitudinous,
accessible to a fault. Both audience and singers, through their intimate knowledge of works such as Spohr's *Jüngsten Gericht*, would have found the music
utterly familiar and thus a mode of access to the perceived profundity of the
text. In short, the listener's comprehension is 'pre-packaged' from the start
and the piece as a whole represents the highpoint (or nadir) of German bourgeois trivial music.

It is against this background and Mendelssohn's own 'Classical' disposition

29 M. Geck, 'Friedrich Schneiders "Weltgericht": Zum Verständnis des Trivialen in der Musik', in C.
Dahlhaus (ed.), *Studien zur Trivialmusik des 19. Jahrhunderts*, Studien zur Musikgeschichte des 19
Jahrhunderts 8 (Regensburg, 1967), pp. 97–109.

that the success of his first oratorio *St Paul* (1836) – and the controversy that it engendered – can be measured. The generic propriety of the oratorio was revitalised with the 'Classical' models of Bach and Handel but it was precisely the mixing of these two that caused the aesthetic approbation of the age. While Handel provided the 'correct' model for the religious oratorio in the concert hall, Bach's models were essentially church works that could only 'illegally' be transferred to the concert genre. Thus Mendelssohn's most overt Bachian touch – the inclusion of five chorales – was considered a stylistic *faux pas*, perhaps a naive ignorance of generic convention with its absolute boundaries. This seems to run against Dahlhaus's conception of Mendelssohn as the supreme Classicist, writing music of an entirely different style (and perhaps – to us – quality) according to the generic preconditions of each piece. However, Peter Mercer-Taylor has suggested that Mendelssohn may well have been fully aware of the problem from the start (indeed, A. B. Marx's early decision to withdraw from writing the libretto would have made this abundantly clear to the composer). The final, most elaborate, chorale-setting comes from a number in which Paul condemns the heathens for worshipping idols and material things, 'God dwelleth not in temples made by human hands', and goes on to expose the central Pauline point that God's temple and spirit live in the body and soul of the believer. The ensuing fugal chorus 'But our God is in heaven' together with the Lutheran chorale on the Credo might seem both dramatically and theologically superfluous. To Mercer-Taylor this is a musical symbol of Paul's central point: four of the five parts of the choir provide a contrapuntal housing 'surrounding a musical utterance we have no trouble identifying with the act of Protestant worship'. In the context of the oratorio as a whole the chorale settings have become increasingly elaborate but this is the first and only instance in which the elaboration is vocal (i.e. 'human') rather than instrumental; an otherwise generic call to worship is thus literally housed in a human temple.[30] Mercer-Taylor's point might be extended by the speculation that the inclusion of chorales *in toto* make a specific link between Paul's ministry and the essentially Pauline theology of Lutheranism; the chorales highlight a particular historical connection that renders a New Testament story specifically relevant to a living German tradition and identity. Mendelssohn thus risks generic impropriety in order to achieve a deeper theological involvement, one of particular cultural relevance.

In fact, one of the enduring qualities in Mendelssohn's output may lie in the specific instances where he took risks: in other words, precisely those points that run against what Rosen describes as Mendelssohn's proclivity towards

30 P. Mercer-Taylor, 'Rethinking Mendelssohn's Historicism: A Lesson from *St. Paul*', *Journal of Musicology*, 15 (1997), p. 226.

religious kitsch, a sense of comfortable, conservative piety that makes a virtue out of unremarkable music.[31] For instance, another aspect of the final chorale setting in *St Paul* is the fact that this is the only five-part vocal writing in the oratorio: the composer had to work somewhat harder to create music of a higher 'specific gravity'. The conversion scene in No. 14 is extraordinary for its sonorities, particularly the voice of God presented by four-part female voices. While such scoring and part-writing is hardly intimidating to a composer of Mendelssohn's technique it certainly requires him to think outside the norm and give the passage his fullest concentration.

Much of Mendelssohn's liturgical music shows him working at his most intense compositional level, primarily because of the generic propriety of liturgical music to conform to older, polyphonic norms (whether such music be written for actual liturgy, as in Mendelssohn's settings for the Berlin Cathedral choir or for the officially secular environment of the Singakademie). His skill in multiple part-writing and polychoral textures is evident in the *Te Deum* of 1826 and the sixteen-part 'Hora est' (1828). The 'Tu es Petrus', Op. 111, of 1827 shows his mastery of the Bachian *stile antico* as handed down through the Kirnberger tradition and 'Mitten wir in Leben sind' Op. 23/3 shows a confessional synthesis between the Palestrinian style and the Lutheran chorale (Garratt, pp. 131–41). While many works of this kind might be dismissed as historicist pastiche, there are numerous instances where Mendelssohn couples a polyphonic texture with a contemporary lyrical style, a feature that works to its best in the 'Ave Maria' of 1830. Here the eight-part choral texture demands the fullest skill and attention from a composer over-trained by the standards of his day; the piece is thus perhaps successful in the same way as the early Octet.

The St Matthew Passion revival

However historicist the conditions that made the *St Matthew Passion* revival possible there are many ways in which the entire event, and the way it was presented to the public at the time, is very much part of the concerns of the present in 1829 and of predictions for the future. Influential though Bach's work may have been on Mendelssohn's own oratorios, there is a sense in which the Bachian elements are relatively superficial, and indeed, as Doflein has noted, much of the resemblance between the *St Matthew Passion* and *St Paul* is in fact between Mendelssohn's truncated version of the *Passion* and *St Paul* (especially in the considerable weighting towards choruses at the expense of solo numbers).

---

31 C. Rosen, *The Romantic Generation* (Cambridge, Mass., 1995, and London, 1996), pp. 594–5.

The 'rediscovery' of Bach in 1829 is also something of a special case in that the wider reception of Bach during the first half of the nineteenth century – in terms of actual performances – was still relatively small. After the initial flurry of interest in the *St Matthew Passion*, works such as Mendelssohn's own oratorios enjoyed a far greater public exposure in the later 1830s and 1840s; the records of the Lower Rhine Festivals show Bach as a relatively small presence in the first half of the century.[32] Even within the context of the Berlin Singakademie, participation in the Bach revival was, from the first, a sign of elite status. When Zelter began his rehearsals of the *St Matthew Passion* in 1815 he used a smaller circle of singers outside the regular rehearsal hours. Mendelssohn used 158 of the 354 members for his famous performance of 11 March 1829.[33]

While the Bach revival as a large-scale popular phenomenon is perhaps often over-emphasised it was absolutely crucial as an element in the German self-fashioning of its high culture, a way of consolidating with historical depth an attitude that was already present in the institutionalisation of Beethoven. Much of the mystique surrounding the work was in place before the first performance owing to the 'press campaign' of A. B. Marx in the *Berliner Allgemeine musikalische Zeitung*; this may well be the first example of its kind in music journalism. From the start (21 February), Marx underlined the century's gap in the performance of the greatest and holiest work by the greatest composer, 'a high-feast of religion and art' (*Die Wiederentdeckung*, p. 25).

Moreover, the names of those who attended the first performance virtually constitute a catalogue of the key figures in German liberal culture of the time; the mechanism for the enduring cultural value of the work was thus virtually in place before a note was publicly performed. In addition to the Prussian royal court and the king, figures such as Droyson, Hegel, Heine and Schleiermacher were present (*Die Wiederentdeckung*, p. 34). Geck has shown how the *St Matthew Passion* was related by these writers and others to central issues of the age: an expression of national Romanticism, of Schleiermacher's religion of feeling and of the musical ideal artwork.[34] Within the latter category the work takes on a political dimension that Bach has hardly retained in later reception. Writers such as Marx, in proclaiming it an artwork of the future, employ the rhetoric of liberalism of the time: such art is emancipatory, open to the ideas of all humanity and is thus the corollary of a free political and economic order. Spohr's performance in Kassel some three years later also contributed to the political-liberal connotations of the work, since it was undertaken in the face of royal

32 Hopkins Porter, 'The New Public', pp. 222–3.
33 Geck, *Die Wiederentdeckung der Matthäuspassion*, pp. 20, 34–5.
34 *Ibid.*, pp. 60–74. See also C. Applegate, 'How German is it? Nationalism and the Idea of Serious Music in the Early Nineteenth Century', *19th Century Music*, 21 (1998), pp. 274–96.

opposition, no doubt resulting from Spohr's well-known liberal sympathies (*Die Wiederentdeckung*, pp. 72–4, 109–16).

An obvious question to ask at this point is whether there really was anything about Bach's work that merited this constellation of progressive epithets. One factor might have been its perceived difficulty for the choruses (Mendelssohn's rehearsal schedule gave the work a level of performance preparation that it would never have received before and seldom has since). Although it can hardly be Bach's most demanding choral work technically, its difficulty and apparent inapproachability may have increased its aura of sublimity; moreover the equality of the voices, all being equally difficult and all contributing to the overall harmony, may have evoked an ideal musical republic in a way that little other music of the time could have achieved (see Forkel's idealistic comments on chorus and fugue, quoted above). Furthermore, by the standards of the generic respectability of most choral music of the time, Bach's music is as incorrigible as Beethoven's in its apparent flouting of generic conventions. An oratorio style that seems to develop the operatic medium of recitative together with dance, concerto forms and a large range of indigenous choral styles must, by its very nature, have seemed revolutionary in 1829. Its historical distance may have excused it from the generic conventions in a way that even Mendelssohn could not experience in the reception of his mild generic mixtures in *St Paul*. In Bach's case the mix could be seen as evidence of its universal status, spanning ages vertically as it spanned the genres horizontally.

New conceptions of religion

The *St Matthew Passion* discovery invites the final topic of this chapter, the role and status of religion in the musical culture of the early nineteenth century. Geck relates the fervour surrounding Bach's passion to the religious sensibility of Schleiermacher (who was himself at the first performance). His 1798 *Reden über Religion* places religious consciousness in the qualities of feeling; and art is the essential means of articulating religious feelings. Geck makes the obvious connection between Schleiermacher's emphasis on the congregation as the concretisation of Christian belief and the religious atmosphere felt by those present at the *Singakademie*'s performances of the *St Matthew Passion* (something that was, moreover, already set up in the pre-concert propaganda of Marx). Droyson's reaction also highlights the specifically Lutheran qualities of the experience, distinguishing it from the incomprehensible ceremonial function of Catholic church music: the *St Matthew Passion* performances represented a living participation in Bach's proclamation of the Word. This, above all, separates the *St Matthew Passion* revival from the contemporaneous Palestrina renaissance.

Given the obvious theological context and the evident experience of Christian piety surrounding the *St Matthew Passion* revival, Geck ponders whether the nineteenth-century experience of the *Passion* was in fact closer to Bach's spiritual intentions for the work than most twentieth-century claims for the rediscovery of its historically objective spirit. While there is certainly some truth in this, the equal ranking and intermixing of art and religion was hardly possible in the orthodox Lutheranism of Bach's age. Moreover, it is important to see Schleiermacher's 'Romantic' religious revival in the context of the Enlightenment attitude to religion (something also entirely foreign to Bach); the new piety was, after all, not only a conscious reaction to this but also depended to some degree on the change in religious sensibilities that the Enlightenment brought.

The Enlightenment attitude to religion is perhaps most clearly summed up in Kant's *Die Religion innerhalb der Grenzen der blossen Vernunft* (1793). This presents a negative attitude to religion exactly contemporaneous with the turn away from Christian religion in the French Revolution, most graphically represented by the erecting of the Goddess of Reason in Notre Dame. Kant similarly attempts to reposition practical reason (i.e. morality) within the sacred context that religion vacates. To him, all religions and all religious history point towards a pure moral system from which all the dogmatic baggage of religion can ultimately be jettisoned. The duties of reason, Kant's categorical imperative, thus become divine as if they were the commands of God. His sense of historical progress leads from Judaism to Christianity and latterly from Catholicism to Lutheranism out of which a church of pure rationality is emerging. Such an historical sense is profoundly different from the relativistic branch of historicism that tends to see each age as viable in its own right.[35]

What is perhaps most valuable in Kant's conception as a way of illuminating the emerging choral culture (and concert culture *per se*) of the early nineteenth century is the emphasis on retaining a religious sensibility in a newly enlightened secular culture. It is the traditional spirit of religion that will prevent the imperatives of rational morality from descending into cold calculation and pedantic acquiescence; the religious attitude gives them vitality and an aura that would otherwise be lost. To Kant, mankind has a religious disposition by nature, and it is historical progress that has taught us to direct this to increasingly rational ends. As Beethoven wrote in a conversation book in 1820, some two years before he decided to incorporate Schiller's verses into a symphonic finale, 'The moral law within us and the starry sky above us – Kant!!!';[36] to him

---

35 See Y. Yovel, *Kant and the Philosophy of History* (Princeton, 1980), pp. 201–23.
36 Cook, *Beethoven: Symphony No. 9*, p. 104.

there was thus a connection between our innate moral sensibility and the divine order of the universe.

Virtually all the connections between religion and the secular world, the Enlightenment and Romanticism and their relation to art come together in Goethe's reworking of the Faust legend. It was Lessing who first tried to recast Faust as an enlightened hero by suggesting that Faust's pursuit of knowledge was a worthy cause and by arranging his ultimate reconciliation with God. Just as with Kant, God seems to be redefined as the ultimate truth that automatically lies at the end of rational enquiry. This redemptive approach was taken on by Goethe (1808, 1832), a figure who, in his early years, showed profound revolutionary and nationalist tendencies but who, in the wake of the French Revolution, developed into a more conservative personality who defined the neo-Classical sensibility. Following Herder's doctrine of *Humanität*, Goethe would have believed in the balance and relationship of intellect and the passions. This connection obviously also paralleled Schleiermacher's belief in the importance of feelings in the context of religion and the relation between religion and art.

Goethe's Faust retains something of the poet's youthful interest in constant striving and self-invention, yet he finally finds salvation in devoting himself to the betterment of humanity. Goethe's conception of the hero is so comprehensive and magisterial that it could both encapsulate the major issues of the age yet also appeal to strikingly diverse systems of belief. In addition to the emphasis on fashioning an identity of self, Faust promotes the virtues of activity and striving, at any cost (i.e. the 'Romantic' side) and the view that infinite knowledge will, by definition, bring about a better state of affairs (the 'Classical' side), whatever the horrors encountered along the way. It is within this inevitable progress towards the good that traditional religious concepts can be reinvented. The drama is also a living embodiment of the belief that art should be central to moral education, the belief shared by Goethe and Schiller for literature and Schleiermacher for religion; the contemplation of the beauties of art actually cultivates the moral sensibility. The musical responses to the Faust culture show a diversity of motifs, all of which could loosely belong to the concept of Romanticism: Berlioz capitalised on the dramatic and characterful elements of Goethe's tale, Schumann the more inward points. Liszt achieved a surprisingly dense musical argument for the transformations and moral ambiguity of Faust. His example also suggests that the Faust myth could appeal to those of a more orthodox Christian disposition (evidenced also by Gounod's opera). Moreover, the most monumental setting of all, the second half of Mahler's Eighth Symphony, shows the Faust myth paired with a traditional Christian text of the first half, as if the two were sides of the same noumenal coin. It is perhaps no accident that this work can also be seen as the culmination of the entire chorus tradition inherited from the nineteenth century at the outset of the twentieth.

Art as education, morality and religion lies behind many aspects of the amateur choral phenomenon across Western Europe: a sense of sacredness is transferred from liturgical worship to the group participation of the choral society and concert hall. Thibaut insisted that the director of a singing society must 'with the highest seriousness, ensure that the playfulness and informality that are permitted and permissible in other activities never bring detriment to the singing society'.[37] As Dahlhaus has noted, the religious sensibility that concert music acquired in the early nineteenth century is given architectural expression in the decking out of concert halls with temple façades.[38] The concert hall was in a very real sense a church and the audience a congregation well before the *St Matthew Passion* revival. Schleiermacher's more specifically religious revival could not have succeeded without a broader aesthetic sense of the religious. It was this heightened aesthetic sense that also provided some of the impetus for the revival of older choral foundations throughout the turbulent eddies of the nineteenth century. Forkel's desire that music should again be fundamental to religion and education was somehow fulfilled, but the natures of the religion and education had themselves radically changed; and musical works could now be viewed as aesthetic wholes rather than as components of a liturgy. However sincere the historicist urge and however complete the revival or survival of earlier institutions, the cultural practice of the age was indelibly conditioned by Romantic conceptions of art.

Bibliography

Applegate, C., 'How German is it? Nationalism and the Idea of Serious Music in the Early Nineteenth Century'. *19th Century Music*, 21 (1998), pp. 274–96

Botstein, L., 'Listening through Reading: Musical Literacy and the Concert Audience'. *19th Century Music*, 16 (1992–3), pp. 129–45

Bowen, J., 'The Conductor and the Score: The Relationship between Interpreter and Text in the Generation of Mendelssohn, Berlioz and Wagner'. Ph.D. diss., Stanford University (1993)

Cook, N., *Beethoven: Symphony No. 9*. Cambridge, 1993

Coy, A., *Die Musik der französischen Revolution*, Musikwissenschaftliche Schriften 13. Munich and Salzburg, 1978

Dahlhaus, C., 'Mendelssohn und die musikalischen Gattungstraditionen'. In C. Dahlhaus (ed.), *Das Problem Mendelssohn*, Studien zur Musikgeschichte des 19 Jahrhunderts 41. Regensburg, 1974, pp. 55–60

---

37 A. F. J. Thibaut, *Über Reinheit der Tonkunst*, ed. R. Heuler (Paderborn, 1907), p. 105, trans. from Garrett, 'Palestrina', p. 120.   38 Dahlhaus, *Nineteenth-Century Music*, p. 164.

Nineteenth-Century Music, trans. J. B. Robinson. Berkeley and Los Angeles, 1989

Dixon, G., 'The Performance of Palestrina: Some Questions, but Fewer Answers'. *Early Music*, 22 (1994), pp. 667–75

Ellis, K., *Music Criticism in Nineteenth Century Paris: 'La Revue et Gazette Musicale de Paris'*, *1834–80*. Cambridge, 1995

Forkel, J. N., *Allgemeine Geschichte der Musik*. 2 vols., Leipzig, 1801

Garratt, J., 'Palestrina and the German Romantic Imagination: Interpreting Historicism in Nineteenth-Century Music.' Ph.D. diss., University of Wales Cardiff (1999)

Gatens, W. J., *Victorian Cathedral Music in Theory and Practice*. Cambridge, 1986

Geck, M., 'Friedrich Schneiders "Weltgericht": Zum Verständnis des Trivialen in der Musik'. In C. Dahlhaus (ed.), *Studien zur Trivialmusik des 19. Jahrhunderts*. Studien zur Musikgeschichte des 19 Jahrhunderts 8. Regensburg, 1967, pp. 97–109

Die Wiederentdeckung der Matthäuspassion im 19. Jahrhundert, Studien zur Musikgeschichte des 19 Jahrhunderts 9. Regensburg, 1967

Grossmann-Vendrey, S., 'Mendelssohn und die Vergangenheit'. In W. Wiora (ed.), *Die Ausbreitung des Historismus über die Musik*, Studien zur Musikgeschichte des 19 Jahrhunderts 14. Regensburg, 1969, pp. 73–84

Hiller, J. A., *Kurze und erleichterte Anweisung zum Singen*. Leipzig, 1792

Kuzma, M., 'Bortniansky à la Bortniansky: An Examination of the Sources of Dmitry Bortniansky's Choral Concertos'. *Journal of Musicology*, 14 (1996), pp. 183–209

Lichtenfeld, M., 'Zur Geschichte, Idee und Ästhetik des historischen Konzerts'. In W. Wiora (ed.), *Die Ausbreitung des Historismus über die Musik*, Studien zur Musikgeschichte des 19 Jahrhunderts 14. Regensburg, 1969, pp. 41–53

Locke, R. P., 'Paris: Centre of Intellectual Ferment'. In A. Ringer (ed.), *The Early Romantic Era*. Englewood Cliffs, 1990, pp. 32–83

Mercer-Taylor, P., 'Rethinking Mendelssohn's Historicism: A Lesson from *St. Paul*'. *Journal of Musicology*, 15 (1997), pp. 208–29

Plantinga, L., *Romantic Music: A History of Musical Style in Nineteenth-Century Europe*. New York, 1984

Porter, C. H., 'The New Public and the Reordering of the Musical Establishment: The Lower Rhine Music Festivals, 1818–67'. *19th Century Music*, 3 (1979–80), pp. 211–24

Rosen, C., *The Romantic Generation*. Cambridge, Mass., 1995, and London, 1996

Rosselli, J. 'Italy: The Centrality of Opera'. In A. Ringer (ed.), *The Early Romantic Era*. Englewood Cliffs, 1990, pp. 160–200

Temperley, N., *Haydn: Creation*. Cambridge, 1991

Thibaut, A. F. J., *Über Reinheit der Tonkunst*, ed. R. Heuler. Paderborn, 1907

Todd, R. L., *Mendelssohn's Musical Education: A Study and Edition of his Exercises in Composition*. Cambridge, 1983

Weber, W., 'The Muddle of the Middle Classes'. *19th Century Music*, 3 (1979–80), pp. 175–85

Wiora, W., 'Grenzen und Stadien des Historismus in der Musik'. In W. Wiora (ed.), *Die Ausbreitung des Historismus über die Musik*, Studien zur Musikgeschichte des 19 Jahrhunderts 14. Regensburg, 1969, pp. 299–327

Yovel, Y., *Kant and the Philosophy of History*. Princeton, 1980

9

The consumption of music

DEREK CAREW

Social background

For most Europeans and North Americans at the beginning of the nineteenth century, the legacy of the French and the Industrial Revolutions was a social and economic transformation which saw the virtual destruction of one social class, the peasantry, and the hegemony of a newer one, the bourgeoisie. In the ensuing 'age of capital' the rise of the bourgeoisie and its relationship with the nobility is as complex as it is important, and a degree of generalisation must be forgiven in what is a musical, rather than a social, history. The pace and the precise nature of this transformation differed from region to region; this chapter, however, is concerned only with the principal areas of Europe in which it is evident: Great Britain, France and the German-speaking lands. And although the bourgeoisie was by no means exclusively citified, my focus will be London, Paris and Vienna, as it is in these, the major European capitals of the early nineteenth century, that the developments can be seen at their most concentrated.

Because Britain had had her political revolution at an earlier date, the power of the monarchy posed no great threat, and, for the most part, little inconvenience. Nor did the rise of the bourgeoisie significantly challenge the nobility, since new industrial capital soon formed the main component in national capital, overtaking landed inheritance, and leaving the latter safe in the hands of its hereditary owners for their own posterity. This also meant that surplus aristocratic capital could be invested in new and exciting ventures such as the railways[1] which had the advantage of being not only British, but on home ground, as opposed to some of the more distant foreign ventures, where the volatility of local conditions could, and often did, jeopardise investments; the loss of the American states was a sobering lesson, in terms of national imperial pride as well as of economics. As a corollary, the wealthier members of the bour-

---

[1] 'In what path of life can a man be found that will not animate his pursuit from seeing the steam engine of Watt? It . . . gives nerve and vigour to our own endeavours.' A. Young, *Tours in England and Wales (selected from the Annals of Agriculture)*, School of Economic and Political Science (London, 1932), p. 269.

geoisie could – and did – buy estates which gave parliamentary entry and, frequently, ennoblement; thus, the possession of any of the three requirements of influential status – wealth, land, a title – almost automatically implied, or soon attracted, the remainder. The ease, in spite of their differences (and these became less and less apparent as the century wore on), with which aristocracy and bourgeoisie could work together was, in effect, an alliance; it was to the advantage of all but the emergent working class and put Britain, even in the later eighteenth century, in the vanguard of capitalism. Carefully regulated intermarriage between 'blood and money' could not but hasten the eventual interchangeability of the two classes.

Any such cosiness between the middle class and nobility in France was historically impossible and effectively ruled out by the Revolution. The French middle class looked for its support not upwards, but downwards, towards the petty bourgeoisie of traders and artisans, and to the poor, but still extant, peasantry, although it was as capable of subduing the latter, in its later guise of a proletariat, as it had been of harnessing its help against the aristocracy and church.[2] But, in a vague analogy with its British counterpart, it also looked across, so to speak, fraternising with the lesser aristocracy. These were the Orleanist nobility, middle-class members who had more recently been ennobled for the purposes of filling administrative office, the so-called *noblesse de robe*, as opposed to the Legitimist *noblesse d'epée*; this fraternisation only served to isolate the latter even more. Thus, the rise of capitalism and the more extreme effects associated with it were delayed in France until later in the nineteenth century.

Unlike Britain and France, there was no buffer between the Austrian high nobility and the middle classes. In the case of Vienna, the very recent acquisition of capital status resulted in a bourgeoisie of lesser means and lineage which tended to look inwards to itself and to remain more cohesive and perhaps less opulent (given the lateness of the spread of industrialisation) than that in London or Paris. Vienna, however, was always a city of paradoxes, no less in this than in other matters.

In spite of the obvious geographical and linguistic distinctions, as well as the differences in the pace and manner of its emergence, the bourgeoisie showed sufficient homogeneity to warrant it being regarded internationally as a class or caste. Given the widespread volatility in all fields during the first half of the nineteenth century, its position as the filling of a social sandwich between an oppressed and overworked peasantry (or working class) on the one hand, and a self-sufficient aristocracy with residual, though reduced, privileges on the

2 M. A. Beaud, *A History of Capitalism 1500–1980*, trans. T. Dickman and A. Lefebvre (London and Basingstoke, 1984), chapter 3.

other, might on the face of it be viewed as precarious. This, however, was far from the reality. Fulfilling, at the time of its first glimmerings, a largely entrepreneurial function – in the commercial world as merchants and traders, in the financial world as bankers and money-lenders,[3] in the legal world as jurists and advocates, and in the administrative world of the state as bureaucrats – this bourgeois class became a pro-active one which rapidly gained controlling interests. Once the French and Industrial Revolutions had seen to the end of its frustration at having wealth and a good degree of control but little legislative say or power, the familiar traits which characterised it – self-confidence, affluence, prudence (perhaps prurience) and self-sufficiency – asserted themselves. This was a class whose wealth and status came, in most cases, not from inherited lands, and the attendant assumptions of priority and privilege, but from good management and prudent investment of finances, and a dedication to hard work and self-improvement. In these, members saw themselves as being – and with justification – the antithesis of aristocratic extravagance, indolence and lasciviousness, and the fact that their own efforts, rather than their caste privileges, were responsible for their well-being gave them a great sense of the value of the individual and a pride in that individuality.

It would be surprising if, as with all other classes and cadres, the preoccupations of this one were not to be discoverable in its artefacts, cultural and physical, and, more importantly, if its image of itself were not also carefully projected. The furniture of the bourgeoisie was more functional and relatively more informal than its aristocratic counterpart, which was elegant, but stilted and very occasional, designed with formality of gesture and conversation in mind, rather than interaction. Bourgeois drapery was heavy and dark, calculated to exclude, thereby emphasising the closeness and cohesion of the family unit; and its pastimes followed suit – the communal entertainments of parlour or drawing-room in which everyone joined and to which everyone contributed, the vital element of which was music.

Musical taste

The music or entertainment-with-music which one heard, even in some of the more up-market concert venues cited in chapter 3, varied with the day of the week and the season of the year: with, perhaps, the exception of the purpose-built concert room or hall, the same venue was happily used for grand opera, vaudeville, symphony concert, masquerade, play, melodrama, ball or oratorio. Concert programmes frequently exhibited this catholicity of taste, with a

3 The power of this function can be seen in the case of, for example, the Rothschild dynasty, which could financially bail out whole countries after the Napoleonic Wars.

definite shift towards the popular. Singers, solo pianists, orchestral items, sacred extracts, improvisations, concertos, chamber pieces, folk troupes, and 'novelty turns' (such as playing the violin upside-down) could be found sharing the limelight with a Beethoven or Haydn symphony or two. Works, including those by composers who were already being groomed for the musico-social canon, were paraphrased, simplified and even rewritten. On 6 March 1819, the Theatre Royal, Covent Garden, offered the *Marriage of Figaro*: 'The Overture and Musick selected chiefly from Mozart's Opera / The new Musick composed, & the whole arranged & adapted to he English Stage, by Mr. BISHOP', and as late as August 1843, Ronzi De Begnis appeared '"for this one night only" in *Norma* "compressed into one act"'.[4] But the shift to the popular can also be seen in opera subjects, with the trend away from the aristocratic preference for the Classical towards more recent – in some cases very recent – history, which went hand in hand with a penchant for the darker side of human nature, the supernatural, and the military and bellicose. This was aided by large casts and orchestras, with great emphasis on spectacle and elaborate settings, effects and scenery, especially after gas lighting was introduced in 1822.

The catholic concert programmes described above, together with the performance conditions characteristic for the operatic repertory, are a warning against any attempt to apply our careful present-day compartmentalisation of musical styles: Classical (or art), popular, pop, folk, light Classical, not to mention the divisions which reside within these generalities. These can obscure the fact that such oppositions between 'Classical' and 'popular', or 'high' and 'low' styles carried little weight until around the middle of the century and were themselves an indication of the bourgeoisie's ascendancy to a semi-autocratic cultural elite. Contrasts there certainly were, and awareness of those contrasts, but they were viewed as complements, not as oppositions or as mutually exclusive. Carl Dahlhaus has drawn attention to some of them, and especially the Beethoven–Rossini polarisation, discussed already in this volume:[5] the one based on what was perceived as spontaneous, vocal melody, approachable and moving, and which anyone could hum; the other the carefully crafted instrumental music of a genius, cerebral and rarely hummable, the object of aesthetic wonder. This divide is also to do with texted music as opposed to 'absolute' music, which was the epitome of 'Classical' music and to which we will return in discussing domestic music.

Another result of this polarisation was a kind of creative schizophrenia, which was revealed by the differing quality of the music composers produced

4 Quoted in S. Sadie (ed.), *The New Grove Dictionary of Music and Musicians* (London, 1995), XI, p. 174.
5 C. Dahlhaus, *Nineteenth-Century Music*, trans. J. B. Robinson (Berkeley and Los Angeles, 1989), pp. 8–15.

for different markets. The trite variation sets of such figures as Hummel, Moscheles and Czerny give little idea of the quality of their sacred music or piano sonatas, for example. And even Beethoven was not immune, as we shall see. The inclusion of popular styles and genres in more serious works could be seen, perhaps, as an attempt to bridge the gap. Beethoven is a powerful instance in the extreme vacillations of styles between high seriousness and low comedy – frequently within a few bars – in late instrumental works such as the String Quartet in C sharp minor, Op. 131, and even in his use of variations in the late piano sonatas, and in movements such as the Alla danza tedesca fourth movement of the B flat major String Quartet, Op. 130. Such stylistic apostrophes would reach one extreme later in the century in Mahler's savage parodies. In the first half of the century, only Chopin consistently managed to write great music while at the same time not seriously compromising the swing of the waltz or the spirit and folkiness of the mazurka.

Folk music

Indeed, the most compelling expression of the high–low, emotional–cerebral, instrumental–vocal axes was the great consumption of 'folksong' during the early nineteenth century. An interest in this area had been evident for some time; already the cultural ground had been cleared for the riot of vernacular vegetation which would spread so lushly in our period. The formalism of the *ancien régime*, with its stiff deportment and codification of dress, conversation and manners, was more and more seen as artificial. Rousseau was not alone in pointing to this, when he linked nature to human nature and contrasted both with the artificiality of aristocratic behaviour, and the crushing of spontaneity in children by extant educational practice. The contrast with the homely, rugged, honest vulgarity of the peasant and artisan was one that became more apparent with the developing interest in the activities of those classes; scenes of low, indoor life, most of them with a moral message (warning against seduction, etc.), had already become fashionable in genre painting; stories, lore and music were collected, and laundered, for drawing-room use. The substitution of a north-western (chiefly Celtic) pantheon for the familiar Hellenic one was a threat to the status of Classical literature, the cornerstone of eighteenth-century education with which the aristocratic class particularly associated itself.[6]

The revolt against social, political and religious strictures was seen as one against old, entrenched and stagnant institutions carried out by the young, the

6 Offenbach was to satirise this as late as 1856 in *Orphée aux enfers*.

dynamic and the creative. The immediacy and freshness of art became germane; less importance was to be attached to submission to academic or theoretical strictures than to the spontaneous flights of the unfettered imagination,[7] occasionally at the expense of certain residual awkwardnesses, even 'barbarisms'. These awkwardnesses were very much part of the 'Sublime', the awe-inspiring aesthetic category of the previous century, associated with mountains and wild places, which would undergo an easy transformation into the more Romantic view of nature as organic, and inhabited by a spirit or personality, a country cousin to Hegel's *Weltgeist*. This is clear in the depiction of nature in such works as C. D. Friedrich's painting *The Wanderer above the Mists* (*c.* 1817–18), in the popularity of Scott's novels and Shakespeare's plays and, in music, with Beethoven, particularly the orchestral works.

Another important aspect of the consumption of folk music and lore can best be seen in Britain. The land enclosures – in effect a calculated disenfranchisement of the peasant class in the name of large-scale farming efficiency – were intensified in the period between 1760 and 1830, and, aggravated by the New Poor Law of 1834 – 'a statute of quite uncommon callousness'[8] – they forced peasant migration and decimated not only farming communities but, because of the dependence of many villagers on the commons, much village life and indeed the villages themselves. One result of this was the great nostalgia engendered, for different, very often opposite, things; for the perceived and perhaps imperfectly remembered stability of the pre-revolutionary systems; for the slow rate of change that characterised those times, making them seem, in an age of rapid change and unrest, like a golden age; and for the agrarian life based on slow seasonal change which seemed unaltered for millennia, as opposed to the grime, poverty, disease and overcrowdedness of the industrial city. This last was felt most keenly by the inflowing migrant peasantry, which made their previous lives seem like idylls of freedom and self-sufficiency. Even the righteous fury of John Clare could be momentarily checked by nostalgia:

> And w[h]ere[']s that lovley maid in days gone by
> The farmers daughter unreserved tho shye
> That milked her cows and old songs used to sing
> As red and rosey as the lovely spring
> Ah these have dwindled to a formal shade
> As pale and bed[-]rid as my ladys maid[9]

---

7 Madame de Staël puts this well: 'Les règles de l'art sont un calcul de probabilités sur les moyens de réussir; et si le succès est obtenu, il importe peu de s'y être soumis'. G. de Staël, *De la littérature considerée dans ses rapports avec les institutions sociales* (Paris, 1872), p. 176.

8 E. J. Hobsbawm, *The Age of Revolution: Europe 1789–1848*, rep. edn (London, 1977; original edn 1962), p. 203.

9 J. Clare, *The Parish: A Satire*, ed. E. Robinson (Harmondsworth, 1986), II, pp. 143–8. The orthography has been preserved, except for bracketed additions. Clare was here remembering people he had known.

In the previous century, such feelings had already been at the root of what was effectively a 'folk' industry, with collections such as Bishop Percy's *Reliques of Ancient English Poetry*, in 3 volumes (1765, with its fourth edition appearing in 1794); Chatterton's 'Rowley' forgeries; Robert Burns's *Poems, chiefly in the Scottish Dialect* 1786 (two editions). Herder's conviction that a people's soul resided in its natural vernacular music was of great influence on the first wave of the German Romantics and the Sturm und Drang movement – which embodied a return to naturalness and a revolt against literary conventions – and led him to coin the word 'folksong'. His *Volkslieder* (2 vols. 1778–9) provided a rich loam in which German nationalism would thrive, giving rise to the Berlin lied school of Schulz and Reichardt, whose influence on later composers such as Schubert and Weber is well attested. MacPherson's famous forgeries of the 1760s, the earliest being *Fragments of Ancient Poetry, Collected in the Highlands of Scotland, and Translated from the Galic or Erse Language* purporting to be the remains of the poetry of the bard Ossian (the Goidelic Oisín), was the first of several Celtic sallies on European artistic consciousness. The very title is an eighteenth-century publisher's dream, full of the 'buzz-words' of the time: 'Fragments' suggesting a great lost (in the sense of untranslated) literature; the painstaking labour-of-love of collecting and translating; the recourse to the Sublime in 'Highlands', mountains being ever the places of the spirit; and the Galic/Erse, suggesting the wildness and isolation of the Celtic countries at this time. It must not be forgotten that Scottish Celtic civilisation was all but destroyed after the battle of Culloden (1746), and the subsequent 'Clearances' of the Highlands were almost literally that, being much more efficient than their English equivalents.

MacPherson's *Fragments*, and his subsequent *Fingal, an Ancient Epic Poem in Six Books* (1762), had a huge and widespread influence on the Continent, inspiring, among others, Klopstock, Schiller, the Goethe of *Werther* and beyond, Schubert, Berlioz and Napoleon, besides spawning works in various genres in various countries.[10] Also important, though less in its own terms, as we shall see, was *A General Collection of Ancient Irish Music*, transcribed and published by Edward Bunting from the few remaining traditional Irish harpers at their meeting in Belfast in 1792.

Such ventures would continue with renewed energy in the nineteenth century. Sir Walter Scott's *Border Minstrelsy* (1802–3) captivated Europe, as did the chivalric Gothic romance of his novels, with their high adventurousness set in wild landscapes, yet their ability to draw the reader in with their immediacy. The aim of Edinburgh publisher George Thomson's various collections of

---

10 See Dahlhaus, *Nineteenth-Century Music*, p. 21.

Scottish, Welsh and Irish airs (Edinburgh, 1792–1816) was to provide a series of arrangements which, because of their instrumentation – various combinations and substitutions of voice, piano, flute, violin etc. – and their lack of technical difficulty, could be performed in the average middle-class drawing-room. The spectacle of no less than Beethoven taking time off from the composition of one of his most cerebral works, the 'Hammerklavier' Sonata, to set Irish, English and Scottish folksongs for these volumes, is a reminder that such work had become acceptable as well as lucrative.[11] Other composers whose talents Thomson enlisted were Josef Haydn, who produced some 400 settings – including work for other Scottish publishers in a similar vein who jumped on the folk bandwagon – Weber, Hummel, Pleyel, Kozeluch and Bishop.

The fact that Thomson's airs were almost all taken from earlier collections did nothing to diminish their popularity or saleability, and recycling of the more popular airs was a feature of the whole movement. Other collections of folk or folk-influenced material included those of Arnim and Brentano (*Des Knaben Wunderhorn*, 1805–8) and the Grimm brothers' *Kinder- und Hausmärchen* (1812–15), which were translated into English with atmospheric illustrations by George Cruikshank as *German Popular Stories* and published in 1823.

Inevitably, traditional material suffered at the hands of the redactors, the songs particularly, with the removal of what were seen as literary and musical crudities and the substitution of drawing-room sensibility. A rather neat way of circumventing the textual problems, especially when excision would distort the sense or narrative flow, or necessitate wholesale restructuring, was simply to compose a new text. Thomson, as well as engaging composers, also drew on the services of poets, of whom Robert Burns was one. But the most famous of all such collections was that of the Classicist,[12] folkloric polymath and composer, Thomas Moore, exhibiting his talents as poet,[13] folk-collector (to a small degree) and arranger. This was the *Irish Melodies*, in ten volumes and a supplement, issued between 1808 (the first number of twenty-four songs including twelve taken from Bunting's collection) and 1834 with 'symphonies and accompaniments' by Sir John Stevenson, and, after his death in 1833, by Bishop. With the songs of Stephen Foster, *Moore's Melodies* (as they soon

11 The settings (by leading composers of the day) ranged from vocal to instrumental, including piano trio, flute trio and flute and piano.

12 He was nicknamed 'Anacreontic' Moore because of his published translation of Anacreon's odes while still a student at Trinity College, Dublin. Moore was one of the first students to enrol after the university was opened to Catholics.

13 An indication of the tremendous popularity and high status of Moore as a littérateur can be seen from his widespread publications – many in the original English – in France and the German-speaking lands. The 'Advertisement' to T. Moore, *The Works of Thomas Moore, Esq. accurately printed from the last original editions. with additional notes. complete in one volume* (Leipzig, 1826) ends: 'We beg leave to inform the friends of English literature, that new, complete, and critical editions of "Milton's Works" and "Ossian's Poems" are now preparing for publication'.

became known) were 'the most popular, widely sung, best-loved, and most durable songs in the English language of the entire nineteenth century'.[14] The staple vocal diet of the middle-class drawing-room from the Georgian through the Victorian and well into the Edwardian eras, they were also an important model for popular music in America.[15] Extra immediacy was lent to them by Moore's own performances, frequently with his own guitar accompaniment.

It is interesting, though perhaps understandable, that Moore should counter the occasional accusations that there was a 'mischievous' political message in his Irish-orientated publications (by no means his only class of publication) when he distanced himself, to put it mildly, from 'those who identify nationality with treason . . . nursed in the gloom of prejudice . . . an ignorant and angry multitude' and, most revealingly, continued:

> it is not through that gross and inflammable region of society [that] a work of this nature could ever have been intended to circulate. It looks much higher for its audience and its readers – it is found upon the piano-fortes of the rich and the educated – of those who can afford to have their national zeal a little stimulated, without exciting much dread of the excesses into which it may hurry them . . .[16]

It is difficult not to perceive here a cultural analogue of the politico-commercial appropriation of property and the means of livelihood of the classes which Moore evidently abhorred. It is even more surprising, if not ironic, however, to find him criticising the very carriers of the culture which was the basis of much of his considerable wealth, for

> foreign innovation . . . the chief corruptions of which we have to complain, arise from the unskilful performance of our own itinerant musicians, from whom, too frequently, the airs are noted down, encumbered by their tasteless decorations, and responsible for all their ignorant anomalies . . . yet, in most of them . . . the pure gold of the melody shines through the ungraceful foliage which surrounds it – and the most delicate and difficult duty of a compiler is to endeavour, as much as possible, by retrenching these inelegant superfluities, and collating the various methods of playing or singing each air, to restore the regularity of its form, and the chaste simplicity of its character.[17]

In a few sentences, the preservers of one of the great traditional cultures of Europe are dismissed. The passage neatly encapsulates the chauvinism so prevalent in the period in its portrayal of the middle-class folk arranger/collector as one who rescues an Old Master from a daubing child. And Moore was one of the more sensitive and careful.

---

14 C. Hamm, *Yesterdays: Popular Song in America* (New York, 1979), p. 44.   15 *Ibid.*
16 'Letter to the Marchioness Dowager of Donegal', prefixed to the Third Number, in Moore, *Works*.
17 *Ibid.*

Given the laundering, it is hard to expect anything distinctive of the 'origi-nals' to be left, and yet there are 'folk' characters in many of the pieces in all the main collections, and they were paramount in the songs' popularity. Commentators frequently talk of 'wildness', and even 'barbarity', referring to what, in the surprised eyes of their modern counterparts, seems, often, not far removed from a Donizetti melody. The comparison, however, is not inapt. The primacy of melody in the eighteenth century continued in the nineteenth and can be seen by the prevalence of genres which highlight melody: vocal and choral music in general, opera and song, and a preference for the characteristic piano piece, particularly the nocturne and its relatives. Furthermore, operatic melody itself had undergone a simplification and, to a degree, a vernacularisa-tion process. Bellinian bel canto, the period's highest melodic ideal, and most clearly evident in the music of the piano virtuosi, particularly Chopin, was itself conditioned by elements of his native Sicilian folk music – although refined – in the use of small intervals and the overall impression of a music generated by the words, or at least the verbal accents. There is also the high frequency of com-pound time-signatures, a characteristic of southern European folk dance in general, and particularly of that of Italy and Sicily. That these characteristics are generally so prevalent in Italian opera of the period only serves to underline the connections.

With the collections of folk music, especially the northern European ones, many of these traits can, of course, be seen. But no one would mistake the jig for the tarantella in spite of the rhythmic similarity. Idiomatic touches such as the preference for octave leaps, the approach to a leap (commonly a sixth or a seventh) by conjunct movement in the same direction, and the progression towards a climactic pause, often with considerable emotional impact, undi-minished by strophic repetition, gave the melodies a distinction which greatly impressed the drawing-room listeners. The remnants of the original modality which were not excised or 'corrected' also fascinated: flattened sevenths and/or sixths, major/minor switches, sharpened fourths and, even in the diatonic Ionian, or Doh mode, the different emphasis given to the degrees, frequently ending off-tonic. There were also the eccentric rhythms and phrase-structures, which veered between the very regular and the tantalisingly irregular. Decorations – again, those few which escaped the censor – remained as quaint-nesses, although they rarely went beyond the kind of decorative addition to be found in any self-respecting prima donna's technical bag of tricks.

Such features, together with the songs' widespread familiarity, also made these tunes unusually amenable for variation-sets, as the tens of thousands of published examples testify. The vast majority of these were free-standing sets for solo piano such as Clementi's *The Black Joke*, Mendelssohn's *Fantasia on a*

Favorite [*sic*] *Irish Melody* (a set of variations, in spite of its name) and the three sets of Scottish tunes which comprise Ries's Op. 101, together with those which Beethoven set in his Op. 107, etc. But there are also many examples occurring as movements of sonatas and for chamber ensembles, such as Hummel's on the Russian folksong popularly known as 'Schöne Minka'.[18] The simpler airs were also ideal for teaching children.

Rondos based on folksongs and the popular tunes which emulated them were also prodigiously in vogue, both as free-standing pieces or as parts of larger cyclical works. The advertisement 'Rondo on the Celebrated Air . . .' was bound to sell, and also infected the 'higher' forms, as in Cramer's *Sonata (Letter C) in which are Introduced the favorite* [*sic*] *Airs of Lochaber & The Graces* and, of course, the concerto finale. It is also not surprising that the piano-and-orchestra repertory should be affected by these two forms, and among the relatively new forms were those comprising an introduction (usually slow) followed by a rondo or a set of variations based on a folk or popular tune. There was also a brisk trade in folk-emulations, particularly popular in Britain, such as those by Arne, Hook and Bishop, for example. Arne's melodic style, though not in the folk tradition, was characterised by Burney as 'an agreeable mixture of Italian, English and Scots'; his frequent visits to Dublin – where his estranged wife settled – may have been part of the equation too. The titles of many of his stage works are interesting, and show a marked penchant for the pastoral. They include *The Country Lasses*, *The Sheep-Shearing*, *Squire Badger*, and the much admired *Love in a Village*. Hook also affected a kind of Scottish-pastoral idiom, so successfully that his best tunes were thought to be folksongs, the most famous being *The Lass of Richmond Hill*.

Often the basis is not a particular tune – 'genuine' or not – but a national style. This is another relatively new feature emerging in the first half of the nineteenth century. The view of the *ancien régime* was one in which the ruling houses all seemed to a great extent to be related – as many in fact were – sharing, in French, a common language (literally the *lingua franca* of the Enlightenment) rather than the vernacular (which was usually reserved for servants and animals), and in which music was dominated by opera seria in Italian. This was contrasted with the emergence of regional nationalities, whose individuality – the prime bourgeois trait – was to be expressed in its national language, culture, architecture and music, of which the vernacular forms were, naturally, the most cogent and distinctive. The ironic fact that folk music and lore are usually regional rather than national, and that the folk traditions of many nations had supranational traits in common, was not a factor in the heady

---

18 Weber also wrote a set of variations on this tune for piano solo.

period following the French and other revolutions, where nationality became an issue. Not surprisingly, most of the older national anthems date from the late eighteenth and early nineteenth centuries.

In many cases a suggestion of a rather simple kind would suffice for folkiness, nationality or distinctive regionality being expressed in characteristic dance-rhythms – the tarantella or saltarello of southern Italy, the bolero of Spain, the Irish and Scottish jig – or symbolised in sound and representation by national instruments – harp, guitar, zither, bagpipes etc. – or by characteristic vocal techniques, such as the yodelling of the Austrian or Swiss Alpine regions.

The travelling virtuosi certainly realised the value of national compliments by including national material in works composed for their visits to a particular country or area. Moscheles was gently lampooned for this in connection with his visit to Scotland in February 1828, when a critic wrote of his playing:

> 'Anticipations of Scotland', a new composition, in which he, perhaps introduced the old song, 'I dreamt a golden dream'. He will, doubtless, publish this, and, most probably write another under the title of *Le retour de l'Ecosse* [*sic*], wherein he may give us the beautiful Scotish [*sic*] air, 'There's nae luck', followed by another almost as good, 'Todlen hame'.[19]

Music in private

But there were other, social, functions which music also fulfilled. In particular, the more intimate aspects of music-making formed a gentler foil to the hurly-burly and giddy virtuosity of the public concert. A self-protectiveness, manifesting itself in public in the various clubs, societies and alliances which mushroomed at this time, was even more clearly seen in an institution which took on its distinctive shape and importance during this period – the enclosed family in the private home. The early nineteenth-century bourgeois patriarch could relax in the bosom of his family to the adoration and attendance of dutiful wife and well-behaved children and servants, wielding a benevolent authority frequently reinforced by the birch.[20] Although the first half of the nineteenth century saw a polarisation in musical genres and in scale of performance, a paradoxical drawing together of the public and private manners also became apparent: that which distinguished, say, a string quartet from a symphony or a sonata from a concerto during the eighteenth century, became much less discernible in the next, especially when chamber music began to partake of both manners; also, the same sentimental song performed from sheet-music in

---

19 *The Harmonicon*, 6/2 (February, 1828), p. 135.
20 See the rather poignant paintings by the children of the wealthy banking family Drummond *c.* 1828 in S. Lasdun, *Victorians at Home* (London, 1981), pp. 36–7.

the drawing-room of Victorian London, Biedermeier Vienna or Paris between the revolutions, was equally likely to feature in the vocal insertions of an orchestral concert. The closedness and cohesion of the bourgeois family of the period, and its reflection in the ambience of the [with]drawing-room, has already been remarked. Music in general, and the piano in particular, was literally as well as figuratively central here, and all the latter's versatility would be called into play. It would take pride of place in the performance of rondos and variations, with both genres frequently based on well-known folk, popular or operatic tunes and with the added advantage that the looseness of the average set of variations would permit selection based on technical difficulty or general mood, while many of the impressive-sounding ones could be mastered by overcoming a particular point of technique. For the more musically literate gatherings, a sonata or sonata-extract would feature, but the new early nineteenth-century favourite genre, the character piece, including nocturne, ballad, or song-without-words, would predominate. All three were the solo-piano analogues of the most important form of entertainment, the song, combining sentimental, or sentimentalised, and on occasion religious, poetry couched in appropriate music featuring the piano as an accompanying instrument, and showing the young ladies of the house at their most fetching, affecting, non-cerebral and submissive. Instrumental chamber groups were also popular, with the same or similar musical fare, combining piano with – most commonly – flute, violin and/or cello, and, occasionally, harp.

Larger, more prosperous houses had rather bigger ideas: their salons were imbued with the spirit of the court and became meeting-places for artists, thinkers, writers and other professionals as well as the local intelligentsia. Presided over by women, their organisation and planning was, with few exceptions, the closest to a profession a woman of the period could approach. The Mendelssohn salon in Berlin was atypical only in the voluminous amount and sterling quality of its music and in the case of its guiding light after 1831, Mendelssohn's sister Fanny, was indeed a substitute for the professions of composer and performer which she was so sadly denied.[21] At the Sunday morning meetings (Sonntagsmusiken), often a hundred-strong and featuring a choir and the hired opera-orchestra when concerto performances were included, one could meet Paganini, Weber, Liszt, Ingres,[22] Heine, E. T. A. Hoffmann, Tieck,

21 She wrote ruefully to her fiancé, shortly before their wedding in late 1829: 'Art is not for women, only for girls; on the threshold of my new life I take leave of this child's playmate'. M. J. Citron, 'The Lieder of Fanny Mendelssohn Hensel', *Musical Quarterly*, 69 (1983), p. 571.

22 Charles Hallé recalls accompanying Ingres in Mozart violin sonatas at Armand Bertin's salon in Paris in the early 1840s: 'Great artist that he was, with an immense reputation, he thought less of his painting than of his violin playing, which, to say the least of it, was vile'. C. Hallé, *The Autobiography of Charles Hallé with Correspondence and Diaries*, ed. M. Kennedy (New York, 1981), p. 97.

Goethe, La Motte Fouqué, Clemens Brentano and Hegel. These occasions were
the continuation of a long tradition in the Mendelssohn family, which was
renowned for its generations of strong intellectual women, including those of
the well-established Salomon family and the formidable Itzigs. Salons were a
halfway house between the drawing-room and the concert hall, and were
important venues for introducing new talent of all kinds, as well as being a
good entrée into high society and invaluable for the furtherance of all kinds of
career.

The dissemination of music

The proliferation of domestic and semi-domestic music-making gave rise to the
consumption of music on an unprecedented scale and provided a market which
had a predictable effect on music-production, a market to which composers
were not slow to respond. But the dissemination of this product was a problem
which required drastic measures, involving compromises between print-
quality, speed of production, and size of print-run. The extant methods of
printing music – type and engraving – were used but, typically for this period,
underwent important new developments, while, again typically, a new method
was invented: lithography. Musical type was used in the same way as letters,
each note or rest having its own type. This was time-consuming, especially
as the number of different kinds of notes and symbols grew during the late
eighteenth and nineteenth centuries; it required the luxury, for most printing-
houses, of a musically literate compositor and often needed several impressions, one each for notes, staves, texts and other features. This was excellent for
music examples included in books, but streamlining was necessary for music
scores.

   Already fine-tuned to the needs of art and map-making, engraving was used
for music and brought to a fine art in the second half of the eighteenth century.
Its development in Vienna by Artaria and Torricella was in response to an
increase not only in large-scale forms but to the expansion of the orchestra and
the increase in their numbers, larger numbers of parts being required. Type was
too slow and cumbersome for this, and the copper or pewter plate, with its
drawn staves and symbols and its punched notes, allowed for ease of correction
and could be used for printing larger numbers of copies. Furthermore, the
plates could be stored for later editions. This method was responsible for the
dissemination of, especially, the Viennese Classics, and the early Romantics. A
further advantage was the ability to include illustrations for title-pages and
frontispieces.

   But it was lithography, the revolutionary method invented by Alois

Senefelder as a cheaper way of publishing his own plays, which solved most of the music publisher's problems. It was closely associated with music from the beginning and was rapidly improved so that the cumbersome stones were replaced by metal plates, and manuscript, if written on the right kind of paper with the right kind of ink, would transfer directly to the plates. This gave composers direct control over their works and allowed for self-publication. Among composers who, for different reasons, resorted to this particular expression of self-sufficiency were Weber – his Op. 2 piano variations – and, famously, Wagner, who wrote out the 450 pages of *Tannhäuser* in full score in 1845, ready for immediate transfer to the plates. Lithography, as it continued to be called, was adopted by all the major music printers, though it lacked the clarity of engraved music, which continued to be used extensively. It was, however, a quarter of the cost of engraving, and was ideal for illustrations, and multicoloured ones at that. Such illustrations, gracing the publications of sentimental or patriotic ballads, made them even more acceptable in the drawing-room. Many of the new publishing firms founded in this period are still trading today, among them Chappell, Boosey, Cramer, Novello and Eulenberg. Furthermore, quicker and, above all, safer modes of transporting goods and people, including the new railways and steamships, contributed to satisfying the greatly increased demand for music.

Dance

Another prominent feature of domestic music-making was music for dancing. The situation in the late eighteenth century is illustrated neatly and with customary unforced genius in the ballroom scene from the finale of the second act of Mozart's *Don Giovanni* (1788), where, simultaneously, three separate bands play a minuet in $\frac{3}{4}$ for the aristocrats' masked ball, a *contredanse* in $\frac{2}{4}$ for the bourgeoisie, and a *Deutsche*, or German dance in $\frac{3}{8}$ for the lower orders. The long history of the courtly minuet – it was still the foremost dance in aristocratic balls in the first quarter of the nineteenth century – had much to do with its grace and versatility. Danced by a series of individual couples who met and touched only occasionally, it gave opportunity for spectacle and appraisal, while a relatively simple floor-pattern allowed for the incorporation of various different kinds of step, all complex, and frequently borrowed from other dances.

But its formality and relative gentleness of pace and demeanour were at odds with the social climate of our period, and the preference grew for simpler round dances with closer proximity of dancers and less of a competitive sense – at least as far as the dancing was concerned. Again, as with the drawing-room ballad, the impetus came from below, socially. The English country dance, which comprised various types of figures and steps, was not confined to the country, nor to the lower social classes. In its most common form two unisex lines provided the couples. However, unlike the minuet, in which the pairing of the couples and the order in which they appeared on the floor was predetermined in accordance with a protocol of precedence, the country dance's figures allowed for varied couplings and even (in a family setting) solo dancing.[23] This continued into the nineteenth, and, indeed, twentieth centuries and is represented in North America in the square dance and in line dancing. It was also imported into France during the eighteenth century and the generic name was transferred directly into French as *contredanse* and although it was furnished with more graceful steps, it was still seen as a lighter form than the minuet, and it became even lighter in the nineteenth century.

It was from Vienna, however, that a dance which was both national and truly international was to spread across Europe – national, in that it was associated always with Austria, but especially Vienna, and international, in that its ethos could not be subjected to localised influences. Unlike all other public dances, and in marked contrast to the noble dances, the waltz had no characteristic figuration. Individual self-absorbed bourgeois couples whirling in and out of a mêlée of others similar was the absolute antithesis of the carefully structured formalism and social placement of the aristocratic ballroom. The waltz was another example of middle-class appropriation of a lower-class form. It began as one of the many types of *Deutscher* (German dances) mostly in triple time danced by embracing twosomes, with names – Dreher, Spinner, Schleifer, Weller – suggestive of the predominating twisting or twirling movement, as, indeed, was the occasionally used *Walzen* which would share with, and eventually supersede, the *ländler* as the generic title for the popular triple-time dance.

These dances were popular in the Vienna Woods and suburbs in the Heurigen, the vineyard inns which kept their country simplicity in spite of their proximity to an increasingly glittering capital; they soon began to encroach on the dance-crazy city, however. To the extant Redoutensäle, comprising a larger and a smaller ballroom, catering for some 3,000 people between them, two splendid new dance halls had been added by the first decade of the nineteenth century. These were the Sperl in 1807, which, with integral beergarden, became one of the great tourist attractions, and the Apollo-Säle in 1808. This last, a sumptuous addition to the city, has been described by one commentator as accommodating:

---

23 As in Diana Sperling's watercolour *Newport Pagnell. Mrs. Hurst dancing. Sepr. 17. 1816.*, in D. Sperling, *Mrs. Hurst dancing & other scenes from Regency life 1812–1823*, G. Mingay (text) (London, 1981), pl. 33.

4000 dancers[24] in five huge halls lined with graceful marble pillars arrayed against mirrored walls that multiplied the brilliance of the crystal chandeliers. For the foot-weary, or those in search of privacy, there were forty-four intimate drawing rooms furnished in rococo style, three flower-filled garden pavilions domed with glass, artificial grottos with waterfalls and live swans, and thirteen kitchens. Half a dozen other establishments vied with each other in lavishness.[25]

This bears out the versatility of use for entertainment-orientated public buildings, mention of which has already been made. When Paganini, who enjoyed gambling, was inveigled into parting with a large sum of money for a venture in Paris, the intention was to provide a complex which would combine a ballroom, a concert hall, billiard, gaming and reading rooms, and a flannel-lined retiring room for the principal artists.[26]

Vienna, untroubled (until 1848) by the revolutions which disturbed much of Europe, had decided, under the iron rule of Metternich, that hedonism, at least from the middle class upwards, was a much-preferred alternative to insurrection, and the spurious equality of the dance hall preferable to political democracy. It was little wonder that this gay and politically stable city should have been chosen to host the Congress of Vienna (1814–15), where the remaining crowned heads of Europe joined their representatives to reorganise the Continent in the wake of Napoleon. And given the city's main distractions, it is also little wonder that, when asked about the Congress's progress, one of those involved replied, famously, '[It] doesn't go; it dances'. [Le Congrès ne marche pas – il danse.]

Several eminent composers had provided music for these balls, illustrating, once again, that lack of snobbish hierarchisation which would characterise music later in the century. Mozart, in accordance with his sole duty when appointed imperial *Kammermusicus* in 1787, had provided sets of *contredanses* and *Deutscher* for the court balls, no less than seven in his last year, excluding single numbers and several sets of minuets. Haydn provided similar music after Mozart's death, and Beethoven's first Viennese orchestral work was such a set: the *Redoutensaal Dances* (1795). Schubert also produced dance music, most of it for the domestic piano, and the lucrative trade in piano arrangements of dances associated with the glittering balls is attested by the works of Hummel, who composed the dances for the opening of the Apollo-Säle.

Music at the Sperl, which included, for variety, some of the rustic *Deutscher* mentioned, was provided by Michael Pamer's more-or-less resident orchestra, but it was two talented young fiddlers, sharing the same desk, who would put

24 Grove V (vol. xx, p. 203) gives 6,000.
25 H. Fantel, *Johann Strauss Father and Son and Their Era* (Newton Abbott, 1971), p. 32.
26 G. I. C. de Courcey, *Paganini, the Genoese*, rep. edn (New York, 1977), II, p. 257.

the new dance on the musical map. Josef Lanner and Johann Strauss I soon formed their own chamber group (two violins, viola and guitar) and began to play in the taverns. The ensemble soon expanded into a more regular-sized orchestra of about twenty, and the waltzes and *ländler* which Lanner composed, especially when grouped in miniature suites with introductions and codas, became very popular. When Strauss also began composing, the contrast between Lanner's lyrical pieces and Strauss's more racy ones made for well-balanced entertainment.

Unfortunately, the public, as always, could never resist partisanship, and the resulting factions placed a wedge between the friends. When they went their separate ways, Strauss's ascendancy was assured. In a stunningly accurate reading of the market worthy of the most hard-nosed British industrialist of the period, Strauss contracted extra players and by 1830 commanded some two hundred, whom he would send out in groups of about twenty-five to play in several venues simultaneously. Aware, from audience reaction, of his personal charisma, he would contrive to make a personal appearance in as many as possible of the dance halls each evening. Hans Fantel describes his frenetic life at this time:

> On a typical evening he would race by fiacre from place to place, conduct the same meticulously rehearsed sequence of waltzes in each location, fight his way out through adoring crowds, and hurry on to the next assignment.
> By about three in the morning he would arrive home, not exhausted, but tingling with the excitement of the hours just passed. In this state of feverish stimulation he would cover his notebooks with ideas for the new waltzes his public constantly demanded. A brief sleep around daybreak sufficed to refresh him for the next rehearsal.[27]

Not even a cholera epidemic in which hundreds died daily could dampen the Viennese enthusiasm for the waltz. While Lanner was honoured with the appointment of Director of Imperial Court Balls in 1829, Strauss managed to engineer an exclusive contract, at a huge fee, with the Sperl. It was here, because of the frequent foreign visitors, that his fame began to spread to the rest of Europe. Wagner, then a teenager, describes Strauss's popularity during a visit to Vienna in the early 1830s:

> I shall never forget the almost hysterical response evoked by every piece of Strauss's in these curious people. A demon within the Viennese populace seems to be summoned anew at the beginning of every waltz. The shudders of sheer pleasure in the audience are unquestionably due to the music rather than the wine, and the frenzied enthusiasm for the magic music master struck me as frightening.[28]

27 Fantel, *Strauss*, p. 41.   28 Quoted in *ibid.*, p. 42.

Much of the effect of this music was the orchestral precision which Strauss had instilled into his players, and this was a major point of comment when Strauss began to take his twenty-eight-strong orchestra abroad in the 1830s. The critic of the London *Morning Post* noted: 'The perfection of such an ensemble our orchestras have never yet reached. The accuracy, the sharpness, the exquisite precision with which every passage is performed, can be the result only of the most careful and persevering practice...'[29] and Berlioz recalled the 'piquant and fanciful waltzes [of] novel rhythm'.[30] In Paris, the aged Paganini, attending one of Strauss's concerts paid him a generous compliment: 'I am so glad to meet a man who has brought so much joy into the world'.[31]

But there were obstacles to overcome and a certain amount of winning-over to be done. The fame of the waltz was tinged with scandal; the close embrace of the couples and the giddy whirling led to outrage and charges of lewdness. As early as 1813, Byron – whose club foot condemned him to the spectator's seat – wrote, in an anonymously published satire

> Imperial Waltz! imported from the Rhine
> (Famed for the growth of pedigrees and wine),
> Long be thy import from all duty free,
> And hock itself be less esteem'd than thee;
> In some few qualities alike – for hock
> Improves our cellar – thou our living stock.
> The head to hock belongs – thy subtler art
> Intoxicates alone the heedless heart:
> Through the full veins thy gentler poison swims,
> And wakes to wantonness the willing limbs.[32]

And, later:

> Endearing Waltz! – to thy more melting tune,
> Bow Irish jig and ancient rigadoon.
> Scotch reels, avaunt! and country-dance, forego
> Your future claims to each fantastic toe!
> Waltz – Waltz alone – both legs and arms demands,
> Liberal of feet and lavish of her hands;
> Hands which may freely range in public sight
> Where ne'er before – but – pray 'put out the light.'[33]

The impression of the waltz as a choreographic rape was compounded by several sallies from the medical establishment, since, in the heat and congestion

29 *Morning Post*, 17 April 1838.
30 Letter of 1842 in H. Berlioz, *The Memoirs of Hector Berlioz*, trans. and ed. D. Cairns (London, 1970), p. 323.   31 Quoted in Fantel, *Strauss*, p. 63.
32 G. Gordon (Lord) Byron, 'The Waltz: An Apostrophic Hymn', in *The Works of Lord Byron* (Ware, 1994), p. 143.   33 *Ibid.*, p. 144.

and in speed of movement, faintings were common, especially among the ladies, and there were several deaths, resulting in laws prohibiting the dance in some northern areas of Europe. But Strauss's progress was a triumphal conquering of most of these bastions, and one of the highlights of his career was when the nineteen-year-old Princess Victoria waltzed to his band at her precoronation court ball in Buckingham Palace.

Strauss brought back to Vienna not only increased fame and riches – he earned £200 for each night's work in England, including the provincial cities – but also the quadrille from France and the polka from Bohemia, which added extra variety. His homecoming, however, was marred by the fact that his homesick orchestra deserted him for Vienna, and he was forced to stop off, at several points on the way back, by a near-terminal fever. He recovered in Vienna and all seemed back to normal. But he now had a rival: his nineteen-year-old son, Johann II, to whose musical talent, in a cruelly ironic echo of his own relationship with his father, he had forbidden any advancement, forcing him to study in secret. The two were to remain in bitter estrangement; they were even on opposite sides in the Revolution of 1848, the father writing the much-loved *Radetzky March*, Op. 228, for the Royalists, and the son the *Patriots' March*, Op. 8, and *March of the Students*, Op. 56, for the rebels. Johann Strauss I died a few months before the end of the first half of the century; his son's triumphs belong to the second half.

A note on community music

A further expression of cohesion between members of the new classes, and one which, because it needed neither instruments, specialised venue, nor anything more than basic musical literacy, seemed to mirror the self-sufficiency of its progenitors, was choral singing. The scale extended from the small group of friends singing partsongs to the massed choral singing which characterised the larger festivals which, as indicated in the previous chapter, became a feature of the nineteenth century. Several smaller bodies had persisted from the eighteenth century. The principal material of The Noblemen and Gentlemen's Catch Club (founded 1761) was the simple canonic catch for a small number of voices, celebrating sport, drinking and sexual matters with suggestive or obscene texts.

This form died out in the early nineteenth century, or became transmuted, under the influence of the rediscovery of the English madrigal, into glees. These were mostly in simple harmony in three or four parts with some imitative writing. Preserving this form were the Civil Club (founded in the late seventeenth century) and the Glee Club (founded 1783), both still meeting in the first half of the nineteenth century. These institutions were, in effect, semi-private men's clubs with restricted entry, and the inevitable – and for many unthinkable – participation of women on ladies' evenings necessarily occasioned rather more sober lyrics. Many of those clubs which began with more democratic ideals, drifted with the same tide. One of the most long-lived was the Madrigal Society, founded in 1741 with a small number of members, mostly artisans. The increase in aristocratic members with a concomitant improvement in venue eventually forced out the lower orders. The glee in turn gave way to the simpler partsong, intended for amateur choral singing, with a mostly homophonic texture enlivened by imitative entries and in which the emphasis was on beauty of sound and equal partnership. This form was ideal for setting folksongs and developed into barber-shop style later in America.

Also the prerogative of men, partly because of its military origins, was the brass band movement in Britain, which included woodwind as well as brass and percussion. This began in the factories of the industrial north-west and the first band is thought to be the Stalybridge Old Band in Lancashire, founded in 1814. The players were amateurs, and met during leisure periods. These bands were supported by subscriptions from the other workers and became a source of pride for the factories and mines which gave rise to them; the goodwill of employers generally was an important factor in their promulgation. Several timely developments also contributed: the addition of valves to most brass instruments meant that the same fingering could be used, allowing for substitutions and variety; the invention of others, such as the saxhorns; and the later adoption of the treble clef for all but the lowest instruments. From the outset, standards were maintained by competitions, which, after the middle of the century, became institutionalised and of national importance, the principal ones being Belle Vue, Manchester (instigated in 1853) and the National Brass Band Festival, Crystal Palace (1860). Similar developments took place rather later in the century in other countries, and tended to favour the military band, although in North America, the first bands appeared in the 1830s in Boston and New York.

Repertory was predictable enough for the period – arrangements of operatic overtures and extracts, and of symphonic movements as well as more popular fare. Technical and interpretative standards were usually very high and these bands – with their high local profiles associated with civic, religious and industrial ceremonial, as well as in their free bandstand recitals – performed a valuable service in introducing music to those who had neither the leisure, transport nor funds for concert attendance. Together with the choral societies, they were of major importance as early examples of the kind of communal music-making organised by and for the emergent working classes which will be examined in chapter 19.

Bibliography

Beaud, M. A., *A History of Capitalism 1500–1980*, trans. T. Dickman and A. Lefebvre. London and Basingstoke, 1984

Berlioz, H., *The Memoirs of Hector Berlioz*, trans. and ed. D. Cairns. London, 1970

Byron, (Lord) G. G., 'The Waltz: An Apostrophic Hymn'. In *The Works of Lord Byron*. Ware, 1994, pp. 143–6

Clare, J., *The Parish: A Satire*, ed. E. Robinson. Harmondsworth, 1986

Dahlhaus, C., *Nineteenth-Century Music*, trans. J. B. Robinson. Berkeley and Los Angeles, 1989

Citron, M. J., 'The Lieder of Fanny Mendelssohn Hensel'. *Musical Quarterly*, 69 (1983), pp. 570–94

de Courcy, G. I. C., *Paganini, the Genoese*, rep. edn. 2 vols., New York, 1977

Fantel, H., *Johann Strauss Father and Son and Their Era*. Newton Abbott, 1971

Hallé, C., *The Autobiography of Charles Hallé with Correspondence and Diaries*, ed. M. Kennedy. New York, 1981

Hamm, C., *Yesterdays: Popular Song in America*. New York, 1979

The Harmonicon: A Journal of Music, ed. W. Ayrton. London, 1823–33

Hobsbawm, E. J., *The Age of Revolution: Europe 1789–1848*. Rep. edn., London, 1977; original edn 1962

Lasdun, S., *Victorians at Home*. London, 1981

Moore, T., *The Works of Thomas Moore, Esq. accurately printed from the last original editions with additional notes complete in one volume*. Leipzig, 1826

Sperling, D., *Mrs. Hurst Dancing & other scenes from Regency life 1812–1823*, G. Mingay (text). London, 1981

De Staël, Mme. G., *De la Littérature considerée dans ses rapports avec les institutions sociales*. Paris, 1872

Young, A., *Tours in England and Wales: (selected from the Annals of Agriculture)*. School of Economic and Political Science, London, 1932

10

The great composer

JIM SAMSON

On canons and spearheads

A focus on greatness is one of the markers of nineteenth-century culture. Indeed it was the nineteenth century that fostered and nurtured that fetishism of greatness – of the great artist, the great work – so familiar to us today. The language of music criticism in the early nineteenth century tells part of that story, registering a subtle shift from the acknowledgement of excellence to the recognition of greatness. This shading of meaning is worth elaborating. Excellence suggests pre-eminence in an enterprise whose terms of reference have been validated by convention. Greatness, on the other hand, implies an achievement or an aptitude so far beyond the ordinary that it is capable of remaking the conventions – resetting the terms on which future evaluations might be made. Excellence carries with it the sense of an object well made, a task well done. Greatness transcends the making, as also the function. It imposes itself on the world. It goes without saying that the nineteenth century did not initiate the concept of greatness. It flourished in the ancient world, and it was reinvented (partly through the mediation of Islamic culture) for the thinkers and makers of Renaissance humanism. And humanism is to the point, for it is the purely human that is honoured in a project of greatness, that capacity of the exceptional mind to speak for all, to celebrate our potencies, to express our emotions through the mystery of creative genius. It was above all during the Renaissance that creativity took on something of its modern, elevated, sense, not least through a swerve towards secular themes, which proved no less susceptible to the aura of creative genius than their sacred counterparts. For the artist was no mere medium, 'making' to divine specifications. He could bring into being his own world. As Tasso put it (*Discourses on Poetic Art*): ' the poet... resembling the supreme Creator in his work, partakes of the divinity of God'.[1]

In this way much of the ground was laid out for a later age of Romanticism in

---

1 Torquato Tasso, *Prose*, ed. Ettore Mazzali (Milan and Naples, 1959), p. 387.

imaginative culture. But the Romantics had of course a more immediate inheritance. What changed the picture in the nineteenth century, effectively redirecting humanist thought, was the impact of Enlightenment thinkers. A sea-change occurred in post-Renaissance intellectual history, separating reason and revelation, elevating critique, and dividing knowledge into those specialised categories of which the *Encyclopédie* was such a powerful symbol. Whatever the mysterious engines driving such shifts in the history of ideas, and however much they were fuelled by social and political change, the effect was a change of orientation in thought and creativity. Out of that an increasingly specialised aesthetic discourse took shape, and it was both subject to (and structured by) reason and at odds with (or, more accurately, a counterpart to) reason. In due course it invested the whole sphere of art, already carving out its own niche in the social world, and also in the intellectual world (as something separated from 'science' by its focus on subjective perception), with an enhanced sense of dignity. Where music is concerned, this marked the point at which critics and historians alike began to hand out their accolades to the 'great men' who 'made history'. And from the start there were two sides to this. There were the great men of the past, increasingly promoted as the validators of culture, and there were the great men of the present, cutting a new path for others to follow.

In the former case greatness was an attribute applied *post hoc* to a handful of composers from an earlier generation, composers working within a patronal culture, for whom the invention of music had been first and foremost a craft to be learned and practised to a high degree of excellence. To have established this small group of (mainly) eighteenth-century composers as the nucleus of a musical pantheon, cut loose from the particulars of time and place, was a central achievement of the nineteenth century, and one that found its appropriate context in the developing historicism of the age. In its performance culture, if not its compositional culture, the nineteenth century was, after all, as much a Classical as a Romantic era. However, greatness was also an intentional project of nineteenth-century composers, a by-product of the growing autonomy of the aesthetic. And a considerable pretension attended this project. Music was much more than an object of beauty; it was a mode of cognition, a discourse of ideas, whose 'truthfulness' should be protected. In an age of revolution, an age of liberalism and nationalism, the composer, no less than the poet, would have his word for mankind, and in formulating it would stretch the existing boundaries of taste and convention, spearheading a notionally unified (and often reluctant) musical culture into unknown territory. In this sense the nineteenth century was a modernist as well as a Romantic age. The counterpart to canon formation was the emergence of an avant-garde, and here I use rather loosely a term which will gain sharper definition and subtler nuancing in the next chapter.

The bridge between the two was the concept of genius, to return to a word (discussed already in chapter 7) that only began to acquire its present meaning, where it is distinguished from talent rather as greatness is from excellence, in the eighteenth century. Etymologically, the key lies in a derivation from 'spirit', or 'breath', from which comes 'inspiration', a concept well recognised but often treated with suspicion by the Ancients. A capacity for creativity (creating rather than making or inventing) was presumed to be the province of genius. That in turn engendered a subtle shift in the relation of the artist towards both nature and history, towards (respectively) rules and conventions. Thus we have (in 1797) a suggestion from Joshua Reynolds (though he qualifies it) that genius is 'a power which no precepts can teach, and which no industry can acquire', that it is 'out of the reach of the rules of art'.[2] And from Kant the proposition that 'genius is a talent for producing that for which no definite rule can be given',[3] that imagination can create 'a second nature out of the material supplied to it by actual nature' (*Critique*, p. 176). 'Where an author owes a product to his genius, he does not himself know how the ideas for it have entered his head' (p. 169). Moreover if genius can break with the rules (mastering or transforming nature), so it can with the conventions (transcending or denying history). As Edward Young put it, 'the less we copy the renowned Ancients, we shall resemble them the more', and again, 'As far as a regard to Nature, and sound Sense, will permit a Departure from your great Predecessors; so far, ambitiously, depart from them'.[4] Likewise for Kant 'originality must be [the] primary property [of genius]' (*Critique*, p. 168). At the same time, in defying the existing rules, the work of genius makes its own rules, as Hans Sachs suggests in the first act of *Die Meistersinger*. 'Even works of genius ... must likewise have their rules' (Reynolds, p. 97). And in doing so, it establishes an exemplary model for future imitation. 'Though not themselves derived from imitation, [works of genius] must serve that purpose for others' (Reynolds, pp. 168–9). For if genius is dependent on originality, it is also formative of tradition.

Given that exceptional talent is ever present, we are bound to probe the historical nature of creative genius as a perceived category, from its rise in Early Modern Europe, through its flowering in the age of Romanticism and culmination in the modernism of the early twentieth century, to its decline in our own age. It goes without saying that such a reading is boldly, if not dangerously, reductive. But it is with good reason that Reinhard Strohm called his study of

---

2 Joshua Reynolds, *Discourses on Art*, ed. Robert R. Wark (New Haven and London, 1975; based on edition of 1797), p. 96.

3 Immanuel Kant, *Critique of Aesthetic Judgement*, trans. J. C. Meredith (Oxford, 1911; original edn 1790), p. 168.

4 Edward Young, *Conjectures on Original Composition*, Scolar Press facsimile (Leeds, 1966; original edn 1759), pp. 21–2.

fifteenth-century music *The Rise of European Music*, and included within it a chapter sub-titled 'The Invention of the Masterwork'.[5] And that Paul Griffiths, in a book called *Modern Music and After*, seems to have regarded 'the demise of the great composer' as a default critical position for the analysis of late twentieth-century culture, albeit a position open to challenge.[6] First causes will no doubt elude us, but it seems obvious enough that the curve of 'great music' maps well on to other aspects of European singularity: political, intellectual and social. Thus it is in Early Modern Europe, at a time of expanding trade and emergent capitalism, that we find the beginnings of an essentially bourgeois civil society, coherent in itself but separate from the State. The extent to which modes of thought and feeling associated with this bourgeois class were products of capitalist economics, or conversely may have helped shape those economics, has long been a debating point. In any event both the progressive (instrumental) rationality of European thought in subsequent centuries, and the increasing investment in subjectivity that was formalised by the rise of aesthetics, were closely tied to middle-class interests. And both tendencies reached a culminating point in the late eighteenth century.

It was at just this time that middle-class aspirations to political, as well as economic, power began to be realised. That process continued through the nineteenth century, and as middle-class power was consolidated, it was increasingly bolstered by the twin ideologies of liberalism and nationalism, by a belief in individual freedom and a commitment to the idea of the nation and its (constructed) history. The new status quo went on to define itself, moreover, through a formal culture deeply imbued with these very same values, powered by ambitious individualism on the one hand and by the weight of an (invented) past on the other – originality and tradition. It is perhaps not too trite to suggest that where Kant gave aesthetic standing to the first of these values, Hegel did the same for the second. They were middle-class values, yet they claimed to speak on behalf of all. For the middle-class establishment represented itself as a kind of universal subject, with art functioning as its mode of expression and its badge of identity – and even in some quarters as something rather like its belief system. Hence the high seriousness attributed to artistic creativity in the nineteenth century, and the social and ethical burdens with which it was increasingly freighted. In music, one result was the ceremony of the public concert, whose rituals were designed to install and maintain the pantheon of great composers. Another was the emergence of the 'modern' composer, pursuing the inherent tendencies of his musical material and expecting his audience to fall in step as best it could.

5 Reinhard Strohm, *The Rise of European Music 1380–1500* (Cambridge, 1993), pp. 412–88.
6 Paul Griffiths, *Modern Music and After: Directions since 1945* (Oxford, 1995), p. 324.

Both categories were in a sense prepared by the growing 'composer-centredness' (to use Michael Talbot's term) of musical culture from around 1800.[7] Composer-centredness was manifest in the programming of the subscription concert series that sprang up in Europe's cultural capitals, from the Philharmonic concerts in London to Habeneck's concerts du conservatoire in Paris and Mendelssohn's Gewandhaus concerts in Leipzig. With their 'Classical' repertories spiced by ambitious modern works, these series – unusual and elitist at the time – were prototypes of the kind of concert that would become more common in the later nineteenth century, similar in broad outline to our concerts today. In much the same way, Liszt established (around 1840) the prototype for the solo piano recital, though the carefully structured programmes of today's recitals did not crystallise until the late nineteenth century. Composer-centredness was also manifest in the shifting tastes and concealed ideologies revealed by journals such as the *Revue et Gazette musicale* and *Allgemeine musikalische Zeitung*, where canon formation can be rather easily traced; and, most importantly, in the changing patterns of music publishing, where single-composer collections began to take precedence over genre-based or medium-based anthologies, culminating in the series of collected editions of the great masters that began to gather around 1800.

Of course geographical difference produced its variations on the theme of creative genius. Ironically enough, given the political and social conservatism and the intellectual repression of the German states and the Habsburg Empire, it was German Idealism that most obviously nurtured the concept of genius in the early nineteenth century, and in both the senses described above. Taking his cue from Kant, Schelling (in *The Philosophy of Art*) distinguished genius from talent by the 'absolute necessity' of the 'true work of art'.[8] In his *System of Transcendental Idealism* 'the obscure concept of genius' is represented as a power through which 'conscious and unconscious activity' are combined to produce more than the artist can consciously intend, bringing 'completion or objectivity to the incomplete work of freedom'.[9] Such ideas were given more informal representation in the musical press, and it is perhaps no surprise that they were very often personified in Beethoven. In particular Beethoven came to be viewed as the epitome of the engaged or committed artist, one who expressed through music his affinity with the radical, humanitarian thought of the age of

7 Michael Talbot, 'The Work-Concept and Composer-Centredness', in M. Talbot (ed.), *The Musical Work: Reality or Invention?* (Liverpool, 2000), pp. 168–86.

8 F. W. J. Schelling, *The Philosophy of Art*, trans. Douglas Stott (Minneapolis, 1989; original edn 1802–3). The relevant discussion is at the beginning of section 3, 'Construction of the Particular or of the Form of Art'.

9 F. W. J. Schelling, *System of Transcendental Idealism (1800)*, trans. Peter Heath (Virginia, 1978), pp. 219–24.

revolution, and bequeathed to his successors an unprecedented sense of the ambition and pretension of the musical work, its quest for an epic status. He marked in that sense the beginnings of an historical avant-garde in music. At the same time his symphonies played a crucial symbolic role in forging an aesthetic of absolute music, and a pivotal role in establishing the German symphonic tradition as the highest expression of that aesthetic. Indeed the symphonic tradition – already a reality in the 1830s and 1840s – was to become a central building-block not only of the musical canon but of the idea of the German nation, two concepts that were brought into ever closer and ever more potent association (see chapter 5). By the mid-century, then, the ground was prepared in Germany for the consolidation of a canon and for the establishment of an avant-garde.

The picture was very different in France, whose political thought and action had provided much of the ideological impetus for both these categories. Here the concept of absolute music was only weakly developed in the early nineteenth century, just as canon formation (in the final stages of the concert spirituel and later in the concerts du conservatoire) carried a less potent ideological charge. The most representative sites of music-making – grand opera and the benefit concert – were monuments to the commodification of culture in post-1830s France, and the one truly significant avant-garde voice was developed at least partly in opposition to such commercial imperatives. 'Offer me a hundred thousand francs to put my name to some of the most successful works of the day, and I would angrily refuse', said Berlioz.[10] Following the mid-century France favoured a 'juste milieu', relativistic and eclectic, of a kind implicitly advocated by Fétis in his later criticism, and in the commentaries of his *Histoire générale de la musique*.[11] Even Schelling's pronouncements on genius were reworked by Fétis in ways that militate against an avant-garde. True genius will be expressed through existing means of expression, argued Fétis, not through self-conscious manifestos of change. The development of lyric opera, carving out a space for French opera somewhere between Meyerbeer and Wagner, would later epitomise this middle ground during the Second Empire. And it is surely significant that it was a German canon and a German avant-garde that were represented in Paris during these years, prior to the wave of nationalism and cultural ambition that followed in the wake of the Franco-Prussian War.

By then (the 1870s) a dialectic of performance culture (canon formation) and

10 *The Memoirs of Hector Berlioz*, trans. and ed. David Cairns (London, 1970), p. 586.

11 F.-J. Fétis, *Histoire générale de la Musique* (Paris, 1876); see especially the preface and first section of the Introduction. For a discussion of the German roots of Fétis's philosophy, see Rosalie Schellhous, 'Fétis's *Tonality* as a Metaphysical Principle: Hypothesis for a New Science', *Music Theory Spectrum*, 13/2 (1991), pp. 219–40; also Katharine Ellis, *Music Criticism in Nineteenth-Century France: 'La Revue et Gazette musicale de Paris' 1834–80* (Cambridge, 1995), pp. 35–44.

compositional culture (emergent modernisms) was developing across much of Europe, including the eastern Habsburg Empire, whose major capitals were poised precariously between their shared dynastic culture and their strengthening nationalist – and in practice that tended to mean anti-German – voices. Even in Italy there was a refocusing of the operatic tradition along similar lines. Just as the repertory of the major opera houses was becoming increasingly standardised, centred on a small number of popular masterpieces, so the major creative impulse in Italian opera was channelled into a handful of ambitious, epic works by a single innovatory genius. But perhaps the most telling development of all was the separation and polarisation of the two strands of our dialectic in two socially and geographically polarised countries on the edge of Europe. In industrialised England there was a musical life (and for that matter a music) which affirmed and legitimised, with no significant critical element, the bourgeois ascendancy, leaving little space for independent aesthetic values, and thus for a project of greatness. In feudal Russia, on the other hand, there was a pioneering, implicitly critical modernism, a music responsive neither to the professional establishment nor to public taste and taking as its sole authority the urge to self-expression of the individual creative genius.

But this is to jump ahead – specifically to the agenda of chapter 20, where these ideas will be developed more fully. It is enough to note here that already by the mid-nineteenth century at least some of the core repertory of the modern canon was established, with Bach and Handel as the foundation stones, and the 'Viennese Classics' forming a second tier (see chapter 7). Implicitly linked to such canon formation was an aesthetic of absolute music, perfectly attuned to the early Romantic ideology of organicism. Thus, it was rather easy to represent a developing (mainly Austro-German) symphonic tradition as the culmination of music's quest for autonomy, and this perception in its turn influenced the subsequent expansion of the canon. Of the Romantic generation, for example, Mendelssohn and Schumann were more readily aligned to a developing tradition than Berlioz, Liszt or Chopin. Indeed the whole process by which the great original was translated into the Classical master became an increasingly protracted one as the century unfolded, a measure of the widening distance between an exemplary past and a modernist present. That distance, along with the continuing need for historical validation of the present, had the effect of supplementing, if not replacing, the sense of a continuously evolving tradition with a growing awareness of the more distant past – the 'roots' of the tradition. It was a tendency that would continue through into the early twentieth century, culminating in the applied historicism of compositional praxes in the 1920s, involving, it should be said, Schoenberg as much as Stravinsky.

We are of course familiar today with the practical and ideological force of the canon, the German canon in particular. Practically it allowed the significant to push into obscurity the only marginally less significant (the Berlioz symphony obscures the Berwald symphony), and this authoritarian quality became even more pronounced in the later nineteenth century, as Classical repertories were placed in a polarised relation not only to avant-garde but (as I shall shortly argue) to commercial repertories. Ideologically it manipulated an innocent music to confirm the social position of a dominant group in society. It is this ideological quality, the 'constructedness' of the canon, that has especially interested critics in more recent years. Thus, the canon has been viewed increasingly as an instrument of exclusion (of women, for example, or of particular social orders, or of countries on the periphery of Europe), one which legitimates and reinforces the identities and values of those who exercise cultural power. For this reason, in our present age the authority of the canon as a measurement of quality in some absolute sense has proved increasingly difficult to sustain. It is threatened above all by a growing sense (it may be disillusioning or cathartic) that any notion of a single culture, of which the canon might be regarded as the finest expression, is no longer viable.

Yet this is not the whole story. To demonstrate the contingency of the canon is not to devalue it, nor to diminish our wonder at the ineffable greatness of a Schubert quintet, a Brahms concerto. Social historians of music have demonstrated that canon formation is not unique to the West, that an *ars classica* (like an *ars nova* and an *ars subtilior*) is common to the musical cultures of many social communities.[12] Even in performance- and genre-orientated musical cultures such as those of sub-Saharan Africa, or the sub- and counter-cultures of North American and British teenagers since the 1960s, there has been a tendency to privilege particular repertories as canonic. All the same we may perhaps claim two things. First, that it is only within the traditions of West European art music that a sense of the canonic has been built centrally and formally into an unfolding history of music. And secondly, that the newly privileged status of art within European middle-class culture, however socially and politically contingent, resulted in ideal conditions for a unique flowering of creative genius, promoting those very qualities that refuse to yield to contingent explanation – the atemporal and disinterested, as against the temporal and functional. In the end we cannot quite explain away, though we may seek to explain, the presence and greatness of the Western canon. Indeed for some critics, its very existence – its independence of the changing fashions of time – is enough to demonstrate

---

12 See Walter Wiora, 'Of Art Music and Cultural Classes', in Edmund Strainchamps and Maria Rika Maniates (eds.), *Music and Civilisation: Essays in Honour of Paul Henry Lang* (New York and London, 1984), pp. 472–7.

that aesthetic value can only be understood in an essentialist way, something we perceive intuitively, but (since it transcends conceptual thought) are unable to describe.[13]

What, then, of the other side of the coin, the avant-garde? One should say, perhaps, the other side of middle-class values – that individualism and subjectivity of which the aesthetic formed a model. A focus on subjectivity – on the independent, desiring subject – inevitably meant a focus on freedom, and that in turn had some potential not only to generate an avant-garde, but to challenge rationality itself. In mapping out the course of the aesthetic, we can identify from the start an element that refused to accommodate itself to reason, notably through the category of the 'sublime', which, unlike the 'beautiful', would simply crush its audience into submission. It is hard to resist invoking Beethoven here (see the discussion in chapter 5). Beethoven's Promethean image was indeed liberating – itself a source of the avant-garde. But it was also inhibiting, a challenge to the future of art just as potent as the challenge of Hegel's *Geschichtsphilosophie*. How, after all, was one to follow Goethe and Beethoven, the two figures in whom Schiller's ideal of the artist ('cleans[ing] and purify[ing]' his age through a 'union of what is possible with what is necessary'; borrowing his form 'from beyond time altogether, from the absolute, unchanging unity of his being') seemed to be the most fully and most perfectly realised?[14] As Brendel put it in 1852, 'With the Ninth Symphony, the last symphony was written'.[15] It was Schopenhauer who put a different spin on the challenge to art, as also the challenge to reason, and one that allowed the modern artist something of an advantage. For Schopenhauer the great artist was a seer or 'diviner', knowing unknowingly, indicating to others the path to revelation. As such he was a redemptive figure in a scientific and commercial world. And in the post-Beethoven era it was above all Liszt and Wagner who aspired to this status.

As the next chapter will demonstrate, Liszt and Wagner went a long way towards building this sense of privilege into something like an avant-garde in the modern sense, with all those connotations of frontiers, leadership, unknown territory, and risk that were associated with the term in its original military meaning. In doing so they brought to fruition an essentially Romantic view of the creative genius as a potential rival to, rather than a medium for, both Nature and God. The Romantic artist, privileged by his genius, revealed the world in expressing himself, since the world was ultimately grounded in

13 For example, G. Steiner, in *Real Presences* (London, 1989).

14 Friedrich Schiller, *On the Aesthetic Education of Man*, trans. and ed. E. M. Wilkinson and L. A. Willoughby (Oxford, 1967), p. 57.

15 Franz Brendel, *Geschichte der Musik in Italien, Deutschland und Frankreich* (Leipzig, 1852), p. 517.

subjectivity, in the self. Hence the growing importance of expression, overriding the claims of formal propriety and convention, and foregrounding originality as a primary aesthetic value. If any single figure – any single Romantic hero, we might say – seemed to embody this expressive imperative, it was the Faust of Goethe's masterpiece, which had a unique significance for nineteenth-century composers, including Liszt and Wagner. As chapter 8 has already suggested, Faust seemed to encapsulate all the most characteristic qualities of the Romantic artist, through his visionary quest for knowledge of the world and of himself, including his darker (demonic) self, through his belief in progress, and through his acknowledgement that such progress (by no means equatable with innovation or novelty) could scarcely be compatible with any suggestion of limits or boundaries to knowledge or experience. This is the rhetoric of modernism, of a 'progressive' art – a campaigning and dissenting 'music of the future'.

Models of greatness

Even as canonic and avant-garde repertories separated out on one level, they drew closer together on another. In no previous era did new composition claim so heavy a dependence on exemplary models from the past, as the polemics of the 1850s testify. Of course composers have always collaborated with their immediate inheritance by taking compositional models. The practice was well established in the Renaissance and Baroque periods. It could involve simple pastiche, designed as compositional exercises, or various kinds of transcription and recomposition, designed to 'make available' (by enlarging or reducing) the inaccessible, to publicise the unfamiliar, to pay tribute to the exemplary composer or the exemplary work, to cultivate an earlier idiom, or to interpret, critique or parody material already in the public domain. In periods less preoccupied with originality, it could – quite simply – save composing time. Compositional modelling of this kind continued into the nineteenth century (and beyond), but in these later stages of music history its status changed, and it is perhaps not surprising that historians of nineteenth-century music have had relatively little to say on the subject. For one thing, a canonic view of music history tends to demote the importance of models, just as it demotes the role of pedagogy, since it fosters the notion that genius will somehow find its own path. And for another, there is a significant difference in the definition of 'the past'. Very broadly, the tendency of the nineteenth-century composer was to look beyond the recent past (in some cases cultivating a certain ambivalence or hostility towards it) to the more distant past. In other words the past was remodelled from a strategic distance rather than as an immediate inheritance.

There was also a significant change in the nature of the borrowing process in the nineteenth century. Transcription was more common than simple modelling, but even transcription stood in a somewhat uneasy relationship to the prevailing Romantic ideology. Romanticism, after all, privileged the singular and the inimitable, qualities that seem on the face of it at some remove from the translation or transcription of another's work. Thus the Romantic premium on originality brought into sharp focus ethical as well as ontological questions which had seemed less pressing (though they were indeed raised) during earlier periods. Not only was the status of the transcription at issue in a medium-sensitive, work-orientated age; its propriety was also at stake. If there was a single validating presence it was Bach, whose exemplary value for the nineteenth century (to which I will return) not only licensed the transcription but provided a model for its development. As Lawrence Dreyfus has potently demonstrated, Bach wrested from his pre-existent materials statements that were not just unique, but were registered 'against the grain' of the borrowed style.[16] This formed one pole of attraction for the nineteenth-century transcriber, who was often more inclined to intervene – commenting, extending, developing, renewing – than to copy or translate. At the same time, this tendency was countered by a no less powerful impulse to give due respect to an original, highly valued and 'untouchable' masterpiece.

To some extent the generic categories mediate between these two poles. Thus we may consider a spectrum journeying from literal translation to free composition. In some readings of genre this would take us from the arrangement through the transcription, paraphrase, and fantasy, to the variation set, though these categories can only be indicative and there is substantial overlap and shading of function between them. Thus the transcription may involve free composition, just as the variation set may involve literal arrangement. More importantly, the tension between the conflicting claims of fidelity and intervention could, and often did, form a vital part of the aesthetic property of the nineteenth-century transcription. Liszt in particular steered a dangerous and exhilarating path between commentary and tribute in a series of remarkable, and often under-valued, transcriptions of everything from Beethoven symphonies to Schubert songs and extracts from Wagner operas. In this sense a transcription might even be compared to a performance, though the intervention involved in a performative interpretation usually leaves the notes themselves more-or-less intact. Busoni later developed this comparison and in doing so he usefully relativised the concept of a transcription, and at the same time dignified it. Not only is the performance a kind of transcription; so too is the

---

16 Lawrence Dreyfus, *Bach and the Patterns of Invention* (Cambridge, Mass., 1996).

notated form of a work, which 'transcribes' an unavailable original, a (Platonic) ideal form. For Busoni, then, the distance between a work and a transcription is not a great one; nor should the one be valued more highly than the other.[17]

Recomposition on the basis of pre-existent models was less common than transcription in the nineteenth century, but it continued to play a significant role nonetheless. Very often the extent, or even the fact, of the modelling process was not made explicit in such cases (as in several of Brahms's recompositions of pieces by Bach), perhaps indicating a more general ambivalence about intertextuality in the Romantic age. Alternatively, and more commonly, the model would be a general style rather than an individual work, as in Chopin's or Grieg's 'Baroque' pieces. Such neo-classicism was present in various forms right from the beginning of the Romantic era, but by the early twentieth century the distance between background and foreground – between model and parody – had become large enough to generate a calculated heteronomy of style. More commonly still, the modelling process would operate at a broad, conceptual level rather than, or as well as, a concrete compositional level, as in Wagner's reception of Beethoven. In such cases, the correspondences were of aims, strategies, ideologies and symbolic meanings as much as of techniques and constructive methods. On all three levels – very loosely, the work, the style and the aesthetic – we can identify a select group of earlier composers who acted as unseen presences in the compositional history of music from around 1830 onwards. The reception of these composers – Beethoven and Schubert, Mozart, Bach and Handel, Palestrina – was directly instrumental in shaping nineteenth-century styles.

In the *New Oxford History of Music* vol. VII the first few decades of the nineteenth century are identified as 'The Age of Beethoven' – a manifesto of 'great man' history if ever there was one. If we are to insist on an 'age of Beethoven', it should arguably begin rather than end in 1830, for while it is true that he achieved legendary status during his lifetime, it was after his death that he became a truly inescapable shaping presence. As already noted, his symphonies and quartets were regarded by a later generation as the embodiment of absolute music, investing in the expressive possibilities of the self-contained, closed work of art. The myth of 'Beethoven', already extensively discussed in this volume (see chapter 5), contributed massively to the consolidation of a work-concept in just this sense. The work was assumed to embody an 'idea' from which it derived its singular meaning, and the integrity of this idea supposedly justified exceeding norms of taste and beauty, as it justified flaunting the expec-

17 Thus, 'Every notation is, in itself, the transcription of an abstract idea'; Ferrucio Busoni, *Sketch of a New Aesthetic of Music*, trans. Th. Baker, in *Three Classics in the Aesthetics of Music* (New York, 1962; original edn 1907), p. 17.

tations of an audience. For the Romantic generation the idea behind a work might well have an autobiographical resonance, either directly programmatic, as in Berlioz (and eventually Richard Strauss), or implicit and attributed, as in Chopin (and eventually Mahler). For the notion that a composer might 'live' in his music, composing out his inner life, was a powerful one in the nineteenth century, signalling music's putative expressive powers, while at the same time securing its greater status or dignity.

The latter point is important. It was a key motivation underlying the marked inclination of post-Beethoven composers to look outwards to the other arts, and especially to poetry. And again Beethoven was viewed as the pioneering figure. It was partly in conscious tribute to Beethoven that the category 'poetic' became a part of Liszt's renovative programme for an instrumental music which might itself become the highest form of poetry through its association with a poetic idea. Liszt's conflation of music and the poetic required well-known topics – real or fictional heroes from world literature and known legend – so that the programme might take on the character of an essential and famil-iar background, orientating communication rather in the nature of a genre title. Yet poetic programmes were by no means confined to the heroes of world literature. For some composers, the licence of the programme invited music to 'express' the beauties and terrors of Nature, now sublime and ordered, now destructive and irrational; for others it was the invocation of a glorious, ideal-ised past which appealed, either as a nostalgic retreat from, or a necessary vali-dation of, the present; for yet others an exotic dream-world of folk-tale and legend, of grotesquerie and fantasy, became their alternative reality. And most common of all were nationalist themes. As we shall see in a later chapter, the attempt by so many composers to lend their support to nationalist causes is revealing both of the unprecedented ambition of music in the Romantic era, and of a widespread belief in its expressive competence.

In more concrete terms, Beethoven bequeathed to the nineteenth century a radical approach to inherited materials and practices – to the length of works and movements, for example, as also to the working through of already estab-lished (if not always fully theorised) formal and tonal models. This 'deforma-tion' of conventional models was part and parcel of his compositional method, as indeed it was to become for many later symphonists (see chapter 15). In Beethoven it was often motivated by larger narrative strategies, including 'plot archetypes' of heroic conflict and triumphant resolution, or of suffering and redemption, that would themselves form models for a later generation, with major implications for the 'weighting' of musical structures – in particular finales. It has been argued that this established a peculiarly masculine archetype of musical composition, which was – it need hardly be said – a predominantly masculine activity in the nineteenth century (the point is elaborated in chapter 5). The Romantic hero was just that – a hero, not a heroine. Even the goal-directed nature of Beethoven's music, its metrical insistence and its tonic–dominant polarity, together with the dynamic, assertive qualities of its developmental motif working, have suggested to some a gendered reading of compositional processes. Man 'becomes', in Hegel's reading, where woman 'is'. Naturally such easy stereotyping carries its own difficulties. But it is partly in this sense that Schubert came to be viewed as an alternative model for nine-teenth-century composers, initially through his influence on the later develop-ment of the lied.

The art-song might well sustain a claim to be the quintessential Romantic genre, born with the early Romantics, fading with the rise of modernism and surviving in the twentieth century where the spirit of Romanticism survives. In its intimate, confessional character it epitomised the autobiographical charac-ter of Romantic art. In its narrative, descriptive aspects it reflected the prog-rammatic, referentialist tendencies of the music of the period. In its evocation of folksong it echoed a wider nineteenth-century idealisation of the *Volksgeist*. And above all in its response to the new, 'singable' lyric poetry of the early nine-teenth century it provided a model of the Romantic impulse towards a fusion of the arts, an impulse which would be given theoretical, if not always practical, formulation in Wagner. As a lied composer, Schubert's impact was immediate, and, as we learn in chapter 16, it remained a shaping presence throughout the nineteenth century. His major instrumental works took rather longer to regis-ter (partly, as chapter 7 suggests, because of their tardy publication history), though some of the later sonatas and quartets were much admired by the *cog-noscenti*, and were 'noticed' in the press. It is true of course that he himself responded in his own way to the Beethovenian model, but at the same time he proposed very different ways of conceiving extended cyclic works, avoiding dynamic goal-directed narratives in favour of more leisurely scenic routes, where essentially similar melodic-motivic materials ('breathing the same life', as Schumann put it)[18] are allowed to drift freely through third-related regions in a gradual, spacious, and in a sense anti-heroic, teleology.

There is little evidence that Schubert's music attracted the kind of blatantly feminine connotations that attended Chopin reception in the nineteenth century, to say nothing of the 'gay' readings of recent musicology.[19] Yet he did come to embody for some later composers a less virile approach to sonata-

18 In his review of Schubert's Piano Sonata in G major, D.894, *Neue Zeitschrift für Musik*, 29 December 1835.
19 Susan McClary, 'Constructions of Subjectivity in Schubert's Music', in P. Brett, E. Wood and G. C. Thomas (eds.), *Queering the Pitch: The New Gay and Lesbian Musicology* (New York and London, 1994), pp. 205–34.

symphonic composition. Where Beethoven had shifted the melodic-motivic balance characteristic of late eighteenth-century practice in the direction of an ever more closely integrated motivic process, Schubert looked in the opposite direction, demonstrating that sustained song-like melody might be no less amenable to symphonic treatment. His impact in this regard really belongs to the history of late nineteenth-century symphonism, where he joined Beethoven as a mandatory historical reference point. Thus in their entirely different ways, Brahms, Bruckner and Mahler all explored meeting-points between the two composers, and in some cases even brought together specific gestures from specific works as recurring *topoi* – as though to emphasise their exemplary status. Even the compositional methods of the two composers – at least as they were understood in the nineteenth century – seemed to suggest two very different profiles of creative genius. In Beethoven reception, musical material became the recalcitrant stuff from which a composer might slowly and painfully wrest a great work; in other words the creative process itself, as well as the resulting product, was viewed in heroic terms. Schubert, on the other hand, was regarded as a composer of effortless facility, his pen flowing easily all day every day, the new work begun as soon as the last was complete. In this he recalled Mozart.

For the nineteenth century Mozart was transformed into an image of the archetypal Romantic artist, exuberant, spontaneous, intuitive; opposed – or so it seemed – to the conventional, the predictable, even the rational. In the myth-making of the age, it was precisely these qualities that were elevated to the status of a compositional ideal. Indeed it was an idealised reception of Mozart that was partly instrumental in promoting one of the most enduring myths of the century – a near-equation of invention and inspiration, where the latter would appear 'sudden, complete, sublime', and largely untrammelled by the operations of reason. This image of the creative process acted as a counterpole to the Beethovenian struggle, and it played a major role in the construction of the prodigy, often viewed as the most visible manifestation of genius. And Mozart was of course the prodigy *par excellence*. It should be stressed that what was new in the nineteenth century was the significance attributed to prodigious talent, not the talent itself. Thus the fusion of youthful skills and creativity with essentially Romantic concepts of inspiration and genius resulted in a product – almost an institution – which proved eminently marketable in the nineteenth century, and retains much of its spell today. Indeed, following Mozart, the cultivation of the child prodigy was especially assiduous, both by parents and by teachers, with Czerny playing a major role. In Vienna evening concerts featuring prodigies became an institution in their own right in the formal culture of the 1830s and 1840s.

Mozart's legendary feats of improvisation and memory (the stories, apocryphal or not, abound) bolstered a developing image of creativity as imbued with mystery and magic, the gift of God or of nature. Hence the appellation 'heir of Mozart' attributed to those subsequent *Wunderkinder*, Chopin and Liszt, both of whose prodigious talents as performers (and above all improvisers) were the subject of myth-making in their own right. Hence too the 'divine' mystery attached to the privileged moment of creative inspiration – the sense that an entire musical universe might be brought into being in an instant. Wagner's account of the conception of *Das Rheingold*, like Stravinsky's description of the genesis of *Le sacre du printemps*, elaborates just this notion of creativity. However in Mozart reception there was a corollary to this Romantic image of the creative process. Not only did the musical idea emerge in a single moment; it appeared in all its Classical perfection, somehow achieving a proper sense of detachment from its (far from perfect) composer. Mozart became in that sense the model of that most elusive of all aesthetic properties, good taste, where all is in balance, nothing out of place. Even at the grassroots level of constructing a musical period or a musical sentence, Mozart was the favoured model of pedagogues. As Chopin, who learnt many a good trick from Mozart, once put it: 'Where [Beethoven] is obscure and seems lacking in unity . . . the reason is that he turns his back on eternal principles; Mozart never'.[20] Half a century later Tchaikowsky echoed these sentiments (he referred to Mozart as 'the Christ of music . . .'), and his own music – extravagantly emotional though it may appear – borrowed much of its clarity and its lucidity from the Mozartean model.[21]

Mozart seemed chronologically close enough to the Romantics to be perceived almost as an immediate inheritance. Indeed he was classified in some quarters as the first of the Romantics, and his direct compositional influence, especially on the development of the concerto and on opera, was immeasurable. Bach and Handel, on the other hand, were sufficiently distanced in time to take on the status of 'origins', the combined foundation layer of the great German tradition. Of the two, it is perhaps Handel who has had the more complex reception history, not least in relation to national affiliation. Much more than Bach, he was prey to appropriation by a kind of 'mass culture' in the nineteenth century, as epitomised by the great Handel performances at London's Crystal Palace in the 1850s (see too the massed forces assembled by Liszt for a performance of *The Messiah* at the Lower Rhine Festival in 1857), and by the subsequent history of choral associations in England, Germany and the Bohemian lands, though it should be stressed that these associations had a lengthy pedigree. Yet he was admired too by the *cognoscenti*. From Reichardt onwards there

20 Reported by Delacroix. See Hubert Wellington (ed.), *The Journal of Eugène Delacroix*, trans. Lucy Norton (London, 1951), pp. 194–5.   21 See John Warrack, *Tchaikovsky* (London, 1973), p. 27.

was a constituency for the view that the inspired simplicity of his music, and the sheer grandeur of its conception – its 'manliness' – made him an even greater figure than Bach, who was admittedly 'more painstaking and technically skillful'.[22] Even Chopin, on hearing a performance of Handel's *Cäcilienfest* at the Singakademie in 1828, wrote: 'It came nearest to the ideal which I had formed of great music', echoing Beethoven's remarks a few years earlier ('the greatest composer who ever lived').[23] Yet unlike Bach, Handel was widely regarded as a traditionalist, and while his direct influence was powerful, it was associated especially with conservative styles.

Bach, on the other hand, came to be viewed as a great original. There can be no more fascinating reception history than his. An eighteenth-century composer working in the provincial, albeit culturally rich, world of the North German church and court was transformed during the nineteenth century into nothing less than the fountainhead of universal values in music. The much-vaunted 'rediscovery' of Bach in the early nineteenth century was in reality something of a misnomer (see the discussion in chapter 8). Among composers and practical musicians Bach needed no rediscovery. During the second half of the eighteenth century more and more of his music became available for study, and its impact on the so-called 'Viennese' Classical composers is well known. But we should note that he was regarded primarily as an 'old master', whose works were to be admired and studied as models of compositional technique and practical instrumental writing. The 'rediscovery', associated especially with Mendelssohn's performance of the *St Matthew Passion* in 1829 but following on too from Forkel's pioneering biography of 1802, was partly a matter of making public (literally moving from church to concert hall, and with augmented forces to match), but it also involved a transformation of meaning, as Bach came to be viewed as a composer of intensely spiritual, profoundly emotional qualities. His music was also viewed as 'modern' and 'national' ('This great man was a German . . . His works are an invaluable national patrimony with which no other nation has anything to be compared', wrote Forkel in his biography), and its potent and unique blend of expression and intellect was directly influential on the most progressive music of the nineteenth century.

At the time of that *St Matthew Passion* performance the early music revival was already well under way (figures such as Reichardt, Thibaut and Moscheles were instrumental). But Mendelssohn gave it considerable impetus through his entrepreneurial activities at Leipzig, motivated in part by what he took to be

22 In Reichardt's *Musikalisches Kunstmagazin*, 1 (1782), p. 196. Quoted in H-J. Schulze (ed.), *Bach-Dokumente*, III (Leipzig, 1972), p. 357.
23 A. Hedley (trans. and ed.), *Selected Correspondence of Fryderyk Chopin* (London, Melbourne and Toronto, 1962), p. 17. See also Maynard Solomon, *Beethoven Essays* (Cambridge, Mass., 1988), p. 291.

the excesses and triviality of the benefit concerts. The programmes for his Gewandhaus historical concerts in 1838 are telling, conceived 'according to the chronological order of the great masters from one hundred years ago to the present day' – in other words, from Bach to Beethoven. Mendelssohn conveyed much of his enthusiasm for Bach and early music to Schumann when they met in 1835, and he too played a proselytising role, not least through *Neue Zeitschrift für Musik*, whose mission was in part 'to acknowledge the past and to draw attention to the fact that new artistic beauties can be strengthened by the past'. When, in 1840, the two men established a syllabus for the teaching of music history at the newly opened conservatoire in Leipzig, they effectively period-ised an emergent canon: Bach and Handel; Haydn, Mozart and Beethoven; Schubert; Mendelssohn and Chopin. Moreover, in compositional terms their own music responded explicitly to Bach: from Mendelssohn's oratorio *St Paul* and 'Reformation' Symphony to his Six Preludes and Fugues, Op. 35; from the 'combination fugues' of Schumann's cyclic finales, to the *stile antico* of the penultimate movement of the 'Rhenish' Symphony, and the Fugues of Op. 60 and Op. 72, composed (most of them) after his study of Cherubini's well-known counterpoint treatise in 1845.

Just a few years earlier Chopin had asked for that same treatise to be sent to him from Paris while he stayed at George Sand's chateau in Nohant, and the results are apparent in the contrapuntal working of some of his later music. Yet in a sense Bach had always been with Chopin. 'Above all he prized Bach, and between Bach and Mozart it is hard to say whom he loved more', was Karl Mikuli's verdict.[24] In a way Chopin's major achievement was to translate Bach's equal-voice counterpoint, perfectly suited to eighteenth-century instruments, into a differentiated counterpoint moulded to the idiomatic nature of the piano, and that achievement in turn influenced the whole future course of piano music. There is also a sense in which Chopin shared with Liszt (whose Bach transcriptions played their own publicising role) and other early Romantic composers a tendency to reach back across the Classical era to recover something of Baroque formal thinking, a unitary process of departure and return rather than a dialectic of tonal and thematic contrast. As Schumann put it, 'the whole so-called Romantic school . . . is far nearer to Bach than Mozart ever was'.[25] In all of this Bach stood as the exemplary model. 'I . . . endeavour to purify and strengthen myself through him', wrote Schumann, 'To my mind [he] is unapproachable – he is unfathomable . . .' (*On Music*, 93). Nor was this a passing phenomenon. Right through into the twentieth century,

24 In the Preface to his edition. See Jean-Jacques Eigeldinger, *Chopin, Pianist and Teacher*, trans. N. Shohet, with K. Osostowicz and R. Howat, ed. R. Howat (Cambridge, 1986; original edn 1970), p. 276.
25 Robert Schumann, *On Music and Musicians*, trans. P. Rosenfeld, ed. K. Wolff (London, 1946), p. 93.

Bach sustained his reputation as 'the essence of all music', to use Debussy's phrase,[26] until in the 1920s he would be appropriated as the model for a kind of international neo-classicism.

That movement was motivated in part by an early twentieth-century tendency to associate Bach with an idealised image of aesthetic purity, cleansing music of late Romantic excesses. To some degree Bach reception in the nineteenth century already carried with it something of this association, invoking an earlier golden age as a counterweight to the perceived failings of contemporary culture. Thus the values associated with his music were order, devotion and stability, neatly embodied in fugue, chorale and characteristic bass line. These values were even more clearly assigned to Palestrina.[27] Indeed the Cecilian ideal of an *a cappella* church music (discussed more fully in chapter 18) was promoted right at the outset of the nineteenth century by such as Reichardt through his editorship of the *Berlinische musikalische Zeitung*, founded in 1805, and later in his specialist *Musikalisches Kunstmagazin*, which was avidly read by Schumann and his circle (one might also mention of course Hoffmann's *Alte und neue Kirchenmusik*). In France too an enthusiasm for Palestrina and the 'Palestrina style' dated from early in the century, associated with Choron in the 1820s, and bolstered by the appearance of the Baini biography in 1828, and by a cluster of editions. In due course the Palestrina revival fed into the North German Protestant traditions associated with the activities of the Berlin Domchor and Singakademie. Mendelssohn was of course caught up in this movement, and was introduced to other late Renaissance repertories, including music by composers such as Lotti and Vittoria, in part through his contacts with those great proselytisers for early music, Zelter and Thibaut (see chapter 8). Likewise the 'Palestrina style' became a focus for debate between new and old in the later South German Catholic traditions associated with the *Allgemeine deutsche Cäcilien-Verein*.

Performance traditions through the century preserved the image of Palestrina as the paradigmatic composer of church music – a composer of almost mystical purity ('devoid of worldly passions', was how Fétis put it), second only to Gregorian plainsong, whose revival in the nineteenth century is a story all of its own (see chapter 18), as an image of timeless perfection in sharp contrast to the contemporary world. And something of this resonance is captured in the direct influence of Palestrina on nineteenth-century composers, ranging from the quasi-liturgical music composed by Mendelssohn for the Singakademie and his liturgical compositions for the Domchor to the sacred works of Liszt and

---

26 *Debussy on Music*, coll. François Lesure, trans. and ed. Richard Langham Smith (New York, 1977), p. 277.

27 See James Garrett, 'Palestrina and the German Romantic Imagination: Interpreting Historicism in Nineteenth-century Music', Ph.D. diss., University of Wales Cardiff (1999).

Bruckner associated with the Catholic tradition. The Palestrina style also played a major role within secular music of the nineteenth century, either as a generalised sacred trope or just as a symbol of nostalgia or reclamation. As such it could carry the connotative values of a kind of mock-medieval Arcadianism, or alternatively of an archaism, or elementalism, suggestive of aesthetic purity. Bruckner's symphonies furnish us with numerous instances, but even Verdi's *Aïda* allows the Palestrinian polyphony of its priests to sit alongside the orientalisms of its priestesses. It was above all in northern Europe in the early twentieth century that such connotations came into their own. In Nielsen (and occasionally in Sibelius) a Palestrinian polyphony, along with a reconstituted diatonic practice, functioned as a powerful symbol of Volkish cosmology. As such it contributed to a larger kind of idealism that enabled the Nordic symphony – in a magnificent second growth of that genre – to recapture something of Beethoven's lofty humanism in ways that seemed no longer available to composers in central Europe.

The culture industry

By way of this pantheon of great composers the past loomed ever larger in the nineteenth century. As it did so it became closely entwined with ideas of the new, and in ways that reached a culminating point immediately following the mid-century. Indeed the whole question of an indebtedness to the past was central to those debates and controversies about 'the new' which took place in the 1850s. They will be discussed in our next chapter, but it should be pointed out here that while the conservative critic was at pains to stress, and deplore, the novelty of the new, the progressive (notably 'New German') composer was anxious to demonstrate his links with the old, his affinities with the great masters. This went beyond competing claims for the mantle of Beethoven to embrace those more abstract qualities that were increasingly (following A. B. Marx) assumed to be the mark of the great composer. The notion of wholeness, of the organic nature of great art, was of central importance, and it related rather specifically to the claims of German Idealism about the relation between art and the world. It was, as noted in chapter 1, the principal ground for an aesthetic of absolute music. Surprisingly, however, the proponents of programme music took their stand on this very same ground. Hence the attempts, especially pertinent in relation to the 'poetic' character of New German music, to demonstrate that the great works of the present – the avant-garde – were no less organically conceived than the great works of the past – the canon.[28]

28 See James Deaville, 'The Controversy Surrounding Liszt's Conception of Programme Music', in Jim Samson and Bennett Zon (eds.), *Nineteenth-Century Music: Selected Proceedings of the Tenth International Conference on Nineteenth-Century Music* (Aldershot, forthcoming).

Our two categories of 'greatness' shared further common cause in what we might call the politics of culture. Above all they were as one in their opposition to a cluster of commercial repertories that were given ever sharper definition through the century. It goes without saying that a clean division between 'art' and 'entertainment' makes for crude historiography. There is within any art form in any culture of any period an interaction – even at times a competition – between aesthetic and functional claims or imperatives. All the same there is a certain historical logic to the ideological privileging of the aesthetic over the functional in the nineteenth century. It resulted in large part from the strengthening mercantile principle at work in middle-class culture, a principle that in some ways forced a separation of the significant and the popular. In social-historical terms this was already signalled by the transformation of court institutions into public institutions in the early nineteenth century, and by the attendant professionalisation of musical life. The effects on concert life and the opera house have already been described. In a nutshell the early decades of the century saw a remarkable synthesis of artistic skills and commercial enterprise as musical culture was increasingly commodified, its products tailored to the demands of a new middle-class establishment. It is against this background that the emergence of a canon and an avant-garde should really be understood. Even as they identified and validated bourgeois culture, these categories challenged its modes of production and reception. Essentially it was the challenge of the aesthetic to the marketplace, though the latter threatened always to embrace the former. The category of greatness, then, took shape in opposition to an emerging 'culture industry'.

The previous chapter has already given some indication of the vast backcloth of music and music-making against which any profile of the 'great composer' needs to be projected. The music that most people performed and to which most people listened was neither canonic nor modernist, though, as Derek Carew reminds us, today's categories were not yesterday's. The nineteenth century, after all, had several 'canons'. There was the canon of the drawing-room, where certain works (piano pieces by Challoner, Henselt and Hünten for example) were popular enough to run to multiple editions throughout the century. Or the canon of the ballroom, dominated by the Strauss dynasty, whose music later crossed the boundaries to the bourgeois concert platform. Or the canon of the choral association, where popular ephemera by Methfessel and even Reichardt took their place alongside Handel and Mendelssohn. The German term *Trivialmusik* is one of the least happy in the lexicon, but it does at least serve as a pointer to some of the relevant associations. Now it goes without saying that a social history of music will seek to do justice to any music that played an important role in people's lives. That said, it is hard to make useful generalisations about so-called *Trivialmusik* in the nineteenth century without exploring more fully the diversity of social and regional contexts within which domestic and community music-making took place. A general history such as this is not the place to attempt such an exploration. But we should at least recognise that music history has stories to tell beyond Europe's major cultural capitals, and beyond the familiar genres of opera, song and bourgeois concert music.

It is interesting to reflect on the approaches of social historians of music in this respect. Undoubtedly we learn much about the dynamics of music history from comparative studies such as William Weber's analysis of concert life in London, Paris and Vienna, where the close investigation of newspaper reports, sponsorship patterns, concert categories, ticket prices and the like enables determinate conclusions to be drawn about the links between music and social class in the early nineteenth century.[29] But this tells only a partial story. Consider London. Its musical life is indeed illuminated by Weber's parallels with European capitals. But it is also illuminated by shading in something of the national context. In other words, Weber's approach needs to be set along-side that of Cyril Ehrlich, whose book on the music profession in Britain as a whole expands the field laterally, so to speak.[30] Then again, the patterns of music-making in Britain exhibit such major local variation as to demand yet more specialised studies. Just what had music in Cornwall to do with music in London? Or even with music in Bradford?[31] Would it be more instructive to compare Cornwall with Brittany?[32] As my references for these regions suggest, studies of 'local' music history are frequently pursued these days, and in just about every European country. Yet they are usually undertaken within a national frame of reference, as implicit contributions to the larger 'national history', and it is far from certain that this is their most helpful context. Paradoxically, the collective impact of such studies may well be to point up the cosmopolitan, class-based and largely urban character of cultural nationalism in Europe as a whole. All we can do here is to signal that the bold patterns in music history outlined by a volume such as this are at the very least nuanced by a mass of contradictory local detail. The rise in professional music-making in England – quite simply an exponential increase in the number of musicians throughout the nineteenth century – might be regarded as one such pattern,

29 William Weber, *Music and the Middle Class* (London, 1975).

30 Cyril Ehrlich, *The Music Profession in Britain since the Eighteenth Century: A Social History* (Oxford, 1985); this is supplemented by later studies of the Performing Rights Society and the Royal Philharmonic Society: *Harmonious Alliance: A History of the Performing Rights Society* (Oxford, 1989); *First Philharmonic: A History of the Royal Philharmonic Society* (Oxford, 1995).

31 See, for example, R. McGrady, *Music and Musicians in Early Nineteenth-Century Cornwall* (Exeter, 1991). Also D. Russell, 'Provincial Concerts in England 1865–1914: A Case Study of Bradford', *Journal of the Royal Musical Association*, 114/1 (1989), pp. 43–55.

32 Marie-Claire Mussat, *Musique et Société à Rennes aux XVIIIè et XIXè siècles* (Geneva, 1988).

but we should note that it bypasses Cornwall almost entirely, with implications for musical taste and musical awareness in the region. On the other hand, the dramatic fall in the price of instruments (violins and pianos especially) and of printed music, together with a vast increase in the supply of both, promoted amateur music-making as much in Cornwall as in London, and that, or so it might be argued, provided some of the educative foundation on which a cross-community musical culture might be built.

This latter point invites some rather bolder generalisations. The commodification of music described in the last chapter provoked, from around the time of the French Revolution onwards, two quite different responses. The first, prevalent especially in the first half of the nineteenth century but extending through to Matthew Arnold and well beyond that, grew out of a utopian liberal belief in the elevation of the masses through culture and education (see chapter 19). This belief, which carried of course certain political advantages for a liberal, or liberal-conservative, establishment, implicitly celebrated the past as a model which might be approached by way of less rounded, but commercially viable, cultural forms, some of which might best be described as kitsch; this may even describe, at least in part, the endeavours of some of our amateur musicians in Cornwall. The assumption underlying this response was that high culture in the fullest sense would develop only when the general standard of education had been raised to an acceptable level in a process of progressive enlightenment, of liberation from superstition (and for many of the *philosophes* the latter category included religion). The consumption of music then came down to questions of freedom and 'rights' – the rights of all to have access to learning and culture, and practical efforts were indeed made in that direction. In practice, however, this democratisation of culture could only proceed so far, such were the barriers of social class in the nineteenth century. It was one thing to disseminate high culture among lower middle-class burghers; quite another to introduce it to the factories. And it is perhaps not surprising that the idealism of the liberal intelligentsia could turn all too easily to an intolerant elitism when the 'ordinary people' seemed unworthy of their efforts.

The second response was to view the commodification of music as a measure of social and cultural decline. Patrick Brantlinger has demonstrated that this attitude – in essence the belief that forms of mass entertainment tend inevitably towards a debasement and trivialisation of culture – was already alive and well in the ancient world, citing the Heraclitean axioms that virtue is rare and the multitude is bestial.[33] However it was above all in post-French Revolution Europe that it gained decisive momentum, as the secularisation

33 Patrick Brantlinger, *Bread and Circuses: Theories of Mass Culture and Social Decay* (Ithaca and London, 1983).

and commercialisation of European societies promoted a sharper polarisation of attitudes, and creative elites increasingly protected themselves from the forces of massification. Already in the early nineteenth century 'progress' was identified in some quarters with decadence, as processes of industrialisation and early forms of mass production were seen to be destructive of art and culture. Such attitudes were already articulated by Blake and the Romantic poets in England, as also by Stendhal and Balzac in France, well before the more characteristic articulations of the decadent movement in the later nineteenth century. Already in Gautier's *Mademoiselle de Maupin* (1835) analogies between contemporary mores and the declining years of the Roman empire were made explicit.

That high culture should have felt itself more threatened than enriched by the beginnings of what would later be described as 'mass culture' – already in the early nineteenth century – is a matter of historical record. Later critical theory – Nietzsche, the Frankfurt School – would read into this historical record severe, modernist messages about the undoing of culture, just as more recent postmodern commentators would in their turn, and by an adroit sleight-of-hand, neutralise these messages by identifying modernism as just another stage of cultural history. But the record itself reveals both an increasingly sharp definition of the once fluid boundaries between high art and popular culture, and an increasing alienation of the latter from the former. That process seemed to reach a defining moment just after the mid-century. It operated both within middle-class cultural forms (Wagner, Offenbach) and between those forms and the emergent forms of an increasingly literate and increasingly politicised working class (opera house, music hall). Put baldly, it was a separation between music that rejected, and music that accepted, its commodity status in a mercantile culture – between great composers (Classical music, the avant-garde) and commercial repertories (the sheet-music industry, choral societies, brass bands, professional 'light music' for ballroom and theatre). As repertories were increasingly prised apart in the later nineteenth century, three broad categories of music and music-making (broadly speaking, avant-garde, Classical and commercial) stood out in ever clearer relief, standing in a mutually dependent, polarised relation to each other. All three will be examined more fully in Part II of this book. The concept of an avant-garde – a 'music of the future' – will be scrutinised in our next chapter. The crystallisation of classical repertories – the 'imaginary museum' – will be traced in chapter 13. It should be recognised, however, that neither of these would have been possible without our third category, which I have very loosely described as commercial. This category – a product of the emergence of a 'culture industry', responsive only to an anonymous mass market and, in some readings at least, manipulative of conventional language – will be examined in chapter 19.

Bibliography

Berlioz, H., *The Memoirs of Hector Berlioz*, trans. and ed. D. Cairns. London, 1970

Brantlinger, P., *Bread and Circuses: Theories of Mass Culture and Social Decay*. Ithaca and London, 1983

Brendel, F., *Geschichte der Musik in Italien, Deutschland und Frankreich*. Leipzig, 1852

Busoni, F., *Sketch of a New Aesthetic of Music*, trans. Th. Baker. In *Three Classics in the Aesthetics of Music*. New York, 1962; original edn 1907

Deaville, J., 'The Controversy Surrounding Liszt's Conception of Programme Music'. In Jim Samson and Bennett Zon (eds.), *Nineteenth-Century Music: Selected Proceedings of the Tenth International Conference on Nineteenth-Century Music*. Aldershot, forthcoming

Debussy, C., *Debussy on Music*, coll. François Lesure, trans. and ed. Richard Langham Smith. New York, 1977

Delacroix, E., *The Journal of Eugène Delacroix*, ed. H. Wellington, trans. L. Norton. London, 1951

Dreyfus, L., *Bach and the Patterns of Invention*. Cambridge, Mass., 1996

Ehrlich, C., *The Music Profession in Britain since the Eighteenth Century: A Social History*. Oxford, 1985
   Harmonious Alliance: A History of the Performing Rights Society. Oxford, 1989
   First Philharmonic: A History of the Royal Philharmonic Society. Oxford, 1995

Eigeldinger, J.-J., *Chopin, Pianist and Teacher*, trans. N. Shohet, with K. Osostowicz and R. Howat, ed. R. Howat. Cambridge, 1986; original edn 1970

Ellis, K., *Music Criticism in Nineteenth-Century France: 'La Revue et Gazette musicale de Paris' 1834–80*. Cambridge, 1995

Fétis, F.-J., *Histoire générale de la Musique*. 5 vols., Paris, 1876

Garrett, J., 'Palestrina and the German Romantic Imagination: Interpreting Historicism in Nineteenth-century Music.' Ph.D. diss., University of Wales Cardiff (1999)

Griffiths, P., *Modern Music and After: Directions since 1945*. Oxford, 1995

Hedley, A. (trans. and ed.), *Selected Correspondence of Fryderyk Chopin*. London, Melbourne and Toronto, 1962

Kant, I., *Critique of Aesthetic Judgement*, trans. J. C. Meredith. Oxford, 1911; original edn 1790

McClary, S., 'Constructions of Subjectivity in Schubert's Music'. In P. Brett, E. Wood and G. C. Thomas (eds.), *Queering the Pitch: The New Gay and Lesbian Musicology*. New York and London, 1994, pp. 205–34

McGrady, R., *Music and Musicians in Early Nineteenth-Century Cornwall*. Exeter, 1991

Mussat, M.-C., *Musique et Société à Rennes aux XVIIIè et XIXè siècles*. Geneva, 1988

Reynolds, J., *Discourses on Art*, ed. Robert R. Wark. New Haven and London, 1975; based on edition of 1797

Russell, D., 'Provincial Concerts in England 1865–1914: A Case Study of Bradford'. *Journal of the Royal Musical Association*, 114/1 (1989), pp. 43–55

Schellhous, R., 'Fétis's *Tonality* as a Metaphysical Principle: Hypothesis for a New Science'. *Music Theory Spectrum*, 13/2 (1991), pp. 219–40

Schelling, F. W. J., *The Philosophy of Art*, trans. Douglas Stott. Minneapolis, 1989; original edn 1802–3
   System of Transcendental Idealism (1800), trans. Peter Heath. Virginia, 1978

Schiller, F., *On the Aesthetic Education of Man*, trans. and ed. E. M. Wilkinson and L. A. Willoughby. Oxford, 1967

Schulze, H.-J. (ed.), *Bach-Dokumente*, III. Leipzig, 1972

Schumann, R., *On Music and Musicians*, trans. P. Rosenfeld, ed. K. Wolff. London, 1946

Solomon, M., *Beethoven Essays*. Cambridge, Mass., 1988

Steiner, G., *Real Presences*. London, 1989

Strohm, R., *The Rise of European Music 1380–1500*. Cambridge, 1993

Talbot, M. (ed.), *The Musical Work: Reality or Invention?* Liverpool, 2000

Tasso, T., *Prose*, ed. E. Mazzali. Milan and Naples, 1959

Warrack, J., *Tchaikovsky*. London, 1973

Weber, W., *Music and the Middle Class*. London, 1975

Williams, R., *Keywords: A Vocabulary of Culture and Society*. London, 1976

Wiora, W., *The Four Ages of Music*, trans. M. D. Herter Norton. London, 1966

'Of Art Music and Cultural Classes.' In E. Strainchamps and M. R. Maniates (eds.) *Music and Civilisation: Essays in Honour of Paul Henry Lang*. New York and London, 1984, pp. 472–7

Young, E., *Conjectures on Original Composition*. Scolar Press facsimile. Leeds, 1966; original edn 1759

· PART TWO 1850–1900 ·

11

Progress, modernity and the concept of an avant-garde

JOHN WILLIAMSON

Progress: theories and discontents

During a series of articles published in the *Allgemeine musikalische Zeitung* in 1848, the editor J. C. Lobe expressed his misgivings about the problem of progress in music, a concept that seemed particularly urgent to the German musical press in the Year of Revolutions. In response to the slogan, 'our age is the age of progress', he could find only this much meaning:

a. If the phrase means, music has made more strides forward in our time than in any other, it is emphatically contradicted by a glance at the period from Haydn to Beethoven. The era after Beethoven has not made the tremendous progress of that epoch.

b. If the phrase means, our age needs to progress in music, for we no longer have works that correspond to the needs of the times and everything available is founded on tired and outmoded points of view, then this is contradicted by the flourishing world of splendid compositions by masters past and present by whom a truly musical soul can be and is delighted.

c. If the phrase means, in our age much that is mediocre, hollow and empty is being produced that should be got rid of, then we claim what was claimed in all ages and goes without saying.

I cannot find a meaning other than these three with reference to the progress of practical music in general, and none of them seems to me to justify the never-ending talk and writing about progress.[1]

Here the idea of progress exists in an uneasy relationship with the notions of the musical artwork and the musical genius. In recent years, Carl Dahlhaus has promulgated the thesis that 'The concept of the avant garde is a historical category which arose in the eighteenth century together with the notion of

---

1 Helmut Kirchmeyer (ed.), *Situationsgeschichte der Musikkritik und des musikalischen Pressewesens in Deutschland dargestellt vom Ausgange des 18. bis zum Beginn des 20. Jahrhunderts*, Part 2, *System- und Methodengeschichte*, IV, *Quellen-Texte 1847–1851 (1852)* (Regensburg, 1996), p. 231. Translations mine, except where otherwise noted.

originality and the idea of the autonomous work'.[2] If the need to distinguish clearly between 'progress' and its most extreme formulation (the avant-garde) is set to one side for the moment, Lobe's little catechism casts a somewhat questioning light on Dahlhaus's widely accepted grouping. It is hardly a matter of a refutation, since Dahlhaus has left the degree to which the three notions of progress, originality and autonomy are dependent intentionally vague (at least within the quotation). In Lobe's account, however, the existence of works (whose autonomy and originality is taken for granted) and the need for progress are thrown into a conflict that points to the disparate sources of musical avant-gardes.

More sharply, progress and 'splendid compositions by masters past and present' are by no means the same thing, a conclusion with which the idea of the avant-garde is by no means unfamiliar. In the writings of the historians of the interrelated groups of ideas loosely associated with modernism, the avant-garde is the point at which notions of the original creative genius and progress start to come apart; indeed this is one of its chief distinguishing features from modernism itself. Matei Calinescu has drawn attention to the manner in which the major figures of modernism (his examples, entirely literary, include Joyce, Kafka and Proust) have been accepted with their works into the canon of original masters, while the avant-garde has tended to survive as movements (e.g., Dada and Surrealism), as 'a deliberate and self-conscious *parody of modernity* itself'.[3] Such a perspective was obviously lacking to Lobe, whose feeling for intellectual movements tended to move within the confines of progress, Classicism and Romanticism; for him the problem of progress was essentially that a journalistic slogan had become destructive of the need for a canon of models for young composers. Opposing the creative spirit to the critical, Lobe came close to identifying progress (at least in its loudly proclaimed contemporary aspect) as an aspect of politics and warned against limiting music (and art in general) by ignoring the past. For him, the critical spirit was an irrelevance to the self-driven creative genius. As a statement of the autonomy of the musical master (and by extension, the musical masterwork), this seems quite emphatic. It is all the more striking in that Lobe was aware of the phenomenon of the artist-critic; indeed the need for the artist to be a critic was shortly to become one of the central points of Franz Liszt's programme for musical reform. That art might have its 'critical' epochs, that with Romanticism it had moved into a

<hr>

2 Carl Dahlhaus, *Schoenberg and the New Music*, trans. Derek Puffett and Alfred Clayton (Cambridge, 1987), p. 24.

3 Matei Calinescu, *Five Faces of Modernity: Modernism, Avant-Garde, Decadence, Kitsch, Postmodernism*, 2nd edn (Durham, NC, 1987), p. 141.

'philosophical' age, were insights that Lobe left to the varied perspectives of Hegel, Young Germany and the Saint-Simonians. Yet in the coming together of social and political ideas of progress in art and the notion of the autonomous artwork, progress gradually gave birth to modernism and to the idea of the avant-garde.

A word of caution is necessary here, inasmuch as concepts of progress and the historicist baggage that they carry do not sit easily alongside the more radical side of modernism. Frederick Karl has put the problem most clearly:

> Modernists in nearly all their innovative phases view themselves not as part of a tradition but as ahistorical, as dissociated from the historical ties one expects in marketplace ideas. At any given stage, Modernism is to break not only with traditional art but with traditional humanistic culture, what is connected to historical process. The avant-garde, especially, is based on this assumption: to move so far outside the mainstream that historical development no longer applies. The militant avant-garde or vanguard – a martial term – may be connected by a thread to the main body, but it conceives of itself as separate, isolated, endangered, as having exposed itself to such danger that it can command its own rules. Thus, it floats free, secedes, becomes ahistorical.[4]

Ideas of progress, such as Lobe and his contemporaries discussed, had not yet taken that vital step of cutting the knot with history; models drawn from history were regularly cited by friends and foes of musical progress alike. The crisis with which they dealt did not yet acknowledge modernism, but was rooted in a more general idea of modernity, one that was not synonymous with avant-gardes and was often deeply opposed to them.

Historians of modernism have drawn frequent attention to the degree to which radical modernism grew out of disaffection with the perceived shallowness of the worship of progress and modernity. This was reflected in a fractured perception of the past: rejected all too often along with its traditional forms and modes of perception, it still retained the glamour of a more aristocratic age and, more distantly, the idea of man and art before the curse of specialisation that lay at the root of Wagner's Hellenism (and also its weaker relative in Liszt). The idea of a radical anti-modern position within modernism is familiar enough to the music historian and to the historian of ideas, and is an important strain in perceptions of Wagner, whether viewed positively (as by Baudelaire) or ultimately judged decadent (as in the later Nietzsche).

The perception of Wagner shared by writers such as Baudelaire and Nietzsche depends heavily on the ideas that modern became as much a critical judgement on quality as a historical description, that it became the embodiment

---

4 Frederick R. Karl, *Modern and Modernism: The Sovereignty of the Artist, 1885–1925* (New York, 1985), p. xii.

of 'the spirit of modern negativity, of pure process, of the constant alteration of all structures and systems' at least as much as of a utopia.[5] Much the same might be said about the debate over musical progress, except that the process ceased to be merely an antithesis between conservatives and reformists, between partisans such as Lobe and Robert Griepenkerl (the only antagonist identified in his articles) or Franz Brendel (the editor of the *Neue Zeitschrift für Musik*, and the leading theoretician in the camp of progress), but was turned to a subtler end. The merely modern became downgraded in the face of the appropriation of the Romantic ideas of utopia that were particularly associated with French writers of the first half of the century. The myth of man made whole, socially conceived earlier in the nineteenth century, took an aesthetic turn in Baudelaire and Wagner. This was an essential element in separating Wagner's intensely individualistic modernism (or perhaps decadence, to speak in terms familiar from both Baudelaire and Nietzsche) from the progressives of the mid-century, whose truest musical representative, Franz Liszt, served best to define the problem that Lobe deplored; yet both Wagner and Liszt, in different ways, dreamt of redemption and utopias.

Liszt as forerunner of the avant-garde

Liszt and his circle seldom wrote of modernism (a term that in any case hardly existed with its later nuances) or of the avant-garde. Where the latter term has been applied to Liszt, it has usually been with the intention of labelling him as a forerunner. In this, musicology has been consistent with its normal usage, which is best represented by the work of Johannes Piersig.[6] In reviewing the problems of musical progress, he allows its history to run fairly seamlessly into a concept of avant-garde that is partially equated with Schoenberg's 'New Music', but more emphatically with the European avant-garde since 1945. The use of the term in the title of a symposium on Liszt looks forward directly to the tradition of the new music from Schoenberg to the avant-garde of the 1950s. In contrast to a standard *topos* in Liszt scholarship, the authors of the symposium do not confine their view of Liszt the forerunner to his later music, but are fully aware of the degree to which his early works and those of the Weimar period experiment with unusual and irregular scales and harmonic configurations; nonetheless, the traditional musicological interpretation of avant-garde in

---

5 Andrea Gogröf-Voorhees, *Defining Modernism: Baudelaire and Nietzsche on Romanticism, Modernity, Decadence, and Wagner* (New York, 1999), p. 36; Richard Klein, 'Wagners plurale Moderne: Eine Konstruktion von Unvereinbarkeiten', in Claus-Steffen Mahnkopf (ed.), *Richard Wagner: Konstrukteur der Moderne* (Stuttgart, 1999), pp. 190–1.

6 Johannes Piersig, *Das Fortschrittsproblem in der Musik um die Jahrhundertwende: Von Richard Wagner bis Arnold Schönberg* (Regensburg, 1977).

relation to Liszt is best represented in relation to his final period.[7] By placing Liszt in the role of mere forerunner to a real, historically self-aware avant-garde, musicology anticipated Peter Bürger's wider strategy of confining the label avant-garde to artistic movements that postdate the rise of aestheticism in the later nineteenth century; thus he separates it from modernism and from the roots of modernism in the era after the French Revolution. By doing this, he also tacitly condones Calinescu's essential insight that a true avant-garde was characterised above all by self-awareness of its role.[8]

One conspicuous exception to this strategy, however, is to be found in the writings of Carl Dahlhaus, for whom the term loses its narrower definition and becomes linked to (but not synonymous with) that vaguer progress to which more than one musical movement has subscribed and which the party of Liszt and Wagner in the 1850s thought of as 'music of the future'. In Dahlhaus's scheme, musical avant-gardes existed in a characteristic grouping of antithetical positions. On the one hand, they represented the opposite to *Volkstümlichkeit* (though concepts of the 'folk' were part of Wagner's idea of a future music, and folk traditions have often been seen as progressive within nationalist revivals in both the nineteenth and twentieth centuries) and in this lay the roots of the increasing gap between new music and popular taste in the later twentieth century. On the other, they stood for the aesthetic of autonomy (or the idea of absolute music in Dahlhaus's system) even at a time when progress had opted, as with Brendel and Liszt, for heteronomy (crudely, 'programme music'). 'Music of the future' was portrayed by Dahlhaus as a refuge for the mid-nineteenth-century avant-garde from the mockery of its triumphant antagonists in the political aftermath of 1848 and in the wake of the decline of Hegelianism. Yet the refuge preserved the avant-garde notion that 'art has to be new in order to be authentic', together with 'the idea of the autonomous work'. The glue that held avant-garde and 'music of the future' together seemed to be a matter in Dahlhaus of an 'extreme form of . . . individualisation', 'dissolution of genre', and a 'tendency to favour the exceptional', that he believed to be present as much in Berlioz as in Wagner (and, he might have added, in Liszt, albeit differently expressed). Dahlhaus's location of Liszt and Wagner as a form of avant-garde fits with more general perceptions of modernism beyond Bürger's definition and reflects a vague feeling that in a sense the modernist adventure has its historical roots rather earlier than is sometimes thought, that it is a Romantic conception, or even a 'romantic illusion' in Roger Scruton's harsher

---

7 Zsolt Gárdonyi and Siegfried Mauser, *Virtuosität und Avantgarde: Untersuchungen zum Klavierwerk Franz Liszts* (Mainz, 1988); see also Alan Walker, *Franz Liszt* (London, 1983–96), III, pp. 437–56.

8 Peter Bürger, *Theory of the Avant-Garde*, trans. Michael Shaw (Minneapolis, 1984), p. 17; Calinescu, *Five Faces*, p. 100; for doubts as to Bürger's approach, see also Max Paddison, *Adorno, Modernism and Mass Culture: Essays on Critical Theory and Music* (London, 1996), p. 37.

verdict.[9] Moreover the term, 'avant-garde', was undoubtedly known to Liszt and his contemporaries.

Calinescu has shown that, although the word was used with something like its present meaning in the sixteenth century in literature, its permanent extension from an explicitly military to a political term came during the aftermath of the French Revolution, and the writings of the Saint-Simonians helped to preserve this while extending its use to aesthetics and artistic matters in general.[10] In this context it was part of a general language of modernity that included various other concepts. In the first half of the nineteenth century, at least until Baudelaire, modern and Romantic tended to be synonymous, however much this varied in emphasis or weakened with the passage of time. In this nexus of ideas, the antithesis between Greek and Roman antiquity on the one hand and modern Christian Romanticism on the other was an essential component. But the poetic dimension to this view of Romanticism already contained the seed of that anti-modern modernism, in which a rejection of mindless belief in progress, particularly the technological, went alongside revolutionary, utopian, and even nihilistic ideas. In view of the particularly strong emphasis that Liszt's theories laid on the poetic, Christian dimension of this Romantic modernism (an area that separated him in the most drastic fashion from Wagner, including *Parsifal*), it is worth stressing Calinescu's account of its phases. That the condition of modernity for the individual involved increasingly the claim to be a freethinker was to pose intense problems for Liszt (and also for his master Lamennais in even more drastic fashion). The location of the modern 'spirit of Christianity' in the area of aesthetics from Chateaubriand onwards led to a separation of pagan and Christian ideals of beauty, 'a truly revolutionary moment' that fostered Calinescu's picture of the 'idea of total discontinuity between cultural cycles' and the avant-garde's sense of separateness from previous ages; in turn, a sense of the decline of the Christian era became part of modernism's feeling of despair that sent artists such as Wagner in search of their own form of utopia. With Wagner, the antique ideal even reasserts itself over Christian Romanticism as an agent for change, though it is a model that cannot truly be recovered; his Hellenism, like Nietzsche's, is a declaration of the 'untimely', un-modern (and eventually anti-modern) side of modernism that is one of its characteristically paradoxical qualities.[11]

How far Liszt travelled along this path is uncertain. There is undoubtedly some truth in the frequently encountered proposition that in the history of the

9 Dahlhaus, *Schoenberg and the New Music*, pp. 14–31 and 43; Roger Scruton, *The Aesthetics of Music* (Oxford, 1997), p. 471.

10 Calinescu, *Five Faces*, pp. 97–100

11 *Ibid.*, pp. 37–42 and 59–61; see also Louis A. Ruprecht, jr., *Afterwords: Hellenism, Modernism, and the Myth of Decadence* (Albany, 1996), pp. 23–53.

idea of musical progress he played a reformist role in contrast to Wagner the revolutionary. Yet the discontinuity of historical cycles implicit in the idea of an avant-garde is a tenet that he would have encountered among the Saint-Simonians and also in Fourier. It is arguable that it was only in Liszt's period of close contact with the Saint-Simonians that he came near to being part of a sect strongly imbued with its own sense of mission. That at least is the interpretation of Ralph Locke, which seems more substantial than that of previous Lisztians, who tended to take the composer's apparent later repudiation of the Saint-Simonians at face value. That the condition of being avant-garde involved an element of submission to a party line is evident from its Saint-Simonian origins and helps explain the dislike of the term that Calinescu notes in Baudelaire. That it was an elite against elites, characterised by discipline and aiming for a radical utopia, was an essential part of its self-awareness; in this phase, it had no intrinsic belief in the idea of 'l'art pour l'art' (whose advocates, such as Théophile Gaultier, were more likely, in Donald Egbert's estimation, to be admirers of Fourier).[12] In time the avant-garde would come to exhibit a high regard for technological metaphors, and would preach an outlook of permanent cultural crisis, but these positions were not as yet completely implicit, though the former is at least hinted at in the Saint-Simonian exaltation of industry. Baudelaire's suspicion was in all probability widely shared at the mid-century. The only use of the term in Liszt, in his major essay on Schumann, remains at the loosely metaphorical stage and has an essentially negative flavour, implying at least as much the tyranny of fashion as of elites: 'die ganze Avant- und Arrièregarde der Dilettanten und Liebhaber . . .' (GS IV, 159).[13]

The French models of Liszt's early writings

Liszt's debt to the Saint-Simonians has been variously interpreted. In estimating it, it is often hard to extricate the Saint-Simonian doctrine (to use the movement's own term) from other ideas that Liszt derived from French thinkers and that the followers of Saint-Simon (as distinct from the master himself) shared with many writers of the period. The first editor of Liszt's early writings, Jean Chantavoine, footnoted the moment in Liszt's first major essay, De la situation des artistes et de leur condition dans la société, where the ideas of the

---

12 Calinescu, Five Faces, pp. 104–25; Donald Drew Egbert, 'The Idea of "Avant-garde" in Art and Politics', American Historical Review, 73 (1967), p. 344.
13 All references in the text to the prose works and letters of Liszt follow these conventions: GS = Franz Liszt, Gesammelte Schriften, ed. Lina Ramann (Leipzig, 1880–83); Pr = Franz Liszt, Pages romantiques, ed. Jean Chantavoine (Paris and Leipzig, 1912); AJ = Franz Liszt, An Artist's Journey: 'Lettres d'un bachelier ès musique', 1835–1841, ed. and trans. Charles Suttoni (Chicago, 1989); SS = Franz Liszt, Sämtliche Schriften, ed. Detlef Altenburg, vols. III, IV and V to date (Leipzig, 1989–); SL = Franz Liszt, Selected Letters, ed. Adrian Williams (Oxford, 1998).

Saint-Simonians give way to the influence of Lamennais; it is the point where Liszt introduces the idea of musicians as '*priests* of *art*, charged with a mission and a sublime *profession to educate*' (Liszt's emphases; *Pr*, 17). But the musician-priest is not unknown in the Saint-Simonian doctrine, which makes Chantavoine's certainty slightly puzzling. The whole question of Liszt's debt to French thinkers and writers of the 1830s may be divided into those who separate it into discrete packages and those who see a more coherent intellectual picture. The stages in both approaches were defined by Heine in a famous squib that satirised Liszt's seemingly aimless drift from the Saint-Simonians through the thoughts of Pierre Simon Ballanche to the position of the Abbé Lamennais, a description that brought a swift rejoinder from the composer; but Heine's list has stood up well to scrutiny, even if the conclusions drawn from it have been very different (*AJ*, 101–7 and 219–26).

The most substantial treatment of the Saint-Simonians and music is Locke's monograph. In his argument, it is precisely the idea of the artist as priest (in a utopian 'vision of a divine community on earth, ruled by the dictates of brotherly love') that attracted Liszt. By priest, Locke understands the 'conception of the modern artist as an inspired being who is unappreciated and even mistreated by the "critical" society in which he lives'. When reading Liszt's prose works, it is at times hard to avoid the impression that the notion of the misunderstood genius is almost as important as the redeeming message that he brings. But, as Locke notes, other ideas of the Saint-Simonians struck a chord in Liszt, ranging from the general to the quite specific. Music's mission as an ennobling 'social' art was a notion shared by Liszt with more than a few musicians who took a more direct part in the movement (Adolphe Nourrit, Fromental Halévy, Félicien David, Jules Vinçard and Dominique Tajan-Rogé), but Locke's main point is that not only his religious music and his directly political pieces (such as *Lyons*) but also 'his insistence that instrumental music, too, must have a poetic vision or message if it is to rise above the level of simple entertainment' was a reflection of the Saint-Simonian to whom Liszt was closest, Emile Barrault. The indifference to entertainment in music would later be a common bond between Liszt and Franz Brendel. In this context, Saint-Simonian ideas underlay piano cycles such as *Années de pèlerinage*, the symphonic poems and the symphonies. Specific doctrines that Liszt derived from the Saint-Simonians include 'the unhealthy isolation of artists . . . the image of the artist as bringer of heavenly fire, [and] the proposal that music leave the church and spread its new religious message in the theatre'.[14]

14 Ralph P. Locke, *Music, Musicians and the Saint-Simonians* (Chicago and London, 1986), pp. 101–4 and 229.

The cult's enthusiasm for a new kind of 'music for the masses' finds its reflection in the apocalyptic section of *De la situation des artistes* on 'Religious Music of the Future', which is often read as a reflection of Lamennais's influence, but reveals Saint-Simonian leanings in its vision of church music revivified in a humanist spirit by hymns whose models are songs of the people, fashioned after the *Marseillaise*.[15] That artists will lead the way is implicit in the scope of this new 'humanistic' religious music that 'will sum up both the *theatre* and the *church* on a colossal scale', and is made explicit in its definition of the hymns and their provenance: 'patriotic, moral, political, and religious in nature, *written* for the people, *taught* to the people, and *sung* by the . . . *people*' (Liszt's emphases: *AJ*, 237). In this world of hymns and ennobling toil, the artist clearly is part of the vanguard.

Whether or not Liszt truly responded to the Saint-Simonians to this extent, Locke is right to note the manner in which he was attracted by their sense of mission. It was almost certainly this that drove him towards Ballanche and Lamennais in turn. What Ballanche had to say about art and its works cannot have had the immediate clarity of a call to action for Liszt, inasmuch as his aesthetics do not go much beyond the ideas of Romanticism with a particularly strong leaning on symbolism. That Liszt was drawn on to Lamennais's vision of art in the service of truth may thus have been a return to, and a consummation of, a strain in Saint-Simonianism or his own Catholic faith. Whatever the reason, in becoming a personal friend and disciple of Lamennais, Liszt was confirmed in the idea that art had a social and religious mission. 'Art for art's sake' and indeed 'absolute music' had little part in this worldview. The artist-priest legislated for humanity rather than art. Modernism's break from the idea of progress remained as yet unaccomplished. But in Ballanche, it has been recently argued, Liszt found the essential stage of transformation through which the idea of the artist-priest could be perfected; whereas the Saint-Simonians had spoken of the artist-priest, but truly meant the artist as mouthpiece for the priest, Ballanche placed the two on an equal footing.[16] It is where Liszt elevates art and music in particular above the role of handmaiden to politics that the influence of Ballanche is probably strongest:

> [Art] exists in humanity, just as it does in the Word, because art is the supreme expression of society; it is the voice of genius, of those men who exist, so to speak, in the confines of two different worlds, and who contemplate the things of the one as illuminated by the divine light of the other.   (*AJ*, 119)

15 Paul Merrick, *Revolution and Religion in the Music of Liszt* (Cambridge, 1987), pp. 19–22.

16 Arthur McCalla, 'Liszt *Bricoleur*: Poetics and Providentialism in Early July Monarchy France', *History of European Ideas*, 24 (1998), pp. 71–92.

The tensions in Liszt's viewpoint then are considerable and founded on this trinity of opposing but not unrelated thinkers. In the Saint-Simonians and even more in Lamennais, he found a revolutionary social doctrine in which music, however important, acted as the voice of ideas – a kind of heteronymous aesthetic that would soon be rendered familiar to his readers and listeners. Ballanche espoused a reformist approach to social conditions and extolled art in a manner that recalled the Romantics. The progressive polemics of Liszt's Weimar years inherit these tensions, flavouring the aesthetic of programme music with the exalted claims of 'absolute music', interpreted not as music complete and 'pure' in itself but as a vehicle for revealing the absolute, an idea that had ramifications beyond French political and social thinking.

Liszt, Idealism and reform

Liszt's programme for the reform of music was at all times aimed at the condition of performers, at the function of critics, and at the education of audiences; that it was not simply an aesthetics of composition was an inheritance reaching back to the Saint-Simonians. But at its heart was a clear, Idealist concept of art, that is decidedly more Germanic than French. It is well known that concepts from the mainstream of German Idealism were absorbed by a variety of French writers on subjects ranging from society to the philosophy of history. Jeffrey Sammons has claimed, 'As a philosophy of history, Saint-Simonianism bears a general resemblance to Hegel', and noted the difficulty for the biographer of Heine in separating ideas from the two sources. Katharine Ellis has also demonstrated the prevalence of ideas from German Idealism in Victor Cousin and in Fétis, the antagonist of Liszt.[17] The key texts in Liszt are the *Lettres d'un bachelier ès musique* that he published in Maurice Schlesinger's *Revue et Gazette musicale* between 1835 and 1841 and the preface to *Album d'un voyageur* of 1842:

> The inner and poetic sense of things, that ideality which exists in everything, seems to manifest itself pre-eminently in those artistic creations that arouse feelings and ideas within the soul by the beauty of their form. Even though music is the least representational of the arts, it nonetheless has its own form and has been defined not without reason as an architecture of sounds. But even as architecture not only has Tuscan, Ionic, Corinthian, etc., orders, but also embodies ideas that are pagan or Christian, sensual or mystic, war-like or com-

---

17 Jeffrey L. Sammons, *Heinrich Heine: A Modern Biography* (Princeton, 1979), p. 159; Katharine Ellis, *Music Criticism in Nineteenth-Century France: 'La Revue et Gazette musicale de Paris' 1834–80* (Cambridge, 1995), pp. 35–44.

mercial, so too, and even more perhaps, music has its hidden meanings, its sense of the ideal, which the majority of people, truly speaking, do not even suspect, because where a work of art is concerned, they rarely rise above the comparison of externals, the facile appreciation of some superficial skill.

The more instrumental music progresses, develops, and frees itself from its early limitations, the more it will tend to bear the stamp of that ideality which marks the perfection of the plastic arts, the more it will cease to be a simple combination of tones and become a poetic language, one that, better than poetry itself perhaps, more readily expresses everything in us that transcends the commonplace, everything that eludes analysis, everything that stirs in the inaccessible depths of imperishable desires and feelings for the infinite.

(*AJ*, 202)

Works of art are to be understood as particular forms of the ideal, amongst which music is of necessity the most elusive and immaterial manifestation. Viewing art as a necessary balance between ideality and reality, Liszt inevitably follows a path that the central German Idealist tradition had already taken. This appropriation, through whatever channels, exposes the difficulty of simply writing off Liszt's resort to Hegelian ideas in his Weimar period, in spite of his known antipathy to reading Hegel, as the malign influence of the Princess Carolyne von Sayn-Wittgenstein or the clumsy editing of Lina Ramann.[18]

This strain of Idealism in Liszt's thinking had an inevitable effect on his notion of musical progress. It may even pose a severe problem for Dahlhaus's idea that the evolution of the avant-garde was linked to the idea of absolute music. An article by Mark Evan Bonds raises the real possibility that 'the revival of idealism as a philosophical and aesthetic principle' at the end of the eighteenth century, and with it, 'the first extended use of poetic imagery to describe works of instrumental music that give no outward indication of a poetic "content", place a serious question mark against the picture of autonomous music suggested by Dahlhaus up to the age of Hanslick'.[19] In Liszt, this element of Idealism is at the core of the 'grande synthèse religieuse et philosophique' that he advocated in *De la situation des artistes* (*Pr*, 3). The synthesis was at once progressive (the clause, 'Une nouvelle génération marche et avance' preserves the essential military metaphor in which the idea of an avant-garde is latent) and imbued with the now familiar distrust of modernity that pointed towards utopia (*Pr*, 17). Modern civilisation (critical rather than

18 As in Ernst Günter Heinemann, *Franz Liszts Auseinandersetzung mit der geistlichen Musik* (Munich and Salzburg, 1978), p. 52; see also Ben Arnold, 'Liszt as Reader, Intellectual, and Musician', in Michael Saffle (ed.), *Analecta Lisztiana I: Liszt and his World* (Stuyvesant, N.Y., 1998), pp. 37–60.

19 Mark Evan Bonds, 'Idealism and the Aesthetics of Instrumental Music at the Turn of the Nineteenth Century', *Journal of the American Musicological Society*, 50 (1997), pp. 389 and 413–14.

organic in the Saint-Simonian alternating scheme) lost its sense of wholeness in the face of the perfection of detail, which in art led to the increasing separation and specialisation of the individual arts, an idea that Liszt returned to in Weimar. The links from this to certain elements of Wagner's later programme of reform are suggestive, as is Liszt's recourse to antiquity for a vision of a time when music and the other arts stood in an integral relationship. If progress was not to be equated with modernity, it was to be found 'in God and humanity, of which art is the organ, the sublime word' (*Pr*, 37). In keeping with Lamennais's belief that 'The rebirth of art is a social rebirth', Liszt then launched his demands for the reform of concerts, for chamber music evenings, a chair of the literature and philosophy of music, the renovation of theatres, philharmonic societies, schools, orchestras and choirs, and the encouragement of the composition of sonatas over the virtuoso genres in which he himself had proved so expert (*Pr*, 21). To counter their ignorance of the concepts of progress and the social mission of music, he concluded by calling for an examination and diploma for would-be music critics.

This programme, which ranges widely over virtually the entire field of music as Liszt knew it, and which blends grand theoretical ideas and practical recommendations into an authentic manifesto of the age, formed the blueprint for Liszt's later Weimar theory (which argues at the very least for his writings, both in the 1830s and in Weimar, as the reflection of his own ideas even if their composition was heavily coloured by the style of his various collaborators). Detlef Altenburg, the editor of the modern series of Liszt's complete prose works, has attempted to order the frequently overblown content of the Weimar period into a coherent scheme (as curiously dependent on trinities of ideas as the Saint-Simonians).[20] This ranges widely over the perceived difficulty of the public with music, the conditions for a future music, and how art should achieve them. In these, the aesthetic background to the practical demands of the earlier period is elaborated on a grander scale. The material differences between the arts, formerly seen as a reflection of modern civilisation's loss of an 'organic' life, now becomes a difficulty for audiences' appreciation. The grand synthesis operates on a more restricted aesthetic level. Music in particular suffers from the lack of immediacy in its material (an idea carried over from the *Lettres d'un bachelier ès musique*), and from the failure of composers and interpreters to recognise their mission (a reflection of a central point in *De la situation des artistes*). The mission of achieving a 'music of the future' depends on the individual composer's recognition of the sublimity and richness of the ideas

---

20 Detlef Altenburg, 'Eine Theorie der Musik der Zukunft: Zur Funktion des Programms im symphonischen Werk von Franz Liszt', in Wolfgang Suppan (ed.), *Kongress-Bericht Eisenstadt 1975*, Liszt-Studien, I (Graz, 1977), pp. 9–25.

and images that music can achieve, his grasping of the poetic (and hence communicative) dimension to music, and facilitating communication (with its own musical semantic code) by means of a programme. The programme in the sphere of instrumental music reflects the poetic idea, as do tone painting and the leitmotif in the area of opera. In recognition of this common origin, Liszt's programme for a 'music of the future' was a campaign for Wagner's idea of music drama as much as for his own works.

The specific task of elaborating this programme was carried through in a variety of documents. Thus the need for reform of the theatre was addressed in a series of articles and pamphlets that climax in the extended essays on *Tannhäuser* and *Lohengrin*. Instrumental music was addressed in various ways, but most comprehensively in the famous essay on Berlioz and *Harold en Italie*. The need of the artist to uphold true standards of criticism is an important theme in it and in the essay on Schumann. The campaign for a Goethe Foundation includes a more general attempt to establish the correct idea of progress:

> The ideas destined to exercise the most astonishing and important influences on the condition of societies have risen from period to period since the beginning of history in different spheres of understanding without apparent order, without visible regularity, a play of unanticipated circumstances. Nevertheless, in spite of passing through countless errors, ceaseless wrongs, and committing unlimited inconsistencies, those ideas inevitably lead sooner or later, as a result of their strange, adventurous, dangerous, and at times terrible trajectory, to some conquest in the realm of the true, beautiful, and good that we term in its entirety, 'Progress'. We cannot deny a recognised fact: that ideas modify themselves in steady progression like the forms that express human thoughts and sentiments. To spare these modifications and sadly groping progressions a useless expenditure of energy in untried and inadvisable attempts, in experiments where bad taste often disfigures the profound, in research where error in application frequently disguises for a long time the truth of the starting-point, in damaging persistence on paths of error on which so many first-rate intellects have sometimes roamed in the absence of complete truth and sincere justice in the criticism they receive – to avoid this long, sad detour of progress, as far as it rests in man's power, would certainly be one of the fairest tasks for noble-minded efforts as well as one of the most valuable effects of the propagation of intellectual enlightenment.   (*SS III*, 70–3)

But it is also an educative project (in which the Saint-Simonian goal of the education of women is a parenthetical strain), specifically aimed at composers and also synthetic in its vision of public music festivals and unique prize compositions. Finally, the much revised book on the gypsies 'emphasized the mystic, fraternal, almost cultic ramifications of gypsy music and thus promoted a myth of the bohemian as artist-prophet-priest' and 'directly reflected Saint-Simonian and Fourierist aesthetic notions of the sentimental value of "avant-garde" art as an agent of social harmony'.[21]

Franz Brendel and progress

In spite of these aims, Liszt's Weimar prose works actually spend more time defining musical progress in terms of the genius and his works, as Altenburg's derived schema clearly recognises, and this aspect is also apparent in the writings of Liszt's Weimar circle. In this may be seen the influence of Franz Brendel, with whom Liszt kept in fairly constant contact and whose opinions were sufficiently close to his own to encourage the idea that here was a genuine musical party, always a defining element in a nascent avant-garde. Although Brendel's views on musical progress depended on the history of works and genres, he did share Liszt's enthusiasm for the artist-critic, a feature that has perhaps been slightly overemphasised. Nonetheless, Brendel, more than most, points to an important moment around the mid-century when music criticism and theory became yardsticks of progress, almost to the composer's disadvantage (and here Lobe's carefully impersonal critical spirit takes on flesh and blood). In the spirit of Young Hegelianism, Brendel overturns the emphasis of Hegel's theory. Where Hegel had viewed the early nineteenth century as the point at which thought and criticism disturbed the Classical equilibrium to art's disadvantage but philosophy's gain, Brendel took this new critical self-awareness as a sign of progress. In this he was followed by other members of Liszt's Weimar circle. Even Peter Cornelius, the 'belated Romantic' of the group, urged composers to acknowledge 'that the times of naïve creation, of sweet dreams of music, are past, that they have acquired reflection and self-criticism, that after years of wandering in various stylistic regions they should now settle and prove themselves as masters in the German homeland, that they should compose after the model of Wagner's *Lohengrin*, that their composing and striving has thus to be "post-March", not "pre-March".'[22]

In Brendel's case, the pursuit of a valid aesthetic of music was an essential tool in the development of a proper progressive perspective:

> The value of the aesthetics of music is not simply scientific, in the strict sense. It
> is not exclusively an intellectual inquisitiveness that it satisfies: its practical sig-

---

21 Marilyn Ruth Brown, *Gypsies and Other Bohemians: The Myth of the Artist in Nineteenth-Century France* (Ann Arbor, 1985), p. 26.

22 Magda Marx-Weber, 'Cornelius' Kritik des Liedes', in Hellmut Federhofer and Kurt Oehl (eds.), *Peter Cornelius als Komponist, Dichter, Kritiker und Essayist* (Regensburg, 1977), p. 215; Peter Cornelius, *Literarische Werke*, III, *Aufsätze über Musik und Kunst*, ed. Edgar Istel (Leipzig, 1904), p. 100.

nificance can be enormous, when it has come to maturity. Can there really be any doubt that a large proportion of our present disagreements would automatically cease immediately with the establishment, or more public familiarizing, of the aesthetic principles concerned?

Here Brendel is thinking of Liszt's departures from historically sanctioned forms through his realisation of the ways in which 'musical content creates its own form and is thus the primary element'; he imagines this progress to be an organic growth (hence Dahlhaus's sceptical judgement of it as 'a curious mélange of classicism and a faith in progress'), arguing that the avant-garde of today creates the classicism of the future, an idea to which Liszt also subscribed in his essay on Adolf Bernhard Marx (*GS V*, 190–1).[23]

Brendel's theory of music history initially crystallised the idea of musical progress in the music dramas of Wagner. Its essential elements were that instrumental music had achieved its peak in the age of Viennese Classicism. The ensuing period was marked by the struggles of theatre music to rise to the same level; while Italian opera declined and French grand opera became ever more preoccupied with 'inartistic' extremes (the equivalent of Meyerbeer's mastery of 'effect' in Liszt's theories), Wagner not only marked an advance in German opera but pointed to it as the 'artwork of the future'. Liszt's task was to achieve a similar goal in the sphere of instrumental music, sharing with Wagner the drive towards 'the unity of the poetic-musical', an insight to which Brendel came only gradually, having at first shared in the general perception of Liszt in the 1840s as a virtuoso rather than a composer; his appreciation of Liszt's 'second epoch' in Weimar accordingly required large-scale revision to his most influential work, the *Geschichte der Musik in Italien, Deutschland und Frankreich*.[24]

How Liszt was to achieve this in view of the overpowering achievements of Viennese Classicism was metaphorically suggested by Liszt himself in his essay on Schumann: the age of Mozart and Haydn was music's achievement of the 'Freiheit ihrer Kraft'; with Beethoven, it then put on its *toga virilis*, achieving a first maturity (*GS IV*, 162). In developing this position, Brendel did not deviate from the earlier Romantic view that the highest form of music was instrumental but viewed it in the perspective of the true historicist. His claims for opera were a recognition that Wagnerian music drama had opened up a rich new field in which even instrumental and symphonic music might operate. In any

---

23 Bojan Bujić (ed.), *Music in European Thought 1851–1912* (Cambridge, 1988), p. 130; Carl Dahlhaus, *Nineteenth-Century Music*, trans. J. B. Robinson (Berkeley and Los Angeles, 1989), pp. 246–7.
24 See Michael Saffle, *Liszt in Germany 1840–1845: A Study in Sources, Documents, and the History of Reception* (Stuyvesant, N.Y., 1994), pp. 208–11; Franz Brendel, *Geschichte der Musik in Italien, Deutschland und Frankreich: Von den ersten christlichen Zeiten bis auf die Gegenwart*, 3rd edn (Leipzig, 1860), pp. 594–609, in particular 601.

event, music independent of the word in the case of Beethoven involved an element of psychological tone painting that was also present in Berlioz, though without the essential German innerness (thereby giving a grudging recognition of Berlioz's role that other members of Liszt's circle would judge more highly). The 'poetic' programme in Beethoven, allied to the search for a deeper unity of poetry and music in Wagner, gave Liszt an importance that transcended the national. In this, he is not merely the 'purely German' Wagner's ally but the successor to Berlioz, for whom as a Frenchman instrumental music on the whole was a new adventure marked by exaggeration to the point of caricature and lack of 'Innerlichkeit'. Rather, Liszt 'took a universal position in that he organically blended various nationalities, in this way providing a new stimulus for German inwardness, which now and then, at least temporarily, runs dry . . .'[25] Seen in this essentially Germanic perspective, Brendel effectively created the notion of a New German School whose achievements embraced a pioneering Frenchman (Berlioz, whom Liszt had enrolled among the militants in his earlier writings) and a cosmopolitan Hungarian, as well as Wagner.

Several critics have noted in Brendel's theories (and in those of his contemporaries) the abandonment of the Romantic view of music, which lingered on as Dahlhaus's idea of neo-romanticism. His commitment to a critical theoretical position was allied to Liszt's music 'as an outgrowth of "intellect in music" and a triumph over the "standpoint of sensuality"', a viewpoint that modified the Saint-Simonian view of progress as a synthesis of the spiritual and the sensuous. That Brendel was (according to Sanna Pederson, who subtly modifies 'neo-romanticism' to a lingering sense of music's unchangeably Romantic nature) the enemy of 'harmless pleasure in art' bears negative witness to the high intellectual purpose that he saw in it.[26] He fully recognised with Liszt the idea of the artist's mission, but located that mission in a liberal and rational interpretation of history, a change that is also partly characteristic of Liszt's writings. But the practical side to this emerges clearly when, in his essay on Adolf Bernhard Marx, Liszt denied that music was exclusively the property of feeling, and that it had more than a few points of contact with ideas; this was the essential link to his view that instrumental music could achieve heightened expression through programmes in a similar manner to the texts of the Wagnerian music drama (*GS V*, 204).

25 Franz Brendel, *Grundzüge der Geschichte der Musik*, 5th edn (Leipzig, 1861), pp. 64–6; *Geschichte der Musik in Italien, Deutschland und Frankreich: Von den ersten christlichen Zeiten bis auf die Gegenwart*, 1st edn (Leipzig, 1852, repr., Vaduz, 1985), pp. 512–13; later editions judge Berlioz more harshly as an exaggeration of tendencies in Beethoven: *Geschichte der Musik*, 3rd edn, pp. 522–38.

26 Sanna Pederson, 'Romantic Music under Siege in 1848', in Ian Bent (ed.), *Music Theory in the Age of Romanticism* (Cambridge, 1996), pp. 66 and 73; Dahlhaus, *Nineteenth-Century Music*, p. 243.

Liszt's Weimar aesthetic

Liszt's aesthetic of progress rested firmly on the cult of genius, whose mission was 'to invoke a new ideal and create new forms' (*GS I*, 1). That genius and progress were inextricably interlinked is strongly suggested in the Schumann essay:

> Whoever speaks the words 'progress' and 'perfection' also simultaneously pronounces the *unforeseen*, the *unsuspected*.

> *Invention* and *innovation*, accomplished by genius and developed by talent, are only so called because they make us familiar with the unfamiliar, because they reveal the undreamt-of   (*GS IV*, 165).

Schumann himself represented to Liszt a tragic figure whose 'quarrelling with his genius' could be heard in those places where he attempted to capture the modern spirit in traditional art forms (*GS IV*, 113). Neither art nor progress was to be seen as an absolute, however, and here Liszt remembered the ideas he inherited from French utopian and socialist movements. From Lamennais came the rejection of art as an absolute, from the Saint-Simonians the notion of its social mission, and these were blended with his native Roman Catholicism. More surprisingly, it was his later reading of Proudhon that best exemplified to him that ceaseless striving for change could never be an end in itself. The letter of 1 August 1855 to Carolyne von Sayn-Wittgenstein offering this revelation makes quite clear that theories of the 'collective man' for Liszt were 'the shadow and the reverse' of his belief in the 'Man-God' (*SL*, 385).

If the absolute were so uncompromisingly located in the truths of religion, it followed that the autonomy aesthetic had no claim on Liszt the composer. But just as man was the corporeal form of the ideal type, created by God as artist, so works of art were lesser forms of ideal types that Liszt the historicist regarded as characteristic of the *Zeitgeist*. He held firmly to the widespread view (shared in different ways by Schopenhauer, Hegel and Hegelians such as Vischer) that music expressed feelings and ideas. 'Pure music' was the incarnation of feeling (as he noted in his essay on 'Berlioz und seine Harold-Symphonie') and held at bay 'the demon, Thought' (*GS IV*, 30). The ideal type held the paramount position over mere matters of musical form, which were subservient to more indefinite experiences of the ideal:

> To cultivate form for its own sake is the business of industry, not art. Whoever does so might call himself an artist but pursues only a profession.
> To practise art means to create and use a form to express a feeling, an idea.
>   (*GS IV*, 140–1)

The duty of the genius was to create new forms suitable to the ideal of the age.

> Art is not absolute. Neither in music in particular, nor in architecture, with which it is so often compared, can one ignore the style to which it belongs in order to judge its products. It would neither be fair, nor indicate knowledge and real insight, if we were to judge a musical artwork regardless of the age and medium in which the composer created it, since the judges themselves equally little can be taken out of the time and age in which they find themselves. But each age and medium permits an ideal to be created which the greatest artists that belong to it strive and seek after, and regard every time as the most perfect. Probably such an ideal never lacks a poetic spark and it is the task of the genius or talented to kindle the fire. If the magic that it exerted disappears from some form, works that belong to it have as often suddenly incurred resentment, just as their agreement with the taste of earlier times redounded to its credit. But to whichever form they might belong, they survive this as long as they contain a mere fragment of art's eternal fire, by which means it forms one of humanity's uncontested claims to its own high esteem. One must only imagine it . . . in the ideas of the time and in the medium of such works to understand its consequences correctly, to comprehend the origin of that form from itself to discover whether it was not an advance on earlier forms, and to discern the gradations through which this form was gradually produced.   (*SS V*, 34–5)

In such passages, however ponderous their style, Liszt also clarifies his reformist position. Laying no claims to understanding the rise and fall of ideals, ideas or forms, he upholds Leibnitz's claim, 'The present, generated by the past, gives birth to the future' (*SS III*, 71), while accepting that the new ideal was as yet imperfectly discernible.

Liszt leaves open the degree to which one art will come to hold sway over the others in an era. As a musician who had first sprung to fame in the age of Romanticism, however, he made high claims for his art. In the essay on Schumann, melody was accorded the status of the '*universal language* of humanity' in view of its limitless supply of idioms (*GS IV*, 161). From there it was not even a short step to regarding music itself as 'the universal language' and grudgingly conceding that it was 'even to a certain extent able to dispense with ideas' in a letter of 25 September 1854 to his daughters (*SL*, 366). But he was unable to overlook the degree to which the age seemed to express itself through the 'modern epic', whose characteristic representatives were to be found in Goethe's *Faust*, Byron's *Cain* and *Manfred*, and Mickiewicz's *Dziady* (*GS IV*, 52–3). Their appeal to Liszt was twofold. On the one hand their heroes were figures apart, embodiments of modern alienation. They became the protagonists of the modern epic as 'a narrative of inner events, whose seeds live in this or that nation and epoch as common nutrients', a notion that led Liszt to his idea of the modern epic as embodiment of a philosophical, rather than an antique 'quasi-statuary', spirit. On the other, this epic was unsuited to the theatre, and thus to the opera house (*GS IV*, 53–6).

Yet modern music drama in Wagner's hand had shown itself capable of the striking reform embodied in the 'characteristic melody': Wagner's 'melodies are in a certain sense personifications of ideas; their return expresses feelings at which the words at best hint; Wagner leaves them to reveal to us all the secrets of the heart' (*SS IV*, 34). In his celebrated propaganda essays for Wagner's operas, the ideal is often to be found in instrumental music as a consequence of Wagner's tendency, apparently against his theories, to produce 'a beautiful symphonic work' such as the prelude to *Tannhäuser* (*SS IV*, 121). Thus the 'secret' on which *Lohengrin* stands is the Holy Grail, for which the prelude is 'a magical formula . . . a secret consecration' (*SS IV*, 29–31). Individual ideas are encapsulated in the 'melodies', which had not yet acquired the name of Leitmotif. Thus Wagner had already achieved an expression of the ideal of the age, which, if still partially obscured, was rendered clear even to the amateur by musical symbols.

Symphony and symphonic poem: programmes and prefaces

Liszt's own symphonic works were intended to achieve something similar but in 'a more absolute form', here deploying 'absolute' more in the spirit of 'absolute music' than in the other metaphysical sense that he tended to favour. Liszt at this point was confronted by a conundrum not of his own making:

> From the moment that [music] completely mastered the material to be used (harmony) and developed into a completely formed language, it lost a dependence under which it must often have suffered. But oddly enough it reached everything that it seemed to lack in comparison with the other arts precisely through this evil.   (*GS IV*, 159)

This was its dependence on the word (and on the other arts generally) for expression of its content; in freeing itself from the need to communicate through the word, it ceased to communicate to the mass audiences on which it depended. At this point Liszt brought in the concept of the programme, in the classic nineteenth-century form of the guide to content, not as content itself. Yet at the same time, he laboured the point sufficiently that 'a higher intellectual culture is necessary to fulfil all the requirements of a programme rather than to create specific music' that it was hardly surprising when the view arose that his music somehow depicted its programmes. There is a dichotomy here between the programme as a mere clue, the 'red thread' or 'thread of Ariadne' so often encountered in writings of the period, and the high-minded symbolic rambles that Liszt provided as prefaces to some of his symphonic poems and that later earned the condemnation of Hanslick (*GS IV*, 183).[27] The programme that prompted Liszt to his most extended treatment of the subject was merely the symbolic allusions in the title and movement headings of Berlioz's *Harold en Italie*, a feature that also held a prominent place in the keyboard works of Schumann, as he openly acknowledged; many of his most successful pieces are those that achieve a similar relationship to a mythic or symbolic figure such as Faust or Dante *(GS IV*, 178). This confusion in Liszt's idea of the programme helps to explain the attempts of his disciple Richard Pohl to provide a taxonomy of the symphonic poems.

That the programmes to Liszt's symphonic works are symbols rather than narratives to be followed in the music is borne out by examination of a few instances. In *Orpheus*, the content of the preface is for much of the time virtually irrelevant to the course of the music, in which the listener finds little that obviously relates to beasts, birds, Eurydice and the underworld. The song and the singer (with his harp as the most obvious pictorial device) are captured, as the title promises, but the preface elaborates on the legend in ways that are mere chat beside the music itself. Only when it turns to Orpheus as symbol of art, does the preface come to the heart of Liszt's 'ideal type'. The preface to *Prometheus* draws attention to Herder (to whose *Der entfesselte Prometheus* the work originally acted as overture) almost as equal ideal type to the titular hero, and its reference to 'mysterious ideas and vague traditions' tantalises the listener or reader before pointing to 'adversity and glory' as the essence of the myth. In this, its poetic idea is hardly different from that of *Tasso*, and the two are more to be distinguished at the ideological level by the need to celebrate Goethe and Byron or Herder than by precise programmatic (as opposed to musical) details. But the two, taken as a pair, may be seen as a contrast between the Greek ideal (as reinterpreted and rendered contemporary by Herder) and the modern spirit that Tasso exemplified in those creators of the 'philosophical epic', Goethe and Byron. In such cases, the preface and the poetic idea are related but not identical.

Elsewhere, the printing of a poem (as in *Ce qu'on entend sur la montagne* and *Mazeppa*) amplifies the title but fails to provide a map of the musical work; that is left to the imagination of the audience. That some element of re-creation is necessary to the listener is suggested by the related case of *Die Ideale*, which reorders Schiller's poem and scatters elements of it around the score, a reminder that the logic of the poem and the musical work do not run in parallel but

---

27 See Thomas Grey, '. . . *wie ein rother Faden*: On the Origin of "Leitmotif" as Critical Construct and Musical Practice', in Ian Bent (ed.), *Music Theory in the Age of Romanticism*, pp. 187–210.

have a higher, appropriately ideal relationship. Even the incorporation of lines from a work of literature as clues to performers and audiences, as in the 'Dante' Symphony, does not constitute a narrative in any precise sense, but draws attention to episodes from the 'Divine Comedy' as moments in which certain poetic ideas are paramount: the gate as symbol of hopelessness, Francesca da Rimini as the even more desolate symbol of memory to the hopeless. The attempts by commentators from Pohl onwards to offer elucidations have essentially annotated symbolic allusions rather than revealed hidden narratives.

There has been a measure of agreement that the symphonic poem is neither 'fixed form-category' nor 'a principle of alliance between music and literature' but 'an aesthetic postulate: that music has the status of poetry'.[28] Carl Dahlhaus, however, has shown how doubts about the aesthetic can lead to highly qualified evaluations of the works: 'while the compositional techniques of the symphonic poems Liszt wrote in the 1850s are undoubtedly representative of the "new music" of their time – the "music of the future" – their spiritual and intellectual structures were essentially informed by the French Romanticism of the 1830s, to whose ideas and attitudes Liszt remained unshakably loyal, passé though they were by 1850'. Even if one quibbles about the reference to French Romanticism as essentially a partial synonym for radical utopias, this is still a powerfully expressed negative reading of Liszt's subscription to reform rather than revolution (let alone the permanent crisis of the avant-garde). It is all the more striking in view of the insight that Dahlhaus brings to Liszt's conception of form as mediation between the symphonic and the character piece. Only thus could Liszt achieve the goal that Dahlhaus defines:

> Liszt does not illustrate the text of Shakespeare's *Hamlet* or Goethe's *Faust* with musical themes and thematic constellations, but extracts from a poetic work the myth to which he poeticises further, so to speak, in the language of music.

Elsewhere in Dahlhaus's monumental output, this takes on decidedly ambiguous features that seem disastrous for a musician of the future. In the estimate of Martin Geck, Dahlhaus consigns a work like *Prometheus* to 'paper music' for *Kenner* and to 'mere entertainment music' for *Liebhaber*; its historical value is far in advance of its aesthetic quality. There is in this dispute between Dahlhaus and Geck a point of some importance for Liszt as forerunner of the avant-garde. Expressed in an extreme form, Geck notes that 'Dahlhaus's verdict on the programmatic factor in Liszt's *Prometheus* in the final resort is aimed at no *specific* content, but at the worry that any kind of discussion about content must

28 Wolfgang Dömling, *Franz Liszt und seine Zeit*, 2nd edn (Laaber, 1998), p. 102.

encourage an uprising of the musical lower ranks'.[29] Geck's challenge to Dahlhaus's 'idea of absolute music' is to invoke the rather different estimate of the artwork as a system of differences to be found in Adorno and Derrida in the twentieth century, and as a Romantic aesthetic of confusion in Friedrich Schlegel in the nineteenth. If Liszt is not to be accorded a place in the equation of genius, integral work and absolute music, then he becomes at the level of ideas, as in the sphere of musical techniques, a forerunner of the avant-garde, and inescapably a politically engaged composer.

Dahlhaus's reference to Liszt's ideas as 'passé' points to a deep problem with Liszt's view of progress. That his position had always been a peculiar one, even in the 1830s, is partly a product of his mixture of progressive elements from his French masters and his dependence on an aristocracy for patronage and audiences. Liszt, then, was never simply a progressive, nor a mere reactionary. When Norbert Nagler asks whether 'the paradox of a retrograde music of the future, in which an aristocratic-bourgeois composer transcends his social status' is thinkable, a problem as challenging as, and directly related to, that of an anti-modernist modernism arises (even if his language creaks with the categories of academic neo-Marxism). With the collapse of the revolutions of 1848 Liszt was confronted with a situation that Nagler rhetorically exaggerates but does not completely falsify as 'well-nigh unimaginably desolate circumstances'.[30] In the surroundings of a bourgeois town ruled by an archduke, Liszt carried out a duty that admitted of several interpretations. To see him as *praeceptor Germaniae* in Geck's view is to take the progressive message at face value. But under Dahlhaus's rather mandarin judgement lurks a related but subtler view in which prophetic elements separate themselves at the level of technique. The progressive elements are less in the individual work, which is subverted by anachronisms and banalities in thematic material and 'developmental' figuration, than in individual ideas. Liszt, the forerunner of the avant-garde, the advocate of an aesthetic of expression that was about to meet its nemesis in Hanslick, separates in spite of himself the notion of progress and the integral work.

The 'New German School': goals and divisions

Liszt's aesthetic touches on Calinescu's conditions for an avant-garde artist most obviously in the manner in which he surrounded himself with a set of col-

29 Carl Dahlhaus, *Between Romanticism and Modernism: Four Studies in the Music of the Later Nineteenth Century*, trans. Mary Whittall (Berkeley and Los Angeles, 1980), p. 17; *Klassische und romantische Musikästhetik* (Laaber, 1988), pp. 396–8 and 401–13; Martin Geck, *Von Beethoven bis Mahler: Die Musik des deutschen Idealismus* (Stuttgart and Weimar, 1993), pp. 252–5.

30 Norbert Nagler, 'Die verspätete Zukunftsmusik', in Heinz-Klaus Metzger and Rainer Riehn (eds.), *Musik-Konzepte 12: Franz Liszt* (Munich, 1980), pp. 4–41.

leagues and disciples. How this party is to be characterised is problematic because of the various rifts within it, divisions characterised partly by personalities but also by genuinely different outlooks. The idea that they constituted a 'New German School' is itself a problem, in that they were certainly new in all manner of ways, but only debatably German, and certainly not a school in any real sense. For Brendel, it was only a school in that it was 'a great world-historical phenomenon' with 'the vocation of completely absorbing the old'. Yet he thought enough of the term to prefer it to the Princess von Sayn-Wittgenstein's *Zukunftsmusik* at the *Tonkünstler-Versammlung* of 1859.[31] When the term first began to become current, it seemed to Brendel still inextricably linked with the fight for Wagner's music dramas, and thus less involved with Liszt save in that he too was of the Wagnerian party. In keeping with its sense of embattled mission, Liszt himself was not above referring to it in terms that suggested the church militant, complete with its heretics, such as the dying Schumann, who constituted 'a kind of *Arius* in the little church we are trying to build' (*SL*, 355; Liszt's emphasis).

This aggressive sect of the future, however, was also trying to resurrect the glories of Weimar's Classical past, with the result that there was a deep rift within it that found expression in quite different directions. The Neu-Weimar-Verein of 1855 was instituted by Liszt and his colleagues to reflect the town's historic status (which was an obvious factor in the project of the Goethe Foundation) and simultaneously to gather together the advocates of musical progress. As a result, non-musical figures such as Hoffmann von Fallersleben, Bonaventura Genelli and Alexander von Humboldt were included at various times, as well as foreign musicians from beyond Weimar like Berlioz. But such an alliance of different specialisms was far removed from Wagner's ideal of the *Gesamtkunstwerk*.

The presence of Berlioz in Weimar for well-publicised concerts and his remote membership of the Verein helped to perpetuate a subtly different picture of the New German School as a kind of trinity. This has led to some remarkably dogmatic (possibly even naïve) writing in which certain scholars have claimed that the school was essentially founded upon French doctrine, and that it is possible to quantify degrees of 'New German-ness' in both Berlioz and Liszt according to historical periods. The position of Berlioz in relation to the school caused problems at the time. In Germany in general, Berlioz stood for progress to writers of many parties, including Lobe, with the obvious reservation that such progress was subject to wildly fluctuating evaluations. The most recent exponent of the 'French theory' of the school sees the element that

31 Brendel, *Grundzüge*, p. 61; Walker, *Franz Liszt*, II, pp. 336–7 and 511.

Berlioz brought to the school as a certain 'dramatisation' of music, but that is not quite the importance that Brendel ascribed to him, which was rather that of the half-formed forerunner in the sphere of instrumental music who had also composed a remarkable opera; *Benvenuto Cellini* as a new *Fidelio* was almost a dogma of the group.[32] None of the Weimar circle expressed this view of *Benvenuto Cellini* more forcefully than Peter Cornelius, who subscribed totally to the view that Berlioz constituted the third in the New German trilogy and offered in *Benvenuto Cellini* a 'glowing realism' to the high Idealism of *Lohengrin*; but Cornelius was hardly the true mouthpiece of the school and was fairly frank about his debt to Berlioz's opera in composing *Der Barbier von Bagdad*.[33]

Amongst the Weimar circle, individuals tended to take up subtly different positions in relation to the central trinity. Thus Raff never really recognised Liszt as a major composer, for all his gratitude to him on a personal level. It took Peter Cornelius a number of years to appreciate Liszt's music fully, and only then through a work like *Die Legende von der heiligen Elisabeth* that appealed both to Cornelius's Catholicism and to his patriotism. Cornelius provided the most eloquent instance of the tensions between French and German elements in the group when he noted that the 'eternal juxtaposition of Goethe and Victor Hugo, of Schiller and Lamartine, is bitter for a German'.[34] The combination of German and Roman elements in Liszt's cultural make-up helped to explain to Cornelius the problematical nature of his symphonic work, while on the other hand Berlioz was accorded the status of an honorary German. Wagner in turn was deeply distrusted by Raff, who admired his music but dismissed his theories. In the face of such disunity among key members of the school, it is hardly surprising that Liszt was later content to use the label for his more faithful pupils of the 1840s, a change in outlook that reflects the failure of the Weimar enterprise and his growing estrangement from Wagner. With this, the 'New German School' acquired its definitive fractured status: an avant-garde fighting for Berlioz, Liszt and Wagner, or a group of epigoni.

Liszt and Wagner: avant-garde and modernism

That the whole Weimar enterprise was linked to the need to provide a forum for Wagner's theatrical works was at once the strength and weakness of Liszt's

32 Serge Gut, 'Berlioz, Liszt und Wagner: Die französischen Komponenten der Neudeutschen Schule', in Serge Gut (ed.), *Franz Liszt und Richard Wagner: Musikalische und geistesgeschichtliche Grundlagen der neudeutschen Schule*, *Liszt-Studien*, III (Munich and Salzburg, 1986), pp. 50–3; see also Fritz Reckow, '"Wirkung" und "Effekt": Über einige Voraussetzungen, Tendenzen und Probleme der deutschen Berlioz-Kritik', *Die Musikforschung*, 33 (1980), pp. 1–36.

33 Cornelius, *Aufsätze über Musik und Kunst*, p. 110; Hans-Josef Irmen, 'Cornelius und Hector Berlioz', in *Peter Cornelius als Komponist, Dichter, Kritiker und Essayist*, pp. 77–9.

34 Max Hasse, *Der Dichtermusiker Peter Cornelius* (Leipzig, 1922–3), I, p. 167.

position. In many ways their outlooks were linked in the 1830s and 1840s by their views on social and political issues. One writer has attempted to distinguish Wagner from Liszt on the ideological level by contrasting the latter's Catholicism with Wagner's use of ideas culled from Saint-Simon, Young Germany and Bakunin.[35] Leaving Bakunin aside as an irrelevance to any comparison with Liszt, there is an element of intellectual confusion here that goes beyond the writer's overlooking of Liszt's own link to the Saint-Simonians (who, it is worth emphasising, are not to be equated absolutely with Saint-Simon himself). Wagner's debt to the writers of Young Germany is fairly well established and includes an opposition to the idea that art expressed the absolute, an emphasis on Hellenism, and a turning from the tenets of Romanticism. At the time when Young German writers like Karl Gutzkow, Ludolf Wienbarg, Theodor Mundt and Heinrich Laube (Wagner's closest acquaintance of the group) first appeared in print, it was a frequent charge against them that they imported ideas from the Saint-Simonians. Nowadays, it is normal to view this connection with more reservations, judging each member of the group on its merits.[36] Wagner and Liszt in this perspective probably shared in a group of ideas that included strains from religion, the critique of religion and a quasi-religious utopia. However differently they developed, Liszt and Wagner in 1848 had real intellectual ties that developed in similar aesthetic directions. At the point of their closest contact in the aftermath of 1848, their views on absolute art and music probably were in fairly close agreement.

Yet there were clear musical differences between the two, as Liszt's writings on musical drama reveal. In announcing his programme for the revival of dramatic music, Liszt laid more stress than Wagner on the revival of neglected masterpieces (including *Genoveva* and *Benvenuto Cellini*, at a time when Wagner had consigned Schumann and Berlioz to the category of the outmoded). The theatre of which Liszt dreamed in Weimar was to embrace the new regardless of school, genre or nationality. Liszt's generous openness to influences went along with his by-now familiar historicist approach, though the details of the historical process constituted another dividing point with Wagner. Opera's development in Liszt's view passed through reform of the expression of feeling in Gluck, the mastering of situations in Meyerbeer, to the triumph of characterisation in Wagner (*SS V*, 6 and 40). This picture of a steady reformist acquisition of traits ran counter to Wagner's outlook most blatantly on the inclusion of Meyerbeer. Nor did Liszt take account of Wagner's claim that music drama was

35 Friedrich W. Riedel, 'Die neudeutsche Schule: Ein Phänomen der deutschen Kulturgeschichte des 19. Jahrhunderts', in *Franz Liszt und Richard Wagner*, pp. 14–15.

36 See Jean-François Candoni, *La Genèse du drame musical wagnérien: mythe, politique et histoire dans les œuvres dramatiques de Richard Wagner entre 1833 et 1850* (Bern, 1998), pp. 109–98; Helmut Koopmann, *Das Junge Deutschland: Eine Einführung* (Darmstadt, 1993), pp. 47, 106 and 120.

the true heir to the Beethovenian symphony, a point that Liszt could hardly recognise since he was already set on regenerating the symphony as Beethoven had left it by his own means. There were also potential areas of debate as to the consequences of Wagner's reforms, since Liszt envisaged the possibility of a Wagnerian school of opera composers almost as a matter of course. Whether this thought chimed with Wagner's essential egoism must remain a matter of doubt.

These specific disagreements reflected deeper ideological divisions. On the question of absolute music, Liszt still held to the view that music was not an end in itself but a vehicle through which the absolute, whether understood in Hegel's or a Catholic sense, could be perceived. The degree to which Idealism influenced Wagner's thinking has never been accurately estimated, though most recent writers have allowed that some of his thinking after 1848, in the period of his life that produced the majority of his theoretical texts, took place as a dialogue with Hegel in which he came to dissent from certain key Idealist positions (indeed, his doubts about Brendel may have sprung from this). That Wagner replaced the Hegelian idea as the basis of art with quite different concepts that could be characterised as life or nature according to the source taken was entirely in accord with his turning to the philosophy of Feuerbach and its key concept of *sinnlich*. Not until his encounter with Schopenhauer's *Die Welt als Wille und Vorstellung* did his ideas on absolute music change, and Dahlhaus's often repeated mantra about his adoption of that philosopher's 'metaphysics of absolute music' can only really be accepted with heavy qualifications (that Dahlhaus, in fairness, does note).[37] When Liszt produced his brochure on *Lohengrin und Tannhäuser*, Wagner's theories on music drama and the impossibility of absolute art of any kind hardly chimed with Liszt's picture of the operas as 'ideal dramas', nor with the Romanticised language in which Liszt spoke of their preludes.

The central Wagnerian concept of the *Gesamtkunstwerk* proved to be the essential theoretical stumbling-block for Liszt. Indeed Liszt's reference to the concept is hedged around with such reservations as to more-or-less admit the impossibility of realising it: beautiful in principle, probably erroneous in practice, but worthy of a genius (*SS IV*, 25). This is of a piece with Liszt's ignoring of Wagner's claim to be Beethoven's true successor. The idea that Liszt propagated a misunderstanding of Wagner's music drama, encouraging the belief that music served the text, became a sharper point of difference once Wagner

---

37 Geck, *Von Beethoven bis Mahler*, p. 303; Monika Lichtenfeld, 'Gesamtkunstwerk und allgemeine Kunst: Das System der Künste bei Wagner und Hegel', in Walter Salmen (ed.), *Beiträge zur Geschichte der Musikanschauung im 19. Jahrhundert* (Regensburg, 1965), pp. 172 and 176; Riedel, 'Die neudeutsche Schule', pp. 17–18; Carl Dahlhaus, *The Idea of Absolute Music*, trans. Roger Lustig (Chicago, 1989), pp. 10 and 26; *Between Romanticism and Modernism*, pp. 34–5.

started to move in the direction of Schopenhauer. Liszt's limited understanding of Wagner was complemented by the reverse, since Wagner's acknowledgement of Liszt's symphonic poems, as Dahlhaus has noted, is also qualified, acclaiming those works in which figures 'partially petrified into allegorical symbols', such as *Orpheus*, *Prometheus*, and the two symphonies. At the level of absolute music, comparison of Liszt and Wagner remains fraught with confusions and contradictions as their ideas shifted over a period of some twenty years. Recent research on Wagner's later ideas has taken refuge in the idea of the 'metaphysics' of absolute music (that Liszt would have emphatically rejected) alongside its dependency in practice on dramatic, formal and poetic ideas (which Liszt would have accepted).[38]

In the last resort, differences between Liszt and Wagner rest on an absolutely irreconcilable difference between their most basic assumptions about ideas and history. Both men subscribed to the central nineteenth-century antithesis of antique and modern and both saw in Classical antiquity an image of a wholeness of art and humanity that had to some degree been lost. But they interpreted this situation rather differently. For all the references to Greek art and ideas in his writings, Liszt claimed to Nietzsche in 1872 that he was ignorant of Hellenism and that the finest achievement of the Athenians was the altar 'deo ignoto': 'And my eyes do not wander around Parnassus and Helicon; rather does my soul turn unceasingly to Tabor and Golgotha' (*SL*, 742). As has recently been restated, Wagner's vision of the *Gesamtkunstwerk* was in essentials a redeeming work for composer and audiences alike that rested on a vision of the union of Greek art in tragedy. With the period of Roman antiquity a decline had set in that led to the modern fragmentation and specialisation of the arts. The corollary, that Catholic Christianity participated in this decline, could never have been accepted by Liszt; as he instinctively rejected the *Gesamtkunstwerk*, so Wagner had no sympathy with that essential part of Liszt's programme that envisaged the reform of church music. The 'ideal drama' or 'epic' that Liszt created in this spirit, *Die Legende von der heiligen Elisabeth*, contained no grand dialectic of sacred and sensual such as Wagner envisaged in *Tannhäuser*, and was consistent with a picture of *Lohengrin* that rested content with admiring its mediaeval poetic spirit, as though a more elemental human drama did not reside within it.[39] Here Wagner is clearly more in tune with an essential strain of modernism than Liszt and this indeed justifies the idea that there is a change of sensibility in Wagner that eluded Liszt. In the contrast

38 Carl Dahlhaus, 'Wagner and Program Music', *Studies in Romanticism*, 9 (1970), pp. 3–20; Dieter Borchmeyer, *Richard Wagner: Theory and Theatre*, trans. Stewart Spencer (Oxford, 1991), chapter 10.

39 Udo Bermbach, *Der Wahn des Gesamtkunstwerks: Richard Wagners politisch-ästhetische Utopie* (Frankfurt am Main, 1994), pp. 146–67; Frank Reinisch, 'Liszts Oratorium *Die Legende von der Heiligen Elisabeth*: Ein Gegenentwurf zu Tannhäuser und Lohengrin', in *Franz Liszt und Richard Wagner*, pp. 131–3.

between Wagner and Liszt, the latter remained committed to progress and modernity to the extent that he prefigures the role of the avant-garde, but the former more acutely defines the broader climate of modernism.

With the passage of time, certain of Liszt's major works have established themselves in the concert hall and in the canon of 'masterworks', most obviously the Sonata and the *Faust-Symphonie*. The major part of his output, however, is probably valued less in itself than for the remarkable pre-echoes of Debussy and Ravel, Bartók, Messiaen, and even the Second Viennese School. In all of this his technical originality is acknowledged. Forever the forerunner, he is also clearly the godfather to national schools that arose in the late nineteenth century, often espousing aesthetic points of view that borrowed eclectically from Wagner and the New German polemics on musical progress. None of this clearly marks him out as a truly avant-garde artist, which has been defined here and elsewhere in terms that are neither exclusively technical nor historicist. If Liszt's view of progress and of the music of the future is compared with the characteristics of an avant-garde in Calinescu's sense, they overlap but do not coincide. That Liszt's ideas were urged with a militant vocabulary may be granted, but his church had always been 'militant', long before Lamennais. The utopia that Liszt perceived in his Paris period became qualified after 1848, even if it was never quite overtaken by the quietist austerity of his later church music. Dogmatic Liszt appears in his prose works, but his dogma was sufficiently flexible to attract such disparate personalities as Pohl, Cornelius, Raff and Hans von Bülow, and the element of strident self-assertion in the group's reactions never threatened to develop a nihilistic or consciously self-parodying strain. That Liszt and Brendel sharpened Romanticism's belief in the poetic with a more strident historicism to the point that it rendered Romanticism itself outdated helped to create a sense of panic in their critics. They did not seriously wish to imperil society (unlike Wagner in his more apocalyptic imaginings), even when they talked of the fragmentation and specialisation of the modern age. But they did train a critical eye on notions of absolute music and weakened, more by Liszt's works than his theories, the idea that a progressive artist should be judged in the light of genius and a canon of works. Inasmuch as Liszt involuntarily represents a critical moment within modernity, he is perhaps more avant-garde than some of his contemporaries.

To Dahlhaus's catalogue of avant-garde traits in Liszt might be added the notion of the transcription as work, which flies in the face of the picture of absolute music that is current. In this Liszt is yet again the precursor, of the image of an absolute music without architectonics that Busoni expressed in his *Entwurf einer neuen Ästhetik der Tonkunst*. Liszt and Busoni both represented radical readjustments of the modern trinity of work, genius and innovation. They did not overtly attack the notion of the artwork inasmuch as their careers unquestionably aimed for major works of summation such as *Christus* and *Doktor Faust*. As a result they do not qualify strictly for the definition of avant-garde offered by Bürger, but they do render art questionable and blur its boundaries. It is the final paradox of the search for wholeness and the union of the aesthetic with the absolute that the nineteenth-century debate on musical progress helped to sharpen the distinction between an avant-garde and other varieties of music. Of this, Liszt the virtuoso and composer of salon music should at least have approved.

Bibliography

Altenburg, D., 'Eine Theorie der Musik der Zukunft: Zur Funktion des Programms im symphonischen Werk von Franz Liszt'. In W. Suppan (ed.), *Kongress-Bericht Eisenstadt 1975, Liszt-Studien*, I. Graz, 1977, pp. 9–25

Arnold, B., 'Liszt as Reader, Intellectual, and Musician'. In M. Saffle (ed.), *Analecta Lisztiana I: Liszt and his World*. Stuyvesant, N.Y., 1998, pp. 37–60

Bermbach, U., *Der Wahn des Gesamtkunstwerks: Richard Wagners politisch-ästhetische Utopie*. Frankfurt am Main, 1994

Bonds, M. E., 'Idealism and the Aesthetics of Instrumental Music at the Turn of the Nineteenth Century'. *Journal of the American Musicological Society*, 50 (1997), pp. 387–420

Borchmeyer, D., *Richard Wagner: Theory and Theatre*, trans. S. Spencer. Oxford, 1991

Brendel, F., *Geschichte der Musik in Italien, Deutschland und Frankreich: Von den ersten christlichen Zeiten bis auf die Gegenwart*. Leipzig, 1st edn 1852, repr. Vaduz, 1985; 3rd edn Leipzig, 1860

Grundzüge der Geschichte der Musik. 5th edn Leipzig, 1861

Brown, M. R., *Gypsies and Other Bohemians: The Myth of the Artist in Nineteenth-Century France*. Ann Arbor, 1985

Bujić, B. (ed.), *Music in European Thought 1851–1912*. Cambridge, 1988

Bürger, P., *Theory of the Avant-Garde*, trans. M. Shaw. Minneapolis, 1984

Calinescu, M., *Five Faces of Modernity: Modernism, Avant-Garde, Decadence, Kitsch, Postmodernism*. Durham, NC, 2nd edn 1987

Candoni, J.-F., *La Genèse du drame musical wagnérien: mythe, politique et histoire dans les œuvres dramatiques de Richard Wagner entre 1833 et 1850*. Bern, 1998

Cornelius, P., *Literarische Werke*, vol. III, *Aufsätze über Musik und Kunst*, ed. Edgar Istel. Leipzig, 1904

Dahlhaus, C., 'Wagner and Program Music'. *Studies in Romanticism*, 9 (1970), pp. 3–20

Between Romanticism and Modernism: Four Studies in the Music of the Later Nineteenth Century, trans. M. Whittall. Berkeley and Los Angeles, 1980

Schoenberg and the New Music, trans. D. Puffett and A. Clayton. Cambridge, 1987

Klassische und romantische Musikästhetik. Laaber, 1988

Nineteenth-Century Music, trans. J. B. Robinson. Berkeley and Los Angeles, 1989

The Idea of Absolute Music, trans. R. Lustig. Chicago and London, 1989

Dömling, W., *Franz Liszt und seine Zeit*. Laaber, 2nd edn 1998

Egbert, D. D., 'The Idea of "Avant-garde" in Art and Politics'. *American Historical Review*, 73 (1967), pp. 339–66

Ellis, K., *Music Criticism in Nineteenth-Century France: 'La Revue et Gazette musicale de Paris'*
    1834–80. Cambridge, 1995

Gárdonyi, Z. and Mauser, S., *Virtuosität und Avantgarde: Untersuchungen zum Klavierwerk*
    Franz Liszts. Mainz, 1988

Geck, M., *Von Beethoven bis Mahler: Die Musik des deutschen Idealismus*. Stuttgart and
    Weimar, 1993

Gogröf-Voorhees, A., *Defining Modernism: Baudelaire and Nietzsche on Romanticism,*
    Modernity, Decadence, and Wagner. New York, 1999

Grey, T., '. . . *wie ein rother Faden*: On the Origin of "Leitmotif" as Critical Construct and
    Musical Practice'. In I. Bent (ed.), *Music Theory in the Age of Romanticism*. Cambridge,
    1996, pp. 187–210

Gut, S., 'Berlioz, Liszt und Wagner: Die französischen Komponenten der
    Neudeutschen Schule'. In S. Gut (ed.), *Franz Liszt und Richard Wagner: Musikalische*
    und geistesgeschichtliche Grundlagen der neudeutschen Schule, Liszt-Studien, III. Munich
    and Salzburg, 1986, pp. 48–55

Hasse, M., *Der Dichtermusiker Peter Cornelius*. 2 vols., Leipzig, 1922–3

Heinemann, E. G., *Franz Liszts Auseinandersetzung mit der geistlichen Musik*. Munich and
    Salzburg, 1978

Irmen, H.-J., 'Cornelius und Hector Berlioz'. In H. Federhofer and K. Oehl (eds.), *Peter*
    Cornelius als Komponist, Dichter, Kritiker und Essayist. Regensburg, 1977, pp. 65–79

Karl, F. R., *Modern and Modernism: The Sovereignty of the Artist, 1885–1925*. New York,
    1985

Kirchmeyer, H. (ed.), *Situationsgeschichte der Musikkritik und des musikalischen Pressewesens in*
    Deutschland dargestellt vom Ausgange des 18. bis zum Beginn des 20. Jahrhunderts, Part 2,
    System- und Methodengeschichte, IV, *Quellen-Texte 1847–1851 (1852)*. Regensburg, 1996

Klein, R., 'Wagners plurale Moderne: Eine Konstruktion von Unvereinbarkeiten'. In
    C.-S. Mahnkopf (ed.), *Richard Wagner: Konstrukteur der Moderne*. Stuttgart, 1999, pp.
    185–225

Koopman, H., *Das Junge Deutschland: Eine Einführung*. Darmstadt, 1993

Lichtenfeld, M., 'Gesamtkunstwerk und allgemeine Kunst: Das System der Künste bei
    Wagner und Hegel'. In W. Salmen (ed.), *Beiträge zur Geschichte der Musikanschauung*
    im 19. Jahrhundert. Regensburg, 1965, pp. 171–7

Liszt, F., *Gesammelte Schriften*, ed. L. Ramann. 6 vols. Leipzig, 1880–83
    Pages romantiques, ed. J. Chantavoine. Paris and Leipzig, 1912
    An Artist's Journey: 'Lettres d'un bachelier ès musique', 1835–1841, ed. and trans. C.
        Suttoni. Chicago and London, 1989
    Selected Letters, ed. A. Williams. Oxford, 1998
    Sämtliche Schriften, ed. D. Altenburg, vols. III, IV, & V to date. Leipzig, 1989–97

Locke, R. P., *Music, Musicians and the Saint-Simonians*. Chicago and London, 1986

Marx-Weber, M., 'Cornelius' Kritik des Liedes'. In H. Federhofer and K. Oehl (eds.),
    Peter Cornelius als Komponist, Dichter, Kritiker und Essayist. Regensburg, 1977, pp.
    169–77

McCalla, A., 'Liszt *Bricoleur*: Poetics and Providentialism in Early July Monarchy
    France'. *History of European Ideas*, 24 (1998), pp. 71–92

Merrick, P., *Revolution and Religion in the Music of Liszt*. Cambridge, 1987

Nagler, N., 'Die verspätete Zukunftsmusik'. In H.-K. Metzger and R. Riehn (eds.),
    Musik-Konzepte 12: Franz Liszt. Munich, 1980, pp. 4–41

Paddison, M., *Adorno, Modernism and Mass Culture: Essays on Critical Theory and Music*. London, 1996

Pederson, S., 'Romantic Music under Siege in 1848'. In Ian Bent (ed.), *Music Theory in the Age of Romanticism*. Cambridge, 1996, pp. 57–74

Piersig, J., *Das Fortschrittsproblem in der Musik um die Jahrhundertwende: Von Richard Wagner bis Arnold Schönberg*. Regensburg, 1977

Reckow, F., '"Wirkung" und "Effekt": Über einige Voraussetzungen, Tendenzen und Probleme der deutschen Berlioz-Kritik'. *Die Musikforschung*, 33 (1980), pp. 1–36

Reinisch, F., 'Liszts Oratorium *Die Legende von der Heiligen Elisabeth*: Ein Gegenentwurf zu Tannhäuser und Lohengrin'. In S. Gut (ed.), *Franz Liszt und Richard Wagner: Musikalische und geistesgeschichtliche Grundlagen der neudeutschen Schule, Liszt-Studien*, III. Munich and Salzburg, 1986, pp. 128–51

Riedel, F. W., 'Die neudeutsche Schule: Ein Phänomen der deutschen Kulturgeschichte des 19. Jahrhunderts'. In S. Gut (ed.), *Franz Liszt und Richard Wagner: Musikalische und geistesgeschichtliche Grundlagen der neudeutschen Schule, Liszt-Studien*, III. Munich and Salzburg, 1986, pp. 13–18

Ruprecht, jr., L. A., *Afterwords: Hellenism, Modernism, and the Myth of Decadence*. Albany, 1996

Saffle, M., *Liszt in Germany 1840–1845: A Study in Sources, Documents, and the History of Reception*. Stuyvesant, N.Y., 1994

Sammons, J. L., *Heinrich Heine: A Modern Biography*. Princeton, 1979

Scruton, R., *The Aesthetics of Music*. Oxford, 1997

Walker, A., *Franz Liszt*. 3 vols., London, 1983–96

12

Music as ideal: the aesthetics of autonomy

MAX PADDISON

By the second half of the nineteenth century music had achieved a central position among the arts, to the extent that, as Walter Pater put it in 1877 in his now celebrated *aperçu*, 'all art constantly aspires towards the condition of music'.[1] This registered a remarkable change in the aesthetic status of music in the hundred years from the 1780s to the 1880s. From an art form regarded as a pleasant but meaningless entertainment without cognitive value, music had come to be viewed as the vehicle of ineffable truths beyond conceptualisation. Although the idea of art music as an autonomous, non-conceptual reflection of inwardness upon itself had remained a constant throughout this period, what had changed was the perception of music by the other arts and the interpretation of this non-conceptuality, particularly in philosophical aesthetics. While the focus in this essay is on music and ideas in the period from 1848, the centrality of the concept of autonomy to the other arts by the late nineteenth century also provides other vantage points from which to view a phenomenon which was to become largely naturalised within music itself. It can be argued, indeed, that for this very reason music calls for awareness of its reflections outside itself, in particular in literature and philosophy, in order for the implications of its autonomy and non-conceptuality to be recognised more fully. An example to illustrate this point is to be found in Joris-Karl Huysmans's infamous novel *A Rebours* of 1884, a work which takes to its extremes the retreat into the inner world and the rejection of the dominant Realism and Naturalism of its time.

Huysmans's novel has a single character: le Duc Jean des Esseintes, an aristocratic recluse and aesthete modelled on the eccentric and decadent Comte de Montesquiou. Des Esseintes conducts a bizarre and extended experiment: he withdraws from society and sets about a solitary and intensive exploration of each of the senses in turn, which he pursues in a manner that takes to its ultimate extreme the 'art for art's sake' aesthetic of the late nineteenth century, the paradigm for which was music. Within his artificially sealed-off world (he even has his servants wear special costumes, so that their silhouettes cast on the

1 Walter Pater, 'The School of Giorgione', in Jennifer Uglow (ed. and intro.), *Essays on Literature and Art* (London, 1973), p. 51.

blinds at the windows to his rooms should not remind him of the real world outside) des Esseintes aims to give himself up exclusively, as a man of private means free from the distractions of family and the need to make a living, to the contemplation and exploration of the aesthetic experience and of works of art. He exhaustively considers each art form in isolation, its distinguishing features and inner logic, and analyses and experiments upon his own aesthetic sensibilities with all the precision of the natural scientist and the refined sensitivity of the artist. Not only does he reflect upon the treasures of art and philosophy of the past in his extensive private library and art collection: he also explores the new and the previously uncharted. Where an appropriate art form corresponding to a particular sense is lacking, he invents it. He conjures up whole poetic landscapes from the art of perfumery, studying its syntax, developing its history and refining its analysis. But his *pièce de résistance* is what he calls his 'mouth organ': an elaborate instrument which enables him to compose

> a music of liqueurs [upon his tongue] . . . playing internal symphonies to himself, and providing his palate with sensations analogous to those which music dispenses to the ear . . . to hear inside his mouth crème-de-menthe solos and rum-and-vespetro duets . . . mixing or contrasting related liqueurs, by subtle approximations and cunning combinations.[2]

This extravagant metaphor from the literature of the end of the nineteenth century indicates powerfully the extent of music's penetration across the arts – music as an *ideal*, as the touchstone for all aesthetic experience. Contained here are also the two conflicting tendencies which mark the nineteenth century as the watershed of modernity: Idealism and Positivism, the aesthetic escape from reality and the scientific analysis of reality. Des Esseintes rejects the outer world of empirical reality – the dominant scientific Positivism of the nineteenth century – only to apply its systematic methodology to the inner world of aesthetic experience and to the exquisite refinement of the senses. The ultimate fulfilment of art, the expansion of the aesthetic domain to include all aspects of sensual experience, also spells the end of art in its traditional sense, and certainly the end of Romanticism, and it is tempting to see in it the apotheosis of Hegel's prediction of the end of art and his diagnosis of the decadence of Romanticism. In its combination of historicism (the systematic survey of the store-house of the art, literature, music and philosophy of the past) and the New (the exploration of the limits of the senses and of aesthetic experience) it shows itself not only to be in tune with the spirit of its age (for example, the refined mediaevalism to be seen in the art of the 1880s – the Pre-Raphaelite

---

2 Joris-Karl Huysmans, *Against Nature*, a translation of *A Rebours* by Robert Baldick (Harmondsworth, 1959), pp. 58–9.

painters and poets, and works like Debussy's *La damoiselle élue* and Satie's Rosicrucian pieces), but also the extent to which it belongs to the anti-Romantic spirit of the avant-garde. Above all, it shows itself to be the heir to the dominant idea of nineteenth-century aesthetics, and the concept to which all others can be seen to relate: the autonomy-character of music. It is the aim of this chapter to explore this concept and its cluster of related ideas.

Autonomy, expression and the decline of Romanticism

Art music, which had detached itself historically from any direct social function, was generally understood as the ultimate vehicle for a free-floating, inward-looking subjectivity which, in the absence of concepts and representation, referred only to itself. Hegel, whose influence spanned the century, and whose attitude to Romanticism was distinctly ambivalent, had proposed that 'the keynote of Romantic art is *musical*'.[3] As Sanna Pederson has pointed out, however, 'Hegel seemed to distrust this emancipation from external reference, which could also imply a lack of spiritual content'.[4] For Hegel, music was problematical because of its indeterminateness, and it was 'concerned only with the completely indeterminate movement of the inner spirit and with sounds as if they were feeling without thought'.[5] The problem articulated by Hegel in his Berlin Lectures on Aesthetics in the 1820s (which were published posthumously in 1842 and continued to resonate in the second half of the century) had a considerable legacy for all the arts, as the example from Huysmans's novel shows. It also had a pre-history (see chapter 2) which is of relevance to the later part of the century, and with which there are certain parallels.

While in the first half of the nineteenth century there arose the notion of absolute music which laid claim to the metaphysical peaks of human experience as a language of the emotions beyond the reach of conceptual thought, it is also important to recognise that the dominance of the concept of autonomy and of the idea of absolute music were by no means total. Opera, oratorio, ballet, salon and 'trivial music' continued to occupy proportionately far greater numbers than symphonic and chamber music for the mass of the nineteenth-century music-loving public. To an extent, therefore, it must be argued that the idea of music as an art existing in and for itself has to be understood in this period not simply as the dominating aesthetic ideal, but as a metaphysi-

---

3 G. W. F. Hegel, *Ästhetik*, vols. I/II (Stuttgart, 1971), p. 578. Cited in Sanna Pederson, 'Romantic Music under Siege in 1848', in Ian Bent (ed.), *Music Theory in the Age of Romanticism* (Cambridge, 1996), pp. 59–60.
4 Pederson, 'Romantic Music', p. 60.
5 Hegel, *Ästhetik*, vols. I/II. Cited in Pederson, 'Romantic Music', p. 60.

cal aspiration, rather than as a social fact, an ideal which had ramifications beyond music itself, and which owes its success as a paradigm as much to its contradictory relation to the social context of the nineteenth century as to its origins in late eighteenth-century German Idealist philosophy and French Enlightenment rationalism.

As the century proceeds, music as an art form becomes increasingly self-contained and self-reflective. This applies not only to so-called 'absolute' music, as instrumental music without words, but also to its extension into the theatre in the form of the Wagnerian music drama, where the expansion through concepts is designed to achieve a cognitive status previously denied to music by Kant and Hegel. Indeed, one can even include here the involvement of autonomous music in nineteenth-century Nationalism in the context of the creation of national identities. To put it in Wagner's terms, music 'comes of age', becomes mature and aware of itself and its context – a context which includes both an involvement of art with politics and society and, equally, the retreat from any obvious sense of social involvement. Wagner, unlike Hegel, saw Beethoven as the touchstone for this process of 'coming of age', calling him in his essay 'The Art-work of the Future' (1849), 'the Master, who was called to write upon his works the *world-history of Music*', and who saw the necessity '*to find out for himself the country of the Manhood of the Future*'.[6] Music, with its long association with metaphors of language, becomes regarded as a kind of language without concepts, a form of 'conceptless cognition'.

While for much of the century this process also goes in parallel with the aesthetics of expression, as is seen in the rapturous claims of Wackenroder, Herder and E. T. A. Hoffmann and in the music journalism of composers like Weber, Berlioz and Schumann, it also led to a tension between 'form' and 'expression', between the immanent formalist relations of musical structure and the need to justify music's free-floating, dynamic expressivity with reference to an object exterior to it. By the mid-century composers were seeking to anchor musical expression in more concrete terms in the extra-musical – in literary programmes, dramatic narrative, gesture, Romantic notions of nature and of national identity (the two latter frequently linked through evocations of folk and community). Wagner's theories of music drama and *Gesamtkunstwerk* played a key role in this process, which was essentially the attempt to solve the problem of absolute music's non-conceptual character. Nietzsche, who initially took his cue from Wagner in *The Birth of Tragedy* (1872) but then rejected him, together with their mutual source of inspiration Arthur Schopenhauer, went on to contribute further thoughts towards the clarification of this

6 Richard Wagner, *The Art-work of the Future and Other Works*, trans. W. Ashton Ellis (Lincoln, Nebr., and London, 1993), pp. 123, 125 (italics in original).

problem in his *Human, All Too Human* (1878). I shall discuss this in more detail later in this chapter.

Right from the beginning of the century, however, there are two distinctly different emphases that can be identified, each with quite different implications for the second half of the century. The first of these is located around the new aesthetics of expression (as opposed to the older aesthetics of music, like that of Sulzer, which was really a development from the doctrine of affections, a theory which had lasted right up to the late eighteenth century). This new aesthetics of expression from the early nineteenth century is essentially an aesthetics of content, where the content in question could be understood as the sensitive listener's own emotional response to the music, or, to put it another way, as the inner world of the listener shaped by the dynamic temporal unfolding of the music, as 'sounding inwardness'. It is first associated with Wackenroder, then with the powerful twist given to the idea by Schopenhauer. The second emphasis from this period is located around a new aesthetics of musical form, and is initially associated with Friedrich von Schlegel, and later at the mid-century with the decisive contribution of Eduard Hanslick.

The delayed influence of Schopenhauer's dualistic metaphysics of expression, together with Hanslick's formalist critique of musical expressivity, also served paradoxically to reinforce the autonomy-character of music, in spite of the fierce debates to which the two positions gave rise at the time. By the end of the century the concept of autonomy had also come to embrace literature in its retreat from referentiality, particularly through the contradictory but all-encompassing influence of Wagner on the Symbolists reinforced by the reception of Baudelaire and the *Revue Wagnérienne*. Subsequently painting is also drawn into the orbit of music in a seemingly inexorable move from representation towards increasing abstraction (something to be seen in the paintings of Klimt and in particular in the *Blue Rider Almanac* of 1911 and the interaction between Kandinsky and Schoenberg).[7]

It would, however, be a considerable oversimplification to see the progress of the idea of autonomy, of absolute music, as an unbroken line of development which swept through the nineteenth century without disruption and without any change of character, from the Idealism of Wackenroder and Schelling at its beginnings to the muted poetic Symbolism of Mallarmé and Pater at its *fin de siècle*. The concept of autonomy, central as it is to nineteenth-century music, needs to be understood as one of a cluster of ideas which can best serve to illuminate the underlying music aesthetics of the period when taken as an ensemble, albeit an ensemble of oppositions. The nineteenth century, particularly

---

7 Cf. Jelena Hahl-Koch (ed.), *Schoenberg–Kandinsky: Letters* (London, 1980).

given the remarkable dissemination of German philosophical thinking throughout Europe and North America, is the age of the dialectic. The philosophy of Hegel, which had itself grown out of the attempt to systematise the fragmentary speculative insights of the early Romantics on the nature of subjectivity through a fusion with the critical rationality of Kant's philosophy, taught the century to think of unity and totality in terms of a dynamic logic of contradiction and opposition. Given the all-pervading presence of Hegel's thinking, and the extent to which it functions as the *modus operandi* of Romantic aesthetics and music theory, it would therefore seem entirely appropriate to take a dialectical approach to the discussion of the ideas themselves, and to the uncovering of their underlying ideology, that of organicism. Thus it is the complex, frequently contradictory, but extremely fruitful interaction of these ideas that is striking in the musical aesthetics of this period. As well as embracing such apparently polarised extremes as the aesthetics of expression and the mid-century arguments in support of formalism, they are also characterised by the extreme singularity of autonomous music and the ambitions for the fusion of the arts; the aesthetics of 'inwardness', for which autonomous music serves as the paradigm, and an outer world dominated increasingly as the century progresses by the commercialisation and industrialisation of the public arena. Connected with this, there are the spiritual claims made for art, and for music in particular, contrasted with the materialism of society at large and the positivism of scientific method. And importantly, there is the social context of all this to be taken into account: the new class relations which emerge with Romanticism, associated with the rise of the bourgeoisie, whose view of the world it initially celebrates, but which it then turns against after the mid-century.

Romanticism, in the metaphysical sense in which it had been understood at the beginning of the nineteenth century, was already in decline by the 1840s. The two opposing aesthetic positions identified here as the aesthetics of expression and the aesthetics of form persist through this decline, but take on a different character. The first becomes, in effect, a refocusing of the aesthetics of feeling towards what has been called variously neo-romanticism and emotional Realism, characterised by erotic sensualism and the attempt to attach the expression of definite emotions to the extra-musical. The second gives rise to the apparently anti-expression aesthetic of formalism, with its insistence that music is incapable of the direct expression of emotions, whether definite or indefinite (although it is debatable that this ever really constituted a genuinely anti-expression stance, in the sense in which this became important, for example, in the neo-classicism of the twentieth century). I shall address this second position, the formalist, in detail later through an examination of

Hanslick's argument in *On the Beautiful in Music*. First I shall consider the extension of the aesthetics of expression at the mid-century.

The subsequent development of the aesthetics of expression from a metaphysical into a more literal and, indeed, 'physical' or concrete form is associated with the New German School of Wagner and Liszt, and with the development of the music drama and the symphonic poem (see chapters 11 and 14 for fuller discussion). The musical origins of this so-called neo-romanticism and Realism lie in Berlioz's literary programmatic symphonies and the influence of Weber's operatic use of reminiscence techniques, together with his evocation of nature and the supernatural. An important aspect of the new materialism and sensuality which characterises the aesthetics of expression in mid-nineteenth-century music is an emphasis on the erotic. A key work in this development is Wagner's *Tannhäuser* (1845), and as Edward Lippman points out, a parallel philosophical argument for this position can be found in Søren Kierkegaard's *Either/Or* (1843).[8] Kierkegaard, in his discussion of 'The Musical-Erotic' in Mozart's *Don Giovanni*, proposes that it is music's very abstractness that enables it to express erotic sensuousness, to give it concrete form and immediacy: 'The most abstract idea conceivable is the sensuous in its elemental originality. But through which medium can it be presented? Only through music.'[9] What makes *Don Giovanni* a great work for Kierkegaard is its unity of poetry and music and its fusion of form and content. Mozart's genius is to have unified a subject-matter (Don Juan as the embodiment of the sensuous) with music which is also the embodiment of the sensuous. The dominating idea of the work – that is, Don Juan as the epitome of the sensuous – is both its form and its content. As Kierkegaard puts it: 'its idea is altogether musical in such a way that the music does not help along as accompaniment but discloses its own innermost nature as it discloses the idea'.[10] Such a notion of the absolute unity of drama and music would appear to restore the opera to the sphere of autonomous music.

However, striking as this parallel is, there is no suggestion, of course, that Wagner himself was in any sense influenced by Kierkegaard. But what is significant for any discussion of the wider influence of the concept of autonomy is the position taken by the philosopher himself – his existential predicament, which is one of isolation and alienation. An important theme in the essay on *Don Giovanni* concerns what it is to live aesthetically – that is, to live the aesthetic life. Kierkegaard represents an extreme case of the 'inwardness' which characterises German Idealist philosophy (and to which tradition the Danish

8 Edward Lippman, *A History of Western Musical Aesthetics* (Lincoln, Nebr., and London, 1992), p. 240.
9 Søren Kierkegaard, *Either/Or*, Part I, ed. and trans. Howard V. Hong and Edna H. Hong (Princeton, 1987), p. 56.   10 *Ibid.*, p. 57.

philosopher essentially belongs). Kierkegaard is of interest in this context because he is a philosopher who has rejected systematic philosophising, and aspires towards artistic praxis, but is nevertheless not an artist. The existentialist abyss he faces represents an impasse at the mid-century which is bridged by art with, it can be argued, the assistance of Schopenhauer's philosophy. Adorno, in his first published book *Kierkegaard: Construction of the Aesthetic*, writes: '[Kierkegaard] gives testimony to the isolation of an intellectual, living on private income, shut in on himself; an isolation that, in this period of late German Romanticism and late idealism, was expressed in philosophy only by Schopenhauer'.[11] This aspiration of philosophy towards art, with its accompanying rejection of academic systematising and tendency towards the aphorism, is also in part provoked by the encounter with music and the version of an isolated, self-reflective inwardness it was felt to embody. It is a line of development which runs through Schopenhauer and Kierkegaard via Nietzsche to Ernst Bloch and Adorno in the twentieth century.

1848: revolution, disenchantment and the retreat into inwardness

The significant turning-point in the mid-century which marks the character of that 'inwardness' as alienation is represented by the failed revolutions of the years 1848–9. Already from the early 1840s the ground was being prepared for this upheaval, and the manifestations were evident in the arts as elsewhere, with a move in the direction of Realism and Naturalism. Sanna Pederson puts this succinctly:

> As the political landscape began to change in the 1840s, the attitude towards Romantic art became more hostile. Liberal intellectuals who now focused on how to seize governmental power blamed Germany's political and economic backwardness on the people's fascination with Romanticism. Subjective inwardness was equated with passive, ineffective and escapist behaviour. Music did not escape the increasing tendency to treat Romanticism with suspicion.[12]

Whereas the early Romantics had managed to combine their retreat into subjectivity with the moderate engagement with society available to the rising bourgeoisie and its aspirations in the wake of the French Revolution, the disillusion following the failure of the political aspirations of 1848 led to disengagement and alienation. This was keenly felt in Germany with the dashing of the utopian hopes raised by the Frankfurt Parliament of 1848, an assembly dominated by liberal intellectuals who perhaps naïvely underestimated the forces of

11 T. W. Adorno, *Kierkegaard: Construction of the Aesthetic*, trans. Robert Hullot-Kentor (Minneapolis, 1989), p. 8.   12 Pederson, 'Romantic Music', p. 64.

political reaction ranged against them. The result was despair, a bitter retreat from involvement in political life, and, it can be argued, a marked political reaction contrasting sharply with the radical political involvement among artists and intellectuals which led up to 1848. The suppression of the revolution in Paris was particularly brutal. The account by the Russian liberal exile Alexander Herzen, who witnessed the 'June days' of 1848 in Paris, when the socialist working classes in the city rose in defiance of the bourgeois national legislature, and were bloodily slaughtered, brings home the cataclysmic effect of the failure:

> No living man can remain the same after such a blow. He either turns more religious, clinging desperately to his creed and finding a kind of consolation in despair, and, struck by the thunderbolt, his heart yet again sends forth new shoots. Or else, manfully, though reluctantly, he parts with his last illusions, taking an even more sober view and loosening his grip on the last withered leaves being whirled away by the biting autumnal wind. Which is preferable? It is hard to say. One leads to the bliss of folly, the other to the misery of knowledge.[13]

These extremes are epitomised in the poetry of Baudelaire in France and – to an extent – in the music of Wagner in Germany. The change is strikingly evident in the jaundiced modernism of Baudelaire's *Fleurs du mal* (1857), with its combination of disillusion and utopian aspiration, the visionary search for the new and unknown, for inner distant shores to escape the dull passage of time and the mundane experience of the everyday, to be seen in a poem like 'Le voyage':

> Amer savoir, celui qu'on tire du voyage!
> Le monde monotone et petit, aujourd'hui,
> Hier, demain, toujours, nous fait voir notre image:
> Une oasis d'horreur dans un désert d'ennui!
>
> [What bitter wisdom does the voyage give!
> The world, small, dull, today and yesterday,
> Tomorrow, will our likeness still revive:
> Oasis grim in our Sahara grey!][14]

The ecstatic desperation of the final stanza of the poem, with its imagery of death and deliverance, can hardly help but call to mind that other passionate retreat into inwardness and extinction of the same year – Wagner's *Tristan und Isolde*:

---

13 Alexander Herzen, 'After the Storm', *From the Other Shore*, trans. L. Navrozov, in Roland N. Stromberg (ed.), *Realism, Naturalism and Symbolism: Modes of Thought and Expression in Europe, 1848–1914* (New York, 1968), pp. 4–5.

14 Charles Baudelaire, 'Le voyage', *Selected Poems*, trans. Joanna Richardson (Harmondsworth, 1975), pp. 214–15.

Verse-nous ton poison pour qu'il nous réconforte!
Nous voulons, tant ce feu nous brûle le cerveau,
Plonger au fond du gouffre, Enfer ou Ciel, qu'importe?
Au fond de l'Inconnu pour trouver de *nouveau*!

[Pour forth your poison, our deliverance!
This fire consumes our minds, let's bid adieu,
Plumb Hell or Heaven, what's the difference?
Plumb the Unknown, to find out something *new*!][15]

In this respect Carl Dahlhaus has commented: 'As chary as we should otherwise
be of historiological speculations based on dates, the temptation is well-nigh
irresistible to see more than a mere coincidence in the fact that *Tristan* was
written at the same time as Baudelaire's *Fleurs du mal* (1857), the *fons et origo* of
the modern movement in poetry'.[16] Wagner's own involvement in the May revolution of 1849 in Dresden, and his subsequent exile and retreat into the sphere
of art provides support for those who argue that the birth of modernism and
the European avant-garde lies in the ruins of the 1848–9 uprisings. Adorno
argued that 'the category of "the modern" . . . emerges for the first time with
Baudelaire, and indeed in the emphatic sense in which it is now used', citing 'Le
voyage' as the key manifesto of the beginnings of aesthetic modernism.[17] And
in his monumental history of the nineteenth century Eric Hobsbawm draws
the contrast between the art for art's sake position before 1848 and the change
that followed after:

> 'Art for art's sake', though already formulated, mostly by conservatives or dilet-
> tantes, could not as yet compete with art for humanity's sake, or for the nations'
> or the proletariat's sake. Not until the 1848 revolutions destroyed the
> Romantic hopes of the great rebirth of man, did self-contained aestheticism
> come into its own.[18]

The disenchantment following the failure of the 1848 revolutions across
Europe, and the general retreat of the arts from social engagement into the
inwardness which had characterised the German Romantic aesthetic from the
earlier part of the century, sows in the period of late Romanticism the seeds of
modernism and the avant-garde. The growth of an 'ideology of organicism' can
also be seen as a product of the project of autonomy and of the aesthetics of
inwardness. This, however, needs to be understood in relation to the parallel
(and apparently conflicting) growth of positivist scientific method, which was
reflected in the development of musicology and music historiography as

15 *Ibid.*, pp. 216–17.
16 Carl Dahlhaus, *Nineteenth-Century Music*, trans. J. B. Robinson (Berkeley and Los Angeles, 1989), p.
203.   17 T. W. Adorno, *Vorlesungen zur Ästhetik 1967–68* (Zurich, 1973), p. 50.
18 Eric Hobsbawm, *The Age of Revolution 1789–1848* (London, 1962), p. 325.

detached, positivistic disciplines, and also in the development of the physiology and psychology of music. This had already begun with the distinctly non-Positivist, Hegelian Idealist A. B. Marx, who played a central role in the establishment of music theory in the mid-century, but whose plans for the rationalisation and development of music pedagogy in schools had the official support of the Prussian state. The consolidation of musicology as an independent discipline continues in the later part of the century through the efforts of Friedrich Chrysander and Philip Spitta, culminating in the systematic musicology of Guido Adler and in the new music theory associated with Hugo Riemann and his circle. The search for the origins of music in primitive forms of communication and animal cries, together with the development of the psychology of music showed the immediate influence of Charles Darwin's evolutionary theories – music's biological origins and its relation to language[19] – as well as the extension of Darwinism in the psychological and philosophical writings of Herbert Spencer.[20] This is manifest in a diverse range of theorists at this period, notably Edmund Gurney, probably the most significant English writer on music in the nineteenth century, and Richard Wallaschek, whose debates with Spencer on the origins of music appeared in the journal *Mind* in the 1890s.[21]

The apparently irresistible confidence and dominance of the natural sciences and their conviction that the world can be controlled and explained through the power of rationality, together with the increasing industrialisation and commercialisation of Western society, are the counterpole to what are, in effect, two different versions of the artistic retreat into inwardness and autonomy. This contradiction is that between, on the one hand, a turning inwards of the arts, and, on the other hand, their unavoidable participation in the bustle of the commercial free market in a rapidly industrialising society. This tension is neatly encapsulated by Hugo von Hofmannsthal, who wrote in 1894: 'Today, two things seem to be modern: the analysis of life and the flight from life . . . One practises anatomy on the inner life of one's mind, or one dreams.'[22]

There is at the same time a convergence of highly influential ideas which impinge on the neo-romantic aesthetics of expression and draw it in the direction of the extra-musical and associations with the turbulent political context

19 See for instance Charles Darwin, *The Expression of the Emotions in Man and Animals* (1872), 3rd edn, with an Introduction, Afterword and Commentaries by Paul Ekman (London, 1998), pp. 91–5, with references to Herbert Spencer.
20 See especially Herbert Spencer, 'The Origin and Function of Music' (1857), in *Literary Style and Music: Essays on Literary Expression, the Origin of Music, and Gracefulness and Beauty* (New York, 1951), pp. 45–106.
21 See Bojan Bujic (ed.), *Music in European Thought 1851–1912* (Cambridge, 1988), pp. 322–6, for extracts from Wallaschek's response to Spencer.
22 Hugo von Hofmannsthal, cited in James McFarlane, 'The Mind of Modernism', in Malcolm Bradbury and James McFarlane (eds.), *Modernism 1890–1930* (Harmondsworth, 1986), p. 71.

of the time. That these all have great resonance in Wagner's writings and in his music is undeniable. But what is equally evident, as Dahlhaus has observed,[23] is the stylistic *divergence* of the music of these years, and the absence of a single dominant style. While it is clear that the conception of an absolute music, free-standing and autonomous, continues to act as centre of gravity for the mid-century, the resistance to the idea also belongs to its force-field. Nationalism and Realism in music would appear at first sight to be pulling in the opposite direction to that of absolute music, towards extra-musical referentiality at the very least, and towards the functional context of music and the shaping of national identities. Having said this, however, there is no doubt that the dominant paradigm remains that of German instrumental music, with Beethoven's symphonies and overtures read as 'programmatic', and German Romantic opera with its evocation of the mysterious and supernatural, but particularly Weber's operatic overtures, as its exemplars. Vladimir Stasov, the highly influential nineteenth-century Russian music critic and protagonist of the Russian nationalist school, emphasises this reading in relation to Glinka when he writes:

> What are most of Beethoven's overtures (*Leonora, Coriolanus, Egmont*, etc.), certain parts of his last quartets, many of his sonatas, and all save his first two symphonies if not 'programme music'?...The overtures of Weber, Mendelssohn, and Berlioz are also programmatic. All of this music is far, far removed from the 'absolute music' of earlier days.[24]

The rejection of the idea of absolute music in this case merely serves to perpetuate its technical means, albeit ostensibly towards other ends. Furthermore, it is also striking that French and Italian music, dominated as they were by grand opera and music for the theatre, also demonstrate a certain convergence with German absolute music by the 1870s and 1880s, with Saint-Saëns's project to introduce instrumental musical forms and genres to France after the Franco-Prussian War (admittedly also for reasons to do with the bolstering of French national self-esteem), and the evident influence of Wagnerian music drama on the late works of Verdi. Indeed, the influence of Wagner increasingly dominates all the arts by the 1870s, in large part due to his remarkable achievement in calculatedly imbuing the apparently abstract material of autonomous music, the symphonic tradition, with a sensuous symbolism which opens it up as never before to extra-musical correspondences. Paradoxically, the vital inspiration for Wagner in the achievement of this aim was Schopenhauer, a philosopher who, in his philosophy at least, taught the renunciation of the world of appearance and detachment from the Will.

23 Dahlhaus, *Nineteenth-Century Music*, pp. 193–4.
24 Vladimir Stasov, *Selected Essays on Music*, trans. Florence Jonas (London, 1968), pp. 74–5.

The aesthetics of feeling: Schopenhauer and Nietzsche

Although Schopenhauer belongs firmly to the Idealist tradition of the first half of the nineteenth century, the full effect of his *Die Welt als Wille und Vorstellung* (*The World as Will and Idea*) (1818; 2nd edn 1844) was not really felt until the period following the 1848 revolutions. Indeed, he is probably, next to Nietzsche, the most influential philosopher of the second half of the century. For Schopenhauer the power of art is the joining of the sensuous particular and the world of universal Ideas (and in this we see a return to the Platonic Ideal Forms). It is through art that we are able to gain some respite and calm from the restless striving of the world of sense and know the universal for an instant in a state of will-less contemplation. It is music which he sees as the most direct representation or expression of the Will, and simultaneously as the art form most immediately capable of freeing us from the force of the Will. But more than this, music constitutes for him a kind of philosophising without concepts, and furthermore, he claims, if one were to succeed in conceptualising music accurately, then one would have succeeded in conceptualising and explaining the world, as music is its essence, its in-itself. Towards the end of his lengthy discussion of music in *The World as Will and Idea* he summarises his argument in the following terms:

> In the whole of this exposition of music I have been trying to bring out clearly that it expresses in a perfectly universal language, in a homogeneous material, (that is, in mere tones), and with the greatest distinction and truth, the inner nature, the in-itself of the world, which we think of under the concept of will, because will is its clearest manifestation. Further, according to my view and contention, philosophy is nothing but a complete and accurate reproduction and expression of the nature of the world in very general concepts, for only in such is it possible to gain a perspective on that whole nature which will be adequate and applicable everywhere. Thus anyone who has followed me and entered into my mode of thought will not be surprised if I say that, supposing it were possible to give a perfectly accurate, complete, even detailed, explanation of music – that is to say, to reproduce minutely in concepts what it expresses – this would also be a sufficient reproduction and explanation of the world in concepts, or at least equivalent to such an explanation, and thus it would be the true philosophy. Consequently Leibnitz's words . . . may be parodied in the following way to suit our loftier view of music: 'music is the unconscious exercise in metaphysics in which the mind does not know that it is philosophising'.[25]

25 Arthur Schopenhauer, *The World as Will and Idea*, ed. David Berman, trans. Jill Berman (London, 1995), pp. 171–2.

Schopenhauer brings the theory of expression to the point where it becomes, in a sense, a version of the theory of imitation or representation. But what is being represented is not the outside world of nature, which Schopenhauer sees as *Schein*, mere illusion or appearance. Instead it is inner nature, the force of the Will itself, as a kind of life force, which, through the transfiguring power of music and the detached self-reflectivity which results, gives immediate access to the world of ideas behind the world of appearance. This is a kind of pure knowledge, characterised by aesthetic disinterestedness and detached from the blind force of the Will, a form of 'cognition without concepts'. But, as Dahlhaus suggests, 'this esthetic "rescue" of ideas is precarious and threatened: the realm of esthetics is a realm of appearance and even ideas sink to this realm if they are entrusted entirely to esthetic contemplation'.[26] This extreme version of the theory of expression as immediate manifestation of the inner world of feelings leads, in fact, to the contemplation of pure form. That is to say, it leads paradoxically back to formalism and the theory of form. Thus we arrive at a point where the idea of pure expression, as put forward by Schopenhauer, becomes what is sometimes mistakenly regarded as its opposite: formalism. Before taking this position further, however, and examining the formalist theory put forward by Eduard Hanslick, I should first like to consider some aspects of Schopenhauer's philosophy in relation to Wagner and Nietzsche.

In his writings from the years 1849–51 we know that Wagner had not yet read Schopenhauer: even so, the late nineteenth-century English translator of his prose writings, William Ashton Ellis, goes so far as to suggest that there is already a remarkable affinity with the philosopher's thought even before he had read him. He notes that 'an attentive perusal [of "The Art-work of the Future" (1849)] cannot fail to bring home to those conversant with Schopenhauer's *Die Welt als Wille und Vorstellung* the remarkable fact that two cognate minds have developed an almost identical system of philosophy'.[27] When in 1854 Wagner did become familiar with Schopenhauer's monumental work it caused him to relinquish his conviction that music should be at the service of the drama (which he had never really put into practice anyway), and instead to place music at the centre of the music drama (*Tristan und Isolde* is the obvious outcome of this conversion). In a sense, therefore, Schopenhauer's influence also sends Wagner some way back in the direction of absolute music. The effect on Wagner was radical, and is felt not only in *Tristan*, but also in his subsequent theoretical writings, particularly the essay 'Beethoven' (1870). The effect of Schopenhauer on the young Nietzsche was, if anything, even more dramatic, particularly as it was so strongly associated with Nietzsche's infatuation with

---

26 Carl Dahlhaus, *Esthetics of Music*, trans. William Austin (Cambridge, 1982), p. 46.
27 *The Art-work of the Future and Other Works*, translator's note, p. 69.

Wagner's music and with the composer's own distinctly uncritical reading of Schopenhauer.

Nietzsche first read Schopenhauer's *The World as Will and Idea* in 1865, and appears, like Wagner before him, to have succumbed initially to the power of its literary style rather than seeing the problems it presented at a philosophical level. At this stage, now an enthusiastic Schopenhaueran, he remained unconvinced by Wagner's music. In 1868, however, having heard *Tristan*, he was won over, and shortly after had the opportunity to meet the composer. By 1869, when he took up his professorship at Basle University, he had become a close member of the Wagner circle and a frequent visitor to the family home at Tribschen. It is this intoxicating combination of the experience of Wagner's music, the reading of the composer's theoretical works, and the mutual enthusiasm for Schopenhauer that led directly to Nietzsche's first important philosophical book, *The Birth of Tragedy out of the Spirit of Music*. In it he attempted to demonstrate the origins of tragedy (which, like Wagner, he ties to music) in the Dionysian rites of the ancient Greek world, and at the same time to derive from this a general theory of artistic creation. He outlines this position at the start of the book – a passage I cite at length to give the flavour of Nietzsche's rhetoric at this stage, and his at times extreme use of somewhat misleading metaphors:

> We shall have gained much for the science of aesthetics when we have come to realize, not just through logical insight but also with the certainty of something directly apprehended [*Anschauung*], that the continuous evolution of art is bound up with the duality of the *Apolline* and the *Dionysiac* in much the same way as reproduction depends on there being two sexes which co-exist in a state of perpetual conflict interrupted only occasionally by periods of reconciliation. We have borrowed these names from the Greeks who reveal the profound mysteries of their view of art to those with insight, not in concepts, admittedly, but through the penetratingly vivid figures of their gods. Their two deities of art, Apollo and Dionysos, provide the starting point for our recognition that there exists in the world of the Greeks an enormous opposition, both in origin and goals, between the Apolline art of the image-maker or sculptor [*Bildner*] and the imageless art of music, which is that of Dionysos. These two very different drives [*Triebe*] exist side by side, mostly in open conflict, stimulating and provoking [*reizen*] one another to give birth to ever-new, more vigorous offspring in whom they perpetuate the conflict inherent in the opposition between them, an opposition only apparently bridged by the common term 'art' – until eventually, by a metaphysical miracle of the Hellenic 'Will', they appear paired and, in this pairing, finally engender a work of art which is Dionysiac and Apolline in equal measure: Attic tragedy.[28]

28 Friedrich Nietzsche, *The Birth of Tragedy and Other Writings*, eds. Raymond Geuss and Ronald Spiers, trans. Ronald Spiers (Cambridge, 1999), p. 14.

While much has been made of the dualistic opposition Nietzsche puts forward between Dionysos and Apollo, which is itself a variation on the dualism of Schopenhauer's *The World as Will and Idea*, *The Birth of Tragedy* was badly received by fellow scholars at the time. It was widely regarded as lacking any firm scientific or scholarly foundations (the work was regarded as a philological rather than philosophical study, given Nietzsche's post as Professor of Classical Philology at Basle) and was seen as amounting to little more than a propaganda tract in support of Wagner.[29] Nietzsche later repudiated the book, and by 1878 had rejected both Wagner and Schopenhauer. I shall return to a consideration of Nietzsche's position regarding the relation between form and expression after an examination of Hanslick's concept of form.

The aesthetics of form: Hanslick and Nietzsche

Well known for his criticism of Wagner and support of Brahms, Hanslick published the first edition of his influential book *Vom Musikalisch-Schönen* (*On the Beautiful in Music*) in 1854, and it was a work which was to go through many further editions over the next half century, reaching its eighth edition in 1891. In it, through a critique of the expressivist position in music, he put forward what is often regarded as a purely formalist aesthetic, a position which argues that music is totally autonomous and self-referential, that is, free-standing, not contingent or dependent upon anything outside itself for its meaning, and, importantly, that music is incapable of expressing definite emotions. It is worth considering his position in some detail here, as it represents the autonomist position in music at its most extreme and offers what still remains one of the clearest and most coherent arguments for it. I shall take key stages of his argument one at a time.

Hanslick step by step refutes the expression theory of music. The first stage is through negation. He starts from the position that all musicians assume that music represents definite feelings, but when pressed, they have to admit they cannot say what feelings precisely are being expressed. So they fall back on the position that music can only represent indefinite feelings.

> Although . . . all music theorists tacitly accept and base their arguments on the postulate that music has the power of representing definite emotions, yet their better judgment has kept them from openly avowing it. The conspicuous absence of definite ideas in music troubled their minds and induced them to lay down the somewhat modified principle that the object of music was to awaken and represent indefinite, not definite, emotions.[30]

29 See R. J. Hollingdale, *Nietzsche: The Man and his Philosophy* (Cambridge, rev. edn 1999), pp. 56–85, for an excellent account of *The Birth of Tragedy* and its reception.

30 Eduard Hanslick, *The Beautiful in Music*, trans. Gustav Cohen, ed. Morris Weitz (New York, 1957), p. 37.

But, he argues, this can only mean that music traces the dynamic motion of a feeling, and this is not the same as expressing an indefinite emotion, for to represent an indefinite emotion is a contradiction in terms. The question is *what* is being represented? and this cannot be answered.

> Rationally understood, this can only mean that music ought to deal with the *motion* accompanying a feeling, regardless of its essential part, with what is felt; in other words, that its function is restricted to the reproduction of what we termed the dynamic element of an emotion, a function which we unhesitatingly conceded to music. But this property does not enable music to represent indefinite feelings, for to 'represent' something 'indefinite' is a contradiction in terms. Psychical motion, considered as motion apart from the state of mind it involves, can never become the object of an art, because without an answer to the query, What is moving, or what is being moved? an art has nothing tangible to work upon. That which is implied in the proposition – namely, that music is not intended to represent a definite feeling (which is undoubtedly true) – is only a negative aspect of the question.   (p. 37)

Hanslick recognises that thus far his argument has had to focus on the negative task of demonstrating that, in spite of the long-standing conviction to the contrary, music does not represent feelings at all, whether definite or indefinite. His argument hinges on the point that artworks are concerned with individualising the particular out of the general – the concretising of its individual form out of the generalised state of the musical material. To represent an indefinite feeling would therefore be to attempt to move in the opposite direction, from the particular to the general, leaving the question as to what form the general could possibly take under such circumstances. He puts his argument with great clarity in the following terms:

> But what is the positive, the creative, factor in a musical composition? An indefinite feeling as such cannot supply a subject; to utilise it an art would, first of all, have to solve the problem: what *form* can be given to it? The function of art consists in *individualising*, in evolving the definite out of the indefinite, the particular out of the general. The theory respecting 'indefinite feelings' would reverse this process. It lands us in even greater difficulties than the theory that music represents something though it is impossible to define what. This position is but a step removed from the clear recognition that music represents no feelings, either definite or indefinite. Yet where is the musician who would deprive his art of that domain which from time immemorial has been claimed as belonging to it?   (pp. 37–8)

Viewed positively, however, the one certainty we are left with is that music in the final analysis is *form*. The first problem of music, therefore, is to give *form* to such dynamic motion. Thus he concludes that music expresses neither definite nor indefinite emotions. The second stage, in chapter III of his book, is to present the positive aspect of music's lack of expression. So, what then is the beautiful in music according to Hanslick? He writes:

> *Its nature is specifically musical.* By this we mean that the beautiful is not contingent upon nor in need of any subject introduced from without, but that it consists wholly of sounds artistically combined. The ingenious co-ordination of intrinsically pleasing sounds, their consonance and contrast, their flight and reapproach, their increasing and diminishing strength – this it is which, in free and unimpeded forms, presents itself to our mental vision.
>
> (p. 47, italics in original)

Thus, for Hanslick, music is a play of sounds, a kind of sonic equivalent of the kaleidoscope, as *forms*, symmetries, structures (although the metaphor of the kaleidoscope is in many respects an unfortunate and misleading one, as it introduces an unintended element of arbitrariness into Hanslick's argument). The composer shapes the material of music – sounds as rhythm, melody, harmony, timbre. And Hanslick goes on:

> To the question: What is to be expressed with all this material? The answer will be: Musical ideas. Now, a musical idea reproduced in its entirety is not only an object of intrinsic beauty but also an end in itself, and not a means of representing feelings and thoughts. The essence of music is sound and motion.   (p. 48)

So there we have it *en nuce*: music is not the expression of feelings at all, but instead is the shaping of the musical *idea* – in purely *musical* terms, as form. Indeed, Hanslick shows himself to be in a direct line of descent from the Idealist philosophers of the early years of the nineteenth century, and appears in particular to be referring back to Hegel, who had argued that art is the shaping of the 'Idea' in sensuous material. But for Hanslick music is not empty form. It is material animated by a mind working within it – the term he uses here is the German word *Geist*, a term which does not translate properly into English, but which can mean variously 'mind', 'spirit' or 'intellect', and which was central to Hegel's dialectical philosophy. Hanslick writes:

> The act of composing is a mental working on material capable of receiving the forms which the mind intends to give. The musical material in the hands of creative genius is as plastic and pliable as it is profuse. Unlike the architect, who has to mould the coarse and unwieldy rock, the composer reckons with the ulterior effect of past sounds . . . A musical composition, as the creation of a thinking and feeling mind, may, therefore, itself possess intellectuality and pathos to a high degree.   (pp. 51–2)

For Hanslick, this process, as relation between composer and material, is entirely a *musical* interaction, and the 'idea' of the resulting work is to be understood in purely immanent terms; it cannot be articulated adequately in words because it is a purely musical matter. But having dismissed expression in music, or at least, having argued that what music expresses is not particular emotions but rather the Idea, Hanslick still avoids confronting the problem of 'meaning' in music. As John Daverio has put it:

> there is at least one fact that Eduard Hanslick's protoformalist aesthetic makes abundantly clear: it is far easier to prove a negative thesis than to forward a positive account of how music, given its discontinuous relationship with objective reality, interacts with meaning. To do so requires a kind of leap over an abyss, a foray, nolens volens, into the murky territory of musical metaphysics.[31]

But Hanslick, anticipating the new Positivism of the second half of the century (he is referred to approvingly by Helmholtz) and the rise of the more sober and systematic ethos of *Musikwissenschaft*, was perhaps understandably reluctant to indulge in excessive metaphysical speculation. At the same time, however, he hints – although he does not draw the necessary conclusions from his theory – that the composer, unlike the architect, in dealing with the material also has to reckon with the effects of past usage. Thus he suggests, without really taking this up, that the material itself is not purely natural, raw material, but is historical, the product of previous interactions between composers and material. The implications of this are also far-reaching, even though not pursued until the twentieth century (for example, in the music aesthetics of T. W. Adorno). If the material is imbued with *Geist*, and possesses 'intellectuality and pathos to a high degree', it is presumably meaningful in the very concrete sense of the musical gestures and genres which form the material itself. Hanslick does not probe deeper, however, leaving his discussion at a disappointingly abstract level.

It is interesting at this juncture to return to Nietzsche, because in the next stage of his development after *The Birth of Tragedy* he addresses the very point where Hanslick leaves off, although without referring to Hanslick's aesthetics. This coincides with Nietzsche's rejection of both Wagner and Schopenhauer after 1878, and thus it also sees a change in his style of philosophising and a shift in his position in relation to music. The new aesthetic is clearly formulated in *Human, All Too Human* (1878), the book which provoked the rift with Wagner, in that section entitled 'From the Soul of Artists and Writers'. What Nietzsche argues here is the recognition of the historical process through which musical figurations, conventions, gestures acquire their apparently immanent musical meanings – that is, largely through former, but now naturalised, associations with drama, poetry, dance and physical gesture. In Aphorism 216 he writes:

---

31 John Daverio, *Nineteenth-Century Music and the German Romantic Ideology* (New York, 1993), pp. xi–xii.

It seems that in earlier times, something must often have occurred much like what is now going on before our eyes and ears in the development of music; namely of dramatic music: while music without explanatory dance and miming (language of gesture) is at first empty noise, long habituation to that juxtaposition of music and gesture teaches the ear an immediate understanding of the tonal figures. Finally, the ear reaches a level of rapid understanding such that it no longer requires visible movement, and *understands* the composer without it. Then we are talking about absolute music, that is, music in which everything can be understood symbolically, without further aids.[32]

Of course, this clearly owes much to Wagner's theory of the leitmotif, but at the same time it seeks to demystify the process and generalise it towards an account of the way in which autonomous music really has its origins in association and representation, the traces of which it carries with it in quite concrete terms. In the previous aphorism in *Human, All Too Human*, Nietzsche hints at the manner in which the essentially empty, non-conceptual formalism of absolute music has come to acquire a type of conceptuality by association:

'Absolute music' is either pure form, in the raw state of music, where sounds in rhythm and at various volumes are enough to give joy; or else it is the symbolism of forms that, without poetry, can speak to our understanding (since, after the two arts had undergone a long development together, musical form was finally woven through and through with threads of concepts and feelings).[33]

These aphorisms point in the direction of symbolism by suggesting that the material of music is itself permeated by figures and gestures which are redolent with meaning, but which are sublimated through the form of the work. This gives a sophisticated twist to the aesthetics of expression through bringing it into conjunction with a concept of form. The apparent meaninglessness of autonomous music is thus seen to be a sublimation of meaning in a very material sense. This is hinted at in Hanslick, but is only formulated clearly, albeit briefly and without elaboration, by Nietzsche. And just as such reflections begin to nudge music out of its isolated state of autonomy, so literature and poetics at this period move even more decisively in the direction of music's idealised state of abstraction.

Symbolism, *l'art pour l'art*, and the triumph of the aesthetics of autonomy

In the chapter devoted specifically to music in *A Rebours*, Huysmans reveals the distaste his hero des Esseintes feels for the rude distractions of the concert hall

---

32 Friedrich Nietzsche, *Human, All Too Human*, trans. Marion Faber and Stephen Lehmann (Harmondsworth, 1994), p. 129.   33 *Ibid.*, p. 128.

and the unfortunate necessity in the pre-recording age of having to have one's solitary musical aesthetic experience in public in the company of hundreds of others. It is as if, in the retreat from society, and thus inevitably from music as a public art, music itself suffuses all else in the seclusion of the inner world. The logic of music and its 'meaningful meaninglessness' now pervades all the arts and acts as a model for the cultivation of the senses characterised by the strictest autonomy and separation from usefulness, functionalism and utility.

Huysmans's hermetic exploration of the limits of art and of aesthetic experience in *A Rebours* raises a number of definitive issues which can serve as reference points for discussion of the contradictions inherent in the concept of autonomy and the ideal of music. Not least it reveals the extent to which this period looks both ways: it anticipates the rise of modernism and the avant-garde while extending to their extreme the ideas of autonomy, expression, form and fragmentation which were so central to early Romanticism. Pivotal is the connection between the autonomy aesthetic which characterised the French Symbolists and the corresponding musical Impressionism of the *fin de siècle* and the German Idealism and Romanticism of the early part of the century (des Esseintes mentions in passing at the end of the novel, when his self-imposed isolation has been breached and his enclosed world is collapsing under the pressure both of the outside world and of his medical condition, the consolation he derives from reading Schopenhauer). There is the uneasy fascination with religion and religiosity which characterises both parts of the century. For des Esseintes, as we have seen, it is Catholic mysticism and monasticism, combined with a fascination with mediaevalism which has its origins in part in Wagner, but which is also to be seen much in evidence in the Debussy of the 1880s and 1890s. For the Idealists it is the residues of Pietism and a liking for metaphysics, with the tendency for art to elevate itself to the status of an art-religion. These are associated with a number of other developments from which I here identify five. First, and most importantly, there is the retreat from everyday life and the mundane into the inner world of aesthetic subjectivity and its corresponding objectification as the autonomous, hermetically sealed artwork. This is a form of solipsism impossible to defend philosophically but easy to understand historically in view of the disillusion of art and its retreat from engagement after 1848. By the late nineteenth century this is epitomised in Paul Valéry's view of art as 'a closed world', *un monde fermé*, and his wish to transcend what he called 'the monotonous disorder of exterior life'.[34] It can be understood as an extreme version of the early German Idealists' concept of 'inwardness'. Secondly, there is the withdrawal from utility, from means-ends

---

34 Cf. W. N. Ince, *The Poetic Theory of Paul Valéry: Inspiration and Technique* (Leicester, 1970), p. 71.

rationality, and the elevation of uselessness to the ultimate aesthetic value. In Oscar Wilde's famous epithets from the preface to *The Portrait of Dorian Gray* (1891) we find: 'From the point of view of form, the type of all the arts is the art of the musician . . . All art is quite useless.'[35] This, in effect, can be understood as a return to Kant's argument in *The Critique of Judgment* that art is characterised by 'purposiveness without a purpose': art has the form of purposiveness, but does not have a purpose outside itself. Valéry, who was first associated with Mallarmé and Verlaine in the 1890s, and whose *Monsieur Teste* (1896) was the model for Debussy's music criticism in his *Monsieur Croche* (1901), later wrote:

> The most evident characteristic of a work of art may be termed uselessness . . . In the life of every individual we can . . . circumscribe a peculiar realm constituted by the sum of his 'useless sensations' and 'arbitrary acts'. *Art* originated in the attempt to endow these sensations with a kind of *utility* and these acts with a kind of *necessity*.[36]

And in *Monsieur Teste* we find the original thought for this – the idea that music is the art above all others which gives coherence to the otherwise fleeting and ephemeral, and gives meaning to the otherwise meaningless through providing it with a structural context – that of its autonomous form – thus rendering it conscious and aware of itself:

> Music alone can do it. A sort of *field* controlling these phenomena of consciousness – images, ideas, which without that field would be simply *combinations*, a symmetrical group of all the combinations.[37]

Debussy's own aesthetic, although seldom articulated at any length or with any seriousness, clearly reflects that of the Symbolists in this respect. The idea of the illusory character of art, and of the hermetically sealed inner necessity of music which resists the incursions of the outside world to construct its own context, is plainly evident in a statement he published in *Musica* in October 1902:

> Art is the most beautiful deception of all! And although people try to incorporate the everyday events of life in it, we must hope that it will remain a deception lest it become a utilitarian thing, sad as a factory.[38]

Thirdly, there is the problem of meaning already alluded to. What is striking about the work of the Symbolist poets and writers, including Verlaine, Rimbaud, Mallarmé, Valéry, Maeterlinck and Huysmans, is the extent to which

---

35 Oscar Wilde, *The Portrait of Dorian Gray* (1891) (Harmondsworth, 1949), pp. 5–6.

36 Paul Valéry, 'The Idea of Art', in *Aesthetics*, trans. R. Manheim, vol. XIII of *The Collected Works of Paul Valéry*, ed. J. Mathews (London, 1964), p. 71.

37 *The Collected Works of Paul Valéry*, ed. J. Mathews, vol. VI, (London, 1973), p. 74.

38 Claude Debussy, 'The Orientation of Music' (1902), in *Debussy on Music: The Critical Writings*, coll. François Lesure, trans. and ed. Richard Langham Smith (New York, 1977), p. 85.

their highly self-aware art sought to distance itself from the everyday meanings of language and to draw on the allusiveness and indirectness of music, a significant aspect of which concerns the sensuous immediacy of words as *sound*. This leads on directly to the fourth point: the rational control of sensuous material, as *matière*, the espousal of formalism, and the rational exploration of the irrational, are central to this – this is Valéry's dialectical oscillation between inspiration and technique, and Mallarmé's exploration of the boundaries of control and chance in his later writings. In weakening the referentiality of language the Symbolists sought to discover an internal rationale for the structuring of the artwork: what Valéry means by 'utility' and 'necessity' implies a purely immanent logic of poetic syntax which at the same time stimulates an endlessly subtle web of allusiveness. At its most experimental extreme, the Symbolist poem comes to parallel in certain respects a musical score, and thus calls for performance. In the prose 'Preface' to the remarkable late poem 'Un coup de dés' ('The throw of the dice') (1897) Mallarmé writes:

> narrative is avoided. Add that from this stripped-down mode of thought, with its retreats, prolongations, flights, or from its very design, there results, for whoever would read it aloud, a musical score. The difference in the type faces, between the dominant motif, a secondary, and adjacent one, dictates their importance for oral expression, and the range or disposition of the characters, in the middle, at the top, or at the bottom of the page, marks the rising and falling of the intonation . . . [Free verse and the prose poem] are joined under a strange influence, that of Music, as it is heard at a concert; several of its methods, which seemed to me to apply to Literature, are to be found here.[39]

And finally, there is the idea of the indivisible fusion of form, content and material represented by music. Indeed, to return to the starting-point of this chapter: Walter Pater had argued that 'all art aspires to the condition of music' precisely because of the general tendency of all art to try to obliterate the distinction between form, content and subject-matter, and increasingly to retreat from representation into abstraction. In 'The School of Giorgione' he writes at length on this aspiration, and even proposes it as an aesthetic criterion of success in all the arts:

> It is the art of music which most completely realises this artistic ideal, this perfect identification of matter and form. In its consummate moments, the end is not distinct from the means, the form from the matter, the subject from the expression; they inhere in and completely saturate each other; and to it, therefore, to the condition of its perfect moments, all the arts may be supposed constantly to tend and aspire. In music, then, rather than in poetry, is to be found

39 Stéphane Mallarmé, *Collected Poems*, trans. with a commentary by Henry Weinfield (Berkeley and Los Angeles, 1994), pp. 122–3.

the true type or measure of perfected art. Therefore, although each art has its incommunicable element, its untranslatable order of impressions, its unique mode of reaching the 'imaginative reason', yet the arts may be represented as continually struggling after the law or principle of music, to a condition which music alone completely realises; and one of the chief functions of aesthetic criticism, dealing with the products of art, new or old, is to estimate the degree in which each of those products approaches, in this sense, to musical law.[40]

Music had arrived at last as the *prima inter pares*, not only accepted as equal in significance to poetry or painting, and indeed to philosophy, but regarded as the model of perfection for all the arts. Verlaine's poem 'Art poétique' ('The Art of Poetry') of 1884, which, as Martin Sorrell suggests, can be taken as his poetic manifesto,[41] speaks not only for the whole Symbolist movement on the centrality of the model provided by autonomous music, but for the triumph of the autonomy aesthetic in its most solipsistic form in all the arts at the *fin de siècle*:

> De la musique avant toute chose,
> Et pour cela préfère l'Impair
> Plus vague et plus soluble dans l'air,
> Sans rien en lui qui pèse ou qui pose.

> [Let's hear the music first and foremost,
> And that means no more one-two-one-twos . . .
> Something more vague instead, something lighter
> Dissolving in air, weightless as air.][42]

Bibliography

Adorno, T, W,, *Kierkegaard: Construction of the Aesthetic*, trans. Robert Hullot-Kentor. Minneapolis, 1989

Vorlesungen zur Ästhetik 1967–68. Zurich, 1973

Baudelaire, C., *Selected Poems*, trans. Joanna Richardson. Harmondsworth, 1975

Bradbury M. and McFarlane J. (eds.), *Modernism 1890–1930*. Harmondsworth, 1986

Bujic, B. (ed.), *Music in European Thought 1851–1912*. Cambridge, 1988

Dahlhaus, C., *The Idea of Absolute Music*. Chicago, 1989; original edn 1978

Esthetics of Music, trans. W. Austin. Cambridge, 1982

Nineteenth-Century Music, trans. J. B. Robinson. Berkeley and Los Angeles, 1989; original edn. 1974

Between Romanticism and Modernism: Four Studies in the Music of the Later Nineteenth Century, trans. M. Whittall. Cambridge, 1980

Darwin, C., *The Expression of the Emotions in Man and Animals* (1872), 3rd edn, with an Introduction, Afterword and Commentaries by P. Ekman. London, 1998

Daverio, J., *Nineteenth-Century Music and the German Romantic Ideology*. New York, 1993

40 Walter Pater, 'The School of Giorgione', p. 53.
41 See Martin Sorrell, 'Introduction', Paul Verlaine, *Selected Poems*, trans. Martin Sorrell (Oxford, 1999), p. xix.   42 *Selected Poems*, p. 123.

Debussy, C., *Debussy on Music: The Critical Writings*, coll. F. Lesure, trans. and ed. R. Langham Smith. New York, 1977

Hahl-Koch, J. (ed.), *Schoenberg–Kandinsky: Letters*. London, 1980

Hanslick, E., *The Beautiful in Music*, trans. G. Cohen, ed. M. Weitz. New York, 1957

Hegel, G. W. F., *Ästhetik*, vols. I/II. Stuttgart, 1971; trans. as *Aesthetics: Lectures on Fine Art*, 2 vols., trans. T. M. Knox. Oxford, 1975

Herzen, A., *From the Other Shore* (1849), trans. L. Navrozov, in R. N. Stromberg (ed.), *Realism, Naturalism and Symbolism: Modes of Thought and Expression in Europe, 1848–1914*. New York and London, 1968, pp. 1–9

Hobsbawm, E., *The Age of Revolution 1789–1848*. London, 1962

Hollingdale, R. J., *Nietzsche: The Man and his Philosophy*. Cambridge, rev. edn 1999

le Huray, P. and Day, J. (eds.), *Music and Aesthetics in the Eighteenth and Early-Nineteenth Centuries*. Cambridge, 1985

Huysmans, J.-K., *Against Nature*, a translation of *A Rebours* by Robert Baldick. Harmondsworth, 1959

Ince, W. N., *The Poetic Theory of Paul Valéry: Inspiration and Technique*. Leicester, 1970

Kant, I., *Critique of Judgment*, trans. W. S. Pluhar. Indianapolis, 1987

Kierkegaard, S., *Either/Or*, ed. and trans. H. V. Hong and E. H. Hong. Princeton, 1987

Lippman, E. (ed.), *Musical Aesthetics: A Historical Reader*, vol. II: *The Nineteenth Century*. New York, 1986

   A History of Western Musical Aesthetics. Lincoln, Nebr., and London, 1992

Mallarmé, S., *Collected Poems*, trans. with a commentary by H. Weinfield. Berkeley and Los Angeles, 1994

Nietzsche, F., *The Birth of Tragedy and Other Writings*, ed. R. Geuss and R. Spiers, trans. R. Spiers. Cambridge, 1999

   Human, All Too Human, trans. M. Faber and S. Lehmann. Harmondsworth, 1994

Pater, W., *Essays on Literature and Art*, ed. and intro. J. Uglow. London, 1973

Pattison, G., *Kierkegaard: The Aesthetic and the Religious*. London, 2nd edn 1999

Pederson, S., 'Romantic Music under Siege in 1848'. In Ian Bent (ed.), *Music Theory in the Age of Romanticism*. Cambridge, 1996, pp. 57–74

Schopenhauer, A., *The World as Will and Idea*, ed. D. Berman, trans. J. Berman. London, 1995

Spencer, H., 'The Origin and Function of Music' (1857). In *Literary Style and Music: Essays on Literary Expression, the Origin of Music, and Gracefulness and Beauty*. New York, 1951, pp. 45–106

Stasov, V., *Selected Essays on Music*, trans. Florence Jonas. London, 1968

Strunk, O. (ed.), *Source Readings in Music History: 5. The Romantic Era*. London and Boston, 1981

Valéry, P., 'The Idea of Art'. In *Aesthetics*, trans. R. Manheim; vol. XIII of *The Collected Works of Paul Valéry*, ed. J. Mathews. London, 1964

   Monsieur Teste, trans. with an introduction by J. Mathews; vol. VI of *The Collected Works of Paul Valéry*, ed. J. Mathews. London, 1973

Verlaine, P., *Selected Poems*, trans. and ed., with an Introduction by M. Sorrell. Oxford, 1999

Wagner, R., *The Art-work of the Future and Other Works*, trans. W. A. Ellis. Lincoln, Nebr., and London, 1993

Wilde, O., *The Portrait of Dorian Gray* (1891). Harmondsworth, 1949

Young, J., *Nietzsche's Philosophy of Art*. Cambridge, 1992

13

The structures of musical life

KATHARINE ELLIS

In the sphere of art music, the second half of the nineteenth century saw the consolidation and wider dissemination of many of the structures and institutions which had been set up in Europe during the preceding decades, and which were now developing worldwide and gaining in status. Models for operatic, orchestral, educational, publishing and journalistic institutions provided by the major European centres – particularly Paris, Vienna and London – became established in the New World to the extent that cities such as Boston and New York emerged as their potential rivals on the increasingly intercontinental stage of middle-class musical life. Such consolidation took various forms: nationalist drive and the breakdown of court culture lay behind the emergence of municipal musical culture in much of what now constitutes the Czech Republic, Poland and Hungary; in North America, the 'European' musical traditions of cities such as New York and Boston were initiated by immigrant German musicians and embraced by a wider middle class hungry for cultural status. The pace of consolidation also varied: in France and Britain, for instance, it was leisurely in comparison with the breathless rush from urbanisation to the establishment of Europeanised cultural institutions in a new city such as Los Angeles, in which the developments of a century in Europe took place in just a few decades, starting in the 1880s.[1] Nevertheless, the relatively late appearance of now-familiar pillars of musical life in some European cities should not be forgotten: through the entire period under consideration Paris lacked a purpose-built orchestral concert hall and Vienna a permanent civic symphony orchestra. In these areas respectively each city lagged well behind Chicago and Boston, for example.

By way of discussions of urban musical life, repertory and canon, elitism, moral improvement, gender and education, this chapter examines the institutions, practices and – perhaps most importantly – assumptions which underpinned an increasingly globalised culture in which particular repertories of Western art music were canonised as pinnacles of musical achievement and set

---

1 C. P. Smith, 'Inventing Tradition: Symphony and Opera in Progressive-era Los Angeles', in M. Saffle (ed.), *Music and Culture in America, 1861–1918* (New York, 1998), pp. 299–321, at p. 300.

apart from other forms of musical entertainment. Since negotiation of the component parts of such a canon was undertaken primarily by bourgeois society, this chapter concentrates essentially on the middle-class experience, both in itself and in the cultural relations which existed between the middle classes and those above and below them in the social hierarchy. It goes without saying that in a chapter of this size complete coverage – both geographical and institutional – is impossible, and that the extent of local variation can only be hinted at. Because of their centrality to the questions under review and the richness of their musical institutions, study of Paris, Vienna and London forms the kernel of this chapter, triggering comparative glances at other urban centres.

The reasons for the globalisation of European musical culture are multifarious but intimately linked with colonialism, industrialisation, the expansion of international trade and the establishment of significant expatriate communities, and relatively large-scale migrations provoked in particular by the revolutionary uprisings of 1848–9. This is not, however, to imply that art music was globalised to the point where it became the most widespread form of musical expression everywhere it was introduced. In many cases, cultural imperialism produced only pockets of Europeanised activity, leaving the majority of the population untouched. China, for instance, was exposed to European influences from the late eighteenth century onwards. Diplomatic missions from England, and in particular the Opium War of 1839–40, forcibly opened Chinese cities to Western influences, including Christianity and Mozart. Spurred by perceptions of backwardness in relation to Japan (whose first Conservatoire was founded in the 1880s), and by a growing expatriate community in Westernised cities such as Shanghai, the Chinese middle classes began to adopt Western art music as a sign of modernity and cosmopolitanism – which led, in 1907, to the foundation of the Shanghai Municipal Symphony Orchestra.[2] It is of course significant that in an extension of ideological processes relating to universality and supreme value which were taking place in Europe itself, its art music should be adopted as a symbol of both cultural refinement and anti-parochialism; equally, we should not forget that Westernised cities such as Shanghai were isolated oases in a country whose population was otherwise steeped in its own ancient, highly aestheticised, complex and class-based modes of musical expression ranging from courtly Pipa music down to the tea-shop rowdiness of Peking Opera.

The consolidation of norms implies a concomitant hardening of boundaries – whether real or assumed – the transgression of which may be fraught with difficulty. In a broadly conservative late nineteenth century in Europe, such

---

2 R. K. Kraus, *Pianos and Politics in China: Middle-Class Ambitions and the Struggle over Western Music* (New York and Oxford, 1989), pp. 4 and 7.

boundaries had significant impact on the reception of composers and performers, on the types of musical experience available to men and women respectively, on the definition of musicians (and the spaces in which they traditionally performed) as either amateur or professional, private or public, and on the relationship between 'serious' and 'popular' music and its practitioners. Yet alongside the sharper delineation of boundaries which heightened the sense that a professional, canonic, male-dominated mainstream of large-scale instrumental music and opera topped the hierarchy of musical activity, there was room for considerable diversity not only in the form of thriving amateur musics but also in the proliferation of specialist and often privately funded societies devoted to lesser-known composers and repertories. It is nevertheless a measure of the tenacity of the musical canon as configured in the late nineteenth century that its primary institutions of the symphony orchestra and the opera/ballet company continue to receive large public subsidies in cultural centres worldwide.

The rhythms of urban musical life

The principle of the 'season' dominated the musical life of cities in which instrumental traditions were strong. Where opera companies might observe only a short summer recess, with a break for religious festivals, concert societies and touring virtuosi crammed their offerings into a much shorter period – usually October/November to April/May – after which their more affluent patrons could be found relaxing in the country, at the seaside, or at increasingly popular spa resorts such as Baden Baden or Cheltenham. The significant increase in public concert activity in centres such as London and Paris during the second half of the century put the season under severe strain. Despite a concomitant expansion of the musical press, critics began to complain that they could be only selective in the events they covered. In 1893 the *Daily News* and *Saturday Review* quoted an estimated figure of fifty concerts per week during the London season, which extended into June (in Paris the season frequently continued into May; in 1890s Vienna the season was shorter, ending in April).[3] For orchestral musicians the consequence of such patterns of activity was that many of them had to find alternative employment (at the very resorts frequented by their winter patrons, with touring opera companies or in dance-music orchestras playing outdoor summer events) for up to seven months of the year. For opera singers seeking summer employment the European spa towns were an obvious destination; but South America and the United States

---

3 C. Ehrlich, *The Music Profession in Britain since the Eighteenth Century: A Social History* (Oxford, 1985), p. 61; S. McColl, *Music Criticism in Vienna, 1896–1897: Critically Moving Forms* (Oxford, 1996), p. 33.

could be vastly more lucrative, and the fact that the American and European seasons did not fully coincide made for such easy dovetailing of engagements that entire companies set sail each summer.[4]

In many northern cities of the USA the concept of 'season' was as strong as in Europe, not least because so much of the impetus for the setting up of art-music institutions came from German musicians who had fled the uprisings of 1848–9 and who re-established familiar customs in the New World. Old traditions died hard: throughout its first fifty years at least (to 1892), the New York Philharmonic, the USA's first permanent orchestra, kept to a season spanning roughly November to late April.[5] The familiar Western European division between the 'serious' winter season and traditionally 'lighter' summer fare was made explicit in Henry Lee Higginson's plans for the Boston Symphony Orchestra, as set out in 1881, in which he took the unprecedented step of offering his musicians annual salaries.[6] Higginson aimed to pay his players enough to secure their full-time devotion to the orchestra; for other instrumentalists, multiple employment was the norm, since no single position yielded a full living wage. The situation in Vienna was typical: members of the Vienna Philharmonic came from the ranks of the Court Opera but also, in some cases, took part in the rival series of concerts presented by the Gesellschaft der Musikfreunde. In addition, eminent players formed chamber ensembles and taught at the Vienna Conservatoire. The violinist Joseph Hellmesberger (1828–93) provides an admittedly extreme case: director of the Gesellschaft concerts from 1851 to 1859, he then led the Court Opera orchestra from 1860, becoming its music director in 1877. During that time he also led the Hellmesberger Quartet (1849–91) and both directed and acted as professor of violin at the Conservatoire. The net result of such fragmented existences on the part of professional musicians was that during the season concert and operatic life was structured around their availability. The proliferation of afternoon concert series in major European cities in the latter part of the century was not simply an unthinking continuation of earlier traditions, but evidence of the continued use of musicians who had to be ready for another performance –

4 In 1889, an estimated 1,200 opera employees left Milan for more gainful summer employment in South America, with Rio, Buenos Aires, Havana, Lima, Caracas and Santiago de Chile the favourite destinations. In the United States the favoured cities were New York, Chicago, Philadelphia and San Francisco. Fiamma Nicolodi, 'Opera Production from Italian Unification to the Present', in L. Bianconi and G. Pestelli (eds.), *Opera Production and its Resources*, trans. L. G. Cochrane (Chicago and London, 1998), pp. 165–228, at p. 170.

5 H. E. Krehbiel, *The Philharmonic Society of New York: A Memorial* (New York, 1892), pp. 95–163. Over the same fifty years the orchestra's membership remained overwhelmingly Germanic and in particular German–Jewish: a cumulative list of eighty-four orchestral members contains just four non-Germanic names (*ibid.*, p. 173).

6 H. L. Higginson, cited in M. DeWolfe Howe, *The Boston Symphony Orchestra, 1881–1931*, rev. edn with J. N. Burk (Boston and New York, 1931), pp. 16–17.

most likely operatic – the same evening. In Paris, major orchestras such as the Société des Concerts or Jules Pasdeloup's Concerts Populaires held their concerts on Sunday afternoons starting at 2 p.m. or 2.30 p.m.; in Vienna the start time for the Gesellschaft concerts was even earlier – 12.30 p.m. – in order to ensure that the musicians were released in time to return to the Court Opera. For singers in particular the working day might even be extended beyond an operatic performance to an appearance at a private soirée.

Operatic activity mirrored the progress of the season in more subtle ways, and with considerable variation between particular theatres within one city. In Paris, the Opéra rarely scheduled first nights after the end of June or before the beginning of October, though it might begin a reprise of even such a prominent work as Meyerbeer's *Le prophète* in August, as indeed it did in 1876. The Opéra-Comique continued to put on first nights throughout the summer, filling its schedules with lesser names. One can only pity a composer such as Justin Cadeaux, whose one-act *Les deux Jaket* was premièred on 12 August 1852, the epicentre of Paris's 'dead' season. As national, subsidised theatres, both establishments were bound by the terms of their contract (the *cahier des charges*), which regulated the number and type of works to be presented during the year in question. Major Italian theatres such as the San Carlo in Naples and La Scala, Milan, were bound by similar contracts. But the prevalence of the impresario system – by which a privately owned or municipal opera house was leased to a single individual contracted to provide nothing more specific than a minimum number of performances of a minimum number of operas – resulted in less regulated programming driven entirely by public demand.

Repertory and canon

The relationships between public demand, commerce and idealism in the second half of the century were as complex as they were far-reaching, influencing not only the dominant repertories of Western music with which musicians and musicologists continue to work, but also the very institutions and buildings within which such activity took place. William Weber highlights the years around 1870 as the crucial period during which a repertory of model works reached the centre of international musical life, increasingly dominating education and public performance, and living in uneasy coexistence with new music, as it would for at least the next century.[7] It was at this point in the nineteenth century, he argues, that after several decades in the making a performing canon became an incontrovertible fact of musical life. For while there had

7 W. Weber, 'The History of the Musical Canon', in N. Cook and M. Everist (eds.), *Rethinking Music* (Oxford and New York, 1999), p. 341.

been striking examples of isolated performing canons in seventeenth- and eighteenth-century France (Lully) and eighteenth-century England (Handel), and while a teaching canon whereby composers emulated models of older music had been in operation for centuries, it took a constellation of early nineteenth-century preoccupations, including respect for history, philosophies of universal beauty and the elevation of the artist to the status of genius to bring the values underpinning the pedagogical canon to the forefront, to inflect them with bourgeois ideals and to render them nearly indispensable to concert and opera audiences. Governments, musicians, teachers, musical patrons, entrepreneurs and critics all participated in the development of a canonic performing repertory the peripheries of which were negotiable but at the centre of whose concert hall tradition stood Beethoven. The centrality of Beethoven to the Western canon and the nature of his reception in the earlier part of the century implied that certain types of music-making should be given priority over others as the cornerstones of musical culture. His 'hallmark' genres of symphony, string quartet and piano sonata appeared naturally predominant over those of choral music and opera, with the result that the arenas in which canonic values became entrenched earliest were the orchestral concert, the chamber concert and (though later) the solo piano recital.

The very structures within which professional musical activity took place reflected such concerns and mark one of the defining features of the institutionalisation of musical life in the second half of the century. Purpose-built orchestral concert halls, some of them publicly funded and seating up to 3,000 people, were erected in Liverpool (Philharmonic Hall, 1849), New York (Steinway Hall, 1854, rebuilt 1866; and Carnegie Hall, 1891), Manchester (Free Trade Hall, 1856), London (St James's Hall, 1858, and Queen's Hall, 1893), Chicago (Bryan Hall, 1860, Central Music Hall, 1879, and Orchestra Hall, 1904), Frankfurt (1861), Vienna (Grosse Musikvereinssaal, 1870), Amsterdam (Concertgebouw, 1888) and Boston (Symphony Hall, 1900). A practice of appending one or more smaller halls for chamber music, typically seating around 500, is also apparent in Vienna (Kleine Musikvereinssaal), Leipzig (the new Gewandhaus complex, 1884), Copenhagen (Odd-Fellow Palace concert halls, 1888) and London (Queen's Hall).

Piano manufacturers added to the available concert spaces by providing dedicated halls available for hire and in which concert artists might conveniently demonstrate their pianos to the general public. The tradition was already well established in Paris, with the Salles Pleyel, Erard, Pape and Herz; the second half of the century saw the standardisation of the practice, with the building or appropriation of halls by Bösendorfer (1872) and Ehrbar (1877) in Vienna, Steinway (1854) and Chickering (1875) in New York, and Steinway (1878) and

Bechstein (Wigmore Hall, 1901) in London. While the business practices of piano manufacturers emphasised the links between bourgeois music-making and commerce, the act of concert-going itself increased in aesthetic serious-ness, its dedicated spaces, many of which had façades reminiscent of ancient Classical temples, becoming shrines for the silent appreciation of acknowl-edged masterpieces.[8]

One does not have to look far for evidence of Beethoven's centrality to the canon of masterworks traditionally presented in such spaces – even in contexts, such as the setting up in 1849 of the Paris Société des Derniers Quatuors de Beethoven, in which the aim was to cultivate appreciation of works hitherto denied public acceptance. His symphonies and overtures provided the reperto-rial backbone for every status-conscious orchestral society in Europe and America.[9] Telling also was the tendency for the organisers of cheap popular concerts in Europe to programme the early- and middle-period works: the first concert of the Vienna Radfahrcapelle, an orchestral society for popular con-certs founded in 1897, included both the 'Egmont' Overture and the First Symphony (McColl, pp. 52–3). By the second half of the century, pianists looking to enhance their reputations as serious artists had no option but to master the sonata repertory; and those, such as Hans von Bülow and Busoni, who regularly performed the late sonatas, achieved almost god-like status on that account. Within these traditions, Herculean efforts such as Marie Jaëll's complete sonata cycle of 1893 in six concerts at the Salle Pleyel-Wolff in Paris represented an extreme manifestation of a general trend.

Canonic pressures relating to respect for the composer's work fundamen-tally affected concert programmes. Increasingly, the old pot-pourri tradition featuring extracts from substantial works gave way to programmes including fewer, but complete, items. By the end of the century the now-familiar sym-phony concert tradition of overture – large-scale concerto – symphony, was well enough established to be reversed when the occasion demanded that audi-ence attendance be secured for the entire duration of a new work. Nevertheless, older traditions, such as that of framing a concert with overtures and situating longer works in the middle, were still prevalent towards the century's end: the first concert of the Boston Symphony Orchestra, on 22 October 1881, began with Beethoven's overture 'The Consecration of the House' and ended with

8 For a stimulating polemic on the public concert as ritual, see C. Small, *Music of the Common Tongue: Survival and Celebration in Afro-American Music* (London and New York, 1987), pp. 357–61.

9 Comparative figures for performances of symphonies by London's Philharmonic Society during the period reveal that, on average, Beethoven's works were given between twice and three times as often as those of any other composer. By contrast, his overtures declined in popularity, ceding to those of Mendelssohn and Weber. See C. Ehrlich, *First Philharmonic: A History of The Royal Philharmonic Society* (Oxford, 1995), pp. [244–5] (Appendix 1).

Weber's *Jubel-Ouverture*, with a Haydn symphony in B flat in the middle; Manns's concert to commemorate the 125th anniversary of Beethoven's birth, held at the Crystal Palace on 14 December 1895, flanked the 'Emperor' Concerto and the *Eroica* Symphony with the 'Prometheus' Overture and, to end, the overture 'Leonore' No. 3. In Paris, Ernest Deldevez, conductor of the Société des Concerts from 1860 to 1885, frequently placed the weightiest work (usually a Beethoven symphony) at the beginning of the programme, ending it with an overture or rousing chorus.[10]

The programming of solos also reflected new concerns about the relationship between the virtuoso and his or her chosen repertory. Despite notable exceptions, such as the pianist Anton Rubinstein and the cellist Karl Davidov, who often toured with their own concertos, it is the virtuoso-interpreter who emerges as the norm, in contrast to the virtuoso-composer. To take Deldevez's quarter-century of Paris Conservatoire programmes as an example once more, we find the pianist Caroline Montigny-Remaury playing Mendelssohn (1863), Beethoven (1868, 1877 and 1883), and Saint-Saëns (1869), and the violinists Wilhelmine Norman-Neruda playing Rode (1868), Sarasate playing De Baillot (1861), Bruch (1873), Beethoven (1875 and 1884) and Mendelssohn (1881), Ysaÿe playing Vieuxtemps (1884), and Wieniawski playing Mendelssohn (1867) and Beethoven (1876). Comparison with concerto choices in the second quarter of the century reveals the male virtuoso-composers moving away from performance of their own works and conforming to a paradigm established largely by female pianists who because of social taboos regarding large-scale composition did not have a work of their own to play.[11] Around the Beethovenian axis, canonic repertories were inevitably inflected according to national preferences and established repertorial traditions. The historical reasons for the canonic status of Handel and Mendelssohn in England are firmly situated in its nation-wide choral tradition; those for Bach in Germany were related not only to an equally flourishing choral tradition but to nationalist concerns about cultural origins. Inevitably, the process of extension edged backwards through revivals of earlier music and forwards through the gathering up of post-Beethovenian repertories. Both currents were debated, sometimes hotly, in the musical press, not least because the increased emphasis on repeat performances of familiar repertory narrowed opportunities for the performance of music by living composers and tended to blunt audiences' tolerance levels in respect of the unknown. It

10 See the concert programmes listing in E.-M.-E. Deldevez, *La Société des Concerts, 1860 à 1885 (Conservatoire Nationale de Musique). Nouvelle édition*, ed. G. Streletski (Heilbronn, 1998), pp. 81–223. A comparison with the programmes for the Philharmonic Society of London, given in M. B. Foster, *History of the Philharmonic Society of London, 1813–1912* (London, 1912), is instructive.

11 See my 'Female Pianists and their Male Critics in Nineteenth-Century Paris', *Journal of the American Musicological Society*, 50 (1997), pp. 353–85.

was here that the role of the critic was of paramount importance, since he (almost invariably 'he') acted as intermediary between a potentially sceptical audience and a composer whose work demanded explication, either before or after the event. The extent to which influential critics could inflate or destroy a composer's reputation may be gauged via the anecdote of Bruckner's half-serious suggestion to the Emperor Franz Joseph – after the five most powerful Viennese critics wrote in hostile terms of his Seventh Symphony – that he might find it possible to 'forbid Hanslick to write'.[12]

The relation of opera to the Beethovenian canonic paradigm was fraught, and has yet to receive the musicological attention it deserves. As the older art form it commanded respect and still operated as a proving ground for aspiring composers; but as a potentially lucrative art form it was vulnerable (as were its composers) to charges of unworthy, materialist, speculation; and as a genre, like ballet, whose music was routinely cut to shape to meet the needs of people other than the composer, it lacked the authorial integrity of instrumental music. With the exception of Wagner's attempt to appropriate the aesthetics of instrumental music for opera (discussed below), opera's canonic traditions operated on different lines. In many European centres, its compartmentalisation in different theatres according to genre and language was key (even though repertorial boundaries were sometimes fluid), and competition between national traditions was rife. In St Petersburg, the century-long dominance of Italian opera was fatally weakened by the Russian tradition of opera and ballet presented at the Mariinsky Theatre, whose foundation in 1860 formed part of a conscious renewal of Russian musical culture led by Anton Rubinstein (even though Rubinstein's efforts were condemned as 'too Germanic' by outright nationalists such as the critic Vladimir Stasov).[13] Nationalist operatic canons resulting from national segregation are particularly visible in Habsburg Eastern Europe, where state repression after the warnings of 1848–9 served to increase nationalist fervour among an occupied populace. The institution of Prague's Provisional Theatre in 1862 antedated the first nationalist Bohemian opera – Smetana's *The Brandenburgers of Bohemia* – by four years, but thereafter provided a home for a flourishing nationalist tradition which defined itself against the German repertory presented at the city's German Theatre. The fact that the Provisional and then the National Theatre mounted performances of French and Italian operas as well as Czech repertory merely highlighted the antagonism towards specifically Germanic traditions. Indeed, the Othering of

12 H.-L. de La Grange, *Vienne: Histoire musicale, 1848 à nos jours* (Arles, 1991), pp. 80–1.

13 Rubinstein founded the Russian Musical Society in St Petersburg in 1859; the city's Conservatoire, established the same year, was opened in 1862 with Rubinstein as director. On Stasov's objections, see R. Taruskin, *Stravinsky and the Russian Traditions: A Biography of the Works through 'Mavra'* (Oxford, 1996), I, pp. 23–9.

Austro-German repertory was a defining feature of concert life more generally, both here and in other musical centres east of Vienna, including Pest and Brno (where there was official segregation of German and Czech concerts from 1860 onwards).[14] The Polish territories – shared between Prussia, Austria and Russia – showed varying degrees of repertorial segregation along national lines: Lwów, in the relatively relaxed Austrian sector, had an exclusively Polish opera; Warsaw's opera, state-controlled and on that account the only musical institution to survive the failed 1830 uprising against the Russians, was fought over by Tsarists importing Italian singers and Italian repertory, and Poles keen to institute their own language and traditions; Poznań, in the highly 'denationalised' Prussian sector, had little Polish musical life at all; nevertheless, Poles boycotted Prussian-organised musical events.[15]

In those parts of Italy which were under Habsburg rule, the role of Italian-language opera – especially in Verdi's hands – was similar to that in countries just beginning to forge national traditions. But in other ways Italy's position was anomalous, especially regarding the relationship between instrumental music and opera. It was only in the years immediately preceding the First World War that instrumental repertories had gained anything approaching the supreme status they had enjoyed in France, Austro-Germany and England for around seventy years.[16] Yet in Italy's operatic traditions there developed similar phenomena of a narrowing of repertory and the establishment of a clear and canonic hierarchy among composers, the essential differences being that its figurehead – Verdi – was a living composer, and that the selection of works was more overtly connected to social and financial, rather than aesthetic, considerations. As John Rosselli has argued, the revolutions of 1848–9 served to accelerate changes in operatic life which had detectable roots in the preceding decade. Many of its impresarios lost their fortunes; its traditionally upper-class audience was gradually replaced by a wealthy bourgeoisie with different tastes and demands; contracts for major theatres showed a reduction in the number of new operas required each year; finally, choice of older repertory rested with star singers who might carry with them a 'portfolio' of around twenty roles and who exercised their right to select the opera in which they first appeared at the price of being expected to cover any of their portfolio roles at short notice if the need arose.[17] Such a system of 'repertory opera', which was well established by

14 See J. Samson, 'East Central Europe: The Struggle for National Identity', in J. Samson (ed.), *The Late Romantic Era* (London and Basingstoke, 1991), pp. 205–39, at p. 214.

15 Zofia Chechlińska, 'Musical Culture in the Polish Territories in the Second Half of the Nineteenth Century', in Rudolf Pečman (ed.), *Colloquium Dvořák, Janáček and their Time* (Brno, 1985), pp. 121–6, at pp. 122–5.

16 J. Rosselli, *Music and Musicians in Nineteenth-Century Italy* (London, 1991), p. 122.

17 J. Rosselli, *The Opera Industry in Italy from Cimarosa to Verdi: The Role of the Impresario* (Cambridge, 1984), pp. 169–70.

the mid-1850s, inevitably resulted in regression to the mean as far as programming was concerned. Just as there was little point in singers learning roles in which they would be unlikely to gain employment, there was little incentive for impresarios to experiment, thereby requiring them to engage yet more new singers for a particular opera during the season. A core repertory developed around Verdi's operas of the 1850s and later, and selected works of Donizetti, Meyerbeer (temporarily), Massenet, Bizet, Gounod, Rossini and Bellini.

Although the first use of the term 'repertory opera' can be traced to contractual dealings of 1845 relating to the Italian soprano Tacchinardi Persiani (Rosselli, *Opera Industry*, p. 170), the practice itself was not restricted to Italy; indeed it became standard in both the Old and New Worlds. At Covent Garden during the directorship of Frederick Gye, repertory of the 1860s and 1870s was all but dictated by the predilections of two leading sopranos, Adelina Patti and Gye's wife Emma Albani; in Berlin, the Royal Opera under Botho van Hülsen relied on the same diet of Meyerbeer, French operas and Italian repertory for three decades from his appointment in 1851. His attempts to introduce increasingly conservative audiences to Verdi (from 1857) were not enthusiastically welcomed; his first Wagner production (*Die Meistersinger*, 1870) 'caused a scandal'.[18] The system of repertory opera served as a convenience to maximise profits, but had an effect on audience attitudes towards the unfamiliar which mirrored that produced by the move towards a canonic repertory within instrumental music. Moreover, it often resulted in low performance standards due to a lack of rehearsal, singers arriving with their own costumes and assumptions about choreography on stage, and the absence of a single authoritative figure to guide participants towards a shared understanding of the work.

The situation in Paris appears distinctive, due to the relatively stable composition of its opera companies (though there were periodic complaints in the press about the tyranny of the 'repertory' system) and, in the case of grand opera, the long experience of the Opéra staff with a multi-faceted genre in which the singing was one element among many and directorial corners could not be cut with impunity. Here it was the theatre directors, not the singers, who held sway, demanding in accordance with a time-honoured tradition that composers either adapt their works to French taste (Verdi's *Jérusalem*, Wagner's *Tannhäuser*) or write with French traditions in mind (Verdi's *Les vêpres siciliennes*, *Don Carlos*). And if the composer happened to be deceased, directorial prerogatives were still customarily exercised to the point of significantly altering the character of the work. The three simultaneous productions of *Don Giovanni* at the Opéra, Théâtre-Italien and the Théâtre-Lyrique in 1866

---

18 H. Becker and R. D. Green, 'Berlin', *New Grove Dictionary of Music and Musicians*, ed. S. Sadie (London, 1980), II, p. 573.

each presented a different version and vision of the work, that at the Opéra being founded on a five-act Hoffmannesque reinterpretation (some might say mutilation) of the work, dating from 1834. Yet if the French were unable to leave scores alone, the current state of research suggests that they were nevertheless more enterprising than other nations in respect of mounting productions of pre-Mozartian works. Léon Carvalho, who directed the Théâtre-Lyrique from 1856 to 1868, presided over Berlioz's adaptation of Gluck's *Orphée* (1859) and a revival of Pergolesi's *La serva padrona* (1862, followed by a production at the Théâtre-Italien, 1863); the Opéra produced Gluck's *Alceste* (1861); the Théâtre-Français regularly staged Molière's *Le bourgeois gentilhomme* using Lully's incidental music in one form or another. Such enterprises went against the commercialised grain of repertory opera, bringing the selection criteria of operatic works closer to those of the concert hall tradition.

However, it was Wagner who effected the closest rapprochement between the conflicting repertorial traditions of opera and instrumental music. For all his protestations against repertory opera in his writings of the 'revolutionary' period of 1849–51, the vehemence of which serves only to indicate how quickly the system had become entrenched, Wagner's Bayreuth Festival took to extremes the narrowing of repertory which repertory opera brought with it. The essential differences lay in modes of preparation and presentation: his meticulous and extended rehearsals contrasted starkly with repertory opera's capacity for 'instant' productions, and presented the finished products in a canonising framework redolent of the Beethovenian concert hall. With most of the traditional operatic distractions discarded (boxes, anterooms and sightlines towards the rest of the audience) and the lights down, Wagner's serried ranks of pilgrims had little option but to devote themselves to silent contemplation of that which unfolded before them: the work itself.

Of course, 'canonic activity' embraced considerably more areas of musical life than the public concert hall tradition and the distinct, though related, phenomenon of 'repertory opera': it encompassed the preparation of collected editions and anthologies, popular arrangements and other publications for domestic consumption, and music criticism (both journalistic and in the form of detailed programme notes). It was during the second half of the nineteenth century that these diverse forms of canonic activity accelerated throughout Europe and the New World, sometimes fuelled by nationalistic rivalries which led to the embedding of certain repertories within strictly national, rather than shared, canons. Collections of music representing the sources of national traditions began appearing, often published in small numbers by subscription, from the 1840s: the English attempted to produce a Handel edition from 1843 onwards; the Bach-Gesellschaft editions were published in Leipzig from 1851 to 1899; Spain's *Lyra sacro-hispanica* was published in Madrid in 1869; the Purcell Society began a complete edition of his works in 1876; the French published a collection of over thirty early stage works under the title *Chefs-d'œuvre classiques de l'Opéra français*, from 1877 to 1884.

Although the expense of such large-scale publications necessarily meant that their dissemination was limited, the increased mechanisation of the publishing industry, including that of music publishing, brought significant expansion in production and consumption of sheet music. The availability of cheap editions of major works, whether in their original form or transcribed for the increasingly ubiquitous domestic piano, transformed musical life within thousands of middle-class households for whose occupants keyboard arrangements of orchestral and chamber music for two or four hands might well represent their sole means of access to such music. As befitted her status as the most industrialised country worldwide, Britain's publishing industry was well developed; through the endeavours of Alfred Novello, who held the view that wealth should not be a prerequisite for the acquisition of knowledge, it also provided a symbol for the democratisation of the choral canon nationwide. George Grove recollected in his preface to an in-house history of the Novello firm 1887 that in the space of fifty years the price of a vocal score of *Messiah* had gone down twentyfold, from a guinea to a shilling.[19]

The result of the acceleration of activity in printed media was that the idea of a canon encompassing the only partially overlapping categories of monumental music to be performed and musical monuments to be revered was supported economically by the central constituent elements within musical life: the publishing industry, teaching institutions with libraries to stock, the press, the paying public, and the musicians themselves, who programmed certain works in preference to others. Such symbiotic relationships with the market are worth stressing, because although the aesthetic idealism which led to the establishment of the late nineteenth-century concert hall canon is historically significant, the most important element in its success came through the intersection of that idealism with bourgeois mercantilism. The very circularity of a canonic, bourgeois culture being the product of such an intersection explains its enduring nature in capitalist societies: the middle-class providers of the culture in the form of teachers, editors, publishers and musicians, were also its main consumers. The market for the musical canon became self-perpetuating.

19 *A Short History of Cheap Music as Exemplified in the Records of the House of Novello, Ewer and Co.* (London and New York, 1887), p. vii.

Elitism and exclusion

All canons exclude: indeed, they are defined as much by that which they exclude as by that which they admit. It is one of the ironies of late nineteenth-century culture (though perhaps a predictable one) that as increased industrial-isation attracted ever-greater numbers of workers to urban centres in search of employment, high-cultural values were becoming increasingly socially elitist. Distinct working-class traditions – music hall entertainments, popular song, brass bands and male-voice choirs – emerged, with segregation between the entertainment preferences of different social strata resulting in a split between 'Classical' and 'popular' musics that characterised most of the twentieth century. Once art-music repertories had been elevated in status such that one was constrained to listen to them with quasi-religious attention in a dedicated, temple-like space, the idea that those who might not 'understand' such works nevertheless had rights of access became problematic for some and a vision-filled opportunity for others. Berlioz presents a particularly severe case of a Romantic elitist fulfilling a self-appointedly educative role through his music criticism but given to venting frustration at the unworthiness of the Paris public; Britain's bourgeois Victorians offer shining examples of exercises in the moral purification of the lower classes through the participation in and experi-ence of 'serious' music.

The elitism of musical high culture in the second half of the century took various forms, the winter season including events which each implied a differ-ent level of public access dictated by the size of the hall, ticket prices and modes of ticket availability. Subscription-only concerts were unquestionably the most elitist, often open only to those who could afford to pay in advance for the entire series. In some cases, such as the Société des Concerts du Conservatoire, first option on subscriptions could be kept for life and bequeathed to the next generation in the manner of an opera box, thereby ensuring minimal turnover within the audience; in others, such as the concerts of the Vienna Philharmonic, priority for subscriptions was given to members of the Gesellschaft der Musikfreunde in whose hall the Philharmonic played from 1870 onwards, with similar consequences (McColl, p. 46). Of the population of Vienna (around 1,000,000 people in the 1890s), only 2,000 had access to these performances, which were nevertheless covered assiduously in the musical press, thereby allowing vicarious enjoyment of each concert among those (if indeed they were minded to read about them) whose experience of such music was restricted to piano reductions. By contrast, the Saal Ehrbar, a venue for cheap 'people's' concerts, on the outskirts of the city, was little frequented by critics, who thus helped marginalise it in the consciousness of the press-reading public (McColl, pp. 40, 82). Even in cases where entrepreneurs tried to avoid elitism, the market conspired to foster it: with typical foresight, Higginson and the management of the Boston Symphony Orchestra tried to widen access to its subscription series by pricing some tickets as low as 25c, only to find that as early as the first season of 1881–2 ticket touts instituted a secondary market which inflated prices beyond the reach of those for whom they were intended.[20]

However, canons do not exclude only in relation to public access; they also exclude on grounds of the perceived quality of the artwork itself, thereby encouraging hierarchies of genres and styles based on particular criteria of aesthetic value. Germanic symphonic ideals as epitomised in Beethoven's expansive, highly integrated, developmental and goal-directed music, became and remained the supreme qualitative yardstick by which all else was judged. Communities keen to assert or develop their cultural status tended to do so by supporting Germanic forms and/or sending their young composers to Germany (Leipzig, Berlin and Frankfurt in particular) for training. Of the early New England 'five' – Paine, MacDowell, Foote, Parker and Chadwick – only Foote did not receive training in Germany.[21] The British – including Smyth, Delius, Stanford and Sullivan – also attended German conservatoires. Since the French trained their own composers, the founders, in 1871, of France's Société Nationale de Musique, may have thought they had headed off such charges when they adopted the slogan *ars gallica* to characterise the Society's celebration, in private meetings, of new chamber and orchestral music; but in the wake of defeat at the hands of the Prussians in 1870–1, the Society's avowed aims to create a worthy body of instrumental music in a country best known for its opera are more plausibly seen as attempts to provide a French response to established Germanic achievement.

Perhaps because of the inevitable cosmopolitanism that results from being a nation of immigrants, America provides a wealth of examples of struggles to defend the prioritising of one type of musical expression over another. In late nineteenth-century New York, members of the intellectual elite, including the critic George William Curtis and the poet Walt Whitman, presented the Germanic instrumental and operatic repertories as the only means through which America might appear recognisably musically cultured. Whitman argued in a report on New York's opera – the Academy of Music – in 1855, that by contrast Italian opera attracted nothing but social climbers and wealthy

---

20 P. Charosh, '"Popular" and "Classical" in the Mid-Nineteenth Century', *American Music*, 10 (1992), pp. 131–2.

21 However, his studies with Paine took place in a Boston dominated by Germanic music performed by immigrant German musicians. See N. Tawa, 'Why American Art Music First Arrived in New England', in Saffle (ed.), *Music and Culture in America*, pp. 141–65 at p. 147.

philistines. Curtis's satire *The Potiphar Papers* (1853) did likewise, lampooning operatic snobbery at the Academy, at which Italian repertory dominated, and thereby tarring the genre itself with the brush of an unworthy audience.[22] From 1884 to 1891, the Metropolitan Opera under Leopold Damrosch instituted a rival tradition of presenting all-German repertory, with Wagner's music at its head, at low cost. The idea – to educate an appropriately 'cultured' audience free of Italianist philistinism – was nevertheless combined with a wish to ensure wide public access.[23]

In the latter part of the century, the development of women's music clubs, for the promotion of chamber and orchestral series, had a similar effect. Clubs such as the Rossini Club of Portland, Maine (1869) – the first of its kind – began as salon-like meetings for women to perform to each other in a culture of self-improvement. Their expansion into concert promotion was a bold move justified by a similar aim: to elevate public taste through the presentation of uniquely 'high-class' music at prices low enough to enable entire families to attend.[24] The underlying belief, to quote Linda Whitesitt, was that instrumental music was 'the ultimate means of elevating the soul' (Whitesitt, p. 65). Determined entrepreneurship brought musical successes such as the presentation, by the Cleveland Fortnightly Musical Club, of Theodore Thomas's orchestra and the violinist Eugène Ysaÿe for four concerts in 1894–5, and the establishment in 1894 of the Cincinnati Symphony Orchestra by the Ladies' Musical Club, headed by the redoubtable Helen Herron Taft; arguably, as with all such ventures such success was not free of irony, since the activities of such women patrons helped institute and uphold a canonic system which created obstacles to members of their own sex achieving recognition as composers or (with some notable exceptions) as professional performers (Whitesitt, p. 78).

There were, of course, those who refused to accept the hegemony of the canon and the institutions which came with it. Towards the end of the century, the urban traditions of *café-concert* and variety show gave rise to a form of counter-culture which in its atmosphere of the private club nevertheless mirrored the elitism of establishment institutions: cabaret. Paris's *Le chat noir* (1881) provided a forum for a small group of renegade artists, Erik Satie among them, to poke fun at the pomposity of art-music traditions. Satire – both cultural and socio-political – characterised a new tradition which spread from Paris to Amsterdam (1895), Barcelona (the Paris-inspired *Els Quatre Gats*, 1897),

---

22 K. Ahlquist, 'Mrs. Potiphar at the Opera: Satire, Idealism, and Cultural Authority in post-Civil War New York', in Saffle (ed.), *Music and Culture in America*, pp. 29–51, at pp. 38–40. Whitman's report was published in *Life Illustrated*.   23 *Ibid.*, p. 42.

24 L. Whitesitt, 'Women as "Keepers of Culture": Music Clubs, Community Concert Series, and Symphony Orchestras', in R. P. Locke and C. Barr (eds.), *Cultivating Music in America: Women Patrons and Activists since 1860* (Berkeley, Los Angeles and London, 1997), pp. 65–86.

Berlin, Munich and Vienna (1901), Kraków (1905), Budapest (1907), Warsaw, Moscow and St Petersburg (1908).[25] And there were the disenfranchised: not just the impoverished, but also those whose race was a barrier to participation. In the late 1870s, southern African-Americans found themselves increasingly the object of discriminatory State laws designed to marginalise, intimidate and oppress them through the imposition of racial segregation. Such disenfranchisement fostered the separation of black musical traditions from those of whites (spirituals, blues, ragtime), even though these traditions were inevitably shaped by life in a dominant white environment. In the more liberal North, a rising middle class of American blacks gradually negotiated its way into white culture, buying pianos for its daughters and helping catalyse the twentieth-century debates of the middle-class Negro Renaissance on the extent to which blacks should assimilate the traditions and structures of white culture in their attempt to gain recognition as a creative artistic community.[26]

Gender and education

The late nineteenth century presents a bewildering richness of tensions regarding music and gender, in terms of attitudes towards music itself, and towards those who aspired to practise it as either amateurs or professionals. Socially- and ideologically-based lines of segregation defined types of musical activity suitable for men or women or (rarely) both. And while many middle- and upper-class women were taught at home by a visiting teacher, those with higher ambitions could seek a more formal education. In addition to established institutions such as those at Paris, Leipzig and Prague, a plethora of secular conservatoires, many of them based on German or French models and drawing international students, was founded in the second half of the century: in Berlin (1850; first state-funded conservatoire, 1869), Dresden (1856), Florence (1861), Warsaw (1861), St Petersburg (1862), Moscow (1866), Hamburg (1873), New York (1878), Brno (1882), Adelaide (1883), Oslo (Christiania) (1883), London (1880, 1883), Tokyo (1887) and Melbourne (1894, 1895). Unlike institutions devoted to church music, all had to negotiate the issue of women's education as compared with men's.

Sometimes discrimination was explicit, such as in the division of men and women into separate classes, and the administering of different curricula; at others its very existence went unnoticed until challenged. A striking case of the

25 H. Segel, *Turn-of-the-Century Cabaret: Paris, Barcelona, Berlin, Munich, Vienna, Cracow, Moscow, St Petersburg, Zurich* (New York, 1987), pp. xiii–xiv.

26 J. C. Djedje, 'African American Music to 1900', in David Nicholls (ed.), *The Cambridge History of American Music* (Cambridge, 1998), pp. 103–34, and J. Magee, 'Ragtime and Early Jazz', in *ibid.*, pp. 388–417.

latter occurred in Paris in 1874, when a composition student at the Paris Conservatoire student named Maria Isambert applied to the Direction des Beaux-Arts for permission to enter the prestigious *Prix de Rome* competition, which the Conservatoire administered on behalf of the Académie des Beaux-Arts. Her request caused some embarrassment, since as she pointed out, no regulation explicitly barred women's entry to the competition; nevertheless, within two days the Académie set a precedent (while not, it seems, altering the regulations) by formally denying her entitlement to compete.[27]

Social constraints on women's music-making in particular were considerable, upheld not only in private from within the family, but also in public through male-dominated media such as the press. For the vast majority of young middle-class women, the practice of music – invariably in the form of playing the piano – remained no more than a social skill. Yet the social necessity for them to attain some degree of musical competence served to sustain and expand several markets: in upright pianos; in the composition and publication of salon music for piano, or 'brilliant but not difficult' arrangements; and in music teaching, which was, during the period, a female-dominated profession of significantly lower status than that of a professional musician. Census figures for England and Wales reveal a shift in the balance of female participation in music teaching around the decade of the 1850s: the 1851 census yielded 2,800 male music teachers as against 2,300 women; for 1861 the figures were, respectively, 2,400 and 3,100; in 1921 the gender imbalance had increased considerably: 4,900 men to 16,400 women. By contrast, for professional musicians the 1851 census yielded 7,800 men and just 600 women.[28]

Although comparative research on the training of musicians is at an early stage, one can see the sources of such imbalances in the practices of conservatoires across Europe. For Frederick Corder, writing of his experiences as one of a tiny minority of male students at the Royal Academy of Music, the institution was essentially a teachers' training school.[29] The Weimar Conservatoire, which developed out of an orchestral training school set up by Liszt in 1872, offered its relatively small proportion of women students a limited syllabus specifically 'with a view to [their] training as music teachers, singers and solo pianists'.[30]

---

27 A. Fauser, '*La guerre en dentelles*: Women and the *Prix de Rome* in French Cultural Politics', *Journal of the American Musicological Society*, 51 (1998), pp. 90–91.

28 Figures taken from Ehrlich, *The Music Profession*, p. 53. The interpretation of such figures is, of course, fraught, especially given the possibility of censorship or self-censorship by those supplying the information: it was not unknown, for instance, for a woman with an established concert career to appear on legal documents as a mere 'music teacher'. Nevertheless, the significant increase in women's involvement in music teaching is clear.

29 F. Corder, *A History of the Royal Academy of Music from 1822 to 1922* (London, 1922), pp. 74–6.

30 Elgin Strub-Ronayne, 'Liszt and the Founding of the Weimar Conservatory', *The Hungarian Quarterly*, 34 (1993), pp. 148–54, at p. 151.

Table 1[a]   1883/4   Total students: 193, of whom 139 women; 54 men

	Pf	Vce	Vn	Vc	H+C	Comp	Org	Hp	Fl	Cb
Women	73	58	2	–	3	1	1	–	–	–
Men	9	10	23	8	15	1	1	–	1	–

1885/6   Total students 185, of whom 121 women, 64 men

	Pf	Vce	Vn	Vc	H+C	Comp	Org	Hp	Fl	Cb
Women	72	50	7	–	2	2	–	1	–	–
Men	19	4	31	11	8	3	2	1	1	1

Notes:

[a] Taken from Cahn, *Das Hoch'sche Konservatorium in Frankfurt am Main*, p. 104

However, figures relating to the student population at the Frankfurt Hoch'sche Konservatorium from its institution in 1878 to the end of World War I are particularly telling. Women outnumbered men by around 2:1 during the entire period.[31] The distribution of students by class indicates the restricted nature of women's available curriculum (see Table 1).

With the exception of their training of female opera singers, European conservatoires reinforced bourgeois concerns about women's propriety in the practice of music, restricting them to the study of instruments with domestic associations (piano, harp, voice) for much of the century. Within bourgeois society, low, loud, military or wind and brass instruments were deemed inappropriate – a threat to a woman's decorous allure – particularly when they necessitated contortion of the face. As one New York commentator wrote in 1881, 'A lady with a cornet would be a *monstrum horrendum*'.[32] There were also doubtless practical considerations to be taken into account: there was little point in training women to play the clarinet while they remained unemployable as clarinettists. For the female musician in the late nineteenth century, the irony lay in the absence of a glass ceiling in soloistic spheres of activity and the near omnipresence of barriers to modest success in more anonymous ones. Societal norms encouraged the idolisation of opera singers such as Jenny Lind, who could command fees far higher than their male counterparts (though like dancers they paid the price of moral opprobrium), and allowed female concert

31 P. Cahn, *Das Hoch'sche Konservatorium in Frankfurt am Main (1878–1978)* (Frankfurt, 1979), p. 377.
32 Given in R. P. Locke and C. Barr, 'Patronage – and Women – in America's Musical Life: An Overview of a Changing Scene', in Locke and Barr (eds.), *Cultivating Music in America*, pp. 24–53, at p. 35, n. 47.

pianists such as Clara Schumann or the St Petersburg Conservatoire-trained Anna Esipova to carve out international careers. Both activities involved levels of display and attention-seeking which transgressed bourgeois codes, and the role of concert pianist – far less comfortably familiar than that of prima donna – provoked ambivalent reactions among critics; yet there was little hope of regular employment for a female violinist of rank-and-file standard within an orchestra otherwise populated by males. Since, in England at least, women and men played alongside each other in amateur and mixed amateur–professional orchestras from the 1880s onwards, the central problem appears to have been that of according a woman professional rights and status, rather than any *a priori* objection to her choice of instrument.[33]

One solution for women who sought careers playing the 'wrong' kind of instrument, was to form all-female groups. A phenomenon of the second half of the nineteenth century, these groups ranged from chamber ensembles such as the Soldät-Roger Ladies' Quartet (Vienna) or the Shinner String Quartet (London), to the Vienna Damen-Orchester of the 1870s, Rosabel Watson's Aeolian Ladies' Orchestra (1890s) and the Los Angeles Women's Orchestra (also 1890s), and military or dance bands playing lighter music. For women who aspired to professional conducting, the larger among these all-female ensembles offered virtually the only opportunity to develop their skills. Yet such enterprises involved both struggle and compromise: finding women willing and able to fill places in a brass section was a perennial difficulty sometimes unresolved (press reports reveal that instruments were sometimes missing or that male players were used); pay was low in comparison with men's orchestras and the overwhelmingly male press tended to damn with faint praise a genre of spectacle which was born of social, rather than artistic, necessity, and which became increasingly enmired in wider debates about women's rights, the 'real' versus the 'new' woman, and suffrage. Despite undeniable widening of opportunity for women instrumentalists, enforced segregation in the professional arena left them vulnerable.

Class, populism and democratisation

However, segregation within musical life was at least as much class-based as it was gender-based. During the earlier part of the period, upper-class English men had to overcome considerable social obstacles if they wished to acquire more than a merely dilettantish musical education, and even greater ones if they intended to use that education professionally (Ehrlich, *Music Profession*,

---

[33] S. Fuller, 'Women Composers during the British Musical Renaissance, 1880–1918', Ph.D. diss., University of London (1998), p. 64.

pp. 71–2). Similar constraints applied to upper-class and aristocratic women, whose rank and leisured status condemned them officially to the role of musical amateur, even if, like the Comtesse de Grandval, they published their compositions regularly on the open market. Yet the heat of debate about music and class in the latter part of the century centred not around the upper classes but around the activities of the working people. A mixture of segregationist and integrationist traditions, including brass bands, male-voice choirs, oratorio festivals, Italian 'cowshed theatre' and 'popular' concerts offered working- and lower-middle-class people direct contact with musical experience of a kind sanctioned and usually organised by their economic and social superiors, while demanding relatively little in the way of conventional musical literacy.

It was in response to a perceived demand for wider access to an increasingly accepted canonic repertory that new concert series, often marketed specifically as 'popular' or 'people's' concerts, were established. An early example, that of the London Popular Concerts (1858–98), was founded in order to attract audiences to London's first full-size concert space – St James's Hall – which seated over 2,000 people; but such events often took place outside of purpose-built halls because the low ticket prices required to ensure wide access also meant that entrepreneurs had to maximise audience numbers. For Jules Pasdeloup, founder and conductor of the Concerts Populaires in Paris from 1861 to 1884, the Cirque Napoléon, which seated nearly 5,000, provided a solution to the equation so long as he did not need to pay a choir; in this latter instance, public subsidy was required. Pasdeloup's venture differed substantially from that of earlier 'popularisers', such as Henri Valentino in Paris or Louis Jullien in England, who each presented programmes mixing dance music with well-known symphonic items. By contrast, Pasdeloup routinely challenged his audience with avant-garde repertory, his concerts sometimes descending into audience riots over the merits or otherwise of Schumann and, particularly, Wagner.

Pasdeloup's refusal to pander to the supposedly un(in)formed tastes of the relatively impecunious earned him respect not only among musicians and writers associated with the art-musical press, but also among those who devoted their time to working-class musical culture in the form of the male-voice choirs (orphéons) and wind and brass bands which flourished right across France in the second half of the century. Although several of its leading figures (including Gounod and Pasdeloup himself) were active in both musical spheres, the degree of separation between elite and popular cultures was high: the art-musical press took relatively little interest in what its writers considered a 'social', rather than a musical phenomenon; writers for the orphéon press had no reason to cover elite concerts from which its readers were effectively barred. The results of such separation within musical culture are nowhere better illustrated than by the unusually warm reception which Wagner received in orphéon journals during the 1850s and 1860s while the 'music of the future' was being attacked as both debased and beyond comprehension as music in many elite musical papers. With few exceptions, as far as writers for the orphéon press were concerned the championing of Wagner by one of their own kind was enough to ensure their support.

Though the most familiar ventures into 'popular' concerts centred on orchestral repertory, chamber ensembles fulfilled a similar function on a smaller scale. In 1890s Vienna, the Duesberg Quartet gave low-cost recitals in the hall of the Society of Architects and Engineers (the choice of venue itself constituting a statement of intent), often playing new music, but also giving a new audience the chance to hear repertory recently performed at the Bösendorfer-Saal or the Kleine Musikverein (McColl, pp. 55–6). In 1863, the violinist Charles Lamoureux was inspired by Pasdeloup's example to turn his series of Parisian quartet concerts into 'Séances Populaires de Musique de Chambre'. Lamoureux kept his prices low and replaced series subscriptions with tickets for individual concerts. The venture was so successful that he soon had to move out of the Salle Pleyel into the larger Salle Herz, which seated over 1,800 people. Even the institution of a second series of concerts in 1864 did not satisfy demand: 200 people were turned away from the last 'supplementary' concert of the series.[34]

Germany, England and Belgium provided some of the most spectacular examples of integrationist ventures in the democratisation of art music. Choral festivals usually extending over three or four days brought together the massed forces of numerous local choirs to perform oratorios with professional soloists and semi-professional orchestras. In Germany, the Lower Rhine Music Festival, which was peripatetic between Kassel, Aachen, Cologne and Düsseldorf in the manner of the English Three Choirs Festival between Hereford, Worcester and Gloucester, attracted as conductors some of the finest musicians the Germanic lands could offer, including Liszt, Richter, Brahms, Rubinstein and Joachim. Part of the populist allure of such events lay in the sheer size of the amateur choirs involved, and the concomitant impression of collective unity within a diverse society: over 400 singers for the Lower Rhine Festival of 1864 at Aachen; over 600 for the 50th anniversary festival at Cologne in 1868; 1,300 for the Belgian festival of 1870. Indeed, it is a measure of the populist nature of such gatherings that they attracted close scrutiny from government forces concerned about the potential of singing societies as sources for the fomenting of social

34 J.-M. Fauquet, *Les sociétés de musique de chambre à Paris de la Restauration à 1870* (Paris, 1986), pp. 160–1.

unrest.[35] Handel Festivals of the late 1850s, presented by the Sacred Harmonic Society at the Crystal Palace's new site in Sydenham, created a precedent for still larger ventures later in the century: the first 'trial' festival of 1857 offered audiences of 11,000–18,000 a choir of 2,000 drawn mainly from London but also from major towns across Britain; in 1858 the choir had increased in size to 2,500; in the commemorative year 1859, to 2,765 – with orchestral forces to match.[36] The 1857 'trial' festival and those that followed marked a turning-point in British musical life, not only because of extended press coverage both in Britain and abroad, but because the social mix of classes among the performers and audience signalled a new celebration of Handel as a national symbol who could cut across traditional class divides (Musgrave, p. 37). These large-scale concerts were part of a late nineteenth-century fashion for 'monster' events' involving massed male-voice or mixed-voice choirs, where bigger seems to have meant better. It was in America that the phenomenon reached its apogee (and its breaking-point): for sheer size, nothing could compete with the Patrick S. Gilmore's Peace Jubilee concert of 1869 in Boston (a 10,000-strong choir; a 1,000-strong orchestra) and its successor, the opening concert of the World Peace Jubilee, also in Boston (1872), at which Gilmore unwisely doubled the numbers.

Common to most large choral events in Britain was the backdrop of 'moral improvement'. In the northern mill towns, other manufacturing towns and mining communities, where working-class population densities were high and wages paid weekly in cash on Fridays, the Victorian middle classes, often in the guise of Temperance societies, missions or other religious groups, were anxious to provide healthier pleasures than those offered by beer, gambling and, in the second half of the century, music hall.[37] In England, The Ten-Hour Act of 1847 offered workers guaranteed leisure time. Allotments, public parks, reading rooms and regulated, employer-built towns such as Saltaire (near Bradford, constructed 1851–72) all attest to the Victorian philanthropic determination to improve the lives (and thereby the morals) of the working-class population. Mixed-voice choral singing, male-voice choirs and brass bands associated with particular manufacturers, quarries or collieries were no exception. However, where oratorio singing provided an integrationist approach to the moral improvement of lower-middle- and working-class populations, male-voice choirs and brass bands across Britain and in Europe tended to be both more separate and more separatist in their traditions.

35 J. Deathridge, 'Germany: The "Special Path"', in J. Samson (ed.), *The Late Romantic Era*, pp. 50–72, at pp. 57 and 59. It was, in particular, male-voice singing societies (Männerchoren) which came under scrutiny; the same applied to their orphéon counterparts in France.

36 M. Musgrave, *The Musical Life of the Crystal Palace* (Cambridge, 1995), pp. 35–9.

37 For discussion of the sociological aspects of music hall, see D. Kift, *The Victorian Music Hall: Culture, Class and Conflict*, trans. R. Kift (Cambridge, 1996).

The central differences related to repertory and performance context: the male-voice choir movement had a distinctive repertory characterised by hymnic and militaristic styles which showed little overlap with art-musical culture. Texts for choral music tended to emphasise comradeship, the defence of justice, morality and one's country, and religious sentiment, set to largely homophonic music which was in some cases based on hymn tunes or other well-known melodies: 'pieces of vocal artillery', as Gwyn Thomas pithily described them.[38] For brass bands, marches, dances and patterned variation sets for cornet were typical fare, though here the overlaps with art music were more significant in that arrangements of operatic and lighter symphonic music were a common feature. For choirs, the main performing context was not philanthropic festivals, but competitive ones. In France during the second half of the century, orphéon festivals became a summer-long feature of regional musical life, with choirs and bands travelling *en masse* on specially negotiated low-price rail tickets to compete. Similar festivals are still traditional in Wales in the form of the more generically varied *eisteddfod*, which in the late nineteenth and early twentieth centuries shared many of the features (and some of the repertory) of the French orphéon and German Männerchore movements (Williams, pp. 182–3). And although brass bands had more varied civic functions than male-voice choirs, in England, brass band competitions at Belle Vue, Manchester (from 1853) and at the Crystal Palace from 1860 (this latter developing into the National Brass Band Festival) were important focal points.

For each host town, a competitive festival was a major civic event, demanding considerable outlay and organisational acumen (the array of classes for bands and choirs was bewilderingly complex) but bringing prestige and, above all, business: it was not uncommon for the population of a small French town to double for the duration of an orphéon festival. As with the Männerchore tradition, music formed only part of each festival's attractions: street processions, banners, elaborate prize-giving ceremonies and, for the organisers, banquets and self-congratulatory speeches were part and parcel of the festival experience. The organisers of such events routinely cited the 'spirit of association' and the promotion of fraternity as the civilising forces underpinning the male-voice choir and brass band movement. Such dilution of their musical rationale, combined with the tenuous links between their repertories and those of elite and populist-integrationist music-making, and separatist behaviour on both sides of the art and popular music divide, rendered them vulnerable to disparagement as healthy recreations of merely

38 G. Thomas, *Fountains of Praise: University College of Wales, Cardiff, 1883–1982* (Cardiff, 1983), p. 32, given in G. Williams, *Valleys of Song: Music and Society in Wales 1840–1914* (Cardiff, 1998), p. 185.

social import. Yet casting the net wider reveals that similar charges were levelled at other forms of music-making which did not conform to the canonic
paradigms established or desired by arbiters of taste. In the context of
increased demands for the imposition of professional standards in public
music-making, the philanthropic English oratorio tradition was itself susceptible to the charge that it was more a social phenomenon than an artistically
meritorious one, especially towards the end of the century.[39] Vulnerable, too,
were professional ladies' ensembles, which in addition to being marginalised
as of primarily social interest, were also frequently misrepresented as amateur
groups.

Conclusion

Many of the structures which became accepted as staples of musical life in the
late nineteenth century had their roots in earlier traditions – in the case of
public opera, a tradition stretching back two centuries. Yet it was the consolid-
atory power wielded by a confident and essentially conservative post-1848
bourgeoisie that gave them a sense of permanence (and, until relatively
recently, unquestioned normalcy), and with whose legacy we still live. The civic
authorities and private patrons who funded conservatoires, symphony orchestras, performing societies and concert halls worldwide shared the belief that
the kind of music practised therein was a civilising force worthy of subvention.
Equally, the early patrons of performing institutions in America had the prescience to realise that such ventures would run at a loss in the absence of either
public funding or regular donations.[40] In contrast to the traditions of repertory
opera, in which the works presented were selected to ensure profitability
despite the 'star singer' system, and those of the British philanthropic oratorio
tradition, new structures underpinning concert and orchestral music seem to
have had expectations of unprofitability factored into the accounts, thereby
inevitably creating a division between music that was commercially viable and
that which, on account of its superior civilising force, could be argued as war-
ranting special treatment. What even the most prescient of late nineteenth-
century patrons – private and civic – could not have predicted was the speed
which the spread of popular musics from the USA would render the objects of

---

39 I am grateful to Maria McHale for drawing this point to my attention.

40 Contrasts between the Old and New Worlds may be instructive here, though more research needs to
be done: while Old World men with a mission, such as Jules Pasdeloup and Charles Lamoureux, risked
financial ruin in the running of their own orchestral and choral concert series, those who ran America's first
orchestras recognised the need for financial stability independent of ticket sales. Higginson's arrangement
with the Boston Symphony Orchestra is an extreme case. See also Whitesitt, 'Women as "Keepers of
Culture"', esp. pp. 74–6.

their philanthropy marginal to the leisure activity of urban dwellers, thereby afflicting not only orchestras and concert halls, but also opera companies and opera houses, with commercial unviability. Indeed, one of the most politically charged consequences of late nineteenth-century canon formation and the structures to which it gave rise was that of the public subsidy through taxation of institutions of high musical culture by a majority which has no connection with them.

Although within the 'academy' the traditions and assumptions which lie behind much of the preceding discussion are coming under increasingly close scrutiny as world and popular musics take their places as core subjects in secondary and tertiary curricula, in the structures of today's art-music culture they remain strong. Even with the benefit of (dwindling) subsidies, both resident and touring opera companies tend to rely on a restricted core of familiar operas sung by 'star singers'; despite women's suffrage and feminism the Vienna Philharmonic Orchestra has still, at the time this chapter is written, to employ a female musician other than a harpist; despite sartorial challenges from the early music and new music wings within performance, concert hall stages still feature men wearing late nineteenth-century dinner dress. Moreover, new performing spaces continue to be designed as symbols of civic regeneration (compare Birmingham's Symphony Hall with the Vienna Musikverein), featuring ever-more-sophisticated means of insulation from the outside world (the earthquake-proof suspension system of the Bridgewater Hall in Manchester is a case in point), thereby enhancing the transcendent, unworldly, aura of the artistic experience, and preserving its ritual significance. We may have ceased to build our concert halls and opera houses as overt reinterpretations of Graeco-Roman temples, but, once inside, the aesthetic imperative of silent, collective worship remains.[41] Whether we like it or not, the structures inspired by the late nineteenth-century musical canon live on.

Bibliography

Bianconi, L. and Pestelli, G. (eds.), *Opera Production and its Resources*, trans. L. G. Cochrane. Chicago and London, 1998
Botstein, L., 'Gustav Mahler's Vienna'. In D. Mitchell and A. Nicholson (eds.), *The Mahler Companion*. Oxford, 1999, pp. 6–38
Brody, E., *Paris: The Musical Kaleidoscope, 1870–1925*. London, 1987
Charosh, P., ' "Popular" and "Classical" in the Mid-Nineteenth Century'. *American Music*, 10 (1992), pp. 117–35

41 The official record of the construction of the Bridgewater Hall celebrates its insulation from all external noise and vibration, and invokes the image of a secular cathedral with faint Classical echoes in its architecture. Such 'vessels of contemplation', writes Philip Thomas, help 'open a window on the infinite'. See L. Grant and P. Thomas, *Built to Music: The Making of the Bridgewater Hall* (Manchester, 1996), pp. 4–6.

Chechlińska, Z., 'Musical Culture in the Polish Territories in the Second Half of the Nineteenth Century'. In Rudolf Pečman (ed.), *Colloquium 'Dvořák, Janáček and their Time', Brno 1984*. Brno, 1985, pp. 121–6

Cooper, J., *The Rise of Instrumental Music and Concert Series in Paris, 1828–71*. Ann Arbor, 1983

Crittenden, C., *Johann Strauss and Vienna: Operetta and the Politics of Popular Culture*. Cambridge, 2000

Ehrlich, C., *First Philharmonic: A History of the Royal Philharmonic Society*. Oxford, 1995
  The Music Profession in Britain since the Eighteenth Century: A Social History. Oxford, 1985
  The Piano: A History. Rev. edn Oxford, 1990

Ellis, K., 'Female Pianists and their Male Critics in Nineteenth-Century Paris'. *Journal of the American Musicological Society*, 50 (1997), pp. 353–85

Fauser, A., '*La guerre en dentelles*: Women and the *Prix de Rome* in French Cultural Politics'. *Journal of the American Musicological Society*, 51 (1998), pp. 83–129

Harwood, G. W., 'Verdi's Reform of the Italian Opera Orchestra'. *19th Century Music*, 10 (1986–7), pp. 108–34

Haskell, H., *The Early Music Revival: A History*. London, 1988

Huebner, S., 'Opera Audiences in Paris, 1830–1870'. *Music & Letters*, 70 (1989), pp. 206–25

Kift, D., *The Victorian Music Hall: Culture, Class and Conflict*, trans. R. Kift. Cambridge, 1996

Kraus, R. K., *Pianos and Politics in China: Middle-Class Ambitions and the Struggle over Western Music*. New York and Oxford, 1989

Locke, R. P., 'Music Lovers, Patrons, and the "Sacralization" of Culture in America'. *19th Century Music*, 17 (1993–4), pp. 149–73

Locke, R. P. and Barr, C. (eds.), *Cultivating Music in America: Women Patrons and Activists since 1860*. Berkeley, Los Angeles and London, 1997

McColl, S., *Music Criticism in Vienna, 1896–1897: Critically Moving Forms*. Oxford, 1996

Musgrave, M., *The Musical Life of the Crystal Palace*. Cambridge, 1995

Nicholls, D. (ed.), *The Cambridge History of American Music*. Cambridge, 1998

Notley, M., '*Volksconcerte* in Vienna and Late Nineteenth-Century Ideology of the Symphony'. *Journal of the American Musicological Society*, 50 (1997), pp. 421–53

Peyser, J. (ed.), *The Orchestra: Origins and Transformations*. New York, 1986

Porter, C. H., 'The New Public and the Reordering of the Musical Establishment: The Lower Rhine Music Festivals, 1818–67'. *19th Century Music*, 3 (1979–80), pp. 211–24

Prawy, M., *The Vienna Opera*. London, 1970

Rosselli, J., *The Opera Industry in Italy from Cimarosa to Verdi: The Role of the Impresario*. Cambridge, 1984
  Music and Musicians in Nineteenth-Century Italy. London, 1991

Saffle, M. (ed.), *Music and Culture in America, 1861–1914*. New York, 1998

Samson, J. (ed.), *The Late Romantic Era*. London and Basingstoke, 1991

Segel, H., *Turn-of-the-Century Cabaret: Paris, Barcelona, Berlin, Munich, Vienna, Cracow, Moscow, St Petersburg, Zurich*. New York, 1987

Small, C., *Music of the Common Tongue: Survival and Celebration in Afro-American Music*. London and New York, 1987

Taruskin, R., *Stravinsky and the Russian Traditions: A Biography of the Works through 'Mavra'*. Oxford, 1996

Taylor, R., *Berlin and its Culture: A Historical Portrait*. New Haven and London, 1997
Temperley, N. (ed.), *The Athlone History of Music in Britain, V: The Romantic Age, 1800–1914*. London, 1981
Walsh, T. J., *Second Empire Opera: The Théâtre Lyrique, Paris, 1851–1870*. London and New York, 1981
Weber, W., 'The History of the Musical Canon'. In N. Cook and M. Everist (eds.), *Rethinking Music*. Oxford and New York, 1999, pp. 336–55
Wiley, R. J., *Tchaikovsky's Ballets: 'Swan Lake', 'Sleeping Beauty', 'Nutcracker'*. Oxford, 1985
Williams, G., *Valleys of Song: Music and Society in Wales, 1840–1914*. Cardiff, 1998

14

Opera and music drama

THOMAS GREY

Paris, 1850: Wagner and Meyerbeer

In the winter months of 1850 Richard Wagner found himself once again in Paris – and not for the last time – with the aim of improving his fame and fortune. Around the middle of February he heard a performance of Meyerbeer's latest sensation, *Le prophète*, which had received its première ten months earlier (16 April 1849), although the origins of the work stretch back to the 1830s. In his autobiography Wagner recounts how he noisily exited the theatre in revulsion at the stock operatic roulades to which the false prophet's mother, Fidès, pours out her grief in the famous Act IV finale.[1] In this new opera he perceived the 'ruins' of all the noble aspirations of the 1848 revolution; he read it as a sign of the complete moral and aesthetic bankruptcy of the French provisional government, the 'dawning of a shameful day of disillusionment' for art, society and politics alike. For Wagner, a rather more hopeful dawn was soon to be signalled by the première of his own *Lohengrin* under Franz Liszt's direction at Weimar in August 1850, if under musical conditions rather less auspicious than those enjoyed by *Le prophète* in Paris.

This nexus of events provides an apt starting-point for surveying operatic developments of the following half-century. The dialectic of Wagner vs. Meyerbeer, as manifested in the examples of *Lohengrin* and *Le prophète*, informs a broad spectrum of the operatic repertory to nearly the end of the century – certainly well into the 1880s, when Wagner's mature 'music dramas' gradually displaced the influential spell of his 'Romantic operas' *Tannhäuser* and *Lohengrin*. Wagner's *Lohengrin* and Meyerbeer's *Le prophète* were both completed during the revolutionary years of 1848–9, the century's political-historical axis. According to a traditional – i.e., Wagnerian – historiographical perspective, these two works mark the crossroads of (Parisian) grand opera and (Wagnerian) music drama, a crucial choice facing composers of opera after the

---

1 Richard Wagner, *My Life*, trans. Andrew Gray (Cambridge, 1983), p. 436. For a somewhat different account of the incident, see the letter of 24 February 1850, in Richard Wagner, *Sämtliche Briefe*, ed. G. Strobel and W. Wolf (Leipzig, 1975), III, p. 240.

middle of the century. A comparison of the two works, however, could just as well demonstrate the deep roots of Wagner's music drama in the musical dramaturgy of French grand opera, roots that are still conspicuously exposed in *Tannhäuser* and *Lohengrin*. The vehement, even slanderous protests against the Meyerbeerian hegemony voiced by Wagner around 1850 can scarcely conceal an obvious anxiety of influence.[2]

The dialectical influence of Wagner and Meyerbeer across the later nineteenth century is revealed in the ease with which composers could turn from one to the other model within the space of a number or scene with almost no risk of stylistic, structural or dramaturgical incongruity. But there are other factors involved, outside the works themselves (as Wagner's anti-Semitic diatribes remind us). Where one side represents opera as commercial success, carefully calculated to gratify the desires of an urban bourgeois public, the other side is firmly aligned with Romantic-modernist notions of the uncompromising, autonomous artwork, conceived in protest against existing conditions and in the desire to transform or 'redeem' and thus transcend them. For Wagner, Meyerbeer fails to insist upon the status of opera as art at all (dragging it down to the level of 'Jewish' speculation in entertainment commodity), while with its righteously reforming mission, Wagner's own musical-dramatic *Gesamtkunstwerk* anticipates, quite against its own theoretical principles, the fracturing of modern art and modern public in the next century.

Meyerbeer's and Scribe's *Prophète* is a melodramatic historical fiction that strives for a quasi-realistic historical 'texture' in elaborating an episode of social and religious unrest during the Reformation in Holland and the northern Rhineland, while also transporting Netherlandish pastoral landscape and genre-painting types to the modern operatic stage. The opera is of course constituted of discrete 'numbers' of varying size and complexity: the characteristic tableaux (cowherds and milkmaids, dancing and singing at the village tavern, marching soldiers, and the famous ballet of 'ice-skating' peasants furnishing provisions to an army encampment, performed on roller-skates) alternate with narrative romances, dramatic duets, comic-sardonic trios, elaborate ensemble finales (the 'coronation scene' of Act IV), and dramatic spectacle (the electric-light sunrise greeting the Prophet's troops as they approach the city of Münster, which excited Wagner's opprobrium in *Opera and Drama*,[3] and the catastrophic final tableau in which the heretics carousing in the Münster palace are blown up by the conspiring principals down in the basement). Finally, certain roles were

---

2 Wagner's polemical denunciations of Meyerbeer (aside from those in his private correspondence) are contained in the article 'Judaism in Music' (printed by Franz Brendel in the *Neue Zeitschrift für Musik* in 1850) and in Part I of *Opera and Drama* (Leipzig, 1852).

3 Richard Wagner, *Gesammelte Schriften und Dichtungen* (Leipzig, 1887–8), III, pp. 302–5.

written with specific performers in mind – most significantly, the role of Fidès, for the celebrated dramatic mezzo-soprano Pauline Viardot-Garcia.

Wagner's *Lohengrin*, on the other hand, treats a chivalric legend as myth or sacred mystery, and its setting in early medieval Brabant has little direct bearing on the character of the music. The score eschews the circumscribed, characteristic 'number' in favour of more loosely structured scenes pointing towards the 'naturalistic' continuity fundamental to the idea of 'music drama'. Soliloquies, dialogues and other dramatic confrontations occupy most of the stage action, with choral-ceremonial activity reduced to a framing function. The varied, characteristic 'spectacle' of grand opera is present, though relatively understated, in Lohengrin's miraculous appearance drawn by the swan, the wedding procession of Act II, and the gathering of the Brabantine troops and populace in Act III. As with virtually all his subsequent works, Wagner had no clear idea, when composing the demanding vocal parts of his opera, precisely who would end up creating them on stage.

The dramatic exposition of both *Le prophète* and *Lohengrin* hinges on the narration of a prophetic dream. In each case, the narration of the dream involves a 'cross-referencing' of musical motifs that figure significantly later in the drama (the background to the 'leitmotif' procedure of Wagner's later music dramas). The two dreams also point up some important differences between the two composers and their legacies, however. Jean's dream is all too clearly a contrivance on the part of the authors of *Le prophète* to allow the character to fall in with the opportunistic schemes of the Anabaptists. It is scarcely possible to determine the ontological status of this 'prophecy' through all the layers of explicit cynicism and deception in Scribe's drama. If Jean is merely the dupe of the self-serving, rabble-rousing Anabaptist trio, what are we to make of this dream of glory, damnation and forgiveness that comes to Jean, apparently unprompted, in Act II? And what of the musical anticipations here that 'truthfully' predict the future course of events? Wagner might justifiably have cited this confusion as evidence of the calculated contrivance inherent in the genre (though oddly enough, he didn't think to comment on it). Elsa's dream-narration in *Lohengrin*, by comparison, demands complete, unquestioning faith on the part of the audience – the same as Lohengrin demands of Elsa. Intentionally or not, the grand opera exposes the artifice of its construction, while Wagner's dramas do all they can to mystify the authorial hand and to mimic the manner of sacred revelation.

The same contrast applies to the large-scale concerted finales, where in many ways Wagner and Meyerbeer remain most closely related. The coronation scene in *Le prophète* (the Act IV finale) is a chain of highly disparate characteristic types: ceremonial march, archaic Latin hymn, coloratura prayer, and an animated lyrical *complainte* introducing the 'big tune' of the ensemble-stretta. This catalogue of the finale's contrasting contents underscores the highly 'constructed' nature of the operatic situation. The situation in the closing scenes of Act II of *Lohengrin* is in many ways just as artificial and 'stagey' (the interrupted royal wedding ceremony was by now a familiar gambit). But Wagner is at pains to smooth over some of the joints between the sections of procession, dramatic confrontation, contemplative ensemble and resumed procession. The result is a stylised musical-dramatic 'action' that partakes more of ritual than melodrama – a contrast that applies to the contending legacies of Wagnerian 'music drama' vs. Meyerbeerian grand opera over the rest of the century.

Verdi's 'middle period' (1849–1871)

Verdi, too, had been spending time in Paris in the years just prior to 1850. His grand-operatic redaction of *I Lombardi*, as *Jérusalem*, introduced him to the audience of the Opéra towards the end of 1847, and he returned to the French capital for some months during each of the following two years. Unlike Wagner, Verdi would succeed in producing several original works for the Paris stage (*Les vêpres siciliennes*, 1855, and *Don Carlos*, 1867) in addition to several adaptations of Italian works. The experience would leave its mark on other works from the 'middle' period of his career, notably *Aïda* (cf. pp. 398–9 below). But the most characteristic works of the 1850s were those that turned away from epic-historical spectacle and explored a newly intimate and intense mode of expression, refining the leaner, more direct manner of the Italian lyric tradition even where the subjects were drawn from French dramatic sources, as in *Rigoletto* (1850–51, after Victor Hugo's *Le roi s'amuse*), *La traviata* (1853–4, after *La dame aux camélias* by Alexandre Dumas, *fils*), or *Un ballo in maschera* (1858–9, after Scribe's grand opera libretto for Auber, *Gustave III, ou le bal masqué*).

The three masterpieces that marked the emergence of a distinctive, personal operatic 'voice' between 1851 and 1853 (*Rigoletto*, *Il trovatore*, *La traviata*) are not self-consciously 'revolutionary' works in terms of style or subject-matter, for all their innovative touches, and despite received notions of the composer as a symbol of the Italian *Risorgimento*.[4] Aside from the unusual 'naturalism' of the modern Parisian high-society setting of *La traviata* (the original designation of '*c.* 1700' is not to be taken seriously), there is little in the overall conception of these works that breaks radically with the practices of Italian *melodramma* of the

---

4 As Roger Parker points out in chapter 4 above, the familiar association between Verdi and the *Risorgimento* is essentially a product of later nineteenth-century historiography (and mythography). See also Parker, '"Va pensiero" and the Insidious Mastery of Song', in *Leonora's Last Act: Studies in Verdian Discourse* (Princeton, 1997), pp. 20–41.

preceding decades. Indeed, the rapid and lasting success of this famous trio of works owes much to the ways in which Verdi freely adapted the well-established musical-dramaturgical formulas or *convenienze* of *primo ottocento* opera to material that he and his librettists had carefully selected and crafted for maximum dramatic impact. While the roles of Rigoletto, Gilda, the Duke of Mantua, Leonora, Manrico, Azucena, the Count di Luna, Violetta Valery and the Germonts (*père et fils*) all continue to provide indispensable vehicles for operatic auditions and recitals, these three signal works of Verdi's maturity decisively tip the balance of the Italian operatic tradition from vocal display towards musical theatre.[5]

The very success of Verdi's operas from *Rigoletto* onwards – both in terms of their ongoing popular appeal and their status as significant works of art – is in itself a phenomenon of historical significance. With the single exception of *Aroldo* (an 1857 reworking of the 1849 *Stiffelio*, motivated by recurring trouble with the censors), every one of Verdi's operas composed after 1850 has remained in the repertory, allowing for some fluctuation of individual reputations. This situation, which also applies to Wagner's works after *The Flying Dutchman* (1841), has almost no parallel in the work of earlier Italian opera composers. (Only a small proportion of Rossini's or Donizetti's operas continued to be performed regularly into the twentieth century, as was true, to a lesser extent, even of the operatic oeuvres of Mozart and Bellini.) Most of the credit must go to the individual genius of Verdi, of course. But it is also symptomatic of a large-scale shift in the culture of operatic production, from a time when new operas were provided on a regular, seasonal basis with little or no expectation of their entering a fixed canon, to a time when 'serious' opera (at least) was composed – like other 'serious' art works – with an eye to posterity, even if some details were still conditioned by the circumstances of a première or a revival (see chapter 13). Paradoxically, the very *in*stability of the texts of Verdi's later middle-period works – as with the extensively revised operas *Simon Boccanegra*, *La forza del destino* and *Don Carlos* – reflects this shift from seasonally commissioned 'event' to canonic musical 'work'. If Verdi's revisions leave open questions as to the definitive text, they are symptomatic of a changing attitude towards operatic production: after this point, composers were less concerned with providing disposable novelties, and more concerned with creating operas that might gain a permanent foothold in the repertory.

Rigoletto, premièred at La Fenice in Venice on 11 March 1851, was the first of Verdi's operas to find a permanent place in the international repertory. Here we can find relatively pure examples of the structures inherited from Bellini and

5 This is not to say, of course, that Italian opera disdained dramatic values before Verdi; on Italian opera as 'music theatre' in the bel canto era, see chapter 4.

Donizetti side by side with elaborations and transformations of these (though not, on the whole, significantly expanded dimensions, as Verdi swore by the virtues of brevity, directness and concision). Thus, for example, the Duke of Mantua opens Act II with a *scena ed aria* completely by the book. In conventionally agitated accents of recitative and lyrical arioso sighs, the Duke (1) expresses his anguish at the thought of having lost the simple young girl (Gilda) whom he was courting as his next mistress ('Ella mi fu rapita!'); (2) he sympathises with her plight, as he imagines it, in a cleanly wrought G flat cantabile ('Parmi veder' le lagrime'); (3) the chorus of male courtiers narrates the previous evening's escapades ('Scorrendo uniti rcmota via' – a formally organised narrative song in place of the usual scena/recitative intervention at this point); learning in this way that Gilda has been abducted to his very own palace, he then launches into (4) a vigorous, joyful cabaletta in D major ('Possente amor mi chiama') in the usual two strophes with brief choral interlude. The Duke's callow hedonism, famously embodied in his signature ditty, 'La donna è mobile', suggests that the emotions expressed in the present number, too, are ultimately superficial – as schematic and unreflexive as the structure itself, even if they possess a high degree of attractiveness and even intensity. The chorus's response to the Duke's behaviour – perfectly normal behaviour, in operatic terms – could almost be taken as an ironic persiflage of the whole convention of the double aria, with its sudden, often covertly motivated central mood swing: 'O, qual pensier or l'agita? come cangiò d'umor!' ('Oh, what thought now agitates him? How he changes humour!').

The *scena ed aria* of Rigoletto immediately following, on the other hand, is unquestionably genuine of expression. The situation itself would lead us to suppose this, and the freer, more spontaneous unfolding of lyric forms here seems to confirm it. The *parlante* exchange between Rigoletto and the courtiers is backed by leisurely, *galant*, harmonically uncomplicated gestures in the orchestra, typical for such an introductory scena, but given a bitter, sardonic spin by Rigoletto's obviously constrained behaviour, which finally explodes into rage and abuse ('Cortigiani, vil razza dannata!'). Instead of parcelling Rigoletto's unleashed emotions into lyrical lament and rhythmic vengefulness, as might be expected, Verdi creates a continuous movement of three distinct phases. The opening (1) is agitated and more declamatory than lyrical ('Cortigiani', Andante mosso agitato, C minor). When this outburst proves ineffective, Rigoletto shifts (2) to a more pathetic, beseeching mode ('Ah! Ebben piango . . . Marullo . . . signore', meno mosso, F minor), and only after that does Verdi indulge him with a broad, lyrical cantabile (3), as a last-ditch effort to wring some sympathy from his auditors ('Miei singori . . . Ah perdono, pietate', D flat).

This is not to say that conventional lyrical models necessarily signify a lack of sincerity in Verdi's middle-period *oeuvre*, however. The *scena e cavatina* that introduces the heroine Leonora in *Il trovatore* is a recitative and double-aria (cantabile/cabaletta pair) every bit as regular as the Duke's in *Rigoletto*. Yet we are certainly not meant to distrust Leonora's confessions of love for the mysterious troubadour. She is a well-bred, aristocratic (or quasi-aristocratic) character who expresses herself in a decorous, elegant manner in keeping with her station. Her cantabile, 'Tacea la notte' (unsurpassed in Verdi's music for its 'concentration of lyrical poetry' and 'melodic craftsmanship', for Julian Budden),[6] establishes Leonora as a paragon of delicacy and refinement, a suitable object of chivalrous or melodramatic contest (Manrico vs. the Count), while her florid cabaletta, 'Di tale amor', hints at hidden reserves of vitality and passion.

Rigoletto and *Il trovatore* present a Janus-faced perspective of Italian opera at mid-century: a masterful consolidation of the rich legacy of the *primo ottocento* with enough that was both novel and durable to maintain these pieces as repertory favourites into the age of *verismo*, modernism and beyond. *Trovatore* in particular – with its far-fetched, ultra-condensed dark and extravagant plot, its finely turned cantabiles and classic cabalettas, and its ensembles packed with melodramatic incident – is the quintessence of everything contrived and preposterous in nineteenth-century opera, but irresistibly effective, for all that. It was ripe for parody already by the time of the Gilbert and Sullivan operettas (cf. pp. 383–5). And yet Verdi's brilliantly calculated expansion of the solo scene and aria in the 'Miserere' episode that opens Act IV, where Leonora's cantabile 'D'amor sull'ali rosee' yields to the lugubrious chanting of the monks and the distant song of Manrico prior to her cabaletta, invests the old formula with new life and even a compelling 'theatrical' plausibility.[7] *Il trovatore* remains a testament to the vigour and polish, as well as the endearing *naïveté*, of a bygone operatic age.

It was, naturally, the 'scene and duet' type that offered Verdi the most scope for investing traditional designs with a new sense of dramatic life and urgency. (A narrative of operatic history orientated towards this progressive loosening of formal numbers need not be seen as an exclusively Wagnerian construct: the potential for dialogic confrontation to expand the horizons of operatic form beyond the static, monologic paradigm of the solo scene and aria was something already glimpsed by French and Italian composers well before the advent of Wagner's international

6 Julian Budden, *The Operas of Verdi*, II (New York, 1978), p. 75. For an even more fulsome tribute to Leonora's melody, see also David Kimbell, *Verdi in the Age of Italian Romanticism* (Cambridge, 1981), p. 437.
7 It was actually Verdi who suggested to his librettist Cammarano the configuration of Leonora, Manrico and the chanting chorus in the 'Miserere' scene (see Budden, *Operas of Verdi*, II, p. 62).

influence.) Duet scenes in *Trovatore*, *Traviata* and *Ballo in maschera* – all composed before Wagner was anything but a suspicious name to Verdi – testify to the impulse to animate the lyric forms of Italian opera in this way.

The atmospheric 'duet' between Rigoletto and Sparafucile that follows the Act I *introduzione* of that opera exemplifies the construction of a quasi-naturalistic dialogue over a clearly structured periodic accompaniment (basically a *parlante* idiom over a ternary orchestral framework), though in its brevity and simplicity the scene remains *sui generis*. At the other end of the spectrum, the 'scene and duet' for Violetta and the senior Germont in Act II of *La traviata* multiplies the number of alternating recitative and lyrical sections to achieve a new dramatic breadth. The constituent sections themselves are not longer than usual – some indeed are quite short, such as Germont's 'Pura siccome un angelo' or Violetta's distressed, cabaletta-like response to it, 'Non sapete qual affetto'. The dramatic 'realism' of Verdi's approach here, which is responsible in some part for the length of the scene, lies not in dispensing with self-contained lyric utterances (nor in expanding them to new lengths), but in devising a longer chain of these utterances, 'realistically' reflecting the stubborn contest of wills played out here. Germont persists in his plea that Violetta renounce Alfredo in a second cantabile ('Un dì, quando le veneri'), answered by a 'dissimilar' response from her, and she finally acquiesces in yet another cantabile movement ('Dite alla giovane'), with encouraging participation from him in the second half. Only after this, and some intermediate scena material, does Violetta initiate the duo-cabaletta proper to the scene ('Morrò! . . . la mia memoria'), whose resolute tread, in accented crotchets, will return at Violetta's final moment of resistance in Act III ('Gran Dio! morir si giovane'). Instead of concluding the scene in the usual burst of loudly accompanied cadential flourishes, Verdi allows the voices and their text to come to the fore in an extended embrace – vocal and gestural – between the two characters.

From the time of *La traviata* up to the caesura in Verdi's career marked by *Aïda* (1871), dramatic confrontations continue to elicit broad designs of this sort, freely compounded of flexible melodic elements, while solo scenes tend to centre on a single extended lyric utterance (without cabaletta). In other words, while duets or other ensembles aim for more dynamic, flexible trajectories, moments of subjective expression or self-reflection become more concentrated and more introspective, avoiding the sudden affective swerves motivated by the intrusion of other characters, typical before 1850.

Examples of the latter would include the famous baritone aria from Act III of *Un ballo in maschera*, 'Eri tu', in which Renato meditates on his wife's supposed infidelity, and Amelia's solo scene at the beginning of Act II of *Ballo*, similarly built around a single cantabile movement, 'Ma dal'arido stelo divulsa'. Amelia's scene is extended by an instrumental prelude during which she appears at the dark and desolate gallows-field, and by a sizeable dramatic coda precipitated by the tolling of midnight and concluding with a great arching phrase in F major ('Deh! mi reggi, m'aita, o Signor'), imploring heaven for support and pity. Such phrases are a hallmark of Verdi's middle-period heroines (*vide* Leonora's 'Deh! non m'abbandonar, pietà, pietà di me, Signore!' in *La forza del destino*, Elisabeth's prayer-like aria, 'Toi qui sus le néant . . . si l'on répand encore', in Act V of *Don Carlos*, and the heroine's reiterations of 'Numi, pietà' in Acts I and II of *Aïda*), showcasing the soprano in a very different way than the *fioritura* of the bel canto generation, but one that is just as vocally demanding, and as effective.

Among numerous examples of expanded/intensified duets, that between Amelia and Riccardo at the centre of *Un ballo in maschera* takes the traditional 'scene and duet' model and expands it from within. The 'slow' movement is actually a fairly urgent $\frac{6}{8}$ Allegretto un poco sostenuto in F ('Non sai tu che se l'anima mia') with a 'dissimilar' response from Amelia in D flat, broadening out *più lento* in the opposite tonal direction, to A major, when at Riccardo's bidding Amelia haltingly articulates her love ('Ebben . . . sì . . . t'amo . . .'). An even more expansive and intense version of this lyrical confession erupts, in E major, between the solo and duo verses of their C major cabaletta, 'O qual soave brivido'. This is an 'expansion' solely by means of expressive intensity, not actual length: where traditionally the verses of the cabaletta are punctuated by a bit of noisy orchestral filler holding the dominant (sometimes with chattering confidante or chorus), here the structural joint blossoms into an unexpected lyrical outpouring over a harmonic parenthesis on the major mediant, completely transforming the effect of the concluding duo-verse that follows.

The *Grande scène et duo* for Don Carlos and Elisabeth de Valois, in Act II of *Don Carlos* (1867), achieves similar, if not greater, dramatic intensity with very different means. Influenced in part by the looser designs of French opera, but also anticipating the methods of his own last two operas and Puccini's generation, Verdi constructs the duet from a series of small, independent musical paragraphs with only a minimum of declamatory recitative or *parlante* material. At first these 'paragraphs' are highly contrasted, reflecting the fraught rhetorical dialectics of the drama (Carlos requests to leave the Spanish court, but cannot help pressing Elisabeth to acknowledge her feelings for him and confessing his own for her). Elsewhere they share the same phrases to create a larger melodic period, either in nostalgic, lyrical accord ('O bien perdu' / 'O Dieu clément') or in tormented mutual recriminations ('Que sous mes pieds me déchire la terre!'/'Eh bien, donc, frappez votre père!'); the contrast between these two sets of paired phrases suggests a faint trace – but no more than that – of the traditional cantabile–cabaletta paradigm.

An ambition that Verdi continued to cultivate throughout his maturity, rooted in the legacy of Victor Hugo and French Romantic drama, was to infuse opera with a 'Shakespearean' diversity of character, tone and dramatic levels (whether using Shakespeare material or not). It was this impulse, of course, that elicited the masterpieces of his final years, *Otello* and *Falstaff*, although there he ended up maintaining the autonomy of tragedy and comedy. The great unrealised project of his middle years, a *King Lear* opera,[8] would have a been a wholly tragic work, too. But in *Un ballo in maschera* and *La forza del destino* Verdi did manage to realise something of this integration of comic and tragic elements. As a dramatic and musical counterpoint to the tragic plot of *Ballo* an element of ironic black comedy is furnished by the awkward surprises of Scribe's scenario (as adapted by Antonio Somma). Thus in the quartet-finale to Act II the sardonic, laughing refrain of the conspirators Sam and Tom ('Ve' se di notte ... Ah! ah! ah!') alternates with Renato's suppressed rage at the discovery of his wife in an apparent tryst with the governor Riccardo, and with Amelia's similarly suppressed anguish. Through contrasts of rhythm, contour and (of course) text, Verdi manages briefly to bring their tragic accents into a literal, musical counterpoint with the comic ones of their antagonists. The *travesti* role of the page, Oscar, imports the idiom of Auber's *opéras comiques* in the form of pert, insouciant 'couplets' for a soubrette-style voice, easily blending with the *faux-galant* idiom of the masked-ball music in the final scene. In *Forza* Verdi attempted something more like the history plays of Shakespeare: a far-flung epic action with light or comic 'character' roles, such as the gypsy camp-follower Preziosilla or the friar Melitone, who provide a foil to the inexorable, tragic 'force of destiny' while also interacting with the principals to some extent. Verdi's grafting of details from the encampment scene of Schiller's *Wallensteins Lager* – an early instance of Romantic 'realism' à la Shakespeare – on to the Duke of Rivas's melodramatic potboiler is another indication of his striving for such a 'universal' Shakespearean canvas.

Comic opera: high and low

'Ve' la tragedia mutò in comedia . . .' ('Lo, the tragedy has turned to comedy . . .'). Thus the conspirators Sam and Tom remark cruelly on the discomfiture of Renato and Amelia in the final scene of Act II of *Un ballo in maschera*, mentioned above. Writ large, so to speak, their remark might well be applied to a famous parallel irony in the *oeuvres* of Verdi and Wagner: the surprising emergence of a major comic opera (*Falstaff* and *Die Meistersinger*, respectively) on the heels of

8 On Verdi's plans for *Il Re Lear*, see Gary Schmidgall, 'Verdi's *King Lear* Project', *19th Century Music*, 9 (1985), pp. 83–101, as well as *Shakespeare and Opera* (New York and Oxford, 1990), pp. 251–7.

what many would call each composer's greatest tragedy (*Otello* and *Tristan*, respectively).[9] Because these two composers so completely dominate the operatic canon after 1850 we tend to think of the later nineteenth century as altogether an era of tragic or otherwise 'serious' opera, whether based on popular melodrama, historical drama, mythology and legend, national historical epic, novel or other literary sources. Verdi's and Wagner's unique comic masterpieces appear as magnificent exceptions, both within their own *oeuvres* and within the repertory at large. Digging just a little way beneath the canonic stratum, of course, we can find others. Reasonably ambitious comic operas were attempted by the likes of Peter Cornelius (*Der Barbier von Bagdad*,1858), Hermann Goetz (*Der Widerspenstigen Zähmung*, 1868–72, after *The Taming of the Shrew*), Hector Berlioz (*Béatrice et Bénédict*, 1862, after *Much Ado about Nothing*), Emanuel Chabrier (*Le roi malgré lui*, 1887). Around the turn of the century there appeared a number of comic one-acters, including Eugen D'Albert's *Die Abreise* and *Flauto solo*, Richard Strauss's *Feuersnot*, Ermanno Wolf-Ferrari's *Le donne curiose* and *Il segreto di Susanna* and Puccini's *Gianni Schicchi*.

It would be tempting to attribute the decline of traditional comic opera to a more serious collective cultural frame of mind in the wake of the 1848–9 revolutions: preoccupations with national identity and autonomy, a new orientation to positivistic ideals of scientific and technological progress, and eventually even the reaction against these things in the form of aestheticism, decadence or utopian mythologising (the climate of late-century 'Wagnerism'). More important, though, was the significant increase of urban middle- and working-class populations throughout Europe and America between 1850 and 1900, creating a large new audience for popular entertainment and encouraging a greater division between the more costly, pretentious forms of 'grand' opera and light or comic genres aimed at this emerging mass market. The growing polarisation is signalled by the fact that by around 1900 'grand opera' comes to refer, in common parlance, not to the tradition of Spontini, Meyerbeer and Halévy specifically, but to the entire repertory of theatres such as La Scala, Covent Garden, the Vienna Court Opera or the Metropolitan Opera as opposed to the types of operetta, musical comedy and revues that flourished in innumerable smaller theatres throughout Europe and America. The generic and institutional gap that grew up between 'opera' as such and 'light opera' or operetta from the 1850s and 1860s on signals the beginning of an even broader polarisation between high and low, 'Classical' and popular musical cultures that becomes a defining trait of the next century (see also chapter 19).

---

9 To complete the parallel, both Verdi and Wagner boasted – if that is the word – one comic-opera fiasco towards the very beginning of their careers: *Un giorno di regno* (1840) and *Das Liebesverbot* (1836), in both cases the composer's second completed opera.

The split between traditional comic opera and a new genre of operetta begins in Paris, setting a model for the rest of Europe in this as in so many nineteenth-century cultural fashions. Already much earlier, Paris had set the precedent for distinguishing between an officially designated Opéra and other institutions of musical-theatrical entertainment – pre-eminently the Opéra-Comique, but also the many 'Boulevard' theatres of the early nineteenth century. (The initial equality of buffa and seria as two species of a single genus, 'opera', is mainly an Italian paradigm, on the other hand.) Jacques Offenbach, having failed to make inroads at the Opéra-Comique, established his own small theatre, the Bouffes Parisiens, where he produced a steady stream of popular works through the end of the Second Empire (1870), falling off somewhat after the hiatus of the Franco-Prussian War and the Paris Commune. Offenbach's earlier products for this theatre were distinguished from opéra comique by their limited dimensions (mainly in one act, with only three or four roles, and a small pit orchestra). This was due in part to bureaucratic restrictions, but also dictated by the small size of the theatres: one of Offenbach's two Parisian venues, the Salle Lacaze, seated only about 300, and the summer theatre at Bad Ems, for which he also composed, could not have been much larger. Even when the scope of his works grew, with *Orphée aux Enfers* (1858) and pieces premièred at other Parisian theatres, such as *La belle Hélène* (Variétés, 1864), *La vie parisienne* (Palais-Royal, 1866), *Fantasio* (Opéra-Comique, 1872), or his posthumous magnum opus, the 'opéra fantastique' *Les contes d'Hoffmann* (Opéra-Comique, 1881), they retained an element of vivacity and spontaneity that seems to derive from the intimate, informal conditions of his early career.

Nonetheless, the basic ingredients of Offenbach's operettas do not differ radically from those of the traditional opéra comique (also true of most German- and English-language operettas of the later nineteenth century with respect to the comic opera traditions they replaced). All make use of spoken dialogue, strophic songs (often with choral refrains), sentimental ballads and romances, a large variety of dance-based numbers, ensembles of varying complexity, and usually at least one extended finale combining solo, ensemble and choral forces. Offenbach and his collaborators appeared little concerned with establishing a consistent generic identity, however. Apart from 'opéra bouffe' or 'opéra bouffon' they sometimes retain the term 'opéra comique', or simply 'opérette' (also 'opérette bouffe'); other designations are whimsical, participating in the satiric enterprise of the works themselves: 'pièce d'occasion', 'anthropophagie musicale' (*Oyayaie, ou la reine des îles*, 1855), 'chinoiserie musicale' (*Ba-ta-clan*, 1855), 'conversation alsacienne' (*Lischen et Fritzschen*, 1863). If anything, it was the predominantly satirical, even cynical tone of the *oeuvre* that set these apart from the earlier opéra comique, which had never been wholly comic and which, with the decline of Auber's output, was increasingly turning to serious, sentimental, melodramatic or exotic subjects (tendencies that find a radical culmination in Bizet's *Carmen*).

Vienna and London had by no means lacked for popular theatrical entertainment, including much music, since the beginning of the century, but it was the example of Offenbach's *opéras bouffes*, successfully exported to both cities since about 1860 (starting with the Carltheater in Vienna in 1858) that engendered a more substantial and durable native repertory of operetta in these centres. A first result of this catalyst were the operettas of Franz von Suppé: for example, *Das Pensionat* (1860), *Pique Dame* (1862) and *Die schöne Galathee* (1865). By the time of Suppé's later successes, *Fatinitza* in 1876 and *Boccaccio* in 1879, Johann Strauss had entered the field with *Die Fledermaus* (1874), based on a text by Offenbach's own librettists Henri Meilhac and Ludovic Halévy, and eventually outstripping any of its Parisian prototypes in terms of international popularity. When the impresario John Mitchell brought Offenbach's operettas to London, they provided a point of departure for Arthur Sullivan's early musical comedies, *Cox and Box* (with F. C. Burnand, 1866), *Thespis, or the Gods Grown Old* (the first collaboration with W. S. Gilbert, incompletely preserved), and the first canonic 'Gilbert and Sullivan' operetta, *Trial by Jury* (premièred in 1875 as a curtain-raiser to a London production of Offenbach's *La Périchole*).

Where Johann Strauss's operettas naturally capitalised on the Viennese waltz idiom, of which he was already the acknowledged master, Sullivan naturalised the genre for Great Britain by incorporating a broad range of native ingredients, from allusions to Handel or the Elizabethan madrigalists (and the enduring tradition of catches and glees) to sentimental parlour songs, Scottish ballads, marching tunes, music-hall ditties, and his signature patter-songs showcasing Gilbert's brilliant verbal wit. Sullivan often inserts such overt regionalisms in stylised 'exotic' settings, such as a 'Fa-la' refrain à la Morley and Weelkes in the Japanese court of *The Mikado* or a rustic children's game-song with eminently British trochees in the picture-book Venice of *The Gondoliers*, to create an amusing cognitive-cultural dissonance.

It is characteristic of these three most successful cultivators of the new type of light opera in France, Austria-Germany and England, respectively, that each harboured ambitions to succeed in 'legitimate' opera. Even though these ambitions were at best partially realised (*Les contes d'Hoffmann*, or Sullivan's *Ivanhoe* of 1890–1), they left their mark on the scope of some of these composers' later comic opera scores, in terms of orchestration, harmonic palette, extended ensemble writing, and deepened 'expressive' vocal writing that sometimes – with Sullivan, for instance – is wilfully at odds with the satirical manner of the texts.[10]

---

10 Carl Dahlhaus makes this point with respect to Offenbach in *Nineteenth-Century Music*, trans. J. B. Robinson (Berkeley and Los Angeles, 1989), p. 230. I would argue that it applies even more to Sullivan – sometimes with Gilbert, but sometimes despite him.

One place where the relation of operetta to the operatic tradition can be appreciated in all its dynamic ambivalence is in the ensemble-finale, precisely where comic and serious opera had joined hands back in the later eighteenth century. The grandiose, inflated finale structures of French and Italian Romantic opera (or Wagner's 'Romantic operas'), with their stylised and schematic dramaturgy, were by now ripe for parody. Effective as these could be, as musical-dramatic tableaux or set pieces, they also epitomised the fine line between the venerable operatic aesthetic of the 'marvellous', on one hand, and the dramaturgically incredible or preposterous, on the other. Here was an opportunity for operetta composers to satirise the excess of grand opera and operatic melodrama while at the same time indulging their own ambitions to create longer, more complex ensembles. The central finales to Offenbach' s *La Périchole* (1868, libretto by Meilhac and Halévy) and Gilbert and Sullivan's *Ruddigore* (1887), for example, both generate parody from a stylistically inverted response to a stock 'grand finale' situation, touched off by some shocking peripiteia. At the same time, both use the object of operatic parody as a means to infuse the operetta genre with greater aesthetic weight or substance.

In *La Périchole*, the humble protagonist Piquillo has discovered that his sweetheart and fellow street-singer ('La Périchole') has become the mistress of the Viceroy of Peru, while he has been hoodwinked into a sham marriage with her to provide a shield of legal respectability. After Piquillo agrees to present his new 'wife' at court (in a short, animated 'Rondeau de bravoure'), he thrusts her to the ground before the Viceroy in a gesture reminiscent of Alfredo's frenzied denunciation of Violetta in the Act II finale of *La traviata*. The *grand mouvement d'indignation* that greets this gesture, however, does not take the expected 'operatic' form of a broad, slow-tempo *concertato* of general stupefaction – but quite the opposite: Don Andrès, the courtiers, and the insulted Périchole join in a lively *galop*, sharply profiling the rhythm of the words 'Sautez dessus/Sautons dessus' ('Seize him/Let us seize him'). This gives way to a slower ensemble, but every bit as lighthearted, in which the phrase 'aux maris récalcitrants' ('to stubborn husbands') is humorously dissected to a lilting waltz tune, with a suggestive kick to each dismembered syllable of the word *récalcitrants*. An up-tempo *stretta* follows, preserving something of the conventional finale dynamic. Still, the whole series of movements (including Piquillo's *rondeau*) conveys the determination of Offenbach's comic characters not to let any situation get the better of their indomitable high spirits.

The Act I finale of Gilbert and Sullivan's *Ruddigore* centres on the revelation by the caricatured melodramatic villain, Sir Despard, that the apparently humble protagonist of this piece, Robin Oakapple, is none other than the rightful heir to the 'cursed' baronetcy of Ruddigore, Sir Ruthven Murgatroyd.[11] Like the *Périchole* finale, it is compounded of short solos, choral songs and dance numbers (with some parodied dramatic recitative and scena connectors). Following another of Sullivan's neo-Elizabethan madrigals, a pastoral gavotte is drastically interrupted by Sir Despard, to a shrieking diminished-seventh chord. (Both madrigal and gavotte are further examples of the composer's fondness for historical pastiche.) But, as in Offenbach, the agitated scena to which the revelation unfolds fails to prompt the appropriate operatic response of broad-paced lyrical stupefaction. Instead, characters take turns responding to the situation in simple song-like movements, while Robin engages the chorus in a quick ensemble whose dactylic metre naturally takes the form of a lively jig ('When I'm a bad Bart. I will tell taradiddles, / I'll play a bad part on the falsest of fiddles').[12] The finale is extended by various ruses, such as rapidly shifting marital configurations to keep the omnipresent chorus of Bridesmaids occupied, and it concludes with another jig-like ensemble and general dance. The parodistic targets of melodrama and 'grand opera' are thus played off against the other generic ingredients of the piece: pastoral comedy and the folkloric 'pageant'.

The Act II finale of Johann Strauss jr.'s *Zigeunerbaron* (1885, libretto by Ignatz Schnitzer, after Maurus Jókai) shares with the first-act finale to *Ruddigore* a tendency towards pageant or revue of patriotic and nostalgic *topoi*, while further approaching grand-operatic dimensions. In Gilbert and Sullivan this is usually linked to an affectionate parody of national institutions, such as the army or the navy, parliament, the legal system, banking and finance, or, above all, the aristocracy. Here, the incidental mention of Vienna by the Imperial Commissioner for Morality (*Sittenkommissar*) touches off the finale with a waltz-song in praise of the city's seductive charms, while much of the rest of the scene is devoted to a staging of the alleged origins of the Hungarian national dance type, the *Verbunkos* or 'recruiting song'. Rather than the 'moral' shock that initiates dramatic ensemble finales, this one parodies the comic expedient of a suddenly disclosed identity, when the assembled cast reacts with an implicit wink and a nudge to the piece of paper ('Ein Dokument, das niemand kennt!') revealing the gypsy girl, Saffi, to be the daughter of the 'last Pasha of Temesvar'. The slightness of the dramatic material and the tendency of the score – despite its lavish craftsmanship – to regress towards revue or pot-pourri are what mainly distinguish Strauss's most ambitious operetta from examples of 'high' operatic comedy in the later Romantic era.

11 Apart from parodying the spoken melodrama that remained popular in Victorian Britain, *Ruddigore* includes more-or-less explicit send-ups of elements from *Il trovatore*, *Lucia di Lammermoor* (in the character of 'Mad Margaret'), and Marschner's *Der Vampyr* (in 'Sir Ruthven').

12 Robin's lines satirise the melodramatic convention of the villainous minor aristocrat: here, the 'bad Baronet (Bart.) of Ruddigore'.

The two outstanding examples of 'high' or serious comic opera in the later nineteenth century, *Die Meistersinger* and *Falstaff*, are exceptional products within their own authors' respective *oeuvres*, who were anything but specialists in comic opera. In each case, a considerable period of time elapsed between the composer's first notion of a comic 'experiment' and the final realisation of the project. Both composers felt self-conscious, in some degree, about embarking on a comic opera in the period of their artistic maturity. Wagner sketched his ideas for a comedy on Hans Sachs and the mastersinger guilds of Renaissance Germany in August 1845, just after completing *Tannhäuser*. (It was to have been a comic pendant, or 'satyr-play', to the serious treatment of the song-contest motif in the earlier opera.) Verdi claimed to have first turned his thoughts towards opera buffa sometime between 1850 and 1860, if not earlier.[13] The public finally heard *Die Meistersinger* on Midsummer Day (21 June) 1868 at the Munich Court Opera. *Falstaff* took longer still, premièring at La Scala on 9 February 1893.

Neither work owes anything, or anything significant, to existing examples of comic opera. Both Wagner and Verdi seem to have concocted from the ingredients of their own mature operas a supple, flexible idiom perfectly suited to their needs. (In both cases they had done *some* prior experimentation along these lines: Wagner in parts of *Das Rheingold* and the first two acts of *Siegfried*, Verdi in the role of Melitone in *La forza del destino* and parts of *Ballo in maschera*, for example.) The results of these 'experimental' comedies were also immediately fruitful in their impact on younger contemporaries.[14] More than the *Ring* operas or *Tristan und Isolde*, Wagner's *Meistersinger* furnished a whole generation of German composers (Hermann Goetz, Heinrich Hoffmann, Engelbert Humperdinck, Eugen D'Albert, Richard Strauss, Hugo Wolf in *Der Corregidor*, and Hans Pfitzner in his early operas and parts of *Palestrina*) with a practical model for reconciling naturalistic declamation and pacing of dialogue with melodic lines maintaining musical interest, continuity, character and variety. And as antithetical as the ebullient wit of *Falstaff* might seem to the aims of the *verismo* generation, the quickly shifting, mosaic-like surfaces of the score and the short, highly contrasted musical paragraphs from which the score is constructed had an evident impact on Puccini (parts of *La bohème* and *Madama*

---

13 On the first conception of the *Meistersinger* project see Wagner, *My Life*, pp. 302–3; on Verdi's initial thoughts of an opera buffa, following the great successes of *Rigoletto* and *Trovatore*, see Julian Budden, *Operas of Verdi*, III (New York, 1981), pp. 417–18.

14 The influence of both these 'exceptional' works did not extend to establishing a new genre of comic opera, however, as Sieghart Döhring and Sabine Henze-Döhring point out (*Oper und Musikdrama Um 19. Jahrhundert*, Handbuch der musikalischen Gattungen 13 [Laaber, 1997], p. 305); their influence was rather a matter of creative responses to the individual works as such.

Butterfly, for instance, and the comedy *Gianni Schicchi*), the comedies of Ermanno Wolf-Ferrari, and the sparkling, sociable backgrounds that serve as a foil in veristic dramas by Cilèa (*Adriana Lecouvreur*) or Giordano (*Fedora*).

While *Die Meistersinger* and *Falstaff* create musical worlds entirely unlike one another, they do exhibit certain parallels (beyond biographical circumstances) that might be symptomatic of the position of a high, 'Classical' genre of operatic comedy in the era of incipient modernism. Both inhabit a historically precise setting that is, from a modern perspective, a kind of fantasy realm, a bourgeois arcadia or golden age (Renaissance Nuremberg, Tudor England). Operetta or 'realist' drama are at home in the modern city, as comedy of this sort is not. This element of Romantic fantasy is epitomised in each work by a dream-like nocturnal contretemps: Walther and Magdalena's foiled elopement, Falstaff's foiled double-rendezvous in Windsor Forest. Both episodes constitute a crux in the structure of the comedy, and at the same time signal its rootedness in the customs and artifice of a vanished world of serenades, masquerades, and the premodern night in which identities could be traded at will. If Wagner's comedy develops loftier themes (the quarrel of ancient and modern art, Sachs's Schopenhauerian resignation) than the elegant farce of Boito and Verdi, the libretti of both works revel in similarly recondite vocabulary: Wagner's quaintly archaic *Meister*-babble and Boito's latinised 'Shakespeare'. The musical setting of this language, often at lightning speeds and/or in fabulously complicated contrapuntal and harmonic textures, further removes it from easy accessibility. Wagner's and Verdi's scores transmute this elaborate comic verse into an astoundingly detailed, ornate musical *objet d'art*, like the work of some master craftsman out of Sachs's Nuremberg. Comic opera becomes 'serious art' not so much by virtue of treating weighty themes (*pace* Hans Sachs) alongside the usual Romantic escapades, but by lavishing on the realisation of stock plot ingredients a degree of creative finesse virtually unknown since Mozart.

Wagner and the 'music drama'

Richard Wagner's initial aims to reform the world of opera, and thereby the world itself, happen to conform to a neat chronological boundary around 1850. This is due in part to the impact of the 1848–9 revolutions and Wagner's role in them. It was upon finding himself suddenly a political exile from Germany, following his involvement in the May 1849 insurrection in Dresden, that Wagner paused to take stock of his career, as well as the situation of opera and the arts generally in modern society. But it was also the utopian pamphleteering spirit of 1848–9, the loquacious philosophising that gripped so many of this post-Hegelian generation, that moved Wagner to formulate his ideas in the trilogy commonly referred to as the 'Zurich writings' or 'reform essays': *Art and Revolution* (1849), *The Art-Work of the Future* (1849), and *Opera and Drama* (1850–51). In the first two of these essays Wagner nearly outdoes Hegel in the breadth, not to say vagueness, of his world-historical imaginings. It is not so much the immediate revolutionary movement of mid-century Europe that concerns him, but an ongoing 'Great Revolution of Mankind', traced back to the disintegration of Greek tragedy into the 'separate arts' and forward into a utopian future.[15] Society and culture have a common mission to free themselves from existing economic and political structures, along with the compromised artistic institutions predicated on these, and to reconstruct a new order in harmony with Nature, the human body, and 'natural' ideals of human love and brotherhood.

The Zurich writings as a group offer ample testimony to Wagner's consciousness of having embarked on a revolutionary 'new path' after 1850. The central and longest essay, *Opera and Drama*, is principally concerned with explaining how and why his musical-dramatic 'total artwork of the future' would render the whole concept of 'opera' obsolete. In the subsequent *Communication to my Friends* of 1851, a kind of artistic autobiography connecting his theories of operatic and cultural reform to his own career, he again insisted on the break from opera as a genre and an institution (prefacing his plans for a drama on the *Nibelungenlied* and related Siegfried myths): 'I will write no more operas; [but] since I do not wish to invent any arbitrary designation for my works, I call them simply dramas, since this at least makes clear the perspective from which they should received' (*Gesammelte Schriften*, IV, p. 343n.). Yet Wagner preferred not to think that he was providing models of a new genre of 'music drama' that *other* librettists and composers might readily emulate. Reflecting in 1872 on the designation now commonly applied to his works ('On the Term "Music Drama"') he famously, and somewhat coyly, advanced the phrase 'deeds of music become visible' (*ersichtlich gewordene Taten der Musik*) as an apt locution, shifting the accent from words to music, or rather, to music as the idealised quintessence of dramatic 'action' ('deeds') (*Gesammelte Schriften*, IX, p. 306). But as that term was too grandiloquent even for Wagner to consider seriously, 'music drama' has remained the generic rubric of choice for his works starting with *Das Rheingold* (completed 1854) and, to a lesser extent, for those operas up through the turn-of-the-century most perceptibly orientated towards the Wagnerian model.

The defining attributes of this new genre, or quasi-genre, are easily enough enumerated, whether or not it was indeed so entirely different from 'opera' as

---

15 Wagner, *Die Kunst und die Revolution*, in *Gesammelte Schriften und Dichtungen* (Leipzig, 1887–1911), III, p. 29.

Wagner would have it. Most familiar, perhaps, is the aim to replace the conventional economy of recitative or scena and formal musical 'numbers' with a more naturalistic, continuous musical discourse built around the principle of dramatic dialogue. Like most of the other features of the Wagnerian music drama, this can be seen as a radical application of existing tendencies. As foreshadowed in *Lohengrin*, for example, the musical dialogue of Wagner's later dramas is clearly indebted to the increasingly free alternation of declamatory and lyrical segments within the 'scene and duet' of the international operatic styles of the 1830s and 1840s. The extension of such techniques within Wagner's music dramas, however, is predicated on another central, defining attribute: the 'symphonic' conception of the orchestral accompaniment. This does not signify so much an autonomy of musical structure (which Wagner had criticised, after all, in the lyric forms of conventional opera), but a kind of developmental musical logic or coherence that could be heard as responding to, and amplifying, the dramatic text of the vocal lines.[16]

A key factor linking these levels of orchestral and vocal-dramatic discourse is the 'leitmotif', another term attached to Wagner's methods independently of his own writings, but one that remains indispensable in denoting the thematic ideas associated with various aspects of the drama and its characters, binding together the musical score at many levels.[17] By elevating the existing practice of the 'reminiscence motif' to a system of musical-dramatic reference embracing the entire thematic substance of the score, this 'symphonic' accompaniment remains in constant dialogue with the dramatic text, rather than reverting to a musical-formal autonomy of the kind Wagner had denounced in his writings. Finally, Wagner claimed that mythology provided the subject-matter best suited to his ideal musical-dramatic artwork because of its foregrounding of symbolically and psychologically charged figures, situations and plots, eschewing the prosaic, 'arbitrary' complications of historical-political intrigue or the comedy of manners that merely distract from music's transcendental expressive vocation. The pedigree of the *Gesamtkunstwerk* in the ancient Greek tragedy was another factor, as was presumably the ethos of the 'marvellous' going back to the origins of opera. If we consider *Die Meistersinger* a music drama, of course, then myth (strictly defined) cannot be included as a defining feature, though most of those who emulated Wagner later in the century did turn to mythological or legendary material of one kind or another.

16 Carl Dahlhaus connects this symphonic principle (which he speaks of in terms of motivic 'logic' predicated on a Beethovenian model) with other pretensions to high cultural significance as what distinguishes Wagner's music drama from 'opera', taking 'a genre previously half ceremonial pomp, half entertainment' and declaring it to be 'the *ne plus ultra* of art' (*Nineteenth-Century Music*, p. 195).

17 See T. Grey, '... *wie ein rother Faden*: On the Origins of "Leitmotif" as Critical Construct and Musical Practice', in Ian Bent (ed.), *Music Theory in the Age of Romanticism* (Cambridge, 1996), pp. 187–210.

Wagner's theorising about the ideal musical drama or *Gesamtkunstwerk* had as its conscious object the *Ring of the Nibelung* project. The first idea for a *Nibelung* opera had been sketched in 1848, as had the complete poetic draft of *Siegfrieds Tod* (Siegfried's Death), which would eventually serve (with relatively few textual changes) as the libretto of *Götterdämmerung*. Within a few months of completing *Opera and Drama* Wagner went on to expand his Siegfried drama into the tetralogy as we know it, completing the poetic text before the end of 1852. Hence *Götterdämmerung* still contains traces of the 'grand heroic opera' Wagner had first conceived, presumably, to be set in a style resembling that of *Lohengrin*: Siegfried and Gunther sing an operatic oath-swearing duet in Act I, for example, and Gunther, Hagen and Brünnhilde swear vengeance on Siegfried's (rigged) betrayal of his oath in parallel poetic verses, darkly juxtaposed with the celebration of Siegfried's marriage to Gutrune – a piece of pure grand-opera dramaturgy for the conclusion of Act II. Working his way backward to the drama's mythical prologue, *Das Rheingold*, Wagner divested this last conceived (though first composed) instalment of the tetralogy of any such 'operatic' traces. Apart from the Rhine-maidens' song to the Gold in scene 1 and its lamenting counterpart near the conclusion, it consists strictly of dialogue and monologue, the latter not generally in the form of reflective aria-like soliloquies, but in narratives or speeches addressed to other characters.

The musical-dramatic ideal towards which Wagner was groping, conceptually, in *Opera and Drama* seems to be fully realised first in *Die Walküre* (completed in March 1856). The first act of the drama traces a steady dramatic trajectory from the chance meeting of the Volsung twins Siegmund and Sieglinde through the gradual process of mutual recognition. The basic conflict propelling the action is Hunding's instinctive suspicion of his uninvited guest and subsequent realisation that this is the very enemy he and the Neidings have just been pursuing (another recognition process). After the vigorous, 'naturalistic' prelude depicting the storm that drives Siegmund on to the scene, the musical realisation of this broadly paced recognition process moves from (1) hesitant, fragmentary gestures of emotional sympathy between the twins through (2) extended narratives that accumulate important layers of personal and musical (leitmotivic) history, to (3) the ever-widening arcs of lyrical passion unleashed with Siegmund's so-called 'Spring Song' ('Winterstürme wichen dem Wonnemond'), culminating in (4) the ecstatic moment of explicit mutual recognition as Siegmund draws the sword 'Nothung' from the ash tree. Throughout all this, tempo, rhythmic activity and orchestration increase by fits and starts, responding to the shifting contours of the dramatic situation, but sometimes seeming to prompt the action, too. The whole can be viewed as a kind of dynamic concatenation of mostly brief musical 'periods', loosely cohering in terms of tonal and motivic content, and thus corresponding to the notion of the 'poetic-musical period' Wagner had tried to describe in Part 3 of *Opera and Drama* as the basic dramatic-musical building blocks of his new kind of musical drama.[18] Dramatic and musical interest are cultivated in tandem, rather than in alternation: this would express, in a nutshell, the distinction (in Wagner's critique) between opera and his own ideal of 'musical drama'.

The deployment of a network of referential 'leitmotifs' – restated, developed and transformed in accordance with the needs of the drama – to generate some loosely construed 'symphonic' quality in Wagner's scores was surely among the most influential features of his legacy, although few composers applied the technique so consistently as Wagner did in the *Ring*, for fear of appearing derivative, perhaps, or because over-reliance on the method was suspected of leading to mechanical, inartistic results.

The versatility of leitmotif, in Wagner's hands, can be illustrated by the motif associated with Wotan and Valhalla, one that maintains a steady presence almost from beginning to end of the cycle. This motif is given a formal exposition at the beginning of scene 2 of *Das Rheingold*, where it appears in its characteristic key of D flat, regally but quietly in middle-to-low brass, accompanied by harps and low string tremolo. The motif has elements of fanfare and march, but its slow $\frac{3}{4}$ metre inflects these with a flowing, meditative quality. It has often been remarked how this motif can be heard to derive from the slow iterations of the 'Ring' motif across the preceding transition, thus creating a semantic link between the Ring's corrupting force and the image of power represented by the fortress Valhalla. While here and throughout *Das Rheingold* this motif is chiefly associated with the fortress itself, and the desire for a secure, invincible power It represents, its field of reference will extend to the character of Wotan in all the subsequent dramas. (Such transferability of reference obtains to many motifs throughout the cycle.) The Valhalla motif and its meanings are parodied by Loge in scene 3 of *Rheingold* when he mocks Alberich's fantasies of world-domination to a *scherzando*, A major transformation and fragmentation. Wotan eventually recapitulates it in D flat against shimmering high string tremolos as the gods prepare to take up residence in Valhalla at the end of the opera ('Abendlich strahlt der Sonne Auge'), reinforcing the idea that this, like other central motifs, is identified with a certain tonic or home key from which appearances in other keys might be heard as significant departures. In the narratives of the Volsung twins in Act I of *Die Walküre*,

---

18 See T. Grey, *Wagner's Musical Prose: Texts and Contexts* (Cambridge, 1995), chapter 4 ('The "Poetic-Musical Period" and the "Evolution" of Wagnerian Form'), where the 'Annunciation of Death' scene (the confrontation between Brünnhilde, as valkyrie, and Siegmund) is also interpreted as an evolving series of 'poetic-musical periods'.

for instance, the Valhalla motif, sonically 'disguised' by E major harmony and subdued string timbres, underscores allusions to Wotan's mortal disguise, a secret even to the narrators themselves. When in *Siegfried* Wotan adopts the incognito of 'the Wanderer' his motivic identity is traded for a wholly new one (the so-called 'Wanderer chords'). But Wotan is able to maintain a numinous or 'virtual' musical presence even throughout *Götterdämmerung* – where his character as such is entirely absent – through the original Valhalla motif in various tonal and timbral guises, at last returned to its 'tonic' D flat, in the full orchestra, as we glimpse the destruction of Walhalla prior to the final curtain.

This capacity of leitmotifs to signal the continuing presence of the past was one that especially attracted Wagner, even on a theoretical level, as demonstrated by his remarks on an unrealised plan for a Buddhist drama involving the theme of reincarnation (*Die Sieger*, or 'The Victors', sketched in 1856). 'The simple story owed its significance to the way that the past life of the suffering principal characters was entwined in the new phase of their lives as being still present time', Wagner recalled in *My Life*. 'I perceived at once how the musical remembrance of this dual life, keeping the past constantly present in the hearing, might be represented perfectly to the emotional receptivities' – that is, through the use of leitmotifs.[19] In *Die Sieger*, the Buddha would have been depicted in the position of the audience of Wagner's dramas, able to read the traces of characters' past lives and ancestry from the musical 'aura' surrounding them.

Finally, the deformation and recombination of leitmotifs provided an important expressive and semantic resource in the music drama to which non-dramatic music had no legitimate claim, in Wagner's view. When Wotan, in the peroration of his great monologue in Act II of *Die Walküre*, despairingly abdicates his 'will to power' in favour of Alberich's misbegotten son (Hagen), the orchestra spits out a fierce diminished-seventh harmonisation of the Valhalla motif superimposed on the 'Rhine-Gold' motif, led from C minor to V of A minor and back ('So nimm meinen Segen, Niblungen Sohn!'). Because the two motifs have been heard originally in consonant triadic form (as Wagner explains in the 1879 essay 'On the Application of Music to the Drama'), and associated – textually and scenically – with Valhalla and the Rhine-Gold, respectively, the listener is in a position to interpret the expressive significance of this distorted combination, elicited by the tortured confessions of Wotan's text (cf. *Gesammelte Schriften*, vol. 10, pp. 187–8).

If the music drama could boast of having absorbed the techniques and aesthetic prestige of the symphony, after Beethoven, it was the absorption of these

---

19 Wagner, *My Life*, p. 528. On the significance of leitmotif technique as a means of externalising the dramatic past within the dramatic present, see also Dahlhaus, *Nineteenth-Century Music*, pp. 201–2.

things into a dramatic-linguistic context that was seen as giving symphonic technique a new lease on life and a newer, higher claim to cultural significance. For Wagner, symphony and opera alike were 'redeemed' for the future in the musical-dramatic *Gesamtkunstwerk*.

The grand opera legacy and the colonisation of the exotic

From an historical perspective the period from the 1850s to the 1880s was clearly dominated by the figures of Verdi, the acknowledged master of 'traditional' opera, and Wagner, the icon of operatic revolution, reform and 'progress'. Yet Meyerbeer's grand operas up through *Le prophète* continued to provide an influential model for large-scale works in many areas of style and subject, whether historical, nationalistic, mythical-legendary or exotic-orientalist.[20] Meyerbeer's own long-deferred and final collaboration with Eugène Scribe, *L'Africaine* (posthumously premièred 28 April 1865 at the Paris Opéra), preserves many of the familiar ingredients of their earlier 'classics' of the genre, while its marriage of semi-historical plot with exotic local colour points towards much repertory of the following decades.

Indeed, just as rapid economic and population growth fuelled the immense colonial expansion of European powers over the later nineteenth century, Parisian-style grand opera (itself a potent symbol of nineteenth-century European power, at many levels) increasingly turned to exotic, 'oriental', antique, or otherwise fantastic material during this period to supply itself with novel and appealing elements of spectacle and dramatic conflict. Many of Jules Massenet's works in the 'grand' manner are paradigmatic in this regard: for example, *Le roi de Lahore* (1877), *Hérodiade* (1881), *Le Cid* (1885), *Esclarmonde* (1889) and *Thaïs* (1894). The Carthaginian acts of Berlioz's otherwise *sui generis* masterpiece, *Les Troyens* (composed 1856–8, partial première 1863) already participate in the 'orientalisation' of grand opera, even if the colonial trajectory of Virgil's epic moves from east (Troy) to west (Rome), via North Africa. The general tendency for works in the tradition of grand opera to explore the geographically and/or chronologically remote is evident in a wide range of post-1850 operas by the likes of Charles Gounod (*Sappho*, 1851; *La reine de Saba*, 1862), Félicien David (*La perle du Brésil*, 1851, rev. 1859–61; *Herculanum*, 1859), Ernest Reyer (*Sigurd*, 1884; *Salammbô*, 1890), as well as many non-French

20 Cf. Döhring and Henze-Döhring, *Oper und Musikdrama*, p. 217, who point out how *Le prophète* represents the culmination of the classical age of Parisian grand opera, while the opera's musical characterisations, scene construction, its 'intense dramatic flair', and the high level of production values it presupposes made it a benchmark for the later nineteenth century.

works influenced by the genre: Boïto's *Mefistofele* (1868, rev. 1875), Carlos Gomes's *Il Guarany* (1870), Verdi's *Aïda* (1871), Borodin's *Prince Igor* (composed 1869–87, performed 1890), Karl Goldmark's *Königin von Saba* (1875), the 'biblical' operas of Anton Rubinstein (*Die Maccabäer, Sulamith, Moses*) or his *Neron* (1879), down through Alberto Franchetti's *Cristoforo Colombo* (1892). Even as he was trying to complete *L'Africaine* in the early 1860s, Meyerbeer confided to Camille Du Locle his fear that 'the old forms are wearing out, [and] the five-act opera is no longer possible'.[21] But if Parisian-style grand opera seemed in imminent danger of becoming moribund and collapsing under its own, ever-accumulating weight, it still remained the most influential, prestigious international style up to the end of the century and the rise of Wagnerism, *drame lyrique* and *verismo*. (Another factor in this prolonged afterlife of grand opera, discussed further below, was the suitability of the genre to the staging of nationalist epics.)

   L'Africaine preserves the attributes of traditional grand opera in relatively pure form – scarcely surprising, as a product of the Scribe–Meyerbeer team, with roots stretching back to the 1840s. The hero, Vasco da Gama, is embroiled in a conventional love-triangle when his beloved Inès is promised to Don Pédro, head of the Portuguese royal council and thus Vasco's social superior. But Scribe adds a second, more interesting complication in the infatuation of Sélika (queen of an indeterminate Brahmin domain in the Indian Ocean, and sold into slavery) with the Portuguese explorer Vasco, along with hints of jealousy on the part of her companion Nélusko. These amorous affinities are channelled into the usual variety of *romances*, grand duets and ensemble finales in which (respectively) the characters express their emotions privately, confess them to each other, and react to the varied impediments to their love (or ambition, in Vasco's case). Assemblies of state, priests, a grand inquisitor, sailors, a great tempest at sea (culminating in an attack on the Portuguese vessel by Sélika's countrymen), Brahmin ritual, and the spectacle of tropical paradise (the famous tenor aria, 'O paradis, sorti de l'onde') form diverse characteristic backdrops to the intrigue, providing related musical opportunities for ceremony, *divertissement* and *couleur locale*. Acts I and II culminate in the type of grand concerted finale typical for opening and/or central acts in this genre. The third-act finale is a more concentrated scenic *coup de théâtre*, with plenty of action (the storm and attack on Don Pédro's ship).

   A novel and influential piece of dramaturgy is introduced in the last act of *L'Africaine*. Fifth-act finales in grand opera had traditionally favoured a terse,

---

21 Henri Blaze de Bury, *Meyerbeer et son temps* (Paris, 1865), p. 297. Cf. Döhring and Henze-Döhring, *Oper und Musikdrama*, p. 220, and A. Gerhard, *The Urbanization of Opera: Music Theater in Paris in the Nineteenth Century*, trans. M Whittall (Chicago, 1998), p. 397.

clinching action. As in Italian *melodramma*, the last-act finale often involved a murder, suicide or other violent action that served as an emphatic punctuation to the concluding scene. A long-standing feature was of course the spectacular catastrophe, with the tumult of chorus and orchestra accompanying some local or global apocalypse. (Last Judgement scenes concluding Halévy's *Le juif errant* of 1852 and David's *Herculanum* of 1859 seem to mark the last gasp of this effect.) But in *L'Africaine*, the brief encounter of Nélusko and the dying Sélika (followed by a perfunctory choral catharsis of some dozen bars) is quite over-shadowed by an extended dramatic-lyrical monologue for the heroine *in extremis*: the 'Grand scène du mancellier'.[22] Other late transformations of grand opera – such as *Les Troyens*, *Götterdämmerung* and *Aïda* – likewise feature such a climactic scena for the expiring heroine; but it is also found in works quite independent of that prototype (*Tristan und Isolde*, Massenet's *Manon*, or even Puccini's *Madama Butterfly* and Strauss's *Salome*).

The exotic subject-matter of *L'Africaine* belongs to the type James Parakilas calls the 'Age of Discovery' opera,[23] more characteristic of the early nineteenth century (Spontini's *Fernand Cortez*, Spohr's *Jessonda*), although it continued with David's *Perle du Brésil* (1851) and Gomes's *Il Guarany* (1870, discussed below). Unlike the feminisation of the exotic that typifies operatic 'orientalism' in the later nineteenth century (Saint-Saëns's *Samson et Dalila*, Delibes's *Lakmé*, Goldmark's *Königin von Saba* or even Bizet's *Carmen*), it is the male-dominated religious/political collective that carries the musical markers of the exotic in this older tradition (with roots in the 'Turkish' themes of the previous century). Where in the later repertory, the wild, strange 'otherness' of the exotic female is the essence of her allure for the European protagonist (and audience), the heroines in this older tradition become suitable objects of desire only insofar as their music manifests more 'universal' feminine values and virtues: purity, modesty, steadfastness, noble bearing and poetic sensibility.

Apart from the fact that European colonialism was reaching its peak between the 1870s and 1890s, the transportation of grand opera to 'oriental', tropical or wholly fantastic climes is logically motivated by the dramaturgy of spectacle and tableau, as well as by the perennial gambit of lovers thwarted by opposing allegiances. While it might be argued that the impulse to represent foreign, exotic cultures within the aristocratic European genre of opera was an inherently imperialistic one (analogous to importation of Egyptian, Greek or Middle-Eastern artefacts or whole archaeological sites to the museums of the

22 Döhring and Henze-Döhring give a philological as well as music-dramaturgical analysis of Sélika's final scene in *Oper und Musikdrama*, pp. 220–3.

23 J. Parakilas, 'The Soldier and the Exotic: Operatic Variations on a Theme of Racial Encounter', *The Opera Quarterly*, 10/2 (1992–93), pp. 33–56 (here 35–8); and 10/3 (1994), pp. 43–68.

modern European metropolis), the operatic 'colonisation' of the Orient, Africa and the New World was also simply a matter of expanding the repertory of scenic-musical spectacle. Of the available cultural media, opera was the best suited to realising the image of these new – or archaic – worlds for the modern Western public, however stylised and imaginary the results. The realisation of feudal and early modern life on the operatic stage of the 1830s and 1840s in courtly, ecclesiastical, military and pastoral scenes or other natural landscapes found ready equivalents in exotic (as well as archaic and legendary) materials of later grand operas.[24] The political or class differences that divide tenor and soprano in medieval and Renaissance European settings were also easily transposed to racial and cultural differences between European and 'other'. Religion provides an important thread of continuity, too. The dilemmas of Catholic vs. Protestant or Jew (*Les Huguenots*, *La Juive*) translate smoothly into those of European Christians vs. Buddhists, Muslims or, more generally, the supernatural realm. In any of these contexts, religious dogma and the ceremonial pomp representing it also symbolise the rigid social and moral norms against which the Romantic subjectivity of operatic hero and heroine rebels – usually in vain.

Two of the relatively few operas by Jules Massenet to receive premières on the stage of the Paris Opéra itself (housed in the splendid Palais Garnier since 1875) are good examples of the grand opera genre in its post-Meyerbeer phase: the 'breakthrough' work of Massenet's career, *Le roi de Lahore* (1877), and *Le Cid* from 1885, when the composer's reputation was reaching its zenith.

Le roi de Lahore, to a text by Louis Gallet (who would furnish the composer with several more exotic and biblical subjects), picks up and amplifies the Indian/Brahmin ambience of *L'Africaine*. The fact that the score may draw on an earlier, uncompleted project set during the crusades (*Les Templiers*) suggests how easily the basic musical framework of 'historical' grand opera could be adapted to new exotic or legendary settings, with the appropriate local colour inserted or adjusted as necessary. The signal success of this early Massenet opera owes much to Gallet's expertly crafted libretto, which offered the composer all the classic ingredients of grand opera freshly conceived in a picturesque-exotic setting well-suited to Massenet's talents for orchestral mood- and tone-painting (for example, the extensive Act III divertissement representing the Paradise of Indra, a Hindu 'Elysian Fields' from whence the eponymous King, Alim, is sent back to earth as a beggar to reclaim his love, the priestess Sîta). Ritual scenes, the tableau of public shock and indignation (when the jealous royal minister Scindia reveals the King's dalliance with the priestess in the Act I finale), the counter-

---

24 Carl Dahlhaus remarks that local colour, whether as the contribution of stage designers or as a musical category, represents 'a confluence of characteristic nineteenth-century trends towards archaism, folklorism, and exoticism' (*Nineteenth-Century Music*, p. 128).

point of offstage battle with onstage evening idyll in Act II, the stupefaction of the crowd when Alim returns from the dead to his own court at Lahore, the usual duet scenes of attraction and repulsion – all of these are handled by Massenet with a fine instinct for how best to fulfil the requisites of the genre without, as Norbert Miller puts it, 'trying to overcome it'.[25]

Massenet's *Le Cid*, first produced at the Paris Opéra on 30 November 1885, exemplifies the longevity of historical grand opera in the nineteenth century. The material is drawn from Corneille's 1636 drama and an earlier Spanish prototype by Guillén de Castro y Bellvís, and offers all the standard requisites: a medieval, chivalric milieu with abundant opportunities for regal, hieratic and folkloristic spectacle, and a pair of high-born lovers whose dilemma (Rodrigue is forced to slay Chimène's father to sustain the honour of his own, Don Diègue) is more intense and more volatile than usual. Massenet's realisation of the Spanish-Moorish local colour, especially in the rich-hued ballet music for Act II, is one decidedly contemporary aspect of the score. As with other late grand operas (those of Saint-Saëns, for instance, or Verdi's *Aïda*), the score is divided into acts and scenes, or tableaux, but not formally defined numbers. Even so, it is easy enough to discern the outlines of the traditional types, ranging from large introduction and finale complexes to the 'grand scene and aria' of Chimène in Act III, scene 1, the dramatic scene and duet that follows, the short *preghiera* with chorus (the apparition of St Jaques to Rodrigue), or, of course, the instrumental overture, *entr'actes* and dances.

It is the fairly conservative observance of grand operatic dramaturgy in Massenet's *Le Cid* that guarantees an effective pacing of the whole. Precisely this sense of pacing, proportion and contrast is what is lost when ambitious but less experienced composers set out to 'liberate' opera from its conventions, as can be seen, for example, in Peter Cornelius's treatment of the same material in his 'lyrical drama in three acts', *Der Cid* (1860–3, premièred Weimar, 1865). As one of the more gifted protégés of Liszt and Wagner, Cornelius naturally took the latter's *Lohengrin* as a point of orientation, suggested also by the charismatic chivalric hero and the early feudal setting. On to this example he grafted some fruits of the harmonic experimentation carried out by Wagner and Liszt over the 1850s. Through his choice of material, Cornelius necessarily engaged with the spirit of historical grand opera, even as he sought to challenge it, rather as Wagner had done in *Tannhäuser* and *Lohengrin*. Yet, lacking the 'symphonic' impetus of Wagner's later dramas and Wagner's own intimate familiarity with the original grand opera prototypes, the result is eminently less stage-worthy than Massenet's more conservative treatment of the same drama.

25 Norbert Miller, 'Massenet: *Le Roi de Lahore*', in *Pipers Enzyklopädie des Musiktheaters*, ed. Carl Dahlhaus and Sieghart Döhring, 7 vols. (Munich and Zurich, 1986–97), III, p. 736.

In Italy the legacy of Meyerbeerian grand opera proved to be even more long-lived, perhaps because it did not really take root there until the 1850s and 1860s, several decades later than its beginnings in France. At the same time as Verdi was fulfilling commissions for the Paris Opéra (*Les vêpres siciliennes*, 1855; *Don Carlos*, 1867), the Meyerbeer 'trilogy', Halévy's *La juive* and other proven successes of the Paris stage were finding their way into the repertory of Italian houses.[26] One successful Italian response to the grand opera influx – and exoticist initiatives in France – was *Il Guarany*, the work of Brazilian-born and Milan-trained composer Carlos Antonio Gomes, enthusiastically received at its La Scala première 19 March 1870. Like Verdi's *Aïda* of the following year, *Il Guarany* (based on a Brazilian novel dealing with collisions between Portuguese colonisers and Amazon tribes) synthesises the grand opera model, in four acts, with the 'tone' and rhythms of Verdian melodramma, set intermittently against an Amazonian jungle background. As in *Aïda*, the setting provides a premise for an 'integrated' ballet, in which the piquant orchestration of French operatic ballet is applied to the imaginary construction of ethnic-archaic ritual. In a reversal of the orientalist trope, however, it is the tenor hero who is the exotic 'savage' in this opera (Pery, the chief of the Guarany tribe), while his love-object, Cecilia, is the daughter of Portuguese colonists, with a musical pedigree suggesting the Elivras of Bellini's *Puritani* or Verdi's *Ernani*.

The centrality of the ballet led to the occasional designation of such French-influenced works in Italy as *opera-ballo*. As in the French prototype, the ballet generally figures within the largest act finale, preceding the *coup* that interrupts the ceremony or festivities and triggers an elaborate *concertato* movement. The exotic eastern-Mediterranean ballet music inserted in the Act III finale of *Otello* creates just such a structure, and would have given the piece a familiar aura for the French audience who heard it this way in 1894. (In *Aïda* Verdi spreads his ballet numbers between several scenes of Acts I and II, and frames the ballet of the 'grand finale' to Act II with the famous triumphal march in the style of Meyerbeer's *Prophète*.) One of the most successful operas of the 'interregnum' between Verdi's middle and late periods – Amilcare Ponchielli's *La Gioconda* (Milan, 1876) – applies the *opera-ballo* formula to a melodramatic subject drawn from Victor Hugo; the famous 'Dance of the Hours' provides a piece of courtly

26 On the influence of Meyerbeer and Parisian grand opera in Italy, see Döhring and Henze-Döhring, *Oper und Musikdrama* pp. 238–46, and Fabrizio della Seta, 'L'immagine di Meyerbeer nella critica italiana', in M. T. Murano (ed.), *L'Opera tra Venezia e Parigi*, I (Florence, 1988), pp. 147–76. Two ambitious operatic cycles from the turn of the century – Leoncavallo's Renaissance trilogy *Crepusculum* (of which only *I Medici*, 1893, was completed) and August Bungert's *Homerische Welt* (of which four out of a projected six or seven were completed between 1896 and 1903) – were still stylistically orientated as much to the traditions of Parisian historical grand opera as they were, conceptually, to Wagner's tetralogy. From a historical perspective, the incompletion of these projects is probably as significant as anything else about them.

decadence as a backdrop to the attempted poisoning of Laura Badoero by her jealous husband Alvise.

Typically, the last act returns to a more intimate focus on the principals within a short sequence of solos (Gioconda's 'Suicidio!'), duets (Radames–Aïda in Verdi's opera), or trios (Antonio–Cecilia–Pery in *Il Guranary*, Gioconda–Laura–Enzo in *La Gioconda*), often followed by a quick and drastic finale curtain – *Gioconda* being one of the most egregiously melodramatic instances. *Il Guarany* concludes with a late manifestation of the Meyerbeerian catastrophe, as Antonio detonates a cache of gunpowder in the vaults of the Portuguese fortress. In *Aïda*, Verdi opted for a different kind of catharsis: a serene 'transfiguration' recalling the demise of some of his earlier heroines in a setting that is, in a grimly ironic way, intimate and monumental at once. The mix of exotic, hieratic ritual and of regal pomp with elements of the picturesque and the fantastic in the repertory of late grand opera suggests that authors and audiences alike embraced the genre as a relic, of sorts, of *ancien régime* courtly spectacle. As such, it seems to have provided a vehicle of escape from the realities of the modern era into an imagined past or a distant, primitive society that preserved the simple, monumentally stable structures of life increasingly lost to the present-day world.

Nationalism, realism and natural song: Russian opera and 'the voice of the people'

The ingredients of grand opera also served very well as a framework for representing various European nationalist cultural agendas in the later nineteenth century. Foundational works of the genre such as *Guillaume Tell* and *La muette de Portici* had been concerned with historical or quasi-historical episodes of popular rebellion against tyrannical oppression. These were easily adapted to key episodes of different national histories, as were themes of religious conflict (*Les Huguenots*, *La juive*) or dynastic (Halévy's *Reine de Chypre* and *Charles VI*). Of course, the private love interest at dramatic cross-purposes with public political or religious affiliations could be worked into almost any such episode with minimal strain, if history itself did not provide it. The element of spectacle and grandiose display that betrayed (even magnified) the roots of the genre in the self-celebration of absolutist regimes now served to validate the dignity and splendour of 'peripheral' nations and cultures, assimilating them into a modern cultural mainstream in the same way that grand squares, boulevards, parks, Beaux-Arts government buildings, museums and (not least) opera houses allowed far-flung capital cities such as Sofia or Bucharest, Cairo or Buenos Aires to inspire the same feeling of national dignity as did the Paris of

Napoleon III, the Berlin of Kaiser Wilhlem, or the London of Queen Victoria. Like such urban architectural monuments, a grand opera treating themes of national history (or mythology) was a sign that a nation had 'arrived' in the modern world. Most of all, the role of local colour that had been characteristic of grand opera provided an opportunity for grafting national (folkloristic) elements on to the historical-tragic core of the drama. These folkloristic elements – generally in the form of characteristic dances, songs and choruses, but also inflecting scenes of state and religious ceremony – served a dual function. Ostensibly they spoke to feelings for 'blood and soil' in native audiences; but for foreign audiences they could assume the same exotic appeal generated by 'oriental', African or New World settings. This was part of the appeal, for instance, of the Russian repertory so influentially exported to Paris by Sergei Diaghilev around 1900 (a repertory already infused with its own brand of Central Asian orientalism, in turn).

The more educated, affluent portion of audiences in Moscow, St Petersburg, Warsaw or Prague very likely experienced the operatic celebration of folk-peasant culture and national history or legend as nostalgic and exotic in equal parts, being aware of such a heritage only at some remove. Even a prototypical 'nationalist' composer such as Bedrich Smetana found himself forced to put some distance between himself and his national subject-matter, initially: Smetana started out working with German-language texts by Josef Wenzig for his operas drawn from national legend – *Dalibor* (1865–7, premièred 1868) and *Libuše* (1868–72, premièred 1881) – and had the librettos translated into Czech only at a later stage. Antonin Dvořák's operas in the 'grand-historical' manner take place not in Czech but in Polish and Russian settings, respectively (*Vanda*, 1875, rev. 1879, 1883, and *Dimitrij*, 1882). In his last opera, *Armida* (1904) he even turned back to the Classical opera seria material of Tasso's Armida and Rinaldo, translating it into the idiom of late nineteenth-century fantastic exoticism. As with Smetana's *Bartered Bride* (1866), Dvořák's more concretely Czech-styled stage works are comedies (*King and Charcoal-Burner*, 1871, rev. 1874 and 1887), or lyrical dramas involving common folk as well as high-born characters (*The Jacobin*, 1889, and the Romantic fairy-tale *Russalka*, 1900). By the end of the century, of course, the model of grand operatic framework with local-colouristic insertions had to vie with Wagnerian mythical music drama. Zdeněk Fibich's *Sarka* (1897) exemplifies this contest of traditional and progressive genres (the heroine is a type of Ur-Bohemian Brünnhilde, like her cohort Vlasta, but crossed with elements of Isolde and even Kundry). Like Smetana's *Libuše*, to which *Sarka* is a sequel of sorts, Fibich's opera contributes to the construction of a national cultural legacy by applying an elevated musical-dramatic discourse to the 'local' mythology of the libretto (by Fibich's young mistress, muse and collaborator Anezka Schulzova, née Agnes Schulz). In *Sarka* this 'elevated' style is that of post-Wagnerian music drama. In Smetana's *Libuše*, grand-operatic ceremonial and pathos are applied to a native mythological subject with no notable citation or elaboration of folk-based material.

However, most operas responding to agendas of cultural nationalism in the later nineteenth century did, for obvious reasons, make extensive use of 'natural song' (and, if one can extend the concept, 'natural dance'). Nowhere is this more evident than in Russian opera from the 1860s to the 1890s, a period encompassing the great majority of the Russian canon as a whole. 'Natural song' ('phenomenal' or 'diegetic' music, in the vocabulary of film theory) is that understood to represent 'actual' singing within the fictional framework of the opera. This mode of 'naturalised' performance had long played a significant role, of course, in the mainstream genres of French grand opera, Italian *melodramma*, Singspiel and German Romantic opera. In these repertories, natural song generally occurs in the form of ballads and romances outlining character, affective state or plot background, as well as in many sorts of 'characteristic' choruses (pastoral, religious, bacchanalian, military, etc.). Dancing, too, whether as formal ballet or *chœurs dansés*, was frequently integrated into the specifics of plot and setting, even more so as these moved away from European courts and into rustic or exotic locales.

Extensive use of characteristic, picturesque national song and dance elements might seem to run counter to the progressive imperatives of Wagnerism and naturalism later in the century, thwarting the ideal of a continuous, dramatically 'developing' musical–verbal discourse. Yet in Russia, the use of self-contained song material borrowed from or styled after the vernacular co-existed with an ideal of operatic 'realism' already since the 1850s and 1860s, the period when the critic Vladimir Stasov and the composer Alexander Dargomïzhsky (along with the young Musorgsky) made 'realism' the watchword of Russian operatic aesthetics.[27] The operatic *œuvre* of the quasi-Wagnerian theoriser, critic and composer Alexander Serov (youthful friend of Stasov, and later his nemesis) set an influential example in the 1860s of how historical grand opera might be 'naturalised', so to speak, through the incorporation of folksong elements, and at the same time 'modernised' through a new emphasis on what he – just as much as Stasov, Dargomïzhsky or Musorgsky –

---

27 In part because of its relevance to twentieth-century operatic aesthetics and criticism (and of course to Musorgsky's *Boris*), 'realism' has dominated the historiography of Russian opera. Significant recent literature includes Carl Dahlhaus's *Realism in Nineteenth-Century Music*, trans. Mary Whittall (Cambridge, 1985), chapter 9; Richard Taruskin, *Musorgsky: Eight Essays and an Epilogue* (Princeton, 1993), esp. chapters 2, 3 and 4; and Döhring and Henze-Döhring, *Oper und Musikdrama*, pp. 312–27 ('Opéra-dilaogué: von Dargomizskijs *Kamennyj gost'* zu Rimskij-Korsakovs *Mocart i Sal'eri*').

construed as 'dramatic truth' (involving meticulous declamation of text, unconstrained harmonic experiment and other means of psychological portraiture in music).[28] The symbiosis of ethnic-vernacular song with self-conscious technical experimentation in Serov, Musorgsky or numerous operas by Rimsky-Korsakov anticipates the manner in which Stravinsky and Bartók generated their ethnically inflected modernist languages in the early twentieth century.

Natural song and dance can serve a variety of aesthetic ends in opera, even apart from the basic one of inscribing the 'spirit' of the nation, as 'folk', into the musical and poetic fabric of the work. In historical epics like Musorgsky's *Boris Godunov*, Borodin's *Prince Igor* or Rimsky-Korsakov's *Pskovityanka* (The Maid of Pskov) natural song represents the ordinary people – good, bad or indifferent – whose presence provides a contrapuntal perspective on public affairs of state and the private affairs of the nobility. In *Boris*, and to a certain extent in *Pskovityanka*, the abundance of solo and choral songs contributes to a broadly 'naturalistic' conception: natural singing to authentic (or authentistic) melodic idioms provides an alternative 'naturalism' to that of studied musical declamation in dramatic monologues and dialogues underscored by expressive or mimetic orchestral gesture. In *Prince Igor* the opulent array of songs and dances serves to outline the native Russian element, on one side (the comic dance-songs of the dissolute minstrels or *gudok*-players Skula and Yeroshka, the lament of Yaroslavna in Act IV and the heterophonic choral lament that follows it, the choral acclamations of Igor in the Prologue and final act), and the colourfully 'savage-oriental' Polovetsian tribe, on the other (the choral songs and celebrated dances of the Polovetsians that run throughout Act II and the stylised 'barbaric' march of the Polovetsians in Act III – one of many features reminiscent of Glinka's *Ruslan and Lyudmila*).

The protracted genesis and troubled textual history of all three of these works – *Boris*, *Pskovityanka* and *Igor* – typifies the operatic production of the 'mighty *Kuchka*', the nationalist pentad completed by Mili Balakirev and César Cui, as christened by their critical apologist Vladimir Stasov. Musorgsky's masterpiece was first completed in 1869, underwent a major revision in 1872, but only become widely known in Rimsky-Korsakov's thorough redaction of 1896.[29] Borodin's sprawling epic occupied him for almost twenty years (from 1869 to his death in 1887) and was likewise put in 'working order' by Rimsky,

---

28 Serov is the central figure in Richard Taruskin's study of Russian opera in the period preceding *Boris Godunov*, *Opera and Drama in Russia as Preached and Practiced in the 1860s* (Ann Arbor, 1981). See also 'Serov and Musorgsky', in Taruskin, *Musorgsky: Eight Essays and an Epilogue*, pp. 96–122.

29 For an extensive account of the genesis and textual history of *Boris Godunov* (and a penetrating critical analysis of these), see R. Taruskin, 'Musorgsky vs. Musorgsky: The Versions of *Boris Godunov*', in *Musorgsky: Eight Essays and an Epilogue*, pp. 201–99.

with the assistance of Alexander Glazunov, for a posthumous première in 1890. While Rimsky-Korsakov became the one thoroughly professionalised member of the *Kuchka*, the original version of his first opera, *Pskovityanka*, was a product of his 'pre-professional' life, in the late 1860s, and dedicated to his fellow Kuchkists in 1872. On the basis of his growing experience in operatic composition and orchestration, Rimsky revised the work in 1876–7 and again in the 1890s, with an additional prologue in 'veristic' style explaining the circumstances surrounding the birth of the heroine, Olga, as illegitimate daughter of Ivan the Terrible and one Vera Sheloga.

In Rimsky's *Snegurochka* (The Snow Maiden, 1880–1) and *Sadko* (1895–6), on the other hand, natural song figures so prominently and, indeed, thematically (both works are in some part celebrations of the 'power of song') as nearly to challenge the primacy of the normal operatic ingredients. 'Joy reigns in the fortunate realm we inhabit, and across our countryside one hears nothing but song.' These lines sung at the opening of Act II of *Snegurochka* by a bardic chorus of blind *gusli* players (a kind of psaltery that shares the iconic status of harp or lyre) seem appropriate to the world of this opera as a whole, or that of *Sadko*, and to some extent to the whole corpus of Russian opera during its golden age in the later nineteenth century. In these two operas the omnipresence of natural song would seem to have little to do with dramatic naturalism (even if, as Richard Taruskin points out, *Snegurochka* uses Alexander Ostrovsky's verse-fable in its original textual state as prescribed by the aesthetics of operatic 'realism' – barring some necessary abridgements).[30] The predominance of song here seems, on the contrary, to relate to a world of fable, fantasy and the 'marvellous' in which much of the action takes place (again like *Sadko*), and where song is the standard currency of expression and communication. Yet the poet-playwright Ostrovsky had made 'natural' singing as much an integral part of his realist dramas – for example *Live Not the Way You'd Like*, concerning the Moscow petty bourgeoisie – as of this folkloric fable. In this he followed the creed of the early theorist of Russian realism, Nikolai Chernïshevsky, who, in his *Aesthetic Relations of Art to Reality* (1855), advocated 'natural singing' (in contradistinction to trained operatic singing in the Italian manner) as a key to grounding drama of any sort in the spirit and texture of popular life.

The abundance of natural song in *Snegurochka* forms one side of the opera's celebration of the themes of nature, springtime and youthful love (the other side consisting in episodes of lush orchestral tone-painting that was a specialty

30 R. Taruskin, 'The Snow Maiden', in *The New Grove Dictionary of Opera*, ed. Stanley Sadie (London and New York, 1992), IV, p. 428. The predominance of song and other 'natural' music in the play is testified by the fact that Tchaikovsky's incidental music (Op. 12) for the original production of Ostrovsky's play in 1873 equals the length of a large one-act opera.

of the composer). Rimsky-Korsakov drew on his own 1877 collection of folk melodies, as well as those of Mili Balakirev and Mikhaíl Stakhovich, for his setting of (1) the birds' dance-song in the prologue; (2) the Shrovetide or carnival song for chorus there; (3) three separate songs for the Orphic shepherd *en travesti*, Lel' (the first in the rhythmically free melismatic style of the *protyazhnaya*, suggesting a kind of natural lyric effusion); (4) the folk-ritual of the Snow Maiden's betrothal of Mizgir; (5) three different *khorovodi* or round-dance tunes (two of them in the nocturnal festivities opening Act III, the first with various Mixolydian and Lydian inflections); and (6) the frequently excerpted dance of the Tsar's *jongleurs*. In addition, the score includes three newly invented hymns that draw on traditional ecclesiastic and folk idioms: the above-mentioned hymn of the blind *gusli* players, an *a cappella* hymn to Tsar Berendey, and a concluding hymn to the sun-god Yarilo in the extravagant, 'hieratic' $\frac{11}{4}$ metre.[31]

Sadko inhabits the world of natural song even more directly, in that it is derived from a collection of early Russian epic ballads or *bïlini* dealing with the merchant Sadko who, in the legendary telling, begins his career as a *gusli*-playing minstrel. The first of the opera's seven scenes or tableaux is a veritable riot of minstrelsy, with a paean to sea-trading from Sadko, boasting of his own ambitions in this line. This is followed by a fantastical legend sung by the younger, contralto *guslyar* Nezhata and a pair of songs mocking Sadko's boastful pride sung by the clownish entertainers Duda and Sapel (cousins to the shiftless minstrel pair Skula and Yeroshka in *Prince Igor*), with dancing and singing back-ups. All of this is sandwiched between drinking and feasting songs and hymns to the city of Novgorod from the general chorus. In the next scene Sadko entices the Sea-Princess from the depths of Lake Ilmen with a song in the rhapsodic-melismatic *protyazhnaya* idiom, then entertains her and her sinuously chromatic nixies with an animated strophic *khorovod* dance-song. And so it goes, with Sadko singing and playing his way (to variously realistic and fanciful orchestral simulations of his *gusli*) through almost every scene. (Other characters respond in kind, such as the foreign traders in scene 4, featuring the once-ubiquitous 'Song of India'.)

Even more than Lel' in *Snegurochka*, Sadko becomes an Orpheus figure when, later on, he descends into the underwater kingdom and sings his way back to earth, having won the hand of the Sea-King's daughter (the Sea-Princess of scene 2), though not before being regaled with a sumptuous aquatic ballet with songs by the denizens of the deep. *Sadko* is exceptional in the degree to

---

31 Rimsky glosses the use of borrowed and 'simulated' folk themes in *Snegurochka* at some length in his autobiography, noting how he had initially been criticised for failure of invention on this account (*My Musical Life*, trans. Judah A. Joffe [New York, 1923; rpt. London, 1974], pp. 236–44).

which natural song overshadows the operatic discourse of recitatives, arias (Chernïshevsky's 'artificial' singing), or through-composed dramatic exchanges in the modern style. (Rimsky-Korsakov's designation of the piece as an *opera-bïlina* – an opera based on, or in the manner of, old heroic lays – indicates his awareness of this exceptional quality.) But the very fact that he felt it possible to write such a work in the age of high Wagnerism and incipient *verismo* testifies to the fundamental, ingrained role of natural song in Russian operatic culture.

Unique as it is in many respects, that colossus of the nineteenth-century Russian repertory, Musorgsky's *Boris Godunov*, perhaps best exemplifies the interactions of historical grand opera, experimental 'realism' and natural/vernacular song typical of this whole era of Russian opera. As the original version of 1869 demonstrates, Musorgsky was at first intent on applying the fruits of his 'experiment in dramatic music in prose', a fragmentary setting of Nikolai Gogol's naturalistic comedy *Marriage* from 1868, to the project of turning Pushkin's neo-Shakespearean historical canvas *Boris Godunov* into the paradigm of a new 'realist' historical opera. Even in the 1872 revision (and even in Rimsky-Korsakov's diplomatically tempered arrangement of it), the ideal of a dramatically uncompromising, musically intensified speech resonates throughout the scene in Pimen's monastic cell (Act I, scene 1), Boris's great, self-searching monologue ('recitative and aria') in Act II, the following tormented interview with Prince Shuisky, and Boris's hallucination to the chiming tones of the clock at the culmination of the act – a detail of Musorgsky's own invention.

The 'Polish act' (Act III), added in 1872 to provide a leading female role in the part of Marina Mnishek, is the most obvious concession to the conventional grand opera idiom the composer had at first been resisting, with its chorus of maidens serenading their mistress with Romantic verses, its grand aria *alla mazurka* for Marina, its festive polonaise with chorus, and its passionate (if cynically compromised) scene and duet for Marina and Grigory/Dmitry. But also in the famous Coronation Scene of the Prologue, or the Council of Boyars culminating in Boris's death, one can easily recognise the lineaments of grand-operatic ceremonial, counterpointing public ritual and private anguish. Both scenes are invested with an intensity of musical invention and a rich texturing of dramatic pathos, irony and (indeed) 'realism' that sets them apart from nearly any example of the original 'Western' genre, or from Alexander Serov's attempts at a Russian naturalisation of it. The alternative of ending the opera with the 'Kromy Forest' scene and the pathetic tonal and metrical divagations of the *yurodivïy* or 'holy fool' (ambiguously situated between natural and operatic song) makes, of course, for a still more pointed contrast to the conventions of historical opera. The interpolation of natural song throughout the opera tends to serve 'naturalistic' rather than simply picturesque ends, whether by virtue of the authentic 'intonations' of the material (the traditional 'Slava!' tune of the Coronation Scene deriving from the influential Lvov-Pratsch collection of 1790, the studied coarseness of Varlaam's singing in the scene at the Lithuanian border, the surrealistic nonsense of the Nurse's and Feodor's 'clapping songs' in Act II) or by the integration of these songs into the texture of the drama, by means of realistic promptings and interruptions, for example.

A similar spectrum of history, folklore, dramatic 'realism' and abundant natural (folk-based) singing informs the operatic *oeuvre* of Pyotr Illyich Tchaikovsky, which rivals that of Rimsky-Korsakov in magnitude and quality. He began with essays in historical opera at the same time as Rimsky and Musorgsky, with *Voyevoda* (1867-8) and *Oprichnik* (1870-2), both cleaving much more conscientiously to the Meyerbeerian model than did the work of the young Kuchkists, while dealing with some of the same historical episodes from the epoch of Ivan the Terrible that had preoccupied that group. As late as 1880 he was composing a relatively pure example of French historical grand opera, with a distinct Russian accent, in his *Maid of Orleans* (after Schiller's *Jungfrau von Orleans*, filtered through an actual Parisian opera on the subject by Auguste Mermet to a libretto by Jean-Paul Barbier). Certainly this model gave Tchaikovsky greater scope for his lyrical and symphonic talents than did the *opéra dialogué* touted by Dargomïzhsky, Stasov and the Kuchka. Perhaps he also hoped that the subject would prove more readily exportable.

One could argue that in the more characteristic operas of his maturity – *Yevgeny Onegin* (1877-8), *Mazepa* (1881-3) and *Pikovaya dama* (The Queen of Spades, 1890) – Tchaikovsky perfected the very ideal of naturally flowing, musically persuasive 'melodic recitative' that César Cui (among the composer's severest critical antagonists) had long preached as the great virtue of operatic realism in the Russian manner. Examples can be found in passages of casual conversation, but equally in the linking portions of Tatyana's famous 'Letter Scene'. Another sort of 'lyrical realism' is generated by consistent stylistic allusion (as Richard Taruskin has argued) to a genre of middle-class domestic romance contemporary with Pushkin's verse-novel.[32] This idiom, with a marked emphasis on contours of a major or minor sixth, is adumbrated in the romance sung offstage by the sisters Olga and Tatyana in the opening scene, in counterpoint to a conversation between their mother and their nursemaid; it returns in several lyrical themes of the Letter Scene, among many other passages. When the peasants of Mme. Larina's estate entertain her with a

32 See Taruskin, 'P. I. Chaikovsky and the Ghetto', in *Defining Russia Musically* (Princeton, 1997), pp. 48-60, as well as his entry on *Yevgeny Onegin* in *The New Grove Dictionary of Opera*, IV, pp. 1190-5.

vernacular harvest song and dance, the contrast of this earthier music to the girls' delicate romance, and to the gently ironic depiction of Mme. Larina's 'educated' conversation with her servant, creates a wonderful layering of musical-dramatic tone that is carried through the opera in diverse ways. Tchaikovsky's transformation of his famous literary source thus achieves a sophisticated kind of operatic realism quite unlike anything attempted by his colleagues. It, too, is pre-eminently national by virtue of its source and the various stylistic 'intonations' of the score. But it also benefits in a crucial way from the composer's affinity with the likes of Gounod and Bizet – the same kind of *mondaine* urbanity to which Pushkin's characters aspire within the social-historical framework of an earlier generation.

Drame lyrique and *verismo*: opera, literature and naturalism

The use of a novel (of sorts) as source material in Tchaikovsky's *Yevgeny Onegin* was still a relatively unusual practice in 1879. For obvious reasons pertaining to convenience of adaptation, stage plays had been the favoured literary sources for operas through most of the nineteenth century. (When a novel or story *did* serve as the basis for an opera, a spoken theatrical adaptation of the source not infrequently served as an intermediate step.) The use of prose fiction as a dramatic source, in modern or quasi-modern settings, does not define any particular operatic genre of the later Romantic era, but it is indicative of a certain temperament characterising much important repertory, beginning with a loosely conceived genre of *drame lyrique* that emerges in the 1860s, and culminating in the Italian *verismo* of the 1890s along with some international echoes of that: Massenet's *Werther* (1892), Puccini's *La bohème* (1896), J. B. Foerster's *Eva* (1899), Gustave Charpentier's *roman musical* of 1900, *Louise*, Eugen D'Albert's *Tiefland* (1903), and the operas of Alfred Bruneau on librettos by or after Emile Zola. Not all of these later works were based on original prose sources, nor were most of the French works of the 1860s and 1870s now often categorised as *drames lyriques*. But whether based on classic dramas from Shakespeare through Goethe, popular fiction of the eighteenth and nineteenth centuries, or contemporary naturalistic dramas, a large number of operas from the period share certain broad aims: a focus on individual characterisation and psychology (as opposed to grandiose spectacle, stage effects and exotic *divertissement*); a concern for what we might describe as 'literary flow' (whether construed as narrative or dramatic) through the flexible deployment of arioso and declamatory styles with evocative scenic music; and a more thoroughgoing integration of 'local colour' into details of the dramatic action.

The term *drame lyrique* was revived at the end of the century by the likes of Massenet (*Werther*, 1892), Chabrier (*Briséïs*, only first act composed, 1888–91), Chausson's *Le roi Arthus* (1885–95), and Bruneau (*L'attaque du moulin*, 1893; *Messidor*, 1897) to designate works of widely diverse subject-matter, but with a common aim to merge Wagnerian influences with a type of lyrical naturalism.[33] The term had originally been applied to the more serious, suspenseful or overtly 'dramatic' works that emerged in the opéra comique genre between the time of Monsigny's *Le déserteur* (1769) and Revolutionary-era works by Grétry, Méhul and Le Sueur.[34] By 1885 Arthur Pougin noted that the term *drame lyrique* – which had in the meantime been indiscriminately applied to almost any opera of 'dramatic, pathetic, passionate' or otherwise serious sentiment – had become increasingly appropriated for the works of Richard Wagner and those in his orbit.[35] In his influential history of nineteenth-century music, Carl Dahlhaus backdated the term to apply to works that might be loosely viewed as stylistic antecedents of *Werther*, such as Gounod's *Faust* and Bizet's *Carmen*. Sieghart and Sabine Henze Döhring follow his example by discussing the repertory of Léon Carvalho's Théâtre Lyrique (1851–70) under this rubric, notably Bizet's *Les pêcheurs de perles* (1863) and *Mireille* (1864), while David Charlton avoids the terminological confusion with those works of the 1890s actually called *drames lyriques* by coining the term *opéra lyrique* to refer to the repertory of Carvalho's theatre.[36] None of these operas of the 1860s through to Bizet's *Carmen* was specifically designated as a *drame lyrique* by composer or librettist, any more than those other contemporary operatic treatments of literary classics, such as Gounod's *Roméo et Juliette* (1867) or Ambroise Thomas's *Mignon* (1866) and *Hamlet* (1868).[37]

The question of whether to use spoken dialogue or recitative that bedevilled the performance history of many of these operas (*Faust*, *Les pêcheurs*, *Mireille*, *Mignon*, *Carmen* or later Offenbach's *Contes d'Hoffmann*) is symptomatic of a larger shift away from the conventions of opéra comique since the time of

---

33 On this end-of-the-century repertory, see Steven Huebner, *French Opera at the Fin de Siècle: Wagnerism, Nationalism, and Style* (Oxford, 1999).

34 M. Elizabeth C. Bartlet, 'Drame lyrique', in *The New Grove Dictionary of Opera*, I, p. 1242.

35 A. Pougin, *Dictionnarie historique et pittoresque du théâtre* (Paris, 1885); cited in Hervé Lacombe, 'Définitions des genres lyriques dans les dictionnaires français di XIXe siècle', in P. Prévost (ed.), *Le Théâtre lyrique en France aux XIXe siècle* (Metz, 1995), pp. 301–2.

36 C. Dahlhaus, '*Drame lyrique* and Operatic Realism', in *Nineteenth-Century Music*, pp. 276–83; Döhring and Henze-Döhring, 'Das Drame lyrique des Second Empire', in *Oper und Musikdrama*, pp. 190–98; D. Charlton, 'Opera 1850–1890: (b) France', in *New Oxford History of Music* 9 ('Romanticism, 1830–1890'), ed. Gerald Abraham (Oxford and New York, 1990), pp. 327–409 (esp. p. 328).

37 Some of the criteria by which Dahlhaus and the Döhrings identify works as belonging to, or tending to, this 'phantom' genre seem somewhat arbitrarily chosen, as generic 'markers', even if they may well apply to individual works or composers. Dahlhaus, for instance, stresses a kind of sentimental *religioso* tone he finds characteristic of *Faust* and Gounod's compositional 'voice' generally. The Döhrings identify an ideal (partially realised in the examples of *Les pêcheurs de perles* and *Mireille*) by which milieu and local customs – Hindu-oriental in *Les pêcheurs*, Provençal in *Mireille* – play an active role in the constitution of the drama as well as the character of the musical score.

Auber and Adam. Institutional restrictions on which Parisian theatres could perform opera with or without dialogue were dropped in 1864, which was a major factor in the blurring of generic identity around this time. Despite Döhring's contention that 'grand opera had no influence on the emergence of *drame lyrique*', which he aligns instead with the serious-dramatic side of the opéra comique tradition (*Oper und Musikdrama*, 191), there seems to be no reason not to view works such as *Faust, Mireille, Roméo et Juliette* or *Les pêcheurs de perles* precisely as a hybridisation of the most successful traits of the grand and comique genres: the fleet, conversational ensembles and audience-pleasing *couplets* of the latter, for example, mingled with a certain number of large choral tableaux, some element of ballet and stage spectacle, and a few large-scale arias and duets for the lead characters all in the grand opera manner. The exotic Indian milieu of Delibes's *Lakmé*, with its Brahmin priests and priestesses and dancing *bayadères*, would have almost certainly assumed the framework of grand opera ten or twenty years earlier. But by 1883, Delibes was able to marry exotic lyricism and spectacle to a modern, novelistic action loosely based on the Polynesian novel *Le Mariage de Loti* by Julien Viaud (pseud. Pierre Loti).

The phenomenal worldwide success of Gounod's *Faust* for at least fifty years after its première probably has something to do with just this judicious mixture of elements. (Indeed, the opera's complex textual history reflects an attempt to fine-tune this balance.)[38] The colourful *Kermesse* scene and the famous waltz-chorus that frame Act II have the structural density of grand opera introduction or finale ensembles, but a lightness of tone that recalls Auber and Adam. At the centre of the act Mephistopheles's 'Ronde du Veau d'or' is a straight example of comic opera *couplets*; but when his shady magic-tricks provoke the sign of the cross from Siébel, Valentin, Brander and the chorus, the 'shadow' of a dramatic grand opera ensemble passes over the scene (only to be dispersed into the waltz-chorus). Valentin's brief cavatina, 'Avant de quitter ces lieux' (still a baritone recital favourite), was added later by Gounod to flesh out the act. The straight-forward yet memorable lyricism of the number is a hallmark of the composer's personal style, and to that extent becomes an important ingredient of the whole. Marguerite's casual entrance, during the waltz-chorus, acquired an accidentally 'naturalistic' touch, *vis-à-vis* the more elaborate means by which leading sopranos were commonly introduced in grand opera, when the composer cut a full-scale duet for Marguerite and Valentin in Act II during the rehearsals for the 1859 première.[39] She is still afforded a solo scene, as any grand opera heroine

---

38 See Stephen Huebner, *The Operas of Charles Gounod* (Oxford, 1990), chapter 7 (pp. 99–132), which also discusses the sources of the Barbier and Carré libretto in popularised theatrical adaptations of Goethe's *Faust* on the Parisian stage from *c.* 1825 to 1850 (principally Carré's own *Faust et Marguerite*).

39 Huebner, *The Operas of Charles Gounod*, p. 124.

would rightly expect, culminating in her 'Jewel Song'. By incorporating Goethe's 'King of Thule' ballad as the slow movement of this overall scene complex, however, Gounod minimises the artificiality of the traditional 'grand scène et air', reconciling it with a familiar component of the literary source, which also (as 'natural song') provides an element of realistic dramaturgy.

The enduring appeal of Georges Bizet's *Carmen* (1875) has also, perhaps, something to do with the way it negotiates between 'realistic' appearances and escapist operatic fantasy. Spoken dialogue and a relative freedom of subject-matter had always allowed opéra comique a greater proximity to 'real life' than could be expected from grand opera, with its courtly genealogy and dedication to the ideal of a 'high style'. The role of the librettists Henri Meilhac and Ludovic Halévy (experienced collaborators of Jacques Offenbach) and the nature of the source text by Prosper Mérimée contributed much to the exceptional vitality of the resulting work. The opera's setting is an effective blend of the ordinary and the Romantic (with its soldiers, *gamins*, cigarette-factory workers, Spanish gypsy smugglers, country-girl sweetheart, young officer, and swaggering bullfighter), providing a perfect framework for the morally ambivalent title character. Because it began life as an opéra comique with spoken dialogue, the realism of the opera's musical conception has little to do with issues of naturalistic vocal declamation along the lines of Wagnerian or Russian aesthetics. Rather, it is to be found in Bizet's felicitously textured realisation of milieu and local colour. Individual popular Spanish-style numbers like Carmen's celebrated Habañera ('L'Amour est un oiseau rebelle), her Seguidilla ('Près des remparts de Seville'), Escamillo's *toréador* song or Carmen's improvised castanet song are all highly effective touches of local colour in their own right. But the true measure of Bizet's success is how naturally these pieces co-exist with the rest of the score – a coherent spectrum of characteristic and local styles, buoyant light-opera ensemble (the gypsies), lyrical cavatina (Micaëla, Don José), and proto-veristic melodrama (Carmen, Don José).

Two of Jules Massenet's most characteristic operas, *Manon* and *Werther*, translate eighteenth-century novels of sentiment into works that can indeed be well described as 'lyrical dramas', even if only *Werther* is actually termed as such. *Manon* premièred 19 January 1884 at the Opéra-Comique and is a late example of an opera still bearing the name of that institution as a generic designation – many works premièred or otherwise performed there by this time were no longer called so. (Spoken dialogue is largely confined to passages of orchestrally accompanied 'melodrama'.) *Werther* was turned down by the director of the Opéra-Comique, Léon Carvalho – formerly of the Théâtre-Lyrique – at the time of its completion in 1887, and it did not reach the stage until 1892, in Vienna and in German translation.

The score of *Manon*, unlike *Werther*, makes extensive use of historical pastiche, working seventeenth- and eighteenth-century French dance idioms into a stylised period background for its eminently late-Romantic characterisation of the amorous protagonists of Abbé Prévost's 1731 novel, *L'Histoire du chevalier des Grieux et de Manon Lescaut*. Not long after the première of Massenet's *Manon* in 1884 Giacomo Puccini would begin to work on his *dramma lirico* based on the same material, in 1890, first performed early in 1893.[40] Puccini's more condensed and in some respects more refined setting makes less attempt to capture the full sweep of the heroine's fickle history; Massenet's, by contrast, is more overtly episodic. The abundance of crowd scenes and action ensembles, deftly choreographed by the music, combine to create the operatic prototype of a Hollywood period-costume romance from the 1930s or 1940s: the guest appearance of the 'Ballet de l'Opéra' at the pleasure-gardens of Cours-la-Reine, the lively public scenes of the inn at Amiens in Act I and the gambling den of the Hôtel de Transylvanie in Act IV, and the musical masks of Manon as ingénue, coquette and impassioned lover. In Massenet – as will be true in much of Puccini – traditional aria and duet situations are distilled into fleeting, passionate 'moments' that are analogous to, and perhaps in some part the inspiration for, cinematic close-ups at key moments of those romance films of a later generation.

The distinctively personal touch in both *Manon* and *Werther* seems to lie in a feeling for the domestic idyll, or melancholy recollections of it. Des Grieux's ethereal vision of 'a little white house, deep in the woods' – imagined through the aural scrim of muted violins playing a musette-like figure to the notes of diatonic D and A major scales – is all the more touching for following almost immediately (though unbeknownst to him) upon Manon's even simpler 'Adieu, notre petite table', haltingly declaimed against a slow series of shifting chords in the same high register, as she bids farewell to the very domestic bliss Des Grieux hopes to rescue by transplanting it from Paris to an idyllic pastoral landscape. In *Werther*, intimate domestic scenes provide both the background foil of small-town, bourgeois contentment and the immediate context of the drama's emotional core: the encounters between Charlotte and Werther in each of the four acts. The tableau of domestic felicity that first greets Werther's eyes when he arrives at the bailiff's house in Wetzlar sparks his infatuation with Charlotte, quite as much as her own personal attributes or their vocal expression. When the two meet again in Act III, on the eve of Werther's suicide, it is the sight of 'everything in its accustomed place' – the clavier at which they sang, the books they read together, and, not least, Albert's fateful set of pistols – that

---

40 This material had already furnished the subject of the first *opéra comique* to conclude with the heroine's tragic death, an adaptation by Eugène Scribe for the septuagenarian Auber from 1856.

initiates the climactic duet-scene, centred around Werther's 'Lied d'Ossian'. The balance struck between 'natural' dramatic continuity and well-defined moments of melodic-harmonic expressivity is similar to the works of Puccini's early operatic maturity (stylistically, Puccini's *Manon Lescaut* is closer to *Werther* than to Massenet's *Manon*), and to the works of the *verismo* composers of the 1890s.

The prolific generation of Italian composers born after the middle of the century (often identified as the *giovane scuola* or 'young school' in distinction to Verdi and his contemporaries) owed a good deal to the example of Massenet altogether. Their debt was not just to the intimate and explosive passions of *Werther*, but also to the composer's refinement of the grand opera style with new attention to elements of exoticism and local or historical colour (*Le roi de Lahore*, *Le Cid*, *Esclarmonde*), and to the example of his free-flowing, non-periodic lyricism embedded in suave, multi-hued orchestral drapery. After Ponchielli, most Italians, including Verdi, eschewed the well-defined framework of solo, ensemble and choral set-pieces that had remained operative in Verdi's *oeuvre* up to *Aïda*, and only nominally abandoned there. The standard now became the through-composed scene, which might take either Wagner or later examples of grand opera (including, indeed, *Aïda*) as a point of orientation. Verdi's notion of the *parola scenica* – a pregnant word or phrase, strikingly declaimed and accompanied – was a key element within the native Italian legacy absorbed by the *verismo* generation. In *Otello* and *Falstaff* Verdi was working along parallel lines with these younger composers (though with very different dramatic material) in discovering new ways of accommodating the traditions of Italian cantabile and dramatic aria within the freer outlines, and often smaller segmentations, of a modern type of 'musical drama'.

Whereas *Carmen* had met with a relatively disappointing reception in 1875, only gradually making its way into the repertory, Pietro Mascagni's *Cavalleria rusticana* was an overnight sensation, suggesting that by 1890 the time was ripe for this brand of operatic naturalism. ('Naturalism' would be the appropriate rendition of the term *verismo*, since Mascagni's source, a story and dramatic adaptation by Giovanni Verga, represents a direct outgrowth of the so-called 'naturalist' fiction of the Goncourt brothers and Emile Zola from the 1870s and 1880s, as distinguished from more general debate over 'realism' in the arts that had been waged since the 1850s.) Mascagni's career was launched at the age of twenty-six when *Cavalleria*, his second completed opera, took first prize in a competition for one-act operas sponsored by the publisher Edoardo Sonzogno, rival to the leading firm of Ricordi. The fact that Mascagni had seventy-two competitors for this prize indicates the robust state of Italy's operatic culture at the end of the century. It was not so much the prize jury, however, as the public, as well as impresarios and singers (the likes of Caruso, Gigli, Melba, Geraldine Farrar and Licia Albanese), who accorded the young composer fame and immortality. *Cavalleria* enjoyed no fewer than nine separate productions, both inside and outside Italy, in the first year of its existence. Within two years it had travelled to theatres in North and South America, to Bucharest and St Petersburg, Lisbon and Barcelona, and all the major European stages. (By 1892 the opera's repertory-twin, Leoncavallo's *I Pagliacci*, had also been born, and it followed a similarly rapid international trajectory.)

Cavalleria rusticana, rather than Puccini's *Tosca*, is actually (*pace* Joseph Kerman) the original 'shabby little shocker', or at least it has suffered this reputation in over a century of operatic criticism. The piece is manifestly littler and shabbier than Puccini's opera, both in dimension and compositional finesse. (However, the 'gushing' cantabile of the Santuzza–Turiddu duet, the *intermezzo sinfonico*, and the musical expression of abjection, crisis and despair all left a profound mark on Puccini's style.) Critics have perhaps insufficiently appreciated the seemingly obvious relation between the opera's blunt, direct expressivity, its unpretentious (though by no means amateurish) texture and orchestration, on one hand, and its status as the foundational work of operatic *verismo*, on the other. A late Romantic opera with aspirations to popular success could scarcely be expected to emulate the naturalism of Zola or Verga in prosaic, unflinching reportage of the tribulations of working-class life in late nineteenth-century Paris or subsistence tenant farming in rural Sicily. Yet the very terms of critical censure so often levelled against *Cavalleria* – the 'vulgarity' or 'brutality' of its musical invention – would seem to indicate a precise analogue, in terms of musical effect, for the social 'reality' that the opera otherwise palliates with picturesque renditions of folksong and Catholic church music, folkloric festival, drinking songs, and the like. From the perspective of contemporary stylistic options, the musical idiom of *Cavalleria* is far more 'realistically' suited to its setting and subject-matter than would be the more 'sophisticated' brutality of Viennese expressionism, for instance.

Because *Cavalleria rusticana* and its invariable double-bill companion, *I Pagliacci*, have proved so durable, they have come to define the notion of operatic *verismo* altogether. Thus, for example, they appear to establish the one-act structure as a requisite of the genre, though there are no clear theoretical grounds for it. (*Pagliacci* is nominally in two acts, although performance tradition has turned it into a one-acter with orchestral intermezzo preceding the 'play within the opera', positioned analogously to the intermezzo preceding the climactic public scene and dénouement of *Cavalleria*.) Continuity of presentation does perhaps contribute to what is perceived as 'veristic' about these two paradigmatic works. The drastic final moment – murder committed in an access of jealous passion – influences our experience of the drama at every step. The outcome is so strongly foreshadowed by the unfolding situations that, even if the works were not so universally familiar (and even if opera plots were not routinely glossed for the audience in advance), we could not help but hear the lighter decorative elements or moments of tranquil reflection as existing under the pall of imminent disaster. This lends to those passages one might be tempted to write off as gratuitous, or at least as anti-realistic picturesqueness (in *Cavalleria*: the peasants' Easter-morning chorus, Alfio's 'Il cavallo scalpita', the large ensemble *preghiera*, the orchestral intermezzo, Turiddu's *brindisi*), a certain ironic, even suspenseful edge they would lack if the same violent dénouement were partitioned off in a separate, final act buffered by one or more intermissions. Likewise in *I Pagliacci*: the 'bell' chorus juxtaposing the picturesque topics of church-bells and bagpipes, or the extensive, sentimentalised rococo-pastiche of the *commedia dell'arte* performance setting the stage for the opera's climax are utilised (as Egon Voss notes of similar picturesque and lyrical items in *Cavalleria*) as tension-building deferrals of the melodramatic revenge simmering in the background.[41] Indeed, the whole idiom of Baroque-rococo pastiche that became increasingly popular in the late nineteenth century is almost invariably designed, in opera, to invite suspicion, or to provide a foil for darker melodramatic currents (*vide* Tosca's 'cantata' in Act II of Puccini's opera). The pointed ambiguities of 'play' vs. 'real life' plotted out through the imagery of comic 'masks' anticipate hallmarks of early modernist aesthetics, as in the work of Pirandello, Picasso, Stravinsky and others from the ensuing decades. Most of all, the self-consciously artificial idiom of gavotte and minuet provides an obvious contrast to what is understood as the music of 'truthful' dramatic expression. The chromaticised E flat minor *canto appassionato* of Canio's violent outburst that marks the turning-point of the performance ('No! Pagliaccio non son') is clearly to be heard by the opera audience as unleashing the 'actor's' genuine emotions, inhabiting an entirely different representational plane than the comically affected C major *tempo di minuetto* and F major trio that open the comedy. Even the naïve stage-audience is moved to wonder about the difference, remarking that Pagliaccio's acting 'moves them to tears', and that his scene seems 'like the real thing' ('Comare, mi fa piangere!', 'Par vera questa scena!').

Significant imitations of the Cavalleria/Pagliacci duo were few. Puccini's *Il tabarro* – the first in his triptych of one-acters, *Il trittico*, premièred at the Metropolitan Opera in 1918 – is one of the rare examples, a melodrama of

---

41 See Egon Voss's entries for Mascagni's *Cavalleria rusticana* and Leoncavallo's *I Pagliacci* in *Pipers Enzyklopädie des Musiktheaters*, III, pp. 705–8 and 468–71.

adultery and jealous revenge among barge-workers in contemporary Paris.[42]
But even if one resists applying the *verismo* label to other, larger-scale works
from the end of the century, there is no doubt as to the significant stylistic and
dramaturgical affinities between Mascagni's and Leoncavallo's signal works of
1890–2 and much of the post-Verdian repertory. Puccini, Cilea, Giordano and
others followed the example of the original *veristi* in definitively replacing the
extended, multi-partite 'scene and aria' or 'scene and duet' with a freely, naturally paced musical action within which shorter, well-defined lyrical moments
were embedded, usually of not more than several minutes' duration. The tendency is already evident in the early works of Puccini (*Le Villi*, *Edgar*) and
Alfredo Catalani (*Elda* [rev. as *Loreley*], *Dejanice*, *Edmea*) from the 1880s. The
affinity with Germanic-Gothic Romanticism, legend and symbol in these
works of Puccini and Catalani, and in the latter's one mature masterpiece, *La
Wally* (1892), might suggest an incipient Italian Wagnerism. It also reflects,
however, a more general ultramontane orientation inherited from the so-called
scapigliati (principally Arrigo Boito and Franco Faccio) who had influenced the
discourse of cultural 'progress' in Italy since the 1860s.

Along with Puccini, other more-or-less successful composers of the turn of
the century built on characteristic features of *verismo* opera. Francesco Cilea's
L'arlesiana (1897), for example, sets a classic example of French 'naturalism'
(Alphonse Daudet's *L'arlésienne*) in a style of simple lyrical conversation with
intermittent expressions of amorous or distraught emotion, building gradually
towards the heavily foreshadowed suicide of the young protagonist, Federico.
Adriana Lecouvreur (1902) applies the lyrical conversation tone to the more rar-
efied ambience of the Comédie-Française in the early 1700s. Here the dichotomy of historical pastiche and 'verisitic' cantabile or *appassionato* outbursts
noted in *I Pagliacci* operates even more extensively. A realistic conversational
tone and pace, within a 'modern' historical setting, also characterises Umberto
Giordano's 'dramma di ambiente storico in quattro quadri', *Andrea Chenier*,
premièred in 1896, and even more so his up-to-the-minute drama of international politics and intrigue, *Fedora*, of 1898. The density of dramatic incident in
these works, their extensive casts of characters and 'extras', the specificity of
historical and geographical locale (post-Revolutionary France in Chénier, the
salons and country villas of the international aristocratic set in *Fedora*), and not

---

42 Impressionistic evocations of the nocturnal urban riverscape à la Whistler provide the foil to the
darker elements of the drama here (in place of the classicising artifice that fulfils that role in works like *I
Pagliacci* or Giordano's *Andrea Chenier*). This aspect of the score marks it as distinctively modern, when compared to its *verismo* antecedents. For reasons of economy, this chapter largely relegates the *oeuvres* of both
Puccini and Richard Strauss to the twentieth century (and hence another history), despite the irrefutable
stature of Puccini's pre-1900 operas, *Manon Lescaut*, *La bohème* and *Tosca*. For further discussion of Puccini,
see chapter 21.

least, the fleet tracking of action, dialogue and expressive gestures big and small by the orchestral score all contribute to a style one could describe as 'proto-cinematic'. Indeed, stage melodrama, operatic *verismo* and early film would seem to inhabit a very similar cultural space in the years around 1900. On the other hand, the fact that Giordano lived on until 1948 and Cilea until 1950 without producing any more significant works is one sign that the operatic culture that nurtured them was not sustained across the next century.

From Wagnerism to modernism

Opera, like European culture at large, was haunted by the spirit of 'Wagnerism' from around the time of Wagner's death in 1883 across the *fin de siècle*. It was, indeed, precisely the 'spiritual' nature (in several senses) of the Wagner phenomenon that led to this pervasive cultural haunting. For one thing, Wagner's presence in opera or other cultural precincts towards the end of the century was often more spiritual than tangible in any practical or technical way. In opera, the use of referential or associative leitmotifs, the role of orchestra in depicting interior and exterior action, the 'symphonic' continuity of the musical score, the exploitation of archaic (or pseudo-archaic) myth and legend to psychological and symbolic ends – all of these were readily perceived as Wagnerian traits. Yet to distinguish the direct influence of the *Meister* from more global tendencies of nineteenth-century operatic practice was a difficult and contentious matter. Furthermore, from the time of reform writings around 1850 to the enthusiastic reception of his aesthetic 'synthesis' among the French Symbolists and the burgeoning of a chauvinistic-ideological Wagnerism around the First World War, Wagnerism was above all a matter of interpreting the 'spiritual legacy' of the composer's writings and his preoccupation with the 'redemptive' role of art in modern society. 'Spiritually' as well as musically, however, the Wagnerian influence leads (together with Italian *verismo*, French symbolism and naturalism, and dramaturgical and musical experiment in Russian opera) directly to the modernist turn of the early twentieth century.

'Wagnerism' as a movement or, more broadly, a discursive field is associated above all with France in the last two decades of the nineteenth century. Wagner's cultural impact was more long-standing in Germany and more ubiquitous, naturally, but for that very reason partook less of the character of a self-conscious cultural movement. The first familiar tenet of French Wagnerism is that it was principally a literary movement; or at least, that the French composers who *did* come heavily under the sway of Wagner – César Franck, Ernest Chausson, Emmanuel Chabrier and Vincent D'Indy – had little to do with the poets, critics and the occasional amateur musicologist who wrote for Edouard

Dujardin's short-lived but influential *Revue wagnérienne* (1885–8). The literary prestige of Wagner's ideas – or Wagner as 'idea' – is an incontrovertible fact of French cultural history, starting with the writings of Gérard de Nerval and Baudelaire in the 1850s and 1860s.[43] A second tenet of French Wagnerism would be that even the most Wagnerian of French composers (not to mention more ambivalent Wagnerians such as Massenet, Saint-Saëns or Debussy) tended to avoid Wagner's influence at an audible level, remaining loyal to French musical tradition in many points.

It would be a mistake, though, to ignore the role of poets, essayists and critics in making French composers keenly aware of the figure of Wagner. The critical discourse on opera in France had always been a strongly literary one, after all. And certainly some literary figures played an active role in fostering a specifically operatic Wagnerism in France – for example the Parnassian poet and sometime Wagner disciple Catulle Mendès, who provided Chabrier with the libretti for his opera *Gwendoline* and the ambitious fragment *Briséïs* (likewise the text of Debussy's uncompleted *Rodrigue et Chimène*).[44] The palpable presence of Wagner in the scores of even acknowledged *wagnéristes*, on the other hand, remains more the exception than the rule. Neither Chabrier's works nor Chausson's overtly Wagnerian *Le roi Arthus* could easily be mistaken for one of Wagner's own works, even for a few bars (with a few exceptions). Likewise César Franck's *Hulda* (posthumously premièred in 1894) – for all its chromatic harmony, continuous scenes and archaic-Nordic setting – displays a strong solidarity with the lyrical idioms of Gounod and Massenet. *Hulda* even includes a large-scale formal *divertissement* for chorus and ballet occupying much of the fourth act, entirely in the 'grand' tradition of the Opéra. Vincent D'Indy, perhaps the most unabashedly epigonal Wagnerian, nevertheless evokes the style of the German *maître* only sporadically.[45] D'Indy's major operatic effort, *Fervaal* (first performed 1897), was, it is true, widely perceived as the French answer to *Parsifal*.[46] But like most of his colleagues he avoids an extensive, structural reliance on leitmotifs, and, like Franck, mingles his

43 As Richard Sieburth puts it, the history of French Wagnerism through the 1890s was 'largely a working out of the intellectual and artistic implications of Baudelaire's 1861 pamphlet', *Richard Wagner et Tannhäuser à Paris* (Sieburth, 'The Music of the Future: 1885, February – Symbolist Poets Publish *La Revue wagnérienne*', in Denis Hollier (ed.), *A New History of French Literature* [Cambridge, Mass., 1989], p. 792).

44 In the epilogue to an 1886 monograph on the composer, Mendès recommended the cultivation of a national French *drame musical* that would develop Wagner's *theories* without trying to imitate his librettos or scores as such ('Le jeune Prix de Rome et le vieux Wagnériste', in *Richard Wagner* [Paris, 1886], p. 287).

45 In the early 'dramatic legend' *Le chant de la cloche* (1879–83), a series of dramatic tableaux based on Schiller's *Lied von der Glocke*, D'Indy did indulge in some explicit homages to Wagner's scores: scene 2 is a kind of 'village *Tristan und Isolde*', paraphrasing 'Sink hernieder, Nacht der Liebe', and scene 3 a colourful remake of the final scene of *Die Meistersinger* in miniature, with a certain French peasant accent.

46 See Manuela Schwartz, *Wagner-Rezeption und französische Oper des Fin de Siècle: Untersuchungen zu Vincent D'Indy's 'Fervaal'* (Berlin, 1999), and Steven Huebner, *French Opera at the Fin de Siècle* (cf. n. 14).

chromatic harmony with a large dose of modal experimentation deriving from practices of French sacred music and folksong, and quite alien to Wagner's melodic-harmonic language.

Thanks to the role of Wagner in the cultural discourse of the 1880s, sponsored above all by the *Revue wagnérienne*, audiences and critics often read more of Wagner into the operatic production of the time than could be supported by objective criteria. When Ernest Reyer's grand opera *Sigurd*, based on material from the *Nibelungenlied*, finally had its première in Brussels at the beginning of 1884, it could not help but appear as a product of the nascent Wagnerian obsession of that decade. But in fact, it had been composed largely in the 1860s, and in a style that mixes Gounod with modest hints of the Berlioz of *Les Troyens*. The work's closest relative would be Massenet's *Esclarmonde*, with which it shares voluptuously scored 'magical' music for the heroine, pompous ceremonial music in the Opéra tradition, and much colourful ballet music for all manner of elves, sylphes and ondines (like Franck's *Hulda*), suggesting how the French image of Germanic myth and legend can be traced as much to the world of Adam's *Giselle* as to Weber or Wagner.

If *Sigurd* gave the appearance, however unintended, of aiming to be a French *Ring of the Nibelung*, Ernest Chausson produced more consciously (though at the same time *malgré lui*) the French *Tristan und Isolde* in *Le roi Arthus*, a *drame lyrique* composed between 1885 and 1895 and posthumously premièred in Brussels in 1903. The large-scale love duet at the centre of Act I, scene 2 of Chausson's *Roi Arthus* unabashedly emulates the *Tristan* love duet, with the Brangäne figure supplied by Lancelot's faithful vassal Lyonnel, and Mordred in the role of Melot, the jealous antagonist who surprises the trysting couple as day breaks. When the music sinks into A flat for the duet, after a period of sinister-agitated chromatic wandering around A major, Chausson makes the musical allusion to *Tristan* as unmistakable as that of the dramatic situation: softly undulating strings pass repeatedly from the added sixth of A flat (F) through flat-6 (F♭, E♮) to the dominant and back. (Franck, incidentally, tried his hand at the *Tristan* Act II duet model in the duet-scene for the title character and her illicit lover, Eiolf, in the third act of *Hulda*, with a D flat 'centre' in place of Wagner's A flat, but similar episodic excursions away from this centre, and a similar ambush of the lovers by jealous, scheming antagonists at the close of the act.) Even more explicitly allusive is a four-note rising chromatic figure in the preceding orchestral transition, to the same rhythmic profile as the 'desire' motif of *Tristan* (especially the version in the Prelude to Act II). Yet the bright, harmonically enriched C major of the dawning day that concludes Act I of *Le roi Arthus*, though it could be thought to recall the end of *Tristan*'s first act, returns us rather to the musical world of the Prelude and first scene of Chausson's own opera, where Wagner's musical fingerprints are scarcely detectable. On the whole, the opera (like D'Indy's *Fervaal*) seems intent on exorcising the very Wagnerian spirit it invokes.

Wagnerism is even more a matter of 'spirit' than technique in *Fervaal*. D'Indy's tonally deracinated style of chromaticism, modal inflections (some deriving from direct Catholic chant borrowings, some from folksong) and frequent impressionist touches (in timbre, harmonic sonority and choral effects) would likely have struck Wagner as incomprehensible. Where other composers were fascinated with Wagner's depiction of passionate, erotic love and psychological motifs of conflicted allegiance, guilt and vengeance, D'Indy was preoccupied with the themes of revelation and redemption. If *Fervaal* borrows something of these impulses from *Parsifal*, it leaves Wagner's musical means almost entirely behind in favour of a highly varied, if often overwrought, late-chromatic language very much of D'Indy's own devising. A logical culmination of the ambivalent love–hate relationship characteristic of French Wagnerism as a whole is perhaps Debussy's *Pelléas et Melisande* (1903), where Wagner is reduced (musically) to a dim 'spiritual' presence, a kind of repressed memory inhabiting the same psychological netherworld as so much else in the enigmatic realm of Maeterlinck's 'Allemonde'.[47]

Back in Germany, Wagnerism also divided into a literary-ideological branch (centred in Cosima Wagner's circle at Bayreuth and Hans von Wolzogen's *Bayreuther Blätter*) and a more diffuse branch of practical influence manifest in any number of neo-Wagnerian music dramas, from the stillborn efforts of such younger 'New Germans' as Felix Draeseke and Wendelin Weissheimer up through the works of Engelbert Humperdinck, his pupil Siegfried Wagner, and the earlier operas of Richard Strauss, Hans Pfitzner and Alexander von Zemlinsky. (Often the two branches would intermingle, as for example in the cultural and musical education of Gustav Mahler in Vienna around 1880.) Without the conflict of national loyalties that burdened French Wagnerites, the impact in Germany seemed natural and inevitable, only to be resisted on the grounds of originality or temperament.

The fate of two operas premièred at the Weimar court theatre within half a year of one another has often been read as an object-lesson in the pitfalls of Wagnerian epigonism.

On 23 December 1893 the young Weimar Hofkapellmeister, Richard Strauss, conducted the first performance of Engelbert Humperdinck's *Hänsel und Gretel*, in its full operatic dress. The work had begun as a simple collection of folk-like song settings for a dramatisation of the familiar fairy tale put

47 Eliot Zuckerman aptly describes *Pelléas* as a 'negative image' of *Tristan* (*The First Hundred Years of Wagner's Tristan* [New York, 1964], p. 121).

together by the composer's sister Adelheid Wette. In amplifying the material into a Singspiel and finally a through-composed opera, Humperdinck arrived at a workable compromise between Wagnerian 'symphonic' music drama and the *Spieloper* legacy of Weber and Lortzing, imbued with a folksong element appropriate to the subject-matter. The result was an instant success: a new genre of *Märchenoper*, or fairy-tale opera, that appeared to provide a 'healthy' but equally accessible alternative to the contemporary craze for Italian *verismo*, combining the best of old and new, of populist and 'high art' elements of the German tradition.

A few months later (10 May 1894) Strauss conducted the première of his own first opera, *Guntram*, also at the Weimar Court Theatre. This work was more obviously a Wagnerian pastiche, above all in its libretto (by the composer himself), which blended elements of *Tannhäuser* and *Parsifal* while tending to displace Wagner's dialectic of aesthetic hedonism and Christian mysticism with modern messages of socialism, free-thinking and Nietzschean individualism. (In his provocative *Minnelied* in Act II, Guntram is more a descendant of Walther von Stolzing than of Tannhäuser.) Although Strauss was already an accomplished and respected composer, the opera was a failure in the long run, especially when a revival was attempted in Munich. The serious, somewhat plodding text produced a score lacking in pacing and variety. Strauss sought to remedy these factors in his next opera, *Feuersnot*, a Romantic comedy set in old Munich (and taking aim at the Munich 'philistines' who had failed to appreciate *Guntram*). The *Meistersinger* tone suggested by this material was more congenial to Strauss's talents and musical personality (this is the operatic counterpart to *Till Eulenspiegel*, as *Guntram* is to *Tod und Verklärung*). But the masterful score suffers again from an insufficiently interesting libretto, and both text and music indulge in the private jokes and self-referentiality that were among the composer's besetting sins.

After 1900 Humperdinck went on to compose a more fully Wagnerian *Märchenoper* in his *Königskinder*, first performed at the Metropolitan Opera (1910) with Geraldine Farrar and Hermann Jadlowker in the leading roles. Opulent, motivically dense textures and symphonically elaborated structures, along with the somewhat vague symbolic pretences of the fairy-tale libretto, signal this as Humperdinck's principal bid to perpetuate the Wagnerian tradition. But despite an initial success in the US and in Germany, the work disappeared from the repertory after World War I. In the meantime, Richard Strauss discovered in Oscar Wilde's *Salomé* and Hugo von Hofmannsthal's *Elektra* dramatic material perfectly suited to his high-voltage musical imagination. These subjects allowed him to shake off the more constraining aspects of Wagnerian music drama, too evident in *Guntram*, while reinventing the distinctly profiled vocal declamation, complex motivic 'orchestral melody', and psychological intensity of Wagner in a striking, concise, and thoroughly modern manner.

Strauss felt the need to retreat from this 'thoroughly modern manner' in order to continue his career as a successful opera composer into the centre of the twentieth century, starting with the neo-classicising *volte-face* of *Der Rosenkavalier* and *Ariadne auf Naxos*. His later works, like those of Puccini, Mascagni and other Italians after 1900, remain in some sense products of a century-long momentum of operatic culture in Germany and Italy, respectively. Without entering into polemics on the state of opera in the twentieth century, it seems fair to say that the modernist aesthetic after World War I, and above all the various techniques of composition pioneered since that time in response to the perceived demise of Classical–Romantic tonality, have been inimical to the high Romantic styles in which the genres of opera and symphony had flourished. *Verismo*, expressionism or the decadent psychological 'portrait' à la *Salome* and *Elektra* are all examples of opera nourishing itself from broader cultural phenomena of the moment, as it would naturally continue to do. But one could argue that opera – as a genre and as an institution – was not well adapted to survive in the twentieth century as a living organism (as opposed to a 'museum culture'). From this perspective, 'Wagnerism' was a symptomatic after-effect of opera's apotheosis in the later nineteenth century, when it reached the height of its cultural ambitions and, indeed, prestige. This original 'apotheosis' of the genre was embodied above all in Wagner's own *oeuvre*, perhaps; and it is one from which opera as a whole has never quite recovered.

Bibliography

Abbate, C., *Unsung Voices: Opera and Narrative in the Nineteenth Century*. Princeton, 1991

Abbate, Carolyn and Roger Parker (eds.), *Analyzing Opera: Verdi and Wagner*. Berkeley and Los Angeles, 1989

Abraham, G. (ed.), *New Oxford History of Music*, vol. 9: *Romanticism (1830–1890)*. New York, 1990 ('Wagner's Later Stage Works', pp. 257–321; 'Opera: 1850–1890', pp. 322–488)

Adorno, T. W., *In Search of Wagner*, trans. Rodney Livingstone. London, 1981

Becker, H. (ed.), *Die 'couleur locale' in der Oper des 19. Jahrhunderts*. Regensburg, 1976

Bellman, J. (ed.), *The Exotic in Western Music*. Boston, 1998

Blaze de Bury, H., *Meyerbeer et son temps*. Paris, 1865

Budden, J., *The Operas of Verdi*: I, *From 'Oberto to 'Rigoletto'* (New York, 1973); II, *From 'Il trovatore' to 'La forza del destino'* (New York, 1978); III, *From 'Don Carlos' to 'Falstaff'* (New York, 1981)

   Verdi. London and Melbourne, 1985

Burbidge, P. and Richard Sutton (eds.), *The Wagner Companion*. New York, 1979

Charlton, D. (ed.), *Cambridge Companion to Grand Opera*. Cambridge, 2001

Crosten, W., *French Grand Opera: An Art and a Business*. New York, 1948; rpt. New York, 1973

Dahlhaus, C., *Richard Wagner's Music Dramas*, trans. M. Whittall. Cambridge, 1979

Nineteenth-Century Music, trans. J. B. Robinson. Berkeley and Los Angeles, 1989

Vom Musikdrama zur Literaturoper: Aufsätze zur neueren Operngeschichte. Munich and Salzburg, 1983

Realism in Nineteenth-Century Music, trans. M. Whittall. Cambridge, 1985

Dizikes, J., *Opera in America: A Cultural History*. New Haven and London, 1993

Döhring, S. and Henze-Döhring, S., *Oper und Musikdrama im 19. Jahrhundert*. Handbuch der musikalischen Gattungen, 13. Laaber, 1997

Fauser, A. and M. Schwartz (eds.), *Von Wagner zum Wagnèrisme: Musik, Literatur, Kunst, Politik*. Leipzig, 1999

Fulcher, J., *The Nation's Image: French Grand Opera as Politics and Politicized Art*. Cambridge, 1987

Gerhard, A., *The Urbanization of Opera: Music Theater in Paris in the Nineteenth Century*, trans. M. Whittall. Chicago, 1998

Grey, T. S., *Wagner's Musical Prose: Texts and Contexts*. Cambridge, 1995

Grout, D. J., *A Short History of Opera*. New York, 2nd edn 1965

Hadlock, H., *Mad Loves: Women and Music in Offenbach's 'Les Contes d'Hoffmann*. Princeton, 2000

Hanslick, E., *Die moderne Oper*. 9 vols., Berlin, 1875–84 and Allgemeiner Verein für deutsche Literatur, 1888–1900

Huebner, S., *The Operas of Charles Gounod*. Oxford, 1990

French Opera at the Fin de Siècle: Wagnerism, Nationalism, and Style. Oxford, 1999

Kimbell, D. R. B., *Verdi in the Age of Italian Romanticism*. Cambridge, 1981

Matz, M. J. P., *Verdi: A Biography*. New York, 1993

McClary, S., *Bizet: Carmen*. Cambridge, 1996

Müller, U. and Wapnewski, P., *Wagner Handbook*, trans. and ed. J. Deathridge. Cambridge, Mass., 1992

Murano, M. T. (ed.), *L'Opera tra Venezia e Parigi*. Florence, 1988

Newman, E., *The Life of Richard Wagner*. 4 vols., New York and London, 1937–46

Nicolaisen, J., *Italian Opera in Transition, 1871–1893*. Ann Arbor, 1980

Parker, R., *Leonora's Last Act: Essays in Verdian Discourse*. Princeton, 1997

Parker, R. and Groos, A. (eds.), *Reading Opera*. Princeton, 1988

Petrobelli, P., *Music in the Theater: Essays on Verdi and other Composers*, with translations by R. Parker. Princeton, 1994

Rimsky-Korsakoff, N., *My Musical Life*, trans. Judah A. Joffe (1923). Rpt., London, 1974

Rosselli, J., *The Opera Industry in Italy from Cimarosa to Verdi: The Role of the Impresario*. Cambridge, 1984

Music and Musicians in Nineteenth-Century Italy. Portland, Oreg., 1991

Sala, E., *L'opera senza canto: Il mélo Romantico e l'invenzione della colonna sonora*. Venice, 1995

Samson, J. (ed.), *The Late Romantic Era*. Englewood Cliffs, 1991

Schmidgall, G., *Shakespeare and Opera*. New York and Oxford, 1990

Schwartz, M., *Wagner-Rezeption und französische oper des Fin de Siècle: Untersuchungen zu Vincent D'Indys 'Fervaal'*. Berlin, 1999

Smart, M. A. (ed.), *Siren Songs: Representations of Gender and Sexuality in Opera*. Princeton, 2000

Taruskin, R., *Opera and Drama in Russia*. Ann Arbor, 1981
  Musorgsky: Eight Essays and an Epilogue. Princeton, 1993
  Defining Russia Musically. Princeton, 1997
Tomlinson, G., *Metaphysical Song: An Essay on Opera*. Princeton, 1998
Tyrrell, J., *Czech Opera*. Cambridge, 1988
de Van, G., *Verdi's Theater: Creating Drama Through Music*, trans. G. Roberts. Chicago, 1998
Wagner, R., *Gesammelte Schriften und Dichtungen*. 10 vols., Leipzig, 1887–8
  Richard Wagner's Prose Works. 8 vols., trans. W. A. Ellis. London, 1893–9
  My Life, trans. A. Gray. Cambridge, 1983
Walsh, T. J., *Second-Empire Opera: The Théâtre-Lyrique, Paris 1851–1870*. London and New York, 1981
Weaver, W. and Chusid, M. (eds.), *The Verdi Companion*. New York, 1979
Zoppelli, L., *L'opera come racconto: Modi narrativi nel teatro musicale dell'Ottocento*. Venice, 1994

15

Beethoven reception: the symphonic tradition

JAMES HEPOKOSKI

Symphonic practice in later nineteenth-century Europe was no unitary activity that we should collapse into a crisp, linear narrative. The reality was messier. It would be more accurate to regard the world of orchestral composition as an arena of competing ideologies and diverse aims, a field of energy and circulation. To be sure, the energy was anything but random. Composers, performers, publishers, critics, academics, students and audiences channelled it through a flurry of enabling and constraining preconditions, historical and cultural circumstances sorted out differently by different groups. Among the most significant precondition was the idea of tradition – or, more to the point, the struggle over the presumed ownership of that tradition. By the second half of the century the European idea of the symphony as a high-status cultural achievement was nourished by lovingly shaped readings of the genre's Austro-Germanic past. Commonly enough, the grounding shape was reinforced by a heroic tale: the ascent to the apex, Beethoven – embodying the long-sought liberation of the modern idea of greatness in instrumental music, the definitional moment of full symphonic adequacy, the 'undeniable' launching of 'the new era of music' (as Liszt put it in 1855)[1] – followed by a crisis of continuation in subsequent decades.

Spurred also by external factors – technological, economic, political, ethnic-national – the symphonic crisis invited a number of solutions: it had been disseminated to several different publics on several different terms.[2] As a result, by mid-century no central authority was able to establish a consensus concerning the best way to continue the tradition while still honouring its past. Consequently, the tradition shattered into individualised solutions and partisan controversy. Like the emerging marketplace with which it was implicated, European symphonic activity came to be moulded in significant measure

---

1 Liszt, 'Robert Schumann' [1855], in *Gesammelte Schriften* (henceforth *GS*), ed. L. Ramann [1882] (rpt. Hildesheim, 1978), IV, p. 163.

2 An overview of symphonic monuments is provided in D. Kern Holoman (ed.), *The Nineteenth-Century Symphony* (New York, 1997). A more extensive inventory may be found in selected volumes of A. Peter Brown's *The Symphonic Repertoire: The European Symphony from 1800–1930* (vol. III, Bloomington forthcoming in 2001); and *The Second Golden Age of the Viennese Symphony: Brahms, Bruckner, Dvořák, Mahler, and Selected Contemporaries* (vol. IV, Bloomington forthcoming in 2001).

by an 'invisible hand', generated by the choices of thousands of pivotally placed individuals and the interplay of dozens of small, often powerful interest groups. Several of these groups sought to impose a 'real' configuration on to this tradition according to the promptings of their own self-interests. For such reasons as these it is futile to seek a mythical consistency among the musical styles and dissimilar achievements of the period's most celebrated figures. Instead, the contestations of the age may be rendered approachable only by reawakening the central problems faced by its composers and audiences – the questions to which individual compositions sought to provide answers.

Dilemmas of symphonic practice at mid-century

It may seem one of the ironies of nineteenth-century music that the perception of a crisis within Austro-Germanic sonata construction set in at almost precisely the same time as the emergence of the academic recognition and honouring of this tradition, most notably in A. B. Marx's University of Berlin lectures and instruction in the 1830s, leading to his extensive, Beethoven-based text-book-codification of musical forms, *Die Lehre von der musikalischen Komposition, praktisch-theoretisch* (1838, with several subsequent, expanded editions). But the two issues – crisis and methodical systematisation – are interrelated. Once precipitated into such detailed language, sonata-symphonic practice and its most prestigious constituent, 'sonata form' (the term famously coined by Marx), became objects open to quasi-scientific classification. It is true, of course, that a broad array of flexible 'first-movement-form' procedures had circulated as common currency among composers several decades before Marx's systematic enquiry. A few quick descriptions of some nodal points of this complex structure had even found their way into print (Koch, Galeazzi, Kollmann, Reicha, and so on). Heinrich Birnbach's essays in 1827 and 1829 had marked an especially important stage in the 'verbal' understanding of the form.[3] (Influential twentieth-century German-language discussions of the subject have viewed Birnbach as part of a broader effort in the early nineteenth century to articulate a prescriptive or 'pragmatic' sonata form. Ever more insistently the concept of a 'form-schema' displaced the earlier idea of an 'open architectonic model'.)[4] But certainly after Marx, whose discussions

3 Heinrich Joseph Birnbach, 'Ueber die verschiedene Form größerer Instrumentaltonstücke aller Art und deren Bearbeitung', an essay in six instalments in the *Berliner allgemeine musikalische Zeitung* [hereafter *BamZ*], 4 (1827), nos. 34–7, 45–6 (pp. 269–72, 277–81, 285–7, 293–5, 361–3, 369–73); expanded with a different title in *Cäcilia* 10/38 (1829), pp. 97–120.
4 Fred Ritzel, *Die Entwicklung der 'Sonatenform' im musiktheoretischen Schrifttum des 18. und 19. Jahrhunderts*, 2nd edn (Wiesbaden, 1969), pp. 213–23. For 'form-schema' see, for example, Ulrich Konrad, 'Der Wiener Kompositionswettbewerb 1835 und Franz Lachners Sinfonia passionata: Ein Beitrag zur Geschichte der Sinfonie nach Beethoven', *Augsburger Jahrbuch für Musikwissenschaft* (Tutzing, 1986), p. 222.

were subsequently imitated, and often condensed, by other writers, there can be no doubt that an abstracted, idealised sonata form existed even more concretely as a reified, conceptual 'thing' – something like a 'regulative idea' (in Kant's sense) or an 'ideal type' (in Max Weber's sense), no matter what elasticity it allowed or what variants from it might be observed in actual practice. By this time the fear of the strongest composers was that it had already devolved into empty formula.

In the 1830s Schumann judged contemporary symphonic composition to be hampered by the false comforts of 'old', 'traditional' or 'received' forms – meaning especially, self-satisfied, rule-of-thumb conceptions of what Marx was calling sonata form. Following the heaven-storming gigantism of Beethoven's Ninth Symphony, for a composer to continue to embrace the older proportions and contained politeness of traditional composition ran the risk of seeming pallid. Now was the time for monumentality, for formal progress, for bold reinterpretations of past habits. Stirring up issues that would dominate the rest of the century, Schumann laid out the difficulty in his 1835 review of Berlioz's *Symphonie fantastique*:

> Form is the vessel of the spirit. Greater spaces require greater spirit to fill them. The word 'symphony' has hitherto designated instrumental music of the greatest proportions . . . It is enough for second-class talents to master the received forms; those of the first rank are granted the right to enlarge them. Only the genius may range freely.
>
> After Beethoven's Ninth Symphony, in external dimensions the greatest of all instrumental works we have, moderation and limit seemed to be exhausted . . . The later symphony composers realized this, and a few even fled back to the traditional forms of Haydn and Mozart . . . None . . . dared make any substantial changes in the old forms with the exception of isolated [programmatic] experiments like Spohr's latest symphony [and Berlioz's *Symphonie fantastique*].[5]

Schumann's anxiety about the vacuity of 'traditional form' (*hergebrachte Form*) in the hands of post-Beethovenian epigones surfaced again in 1836, in a sharp criticism of a recent prize-winning symphony by Franz Lachner (*Sinfonia passionata* in C minor, 1835). This lengthy work, he charged, was eclectically 'Meyerbeerian' and 'lacking in style' (*stillos*), 'put together out of German, Italian, and French [traits]' instead of continuing the more purely Germanic path set forth by Beethoven. Moreover, its extraordinary length lacked a seri-

---

5 Schumann, *Neue Zeitschrift für Musik* (henceforth *NZfM*) (3 and 31 July, 4, 7, 11 and 14 August 1835); rpt. of revised essay in Schumann, *Gesammelte Schriften über Musik und Musiker* [1854, henceforth *GS*] (rpt. Wiesbaden, 1985), I, pp. 118–51 (quotations from pp. 118–19). The translation used here is that of Edward T. Cone in *Berlioz: Fantastic Symphony* (New York, 1971), pp. 226–7. Cone noted that the Spohr symphony in question was No. 4 in F major, a programme symphony subtitled *Die Weihe der Töne* (The Consecration of Sound).

ousness of content; the result was a 'diluted' work, an ongoing dissipation into thinness that, by the finale, 'disappeared into complete tediousness and emptiness' (*Öde und Leere*).[6] Similar remarks may be found in a series of essays from summer 1839, on the heels of his discovery of Schubert's Great C Major Symphony and its 21 March première under Mendelssohn.[7] Recent piano sonatas, he insisted, had declined into mere 'examples, or studies in form': 'Single beautiful examples of this genre will surely show up here and there, and already have, but in general it appears that the form has run its course'.[8] As for the symphony (in this case, ones by Preyer, Reissiger and, again, Lachner): 'When the German speaks of symphonies, he means Beethoven. The two names are for him one and indivisible – his joy, his pride . . . For the most part the more recent symphonies decline intellectually into the overture style – the first movements, that is to say; the slow [movements] are only there because they cannot be left out; the scherzos are scherzos in name only; the finales no longer know what the preceding movements contained'. Modern works fail to measure up to the Beethovenian standard, in which the rapidly changing ideas are 'linked through an inner, spiritual bond'.[9]

Schumann's writings from the later 1830s brought together three convictions: (1) the Germanic post-Beethovenian symphony must retain a strong, ethical component; it needed to be underpinned with moral seriousness and consistency of national character and not lose itself in special effects, amusement or divertissement; (2) in the absence of a foregrounded problematisation or transformation in individual works, 'traditional form' decayed into insipid formula; and (3) the resulting formal shapes, whatever their relationship to tradition might be, needed justification through a strong expressive content, implicit or explicit, that could draw the movements together under a single conception. His subsequent four symphonies (1841–51) were doubtless intended as object-lessons. In beguilingly ingenious ways each of them seeks to reconcile earnest, Beethovenian (self-consciously 'Classical') sonorities with formal experimentation. (See the discussion in chapter 7.)

6 Schumann, *NZfM* (8 November 1836). Reprinted in 'Die Preissymphonie', in Schumann, *GS*, I, pp. 230–5. On Lachner's music and Schumann's criticism, see Konrad, 'Die Wiener Kompositionswettbewerb'. Konrad additionally argues that Lachner may have been aware of and influenced by Schubert's (as yet 'unknown') 'Great' C Major Symphony.

7 Schumann's essay on the newly uncovered Schubert symphony and its 'heavenly lengths' appeared a year later, in 1840. Reprinted in Schumann, *GS*, III, pp. 195–203.

8 *NZfM* (26 April 1839); Schumann, *GS*, III, p. 80.

9 Schumann, *NZfM*, (2 July 1839), 1; *GS*, III, pp. 133–44. The translation of most of this passage is that of Linda Correll Roesner, 'Schumann', in Holoman, *The Nineteenth-Century Symphony*, p. 43. Cf. the translation in Robert Schumann, *On Music and Musicians*, ed. Konrad Wolff, trans. Paul Rosenfeld (New York, 1969), p. 61; and Jon W. Finson, *Robert Schumann and the Study of Orchestral Composition* (Oxford, 1989), p. 19. Cf. also Walter Frisch, *Brahms: The Four Symphonies* (New York, 1996), pp. 3–4; and Frisch, "Echt symphonisch": On the Historical Context of Brahms's Symphonies', in David Brodbeck (ed.), *Brahms Studies II* (Lincoln, Nebr., and London, 1998), pp. 113–33.

The same concerns for a historically appropriate balance between preservationist and progressive impulses – though filtered through a different personality and sense of poetic elegance – might be claimed for the other main set of Classicising symphonies that saw publication in the period 1840–51, those of Mendelssohn. No. 2, the large-scale 'Lobgesang' from 1840, paid obvious homage to Beethoven's Ninth. This highly polished 'symphony-cantata' merged three instrumental symphonic movements (linked without pauses) with a forty-minute, socially affirmative cantata finale, complete with arias, choruses, recitative and even an interior chorale. No. 3, 'Scottish' (1842), displayed tidier, more Classical proportions but might have been planned, in part, as a metaphor and proposed solution for the current symphonic dilemma. Among its remarkable features is a phoenix-from-the-ashes epilogue ('finale maestoso'), which, at least on a broader plane of interpretation, may be construed as representing a grand hope, a swelling declaration of the historically conscious renewal of the symphonic tradition itself, whose 'death' had just been enacted in the preceding movements.[10] No. 4, 'Italian' (published only in 1851, posthumously – though completed and performed in 1833), is a more traditionally formatted work. Compactly brilliant and filled with masterly details and characteristic touches, it is less structurally adventuresome as a whole than either No. 2 or No. 3. (Mendelssohn's 'Fifth' Symphony, the 'Reformation', had been composed in 1830 but would not see publication until 1868.)

Mendelssohn's Fourth and Schumann's Third, both emerging in the early 1850s, brought this phase of post-Beethovenian symphonic composition to a close and precipitated a new crisis of continuation. On the one hand, throughout the 1850s and 1860s self-styled progressives and their supporters claimed to have supplanted the more abstract symphony with the new genres of the music drama (Wagner) and the symphonic poem (Liszt). On the other hand, conservative partisans of the official or mainline mid-century style, honouring the proportions and textures of Mendelssohn and Schumann, decried the radicalism of Liszt and the 'New German School' and looked in vain for worthy successors to the more restrained, more abstract symphony. Finally appearing in 1876 – perhaps in part spurred into existence by the appearance of Max Bruch's Symphonies Nos. 1 and 2 in 1868 and 1870 – Brahms's magisterial First Symphony addressed a long-felt need and shored up a traditionalist position that many on all sides had assumed was no longer viable. [11]

10 This interpretation – according to which performances of this symphony enacted what the work itself may have sought to declare – differs in some respects from that offered in Peter Mercer-Taylor, 'Mendelssohn's "Scottish" Symphony and the Music of German Memory', *19th Century Music*, 19 (1995), pp. 68–82.

11 David Brodbeck, *Brahms: Symphony No. 1* (Cambridge, 1997), pp. 11–15, 84–5; and Walter Frisch, *Brahms: The Four Symphonies* (New York, 1996), pp. 20–7.

These controversies were played out in the context of a more fundamental dilemma, one that may be regarded as the foundational paradox of mid-century symphonic practice. Briefly put, the seeming compositional imperatives towards complexity, individuality and emancipation from an uncritical reliance on inherited traditions worked at cross-purposes to the cultural conditions required for this music's widespread public success. These conditions encouraged participants to promote the impression of symphonic music's ready accessibility to an international, liberal-humanist public whose musical literacy was often shaky. This illusion needed to be underpinned by strategies of reassurance. For some, it was the quasi-religious conviction that in the hands of its greatest masters instrumental music could express transcendental essences by taking on the role of an idealised 'spirit' or metaphysics. (Here the additionally implied aesthetics of immediacy offered an easy dispensation from cognitive grapplings with music's history, genres and structures by declaring that these concerns were either fussily academic or irrelevant.) For others, it was the claim that instrumental music could reach a wider audience through a merger with high-prestige literary, national or philosophical programmes. For still others it was harboured in the growing cult of the performer. Additional fuel for the enterprise was furnished by a marked upsurge in superficial music criticism in the press, buttressed by the simplified music-guide or programme-note for the lay listener.[12]

Such considerations led to two features characteristic of later nineteenth-century orchestral music. The first was a heightened personalisation of symphonic style and content. In principle, each composer, spurred onward by the doctrine of originality, was to construct an individual (or national) voice to carry on a provocative dialogue with the official mid-century style. Some solutions, while by no means lacking distinctiveness and savour, remained more loyal to the proportions of the Mendelssohn–Schumann tradition – Gade, Bruch, Rubinstein, Svendsen, Goldmark, Parry, Fibich, much of Dvořák. Others insisted on their own uniqueness and innovation counterpointed against the ever-accumulating tradition – Liszt, Tchaikovsky, Bruckner, Strauss, Mahler, Nielsen, Sibelius. The second feature was an increasing attention to orchestral music's lush, emotional power – intense sonic surfaces designed to sweep one away or to suffuse the whole with an aura of elevation. This became all the more possible with the dynamic and colouristic resources provided by the modern orchestra. The important point, though, was that these experiences helped to provide audiences, critics and performers with a gratifying sense of devotional participation in profundity while relieving most

12 Cf. Leon Botstein, 'Listening through Reading: Musical Literacy and the Concert Audience', *19th Century Music*, 16 (1992), pp. 129–45.

of them from the burden of investigating the details of the actual musical thought at hand.

Ardent debates and new aesthetic ideologies now swirled around symphonic composition. One senses everywhere in them the old eighteenth-century fear that non-texted instrumental music might mean nothing at all, that it would collapse into empty pretence unless shored up with readily absorbed articles of faith. Before long the various factions would come to accuse each other of trivial composition, of sensationalism or decadence, of betraying the tradition, while maintaining that it alone was not squandering the cherished legacy of Beethoven. After 1850, in an age of expanding technical materials and sumptuous orchestral resources, one persistent symphonic problem was to keep the fear of emptiness at bay through acts of artistic compensation buttressed by earnestly promulgated networks of prestige. As larger Europe raced towards commercial, urban, technological, political and military modernity, the continued viability of the artistic tradition could not be taken for granted.

Poetic content: the challenge of Liszt

With their Shakespearean, 'Hebridean', 'Scottish' or 'Italian' tints and lyrical landscapes, Mendelssohn's concert overtures and symphonies helped to nurture the idea that orchestral music should take a more decisive literary-poetic turn, and it was a simple matter for non-Austro-Germanic composers to adapt such precedents into *völkisch* evocations of their own homelands. Still, the issue of extra-musical representation extended beyond matters of local colour. Berlioz's programme symphonies from the 1830s posed a special challenge, but many earlier works also spoke to this generalised impulse. Foremost among them were Beethoven's and Weber's overtures, along with the former's much-discussed 'Pastoral' Symphony. Many of Beethoven's other works were also given early and mid-nineteenth-century poetic interpretations. In 1825, for instance, an article signed by 'C. F. Ebers' in the periodical *Cäcilia* suggested that the whole of Beethoven's Seventh Symphony, movement by movement, represented a wedding celebration. Schumann would pass on the interpretation – recasting the image as a 'peasant-wedding' – and the reading was also mentioned by Wagner, A. W. Ambros, and others.[13] (In 1877 Karl Goldmark would conflate the reception traditions of Beethoven's Sixth and Seventh, producing the five-movement symphonic poem 'Rustic Wedding'.)

The drive to interpret textless compositions poetically had been intellectu-

13 See Thomas Grey, 'Metaphorical Modes in Nineteenth-Century Music Criticism: Image, Narrative, and Idea', in Steven Paul Scher (ed.), *Music and Text: Critical Inquiries* (Cambridge, 1992), pp. 93–117 (on Beethoven's Seventh, pp. 99–110).

ally fortified in part by A. B. Marx's advocacy in the 1820s of programmatic or 'characteristic' music, along with his parallel insistence in the *Berliner allgemeine musikalische Zeitung* that to understand Beethoven's major works is to grasp the *Grundideen* or fundamental ideas that had motivated them.[14] By mid-century Wagner raised the pitch of the issue by publishing his often self-serving interpretations of a few of Beethoven's orchestral works. 'The plastic subject of almost all the master's symphonic works [is that of] scenes between man and woman', he claimed in 1852 in a much-cited, if dubious, reading of 'Beethoven's Overture to "Coriolanus".[15] Such powder-kegs exploded into the programme-music debate that preoccupied much of the later nineteenth century.

That debate was sparked in the 1850s by Liszt and his supporters in and around Weimar, the self-styled 'New German School'. Marching under the banner of a historically necessary musical progress (*Fortschritt*, literally a 'step forward'), Liszt argued that the vehicles for this advancement were the 'symphonic poem' (*symphonische Dichtung*) – a term of his own coinage – and the programme symphony. These, he claimed, were the main orchestral replacements for the now-enervated abstract symphony. In both, purely musical effects (potentially new musical forms, motivic and thematic transformation, sensational orchestration) fused with high-prestige literary or historical images conveyed in the title or other supplementary material, such as interior subtitles, appended texts or other composer-authorised programmatic commentary. Poetic ideas were now to serve even more decisively as the wind in orchestral music's sails.

To that end, in the 1850s Liszt completed twelve symphonic poems: *Ce qu'on entend sur la montagne, Tasso, Les préludes, Orpheus, Prometheus, Mazeppa, Festklänge, Héroïde funèbre, Hungaria, Hamlet, Hunnenschlacht (The Battle of the Huns)* and *Die Ideale*. Most of these were expansions and adaptations of the one-movement format and sonata-form basis of the operatic and concert overture – the Beethoven, Weber, Mendelssohn or Berlioz precedent shorn of the generic designation 'overture', swollen to larger proportions, and provided, usually, with an even less orthodox formal treatment. He complemented these with two programme symphonies, marked by ever-transforming representational themes or motifs: the '*Faust* Symphony in

14 E.g., Marx, 'Etwas über die Symphonie und Beethoven's Leistungen in diesem Fache', in *BamZ* 1/19–21 (1824), pp. 165–8, 173–6, 181–4); and Marx, *Über Malerei in der Tonkunst* (Berlin, 1828). See also Scott Burnham, 'Criticism, Faith, and the *Idee*: A. B. Marx's Early Reception of Beethoven', *19th Century Music*, 13 (1990), pp. 183–92; and Judith Silber Ballan, 'Marxian Programmatic Music: A Stage in Mendelssohn's Musical Development', in R. Larry Todd (ed.), *Mendelssohn Studies* (Cambridge, 1992), pp. 149–61.

15 My emendation of the translation found in *Richard Wagner's Prose Works*, trans. William Ashton Ellis [1894], rpt. (New York, 1966), III, p. 225.

Three Character Pictures' (1854–7), with its choral finale setting the conclusion of the second part of Goethe's masterwork; and the 'Symphony on Dante's *Divina commedia*' (1855–7). It is difficult to overestimate the impact of Liszt's orchestral output and the aesthetic ideology that it exemplified. These works served as incitements to personal experimentation and as sources of analogous ideas and even rival compositions for many in the next two or three generations.

Liszt's polemical version of the idea of programme music was instantly surrounded by partisan controversy. Spearheading the traditionalist counterattack to it on behalf of 'the independent meaning of music', the Viennese critic and aesthetician Eduard Hanslick – by 1862 a friend and supporter of Brahms – saw in it little but mistaken, schismatic ideas, an arrogant betrayal of the tradition, and a ready-made pack of excuses for inadequate talent. For Liszt and his followers the fusion of a unique musical process with a clearly indicated poetic concept was to be permanent and inseparable. As Franz Brendel, a leading spokesman for the New German School, insisted in 1859, both belonged 'up to a certain point' to what aesthetic philosophers call 'the work itself'.[16] This meant that to subtract the programme and to hear these compositions only as 'absolute music' – originally the Wagnerian-Lisztian term for the non-representational work – or to try to imagine conceivable, alternative programmes, was an aesthetic error. One would violate the very conditions of the genre, refusing to play the intended aesthetic game by its rules.

The conviction that the 'poetic solution' was the key to the problem of an otherwise blocked musical progress lay behind Liszt's galvanising manifesto, *Berlioz and His 'Harold' Symphony* (1855) – an essay stretching to around a hundred pages, already discussed in another context in this volume (see chapter 11). For polemical purposes he divided current instrumental composition into two camps, non-programmatic and programmatic. The former he referred to in various ways: the 'specifically musical' composers, the 'independent style', the work of the 'formalists' or 'mere musicians', and so on. This position he arraigned as unimaginatively committed to orthodox formulas, as embracing aesthetic stasis, opposed to the inevitable march of history and aesthetic renovation. As Schumann had done almost two decades earlier, Liszt dismissed recent work in non-representational music as lacklustre, imitative, empty. Worse, he claimed, such compositions eluded the understanding of mid-century audiences. Because non-programmatic music conveyed merely 'an abstract ideal' or only loosely generalised 'ideal regions', the listener in

---

16 Brendel, *Franz Liszt als Symphoniker* (Leipzig, 1859), p. 13. Cf. Vera Micznik, 'The Absolute Limitations of Programme Music: The Case of Liszt's "Die Ideale"', *Music and Letters*, 80 (1999), pp. 207–40.

search of more concrete meanings was obliged to fill in the details arbitrarily, pursuing the whims of his or her own fantasy.[17]

As opposed to this, 'tone-poets' (*Tondichter*) were answering 'the call of the times'. They were the 'New Testament' heirs to Beethoven's tradition by producing 'poetic' works that served at least three practical purposes. First, inspired by literary masterpieces, such pieces revealed the 'innermost relationships' between music and great ideas, 'the totality of human feeling, thought, poetry, and aspirations', laid out in 'a succession of soul-states' (*eine Folge von Seelenzuständen*). Second, by providing the programme the composer furnished a much-needed anchor to stabilise the perception of the listener who, lacking this, was in danger of experiencing a free-floating bewilderment. Third – and most revolutionarily – poetic music, unlike traditionalist abstractions, liberated the composer from blindly following eclipsed formal conventions. This was Liszt's clarion call to the future:

> In so-called Classic Music the return and thematic development of the themes is determined [*bestimmt*] through formal rules that one [erroneously] regards as inviolable, even though its composers had no written rule in front of them other than that of their own fantasy. (They themselves drew up the formal layouts that some today wish to regard as law.) On the other hand, in programme music the returns, alternations, modifications, and modulations of the motif are conditioned [*bedingt*] by their relationship to a poetic idea. Here one theme does not call forth another by rule of law. Here the motifs are not a succession of stereotyped similarities or oppositions of tone-colours . . . Although they are by no means ignored, all exclusively musical considerations are subordinated to the treatment of the given subject.[18]

Here Liszt separated himself from the conservatives. Today's geniuses 'create new forms for new ideas, new skins for new wine'; they drive their musical thoughts 'to new and bold, unusual and intricate combinations'.[19] (Nearly ninety years later, Richard Strauss, almost a half-century past his own programme-music battles of the 1890s, would recall the invigorating challenge

---

17 *Berlioz und seine 'Harold-Symphonie'*, in Liszt, *GS*, IV, pp. 3–102. On the issue of Liszt's authorship of this essay (some of which was probably penned by Carolyne von Sayn-Wittgenstein, perhaps as part of 'a collaborative effort'), see, e.g., Oliver Strunk (ed.), *Source Readings in Music History: The Nineteenth Century*, ed. Ruth Solie (New York, 1998), pp. 116–17. (Some translated extracts from the essay appear on pp. 117–32, attributed to both Liszt and Sayn-Wittgenstein; several of the passages mentioned in the present text do not appear in the *Source Readings*.) Whatever the nuances surrounding the authorship, Liszt obviously endorsed both the ideas and the way that they were articulated, and the declarations were embraced as characteristically Lisztian throughout the rest of the century. All of the translations in the present text are my own. Page-sources in the *Gesammelte Schriften* for the quotations: 'poetic solution', p. 44; 'specifically musical', pp. 49, 50, 56; 'independent style', p. 56; 'formalists', p. 50; 'mere musicians', p. 48; 'abstract ideal', p. 57, quoting Fétis; 'ideal regions', etc., p. 56.

18 Liszt, *Berlioz*; 'tone-poets', p. 47; 'call of the times', p. 42; 'New Testament', p. 59; 'poetic', p. 44; 'innermost relationships . . . totality', p. 57; 'soul states', p. 50; 'In so-called', p. 69.

19 Liszt, *Berlioz*; 'create', p. 60; 'to new and bold', p. 48.

of the Lisztian agenda, whose slogan he recalled as 'New ideas must seek new forms for themselves' [*Neue Gedanken müssen sich neue Formen suchen*].)[20] Even those threatened or scandalised by Liszt could hardly avoid being affected by such ideas. In retrospect it is clear that many of the formal experiments of the later nineteenth century sought to modify existing practice on the basis of some sort of conceptual idea (not necessarily extra-musical) working dialectically with the traditional demands of the material itself. And by the 1860s Northern and Eastern European nationalists of various stripes would seek to merge aspects of Liszt's demands with the validation also conferred by what remained of the claims of traditional form. For both sides, more was at risk than matters of aesthetics and personal taste. 'Form under siege' became a moral battle – for some, a metaphysical one – in which the cultural stakes were high.

The ways in which the reception history of Liszt's ideas was played out in subsequent orchestral music may be complex, but this very complexity afforded later composers a variety of defences as they sought ways of justifying themselves against the equally intricate arguments of sceptics. One significant strand of the reception history, as Carl Dahlhaus has pointed out, lay in Wagner's acknowledgement ('On Franz Liszt's Symphonic Poems', 1857) that a casual examination of Liszt might tempt composers and audiences to lose sight of the self-standing, metaphysical supremacy of music. Consequently, he argued, a literary or extra-musical programme, while necessary as an initial step for both composer and listener, existed primarily as a 'form[al] motif' that the greatest music, following its own inner dictates, will eventually transcend.[21] The metaphysical substance of music, that is, will at some point cast aside the lift-off programme – which had functioned as a mere booster rocket – on the way to the stars. Such a paradoxical position had its self-evident uses against the charge of producing mere, musically empty *Literaturmusik*: it permitted a composer simultaneously to avow and disavow the programme, depending on the circumstances at hand. Yearning for an ever-elusive metaphysical saturation, Mahler, in particular, would be much drawn in the 1890s to the tensions inherent in this argument.

Between absolute and programme music

It is counter-productive to collapse post-1850 instrumental music into two polarised types. The supposed opposition of absolute and programme music is

---

20 Strauss, 'Aus meinen Jugend- und Lehrjahren', *Betrachtungen und Erinnerungen*, ed. Willi Schuh, 1st edn (Zurich, 1949), p. 168. A differing translation is found in *Recollections and Reflections*, trans. L. J. Lawrence (London, 1953), p. 139.

21 See, e.g., Dahlhaus, *The Idea of Absolute Music*, trans. Roger Lustig (Chicago, 1989), p. 135; Dahlhaus, *Nineteenth-Century Music*, trans. J. B. Robinson (Berkeley and Los Angeles, 1989), pp. 237, 361; Thomas S. Grey, *Wagner's Musical Prose: Texts and Contexts* (Cambridge, 1995), pp. 308–11.

a false dichotomy, one forged in the heat of nineteenth-century polemics. Nor are such terms to be regarded as verifiable properties of the works themselves. All such classifications serve overwhelmingly as hermeneutic genres – differing modes of interpretation that, for differing purposes, seek to supervise the interplay between a piece and its listener. Hermeneutic genres provide the guidelines encouraging certain kinds of communication to occur while discouraging others; they are lenses through which selected aspects of culturally complex compositions may be called forth for analysis, discussion and commentary. The seemingly mutually exclusive extremes – absolute versus programmatic understandings – are not our only choices. Between them lies a flexible middle ground, a vast zone of nuanced implication that may be tapped in various ways, depending on the desired point of view. Consequently, what we encounter is a spectrum of possibilities under which any single piece might be framed for understanding. There is no single, objectively 'correct' approach to any composition. All symphonic works house multiple strata of potential meaning; some are musical, some are extra-musical. Nevertheless, in their interactions with the public, composers sometimes highlighted one or two of these meaning-strata while downplaying the others. Some works do invite richer speculation about representational allusion than do others. With these caveats, we might explicate the broad categories of interpretive possibility as follows:

1. The purely abstract symphony

The hallmarks of the symphony that seeks to call attention to its pure musicality are its declaration on behalf of an abstract generic category in the title ('Symphony No. X in Y major/minor, Op. Z', without further subtitle), its self-evident deployment of recognisably standard theme types operating within a set of more or less standard formal conventions and proportions (however strained they might be in practice), and its pointed avoidance of any explicit programmatic suggestion regarding non-musical references. One is consequently encouraged to hear the musical ideas as the most obvious topics at hand, although those ideas were nearly always crafted to intersect with traditions established in esteemed works of the past.

In its strictest conception, this may be an 'ideal type' unattainable in practice – if by that we mean a work that excludes other types of meaning. Grounded in a rich 'musical logic', Brahms's four symphonies have occasionally been considered under this rubric. Recent research, though, suggests that they are also open to the mixed interpretation suggested in the subcategories of No. 2 below. Functioning as a regulative idea, however, the purely abstract symphony's demands for inner coherence exercised an enormous influence on all orchestral composition. Hanslick's celebrated embrace of formalism is relevant

here. In *On the Beautiful in Music* (*Vom Musikalisch-Schönen*, 1854 with many subsequent, differing editions) he argued that music consisted essentially of
self-referential 'sounding forms in motion' (*tönend bewegte Formen*). In this view
the only genuine subject of any instrumental piece is the quality and implications of its themes – its own explorations of musical language, its own possibilities for self-reflective coherence and commentary, its own autonomous
tradition. As for the role of orchestral music in all this, Hanslick would declare
in 1886 (following the première of Brahms's Fourth) that 'the symphony . . . is
the most inexorable touchstone and the supreme consecration of the instrumental composer'.[22]

2a. Dialogues with the musical tradition

At times verging on category No. 1 – and sharing most of its concerns – this
more inclusive hermeneutic category stresses the purely musical but leaves
room for provocative intersections with larger aesthetic and generic issues
outside of the specifics of the immediate work. An otherwise abstract symphony usually invites its listeners to hear allusions to a community-shared collection of referential pieces lodged in the mind and memory – intertextual
allusions of differing degrees of verifiability to the canon of accepted masterworks. Such self-conscious historicism underscores the composition's situat-
edness in a web of traditions. Correspondingly, it encourages us to
contextualise what we hear by appealing to a historically grounded conceptual
apparatus transcending the individual work. From this perspective an orchestral piece might embody a composer's declaration *vis-à-vis* the status of the tradition or how that tradition was to be absorbed into current composition.

Even if we were to overlook the possibility of their intersections with more
programmatic ideas, Brahms's four symphonies are overwhelmingly allusive in
this manner. All four have a valedictory sense of 'the Austro-Germanic musical
tradition' very much on their minds. Listeners have long known, for instance,
that the first theme in the exposition in the finale of the First Symphony alludes
to the 'Ode to Joy' from Beethoven's Ninth. (Recent scholarship has deepened
the issue by also suggesting that, simultaneously, it recomposes the comparably placed finale-theme from Bruch's Symphony No. 2 in F minor, which had
appeared in 1870, only a few years earlier.)[23] There are dozens of similarly allusive passages throughout Brahms's works – or so it seems. From this point of
view, Brahms's four symphonies are symphonic retrospectives demanding the

---

22 Hanslick, rev. of Brahms, Symphony No. 4, *Wiener allgemeine Zeitung* (21 January 1886), cited in
Margaret Notley, '*Volksconcerte* in Vienna and Late Nineteenth-Century Ideology of the Symphony', *Journal
of the American Musicological Society*, 50 (1997), p. 425.

23 Frisch, *Brahms: The Four Symphonies*, pp. 24–5.

attention of a historically educated listener. Indeed, a significant sector of current Brahms scholarship has been devoted to proposing and debating the significance of these potential allusions.[24] It may be, though, that haggling about precise identifications misses the point. More germane than disputing whether this or that allusion is 'really there' is the task of attuning ourselves to the generalised aesthetic invitation to hear ad hoc allusions at all – and recognising that invitation as a central component of the music. (One might call it an all-pervading aesthetics of the secret, rooted in part in Schumann.) The same concerns apply to other allusive composers – for instance, to Dvořák, Strauss, Mahler and Elgar. Here, too, impressions of referentiality seem omnipresent.

Along the same lines, symphonic works in the second half of the nineteenth century were also concerned with recycling a limited collection of appropriately serious moods, effects, poses or compositional 'topics' – the point being to recast and mix them in ingenious, profound or progressive ways. There were many dozens of these generalised topics – a grand topic tradition – nearly all instantly recognisable and almost all traceable to precedents in Mozart, Beethoven, Weber, Schubert, Schumann or Mendelssohn. But the legacy of Beethoven was uppermost, even though the later nineteenth-century understanding of these effects had been mediated by the accomplishments of his successors. The desire to create a 'finale-symphony', for instance – one that drove towards a culminating final movement – was grounded in Beethovenian precedent. Any symphony with a minor-to-major narrative trajectory of struggle-to-victory (there were many of them) inevitably conjured up memories of the same effect in several of Beethoven's works. C minor symphonies with C major finales claimed a special resonance with the Fifth Symphony and D-minor-to-D-major symphonies with the Ninth, but the pattern could occur, or be denied, within any symphony that began in – or at some point collapsed into – the minor mode.

Especially in the last decades of the century, an Adagio slow movement carried a Beethovenian connotation – a sign of contemplative inwardness and soul-searching depth. (It would become a specialty of Bruckner and Mahler.)[25] Similarly, funeral-march slow movements unfolded in the shadow of the *Eroica*. This was especially the case with C minor funeral marches within E flat symphonies, as in the slow movements of Bruckner's Fourth (1874, rev. 1878–80) and Elgar's Second (1911), although other funeral-march keys were also possible: C sharp minor for the slow movement of Bruckner's Seventh (1881–3)

---

24 See, e.g., Kenneth Ross Hull, 'Brahms the Allusive: Extra-Compositional Reference in the Instrumental Music of Johannes Brahms', Ph.D. Diss., Princeton University (1989); Raymond Knapp, *Brahms and the Challenge of the Symphony* (Stuyvesant, N.Y., 1997).

25 Margaret Notley, 'Late-Nineteenth-Century Chamber Music and the Cult of the Classical Adagio', *19th Century Music*, 23 (1999), pp. 33–61.

and the opening movement to Mahler's Fifth (1901–2, generically a vastly expanded introduction to the first Allegro movement proper); D minor for the ironised nightmare-march in the slow movement of Mahler's First (1884–8 with subsequent revisions; in its initial stages, this seems to have been planned as a programme symphony). In addition, Bruckner typically began his symphonies by reworking the cumulative, *creatio ex nihilo* opening of Beethoven's Ninth (and Wagner's *Das Rheingold*).

One might also cite the penchant for passages, movements or entire works with a pastoral, forest-centred, or idyllic tint – touching upon not only the precedent of Beethoven's Sixth Symphony but also the larger tradition of nature-representation to which it had belonged. The effect of encountering a spacious, relaxed, resonantly pulsating nature – inner motion within stasis, sometimes evocative of an Edenic goodness and purity, sometimes coupled with reflective melancholy, sublime majesty or hearty rusticity – may be experienced in dozens of 'nearly abstract' symphonies: in Bruckner's Fourth (the 'Romantic', with its opening horn-call and 'Hunt' scherzo), in Brahms's Second (1877), in the Swedish composer Wilhelm Stenhammar's quasi-Brucknerian First (1902–3), in Glazunov's Seventh (1902), and the like. Lyrical, idealised landscape was also a primary attraction to the nationalist composers: the opening of Dvořák's Fifth (1875), the slow movement of Dvořák's Eighth (1889), the opening of Sibelius's Second (1901–2) and virtually all of his subsequent symphonies (Nos. 3–7, 1907–24, although the Fourth, still nature-centred, might be considered something of an anti-pastoral), and so on. Not surprisingly, one also encounters this idyllic strain in symphonic poems (as in much of Smetana's cycle, *Má Vlast*, ['My Country'], 1872–9, orchestrated 1880–94) and in programme symphonies. Joachim Raff gave his Third Symphony the subtitle, 'Im Walde' ('In the Forest', 1869); the Seventh, 'In den Alpen' ('In the Alps', 1875; cf. Richard Strauss's 'Eine Alpensinfonie' of 1911–15). Raff's Symphonies Nos. 8–11 (1876–9) comprised a cycle of the seasons.

Even the breadth of a symphony and its deployed instrumental and harmonic resources carried extra-musical resonances. In the last quarter of the nineteenth century Wagner- and Liszt-supporters came to regard monumentality as a virtue not only of music drama but of the late nineteenth-century symphony, even when that symphony, as was the case with Bruckner's, was largely abstract (or more precisely in this case – as with Franck – a work that conflated musical production with Roman Catholic devotional practice). Bruckner was a dedicated Wagnerian, and his personalised style of massive gestures, broad chromatic sequences, self-conscious counterpoint, and vast time-scale divided Viennese audiences along cultural and political lines. Progressives sometimes linked this monumentality to a claim of universality, as opposed to the mere 'Romanticism' or lyrical, fussily detailed subjectivity that these partisans suspected in Mendelssohn, Schumann and Brahms. Grand symphonies, argued Hans Paumgartner in 1882, were the equivalent of a public oration before an assembly of the Austro-Germanic *Volk* (a *Volksversammlung*) – and through them, by extension, to all humankind. To that end they relied on cumulative effects of long-range intensification to a climax (*Steigerung*). Moreover, for some the post-Beethovenian monumental symphony needed to be bold and 'manly' (a term with which Paul Marsop praised Bruckner in 1887, opposing him to the 'ladylike' Mendelssohn of the 'perfumed handkerchief').[26] In such a context the drive towards the Germanic orchestral *magnum opus* becomes more understandable – in Bruckner, in Mahler, even (from a more explicitly programmatic standpoint) in the later tone poems of Strauss and some of the early works of Schoenberg.

2b. 'Nationalistic' symphonies

These were works which made a *primary* appeal to national pride, national ownership and a privileged access of understanding possessed by a clearly identifiable regional audience. Crucial here was the invitation to hear the work as capturing an ethnic/national/political essence – as a symphony preceded by a national adjective, 'Russian', 'Swedish', 'Czech', and so on. This feature alone guaranteed a contextual framing of the music along extra-musical lines, regardless of the degree of supplementary programmaticism in which the piece might be engaged. Strengthened forms of this appeal relied on 'national' turns in the music – melodic, rhythmic (dance-based), textural, harmonic or modal quirks that called attention to themselves as standing out from normative Austro-Germanic practice. These aspects of musical difference need not have been uniquely indigenous to the region in question: it sufficed that audiences and critics were willing to hear them in this way and that the composer encouraged them to do so.

The Austro-Germanic symphony, of course, was anything but innocent of implication in the game of 'national' meaning. As early as 1824 A. B. Marx had written in the *Berliner allgemeine musikalische Zeitung* that the serious, *Eroica*-like symphony as a genre was to be regarded as 'virtually the exclusive property of the Germans' (*ausschliessliches Eigenthum der Deutschen*).[27] All post-Beethovenian Austro-Germanic symphonies paid homage to this cultural

---

26 See the discussion of the ideological currents surrounding the late nineteenth-century symphony ideology in Margaret Notley, '*Volksconcerte*' (on Marsop, pp. 428–9; on Paumgartner, pp. 431–2).

27 28 April 1824, cited in Sanna Pederson, 'A. B. Marx, Berlin Concert Life, and German National Identity', *19th Century Music*, 18 (1994), p. 96.

undertow, although one often sublimated into philosophical claims of a presumed universality within the Germanic particular. At times Teutonic nationalism could be more explicitly foregrounded, especially in the fervent years surrounding the Bismarck-led drive towards the establishment of the Prussianised *Deutsches Reich*, the unified nation-state of Germany, in 1871. One relatively early example is Raff's celebratory, spacious and occasionally proto-Brucknerian Symphony No. 1 (1859–61), subtitled 'To the Fatherland'.

Nor would it be wrong to presume that some French symphonies in the decades after the Franco-Prussian War (1870–1) were concerned with projecting an aura of French difference within a more self-conscious, 'modern' system of bureaucratically administered concert life. Some, like Saint-Saëns (Symphony No. 3 in C minor, with organ, 1886) grounded this in the production of clear-eyed, crystalline musical ideas and spacious textures coupled with what was frequently a schematic-modular conception of formal sections. This approach contrasted with the reigning metaphysical heft and opacity of Germanic practice while still holding on to refined residues of Romantic emotion and Lisztian chromaticism, thematic transformation over broad expanses of musical space, experimentation with larger forms, and the concept of the splashy apotheosis-finale that revisited motifs from earlier movements. César Franck's devotionally earnest Symphony in D minor (1886–8) – which also featured the 'cyclic' return of earlier themes in the finale – took a different direction, one emphasising intense chromaticism, thicker textures and a drive towards a radiant spiritual uplift within what was typically regarded as a Roman Catholic or culturally conservative 'message symphony'. Several other symphonic works were composed in the general orbit of Franck, including Vincent d'Indy's colourful, regionalistic 'Symphony on a French Mountaineer's Song' or *Symphonie cévenole* with piano obbligato (1886), Ernest Chausson's Symphony in B flat (1889–90), and d'Indy's later Symphony No. 2 in B flat (1902–3). Other French symphonists included Edouard Lalo (Symphony in G minor, 1886) and Paul Dukas (Symphony in C major, 1895–6).

The self-assured power-centres of music-historical practice, however, relegated the term 'nationalistic', with its unmistakably deprecatory flavour, to use in conjunction with Eastern and Northern European composition, particularly from regions that prior to the 1840s had staked either modest claims with regard to art music or none at all. One of the local drives behind such music was political: the celebration and validation of an outsider culture in the face of artistic or political forces that had previously sidelined, ignored or suppressed it. In the later nineteenth century, new schools of composers in Eastern and Northern Europe negotiated between two conflicting motivations. On the one hand, musicians from Russia, Norway, Sweden, Denmark, Finland, Bohemia,

Poland, Hungary and so on, sometimes asserted the independent legitimacy of their region's modes of cultural experience by claiming that these wellsprings were more pure and uncompromised than the supposedly overripe Austro-Germanic or French traditions. On the other hand, by adapting local ideas to the most prestigious genre of instrumental music – the post-Beethovenian symphony – they sought to bring honour to themselves and their country by proving worthy of entering an existing international marketplace of music on its own terms.

A composer's assimilation into the Austro-Germanic tradition could occur in varying degrees. Depending on one's aesthetic convictions, the official-style symphonic language could be spoken with either a weak or a strong regional accent. Well-wrought, though only modestly inflected nationalism sought acceptance on more international grounds. This tack stressed tightly knit adaptations of Mendelssohn–Schumann syntax, although that base, after 1860, was typically intermixed with the sweeping, texturally rich style found in the music of Liszt, Wagner, Brahms and others. In such blends room was usually left for the occasional characteristic or folk-styled thumbprint, which might turn up in any of a number of sections: in introductions, in 'lyric-piece' slow-movement themes, in scherzos, or perhaps in culminatory finales. This was the more Classical solution preferred by the Dane Niels Gade (eight symphonies, 1842–71); by the Russian Anton Rubinstein (six symphonies, 1850–86); by the Norwegians Johan Svendsen (two symphonies, 1865–6, 1877) and Christian Sinding (three published symphonies, 1890–1936); by the Bohemian Zdeněk Fibich (three symphonies, 1877–98); by the Englishmen Hubert Parry (four symphonies, 1882–9) and Charles Villiers Stanford (seven symphonies, 1875–1911).

But the models could also be pushed towards a heightened personalism. A heartier local flavour would be overlaid on to the official style by the Bohemian Antonin Dvořák (nine symphonies, 1865–93); an even stronger, more sonorously radicalised one was devised by the Russian Peter Tchaikovsky (six completed symphonies, 1866–93). All strongly accented nationalisms called primary attention to their projection of ethnic difference. In the presence of those regionalisms lay both the attraction and the risk of the more combative strains of nationalism. From the Germanic standpoint, could these accents be welcomed into the tradition? Or were these merely 'folkloristic symphonies' (as Schoenberg would claim in 1947) trying to fill the symphony with melodic material at odds with the presumably more exalted demands of the genre?[28] In

---

28 Schoenberg, 'Folkloristic Symphonies' (1947), in *Style and Idea: Selected Writings of Arnold Schoenberg*, ed. Leonard Stein, trans. Leo Black (Berkeley and Los Angeles, 1984 [originally published 1975]), pp. 161–6. 'The discrepancy between the requirements of larger forms and the simple construction of folk tunes has never been solved and cannot be solved. A simple idea must not use the language of profundity, or it can never become popular' (p. 163).

the later nineteenth century the principal challengers here, in addition to Tchaikovsky, were the St Petersburg Russians with their iridescently colouristic, non-developmental (in the Germanic sense), and often exotic symphonies: Mili Balakirev (two symphonies, 1897, 1908); Alexander Borodin (the most successful: three symphonies, 1867–87); and Nikolai Rimsky-Korsakov (three numbered, completed symphonies in multiple versions, from 1865 onward, in addition to a nearly completed Fourth [1884] and the symphonic suite, *Scheherazade*, 1888). A second St Petersburg generation would be ably represented by the professionally polished Alexander Glazunov (eight completed symphonies, 1882–1906, among the central models for the young Stravinsky's Symphony in E flat, 1905–7). More self-consciously 'modern' symphonies would be produced by other members of this younger generation: by the Dane Carl Nielsen (six symphonies, 1892–1925); by the Swede Wilhelm Stenhammar (two symphonies, 1902–3, 1911–15); by the Englishman Edward Elgar (two completed symphonies, 1908, 1911); by the Finn Jean Sibelius (seven symphonies, 1899–1924); by the Russians Sergei Rachmaninoff (three symphonies, 1895, 1908, 1936) and Alexander Scriabin (three numbered symphonies, 1899–1904, followed by the modernistically striking successors, *Le poème de l'extase*, 1908, and *Prométhée*, 1910).

From about 1865 onward composers from outlying areas sometimes rallied around what may be regarded as one of the nationalistic formulas for a symphony or concerto. Deployed over the course of a work, this formula suggested the ongoing distillation of an ever purer ethnicity, one that finally achieved its liberated centre-point in the final movement. There are many virtually perfect examples of it familiar from the standard repertory: Grieg's Piano Concerto; Tchaikovsky's Second Symphony and Violin Concerto; Dvořák's Symphony No. 8; Sibelius's first three symphonies along with the Violin Concerto; and several others. Within the formula, the first movement was to provide a regionally accented adaptation – perhaps strongly accented – of Western European sonata procedures. (The first movement could be preceded by a slow introduction that invited a politicised understanding as representing the folk-soul of the ethnic group at hand; if so, it was to be taken as the wellspring of all that followed. Not infrequently, the folk-soul source reappeared from time to time throughout the work.) The second and third movements – often a 'national' lyrical song and scherzo – pressed closer towards the goal. That goal was the finale, which, in varying degrees, was to feature the folk-reduction down to its essence. As the most folk-like of the movements, the finale could be understood as representing the full emergence of the group, more or less on its own terms. Towards that end these finales often featured vigorous dance-like music, or, especially, the tracking of thematic, repetitive loops, as if finally centring around a core of ethnic being within an otherwise linear work – a centring that might involve variation procedures (Dvořák's Eighth Symphony, which even precedes the variations with an annunciatory fanfare) or, more commonly, a circular, obstinately repetitive second theme (Tchaikovsky's Violin Concerto; Sibelius's Second Symphony).

2c. Tacit, implicit or suspected programmes throughout or for substantial sections

From time to time one learns, or is given to suspect, that ostensibly abstract symphonies include momentary passages that are subjectively emblematic or even quasi-programmatic, such as the spacious horn call in the finale of Brahms's Symphony No. 1 (première, 1876; Brahms had initially written down the call and provided it with a personal text on a postcard sent to Clara Schumann in 1868). More broadly, we might encounter what amount to instances of the programme symphony (no. 3 below) that were initially (or eventually) presented to the public as non-programmatic works. These include nearly abstract symphonies or concertos with more elaborate, but private, hidden or suppressed narratives. In some cases our suspicion that such a programme exists, or our suggestions concerning their details, remains speculative. In the past two decades, for instance, some have sought to propose that Brahms's First conceals a declaration of the composer's feelings towards Clara Schumann – one that she alone was likely to have understood. Such claims rest on the postcard horn-call in its finale and the conviction that Schumann's 'Clara cipher', a specific changing-note figure, is a central element in all four movements. It has also been suggested that at least the first two movements contain reminiscences of Schumann's *Manfred* music (based in part on Byron's idea of forbidden and tormented love).[29]

Tchaikovsky's emotionally edgy, often anguished symphonies have always offered temptations along these lines, and opinion has been sharply divided about the autobiographical significance of, especially, his final three symphonies – by which has been meant the relationship of the music to his homosexuality. With the recent onset of a politicised gender-studies movement in musicology, these questions and the manner in which they are addressed have taken on a new urgency. Here we confront: a programme symphony (No. 4) whose provided programme (a standard grappling with 'Fate') might be taken as a prop for a more concealed statement; a programme symphony (No. 5) – apparently – whose specifics (again dealing with 'Fate') were for the most part abandoned or suppressed; and a desperately depressive symphony with a

---

29 Michael Musgrave, 'Brahms's First Symphony: Thematic Coherence and Its Secret Origin', *Music Analysis*, 2 (1983), pp. 117–33. Brodbeck, *Brahms: Symphony No. 1*, pp. 31–58.

provocative subtitle furnished by the composer's brother (No. 6, 'Pathétique') and a self-evidently confessional content, but with no other explicit programme. Interpretations of the 'Pathétique' have ranged from a sceptical rejection of all 'fanciful' programmes (thus seeking to focus attention instead on its impressive musical integrity) to considerations of the possible programme ranging from the general to the recklessly specific.[30]

The suppressed programme became a commonly encountered feature of much later nineteenth- and early twentieth-century music. Elgar would elevate personalised secrets and 'enigmas' into a central attribute of his music in general. And we now know that Dvořák's Symphony No. 9 in E minor ('From the New World', 1893) conflated the composer's limited awareness of a handful of published African-American melodies (including 'Swing Low, Sweet Chariot') with a narrative personally extracted from at least chapters 10, 11 and 20 of Longfellow's *The Song of Hiawatha*.[31] With the recently uncovered evidence for all this in hand, the larger question may now shift to the mechanism and purpose whereby substantially differing African-American and American Indian representations became overlaid or fused with one another – and then merged with the European conception of the abstract symphony, ultimately to be presented to international public audiences without an official programme.

That Mahler's early symphonies – and possibly some of the later ones as well – also belong in this category seems clear. In the mid- and late 1890s Mahler, recalling Wagner's and Schopenhauer's claims about music's independence from the phenomenal world, was troubled by the supposed limitations that literary programmes seemed to place on what he wished to regard as the boundlessly metaphysical nature of music. Drawing a line of difference between himself and Strauss, he now insisted that his works stemmed from musical impulses, not literary ones; to emphasise any programme, except as perhaps a

30 See, e.g., Joseph C. Kraus, 'Tchaikovsky', in Holoman, ed., *The Nineteenth-Century Symphony*, pp. 299–326, including criticism of those who believe that 'Tchaikovsky had foretold his own death' in the 'Pathétique' and a warning to any others who harbour similar 'fanciful notions (particularly his supposed suicide and his image as a "tragic soul tormented by his homosexuality")', p. 323. The opposite viewpoint is provided by the indulgent programmaticism of Timothy L. Jackson, *Tchaikovsky: The 'Pathétique' Symphony* (Cambridge, 1999).

31 The programmatic issue resurfaced provocatively in Michael Beckerman, 'Dvořák's "New World" Largo and *The Song of Hiawatha*', *19th Century Music*, 16 (1992), pp. 35–48; and Beckerman, 'The Dance of Pau-Puk-Keewis, The Song of Chibiabos, and the Story of Iagoo: Reflections on Dvořák's 'New World' Scherzo', in John C. Tibbetts (ed.), *Dvořák in America: 1892–1895* (Portland, Oreg., 1992), pp. 210–28. Most recently, Beckerman established the African-American connection in 'A New Source for the "New World" Symphony', currently unpublished paper presented at the Annual Conference of the American Musicological Society, Kansas City, 6 November 1999; an article in the Chicago periodical *Music* (December 1892), 'Negro Music', with musical examples, 'was the primary stimulus for the symphony's composition'. A broader Hiawatha reading of the work had also been provided by Hepokoski, 'Culture Clash', *The Musical Times*, 134 (1993), pp. 685–8; and Robert Winter, *Antonin Dvořák: Symphony No. 9 in E Minor, 'From the New World'*, CD-ROM (Irvington, N.Y., 1994).

'last, ideal clarification', led one away from what should be a composition's essential spirituality.[32] Accordingly, beginning in the late 1890s he stripped away most of the programmatic titles and subtitles that he had given to what would become his first three symphonies and published them, with differing degrees of nuance and suggestion, as more objectively symphonic works. (Before its publication the First Symphony had been billed in 1893–4 performances, for example, as '"Titan", a Tone Poem in Symphony Form', with separate evocative titles for each of the movements; the first movement of the Second was once offered as a separate symphonic poem, *Todtenfeier* ['Funeral Rites', 1888], based on Mickiewicz; and so on). Knowledge of the varying states of the original titles has long since been restored by scholars.[33]

3. Programme symphony/suite, symphonic poem and overture

This category is defined through a gateway title (such as Strauss's *Don Juan* or *Death and Transfiguration*) that prepares the listener to interpret the work through that conceptual framework. Here, too, we find a range of strengths to the representational suggestion at hand. An only modestly programmatic symphony, for example, may be assigned a brief subtitle or nickname – Rubinstein's 'Ocean' Symphony (No. 2, three versions, 1851, 1863, 1880, the last with seven untitled movements corresponding to each of the seven seas); Bruckner's 'Romantic' Symphony (No. 4); Nielsen's Symphony No. 2, 'The Four Temperaments' (1901–2: choleric, phlegmatic, melancholic, sanguine); and so on. Nor need the presence of a title imply a radicalisation of style. Many of Raff's symphonies sought, at times controversially, to seek a compromise between traditional form and the notion of a programme.[34] And Goldmark's symphonic-poem set, 'Rustic Wedding' (1877) – which includes subtitles (such as 'Bride's Song: Intermezzo') for each of the five movements – is a lyrical, relatively conservative work. Similarly, later nineteenth-century concert overtures harked back to a tradition before the advent of the symphonic poem: they bore a poetic title (along with the genre-identifier, 'overture') but were typically

---

32 Mahler, letter to Arthur Seidl, February 1897 (Mahler was quoting Seidl's words, 'the last, ideal clarification'). See the translation and further discussion in Stephen E. Hefling, 'Miners Digging from Opposite Sides: Mahler, Strauss, and the Problem of Program Music', in Bryan Gilliam (ed.), *Richard Strauss: New Perspectives on the Composer and His Work* (Durham, NC, 1992), pp. 41, 50, note 1.

33 For overviews of such issues see Constantin Floros, *Gustav Mahler: The Symphonies*, trans. Vernon and Jutta Wicker (Portland, Oreg., 1993); Stephen E. Hefling, 'Mahler: Symphonies 1–4', in Holoman (ed.), *The Nineteenth-Century Symphony*, pp. 369–416; Peter Franklin, *Mahler: Symphony No. 3* (Cambridge, 1991); Donald Mitchell and Andrew Nicholson (eds.), *The Mahler Companion* (Oxford, 1999).

34 Hugo Riemann, in his *Geschichte der Musik seit Beethoven* (Berlin, 1901), p. 432, criticised Raff on precisely this point. Programme music demanded a poetic transformation of form, he argued, and 'history breaks its staff pitilessly on indecisive attempts [*Halbheiten*] like those Raff-like compromises, because they are not completely honest . . . It is an aesthetic lie to write programme music that at the same time is to be taken as absolute music'. Quoted in Markus Römer, *Joseph Joachim Raff (1822–82)* (Wiesbaden, 1982), pp. 59–60.

briefer and more modest in their representational claims. Brahms's complementary pair from 1880 provided the strongest examples: the *Academic Festival Overture* (a celebratory work featuring a few quoted themes and rising, in the manner of Weber's *Jubel* or 'Jubilee' Overture, to the final, climactic inbreaking of a 'publicly' significant tune, here the college-song 'Gaudeamus igitur'); and the *Tragic Overture* (evoking recollections, surely, of moods found in Beethoven's *Coriolan* and Schumann's *Manfred* Overtures).

Symphonic poems proper were normally works that declared themselves to be ideologically Lisztian in their embraces of titles and specific representational images. They tended to follow three main lines. The first was the 'radical' Austro-Germanic line proper, beginning with Liszt in the 1850s and reinvigorated mightily in the late 1880s and 1890s by the dazzling early modernist Richard Strauss, who often called his works 'tone poems' to distinguish them from those of his predecessor. The second was the highly differentiated 'nationalist' track from the later 1850s onward: the genre's natural affinities for history, landscape and national literature would virtually guarantee its eager acceptance by these composers. The third was to be found in French orchestral composition after 1871: Saint-Saëns (*Le rouet d'Omphale*, *Danse macabre*), Franck (*Le chasseur maudit*, *Psyché*), Chausson (*Viviane*), Dukas (*L'apprenti sorcier*), Debussy (*Prélude à 'L'après-midi d'un faune'*) and others.

Successful examples of the aggressive, post-Lisztian programme symphony proper – as opposed to the mere symphony or suite with a representational title or nickname – were not as common as might be supposed. Tchaikovsky's *Manfred* Symphony (1885) makes a strong claim here, as do Richard Strauss's *Aus Italien* ('symphonic fantasy', 1886) and Sibelius's early *Kullervo* (a five-movement 'symphonic poem', 1891–2, not published until 1961, based on texts from the Finnish epic, *Kalevala*, and including two vocal movements). Had he not suppressed their original programmes, Mahler's First and Third Symphonies would qualify unequivocally. Even with the suppression of its first-movement *Todtenfeier* programme, however, his Second Symphony, 'Resurrection' – with its de-texted *Wunderhorn* song as the scherzo and its literally texted two final movements – still stands as an unmistakable programme symphony. A similar argument might be made for the Fourth.

Closely related, though less ambitious in their generic claims, are cycles or suites of symphonic poems – individual tableaux bound together into a single, larger work. Rimsky-Korsakov's *Scheherazade* (1888), billed as a 'symphonic suite', is in effect a colouristic programme symphony. The same is true of Sibelius's *Kalevala*-based *Four Legends*, (1893–7, with later revisions; originally called the *Lemminkäinen Suite*, it includes 'The Swan of Tuonela' as the slow movement and 'Lemminkäinen's Return' as its finale). From this perspective – and notwithstanding its self-consciously anti-symphonic ambience – Debussy's *Nocturnes* of 1897–9 ('Clouds', 'Festivals', 'Sirens') seems to be something of a programme symphony shorn of an initial movement. Debussy's three-movement set of 'symphonic sketches', *La mer* (1903–5), also fits comfortably into this general tradition.

Structural deformation

Dissatisfied with formulaic tradition and driven by mid-century demands for originality, composers now often sought to produce what we may call sonata deformations – individualised adaptations of the regulative ideas that sonata form and the multi-movement sonata had become. A sonata deformation is an individual work in dialogue primarily with sonata norms even though certain central features of the sonata-concept have been reshaped, exaggerated, marginalised or overridden altogether. What is presented on the musical surface of a composition (what one hears) may not be a sonata in any 'textbook' sense, and yet the work may still encourage, even demand, the application of one's knowledge of traditional sonata procedures as a rule for analysis and interpretation.

Needless to say, there had been no shortage of sonata-deformational structures prior to the 1850s, particularly in the hands of the master composers, whose presence loomed large in the new age of canonical repertory. After 1850, however, creatively *ad hoc* designs came to be even more normative, sometimes more eccentric, often to the consternation of later analysts confronting the dizzying variety of individualised shapes and the seeming crisis of form to which they appeared to attest. Such a scattering of procedures has made it notoriously difficult to generalise about the history of sonata form in the later nineteenth century – except to remark that it came to be treated freely, loosely or expansively. And yet, despite the wealth of exceptional compositions, the sonata form *idea* remained venerated as the structural root of the symphonic tradition. As such, it continued to hold sway as a community-shared rule for interpretation, even when it was written *against*. In such instances the normative thing that does not happen, or that is kept from happening (what the literary critic Wolfgang Iser called the 'minus functions' of a text) can be as important as what does occur.[35] For this reason the appropriate formal question to be asked of such a piece – more often, of one of its movements – is not the blunt, reductive one, 'Is it in sonata form'?, but rather, 'Are we invited to apply the norms of the traditional sonata in order to interpret what does (or does not) occur in this individualised work?' In many of the *ad hoc* shapes of the later nineteenth century, the answer is obviously affirmative.

35 Wolfgang Iser, *The Act of Reading: A Theory of Aesthetic Response* (Baltimore, 1978), pp. 206–10.

Certain types of deformational procedures may be grouped into families. Omitting the expositional repeat within Allegro sonata movements, for instance – a practice increasingly common from the 1840s onward (although it may be occasionally found in middle- and late-Beethoven, for instance, in the first movements of the Appassionata Sonata and the Ninth Symphony and in the finale of the Eighth) – in effect treated quick-tempo movements as though they were overtures. (Overtures – and their successors, symphonic poems – always lacked this repeat.) By mid-century the trimmer overture-format had become the norm, no longer an exceptional practice. Any 'archaic' reinstating of that repeat, as in the opening movements of Brahms's first three symphonies, was probably to be taken as a purposeful gesture harking back not only to older traditions but also to the more abstract or absolute idea of the symphony. (A parallel is to be drawn, of course, to the reinstating of the increasingly archaic orchestral 'tutti' at the opening of concerto first-movements, as opposed to beginning directly with the solo exposition – as commonly happened by the mid- and later nineteenth century.)

But deformational practice extended beyond mere repeat-conventions. After about 1840 one influential treatment of sonata form centred on the idea of creating a stark, maximal opposition between the two 'halves' of an exposition. This procedure was the one most amenable to the then-emerging possibility of more or less explicitly gendered themes.[36] Most commonly, the two-block exposition opened with a tormented, driven, 'masculine' first theme, typically thrashing about in the minor mode and sometimes bonded to a continuation or transition, although one similar in distressed urgency. To this would be immediately counterposed a contrasting block, an angelically redemptive, lyrically 'feminine' second theme in the non-tonic major mode and not infrequently in a slower tempo as well. Interpretable within the exposition as the prediction of a hope, this alternative theme was often treated in the recapitulatory space or coda to a grandiosely salvific, major-tonic-grounded 'Weber apotheosis'. This minor/major binary-exposition type often featured only the briefest – and thinnest – of connective material between the first and second static-blocks (a mere panning from one tableau to another, a clearing of space for the emergence of the second theme). Such an exposition could be implicitly or literally linked to any number of extra-musical contraries: masculine/feminine; tormented hero/redemptive agent; active struggle/withdrawal into the erotic; tyrannical oppression/projected political emancipation; and the like.

One of the earliest occurrences of the gendered two-block exposition is

---

36 Hepokoski, 'Masculine–Feminine', *The Musical Times*, 135 (1994), pp. 494–9.

found in Wagner's Overture to *The Flying Dutchman* (first version, 1841), with its representations of the Dutchman and Senta. (As a whole, the overture unfolds as an extraordinarily provocative sonata deformation.) Whether or not Wagner's overture was the principal model for later composition, variants and large-scale expansions of the sure-fire *Dutchman*-exposition-formula, along with its electrifying recapitulatory dénouement, soon became a familiar symphonic option in orchestrally lavish Allegro-tempo compositions or movements (especially finales). It could be readily adapted to rondo-orientated compositions as well. With its built-in struggle-to-victory trajectory, this 'new' sonata-subtype itself became amenable to later alteration, adaptation and deformation (including the frustration of expectations) for localised purposes.

Built on unmediated clash and contrast, the formula was especially associated with certain strains of the radical, Wagner–Liszt view of things: not surprisingly, the more traditionally orientated Brahms seems to have been little tempted by it. Tchaikovsky, though, would occasionally be drawn to the model, perhaps through the mediating influence of Lisztian practice in the 1850s. We find orchestrally spectacular dialogues with the formula in Tchaikovsky's *Romeo and Juliet* (1869, rev. 1870, 1880, masculine feud followed by a quick-slippage and escape into the forbidden erotic), and in the first movement of Symphony No. 6 in B minor, 'Pathétique' (1893). Here the first theme sets out in B minor (Allegro non troppo) as a tenderly sad, quasi-balletic transformation of the desolate introduction, but in the transition the theme intensifies in texture and tempo into the characteristic frenzy of the *Dutchman*-formula, cresting towards its end and then withdrawing in exhaustion. The maximally contrasting, static second theme in D major, its tempo reined back to an Andante (following a brief link, *rilardando molto* and Adagio), never attains a clear perfect authentic cadence and with it a sense of satisfactory completion and closure: at the end of each thematic module its fifth scale-degree remains frozen in place, immobile. Consequently, the second theme projects not consolation but the unattainability of consolation, the characteristic 'if only!' mood of much music of this period. This non-closed aspect of the secondary theme sets the stage for its later, similarly non-closed B major tonic statement in the recapitulation. The impression here of a recapitulatory incompleteness helps to launch the downward spiral tracked by the subsequent movements.

The two-block exposition formula and its variants persisted to the end of the century and beyond. The finale of Mahler's First Symphony provides a near-perfect illustration of it, although in this case the redemptive apotheosis late in the movement is given not to the 'feminine' second theme but to the threefold appearance of a 'breakthrough' idea that eventually wrenches the musical

process from the 'inferno-key' of F minor to the properly emancipatory
D major, the real tonic of the symphony. Further adaptations are found in the
first movements of his Second and Sixth Symphonies (1888–94, rev. 1903–4;
1906). The *Dutchman* formula is also treated as a background rule for interpretation in the A minor (sonata-deformational) second movement of the Fifth
(1902). Here the emphatically negative point is that what 'ought' to be the
generically redemptive feminine, major-mode second theme is written over by
a grieving lapse into a reference to the minor-mode funeral march from the first
movement. Thus the traditional presence of hope within the sonata-process is
erased, and, as with the First Symphony – obviously a model here – an 'external'
chorale eventually breaks into the texture to suggest a way out.

Of course, not all sonatas were based on expositions that relied on the
starker, two-block model. Another 'new' approach was to produce a loosely
knit, discursive exposition – one also potentially in dialogue with implicitly
gendered elements – interlarded with digressions and interpolations, giving
the impression of a series of contrasting tableaux, only some of which were to
be taken as marking the referential stations of the sonata. This slack,
anti-efficient approach may have been a response to the multi-sectional finale of
Beethoven's Ninth Symphony and perhaps also to the French sonata form tradition and Berlioz's formal experiments. Especially characteristic of some of
Liszt's sonata deformations in the 1850s, it may be found in the first movement
of the *Faust* Symphony and in several of the symphonic poems. Giving the
impression of a leisurely diffusion of thematic materials over musical space, this
exposition-subtype was particularly adaptable to programmatic narratives
seeking the impression of a vastness of canvas or a near-suspension of the press
of time. Such traditionalists as Hanslick saw in it only more evidence of the
insufficiently engaged compositional thought of programme music: it produced works in which the sections 'appear often to be strung together as in a
mosaic, [or] mixed up chaotically'.[37] This approach resurfaced in some of the
larger tone poems of Richard Strauss, such as *Also sprach Zarathustra* (1895–6)
and *Ein Heldenleben* (1897–8). It also may be occasionally found in certain
movements of Mahler, such as the finale of the Second Symphony.

Regardless of their layout-subtype, many expositions after 1850 feature
tonal plans that would have been extraordinary earlier in the century, and these
plans may or may not have complementary tonal consequences in the recapitulatory space. To cite one famous example, the exposition of the first movement of Tchaikovsky's Symphony No. 4 (1877–8) moves upward by minor

---

37 Hanslick, 1857 review of Liszt's *Les préludes*, in *Geschichte des Concertwesens in Wien*, 2 vols. (Vienna,
1869–70), II, p. 119. Quoted, with additional commentary, in Richard Will, 'Time, Morality, and Humanity
in Beethoven's *Pastoral* Symphony', *Journal of the American Musicological Society*, 50 (1997), p. 275.

thirds: F minor, A flat minor, and B major (collapsing to B minor at the beginning of the development). Here the principle at work, eventually partitioning the movement into a full division of the F-tonic octave by minor thirds, is that each locally minor tonic seeks momentary relief by shifting to its presumably *major* mediant; when that mediant is subsequently collapsed into the minor mode, the process replicates itself on a higher pitch level. The exposition of Saint-Saëns's Symphony No. 3 (1886) – a cooler adaptation of the *Dutchman*-formula – moves from a first theme in C minor to a second theme starting on a modally inflected D flat major (♭II) that finally stabilises, and ends the exposition, in F major (IV!). Here the recapitulatory consequences are notable: the re-establishing of C minor leads to a second theme initially suggesting F major (IV) and thence to a rapidly dissolving E major (III!) – thus deferring the C-tonic resolution to a later movement.

As for developments, the main danger was that familiar mid-movement strategies (motivic fragmentation and combination; sequential modulatory patterns; generic storm and stress) ran the risk of seeming emptily academic. Thus we can find middle spaces of sonata deformations invaded by one or two tableau-episodes, which sometimes elbow out much of the 'developmental'-activity proper. This happens occasionally in Liszt and Strauss; another instance may be found in Wagner's *Siegfried Idyll* (1870). The procedure can further the impression that the piece is constructed around a mere linear string of contrasted episodes, perhaps motivically interrelated, up until the point of recapitulation. Another possibility was to produce a sudden 'break-through' of new, seemingly transcendent material within the development that serves to change the course of the whole sonata (finale of Mahler's Symphony No. 1; Strauss's *Don Juan*). Of particular importance were the many adaptations of large-scale 'rotational' procedures (multiple, varied cyclings through the thematic pattern initially laid out in the exposition, a concern especially typical of Bruckner and the later Sibelius; usually, the development begins a second, varied rotation of the expositional materials).[38] Other sonata-based works feature unexpected incursions of what had been introductory material into the sonata-process proper, most often within the developmental space or towards the end of the work, thus in effect informing or framing the whole. This occurs in the finale of Brahms's Symphony No. 1, in Strauss's *Till Eulenspiegel* (which is also in dialogue with rondo-traditions), in many nationalistic works, and so on.

---

38 Warren Darcy, 'Bruckner's Sonata Deformations', in Timothy L. Jackson and Paul Hawkshaw (ed.), *Bruckner Studies* (Cambridge, 1997), pp. 256–77. See also Hepokoski, *Sibelius: Symphony No. 5* (Cambridge, 1993); and *idem*, 'Rotations, Sketches, and the Sixth Symphony', in Timothy L. Jackson and Veijo Murtomäki (ed.), *Sibelius Studies* (Cambridge, 2000), pp. 322–51.

Extraordinary treatments of the recapitulatory space were especially common, perhaps to surmount the non-progressive implication of merely traditional symmetrical repetition, which came to be regarded as the nemesis not only of symphonic poems (must the narrative stop at this point?) but also, eventually, of more abstract compositions as well. Any number of strategies may be found in symphonic works after 1850. Brahms was especially partial to finales that followed a non-repeated exposition with the *immediate* onset of the recapitulation (launched by the first theme in the *tonic*), within whose ordered rotation of thematic materials a large section of first-theme or transition space was expanded freely into a development (as in the finale of the First Symphony).[39]

In another deformational option the composer might decide to omit or reorder some of the important themes. The initial – and most important – elements of the second-theme complex, for example, are suppressed in the recapitulation of the slow movements of Brahms's Symphonies No. 2 and 3, with a concomitant, poignant sense of absence and loss. (Classical models – ones that suggest even more of a hybrid between an ABA′ structure and a partially incomplete sonata – may be found in the slow movements of Haydn's Quartets in G major and D major, Op. 33, nos. 5 and 6, and in that of Mozart's, Quartet in D major, K.575.) In Brahms's Third the 'lost' second theme of the slow movement is reintroduced as an important part of the proceedings of the finale.

Alternatively, it continued to be possible to bypass the tonic recapitulation of the first theme, merging into the 'tonal resolution' only at or around the point of the second theme – usually after a modulatory development that had been based primarily on non-tonic references to the first theme and/or transition. This double-rotational sonata-type also afforded the option of reinstating sometimes prolonged references to the first theme at the end, as if in compensation, in what is best considered coda-space, thus producing the illusion of what has mistakenly been called the 'reversed recapitulation'. With or without the appended tonic-first-theme coda, this was an old 'binary-sonata' formula from the eighteenth century (although one rarely mentioned by the theorists) that managed to breathe new life in isolated pieces in the nineteenth century and beyond: in the finale of Schumann's Fourth Symphony; in Liszt's *Les préludes*; in the finale of Saint-Saëns's Third (an expanded variant with an extra, altered rotation of the materials after the tonal resolution proper) and Mahler's First; in the first movements of Tchaikovsky's and Sibelius's Fourth Symphonies; and elsewhere.

---

39 For a useful discussion of this much-noted structure along with a list of instances of it and a bibliography of earlier treatments, see John Daverio, 'From "Concertante Rondo" to "Lyric Sonata": A Commentary on Brahms's Reception of Mozart', in David Brodbeck (ed.), *Brahms Studies I* (Lincoln, Nebr., and London, 1994), pp. 111–36. Daverio's term for this structure, an 'amplified binary', may be slightly misleading, as might other common terms for it, such as 'expanded sonatina' or 'sonata with displaced development'. Cf. Robert Pascall, 'Some Special Uses of Sonata Form by Brahms', *Soundings*, 4 (1974), pp. 58–63.

Within more or less full recapitulations, though, the composer might substitute new ideas for old ones, or distort or radically curtail the recapitulation as a whole. Around the end of the century Strauss was much taken with the idea of merely touching upon a recapitulatory theme – as if obligatorily to mark its station – then going on to produce other, often 'new' things in the music that follows (*Don Juan*; *Ein Heldenleben*). Mahler's characteristic solution was different. With his heightened aversion to the potential emptiness of unvaried repetition – and unlike most of his predecessors (the main exception being Haydn) – Mahler overturned the convention of predominantly literal, though transposed repetition of the secondary and closing themes in order to submit his recapitulations to a thoroughgoing recomposition and rethinking. This resulted in through-composed works, ones grappling with the 'modern' instability and volatility of the materials at hand.

With regard to tonality, one might find the lack of a clear tonal resolution within the reprise. This could produce any of a number of 'non-resolving-recapitulation' types that, in their purposeful 'sonata failure', deferred resolution either to the coda-space or to a subsequent movement. To cite merely one instance: the recapitulation proper of Brahms's (F Major) Third Symphony concludes in D major–minor (VI–vi), stabilising back to F major only in the coda. By the 1880s and 1890s it even became thinkable to end a composition or a movement in a key other than that in which it had begun. (This is sometimes called 'progressive' or 'directional tonality'. Each occurrence of it demands a local interpretation.)[40] We have already mentioned Saint-Saëns's Symphony No. 3 in this regard, whose first movement begins in C minor and ends in E major. A broader extension of the principle may be found in the whole of Nielsen's Symphony No. 1 (1890–2), the staging of a battle between two keys. Here the first movement decides in favour of G minor (although it begins on a rapidly relinquished C major chord) and the finale moves from G minor to C major. Other examples: the finale of Mahler's First Symphony (F minor to D major); the whole of Mahler's Second Symphony, 'Resurrection' (C minor 'resurrected' to E flat major at the end); the first movement of Mahler's Third (D minor to F major); and some of the later Mahler symphonies as well.

Several composers came to be attracted to the 'double-function' sonata or

40 For the term 'progressive tonality', see Dika Newlin, *Bruckner–Mahler–Schoenberg*, rev. edn (New York, 1978). The term 'directional tonality' stems from the work of Robert Bailey – with particular reference to the concept of a 'double-tonic complex' within an individual piece. See Patrick McCreless, *Wagner's 'Siegfried': Its Drama, History, and Music* (Ann Arbor, 1982), pp. 88–95; Christopher Orlo Lewis, *Tonal Coherence in Mahler's Ninth Symphony* (Ann Arbor, 1984); Robert Bailey, 'An Analytical Study of the Sketches and Drafts', in Robert Bailey (ed.), *Richard Wagner, Prelude and Transfiguration from 'Tristan und Isolde'* (New York, 1985), pp. 121–2 (double-tonic complex).

'multi-movement work in a single movement' (four movements in one, characteristic especially of Liszt, Strauss, and the early Schoenberg); others to hybrid blends of the sonata with other formal principles. Still another procedure was to produce a movement or set of movements that stages the conception, maturation and growth of a single idea that finally rings forth in full at or near the end. Raff's Symphony No. 1 participates in this cumulative logic, as do most of Bruckner's symphonies, with their characteristic chorale- and/or tonic-attainment endings. One of the most inventive treatments of the technique is found in Strauss's *Death and Transfiguration* (1889), devoted to the growth of the secondary theme ('transfiguration'), an idea that is only hinted at in the exposition. (With this mere collapsing-glimpse of the secondary theme, that exposition may be regarded as a deformation of the *Dutchman*-formula.) Several other adaptations of this procedure of 'teleological genesis' – or persistent shaping and re-emergence of an ever-growing idea – are also to be found in the mature Sibelius, who often elevated it into a commanding feature of his style.

Two waves of composers

One of the remarkable features in the history of the symphony is its unforeseen resurgence of vigour and depth in the last thirty years of the nineteenth century. The genre that by mid-century had run aground took sail once more, in what Carl Dahlhaus famously called 'the second age of the symphony', encompassing 'Bruckner and Brahms, Tchaikovsky and Borodin, Dvořák and Franck in the 1870s and 1880s'. Dahlhaus attributed this to several factors, and especially to the symphony's enrichment through the challenges posed by Liszt and the principles of the symphonic poem. In his own compact formulation: 'The reconstitution of absolute music following its mid-century hiatus deserves to be called dialectical in that it emerged in part by abstracting features of its aesthetic opposite, programme music . . . [The essential problem was] how to create a symphonic form equal to the aesthetic claims of the genre and yet consistent with the historical situation of the 1870s.'[41]

In this reading, the 'second age' was called forth principally by a genre-immanent crisis; it emerged as a cluster of solutions to an internal, aesthetic problem. This is surely a valid assessment, and yet a confluence of external pressures was redoubling the urgency of that situation: the near-devotional claims that high-cultural circles conferred on the Beethovenian tradition; the eagerness of outsider cultures ('nationalists') to demonstrate themselves worthy of contributing to the prestige of that tradition; and the looming anxiety, in a

41 Dahlhaus, *Nineteenth-Century Music*, pp. 265, 268. The symphony's 'first age', of course, had been that of Mozart, Haydn and Beethoven.

rapidly modernising world, that the art-music enterprise might be compromised altogether in a world of accelerating commercialism, technology, sceptical 'realism', new social and political movements, and emerging popular culture. An equally telling motivation for the 'second-age' phenomenon lay not in autonomous concerns within the artworks *per se* but in the interests of the material culture that surrounded them – the web of international orchestra concerts, legal contracts, commissions, publishing, advertising, publicity, conservatory life, journalistic criticism and the like. By the 1870s and 1880s a highly diversified 'institution of art music' was propelling towards its zenith. Committed to the advancement and promotion of the ever-solidifying canon, the bureaucratised concert system required successful new compositions as signs of its own legitimacy and continued viability. New works validated the institution and added to its prestige. As a result, both younger and established composers found themselves placed into competition with each other, and often with the giants of the past, for recognition within the sharply limited marketplace of art. In short, internal and external factors worked together to make possible a renewed tide of symphonies, symphonic poems and concertos.

The 'second-age' symphonists appeared in two generational waves, each with different concerns. The first wave comprised composers born between about 1820 and 1845 and included Bruckner, Brahms, Bruch, Saint-Saëns, Franck, Dvořák, Borodin and Tchaikovsky. It fell on the shoulders of this generation to re-establish in the 1870s and 1880s the foothold of the post-Schumann symphony in diverse local circumstances with substantially differing demands – and to do so in a musical Europe supercharged by the music and ideas of Liszt and Wagner.

Of this distinguished group, the works of all of whom had an enormous impact on later composers, Brahms and Tchaikovsky were the giants, although in most respects they were polar opposites. Today Brahms's distinction seems self-evident: his unparalleled compositional skill and multi-levelled richness of thought; his reverential seriousness *vis-à-vis* the symphonic tradition; his ability to synthesise divergent currents of compositional practice; his virtually heroic rescue of the more 'abstract' tradition with the First Symphony (1876) and its successors; and yet his pervasive melancholy, bidding a loving farewell to that tradition.[42] More challenging to convey in academic terms, Tchaikovsky's enduring contribution lay in his tilt away from studied intellectualism and close argument in pursuit of reawakening the presence of sonority on enhanced, more immediate terms – as though some inexpressible, vibrant secret lay in the naked palpability of sound, often deployed in contrasting sonic

42 Cf., e.g., Reinhold Brinkmann, *Late Idyll: The Second Symphony of Johannes Brahms*, trans. Peter Palmer (Cambridge, Mass., 1995).

planes. From one perspective, his debts to the emancipated sound-worlds of Berlioz, Liszt and (sometimes) Wagner could scarcely be clearer. From another perspective, he may be heard as stunningly and poignantly Russian. From another, we notice a prizing of physical movement and the allure of 'staged' or artificial theatrical glitter – the balletic or operatic (or symphonic?) dream-worlds of uncontaminated beauty to whose evanescent perfections the fallen 'real world' could never measure up. From still another, this was subversive music – convulsively emotional, frequently confessional, depressive, manic – that transgressed previously presumed limits of decorum, thematic type and dynamic range.

With the late-century symphonic ground thus prepared, there arose a second wave of younger composers prepared to capitalise upon it, employing all the virtuosity and technology of the now-augmented and well-drilled civic orchestra. This was the first generation of self-styled musical 'modernists', born in the later 1850s and early 1860s, composers deeply aware of their post-Wagnerian, post-Lisztian generational difference from their predecessors.[43] Born into an age of social controversy and ever-advancing modernity and technology – coming to maturity in the age of Edison, Ibsen, Mallarmé, and Nietzsche – this 'generation of the 1860s' included, most prominently, Richard Strauss, Mahler, Debussy, Elgar, Sibelius, Nielsen and Glazunov, all of whom began to establish their careers in the late 1880s and 1890s. The strongly personalised styles within this group could hardly be more distinct from one another. Nevertheless, these styles were all individualised solutions to the problem of seeking to fashion a marketable voice within the 'idealistic' tradition in an urban age in which such earlier aesthetic convictions were rapidly decaying away. That these composers thought of themselves as the first modernists – as something of a youth movement, not as 'late Romantics' – has now been clearly established. The pejorative label 'late Romanticism' (or 'post-Romanticism'), with its faded, pressed-flower connotations, was a polemical term of reproach affixed to them only by the next generation of high modernists, supporters of the dissonant 'new music' in the years before and after the First World War.[44]

Recontextualising Strauss's generation more properly as 'early modernists' is a historical task that has just begun – a central component of a much-needed, larger project to reconstrue early twentieth-century modernism in terms more complex than those typically proposed in the mid-century historical consensus that emerged in the decades after 1945. Dahlhaus has underlined the arrival of

---

43 Issues of generational difference and the concept of modernism are treated in Dahlhaus, 'Musikalische Moderne und Neue Musik', *Melos/Neue Zeitschrift für Musik*, 2 (1976), p. 90; Dahlhaus, 'Modernism as a Period in Music History', in *Nineteenth-Century Music*, pp. 332–9; Hepokoski, *Sibelius: Symphony No. 5*, pp. 1–9.   44 Dahlhaus, 'Musikalische Moderne'.

a 'breakaway mood' beginning with such works as Mahler's First Symphony (first version) and Strauss's *Don Juan*, both completed in 1888,[45] but such observations only invite further reflection on the multiple components of this diversified movement within all of the arts and philosophy. The concept of *die Moderne* in both literature and music of the 1880s and 1890s, for instance, brought together a number of generational issues: the recognition of an emerging 'new world' fundamentally different from that of the earlier nineteenth century; the need to demonstrate a decisive break with the institutionalised past and its now-formulaic traditions, to challenge the socially sanctioned artistic codes; an embrace of a much-enhanced subjectivity in art, in which the demonstration of a focused, powerful individuality became paramount; the reliance on strong emotion and 'nerves' as the source the modern personality (*fin-de-siècle* modernism as *Nervenkunst*); the conviction that the break with decorum led to a higher, more unmediated 'truth' within modern art; and so on.[46] And yet, at least for the early modernist composers, such attitudes were somehow to be simultaneously wedded to the existing institution of art music, resulting in a clash of provocative claims between old and new.

It is under such lights that we shall need to reassess the significance of Richard Strauss's brazen hypertechnique and flamboyant extroversion, his calculated, moment-to-moment shifting between different stylistic registers, and his renunciation of traditionalist Schopenhauerian-Wagnerian metaphysics around 1893–4 to produce such material-world, quasi-Nietzschean manifestos as *Till Eulenspiegel's Merry Pranks* (1895) and *Also sprach Zarathustra* (1896).[47] Or to enquire into the larger implications of Sibelius's frequent abandonment of traditional linear-contrapuntal syntax in search of a revelatory, elemental world of sound-sheet sonority, 'national' melody and motivic compression that in the 1890s he would imbue with the mythic significance of the Finnish pre-Christian epic, the *Kalevala*. Or to re-examine the high-strung tensions and earnest contradictions that tear at the heart of Mahler's all-inclusive symphonies – suggesting that the Austro-Germanic symphony *qua* genre, apparently now in tatters (a metaphor for European society?), was to be held together primarily, if at all, by a force of desperate will. For the most part, the worlds of early modernist orchestral music in the decades around 1900 need not so much

45 Dahlhaus, *Nineteenth-Century Music*, p. 334.

46 Important manifestos of the early phases of Austro-Germanic modernism are reprinted in Erich Ruprecht (ed.), *Literarische Manifeste des Naturalismus: 1880–1892* (Stuttgart, 1962), from which the above features were extrapolated. Another useful discussion may be found in Astradur Eysteinsson, *The Concept of Modernism* (Ithaca, 1990).

47 See, e.g., Charles Youmans, 'The Private Intellectual Context of Richard Strauss's *Also sprach Zarathustra*', *19th Century Music*, 22 (1998), pp. 101–26. Cf. Hepokoski, 'The Framing of Till Eulenspiegel: Strauss's Credo of Musical Modernism?' in Timothy L. Jackson (ed.), *Strauss Studies* (Cambridge, forthcoming).

to be defended as to be rediscovered – and problematised – on new terms, hope-
fully ones emancipated from the misconceptions and partisan bickerings of the
past century.

Bibliography

Adorno, T. W., *Mahler: A Musical Physiognomy*, trans. E. Jephcott. London, 1992
Beckerman, M., 'Dvořák's "New World" Largo and *The Song of Hiawatha*'. *19th Century
     Music*, 16 (1992), pp. 35–48
Bonds, M. E., *After Beethoven: Imperatives of Originality in the Symphony*. Cambridge,
     Mass., 1996
   'Idealism and the Aesthetics of Instrumental Music at the Turn of the Nineteenth
     Century'. *Journal of the American Musicological Society*, 50 (1997), pp. 387–420
Botstein, L., 'Listening through Reading: Musical Literacy and the Concert Audience'.
     19th Century Music, 16 (1992), pp. 129–45
Brinkmann, R., *Late Idyll: The Second Symphony of Johannes Brahms*, trans. P. Palmer.
     Cambridge, Mass., 1995
Brodbeck, D., *Brahms: Symphony No. 1*. Cambridge, 1997
Brown, A. P., *The Symphonic Repertoire*, III, *The European Symphony from 1800–1930*.
     Bloomington, forthcoming; and IV, *The Second Golden Age of the Viennese Symphony:
     Brahms, Bruckner, Dvořák, Mahler, and Selected Contemporaries*. Bloomington, forth-
     coming
Burnham, S., *Beethoven Hero*. Princeton, 1995
Darcy, W., 'Bruckner's Sonata Deformations'. In T. L. Jackson and P. Hawkshaw (eds.),
     Bruckner Studies. Cambridge, 1997, pp. 256–77
Dahlhaus, C., *The Idea of Absolute Music*, trans. R. Lustig. Chicago, 1989.
   'Musikalische Moderne und Neue Musik'. *Melos/Neue Zeitschrift für Musik*, 2 (1976), p.
     90
   Nineteenth-Century Music, trans. J. B. Robinson. Berkeley and Los Angeles, 1989
Floros, C., *Gustav Mahler: The Symphonies*, trans. V. and J. Wicker. Portland, Oreg., 1993
Forchert, A., 'Zur Auflösung traditioneller Formkategorien in der Musik um 1900:
     Probleme formaler Organisation bei Mahler und Strauss'. *Archiv für
     Musikwissenschaft*, 32 (1975), pp. 85–98
Franklin, P., *Mahler: Symphony No. 3*. Cambridge, 1991
Frisch, W., *Brahms: The Four Symphonies*. New York, 1996
Hefling, S. E., 'Miners Digging from Opposite Sides: Mahler, Strauss, and the Problem
     of Program Music'. In B. Gilliam (ed.), *Richard Strauss: New Perspectives on the
     Composer and His Work*. Durham, NC, 1992, pp. 41–53
Hepokoski, J., 'Culture Clash'. *The Musical Times*, 134 (1993), pp. 685–8
   'Fiery-Pulsed Libertine or Domestic Hero: Strauss's *Don Juan* Reinvestigated'. In
     Bryan Gilliam (ed.), *Richard Strauss: New Perspectives on the Composer and His Work*.
     Durham, NC, 1992, pp. 135–75
   'Masculine-Feminine'. *The Musical Times*, 135 (1994), pp. 494–9
Holoman, D. K. (ed.), *The Nineteenth-Century Symphony*. New York, 1997
Knapp, R., *Brahms and the Challenge of the Symphony*. Stuyvesant, N.Y., 1997
Mercer-Taylor, P., 'Mendelssohn's "Scottish" Symphony and the Music of German
     Memory'. *19th Century Music*, 19 (1995), pp. 68–82

Micznik, V., 'The Absolute Limitations of Programme Music: The Case of Liszt's "Die Ideale"'. *Music & Letters*, 80 (1999), pp. 207–40

Mitchell, D. and Nicholson, A. (eds.), *The Mahler Companion*. Oxford, 1999

Musgrave, M., 'Brahms's First Symphony: Thematic Coherence and Its Secret Origin'. *Music Analysis*, 2 (1983), pp. 117–33

Notley, Margaret, 'Late-Nineteenth-Century Chamber Music and the Cult of the Classical Adagio'. *19th Century Music*, 23 (1999), pp. 33–61.

'*Volksconcerte* in Vienna and Late Nineteenth-Century Ideology of the Symphony'. *Journal of the American Musicological Society*, 50 (1997), 421–53

Werbeck, W., *Die Tondichtungen von Richard Strauss*. Tutzing, 1996

Youmans, C., 'The Private Intellectual Context of Richard Strauss's *Also sprach Zarathustra*'. *19th Century Music*, 22 (1998), pp. 101–26

16

Words and music in Germany and France

SUSAN YOUENS

Few generalisations are safe, but the following one is perhaps more defensible than many others: the coming together of words and music is a Hydra-headed phenomenon, changeable from composer to composer, era to era, place to place, and it is always fraught with difficulties. Song is both natural, that is, an innate impulse (to heighten words by singing them precedes recorded history) and unnatural (words and music are two different sign-systems), and its agonistic tensions were the source of continuing debate in the later nineteenth century, especially given the commercial viability of the genre. Songs abounded: by the later decades of the century, the composer Peter Cornelius could rightly speak of an endless stream of *Three Songs* issuing from German music firms, while the immense girth of Ernst Challier's *Grosser Lieder-Katalog* (Great Song Catalogue) of 1885 testifies to the proliferation which prompted Cornelius's half-exasperated, half-rueful comment.[1] He was, after all, a contributor to the floodtide, composing both song cycles (including *Vater unser*, Op. 2; *Trauer und Trost*, Op. 3; *Rheinische Lieder*, Op. 7; and the popular *Weihnachtslieder*, Op. 8) and individual songs. Whatever the assertions of singing 'as the birds sing' – so proclaims Goethe's Harper in 'Der Sänger' (The Minstrel), a ballad replete with ironies – or of folklike *naïveté*, the nineteenth-century lied was never unselfconscious, and by this point it had its own history to contend with as well.

In song, poetry loses its poetic structure but retains its meanings, imagistic associations, and literary pleasures and provocations, while music both insists on its self-sufficiency and is bent to poetic analogy. How these confluences and divergences were calibrated in late nineteenth-century lieder varied according to numerous factors, changeable from one composer to another. For example, song composition entails going outside a composer's bailiwick of music in order to find literary sources, and the choice of poetry speaks volumes about literary fashion and the composer's individual nature. What made so many composers from the 1820s on so attracted to Heinrich Heine's early poetry, for example? What convergence of political disillusionment, Romantic self-

---

1 Peter Cornelius, *Literarische Werke*, II (Leipzig, 1904; repr., New York, 1970), p. 646.

loathing, and the dissection of desire as gall, revulsion and loss drew them in droves to this repertory? What role did the composer's individual personality and psychology play in the attraction to certain poems and the rejection of others? Whether a composer gravitated mostly to contemporary poems by less than stellar poets (Richard Strauss) or detested modern versifying, reverting instead to earlier repertories (Hugo Wolf), was another variable, and so too were musico-literary nationalisms, that is, instances in which a composer was concerned with the peculiarly French (Debussy), Russian (Musorgsky) or Czech (Dvořák) shaping of the words in melody. Furthermore, each composer's musical imperatives – the compositional problems they attempted to solve, the formation of their own stylistic stamp – impinged on song in different ways; for example, Debussy and Wolf both grappled with complex responses to Wagner, with very dissimilar results. To complicate matters even more (but this is what makes the genre so interesting), song was always a locus for cultural teachings about that which society sought to inculcate in its men and women and a mirror held up to history. The Romantic lied tells simultaneously of the individual composer's artistic aspirations (Schubert's ambitious intent to elevate the song cycle to equal stature with symphony and string quartet, for example) and of the political and cultural spheres enveloping the composer. One need only recall the explosion of patriotic songs post-1812 as Napoleon's realm was dismantled or the embedding of messages about gender roles in songs about love, marriage, motherhood and women.

In sum, the conjunction of music and poetry is calibrated anew with the creation of each song *oeuvre*, despite ongoing debates with common threads and recurring themes. Words and music have their own large tales to tell; sometimes they intersect, and sometimes they set off on radically different paths, and all composers drawn to song composition construe the connections anew in their songs.

The German-speaking world: tradition, struggle, homage

Composers who wrote lieder after the European upheavals of 1848 did so against the backdrop of a singularly rich recent history: the burgeoning of the lied in the first half of the century. Their knowledge of what Beethoven, Schubert, Schumann and a host of others had created only a few years before affected what came later in many ways, homage and reference jostling cheek-by-jowl with the desire for difference. The story of German song in the latter half of the century is in part the story of Oedipal love–hate relationships with illustrious predecessors.

For example, the song cycle had already undergone a transformation from the simple, non-operatic style evident in the *Liederspiele* (song-plays) of Johann Friedrich Reichardt at the start of the century to concert song cycles by Schubert, Schumann and others whose music bespeaks the avant-garde in musico-poetic conceptions. Beethoven's *An die ferne Geliebte*, Schubert's *Die schöne Müllerin* and *Winterreise*, Schumann's many cycles, and even such second-rank but interesting works as Conradin Kreutzer's *Frühlingslieder* (Spring Songs) and *Wanderlieder* (Wandering Songs) to texts by Ludwig Uhland, con-stituted a powerful prior repertory, and later composers defined their cyclic enterprises as echoes of and/or divergences from this heritage.

Two of the later nineteenth-century's greatest song composers, both acutely aware of what came before them, tended to shy away from song cycles: Johannes Brahms and Hugo Wolf. Brahms only composed two specimens of the genre, neither one designated as a cycle, although that is what they are; one cycle is an early work, the other near the end of his life, and these works com-posed at almost thirty years' distance from one another are each defined in ways different from those of Brahms's predecessors. (One should point out that Brahms took pains assembling his 'bouquets' of individual songs for publica-tions, and the bouquets often begin or end with grouped songs, such as 'Klage I' and 'Klage II' at the start of Op. 69; the three songs each entitled 'Heimweh' (Homesickness) at the end of Op. 63; and the Heine songs, 'Sommerabend' (Summer Evening) and 'Mondenschein' (Moonlight) of Op. 85, linked by related melodies.) The *Romanzen aus Tiecks Magelone* (Nos. 1–6 published in 1865, Nos. 7–15 in 1868–9), dedicated to the great baritone Julius Stockhausen, is a large composition, eighty-plus pages of score and almost an hour in performance, but its singular stance *vis-à-vis* the textual source has been a factor in its absence from the standard repertory, despite its beauty.

The source is a twelfth-century tale reworked in 1797 by the Romantic writer Ludwig Tieck (1773–1853) for his *Phantasus* of 1812–16, where it is entitled the *Wundersame Liebesgeschichte der schönen Magelone und des Grafen Peter von Provence* (The Marvelous Love-History of Lord Peter of Provence and the Beautiful Magelone). Each of Tieck's eighteen chapters ends with a poem, such lyric inser-tions inspired by Goethe's *Wilhelm Meisters Lehrjahre* (William Master's Apprenticeship), and the songs ostensibly issue from different characters – an unnamed wandering minstrel, the handsome young knight Peter, the princess Magelone of Naples, and the Moorish Sultan's daughter Sulima. Brahms set fifteen of the poems, omitting those at the end of chapters 1, 16 and 17, in order, suggesting that he thought of the work as a narrative, perhaps even as sublimated opera; unless the songs are performed along with readings from Tieck's tale or the audience is given summaries of what transpires in the interim between songs, however, the narrative thread is lost to the experience of Brahms's music. The fifteen songs mediate between sprawling *Romanzen* of balladesque dimensions and more lied-like songs – despite this confirmed bachelor's famous later statement that he would rather marry than compose an opera, this work is larger and bolder than the usual contemporaneous compilation of smaller songs.

Op. 33 is truly cyclic in its musical construction. The tonal relationships from song to song are quite close at the beginning (E flat major, C minor, A flat major, D flat major) and then embark on further travels (F major, A major, D Major, G flat major) as the protagonist sets forth on his adventures. Several of the tonalities one finds early in the work recur later on as the cycle draws to its close; the A flat major of No. 3, 'Sind es Schmerzen, sind es Freuden', comes back as the tonality of No. 9, 'Ruhe, Süßliebchen'; the C minor of song No. 2, 'Traun! Bogen und Pfeil', returns as the key of No. 10, 'Verzweiflung'; and the last song is set in the same E flat major key as the first song. The often lengthy piano postludes serve a dual function as the conclusion of one song and the corridor leading to the next; the unusual absence of any postlude at all at the end of the final song, 'Treue Liebe dauert lange', signals finality. Beyond the architectural logic of the cycle as a whole, the individual songs are filled with felicities, too many to allow more than a representative sampling: the vocal line which twists and winds at the words 'und windet euch rund um mich her' (and twine about me here) in 'Verzweiflung' (Despair); the lulling way in which Brahms so beautifully blurs the $\frac{6}{8}$ time in the left hand at the beginning of 'Ruhe, Süßliebchen' (Rest, Beloved); and the affective use of Brahms's favourite Neapolitan harmony at the words 'Leben ist dunkles Grab' (Life is a dark grave) in the third song, 'Sind es Schmerzen, sind es Freuden' (Are These Sorrows, Are These Joys?). Did Mahler have this song in his mind's ear when he composed the refrains 'Dunkel ist das Leben, ist das Grab' in the first movement of *Das Lied von der Erde*? The similarities seem beyond coincidence.

The second and last cycle by Brahms, the *Vier ernste Gesänge*, Op. 121 (Four Serious Songs – 'serious' is a typically Brahmsian understatement) of 1896, is one of this composer's most important works and one which tells much about him. He was not conventionally religious, but he read Scripture from the Bible he was given as a child throughout his life and chose the texts of these songs from the great gloomy prophet Ecclesiastes (the first two songs), from Jesus Sirach, and from St Paul to the Corinthians. The first three songs are bleak meditations having as much and more to do with life's injustices and miseries as with death; not even Paul's affirmation of Faith, Hope and Love in the final song can obliterate the taste of ashes left behind by the evocations of suffering in the first three. But Brahms's music for these songs exemplifies in a particularly concentrated fashion his late style, which Arnold Schoenberg would later hail as the precursor of certain twentieth-century composers' derivation both of the vertical and horizontal levels of music from the pitches/intervals/motivic figures stated at the beginning. In the third song, 'O Tod, wie bitter bist du' (Oh Death, How Bitter Thou Art), Brahms symbolises the Janus faces of death – unjust when it snatches the young, merciful when it puts an end to the sufferings of the elderly – by turning interlacing intervals of a major and minor third inside out, eliding them, stating them in sequence, inversion and chromatic permutation. The process is unforgettably set into motion with a chain-of-thirds harmonic progression in the piano at the beginning, elided with the singer's acclamation of death, 'O Tod, o Tod' (Oh death, death), the melody descending by alternating major and minor thirds as if into the Valley of Death. Brahms, who had been stung more than once by Wolf's criticisms of his prosody (Wolf dismissed Brahms's setting of Gottfried Keller's 'Therese' as 'yodelling in the noble folksong manner'), had different notions of how to shape verbal rhythms into musical rhythms than his younger contemporary, and there is little of Wagner-derived notions of declamatory melody in this song, but the long, unfurling lines of bars 6–11 and the fragmentation of the vocal line thereafter – 'O Tod . . . wie wohl . . . tust du . . . dem Dürftigen', etc. – are wonderfully expressive in their own way. For example, the phrase 'und dem es wohl geht in allen Dingen und noch wohl essen mag' (and for whom it goes well in all things and who can still eat) is notable for such details as the lift to a higher pitch on the weak half of the beat at the first invocation of the word 'wohl' – bitter emphasis – and the even more emphatic repeated pitches at the end of the phrase. The broad expanse of this phrase begins with convoluted sinews, the 'death'-thirds entwining about each other, and ends in austere finality, as if stating immutable, inescapable laws. Death, we are told, lies in wait for the fortunate even as they enjoy what is good in life.

Most of Brahms's songs are individual lieder, composed in on-again, off-again spurts throughout his entire life. He began, so he later told a friend, with songs to texts by Heine and Eichendorff, the poets forever associated with Schumann; dissatisfied with most of these juvenile efforts, Brahms subsequently destroyed the manuscripts. His reputation as a song composer was once shaped in some measure by Wolf's coruscating disapprobation in the 1880s, by the antinomies critics established between the Wagnerites and the Brahmsians; according to that formulation, Wolf was sensitive as none other to poetic nuance while Brahms was a generalist who responded to poetic atmospheres – often in negligible verse – with pure music and bad prosody. Like many clichés, it does not survive a closer examination of his almost 300 solo songs. If the text-setting aesthetic is not what Wolf would espouse near the end of Brahms's life, neither is Brahms unresponsive to subtleties of verbal meaning. Brahms first looked for poems which invited musical elaboration, then memorised his chosen text, recited it out loud numerous times, studied its form and rhythms intently, and then waited for melodic ideas to come. His compositional process was painstaking, beginning with the vocal part and the bass line (after the fashion of the Baroque music he loved, Brahms felt that the topmost and bottommost voices should be a *Spiegelbild* of one another, that is, equally strong) and concluding with thoroughgoing revisions.

Surveying Brahms's song *oeuvre*, one sees an implicit rejection of identification with one poet in particular or a group of poets after the manner of the Goethe–Schubert, Müller–Schubert or Schumann–Heine nexus. If one remembers that almost eighty of Brahms's 240-or-so songs are settings of anonymous folk poems, the remaining 160-plus are settings of fifty-five different poets, evidence of wide reading and a restless search for suitable song texts. If the reputation of some of his poets did not outlive their own day (the Nobel-prize winning writer Paul Heyse, for example, or the adventurer in exotic realms, Friedrich Bodenstedt), Brahms could not have known this; literary reputations, forever in the process of re-evaluation, are often sorted out after the poets are no more. The Hermann Allmers song 'Feldeinsamkeit' (Meadow Loneliness), Op. 86, No. 2, and the Hermann von Lingg setting 'Immer leiser wird mein Schlummer' (Ever Gentler My Sleep Will Be), Op. 105, No. 2, are on everyone's short-list of Brahms's most beautiful songs, whatever the deficiencies of the poetry. And Brahms *did* set to music poems by great poets such as Ludwig Hölty ('Die Mainacht'), Clemens Brentano ('O kühler Wald'), Heine ('Der Tod, das ist die kühle Nacht'), Eduard Mörike ('Agnes'), Goethe ('Dämmerung senkte sich von oben'), August von Platen ('Nicht mehr zu dir zu gehen'), Eichendorff ('Anklänge'), to name only a few. One notes that he tended to avoid the poems so often set to music before him.

But other reminiscences constitute a powerful presence in his songs, fragments of the past given new contexts. Brahms once said that there was no song by Schubert from which one could not learn something, this by way of defending Schubert's youthful songs, and he remembers Schubert from within his own songs after a fashion one might call 'creative nostalgia'. When Schubert had responded to earlier songs, such as the ballads of Johann Rudolf Zumsteeg, it was both to learn from predecessors' achievement and to surpass it, the latter aim stated openly to his school friends, but Brahms's quotations blend nostalgia, homage, appropriation and revision. One such instance – Brahms's setting of Adolf Friedrich von Schack's 'Herbstgefühl' (Autumn Feeling), Op. 48, No. 7, published in 1868 – is particularly intriguing because the poet also recalled an earlier work, Goethe's 'Ein Gleiches' or 'Wandrers Nachtlied II' (Wanderer's Night Song II). The consolatory injunction at the close of

Goethe's poem, 'Warte nur, balde / Ruhest du auch' (Wait a little, soon you too
will rest), becomes the later persona's gloomier words, 'Gib dich zur Ruh, /
Bald stirbt sie auch' (Be at peace: soon they too will die), 'they' being 'the last
withered joys' invoked in the preceding line. Brahms too quotes the end of a
great work: Schubert's setting of Heine's 'Der Doppelgänger', specifically, the
final clause of the final question which opens up a gap in time between the
present moment and its origins in the past ('Why do you ape love's suffering,
which tormented me at this spot *so many nights in bygone times?*'). The borrowed
gestures are recomposed; Schubert's unforgettable root-position Neapolitan
harmony in the postlude of 'Der Doppelgänger' becomes Brahms's passage on
G major, this in a song set in F sharp minor, in bars 81–4 ('Gib dich zur Ruh'
[surrender to quietude before death]), the G♯ belonging to the key subsequently reinstated at the verb 'stirbt'. Schubert's B–D ambiguities reappear as
voice-exchange mirrors in contrary motion (a signature element of Brahmsian
counterpoint). That the passage is lowered in temperature and tessitura by
comparison with the tension-wracked original model tells of nostalgia, of distance from Schubert's song. It is also obvious: we are meant to recognise the
quotation.

Another instance has gone unrecognised because the Schubertian model is
less well known. 'Der Winterabend' (The Winter Evening), Schubert's 1827
setting of a poem by the Styrian nobleman Karl Gottfried Ritter von Leitner,
includes a series of mediant modulations in the interior of the song as the
musing elderly persona withdraws into contemplative peacefulness, his only
companion the moonlight which steals into the room. From tonic B flat major,
Schubert slips via common-tone motion to G major at the first invocation of
'blessed peace', and from there to E flat major with the arrival of moonlight:
'Nur der Mondenschein kommt leise zu mir in's Gemach' (Only the moonlight
comes softly to me in the room). It is an epiphanic moment which haunts, like
the gentlest of ghosts, Brahms's setting of Goethe's words, 'Nun am östlichen
Bereiche ahn ich Mondenglanz- und -glut' (In the east, I now see hints of the
moonlight's radiance and glow), similarly an announcement of the moon's
advent, in the late poem (1827) 'Dämmrung senkte sich von oben' (Twilight
sinks from on high), Op. 59, No. 1, published in 1873. The octave span of each
of those phrases, the ascent up the scale (albeit with gently curlicued divagations to emphasise the dominant and subdominant pitches in Schubert's song),
the culmination on the newly tonicised E♭, even the location of both on E flat
major, seem too closely related to be coincidental.

One cannot leave the subject of Brahms's songs without mentioning the
influence of German folksong, a lifelong passion of this composer: he harmon-
ised folk melodies from such anthologies as Kretzschmer and Zuccalmaglio's

Deutsche Volkslieder mit ihren Original-Weisen (German Folk Songs with their Original Melodies) of 1838 and 1840 – he defended this collection in the face of charges that it was inauthentic – and set many art-poems in quasi-*volkstümlich* ways. 'Volkstümlichkeit' is not equivalent to simplicity in Brahms's reckoning: beneath an unchanging A minor vocal melody, the piano accompaniment to 'Maria ging aus wandern' (The Virgin Mary Went Forth on a Journey) from his forty-nine *Deutsche Volkslieder* of 1894 becomes increasingly chromatic with each stanza as one draws closer to the crucifixion, and the extreme metric-rhythmic intricacies of 'In stiller Nacht' (In the Quiet of the Night) invest this lament with tensions far from simple. The poet Mörike gives the forester's daughter Agnes in his 1832 novel *Maler Nolten* (The Artist Nolten) a 'folksong' to sing on the archetypal theme of the abandoned maiden as she nears insanity and suicide; Brahms portrays this folklike figure's impending loss of reason by means of metric fluctuations (the song is marked in two metres, $\frac{3}{4}\frac{2}{4}$), harmonic wavering between C minor and G minor/major, and increasing chromaticism in the piano which tells of increasing pain after the same fashion as 'Maria ging aus wandern'. Once again, art song and folksong fuse.

Brahms's antipode in the debates over absolute and programmatic music (a debate which was an artificial construct in many respects) was Richard Wagner (1813–83), who cared little for lied. As a university student in Leipzig, he composed seven works (lieder, melodrama, choral compositions) to texts from Goethe's *Faust*, including a version of 'Gretchen am Spinnrade' notable for its distant trivialised echoes of Schubert's 1814 masterpiece, and in Paris in 1840 he wrote a few French songs (including two on texts from Victor Hugo's *Les orientales* and Pierre de Ronsard's famous monument to *carpe diem* seduction, 'Mignonne, allons voir si la rose') as fodder for famous singers, or so he hoped. The florid, Meyerbeer-like setting of Pierre Jean de Béranger's 'Adieux de Marie Stuart' (Mary Stuart's Farewell) and of François-Adolphe Loeve-Veimar's translation of Heine's 'Die beiden Grenadiere' (The Two Grenadiers), however, demonstrate little more than Wagner's imperfect mastery of French and a version of the Marseillaise more bombastic than the one at the end of Schumann's Heine song. With characteristic chutzpah, Wagner wrote to Schumann in December 1840, explaining that his (Wagner's) Frenchified song had come first and had even garnered him a large pension from Louis-Philippe himself (Wagner was being ironic).[2] After 1844, he found no occasion to compose lieder until 1857, at the time of his affair with Mathilde Wesendonck (1828–1902), the wife of a music-loving silk merchant named Otto Wesendonck. Wagner set five of her sensual-ecstatic or sorrowful poems to

---

2 Richard Wagner, *Sämtliche Werke*, XVII: *Klavierlieder*, ed. Egon Voss (Mainz, 1976), p. xii.

music during the composition of *Tristan und Isolde*; the third and fifth songs, 'Im Treibhaus' (In the Greenhouse, No. 3) and 'Träume' (Dreams, No. 5), are even subtitled 'Studies for Tristan and Isolde'. The piano part of 'Im Treibhaus' subsequently reappears in the Prelude to Act III and at the beginning of Tristan's account of the 'Weiten Reich der Weltennacht' (The wide realm of the world's night), while the last song at its beginning and end anticipates the love-duet, 'O sink hernieder, Nacht der Liebe', in Act II. It is a singularity in the history of the nineteenth-century lied that song should be thus so nakedly conceived as the servant to opera, the songs both self-sufficient works and *maquettes* for a bigger and fundamentally different genre. Wagner himself seems to have been surprised by the success of the dual venture, telling Mathilde in a letter of September 1861 (the affair was over, but the two remained friends) that he had placed a copy of 'Träume' next to the 'night scene' from the opera: 'As God is my witness, the song pleased me more than the noble scene! Heavens, it is more beautiful than everything else I've made! It strikes me right down to the deepest nerve when I hear it!'[3] He was, one guesses, exaggerating in order to flatter her in her role as poet and Muse, but only somewhat, as the songs are indeed beautiful.

Mathilde Wesendonck took her cue from Wagner in these poems; the references to the sun rising 'wie ein stolzer Siegesheld' (like a proud warrior-hero), to 'eternal creation, primal thought, powers of generation', and the cry 'Enough of becoming, let me be!' proclaim his influence, although much else in the poems anticipates Maeterlinck's *fin-de-siècle* moods. The cycle is in part unified by closely related keys (for example, both the second and fourth songs, on either side of the central lied 'Im Treibhaus' in D minor, are in C minor–major), although it is tonally progressive after a fashion sanctioned many years earlier by Schubert; the first Wesendonck song is in G major, the fifth in A flat major. There are other recurring threads as well, such as the gently throbbing repeated chords beneath the words 'selig süßem Vergessen' (blessed sweet oblivion) in the second song which then underlie the entirety of 'Träume', or the fact that the rising figure at the beginning of 'Im Treibhaus' is a slowed-down recollection of the dizzying figures in the piano throughout the first half of 'Stehe still!' The two Tristan studies are usually singled out as the best of the five, although one notes that this is an assessment which privileges opera over the lyrical gestures of song. Certainly the great wheeling, circling, rising figures at the start of the second song, 'Stehe still!' (Stand Still!), with its invocation of the 'Rad der Zeit' (wheel of Time), and the rapturous slowing down throughout the latter half of the song as passion brings Time almost to a

---

3 *Ibid.*, p. xv.

standstill, also the progression from turbulent C minor in the beginning to a triumphal C major when love clarifies 'Nature's riddle' at the end, are remarkable as well.

One of the most notable features of these songs, however, is the interweaving of song style and the declamatory manner fashioned for Wagner's mature operas. If one looks at the gem of the set, 'Im Treibhaus' (the introduction, in which a figure drifts upwards into the treble empyrean and ends, hovering, on a crystalline voicing of the dominant harmony, is unforgettable), one can see the workings of such a fusion. Compound metre or $\frac{6}{8}$ time is a staple of *volkstümlich* art song, its customary crotchet–quaver repeated rhythmic pattern telling more of music's imposed order than of attention to verbal rhythms. Wagner first slows the metre down to a tempo (*Langsam und schwer*) which vitiates any hint of jogtrot and intersperses the $\frac{6}{8}$ with bars of $\frac{9}{8}$, increasing the languor still more. Even where he repeats the standard metrical pattern to induce an appropriately hypnotic or enervated state, he inflects the melodic/harmonic contours in a manner prompted by verbal meaning. For example, in his setting of the words 'Kinder ihr aus fernen Zonen, saget mir warum ihr klagt?' (You children from distant lands, tell me why you lament?), he slips to the flat side at the word 'fernen' (distant) to underscore distance harmonically, while the verb 'steiget' (rises) – 'und der Leiden stummer Zeuge, steiget aufwärts süßer Duft' (and, mute witness to your sorrows, a sweet perfume rises) – impels similar side-slipping motion to the sharp side. Other phrases are expressively broken into fragments, while the final texted phrase is mostly recitation. The way in which the dissonant, heavy droplets ('schwere Tropfen seh' ich schweben an der Blätter grünem Saum') in the piano beneath the final words of the text merge into a repetition of the introduction as postlude is beautifully affective. Wagner clearly knew the conventions of song composition and uses them, but music drama is present here as well (not for the first time, as anyone surveying Zumsteeg's or Schubert's songs rapidly realises).

Franz Liszt (1811–86) was also an avatar of large-scale musical genres (but not opera), and he advised others – notably, Hugo Wolf – to do so as well; we owe Wolf's oratorio *Christnacht* (Christmas Night) and his symphonic tone poem *Penthesilea* in part to Liszt's advice to the teenage composer that he turn to larger forms. Liszt says little about the lied in his letters and essays, but he considered song important in the same way and to the same degree as his works in the big public genres; despite his reticence on the subject, his eighty or so songs constitute a particularly fine body of works and deserve to be better known than they are. In his early years, Liszt transcribed many of Schubert's songs for solo piano, and his knowledge of them is on occasion inscribed in his own lieder; the beginning of Liszt's setting of Ludwig Uhland's 'Die

Vätergruft' (The Ancestral Tomb) recalls the beginning of Schubert's 'An die Freunde' (To his friends), D.654, on a text by Johann Mayrhofer. The often formidable difficulties for both performers, especially in the ballad texts which invited greater virtuosity (such as 'Le vieux vagabond / Der alte Vagabund', a French poem by Béranger translated into German by Theodor Rehbaum, and Nikolaus Lenau's 'Die drei Zigeuner'), are responsible in part for the neglect of Liszt's songs, but the best of the lot are often both short and not technically challenging, the harmonic radicalism and poetico-musical depths all the more potent for their containment in small packages. Brevity is not equivalent to conceptual simplicity, however, and such works have nothing to do with the folklike ideal in song composition. Liszt could indulge his taste for musical sophistication to the end of his life: his late songs on poems by Friedrich von Bodenstedt ('Gebet' [Prayer]; 'Einst' [Once Upon a Time]; and 'An Edlitam' [To Edlitam] – a play on the name of Bodenstedt's wife Mathilde – all three published in 1879) are experiments in music on the brink between tonality's end and whatever would come after. Nothing in 'Einst' ever resolves; in this constricted world of loss (loss of love = loss of tonal certainty), resolution is no longer possible. Liszt's setting in 1855 of Hoffmann von Fallersleben's 'Wie singt die Lerche schön' (How beautifully sings the lark), first published in the *Deutschen Musen-Almanach* in 1856, is even more radical for its time, twenty years before the composer's experiments in old age.

It was especially during his years in Weimar (1848–61) that Liszt was impelled to compose lieder. He had at his disposal in Weimar a vocal ensemble of extraordinary gifts, including the baritone and soprano husband-wife team of Feodor and Rosa von Milde (the first Elsa and Telramund of the 1850 production of *Lohengrin*) and, later, the lighter-voiced soprano Emilie Genast, daughter of the Weimar impresario Eduard Genast. The songs written at this time are among his most profound works in the genre, many of them on melancholy or tragic texts; life for the composer in his forties was fraught with difficulties, including the death of his son Daniel, and his preference for darker-hued verse is understandable. The roster of his poets, including Petrarch, Victor Hugo, Tennyson, Tolstoy, Petöfi, Goethe, Schiller, Heine, Lenau and Uhland, is evidence of a cosmopolitan life, although lieder and therefore German poetry predominate in his song *oeuvre*. If some of his chosen poems, especially in his later years, are the dilettantish products of the *hochadelige* (high nobility) in Liszt's glittering social circle, he is also on the short-list of those nineteenth-century composers who served Heine best. He is truly, as Alan Walker has observed, the 'missing link' between Schumann and Wolf – one can point to direct relationships between, for example, Liszt's setting of Emil Kuh's 'Die Glocken von Marling' (The Bells of Marling) of 1874 and

Wolf's setting of Goethe's 'Sankt Nepomuks Vorabend' (The Eve of St Nepomuk's Day) – and a song composer to be reckoned with in his own right.

Singers often gravitate to Liszt's salon songs, such as 'Kling leise, mein Lied' (Sound Softly, My Song) to a forgettable poem by Johannes Nordmann or 'Angiolin del biondo crin' (Angel with Golden Hair), but the majority of his songs are made of sterner, deeper stuff than these elegant trifles. Hundreds of composers flocked to Heine's *Buch der Lieder* from Schubert's day onward, but this volume might as well have been bound in barbed wire, such are its traps for the unwary. Heine's bitterness and his deceptive simplicity veiling formidable subterranean complexities are less accessible to musical grasp than some have believed, and many composers came to shipwreck in these depths. Not so Liszt: en route to the 1859–60 edition of his collected lieder, he revised the song 'Vergiftet sind meine Lieder' (My Songs are Poisoned), composed in the 1840s, and the final version is a masterpiece etched in gall and black bile. The text is the fifty-first poem in the grouping entitled *Lyrisches Intermezzo* from the *Buch der Lieder*:

Vergiftet sind meine Lieder; –	My songs are poisoned; –
Wie könnt es anders sein?	how could it be otherwise?
Du hast mir ja Gift gegossen	You have injected me with poison
Ins blühende Leben hinein.	in life's blossoming time.
Vergiftet sind meine Lieder; –	My songs are poisoned; –
Wie könnt es anders sein?	how could it be otherwise?
Ich trage im Herzen viel Schlangen,	I bear in my heart many snakes
Und dich, Geliebte mein.	and you, my beloved.

Heine emphasises the crucial participle 'vergiftet' by placing it at the beginning of both the first and second stanzas, and Liszt in turn underlines the word still more by dispensing with any piano introduction such that 'vergiftet' first sounds as a volcanic outburst without preliminaries. When poem becomes song, it is tonality which is poisoned. Liszt deliberately wavers between an implied E major and its relative minor C sharp minor at the beginning, without establishing either one, then hints in his setting of the words 'blühende Leben' (bars 7–8) that E major is the key of 'blossoming life'; the fact that the voice is alone as it sings these words, deprived of instrumental support, implies something now vanished, a memory devoid of substance. Just before, in bars 5–6, we hear the poisoning of E major, injected with chromatic tones, in particular, with the Neapolitan at the word 'Gift' (poison); both the restoration of E major diatonicism for the phrase 'ins blühende Leben hinein' and the refusal of a tonic resting-point (the two-bar phrase is contained between the wistfully prolonged leading tone D♯ and the supertonic degree F♯) are evocative compositional decisions. When the anguished protagonist sings the words 'und dich,

Geliebte mein' at the climax of the song (bars 25–9), we are made to understand that 'Gift' and 'dich' are the same pitch, the same thing, and that the typically Lisztian enharmonic transformation of F into E♯ as the word 'dich' (you) is sustained across the barline between bar 26 and bar 27 signals the end of any possibility of E major 'blossoming life'. Thereafter in the piano postlude (bars 29–36), the right hand wordlessly repeats 'Vergiftet sind meine Lieder' but with the apex pitch altered, E♯ rather than the prior E.

Another aspect of this postlude compels notice as well. Among Heine's repertory of obsessively recurring images is that of serpents gnawing at lovers' hearts, as in 'Ich grolle nicht' (I do not complain) whose poetic 'I' furiously proclaims, 'Und sah die Schlang' die dir am Herzen frißt' (and saw the snake that gnaws at your heart). In 'Vergiftet sind meine Lieder', the beloved keeps company with a nest of snakes in the protagonist's heart, and Liszt makes of their slithering and biting a potent musical emblem. The rising chromatic bass line in bars 5–6 (G♯–A–B–C) returns in the piano interlude at bars 15–18, rhythmically diminished, *accelerando*, and extended, and then speeds up even more for the repeated left-hand figure in bars 19–21, underscoring the sustained D minor harmony (the Neapolitan of C♯) in those bars with its constituent F 'poison' pitch; Liszt accents the C♯ penultimate note in these figures at mid-bar. In the postlude, this same snake-like motif returns, slithering beneath the altered 'Vergiftet' reminiscence in the right-hand part and throwing the postlude off-balance rhythmically, such that the *morendo* resolution to a C sharp major chord – a 'tonic' only achieved at the song's last gasp – occurs on the fourth and weakest beat of the last bar. There is no tie across the barline, no prolongation of the harmony, just this ending that is not really an ending. More horror can be expected from the conjunction of *this* protagonist and *this* beloved, and Liszt tells us so in this eerie, angry conclusion.

Liszt, who was his own most severe critic, composed fully one-half of his songs before 1850 and subsequently revised many of them, often in multiple stages. He seems seldom to have considered a poem over and done with, but instead made a habit of returning to poems and finding in them new possibilities in accord with his latest compositional concerns and text-setting aesthetic. As Rena Charnin Mueller was the first to point out, the act of transposition often led to the recomposition of a text because the new tonality required a different approach to the poetry. The first version of Heine's 'Morgens steh ich auf und frage' is in A major, the second in G major, and the latter, better-known version is a thorough reconceptualisation of the lied.[4] Even where the later setting does not involve a change of tonal venue, Liszt

4 I am grateful to Rena Charnin Mueller for this information in a personal communiqué and for her aid with this chapter.

would still seek different possibilities in the same words, and he would often modify or expunge prior virtuosic elements in the process of revision. For example, he provides the first version of Heine's 'Im Rhein, im schönen Strome' (In the Rhine, in the Beautiful Waters) from the early 1840s with two versions of the piano accompaniment, one a veritable cascade of hand-crossings and the other a slightly less challenging foreshadowing of Wagner's Rhine River music in the *Ring* operas. The later setting, published in 1856, is far more taut, its sophistication having less to do with technical glitz than with harmonic resources, for example, the plunge from tonic E major to a brief passage on an unstable F minor for the invocation of 'meines Lebens Wildnis" (the wilderness of my life). Similarly, the siren who lures the fisher lad into the depths in Liszt's 1840s setting of 'Der Fischerknabe' from *Wilhelm Tell* ('Der Hirt' and 'Der Alpenjäger' complete the set of three songs) at first bathes in a torrent of pianistic water-music, a work-out on the order of the *Etudes transcendantes*, and sings melismatic lures in the vocal stratosphere. This is not empty virtuosity, however (supernatural forces rightly require superhuman music), and Liszt retains certain harmonic aspects of this setting for the version published in 1860. The death-dealing siren born of Homer and multiplied a hundredfold in German mythology declares openly at the end of the poem, 'Ich locke den Schläfer, ich zieh' ihn herein' (I lure the sleeper, I drag him down below), and both in the earlier and the later versions, the shift of worlds – from life to death, from terra firma to watery depths – is signified by the enharmonic transformation of G♯ in an E major context to A♭ in a D flat major context. The darkness of death washes over one in a sudden barrage of flats. Of all later nineteenth-century composers, Liszt was among those most fascinated by the possibilities of enharmony in tonal music, and he made enharmonic tonal metamorphosis a principal vehicle of poetic reading.

But there are also instances in which paring down prior virtuosity was not the impetus for recomposition but rather the exploration of different tonal/chromatic/enharmonic possibilities to be found in the same poetic words. In both of the related versions of Heine's 'Ein Fichtenbaum steht einsam' (A Fir-tree Stands Solitary), Liszt abjures pianistic or vocal fireworks and devises an initial C minor tonal region whose nebulous tonality and austere texture are the late Romantic concomitant to Heine's snowy, barren heights. The bass figures at the start of each version are also somewhat similar (the 'Langsam – düster' descending sequential motifs of the first version are distantly reminiscent of the famous theme at the beginning of the *Faust* Symphony), but there are differences as well which bespeak Liszt's concern for subtleties of poetico-musical reading. For example, Liszt locates the turning-point from cold, harsh reality to a dream of tropical warmth at a different place when he revised the setting. After the chromatic northern climes of the first version fade into near-nothingness on a single sustained E♭, we hear a *pianissimo* patch of diatonic, ethereal, high (this is a *dream*) A flat major harmonies, followed by the brief tonicisation of F sharp major for the Oriental palm. Otherness is spelled out for us in a tonality a tritone away from the fir-tree's tonal realm. In the alternative setting, however, Liszt places the enharmonic change of venue right at the words 'er träumt', returning to the flat side of the tonal wheel at the verb 'trauert' (grieves). Separated from that which it loves, the palm-tree too is desolate, and Liszt implies that it is slated for death as it leans 'auf brennender Felsenwand' (on the burning wall of rock), the *sforzando* descending chromatic bass lines in the final four bars of the first version extended in the second version (but not at the end). It is tempting to think that Liszt knew Schubert's descending chromatic invocation of 'Untergang' (doom) at the end of the 1817 song 'Auf der Donau' (On the Danube) and remembered it when he was setting Heine's poem to music.

Lied was not Liszt's primary medium, but it was Hugo Wolf's (1860–1903). Ironically, it was never Wolf's intention to become famous for song composition alone; his greatest desire was to compose opera. And yet, throughout the long years of his autodidactic musical apprenticeship, from the time of his expulsion from the Vienna Conservatory in 1877 (he was falsely accused of threatening the director's life) until his accession to compositional maturity in 1888, he came to focus more and more on this genre. In nine years from 1888 to 1897, broken by long intervals of compositional drought, he composed some 240 songs in a unique manner – 'Wölferl's own howl', he called it. Sadly, the onset of syphilitic insanity in September 1897 put an end to the creation of more such lieder, whose singular sophistication we are only beginning to understand a century later.

Wolf's myth is that of the 'Poet's Composer', someone who was more responsive to poetry, delved into it more deeply, understood its nuances with greater refinement than anyone else. He helped to create the myth by his much-touted act of placing the word *Gedichte* and the poet's name on the title-page before his own name in the songbooks on poems by Eduard Mörike (fifty-three songs published in 1889), Joseph von Eichendorff (twenty songs published in 1889) and Goethe (fifty-one songs published in 1890), although one notes the verb 'composed' in these titles. Music is the active force. Beyond the myth is an aesthetic of song like no one else's. Wolf delighted in all the resources of extended chromatic tonality at century's end and even believed that certain poems had to await the advent of post-Wagnerian harmony before they could be successfully realised in music. But he contains the complexities of his tonal language within closed lyrical structures, in song forms bordered and boundaried in traditional ways; if there is perhaps a sense of loss evident in his allegiance to the Schubertian–Schumannian past, it is conjoined with the clear-sighted recognition that time (and music) moves on, and so must he. And the myth of his reverence for his poets is in large measure true, although what he sought was verse which lent itself to *his* music, a self-serving enterprise in which poems exist for conversion into something no longer purely literary. Still, he read poetry, much of it allusive and complex, with great perception, and he fashioned both the larger tonal architecture and innumerable musical details – he traffics in multiple nuances – in accord with *his* reading of the poem. If his interpretations were inevitably affected by a personality, circumstances and opinions different from the poet's, that is inevitable in song, where two different artistic purposes are preserved in amber in the same work of art.

The young Wolf had begun by imitating Schumann, including the earlier composer's gravitation to Heine's verse, but by 1888, he had recognised his preference for other kinds of poetry – for example, his discovery of Eichendorff's 'character' poems, such as 'The Gypsy Woman', 'The Scholar' and 'The Mercenary Soldier', rather than the mystic strain Schumann had chosen – and his dislike of contemporary poets. Just as Schumann's name is forever linked with that of Heine, so too is Wolf's with that of Eduard Mörike (1804–75); Wolf's Mörike's songs did much to spread the word about a great poet whose reputation was not yet fully established. 'This is written with blood', Wolf once said in utmost admiration for Mörike's art,[5] and he found in this poet's single anthology of poems a Protean diversity of texts to his taste. If he admired intensity, he did not admire Heine's brand of subjectivity, and Mörike's classicising surfaces over profound, sometimes demonic, depths were the perfect antidote. In particular, Wolf was drawn to Mörike's poems of the fantastic and supernatural (Mörike invented a mythological island realm called Orplid and peopled it with elves, fairies and a tragic king), comic poems, poems of erotic and divine love, poems about death, *Dinggedichte* ('thing poems', in which vast recesses of meaning are glimpsed in seemingly insignificant objects), and figures from folk tradition (hunters, village youths and maidens, a drummer boy, an old woman).

Two examples from the Mörike songs can serve as small demonstrations of Wolf's art of song composition. Mörike, nostalgic for the loss of wholeness in the world, wrote numerous poems about time, including 'Um Mitternacht' (At Midnight), written when he was only twenty years old. In this allegorical tableau, Night is an *Ur*-mother, a primeval figure who leans wearily against the

---

5   H. Wolf, *Briefe an Emil Kauffmann* (Berlin, 1903), letter of 5 June 1890, pp. 13–14. Emil Kauffmann was the son of Mörike's close friend Ernst Friedrich Kauffmann; the poems to which Wolf refers in the letter are 'Erstes Liebeslied eines Mädchens' and 'Besuch in Urach'.

mountainside at midnight, the hour which marks the passing of one day and the beginning of the next. The earth-bound, babbling brooks (poets?) insistently sing to her of the bygone day, of the past – the words 'vom Tage, / vom heute gewesenen Tage' (of the day, of the day just past) are the refrain for both stanzas – although she would prefer that they leave her alone to listen to the resonant heavens and the swiftly flowing hours, whose motion points forward. For this poem, Wolf devised non-stop, murmurous, measured rustling in the piano, the long-breathed $\frac{12}{8}$ metre disposed in such a way as to obscure awareness of metrical units. The higher topmost pitch and the greatest harmonic weight in these pulsations occur on the offbeats, thus vitiating the downbeats of their customary strength in regulating metre. The first half of the first stanza, in which Night appears, is set over a C♯–G♯ ostinato figure whose contours are slightly blurred by the slow neighbour-note trill motion; mode too is made misty by the wavering between major and minor forms of the C♯ and F♯ harmonies of the nocturnal realm. At the words 'stille ruhn' (quietly rest), Wolf continues the same murmuring, rustling figuration, but respells G♯ as A♭ in true Lisztian fashion in order to shift gently downwards a semitone to a passage on an F–C ostinato. One can, somewhat fancifully, think of the sharp side as day/the past/history of which the brooks insist on singing non-stop, the all-too-brief turn to the flat side as night/rest/present time; even when a turn to 'quiet rest' seems possible, the 'Quellen' harp on the enharmonic equivalents of Day (G♭ D♭), those pitches accented, until they finally (bar 16) bring back the sharp side of the tonal spectrum. That Wolf mixes modes as thoroughly as he does in the piano postlude perhaps tells of a poet/composer who muses about both realms, day and night alike, when the words come to an end.

Wolf prided himself on his comic lieder, not childish humour or operetta-style farce but Freudian jests which convert anger, tragedy and darkness into comedy. His setting of Mörike's 'Nimmersatte Liebe' (Insatiable Love), which Wolf described as a 'student song', the implication being that students then as now are obsessed with sex, is a particularly complex example because cultural attitudes (attitudes plural: the persona's, society's, and a hint of the poet's own point of view) are on parade in the poem and because Wolf's setting may have a biographical subtext. It was probably in the summer of 1884 that Wolf began his lengthy affair with Melanie Köchert, the wife of a Viennese jeweller; given the secrecy necessary to protect her reputation, Wolf might have found a certain personal satisfaction in setting to music poems such as this and the even more shocking 'Erstes Liebeslied eines Mädchens' (A Maiden's First Love Song). In 'Nimmersatte Liebe', Mörike's youthful poetic persona brags about what one surmises is recent and novel sexual experience as if he had Solomonic authority. His account in the second stanza of the woman's complacency and masochistic submission are – the poet's 'send-up' of male constructions of the female? his agreement with them? That one cannot tell which predominates is a measure of this poet's complexity. 'Love, love, has amazing new appetites all the time', Mörike writes. 'We bit each other's lips till they bled when we kissed today. The girl stood there patiently, like a little lamb to the slaughter; her eyes asked, "Please keep on! The more it hurts, the better I like it!"' In Wolf's setting, the mimicry of panting is astonishingly graphic, the rapid pulsations in the piano and the persistent offbeat rhythms creating an intense erotic charge and the agonistic impression of two bodies who act upon each other. (Tongue-definitely-in-cheek, the composer marks his setting 'Sehr mässig' [Very moderate]; since the poem asserts that erotic passion is by its very nature *im*moderate, the tempo directive is a typically witty touch.) It is at the words 'guter Ruh'' ('Das Mädchen liegt in guter Ruh'') that Wolf begins to fill the air with augmented triads, combining the near-pornographic pumping rhythms one hears throughout stanza 2 with the rising-and-falling motion from the last half of stanza 1. What the callow speaker proclaims as contentment on the girl's part, Wolf tells us is tension and pain, borrowing from Liszt's thirty-two-year-old *Faust* Symphony to do so. Chain-sequences of augmented triads were harmonies with a history ever since the first theme of the first movement of that mid-century masterpiece, although Wolf arranges *his* augmented triads differently, in block chords rather than linear arrangement and in an intricate sequence whose bass line rises in interlocked minor thirds/augmented seconds (G♭–A, G♯–B, B♭–D♭) while the two-bar vocal sequential pattern rises by whole steps. The right- and left-hand parts in the block chords of bars 32–4 are notated in such a way that the two hands overlap, intertwined and moving up and down between registers in a manner too suggestive to be coincidental. Whether or not one endorses *Zeitgeist* notions about Vienna's *fin-de-siècle* fascination with Eros and Thanatos, one can hear in Wolf's lied a relish in the exposure of sexual truths, including the admission of cruelty in sex considered 'normal'. 'The first principle of art for me is inexorable, harsh, strong truth, truth to the point of terror', Wolf told Kauffmann, and even a comic song which 'goes damned merrily' (Wolf's words) bears out his credo.

Wolf did not insist on great poetry all the time. In 1889–90, he composed forty-four songs to poems from Emanuel Geibel's and Paul Heyse's *Spanisches Liederbuch* of 1852, consisting of translations both of verse by the likes of Cervantes and anonymous folk poetry, the latter predominating. The German paraphrases have any folkish roughness refined right out of them, perfect for a composer uninterested in lieder *im Volkston*; whenever a composer caught what the anti-Wagnerian critic Eduard Hanslick called 'Wagner-Influenza', manifest in challenging piano parts and declamatory vocal lines, this was viewed as antithetical to the folksong repertory which played such a large role in lied history.

(But for all Wolf's vociferously expressed adulation of Wagner, one can find criticisms of his musical god embedded in the songs.) Far from simple, the songs of the *Spanisches Liederbuch* demonstrate some of Wolf's thorniest, most chromatically saturated exercises in extended tonality, especially remarkable in the six songs from the opening section of ten religious songs which tell of the tormented consciousness of sin. For Wolf, who underwent excruciating mental torment when diagnosed with syphilis in 1877, such poems evoked music whose contortions tell of anguish at every turn; so too do the male poems of erotic love in the 'weltliche Lieder' (secular songs) which follow. In 1890–91, Wolf set twenty-two poems from Paul Heyse's *Italienisches Liederbuch* of 1860, similarly polished paraphrase-translations of Italian folk poetry, and was then silenced for more than three years by compositional block, probably a consequence of the silent inroads of syphilis ('I could just as soon begin suddenly to speak Chinese as compose anything at all', he told a friend[6]). When released from his incapacity by work on his one completed opera *Der Corregidor*, he returned to the Italian anthology in 1896 and composed another twenty-four songs, including the beautiful, 'Sterb' ich, so hüllt in Blumen meine Glieder' (When I Die, Wrap My Limbs in Flowers) and the passionate concluding song, 'Verschling' der Abgrund meines Liebsten Hütte' (May the Abyss Swallow Up My Beloved's Cottage). Wolf did not forswear poetry by *Kunstdichter* altogether, however. In 1890, he set six poems by Gottfried Keller (1819–90), better known for his prose works but a fine poet as well, and in his last sane year (1897), he began work on a volume of songs to translations of Michelangelo Buonaroti's poetry by Walter-Heinrich Robert-Tornow, intended, so Wolf said, as a portrait of the artist. He only completed four songs, one of which he destroyed, but the three remaining songs constitute a remarkable conclusion to his song *oeuvre*. The bleak second song, a *memento mori* entitled 'Alles endet, was entstehet' (Everything Created Dies), is fraught with motivic and tonal symbolism. Michelangelo dwells in horror on the thought that death is contained within life, and Wolf, who always makes poetic messages musical, hints that the death of tonality is contained within tonality itself, although he does not cross over the borderline into the afterlife of functional tonal relations.

Gustav Mahler was born the same year as Wolf and, like Wolf, came to the Vienna Conservatory in 1875 from elsewhere in the Austro-Hungarian empire (Wolf from Windischgraz in lower Styria, Mahler from Iglau in Bohemia). The two classmates, however, went in different directions, in song composition as in much else, and ended by disliking one another heartily; Wolf's insanity was first evident in the delusion that he had replaced Mahler as director of the

---

6 Cited in F. Walker, *Hugo Wolf: A Biography* (Princeton, 1992), pp. 323–4.

Vienna State Opera. Mahler was an exponent both of the gigantic-Romantic and of the lied, for which he created his own fusion of art-song and folksong, different from Brahms's. In the wake of two fragmentary Heine songs and three specimens of juvenilia to his own texts, the mature Mahler published six groups of songs, beginning with the first volume of the *Lieder und Gesänge [aus der Jugendzeit]* (five songs composed between 1880 and 1883 [?], printed in 1892); the song 'Hans und Grethe' in this first song collection is a revised version of his *ländler*-song 'Maitanz in Grünen' (May Dance in the Green Meadow) to his own words. The tonally progressive cycle, *Lieder eines fahrenden Gesellen* (Songs of a Wayfarer), composed 1884[?]–96[?], came next,[7] followed by two more small volumes (four songs and five songs) on poems by Clemens Brentano's and Achim von Arnim's famous collection of 'touched-up' folk poems, *Des Knaben Wunderhorn* of 1808 and a larger compilation (thirteen songs, all scored for orchestral accompaniment) in 1899–1900 actually entitled *Lieder aus Des Knaben Wunderhorn* (Songs from The Youth's Magic Horn). The *Sieben Lieder aus letzter Zeit* (Seven Late Songs) of 1905 and 1907 include two *Wunderhorn* songs and five settings of Friedrich Rückert, while the cycle *Kindertotenlieder* (Songs on the Deaths of Children), published in 1905, consists of further Rückert settings from a single grief-obsessed poetic anthology, its creation impelled by the deaths of two of the poet's children. Song and symphony have much to do with one another in Mahler's *oeuvre*: the *Wunderhorn* song 'Des Antonius von Paduas Fischpredigt' (St Anthony of Padua's Sermon to the Fishes) metamorphoses into the instrumental scherzo of Symphony No. 2 in C minor; another *Wunderhorn* song, 'Urlicht' (Primeval Light), becomes the fourth movement of the same symphony; and yet another *Wunderhorn* song, 'Das himmlische Leben' (Life in Heaven) reappears as the finale of the Fourth Symphony.[8]

Mahler's stance *vis-à-vis* words and music, poem and song, is so unlike Wolf's as to constitute a case study in opposites. The singularities of Mahler's approach are represented in extreme form in the four wayfarer songs, that is, his first song cycle. The text of the first song is actually Mahler's trope on the first eight lines of a *Wunderhorn* text, 'Wann mein Schatz Hochzeit macht' (My Sweetheart's Wedding Day – Mahler changed the initial word 'Wann' to 'Wenn'), although he later claimed that he did not realise it at the time of composition. Indeed, he was so steeped in the folk-poetic tradition of the

7 See Z. Roman, 'The Chronology of Mahler's *Gesellen-Lieder*: Literary and Musical Evidence', paper read before the American Musicological Society, Chicago, 10 November 1991, and T. Gish, '*Wanderlust* and *Wanderlied*: The Motif of the Wandering Hero in German Romanticism', *Studies in Romanticism*, 3 (1963), pp. 225–39.

8 See M. Tibbe, *Über die Verwendung von Liedern und Liedelementen in instrumentalen Symphoniesatzen Gustav Mahlers* (Munich, 2nd edn 1971).

Wunderhorn poems that the excuse of unknowing appropriation may well be true. After the first performance in 1896, Mahler wrote a friend to say, 'The words of the songs are my *own*. I did not put my name in the program to avoid giving ammunition to adversaries who would be perfectly capable of parodying the simple, naïve style.'[9] By 'naïve', he meant the feint that the poems transcribe emotional impulses as they occur, with near-hysterical intensity and exclamation marks everywhere – it was this vein of verse that drove Wolf to exasperated mockery of the sort Mahler hoped to deter by hiding his authorship. Poetry and music such as this are autobiographical, but in a sophisticated sense, a probing of the artistic dilemma at the *fin de siècle* rather than a narration of external events.

Even the texts for 'Ging heut Morgen über's Feld' (This Morning I Went Through the Fields), 'Ich hab' ein glühend Messer' (I Have a Burning Knife) and 'Die zwei blauen Augen von meinem Schatz' (The Two Blue Eyes of My Sweetheart) are not imagined *de novo*, but perhaps originate with Mahler's complex response to Schubert: yet again, the theme of the later lied composer wrestling with the ghosts of earlier history. Mahler described 'the idea of the songs as a whole . . . [as] that of a wayfaring man who has been stricken by fate [and] now sets forth into the world, travelling wherever his road may lead him', and this encapsulation, coupled with the impetus for the journey in rejection by a sweetheart who marries another man, will remind many of Schubert's *Winterreise* (Winter Journey), D.911. When the wayfarer finds surcease for his sorrow in 'sleep' – death – beneath the linden tree emblematic of lovers' rendez-vous, one recalls Müller's and Schubert's winter wanderer who almost freezes to death 'unter den Linden', especially since Mahler bids *his* linden tree to shed its blossoms in a snow-fall of flowers around the dying man. The blue flowers and metonymic blue eyes of the eponymous sweetheart which haunt the protagonist are commonplace folk motifs, but they are also images from *Die schöne Müllerin*, in which erotic experience likewise leads to death. The whole enterprise proclaims Mahler's mission to fashion from folk-poetic origins something which is not simple, not naïve, but modern. That there is more than a doff of the hat to an earlier repertory seems only to be expected.

Whether Mahler set his own poems or someone else's (and one notes the avoidance of Heine, Goethe, Schiller, Eichendorff, and others), one finds not Wagnerian-influenced declamation but a complex adaptation of lyrical melody to a complete poetico-musical conception. In the wayfarer-cycle, for example, an artist laments his estrangement from society, love, family and can only find escape from his dilemma in death, the Romantic mystic's pathway to the

---

9 K. Martner (ed.), *Gustav Mahler: Selected Letters* (New York, 1979), p. 178.

infinite. The last song, 'Die zwei blauen Augen von meinem Schatz', begins as a funeral march, the music both replicating the traditional dotted rhythms and march patterns of the genre and expressively moulding them to this context. For example, Mahler inserts an expressive rest in the middle of the first phrase, 'Die zwei blauen Augen . . . von meinem Schatz' (that there is no introduction intensifies the impression of austerity and solemnity); he bids the singer chant '[Da] musst' ich Abschied nehmen' on a repeated pitch while the inner voices slip downwards (this phrase will remind many of Schubert's 'Der Wegweiser' from *Winterreise*); the words 'allerliebsten Platz' impel a leap upwards in massive anguish; and 'Leid und Grämen' are dragged across the barline in syncopation, accented and unforgettably coloured by the heaviness of the flatted second degree. Mahler's characteristic mixture of modes – not separated into separate planes but intermingled – is here bent to the intermingling of pain/mortal life/alienation/loneliness and intimations of peace/death/infinity. Within each of the song's tonal areas, major and minor waver back and forth (E minor, with an admixture of relative major; C major/minor; and F major/minor). After eleven bars of purest diatonic F major when the wayfarer arrives at the linden tree, he sings, 'Da wusst' ich nicht, wie das Leben thut' (I no longer knew what life had done), and the mere mention of life's harshness, even in order to negate it, is enough to bring back dissonance and the darkness of lowered pitches. Thereafter, it is difficult to escape the painful reminiscence; although the protagonist is finally able to banish the troubling notes in the final six texted bars, the minor mode reasserts itself as a *pianississimo* treble echo in the postlude – and there, the song and the cycle end.

The songs of Richard Strauss (1864–1949) tell of yet another and different approach to lied composition. His earliest preserved lied, a Christmas song, was composed at the age of six; thereafter in the 1870s and early 1880s, he wrote a scattering of songs for drawing-room performances and for his aunt Johanna Pschorr, a skilful amateur singer. Almost all of them are settings of poems by the famous poets favoured by earlier lieder composers – Uhland, Hoffmann von Fallersleben, Adelbert von Chamisso, Lenau, Theodor Körner, Justinus Kerner, Emmanuel Geibel, and Goethe (the perennial favourite 'Der Fischer' is one of two youthful Goethe songs), but with the advent of compositional maturity, he set this repertory aside. At the encouragement of his friend Louis Thuille, he began cultivating contemporary poets and continued to do so for fourteen years thereafter, with only the occasional poetic 'golden oldie' (two poems from *Des Knaben Wunderhorn*, Goethe's 'Pilgers Morgenlied', Klopstock's 'Das Rosenband', the two Lenau songs of Op. 26) to be found in Opp. 10, 15, 17, 19, 21, 22, 26, 27, 29, 31, 32, 33, 36, 37, 39 and 41. One notes that a number of Strauss's choices from among the poets of his own day constitute telling commentaries on then-current stereotypes of women, most notably such works as Felix Dahn's cycle of four *Mädchenblumen* (Maiden-Flowers) and the same poet's 'Die Frauen sind oft fromm und still' (Women are Often Pious and Quiet).

It is with the *Acht Gedichte aus 'Letzte Blätter' von Hermann Gilm* (Eight Poems from the 'Last Leaves' of Hermann Gilm), Op. 10 of 1885, that Strauss began to make his mark as a song composer; at only the age twenty-one, he composed what would become three of his most popular songs ('Zueignung' [Dedication]; 'Die Nacht' [The Night] and 'Allerseelen' [All Souls' Eve]) for this set. A few of Strauss's chosen poets were from the generation circa 1815: Gilm zu Rosenegg (1812–64), for example, was a Tyrolean civil servant whose single volume of poetry was published posthumously in 1865, while Brahms had already discovered the virtues of Schack's fluent, elegant, if not profound, poetry for lied composition before Strauss's time. The influential writer Detlev von Liliencron (1844–1909) – he once offered Wolf an opera libretto but was turned down – was both a Strauss poet and the friend and sponsor of other younger Strauss poets, in particular, Gustav Falke (1853–1916) and Richard Dehmel (1863–1920). Other poets of Strauss's own generation whose verse he set to music included Otto Julius Bierbaum (1865–1910) and Carl Busse (1872–1918); two others, John Henry Mackay (1864–1933) and Karl Friedrich Henckell (1864–1929), were left-wing radicals, some of whose works were proscribed as inflammatory, although Strauss gravitated to their gentler, sentimental poems (Henckell's 'Ich trage meine Minne' and Mackay's 'Morgen!', for example). Strauss's preference was for slightly sappy or outright bathetic verse, for humorous character portrayal, and for quasi-Nietzschean rhapsodising of the sort that Wolf detested. At the turn of the century, however, beginning with the Op. 43 *Drei Gesänge älterer deutscher Dichter* of 1899 (Three Songs of Older German Poets), Strauss turned back to the classics of lied poetry, to Rückert (a particular favourite), Uhland, Heine, Brentano and Goethe, although, significantly, not to the poems so often colonised by earlier composers. Wolf's defiant act of placing his Mignon and Harper songs at the beginning of the *Goethe Lieder* of 1890 was not a feat Strauss would emulate.

If Strauss had not described his *modus operandi* in the following famous passage, one could deduce it from the songs themselves.

> Musical ideas have prepared themselves in me – God knows why – and when, as it were, the barrel is full, a song appears in the twinkling of an eye as soon as I come across a poem more or less corresponding to the subject of the imaginary song . . . If I find no poem corresponding to the subject which exists in my sub-conscious mind, then the creative urge has to be rechannelled to the setting of

some other which I think lends itself to music. It goes slowly, though ... I resort to artifice.[10]

This explains why song was not Strauss's foremost field of endeavour, why he composed only some 200-plus songs between the advent of compositional maturity in 1885 and death in 1949, three-quarters of them composed before 1904 (such famous works as the *Drei Lieder der Ophelia*, Op. 67, the *Sechs Lieder nach Gedichten von Clemens Brentano*, Op. 68, and the *Vier letzte Lieder* lie outside the chronological bounds of this study). The statement above is, one notes, curiously defensive, its honesty an invitation to criticism or puzzlement (on his part as well) or both. One guesses that the musical ideas had some connection with a subject somewhere in his mind, and tripping across a poem on the same subject called forth the buried music so that he could put the two entities together. His frank admission that a poem could be 'more or less' on target, that he searched for poems to go with music *after* the fact of musical inception, that artifice was sometimes required to effect the forced marriage of prior music and subsequent poetry, seems not the working method of an innate lied composer. Certainly it is as far removed from the Wolfian aesthetic of song composition as one could be.

Strauss's best early songs demonstrate both the anomalies which result from the compositional process described and the effectiveness with which he could, on occasion, overcome its difficulties. The Gilm song 'Die Nacht', Op. 10, No. 3, is justly famous for its atmospheric evocation of night, for music which steals into audibility at the beginning as quietly as the poet's night glides from her hiding place in the forest to shine on everything around her. But the poem says one thing, the music another, and neither Strauss's deft adjustment of details ('I resort to artifice') nor the beauty of the music as music can entirely obscure the discrepancy. Moonlight is a thief, the poet suggests, robbing all things beautiful of their own hue, and the lover-persona who speaks in this poem fears that night will also take his beloved away from him. The words waver between menace ('Nun gib acht', 'Now beware', the persona says as the moon sneaks out of its hiding place) and the evocation of menaced beauty, but Strauss's music tells us of nocturnal rapture. If there are dark touches, such as the F sharp minor harmonies (in a D major song) at the words 'Alles nimmt sie' (She takes everything), the D minor darkness of 'Ausgeplündert steht der Strauch' (The bushes stand despoiled), and the diminished-seventh harmony and minor chords which invest the words 'soul to soul' with hints of dark danger, the song is nonetheless a study in exquisite lyricism. The rapturously rising scalewise

10 W. Schuh, *Richard Strauss. Jugend und frühe Meisterjahre: Lebenschronik 1864-98* (Zurich, 1976), pp. 412-13.

vocal phrases at the words 'nimmt das Silber weg des Stroms, nimmt vom Kupferdach des Doms weg das Gold' ([the moon] takes the silver away from the stream, takes the gold from the cathedral's copper dome), echoed in the left-hand part and sounding in contrary motion to the piano's topmost voice for additional richness, suggest nothing of danger, theft or despoilment; rather, they foreshadow the quieter rapture with which Strauss ends his setting of Bierbaum's 'Traum durch die Dämmrung' (Dream Through the Twilight) at the words '[I go] through the twilight greyness into the land of love, into a blue, gentle light'. Similarly, Strauss locates the *pianissimo* climax of 'Die Nacht' at the verb 'stehle' (steal), but the C major harmonies at that moment are softest rapture. That the menace is more feigned than real, that sentimentality prevails over fear, are apparent in the poem, but Gilm's trafficking in the *frisson* of fear at the heart of passion is of even less importance in the musical setting. Strauss's lush music is complete unto itself, needing only occasional, nominal, general connection to Gilm's poem (and perhaps that is a good thing).

In Strauss's setting of Henckell's 'Ruhe, meine Seele!' (Rest, my Soul!), Op. 27, No. 1 (1896), however, poetry and music have more to do with one another than is this composer's wont. Henckell was no Hesse or Eichendorff – the two poets of the four last songs – but Strauss's unusually focused response to this poem, with its self-exhortation to inner tranquillity in the midst of threatening times, is revealing. Henckell, engaged in politics to a degree Strauss shunned, was in need of withdrawal from the hurly-burly at times, while Strauss, well in advance of the Nazi rise to power, was averse to such involvement and spun a beautifully crafted song from a poem with which he could wholly concur. (He composed the four songs of Op. 27 as a wedding present for his bride Pauline de Ahna on the occasion of their marriage on 10 September 1894; given the stormy course of their courtship and subsequent married life, the song acquires additional undertones of biographical irony.) Furthermore, his use of sustained harmonies in the piano meant that the prosody of the vocal line could be shaped in a more declamatory fashion than is often the case in his songs, where the purely musical origins act on many occasions to warp verbal rhythms. Most striking of all, the tonal-harmonic cloth is cut to fit the words: is this, one wonders, an exception to his usual method of composing song? The repeated heavy 'sighing figure' at the start of the piano introduction consists of seventh chords on C and F♯, significant pitches because C major – devoid of chromatic turbulence – is the tonal symbol of rest and because F♯ is a tritone distant from it, the two polarities additionally symbolic of Nature and humanity. The invocation of Nature's peace at the beginning of the texted body of the song ('Not a breeze gently stirs; the grove softly reposes; through the leaves' dark veils, bright sunshine steals') is set to F♯-related harmonies, while the human spirit longs for quietude on C. The accented half-diminished chord in bar 3 becomes, once one knows the words to follow, a succinct musical symbol of threat, the C in the topmost voice menaced by interior darkness (A♭). The symbolism becomes even more explicit when the persona sings the entreaty, 'Ruhe, ruhe, meine Seele' in bars 14–16 to pitches belonging to the C-centre while the piano is darkened by persistent B♭s. 'Powerful eras', 'swelling tides', conflict and wildness all elicit telling harmonic responses, especially the diminished seventh on C–E♭–F♯–A occurring twice at climactic points (bars 20–1, 30) to tell us that both Nature and the human soul are endangered at times of tumult. This is one of Strauss's most successful songs; here, he created a true late Romantic document in which poem and music enjoy a less disinterested conjunction than was usual for him.

From *romance* and chanson to *mélodie*: French song and the French language

By the middle of the century, the German-speaking world had a rich, variegated repertory of song, from the smallest folk-like songs to sprawling through-composed ballads, composed both by consummate masters and *Kleinmeister* who could, on the right day, with the right poem in their hands, produce a memorable song. The situation in France, however, was different. Aristocratic salons were the principal performance milieu for the thousands of *romances* composed in the 1830s and thereafter, *romance* being an imprecise designation for mostly strophic songs by the likes of Henri Romagnesi (1781–1850), Pauline Duchambge (1778–1858), Hippolyte Monpou (1804–41), Auguste Panseron (1796–1859), and others.[11] At their best, such as Monpou's setting of Hugo's 'Puisqu'ici bas toute âme' (entitled 'A genoux' [On My Knees]) they are very attractive, but they took a back seat to operatic composition, which was considered a far more important genre, and the French language was often subjected to near-grotesque deformation. While the status of opera would never diminish, song underwent multiple metamorphoses in the last half of the century at the hands of composers no longer content to maul their native tongue in musical setting.

Of all poetry in the Romance languages, French – descended from the Latin of the Decadents, not the Latin of Horace and Ovid – is perhaps the most difficult to set to music because accents in French have nothing to do with beat or metre, but rather with cadence and phrase, with measure governed by syntax.

11 See David Tunley (ed.), *Romantic French Song 1830–1870*, I: *Early Romances by Bérat, Berlioz, Duchambge, Grisar, Meyerbeer, Monpou, Morel, Panseron, and Romagnesi. Selected Songs of Louis Niedermeyer and Ernest Reyer* (New York and London, 1994).

The language is syllabic before it is accentual, and the various roles the mute *e* can assume – elided, omitted, pronounced – account in part for the unique suppleness of French. The weaker syllables – the 'accents mobiles' – are just that, 'mobiles', and their duration varies depending on the context. The very tempo of the language is different from that of metrical languages: August Schlegel observed in one of his essays on poetry and language that the six syllables of 'ir-ri-ti-bi-li-té' can be said more quickly than the German synonym 'Reizbarkeit', doubtless the word of choice for problems of prosody.[12] Rhythm and syntax are interdependent in French; grammatical and syntactical groupings form units of measurement that are often longer than the regular, repetitive disyllabic or trisyllabic divisions in stress-based prosodic structures such as English and German. There is no such thing as an iamb or trochee or a dactyl in French poetry; actually, all such measurements are fictions, invented devices for comprehending poetic rhythm at the most basic level, but most eighteenth- and nineteenth-century German poetry *does* share with music a regular tactus and recurrent rhythmic/metric patterns defined by greater and lesser degrees of accent and weight. French, however, lacks this fundamental relationship between verse and music, and therefore the tension between the internal dynamics of the two is greater than in stress-based languages.

To complicate matters still more, French song in the second half of the nineteenth century stems in part from the French response to the German lied, especially Schubert, whose songs were first sung in France in 1829, the year after the composer's death, and first published in French translation in 1834. After the eccentric Belgian-born composer Chrétien Urhan introduced the young Franz Liszt to the music of Schubert, Liszt became one of the Viennese master's principal European champions, composing transcriptions of Schubert lieder and accompanying the renowned tenor Adolphe Nourrit (1800–39) in performances of the songs.[13] By the late 1830s and 1840s, the vogue for Schubert in French translation was well established, the firm of Richault printing 267 Schubert songs by 1850. Liszt was already complaining about the wretched quality of the French texts in 1838, and, looking at a translation of 'Du bist die Ruh'' (Thou art peace) by Bélanger in one of Richault's editions, one can see the cause of his, and also Heinrich Heine's, displeasure; the German poet, self-exiled in Paris from 1831 until his death in 1856, was appalled at the traductions of his own and others' poetry in singers' translations. The vocal line begins with two lines of maladroit French accented thusly: 'La dou-ce PAIX et LE

---

12 August Wilhelm Schlegel, 'Betrachtungen über Metrik', *Sprache und Poetik* (Stuttgart, 1962), p. 209.
13 See J. G. Prod'homme, 'Les Œuvres de Schubert en France', *Bericht über den Internationalen Kongreß für Schubertforschung* (Augsburg, 1929), pp. 89–110; E. Duméril, *Le Lied Allemand et ses traductions poétiques en France*, 2 vols. (Geneva, 1975); and T. Kalisch, *Liszt und Schubert* (Munich, 1984).

bon-HEUR, L'ES-POIR qui FAIT bat-TRE mon C Œ U R ', the slow tempo of the song prolonging the misaccentuations unbearably.[14] The Procrustean exercise was all the worse because the German original was not given. One thinks of Vladimir Nabokov's poem, directed ironically at his own forays into translation: 'What is translation? On a platter / A poet's pale and glaring head, / A parrot's screech, a monkey's chatter, / And profanation of the dead'.[15]

But who would deny Schubert to anyone? Certainly his influence on French composers was considerable. Already in 1840, the *Revue et Gazette musicale* would publish a New Year's Eve skit in which 'The Romance' and 'The Lied' complain bitterly about one another, 'The Romance' asserting that she is eminently French and desires protection. When Monsieur 1841 enquires 'Against whom?', 'The Lied' replies: 'Mein Gott! Against me, who haf replaced her. I am as light-headed as she, ant more so; I am fresher dan she. I haf peen Schubert's faforite chilt ant now I am de same von Proch ant von Dessauer [Joseph Dessauer and Heinrich Proch]'. When granted civil rights until such time as naturalisation could be conferred, 'The Lied' protests, 'I ton't vant to be naturalizet; I vant to remain Cherman' and yet, at the same time, 'to lif in Paris, zing in Paris, enchant Paris'. Monsieur 1841, exasperated, bids the two litigants marry one another, but 'The Lied' protests, 'She iss too olt'.[16] In the preface to a new edition in 1896 of his first volume of songs, Camille Saint-Saëns (1835–1921) tried to deny charges that his setting of Madame Amable Tastu's 'La feuille de peuplier' (The Poplar Leaf) resembled 'Die Krähe' (The Crow) from *Winterreise*, but the resemblances make the disavowal barely credible. Certainly his awareness of being measured against Schubert, his sensitivity about the matter, are evident.[17] Edouard Lalo (1823–92) was massively influenced by Schubert in his twenty-three songs on poems by Hugo, Alfred de Musset, Théophile Gautier, Lamartine and others, the refined prosody owing in part to Lalo's enthusiasm for Rameau's operas; in 'Marine' on a poem by André Theuriet, the recitative-like declamation and liberal use of triplets foreshadow Debussy's prosody.[18] Virtually everyone of note was affected by German song: it seems indicative that Charles Gounod would set to music an abbreviated and sentimentalised 'translation' by Louis Gallet of Goethe's Mignon poem, 'Kennst du das Land / Connais-tu le pays' (minus the third stanza) and that Giacomo Meyerbeer, half-Italian, half-German and resident in

---

14 *40 Mélodies de François Schubert* (Paris, n.d.), pp. 42–3.

15 Vladimir Nabokov (trans.), *Eugene Onegin: A Novel in Verse by Aleksandr Pushkin*, I (New York, 1964), p. 9.

16 Cited in F. Noske, *French Song from Berlioz to Duparc: The Origin and Development of the Mélodie*, trans. Rita Benton, 2nd edn (New York, 1970), p. 35.

17 Camille Saint-Saëns, *1er recueil, Vingt mélodies et duos, nouvelle édition avec une préface de l'auteur* (Paris, 1896).   18 Edouard Lalo, *Mélodies*, ed. Joël-Marie Fauquet (Paris, 1988), pp. 72–5.

Paris, would publish his lieder to poems by Goethe, Heine, Müller, Rückert and other Schubert poets with both 'paroles françaises et allemandes'.[19]

In 1885, Camille Saint-Saëns wrote of French poetry as being a 'conquered country', vandalised by composers who had stormed through its domains. His chief concern in the essay 'La poésie et la musique' (Poetry and Music) was bad prosody in operetta, and his [jealous?] irritation at Jacques Offenbach's popularity is evident, but his admonitions were sincere.[20] He himself, after all, was a reformed character. His early *mélodies* from the 1850s, despite their frequent musical beauty, are filled with the prosodic sins he would later find condemnable. His well-known setting of Victor Hugo's 'Puisqu'ici-bas toute âme' from the poet's *Les voix intérieures* could by itself have impelled Hugo's snappish dictum that 'Nothing irritates me like the passion for setting beautiful verse to music'.[21] Even the best French songs circa mid-century often exemplify the conundrum whereby music acts upon the poetry to warp the very language that has called it into being. Hector Berlioz (1803–69), in the 'Villanelle' at the beginning of his cycle *Les nuits d'été* (Summer Nights), serves Théophile Gautier's poem beautifully in one sense by making explicit in the constant crotchet tactus the light, throbbing pulsation of new life in spring, but he also wreaks occasional violence on the verbal rhythms (see chapter 6 for a discussion of this cycle). For example, he emphasises the word 'sous' in awkward fashion and then imposes a grid of dactyls and trochees on the words which follow, 'Sous nos pied égrénnant les perles / Que l'on voit, au matin trembler' (shaking free beneath our feet the dewdrops / that one sees atremble in the early morning). But by the end of Berlioz's life, a different aesthetic was evident. One sees in Louis Niedermeyer's (1802–61) settings of Lamartine's méditations 'Le Lac' (The Lake) 'L'Isolement' (Isolation) and 'L'Automne' (Autumn) traits such as through-composition, more complex piano accompaniments, and generally more scrupulous prosody, differentiating these compositions from the mass of contemporaneous *romances*.[22] All poetry set to music is a 'pays conquis' in one sense, but Debussy's generation could no longer accept that it be trampled underfoot altogether.

Wagnerism was another factor in the transformation of French song, given Wagner's overpowering example of an attitude to text quite other than that of French opera and song at the mid-century mark. Despite his reputation during the early 1870s as 'the insulter of France', Wagner's musical fortunes on French

---

19 Giacomo Meyerbeer, *40 Mélodies d'une et à plusieurs voix avec paroles françaises et allemandes* (Paris, n.d.), which includes settings of Heine's 'Hör' ich das Liedchen klingen' and 'Die Rose, die Lilie, die Taube, die Sonne', Rückert's 'Dass sie hier gewesen' and Goethe's Suleika song, 'Wie mit innigstem Behagen'.
20 Camille Saint-Saëns, 'La Poésie et la musique', *Harmonie et mélodie* (Paris, 1885), p. 260.
21 Victor Hugo, 'Carnets inédits', in *Les nouvelles littéraires*, 31 (21 February 1951), p. 9.
22 Reproduced in Tunley, *Early Romances*, pp. 61–91.

soil rose thereafter, and the Parnassians, Symbolists, and Decadents who revolutionised French poetry with *vers libérés*, *vers impairs* and prose poetry often identified themselves with the *wagnéristes*; they were the inheritors of Baudelaire's championship of Wagner after the 1861 Paris première of *Tannhäuser*. The new definitions of what constituted poetry and what was therefore available to progressive composers for musical setting must also be included among the elements of change in the late nineteenth-century *mélodie*. In prose poetry, the tension between the variable rhythms of the *vers* (line of poetry) and the rigidity of traditional forms was no longer a factor, and the prosaicising of poetry impelled a new attentiveness to speech-rhythms in melody, a concern reinforced by the advent of Wagner, 'ce spectre rouge' (this blood-red ghost), as Ernest Chausson called him.

The more perceptive of those poets, composers and prosodists who grappled with the conflicts between music and French realised that the transmutation of verbal rhythms into melody was neither easily done nor fully possible. The rhythmic accents in a line of French poetry are determined, first, by the laws of individual word accent and, second, by syntax and content. The rules of accentuation in single words begin with the *accent tonique* or tonic accent, the last sonorous syllable of any word, excluding the mute e, or *e atone*: mus<u>i</u>que, <u>ta</u>ble, en<u>ten</u>dre, déplace<u>ment</u>, l'au<u>ro</u>re. French opera and song are replete with examples of mistreated tonic accents, in which the most important syllable of a word is set to a weak beat or to a rhythmic value shorter than the remaining weaker syllables; Bizet's 'L'amour est EN-fant de Bohème' in *Carmen* is a classic example. In words of more than three syllables, there is also an *accent contre-tonique* or *accent secondaire* on the first syllable, for example, '<u>ra</u>pidité, <u>fra</u>gilité, <u>cru</u>ellement', with the tonic accent on the last syllable of all three words. Neither the tonic accent nor the secondary accent of the word 'frémissements' in Jules Massenet's song 'Il pleuvait' (It Rained) emerges undistorted in the phrase 'avec des frémissements d'ailes'; the leap of a major sixth to a higher pitch for the tonic accent is insufficient to compensate for its placement at the sixth beat – the weakest rhythmic point – in the $\frac{6}{8}$ bar, while the slight intervallic ascent from the initial syllable (the secondary accent) to the second syllable puts undue emphasis on the latter. Massenet had plenty of company for such prosodic misdemeanours in the latter half of the century.

Composers, like actors and actresses, *did* have recognised rights to expressive distortions. The tonic accent of any word can become an *accent oratoire*, *pathétique* or *d'appui* (a rhetorical or dramatic accent) in musical setting, the emphasis determined by its context within a phrase or line. Gounod, whose prosody often puts his contemporaries to shame in its accuracy, makes the words 'même' and 'plus' at the beginning of Alphonse de Lamartine's 'Le Vallon' –

rightly one of Gounod's best-known songs – into *accents oratoires*: 'Mon cœur, lassé de tout, ME-me de l'espérance, N'ira PLUS de ses vœux importuner le sort!' In a more unusual and subtle instance, Debussy lingers on all three words of the enjambed phrase 'et quasi / Tristes' in his second setting of Verlaine's 'Clair de lune'; the durational emphases on the connective 'et' and the qualifying word 'quasi' make the arrival at the chromatic harmony on 'Tristes' all the more striking. That colourful chord is Debussy's analogue for the poet's enjambment that so beautifully heightens the melancholy of the poem, the ambiguity of mingled loveliness and sadness. There is even a phenomenon in French song that one might call *pauses oratoires*, or the insertion of expressive rests where they would not appear in ordinary declamation. In his setting of Verlaine's lines 'Et que toutes pleuraient dans les hautes feuillées, / Tes espérances noyées!' (and how they wept in the high foliage / your drowned hopes!) at the end of 'L'ombre des arbres' (The Shadow of the Trees), composed in January 1885, Debussy ignores the poet's comma and then separates the noun 'espérances' from its adjective 'noyées' with a rest. One would not do so in speech, even in heightened declamation by an actor, but Debussy's compositional choice makes the adjective the locus of greatest intensity, repeated lest anyone miss its significance.

One of the knottiest problems in French musical prosody is the mute *e*, which Voltaire once described by means of a charming simile: their effect, he said, is 'like a keyboard which resounds after the fingers no longer strike the keys'.[23] Scansion in French poetry is dependent on the number of syllables in a line and therefore on the regulations that govern elisions of the mute *e* with the following word or its inclusion as a separate syllable. For example, the line 'L'aurore apparaissait; quelle aurore? un abîme' would be read and scanned as 'L'auror'apparaissait; quell'auror'? un abîme', that is, as an alexandrine line of twelve syllables. But in any musical setting, that scansion would have to be violated for syntactical reasons. In order to account for the grammatical separation into the question, 'What dawn?' and its answer 'An abyss', within the slower pace imposed by most music, the elision between the two that suppresses the mute *e* of 'aurore' the second time would have to be disregarded and the mute *e* set either as a separate pitch or a repetition of the pitch. The same is true of the mute *e* in 'abîme', thus adding two more syllables to the line and eradicating the alexandrine. Even the elision of 'Auror'apparaissait' might justifiably be set aside by a composer who wished to make that moment especially portentous. Where a composer *does* elide a word ending in a mute *e* with the vowel at the beginning of the next word, it should be for the enhancement of poetic

---

23 Cited in Emile Stièvenard, *Essai sur la prosodie musicale* (Paris, 1924), p. 75.

meaning. When the poetic persona in Verlaine's 'Spleen' goes from despairing lethargy at the beginning to heights of anguish at the end, Debussy elides the words 'campagne infinie' as part of the *crescendo–accelerando* to the climactic words 'Et de tout'; if the downbeat emphasis on the word 'et' (and) is not defensible in ordinary prosodic terms, it is justified in this instance by the atmosphere of high tension in which every syllable is accented. But in most instances in music, the mute *e* is sounded, and the pitfalls in doing so are numerous. According to the prosodists, mute *e*'s should be placed at a weak point in the bar, on a relatively short note, and as an element of melodic descent; Emile Stièvenard whose 1924 *Essai sur la prosodie musicale* draws primarily on repertory from the second half of the nineteenth century, had severe words for those composers who conclude a phrase with ascending motion to a downbeat, especially at the end of a song (Stièvenard, p. 71).

Other prosodic dangers for those setting French to music included the treatment of *diérèses* (two successive but separated vowels, as in 'me-nu-et' or 'di-a-mant') and *synérèses* (compound vowels contracted into a single sound, as in 'roi'). Certain words, such as 'Dieu', 'nuit', 'vierge', 'ciel', 'pied', 'yeux', 'diable' and 'cieux', are always *synérèses*, but other diphthongs are more variable in music, as when Debussy sets the word 'fouet' (whip) in 'Recueillement' from his *Cinq poèmes de Baudelaire* as a monosyllable in order to suggest more graphically the cracking sound of the merciless torturer Pleasure's whip. Furthermore, the organisation of French poetry into units of meaning depends in part on paired dependent words, the weaker of the pair designated by prosodists as *mots proclitiques* or *mots enclitiques*. *Mots proclitiques* are usually monosyllabic words – prepositions, pronominal adjectives placed before the nouns they modify, conjunctions, indefinite and definite articles – which, having no accent of their own, lean on the word following ('*mon* role'), while *mots enclitiques* are dependent upon the preceding word ('sais-je'). Their correct musical realisation depends upon the accurate gauge of proximity to the stronger words on which they lean and an appropriate (weaker) stress – easier said than done. The adverbial compound at the beginning of Victor Hugo's 'Puisqu'ici-bas toute âme' (Since Here Below Every Soul), set to music by Saint-Saëns, Liszt and Reynaldo Hahn, among others, was a *locus classicus* for prosodic sins of this sort. And finally, in those composers most sensitive to prosodic refinements, one sees the beginnings of melodic lines located after the first beat of the bar, in accord with the general law that accentuation in French tilts to the right-hand side of the page. Where an adjective follows a noun, the stress shifts to the adjective; the rhyme words in traditional rhyming verse are placed at the end of the line; and a verb should be closer to the object which follows it than the subject which precedes it – over and over, one finds this Leaning Tower of

Pisa-like incline in the structure of the language. By 1885, for example, Debussy knew that the crucial verb 'Meurt' (dies) in the line 'Meurt comme de la fumée' (dies like smoke) from 'L'ombre des arbres' would be more power-fully rendered when the piano sounds the underlying chord on the first beat and the voice chimes in just after with an accented offbeat pitch, sustained slightly for further emphasis. The result is the perfect marriage of prosodic accuracy and interpretative acuity.

Debussy was not the only composer for whom prosody came to matter more with the passage of time. Liszt first published a group of six Hugo songs in 1844 and then revised the four gems in the set ('Oh! quand je dors' [Oh, when I sleep], 'Comment, disaient-ils' [Tell us how, they said], 'Enfant, si j'étais roi' [Child, were I king], and 'S'il est un charmant gazon' [If there is a lovely lawn]) for his 1860 song collection. (Amidst many lacunae of French song scholar-ship, the story of Victor Hugo and nineteenth-century song remains to be told.)[24] As with some of his lieder, the later version of the justly popular 'Oh! quand je dors' represents a slimming-down of the original version and entailed the expunging of certain more outré harmonic progressions from before. For example, Liszt in the 1840s shifts from tonic E major to a brief heightening of C minor, its chord tone E♭ worlds away from the principal key, at the words 'soudain ma bouche s'entr'ouvrira'. In the later version, Liszt evidently decided that the darkness of minor mode was sufficient sensual intensification without the added jolt of distant harmonic manoeuvres, and therefore turns, simply and briefly, to relative minor (C sharp minor), the effect much smoother than before. If one compares the two settings of the words 'Sur mon front morne où peut-être s'achève un songe noir qui trop longtemps dura', one sees and hears in the later version not only a more powerful economy of har-monic means but a correction of previous prosodic flaws. The initial treatment of what should be, and is in the second setting, an elision of 'morne où' is par-ticularly egregious; if there is still in 1860 a mute *e* on the downbeat ('s'achèvE') which prosodists would not have condoned, Liszt goes right past it to the slight but significant elevation on the important tonic accent of 'soNge' and the even more important adjective 'noir'. The increased sensitivity to French prosody, albeit not to Debussyan nicety, and its harnessing to beau-tiful melody are apparent in the unforgettable ending of the revised song, with its *morendo* (dying away) scalewise ascent into the empyrean and the long-breathed exhalation on the final syllable of Lau-RA, Petrarch's beloved, to whom the persona's love is compared.

A taste for fine poetry is also evident in the tiny *oeuvre* of (Marie Eugène)

---

24 H. Puls, 'Die Musikauffassung der französischen Romantiker dargestellt an Lamartine und Victor Hugo', Ph.D. diss., University of Sarre (1956), is one of the few works on this subject.

Henri (Fouques) Duparc (1848–1933), a pupil of César Franck and an early champion of Baudelaire and Verlaine. Of the seventeen songs composed before a neurasthenic disorder put an end to composition at the age of thirty-six, two of the best-known are settings of Baudelaire (the 1870 song 'L'invitation au voyage' [Invitation to a Voyage], and Duparc's last song, 'La vie antérieure' [My Previous Life] composed in 1884); he would also set poetry by Théophile Gautier, Leconte de Lisle, Jean Lahor, René-François Sully-Prudhomme and François Coppé, all of them contemporaries of the composer. In 'L'invitation au voyage', one can hear both Duparc's harmonic depths, approaching Lisztian or Wagnerian complexity, and his occasional willingness to mangle the prosody somewhat at the behest of strophic song. Having decided to set Baudelaire's poem of passion for the green-eyed actress Marie Daubrun as a barcarolle, with the murmurous sound of the sea assigned to the piano, Duparc omits Baudelaire's second stanza; its description of the lovers' chamber as a sybarite's paradise filled with mirrors, amber and rare flowers would distract from the water-music strains Duparc concocted on the basis of Baudelaire's single reference in the third stanza to vessels sleeping on the canals. An entire symbolism of water = female is at work in the alternation one hears at the beginning between the tonic C minor harmony over an open fifth low in the bass and the chromatic neighbouring chord on the supertonic, a slowed-down harmonic trill that denies forward motion for a suitably languorous atmosphere, a floating sensation that seems not of this world. Thereafter, Duparc uses changing chord colours, often wavering between parallel minor and major, to convey the play of light, with the fluid alternation between the raised leading tone and the modal-sounding, flatted seventh degree, between raised and lowered forms of the second, third and sixth scale-degrees, casting mode in doubt. The prosody betrays both sensitive touches and errors, melodic imperatives at times running roughshod over the inflection of the words, as when the descending phrase and rhythmic pattern at the words 'Songe à la douceur' (Dream of the Sweetness) are repeated to the corresponding words in the second (Baudelaire's third) stanza, 'De tes traitres yeux' (of your treacherous eyes). The pensive, lingering tonic accent of 'Songe' across the barline is beautifully apropos, although there is a slight undue emphasis on the word 'la', but the second time around, the sustained note occurs inappropriately on the preposition 'de'. Even so, Duparc's prosody is considerably finer than that of Gustave Charpentier in his settings of Baudelaire and Verlaine in the 1890s. One need only invoke 'LES sanglots longs DES violons' at the beginning of Charpentier's setting of Verlaine's 'Chanson d'automne' (Autumn Song) to see the difference between occasional negligence in the service of harmonic-melodic, etc. invention and the trampling underfoot of every prosodic sensibility.

One can trace throughout Gabriel Fauré's 1879, 1897 and 1908 song collections, their *mélodies* composed between 1861 and 1907, a progression from works in a style influenced by his teachers Saint-Saëns and Louis Niedermeyer – including the often cavalier treatment of prosody – to a manner uniquely his own. The earlier works demonstrate the continuing hold of Victor Hugo on French composers, although the nine Hugo songs keep company with three on texts by Baudelaire ('Hymne' [Hymn], 'Chant d'automne' [Autumn Song] and 'La rançon' [The Penalty], the last dedicated to Duparc) and a setting of the Gautier 'Chanson du pêcheur (Lamento)' [Fisherman's Song (Lament)] which Berlioz had earlier included in *Les nuits d'été*. If one contrasts the beginning of Fauré's version of this famous lament (Op. 4, No. 1) with his haunting late song 'Prison', Op. 83, No. 1, to a poem by Verlaine, one can see how much more attentive this master of French *mélodie* had become to prosodic subtleties. The meld of recitative and melody in the Gautier song is especially revealing because the cessation of the piano part beneath much of the first two phrases would have permitted greater prosodic accuracy, but that was not the concern circa 1872 that it would become later in the century. The greater emphasis on the tonic accent of the adjective 'belle' rather than the crucial word 'morte', the placement of 'je' on the downbeat and at the apex of a melodic descent, the downbeat prolongation of the preposition 'sous', are all prosodic flaws, although the phrases are of great melodic beauty. 'Prison', composed in 1894, is a different matter, as are all of the other songs of the third volume; the way in which the vocal line of 'Au cimetière' (At the Cemetery), Op. 51, No. 2, turns and winds flexibly, slowly, about the unchanging crotchet tactus – triple metre rendered funereal – of the chords in the piano (bars 1–35, 56–74) is a testament to a lifetime of setting French to music and to the heightened awareness of prosody at the *fin de siècle*. In Fauré's setting of the words 'Le ciel est pardessus le toit, / si bleu, si calme' (The sky above the roof / is so blue, so calm), one can note as particular felicities the leap to the sky ('ciel'), the proper placement of the verb 'est' closer to the dependent phrase which follows it than to the subject which precedes it, and the *accent oratoire* on 'bleu'. Perhaps the loveliest detail in this initial three-bar phrase, its asymmetry another remarkable factor, is not *echt* according to the strictest prosodic rules, but neither is it incorrect, and the expressive effect is justification aplenty: Fauré sets the mute e of 'cal – *me*' to the same pitch as the tonic accent of the word, rather than a melodic descent. The impression is of a state approaching hypnosis, the phrase momentarily too tranced to stir from the spot. When the vocal part ends suspended in mid-air on that same pitch (' . . . de ta jeunes*se*?'), we hear a final statement of the same impossible yearning for bygone possibility, for quietude. At the outbreak of despair in the second half of the poem, Fauré's syncopated stress on '*sim* –

ple' to convey the persona's longing for bygone simpler, tranquil times and the *accent oratoire* on 'CET – te paisible rumeur-là' (That peaceful sound) – prolonged and yet properly placed on an offbeat – heighten the desperation already evident in every other parameter of the music; one notes, for example, the use of the flatted second degree F♭, this in a quasi-modal, thoroughly chromaticised E flat minor, to weigh down the verb 'fait' in the line, 'Dis, qu'as tu *fait, toi que voi*là' – 'What have you *done?*' – at the end. It is no wonder Fauré is hailed as one of the greatest masters of French song.

With Claude Debussy's setting of Verlaine's 'L'ombre des arbres' in January of 1885, a slow, soft battle call was sounded in the war against music's deformation of French. Thereafter, Debussy was responsive to prosodic concerns as few composers of this language have been. The Symbolist literary circles with which Debussy was associated (he attended Stéphane Mallarmé's famous *mardis*, or Tuesday salons) radically reinvented French poetry, and their probing of language affected Debussy, whose sense of responsibility to his native tongue only increased with time. In 1911, when he was asked, 'Should one set good poetry, bad poetry, free verse, or prose to music?', he responded:

> It's difficult . . . to strike the right metre and still retain some inspiration. If you're just putting things together, content to juxtapose, of course it's not difficult, but then it's not worth the trouble either. Classic poetry has a life of its own, an 'inner dynamism', as the Germans would say, which has nothing to do with us.[25]

'Us' are composers, and the 'things' an uncaring composer puts together without heed are words and music. One can trace throughout Debussy's song *oeuvre* a process which led to those troubled musings, uttered not long before the composition of his last significant set of songs (the 1913 *Trois poèmes de Stéphane Mallarmé*). Debussy knew whereof he spoke: he himself began as someone more or less content to juxtapose. For all the sinuous, languid curvature of the 1880 melody for 'Beau soir' (Beautiful Evening) on a poem by Paul Bourget, the prosody is marred by first-beat stresses on syntactically unimportant words. The setting in 1882 of Verlaine's 'Mandoline' is similarly plagued by this early besetting sin; in fact, one can only describe the prosody of the lines, 'Et c'est Damis qui pour mainte / Cruelle fait maint vers tendre' (and it is Damis who for many a / cruel woman makes many a tender verse), as tortured, whatever the delights of Debussy's music for the piano-mandoline.

But by 1887, in songs such as Verlaine's 'C'est l'extase langoureuse', Debussy had almost completely abjured first-beat phrase beginnings; where they *do*

25 Fernand Divoire asked a number of poets and composers to respond to the question, 'Sous la musique que faut-il mettre? De beaux vers, de mauvais, des vers libres, de la prose?' *Musica*, 101–2 (February–March 1911), pp. 38–40, 58–60.

occur, it is either because prosody is momentarily subordinated to the eye-music of the phrase 'le roulis sourd des cailloux' (the muffled rolling of pebbles) or because the first-beat stress is followed by an expressive leap upwards to the proper tonic accent of 'C'est la *no*-tre'. Leafing through the *Cinq poèmes de Baudelaire* of 1890, the 1891 *Trois mélodies* of Verlaine, the *Fêtes galantes* I of 1891, Debussy's own prose-poetry set to music in the *Proses lyriques* of 1895, and the *Chansons de Bilitis* of 1899, one can trace the growing concern with the most sensitive possible moulding of the language in melody. An example from the *Chansons de Bilitis* can serve both to bring us to the century mark and to the end of the chapter. Debussy was in the habit, like Schumann, of selecting individual poems from larger collections and grouping them in a vaguely narrative order; here, his source was one of the most successful literary hoaxes of the nineteenth century, prose-poems purporting to be written by a poet contemporary with Sappho but in fact the creation of Pierre Louÿs (1870–1925). The three poems Debussy chose delineate a lyrical plot beginning with the sexual awakening of a young woman, followed by seduction and a final song in which the woman searches in the winter ice for traces of her lost satyr-lover (this is not the plot of Louÿs's volume taken in its entirety). In the first song, 'La flûte de Pan' (The Panpipes), one finds a sinuously scrolled, long-breathed quasi-recitative-like melodic manner, characterised by episodes of chanting on repeated pitches – there is more of this declamatory style than ever before – and a flexible alternation between duplet and triplet groupings. (An eighteenth-century writer, Michel de Chabanon, in his 'Lettre sur les propriétés musicales de langue française' in the *Mercure de France* for January 1773 [pp. 171–91], criticised composers who set lines of verse as a series of notes of equal value, which he considered to be a condemnable levelling of syllabic quantity, but composers both before and after his day made use of the practice. Certainly it is a commonplace in Debussy's music.) The male poet casts his female persona into a sensuous trance as she recounts a music lesson (an age-old *mise-en-scène* for seduction), a kiss and delicate hints that much more followed that kiss. At the poet's words 'unis avec la blanche cire qui est douce à mes lèvres comme le miel' (joined with the white wax which is sweet to my lips, like honey), Debussy's persona sways back and forth dreamily, outlining the same interval of a third as if in a spell while the piano sounds a slow harmonic trill. The melodic phrase leans all the way to the right to droop languorously at the words 'comme le miel', the singer directed to linger over each syllable of the concluding sweetness. Prosody, one realises, is fundamental to musical interpretation in Debussy's mature *mélodies*.

The history of French song in the late nineteenth century constitutes a singular chapter in the larger tale of words set to music, one in which various composers in various ways grapple with the fundamental problem of the enterprise: the limits of compatibility, all the more difficult where rhythm and accent in the two spheres are differently calibrated. In Alexandre Dumas's words, 'It [poetry] is not a sister of music, but a rival . . . not an ally, but an adversary. Instead of lending its help to the siren, the enchantress struggles against it. It is the fight of Armida and of Fata Morgana, but its victory leaves it exhausted.' The antique battle for primacy was exacerbated at the century's end by what Stéphane Mallarmé called 'an exquisite, fundamental crisis', a challenge that poetry should reclaim its 'rightful place' from music. The poetry born from this assertion was a challenge to those composers who understood it and who could no longer treat the new verse-art with the same fine disdain to which earlier composers had subjected Hugo and Lamartine. This is not to say that the problem vanished altogether at the end of the century; Debussy's dislike of Reynaldo Hahn's music doubtless stemmed in part from the fact that Hahn often wreaks prosodic violence on poets Debussy particularly cherished, such as Verlaine, Gautier and Charles d'Orléans.[26] For Debussy, the difficulties of song in French became more and more unsettling and finally appeared insoluble. With the first year of the First World War, the pre-eminent voice in French song fell silent.

Bibliography

Agawu, V. K., 'The Musical Language of *Kindertotenlieder* No. 2'. *Journal of Musicology*, 2 (1983), pp. 81–92

Beller-McKenna, D., 'Johannes Brahms's Later Settings of Biblical Texts, 1877–1896'. Ph.D. diss., Harvard University (1994)

Bozarth, G., 'Brahms's 'Liederjahr of 1868'. *Music Review*, 44 (1983), pp. 208–22

'The Lieder of Johannes Brahms 1868–1871: Studies in Chronology and Compositional Process'. Ph.D. diss., Princeton University (1978)

Braus, I., 'Textual Rhetoric and Harmonic Anomaly in Selected Lieder of Johannes Brahms'. Ph.D. diss., Harvard University (1988)

Carner, M., *Hugo Wolf Songs*. London, 1982

Daverio, J., 'Brahms's Magelone Romanzen and the Romantic Imperative'. *Journal of Musicology*, 7 (1989), pp. 343–65

Fauser, A., *Der Orchestergesang in Frankreich zwischen 1870 und 1920*. Regensburg, 1994

Finscher, L., 'Brahms's Early Songs: Poetry Versus Music'. In Bozarth (ed.), *Brahms Studies: Analytical and Historical Perspectives*. Oxford, 1990, pp. 331–44

Glauert, A., *Hugo Wolf and the Wagnerian Inheritance*. Cambridge, 1999

Gülke, P., '"Sterb' ich, so hüllt in Blumen meine Glieder . . .": zu einem Lied von Hugo Wolf'. *Musica*, 33 (March–April 1979), pp. 132–40

Hallmark, R. (ed.), *German Lieder in the Nineteenth Century*. New York, 1996

---

26 See also R. Hahn, 'De l'interprétation dans le chant – Le Rythme et la prosodie, conférence de m. Reynaldo Hahn, faite le 16 décembre 1918', *Journal de l'Université des Annales*, 13/1 (1919), pp. 320–33.

Hefling, S. A., '*Das Lied von der Erde*: Mahler's Symphony for Voices and Orchestra – or Piano'. *The Journal of Musicology*, 10/3 (Summer 1992), pp. 293–341

Jacobsen, C., *Das Verhältnis von Sprache und Musik im Liedern von Johannes Brahms, dargestellt an Parallelvertonungen*. Hamburg, 1975

Jackson, T., 'Compositional Revisions in Strauss's "Waldseligkeit" and a New Source'. *Richard Strauss-Blätter*, 21 (1989), pp. 55–82

   'Richard Strauss's *Winterweihe* – An Analysis and Study of the Sketches'. *Richard Strauss-Blätter*, 17 (1987), pp. 28–69

Jefferson, A., *The Lieder of Richard Strauss*. London, 1971

Jost, P., *Brahms als Liedkomponist: Studien zum Verhältnis von Text und Vertonung*. Stuttgart, 1992

Kramer, L., 'Decadence and Desire: The *Wilhelm Meister* Songs of Wolf and Schubert'. In J. Kerman (ed.), *Music at the Turn of Century: A Nineteenth- Century Music Reader*. Berkeley and Los Angeles, 1990, pp. 115–28

Kravitt, E. F., 'The Lied in 19th-Century Concert Life'. *Journal of the American Musicological Society*, 18 (1965), pp. 207–18

   The Lied: Mirror of Late Romanticism. New Haven and London, 1996

   'Mahler's Dirges for his Death: February 24, 1901'. *Musical Quarterly*, 64 (1978), pp. 329–53

Krones, H., 'Der Einfluss Franz Schuberts auf das Liedschaffen von Johannes Brahms'. In S. Antonicek and O. Biba (eds.), *Brahms-Kongress Wien 1983*. Tutzing, 1988, pp. 309–24

Meister, B., *Nineteenth-Century French Song: Fauré, Chausson, Duparc, and Debussy*. Bloomington and Indiana, 1980

Mueller, R. C., 'Reevaluating the Liszt Chronology: The Case of *Anfangs wollt ich fast verzagen*'. *19th Century Music*, 12 (1988), pp. 132–47

Noske, F., *French Song from Berlioz to Duparc: The Origin and Development of the Mélodie*, trans. Rita Benton. New York, 2nd edn 1970

Petersen, B., '*Ton und Wort*': The Lieder of Richard Strauss. Ann Arbor, 1980

Platt, H., 'Jenner Versus Wolf: The Critical Reception of Brahms's Songs'. *The Journal of Musicology*, 13/3 (1995), pp. 377–403

   'Text–Music Relationships in Lieder of Johannes Brahms'. Ph.D. diss., City University of New York (1992)

Rolf, M. and Marvin, E. W., 'Analytical Issues and Interpretive Decisions in Two Songs by Richard Strauss'. *Intégral*, 4 (1990), pp. 67–103

Rumph, S., 'Debussy's *Trois Chansons de Bilitis*: Song, Opera, and the Death of the Subject'. *The Journal of Musicology*, 12/ 4 (Fall 1994), pp. 464–90

Sams, E., *The Songs of Hugo Wolf*. London, 2nd edn 1985

Stein, D., *Hugo Wolf's Lieder and Extensions of Tonality*. Ann Arbor, 1985

Thorau, C., '"In der Frühe": Mörikes "Zeit" in Hugo Wolf's Music'. In H.-K. Metzger and R. Riehn (eds.), *Musik-Konzepte 75: Hugo Wolf*. Karlsruhe, 1992, pp. 83–101

Wenk, A., *Claude Debussy and the Poets*. Berkeley and Los Angeles, 1976

Youens, S., '"Alles endet, was entstehet": The Second of Hugo Wolf's *Michelangelo-Lieder*'. *Studies in Music* (University of Western Australia), 14 (1980), pp. 87–103

   'Debussy's Setting of Verlaine's "Colloque sentimental": From the Past to the Present'. *Studies in Music*, 15 (1981), pp. 93–105

   'Drama in the Lied: Piano vs. Voice in Wolf's Serenades'. *Studies in Music*, 23 (1989), pp. 61–87

'From the Fifteenth Century to the Twentieth: Considerations of Musical Prosody in Debussy's *Trois Ballades de François Villon*'. *The Journal of Musicology*, 2/4 (Fall 1983), pp. 418–33

Hugo Wolf and his Mörike Songs. Cambridge, 2000

Hugo Wolf: The Vocal Music. Princeton, 1992

'Music, Verse, and Prose Poetry: Debussy's *Trois Chansons de Bilitis*'. *Journal of Musicological Research*, 7 (1986), pp. 69–94

17

Chamber music and piano

JONATHAN DUNSBY

The historical challenge and a black and white response

If we were applying the title of this chapter to the period 1800–60, and resorting to the nineteenth century's favoured type of historiography, the 'great-man theory',[1] and focusing on new music rather than all the music that was performed, then household names and lists of canonical works would crowd these pages. We would be navigating through Beethoven's string quartets and piano sonatas, Schubert's too as well as his piano 'miniatures', the Mendelssohn Octet and Songs without Words, Schumann's piano-chamber music such as the Quintet and his piano cycles from the 1830s that have been performed recurrently to this day – *Carnaval* (1835) above all, perhaps – and indeed other piano music of that time, most obviously from Chopin and Liszt, both of whom were prolific, as well as being instantly recognised at the time as outstanding. It would be a considerable challenge to provide a representative picture of a period of such scintillating novelty both in the home, in the salon – from which chamber music was emerging on to the professional stage – and in the concert hall, where the piano had established its prestigious position in the closing decades of the eighteenth century.

In the second part of the century, on the other hand, which is our concern here, it is noticeable how the 'great-man theory' shows a certain retrenchment, since in both chamber and piano music the scene came to be so radically dominated not by a group of composers of different ages and in different countries, but by one figure, that of Johannes Brahms. This dominance was especially marked after the 1860s, when Brahms had become established as a mature master, and when Liszt had turned from the piano solo largely to other genres. In the 1860s too an aesthetic polarisation had seized European musical life: to put it at its crudest, the agenda was divided between those matters which concerned Wagner's music dramas (and, admittedly, Verdi's operas), and those matters, including instrumental music, which did not.

---

1 W. D. Allen, *Philosophies of Music History: A Study of General Histories of Music 1600–1960* (New York, 1962), pp. 86–91.

The Wagner/Brahms aesthetic schism – and this is not too strong a word for such a sharp and hotly debated polarisation in the attitudes of the time towards new music (as chapter 11 demonstrates) – explains at least in part why historians of later nineteenth-century music have always tended to favour geographical, national categorisation over generic distinctions. Critics were as certain at the time as they continued to be in the twentieth century that if Brahms had written the opera he so genuinely wished he could, it would have been so different from Wagnerian music drama (and the mature Verdi) as to open an entirely distinct story in the history of musical composition at its highest, or let us say most elaborate, level; and the same would have been true had Wagner composed the symphony of which he merely dreamed while working dutifully and relentlessly on *Parsifal* in 1877–82, as his life was drawing to its close. Even though it may seem slightly ridiculous to marginalise Verdi in this picture, the great debate, the fundamental movement in Western musical art, was taking place in the German-speaking world, and the music of contemporaneous 'languages', be they Bohemian, French, Russian or other, has perhaps inevitably tended to be seen as a reflection of or response to that debate.

To the general historian of chamber and piano music of this period, then, there has always been the temptation to go 'native' and adopt the slightly sour pose of much of the polemical writing of and on the later nineteenth century, which is weighed down by the aesthetic prejudices of one or the other camp; and our chosen task is to avoid this. For example, one cannot but ask whether there is an inappropriate lack of forensic detachment in the following distillation from Grout and Palisca's *A History of Western Music*:

> The medium of chamber music was not congenial to many Romantic composers; it lacked on the one hand the intimate personal expressiveness of the solo piano piece or the Lied and on the other the glowing colors and powerful sound of orchestral music. It is therefore not surprising that the arch-Romantics Berlioz, Liszt, and Wagner contributed nothing to chamber music, nor that the best works in this medium in the nineteenth century came from those composers who had the closest affinity with the Classic tradition.[2]

Even if 'sour' is found to be too strong a word in characterising Grout and Palisca's comment, it is certainly possible to take an entirely different view of those 'glowing' and 'powerful' aspects of orchestral music, if one can get to some sense at all behind these hyperbolic and no doubt unwittingly gendered adjectives.

We can learn a lot about this different view from a contemporaneous witness to the music and times, Dublin-born Charles Stanford. In reviewing the

---

2 D. J. Grout and C. V. Palisca, *A History of Western Music* (London, 4th edn 1988), p. 697.

progress of European musical life during his long years as an accomplished composer and highly educated scholar, beginning in the 1850s, Stanford takes an aesthetic position that could be understood (in 1914) as merely an old person's tirade against the modernism that can be said to have shaken musical composition of the early 1900s to its foundations, yet it is a position that takes on an authentic subtlety when viewed sympathetically and in some of its ramifications. 'The worship of colour for its own sake', he writes, fully expecting his reader to know to whom he is referring, Berlioz-lovers for instance, 'is the rock upon which modern superficial taste is in danger of splitting'.[3] What is most interesting for our purposes, however, is the test Stanford offers of orchestral works, and this test is simply to play them on the piano: 'if they give real pleasure to listen to as music under these black and white conditions they will have proved their inherent value'.[4] This is a most instructive notion since, without going into all the keen aesthetic issues Stanford is apparently raising, we can look through these contemporaneous eyes at some of his perhaps unintended implications.

First, there is the rather obvious implication that piano music, and one may infer all species of chamber music, are somehow inferior. The analogy Stanford uses is the photograph, which he believes gives a true image through what he calls 'the inexorable camera', but of course it is a defective, monochrome image. Thus, to consider chamber music of the period, we might surmise that Debussy's String Quartet (1893) is of an inherently lower order than his *Prélude à L'Après-midi d'un faune* of the following year; but even though the *Prélude* is undoubtedly a milestone in the early history of the 'big' impressionistic European soundscape works of the 1890s and beyond, the Quartet has always been described as a pioneering masterpiece in which Debussy broke away from the generic constraints of a century and more of quartet composition, freeing himself from the very 'Classic tradition' mentioned above by Grout and Palisca as, they believe, the wellspring of the 'best works in this medium' (into which hall of fame Debussy's Quartet is presumably not invited). And in general, even if no one is likely to claim that this period is some sort of 'great age' of chamber music, nevertheless composers did use the medium to make some of the most significant steps in their individual development.

Secondly, what does it really mean to call piano music 'black and white'? We do not need to recount here the number of music historians in the following century who found different ways of saying that the nineteenth century was the 'age of the piano'. The piano was not only the compositional workhorse that to some extent it remained in post-Romantic music, and not only the educational

---

3 C. V. Stanford, *Pages From an Unwritten Diary* (London, 1914), p. 302.   4 *Ibid.*, p. 303.

route through which most composers learned the language of Western music, but also an artistic medium of the highest level, considered worthy by one composer after another to carry their most significant compositional acts. There are obvious exceptions – Berlioz, Wagner, Verdi – but they are rather few, and some careers built in other mediums – Wolf's in particular – did of course rely fundamentally on the piano, for without the piano there is no lied. We should not forget, either, that the piano was a favoured point of contact between audiences and 'star' music-making, and following the establishment of the piano tradition in early Romantic musical life, and the standardisation of the iron-framed instrument that has changed little since about 1860, the centre-stage place of the piano virtuoso in Western concert life is one of the various features that rendered the last four decades of the nineteenth century a remarkably stable one musically. History has shown that Stanford's actual analogy of piano music being a kind of black and white photograph of the 'real' world of colour heard in the symphony hall and the opera house was both mistaken and, as it were, uncannily accurate. It was mistaken because it sets up a false aesthetic hierarchy; after all, if Brahms, say, had actually considered symphonic writing to be inherently 'better' than solo piano writing or chamber music, it is certain that someone with his dogged commitment to artistic integrity would not have wasted so much of his muse on a peripheral activity. What was uncannily accurate concerning Stanford's metaphor of non-orchestral, instrumental music as the equivalent of black and white photography is that black and white photography did persist as a highly valued art form even in the century after Stanford's life when colour photography became commonplace; so did chamber and piano music.

Thirdly, we should notice how Stanford takes it as read that a work for orchestra can validly be played on the piano, and he recounts an actual case in this delightfully anecdotal but thoughtful volume,[5] written at a period when the piano transcription was common in solo piano performance, as incidentally it began to become again in the later twentieth century after many decades of being out of fashion. In the later nineteenth century the transcription and especially the 'arrangement' remained the serious artistic phenomenon that it had always been in Western music, and most recently then in the successful campaign of Liszt in the 1830s and 1840s to 'make the solo piano, under his hands, a rival of the orchestra',[6] not only through original composition, but also by letting the piano substitute for the orchestra in established repertory. Fluidity of medium was a cultural fact of the period, so that for example Brahms's Op.

5 *Ibid.*, pp. 303–4.
6 L. Plantinga, *Romantic Music: A History of Musical Style in Nineteenth-Century Europe* (New York, 1984), p. 183.

34 was a sonata for two pianos, but also, in a quasi-literal transcription, the F minor Piano Quintet (1864), and Wagner's *Siegfried Idyll* could capture for chamber orchestra not just a 'version' of some of the large 1871 music-drama score, but some of its orchestral essence.

As a momentary, but relevant, diversion, to be fair to Stanford, he finishes his complaint about where music has ended up at the close of the nineteenth century with a little story to back up his analogy, which can maybe remind us of the centrality of chamber and piano music in representing the essence of Romantic composition. He had complained to a friend that a photograph of himself was disappointing. 'Don't flatter yourself', he was told, 'It's exactly like you'.[7]

The core compositions

It might seem that the simplest account of chamber and piano music of the later nineteenth century, in a period when music taken seriously was music written down rather than improvised, but before the time when music could be stored electronically more or less as it sounds, should include a list of all known, relevant publications. This would be a daunting task, as the following quotation concerning chamber music of the period indicates:

> The following selective list gives some idea of the numbers of composers and work involved; the summations after each composer are of mature completed works in the genre titled by specific performing forces. Significant composers of chamber music in [Germany and Austria] from the 1850s on included: Woldemar Barfiel (9), Brahms (24), Bruch (6), Eduard Franck (18), Goldmark (11), Friedrich Kiel (20), Raff (25), Reinecke (24) and Volkmann (12). In the 1860s the following composers began their production in the genre: Friedrich Gernsheim (19), Goetz (4), Rheinberger (14); in the 1870s: Brüll (6), Robert Fuchs (40), Heinrich von Herzogenberg (21), August Klughardt (10); and in the 1880s: Wilhelm Berger (12), Felix Draeseke (10), Richard von Perger (6), and Richard Strauss (4).[8]

One naturally wonders what of France, Italy, Russia, the United States? However, it is not so much the sheer difficulty of such a task that is striking, but rather the underlying question of the extent to which, other than as an information database, an inventory of compositions would be worthwhile. Pascall rightly cautions that he aims to provide only 'some idea'; and Treitler has invited us to think clearly about the 'failure of the idea of history as an objective

---

7 Stanford, *Pages*, p. 304.
8 R. Pascall, 'Major Instrumental Forms: 1850–1890', in G. Abraham (ed.), *The New Oxford History of Music IX: Romanticism (1830–1890)* (Oxford, 1990), p. 625.

account of what happened in the past'.[9] Even a would-be comprehensive list of works published, fascinating though it is,[10] and even though the compiler claimed with a certain understandable historian's pride that it was unprecedented, provides us only with raw data for interpretation. For example, one can easily see that there are dozens of newly composed string trios listed by Altmann, while there are only a handful of quintets for clarinet and string quartet: however, one of the clarinet quintets is Brahms's Op. 115 of 1892, which by anybody's reasonable standards (privately, perhaps even those of the most committed Wagnerians) is one of the masterpieces of late nineteenth-century music in any medium.

Brahms's domination of chamber music of this period is undoubted. In the *Norton Anthology of Western Music* section of 'Solo, Chamber, and Vocal Music in the Nineteenth Century',[11] twelve works or movements by eight different composers are offered, of which only one is chamber music, the Scherzo from Brahms's Piano Quintet, Op. 34. Brahms produced an extensive repertory covering some forty years until shortly before his death in 1897, with between one and three examples of familiar genres (such as violin sonatas and string quartets) and the relatively unfamiliar (for example the horn trio, and for bigger forces the two string sextets): twenty-four works in all. Much has been written about the continuity of Brahms's compositional approach from the 1850s to the 1890s, and the fact that in 1891 he was inspired to revise the Piano Trio in B major, Op. 8, of 1854 in an admittedly radically rewritten version nevertheless indicates how comfortable he felt with the archive of his own creative portfolio. Yet the twentieth century took a somewhat collapsed view of the Brahms story, and in contrast we find in authoritative contemporaneous criticism, by writers without the benefit of hindsight, accounts of his new works as truly bold innovations. For example, in the following comments from 1889, discussing the second Cello Sonata, Op. 99, and the third Violin Sonata, Op. 100, both of which had first been performed in Vienna in 1886, the philosopher and critic Eduard Hanslick conveys a sense of Brahms as genuinely progressive as well as giving us some indication of why he was thought to tower above his younger contemporaries:

> As works of art, both sonatas are offspring of the same strong, manly, and healthy spirit that, nicely mixed with intimate, not too tender-hearted feelings, characterizes and distinguishes all of the late works of Brahms. The unexpected nature of their phrases, combined with the strictly unified character of these

9 L. Treitler, 'The Historiography of Music: Issues of Past and Present', in N. Cook and M. Everist (eds.), *Rethinking Music* (Oxford, 1999), p. 357.
10 W. Altmann, *Kammermusik-Katalog: Ein Verzeichnis von seit 1841 veröffentlichten Kammermusikwerken* (Hofheim, 1910 and 1967, reprint of 6th edn, ed. J. Richter, 1944).
11 C. V. Palisca (ed.), *Norton Anthology of Western Music* (New York, 1996).

new musical works, lends them an inexhaustible charm. Their brief form is noteworthy. May those young composers who no longer know the difference between a sonata and a symphony observe here that profound thoughts and passionate emotions can also be expressed in a condensed way, without verbosity. To attempt to describe this in words is admittedly quite useless. Even if we were to print the themes of the individual sonata movements of Brahms here, as the English concert programs do – what does one know of Brahms if one only knows his naked themes? The principal motif of the first and of the third movement of the new violin sonata, of the finale of the cello sonata – couldn't they, taken by themselves, almost be by Haydn?[12]

The 'poetic' is never far away in Brahms's chamber music, and arises explicitly in the song-derived finale of the first Violin Sonata, Op. 78 (1879) – and despite what Hanslick says, Brahms certainly at times wrote chamber music on a symphonic scale, especially Op. 34 (see above). But Pascall is accurate in stating that 'the chamber work', in general, not only in Brahms, 'was not greatly used for programmatic expression'.[13] It was only later, particularly with one of the chronologically and one might say spiritually final masterpieces of the century, Schoenberg's string sextet *Verklärte Nacht* (1899: see below), that programme and construction pointed the way to the chamber music of the future. Brahms's hegemony of chamber music is nowhere more evident than in contemporaneous and subsequent judgement of his virtual simulacrum, Dvořák, who, bear in mind, and notwithstanding some critical faint praise from the last century, stands on his own as the composer of the Ninth Symphony and the Cello Concerto, at least if the test is works that are performed nearly as often as those of a Bach or a Beethoven and have been heard throughout the shifting tastes of late Romanticism, modernism and post-modernism. The same endurance was already true in 1913 of Dvořák's String Quartet No. 12, Op. 96, which Dunhill referred to as 'one of the most successful chamber works of modern days'.[14]

If Brahms also dominates the period to some extent as a master of piano music, there are two caveats. First, it is probably through the two Piano Concertos, Op. 15 in D minor (1861) and Op. 83 in B flat major (1881) rather than through solo piano music that Brahms the virtuoso pianist became best known, even though Op. 15 took some years to settle into the repertory. Secondly, Brahms wrote relatively little piano music. The early three piano sonatas completed in 1853, although important in helping to launch his career, were in the wider scheme inevitably eclipsed by a visionary work by a composer of the elder generation, Liszt, whose B minor Sonata was completed in the

---

12 E. Hanslick, 'Brahms's Newest Compositions', in W. Frisch (ed.), *Brahms and His World* (Princeton, 1990), pp. 145–50; original edn 1889, *Die Moderne Oper, Part V*, p. 146.
13 Pascall, 'Major Instrumental Forms', p. 623.
14 T. Dunhill, *Chamber Music: A Treatise for Students* (London, 1913), p. 70.

same year: 'Liszt's ability – especially evident in the Piano Sonata – was to construct a thrilling tonal and thematic drama by challenging, but ultimately confirming, the most essential characteristics of goal-directed symphonic organization'.[15] Brahms's other major contributions are two sets of piano variations on themes by Handel, Op. 24 (1861), and Paganini, Op. 35 (1863) – these are the variations lionised by history, although the Variations on a Theme of Schumann, Op. 9 (1854), offer a combination of soaring imagination with compositional ingenuity and historical moment that some would say is not to be found elsewhere in Brahms; and a variety of shorter works from later periods, some all-time favourites, such as the Op. 117 Intermezzos, some, such as the Intermezzo, Op. 116, No. 5, modernistic in a way that came to be appreciated only during the next century by those who developed a taste for Second Viennese music.

One 'fact' concerning repertory that can make a reasonable claim on our attention is not only the domination of Austro-German composers of instrumental music, but also during the 1870s in Paris, in the onset of a period of political stability, the rise of what has been called a 'French Musical Renaissance', which plays a central part of our picture of what one historian calls 'the rebirth of absolute music'.[16] César Franck was not only the leading figure in this creative push, but is an interesting case of a composer who flowered late, when the time was right culturally. Works such as the Prelude, Chorale, and Fugue for piano (1884), the Violin Sonata (1886) and the Piano Quintet (1879) would have been inconceivable in the 1850s, when Franck was in his thirties, not only in terms of their advanced chromaticism, much-discussed in the literature, but also their 'Germanic' characteristics, especially Franck's brilliant solutions in adapting sonata procedures and forms to a rich tonal palette. It is also remarkable how carefully he considered the generic options available: the three works listed above involve personnel of one, two and five, but Franck also wrote for trio and quartet, and took his place in the pantheon of composers who have used the piano in its most 'colourful' and 'powerful' (see above, p. 501) setting, the concerto, which is the genre of his Symphonic Variations (1885), albeit in a single-movement contribution. Typically, Franck in the 1880s uses each genre once, and this is clearly not because he was ever in danger of running out of ideas, but because he was exploring systematically the range of solo and chamber music of his times, as he saw them. One may even feel there is some irony in his conservatism, from this point of view, even compared with the dominant conserving mind of the age, Brahms's, from which there did emerge canonical contributions to otherwise

15 A. Whittall, *Romantic Music: A Concise History from Schubert to Sibelius* (London, 1987), p. 89.
16 R. Longyear, *Nineteenth-Century Romanticism in Music* (Englewood Cliffs, 2nd edn 1973), pp. 130–53.

more or less dormant genres – cello sonatas and clarinet sonatas for example. Yet Brahms never ventured into the world of roving harmony and even on occasion suspended tonality (to use Schoenberg's terms from 1911[17]) that were Franck's stock-in-trade in the 1880s and proved to be a profound influence on such younger French composers as Chabrier, Duparc and d'Indy; and a good thing too, we might think, of Brahms's more cautious approach, if agreeing with Debussy's sardonic, retrospective comment on Franck's structural abilities – 'César Franck was single minded. To have found a beautiful harmony sufficed to make his day happy.'[18]

A crucial figure in the French Renaissance was Fauré. Born in 1845, he was active throughout this period, and was blessed with a long life and a healthy old age ending in 1924. As a composer for piano, he never tried to escape the miniaturism that was a persistent feature of Romantic composition (and Fauré's impromptus, nocturnes and barcaroles of the 1880s pre-dated Brahms's Opp. 116–19 by a few years). In the twentieth century historians were seemingly unable to mention Fauré's piano writing without mentioning that of Chopin as an obvious, direct influence, and although this is true, it needs to be said that Chopin's restlessly experimental approach to all aspects of musical language and his Beethovenian flair for large-scale construction eluded Fauré at every turn. The Brahms influence makes Fauré a doubly derivative composer, although in specific cases, such as the heavy reliance of his Piano Quartet in C minor (1879) on Brahms's third Piano Quartet, Op. 60 (1875), one can admire the way in which Fauré overcame the anxiety of influence to produce music that manages to be at the same time relatively non-Wagnerian but also stylistically coherent. Every account of music in Paris in the closing decades of the nineteenth century is rippling with references to Fauré, and his songs never did go out of fashion. Perhaps one strong historical interpretation of his flagging reputation in the mid-twentieth century[19] is that he and others of his age and cultural location were an easy act for Debussy and Ravel to follow.

If we have tried to see a structure to the idea of 'repertory' in this context, it does tend to break down when we consider cases that have to be treated with at least as careful interpretation, of which three – Dvořák, Borodin and Tchaikovsky – will be considered here, each emblematic of their times. Dvořák is an interesting case of a composer active under the shadow of Wagner, whose influence, if not harmonic language, is patent in the mature operas *Rusalka* (1900) and *Armida* (1903), and of Brahms, to whose style in general his music is

17 A. Schoenberg, *Theory of Harmony*, trans. R. Carter (London, 1978).

18 C. Debussy, 'Monsieur Croche the Dilettante Hater', in *Three Classics in the Aesthetics of Music* (New York, 1962; original edn 1921 from journal articles 1901–5), p. 51.

19 See for example C. Darnton, *You and Music* (Harmondsworth, 2nd edn 1945), p. 108.

so close that he must be admired for his dogged ability to escape into prolific compositional confidence. As Whittall puts it, 'while in no sense an experimenter – he did not seek to create new forms or challenge existing norms of dissonance or periodicity – he was able to move effectively and individually within existing conventions. His distinction lies in the fact that his fluent, fresh, flexible idiom so rarely becomes routine'.[20] What we can also note is his sheer fecundity in chamber and piano music, which indicates the canonical value he placed on this way of spending his creative time: there were no fewer than seventeen works for violin and piano and cello and piano between 1865 and 1895, nine trios for various forces including the famous 'Dumky' Piano Trio, Op. 90, of 1891, fourteen string quartets and two piano quartets, three string quintets and another well-known work, the Piano Quintet, Op. 81, of 1887, and the String Sextet, Op. 48, a relatively early work from 1878; in piano music for two hands we find some thirty identifiable works including collections such as eight Waltzes (Op. 54, 1880), and the eight Humoresques, Op. 101, of 1894, but, so far as is known, not a single piano sonata, and but for an early Theme and Variations (Op. 36, 1876) not a single instance of Classical, 'abstract' forms; apart from Dvořák's duet arrangements of works such as the 'Dumky' Trio (1893) and his Eighth and Ninth Symphonies (1890, 1893), the piano works for four hands are equally devoid of indications of any desire to carry on the tradition of sonatas, variations and the like.

While Dvořák offers a study in how a Bohemian composer, never hesitating to use the rhythms and melodic types of his native folk music, adapted to composition within the German tradition, further east there was much greater suspicion of these influences: 'there are clear indications that some Russian composers regarded the multi-movement chamber music genre as a particularly Teutonic one',[21] and this goes a long way to explaining why Tchaikovsky rarely, as we shall see, ventured into this territory. Borodin, however, in a relatively short and unproductive compositional career (he died in 1887 at the age of fifty-three), consistently worked in the chamber medium. About a dozen finished compositions survive, most notably the two Strings Quartets in A (1879) and D (1881). Time and again historians have referred to the 'Mendelssohnian' style in Borodin's chamber music, but this should be taken perhaps more as a compliment than an accusation: his serene control of musical texture and careful planning of an extensive harmonic palette secured for him a conspicuous place in the chamber music repertory of live and recorded music in the twentieth century. Although Borodin composed one suite for piano, and may well have composed other piano music that has not survived, the piano clearly

20 Whittall, *Romantic Music*, p. 146.   21 Pascall, 'Major Instrumental Forms', p. 636

figured little in his attention, not least perhaps because unlike many late nine-teenth-century composers, and composers of the preceding century or so, he was not himself an accomplished pianist.

Tchaikowsky, in contrast, composed a good deal of piano music, most of it, in this writer's experience, an indication of his capacity for unnerving miscal-culation. This is evident in other genres too, especially the piano concerto, where following the First (1876), which may with justification be called the best-known piano concerto of all time, there followed two more, neither of which is much performed or deserves to be. The second, for example, was instantly disliked. George Bernard Shaw wrote after a London performance in 1890 that the work was 'impulsive, copious, difficult, and pretentious; but it has no distinction, no originality, no feeling for the solo instrument, nothing to rouse the attention or to occupy the memory'.[22] Even Tchaikovsky's notable contribution to chamber music, the Piano Trio in A minor of 1882, although it has always been considered grateful to perform, and admired for its original form (in two sections, the second divided into variations and finale), is never-theless always the object of critical disquiet. Hutcheson's comments are typical: 'this work has moments of fine inspiration, but is long and diffuse . . . some cuts are often made, to its benefit. Usually it turns out to be more inter-esting to the performers than to the audience.'[23]

Interlude: genre/genera

Although chamber music, like piano music, could through the technique of arrangement be made to carry music of any genre – even Wagner's music dramas were rehearsed with piano – it has seemed to many historians of the period that there is something not only generically specific about most of its chamber music, or at least of the best chamber music of the period, but techni-cally or compositionally specific, as if composing chamber music were to work within a particular genus, with species ranging from, say, flute duos (a most popular item in the 1800s, contributed to by dozens of composers whose names are consigned to the mere historical record) to something like Rheinberger's chamber-orchestra-like nonet for wind and strings of 1885; and from formal miniatures to extensive works. Indeed, if Raynor's history is to be believed there was in fact a social role for the piano in professionalising

---

22 G. B. Shaw, *London Music in 1888–89 as Heard by Corno di Bassetto (Later Known as Bernard Shaw) with Some Further Autobiographical Particulars* (New York, 1973; original edn 1937), p. 382. See also M. Musgrave, 'Brahms and England', in M. Musgrave (ed.), *Brahms 2: Biographical, Documentary and Analytical Studies* (Cambridge, 1987), pp. 1–20.

23 E. Hutcheson, *The Literature of the Piano: A Guide for Amateur and Student* (2nd edn rev. R. Ganz, London, 1969), p. 330.

chamber music: 'the piano was so firmly entrenched in amateur musical life that chamber music had drifted out of the home and was becoming the preserve of ensembles of professional players like the Joachim Quartet'.[24] Others would put this trend down more to the rise of virtuosity, which by the 1860s and even earlier was making even routine chamber music mostly out of the reach of the amateur player, since 'some early Romantic music, in its purely physical demands, is more or less at the limits of possible human achievements and is never going to be significantly exceeded'.[25]

Dahlhaus, who refers to the 'intimate discourse of chamber music', argues the musical point with force and clarity that we can identify some special quality in chamber composition after the 1850s, a matter of its genus rather than its genre (tellingly, even a work albeit of very rare quality as 'early' as Brahms's First Piano Quartet, Op. 25 published in 1863, became in Schoenberg's orchestral version of 1937 a different species of work, one that was latent in its deceptive inception: a true symphony):

> Sequential writing on the scale and in the manner in which it occurs in Wagner and Liszt, if found in the exposition of a piece of chamber music, would strike the listener as unwelcome tonal discursiveness and pompous rhetoric. Developing variation, for its part, would fall flat in music drama: it would be nothing but a pedantic self-indulgence by the composer, it would not penetrate the listener's awareness in performance, and aesthetically – in any bearing it might have on the realization of the drama – it would still be ineffectual even for someone reading the score who was able to see the latent associations.[26]

Dahlhaus may well have had Schoenberg's transformation of Brahms's Op. 25 somewhere in his mind in writing this generalisation that naturally marginalises the truly noumenal. One would hardly expect to see the same argument advanced, in any case, about piano music of the period, which is marked by the orchestral and operatic obsessions of the age. Not only is this true in general, but in one specific case – one that stands out from the period, if only because it has been played ever since either as originally on the piano or in Ravel's orchestration, Musorgsky's *Pictures at an Exhibition* (1874) – we see inscribed a whole array of the obsessions of Romantic composition: obsessions with large forms, narrative programmes, the monumental, the supernatural, the natural world, race, virtuosity, dramatic reversal, folk music, antiquity, the gothic, and of course others too. Just how comprehensively the piano could carry the *topoi* of late Romantic music is a recurrent theme in Christensen's vivid account of the piano

---

24 H. Raynor, *Music and Society since 1815* (London, 1976), pp. 61–2.
25 J. Dunsby, *Performing Music: Shared Concerns* (Oxford, 1995), p. 50.
26 C. Dahlhaus, *Between Romanticism and Modernism: Four Studies in the Music of the Later Nineteenth Century*, trans. M. Whittall (Cambridge, 1989; original edn 1974), pp. 50–1.

duet in this period: 'by extricating a piece of music from its physical presence in time and space, the piano transcription is implicated in the process of etherialization that became such a cornerstone of Romantic formalist music aesthetics'.[27]

It must be understood that this 'etherialisation' of the keyboard was in a context where the virtuosi of the day – above all Thalberg earlier on, who was only a year younger than Liszt and died in 1871, and as the inheritors of this tradition Gottschalk (1829–69), Moszkowski (1854–1925) and Godowsky (1870–1938) – played for the most part music of dazzling virtuosity that was compositionally so shallow as to render their recitals little more than circus acts, a phenomenon that was hardly likely to arise within the genus of chamber music, despite the urge to the spectacular that is seen in for instance the very Brahms Op. 25 (especially its finale) mentioned above. Against this virtuoso backdrop in the public mind, 'serious' piano music of which we have mentioned some of the milestones in Liszt, Brahms, Franck and Musorgsky, but which category must also include the contributions of Alkan, Heller, Litolff, Anton Rubinstein and Saint-Saëns, was truly 'high' art. And although it is easy to tend to be dismissive of the 'shallow' it must always be remembered that the cult of virtuosity (which is an inevitable theme of music-history books on the nineteenth century celebrating its greatest flowering in Paganini and typically neglecting the huge and largely unwritten role of Czerny and of the violinist Joachim in linking the virtuosic to the profound) was a resource on which deep-thinking composers could and did draw. One only has to look at the techniques employed in some of Brahms's piano arrangements to begin to imagine what it might have been like to hear him improvising at parties, and to realise that serious music like the Paganini Variations, still regarded as technically difficult even for the greatest piano athletes, found essential nourishment in the developments of the popular repertory, just as was to be the case in such austere later territory as the Debussy Etudes of 1915.

Paths to the future: two case studies

Although the much-discussed outbreak of 'modernism' in the years immediately following the nineteenth century was a real and momentous cultural fact, nevertheless life goes on and evidently the early twentieth century was more a period of transition than of overthrow, much as its vibrancy may lead any commentator to suggest that the leading composers born in the 1860s and 1870s gave European music a wake-up call to which it was still listening ardently a century later. We might say that our period had a sting in its tail; or even

27 T. Christensen, 'Four-Hand Piano Transcription and Geographies of Nineteenth-Century Musical Reception', *Journal of the American Musicological Society*, 52 (1999), p. 290.

indulge in the more fanciful notion that the 1800s, which saw the poetic culti-vation – especially in Heine's work early in the century – of the 'dramatic rever-sal' as closure, formed an age that was itself to undergo a closing reversal rather than fading quietly into the next (as Classical music has often been described as merging into the Romantic).

Perhaps inevitably, the paths to the future laid down in the final years of the 'Romantic' century have tended to be seen principally as those which concern tonality. Thus for example in introducing a history of tonal expansion and ato-nality in early post-Romantic Western music Samson concentrates without ceremony on 'Tonality: its Expansion and Reinterpretation'.[28] On the one hand, there is no doubt that 'tonality' was a vibrant issue to composers of the late nineteenth century, and it is certainly possible, perhaps vital, to write one kind of history of the music of this period with a concentration on tonality as the focus of musical 'language'. On the other hand, many composers knew that the die was cast. The foundations for a radicalisation of tonal musical language had been laid well before the birth of the canonical composers of the late Romantic period. This chronology is not specific to chamber and piano music, the one being a relatively conservative medium perhaps, and the other, as we have not hidden, being susceptible to populist exploitation. Yet the chronology is fundamental to our historical interpretation and, it might be claimed, not sufficiently transparent in the general literature on Romantic music. Simms, discussing Liszt's attitude to tonal language, reminds us in a startling way how early on it was that the seeds of 'expansion and reinterpretation' were sown:

> Throughout his life Liszt maintained a keen interest in ways by which tradi-tional tonality could be expanded or reinterpreted. His imagination was fired by lectures given in Paris in 1832 by the Belgian theoretician François-Joseph Fétis (1784–1871), who spoke of a forthcoming 'omnitonic' era in music history. A work of this period, Fétis theorized, would not be governed by a single key; tonality would instead fluctuate freely among keys linked by dimin-ished chords.[29]

The 'forthcoming' era was certainly imminent.[30] As Abraham describes Wagner's progress, 'it was only natural that a composer who had so accus-tomed himself to chromatic idioms in 1845 [the year of the première of *Tannhäuser*] should have arrived at the musical language of *Tristan* a dozen years later'.[31] Composers were willing to abandon key signatures (for example

28 J. Samson, *Music in Transition: A Study of Tonal Expansion and Atonality 1900–1920* (Oxford, 2nd edn 1993), pp. 1–55.

29 B. Simms, *Music of the Twentieth Century: Style and Structure* (New York, 1986), p. 20.

30 See also T. Christensen, 'Fétis and Emerging Tonal Consciousness', in I. Bent (ed.), *Music Theory in the Age of Romanticism* (Cambridge, 1996), pp. 37–56.

31 G. Abraham, *A Hundred Years of Music* (London, 4th edn 1974), p. 96

Musorgsky's master opera *Boris Godunov*, the first version of which was drafted in 1869), or to abandon the very purpose of key signatures (Liszt's sketch of a piece called *Bagatelle sans tonalité* – 'Bagatelle Without Tonality' – in 1885). It is important to keep this chronology in clear focus as we assess the actual close of the nineteenth century, which has been repeatedly colonised by historians of what used to be called 'modern', twentieth-century music, who have tended to seek proximate historical explanations – a direct and immediate ancestry – for the dissolution of major–minor tonality in the works of Second Viennese and many subsequent composers that set in decisively in 1907–8. The spin they imposed in this historical explanation does tend to marginalise the inherent, multi-dimensional experimentalism that, far from creeping up on the closing decades of nineteenth-century music, was of its essence. So it is not just a matter of key signatures and so on. Let us not forget that one of Chopin's earliest complete compositions, the Piano Sonata No. 1, Op. 4, of 1828, has a slow movement with a $\frac{5}{4}$ time-signature; or that for example from the point of view of virtually unprecedented musical form, within the next few years Schumann was building large cycles for piano out of fragmentary miniatures (not only *Carnaval* as mentioned above, but masterpieces such as the *Davidsbündlertänze* and *Kreisleriana*). In summary:

> The radical differences in style between Schumann and Haydn, Wagner and Mozart, Brahms and Beethoven . . . represent more than matters of mere surface, of emotion becoming more urgent and intense as form became freer and tone colour richer. Romantic music remained tonal, but it became more chromatic, more willing to give priority to melodic structural processes; it remained periodic, but phrase structure became less consistently regular; symphonies, sonatas and string quartets continued to be composed, but the emphasis was increasingly illustrative, the stimulus (however vaguely) increasingly extra-musical. These were the distinctive features of musical Romanticism, and it is perhaps the ultimate indication of that music's tendency to feel rather than think – at least initially – that it should so often seem, to the rational, inquiring mind, confused about its own status . . . uncertain how far its priorities could convincingly be more poetic than abstract, more organic than mosaic, more melodic than harmonic in origin.[32]

Not only does Whittall's conspectus point us to the inherently disintegrative spirit of Romantic music, but it also serves as an intriguing *pro*spectus, for if this is the nature of composition of the period, then presumably these are just the features we should be assessing in particular works. For better or worse, two masterpieces of late Romanticism are chosen here for more detailed attention. Each in a different way betrays our plot. The one,

---

32 Whittall, *Romantic Music*, pp. 13–14.

Debussy's virtuosic piano piece *L'isle joyeuse* of 1904, threatens to do this because it falls, literally if only just, outside the nineteenth century, though it is clearly *fin-de-siècle* music, music that grew out of the 1880s and 1890s, that could not conceivably have been composed much before then, and that could justifiably be taken – of the Debussy who was at just the period of his most radical compositional developments – to be somewhat old-fashioned. As an early commentator recorded, 'the *Masques* [1904] and *L'Isle joyeuse* seem to belong to an antecedent period: to that of the *Suite bergamasque* [1890] rather than to that of the *Estampes* [1903]'.[33] The other, Schoenberg's string sextet *Verklärte Nacht* of 1899, is similarly challenging in this context because, although it is chronologically convenient, it strains at the very concept of chamber music, and has been heard more often in Schoenberg's version for string orchestra, and, as Abraham almost casually mentioned, 'though chamber music, is a symphonic poem in one movement'.[34] Nevertheless, there is much to be learned from taking on these challenges, and the music is so accessible and of such abiding popularity – to date at least – that if these works are not necessarily an obvious choice, they can nevertheless prove to be a worthwhile one.

From the point of view of the musical specialist the apposition of Debussy and Schoenberg suggests, if not sparks of conflict such as there certainly were between Schoenberg and Strauss, Schoenberg and Stravinsky, and Schoenberg and quite a few other creative minds of his time, then some kind of mutual indifference. Schoenberg, although eventually an admirer of Debussy, probably knew little of his music in 1899 and, from what we can glean from his scant early biography and from tracing back the lines that must have led to his known tastes in the 1910s and 1920s, was not particularly interested in non-German music. Debussy was considerably more vociferous in his xenophobia, subscribing persistently and bitterly to the late Romantic climate of open Parisian hostility to all things German. We can read such breathtaking sentiments – as they may seem today – in a retrospective commentary from 1919 that, a year after Debussy's death, compares 'French Music and German Music':

> In the vast musical agitation which has been seething from one end of Europe to the other for the past forty years, what does the original contribution of Germany amount to, if we compare it to the new impressions, the wealth of originality, the substantial provision for our musical enjoyment that have been and are being furnished by the Russian and French schools, by the Scandinavians from Grieg to Sibelius, by the Spaniards from Albeniz to Turina,

---

33 G. Gatti, 'The Piano Works of Claude Debussy', *The Musical Quarterly*, 7 (1921), p. 429.
34 Abraham, *A Hundred Years of Music*, p. 221

Granados and Falla, and by the young Hungarian School with Bartók and Kodaly?[35]

It is not only a matter of indifference, but of distinct intent, for whereas *L'isle joyeuse* is a light and entertaining piece, for all its undoubted technical brilliance and 'symphonic breadth',[36] *Verklärte Nacht* is in every sense fearsomely serious – it is long, complex, heady in its narrative (of which more below) and in the musical demands it makes on even the most sympathetic listener (which can be greatly exaggerated of course – famously, Schoenberg mentioned how 'a Viennese society refused the first performance of my String Sextet . . . because of the "revolutionary" use of one – that is *one* single uncatalogued disso-nance'[37]). Tectonic diffusions, in the age of what Whittall goes so far as to call the 'confused' (see above, p. 514), are, let it be said, endemic to late Romanticism. If there is one overarching point to be made in this chapter it is this: no case of radical contrast can be called a special case; and 'the withdrawal from consensual languages' that Butler finds to be the driving force of 'early modernism' in general[38] is something that one might also see as an entrenched feature of the preceding era – another feature that is being proposed here as 'not sufficiently transparent in the general literature' (see above, p. 513).

There is always, however, synchronicity. Synchronicities are the stock-in-trade of any student of any period, but have recently been a significant fashion in so-called New Musicology; see for example Kramer's research in which pairings such as Beethoven and Wordsworth, or Chopin and Shelley, are investigated with an astonishing commitment to the idea of *Zeitgeist*[39] – an idea that, appropriately enough, the *OED* dates from 1884 (the term 'New Musicology' may have first been used in 1991 by Jean-Jacques Nattiez[40]). The synchronicities of Debussy's island and Schoenberg's night are many. First, for example, these are both works of significant non-musical impulse. Debussy's inspiration was – it has always been assumed – a painting by Watteau, *L'embarquement pour Cythère*, one of three images of this courtly festival he painted between 1710 and 1717, images repre-senting impossible dreams and fantasies buried in the mists of Classical Greece. A passion for the secrets of antiquity was a continual thread in Debussy's creative musings, which consisted of at least as many abandoned projects as there are fin-ished works. 'The enchantment of the "land of love"', writes Schmitz,

---

35 G. Jean-Aubry, *French Music of To-Day*, trans. E. Evans, pref. G. Fauré (New York, 1919; repr. 1976), p. 11.

36 S. Tresize, *Debussy: La mer* (Cambridge, 1994), p. 9.

37 A. Schoenberg, *Style and Idea*, ed. L. Stein (London, 1975), pp. 131–2.

38 C. Butler, *Early Modernism: Literature, Music, and Painting in Europe, 1900–1916* (Oxford, 1994), pp. 4–14.

39 L. Kramer, *Music and Poetry: The Nineteenth Century and After* (Berkeley and Los Angeles, 1984).

40 See D. Puffett, 'Editorial: In Defence of Formalism', *Music Analysis*, 13 (1994), p. 3.

pervades the music, culminating into triumphant dance rhythms, a glorious fanfare in honor of [Venus]. It is veritably the isle of joy and its homage to the Deity of Love never becomes dulled by even the slightest shade of morbidity – Cythère, one must remember, is not an island on the Rhine permeated by legends of the Nibelungen![41]

This Cythère is a site of what Tresize, writing of the kinship between *L'isle joyeuse* and Debussy's large orchestral piece *La mer* (1905), calls an 'ecstatic lyricism',[42] with its generic building blocks: a Spanish-style serenade (from bar 8), a slow, undulating waltz (from bar 61), a whole-tone-based 'development' section from bar 99 that in its right-hand figurations has something of the typical Romantic étude about it, merging into a developed reprise (from bar 160) cast in a rapid triple time that refers perhaps to the 'gigue' archetype and is punctuated by a cascade (bars 182–5) picking up material from the opening (which is marked 'quasi una cadenza'), and culminating in the final grand waltz from bar 220.

Schoenberg too is inspired by love, of a kind much closer, of course, to the Wagnerian. The 'programme' of *Verklärte Nacht* is Richard Dehmel's poem of that title from his collection of lyrics 'Weib und Welt' which had appeared in 1896, causing critical controversy because of its challenge to religious sensibilities and bourgeois values, including its smouldering eroticism. The sentiment that transfigures this night, however, is in fact a lofty, if highly idealised one, as a woman confesses to her lover that she is carrying another man's child, and the lover reassures her that through their love the child will become his own and embraces her. Dehmel, Schoenberg's senior by eleven years, wrote of themes that attracted the twenty-five-year-old composer – who also worked on at least three Dehmel song settings in 1899 – because of their harnessing of stark reality with a transcendental tone. Note that for all the differences between his stimulus and that of Debussy, we can certainly sense the spirit of the times in these works in their Romantic 'tendency to feel rather than think' (Whittall; see above, p. 514). The cerebral (but immaculate) Debussy of the 1915 *Etudes*, say, or the tortured and, some have thought, even tortuous Schoenberg of the 1908 Second String Quartet, Op. 10, were to be part of an as yet unsuspected scenario.

If we are convinced that there really is synchronicity in the 'significant non-musical impulse' mentioned above as a hallmark of each of these works, we may find it too in the lightness of touch with which the world of music and the world of ideas are connected by Debussy and Schoenberg. The literalism of earlier Romantic music (for example one can point to the poetic epithets

41 E. Schmitz, *The Piano Works of Claude Debussy* (New York, 1966; original edn 1950), p. 94.
42 Tresize, *Debussy: La mer*, p. 9.

attached to some of Brahms's piano works, a practice that he abandoned later in his career; or, to go outside the generic brief here for a moment, the highly specific programme of Berlioz's 1830 *Symphonie fantastique*) would now be inappropriate to the generalised late Romantic taste for allusion, implication and, of course, 'impression'. One cannot but be struck by how commentators on *L'isle joyeuse* and *Verklärte Nacht* over the ensuing century or so, even if they were to indulge in the kind of nationalistic hate-history seen above in Jean-Aubry (p. 515–16), unite in their easy acceptance of a relaxed link between impulse and musical result. Reminding us of the heady early days when E. T. A. Hoffman had explained to his captivated readers how Beethoven had emancipated instrumental music from the hegemony of the word (but bearing in mind that this was the Beethoven who in the Ninth Symphony offered a model for how the nineteenth century and beyond would try to unite word and music), and as was philosophised so decisively by Hanslick in *On the Beautiful in Music* of 1854, in late Romantic music, as much in chamber works and the piano repertory as in other instrumental music, pure musical language reasserts itself, ready for the radical modernisation of the 'as yet unsuspected scenario' (see above, p. 517).[43] No surprise that in writing about *Verklärte Nacht* in 1921 Schoenberg's star pupil Egon Wellesz mentioned how 'the present generation has quite rightly turned against external description in programme-music'.[44]

Secondly in this account of synchronicity, it is clear that both *L'isle joyeuse* and *Verklärte Nacht* are able to maintain their musical integrity independently of painting or poem because they draw on the formal resources of late Romantic compositional technique – which is another way in which 'musical language reasserts itself'. In contemporaneous spirit, they are both single-movement pieces, demonstrating the morphology of Romantic form in that both are kinds of disguised sonata form, *L'isle joyeuse* having what Schmitz describes – stretching terminology as is appropriate to Debussy's advanced, almost permutational approach to musical continuity – as a 'condensed and varied recapitulation [bars 189–245]'.[45] Schoenberg's larger canvas offers five continuous 'movements' that more or less do what a Beethoven sonata or, say, a Dvořák Serenade might do, involving organic thematic recurrence and metamorphosis, and, as Samson rightly indicates,[46] tonal coherence and balance: the brooding, slow introduction representing Dehmel's scene-setting will reappear, inevitably transformed, for the middle stanza which returns to third-person narrative ('She walks stiffly onwards . . . her dark face bathed in

43 E. Hanslick, *On the Musically Beautiful: A Contribution towards the Revision of the Aesthetics of Music*, trans. G. Payzant (Indianapolis, 1986; original edn 1854).

44 E. Wellesz, *Arnold Schoenberg: The Formative Years* (London, 1971; original edn 1921), p. 72.

45 Schmitz, *The Piano Works of Claude Debussy*, p. 85.   46 Samson, *Music in Transition*, p. 101.

moonlight'; for the musically equivalent passages see the Dreililien edition, from bar 14 of letter K). This device of varied reprise binds together the entire structure, linking forward to the further transformed fifth section (letter U) where the two lovers embrace and 'go forth into the bright night'. Now, looking briefly at the development and structural role of the first theme alone might give the impression that Schoenberg is imitating the 'thematic recall' he learned from the Schubert 'Wanderer' Fantasy, from many works of Liszt, from Brahms's First Symphony and so on. Thematic recall was a commonplace of Romantic music. But what we see in *Verklärte Nacht* is a comprehensive integration of themes and motifs over five movements forming a giant 'movement', still within the Romantic idiom of tonality in an extended structure.[47] Thus we can judge this work to be a valedictory triumph of Romantic music, as Wellesz eloquently conveys:

> However closely Schönberg has here followed the course of the poem, his unusually strongly developed architectonic sense prevented him from letting the form lapse into a fantasy. There is certainly an excess of climax in the sextet, but that is attributable rather to Schönberg's exuberant fancy, which had so much to say; yet he never loses himself in mere externals, and the description of Nature is never an end in itself. Everything is seen and shaped from a central point. The present generation has quite rightly turned against external description in programme-music. This phase was necessary in order to bring forth the full beauty of orchestral tone, but this aim having been achieved it lost its justification. In both cases, while Schönberg has made use of the poetic outline, he has so conceived the things from within, that the music is fully justified, even if one does not know the 'programme'.[48]

Thus, having begun by concentrating on the thoughts on late Romantic piano music of a very British (albeit Irish) establishment figure, we close with the wise words of a member of the continental-European elite on one of the very last, one of the greatest and one of the most portentous chamber compositions of the period, when Christensen's 'etherialisation' (see above, p. 512) may be said to have found its final mark in the nineteenth century.

Bibliography

Abraham, G., *A Hundred Years of Music*. London, 4th edn 1974
Allen, W. D., *Philosophies of Music History: A Study of General Histories of Music 1600–1960*. New York, 1962
Altmann, W., *Kammermusik-Katalog: Ein Verzeichnis von seit 1841 veröffentlichten Kammermusikwerken*. Hofheim, 1910 and 1967; reprint of 6th edn, ed. J. Richter, 1944

---

47 See the tonal summary in Samson, *ibid*. See also R. Swift, '1/XII/99: Tonal Relations in Schoenberg's *Verklärte Nacht*', *19th Century Music*, 1 (1977), pp. 3–14.
48 Wellesz, *Arnold Schoenberg*, p. 72.

Butler, C., *Early Modernism: Literature, Music, and Painting in Europe, 1900–1916*. Oxford, 1994

Christensen, T., 'Fétis and Emerging Tonal Consciousness'. In I. Bent (ed.), *Music Theory in the Age of Romanticism*. Cambridge, 1996, pp. 37–56

'Four Hand Piano Transcription and Geographies of Nineteenth-Century Musical Reception'. *Journal of the American Musicological Society*, 52 (1999), pp. 255–98

Dahlhaus, C., *Between Romanticism and Modernism: Four Studies in the Music of the Later Nineteenth Century*, trans. M. Whittall. Cambridge, 1989; original edn 1974

Darnton, C., *You and Music*. Harmondsworth, 2nd edn 1945

Debussy, C., 'Monsieur Croche the Dilettante Hater'. In *Three Classics in the Aesthetics of Music*. New York, 1962; original edn 1921 from journal articles 1901–5, pp. 1–71

Dunhill, T., *Chamber Music: A Treatise for Students*. London, 1913

Dunsby, J., *Performing Music: Shared Concerns*. Oxford, 1995

Gatti, G., 'The Piano Works of Claude Debussy'. *The Musical Quarterly*, 7 (1921), pp. 418–60

Grout, D. J. and Palisca, C. V., *A History of Western Music*. London, 4th edn 1988

Hanslick, E., *On the Musically Beautiful: A Contribution towards the Revision of the Aesthetics of Music*, trans. G. Payzant. Indianapolis, 1986; original edn 1854

'Brahms's Newest Compositions'. In W. Frisch (ed.), *Brahms and His World*. Princeton, 1990, pp. 145–50; original edn 1889, *Die Moderne Oper, Part V*

Hutcheson, E., *The Literature of the Piano: A Guide for Amateur and Student*. London, 2nd edn rev. R. Ganz, 1969

Jean-Aubry, G., *French Music of To-day*, trans. E. Evans, pref. G. Fauré. New York, 1919; repr. 1976

Kramer, L., *Music and Poetry: The Nineteenth Century and After*. Berkeley and Los Angeles, 1984

Longyear. R., *Nineteenth-Century Romanticism in Music*. Englewood Cliffs, 2nd edn 1973

Musgrave, M., 'Brahms and England'. In M. Musgrave (ed.), *Brahms 2: Biographical, Documentary and Analytical Studies*. Cambridge, 1987, pp. 1–20

Palisca, C. V. (ed.), *Norton Anthology of Western Music*. New York, 1996

Pascall, R., 'Major Instrumental Forms: 1850–1890'. In G. Abraham (ed.), *The New Oxford History of Music IX: Romanticism (1830–1890)*. Oxford, 1990, pp. 534–658

Plantinga, L., *Romantic Music: A History of Musical Style in Nineteenth-Century Europe*. New York, 1984

Puffett, D., 'Editorial: In Defence of Formalism'. *Music Analysis*, 13 (1994), pp. 3–5

Raynor, H., *Music and Society since 1815*. London, 1976

Samson, J., *Music in Transition: A Study of Tonal Expansion and Atonality: 1900–1920*. Oxford, 2nd edn 1993

Schmitz, E., *The Piano Works of Claude Debussy*. New York, 1966; original edn 1950

Schoenberg, A., *Style and Idea*, ed. L. Stein. London, 1975

Theory of Harmony, trans. R. Carter. London, 1978

Shaw, G. B., *London Music in 1888–89 as Heard by Corno di Bassetto (Later Known as Bernard Shaw) with Some Further Autobiographical Particulars*. New York, 1973; original edn 1937

Simms, B., *Music of the Twentieth Century: Style and Structure*. New York, 1986

Stanford, C. V., *Pages From an Unwritten Diary*. London, 1914

Swift, R., '1/XII/99: Tonal Relations in Schoenberg's *Verklärte Nacht'*. *19th Century Music*, 1 (1977), pp. 3-14

Treitler, L., 'The Historiography of Music: Issues of Past and Present'. In N. Cook and M. Everist (eds.), *Rethinking Music*. Oxford, 1999, pp. 356-77

Tresize, S., *Debussy: La mer*. Cambridge, 1994

Wellesz, E., *Arnold Schoenberg: The Formative Years*. London, 1971; original edn 1921

Whittall, A., *Romantic Music: A Concise History from Schubert to Sibelius*. London, 1987

18

Choral culture and the regeneration of the organ

JOHN BUTT

Most historical accounts of European choral movements in the nineteenth century note a certain loss of intensity and idealistic purpose after the revolutions of 1848. Central to the constellation of possible reasons may be the expansion and liberalisation of economies leading to greater mass production and an increasing division of labour. With an enormous growth in musical consumption and participation in massed singing a dilution in the idealistic zeal displayed by the first amateur choral groups was all but inevitable. The changes in musical production were equally predictable with an increasing distinction between the amateur and the professional that may have resulted in some decline in the musical capabilities of the former.[1] Dahlhaus relates the withering of the seemingly holistic combination of conviviality, educative purpose and bourgeois self-display to the increasing polarisation of the public and private spheres; audiences became an anonymous, cosmopolitan public who no longer fully shared the social brotherhood of the amateur singers.[2] Steady economic growth contributed to a sense of hedonism rather than idealism in some places, such as Napoleon III's France, but also to more authoritarian, centralising regimes. It was not unknown for choral establishments to be subject to police observation and many inevitably swapped their idealism for a more reactionary stance.[3] On the other hand, the very fact that some musical institutions provoked official surveillance suggests that they must have retained some of their radical elements.

Even more palpable than the political transformations was the new scientific climate. The latter half of the century saw not only enormous technological advances in the wake of industrialisation and an increasingly dispassionate empiricism, but also a concomitant positivistic attitude in the arts that spawned numerous collected editions and catalogues of composers' works. This inevitably interacted with an invigorated historicist sense that either

---

1 L. Botstein, 'Listening through Reading: Musical Literacy and the Concert Audience', *19th Century Music*, 16 (1992–3), pp. 129–45.
2 C. Dahlhaus, *Nineteenth-Century Music*, trans. J. B. Robinson (Berkeley and Los Angeles, 1989), p. 174.
3 J. Deathridge, 'Germany: The "Special Path"', in J. Samson (ed.), *The Late Romantic Era* (Englewood Cliffs, 1991), pp. 57–9.

embraced the chimera of understanding and re-creating the past exactly as it had been or saw every element of the past as a necessary evolutionary step towards a more perfect present. The scientific climate posed a threat to religion redoubling that of the Enlightenment years; indeed, the various religious revivals must be viewed against the background of a society in which atheism was a real possibility for an unprecedented number of people. But many of the revivals themselves embraced something of the new positivism and historicism in their painstaking reconstruction of ancient repertories and liturgies.

It is already clear that this seemingly reactionary age was not without its benefits for musical culture. With the new notion of musical classics and a repertory of earlier music to rediscover, music, in effect, experienced its renaissance in a way it could not have done some four centuries before, and only now were there the necessary scientific tools to turn fragments of the musical past into viable works. Moreover, the sheer scale of musical consumption and musical organisations was unprecedented. The number of singing societies in Germany eclipsed that of the earlier part of the century.[4] Britain, as the leading industrialised nation, became one of the largest markets for music and could promote amateur choral performance on an unprecedented scale. Handel still provided the focal point for massed vocal performance, and, at the centennial commemoration of 1859, two of his oratorios were performed at the Crystal Palace with a chorus numbering 2,700 and an audience of over 81,000. The Handel festivals continued as triennial events and reached a numerical peak in the 1880s with a chorus of 4,000.[5] Donald Burrows goes on to observe that such achievements as this would not have been possible without the development of excellent teaching systems from the 1840s onwards and the spread of the choral culture throughout the country (important centres being Manchester, Leeds and Birmingham).

The success of mass musical culture in England was of considerable influence in France too, during the latter part of the century. Spain – Catalonia in particular – experienced its first amateur choral establishments after 1850, partly through the educational zeal of Anselmo Clavé and through a renewed interest in the indigenous folksong culture. By the 1860s choral festivals could involve several thousand singers. As modernisation and the massed organised choral culture of bourgeois society spread eastwards, national folksong repertories became important in Central and Eastern Europe as a means of preserving a distance from German culture. America's growing choral culture was directly

4 *Ibid.*, p. 56; C.-H. Mahling, 'Berlin: "Music in the Air"', in A. Ringer (ed.), *The Early Romantic Era* (Englewood Cliffs, 1990), p. 121; Botstein, 'Listening through Reading'; C. Hopkins Porter, 'The New Public and the Reordering of the Musical Establishment: The Lower Rhine Music Festivals, 1818-67', *19th Century Music*, 3 (1979-80), pp. 211-24.

5 D. Burrows, 'Victorian England: An Age of Expansion', in J. Samson (ed.), *The Late Romantic Era*, p. 277.

related to educational reforms and the adoption of music in public school curricula;[6] Lowell Mason's pedagogical systems were particularly efficient in facilitating the participation of a large cross-section of American society in choral performance.

Not only does the tremendous growth in scale suggest that choral culture in the latter half of the century could hardly have lost all of its impetus, but also that it could be a rich arena for compositional achievement. Indeed, as suggested in chapter 8, compositional innovation was not necessarily a desirable goal during the more politically active phase of the choral movement; verbal content and generic consistency were far more at a premium than the ideology of absolute music. Crudely put, the idealistic culture of the earlier Romantic era engendered a more conservative choral style while the more realist and politically conservative climate after the mid-century at least allowed for a bolder musical idiom. But, as Dahlhaus suggests with his analysis of secular choral works by Brahms, Berlioz and Bruch, composers continued to write music that not only anticipated the listener's detailed acquaintance with the literary content, but also presupposed that such literary breeding would make allowances for any lacunae in dramatic and musical logic or consistency (Dahlhaus, pp. 166–8).

Major composers were more likely than not to write choral music (whether sacred or secular) at some point in their careers: Liszt, Bruckner, Brahms and Mahler in Germany and Austria; Gounod, Franck, Saint-Saëns, Fauré and even Debussy in France; Dvořák in Bohemia; most Russian composers from Glinka to Rachmaninov; and Rossini, Verdi and Puccini in Italy. Virtually all English composers worked in the choral field but English festivals and choral institutions were particularly extravagant commissioners of choral music from abroad: Dvořák provided *The Spectre's Bride* and the Requiem for the Birmingham Festivals in 1885 and 1891 and *St Ludmilla* for the Leeds Festival of 1886. The Birmingham Festival also commissioned two of Gounod's later works, *La Rédemption* (1882) and *Mors et vita* (1885). Only with Elgar's oratorios at the turn of the twentieth century was there native music that could equal or better that commissioned from abroad.

Restoring tradition in music and liturgical practice

What makes the history of the nineteenth century particularly complex is the survival of pre-aesthetic values in areas such as church music and the fact that many of the restorations in both compositional and liturgical practice were

6 C. Hamm, 'The USA: Classical, Industrial and Invisible Music', in J. Samson (ed.), *The Late Romantic Era*, pp. 300–1.

openly defiant towards the imperatives of originality and aesthetic separability. Nevertheless, Dahlhaus is doubtless correct in observing that none of the restorations could be completely immune to prevailing attitudes: church choirs were often refounded along the lines of bourgeois oratorio societies, and even seemingly literal transplantations of earlier church music into the contemporary setting were often governed by bourgeois categories of edification and noble simplicity (Dahlhaus, pp. 180–6).

The increasing interest in restoring earlier repertories and traditions was partly a reaction to the destructive results of revolution and partly a nostalgia for the presumed stability of the past. This was particularly the case in France which underwent a continual string of political restorations and revolutions and where the destruction of institutions and artefacts had happened in such a rapid and 'unnatural' way. The first French restoration of Christian worship and its associated music came with Napoleon in 1801. However, despite the extravagant occasional works of Cherubini, Le Sueur and Berlioz which capitalised on the grandeur of revolutionary genres, the general practice of church music consisted of a debased chant repertory with serpent accompaniment and a motet style derived from popular operatic genres.[7] Choron's attempts at restoring older repertoires of chant and motets have already been mentioned (chapter 8) and the Bach revival began in France with the efforts of Boëly. The latter was also instrumental in restoring works from the French Baroque, a movement that came into its own after France's defeat in the Franco-Prussian war (1870) and which involved such major figures as Saint-Saëns and D'Indy. But the most significant musical restoration in France, if not the whole of Europe, was that of the Gregorian plainchant repertory by the monks of Solesmes. This brought a standard of textual scholarship to the production of its scholarly editions that was largely unmatched even by the collected editions so ubiquitous in the latter half of the century. But it was simultaneously a restoration of performing practice and, most importantly, of the liturgical context of monastic life; in short, it was a restoration on a scale that was possible in no other area of music.

Katherine Bergeron begins her exquisitely perceptive study of the Solesmes revival with a consideration of the disorientation felt by figures who had witnessed the destruction and desecration of churches and other religious buildings throughout France. Chateaubriand compared the historicist delight experienced in beholding ruins caused by the natural effects of time with the horror of contemplating ruins created in a single moment of revolutionary vandalism. Soon new government agencies were charged with overseeing the

---

7 R. P. Locke, 'Paris: Centre of Intellectual Ferment', in A. Ringer (ed.), *The Early Romantic Era*, p. 59.

national heritage, culminating in Viollet-le-Duc's ambitious project to restore Notre Dame in Paris (begun in 1844). This was nothing less than an attempt to reconstruct – in an ideal sense – the entire history of the building, to re-establish it as something that showed the 'natural' and leisurely progress of time, with a multiplicity of layers and styles. Viollet-le-Duc had a very urgent sense of the accelerating advances in modern technology and saw the reclaiming of history, a sense of historical depth and the meticulous cataloguing of individual styles as the means of balancing the vertiginous vista of the future; in other words, this sort of historicism was an archetypally modern conception. However, Prosper Guéranger, soon to be founder of the Solesmes community, noted that the restoration of Notre Dame was a sterile project without a concomitant restoration of the liturgy and the music that gave churches their vitality.[8]

The intimate connection between the Solesmes project and the restoration of ecclesiastical buildings in France (including the ambitious rebuilding of Solesmes itself) shares something with other musical restorations, revivals and renewals: A. B. Marx related Mendelssohn's revival of the *St Matthew Passion* in 1829 to Goethe's celebrated discovery of gothic art in his encounter with Strasbourg Cathedral,[9] Liszt wrote a new Mass to celebrate the restoration of Gran Cathedral in 1855 (ruined by Turkish attacks) and Proske relates his new series of publications of Italian Renaissance polyphony to the belated recognition of earlier buildings and paintings.[10] The revolutionary age exposed the vulnerability of ancient buildings and the threat to one's 'historicity' – that sense of being situated in a cultural tradition. Reciprocally, the recovery of forgotten repertories and the regeneration of ancient genres was a potent way of giving the past a semblance of life, since actual performance achieved an immanence that even architectural restoration could not approach.

The gradual progress of the monks at Solesmes towards re-creating a past they had never known is in many ways a model for most subsequent forms of restoration of repertory and practice. The Solesmes monks sensed how new discoveries and knowledge of a wide range of religious practices could mutually inform one another in a sort of hermeneutic circle that influenced the direction of the next stage of enquiry. They were working to a scholarly standard by the 1860s, initially under the direction of Dom Joseph Pothier, and produced their first edition of chant – the *Liber Gradualis* – in 1883. When, in 1884, Pope Leo

8 K. Bergeron, *Decadent Enchantments: The Revival of Gregorian Chant at Solesmes* (Berkeley and Los Angeles, 1998), pp. 1–11.

9 M. Geck, *Die Wiederentdeckung der Matthäuspassion im 19. Jahrhundert*, Studien zur Musikgeschichte des 19 Jahrhunderts 9 (Regensburg, 1967), p. 66.

10 J. Garratt, 'Palestrina and the German Romantic Imagination: Interpreting Historicism in Nineteenth-Century Music', Ph.D. diss., University of Wales Cardiff (1999), p. 268.

XIII still refused to grant the Benedictines his privilege for the publication of chant (giving it again to Pustet in Regensburg), Dom André Mocquereau's proposed series of facsimiles of important sources of chant, *Paléographie musicale* (from 1889), became a way of tacitly proving the textual superiority of the Solesmes gradual (Bergeron, pp. 64–6). This undoubtedly gave the edition an authority it could have acquired by no other means, but it also raised the stakes in the standard and methodology of editing all kinds of music. The new technology of photography was now at the service of Mocquereau's ambition to recreate the 'truth' of chant within the walls of the monastery, and to put it into the hands of all people.

The conflict between the earlier conception of historical reconstruction undertaken by Pothier and the later approach of Mocquereau provides an extremely illuminating perspective of late nineteenth-century approaches to history: Bergeron suggests that Pothier represents a Romantic ideology while Mocquereau more the modern. Mocquereau saw his facsimile project as a democratisation of scholarship and a use of technology to provide future benefits, but Pothier objected, fearing that the collection would undermine the single authoritative text of his *Liber Gradualis*. The sense of wholeness of the earlier edition and, literally, the faith it implicitly demanded of its users, were being undermined by the secularising influence of science and a sense of ultimate uncertainty.

The final victory in the restoration of Gregorian chant and practice was, ironically, a pyrrhic one for the Solesmes community (which itself was exiled to the Isle of Wight in the face of yet another wave of anticlericalism in France). With a ruling in 1903, the new pope, Pius X, gave detailed directives on the appropriate music for church, re-establishing Gregorian chant as the staple diet of the liturgy. The following year he published an addendum that set in motion the publication of a Vatican 'typical edition' that would establish a universal text to be sanctioned throughout the Church. Ultimately, the pope defined this as the republication of Pothier's Gradual of 1895, thereby relegating Mocquereau's subsequent work and all future efforts by the Solesmes community to a 'free field' of research that would have no affect on the newly established tradition. The Church thus officially severed itself from the umbilical chord of scholarship and modernist historicism (Bergeron, pp. 143–61).

The pope's directives of 1903–4 also re-established the late Renaissance style of Palestrina as the model of church polyphony. This, like the Solesmes revival, represents the culmination of a decades-long revival of Palestrina's music, particularly in German-speaking lands, but also in Italy and France. The interest in Palestrina and his elevation as the supreme model for purity in polyphonic church music is perhaps a more complex phenomenon than first meets the eye.

First, there was a certain degree of continuity in the performance of Palestrina, especially in the Sistine Chapel where it was associated with a particular performing tradition allegedly stretching back to Palestrina's own time. Eighteenth-century performance of Palestrina was by no means uncommon, even in northern Catholic courts such as Dresden,[11] and the tradition survived into nineteenth-century Vienna. For composers, the pedagogical tradition stemming from Fux was ubiquitous in Catholic lands, but also had some influence on the Lutheran tradition through the teaching of Kirnberger. The Fuxian tradition was itself an eighteenth-century distillation and translation of late sixteenth-century rules which certainly had something to do with Palestrina but hardly represented a precise codification of his style.

However extensive the continuity of performance in Italy and Catholic German-speaking lands, Palestrina's music was largely associated with the penitential seasons of Advent and Lent, and thus did not provide the polyphonic staple for the entire year. Moreover, as James Garratt has demonstrated, the two writers who did most to promote the image of Palestrina as the model of noble simplicity – E. T. A. Hoffmann (1814) and Justus Thibaut (1825) – based their opinion on an extraordinarily slim knowledge of his works, reserving their highest praise for homophonic *Responsoria* attributed to Palestrina (but discovered to be by Ingegneri in 1898 – Garratt, pp. 69–74, 110–19). As Dahlhaus notes, not only the concept of 'noble simplicity' but also that of the edification that these writers saw in the music they believed to be Palestrina's are the specifically Romantic elements of the revival, elements that also increased the distance between the sacred and the profane and pushed church music closer towards the status of a 'ghetto' within the wider musical culture (Dahlhaus, pp. 181–2).

The knowledge of Palestrina and, indeed, other Italian and German composers of the early Baroque was greatly enhanced by the *Musica Sacra* series of publications begun in 1839 in Berlin (Garratt, p. 180). Furthermore, Palestrina and other 'old Italians' became the model for a regenerated church music in Prussia under the directives of the Kaiser and Freiherr von Bunsen, begun in 1840. Given that Prussia had been the seat of the amateur choral movement with the work of Zelter's Berlin Singakademie, it is interesting how much this reform of liturgical church music reproduced the values and ethos of the bourgeois institution. With the political success of Bismarck in the 1870s and a greater sense of the cultural difference between Protestant and Catholic areas of the new Germany, the Palestrina revival slowed down somewhat in Lutheran establishments. His style became more a Platonist model than a holy art for Lutherans

11 W. Horn, *Die Dresdner Hofkirchenmusik 1720–1745: Studien zu ihren Voraussetzungen und ihrem Repertoire* (Kassel, 1987).

who now took more specifically German, chorale-based, idioms as the basis for liturgical music (Garratt, pp. 246–8). Carl von Winterfeld's search for a German Palestrina had resulted not in the rehabilitation of Bach (or even Schütz) as the ideal for liturgical music but Eccard. Even Spitta's efforts on Bach's behalf, with a book of 1882, failed, largely because he was thinking more in terms of the aesthetic category of Classical models than of liturgical expediency.[12] Bach's time had truly come, but as an object of aesthetic contemplation in the concert hall; now the religions of concert life and liturgy were truly separated.

Garratt observes that in Catholic areas of Germany and in Austria, the Palestrina revival peaked somewhat later, although here there had been a more continuous performance tradition of Palestrina and works of other selected Italians (albeit in the penitential seasons). The aesthetic stance of 'noble purity' was initially taken over directly from the Protestant writings and some reform movements began relatively early in the century. In 1816 Caspar Ett, the Munich court organist, performed Allegri's *Miserere*, which became a redefining moment in South Germany, and he and the court Kapellmeister, J. K. Aiblinger, subsequently travelled to Italy to study sources of Italian polyphony. While Ett's work helped to consolidate a tradition that was already partly in place, the movement in Regensburg represented more a direct replacement of tradition by historical models. C. Proske was set in charge of improving music in Regensburg Cathedral and he spent much of the late 1830s copying new material in Rome. This resulted in Regensburg becoming a publishing centre for early liturgical music from 1841. Indeed, Proske's series *Musica divina* and *Selectus novus missarum* were most influential in creating the climate of historicist reform in the Catholic realm throughout the latter half of the century and also extended the use of the Palestrina style outside the penitential seasons (Garratt, pp. 256–72).

Many of these movements came together in the so-called 'Cecilian movement', which was consolidated with the founding of the Allgemeine Deutsche Cäcilien-Verein in 1868. This South German branch of the organisation began under the presidency of F. X. Witt (1834–88) and soon had a membership of several thousands. It set itself against most forms of modern music, providing guidelines on the music most suitable for liturgical use and promoting music as a medium of moral education; now the artist's calling required the same moral responsibility as that exhibited by the priest (Garratt, pp. 272–94, esp. p. 277). Its list of 'approved pieces' began in 1870 and the voting system used to determine the list seems to have placed the criterion of liturgical suitability above

---

12 Dahlhaus, *Nineteenth-Century Music*, pp. 182–3.

musical quality; all the music had to be 'objective' and subject to the rules of the Church (Garratt, pp. 331–4). The movement – soon comprising several societies in Bavaria and Austria – was increasingly connected politically with the move to establish a counterweight to the increasing domination of imperial Germany ruled from Berlin.

Witt himself became suspicious of the urge to imitate Palestrina directly and advocated the use of earlier models more as a way of regenerating contemporary compositional styles (Garratt, pp. 284–93). Other Cecilians advocated a stricter adherence to late Renaissance rules, most notably Michael Haller (1840–1915), whose skill in the imitation of Palestrina led him to complete missing voices in the new collected edition of the master's music that began in 1862. His own music represents perhaps the closest literal copy of Palestrina's style throughout the entire century; as Garratt has noted, his obituarist believed that he had achieved true progress within the Palestrinian style to the extent that some of his works surpassed those of the master himself (pp. 310–30, esp. p. 314). After the death of Witt the ACV became more rigid in its proscription of impure elements: even Liszt's *Missa Choralis* was removed from the list of approved pieces in 1890 for going beyond the limits of liturgical expression. Rather like the differences emerging between Pothier and Mocquereau in their work at Solesmes – the Romantic versus the modern – Witt and Haller perhaps represented the Romantic and positivistic sides of the Cecilian movement.

Composers and the religions of the later nineteenth century

A number of extremely prominent composers, who were not otherwise connected with the regular composition of church music, wrote significant large-scale settings of religious texts. Works such as the requiems of Berlioz and Verdi commemorated specific events and people: the death of an important general in the case of Berlioz, and the death of Rossini (for the Offertory) and of the writer Alessandro Manzoni (for the complete *Requiem*) for Verdi. To Dahlhaus, the idea of consecrating a major public event is symptomatic of the bourgeois tendency to turn to religion whenever something happens that demands an effort beyond the 'resources of everyday secular reality' (Dahlhaus, pp. 185–6). Perhaps there is thus a sense in which religious occasional music became part of the relatively modern category of the sublime.

Several composers seem to have shared the imperative of writing the most up-to-date or progressive music for a major public event. This is certainly the case with Liszt's two Masses for specific events – the 'Gran' Mass and the

Hungarian Coronation Mass – which draw heavily on his latest experiments in symphonic form. Verdi is entirely unsparing in employing the devices and expressive gestures of his operatic style in the *Requiem*. If 1874 was still too early for him to have experienced the full force of the growing purification of church music and the restoration of plainchant, it is debatable as to whether he would ever have taken such trends on board in what is so obviously a terrifying subjective vision.[13] The *Te Deum* published in 1898 obviously benefits from a consummate skill and experience in writing for multiple voices, yet any 'pure' or 'churchy' elements serve as a dramatic evocation of ecclesiastical practice rather than as a self-imposed stylistic austerity.

The following sections examine several composers and categories of composer who show a particular affinity with specific trends in religion, or with restorations of religion and religious music.

Liszt and the revolutionary restoration of religion

Liszt's early position on the restoration of religion and re-establishment of church music is unique in that he openly linked it to the revolutionary fervour of the age. His ideas were strongly influenced by Félicité de Lamennais who, more than anyone, tried to unite the various benefits brought by the Revolution into one religious vision; it was with him and his liberal republican bent that the restoration of religion could be separated from the restoration of the monarchy. As the leader of the 'ultramontanes', a party of liberal Christians in the 1830s, he tried to reforge the connections between the French church and Rome (although he was effectively ejected from the Church in 1834).[14] In his support for the restoration of the Roman liturgy he greatly influenced Prosper Guéranger, the founder of the Solesmes community.[15] But his ideas also inspired Liszt towards new composition, of a style and scale that had not so far been experienced in church music. His most articulate expression on the future of church music came in an article of 1834 ('On Future Church Music', published in the *Revue et Gazette musicale* in 1835): taking heart from the recent pledge to establish universal music education in France, Liszt calls for a regeneration of church music with music that 'we would baptize *humanitary*, must be *inspired, strong, and effective, uniting, in colossal proportions, theatre and church; at the same time dramatic and holy, splendid and simple, solemn and serious, fiery and unbridled, stormy and calm, clear and fervid'*. This music is to take *The Marseillaise* as its model and is to be composed for, taught to and sung by the people; all

13 J. Rosselli, 'Italy: The Decline of a Tradition', in J. Samson (ed.) *The Late Romantic Era*, pp. 138–40.
14 P. Merrick, *Revolution and Religion in the Music of Liszt* (Cambridge, 1987), pp. 15–16.
15 Bergeron, *Decadent Enchantments*, p. 11.

social divisions will disappear within the one great religious art of humanity (Merrick, pp. 19–20).

Liszt and Guéranger, at least before 1848, perhaps represented opposite ends of the spectrum of movements for the renewal of church music. While it is clear that Guéranger achieved his aim during the latter half of the century it is arguable as to what extent Liszt fulfilled his youthful ambitions. Paul Merrick is certainly right to suggest that the verbal prescription Liszt makes for the future music could be applied to some of the music he was eventually to write, but there is no sense in which Liszt's idealistic social aims for performance were ever realised. After the ultimate failure of the 1848 revolution in France and some ugly behaviour by the very people in whom he had placed so much hope, Liszt's sympathies came ever closer to Rome and the cultivation of his personal religious development within a conservative canonical Catholicism (Merrick, pp. 33–4). In the early 1860s, now relocated to Rome itself, Liszt referred to his aim to lead a natural life approaching his 'monastico-artistic ideal'. His aims thus became increasingly traditionalist and in many ways came closer to those of Guéranger himself: for a while Liszt aimed to provide chant for the entire Catholic world, together with his own harmonisations (Merrick, pp. 70, 89).

Merrick suggests that the model of Palestrina, at least as he was constructed in the Romantic imagination (largely through the 1828 biography of Giuseppe Baini) became increasingly important for Liszt during the 1860s. His most extended work in the style is the *Missa Choralis*, finished while he was a resident of the Vatican in 1865 (the year he took minor orders). Ironically, it seems that this, the most conservative and ascetic of Liszt's Masses, was never performed in the Sistine Chapel on account of its 'modernity' (Merrick, pp. 95–6, 122–3).

Liszt's original aims for the 'dramatic and holy' restoration of church music had been more clearly fulfilled in the Mass of 1855 commemorating the restoration of the Cathedral in Gran (Esztergom), the centre of the Catholic Church in Hungary. This building had been ruined, not by the anticlerical fervour of the revolution years, but by repeated Turkish attack some two centuries before. The renewal of such a Christian symbol in Liszt's own homeland must have had particular resonance for him. The work, often approaching the genre of symphonic poem, is Liszt's most opulent Mass setting. Its use of recurring themes has drawn comparisons with Liszt's own B minor Piano Sonata, *Faust Symphony* and Piano Concerto in E flat together with cyclic works of Schumann and Berlioz.[16]

The genre of oratorio gave Liszt considerably more leeway to write supremely religious music with many of the expressive devices offered by opera

16 Dahlhaus, *Nineteenth-Century Music*, pp. 187–8.

and instrumental music. The *Legend of St Elizabeth* (1857–62) is based on the life of the thirteenth-century Hungarian princess. Elizabeth's work for the poor was the main attribute of her saintliness before the miraculous happening, so she made an obvious subject for the social side of Liszt's religious programme. Liszt could not only make use of programmatic themes (uniquely listed by him in the score) and thematic transformation, but also achieve a generic and stylistic mix that ranged from the most operatic style (in the diabolical depiction of Elizabeth's mother-in-law) to elements of plainchant and folk melody.

Liszt's increasing interest in the restoration of chant and the 'noble simplicity' of Palestrina is more evident in his second oratorio, *Christus*, which was perhaps the most protracted of his religious projects (1853–68). Much of the texture is closer to the *Missa Choralis* than the more symphonic works and Christ's divinity calls forth a more static, liturgically based approach to form. Indeed, parts of the work were performed alone during the gestation of the work and some movements could be abstracted for liturgical use. More 'modern' elements include the whole-tone storm scene and the deeply chromatic portrayal of Christ's agony at the opening of the third part.

Brahms and the personal definition of religion

Of all the composers writing significant amounts of religious music in the latter half of the nineteenth century, Brahms is unusual in never having been associated with a religious foundation. He had perhaps the keenest interest in works of the Renaissance and Baroque, yet for the most 'modern' of reasons: the cultivation of a sense of historical identity and depth as a composer and a belief in the social value of communal singing. Both of these carry with them implications for the religious nature of bourgeois art which in turn inflect the religious content of the works performed.

Brahms's activity as a choral conductor ranges from the men's chorus he conducted as a teenager, the women's choir in Hamburg, the mixed choral societies at the court of Detmold, and, finally the Vienna Singakademie and the Musikverein of the Gesellschaft der Musikfreunde 1872–5. He wrote an astonishingly wide range of choral music, ranging from the early 'Ave Maria', Op. 12, for female voices to the late motets Op. 110, and, on the secular side, *Rinaldo*, Op. 50, for male voices and tenor soloist, the *Alto Rhapsodie*, Op. 53, and numerous partsongs and folksong arrangements. The repertory of early music that he performed ranges from Isaac, Gallus, Lassus and Palestrina through Gabrieli, Praetorius, Eccard and Schütz to Bach and Handel.[17] Just as his interest in

---

17 V. Hancock, 'Brahms's Performances of Early Choral Music', *19th Century Music*, 8 (1984), pp. 126–7.

history was fostered within the 'modern' institution of the amateur chorus his
work on early church music, particularly of the German Renaissance, came
through a modern patriotic concern for folksong and its historical roots.[18]
Other routes into early music included his desire to give historical depth to his
growing knowledge of Bach, such as his interest in the secular song by Hassler
that eventually became the most important chorale in the *St Matthew Passion*.
Then there was the personal relationship with the Schumanns: during Robert's
illness Brahms spent much time studying and copying both folksongs and chorales from Schumann's library (Hancock, p. 97).

  Rather than taking the past as a matter of poetic inspiration, as did
Schumann, Brahms saw it as something more to be understood on its own
terms, thus becoming a model and challenge for his own creativity. In this
respect, he seems to reflect the change in historical consciousness after the mid-
century, a change that could lead to much stale antiquarianism but that,
through a peculiar form of the anxiety of influence, produced astonishing
results in Brahms's case. His self-education is most graphically depicted in the
'counterpoint exchange' with Joachim, 1856–61.[19] As part of this correspondence course Brahms prepared several movements of a canonic Mass for five
voices which was ultimately to form the basis of his motet 'Warum ist das Licht
gegeben dem Mühseligen?' Op. 74/1, which he finished in 1877. Here he synthesised the Palestrinian style of the Mass movements with the Bachian chorale
tradition by closing the motet with a setting of 'Mit Fried' und Freud'.[20]
Daniel Beller-McKenna recognises a pronounced similarity between this
motet and the Lutheran *Trauermusik* tradition, in particular Bach's symmetrical
cantata, the *Actus Tragicus*, BWV 106. In its departures from Bach's models
though there is a pronounced underplaying of the Christian element: when the
New Testament text appears – following Bach's model – at the central point of
the piece (James 5:11) it refers only to God's mercy and not to Christian salvation. This, together with the acceptance of death in the final chorale suggests a
rather less ambitious form of religion than that traditionally offered by
Christian theology. Beller-McKenna suggests that here Brahms ultimately
'placed himself in a weak relationship to his past, unable to assert a strong sense
of his own identity' by writing so Bachian a movement at the end. The work
could be seen as symptomatic of a growing melancholy, one that drove Brahms

  18 V. Hancock, 'Brahms's Links with German Renaissance Music: A Discussion of Selected Choral
Works', in M. Musgrave (ed.), *Brahms 2: Biographical, Documentary and Analytical Studies* (Cambridge, 1987),
esp. p. 95.

  19 D. Brodbeck, 'The Brahms–Joachim Counterpoint Exchange; or, Robert, Clara, and "the Best
Harmony between Jos. and Joh."', in D. Brodbeck (ed.), *Brahms Studies*, I (Lincoln, Nebr., and London,
1994), pp. 30–80.

  20 R. Pascall, 'Brahms's *Missa Canonica* and its Recomposition in his Motet "Warum" Op. 74 No. 1', in
M. Musgrave (ed.), *Brahms 2*, pp. 111–36.

to use the Bible and historical styles more as sources of pessimism than of hope.[21]

A similar sense of a personally defined religion, but a rather more optimistic one, has often been noted in connection with the *Requiem*, Op. 45 of 1868. Although Brahms's chosen material is biblical it does not conform to any liturgical requiem and specifically Christian elements are minimised. Again, the models of Bach and the Lutheran chorale tradition are easily discerned but there is never a point where Brahms's identity is overwhelmed by historical models. Dahlhaus sees the work as a superlative example of nineteenth-century religious art: specifics of faith are dissolved into intense, but vague, Schleiermachian feelings of utter dependence (Dahlhaus, pp. 184–5). In it, a profound sense of the religious and of individual subjectivity, alluding both to musical and religious traditions, is played out in the interdenominational temple of the concert hall.

The professional church musician

Most composers who worked regularly in both sacred and secular spheres had – to be accepted at all in either – to make some gesture of stylistic differentiation, but in some cases the distinction is very subtle or complex. Fauré, in his famous *Requiem* developed from 1877 to 1900, adopts a very suitable, austere and semi-polyphonic idiom. But the style is not enormously different from that of his simpler song settings and the work is full of lyrical, expressive moments. In some ways, it may be that his style *per se* owes something to what he had learned from the austerity of church music and the implications of the recently resurrected chant and modal systems. What makes the *Requiem* entirely suitable for a liturgical context is a certain stasis of harmonic movement coupled with modal turns and a tendency towards repetition. Thus even one of the most lyrical melodies, that introducing and accompanying the 'Agnus Dei', features as a quasi-ostinato, being repeated, alternating with other material, and returning, in a manner not unlike a Baroque ritornello (although it is tonally much more static). All these elements, so expertly handled, actually become mildly progressive in the wider context of French music at the end of the century.

Bruckner too took much from his experience as a church musician and clearly shared something of the historicist spirit of the Cecilian movement. Some writers make sharp distinctions between Bruckner's purely liturgical writing and the larger occasional church works: the motets thus reflect the

21 D. Beller-McKenna, 'The Great *Warum?* Job, Christ, and Bach in a Brahms Motet', *19th Century Music*, 19 (1996), esp. p. 251.

ethos of purity encouraged by the Cecilian reformers; the Masses in D and F minor, the *Te Deum* and Psalm 150 partake of the symphonic tradition while the E minor Mass represents a successful synthesis of symphonic and Cecilian trends.[22] This view is complicated by, for instance, Dahlhaus's observation that the *Te Deum* is so motivically saturated that it actually undermines the symphonic aesthetic, and that it comes closer to a Baroque ideal than any actual work of the seventeenth century (Dahlhaus, p. 188). Moreover, Baroque motivic saturation would have reeked too highly of needless complexity and instrumental style for a pure Cecilian.

The motets go far beyond the level of weak stylistic imitation or historicist fundamentalism and indeed show such a remarkable eclecticism of style and such a range of gestures and tonality that they are almost a microcosm of the symphonies. Whether in the ecstatic chording of the second 'Ave Maria' setting (1861) or the monumental brass-like textures and third-related progressions of 'Ecce sacerdos', these motets perhaps represent the peak of purely liturgical music in the nineteenth century. The 1884 setting of the Maundy Thursday Gradual, 'Christus factus est', a meditation on Christ's sacrifice for mankind, displays perhaps the greatest tonal ambitus (the opening section modulating from D minor to D flat major to depict Christ's sacrifice: 'Christ became obedient for our sake unto death, even unto death upon the cross') and expressive range. Timothy Jackson suggests that the D♭ of Christ's painful sacrifice is then enharmonically transformed to C♯ as it becomes the means for mankind's redemption.[23]

One striking difference between Bruckner's motets and his symphonies (other than the fact that they display – perhaps somewhat to our relief – his ability to write concisely) is that, however disparate their elements, the motets are highly unified and rounded. Although an intense unification may be discovered at deeper structural levels in the symphonies, these works can sound extremely disjointed and almost disturbingly fragmentary in performance. Moreover, 'churchy' Palestrinian passages can often be so contrasted with their neighbours that they can sound ironic – something that is evident, for instance, in the first movement of the Fifth Symphony (bar 100) where a homophonic, largely root-position Palestrinian topic is played pizzicato (and later by staccato winds) and leads into seemingly incongruous dance music (bar 161). The highly effective, repeated cadential gesture at the end of 'Christus factus est' also appears at the close of the introduction to the last movement (bar 49) of the Eighth Symphony (sketched around the same time). In its symphonic

22 R. M. Longyear, *Nineteenth-Century Romanticism in Music* (Englewood Cliffs, 1969), p. 135.
23 T. Jackson, 'The Enharmonics of Faith: Enharmonic Symbolism in Bruckner's Christus factus est (1884)', *Bruckner-Jahrbuch* (1987–8), pp. 7–20.

environment it thus sounds far more provisional, less final, than in its more beatific guise at the close of a motet. In all, then, the motets – while employing much of the same language – suggest a sense of certainty and stability that contrasts quite strongly with the enormous questions the symphonies seem to pose (Bruckner himself seems to have reflected their uncertainty and 'openness' with his numerous revisions, albeit in the face of savage criticism). The sacred music, far from being an antiquarian throwback, seems to represent a perfected 'Romantic' haven of religious security within Bruckner's uncannily prophetic proto-modernist vision.

The organ and its rehabilitation

The neglect of the organ as an instrument of serious music-making and composition undoubtedly reached its nadir in the first half of the nineteenth century. As Liszt so characterfully described it – 'now prostituting itself with vaudeville airs and even galops' (1835 – Merrick, p. 88) – the instrument was largely used for music abstracted from opera and light entertainment, and this seems to be reflected in the astonishing lack of original organ music from this era. However, it should not be forgotten that, even if its notated repertory shrank drastically in the late eighteenth century, the organ remained a significant medium for improvisation (in the practice of which Mozart, for instance, had been so renowned). The survival of instruments both through and from the early nineteenth century is an important reminder of countless musical institutions and traditions that can never adequately be recalled in a history of the era; a whole body of musical practices and phenomena that we must somehow try and remember whenever we concentrate on the central traditions and repertories of the time. The fact that so many of the older organs survived the entire century without changes to their tonal disposition or temperament suggests that much of what was played on them was either extremely conservative or – as Liszt avers – excruciating (and maybe both). Yet if figures such as Bruckner, Franck and Fauré were serving their musical apprenticeship as organists during this 'dark age' of the organ, it is not necessarily fruitless to speculate as to what liturgical accompaniments and improvisations might actually have sounded like.[24]

Many of these issues come together with one of the few significant publications of organ music before 1850, the Sonatas, Op. 65, of Mendelssohn (1845). As Susanna Grossmann-Vendrey notes, the very choice of the sonata genre implies a sense of transcription, since there was no tradition of sonata

24 A. C. Howie, 'Traditional and Novel Elements in Bruckner's Sacred Music', *Musical Quarterly*, 66 (1981), esp. p. 556.

composition on which the composer could build.[25] Mendelssohn did, of course, write organ works in the more historical genre of prelude and fugue, one that still preserved a weak sense of continuity with the Bach tradition. But the stylistic diversity and unpredictable shape of the sonatas reflect the very ambiguity of the organ and its role in the music culture of the time: traditional fugues and chorale settings sit beside dramatic fantasias and tender lieder, creating a succession of movements and a conscious mixing of historical levels that Grossmann-Vendrey aptly describes as 'collage'. The composer's letter to his German publisher implies that the sonatas represent the notation of his 'art of handling the organ and thinking for it'; moreover, the advertisement for the English edition refers to the pieces 'as specimens of what the composer himself considers his own peculiar style of performance on the organ' (Grossmann-Vendrey, pp. 186–8). This may be a sign of a relatively archaic sense (at least for Germany) of the ontology of music lying more in its performance than its existence as a 'work'.

Robert Schumann enthused about the new sonatas, praising their 'genuine poetic new forms' (Grossmann-Vendrey, p. 190). This is a striking observation in the face of music that is so suffused with conventional and traditional forms and perhaps tells us as much about Schumann as about Mendelssohn. On the one hand, Schumann had admired Bach's fugues from the *Well-tempered Clavier* 'as character pieces of the highest art' and as 'poetic', perhaps the highest accolade he could offer any music. On the other, Schumann increasingly saw Bach as a teacher of the highest musical logic, a technical yardstick for everything he wrote. Even at its most intense, as in 1845, Schumann's concern with the technical implications of Bach's music has a 'Romantic' quality that is not so evident in Mendelssohn's inbred facility with fugal counterpoint as a 'Classical' style. However studied the music might sound, Schumann's efforts in 1845 – the six fugues on BACH for organ, Op. 60, and the six canonic pieces for pedal-piano, Op. 56, being of particular relevance to the organ repertory – are written with a deep sense of personal need and development. This relates directly to his breakdown of 1844 and the concomitant loss of his creative energies. Indeed, Clara seems positively to have encouraged the study of counterpoint and the organ as a way of settling her husband's mind.[26] To the Schumanns the organ and fugal form went naturally together as part of an elevated but purely musical concept, certainly informed by a monumentalist historicism but totally divorced from religious meaning, liturgical function or even, perhaps, current organ practice.

25 S. Grossmann-Vendrey, 'Stilprobleme in Mendelssohns Orgelsonaten op. 65', in C. Dahlhaus (ed.), *Das Problem Mendelssohn*, Studien zur Musikgeschichte des 19 Jahrhunderts 41 (Regensburg, 1974), esp. p. 185.   26 Brodbeck, 'The Brahms–Joachim Counterpoint Exchange', p. 68.

Given that Schumann's encounter with counterpoint and the organ are to some degree associated with personal trauma, it is interesting to observe that Brahms used exactly the same discipline to mollify a related crisis some ten years later. His affections for Clara Schumann reached a peak in the months before her husband's tragic death in 1856. In 1854 Clara had expressed to Brahms her sudden desire to learn the organ to please Robert once he had recovered his health; David Brodbeck sees the organ introduction and accompaniment of Brahms's *Geistliches Lied* as a direct portrayal of this hoped-for scene. By 1856 Brahms desired to become an organ virtuoso specifically to give him something to offer on his prospective tours with Clara. A Prelude and Fugue in A Minor for organ soon came as a present for her and the remarkable Fugue in A flat Minor honoured Robert's birthday. The latter piece, with its possible references to Brahms's name and Schumann's *Manfred* Overture, may well be an allegory on the extremely complex and guilt-ridden situation in which Brahms then found himself. Even more overt are the references to Clara in the Chorale Prelude on 'O Traurigkeit, o Herzeleid', a work that was almost certainly written in the wake of her husband's death (Brodbeck, pp. 64–80). Brahms returned to the genre of the organ chorale at the very end of his life – incidentally around the time of Clara's final illness and death in 1896 – in the remarkable set of eleven chorale preludes, Op. 122, that, in scale and figuration, seem to approach the short chorale forms of Bach's 'Orgelbüchlein'. The second setting of 'Herzlich thut mich Verlangen' is perhaps one of the most beautiful homages to Bach, taking the figuration of Bach's 'Ich ruf' zu dir', BWV 639, extending it in range, and adding a gentle Brahmsian three-note grouping within a quadruple division of the pulse. In all, it is interesting that some of the finest organ music of the century, that of Brahms and Schumann, should stem from a psychological necessity (Clara being, to some degree, the common cause) and from a search for mental and musical discipline that saw the organ as a purifying influence. Taken out of its traditional religious role the organ seems almost to acquire the connotations of a Romantic religion in its own right.

Liszt's three significant organ works also arose from particular issues that were relevant to the composer and not as part of a specifically religious revival or tradition (although Liszt left plenty of largely inoffensive liturgical organ music). The largest work, the *Fantasy and Fugue on the Chorale 'Ad nos, ad salutarem undam'* (1850), was based on a theme from Meyerbeer's *Le prophète* (1849). Given that this was Liszt's first attempt at instrumental fugue it is likely that, like the Schumanns, Liszt made a direct association between fugue and the organ. R. Larry Todd suggests that Liszt's use of the organ for the first time 'encouraged an innovative treatment of form and design': it is part of his ongoing experiments with compressing a sequence of several movements into the span of a single sonata form, in this case one based entirely on a single theme.[27] Todd also discerns several whole-tone elements both in the large-scale harmonic movement (generating, for instance, the F sharp major of the central slow movement) and in some of the transitions in the slow movement itself. These latter descending whole-tone passages might, moreover, represent a specifically Palestrinian *topos*, that of the opening of the 'Stabat mater', which was so significant throughout the century.

The two other works, the Prelude and Fugue on BACH (1855/1870) and the Variations on *Weinen, Klagen, Sorgen, Zagen* (1863), represent more directly Liszt's homage to Bach, although their boldness lies in their departures from Bach's models rather than in any slavish imitation. Liszt, like Schumann in his younger years, saw Bach as a model for fantasy and poetic inspiration rather than a stern fugal taskmaster. Like Mendelssohn, Liszt approached the organ with his own experiences in performance and improvisation in mind. Moreover, for a time at least, these works seem to have been 'works-in-progress' for Liszt where each version represented an alternative 'performance' rather than an imperfect approximation of an ideal model.[28]

The genre of the chorale fantasia was ultimately developed to the point of near-exhaustion by Max Reger. His seven examples from 1898 to 1900 generally consist of a loose sequence of chorale variations and free material culminating in a dense fugue.[29] Here Bachian complexity is developed almost to neurotic density – as Walter Frisch has said in relation to an early chorale prelude 'there is a sense of loss the composer is trying to recover, or a distance he is trying to bridge, by overdetermining the counterpoint'.[30] Reger's exuberance and dramatic use of the organ medium is perhaps best appreciated in the shorter pieces such as the *Dankpsalm*, Op. 145, No. 2, and the more formally controlled *Introduction and Passacaglia* in D minor. It was partly Reger's Bach-obsessed music that helped to make public the link between Bach and the organ, something which contributed towards a new 'organ movement' in Germany during the first decades of the twentieth century.

The rehabilitation of the organ as an instrument for both concert and liturgical life first took place in France. Here again, the increasing importance of Bach contributed to the organ's prestige, first with the pioneering work of A.-P.-F.

27 R. L. Todd, 'Liszt, Fantasy and Fugue for Organ on "Ad nos, ad salutarem undam"', *19th Century Music*, 4 (1981), esp. pp. 250–1.

28 M. Zenck, 'Reinterpreting Bach in the Nineteenth and Twentieth Centuries', in J. Butt (ed.), *Cambridge Companion to Bach* (Cambridge, 1997), pp. 228–30.

29 G. Barber, 'German Organ Music after 1800', in N. Thistlethwaite and G. Webber (eds.), *The Cambridge Companion to the Organ* (Cambridge, 1998), pp. 255–6.

30 W. Frisch, 'Bach, Brahms, and the Emergence of Musical Modernism', in M. Marissen (ed.), *Bach Perspectives*, III (Lincoln, Nebr., and London, 1998), p. 126.

Boëly (1785–1858)[31] and later with the performances and editions of Widor. But up until the middle of the century whatever organs had survived the Revolution were generally played in a manner reflecting current operatic tastes. One significant way in which the organ began to be taken more seriously from the 1840s onwards was through the technological advances in its construction. Aristide Cavaillé-Coll (1811–99) was the organ builder who, virtually single-handedly, made the new French organ school possible. He introduced pneumatic actions that allowed organists to benefit from some of the recent advances in piano technique, he extended the compass of the instrument and made quick changes of registration and dynamic more possible. Not only did the various families of pipes blend in distinctive choruses but the organ also became more capable of imitating orchestral sonorities (Brooks, pp. 267–72).

The first major composer of the school is César Franck (1822–90) who, as someone working in much of the wider field of music, absorbed many of the progressive elements of the day. It is important to note that Franck, like all his younger colleagues in the French organ school, intended his published pieces primarily for concert use, however much they might have derived from the atmosphere of formal liturgy and devotion. In fact, the success of the school rested partly on the secularisation of the organ that, ironically, the Revolution had set in train.

Franck's organ works show the influence of Liszt's monothematic sonata structures in the early *Grande pièce symphonique* (1862), Wagner's chromaticism after he first heard *Tristan* in 1874,[32] and perhaps even something of Chopin's style in his mature fantasy writing.[33] It is perhaps the *Trois chorales* of 1890 that mark the highest point of French achievement in organ composition during the nineteenth century: drawing on the Germanic chorale tradition, particularly in its Lisztian manifestation, these pieces are relatively concise and coherent. While the first (E major) is based around two principal themes melded into a climactic symphonic movement, the other two take more historical forms: passacaglia and fugue (B minor) and toccata and aria (A minor).

Fully fledged organ symphonies – ten of them – were developed by Charles-Marie Widor (1844–1937) who capitalised on the orchestral potential of the instruments. Virtually none of this music competes with the best symphonic and instrumental music of the day, although some of the dynamic gestures must contain an echo of Widor's renowned brilliance as an improviser. One piece stands out – although regularly reviled by connoisseurs of the composer's

---

31 G. Brooks, 'French and Belgian Organ Music after 1800', in Thistlethwaite and Webber (eds.), *The Cambridge Companion to the Organ*, pp. 265–6.

32 L. Plantinga, *Romantic Music: A History of Musical Style in Nineteenth-Century Europe* (New York and London, 1984), p. 443.

33 L. Archbold, 'Franck's Organ Music and Its Legacy', *19th Century Music*, 12 (1988), p. 56.

works – the famous Toccata from the Fifth Symphony, which exploits an almost mesmeric minimalism to tremendously dramatic effect; in all, it is a lucky 'hit', somehow prophetic of several later directions in musical style, and one that Widor doubtlessly developed through improvised experiments with figuration and touch.

The renaissance of the organ in Britain to some degree mirrored that of France, although there had not been the same sequence of revolutions and restorations that brought the church and its music in and out of favour. Mendelssohn's visits clearly had an influence on organ performance and indigenous performers such as S. S. Wesley and Henry Smart became respected as both composers and improvisers. One of the most significant elements of organ performance to develop in England was the use of the instrument to perform transcriptions of orchestral music, an art first perfected by W. T. Best (1826–97).[34] This role, coupled with civic pride in the technological advances of the instrument, caused large organs to be installed in concert halls throughout the land; the concept of the 'borough organist' meant that the instrument was no longer seen purely as a sacred instrument (indeed, organs were common in private residences from the time of the Commonwealth two centuries earlier, so perhaps this was an extension of an inherited tradition). Where no orchestra was available, it was the organ that brought many people their first experience of the European symphonic repertory. Moreover, the trend for transcription meant that the instrument developed sonorities and registrational aids that arguably rendered the instrument more 'orchestral' than even that of France. In some ways, many of the transcriptions surviving from the nineteenth century eclipse much of the original English music for the instrument. Only one new piece stands out – Elgar's Sonata in G, Op. 28 (1895) – which the composer seems to have written as if it were actually a transcription of orchestral sonorities (evidenced, for instance, in the repeated-chord accompaniment in the first bridge passage of the opening movement). Despite its textbook sonata forms this piece shows a degree of imagination, dramatic pacing and ingenious development that renders it one of the most successful works in the European organ repertory of the nineteenth century.

Bibliography

Archbold, L., 'Franck's Organ Music and Its Legacy'. *19th Century Music*, 12 (1988), pp. 54–63

Beller-McKenna, D., 'The Great *Warum?* Job, Christ, and Bach in a Brahms Motet'. *19th Century Music*, 19 (1996), pp. 231–51

34 A. McCrea, 'British Organ Music after 1800', in Thistlethwaite and Webber (eds.), *The Cambridge Companion to the Organ*, pp. 288–90.

Bergeron, K., *Decadent Enchantments – The Revival of Gregorian Chant at Solesmes*. Berkeley and Los Angeles, 1998

Botstein, L., 'Listening through Reading: Musical Literacy and the Concert Audience'. *19th Century Music*, 16 (1992–3), pp. 129–45

Brodbeck, D., 'The Brahms–Joachim Counterpoint Exchange; or, Robert, Clara, and "the Best Harmony between Jos. and Joh."'. In D. Brodbeck (ed.), *Brahms Studies*, I. Lincoln, Nebr., and London, 1994

Dahlhaus, C., *Nineteenth-Century Music*, trans. J. B. Robinson. Berkeley and Los Angeles, 1989

Frisch, W., 'Bach, Brahms, and the Emergence of Musical Modernism'. In M. Marissen (ed.), *Bach Perspectives*, III. Lincoln, Nebr., and London, 1998, pp. 109–31

Garratt, J., 'Palestrina and the German Romantic Imagination: Interpreting Historicism in Nineteenth-Century Music'. Ph.D. diss., University of Wales Cardiff (1999)

Geck, M., *Die Wiederentdeckung der Matthäuspassion im 19. Jahrhundert*, Studien zur Musikgeschichte des 19 Jahrhunderts. Regensburg, 1967

Grossmann-Vendrey, S., 'Stilprobleme in Mendelssohns Orgelsonaten op. 65'. In C. Dahlhaus (ed.), *Das Problem Mendelssohn*, Studien zur Musikgeschichte des 19 Jahrhunderts 41. Regensburg, 1974, pp. 185–94

Hancock, V., 'Brahms's Performances of Early Choral Music'. *19th Century Music*, 8 (1984), pp. 125–41
  'Brahms's Links with German Renaissance Music: A Discussion of Selected Choral Works'. In M. Musgrave (ed.), *Brahms 2: Biographical, Documentary and Analytical Studies*. Cambridge, 1987, pp. 95–110

Hopkins Porter, C., 'The New Public and the Reordering of the Musical Establishment: The Lower Rhine Music Festivals, 1818–67'. *19th Century Music*, 3 (1979–80), pp. 211–24

Horn, W., *Die Dresdner Hofkirchenmusik 1720–1745: Studien zu ihren Voraussetzungen und ihrem Repertoire*. Kassel, 1987

Howie, A. C., 'Traditional and Novel Elements in Bruckner's Sacred Music'. *Musical Quarterly*, 66 (1981), pp. 544–67

Jackson, T., 'The Enharmonics of Faith: Enharmonic Symbolism in Bruckner's Christus factus est (1884)'. *Bruckner-Jahrbuch* (1987–8), pp. 7–20

Longyear, R. M., *Nineteenth-Century Romanticism in Music*. Englewood Cliffs, 1969

Merrick, P., *Revolution and Religion in the Music of Liszt*. Cambridge, 1987

Pascall, R., 'Brahms's *Missa Canonica* and it Reomposition in his Motet "Warum" Op. 74 No. 1'. In M. Musgrave (ed.), *Brahms 2: Biographical, Documentary and Analytical Studies*. Cambridge, 1987, pp. 111–36

Plantinga, L., *Romantic Music: A History of Musical Style in Nineteenth-Century Europe*. New York and London, 1984

Ringer, A. (ed.), *The Early Romantic Era*. Englewood Cliffs, 1990

Samson, J. (ed.), *The Late Romantic Era*. Englewood Cliffs, 1991

Thistlethwaite, N. and Webber G. (eds.), *The Cambridge Companion to the Organ*. Cambridge, 1998

Todd, R. L., 'Liszt, Fantasy and Fugue for Organ on "Ad nos, ad salutarem undam"'. *19th Century Music*, 4 (1981), pp. 250–61

Zenck, M., 'Reinterpreting Bach in the Nineteenth and Twentieth Centuries'. In J. Butt (ed.), *Cambridge Companion to Bach*. Cambridge, 1997, pp. 226–50

19

Music and social class

DEREK B. SCOTT

A chapter of this size cannot provide much more than an overview of music and class in four major cities (London, Paris, New York and Vienna), but will focus on detail whenever this illustrates the broader argument or reveals developments of particular interest. In the second half of the nineteenth century features of musical life associated with a capitalist economy and the consolidation of power of a wealthy industrial bourgeoisie became firmly established. Prominent among such features were the commercialisation and professionalisation of music, new markets for cultural goods, the bourgeoisie's struggle for cultural domination and a growing rift between art and entertainment.

Presented below is a study of music and class in four cities, not four countries. Nevertheless, these were the major commercial cities of those countries, home to the wealthiest commercial families. In each, there was rapid population growth and the creation of a large market for entertainment. The power wielded by the upper class began to weaken earlier in Paris than in London, and was slowest to give way in Vienna where the bourgeoisie mingled least with the aristocracy. In New York, there were no inherited titles, of course, although the 'upper ten' of that city were often disposed to define themselves against the European aristocracy and, at mid-century, were perceived to be not dissimilar to the upper classes of Paris's Faubourg St Germain or London's West End.[1] Paris and Vienna both underwent major reconstruction in the second half of the century. Napoleon III instructed Haussmann to redesign Paris following the 1848 Revolution, and the result was a city of wide arterial boulevards and symmetrical layouts. In Vienna, the Ring developments that replaced the city walls initiated equally important changes and, for some fifty years, property developers were continually at work. The title of Johann Strauss II's *Demolirer-Polka* (1862) refers to the demolition of Vienna's ramparts. In both cities working-class communities were uprooted and displaced. In all four, the demarcation between private and public became increasingly rigid and their boundaries ever more strictly policed.

---

1 See Max Maretzek, *Revelations of an Opera Manager in Nineteenth-Century America*, Part 1 (New York, 1968; original edn as *Crotchets and Quavers*, 1855), p. 25; see also Charles Hamm, *Yesterdays: Popular Song in America* (New York, 1979), p. 69.

Since a great deal of this chapter is concerned with popular music, a warning is needed about mapping high- and low-status music directly on to high- and low-status consumers. While an argument can be made for the effectiveness of different styles in articulating distinct class interests, it should not be forgotten that a French haut bourgeois could enjoy a *café-concert* chanson, and an English factory worker enjoy singing in Handel's *Messiah*. On the other hand, for those who argue there is no relation between musical taste and social class, the empirical data gathered by Pierre Bourdieu are disconcerting.[2] The field of the popular that opened up in the nineteenth century was one in which different classes and class fractions fought over questions of intellectual and moral leadership (in Gramscian terms, hegemony). A class fraction is an identifiable grouping within a particular class whose behaviour or opinions may not be characteristic of the class as a whole and who may even play an oppositional role at times: for example, middle-class temperance campaigners who cut across the dominant middle-class view of a free market. Popular culture was a site for the contested meanings of social experience, and functioned frequently as an area of compromise over values, allowing the working class to adopt evasive or resistant strategies.

In tandem with the growth of a commercial music industry, the term 'popular' changed its meaning during the course of the century, moving from well known to well received to successful in terms of sheet music sales. A song described as a 'favourite air' suggested one widely liked; the words 'sung with tumultuous applause by' indicated a song adopted by a star singer whose choice had been endorsed by an admiring audience; the boast '20,000 copies sold' implied that there could be no better recommendation than that so many people had bought the song. The last type of claim became the key marker of the popular song. A related development was the reluctance to accept as folk-songs anything originating in composed music, an effective means of excluding commercial popular song. Folk music came to mean national music, an ideological shift aligning it with bourgeois aspirations and identity rather than the lower class. In London, during 1855–9, William Chappell felt comfortable publishing a collection of traditional songs under the title *Popular Music of the Olden Time*. In the 1890s, however, Frank Kidson explained that he was driven to collecting the material he published as *English Peasant Songs* by the desire to counter the accusation that England had no *national* music.[3]

To understand matters relating to music and class in the nineteenth century,

2 See Pierre Bourdieu, *Distinction: A Social Critique of the Judgement of Taste*, trans. Richard Nice (London, 1984; original edn Paris, 1979), pp. 14–18. Bourdieu provides an empirical study of musical preferences, and identifies three 'zones of taste' corresponding to educational level and social class.

3 See Dave Harker, *Fakesong: The Manufacture of British 'Folksong' 1700 to the Present Day* (Milton Keynes, 1985), pp. 155–6.

it is important to know how ideas of class were being reformulated. A new perception grew of classes as economic social groupings with the capacity to effect social change. From this perspective, most familiar from the writings of Marx and Engels, some groups were regarded as left over from a previous 'mode of production' (the aristocracy and peasantry as residual feudal elements), while others were seen to represent a modern clash of class interests (capitalists and the working class). Ideas of 'class struggle' and 'class consciousness' developed in the nineteenth century. The crucial determinants of class position in these economic terms were whether or not one had ownership of the 'means of production' and whether one had the ability to purchase labour power, or needed to sell one's own. Economic relations between people were of paramount importance. Class divisions described in terms of lower class, middle class and upper class arose in the period 1770–1840, the time of the Industrial Revolution in Britain, but the new conceptualisation of class saw social position as something that could be, at least partially, attained by anyone. Former ideas were based on notions of hierarchy and rank, linked to a belief that these were determined at birth: hence, the term 'lower orders', though it continued to be used, really belonged to earlier times. Raymond Williams suggested that the 'lower middle classes' were first heard of in the twentieth century (*Culture and Society*, p. 15), but they are already named in Gilbert and Sullivan's *Iolanthe* (1882): the 'March of Peers' contains the command, 'Bow, bow ye lower middle classes'.

Professionalisation and commercialisation

William Weber states that by 1848 a commercial concert world had emerged in London, Paris and Vienna, 'over which the middle class exerted powerful, if not dominant, control' (*Music and the Middle Class*, p. 7). While Britain's population doubled in the sixty years after 1870, the increase in musicians was sevenfold, a fact Cyril Ehrlich puts down to expanded demand 'derived, in large measure, from an efflorescence of commercial entertainment' (*The Music Profession in Britain*, p. 54). Antagonisms provoked by commercial interests in music began in the same period. Richard Leppert relates the 'implicit social antagonism in the ideological foundation of much nineteenth-century aesthetics' to the increased dependence of artists on the cultural market created by capitalism (*The Sight of Sound*, p. 207). Leonard Meyer has commented, 'even as they scorned and mocked the middle class, the artists of the nineteenth century created for it' (*Style and Music*, p. 183). Some composers depended for their livelihood on the wealthy bourgeoisie, and some musicians played low-status music because they could not find employment playing high-status music.

The enforcement of copyright protection on the reproduction and performance of music was an enormous stimulus to the music market, affecting both writers, performers and publishers. In Britain, the Copyright Act of 1842 allowed the author to sell copyright and performing rights together or separately. In France, the law first offered protection to *café-concert* songwriters in 1848-9. The star emerged with the *café-concert*, the first being Thérésa (Emma Valadon). Popular performers could now become very wealthy and those who offered a 'rags to riches' story were 'a formidable instrument of social order, of hope and submission simultaneously.'[4] Paulus (Jean-Paul Habans) became the foremost male star after developing a unique jerky style (*style gambillard*) in the 1880s.

The star system was also a feature of the London music hall: Marie Lloyd, George Leybourne, the Great MacDermott, Albert Chevalier and Gus Elen, were among the most admired. Richard Middleton comments that Marie Lloyd's appeal and relationship with her 'gallery boys' was 'built on an acceptance of secure class definitions and an awareness of common life styles' ('Popular Music of the Lower Classes', p. 87). It perhaps explains her failure to triumph in the USA. The glamorous female star was a feature of operetta: Hortense Schneider became famous in the title role of *La grande duchesse de Gérolstein* after its tremendous success during the Paris Exhibition of 1867. Emily Soldene was Schneider's counterpart in London; Vienna had Josefine Gallmeyer, and New York, Lillian Russell.

The aristocracy began to find themselves unable to afford the high fees of international stars for their private concerts and their salons were on the wane during the second half of the century. Liszt's recitals took on much of the character of the aristocratic salon, involving socialising, drinking and smoking. He appeared at the highest-status public venues at the highest prices. Wagner, attending a recital in Paris, wrote that tickets cost 20 francs, providing Liszt with 10,000 francs for one concert.[5]

Ticket prices were used in each city to produce a class hierarchy of concerts. They ensured a socially exclusive audience at London's Royal Philharmonic Society concerts. The conservatoire concerts were Paris's main 'high' concerts of Classical music, attended by subscribers drawn from the city's nobility and haute bourgeoisie. In 1842, New York's Philharmonic Orchestra was formed, funded by wealthy subscribers. No professionalisation of Classical music, such as that found in London, New York and Paris, occurred in Vienna before mid-century (popular music was a different matter); a major reason was the lack of mingling

4 Jacques Attali, *Noise: The Political Economy of Music*, trans. Brian Massumi (Manchester, 1985; original edn Paris, 1977), p. 77.

5 Richard Wagner, 'Farewell Performances', in Robert L. Jacob and Geoffrey Skelton (eds.), *Wagner Writes from Paris* (London, 1973), p. 124, cited in Henry Raynor, *Music and Society Since 1815* (London, 1976), p. 63.

between the upper middle class and aristocracy. In the second half of the century, change was set in motion by the founding of the Vienna Philharmonic.

Cheap concerts were plentiful in the 1850s. In London, the Saturday Concerts begun by August Manns in the Crystal Palace in 1855 necessitated popular programming and a small admission charge in order to fill the large hall. When the large St James's Hall opened in 1858, programmes of accessible music were put together to attract audiences and, as at Manns's concerts, programme notes were used to build appreciation of Classical music. As the middle-class audience grew so did middle-class domestic music-making. Taken together with the professionalisation of music performance, the result was that amateur music-making lost status.

The commodification of music was most evident in the sheet music trade. Music publishing in Vienna dates from the last two decades of the eighteenth century with Artaria. By 1857, Diabelli's firm had become Spina, which published the music of Strauss II. A hundred plates, each sufficient for 10,000 copies, were needed to satisfy demand for the 'Blue Danube'. Oliver Ditson of Boston was America's biggest popular song publisher until the 1880s. New York's biggest firms were Harms (established 1881) and Witmark (established 1885). The economic potential of popular music was evident in the 1890s when Charles Harris's 'After the Ball' (1892) showed that a hit song could sell millions of copies. The label 'Tin Pan Alley' referred to the area between 14th and 28th Streets where publishers were expanding in the 1890s. Paul Dresser, composer of 'On the Banks of the Wabash' (1897), was a popular early Tin Pan Alley songwriter. There was a new attitude to marketing, along with new strategies for promoting songs. Song-plugging, for example, involved performances in music shops and department stores to boost sales. The song itself had to have a 'punch' – something to make it stand out in a competitive market, like a memorable group of notes, or memorable line in the lyric. In London, Novello made successive reductions in the price of music, and cheap music was also to be had from Davidson, Hopwood and Crew, and Charles Sheard. The halfpenny broadside ballad and street ballad singer both began to disappear in the late 1850s. By 1880 music hall songs had supplanted broadsides as the preferred popular music of the working class.

The status of popular music changed with the development of the music market. There were two stages: when commercialisation was in its early stages, the popular was vulgar only if deemed to be pandering to low taste, but as the music industry grew, the more successful music was commercially, the more it was perceived as low, until all music written for sale was regarded as inferior. Only music not thought to originate as 'music for sale' could sell in huge numbers, as did the vocal score of *Messiah*, the song-sheet of the folksong 'The

British Grenadiers', and the collection *Hymns Ancient and Modern* (1861), and remain popular without being low.

New markets for cultural goods

The ideal for social reformers was a single, shared culture, uniting different classes and ethnic groups; but the reality was that the economics of cultural provision in the second half of the century necessitated focusing on particular consumers. Old markets had to be developed, new ones created and, where necessary, demand stimulated. London's diverse markets for cultural goods were noted by journalist James Ritchie at mid-century: 'The gay have their theatres – the philanthropic their Exeter Hall – the wealthy their "ancient concerts" – the costermongers what they term their sing-song' (*The Night Side of London*, p. 200). Cultural value fluctuates with the consumer's social status and power to define legitimate taste. A cultural struggle occurs when a current market's values are upset by the formation of a new market, as shown in Gilbert and Sullivan's *Patience* (1881), where Bunthorne the fleshly poet and Grosvenor the idyllic poet compete for aesthetic status. Since the latter's arrival, Bunthorne complains, 'insipidity has been at a premium'.

Aristocratic taste in the eighteenth century was for ceremony and formality; the bourgeoisie reacted against that by prizing individual character and feelings.[6] The fondness of the bourgeoisie for virtuosi, suggests Leonard Meyer, is because their gifts 'are understood to be innate rather than dependent on lineage or learning' (*Style and Music*, p. 171). A 'natural' music was preferred that did not rely on previous informed knowledge. The dislike for rules and conventions linked to a new trust in the spontaneous verdict of the people is found in *Die Meistersinger von Nürnberg* (1867) when Hans Sachs claims that if a musician follows nature's path, it will be obvious to those who 'know nothing of the tablature'. Love was a favourite subject because it cut across class, as Earl Tolloller acknowledges in his song 'Blue Blood' in *Iolanthe*. The values of originality and individuality relate to bourgeois ideology, as the virtues prized by 'leaders of industry'.[7] Popular forms with a working-class base are more likely to offer participation (for example, the music hall song's chorus); higher forms are more likely to be objects of aesthetic contemplation. The greater the stress on the aesthetic object, such as the priority of form over function, the more likely it is to cause confusion or attract ridicule. Even in Gilbert and Sullivan's *Ruddigore* (1887), we are told the villagers are odd because they go around singing in four-part harmony.

6 See N. Elias, *The Civilizing Process*, I, *The History of Manners* (Oxford, 1978).
7 Samuel Smiles, *Self-Help* (London, 1859), pp. 35–67.

New markets developed for cultural goods, but certain classes and class fractions could only acquire them if that market was socially suitable. A Viennese aristocrat, for example, might balk at attending a concert in a bourgeois salon. In Paris, a *cabaret artistique* was not an appropriate venue for some. Yvette Guilbert says it was a revelation for the audience at the Divan Japonais when she began singing chansons by Xanrof and Bruant there in 1891; for the first time these songs had left their home in the Chat Noir and, through her, were to become popularised (*La Chanson de ma Vie*, p. 93). Next, the haute bourgeoisie wished to hear her, but could not frequent the *café-concert*. Arrangements then having been made for her to appear at the Théâtre d'Application, the proprietor begged the women in the audience not to be shocked,[8] although that is probably the reason they had come. She successfully 'crossed over' and, by the mid-1890s, had admirers in all classes.

Raymond Williams commended music hall for presenting areas of experience that other genres neglected or despised (*The Long Revolution*, p. 291). An example from operetta is what Henry Raynor calls the 'alcoholic goodwill' of the Act II finale of *Die Fledermaus* (1874).[9] The popular style developed novel musical features. Hubert Parry cites as a conspicuous feature of 'second-rate music', providing examples from 'low-class tunes' (note how the two are conflated), 'an insistence on the independence of the "leading note" from the note to which it has been supposed to lead'.[10] The falling leading-note in a subdominant context (the 'Viennese note') is a feature of Strauss II's waltzes. The tendency for the leading note to fall on to the sixth degree of the scale is part of that note's having attained a new importance. As early as the 'Blue Danube' (1867) it is being added to the tonic chord without resolution as a melody note. It had clearly caught the ear of Wagner when writing for his Rhinemaidens. The major seventh, too, begins to break free of a need to resolve: consider the refrain of Adele's 'laughing song' from *Die Fledermaus* at the words 'ich die Sache, ha ha ha'. Peter Van der Merwe states that composers 'became aware that there were certain features that stamped popular music, and either cultivated these if they were writing for the general public, or avoided them if they were writing for the elect' (*Origins of the Popular Style*, p. 242). The popular style, however, allows for considerable diversity of mood. The end of the verse of 'Champagne Charlie' (Leybourne–Lee, 1867) and the opening of the refrain of 'Wer uns getraut' (from *Der Zigeunerbaron*, 1885) use an almost identical pattern of falling leading-note and chromatically inflected descending scale, but to very different ends.

8 See Y. Guilbert and H. Simpson, *Yvette Guilbert: Struggles and Victories* (London, 1910), p. 207.

9 Raynor, *Music and Society Since 1815*, p. 149.

10 Quotation from Hubert Parry, *Style in Musical Art* (1911), in Peter van der Merwe, *Origins of the Popular Style: The Antecedents of Twentieth-Century Popular Music* (Oxford, 1989), p. 223.

Promenade concerts mixed popular and Classical items. In the first half of the century, 'popular' did not necessarily mean 'low status': some of the virtuoso display pieces heard in salons were popular in style but high status at that time. Vienna hosted more promenade concerts than the other cities. Promenade concerts had a petit bourgeois character, catering to a taste developed in cafés, taverns, parks and pleasure gardens (the latter busiest in summer when the aristocracy were not in town). The haute bourgeoisie went only to the most prestigious of promenade concerts, such as those involving Philippe Musard in Paris, Johann Strauss I in Vienna, and Louis Jullien in London. Strauss and Josef Lanner were each giving musical entertainments three evenings a week in the 1830s, their waltz nights proving the most successful. Their music was thrilling to dance to, but they were also exciting to watch as violinists, with their double-stopping, wide leaps, portamento and idiomatic bowing effects. The violinist style is retained in the waltzes of Strauss II: consider the typical violin grace notes in the theme of the 'Blue Danube'.

The Viennese working class found music at a cheap price in some dance halls, in the Tafelmusik played in local coffeehouses and restaurants, and in public parks. Zither music, which had been popularised in Vienna by Johann Petzmeyer, was a favourite in taverns. In New York, working-class dances, called 'affairs', were held in rented neighbourhood halls. They offered an opportunity for immigrants to enjoy the dances of their homelands. Public dance halls increased rapidly in the 1890s, and attracted different classes (Carnegie Hall the middle class, Liberty Hall the working class).

The diaries of Charles Rice, a comic singer in London taverns during the 1840s, throw interesting light on the years leading up to music hall.[11] The tavern concert room, with its lower-middle-class patrons and professional or semi-professional entertainment, has a more direct link to the music hall than do the song and supper rooms around Covent Garden and the Strand, which were frequented by the aristocracy and wealthy middle class. West End halls, like the Oxford, were the only ones to attract higher-class patrons; suburban halls relied on patronage from the working class and lower middle class (tradesmen, shopkeepers, mechanics, clerks). Charles Morton had difficulty enticing the middle class to attend his grand hall, the Canterbury, in Lambeth.[12] In the 1890s, middle-class attitudes became more favourable to music hall, swayed by the 'new character of the entertainment,'[13] in a word, the respectability striven for by managers (such as encouraging the attendance of married women).

11 Laurence Senelick (ed.), *Tavern Singing in Early Victorian London: The Diaries of Charles Rice for 1840 and 1850* (London, 1997).
12 Dagmar Höher, 'The Composition of Music Hall Audiences 1850–1900', in P. Bailey (ed.), *Music Hall: The Business of Pleasure* (Milton Keynes, 1986), pp. 73–92, at p. 76.   13 *Ibid.*, p. 86.

The *café-concert* took off during the Second Empire (1852–70). The first were established along the Champs-Elysées, the entertainment given in the open air in summer on stages erected between the trees. They then began to open in the city in winter, providing further employment for the same entertainers. Performers' names were indicated on a board to the right of the stage; unlike British music hall, no chairman was used. Another difference was that entrance was generally free; patrons paid only for drinks. There was a certain amount of class mixing in the *cafés-concerts*, but separation was possible by there being best tables (boxes at the Eldorado). The comic songs, smoke and drink gave both music hall and *café-concert* a morally suspect air. The Eldorado remained open during the Commune, showing that the *café-concert* public was still in Paris, even if the theatre-goers had left for Versailles. The *Réveil*, in 1886, described Alcazar patrons as 'a wholly Parisian public of toffs, prostitutes, petits bourgeois with their families, and shop assistants'.[14] The *Figaro illustré* announced in 1896 that *café-concert* songs were the principal cause of the corruption of musical taste in France.[15] Saturday was payday for 85 per cent of Parisian workers and their preferred evening for a *café-concert* or *bal*. It was also the day for leisure activities and a night out for workers in London, especially after Saturday half-day holidays became the norm in the 1870s. As with music halls, there were *cafés-concerts* in poorer areas (commonly called *beuglants*, a reference to the audience singing along).

Charles Hamm remarks that the minstrel song 'emerged as the first distinctly American genre' (*Music in the New World*, p. 183). It began when New Yorker Thomas Rice copied his 'Jim Crow' dance routine from a disabled African-American slave, and introduced it into his act at the Bowery Theatre in 1832. The Virginia Minstrels, four in number, formed in New York in 1842. Rice visited London in 1836, the Virginia Minstrels in 1843, and troupes soon formed in England. Blackface minstrels inscribed racism, but subverted bourgeois values by celebrating idleness and mischief rather than work and responsible behaviour, their blackface mask allowing an inversion of dominant values.[16] They had a broad appeal, however, and London had a troupe in permanent residency at the smaller St James's Hall. The cross-class popularity of the songs of Stephen Foster (1826–64) effectively created a 'national music' for America. His first big success, 'Oh! Susanna' was published in New York in 1848. 'Massa's in de Cold Ground' and 'My Old Kentucky Home, Good Night', published in New York in 1852 and 1853 respectively, were both labelled 'plan-

---

14 Anon., *'Chronique – Le Café-concert'*, *Le Réveil*, 29 September, 1886, quoted in T. J. Clark, *The Painting of Modern Life: Paris in the Art of Manet and His Followers* (London, 1985), p. 214.

15 Victorin Joncières, quoted in François Caradec and Alan Weill, *Le café-concert* (Paris, 1980), p. 30.

16 For a discussion of blackface minstrelsy in England and its meanings, see Michael Pickering, 'White Skin, Black Masks', in J. S. Bratton (ed.), *Music Hall: Performance and Style* (Milton Keynes, 1986), pp. 70–91.

tation melodies', but one is in 'minstrel dialect' the other not. His talent was not only for minstrel songs, as 'Jeanie with the Light Brown Hair' (1854) confirms.

The abolition of slavery after the American Civil War had little effect on theatrical representations of African-Americans. Black minstrel troupes were formed which stressed the values of genuineness and authenticity but, since they adopted minstrel conventions, offered a distortion of black culture and plantation life the more insidious for seeming natural. The first commercially successful black songwriter was James Bland (1854–1911) who worked for Callender and Haverly, and whose songs included 'Dem Golden Slippers' and 'Carry Me Back to Old Virginny'. For black performers minstrelsy was a way of earning a living. Some – for example Sam Lucas, and the Hyers sisters – tried to make a success of other forms of entertainment, but lacked audience support. Lucas was able to shake off minstrelsy in the 1890s, when black performers began to appear in vaudeville and the focus shifted from Southern plantations to Northern cities. In 1890, Sam Jack produced *The Creole Show*, which included black women performers and paved the way for the future development of the all-black musical. In 1898, *Clorindy* by African-American composer Will Marion Cook was the first, and featured the ragtime star Ernest Hogan.

Ragtime was indebted to the 'jig piano' styles of African-American musicians and the European military march. Black musicians, incidentally, were to be found in nearly every regimental band in New York in the 1840s.[17] In 1896, Ben Harney was the first to make an impact playing ragtime piano in New York, and his 'You've Been a Good Old Wagon' was published that year. Ragtime developed as an original and idiomatic piano composition, but there were also ragtime songs and the march rhythm of ragtime was danced to as a two-step or a cakewalk. The two-step was launched in 1889, using Sousa's new march, *The Washington Post*.[18] Although the cakewalk had featured in minstrel shows of the 1870s, it was its performance by Charles Johnson and Dora Dean in *The Creole Show* that led to its becoming a rage in North America and Europe.

Variety began as a free show in a concert saloon or beer garden. After the Civil War, it was more usually found in theatres. It leaned on minstrelsy at first, but developed in its own way. Jokes directed at New York's Irish, Italian and German immigrants were common. Vaudeville came to mean variety fare suitable for the 'double audience', that is, men and women. When F. F. Proctor opened his 23rd Street Theatre in 1892, he made it the home of continuous vaudeville suitable for 'ladies and children'; his slogan was 'After breakfast go to

---

17 See Denja J. Epstein, *Sinful Tunes and Spirituals: Black Folk Music to the Civil War* (Urbana, 1977), pp. 119–20.

18 N. Tawa, *The Way to Tin Pan Alley: American Popular Song, 1866–1910* (New York, 1990), p. 183.

Proctor's, after Proctor's go to bed'. His shows included a range of wholesome entertainment – from a baritone soloist to 'comedy elephants'. Proctor pioneered 'popular prices' from 25 to 50 cents; yet, the capacity of his theatre meant he could afford the high salaries of stars. The *comédie-vaudevilles* performed at Parisian theatres like the Gaîté and the Vaudeville contained songs from operetta, traditional airs and a few original numbers. Such theatres were the domain of actors who sang rather than singers who acted.

The first *opéra bouffe* was *Don Quichotte* (1847) by Hervé, whose Folies nouvelles theatre gave Jacques Offenbach (1819–80) the idea for his own Bouffes Parisiens, opened in 1855. *Orphée aux enfers*, an *opéra bouffe* in two acts, was first performed there in 1858. Such a thing as *Orphée* was not possible earlier because of the strict regulations of the prefecture of police which, in 1855, allowed Offenbach's company only three characters in musical scenes, no choruses without special permission, and restricted the entertainment to one act. *Orphée* pokes fun indirectly at aristocratic Classical learning and the aristocracy's self-identification with Classical figures. Orpheus and Euridice are a bored husband and wife having affairs, though when Orpheus sings 'On m'a ravi mon Euridice', he quotes Gluck's famous melody. The *galop infernal* was a sensation and, later, often used for the cancan. Significantly, the 'Marseillaise' is quoted in the chorus of gods rebelling against Jupiter. Part of Offenbach's popular appeal was his use of 'couplets' (verse plus chorus) instead of arias and cavatinas.

Vienna was the first foreign city to respond enthusiastically to Offenbach. The reader will find a fuller discussion of operetta in chapter 14; here, I will confine myself to some remarks on Strauss's *Die Fledermaus*, composed after he had already established the importance of the waltz in two previous operettas. There is an obvious middle-class subject position in Adele's 'laughing song', which satirises the idea that certain physiognomic features are the preserve of the aristocracy. In general, the satirical bite of Offenbach or Gilbert and Sullivan is absent, but there were no London or New York operettas as sensual or hedonistic. Typical of operetta is the use of musical irony. In *Die Fledermaus*, the 'wrong' musical mood for 'O je, o je, wie rührt mich dies!' in the trio in Act I betrays the characters' real feelings. Irony often works as an appropriation of a style: for example, the bombast of 'When Britain Really Ruled the Waves' (from *Iolanthe*) is strengthened by Sullivan's use of a style associated with stirring, patriotic music. Alternatively, a style may contradict the text, so that the music undermines it: for example, in the refrain of General Boum's 'Piff, Paff, Pouff' (from *La grande duchesse*) Offenbach could have adopted a grand Meyerbeerian manner, but chooses, instead, to provide music that deflates the General's pomposity.

Postbellum prosperity in America came to an end in 1873, and some minstrel troupes went bankrupt; variety entertainment, being more adaptable, survived better. The time was right to try new things. The import of operetta from London, Paris and Vienna met with great success because of its cross-class appeal. A native variety of operetta appeared with *The Pearl of Pekin* (1888) by Gustave Kerker, based on Charles Lecocq's *Fleur de thé* (1868). Kerker's *The Belle of New York* (1897) took London by storm in 1898 and notched up over 700 performances. Edward Harrigan and David Braham are often referred to as the American Gilbert and Sullivan for their musical plays of the 1880s in which Tony Hart performed as Harrigan's partner. Harrigan was the librettist and was first to make substantial use on stage of characters drawn from New York's ethnic minorities, commenting, 'Polite society, wealth, and culture possess little or no color and picturesqueness. The chief use I make of them is as a foil to the poor, the workers, the great middle class.'[19] However, Harrigan and Hart did not go in for political polemic, and their social comment never overrode their comedy and entertainment. The title song from their *Mulligan Guards* of 1879 was known in London, Paris and Vienna, where Karl Millöcker quoted it in *Der Bettelstudent* (1882).

The Montmartre *cabarets artistiques* were designed to attract an informal gathering of musicians, theatrical performers, poets and artists of a bohemian disposition. Cabaret reinvigorated the chanson, bringing back its concern with social issues: for example, 'Le réveillon des gueux' by Jules Jouy warns of imminent conflict between the hungry poor and the wealthy. A chansonnier was originally a singer-poet, though not necessarily a composer. A famous earlier chansonnier was Pierre-Jean de Béranger, who gave politically charged performances in the Caveau Moderne from 1813. Chanson and chansonnier began to separate in the later century as the former began to embrace a wider range of popular material.

The Chat Noir, founded in 1881 in Montmartre by Rodolphe Salis, drew in most of the Club des Hydropathes; they were led by journalist Emile Goudeau, who took the club's name from Joseph Gung'l's Hydropathen Waltz. The Chat Noir was originally advertised as a Louis XIII cabaret (a reference to its bizarre but by no means authentic décor) founded by a *fumiste*.[20] Goudeau's Hydropathes and Jouy's Incohérents were groups of left-bank writers, artists and performers committed to *l'esprit fumiste*. An example was the empty score produced by Alphonse Allais for the 1884 Incohérent exhibition, a silent

19 Quoted in R. C. Toll, *On with the Show: The First Century of Show Business in America* (New York, 1976), p. 185.

20 Phillip Dennis Cate, 'The Spirit of Montmartre', in Phillip Dennis Cate and Mary Shaw (eds.), *The Spirit of Montmartre: Cabarets, Humor, and the Avant-Garde, 1875–1905* (Jane Voorhees Zimmerli Art Museum, Rutgers, The State University of New Jersey, exhibition catalogue, 1996), at p. 25.

funeral march for a great deaf man. Maurice Mac-Nab had sung satirical songs of working-class life at the Club des Hydropathes. A favourite at the Chat Noir was 'Le grand métingue du métropolitain', which celebrates striking workers, pokes fun at the municipal police, and makes ironic use of phrases associated with appeals to patriotism. Erik Satie frequented the Chat Noir, accompanied the chansonnier Vincent Hypsa, and wrote a *fumiste* essay on the musicians of Montmartre.[21]

Aristide Bruant (1851–1925), formerly a *café-concert* performer, was taken to the Chat Noir by Jouy. He decided to remodel his image and repertory to make words, music and persona all contribute to the aesthetic experience. He developed the *chanson réaliste*, influenced by reading Zola. He sang of the dispossessed and disaffected, building a celebrated repertory of songs of the *barrières* ('A la Villette', 'A Grenelle', 'A la Chapelle', 'A la Bastille'), though he was of provincial middle-class origin. 'A la Villette' (1885) has a trite tune and banal rhythm that, along with Bruant's unflinching, deadpan delivery (he later recorded it), act as a perfect match for the impoverished existence of its 'anti-hero' and increase the sense of brutality as the song ends with his neck held ready for the guillotine. Having lived near Mazas prison and visited it regularly, Bruant had acquired a knowledge of criminal language and behaviour. He gave immediacy to his songs about social injustice by singing in the first person. The overall effect was one of authenticity, his listeners feeling that his songs 'take the real life of poor and miserable and vicious people, their real sentiments . . . and they say straight out, in the fewest words, just what such people would really say, with a wonderful art in the reproduction of the actual vulgar accent'.[22] The obvious theatricality of the red scarf, big hat and cape, though they caught the attention of Toulouse-Lautrec, went without comment in this type of reaction. When the Chat Noir moved to larger premises in 1885, Bruant stayed on and created his own cabaret *Le Mirliton*.

Yvette Guilbert (1865–1944) became celebrated as a *diseuse*, giving primary attention to enunciating words expressively. She replaced Thérésa as Paris's star singer-comedian. An article in the *Echo de Paris* claimed, 'Montmartre . . . has made her what she is, cadaverous and intensely modern, with a sort of bitter and deadly modernity which she must have acquired at the Chat Noir'.[23] She sang 'La soûlarde', perhaps the most famous of her Jouy songs, wearing a simple evening dress and long black gloves (well known from Toulouse-Lautrec's

---

21 Erik Satie, 'Les Musiciens de Montmartre' (1900), in Ornella Volta (ed.), *Écrits* (Paris, 1990), p. 47. For a detailed survey of the importance of cabaret to Satie, see Stephen Whiting, *Satie the Bohemian: From Cabaret to Concert Hall* (Oxford, 1998).

22 Contemporary quotation from Arthur Symons, *Colour Studies in Paris* (New York, 1918), pp. 67–8; quoted in H. B. Segel, *Turn-of-the-Century Cabaret* (New York, 1987), p. 63.

23 Cited without date, but *c.* 1891, in Guilbert and Simpson, *Struggles and Victories*, p. 199.

sketches), yet, she was felt to convey more of a sense of realism than costumed performers. She made a big impact with this song in London, seeming to reveal 'something new and hitherto undreamt of in the power of song as a medium of dramatic expression'.[24] It concerns a drunken, wretched old woman dragging herself down a street, enduring jeers and abuse. It avoids sentimentality, and was probably found morally acceptable as a warning of the degrading effects of alcohol.

Her repertory was not unremittingly grim, however. Henry Bauer, in the *Echo de Paris* (1891), writes that there is a 'middle kind' of song taken up by Guilbert that falls between the 'inane' *café-concert* songs and the 'powerful' verses of Jouy and Bruant: 'songs of delicate fancy, pointed without being ill-natured, and not broad enough to be unpleasant. This class of song has its own particular bard, whose name is Fourneau, or in Latin Fornax, whence by anagram, Xanrof.'[25] The artistic cabarets of Montmartre were relying on wealthy middle-class patronage before the century was out and, as Goudeau commented, 'saw at their formerly modest doors the throng of emblazoned carriages and the wealthiest bankers contributing their subsidy to this former Golgotha transformed into Gotha of the silly songs'.[26]

Music, morals and social order

Nineteenth-century bourgeois values were several, as were their ideological functions (thrift set against extravagance, self-help vs. dependence, hard work vs. idleness) but, where art and entertainment were concerned, the key value in asserting moral leadership was respectability. It was something within the grasp of all, unlike the aristocratic values of lineage and 'good breeding'. Lineage was to become the butt of satire: Pooh-Bah in *The Mikado* is incurably haughty because he can trace back his ancestry to a pre-Adamite atomic globule. Respectability is not enforced from on high, however; it operates as part of a consensus won by ideological persuasion. In Offenbach's *Orphée aux enfers*, the outcry against Eurydice's immorality is led by a character called, satirically, Public Opinion (a phrase recently coined by the press).

The fight for respectability was one that religious organisations were eager to support. Nonconformism was a major force behind English choral music in the nineteenth century. London's Sacred Harmonic Society, founded in 1832, began as a nonconformist organisation. Of its seventy-three members in 1834, thirty-six were artisans and twenty-seven shopkeepers, figures that reveal that

24 *Ibid.*, p. 317.   25 Quoted *Ibid.*, p. 206.
26 Emile Goudeau, preface to Victor Meusy and Edmond Depas, *Guide de l'étranger à Montmartre* (Paris, 1900), quoted in Cate, 'The Spirit of Montmartre', p. 39.

it was dominated by the lower middle class.[27] In Paris, William Wilhelm's singing class, called the Orphéon, received state subsidy in 1836 and, because of that, had more prestige and a higher-class membership than the Sacred Harmonic Society. (Offenbach's Orpheus, incidentally, is Director of the Orphéon of Thebes.)

Oratorios dominated the choral scene in London, but took longer to find an enthusiastic response in New York. Walt Whitman remarked of the performance of Mendelssohn's *Elijah* by the Sacred Music Society in 1847 that it gave the audience 'no great degree of pleasure'.[28] There was no mass choral singing movement in Vienna because of the late decline of aristocratic power there and the suspicion that choral societies were covert political organisations.[29] The Gesellschaft der Musikfreunde mounted oratorio performances on a scale similar to the Sacred Harmonic Society, but no regular choral society was relied upon. The large choirs used for these events were, however, comprised largely of the lower middle class, just as in London.

The conviction behind Matthew Arnold's *Culture and Anarchy* (1869) was that only culture could save society from anarchy. In America, similar ideas prevailed, as Nicholas Tawa has explained: 'Prominent educators and social-minded leaders were confident that music could shore up humanity's ethical and emotional being, teach democratic principles, and encourage allegiance to an undivided national society' (*A Music for the Millions*, pp. 21-2). The working class was thought to need 'rational amusement'. It was not a cynical exercise in control: in their own lives the middle class were committed to self-improvement by going to concerts, buying sheet music and performing it at home. Parisian *soirées*, Viennese *Hauskonzerte*, and 'at home' functions in London and New York made demands on those present. A belief in the moral power of music was an all-pervasive ideology: 'Let no one', admonished the great champion of the improving powers of music, the Reverend Haweis, 'say the moral effects of music are small or insignificant' (*Music and Morals*, p. 112). It was the activities that accompanied music that raised suspicion of the unwholesome, not the music itself. Even in Vienna, for example, there were those who worried about the moral propriety of the waltz, its sensuality and the close proximity of the couple dancing.

The British Brass Band Movement, in the second half of the century was, like choirs, an example of 'rational recreation' – hence, the willingness of factory

27 See W. Weber, *Music and the Middle Class: The Social Structure of Concert Life in London, Paris and Vienna Between 1830 and 1848* (New York, 1975), p. 167, Table 21.

28 Cleveland Rodgers and John Black (eds.), *The Gathering of the Forces, by Walt Whitman*, II (New York, 1920), pp. 353-4, quoted in Charles Hamm, *Music in the New World* (New York, 1983), pp. 206-7.

29 On the perceived political threat of choral societies in Vienna, see Heinrich Eduard Jacob, *Johann Strauss: A Century of Light Music*, trans. Marguerite Wolff (London, 1940), p. 188.

owners to sponsor works bands. These bands had their roots in the industrial North, but the steel, ironworks and shipping companies of East London also had bands in the 1860s. Huge annual contests were held at the Crystal Palace during 1860–3. The first of these, a two-day event, attracted an audience of 29,000.[30] The test pieces for the contests at the Crystal Palace placed an emphasis on high-status music: selections from Meyerbeer's grand operas were the favourite choices, as at the Belle Vue contests in Manchester that same decade.

It was meaningless, of course, if the entertainment was respectable but the venue not. Concern about prostitution in theatres and music halls grew in the second half of the century.[31] In Vienna, prostitutes were found at some of the grandest dance halls, such as the Apollo. In Paris, concern about prostitution in cafés developed in the 1860s, previous attention having been on other public spaces, such as boulevards and gardens. Alcohol consumption was another threat to morals and respectability, and music was used as a medium of persuasion by fractional interests within the bourgeoisie, such as the temperance groups in London and New York which promoted songs portraying the destructive effects of drunkenness on the home and family.[32]

The respectability of the bourgeoisie was not beyond challenge, of course. Yvette Guilbert represented bourgeois vices humorously in chansons like 'Le fiacre' (Xanrof) and 'Je suis pocharde!' (Laroche–Byrec). When she sang at the respectable Eden-Concert in 1890, she was allowed to sing the latter (concerning the effects of alcohol), but not the former (concerning marital infidelity). The context of 'Je suis pocharde!' helped it to gain acceptability. Guilbert herself stressed that this is a girl from a 'good family' who has been drinking champagne at her sister's wedding and is 'gentiment grise', or slightly tipsy (*Struggles and Victories*, p. 116).

The labouring poor may have been sung about and even felt to be understood in certain socially concerned drawing-room ballads, but their lives often lay outside the experience of those who sang the ballads. Antoinette Sterling, who so movingly sang 'Three Fishers Went Sailing' (Kingsley–Hullah), confessed that not only had she no experience of storms at sea, but 'had never even seen fishermen'.[33] The subject position such ballads address is that of the middle class. So, too, do the Gilbert and Sullivan operettas, parading middle-class prejudices, albeit in an ironic way, as in Ko-Ko's list of 'society offenders' in *The*

30 See Roy Newsome, *Brass Roots: A Hundred Years of Brass Bands and Their Music, 1836–1936* (Aldershot, 1998), pp. 38–42.

31 See Dagmar Kift, *The Victorian Music Hall: Culture, Class and Conflict* (Cambridge, 1996; original edn Essen, 1991), pp. 136–9, and Dagmar Höher, 'The Composition of Music Hall Audiences 1850–1900', in Bailey (ed.), *Music Hall: The Business of Pleasure*, pp. 74–5.

32 See Derek B. Scott, *The Singing Bourgeois: Songs of the Victorian Drawing Room and Parlour* (Aldershot, 2001), p. 189.   33 Harold Simpson, *A Century of Ballads 1810–1910* (London, 1910), p. 121.

Mikado. The characters of this operetta are, of course, English in fancy dress. *The Gondoliers* (1889) satirises anti-egalitarianism, summed up in the lines: 'When every one is somebodee, Then no one's anybody.' It appeared at a time of anti-monarchist sentiment, and the growth of socialist and republican ideas. The issue of class distinction was especially to the fore, and the buying of titles is lampooned by the Duke of Plaza-Toro. *Iolanthe* satirises the House of Lords more than the Commons. After the first night, a song was removed because a critic accused Gilbert of pathos that 'smacks of anger, a passion altogether out of place in a "fairy opera"', and of 'bitterly aggressive politics'.[34] The song offended middle-class values by sympathising with a wretched pickpocket, suggesting that anyone 'robbed of all chances' would steal in turn.

The subject position of music halls and *cafés-concerts* was that of the upper-working-class or lower-middle-class male. The performers themselves were of a mixed class background: of the *lions comiques* in London, for example, George Leybourne had been a mechanic and the Great MacDermott a bricklayer, but the Great Vance was formerly a solicitor's clerk. The toff or 'swell' character of the 1860s appealed to socially aspiring lower-middle-class males. Leybourne, the most acclaimed of the swells, was given a contract in 1868, at the height of his success with the song 'Champagne Charlie', making it a condition that he continued his swell persona offstage.[35] The swell, however, is double-coded, inscribing admiration for wealth and status, but subverting bourgeois values by celebrating excess and idleness ('A noise all night, in bed all day and swimming in Champagne', boasts Charlie). Some of those at *cafés-concerts*, also, were putting on appearances, like the 'calicots' or 'counter-jumpers'. Hence the appeal of the Parisian swell, or *gommeux*, the most famous being Libert. Henriette Bépoix, a *gommeuse*, appeared the year after. *Gommeuses* were common in the 1890s, wearing extravagant feathered hats, gaudy dresses and lots of jewellery. They presented themselves as fun-loving and giddy, with rich, if unattractive, lovers.

The efforts made by the bourgeoisie in the interests of respectability were not always an unqualified success and, sometimes, failure occurred unexpectedly. It would be easy to assume, given the association of French entertainment with the *risqué*, that London reacted more cautiously to the sauciness of Offenbach's operettas. On the contrary, in England, productions were sometimes lewder. *Punch* remarked of the performances of *La grande duchesse de Gérolstein* and *La belle Hélène* starring Hortense Schneider in 1868: 'Schneider

34 William Beatty-Kingston, critic of the *Theatre*, quoted in L. Baily, *The Gilbert and Sullivan Book* (London, 1966; original edn London, 1952, rev. 1956), p. 238.

35 See Peter Bailey, 'Champagne Charlie: Performance and Ideology in the Music Hall Swell Song', in Bratton, (ed.), *Music Hall: Performance and Style*, pp. 50–1.

was far more vulgar in London than in Paris, though on her native heath her performance was witnessed chiefly by ladies of the faster set'.[36] Once again, this opens up the issue of culture, especially popular culture, as an area of compromise, where no complete dominance can be achieved.

Much of the cultural change during the century can be seen as driven by the power and interests of fractions within the middle class but, as Kathy Peiss points out, 'the lines of cultural transmission travel in both directions', and the working class did not passively consume cultural messages (*Cheap Amusements*, p. 8). In 1899, the *Musical Courier*, with reference to ragtime, proclaimed: 'A wave of vulgar, filthy and suggestive music has inundated the land'.[37] The irony was that ragtime idiomatically suited the instrument most imbued with domestic respectability, the piano. However, the flipside was that pianos were also commonly to be found in New York's brothels and honky-tonks.

The presence of different classes in the same venue did not mean that they mixed. Emile Blémont wrote about *cafés-concerts* in the *Evénement*, February 1891:

> On the one hand you will find the masses, a trifle heavy, a trifle slow, but simple-minded, sympathetic and generous . . . faithful to the old traditional form of song . . . On the other hand . . . you will find another public which is, in some respects, more highly cultivated. They are the rakes, the 'déclassés' of literature or trade, forming the bohemia of the more well-to-do middle class.
>
> (Quoted in Guilbert and Simpson, *Struggles and Victories*, pp. 204–5)

Blémont commented that the two publics sat close together but did not intermingle, and that in some establishments the 'popular element' dominated, while in others it was the 'bohemian element'. In London, socially mixed music halls were in the centre, working class halls in the suburbs. The West End halls attracted bohemian types from the beginning.

When hegemony fails, Gramsci explained, it is replaced by coercion. The music hall audience in London, however, defended its values and behaviour when the law was used in a repressive manner, turning up in large numbers at the halls, at law courts and licensing sessions, and writing letters and petitions. The clearest example of coercive control is censorship. French censorship of songs was relaxed during 1870. An official report of 1872 rails against the shamelessness of *café-concert* songwriters from all points of view, moral, political and religious, stating that a large number of songs are refused absolutely, while 'serious modifications' are required in others.[38]

36 Quoted without date in Baily, *The Gilbert and Sullivan Book*, p. 90.

37 Quoted in Ian Whitcomb, *After the Ball: Pop Music from Rag to Rock* (New York, 1986; original edn 1972), p. 16.

38 Archives nationales, series F21, no. 1338, report of November 1872, p. 2, quoted in Clark, *The Painting of Modern Life*, p. 304, n. 10.

The physicality of some performers was a threat in itself. Thérésa had a loud, low-pitched voice and striking physical presence, an idea of which can be gained from Degas' studies of her performances. There is no doubt that in her early career the censor scrutinised all her songs. However, it was the way she sang that had such an impact – her energy and defiance. No corporeal discipline was to be found, either, in the gestures, winks and knowing smiles that Marie Lloyd used to lend suggestiveness to the most 'innocent' of music hall songs.

Urban ballads were another repository of oppositional elements. 'The new Poor Law', a song about the workhouse that followed that law's passing in 1834 chooses, ironically, the tune of 'Home, Sweet, Home!' Queen Victoria is represented as having very un-Victorian sexual interests in 'Married at Last' (1840). The striking women of 1888 from Bryant and May's match factory sang a parody of 'John Brown's Body' on their marches through the West End.[39] The next year, during the London dock strike, Jim Connell wrote 'The Red Flag' (to the tune of 'The White Cockade'), and Harry Clifton's conservative anthem 'Work, Boys, Work' (to the tune of Root's 'Tramp, Tramp, Tramp') was parodied as 'Strike, Boys, Strike'. In America, the Labor Movement prompted the production of thousands of labour songs. A New York writer of such songs was Mary Agnes Sheridan, a carpet mill operative.[40] They would be sung to traditional airs, hymn tunes or minstrel melodies. The words typically accuse capitalists of betraying republican ideas of democracy and brotherhood. However, the increased use of repressive action by state and federal troops in disputes weakened the Labor Movement in the 1890s.

In France, the Saint-Simonians insisted upon a social art which would contribute to a better society. Rouget de Lisle (composer of the 'Marseillaise') wrote 'Premier chant des industriels' (1821), praising industrial workers, at Henri Saint-Simon's instigation. Jules Vinçard, head of the Famille de Paris, a group of working-class and artisan members in Paris, wrote songs influenced by the political chansons of Béranger, but for which, unlike Béranger, he also composed the music.[41] Eugène Pottier, a woodworker from Lille, wrote the words of one of the most famous political chansons, the 'Internationale', after the suppression of the Paris Commune in 1871 (Pierre Degeyter provided music in 1888). Jean-Baptiste Clément's 'Le temps de cérises' (set to music by Antoine Renard in 1868) was sung by the Communards, interpreting the return of spring as a metaphor for the return of liberty. Clément was one of the elected of the Commune. In 1886, Jouy reworked the song as 'Le temps des crises', making an overtly political statement.

39 Roy Palmer, *The Sound of History: Songs and Social Comment* (Oxford, 1988), p. 108.
40 See Clark D. Halker, *For Democracy, Workers, and God: Labor Song-Poems and Labor Protest, 1865–95* (Urbana, 1991), pp. 55, 70 and 206.
41 Rouget de Lisle's song and five of Vinçard's songs are reproduced with music in Ralph P. Locke, *Music, Musicians and the Saint-Simonians* (Chicago, 1986), pp. 238–9 and Appendix C, pp. 247–50.

Oppositional elements came to the fore in Vienna when the outbreak of the Hungarian Revolution in 1848 triggered an uprising there a week later. Strauss II wrote several pro-Revolution works, including a 'Revolution March' and a 'Song of the Barricades'. His 'Students' March' was confiscated by the police.[42] He played the 'Marseillaise' at the barricades, and was probably saved only by his popularity when the Revolution was crushed; nevertheless, he acquired a police record. A warrant for arrest was also issued on his brother Josef. Their father, who had separated from the family, did not share their republican sentiments; his *Radetzky March* was a tribute to the general in command of the Habsburg army.

The rift between art and entertainment

Culture can be used as a marker of superiority, a taste for the 'refined' over the 'vulgar', which is why Bourdieu remarks that 'art and cultural consumption are predisposed, consciously and deliberately or not, to fulfil a social function of legitimating social differences' (*Distinction*, p. 7). The increase in urban populations and rise of the bourgeoisie brought a need for public demonstrations of social standing, since it was no longer common knowledge who was important. Attending concerts was a means of displaying status. By the second half of the century, a distinction had arisen between 'art music' and 'popular music', even if not expressed in exactly those terms. 'Light music' might be said to have originated in Vienna, in the dance music of Lanner and Strauss I, which combined folk and Classical styles in a new way. The terms 'highbrow', first used in the 1880s, and 'lowbrow', which emerged in the 1900s, relate to the pseudoscience of phrenology: the high brow was a sign of intelligence, especially since it was a feature of the 'civilised' European races.

Carl Dahlhaus has argued that nineteenth-century popular music is lowbrow, and better described as 'trivial music': 'Eighteenth-century divertimentos were also designed to entertain, but no one would wish to place them alongside a nineteenth-century Viennese coffeehouse *pièce*'. Dahlhaus seeks to make a qualitative distinction, but explains it in terms of a betrayal of eighteenth-century philanthropy by nineteenth-century capitalists: the fault for the trivialisation of those 'philanthropic tendencies' lies with industrialisation and the 'compulsion to mass-produce and distribute commodities'. His example of *Trivialmusik*, Lefébure-Wély's piano piece *Les cloches du monastère*, is revealed to be sadly lacking as a musical structure. He then rails against 'trivialised listening' which ignores 'the principle of self-absorption in the work as an

---

42 J. Wechsberg, *The Waltz Emperors: The Life and Times and Music of the Strauss Family* (London, 1973), p. 101.

aesthetic object', so that the music 'degenerates into a vehicle for associations and for edifying or melancholy self-indulgence'. The word 'degenerates', in the context of what Dahlhaus describes as 'a special form of lowbrow music', is not without its significance.[43]

In 1860, a writer in *Macmillan's Magazine* identifies a 'higher class of music'. This is not a kind associated with female accomplishments; it is a serious and quasi-religious 'man's music'. The writer mentions an old friend who 'would as soon have thought of sawing his beloved "Strad" up for firewood as of admitting his wife into the music-room during the celebration of the mysteries'.[44] Composers were soon held to task by high-minded critics for producing low (that is, entertaining) music. The London weekly *Figaro*, commenting on the first night of Gilbert and Sullivan's *The Sorcerer* (1877), expressed its 'disappointment at the downward art course that Sullivan appears to be drifting into'.[45] Another review, in *The World* remarked: 'It was hoped that he would soar with Mendelssohn, whereas he is, it seems, content to sink with Offenbach'.[46] This was a criticism he was to encounter often. The press greeted *HMS Pinafore* (1878) by damning it as undistinguished, disappointing and feeble, despite its success with the audience.

When Lawrence Levine writes of the 'sacralisation of culture', he refers to the idea that culture is not to be vulgarised; it is too sacred. This idea of culture is contrasted with the flexibility evident during one of the earliest New York performances of Rossini's *Il barbiere di Siviglia* in 1825, when Maria Garcia sang 'Home, Sweet Home!' (Payne–Bishop) as an encore in Act II (Levine, *Highbow/Lowbrow*, p. 90). As the decades passed, opera became high-class culture: Italian opera was to be performed in Italian, not English; opera was refined and intellectual; and opera houses were for fashionable society. The progress of a 'sacralised' art becomes evident comparing Adelina Patti's two visits to New York, first in the 1850s, then in the 1880s when some critics took offence at her giving a recital of 'popular ballads', claiming that she had returned to 'another America', an 'intelligent musically developed America'.[47] She had first visited when there was strong support for a popular or 'common man's' culture. The schism between the demands of the lowbrows (which included most of the 'midding classes') and the highbrows had resulted in a

43 Quotations from C. Dahlhaus, *Nineteenth-Century Music*, trans. J. B. Robinson (Berkeley and Los Angeles, 1989), pp. 311, 314–15.

44 J. B. Macdonnell, 'Classical Music and British Musical Taste', *Macmillan's Magazine*, 1 (1860), p. 384.

45 Quoted in Reginald Allen, *The First Night Gilbert and Sullivan* (London, rev. edn 1976; original edn New York, 1958), p. 49, and in Arthur Jacobs, *Arthur Sullivan: A Victorian Musician* (Oxford, 1984), p. 112.

46 Quoted in Arthur Jacobs, 'Sullivan, Gilbert and the Victorians', *Music Review*, 12 (1951), p. 123, and in E. D. Mackerness, *A Social History of English Music* (London, 1964), p. 191.

47 George William Curtis, 'Editor's Easy Chair', *Harper's New Monthly Magazine*, 64 (February 1882), pp. 467–78, quoted in L. M. Levine, *Highbrow/Lowbrow* (Cambridge, Mass., 1988), p. 135.

full-scale riot in Astor Place in 1849 outside the Opera House, then New York's largest theatre. The riot was triggered by rivalry between two actors, a British tragedian admired by the 'better families' and an American; they represented competing claims on the future direction of American culture. After the riot, which left thirty-one dead and 150 injured, the *Philadelphia Ledger* remarked: 'There is now . . . in New York City, what every good patriot has hitherto considered it his duty to deny – a high class and a low class'.[48] It is worth noting that culture has classified them.

The rift between art and entertainment widened in Vienna towards the century's close. The Theater an der Wien thought it could span the gulf, and began to offer opera as well as its traditional fare of *Spieloper*. In 1896-7, facing artistic and financial difficulties, the music critic Richard Wallaschek warned it to make a choice between opera and operetta, 'given the complete separation that exists between these genres today'.[49] This was the period when Vienna witnessed an increase in learned articles on music, an emphasis on theory and analysis, and a preference for abstraction and structural listening among erudite musicians. Yet, when Strauss II died, Hanslick called him Vienna's 'most original musical talent'.[50]

Working-class rational recreations now seemed insufficiently dedicated to the shrine of art. In the summer of 1880, the *New York Times* ran three editorials opposed to the enthusiasm for brass instruments and brass bands. At this time, Sousa increased the number of reeds in his band, bringing it closer to the Classical orchestra and making it more acceptable to the music critics, though not all approved of the way he mixed the 'classics' and the 'popular'. In the first half of the century, popular music was possible in the 'best of homes', but from now on the message of 'high art' was that there was a 'better class of music' and another kind that appealed to 'the masses'.

Bibliography

Allen, R., *The First Night Gilbert and Sullivan*. London, rev. edn. 1976; original edn New York, 1958

Attali, J., *Noise: The Political Economy of Music*, trans. B. Massumi. Manchester, 1985; original edn Paris, 1977

Bailey, P. (ed.), *Music Hall: The Business of Pleasure*. Milton Keynes, 1986

Baily, L., *The Gilbert and Sullivan Book*. London, 1966; original edn London, 1952, rev. 1956

---

48 Quoted in Toll, *On with the Show*, p. 21.

49 *Die Zeit* (9 October 1897), p. 26, quoted in Sandra McColl, *Music Criticism in Vienna 1896-1897: Critically Moving Forms* (Oxford, 1996), p. 83.

50 Eduard Hanslick, *Vienna's Golden Years of Music 1850-1900*, trans. Henry Pleasants (London, 1951), p. 325.

Bourdieu, P., *Distinction: A Social Critique of the Judgement of Taste*, trans. R. Nice. London, 1984; original edn Paris, 1979

Bratton, J. S. (ed.), *Music Hall: Performance and Style*. Milton Keynes, 1986

Caradec, F. and Weill, A., *Le café-concert*. Paris, 1980

Cate, P. D., 'The Spirit of Montmartre'. In P. D. Cate and M. Shaw (eds.), *The Spirit of Montmartre: Cabarets, Humor, and the Avant-Garde, 1875–1905*. Jane Voorhees Zimmerli Art Museum, Rutgers, The State University of New Jersey, exhibition catalogue, 1996, pp. 1–93

Clark, T. J., *The Painting of Modern Life: Paris in the Art of Manet and His Followers*. London, 1985

Dahlhaus, C., *Nineteenth-Century Music*, trans. J. B. Robinson. Berkeley and Los Angeles, 1989

Ehrlich, C., *The Music Profession in Britain since the Eighteenth Century: A Social History*. Oxford, 1985

Elias, N., *The Civilizing Process*, I, *The History of Manners*. Oxford, 1978

Epstein, D. J., *Sinful Tunes and Spirituals: Black Folk Music to the Civil War*. Urbana, 1977

Guilbert, Y., *La Chanson de ma Vie (Mes Mémoires)*. Paris, 1927

Guilbert, Y. and Simpson, H., *Yvette Guilbert: Struggles and Victories*. London, 1910

Halker, C. D., *For Democracy, Workers, and God: Labor Song-Poems and Labor Protest, 1865–95*. Urbana, 1991

Hamm, C., *Yesterdays: Popular Song in America*. New York, 1979
Music in the New World. New York, 1983

Hanslick, E., *Vienna's Golden Years of Music 1850–1900*, trans. H. Pleasants. London, 1951

Hanson, A. M., *Musical Life in Biedermeier Vienna*. Cambridge, 1985

Harker, D., *Fakesong: The Manufacture of British 'Folksong' 1700 to the Present Day*. Milton Keynes, 1985

Haweis, H. R., *Music and Morals*. London, 1912; reprint of 1871 edn

Jacob, H. E., *Johann Strauss: A Century of Light Music*, trans. M. Wolff. London, 1940

Jacob, R. L. and Skelton, G. (eds.), *Wagner Writes from Paris*. London, 1973

Jacobs, A., *Arthur Sullivan: A Victorian Musician*. Oxford, 1984

Kift, D., *The Victorian Music Hall: Culture, Class and Conflict*. Cambridge, 1996; original edn Essen, 1991

Leppert, R., *The Sight of Sound: Music, Representation, and the History of the Body*. Berkeley and Los Angeles, 1993

Levine, L. M., *Highbrow/Lowbrow*. Cambridge, Mass., 1988

Locke, R. P., *Music, Musicians and the Saint-Simonians*. Chicago, 1986

Macdonnell, J. B., 'Classical Music and British Musical Taste'. *Macmillan's Magazine*, 1 (1860), pp. 383–9.

Mackerness, E. D., *A Social History of English Music*. London, 1964

Mackinlay, S., *Origin and Development of Light Opera*. London, 1927

Maretzek, M., *Revelations of an Opera Manager in Nineteenth-Century America*, Part 1. New York, 1968; original edn *Crotchets and Quavers*, 1855

McColl, S., *Music Criticism in Vienna 1896–1897: Critically Moving Forms*. Oxford, 1996

Meusy, V. and Depas, E., *Guide de l'étranger à Montmartre*. Paris, 1900

Meyer, L. B., *Style and Music: Theory, History, and Ideology*. Chicago, 1996

Middleton, R., 'Popular Music of the Lower Classes'. In N. Temperley, *The Romantic Age 1800–1914: The Athlone History of Music in Britain*. London, 1981, pp. 63–91

Newsome, R., *Brass Roots: A Hundred Years of Brass Bands and Their Music, 1836–1936*. Aldershot, 1998

Palmer, R., *The Sound of History: Songs and Social Comment*. Oxford, 1988

Peiss, K., *Cheap Amusements: Working Women and Leisure in Turn-of-the-Century New York*. Philadelphia, 1986

Raynor, H., *Music and Society Since 1815*. London, 1976

Ritchie, J. E., *The Night Side of London*. London, 1857

Satie, E., 'Les Musiciens de Montmartre' (1900). In Ornella Volta (ed.), *Ecrits*. Paris, 1990, p. 47.

Scott, D. B., *The Singing Bourgeois: Songs of the Victorian Drawing Room and Parlour*. Aldershot, 2001; original edn Milton Keynes, 1989

Segel, H. B., *Turn-of-the-Century Cabaret*. New York, 1987

Senelick, L. (ed.), *Tavern Singing in Early Victorian London: The Diaries of Charles Rice for 1840 and 1850*. London, 1997

Simpson, H., *A Century of Ballads 1810–1910*. London, 1910

Smiles, S., *Self-Help*. London, 1859

Tawa, N., *A Music for the Millions: Antebellum Democratic Attitudes and the Birth of American Popular Music*. New York, 1984

   The Way to Tin Pan Alley: American Popular Song, 1866–1910. New York, 1990

Temperley, N. (ed.), *The Romantic Age 1800–1914: The Athlone History of Music in Britain*. London, 1981

Toll, R. C., *On with the Show: The First Century of Show Business in America*. New York, 1976

Van der Merwe, P., *Origins of the Popular Style: The Antecedents of Twentieth-Century Popular Music*. Oxford, 1989

Weber, W., *Music and the Middle Class: The Social Structure of Concert Life in London, Paris and Vienna Between 1830 and 1848*. New York, 1975

Wechsberg, J., *The Waltz Emperors: The Life and Times and Music of the Strauss Family*. London, 1973

Whitcomb, I., *After the Ball: Pop Music from Rag to Rock*. New York, 1986; original edn 1972

Whiting S., *Satie the Bohemian: From Cabaret to Concert Hall*. Oxford, 1998

Williams, R., *Culture and Society 1780–1950*. Harmondsworth, 1961; original edn London, 1958

   The Long Revolution. Harmondsworth, 1965; original edn London, 1961

20

Nations and nationalism

JIM SAMSON

Nationalisms

The French Revolution brought into sharp focus a cluster of ideas about freedom and rights that had been bred in seventeenth-century England and nurtured in eighteenth-century France. Unsurprisingly, it is far from easy to disentangle these ideas – to be clear about causes and effects. Notions of freedom and rights were no doubt promoted by the mode of production of an emergent capitalism in the seventeenth century. But they were promoted too by the Protestant reformation and its influential ethos; and by the philosophical empiricism cultivated by English thinkers. How is one to define a relation between these levels? A (broadly) Marxist position claims that changes in the polity, as also in the cultural and intellectual domains, are invariably motivated by changes in the socio-economic base. Yet this is in competition with the claim (by, for example, Max Weber) that ideas can change the world.[1] Then again, more recent critical theory takes refuge in dialectics, a seductive solution to the chicken and egg problem, but one that may on occasion amount to a failure of nerve. Whatever the underlying causality, it is clear that on a political level strengthening notions of popular sovereignty were given practical meaning and propaganda by the Revolution in France, as earlier by the American War of Independence. These events effectively inaugurated an age of revolution and of liberalism, though it should be noted that from the start liberalism involved a dimension of contractualism as well as of freedom.

It was from this same cluster of ideas that nationalism took much of its impetus; indeed my pairing of French and American histories in the late eighteenth century already says as much. At the same time the relationship of nationalism to a parent ideology of liberalism was bound to be problematical – and turned out to be tragically so in twentieth-century history. The egalitarian premise that fed into and enabled the nationalist enterprises of the nineteenth century was inevitably compromised by the reality of the nation-state. 'Liberty,

---

1 Max Weber, *The Protestant Ethic and the Spirit of Capitalism*, trans. Talcott Parsons (London, 1930).

equality and fraternity' were qualities that translated with difficulty from the individual to the collective levels. The nation-state established a province within which these qualities were active (at least in theory), but without which they had no jurisdiction. Thus the model of civic nationalism that developed in the early nineteenth century implied freedoms and equalities for the citizens within the state, but not beyond its frontiers: to say nothing of the qualified nature of those freedoms and equalities even within the state.[2] Civic nationalisms may have paid lip-service to the individual, but it is rather clear that as the nation-states firmed up in the nineteenth century, it was a contractual model of society that took precedence over any putative freedom of political choice. The nation-state took its stand on communitarian politics – on an identification of the nation with its citizens – but in practice it was constructed 'top-down' by a dominant bourgeois class, and it was careful to insist on obligations as well as rights.

The liberal nation-state, in other words, was the construction of an ascendant bourgeoisie, and it goes without saying that it was in competition with the principle and practice of dynastic government. This relationship between nationalism and social class has been emphasised above all by the historian Eric Hobsbawm and by the social anthropologist Ernest Gellner, though their readings have not won universal acclaim.[3] Crudely, the argument is that the move from a simple agrarian to a complex industrial society promoted communitarianism, in that it necessitated a homogeneous culture under the state. There was, in other words, a strong economic imperative dictating the particular political and social order represented by the nation-state. Yet the exact nature of the interplay between a strengthening industrial-technological base in European societies and a strengthening national consciousness remains something of a moot question, given that the natural tendency of industrialisation was, and is, towards cosmopolitanism. There is, indeed, a perfectly respectable argument for inverting – or at least problematising – Gellner's argument, so that national consciousness is viewed as prior to, or coeval with, the consolidation of bourgeois capitalism.[4] And, as I shall argue later, a comparable ambivalence concerns the centring of both an inclusive cosmopolitan culture and an exclusive national consciousness in the modern city.

However we understand its sources, nationalism rapidly took on something of the character of a belief system, albeit one entirely lacking in transcendental properties. It is presumably no accident, then, that it marched in step with the

---

2 See Liah Greenfeld, *Nationalism: Five Roads to Modernity* (Cambridge, Mass., 1992).
3 Eric J. Hobsbawm, *Nations and Nationalism since 1870: Programme, Myth and Reality* (Cambridge, 1990); Ernest Gellner, *Nations and Nationalism* (Oxford, 1983).
4 Liah Greenfeld, 'The Modern Religion', *Critical Review*, 10/2 (1996), p. 175.

growing secularisation of European societies. As the state divorced itself from the church, an alternative secular image of authority began to emerge, resting on the equation of the polity and the nation: on the assumption that, as Gellner put it, 'the political and the national unit should be congruent'. The effectiveness of this image depended on the belief, largely illusory, that the 'common man' might have some genuine investment in the nation, as he had in the church. But in reality this belief, perhaps like its sacred counterpart, was an easy prey for those interested in imposing control from above. Like the church, the nation could represent a useful mechanism for achieving some measure of social integration, replacing the spiritual relationship of man to God with the political and social relationships of man to man. These two images of authority – church and nation – coexisted in varying degrees of disharmony in the several European states. But whatever the local variation, the shift in balance was very largely in a single direction in Europe as a whole. Premised on the belief that nations had a clear sense of cultural identity, the nationalist impulse gathered increasing momentum. As it did so, it informed existing political structures (notably in France), and in due course generated new structures (in Italy, Germany and much of the eastern Habsburg Empire).

Benedict Anderson used the phrase 'an imagined community' to describe the perceived cultural identity of the nation.[5] It was a community of believers, and as such it was asserted against other communities, by definition those outside the political boundaries, but also those insiders who were perceived to be different. Like its sacred counterpart, moreover, the nation needed its ceremonies, its anthologies and its validating myths. They took their place alongside spoken (vernacular) languages, invented histories and cultural institutions as ways of defining and then bolstering the elusive national essence that was presumed to infuse just about all modes and forms within the boundaries of the nation-state. The arts were naturally included. But we should note that it was in the realm of high culture rather than folk culture that the spirit of nationalism made itself felt. For all the claims made on its behalf, folk culture had in reality little, if anything, to do with the nation, though it was often expressive of a sense of place: a locality. Its value to the larger mission was largely symbolic. Thus folk music was appropriated by bourgeois nationalism rather as that other 'innocent' music, Viennese Classicism, was appropriated by bourgeois historicism. In the end, cultural nationalisms exhibited an oddly paradoxical condition. They staked their claim on a respected contribution to a generalised high culture. At the same time they asserted their distinctiveness, usually by drawing elements of history and myth, together with suitably sanitised compo-

5 Benedict Anderson, *Imagined Communities* (London, 1983).

nents of folk culture, into a synthetic national tradition. There was a sense, then, in which each nation presented a variant on a single bourgeois culture, while at the same time competitively elevating, asserting and promoting its uniqueness.

The ideology of nationalism was forged largely in the German-speaking world. There were pre-echoes in the circumbaltic and northern Slavonic lands, but it was above all in the writings of post-Kantian German philosophers such as Fichte and Herder that the translation of Enlightenment political thought into cultural nationalism was most clearly effected and articulated. Herder in particular identified the nation with its cultural heritage and its language, and in doing so he strengthened the notion that there exists a *Volksgeist*, a genuine 'spirit of the people' that acts as a kind of national glue. Such ideas had special potency in a context where the nation had as yet no political status, and they naturally fed, and at the same time justified, the strengthening impulse towards German unification, even if that aim would eventually be realised on a less idealistic agenda. Herder's '*Volksgeist* hypothesis', as Dahlhaus called it,[6] proved no less seductive in the lands of the eastern Habsburg Empire, where it was quickly distilled into slogans for a political independence premised on a sense of cultural identity. There is perhaps something in the argument that nationalism in Eastern Europe was qualitatively different from that in the west, that it was collectivistic and ethnic rather than individualistic and political in character. Yet it is hard to differentiate it cleanly at least from its German counterpart. Perhaps the real point is that Germany played a key mediating role in the transformation of ideological currents as they migrated from west to east, encountering significantly different social and political conditions *en route*. I shall return to these conditions later.

But for now I will apply a broad brush-stroke to the politics of the later nineteenth century, when the nationalist principle did some of its most energetic work. That in turn will provide the setting for a national perspective on late nineteenth-century institutions and repertories. The decisive event for France and Germany was of course the Franco-Prussian war of 1870–71. In the wake of the 1848 Revolutions the consolidation of middle-class power and influence in both France and Germany had taken place within authoritarian, paternalistic and increasingly centralist regimes, in which the liberal impulses of the early nineteenth century were absorbed into moderate, loosely reformist social policies. Yet as Prussia moved centre stage in the 1860s the common ground was steadily lost. Napoleon, under pressure, liberalised the Second Empire, while Bismarck, in the ascendant, defeated his own liberal opposition. Napoleon

---

6 Carl Dahlhaus, *Between Romanticism and Modernism: Four Studies in the Music of the Later Nineteenth Century*, trans. M. Whittall (Berkeley and Los Angeles, 1980; original edn 1974).

championed the nationalisms of others, while Bismarck consolidated and manipulated nationalism at home. Napoleon rushed into ill-considered foreign adventures, while Bismarck used his wars economically and strategically to further Prussian interests. France, already heavily industrialised, confidently and carelessly enjoyed its status as the first power of Europe, while Prussia, conservative and near-feudal in its social base, steadily mounted its strength, building an economic and military power that was second to none in Europe. The war, when it came, was Napoleon's last hope to save a crumbling empire. It was Bismarck's opportunity to unite or, as one historian put it, to conquer Germany.

It is with Bismarck that the term *Realpolitik* has been inseparably linked. However the term aptly describes a more general loss of idealism in the decades following 1848, when revolution made way for a succession of wars of limited and specific goals and durations. Even Italian unification was achieved somewhat on the German model, and more-or-less in parallel with it – less a populist movement from below than a series of conquests (by Piedmont) from above. By 1871, then, two newly minted nation-states were in place. For the remaining decades of the century, and well into the twentieth century, nationalist hostilities intensified in Europe. Underlying many of them was an increasing tension between the strengthening ethnic identities of the Germans and the Slavs. Leaving aside (for the moment) the positioning of Russia, that tension was interleaved with an even more deep-rooted conflict of interests, as nationalist politics collided with the claims and interests of the dynasties governing Europe, and especially with those of the far-flung Habsburg Empire. The Habsburg defeat in the Austro-Prussian War of 1866 had occasioned concessions to the growing nationalist clamour of northern Italy and the eastern empire, culminating in the historic 'Compromise' of 1867. The resulting so-called Dual Monarchy may have benefited Italy and Hungary, but if anything it served only to strengthen the political nationalisms of the many other groups that remained disadvantaged, notably the Czechs.

Since 1848 the Czechs had been widely perceived as the leaders in liberation movements against the Habsburgs, and their resistance increased following the Compromise. That resistance was expressed through popular movements like the 'Sokols' as well as through the successive political manoeuvrings of the Young Czech Party, the Czech National Party and the Realist Party (under Masaryk), all articulating the hopes of a strong Czech bourgeoisie for Czech rights and ultimately independence. The other front line in this battle was of course the Balkan peninsula, where the Ottoman and Habsburg dynasties came into collision, while the Russian Empire and the Western powers watched, waited and occasionally intervened. It was here, with Slovenia aspiring to freedom from the Habsburgs, Croatia menaced by the Hungarians, Bosnia and Herzegovina annexed by Austria, and Serbia and Bulgaria wrangling over Macedonia, that the spark touching off Europe's conflagration in 1914 was finally ignited, bringing down the Ottoman, Habsburg, Hohenzollern and Romanov dynasties one by one.

Conquering the cities

Our third chapter described how in the early nineteenth century the location of formal musical culture shifted from court to city, a shift closely tied to the professionalisation of bourgeois musical life, and to the gradual emaciation of patronal culture. This, however, was no straightforward replacement of one system by another. The conflicting interests of court and city – the tug-of-war between them – continued in some quarters well into the second half of the nineteenth century. After all, the two leading pioneers of musical modernism after 1848, Wagner and Liszt, both realised their ambitions – or some of them – under the aegis of an aristocratic patronage, albeit in Wagner's case of a rather eccentric kind. And even in the early twentieth century private sponsorship by well-placed and wealthy aristocratic families helped draw the map of musical modernism. Yet the general trend was fairly clear. By the later nineteenth century the institutions of civic music-making, like the bourgeois society which installed them, represented the new order of things. The city was now the principal site for music-making, and as the middle-class cultural base steadily widened, musical life began to stabilise, though at different rates, into structures and practices that were reasonably uniform across Europe and the New World (as noted in chapter 13). Most of these were at base dependent on market forces for their survival.

The cities, in other words, promoted a cosmopolitan musical culture grounded in middle-class, mercantile values. For this reason they represented a tendency somewhat at odds with the thrust of cultural nationalism, though paradoxically this too was largely an urban phenomenon. There was a developing tension, then, between city and nation in the later nineteenth century, just as there was a receding tension between city and court. The issues at stake may perhaps be clarified by focusing on the contrasted destinies of the two cities that were widely regarded as the musical capitals of Europe at the time. Paris and Vienna had much in common following the 1848 Revolutions, not least through the parallel programmes of urban reconstruction inaugurated by Napoleon and Franz Josef. The boulevards and the Ringstrasse, and the impressive public buildings associated with each of them, affirmed and neatly symbolised the ascendancy of bourgeois society under enlightened autocracies in both capitals. Moreover the 'flavour' of the two cities was similar, with political corruption proceeding hand in hand with the extravagance and heedless gaiety of cosmopolitan capitals, where the lavish entertainments of a pleasure-seeking demi-monde could barely conceal the real hardship below. For all their glories, Vienna and Paris were the shop windows of declining empires during the two decades that separated the Revolutions and the Franco-Prussian War.

Yet given the wider political context, the two cities were bound to respond very differently to the challenge of strengthening nationalisms at home and abroad. Vienna had of course a dual status, as a city of the German confederation but also as the seat of the Habsburg Empire, to whose interests developing German nationalism obviously posed a direct threat. As the capital of an empire on the wane, the city was both a hotbed of underground political radicalism (much of it in support of German nationalism and opposed to the liberal bourgeois establishment) and a showcase for imperial display. And it was the latter that was reflected in cultural life after the Revolutions. The Classical legacy was sustained and invigorated in these years by a renewal of energy at the Hofoper, and above all at the Gesellschaft der Musikfreunde, with its newly founded Singverein, its ever expanding conservatory (a new building was established in 1869), and its close links with Brahms and Bruckner, the major creative figures residing in Vienna in the 1860s. Brahms moved there in 1863, but his creativity had already been shaped by North German traditions. Significantly, his epic composition of the 1860s was the *German Requiem*, whose implicit German nationalism could scarcely have been further removed from the ambience of Vienna; Theodor Billroth remarked that it was 'so Protestant-Bachish that it was difficult to make it go down here'.[7] Bruckner arrived in the Habsburg capital a little later, succeeding his teacher Sechter at the Conservatory in 1867, but he too seemed a misfit, a product of provincial Austria moulded by an unlikely blend of South German Cecilian revivalism and Wagnerian late Romanticism.

In general the repertories promoted by the Gesellschaft and at the Hofoper were catholic but conservative. Wagner had a mixed reception. *Lohengrin* was performed in 1861, but attempts to stage *Tristan und Isolde* in the early 1860s, like plans to mount the first performance of *Die Meistersinger* at the opening of the new opera house in 1869, came to nothing. Such hostility towards the new (and Brahms encountered it too, at least in his early years in Vienna) was fuelled by certain sections of the press, but it was already deeply ingrained among the wider music-loving public of Vienna. For many of them the most characteristic and 'visible' Viennese repertory belonged neither to the concert hall nor to the

---

7 See F. May, *The Life of Johannes Brahms* (London, 1905), II, p. 396.

opera house, but to a tradition of professional light music already well established in this, the city of musical Classicism. As early as 1830, just after the deaths of Beethoven and Schubert, Chopin had remarked 'Here they call waltzes *works*',[8] and during the Metternich years – the years of 'Biedermeier Vienna' – it was popular dance music, composed and promoted by Joseph Lanner and the Strauss family, that took centre stage in Viennese musical life (cf. chapter 9). Following the Revolutions, the Strauss dynasty continued to rule, and its members quickly learnt from Offenbach that they could dominate the musical stage as well as the ballroom. Such music was the true mirror of imperial society, and it was given a further boost by the establishment of the Dual Monarchy in 1867.

At this point the empire became 'Austro-Hungarian'. As noted earlier, this move was first and foremost an attempt to quell the growing liberal and nationalist ferment of the Habsburg lands. Yet on another level it involved the recognition that Austria had been obliged to cede to Prussia the leadership of the German-speaking world, following her defeat at Königgrätz a year earlier. Vienna, in other words, was placed on the losing side in the battle between nations and dynasties. The city did, of course, retain its status as a great capital, worthy of its imperial past. There was a rapid modernisation of society in the years following the Dual Monarchy, together with an astonishing resurgence of activity in science, philosophy and imaginative culture. But the unification of Germany, achieved shortly after the establishment of the Dual Monarchy, confirmed that this was an empire under threat. Vienna, then, was effectively sidelined by the swelling tide of German nationalism. In the closing years of the century there was a deepening sense of insecurity about many of its cultural forms, expressed either as satirical critique or in the form of an inward-looking crisis of expression. Indeed much of the surge of artistic creativity at the end of the century was born of a profound sense of alienation. Caught between the German and the Slavonic worlds, and marginalised from the nationalist ambitions of both, Vienna became the major crucible of modernism, not only chronicling a much wider crisis in liberal bourgeois society, but giving voice to highly specific forms of exclusion and dispossession. It is no accident that modernism in Vienna, in almost every discipline including music, was predominantly a Jewish movement.[9]

If Vienna was sidelined by the German nation following 1871, Paris was rather conquered by the French nation. Second Empire Parisian society, ruled

---

8 In a letter to his teacher Józef Elsner, *Korespondencja Fryderyka Chopina*, ed. B. E. Sydow (Warsaw, 1955), I, p. 171.

9 See S. Beller, *Vienna and the Jews 1867–1938: A Cultural History* (Cambridge, 1989); also I. Oxal, M. Pollak and G. Botz (eds.), *Jews, Antisemitism and Culture in Vienna* (London, Boston and Henley, 1987).

by the theatre, and especially by opera, was no less cosmopolitan than its Viennese counterpart. Sites and repertories have been discussed already in this volume, but it may be worth recalling here that the Opéra (still at Le Peletier for most of the Second Empire) was dominated by Meyerbeer, even after the Revolutions, and that French composers, including Berlioz, had only limited access to this most prestigious of all cultural venues. As in Vienna, there was resistance to Wagner, but it should be noted that the notorious disruption of *Tannhäuser* in 1860 was as much a political demonstration against Napoleon as a chauvinistic hostility to anything 'new German'. For the rest, there was something of a realignment in the 1850s and 1860s. The Opéra-Comique at the Salle-Favart, whose characteristic repertory was Auber, Adam and Halévy, broadened its horizons in the 1860s (it would host *Carmen* in 1875), partly because the domain of 'light' opera had been appropriated by Offenbach, following his triumphant debut at the Bouffes-Parisiens in 1855. With their satires on contemporary mores and politics, presented in an idiom at once nostalgic of, and parodistic of, eighteenth-century comic opera, Offenbach and his librettists captured the spirit of Second Empire society with no less authenticity than their counterparts at the Opéra. And importantly, neither the Bouffes-Parisiens nor Le Peletier offered anything akin to those celebrations of nationhood, often interwoven with themes of religious conflict, that had been developed in the Parisian lyric theatre much earlier in the century (from the 1820s onwards), both at the Opéra and at the numerous secondary theatres.

Nationalist sentiment is fed by a sense of inferiority, and this was conspicuously lacking in the Second Empire. Yet although pride in the patria, and the complacency and even chauvinism that often accompany it, are less conducive to projects of cultural nationalism than insecurity and disadvantage, such projects were not entirely lacking during the Second Empire. The relatively short-lived Théâtre-Lyrique was especially significant as the site for a genuinely French 'drame lyrique', with Gounod's *Faust* (presented in 1859) setting the tone, followed by his *Philémon et Baucis* (1860), *Mireille* (1864) and *Roméo et Juliette* (1867), by Ambroise Thomas's *Mignon* (1866), and by Bizet's *Les pêcheurs de perles* (1863) and *La jolie fille de Perth* (1867). The genre title may be in search of closer definition (see chapter 14), but on the back of these achievements Massenet would build a corpus that lent itself well to the overtly nationalist ambitions of French culture in the aftermath of 1871. Likewise, the activities of various concert societies in the 1850s and 1860s, including Pasdeloup's Société des Jeunes Artistes (founded 1852), the Société Armingaud (1856) and Lamoureux's Séances Populaires de Musiques (1859), prepared the ground for the significantly named Société Nationale de Musique, founded by Saint-Saëns and others as part of the major resurgence of French nationalism that followed defeat in 1871. This was the point at which, in the apt words of Nicholas Xenos, 'the forces of the nation triumphed over those of the city';[10] indeed they did so literally, when the Paris Commune was suppressed by a national army. Music in Paris immediately after 1871 – and here the contrast with Vienna is striking – inscribes the history of a strengthening sense of French national identity. It marked the victory of the nation over the urban cosmopolitanism of 'old Paris'.

A similar story was told in different ways by the cities of Germany and Central Europe. The historic cities of Germany had of course very different traditions and they preserved their separate characters in some measure throughout the century. The leading courts were at Berlin, Dresden and Munich: Berlin, a garrison town but with an impressive court establishment and strong, if conservative, musical traditions; Dresden, a cultural centre with pronounced nationalist leanings; Munich, developed by Ludwig I as a 'renaissance city', but with its artistic pretensions utterly remote from the Bavarian peasantry. If we include Leipzig and Thuringian Weimar, with their rich cultural history and reputations for progressive thought and art, and commercially and artistically active 'free' cities like Frankfurt and Hamburg, we may gain some impression of the thriving diversity of cultural life in the German states, prior to unification. Yet in spite of this diversity, a middle-class concert life gradually took shape in Germany, similar in many ways to that developing in Paris and Vienna. The persistence of patronal culture delayed it, but increasingly court institutions were transformed *de facto* into public institutions, with the court functioning as a promoter rather than a sponsor of culture for middle-class consumers. Federal differences, in other words, gave way to modern urban structures, and by the 1860s concert life already had a profile recognisably similar to our own.

The gradual subordination of this urban culture to the idea of the nation is one way of reading German history in the later nineteenth century, not excluding its music history. Liszt was making no pitch for German nationalism when he took his court appointment at Weimar (others had their claims on him). Yet by consciously seeking to re-create the conditions and ambience of Weimar Classicism, and even more by building a bridge between that and Viennese Classicism, he played his part in locating Franz Brendel's 'New German' music ('announced' at Leipzig in 1859) within a national tradition right in the heartland of Germany, in a region forever associated with Bach. Wagner went further. After abortive plans to build his theatre in Munich, he finally realised his objective in Bayreuth in 1872, with the Reich already established. Here the

---

10 Nicholas Xenos, 'Civic Nationalism: Oxymoron?' *Critical Review*, 10/2 (1996), p. 223.

conventions of middle-class institutions were decidedly thwarted, harnessed not only to the cause of Wagner but to the cause of the nation, whose spirit and destiny were intentionally and idealistically locked into the Bayreuth project. A later generation of 'New Germans' likewise sited their activities on a Bavarian–Thuringian axis, and that extended beyond the immediate Liszt circle to include Richard Strauss, whose early career was centred on Weimar and Munich, a city increasingly identified with the modernism of Liszt and Wagner. Even Max Reger, no conventional 'New German' but a discreetly progressive figure whose Brahmsian neo-Classicism has yet to gain favour outside Germany, worked in Munich and Leipzig. Leipzig was especially significant as the home of German music publishing (and therefore of those collected editions that so eloquently spoke of a national canon), and also, through the conservatory, as a major centre of theory and pedagogy. In Hugo Riemann especially ideas of the 'language character' of music both signalled and reflected a nationalist ideology, preparing some of the ground for a tradition of *Musikwissenschaft* that could stand for the nation and at the same time (notionally) for universal values.[11]

In rather different ways the North German cities and their institutions also served the nation. They did so partly through a proliferation of festivals (some, such as the Lower Rhine, dated from early in the century and promoted a near-exclusive German repertory), journals and conservatories (especially Cologne and Frankfurt) that seemed to pronounce Germany the true 'home' of music (see chapter 8). They did so also through music societies (often sponsoring – as in Hamburg – ambitious concert series) and through the voluntary associations that played so central a part in German musical life generally, and especially in the Protestant north. In subtle, and not always positive, ways the choral associations in particular fostered the sense of an almost familial national community among their middle-class participants, and it is notable that leading composers such as Brahms in Hamburg and Bruch in Berlin were closely associated with them.[12] Unsurprisingly, their conservative, even reactionary, inclinations were well attuned to Berlin, and to Prussian society generally. Yet at the same time, as the capital of the new Reich, Berlin hosted a growing band of radical, progressive artists in the later years of the century, including the composers Busoni and Strauss (who arrived there from Munich in 1898), both committed to a probing, exploratory modernism that extended the bourgeois faith in progress. And three years after Strauss, Schoenberg arrived in Berlin for a two-

11 See Alexander Rehding, 'Nature and Nationhood in Hugo Riemann's Dualistic Theory of Harmony', Ph.D. diss., Cambridge University (1998).

12 For a useful discussion of the changing ideology behind choral associations, see John Deathridge, 'Germany: The "Special Path"', in Jim Samson (ed.), *The Late Romantic Era* (London and Basingstoke, 1991), pp. 50–73.

year period, returning to the city in 1911. His high-minded aesthetic – jealous of the integrity of art, protective of its truthfulness, fearful of its debasement – was in reality a product of Viennese modernism, finding its context in the music of Mahler, the campaigns of Karl Kraus, the deliberations of Wittgenstein and the 'Vienna Circle', and the expressionism of Kokoschka. Yet, and here is the paradox, no composer was more preoccupied than Schoenberg with the renewal of German music, and his dual biography in this respect speaks of a wider crisis of identity. In due course the category 'German music' would come to embrace Vienna as easily as Berlin. We would speak of a 'Second Viennese School', and of an 'Austro-German tradition'.

The music of Eastern and Central Europe is often differentiated from that tradition. Yet in the eighteenth and early nineteenth centuries musical life at the Polish, Hungarian and Bohemian courts was not so different from, and was often modelled on, that of the German courts, and its urban modernisation followed a similar pattern. Warsaw was something of a special case in that the promising resurgence of musical life at the beginning of the century was thwarted by the failure of the 1830 rising. There was greater continuity in the Habsburg cities Prague and Pest (later united with Buda). These cities had quite different profiles and traditions in the early nineteenth century, the one with a fine medieval heritage, the other still awaiting its most impressive development as an imperial capital, but they also had much in common. Until the mid-century both were thoroughly German in all but name, with their administrative structures, their artistic organisations and their social mores modelled largely on Vienna, and as in Vienna fashionable society promoted a distinctive repertory of professional popular music as well as a flourishing concert and operatic life. In both cities there were music societies promoting chamber and orchestral series, new teaching institutions (the Prague conservatory opened in 1811, while the Singing School of the Society of Musicians, prototype of the Budapest Academy, was founded in 1840) and opera companies, both German-language and Czech- or Hungarian-language. This tug-of-war between the languages in turn became the key feature of formal culture in these cities – and across East Central Europe as a whole – in the second half of the nineteenth century.

By then the gradually expanding bourgeoisie of the (largely agrarian) eastern Habsburg Empire was mustering its artistic and intellectual energies in support of nationalist causes. Moreover there was an ethnic as well as a nationalist dimension to this. The gathering strength of Slavonic nationalisms, at times articulated in pan-Slavonic movements, became an ever greater challenge not only to the Austrian Germans but to the Germans generally. This was reflected in growing divisions in the organisation of musical life throughout the region. Already at the turn of the eighteenth and nineteenth centuries vernacular Singspiele, such as Stefani's *Cud mniemany* (The Supposed Miracle) in Poland, Ruzitska's *Béla futása* (Bela's Flight) in Hungary and Škroup's *Drátinek* (The Tinker) in Bohemia were hugely popular among native audiences. In the later nineteenth century formal musical culture increasingly reflected the growing rivalry between native and foreign (usually German) communities. At the same time it proclaimed through its institutions a strengthening commitment to nationalism. In several towns the main performing forces were segregated strictly along national lines. In Brno, for example, concerts were organised for the German population at the Deutsches Hags and for a native audience at the Besední Dom. In Ljubljana (Laibach) there was a comparable division between the Philharmonische Gesellschaft and the Glasbena Matica. And often the segregation amounted to something like a cultural war. In Poznań, for instance (especially after 1870), Poles would avoid the German concerts at all costs, attending only the Polish concerts at the Hotel Bazar.

Unsurprisingly, opera was even more clearly segregated. Even where separate venues were not available there would often be two companies, German and native, as in Lwów, Zagreb and Pest. In Prague the division was cleaner still. The Estates Theatre (and in summer the New Town Theatre) continued to offer German-language opera throughout the century, though its leading position was usurped by the establishment of the Neues Deutsches Theater in 1888. The Czech community, meanwhile, was served by the Provisional Theatre, opened in 1861 and designed exclusively for Czech-language productions. It remained the home of Czech opera for some twenty years before the opening of the long-awaited National Theatre in 1882.[13] Indeed the proliferation of so-called 'national theatres' throughout East Central Europe in itself speaks eloquently of the harnessing of the cities to a nationalist cause and of the increasing association of that cause with an emerging bourgeoisie. The example of Prague was followed some two years later by Brno. 'National theatres' had already been established in Warsaw (1765), Pest (1837), Bucharest (1852) and Belgrade (1869), and they would soon appear in Zagreb (1870) and Pozsony (Bratislava) (1886). In each case the enterprise, often involving a lengthy building programme, came to take on powerfully symbolic values. Even where repertories were dominated, as they were almost bound to be, by the mainstreams of European music, the nationalist voice now had a platform. Like the segregation of formal culture, the national theatres were a marker of nationalist agendas in the cities of East Central Europe. And there was a further informal marker in the changing patterns of composer biography. Where native composers

---

13 See John Tyrrell, *Czech Opera* (Cambridge, 1988).

typically drifted abroad in the first half of the nineteenth century – to the German courts, Italy, Paris or Vienna – they now settled in their homeland and involved themselves actively with its institutions as they set about the task of building a repertory of modern national music.

Forging the nations

The Franco-Prussian war of 1870–71 helped define the nationhood of France no less than Germany. The Société Nationale de Musique may have been less ambitious in the scale of its concert activities than several other organisations in Paris, but its revivalist mission was unambiguously nationalist, and as such representative of the wider tendencies of French culture following the war. Thus the revival of French instrumental music associated with the Société, challenging Germany on its home ground, was part and parcel of a quest for national dignity (see chapter 17), as was the search for validating traditions in earlier eras of French music. A figure such as Louis-Albert Bourgault-Ducoudray (1840–1910) neatly linked these two modes of nationalist ambition, as a founding member (along with Saint-Saëns) of the Société Nationale and as a Professor of Music History at the Conservatoire. Like Louis Niedermeyer before him, he set out to raise the general awareness of French Renaissance repertories not only as a teacher and writer but, more directly, through his activities as a choral conductor,[14] where he blazed a trail for the activities of the Schola Cantorum (founded 1896), associated especially with D'Indy (1851–1931) and Bordes (1863–1909). Moreover, Bourgault-Ducoudray touched importantly on yet another dimension of French nationalism, the development of regional identities through an exploration of folksong, tapping into 'la muse populaire'. There were two dimensions to this in late nineteenth-century France. The (French) region could stand as a kind of concentrated, essentialised form of a larger national identity, as exploited in several works by d'Indy, Guy Ropartz (1864–1955) and Déodat de Séverac (1872–1921). Alternatively the exotic (non-French) repertory could serve as a measure of difference, and here Bourgault-Ducoudray's studies of Greek folksong formed a useful model.

Annegret Fauser has demonstrated how several of these nationalist impulses coincided at the Exposition Universale in 1889. There was the appropriation of Massenet's already composed opera *Esclarmonde* as the official representative of present-day French creativity, 'placed' historically by performances of eighteenth- and early nineteenth-century opéras comiques; there was the celebration of republicanism as a French achievement in the spectacular performances

---

14 Donna Marie DiGrazia, *Concert Societies in Paris and their Choral Repertories c. 1828–1880* (Ann Arbor, 1995).

of Augusta Holmès's *Ode triumphale*; and there was of course the music of the French colonies.[15] These latter repertories introduced a note of ambivalence to the nation-building project, helping to define the homeland through cultural difference, but also prone to appropriation in a spirit of eclecticism (as a means of invigoration and renewal) that was common to earlier generations of French music. Russian music served a comparably ambivalent role in later nineteenth-century France. And what of Wagner, promoted so vociferously in French literature and criticism? Thomas Grey has suggested (chapter 14) that even the most Wagnerian of French composers 'remained loyal to the French musical tradition in many points of style'. If the concept of a 'French tradition' has any concrete meaning, it may refer to the melodic priority (subject to ornamental elaboration), the formal lucidity, and, more generally, the cool, poised, Classical quality, essentially latinate, that is detectable in even the most German-influenced music by French composers of the late nineteenth century, and that is firmly reinstated in the music of Fauré and Ravel. It is no doubt significant that neither composer had any truck with Wagner. In contrast, Debussy inherited something of the more general French ambivalence towards Wagner, and the defiant assertion of national values, invoking Couperin and (significantly) Chopin, in his later music in particular was genuinely hard-won.

'We have made Italy. Now we must make Italians.' The well-known tag, popularly but wrongly attributed to Cavour, pinpoints a paradox at the heart of the nationalist enterprise in Italy.[16] The concept of national consciousness was prior to the state, and called it forth. Thus the *Risorgimento* – an Italy-wide movement, and one in which artists played an active part (but see chapter 4 on the tendency to overstate Verdi's role in this) – was predicated on a concept of nationhood and fuelled by quite specific anti-Habsburg sentiment, even on the part of those territories that were not directly ruled by Austria. Yet the accomplishment of the primary political objective could not, and did not, instantly forge the cities and states, which had their different histories and traditions, into a nation. The enormity of that task had been well recognised long before unification, and it motivated the rather particular brand of social and political Romanticism that distinguished imaginative culture in Italy from its North European counterparts. Hence the rash of historical novels, plays, operas and paintings, with their thinly disguised contemporary relevance, associated with the *Risorgimento*. Hence, too, the reform of language, amounting to nothing

---

15 Annegret Fauser, 'World Fair – World Music: Musical Politics in 1889 Paris', in Jim Samson and Bennett Zon (eds.), *Nineteenth-Century Music: Selected Proceedings of the Tenth International Conference on Nineteenth-Century Music* (Aldershot, forthcoming).

16 It seems that it was actually uttered by Massimo D'Azeglio, a Piedmontese intellectual and politician who succeeded Cavour as the second prime minister of the newly formed Kingdom of Italy. I am grateful to Emmanuele Senici for this information.

less than the creation of a national language from a welter of dialects. And hence the attempts – by Verdi and others – to ground implicit nationalist programmes (as in *Nabucco* and *I Lombardi*) in forms and materials that remained accessible to a wide cross-section of the Italian populace.

Following 1848 there was a renewed sense of urgency in nationalist enterprises, in music as in other fields. It seems possible in retrospect to identify several different strands. One was an increasingly possessive attitude to 'national' materials. Again there is a paradox at the root of this. Despite the growing cosmopolitanism of operatic styles, the Italian operatic tradition became the jealously guarded preserve of the Italian composer, and pains were taken to differentiate it from rival national traditions, both French and German. Another, related to the first, was the consolidation of repertory opera, which had the effect of firming up an exclusive tradition based on a group of highly valued figures, past and present. A third, developed largely in the post-unification years, was a renewed interest in early Italian repertories. This of course included Palestrina and his contemporaries. But even more significant (given the appropriation of Palestrina by Europe as a whole) was the new-found enthusiasm for Monteverdi, who would become a giant figure in the musical nation-building of the early twentieth century. In all these respects Italy elaborated themes that were common to nationalist programmes in other European countries. But there was another tendency, born of Italy's long-standing reputation as the heartland of music. The rise of a Romantic aesthetic, German in origin and nature, was profoundly threatening to the prestige of Italian opera, inimical to its entertainment status, to its approach to text and authorship, and even to its performance conditions. The result was a loss of confidence (by Italians themselves) in the primacy of Italian music, as German symphonism increasingly dominated European musical culture as a whole.[17]

This deepening sense of insecurity in relation to German music married with a more general insecurity in Italian culture and society as the century drew to a close. The first flush of national pride gave way in the 1890s to a more fundamental questioning of national identity. Even Verdi responded, as the parodistic tendencies of *Falstaff* suggest. Yet *Falstaff* in its turn pointed to new creative possibilities for younger Italian composers. Busoni in particular saw in the work a way of re-establishing links not only with Rossini and Donizetti but with Mozart, who, like his other mentors, Bach and Liszt, seemed to represent a point of contact between the two great traditions – Italian and German – to which he felt himself heir. Here, in the declining years of repertory opera, and in the context of a belatedly industrialised nation, understandings of an Italian

---

17 See John Rosselli, 'Italy: The Decline of a Tradition', in Samson (ed.), *The Late Romantic Era*, pp. 130–1.

tradition were gradually broadened out. The issue at stake was how an Italian identity might be redefined, in ways that remained essentially separate from the operatic tradition. There were extreme positions, in which art and politics were unhappily wedded. But there was also a more moderate path, marked in particular by Busoni's revival of a long-dormant tradition of instrumental music. Busoni promoted, among many other things, a visionary modernity comparable to Schoenberg's, and a 'Young Classicism' (his term) comparable to Stravinsky's, with whom he shared a discreet detachment from the heritage of folk and Baroque musics he simultaneously invoked. His influence on later Italian music, the *generazione dell'ottanta*, was perhaps more inspirational than compositional, but it should be noted that composers such as Casella (1883–1947) and Malipiero (1882–1973), whose music belonged of course to another century, also defined their national identity in terms that linked progress to the recovery of an ancient heritage.

The projection of German symphonism as a privileged high-status tradition had a clear nationalist resonance in the ninteenth century. Thus, as early as 1824, A. B. Marx, having damned the nations in turn, wrote (in his *Berliner allgemeine musikalische Zeitung*) that 'an alliance is forming in the realm of music, proceeding from Germany as its middle point (as before Italy) in all of higher educated Europe'. The tone reminds us unmistakably of Goethe's celebration of the Strasbourg Minster in *Von Deutscher Baukunst* (1772): 'this is German architecture, our architecture. Something of which the Italian cannot boast, far less the Frenchman . . . ,[18] sentiments echoed by Schlegel in *Briefe auf einer Reise* (1806), by Schinkel in his *Project for a Mausoleum* (1810), and by the neo-medieval pronouncements of the Boisserée brothers at Cologne. The project of completing Cologne Cathedral, whose extension foundation stone was laid in 1842, was powerfully symbolic of this national consciousness, expressing 'the spirit of German unity and strength', as King Friedrich Wilhelm IV remarked on the occasion (Prussia had acquired its Rhine Province in 1815, creating strong cultural links between Berlin and the Rhenish cities Düsseldorf and Cologne). Indeed Sulphis Boisserée proposed at the time that the walls of the aisles should be filled with monuments, and serve as a national Valhalla. This glorification and idealisation of a German past was of course grist to the mill of the nationalist cause, and it had its counterpart in all the arts, not least in the construction of a national canon in music, firmed up in festivals, concert life and publishing enterprises. It is notable, too, that nationalism in Germany carried with it a strong familial quality, grounded in the ideal of the bourgeois family, the myth of community, and the Protestant ethic. Thus in music the

18 For a discussion of the context for this celebration of Gothic architecture, see Richard Friedenthal, *Goethe: His Life and Times* (London, 1963), p. 82.

emergent canon was viewed as a genealogy, headed by Bach; indeed the Bach family was itself a model for the larger genealogy. 'Truly', wrote Spitta in 1880, 'did Sebastian Bach spring from the very core and marrow of the German people'.[19]

The Cologne Cathedral project registered a further aspect of developing nationalism. This was the elevation of the Rhine as a potent symbol of nationhood, the more potent in that it explicitly linked north and south: the Prussian Rhine Province and the Bavarian Rhine Palatinate.[20] Rhenish Romantic nationalism reached its apogee in the remarkable outpouring of Rhinelieder in the 1840s (following the so-called 'Rhine Crisis' of 1840), in the work of the Nazarene painters, and ultimately in Wagner's tetralogy *Der Ring des Nibelungen*, whose poem was begun at the end of that same decade. The folk ethos and nature worship so central to German nationalism (in sharp contrast to its French counterpart) is embodied in much of this Rhenish art. It taps into a rich vein of Romantic nationalism, much of it stemming (musically) from Weber, incorporating poeticised images of the forest, the hunt, the ubiquitous hero-wanderer, and the various mythological figures associated with the Rhine itself, notably the Lorelei and the Nibelungen. This 'animising' of the Rhine was of course given its most sustained expression in Wagner's *Ring*, where the linkage between a mytho-historical subject-matter and the contemporary world is made explicit. The sense of a continuing tradition, where the deeds of an idealised past are the exemplars from which modern Man may draw significant parallels for resolving, personal, spiritual and social problems, links Wagner's enterprise with that of the Nazarenes. It amounts really to the construction of a 'new' mythology based on the old, and it finds its context in the collections of German folklore and myth made by the Heidelberg *litterati* among many others, and in a more general tendency to associate the 'old Germany' revealed in idealised form in such collections with a no less idealised Classical Greece.

This poeticising of the past and of nature to generate an image of Germany (Herder's 'spirit of the nation') was bolstered by the historicism and organicism around which a good deal of idealist thought was gathered. Both these principles, perfectly fused in the biological metaphor of organic growth, worked to forge a concept of the nation as a cultural unity, and at the same time a concept of music – 'absolute music' – as central to the larger national identity. The centrality of music, moreover, united the 'common man' and the philosopher in a manner rather specific to Germany (and reflected even in the nature of

19 Philipp Spitta, *Johann Sebastian Bach: His Work and Influence on the Music of Germany*, trans. Clara Bell and J. A. Fuller Maitland (London, 1899), I, p. 13.

20 For a detailed examination of Rhenish Romanticism in music, see Cecelia Hopkins Porter, *The Rhine as Musical Metaphor: Cultural Identity in German Romantic Music* (Boston, 1996).

the German language, with its singular capacity to link the abstract and the concrete). Thus the cultivation of music as a worthy, improving activity was an important dimension of the down-to-earth bourgeois ethic in Germany. At the same time music was often at the heart of the philosophical debate. 'In the realm of ideas . . . not only inner unity and national independence but also a decided superiority must be granted to the Germans', wrote Karl Kossmaly in *Neue Zeitschrift für Musik*, and he went on to identify music as 'the most sublime . . . of all the arts'.[21] Much more than in Italy, nationalism in Germany was located in ideas, or more precisely in a conjunction of ideas and feeling, a conjunction for which music served as a privileged model. Absolute music not only stood for the unity of the German spirit, then; it expressed the inexpressible, 'made available' the ineffable, and encapsulated that sense of longing and interiority at the heart of German Romanticism.

Just how political and cultural nationalisms intersected in Germany in the later years of the century is a complex and controversial subject. Hegel's legacy in this respect was doubled-edged. It is no surprise that artists were disinclined to embrace the full implications of a philosophy of history that was – to put it mildly – less than sanguine about the future of art. Yet that same philosophy, selectively 'applied' to art, could privilege the contemporary by identifying history as progress, and could even suggest to some a link between artistic progress and political progress. For Hegel, political progress described the modern Prussian state, and the tendency of his political philosophy was towards just the kind of authoritarianism represented by an increasingly militarised Prussia before and beyond unification. Indeed a historian such as Treitschke would later reconcile the Prussian 'conquest' of Germany with a natural, 'organic' process of unification in ways that clearly registered Hegel's influence. Cultural nationalism was not just the seedbed of political nationalism, then. It was also the legitimation of some of its less palatable means and consequences. Self-evidently the forging of the German nation was partly at the expense of its 'others' – political, cultural, and even ethnic; witness all those claims for the superiority of German culture, born of a Hegelian belief that the onus of revelation – the next stage of an unfolding process – now fell to Germany (Prussia). Such claims were symptomatic of a chauvinism directed not just at Italy, France and the Habsburg Empire, but at the Latin and Slavonic races. And of course at the Jews. Here we would note that Wagner's representation of the German nation, its past and its present, was part of a larger story – a separation of German and German–Jewish communities. Yet it is easy to read that larger story (backwards from the holocaust) in too unnuanced a way.

---

21 Karl Kossmaly, *Neue Zeitschrift für Musik*, 19 February 1841, p. 59.

Another story (read forwards from emancipation) told of growing Jewish success and a putative symbiosis between the races. The reception of Mendelssohn (even Wagner's reception of Mendelssohn) tells both stories, and it was only in the first third of the twentieth century that the former prevailed.[22]

Wagner's polemic, characteristic of a widespread and increasing anti-Semitism in the political and cultural life of the new Reich, attracted attention because of his status as nothing less than a cultural icon. By the end of the nineteenth century he had become mystically separated off from the wider operatic context, as to some extent he is even today. His world vision, and the xenophobia it embodied, found temporary favour with the young Nietzsche among others, but for the most part its representation (and reception) at Bayreuth remained aloof from such programmes of narrow nationalism. Bayreuth would be manipulated of course, by Cosima and her circle, and by the Third Reich, but its survival had little to do with the fascism of the future, and everything to do with the idealism of the past. Quite apart from the dignity it assigned to German opera, the Wagnerian music drama, with its projects of unity and synthesis, represented the summation of those ambitious early Romantic claims for music, that through its self-referential, autonomous qualities it had a unique capacity to access the infinite, attain the transcendental. In this sense Wagner, no less than the symphonic tradition, was heir to an aesthetic of absolute music. The realisation of that aesthetic – in Wagner, in Beethoven and the symphonic canon, even in Bach (who, ironically enough, was transformed in a historicist reception into a kind of originating paradigm of absolute music) – marked the larger achievement of German music in the nineteenth century, and before it even the polemics of the 1850s recede from view. Through that achievement music played its major role in building first the nation and then its cultural empire.

Nowhere did the seeds of Herder's cultural-linguistic nationalism fall on more fertile soil than in East Central Europe.[23] His few words on the future of the Slavonic peoples were to become slogans of political nationalism in the eastern Habsburg territories, as they sought to forge independent national states modelled on the bourgeois national states of the West. Yet the societies of East Central Europe were very different from their western counterparts, and

---

22 See Ritchie Robertson, *The 'Jewish' Question in German Literature 1749–1939* (Oxford, 1999).

23 The extent to which the region I have described as 'East Central Europe' had any real identity as an historical unit remains something of a open question. Certainly it would be misleading to project back on to the nineteenth-century map 'Eastern Europe' created by Yalta, together with that sharp sense of separation from the West which characterised the late twentieth-century political history of the territories roughly separating Russia and Germany. Larry Wolff has gone so far as to claim that 'Eastern Europe' is largely an 'invention'. See his *Inventing Eastern Europe: The Map of Civilization on the Mind of the Enlightenment* (Stanford, 1994).

as a result nationalism was promoted not only by an emergent bourgeoisie (as in the West), but by an established class-conscious middle gentry, who claimed to speak on behalf of the *Volkswille*. Because of this divorce between ideology and social realities, nationalism in these lands, even more than in Germany, tended to thrive on myth and dream – the myth of a glorious past, the dream of a glorious future. The historicism common to Europe as a whole in the later nineteenth century began to take on a very special significance in the eastern empire, with constant recourse to historic rights, waves of heritage gathering, and a political struggle for language rights in education and the public domain. In this context the composer, no less than the poet, rummaged history, mythology and folklore to render his nationalist statement, with major initiatives taken in opera by Moniuszko (1819–72) in Poland, by Erkel (1810–93) in Hungary and by Smetana (1824–84) in Bohemia. While opera was the most obvious genre for the nationalist composer, programmatic instrumental music ran it a close second. Indeed the flowering of the symphonic poem in Russia and Central Europe must be understood at least in part as a response to the nationalist imperative. Thus, the poetic or loosely philosophical subject-matter that characterised Liszt's pioneering works gave way to more 'narrative' programmes based on national history, geography and folklore, notably in Russia and the Czech lands. Smetana, Fibich (1850–1900) and Dvořák all celebrated Bohemia in this way.

The most powerful symbol of nationalism in East Central Europe was the music of the 'folk', which had a special richness and vitality in the as yet unmodernised rural communities of these territories. The nationalist movements of the nineteenth century made substantial capital out of folklore, which they viewed – somewhat spuriously – as a collective expression of national (as opposed to social or regional) identities. The general practice was to allow a repertory of generalised folk idioms (modal types, bourdon drones, ornamentations, rhythmic patterns, and so on) to serve as an all-purpose musical signifier of nationalism, while specificity resided in a poetics of intention and reception; and here the equation of folk culture and nationalism was real enough. That equation was already a debating point in early nineteenth-century Poland and it became a compositional reality in the mazurkas of Chopin. By the mid-century it had gained a solid footing in Russia and it quickly spread to the rest of Central Europe. Folksong and dance, then, assumed considerable privilege in the nineteenth century, and the activity of collecting gathered momentum, providing the composer with easily accessible, if less than authentic, sources. In addition there was an upsurge of creativity in popular song, especially associated with the gypsy bands of Hungary and Romania, and this too served the committed nationalist composer. There was of course nothing new in the composer turning to such music. What was new from around the mid-century was the spirit in which it was deployed, as it came increasingly under the sway of a nationalist commitment. No longer a decorative elaboration of existing syntax, it became a means of reshaping that syntax. Even when presented in the form of simple transcriptions, folk and popular musics were now freighted with a nationalist ideology.

In the second half of the century, then, national 'schools' began to develop across East Central Europe, though with the exception of the Czech lands they achieved limited success outside their native lands, at least until the early twentieth century. In this respect, Chopin was a pioneering figure. In the mazurkas and polonaises he composed after he left Poland in 1830 he allowed the dance pieces to stand not as a conventional means of creating Polish colour but as a defiant expression of national identity, integrating indigenous qualities with the most advanced techniques of contemporary European art music. That his achievements were not developed in Poland was due above all to the repressive aftermath to the 1830 rising. It was Moniuszko rather than Chopin who met the musical needs of the country in the post-1830 years. In his 'Home Songbooks' and in his major operas *Halka* and *Straszny Dwór* (The Haunted Manor), Moniuszko dictated the musical formulation of 'Polishness' to later composers such as Żelenski (1837–1921), Noskowski (1846–1909) and Zarębski (1854–85). This really amounted to little more than colouring the European styles of an earlier generation (especially Italian and French opera of the early nineteenth century) with the rhythms of national dances. It was only in the early twentieth century that a younger generation of Polish composers (Karłowicz and Szymanowski especially) succeeded in breaking through the barrier of institutional and stylistic conservatism that isolated Polish music from Europe, regaining some point of contact with Chopin's path-breaking achievement.

Like Moniuszko, those Hungarian composers who remained in Pest and Poszony (now Bratislava in Slovakia) – notably Erkel and Mosonyi (1815–70) – seldom gained access to wider European cultural capitals. Indeed it is tempting to compare Liszt and Erkel in this respect to Chopin and Moniuszko. Where Erkel spoke to native Hungarians in a language accessible to all, Liszt spoke to the world at large about Hungary, and in the language of contemporary European art music. Like Moniuszko's, Erkel's mature operas – especially *Bánk Bán* (1861) and *Brankovics György* (1874) – went some way towards establishing a national operatic style, but they have seldom crossed the national frontier with any success. Liszt, on the other hand, cultivated Hungary only in certain selected works, including *Hungaria* (1856), *Die heilige Elizabeth* (1865) and the Coronation Mass (1867), together with such piano pieces as *Sunt lacrymae rerum* from the third book of *Années de pèlerinage* (1869–72). Yet, like Chopin in his mature dance pieces, he drew on native features to underline a nationalist commitment rather than to cultivate conventional exoticisms. Even in the four late *Rhapsodies hongroises*, where we might reasonably have expected a more popular idiom, Liszt makes it abundantly clear that there need be no incompatibility between nationalism and modernism. In due course that message would be underlined by Bartók, though in Bartók the 'tone' of the nationalist enterprise changed radically, subsumed within a larger project of synthesis between folk and art musics, between East and West.

In the early nineteenth century, Prague was an imperial capital with a reputation for music not far short of Vienna's. Leading Bohemian composers, such as Dussek, Tomášek and Voříšek, were cosmopolitan figures, as much at home in Vienna or London as in Prague. Smetana's career began in a similar way. But in the 1860s, when he finally settled in Prague after extended exposure to the ideas of the Liszt circle, he committed himself to an alliance between national images and symbols on one hand and progressive European music on the other, creating in his tone poems and operas (see chapter 14) a store of devices and associations on which his later compatriots would draw. At the same time, the historical and geographical proximity of Austro-German culture ensured that the nineteenth-century Czech masters maintained a fairly close dialogue with West European traditions. This was especially the case for Smetana's successor, complement and to some extent rival in late nineteenth-century Czech music, Antonin Dvořák, who (rather like Tchaikowsky in Russia) set out deliberately to 'place' national characteristics within the framework of a predominantly cosmopolitan idiom, indebted above all (at least in the instrumental works) to Brahms. And much the same is true of the Romantic nationalism associated with less well-known figures such as Zdeněk Fibich and Josef Bohuslav Foerster (1859–1951), and even Janáček (1854–1928) in his earlier music. It was in the twentieth century (beyond the purview of this volume) that Janáček found a more characteristically innovatory voice, and that in turn was part of a much more general 'renaissance' of music in East Central Europe, associated with Bartók and Kodály in Hungary, and with Szymanowski in Poland.

Music at the edge

During the second half of the nineteenth century the cultural life of Poland, Hungary and the Czech lands stood in a characteristically ambivalent relationship to west European traditions. Even as they embraced the institutional and material forms of a shared imperial culture, these nations or would-be nations set out to construct their individual cultural identities. They began to participate, in other words, in the tussle of competitive nationalisms that characterised cultural life as a whole in the late nineteenth century. The competition – the word is not too strong – was based on geographical difference, on constructed histories and traditions, and on a developing sense of 'mainstreams' and 'peripheries'. Edward Said famously argued that Europe constructed the Orient to its (that is to Europe's) own specifications.[24] This represents, of course, an obvious 'other', but arguably the same analysis can be applied to the Orient within – the cultures of gypsies and Jews – as well as to those less obvious 'others', the cultures around the edge of Europe, further removed from the major centres than anywhere in East Central Europe. In this respect Richard Taruskin echoed Said when he suggested that European musicians constructed their own Russia, as well as their own Orient, and proceeded to demonstrate that our evaluations of Russian music are not at all congruent with those of Russian musicians.[25] All in all, historical justice is hard to come by as we assess the cultures of Europe's periphery. We may skew the plot in favour of the values of a dominant culture, writing a kind of assimilationist history which draws the more highly valued figures into a canon of European Romanticism or modernism, while ignoring measures of difference. Alternatively (and this is probably the greater danger) we may fetishise what we perceive to be the difference. In either case we run the risk of undervaluing, or misunderstanding, the constitutive role of Western Europe as an historical 'presence' in those cultures which sought to establish their separateness. Dialogues with the West were fundamental to the quest for a voice in the East, the South-east, the North, and the far West.

Elsewhere I have argued that this question can be focused by considering two socially polarised countries on the edge of Europe: Britain and Russia.[26] It was a polarity between an 'advanced' industrialised country and a backward feudal one; between a country which tended to reduce European achievements to the status of passing fashions – ideas to be tried for size – and one which agonised over Europe, either embracing it uncritically or rejecting it fiercely; between a culture which (putting it blatantly) collapsed aesthetics into ethics and one which collapsed ethics into aesthetics. Briefly, I suggested that this polarity allowed us to view separately, and with particular clarity, two strands that were held in dialectical opposition in France and Germany, where they generated an increasingly explosive force-field. In Britain bourgeois music-making devoted

24 Edward Said, *Orientalism* (New York, 1979).

25 Richard Taruskin, 'Some Thoughts on the History and Historiography of Russian Music', *The Journal of Musicology*, 3/4 (1984), pp. 321–39. See also *Defining Russia Musically: Historical and Hermeneutical Essays* (Princeton, 1997).

26 Jim Samson, 'Music and Society', in Samson (ed.), *The Late Romantic Era*, pp. 28–33. Likewise some of the material on Eastern Europe draws on my chapter 'East Central Europe: The Struggle for National Identity' in the same book.

itself whole-heartedly to canonic and popular repertories, cultivating the performer and listener at the expense of the composer and accepting more-or-less uncritically the commodity status of music. Only in the twilight of the century did composers of real stature emerge from a musical establishment reluctant to promote original creativity (most composers were trained in Europe). And even here – in the music of Parry (1848–1918), Stanford (1852–1924), Mackenzie (1847–1935) and Elgar (1857–1934), whose 'Enigma' Variations just squeeze into the nineteenth century – the stylistic dialogue with Europe was one-sided, to say the least; only through the idiomatic demands of word-setting was there any real resistance to continental styles. The timely adoption of Elgar as a national figure, together with the creative reclamation by later composers of folksong and the Tudor-Elizabethan inheritance in a circular and self-referential quest for 'Englishness', belongs essentially to twentieth-century history.

In Russia, on the other hand, the equation of nationalism and modernism created a powerful and radical alternative to the forms and conventions of West European music – hardly surprising, given the virtual isolation of Russia from European culture until the late eighteenth century. This alternative already began to emerge in the 1840s in Glinka, but it crystallised in the 1860s in the music of the Balakirev circle. In opera, as in the symphony and the tone poem, these composers promoted a genuine dialogue with Europe, adopting many of the generic conventions of European prototypes, but asserting through them an independence of thought and practice that would serve as an exemplary model for later composers – of several nationalities – who were concerned to challenge the hegemony of an Austro-German tradition. At risk of seeming trite, we might encapsulate that independence into a list of technical points: the development both of modal chromaticism (where folk-derived modalities are built into the substance of harmonic thought) and of chromatic symmetries (notably those based on the whole-tone and octatonic scales); a preference for ornamental melody, which is subject to repetition and decorative variation rather than motivic development; the elevation of timbre and texture to an unprecedented structural status; a radical revision of conventional relationships between harmony and metre. All these are big points, and in search of the kind of detailed exemplification which will not be possible here. The operatic and instrumental music of Russian composers has in any case already been discussed (chapters 14, 15, 17), and it will be enough to add a brief word here on some of their songs. In this genre, perhaps more than in any other, the sense of detachment, of 'difference', from European traditions is patent, and it can be traced through from the derivative salon romances composed by Glinka and Dargomïzhsky in the 1830s and 1840s to the astonishing power and maturity of the later songs of Borodin and Musorgsky in the 1860s and 1870s.

The decade from 1865 to 1875 was indeed the heyday of Russian song. There is really nothing in the lied or *mélodie* tradition prior to that time which could possibly have prepared listeners for the first song 'S nyaney' (With Nanny) from Musorgsky's *Detskaya* (Nursery) cycle (1868–72). Its everyday subject-matter (a sort of domestic version of the 'street corner' realism of earlier songs such as *Svetik Savishna* [Darling Savishna], *Ozornik* [The Ragamuffin] and *Sirotka* [The Orphan]), its harmonic opacities and unorthodoxies, and its replacement of regular phrase and melodic periodicities by a 'realistic' reflection of speech rhythms and inflections ('making my characters speak . . . exactly as people speak in everyday life'[27]), all cut a swathe through the conventions of the art song. The underlying conviction was that art is a component of life and must remain anchored by it, such that even the minutest musical gesture may be validated by experience. The remaining songs in the cycle find greater accommodation with convention. And so do the later cycles, *Bez Solntsa* (Without Sun) and *Pesni i plyaski smerti* (Songs and Dances of Death), though their darker tone of psychological realism continues to 'make strange' the conventional gesture, whether the folk modalities of a 'Serenade', or the Cossack rhythms of a 'Trepak' (the second and third of the *Pesni i plyaski*, both composed in 1875). Musorgsky's songs came as close as any late nineteenth-century music to finding a musical expression for the realist aesthetic that informed so much literature of the period. For Rimsky-Korsakov, in contrast, the 'real' served as a foil for a world of fantasy and imagination – an *un*reality that was most commonly encapsulated in oriental themes and treatments. In *V tyomnoy roshche* (In the Dark Grove) and *El' i pal'ma* (The Fir and the Palm), both of 1866, he allowed oriental arabesques and roulades to weave their magic over relatively unchanging harmonic fields in a manner heavily indebted to earlier Balakirev songs such as *Pesnya Selima* (Song of Seleim) and *Gruzinskaya pesnya* (Song of Georgia) (just as the orientalisms of *Sheherazade* are borrowed directly from *Tamara*). Yet even the best of his songs – *Tayna* (The Secret) and *V tsarstvo rozï i vina* (In the Kingdom of Roses and Wine) – fall some way short of those composed by Borodin between 1867 and 1870. The innovatory harmonies – unresolved major-second pedal points and whole-tone material – of *Spyashchaya* (The Sleeping Princess) have often been linked with Debussy. But other songs – *Penya tyomnogo lesa* (Song of the Dark Forest) and *Morskaya tsarevna* (The Sea Princess) – are hardly less adventurous, as radical in their own very different (more refined and delicate) way as those of Musorgsky.

The reception of nineteenth-century Russian composers, initially favouring their group identity and valuing their collective independence of West European practices, moved in the twentieth century towards selective assimilation, where a

---

27 Quoted in M. D. Calvocoressi, *Mussorgsky* (London, 1946), p. 32.

corpus of works by leading figures was drawn into the canon of Romantic or modernist masterpieces. It may even have been advantageous to Russian music that its traditions were established at a greater distance from Europe, geographically and culturally, than, for example, the Iberian peninsula, Scandinavia or parts of the Balkans. In some of these latter regions it was difficult to escape the predatory cultures of powerful neighbours, especially where there was relatively little in the way of a native music profession or an infrastructure of concerts and conservatories. It was all too easy, then, for French, German or Italian traditions to take on the role of exemplary models – to be closely, even slavishly, emulated, if only in that spirit of rivalry characterised by Gellner (in his typology of nationalisms) as 'imitative but hostile'. Against this background the tendency was for the original genius either to be absorbed by European music or to be packaged as an iconoclast, separate both from the national context and from the European canon. It should also be noted that a self-conscious musical nationalism was delayed in most quarters until the closing years of the nineteenth century, and achieved fruition only in the twentieth. All the same, as historians we should not be let off the hook entirely. It is hard to deny that the construction of 'mainstream' traditions – as much to do with chauvinist politics as with art – has coloured our view of so-called peripheral cultures. That we have identified little of value in some of these repertories is as often as not because we know little about them.

'Who', asks Lionel Salter, 'has ever heard Gabriel Balart's five symphonies, the nine by Nicolau Manent or the five by Berlioz's friend and pupil Miguel Marqués, the symphonic poems of Giner, Ruperto Chapí or Nicolau, the string quartets of Chapí or Bréton?'[28] His rhetorical question leaves open whether the neglect of these Spanish repertories is attributable to inferior music or ignorant listeners. True, concert life and professional music-making in general were underdeveloped in nineteenth-century Spain (hardly surprising, given the political instability), and it may be for this reason that major symphonic composers apparently did not emerge. In any case, as in Italy, it was to lyric theatre that Spanish composers were most naturally drawn. The long-established stranglehold of Italian opera virtually stifled the attempts of Spanish composers to establish a distinctive idiom in the sphere of opera seria, but through the revival of the zarzuela tradition, with its characteristically Spanish settings and popular idioms, some sense of a national voice was preserved. Then, as the new century approached, two major developments, both entirely in line with nationalist movements elsewhere in Europe, began to yield compositional fruit. One was the rediscovery of earlier Spanish repertories, associated above all with Felipe Pedrell (1841–1922), and the other was the collection and transcription of folk

28 Lionel Salter, 'Spain: A Nation in Turbulence', in Samson (ed.), *The Late Romantic Era*, p. 137.

musics. A new generation of composers, several of them pupils of Pedrell, began to attract attention in major European centres, and it is significant that the stylistic allegiance of these composers was no longer to Italy but to France. It is hard not to see a parallel with England in the recovery of earlier 'national' repertories, in the folksong revival and in the role of modern French music as a means of releasing native creativity from a dominant neighbouring tradition. As in England, moreover, the beginnings of the renaissance were already in place before the century turned. Granados (1867–1916) composed his *Danzas españolas* in 1896, Albéniz (1860–1909) his *Peptita Jiménez* in 1896. A few years later, in 1905, Spanish opera entered the world at large with Falla's *La vida breve*.

There was a comparable, if less widely reported, renaissance in parts of southeast Europe at the turn of the century. Nowhere is it more difficult to generalise about nationality than in the Balkan peninsula, embracing present-day Romania, Bulgaria, Albania, the former Yugoslavia and Greece. The entire region was carved up between three faiths (Islam, Orthodox and Catholic) and two empires (Ottoman and Habsburg). In the Ottoman-ruled territories, where the place of music was formally constrained and musicians were considered of low caste, European traditions were naturally slow to infiltrate. The timetable of cultural renewal was thus determined very largely by the expulsion of the Turks. Greece gained its independence in 1829 (following an eight-year War of Independence), while the Union of Wallachia and Moldavia ensured *de facto* freedom for Romania in 1859, though full independence came only in 1878 (Transylvania was part of the Austro-Hungarian Empire from 1867). It was also in 1878 that the Turks were expelled from Bulgaria, Serbia (which had already been ceded a measure of self-government), Bosnia and Herzegovina, and Montenegro. And Macedonia finally followed suit after the two Balkan Wars of 1912–13. In all these regions the development of anything like a national idiom in music was delayed until the twentieth century, and in some cases well into that century.

Even in Greece and Romania it was only the foundations that were laid during the nineteenth century. An institutional base was established in both countries, and a native music profession gradually created. This was accomplished more quickly and easily in the Romanian provinces, whose Latin inheritance promoted close ties to the West, than in Greece. By the second half of the century, there were national theatres in Bucharest, Iaşi and Craiova, state conservatories in Iaşi (1860) and Bucharest (1864), a philharmonic society in Bucharest (1868), and even a special music journal *Musicul român* (The Romanian Musician), founded in 1861. Such activities culminated in the establishment of the Romanian Opera in Bucharest in 1877, and this in turn stimulated a renewed enthusiasm for operatic composition, building on the achievements of Alexandru Flechtenmacher (1823–98) in comic opera and Ion Andrei Wachmann (1807–63) in grand opera. The leading Romanian composers during the second half of the century were Mauriciu Cohen-Lînaru (1849–1928), a pupil of Bizet and César Franck, Ciprian Porumbescu (1853–83), whose early death prevented him from realising his full stature as a composer, and Eduard Caudella (1841–1924). In the end, though, Romania was drawn into the orbit of European music by the single-handed achievements of one composer of exceptional talent, Caudella's pupil George Enescu (1881–1955). And much the same was true of Greece. It was only in Manolis Kalomiris (1882–1962), a composer whose stature has been generally underrated, that mainland Greece found its voice, in direct opposition to the Italian-dominated Ionian school (the Ionian Islands had never been ruled by Turkey) associated with Nicolaos Mantzaros and his pupils.

For reasons which are hard to explicate fully there was no Enescu and no Kalomiris in Habsburg Slovenia and Croatia, though the nationalist ferment in those lands was no less intense, and found powerful enough outlets in literature. In the late nineteenth century musical life in the major capitals, Ljubljana (Laibach) and Zagreb, was institutionalised very much on the pattern of Habsburg cities elsewhere. By the end of the century both cities had their music societies (notably Zagreb's National Illyrian Music Society), their opera companies (Mahler did a stint as conductor in Ljubljana) and their fully fledged philharmonic societies. Yet little of the music composed in these provinces has remained in the repertory. Slovenian composers well into the twentieth century developed a cosmopolitan late Romantic idiom influenced by Brahms and Dvořák and occasionally, as in Risto Savin's 1907 opera *Lepa Vida* (Lovely Vida), by Wagner. In Croatia, on the other hand, there was a lively nationalist (Illyrian) movement, which paralleled rather closely the Hungarian experience in its diffusion into more cosmopolitan tendencies towards the end of the century, associated above all with the arrival in Zagreb of Ivan Zajc (1832–1914). But although Zajc played an important part in encouraging professional standards in Croatian musical life, notably at the Croatian National Theatre, his own musical idiom was conservative and derivative and he offered little of promise to a later generation of Croatian composers.

Compared to the confusing ethnic and cultural diversity of south-east Europe, Scandinavia presents us with a rather different problematic of cultural identity, as between a generalised northern identity, rather than specifically Danish, Norwegian, Swedish or Finnish identities (Finland, despite its different language and mythology, was a province of Sweden for much of its history). Under the banner of national Romanticism, all of these nations (whether or not they had political independence) asserted their cultural identities in the nineteenth century, though they did so in close dialogue with the institutions and traditions of Germany and (later) France. As royal cities, Copenhagen and Stockholm promoted lively operatic and concert activities (at secondary theatres as well as at the court), and to a lesser degree Christiania (Oslo) and (rather later) Helsinki followed suit. Yet the facilities for professional performance and high-level instruction were far from adequate in any of these capitals, and most of the abler professional musicians, including composers, were obliged to study abroad; indeed many never returned. Among the several Scandinavian composers who made their mark in the late nineteenth century were Niels Wilhelm Gade (1817–90) and Emil Hartmann (1836–98) in Denmark; Franz Berwald (1796–1868) in Sweden; Johan Svendsen (1840–1908) and Edvard Grieg (1843–1907) in Norway. Of these composers, only Grieg has been assimilated by our present-day canon, though Berwald occasionally registers as an iconoclastic presence. The neglect of the others might have to do with intrinsic merit; but equally it might result from a critical perspective that seeks and values a distinctive sense of northern identity and is inclined to dismiss as derivative works that hone to perfection an idiom well established elsewhere (Gade would be a case in point). Such a northern identity, associated in some minds with an idealised blend of purity and physicality, was really only achieved at the turn of the century, and then it had less to do with folk music than with what I called in chapter 10 a 'second growth' of the symphonic tradition associated with Stenhammar (1871–1927), Nielsen (1865–1931) and Sibelius (1865–1957).

Furthest removed of all – well beyond the edge – was of course America. The groundwork of institutions for art music, clearly modelled on European prototypes, has already been discussed in chapter 13, and the development of popular cultures in chapter 19. Two later tales unfolded from these nineteenth-century backgrounds: the emergence of a uniquely American voice in art music (Charles Ives and beyond) following generations of German- and later French-influenced compositional styles; and the growth of an Afro-American popular idiom – jazz, blues, Tin Pan Alley and beyond – that remained essentially separate from European traditions, though it went on to colonise them. Much more than in Europe, this twin-track history raises treacherous questions about value, innovation and progress. We may pose one of them as a provocation. Which is the truly 'progressive' composer: Charles Ives, whose radical innovations at the turn of the century were rooted in the Romantic, transcendentalist philosophy of a bygone age, or Stephen Foster, whose accessible ballads of a half-century earlier looked ahead to a popular music that eschewed Romantic pretensions in favour of an easy engagement with the modern culture industry? However we decide to answer, we can agree that the music of both composers spells out its 'American-ness' – its distance from Europe, though it goes without saying they also drew heavily on European traditions. Thus Foster's ballads translated the sentimentality and nostalgia of the Victorian parlour song into both the subject-matter (especially attitudes to slavery) and the 'minstrel' idioms of the New World. Likewise Ives, his roots 'deeply anchored . . . in the European past',[29] drew on Beethoven and the symphonic tradition, as also on the practices of European nationalists (notably through his reliance on national images drawn from history and landscape and on vernacular musical material as a powerful symbol of the nation), while at the same time transforming these, through his frontier spirit, and above all through his untroubled acceptance of a stylistic pluralism that is entirely without ironic intent, into the music of America.

How, then, can we sum up the effects of cultural nationalism on music history as the century turned? There can be no doubt that the quest for a national voice motivated and shaped musical composition in telling ways. Yet from our present perspective it seems rather clear that the distinctiveness of individual national styles was greatly exaggerated at the time. For the most part the ideological input served its customary purpose, which is to trigger rather than fully to determine the creative impulse, even if composers may have assigned greater privilege to it. Nationalism was undoubtedly the essential agent of a musical 'awakening' around the edge of Europe, but once awakened the music very soon entered the wider world. Indeed there is a certain inevitability about this sequence. National 'schools' tend of their nature to have a limited lifespan, developing from the particular towards the universal, and preserving their vitality only when the two are held in balance. Looking back on it now, it seems that the major outcome of musical nationalism in the late nineteenth and early twentieth centuries was less a crop of clearly differentiated national styles than a collective alternative to the styles and aesthetic of German late Romanticism, leading in turn to a polarisation of two lines of development within musical Modernism (Schoenberg, Stravinsky). And even this divergence may prove in the end to have been a surface event in the history of music, given those deeper, more radical changes in musical syntax that embraced *both* modernisms, crossing national boundaries and ignoring political differences. (Nor is this surprising, since the advance of political nationalisms, promoting separatism, could scarcely conceal the ever more homogeneous and *inter*national character of a modern urban culture.) For composers reaching their musical maturity around the turn of the century, then, those major shifts in musical

29 Robert Morgan, '"The Things Our Fathers Loved": Charles Ives and the European Tradition', in Philip Lambert (ed.), *Ives Studies* (Cambridge, 1997), p. 26.

syntax were arguably even more crucial than the issue of nationalism. These composers helped to create, just as they also responded to, the 'waves of innovation' that are the subject of our final chapter.

Bibliography

Anderson, B., *Imagined Communities*. London, 1983

Armstrong, J., *Nations before Nationalism*. Chapel Hill, 1962

Beller, S., *Vienna and the Jews 1867–1938: A Cultural History*. Cambridge, 1989

Breilly, J., *Nationalism and the State*. Manchester, 1982; 2nd edn Chicago, 1993

Calvocoressi, M. D., *Mussorgsky*. London, 1946

Chopin, F. F., *Korespondencja Fryderyka Chopina*, ed. B. E. Sydow. Warsaw, 1955

Cooper, M., *French Music from the Death of Berlioz to the Death of Fauré*. Oxford, 1951

Dahlhaus, C., *Between Romanticism and Modernism: Four Studies in the Music of the Later Nineteenth Century*, trans. M. Whittall. Berkeley and Los Angeles, 1980; original edn 1974

Deathridge, J., 'Germany: The "Special Path"'. In Jim Samson (ed.), *The Late Romantic Era*. London and Basingstoke, 1991, pp. 50–73

DiGrazia, D. M., *Concert Societies in Paris and their Choral Repertories c. 1828–1880*. 2 vols., Ann Arbor, 1995

Fauser, A., 'World Fair – World Music: Musical Politics in 1889 Paris'. In Jim Samson and Bennett Zon (eds.), *Nineteenth-Century Music: Selected Proceedings of the Tenth International Conference on Nineteenth-Century Music*. Aldershot, forthcoming

Friedenthal, R., *Goethe: His Life and Times*. London, 1963

Friedman, J. (ed.), *Critical Review*, 10/2 (Spring 1996)

Gellner, E., *Nations and Nationalism*. Oxford, 1983

Greenfeld, L., *Nationalism: Five Roads to Modernity*. Cambridge, Mass., 1992

Hobsbawm, E. J., *Nations and Nationalism since 1870: Programme, Myth and Reality*. Cambridge, 1990

Kohn, H., *Nationalism: Its Meaning and History*. Princeton, 1955

Lambert, P. (ed.), *Ives Studies*. Cambridge, 1997

May, F., *The Life of Johannes Brahms*. 2 vols., London, 1905

Newman, E., *The Life of Richard Wagner*. 4 vols., Cambridge, 1976

Oxal, I., Pollak, M. and Botz, G. (eds.), *Jews, Antisemitism and Culture in Vienna*. London, Boston and Henley, 1987

Porter, C. H., *The Rhine as Musical Metaphor: Cultural Identity in German Romantic Music*. Boston, 1996

Rehding, A., 'Nature and Nationhood in Hugo Riemann's Dualistic Theory of Harmony.' Ph.D. diss., Cambridge University (1998)

Robertson, R., *The 'Jewish' Question in German Literature 1749–1939*. Oxford, 1999

Rosselli, J., 'Italy: The Decline of a Tradition'. In Samson (ed.), *The Late Romantic Era*, pp. 126–50

Said, E., *Orientalism*. New York, 1979

Salter, L., 'Spain: A Nation in Turbulence'. In Samson (ed.), *The Late Romantic Era*, pp. 151–66

Spitta, P., *Johann Sebastian Bach: His Work and Influence on the Music of Germany*, trans. Clara Bell and J. A. Fuller Maitland. 3 vols., London, 1899

Taruskin, R., 'Some Thoughts on the History and Historiography of Russian Music'. *The Journal of Musicology*, 3/4 (1984), pp. 321–9

   Defining Russia Musically: Historical and Hermeneutical Essays. Princeton, 1997

Tyrrell, J., *Czech Opera*. Cambridge, 1988

Weber, M., *The Protestant Ethic and the Spirit of Capitalism*, trans. Talcott Parsons. London, 1930

Wolff, L., *Inventing Eastern Europe: The Map of Civilization on the Mind of the Enlightenment*. Stanford, 1994

21

Styles and languages around the turn of the century

ANTHONY POPLE

The title of this chapter implies not only a concern with musical style and musical language, but also that a distinction may be drawn between the two. In the paragraphs that follow I shall take this distinction to be roughly equivalent to the point at which the style of a musical passage, work or repertory can be said to be more than simply a matter of how a composer's musical mannerisms, habits or inclinations are identifiable as an emergent property of the music he or she produces. At this point, 'style' – as an attribute of a passage, piece or repertory – becomes something that can be manipulated along with the musical elements that express that style. Such manipulation allows musical language to be deployed as a means to a variety of ends: to express emotion, for example, or to articulate a drama, or to engage in cultural politics.

All of this presupposes that differences of style are actually recognisable as such across the field of contemporaneous musical composition, and indeed by the middle of the nineteenth century this had clearly been the case for some time. What is more, one of the century's most notable attempts to deploy musical language for culture-political ends dates from this time, with the declaration of the New German School. But the most remarkable flowering of this kind of project was to come a little later, in and around the two decades that straddle the turn of the nineteenth and twentieth centuries. A music-lover of catholic tastes who had the time and resources to travel around Europe and North America taking in premières during this period could have heard the first performances of works as diverse as *Don Juan* (1889), *Pagliacci* (1892), the *Variations on America* (1892), *En Saga* (1893), the *Prélude à l'Après-midi d'un faune* (1894), the 'Resurrection' Symphony (1895), *Verklärte Nacht* (1902), Debussy's *Pelléas et Mélisande* (1902), *Jenůfa* (1904), *Salome* (1905), the *Poem of Ecstasy* (1908) and *The Firebird* (1910) – to name a mere dozen.[1] It is this remarkable florescence of styles and languages, of which the above list illustrates merely the tip of an iceberg, that will be the main focus of this chapter.

The impact of the New German School, and in particular of Wagner's music

---

1 The dates given in parentheses are those of first performance.

dramas, created an expectation of something significant to follow, particularly after the deaths of both Wagner and Liszt in the mid-1880s. The century had earlier mortgaged a number of its composers to the ghost of Beethoven, Brahms in particular feeling the anxiety of influence in this regard. Brahms's own musical language was contrived so as to characterise Beethoven as a predecessor, and at the same time, by avoiding both expanded orchestration and any taint of the operatic, made manifest a musically distinctive opposition to Wagner, Liszt and their followers. Composers such as Grieg and Stanford, on the other hand, whose musical styles might seem to later generations to be broadly akin to that of Brahms in a number of respects, should actually be understood rather differently in terms of musical language. In terms of style their core musical idiom was indeed a kind of general-purpose Austro-Germanic one, as befitted their training,[2] but on to this they grafted elements that gave their musical languages a local identity. In Grieg's case, characteristic cadences in which the melodic anacrusis is presented on the downbeat rather than a beat earlier, together with some evocations of Norwegian folk music, served this purpose. Grieg's devotion to sets of 'multi-pieces', notably the groups of *Lyric Pieces*, afforded the opportunity to bring nationally defined elements into individual pieces without undermining the impression of international respectability given by the set when taken as a whole. The same phenomenon is to be seen in Dvořák's incorporation of *dumka*, *furiant* and other folk-music types into multi-movement works.[3]

So rich and varied were the musical innovations of the decades that straddled the end of the century that many historians of twentieth-century music, particularly those writing before about 1970, chose to appropriate them as a starting-point, despite the enormous cultural break that was wrought by the First World War and the subsequent, defining impact both of American popular music and of electrical means of dissemination. The earliest of these waves of innovation was the Straussian tone poem, which reached public view in 1889 in the shape of *Don Juan* (composed in 1888) and continued with *Tod und Verklärung* (1889), *Macbeth* (first performed in the revision of 1889–90), '*Also sprach Zarathustra*' (1895–6) and *Ein Heldenleben* (1897–8).[4] Rightly or wrongly,

2 Grieg studied at the Leipzig conservatory from 1858, and Stanford at both Leipzig and Berlin in the 1870s.

3 Stanford's construction of a local musical identity was made more complex by the fact of his being an Irishman active in a United Kingdom which was dominated by the English. Further consideration of this topic lies beyond the scope of this chapter.

4 *Till Eulenspiegel* (1894–5), *Don Quixote* (1896–7), the *Sinfonia domestica* (1902–3) and *An Alpine Symphony* (1911–15) are generally thought of as tone poems today, though their title-pages denote otherwise. The same may be said of the earlier *Aus Italien* (1886), which Strauss termed a symphonic fantasy (*Symphonische Fantasie*).

the antecedents of these works seemed clear enough to Strauss's supporters and detractors alike: Liszt on the one hand for the genre (though his works in this format had been called *symphonic* poems), and Wagner for harmony – increasingly so as time went on. There was much about Strauss's works that was new, however, and at the same time much that spoke of a perhaps surprising continuity with the past.

In fact, a large proportion of Strauss's harmonic writing did not by any means pick up where Wagner had left off in *Parsifal*, and his use of conventional formal devices was in general far clearer than Liszt's. For example, after the initial flourish is done, the principal theme of *Don Juan* is frankly Mendelssohnian in texture, harmony and phraseology, albeit conceived for a larger and more colourful orchestra, and harmonically at least this is not atypical of Strauss at this time. The modernity of the opening lay precisely in those elements I have just characterised as exceptions: the opening flourish and the orchestration. Strauss's brand of innovation – fully justifying the shift of terminology from 'symphonic' to *tone* poem – stemmed very largely from his use of the orchestra, and from what this came to imply for what is commonly termed the 'musical material' – as if what is musical does not include the sound itself! As John Williamson argues in his illuminating monograph on *'Also sprach Zarathustra'*, it is from this immediacy that Strauss's association of music and poetic ideas comes, and with it the potential for a tone poem to articulate a drama, rather than merely to delineate characters.[5] Strauss's reworking of Wagner's leitmotif technique was implicated in this development, as Williamson goes on to suggest; but the quality of directness in Strauss's most ear-catching musical ideas is such that the flexibility of tonal and contrapuntal treatment on which Wagner's technique had depended became difficult to sustain. At the same time, Strauss had Liszt's technique of thematic metamorphosis at his command – as is evident, for example, in *Tod und Verklärung*. And having been closer in spirit to Brahms than to Wagner in his most youthful works, he was also able to deploy elements of textbook forms to organise, or at least to contain, the musical flow. (This is especially the case in *Till Eulenspiegel* and *Don Quixote*, which are described in terms of their form – rondo and variations, respectively – on their title-pages; but the tone poems proper make use of formal schemata as well.) On those occasions when Strauss was adventurous harmonically, this tended not to show itself in terms of chromatic intensification, as had been the case with Wagner, but in terms of juxtaposed triads and other such configurations that emerge from orchestral and textural thinking, in line with the main thrust of his innovations. This is true even of *Salome* and

---

5 John Williamson, *Strauss: Also sprach Zarathustra* (Cambridge, 1993), pp. 16–18.

Elektra (to be discussed below), which are sometimes said to verge in places on atonality.

The result, all things considered, was an overall expansion of musical means, such that a certain amount of leitmotivic work, a certain amount of thematic transformation and a certain amount of conventional formal patterning were supplemented by a new type of tone poetry that was intimately bound up with the orchestral writing itself. Strauss's expansion of means and scope was indeed a continual one, for as if in response to public expectation, the works of the 1890s grew ever more striking – in ambition, orchestral device and personal aggrandisement – culminating in *Don Quixote* and *Ein Heldenleben*. The next stage, after wrong turnings in *Feuersnot* and the *Sinfonia domestica*, was for Strauss to bring his tone poetry into the opera house with *Salome* (1903–5) and *Elektra* (1906–8, first produced in 1909), thus making his second contribution to the successive 'waves of innovation' under discussion in this chapter. One reason behind the poor critical reception of the *Sinfonia domestica* had been the very apparent lack of comparability between the mundane programme of the work, which was based on domestic events, and the extravagant orchestral means employed to portray it. In this respect, the work simply continued a trend observable in *Don Quixote* and even more so in *Ein Heldenleben*, wherein the pursuit of musical realism – which was a matter of pride with Strauss, though clearly a vain hope – had led not to a refinement of means but to a coarsening of ends. *Salome* and *Elektra* are successful in part because they recapture something of the exotic and the mythical that were an essential part of both Wagner's music-drama project and Liszt's practice in his symphonic poems. One might argue that it is a measure of how far Strauss had departed from this that words and action were necessary to the reversal of his own fortunes.

Describing the actual sound of music is a notoriously difficult enterprise. The most common way of attempting this – beyond merely enumerating the instruments that are playing – is to respond with a flurry of adjectives: dark, glittering, strident and so forth. But when the sonic material is brought into being as a response to a poetic idea, as is the case with these works of Strauss, to translate the sounds back into a probably different imagery is clearly absurd, and the difficulty of establishing a musicological discourse is thus very apparent. Robin Holloway confronts this difficulty head-on in discussing *Salome* under the rubric 'art or kitsch?'[6] He is more than once confined to observe that Strauss provides 'exactly what's wanted': in doing so, he makes plain that the music is above all *successful* – which is to say that it captures the poetry aright. To charge Strauss's *Salome* with being kitsch is to charge Oscar Wilde's play

6 Robin Holloway, '"Salome": Art or Kitsch?', in Derrick Puffett (ed.), *Richard Strauss: Salome* (Cambridge, 1989), pp. 145–60.

with the same offence – and this in itself is a measure of the composer's success as a tone poet.

The possibility of creating and using a musical language which can produce 'exactly what's wanted' is critically dependent on the existence of a rich background of established convention on which the empathy between a new work and its audience can be founded. For this reason if no other, Strauss's innovations are better understood as an outcome of earlier nineteenth-century musical practices than as a quantum leap into the twentieth. The essentially Straussian qualities on which Holloway fastens should not be obscured by the ease with which the musicological discourse of opera studies provides other ways into these two works, and so whilst it would be wrong not to point out that Strauss's somewhat reduced conception of the leitmotif also informs the two operas, one should observe at the same time that Strauss's use of motifs characteristically reflects the popular Wagner criticism of his day. The kind of thematic guide that reduces a Wagnerian network of reminiscences and allusions to a mere catalogue is not inappropriate for Strauss, as one can see from the handbook produced by Otto Röse and Julius Prüwer for the first audiences of *Elektra*.[7] If in this way Strauss effected a popular renewal of Wagnerian music drama for the turn of the century, one casualty was the quasi-religious idea of the *Gesamtkunstwerk*, and together with that went the principle that one creative artist should be at the helm of all aspects of the operatic enterprise. Indeed, Strauss would go on to become a great collaborator, and one can only speculate as to the kind of contribution he might have made to film music in old age had his personal fate matched that of his younger contemporary Erich Wolfgang Korngold.

Another popular renewal in the operatic sphere can be identified in the 'wave of innovation' that is evident in Italian operas of the 1890s and shortly thereafter. In considering the musical language and styles involved, it is important to come to terms with the fact that the first *verismo* operas – of which *Cavalleria rusticana* (produced in 1890) and *Pagliacci* (1892) were immediately successful with the public and have never left the repertory – were in historical terms a catalyst for the emergence of a new type of sentimental opera with Puccini's *La bohème* (1896), followed by *Tosca* (1900) and *Madama Butterfly* (1904). It could be said of Puccini's mature operas as much as of Strauss's that the music always produces 'exactly what's wanted', and that this depended in the same way on Puccini's working against a rich background of conventions – in his case those of Verdian opera. This background obviously extends further than the immediate impact of *Falstaff* (1893), the fast musico-dramatic pace of which is commonly said to have influenced Puccini directly.

---

7 Otto Röse and Julius Prüwer, *Elektra: Ein Musikführer durch das Werk* (Berlin, 1909; English edn 1910).

In consequence, Puccini's art is arguably more discriminating than Strauss's in terms of its control of musical styles for dramatic ends. Whereas the roots of Strauss's musical language lay in musical thought that valued unity, coherence and organicism, the traditions of Italian opera were highly nuanced, despite an overall stylistic range that is easily portrayed as inward-looking to the point of parochialism. A particularly striking feature of Puccini's works is their control of dramatic pace: events can happen quickly, with musical gestures thrown one after the other to give hustle and bustle to the stage business, and on the other hand moments of intimacy, such as that which begins with 'Che gelida manina', are handled in a way that brings an uncanny sense of stillness. This is achieved not simply through deployment of the aria as a musical type, however, but beyond this by the peculiar intensity of Puccini's melodic invention, and his composition of the entire texture – including not only the orchestral writing but also the vocal timbres associated with different melodic registers – in such a way as to give the melody – music and text together – its sole focus. Puccini cleverly mixes conjunct melodic motion and downward leaps of a third, fourth or fifth – all of these being easy to sing along with, silently – with breathtaking leaps into the higher reaches of the voice, the use of *allargando* to dwell on extreme notes placed at points of melodic anacrusis being a mannerism eagerly taken up by singers.

Mosco Carner and other writers have been keen to point out the occasional use of whole-tone writing and other 'advanced' harmonic types in Puccini's works, as if these were an index of his respectability. This is something of a red herring, but it remains true that such passages can be found, despite the fact that continuity with previous operatic tradition was deeply embedded in the medium that was Puccini's message, and that his core harmonic vocabulary was extremely (though no doubt deliberately) limited by the international standards of the late nineteenth century. The question of respectability, if it arises at all, has to be dealt with differently, but it is fair to observe that Puccini's occasional use of modern-sounding harmonies was balanced by the reassuring quality of his post-verist scenarios, just as Grieg's use of local colour was in balance with his 'mainly mainstream' musical style. This balance allowed Puccini to meet expectations of novelty without alienating his audience, and without necessarily admitting such devices into the canon of musical styles that made up his musical language. (Strauss, in *Der Rosenkavalier*, showed that his attitude was the same in this respect, but in a Germanic context it cost him dear in terms of accusations of stylistic cowardice.) It is also worth emphasising the sheer craftsmanship that is evident in the work of both Puccini and his librettists – something which ensured, perhaps in an exaggerated manner, that harmonic audacity was never deployed without some kind of 'justification' either in terms of a specific dramatic situation or, as at the very opening of *Tosca*, as a means of conjuring up an immediately recognisable musical tag that could be used as a motif of reminiscence.

The dialectic of innovation and continuity reached a deeper level of complexity in the case of Debussy. His mature music, beginning with the *Prélude à l'Après-midi d'un faune* (composed in 1892), has frequently been seen as so innovative that it marked a new beginning, Pierre Boulez's comment being not atypical of the mid-twentieth century:

> Just as modern poetry is clearly rooted in certain poems of Baudelaire, one can justifiably claim that modern music began with *L'Après-midi d'un faune*.[8]

Debussy's debt to the Symbolist movement in literature is not difficult to identify, but it is far harder to see his musical precedents, and this is surely the principal reason why his music has seemed so very fresh. The resemblance between the opening of 'Nuages' (from the Nocturnes for orchestra) and a passage in the third song of Musorgsky's cycle *Without Sun* (1874) has been fastened on obsessively as evidence of Russian influence, and one can identify a general kinship in Debussy's early music with his older French contemporaries, but the fact that such observations fall pitifully short of the mark is evidence that something more obscure is afoot. It was again Robin Holloway who in the 1970s brilliantly demonstrated that the greatest influence was that of Wagner, but so hidden, so transmuted, as to be completed dominated by Debussy's own creative persona. This was a staggering achievement on Debussy's part, given the awesome stature that Wagner had in the minds of his contemporaries. At the core of Holloway's analysis lies *Pelléas et Mélisande* (1893–5, 1901–2), which offers ample demonstration of what he terms 'a complex of Wagnerian reminiscence both in music and of subject-matter'.[9] Ultimately, Holloway argues that '[Debussy] must be recognized to be, within the limits of a subtle and specialized relationship, the most profoundly Wagnerian of all composers' (*Debussy and Wagner*, p. 21).

In terms of subject-matter, the points of contact between Wagner and Debussy have much to do with the Symbolist movement, on which Wagner was a clear influence and which in turn provided an aesthetic point of departure for the younger composer. Holloway also identifies numerous points of musical correspondence, all of which are quite brief. This brevity is actually a definitive point of cleavage between Debussy and his Wagnerian models: as Holloway remarks of the correspondence between the first orchestral interlude

---

8 Pierre Boulez, *Stocktakings from an Apprenticeship*, trans. Stephen Walsh (Oxford, 1991), p. 267.
9 Robin Holloway, *Debussy and Wagner* (London, 1979), p. 7.

in Act I of *Pelléas* and the Transformation music in *Parsifal*, 'Wagner [makes] of this rhythm a constantly-evolving structural span, while Debussy's use of it is fleeting and transitory – he evokes a march but does not write one' (p. 77). If one looks closely at the score of the *Prélude à l'Après-midi d'un faune*, there is abundant evidence that Debussy was thoroughly familiar with one of the classic harmonic gambits of *Tristan und Isolde* – involving chromatic voice-leading between half-diminished and dominant-quality chords, and the occasional use of enharmonic changes to send such motion in unexpected directions. What is entirely different, however, is the phraseology: Debussy's music moves in fragments, often hesitatingly and occasionally bursting into a melodic character for a handful of bars – altogether unlike the quasi-symphonic 'endless melody' at which Wagner had aimed. Nor does Debussy employ an ongoing counterpoint of motifs as a textural fallback: his thinking is altogether more homophonic, but does not exclude, in the later orchestral music, dense passages of filigree decoration normally in the upper strings or woodwind. Like the Magic Fire Music of *Die Walküre*, which provides a (for once) clear Wagnerian precedent, such textures amount to an orchestral transcription of the kind of virtuoso upper-register piano writing – common in Liszt above all – that gives body and sustaining power to passages that if presented in undivided longer notes on that instrument would fall utterly flat.[10]

Debussy's musical language, however striking, should not though be regarded as an unchanging point of reference. Compared with *L'Après-midi*, his reliance on chromatic chords in a fluidly modulating tonality was already less marked in *Pelléas* and decreased still further in the later works. Correspondingly, he made increasing use of new modes such as the whole-tone, acoustic and octatonic collections, bound together with the characteristic dominant-quality sonorities that are easily associated with these collections, and also with diatonic melodic fragments that give a veneer of traditional tonality to much of the music.[11] Parallel motion between chords also offered something quite distinct from Wagnerian precedent. This later style of Debussy's perhaps reached its zenith in the piano Preludes (1909–10; 1912–13) and the ballet score *Jeux* (1912–13). Although Russian composers are generally held to have exhibited the closest association with the whole-tone and octatonic collections in the latter part of the nineteenth century, it seems quite possible that the development of Debussy's later harmonic technique was more directly

---

10 For a stimulating study of Debussy's textures, see Derrick Puffett, *Debussy's Ostinato Machine* (Nottingham, 1996).

11 The fullest single analysis of Debussy's technique is to be found in Richard S. Parks, *The Music of Claude Debussy* (New Haven and London, 1989), though the author's approach is somewhat idiosyncratic.

influenced by Paul Dukas, whose *Ariane et Barbe-bleu* (1899–1906) deeply impressed a number of his contemporaries around Europe and uses the whole-tone scale in a manner perhaps more sophisticated than any other work in the repertory.[12] Certainly, a stylistic realm very much the same as Dukas's work is to be heard in the twenty-five minutes or so of music that Debussy left for his unfinished opera *La chute de la maison Usher* (1908–17).[13]

The 'waves of innovation' so far considered have been represented in each case by a composer who was successful at the time and whose works remain in the repertory. In contrast, the later reputations of Mahler and Sibelius – two innovators in the previously central genre of the symphony – have far exceeded the extent of their public and critical success around 1900. The symphony at the end of the nineteenth century was a genre fraught with expectations: simply to entitle a work 'symphony' implicated the composer in the international play of musical languages, and beyond that in the treacherous ongoing debate about absolute and programme music. Peter Franklin has pointed out how, in the case of his Third Symphony, which was performed complete for the first time in 1902,[14] Mahler attempted to suppress its programmatic basis from the public whilst making this abundantly clear to his own friends and associates. As Franklin observes, there was a 'continuing tension between Mahler's . . . public presentation policy and his private conceptual interpretation of the symphony', but at the same time 'none of his public strategies fooled the critics for one moment into thinking that they were hearing anything other than an altogether radical new work, the suppression of whose programme some even denounced as . . . evasion'.[15]

Mahler had already brought texted music into his symphonic output in the Second Symphony, and the presence of 'songs without words' in his First was self-evident. Arguably, the effect, even without words or programme, is to make these works more rich in their associative meanings, not less, than a Straussian tone poem. It is a moot point whether, as is commonly maintained, such meanings readily acquire an ironic tone from being placed in a symphonic frame, or, to the contrary, it is the symphonic framework that is itself ironised. Robert Samuels has shown how the purely instrumental music of Mahler's Sixth Symphony sets up a rich web of meanings that ultimately points to 'the suicide of the Romantic

---

12 See Debussy's appreciation of Dukas's Piano Sonata in 'Monsieur Croche the Dilettante Hater', trans. B. N. Langdon Davies, in *Three Classics in the Aesthetic of Music* (New York, 1962), pp. 20–1. I am grateful to Philip Weller for impressing on me Debussy's high opinion of Dukas.

13 These fragments are published in the version realised by Juan Allende-Blin by Editions Jobert (Paris, 1979).

14 Some movements had been performed in 1896 and 1897. See Peter Franklin, *Mahler: Symphony No. 3* (Cambridge, 1991), pp. 23–5.   15 Franklin, *Mahler: Symphony No. 3*, p. 27.

symphony'.[16] The famous exchange between Mahler and Sibelius in Helsinki in 1907 perhaps suggests, however, that the former view should indeed hold sway more generally – and indeed Samuels is careful to present the Sixth Symphony as a special case – yet in reading Sibelius's account of the famous discussion between the two composers one should not overlook the fact that Mahler was almost totally unfamiliar with Sibelius's music and may simply have been 'talking down' to his younger Finnish contemporary. The conversation in fact took place after a concert at which the only works of Sibelius on the programme had been light-weight items, one of which Mahler described privately as kitsch, 'spiced with certain "Nordic" touches like a kind of national sauce':[17]

> When our conversation touched on the symphony, I [Sibelius] said that I admired its style and severity of form, and the profound logic that created an inner connection between all the motifs. This was my experience in the course of my creative work. Mahler's opinion was just the opposite. 'No!' he said, 'The symphony must be like the world. It must be all-embracing.' (Tawaststjerna, pp. 76–7)

It is interesting to note that Sibelius's apparent belief in 'profound logic' was expressed at the time of his Third Symphony, which commentators normally regard as the first to show the mature Sibelian style in which the previous Russian influence is less evident and the 'profound logic' first shows itself.[18] And yet the opening theme of the symphony seems to me to be very similar in melodic substance to the Danish folk melody 'Under en Bro' ('Under a Bridge'), which has reached the present-day repertory in Percy Grainger's setting.[19] The treatment of this melody in the first movement of the symphony moves strongly in the direction of two linked compositional principles that James Hepokoski identifies most characteristically in the case of Sibelius's Fifth, involving the 'rotational' presentation of material – a kind of 'circular stasis' – and the 'teleological generation' of a new idea that is made apparently to emerge from such rotations – Hepokoski likens this to 'the patient rocking of the cradle . . . preparing for the birth of something new'.[20] Hepokoski actually finds the other movements of the Third more to embody these procedures, yet I mention the first movement and the unacknowledged folksong not only because the admixture of song and symphony begs comparison with Mahler but also because, like it or not, there is a strong point of contact between the

---

16 Robert Samuels, *Mahler's Sixth Symphony: A Study in Musical Semiotics* (Cambridge, 1995), p. 157.

17 Eric Tawaststjerna, *Sibelius, Volume II: 1904–1914*, trans. Robert Layton (London, 1986), p. 76.

18 For example, Robert Layton in *Sibelius*, 2nd edn (London, 1978), pp. 37–8. The oft-cited Russian influence on early Sibelius is brought into focus by Veijo Murtomäki, who points out that 'Sibelius was indeed "a Russian composer", since Finland was part of Russia for most of Sibelius's creative life, until 1917!'; see his 'Russian Influences on Sibelius', in Veijo Murtomäki, Kari Kilpeläinen and Risto Väisänen (eds.), *Sibelius Forum*, Proceedings from the Second International Jean Sibelius Conference, Helsinki, November 25–29, 1995 (Helsinki, 1998), pp. 153–61, at p. 155.

19 *Danish Folk-Music Settings*, No. 12 (1945–6). The melodies are not identical, but they are sufficiently similar to invite comparison.

20 James Hepokoski, *Sibelius: Symphony No. 5* (Cambridge, 1993), pp. 23–7, at p. 26.

'rotational' idea and Constant Lambert's notorious suggestion that 'the whole trouble with a folksong is that once you have played it through there is nothing much you can do except play it over again and play it rather louder'.[21]

In their different evasions of the risk implied by Lambert's scurrilous remark lies a major part of the distinction between the musical languages of Mahler and Sibelius. In Mahler, as Samuels and others have observed, the use of themes is overt, and since when one well-rounded thematic statement comes to an end it has to be followed by something else, this leads to discontinuities in the ostensibly 'symphonic' musical argument. By doing so, it both points up the thematic character of the material itself – along with the connotations it carries in terms of its text or its melodic type (*ländler*, Jewish music, etc.) – and subjects the very idea of the 'symphony' to inordinate stress. (In his last two symphonies, the Ninth [1908–9] and the uncompleted Tenth [sketched in 1910], Mahler frequently employed a harmonic language sufficiently astringent to keep pace with his attack on the symphonic genre from within.) Sibelius, on the other hand, destabilises his melodic materials, so that their motivic elements can be manipulated in ways that make them appear to be the predicates of 'the profound logic'. With his nationalist credentials established by a series of tone poems and other works, it was not necessary for him to advertise any role that folk music might play in his symphonic compositions; the tone painting of austere and cold landscapes was sufficient to provide the 'Nordic touches' that Mahler so disparaged. It was thus that the motivically concise tone poem *Tapiola* would paradoxically come to be seen in the mid-twentieth-century Sibelius literature as the culmination of his symphonic writing.[22]

Arguably, both Mahler and Sibelius occupy a useful median position in terms of the developments surveyed here. The movements led by Strauss, Puccini and Debussy were determined in their substance more by aesthetic or culture-political renewal than by technical innovation. In the case of both Mahler and Sibelius, however, the focus is really neither on one thing nor the other. The following paragraphs address a musical language in which the aspect of technical innovation is more immediately apparent, albeit with a strongly articulated aesthetic and culture-political position occasionally in support. The perceived balance of these factors must be regarded primarily as an aspect of reception: in the case of Arnold Schoenberg, his 'bogy-man'[23] status quite clearly arose from a critical focus on his technique at the expense of his inspiration.

There is in fact clear documentary evidence that Schoenberg was a composer

21 Constant Lambert, *Music Ho! A Study of Music in Decline* (London, 1934), p. 164.
22 See again, for example, Robert Layton in *Sibelius*, p. 78.
23 Letter from Arnold Schoenberg to Werner Reinhart, dated 9 July 1923, in Erwin Stein (ed.), *Arnold Schoenberg: Letters* (Berkeley and Los Angeles, 1964), p. 100.

who composed in an inspirational way: an extraordinary speed of composition, works discarded unfinished because he could not find the thread again after being interrupted by circumstances, and so forth. Critical opinion does not rest on documentary evidence, however, but on perceptions about musical language and compositional intent. To the extent that such perceptions entail a kind of communication, they are dependent on a composer being seen (or, rather, heard) to share in conventions of musical language that allow such communication to take place. Schoenberg was slow to realise the benefits of presenting himself as 'the natural continuer of properly understood good old tradition' (*Letters*, p. 100), but in any case it is questionable whether he would credibly have been able to present himself in this way to his contemporaries beyond about 1907. As late as 1973, the distinguished American theorist Allen Forte could write without much fear of contradiction that 'In 1908 a profound change in music was initiated when Arnold Schoenberg . . . deliberately relinquished the traditional system of tonality, which had been the basis of musical syntax for the previous two hundred and fifty years'.[24] It would appear, then, that there is something of a gulf between Schoenberg's 'properly understood' tradition and the kind of understanding of it that Forte's statement represents.

Although one ought not to take Schoenberg's protestations at face value either, an important aspect of the musical languages that are to be heard in his works around 1900 consists in what they tell us of his relationship with his predecessors and older contemporaries. We are talking here not so much of a single Austro-German tradition – whether 'good' or 'old' or otherwise – as of the tradition-like qualities that might be construed among the stylistic relationships and allegiances that obtained among a large number of composers even within the Austro-Germanic sphere. The divide between, on the one hand, those who counted themselves followers of Liszt and Wagner and, on the other, those who were aligned with the supporters of Brahms, is sufficient to indicate the nature of the issue. Strauss had dealt with his inheritance by starting as a Brahmsian and then, as we have seen, establishing himself as a popular modernist. Schoenberg's personal circumstances in relation to what must be counted as genuinely 'traditional' – that is, the teaching of one generation by another – could hardly have been more different from Strauss's. Whereas Strauss, through his father (a professional horn-player), had personal contact with prominent musicians in his teens and before, Schoenberg was to all intents and purposes an autodidact. In one sense, then, he simply was not in a position to inherit anything in a tradition-like manner. The stress he laid upon his own work as a teacher, by contrast, is indicative of one way in which he immediately

24 Allen Forte, *The Structure of Atonal Music* (New Haven and London, 1973), p. ix.

sought to invent a position for himself within a quasi-traditional structure.[25] In terms of musical language his personal agenda was even more ambitious. Although, as Arnold Whittall has pointed out, Schoenberg later acknowledged that he had felt the impact of Straussian modernism during the late 1890s and that this had led him to compose a number of symphonic poems,[26] only *Pelleas und Melisande* (1902–3) of these can properly be compared with Strauss's output in the genre; of far greater import is that Schoenberg's first symphonic poem was in fact a piece of chamber music, *Verklärte Nacht* for string sextet (1899). In composing this work, then, Schoenberg positioned himself directly across the great divide that apparently existed between the Wagnerian and Brahmsian camps.

There was another aspect of musical language – besides the generic combination of tone poem and chamber music, and the post-Wagnerian harmony – that bore witness to this stance of Schoenberg's. The use of motifs in *Verklärte Nacht*, *Pelleas und Melisande*, and his First String Quartet (1904–5) follows on from Brahms's approach to this issue and reveals it to have been a transcendental piece of anti-Wagnerism. The dense and intricate motivic working in the textures of Brahms's late chamber works, songs and piano pieces is such that accompaniment textures are in many cases almost saturated with motivic fragments related to the thematic material, the sets of piano pieces – Ballades, Intermezzos, etc. – are held together by underlying motivic relationships between expressively disparate movements. The success of these works in terms of musico-cultural politics resides only partly in their having appropriated the Wagnerian idea of the motivic web as an aspect of musical language and then taken it to new heights of complexity. More significantly, and with breathtaking directness, Brahms had separated the idea of motif from the whole edifice of musico-dramatic aesthetics which Wagner had created in justification of his approach. Like Wagner's slogan of 'endless melody' – which he used to describe a kind of vocal writing very much unlike the melodies of mid-century French and Italian opera – this apparent contradiction in Brahms's thought was subversive: there was certainly no reason to believe *a priori* that motivic writing should reserve its full potential for absolute music, but Brahms's late style amounted to a claim that this was the case, bringing it into the sphere of academicism as a touchstone of technical competence, like a latter-day equivalent of triple invertible counterpoint.

The possibility of an entirely motivic music, going beyond even what Brahms had achieved, was one strand in Schoenberg's later thought, but this

---

25 See, for example, his letter to Emil Hertzka, dated 5 January 1910, in Erwin Stein (ed.), *Arnold Schoenberg: Letters*, pp. 23–4.
26 Arnold Whittall, *Schoenberg Chamber Music* (London, 1972), pp. 8–9.

had not been realised in his musical language by the time he dared to dispense with tonal centres. One can see, in works such as *Das Buch der hängenden Gärten*(1908–9) and the Three Piano Pieces, Op. 11 (1909), that the interaction of harmony and melody still generally mimicked the textures of tonal music. The most audible point of innovation in these works, on the other hand, is that traditional consonances are avoided altogether. In this 'emancipation of the dissonance', that allows contrapuntal lines to proceed 'regardless of whether or not their meetings result in codified harmonies',[27] there is a distinction to be drawn between allowing contrapuntal lines to meet haphazardly, and allowing them to meet in harmonies which though they may not be codified are nonetheless carefully weighed as chord-like sonorities. Schoenberg's *Harmonielehre* (Theory of Harmony), a book first published in 1911, makes it plain that in the case of novel configurations such as chords built in perfect fourths, he saw them both as holistic entities with certain sonorous qualities, and as chromatically altered tonal chords that with this important proviso – for the alteration was sometimes quite substantial! – were subject to the norms of tonal voice-leading.[28] A six-note chord of this kind plays a striking role in Schoenberg's First Chamber Symphony (1906), being prolonged at points of formal articulation in place of the dominant-functional harmony that one might expect. Having developed his harmonic language in this same work to the point where, through the use of the whole-tone scale and 'vagrant' chords such as the diminished seventh and the augmented triad which, considered enharmonically at least, could function in several different keys, Schoenberg had within ten years of Brahms's death reached a point at which his music would 'suspend' tonality for many bars at a time. The 'decisive step'[29] of abandoning a return to a tonal centre when to do so seemed perfunctory, was certainly decisive in terms of Schoenberg's long-term critical reception, as the example of Forte's statement quoted above illustrates. But in terms of musical language it was only a small step in what Ethan Haimo has called Schoenberg's 'Odyssey'.[30]

Many twentieth-century writers have seen Schoenberg's 'emancipation of the dissonance' as the logical outcome of Wagner's harmonic innovation in *Tristan*. Like Sibelius's 'profound logic', this seems to misappropriate a domain of mathematical philosophy which can hardly be applied conscientiously to the products of artistic work. Rather, in Schoenberg's case, just as he picked up on

27 Arnold Schoenberg, 'My Evolution (1949)', in *Style and Idea*, ed. Stein, pp. 84, 86.
28 Ernst Kurth's consideration of chromatic alteration, which he conceives in terms of tension and energy, shortly post-dates this phase of Schoenberg's compositional practice, though Schoenberg himself is not the subject of Kurth's enquiries. See Lee Rothfarb, *Ernst Kurth as Theorist and Analyst* (Philadelphia, 1988).
29 Arnold Schoenberg, 'My Evolution (1949)', in *Style and Idea*, ed. Stein, p. 86.
30 Ethan Haimo, *Schoenberg's Serial Odyssey: The Evolution of his Twelve-Tone Method, 1914–1928* (Oxford, 1990).

Brahms's transcendental reworking of the Wagnerian motivic web, his so-called atonal writing may be seen as his own transcendental take on the controversies that dogged the reception of the opening bars of Wagner's great work. (Briefly: the seemingly intractable question was whether the 'Tristan chord' can be regarded by theory as a chord at all;[31] by emancipating dissonances Schoenberg stated in effect that it did not matter one way or the other.) Schoenberg's obsession with the idea of combining the four movements of a traditional symphonic scheme into an expanded, and by implication much diluted, sonata-form structure can likewise be understood as his attempt to encompass both the exaggerated insistence on conventional formats that had formed part of Brahms's musical language, and the attempts to reconcile well-characterised episodes with vestiges of respectable forms that we see in Strauss's tone poems. Though Schoenberg arguably never achieved this most difficult synthesis, the First String Quartet and First Chamber Symphony both bear witness to his desire to bring it about.

Both transcendence and synthesis are represented in the musical languages that will be the last to be surveyed here. Scriabin's case is perhaps most interesting on account of the difficulties his late works set for their twentieth-century reception. (It is this as much as anything that marks them out as cultural products of a previous era.) He began as a conservative composer whose works up until the mid-to-late 1890s bear comparison with those of his less precocious and slightly younger contemporary Rachmaninov. The direct influence of Chopin is evident both in Scriabin's concentration on piano music and in his choice of genres, though at this stage he did not replicate, let alone build on, Chopin's harmonically most adventurous writing. Although one can observe in the works of the subsequent few years a tendency to pack his harmonic language with dominant-quality chords and a habitual progression from the flat supertonic to the dominant as a cadential gambit, it was after Scriabin's awakening to the beliefs and principles of Theosophy around 1903 that his musical language began to develop to the point where by about 1910 he had abandoned traditional cadences and, to judge by the evidence of his final sketches, had proposed to use twelve-note chords in his unfinished *Acte préalable*.[32]

As Richard Taruskin has eloquently pointed out, the difficulty this body of work presented to twentieth-century criticism was that the innovations in

31 See Jean-Jacques Nattiez, 'The Concepts of Plot and Seriation Process in Music Analysis', trans. Catherine Dale, *Music Analysis*, 4/1 (1985), pp. 107–18, and *Music and Discourse: Toward a Semiology of Music*, trans. Carolyn Abbate (Princeton, 1990), pp. 216–33.

32 See Manfred Kelkel, *Alexandre Scriabine: Sa vie, l'ésotérisme et le langage musical dans son œuvre* (Paris, 1978), Annexe III. The 'realisation' of *L'Acte préalable* prepared by Alexander Nemtin, though based on Scriabin's sketches and other authentic material, is best regarded as a composition by Nemtin himself.

terms of compositional technique appealed to the 'race-to-the-patent-office mentality' that was 'characteristic of techno-essentialist historiography',[33] whilst the defining motivation for this musical language was, to put it bluntly, embarrassing. This created the conditions in which Scriabin could be seen merely as a pioneer of atonal music, a little behind Schoenberg chronologically and with his claim to greatness undermined by inflexible principles and an early death – rather in the way that Captain Scott lost out to Amundsen in 1911–12 in their race for the South Pole. But the grand scope of Scriabin's vision should not encourage us to see him as a heroic failure. Rather, the challenge is to understand his highly distinctive musical language as the outcome of his beliefs and motivations. Taruskin has attempted to meet this challenge, outlining a historical basis for understanding the tritone interval as embodying both harmonic tension, through its association with dominant functionality, and also passivity, because, in Taruskin's words, 'The way in which it will seek resolution depends on external stimuli – that is, the notes that accompany it' (Taruskin, p. 329). A harmony such as the French sixth, which is composed of two tritones, could thus achieve 'a quality of hovering, of time-forgetful stasis' (Taruskin, p. 330), since it could be reordered vertically whilst its constituent notes remained enharmonically the same.

Contrasting descriptions of technical phenomena in music might be said not to alter the notes in the score, but they do affect the way those notes are understood. Taruskin extends his discussion to arrive at a way of understanding the harmonic gambits typical of Scriabin's *Poem of Ecstasy* (1905–8) – dominant-quality chords, perhaps over a 'tonic' bass, progressing minimally by way of root movement through a tritone or a whole tone – and *Prometheus* (1908–10) – a characteristic near whole-tone, near-octatonic chord with the notes of a French sixth in the lower register and the upper notes voiced in perfect fourths, typically moving by a tritone or a minor third within the same octatonic framework. The latter, known to musical history as the 'mystic' chord, was actually described by Scriabin to an astonished Rachmaninov as 'the chord of the pleroma' (Taruskin, pp. 340–1). Taruskin explains this as follows:

> The pleroma, a Christian Gnostic term derived from the Greek for 'plenitude', was the all-encompassing hierarchy of the divine realm, located entirely outside the physical universe . . . totally alien and essentially 'other' to the phenomenal world and whatever belongs to it. What we know as the mystic chord, then, was designed to afford instant apprehension of – that is, to *reveal* – what was in essence beyond the mind of man to conceptualise.   (pp. 341–2)

---

33 Richard Taruskin, *Defining Russia Musically: Historical and Hermeneutic Essays* (Princeton, 1997), p. 315.

All of this seems a long way removed from Schoenberg's apparent desire to develop musical technique from within. Whether Taruskin is right to call for that composer's work, too, to be reassessed in similar terms on the evidence of Schoenberg's own occult concerns, is questionable but stimulating (pp. 349–59). Desirable or not, there can surely be little chance of it happening for some time, even though – or perhaps because – the transcendental aspect of Schoenberg's thought is evident even to a broadly 'techno-essentialist' point of view. A similar unity of ends and means has been difficult to establish in Scriabin's case, but the example of Taruskin's discussion gives hope that such a reassessment may gradually come about.[34]

Although Stravinsky was for a while in thrall to the Symbolist poet Balmont, and although some of his early scores have stylistic points of contact with Scriabin's musical idiom – in particular *The Firebird* (1909–10) and the first act of *The Nightingale* (1908–9; the remainder of the opera dates from 1913–14) – these connections must be regarded as indicative not of deep aesthetic affinities but as residues of the cultural milieu from which Stravinsky emerged. There is plenty of evidence to suggest that Stravinsky's talent was seen as being quite ordinary by his fellow-members of Rimsky-Korsakov's circle, and the growth of his reputation to the point that he was regarded posthumously as perhaps the greatest of all twentieth-century composers is an extraordinary phenomenon – though it is one that lies beyond the scope of this book. For a few years at the very outset of his public career, however, Stravinsky's music lay firmly in a line of continuity from Rimsky-Korsakov's operas, though with a comparatively modernist character that seems to have been due to his interest in composers such as Wagner, Dukas, Debussy and Scriabin.[35] Broadly speaking, Stravinsky may be reckoned to have taken as a given the Korsakovian convention that exotic and magical personages, events and scenarios should be associated with 'chromatic' music – very often octatonic – and the sphere of human beings and their actions should be associated with diatonic music. This distinction, rough-and-ready though it is, holds for both *The Firebird* and *Petrushka* (1910–11) – the latter being the first in a series of works exploring Russian folk festivals and customs.[36] In *The Rite of Spring* (1911–13), however, Stravinsky

---

34 See also James M. Baker, 'Scriabin's Music: Structure as Prism for Mystical Philosophy', in James M. Baker, David W. Beach and Jonathan W. Bernard (eds.), *Music Theory in Concept and Practice* (Rochester, N.Y., 1997), pp. 53–96.

35 For a brief account see Anthony Pople, 'Early Stravinsky', in Jonathan Cross (ed.), *The Cambridge Companion to Stravinsky* (Cambridge, 2001). The finest extended studies of Stravinsky's early career are Richard Taruskin, *Stravinsky and the Russian Traditions: A Biography of the Works Through 'Mavra'* (Oxford, 1996) and Stephen Walsh, *Stravinsky: A Creative Spring: Russia and France, 1882–1934* (London, 2000).

36 See Simon Karlinsky, 'Igor Stravinsky and Russian Preliterate Theater', in Jann Pasler (ed.), *Confronting Stravinsky: Man, Musician, and Modernist* (Berkeley and Los Angeles, 1986), pp. 3–15.

and his collaborator, the folklorist Nicholas Roerich, developed their scenario into an account of a pagan fertility rite, lending magical and mysterious qualities to the human participants themselves. In response, Stravinsky's music produced a synthesis of 'human' and 'magical' musics, which in terms of technique led him to combine the diatonic and the octatonic in a manner that, according to Pieter van den Toorn's compendious analysis of the composer's output, would stand as a touchstone for his subsequent music.[37]

The principle of synthesis, by which elements given associative meaning by nineteenth-century aesthetics would be combined into new musical languages, was one that was indeed definitive for a number of composers the bulk of whose output is more properly considered in the context of the later century. In England, Vaughan Williams forged an alloy of English folksong and Tudor church music, in works such as *On Wenlock Edge* (1908–9), *A London Symphony* (1912–13) and above all the *Fantasia on a Theme by Thomas Tallis* (1910).[38] This quietly nationalistic musical language, very different from Elgar's willing celebration of the British Empire, was designed to evoke an idyllic, pre-industrial age, and thereby to promote the virtues of honest labour in an unspoiled rural landscape; it would suffice Vaughan Williams with little modification for nearly another half-century, his reputation being sustained by the British tendency to canonise Establishment figures during their own lifetime. In New England, Charles Ives produced a remarkable series of works in which the synthetic aspect is frequently made overtly audible through the simultaneous presentation of different musical layers. Vernacular musical styles featured in Ives's synthesis as they did in Vaughan Williams's, and were again used to celebrate the everyday lives of unpretentious people, but Ives also had an interest in transcendental philosophy that led him to attempt the articulation of moral and ethical debate in musical terms, most clearly and famously in *The Unanswered Question* (1906). In contrast to Vaughan Williams, however, Ives's work was virtually neglected during his lifetime. In Eastern Europe, Janáček and Bartók also developed synthetic musical languages involving vernacular elements, such as melodies derived from folk music and rhythmic characteristics derived from spoken language. Their fate, in terms of critical reception, was to be regarded in an exaggerated way as national composers: Bartók's emigration to America notwithstanding, the Western image of both these composers was dependent to a perhaps embarrassing degree on the exoticism of their musical sources.

37 Pieter C. van den Toorn, *The Music of Igor Stravinsky* (New Haven and London, 1983). See also the same author's *Stravinsky and The Rite of Spring: The Beginnings of a Musical Language* (Oxford, 1987).

38 See Anthony Pople, 'Vaughan Williams, Tallis, and the Phantasy Principle', in Alain Frogley (ed.), *Vaughan Williams Studies* (Cambridge, 1996), pp. 47–80.

We have seen how the sheer range of musical styles around 1890 – amounting not so much to the 'common practice' of tonality as to an array of common practices – provided the basis for a number of 'waves of innovation' in the two decades or so that followed. Certain common points have been noted: the popular renewal of expectant traditions, transcendentalism, synthesis, the expansion of musical technique, and a new concentration on sonority that manifested itself in a variety of ways. A number of composers who have eluded specific discussion above – Busoni and Reger, for example – may be reckoned nonetheless to fall into this framework in one way or another.

Where one century's music ended and that of the next began is a question to which no answer that is both definitive and useful can really be given. To indulge in list-making for a moment: turn-of-the-century composers who actually lived more than half of their chronological lifetimes in the nineteenth include Janáček, Elgar, Puccini, Mahler, Debussy, Delius, Nielsen, Satie, Granados, Scriabin and Reger; whilst Strauss, Sibelius, Vaughan Williams, Rachmaninov, Schoenberg, Holst and Ravel were among their contemporaries by birth. Even Stravinsky's reputation was made before the outbreak of the First World War, which arguably marked the turning-point, both in terms of aesthetics and in terms of the role of high art in Western society, that most nearly corresponds to the chronological turn of the centuries. Certainly the vast impact of popular music and film through mechanical dissemination post-dates this conflagration, as do the two – often antagonistic – qualities of reaction and rebuilding which set the tone for so much art music of this later period.

In contrast, the waves of innovation that first broke around 1890 were deeply rooted in nineteenth-century aesthetics and practices. Among the composers involved, many of those who achieved longevity – Strauss, Sibelius, Ives and Stravinsky, for example – seemed to be forced by changing circumstances either to attempt a kind of personal renewal, or to retire from creative work altogether, or to work on in their established manner whilst accepting that events had passed them by. Many twentieth-century histories of twentieth-century music have annexed the music of the 1890s as a starting-point, apparently *faute de mieux*; but from a twenty-first-century perspective it seems more reasonable to see as most characteristic of the twentieth century those musical products and practices that were centred on mid-century developments in society and technology, rather than putting the centre of gravity in the first decade, and instead to associate the richness of this 'music in transition' with the 'long nineteenth century'.[39]

39 The debt this chapter owes to Jim Samson's book *Music in Transition: A Study of Tonal Expansion and Atonality, 1900–1920* (London, 1977) will have been obvious throughout.

Bibliography

Block, G., *Ives: Concord Sonata*. Cambridge, 1996

Dahlhaus, C., *Between Romanticism and Modernism: Four Studies in the Music of the Later Nineteenth Century*, trans. M. Whittall. Berkeley and Los Angeles, 1980

 Schoenberg and the New Music, trans. Derrick Puffett and Alfred Clayton. Cambridge, 1987

Dunsby, J., *Schoenberg: Pierrot Lunaire*. Cambridge, 1992

Franklin, P., *Mahler: Symphony No. 3*. Cambridge, 1991

Frisch, W., *The Early Works of Arnold Schoenberg, 1893–1908*. Berkeley and Los Angeles, 1993

Hepokoski, J., *Sibelius: Symphony No. 5*. Cambridge, 1993

Holloway, R., *Debussy and Wagner*. London, 1979

Kelkel, M., *Alexandre Scriabine: Sa vie, l'ésotérisme et le langage musical dans son œuvre*. Paris, 1978

Kerman, J. (ed.), *Music at the Turn of the Century*. Berkeley and Los Angeles, 1990

Layton, R., *Sibelius*. 2nd edn, London, 1978

Mellers, W., *Vaughan Williams and the Vision of Albion*. London, 1989

Nicholls, D., *American Experimental Music, 1840–1940*. Cambridge, 1990

Nichols, R. and Langham Smith, R., *Claude Debussy: Pelléas et Mélisande*. Cambridge, 1989

Pople, A., 'Vaughan Williams, Tallis, and the Phantasy Principle'. In Alain Frogley (ed.), *Vaughan Williams Studies*. Cambridge, 1996, pp. 47–80

Puffett, D. (ed.), *Richard Strauss*: Elektra. Cambridge, 1989

 (ed.), *Richard Strauss: Salome*. Cambridge, 1989

 Debussy's Ostinato Machine. Nottingham, 1996

Sadie, S. (ed.), *Puccini and his Operas*. London, 2000

Samson, J., *Music in Transition: A Study of Tonal Expansion and Atonality, 1900–1920*. London, 1977

Samuels, R., *Mahler's Sixth Symphony: A Study in Musical Semiotics*. Cambridge, 1995

Schloezer, B. de, *Scriabin: Artist and Mystic*, trans. N. Slonimsky. Oxford, 1987

Schoenberg, A., *Theory of Harmony*, trans. Roy E. Carter. London, 1978

Taruskin, R., *Defining Russia Musically: Historical and Hermeneutic Essays*. Princeton, 1997

 Stravinsky and the Russian Traditions: A Biography of the Works Through 'Mavra'. Oxford, 1996

Tyrrell, J., *Leos Janáček: Kát'a Kabanová*. Cambridge, 1982

Van den Toorn, P. C., *Stravinsky and The Rite of Spring: The Beginnings of a Musical Language*. Oxford, 1987

Walsh, S., *Stravinsky: A Creative Spring: Russia and France, 1882–1934*. London, 2000

Williamson, J., *Strauss: Also Sprach Zarathustra*. Cambridge, 1993

Chronology

SARAH HIBBERD

1800   Napoleon takes control of Italy. Publication of F. W. J. von Schelling's *System des transcendentalen Idealismus*, Herder's *Kalligone*, and the second edition of Wordsworth's *Lyrical Ballads* in which he notes 'all good poetry is the spontaneous overflow of powerful feelings', a phrase which becomes a manifesto of Romanticism. Zelter becomes director of the Berlin Singakademie. Franz Anton Hoffmeister and Ambrosius Kühnel set up the publishing house Bureau de Musique in Leipzig (taken over by Peters in 1814). The Musikakademie is founded in Düsseldorf. Premières of Cherubini's *Les deux journées*, Nicolas-Marie Dalayrac's *Maison à vendre* and Boieldieu's *Le calife de Bagdad* in Paris. Beethoven defeats the pianist Steibelt in an improvisation contest in Vienna. Czerny's public debut in Vienna, playing a Mozart concerto. Beethoven holds a benefit concert at the Bergtheater in Vienna; the programme includes his own Piano Concerto No. 1 and Symphony No. 1.

1801   Peace between France and Austria marks the passing of the Holy Roman Empire. The accession of Alexander I in Russia, following the assassination of Paul I, leads to a growth in creative activity. The reinstatement, following the French Revolution, of Christian worship and the Chapelle in Paris under the direction of Giovanni Paisiello, then Paer. The restoration of the Théâtre-Italien, and merging of the Comédie-Italienne and the Opéra-Comique. The dramatic soprano Caroline Branchu arrives at the Paris Opéra. Haydn's *Die Schöpfung* is performed in Vienna. Johann Nikolaus Forkel completes his *Allgemeine Geschichte der Musik*. Publication of Field's Piano Sonatas, Op. 1, dedicated to Clementi. Beethoven completes the music for the ballet *Die Geschöpfe des Prometheus*.

1802   Peace of Amiens between France and Britain. Napoleon becomes president of the Italian Republic and first consul of France. Publication of Chateaubriand's *Génie du christianisme*, a defence of Catholic

Christianity against the rationalist philosophers, and Forkel's pioneering biography of J. S. Bach. The influential Singakademie is established
in Leipzig. The St Petersburg Philharmonic Society is founded, specialising in choral music by Haydn and others. The earliest pocket scores
are published, by Pleyel. Beethoven writes his Heiligenstadt
Testament. Première of Peter von Winter's *Tamerlan* in Paris.

1803   The German states are reconstituted as the Confederation of the Rhine
under French and Russian influence. Subscription concerts in Berlin
are established. The Gewandhaus Quartet is founded in Leipzig. Bach's
motets appear in print, edited by Zelter. Première of Paisiello's
Proserpine in Paris. Beethoven writes his Symphony No. 3, the *Eroica*.

1804   Napoleon is crowned emperor by the pope, and France begins a period
of stability and prosperity, with many aristocrats returning from exile.
Schuppanzigh establishes quartet evenings in Vienna. Schiller writes
Wilhelm Tell. In his lectures on philosophy (1804–5) Schlegel, leader of
the new Romantic criticism and translator of Shakespeare, claims con-
temporary music is in a desolate state because composers are ignoring
its basis in mathematics. Boieldieu is appointed conductor of the
Imperial Opera in St Petersburg (–1810). Publication of Johann
Friedrich Reichardt's *Liederspiele*. Premières of Jean-François Le
Sueur's *Ossian* and Henri-Montan Berton's *La romance* in Paris, and
Paer's *Leonora* in Dresden.

1805   The Russian and Austrian armies are defeated by Napoleon at
Austerlitz; Austria gives up territories including those in Italy. Revival
of the Paris Concerts Spirituels. August Tessier inaugurates the New
Orleans 'quadroon balls', attended by black women and white men.
Reichardt becomes editor of the *Berlinische musikalische Zeitung*
(–1806). Beethoven's Symphony No. 3 and the first version of *Fidelio*
are performed in Vienna. Paganini writes his Twenty-Four Caprices,
Op. 1.

1806   France defeats Prussia at Jena and Napoleon occupies Berlin.
Publication of Schlegel's *Briefe auf einer Reise*, Joseph-Jérome
Momigny's *Cours complet d'harmonie et de composition* and A. F. C.
Kollmann's *A New Theory of Musical Harmony*. Première of Méhul's *Uthal*
in Paris. Beethoven writes his Symphony No. 4, Violin Concerto and
'Appassionata' Sonata.

1807   Treaty of Tilsit; Friedrich Wilhelm III of Prussia cedes possession west of the Elbe and the Polish lands to form a duchy of Warsaw under the King of Saxony. Hegel writes *Phänomenologie des Geistes*, a classic work of Idealist philosophy. Publication of Schelling's *Über das Verhältniss der bildenden Künste zu der Natur*. The reconstruction of Prussia begins, with the merging in Berlin of the management and orchestras of the Hofoper and the Nationaltheater as the Royal Opera. In Vienna the Sperl dance hall opens, where Johann Strauss I later obtains an exclusive contract. The Milan Conservatory is founded by Napoleon's son-in-law Eugène de Beauharnais. The Hungarian Theatre Company of Buda is founded. The first of the Bliesner brothers' subscription concerts in Berlin takes place. Napoleon issues a decree restricting the number of theatres in Paris. The Dreyssigsche Singakademie is established, modelled on the Berlin institution. Premières of Spontini's *La vestale* and Méhul's *Joseph* in Paris. Beethoven's Symphony No. 1 receives its Paris première.

1808   The French army occupies Rome. France invades Spain, installing Joseph Bonaparte as king; Joachim Murat becomes King of Naples. The Portuguese royal family moves to Rio de Janeiro (–1821). Publication of the first of Thomas Moore's *Irish Melodies*, the first part of Goethe's *Faust*, and Clemens Brentano and Achim von Arnim's collection of adapted folk poems, *Des Knaben Wunderhorn* (some of which were later set by Mahler). The publishing firm Ricordi is established in Milan, the Gesellschaft der Musikfreunde in Vienna, and the Philharmonic Society in Brno. Première of Boieldieu's *Les voitures versées* in Paris. Beethoven's Fifth and Sixth Symphonies are performed for the first time, in Vienna. Beethoven writes the *Fantasia* (Choral Fantasy) for piano, chorus and orchestra.

1809   Franz I of Austria, with British support, declares war on France but is defeated; Vienna is taken by Napoleon. Prince Metternich becomes chief minister of Austria. Publication of Schlegel's *Über dramatische Kunst und Literatur*. Founding of the Boston Philo-Harmonic Society, incorporating amateur and professional players. Zelter founds the Liedertafel in Berlin. Barbaia, a gambling magnate, becomes director of the royal theatres in Naples. A riot takes place over raised ticket prices at second opening of Covent Garden. Weber begins a fragmentary novel, *Tonkünsters Leben*. Georg August Griesinger's *Biographische Notizen über Joseph Haydn* is serialised in the *Allgemeine musikalische*

Zeitung. Premières of Spontini's *Fernand Cortez* in Paris and Paer's
Agnese in Parma. Publication of Méhul's first three symphonies.
Beethoven writes his 'Rasumovsky' Quartets, Op. 59.

1810   Start of the Mexican war of independence. Publication of Mme de
        Staël's *De l'Allemagne*, a work that introduces contemporary German
        culture to the French in a positive way. Publication of Schinkel's *Project
        for a Mausoleum*. Publication in the *Allgemeine musikalische Zeitung* of
        E. T. A. Hoffmann's review of Beethoven's Fifth Symphony; his use of
        the term 'Romantic' was to cause much discussion. Publication of
        Reichardt's *Vertraute Briefe geschrieben auf einer Reise nach Wien* (written
        in 1808–9), an account of Vienna's music at the height of its most cele-
        brated era. First performance of Beethoven's *Egmont* Overture. Maria
        Szymanowska makes her debut as a concert pianist in Warsaw and
        Paris. Weber writes his First Piano Concerto, Op. 11, and his 'Romantic
        opera' *Silvana*.

1811   The founding in Sweden of the 'Gothic League' to stimulate national
        feeling. Invention of damper pedals for the piano. Anton Friedrich
        Thibaut founds a Singverein in Heidelberg, which becomes the
        impetus for the Protestant Palestrina revival. The Prague Conservatory
        is established. Publication of Choron and Fayolle's *Dictionnaire des musi-
        ciens*. Premières of Weber's *Abu Hassan* in Munich and Adalbert
        Gyrowetz's *Der Augenarzt* in Vienna. Stepan Anikiyevich Degtyaryov's
        patriotic oratorio *Minin i Pozharsky, ili Osvobozhdeniye Moskvii* (Minin
        and Pozharsky, or The Liberation of Moscow) is published.
        Beethoven's Fifth Piano Concerto, the 'Emperor', receives its first per-
        formance in Leipzig.

1812   Napoleon invades Russia and occupies Moscow; the retreat from
        Moscow is a disaster for the French army. The first two cantos of
        Byron's *Childe Harold's Pilgrimage* and first of Ludwig Tieck's *Phantasus*
        are published. The Gesellschaft der Musikfreunde is founded in Vienna.
        Carl Möser's first subscription concert takes place in Berlin. Beethoven
        and Goethe meet in Teplitz. Publication in St Petersburg of Field's First
        Nocturne.

1813   Wellington drives the French out of Spain. Napoleon is defeated at
        Leipzig by the allied armies, and the Austrians defeat the French,
        regaining a foothold in Italy. The Philharmonic Society is founded by

William Dance, J. B. Cramer and others in London to organise orchestral performances of modern music. Möser establishes quartet *soirées* in Berlin. Weber is appointed opera director in Prague. Premières of Cherubini's *Les abencérages* in Paris, Rossini's *Tancredi* and *L'italiana in Algeri* in Venice, and Mayr's *Medea in Corinto* in Naples and *La rosa bianca e la rosa rossa* in Genoa. Spohr writes his Nonet. Pierre-Jean de Béranger begins his political chanson performances in the Caveau Moderne in Paris. First performance of Beethoven's *Wellingtons Sieg* (Wellington's Victory), written to celebrate the battle at Vittoria.

1814   Napoleon abdicates, Louis XVIII becomes king, and France recognises 1792 frontiers. Russia hands Saxony over to Prussia. The chiroplast, a gadget to ease tension and enhance finger development in piano playing, is patented by Johann Bernhard Logier. Baillot's quartet concert series is founded in Paris. Peters takes over the music publishing house the Bureau de Musique in Leipzig. Founding of the first brass band, the Stalybridge Old Band in Lancashire. The Academia de Música is established in Cuba. Valves for brass instruments are introduced, enabling them to play chromatically. Publication of Walter Scott's historical novel *Waverley* and the Idealist philosopher Johann Gottlieb Fichte's *Reden an die deutsche Nation*. E. T. A. Hoffman's essay on 'Alte und neue Kirchenmusik' appears in the *Allgemeine musikalische Zeitung*. The final version of Beethoven's *Fidelio* is performed in Vienna. Schubert writes his B flat quartet, D.112.

1815   Napoleon breaks his exile but is defeated at Waterloo. The Congress of Vienna redraws the map of Europe and thirty-eight German states become the German Confederation; another one is added later. Prussia acquires a Rhine Province. Andrew Jackson, future president of America, defeats the British at New Orleans and becomes a national hero. E. T. A. Hoffmann writes the *Elixire des Teufels*. Publication of the Grimm brothers' *Kinder- und Hausmärchen*. Johann Nepomuk Maelzel patents the metronome. Leipzig's influential Liedertafel is established. First performance of the Boston Handel and Haydn Society, devoted to choral music. Rossini becomes artistic director of the S Carlo in Naples, and concentrates on writing serious opera. Olof Åhlström publishes the anthology *Traditioner as swenska folk-dansar*. Ignaz Moscheles has great success in Vienna with his virtuoso display piece *La marche d'Alexandre*. Beethoven's final public performance, accompanying his song 'Adelaide', with the singer Franz Wild.

1816   Beethoven writes his song cycle *An die ferne Geliebte*. Kiesewetter organises concerts of early music in his home in Vienna. Publication of Hegel's *Logik*. In Russia the synod forbids the use of manuscript music and the inclusion of such pieces in the service, allowing only pieces composed (or approved) by Dmitry Stepanovich Bortnyansky. Premières of Rossini's *Il barbiere di Siviglia* in Rome and *Otello* in Naples, Spohr's *Faust* in Prague, and E. T. A. Hoffmann's *Undine* in Berlin. Caspar Ett, the Munich court organist, performs Allegri's *Miserere*. The debut performances of Giuditta Pasta in Milan and Laure Cinti-Damoreau in Paris. Schubert writes his lied 'Der Wanderer', D.489.

1817   Publication of Byron's *Manfred*. Choron founds the Institution Royale de Musique Classique et Religieuse in Paris. The Vienna Conservatory is founded. Weber appointed Royal Saxon Kapellmeister in Dresden, where a new Italian Hofoper and Geman Opera are established. William Ayrton becomes musical director of the King's Theatre and stages the first London performance of Mozart's *Don Giovanni*. Publication of Clementi's *Gradus ad Parnassum*. The Vienna Conservatory is founded. Anthony Philip Heinrich directs the first known performance in America of a Beethoven symphony (probably No. 1) in Lexington, Kentucky.

1818   Publication of Goethe's *Italienische Reise*. Caspar David Friedrich's painting *Wanderer above the Mists* is completed, an influential representation of the isolation of the individual. The Niederrheinisches Musikfest and Musikverein are established in Düsseldorf. The *Quarterly Musical Magazine and Review* is founded in England by Richard MacKenzie Bacon. Reicha's *Cours de composition musicale*, an early example of a modern harmony textbook, replaces that of Charles-Simon Catel as the Paris Conservatoire's official theory manual. Beethoven composes the 'Hammerklavier' Piano Sonata, Op. 106.

1819   Publication of Schopenhauer's influential *Die Welt als Wille und Vorstellung* and Byron's *Mazeppa*. Théodore Géricault completes his painting *Le Radeau de la Méduse*. Breitkopf & Härtel publish an edition of Bach's *Das wohltemperirte Clavier*. Publication of Weber's piano rondo *Aufforderung zum Tanz*, raising the status of the waltz from the dance hall to the concert room. Premières of Spontini's *Olimpie* in Paris, and Rossini's *Ermione* and *La donna del lago* in Naples, and first performance in Paris of Rossini's *Il barbiere di Siviglia*. Schubert writes his Piano Quintet, 'Die Forelle'.

1820   The Frankfurt Diet sanctions the Carlsbad decrees: freedom of the press is abolished and revolutionary and liberal movements are suppressed in Germany. Revolts are crushed in Spain, Portugal and Naples. Publication of Walter Scott's *Ivanhoe* and Lamartine's *Méditations poétiques* (later set by Niedermeyer and others). Founding of the music journal *The Euterpeiad* in Boston. The Musical Fund Society is established in Philadelphia. Spohr is engaged as leader of the Philharmonic Society orchestra in London and claims the first use of the conductor's baton. Spontini is appointed director of the royal opera, Berlin, and improves the social lot of the players. In one of his 'musico-dramatic notices' Weber expresses his hopes for a new German national opera. Publication of P. A. Heinrich's *The Dawning of Music in Kentucky*, a collection of songs and pieces for violin and piano. Première of Rossini's *Maometto II* in Naples.

1821   Death of Napoleon. Beginning of the Greek War of Independence, which attracts popular support throughout Europe and inspires the Romantics. Publication of Scott's *Kenilworth* and Byron's *Cain*. Sébastien Erard patents the double-escapement action on the piano. A new theatre for the Paris Opéra is built following the demolition of the previous building after the assassination of the Duke of Berry. Founding of the Warsaw Conservatory. The first report of a concert by a military band (with male voices) in Berlin. Première of Weber's *Der Freischütz* in the new Schauspielhaus in Berlin; its success challenges the pre-eminence of Italian opera in Germany. Claude-Joseph Rouget de Lisle writes 'Premier chant des industriels', at Saint-Simon's suggestion. Moscheles's successful London debut at a Philharmonic concert. Giuditta Pasta's first great triumph, singing Desdemona in Rossini's *Otello* in Paris.

1822   Founding of the Royal Academy of Music in London; William Crotch is appointed director. Zelter founds an institute of church music in Berlin. The Sociedad Filarmónica is established in Buenos Aires. Gas lighting is introduced to the Paris Opéra in Nicolas Isouard's *Aladin, ou La lampe merveilleuse*. Cherubini becomes director of the Paris Conservatoire. Choron begins his historical music concerts in Paris. Konradin Kreutzer becomes Kapellmeister of the Kärntnertortheater,

Vienna. Schubert writes his Eighth Symphony, the 'Unfinished'. Liszt's first public concert in Vienna takes place. Wilhelmine Schröder-Devrient is celebrated in her performances as Agathe in Weber's *Der Freischütz* and Leonore in Beethoven's *Fidelio*. Schubert writes his 'Wanderer' Fantasy, D.760.

1823   Pushkin begins his novel *Evgeny Onegin*. William Ayrton founds the *Harmonicon*, a monthly journal of music news in London. Première of Weber's *Euryanthe* in Vienna. Beethoven begins his 'late' string quartets (−1826). Aleksey Nikolayevich Verstovsky writes his popular dramatic ballad *Chornaya shal'* (The Black Shawl) to a text by Pushkin. Schubert writes *Die schöne Müllerin*.

1824   Death in France of Louis XVIII; he is succeeded by the reactionary Charles X, under whom press and theatre censorship is tightened. Leopold von Ranke publishes *Geschichte der roman und german Völker von 1494−1535*, the foundation of modern historiography. Première of Meyerbeer's *Il crociato in Egitto* in Venice. First performance of Beethoven's Symphony No. 9 at the Kärnthnertortheater, Vienna. Rossini arrives in Paris, as director of the Théâtre-Italien. Habeneck becomes chief conductor at the Paris Opéra. *Der Freischütz* is performed in a French adaptation (*Robin des bois*) in Paris. Beethoven's *Missa solemnis* is performed in St Petersburg. Liszt's debut performances in Paris and London take place. Schubert writes his String Quartet in D Minor, 'Der Tod und das Mädchen', and 'Arpeggione' Sonata. First performance of Schubert's A Minor Quartet, D.804, by the Schuppanzigh Quartet in Vienna.

1825   Decembrist uprisings in Russia (following the death of Alexander I) are crushed by Nicholas I; a new period of reaction and repression follows. Founding of Saint-Simonism following the death of the social thinker Claude-Henri de Rouvroy, Count of Saint-Simon. Johann Strauss (I) establishes his own orchestra in Vienna. Publication of A. F. Thibaut's *Über Reinheit der Tonkunst*, in which he promotes the music of Palestrina and Handel. Première in Paris of Boieldieu's *La dame blanche*. Rossini's *Il barbiere di Siviglia* is given at the new Coliseo Provisional in Buenos Aires (it is the first complete opera to be heard in the city). Maria Malibran gives her debut performance in *Il barbiere di Siviglia* in London. Disastrous London première of Beethoven's Symphony No. 9, conducted by George Smart. Cherubini writes a Mass for the corona-

tion of Charles X at Rheims. Schubert composes his 'Great' C major
Symphony.

1826   The Bourse (stock exchange) is opened in Paris. Lamennais publishes
        De la religion considérée dans ses rapports avec l'ordre politique et civil, which
        influences the foundation of Christian socialism. Eduard Reitz forms
        the Berlin Philharmonic Society (later the Berlin Philharmonic). Weber
        dies in London after the première of *Oberon*. Fyodor L'vov is appointed
        director of the imperial chapel in St Petersburg. Schubert composes his
        String Quartet in G major, Op. 161. Mendelssohn writes his overture to
        A Midsummer Night's Dream. Première of František Škroup's Singspiel
        Dráteník in Prague. Weber's *Oberon* is performed in the house of the
        publisher Schlesinger in Berlin. Liszt writes his *Etude en douze exercices*,
        the original version of the *Douze grandes études*, completed in 1837 and
        dedicated to Czerny. Cinti-Damoreau is engaged at the Paris Opéra,
        where she remains until 1835. Paganini writes his Violin Concerto No.
        2 in B minor.

1827   Publication of Victor Hugo's *Préface de Cromwell*, which consolidates
        ideas about Romanticism in France and has an impact on all the arts,
        and Gérard de Nerval's French translation of Goethe's *Faust*, which
        influences Berlioz and other Romantics. Broadwood patents the iron
        bracing scheme in piano manufacture. Heinrich Joseph Birnbach's
        'Ueber die verschiedene Form grösserer Instrumentaltonstücke aller
        Art und deren Bearbeitung' is serialised in the *Berliner allgemeine
        musikalische Zeitung*. The Stockholm music school is founded. François-
        Joseph Fétis publishes the first issue of the *Revue musicale*, the first
        significant nineteenth-century French journal devoted to music. The
        Berlin Singakademie acquires its own premises and concert hall.
        Halévy is appointed professor of harmony at the Paris Conservatoire.
        Liszt settles in Paris. Schubert composes *Winterreise*. Première in
        Berlin of Spontini's *Agnes von Hohenstauffen*. Catalani visits Berlin,
        singing in concerts and private *soirées*. Rubini creates the title role in
        the première of Bellini's *Il pirata* in Milan. Manuel García introduces
        Italian opera (sung in Italian) to Mexico at the Teatro de Las Gallos.
        Adolphe Nourrit is appointed *professeur de déclamation pour la tragédie
        lyrique* at the Conservatoire, following his success in Rossini's *Moïse*
        and *Le siège de Corinthe*. Chopin writes variations for piano and orches-
        tra on Mozart's 'Là ci darem la mano'. Hummel write his Piano
        Concerto in A flat.

1828   Publication of Johann Aloys Schlosser's short biography of Beethoven, Giuseppe Baini's influential study of Palestrina, and Georg Nicolaus Nissen's *Biographie W. A. Mozart nach Originalbriefen*. Pierre Laporte is appointed manager of the King's Theatre, London. Première of Auber's *La muette de Portici*, the first grand opera, in Paris and Marschner's *Der Vampyr* in Leipzig. Habeneck conducts Beethoven's Symphony No. 3 at the newly founded Société des Concerts du Conservatoire in Paris. Publication of Hummel's *Ausführliche theoretisch-practische Anweisung zum Pianoforte-Spiele* in Vienna. Schubert writes his String Quintet in C major. Kuhlau writes incidental music to *Elver høj* (The Elves Hill). Schubert's 'Invitation Concert' (at which his own pieces are performed) takes place under the auspices of the Gesellschaft der Musikfreunde in Vienna. Malibran gives her Paris debut in Rossini's *Semiramide*.

1829   Greece achieves independence from Turkey. The first complete performance of Goethe's *Faust*, Part I, takes place in Brunswick. Publication of the Saint-Simonian work *Opinions littéraires, philosophiques et industrielles*. Louis Véron founds the *Revue de Paris*. Goethe writes a letter to Zelter in which he considers the relationship between Romantic (chamber) music and its immediate Classical past. Premières of Rossini's *Guillaume Tell* in Paris, Marschner's *Der Templer und die Jüdin* in Leipzig and Bellini's *La straniera* in Milan. Mendelssohn conducts the first performance since Bach's time of his *St Matthew Passion* in Berlin. Mendelssohn's Concerto for 2 Pianos is performed by the composer and Moscheles in London. Schubert's *Schwanengesang* is published. Mendelssohn writes his String Quartet in E flat, Op. 12.

1830   Following the July Revolution and the overthrow of the Bourbons, Louis-Philippe of Orléans, the 'citizen king', comes to the French throne. The French seize Algiers and begin to colonise Algeria. Serbia and Greece gain independence from the Turks. A Polish uprising is suppressed by Russia. A performance of *La muette de Portici* in Brussels is the signal to begin the Belgian revolt against the ruling Dutch. A. B. Marx is appointed professor of music at Berlin University. Publication of Fétis's dictionary *La musique mise à la portée de tout le monde*. The Royal Conservatory is founded in Madrid. Carl Proske appointed canon of the Alte Kapelle in Regensburg, where he devotes himself to church music reform. Premières of Donizetti's *Anna Bolena* in Milan, Bellini's *I Capuleti e i Montecchi* in Venice and Auber's *Fra Diavolo* in

Paris. Berlioz's *Symphonie fantastique* is given its first performance in Paris. Glinka goes to Italy to study. G. B. Velluti, the last castrato opera singer, retires. Debut of the Ukrainian bass Petrov in *Die Zauberflöte* in St Petersburg.

1831 Uprisings in Modena, Parma and the Papal States suppressed by Austria. A revolt of silk weavers in Lyons is brutally quashed by the French government. Censorship is abolished in France. In London Faraday discovers electro-magnetic induction. Delacroix's painting *Liberty Leading the People* is exhibited in the Academy salon in Paris. The entrepeneur Louis Véron is appointed director of the Paris Opéra. Premières of Bellini's *La sonnambula* and *Norma* in Milan, and Meyerbeer's *Robert le diable* and Hérold's *Zampa* in Paris. Publication of Friedrich Kalkbrenner's *Méthode pour apprendre le piano-forte à l'aide du guide-mains*. Paganini gives his debut performances in London and Paris; he effectively transforms concert life in London. Chopin arrives in Paris. Paris première of Beethoven's Symphony No. 9 at the Conservatoire Concerts. The first of the Ganz brothers' popular 'morning diversions' take place in Berlin.

1832 'La Giovane Italia' is founded by Giuseppe Mazzini, with the aim of national independence. The Reform Bill is passed in Britain. The first continental railway is completed, from Budweis to Linz. A canal linking the Rhine and the Rhône is opened. Outbreak of a cholera epidemic in Paris. Publication of Goethe's *Faust*, Part II. The Italian department of the Dresden Opera is closed, although Italian (and French) operas continue to be performed. Theobald Boehm constructs the prototype of the modern flute. The Sacred Harmonic Society is founded in London, specialising in oratorios. The Boston Academy of Music is founded by Lowell Mason and others. The first music publishing firm in America is established by Oliver Ditson in Boston. The first of Fétis's historical concerts takes place in Paris. Premières of Hérold's *Le pré aux clercs* in Paris and Donizetti's *L'elisir d'amore* in Milan. Chopin gives his first public concert in Paris. Johan Peter Emilius Hartmann writes his opera *Ravnen* (The Raven). Field plays his Seventh Piano Concerto at the Salle du Conservatoire in Paris. Moscheles conducts the first London performance of Beethoven's *Missa solemnis*. Mendelssohn's Fifth Symphony, the 'Reformation', is performed in Berlin. The debut of Cornélie Falcon takes place at the Paris Opéra in Meyerbeer's *Robert le diable*.

1833   The first electro-magnetic telegraph is set up in Göttingen. Following
       suppression by the government, many Saint-Simonians (including
       Félicien David) leave France for Egypt. Aristide Cavaillé-Coll wins the
       competition to design the organ for the abbey of St-Denis. The
       Orphéon choral society is established in Paris by G. L. B. Wilhelm. *Le
       Ménestrel* is founded in Paris. Founding of the Philharmonic Society in
       Bucharest. The first American theatre devoted to Italian opera is built
       in New York. Fétis becomes first director of the new Brussels
       Conservatory. Musard's popular promenade concerts begin. Alfred
       Bunn is appointed manager of Covent Garden Theatre, and introduces
       more ambitious productions into the repertory. Reicha publishes his
       Art du compositeur dramatique. Premières of Auber's *Gustave III* in Paris,
       Donizetti's *Torquato Tasso* in Rome, *Parisina* in Florence and *Lucrezia
       Borgia* in Milan, Bellini's *Beatrice di Tenda* in Venice and Marschner's
       Hans Heiling in Berlin. Wagner completes his first opera *Die Feen* (first
       performed in 1888). Chopin's first set of piano Etudes is published.
       Aleksey L'vov is commissioned by Nicholas I to write a Russian
       national hymn, *Bozhe, tsarya khrani* (God Save the Tsar). The first per-
       formance is given of Mendelssohn's Symphony No. 4, the 'Italian'.
       Liszt writes piano transcriptions of some of Berlioz's works, including
       the *Symphonie fantastique.* Moscheles completes his *Hommage à Handel*
       (begun in 1822) for two pianos. The Austrian zither player Johann
       Petzmayer tours Germany.

1834   Passing of the New Poor Law in Britain. Suppression of renewed unrest
       of workers in Lyons and Paris. The Society of British Musicians is estab-
       lished. Schumann co-founds the *Neue Zeitschrift für Musik* in Leipzig.
       Berlioz writes *Harold en Italie.* Publication of Baillot's *L'art du violon.*
       The Handel Commemoration takes place at Westminster Abbey, con-
       ducted by George Smart. Première of Konradin Kreutzer's popular
       Singspiel *Nachtlager von Granada* in Vienna.

1835   The 'Young Germany' movement is banned. Censorship is reintro-
       duced in France (after five years of relaxation), and the satirical paper *Le
       Caricature* is outlawed. Steam-powered cylindrical presses significantly
       increase the circulation of papers in France. Publication of the Finnish
       epic *Kalevala* (which was to inspire composers including Sibelius) and
       Alexis de Tocqueville's *Democracy in America.* Premières of Donizetti's
       Lucia di Lammermoor in Naples, *Maria Stuarda* in Milan, and Halévy's *La
       juive* (Falcon creates the title role) and Bellini's *I puritani* in Paris.

Mendelssohn appointed conductor of the Leipzig Gewandhaus Orchestra. The first part of Liszt's *Lettres d'un bachelier ès musique* is serialised in the *Revue et Gazette musicale* (–1841); his *Harmonies poétiques et religieuses* (later revised) and an essay, *Über die zukünftige Kirchenmusik* (1834), are published in the same journal. Liszt and the Countess Marie d'Agoult move to Geneva, where Liszt teaches at the new Conservatory. Fétis begins work on his influential *Biographie universelle des musiciens* (first edition completed in 1844). Publication of Cherubini's *Cours de contrepoint et de fugue* (on which Halévy has collaborated). The virtuoso Thalberg arrives in Paris. Schumann completes *Carnaval*.

1836 La Fenice in Venice is destroyed by fire, and rebuilt the following year. The *Musical World* is founded in London. The rebuilt Bol'shoy Theatre opens in St Petersburg for opera productions. Weyse founds the Musikforening in Copenhagen to promote Danish music. Premières of Glinka's *Zhizn'za tsarya* (A Life for the Tsar) in St Petersburg (in which the Russian contralto Anna Yakovlevna Vorob'yova creates Vanya), and Meyerbeer's *Les Huguenots* and Adam's *Le postillon de Longjumeau* in Paris. Mendelssohn writes his *St Paul* oratorio. In London Maria Malibran creates the title role in Balfe's *The Maid of Artois*, written for her.

1837 Accession of Queen Victoria in London. A constitution is introduced into Spanish politics. Louis Daguerre invents the first practicable process of photography, the daguerreotype. The first railway-line in France opens between Paris and St-Germain-en-Laye. In England Robert Wornum first uses tape-check action (patented in 1842), which forms the basis of the modern upright piano. Opening of the National Theatre in Pest. Kastner writes his *Traité général d'instrumentation*. Publication of Liszt's article 'R. Schumanns Klavier-Kompositionen' (incl. Opp. 5, 11, 14). Wagner is appointed musical director at Riga. Premières of Auber's *Le domino noir* and Louis Niedermeyer's *Stradella* in Paris, Mercadante's *Il giuramento* in Milan, Donizetti's *Roberto Devereux* in Naples, and Lortzing's Spieloper *Czaar [Zar] und Zimmermann* in Leipzig. Berlioz writes his *Grande messe des morts*. Liszt and Thalberg play in a pianistic duel at the house of Princess Belgiojoso in Paris. The first of Moscheles's 'Historical Soirées' takes place in London. Liszt writes piano transcriptions of Beethoven's Symphonies Nos. 5, 6, 7, dedicated to the painter Ingres. Mendelssohn inaugurates a series of 'historical concerts' at the Gewandhaus in Leipzig. Publication of Mendelssohn's Six Preludes and Fugues, Op. 35. Gilbert

Duprez sings his 'high C' from the chest in Rossini's *Guillaume Tell*, at his debut at the Paris Opéra. Rosine Stoltz gives her Paris Opéra debut as Rachel in Halévy's *La juive*. Fanny Tacchinardi-Persiani makes her Paris debut in *La sonnambula* and *Lucia di Lammermoor*.

1838   Austrians evacuate most of the Papal States. Steamships begin to run regularly between Britain and North America. Founding of the Promenade Concerts in London, modelled on those of Musard in Paris. Building of the Pavlovsky Muzykal'ny Vokzal on the outskirts of St Petersburg, where outdoor concerts and entertainments are given in the summer. First publication of A. B. Marx's *Die Lehre von der musikalischen Komposition*. Premières of Halévy's *Guido et Ginevra* and Berlioz's *Benvenuto Cellini* in Paris. Chopin goes to Majorca with George Sand. Schumann writes *Kinderszenen* and *Kreisleriana*. Donizetti settles in Paris. Oskar Kolberg begins his systematic collection of Polish folktunes. First performance of Cherubini's *Requiem Mass* (1836) at the Paris Conservatoire. Johann Strauss (I) and his orchestra make their first visit to England.

1839   William Henry Fox Talbot produces a photographic negative. Henry Chorley is appointed music reviewer for the *Athenaeum*. Founding of the Russian music journal *Nouvelliste*. The beginning of the *Musica Sacra* series of publications in Berlin, which enhances knowledge of Palestrina and other Italian and German composers of the early Baroque. Publication of Czerny's *Complete Theoretical and Practical Pianoforte School*, Op. 500. Première of Verdi's first opera, *Oberto*, in Milan. Chopin writes his Piano Sonata in B flat Minor. The tenor Adolphe Nourrit commits suicide in Naples. Wagner arrives in Paris. Berlioz writes his 'dramatic symphony' *Roméo et Juliette*. Mendelssohn conducts the posthumous first performance of Schubert's 'Great' C major Symphony in Leipzig. Pauline Viardot makes her stage debut in London as Rossini's Desdemona. Publication of Chopin's Twenty-Four Preludes, Op. 28.

1840   Friederich Wilhelm IV succeeds his father as king of Prussia. Napoleon's remains are interred at Les Invalides. The conservative François Guizot becomes Prime Minister of France. End of the Opium War in China. The Opéra-Comique in Paris moves to the Salle Favart. The Singing School of the Pestbuda Society of Musicians (the prototype of the National Conservatory, 1867) is established under Gábor

Mátray. The 'Rhine Crisis' leads to an outpouring of Rhinelieder. Joseph Danhauser completes his painting depicting Liszt at the piano surrounded by Paris 'Romantics'. Premières in Paris of Donizetti's *La fille du régiment*, *Les martyrs* (Italian version performed in 1848 in Naples as *Poliuto*) and *La favorite*. The 'Tamburini riot' breaks out at Her Majesty's Theatre in London, when the singers threaten to resign unless they are all re-engaged by Lumley and Laporte. Past Italian composers such as Palestrina become the model for a regenerated church music in Prussia under the directives of the Kaiser and Freiherr von Bunsen. First performance of Mendelssohn's Symphony No. 2, the 'Lobgesang'. Publication of Liszt's piano transcriptions of Schubert's *Schwanengesang*, *Winterreise* and *Geistliche Lieder*, and of his *Heroischer Marsch im ungarischen Styl*. Wagner writes an overture to *Faust*, which he later revises and reorchestrates (1855).

1841   Completion of the new Königliches Hoftheater in Dresden. Meyerbeer replaces Spontini as Generalmusikdirektor in Berlin. Louis Jullien conducts the first in his series of popular Concerts d'Hiver in London, which attract a new and broadly mixed audience. A. B. Marx writes *Die alte Musiklehre im Streit mit unserer Zeit*. Premières in Paris of Halévy's *La reine de Chypre*, Weber's *Le Freyschütz*, translated and adapted by Berlioz, and Adam's ballet *Giselle*. Mendelssohn conducts a performance of Bach's *St Matthew Passion* in Leipzig. Rossini completes his *Stabat mater*. First American production of Mozart's *Die Zauberflöte* in Philadelphia, drawing audiences from New York and Boston. First performance of Schumann's First Symphony, the 'Spring', in Leipzig.

1842   Project of completing Cologne Cathedral begins with the laying of the extension foundation stone. Sterndale Bennett's Classical Chamber Concerts begin in London. Stoger's New Theatre is founded in Prague, specialising in Czech-language productions. The Virginia Minstrels form in New York. Publication of Christoph Weyse's *Halviresindstyve gamle kaempeviser* (Fifty Old Heroic Ballads). First concert given by the Philharmonic Society of New York. Nicolai founds the Vienna Philharmonic concerts. The royal Kapelle in Berlin takes over Carl Möser's subscription concerts. Premières of Wagner's *Rienzi* (with Tichatschek in the title role) in Dresden, Verdi's *Nabucco* in Milan, Donizetti's *Linda di Chamounix* in Vienna, and Glinka's *Ruslan i Lyudmila* in St Petersburg. Mendelssohn writes his Third Symphony, the

'Scottish'. Wagner becomes Kapellmeister at Dresden. Publication of Liszt's *Album d'un voyageur* (composed in 1835–6; many pieces are revised and included in the first (Swiss) volume of *Années de pèlerinage* in 1855). Berwald writes his first two symphonies, *Sinfonie sérieuse* and *Sinfonie capricieuse*.

1843   Marx and Engels meet in Paris. The Leipzig Conservatory opens, with Mendelssohn as director. Publication of Kirkegaard's *Either/Or*. The first illustrated magazine in Paris, *L'Illustration*, is published. The London Handel Society begins publication of Handel's complete works (not finished). Founding of the *Signale für die Musikalische Welt* in Leipzig, aimed at the amateur music-lover. The Vienna Männergesangverein is established. Publication of Fétis's *Méthode élémentaire de plain-chant* and W. R. Griepenkerl's *Ritter Berlioz in Braunschweig*. Premières of Wagner's *Der fliegende Holländer* in Dresden, Verdi's *I lombardi* in Milan, and Donizetti's *Dom Sébastien* and *Don Pasquale* in Paris and *Maria di Rohan* in Vienna. Publication of Berlioz's *Grand traité d'instrumentation et d'orchestration modernes*. Moniusko begins his twelve popular *Spiewniki domowe* (Songbooks for Home Use). First performance of Gade's First Symphony (1842) by the Leipzig Gewandhaus Orchestra under Mendelssohn. Opening of the Tivoli Gardens in Copenhagen. The violinist Joseph Joachim is first heard at Fanny Hensel-Mendelssohn's musical Sundays in Berlin. Wagner presents a revised version of Gluck's *Armide* at Dresden. A troupe of singers (including Rubini, Tamburini and Viardot) visits St Petersburg.

1844   Machine-breaking riots take place in Prague. Viollet de Duc begins his plans to restore Notre-Dame in Paris. *The Musical Times* is founded in London. Espín y Guillén establishes Spain's first musical magazine, *La Iberia musical*. A Philharmonic Society is established in Barcelona. Founding of the Hamburger Singakademie, a reconstitution of the Gesellschaft der Freunde religiösen Gesanges. The *Neue Berliner musikalische Zeitung* is founded. Publication of Fétis's *Traité complet de la théorie et de la pratique de l'harmonie*. Première of Verdi's *Ernani* in Venice. The first Hungarian national opera, Erkel's *Hunyadi László*, is staged in Pest. Liszt's connection with the Weimar court begins. Mendelssohn composes his Violin Concerto. Félicien David writes his exotic 'ode-symphonie' *Le désert*. Jenny Lind has great success performing in Berlin.

1845 The Musical Union chamber concerts begin, with analytical programme notes. Mérimée publishes his story *Carmen*. Turgenev comes to Paris with the singer Pauline Viardot. Première of Wagner's *Tannhäuser* in Dresden and William Henry Fry's Bellinian opera *Leonora* in Philadelphia. Schumann composes his Piano Concerto. Kjerulf appointed conductor of the new Norwegian Students' Choir and a male voice quartet in Christiania (Oslo). Mendelssohn writes his Violin Concerto. Berwald writes his *Symphonie singulière* and Symphony in E flat.

1846 Adolphe Sax develops the saxophone family. Asenjo Barbieri founds the periodical *La Espana musical*. Covent Garden Theatre becomes a permanent opera house, the home of the Royal Italian Opera in London. Michael Costa appointed permanent conductor of the Italian Opera at Her Majesty's Theatre (formerly the King's Theatre). Publication of Cavaillé-Coll's *Rapport sur les travaux du grand orgue de l'église de la Madeleine à Paris*. Première of Verdi's *Attila* in Venice. The first Croatian opera, Vatroslav Lisinski's *Ljubav i zloba* (Love and Malice), is given in Zagreb, at the peak of the national Illyrian movement (1835–48). First performances of Mendelssohn's *Elijah* in Birmingham, Berlioz's *La damnation de Faust* in Paris and Schumann's Second Symphony in Leipzig. Chopin completes his *Barcarolle*, Op. 60, and *Polonaise-Fantaisie*, Op. 61. Jenny Lind makes her Viennese debut in Bellini's *Norma*.

1847 In England, the Ten-Hour Act offers workers guaranteed leisure time. Founding of the Opéra-National in Paris, directed by Adolphe Adam (it is forced to close the following year owing to the revolutionary events). The España Musical society founded under Eslava to promote Spanish opera. Nicolai appointed director of the Berlin Opera. Rio de Janeiro Conservatory founded by Francisco Manuel da Silva. A. B. Marx completes his textbook *Die Lehre von der musikalischen Komposition*. Premières of Verdi's *Macbeth* in Florence and *Jérusalem* (an adaptation of *Il Lombardi*, 1843) in Paris, and Flotow's *Martha* in Vienna. Spohr appointed Generalmusikdirektor at Kassel. Liszt completes his first fifteen *Rhapsodies hongroises*. Pauline Viardot sings at a concert given by Clara Schumann in Berlin. Jullien engages Berlioz as musical director at Drury Lane and tries to establish an English Opera. Performance of Mendelssohn's *Elijah* by the Sacred Music Society in New York. Jenny Lind makes her London debut as Alice in Meyerbeer's *Robert le diable* (in Italian). Verdi moves to Paris, where he stays for most of the next two years.

1848　Uprisings in Sicily, Paris, Vienna, Venice, Berlin, Budapest, Milan, Parma, the Papal States, Warsaw, Prague; all suppressed except Paris, constitution granted in Prussia. Metternich resigns. Abdication of Ferdinand I of Austria (succeeded by Franz Joseph). Abdication of Louis Philippe, French Republic proclaimed (Feb.), Louis Napoleon becomes president (Dec.). The Pre-Raphaelite Brotherhood founded in England by Holman Hunt, John Millais and Dante Gabriel Rossetti. Publication of Marx and Engels's *Communist Manifesto*. The Société Alard-Franchomme is founded in Paris, specialising in Classical quartets. Premières of two early Romanian operas, Alexandru Flechtenmacher's *Baba Hîrca* (The Witch Hîrca) in Iaşi, and Ion Andrei Wachmann's *Mihai Bravul în ajunul bătălieri de la Călugăreni* (Michael the Brave on the Eve of the Battle of Călugăreni) in Bucharest. Première of Hervé's opéra bouffe *Don Quichotte* in Paris. Concert performance in Vilnius of Poland's first major national opera, Moniuszko's *Halka* (staged in 1854). Wagner flees to Weimar to escape arrest. Spohr helps man the barricades in Kassel and writes his String Sextet in C, Op. 140. Anton Rubinstein returns to Russia from abroad. Glinka writes his orchestral piece *Kamarinskaya*. Liszt appointed Hofkapellmeister at Weimar; he instigates a modern movement in German music and completes his first symphonic poem *Les préludes* and the cantata *Hungaria*. Brahms makes his solo debut in Hamburg. Aleksey L'vov publishes a complete cycle of liturgical chant used throughout the church year, which becomes a standard work. Publication of Stephen Foster's popular minstrel song *Oh, Susanna*. Strauss (I) writes his *Radetzky-Marsch* as a tribute to the general commanding the Habsburg army, and Strauss (II) writes several pro-Revolution works, including a *Revolutions-Marsch*, and his *Studenten-Marsch* is confiscated by the police. Gottschalk's *Bamboula* ('danse des nègres', 1844/5) and *La savane* ('ballade créole', 1845/6) are heard in public in Paris for the first time. Publication of Alkan's *grande sonate, Les quatres âges*, Op. 33.

1849　Mazzini proclaims a republic in Rome, but Pius IX is restored in July. Friedrich Wilhelm IV declines title of German Emperor offered by National Assembly; attempted German unity fails with the dissolution of the German Assembly. Hungary and Venice submit to Austria. Founding of the London Bach Society. Opening of the Philharmonic

Hall in Liverpool. Wieprecht founds Euterpe in Berlin, an ensemble consisting of former military bandsmen. Premières of Meyerbeer's *Le prophète* (with Viardot in the title role) in Paris, and Verdi's *La battaglia di Legnano* in Rome and *Luisa Miller* in Naples. Nicolai dies in Berlin two months after the première of *Die lustigen Weiber von Windsor*. Chopin dies in Paris. Following his activities fighting on the barricades in Dresden, Wagner is exiled to Switzerland, where he writes *Die Kunst und die Revolution* and *Das Kunstwerk der Zukunft*. A riot breaks out in Astor Place, outside the Opera House in New York, between supporters of 'highbrow' and 'lowbrow' entertainment. Schumann completes his *Manfred* Overture. Gottschalk makes his debut as a professional pianist in the Salle Pleyel in Paris, with a number of his 'creole' compositions then in vogue.

1850   The US Senate enacts 'The Compromise of 1850'. Prussia agrees to Austrian supremacy in the revived Frankfurt Diet. A. B. Marx cofounds the Berlin Musikschule (later the Stern Conservatory). The Bach-Gesellschaft is founded in Leipzig. Wagner's polemic *Das Judenthum in der Musik* is published under a pseudonym in the *Neue Zeitschrift für Musik*. Premières of Wagner's *Lohengrin* in Weimar (conducted by Liszt) and Verdi's *Stiffelio* in Trieste. Jenny Lind goes to the USA on a recital tour (–1852). Liszt completes his symphonic poem *Prometheus* and writes his Fantasy and Fugue for organ on 'Ad nos, ad salutarem undam' (from Meyerbeer's *Le prophète*). Lobe, formerly editor of the *Allgemeine musikalische Zeitung* (1846–8), begins his *Lehrbuch der musikalischen Composition*.

1851   Louis Bonaparte stages a *coup d'état*, and the following year becomes Emperor Napoleon III following a successful plebiscite. In Spain a Concordat severely restricts the number of musical personnel in churches. The Great Exhibition opens in London at the new Crystal Palace. The Opéra-National reopens in Paris, and the following year changes its name to the Théâtre-Lyrique. The Société des Dernières Quatuors de Beethoven is founded in Paris. Founding of the (shortlived) Musical Institute of London. Wagner publishes *Oper und Drama*. Breitkopf & Härtel begin publication of the first complete Bach edition (–1899). Liszt publishes *Lohengrin et Tannhäuser de Richard Wagner*. Premières of Verdi's *Rigoletto* in Venice, and David's *La perle du Brésil* (rev. 1859–61) and Gounod's *Sapho* in Paris. Liszt begins his symphonic poem *Mazeppa* (–1854), based on the fourth of the *Grandes études*

(1837). First performance of Schumann's Third Symphony, the 'Rhenish', in Düsseldorf. Lambillotte publishes a facsimile of the St Gall Codex 359. Publication of Stephen Heller's evocative character pieces *Spaziergänge eines Einsamen*, Op. 78.

1852   First meeting of the Convocation of the Church of England since 1717. Crystal Palace is moved to Sydenham. The New Philharmonic Society is founded in London (partly promoted by the music publisher Cramer). Verdi sees a performance of *La dame aux camélias* by Dumas *fils* in Paris. The Société des Jeunes Artistes du Conservatoire is founded in Paris by Pasdeloup. Opening of the National Theatre in Bucharest. Stephen Foster publishes his minstrel songs under his own name for the first time. Publication in Leipzig of Franz Brendel's *Geschichte der Musik in Italien, Deutschland und Frankreich: von den ersten christlichen Zeiten bis auf die Gegenwart*. Publication of Emanuel Geibel and Paul Heyse's *Spanisches Liederbuch*, containing translations of Cervantes and folk poetry (Wolf sets forty-four songs in 1889–90). Première of Halévy's *Le juif errant* in Paris. First performance of the revised version of Schumann's Fourth Symphony in Düsseldorf. Publication of Liszt's piano transcription of J. S. Bach's Six Preludes and Fugues for organ. Liszt presents a 'Berlioz Week' in Weimar, at which *Benvenuto Cellini*, *Roméo et Juliette* and two parts of *La damnation de Faust* are performed. Publication of Liszt's *Etudes d'exécution transcendentale* (Transcendental Studies), based on the *Douze grandes études* (1837).

1853   As protector of the Christians of the Ottoman Empire, Russia invades the Danube provinces and defeats the Turkish fleet. Georges Haussmann is appointed Préfet de la Seine and begins his programme to redesign Paris. Founding of the New York Academy of Music. Institution of brass band competitions at Belle Vue, Manchester. Steinway & Sons established in New York. Carl Proske begins to publish the collection *Musica divina*. Véron begins publication of his *Mémoires d'un bourgeois de Paris*. Premières of Verdi's *Il trovatore* in Rome and *La traviata* in Venice. Schumann completes his *Szenen aus Goethes Faust*. The pianist Gottschalk returns to America after travelling in Europe, and gives several extended concert tours featuring his own compositions.

1854   Allied victories during the Crimean War at Balaclava and Inkerman. Opening of the Steinway Hall in New York (rebuilt in 1866). Hanslick first publishes his influential *Vom Musikalisch-Schönen* in Leipzig. Simon

Sechter completes *Die Grundsätze der musikalischen Komposition*. Première of Meyerbeer's *L'étoile du nord* in Paris. Liszt publishes his B minor Piano Sonata (1853), dedicated to Schumann, and Brahms publishes his F minor Sonata, Op. 5. Liszt completes his second symphonic poem *Tasso: lamento e trionfo* (begun in 1849).

1855 Death of Tsar Nicholas I of Russia, and the accession of the more liberal Alexander II. The Exposition Universelle takes place in Paris. The popular Crystal Palace Saturday Concerts begin in London under August Mann, organised by George Grove. Chappell's begins publication of *Popular Music of Olden Time* in London. Founding of the Neu-Weimar-Verein by Liszt and his colleagues to reflect the town's historical status and to gather together advocates of musical progress. Publication in the *Neue Zeitschrift für Musik* of Liszt's 'manifesto' *Berlioz und seine Haroldsymphonie*. Publication in Paris of Wilhelm von Lenz's *Beethoven et ses trois styles*. Lobe begins his series *Fliegende Blätter für Musik*. Publication of Nikolai Chernïshevsky's *Aesthetic Relation of Art to Reality*, in which he advocates 'natural' singing. Premières of Verdi's *Les vêpres siciliennes* at the Opéra and Offenbach's *Ba-ta-clan* at the new Bouffes-Parisiens. Rossini settles back in Paris. Bruckner is appointed organist at Linz Cathedral. Liszt completes his Mass commemorating the restoration of the cathedral in Gran (Esztergom), the centre of the Catholic Church in Hungary. Hortense Schneider makes her Parisian debut in a double-bill at the Bouffes-Parisiens, including Offenbach's *Le violoneux*.

1856 The Treaty of Paris ends the Crimean War. In the massacre of Pottawatomie Creek Kansas slavers are murdered by free-staters. Publication of Liszt's symphonic poem *Les préludes* (written in 1848 and later revised), dedicated to Princess Sayn-Wittgenstein. Berlioz elected to the Académie Française. The Dresden Conservatory is founded. Otto Jahn publishes his study of Mozart. Brahms is appointed musical director at Detmold. The Société Armingaud is established in Paris, specialising in string quartets. The Teatro de la Zarzuela is founded in Madrid. Founding of the Tonkünstlerverein in Dresden. Opening of the Free Trade Hall in Manchester. Publication of Théophile Gautier's *Histoire de l'art dramatique depuis vingt-cinq ans*. Première of Dargomïzhsky's *Rusalka* in St Petersburg.

1857 Garibaldi forms the Italian National Association for unification under Piedmont. Ibsen becomes director of the Norske Teatret in Christiana

(Oslo). Charles Hallé begins his Manchester orchestral series. Saint-Saëns is appointed organist at the Madeleine, Paris. Baudelaire publishes *Les fleurs du mal*. The first 'trial' Crystal Palace Handel Festival is presented by the Sacred Harmonic Society, with a choir of 2,000 (including amateur singers). Opening of the Teatro Colón in Buenos Aires. Founding of the Imperial Academy of Music and National Opera in Rio de Janeiro. Première of Verdi's *Simon Boccanegra* in Venice. Liszt completes *Eine Faust-Symphonie* (dedicated to Berlioz) and *Eine Symphonie zu Dantes Divina commedia* (dedicated to Wagner). Wagner sets five of Mathilde Wesendonck's poems while writing *Tristan und Isolde*.

1858   The Franco-Italian pact is drawn up between Napoleon III and Cavour in Plombières; repression intensifies in France following Orsini's failed attempt to assassinate Napoleon III. The Händel-Gesellschaft edition is begun by Breitkopf & Härtel. Franck is appointed organist at Ste Clotilde, Paris. The Singakademie is established in Vienna. The St James's Hall opens in London with a 2,000-seat capacity; Chappell's Popular Concerts begin there. Charles Hallé founds a professional orchestra in Manchester. Premières of Offenbach's *Orphée aux enfers* in Paris, and Cornelius's *Der Barbier von Bagdad* in Weimar under Liszt, who resigns from his post following the hostile reception. Moniuszko's *Halka* (four-act version) is given in Warsaw. Berlioz completes *Les troyens*. Grieg is sent to study at the Leipzig Conservatory (–1862). Publication of Liszt's second (Italian) volume of *Années de pèlerinage* (composed in 1837–49). Brahms completes his Piano Concerto No. 1.

1859   War between France and Austria in Italy; Austria cedes Parma and Lombardy, but Tuscany and Modena are restored; Venice remains Austrian. Ferdinand II of the Two Sicilies is succeeded by Francis II. The Union of Wallachia and Moldavia ensures effective freedom for Romania. A French consortium starts the construction of the Suez Canal. John Stuart Mill publishes *On Liberty*, in which he pleads for individual freedom; Charles Darwin publishes *Origin of Species*. Henry Steinway obtains a patent for an overstrung piano, in which the sound of the instrument is enhanced. Anselmo Clavé founds the first Spanish choral society in Barcelona. Barbieri founds a Madrid orchestra. Institution of the triennial Handel Festival, with the composer's centennial commemoration; two of his oratorios are performed at Crystal Palace with a choir numbering 2,700 and an audience of more than 81,000. The Russian Musical Society is founded in St Petersburg. Publication of Liszt's *Über John Fields* and *Des bohémiens et de leur musique en Hongrie*. Premières of Gounod's *Faust* in Paris and Verdi's *Un ballo in maschera* in Rome. Brahms's First Piano Concerto is performed in Hanover. Wagner completes *Tristan und Isolde* in Lucerne. First performance of Brahms's *Ave Maria* for women's chorus in Hamburg. Brendel launches the idea of the New German School at a conference to mark the twenty-fifth anniversary of the *Neue Zeitschrift für Musik* in Leipzig. Pauline Viardot sings the title role in Berlioz's adaptation of Gluck's *Orfeo* in Paris. Adelina Patti's debut in New York in Donizetti's *Lucia di Lammermoor*.

1860   Garibaldi and the Red Shirts take Palermo and Naples; Victor Emmanuel invades the Papal States and is proclaimed King of Italy by Garibaldi. President Lincoln is elected in America. Paul Heyse publishes the *Italienisches Liederbuch*, consisting of translations of folk poetry (Wolf sets forty-six songs in 1890–1 and 1896). Founding of Lamoureux's Séances Populaires de Musique de Chambre in Paris. State conservatory established in Iaşi. The Vienna Philharmonic is established. Wagner writes his *Zukunftsmusik*. Opening of the Bryan Hall in Chicago. Institution of brass band competitions at Crystal Palace (which later develop into the National Brass Band Festival). Founding of the Opera Lírica Nacional (replacing the Academy) in Rio de Janeiro. Premières of Franz von Suppé's *Das Pensionat* in Vienna and Gounod's *Philémon et Baucis* in Paris. Offenbach 'celebrates' Wagner's arrival in Paris with a parody, *Le carnaval des revues*. In Catalonia the first in a series of massed festivals directed by Clavé is given. Viardot sings in a private performance of Act II of *Tristan und Isolde* in Paris.

1861   Friedrich Wilhelm IV of Prussia is succeeded by Wilhelm I. Outbreak of American Civil War. Emancipation of Russian serfs. Liszt founds the Allgemeiner Deutsches Musikverein for the promotion of modern German music; he moves to Rome. The journal *Musicul român* (The Romanian Musician) is founded. The inauguration of Pasdeloup's Concerts Populaires de Musique Classique in Paris, which promote modern as well as Classical works. Founding of the Frankfurt Conservatory. The founding of the London Academy of Music. Publication in London of the popular collection *Hymns Ancient and Modern*. Première of Erkel's *Bánk bán* in Pest. The Paris première of Wagner's *Tannhäuser* is disrupted by the Jockey Club. Joachim Raff completes his First Symphony, 'To the Fatherland'. Smetana settles in Prague after a period abroad. Patti gives her European debut in Bellini's *La sonnambula* at Covent Garden. Brahms writes twenty-five Variations and a Fugue on a theme by Handel, Op. 24.

1862 President Lincoln declares the freedom of all slaves. Bismarck is appointed Minister-President of Prussia. Turgenev writes *Fathers and Sons*, creating an archetypal nihilist hero. Balakirev founds the Free Music School in St Petersburg. The opening of the St Petersburg Conservatory, founded by Rubinstein. The Provisional Theatre in Prague opens as a home for Czech-language opera and drama. The complete editions of Beethoven and Palestrina are begun. Henry Chorley publishes his *Thirty Years' Musical Recollections*, a chronicle of London musical life. Premières of Berlioz's *Béatrice et Bénédict* at Baden-Baden, Verdi's *La forza del destino* at St Petersburg, Berwald's *Estrella de Soria* (composed in 1841) in Stockholm, and David's *Lalla-Roukh* and Gounod's *La reine de Saba* in Paris. Balakirev begins collecting folktunes in the Caucasus. Pergolesi's *La serva padrona* is revived at the Théâtre-Lyrique in Paris.

1863 The Polish rebellion is suppressed by Russia. Chrysander's *Jahrbuch für musikalische Wissenschaft* is inaugurated. Jesús Monasterio founds a Quartet Society in Madrid, concentrating on German classics. Acts III, IV and V of Berlioz's *Les troyens* are performed in Paris as *Les troyens à Carthage*. Première of Bizet's *Les pêcheurs de perles* in Paris. Brahms moves to Vienna, and is appointed conductor of the Singakademie. Smetana completes *Branibori v Cechách* (The Brandenburgers in Bohemia). Brahms completes twenty-eight Variations on a theme by Paganini, Op. 35. Publication of the *Demolirer-Polka*, Op. 269 by Johann Strauss (II), which refers to the demolition of Vienna's ramparts.

1864 Provincial councils are established in Russia. End of the Danish war against Prussia and Austria. Archduke Maximilian of Austria accepts the crown of Mexico. A state conservatory is established in Bucharest. The Royal College of Organists is founded in London. Première of Gounod's *Mireille* in Paris. Rossini writes his *Petite messe solennelle*. Balakirev writes his Second Overture on Russian Themes and Symphony in C.

1865 Assassination of Lincoln; he is succeeded as president by Johnson. End of American Civil War. Bismarck meets with Napoleon III who agrees to Prussian supremacy in Germany and a united Italy. The Euterpe Society is founded in Copenhagen by Grieg and others to promote modern, especially Scandinavian, music. Theodore Thomas inaugurates a series of popular Garden Concerts in New York. Premières of Meyerbeer's *L'Africaine* in Paris, Wagner's *Tristan und Isolde* in Munich and Morales's *Ildegonda* in Mexico City, with the celebrated soprano Angela Peralta, 'the Mexican nightingale'. Moniusko completes *Straszny dwór* (The Haunted Manor). First performance of Suppé's *Die schöne Galathee*, a work indebted to Offenbach's *La belle Hélène* (1864). Liszt completes his *Missa choralis* while a resident of the Vatican. Rimsky-Korsakov writes his First Symphony. First performance of Liszt's oratorio *Die Legende von der heiligen Elisabeth* (completed in 1862) in Budapest. Publication of Liszt's piano transcriptions of all Beethoven's symphonies, dedicated to Bülow.

1866   Austria cedes Venetia to the Kingdom of Italy, and is excluded from the new German Confederation under Prussia, following defeat at Königgrätz. The régime in Russia becomes stricter following the attempted assassination of Alexander II. The Madrid orchestra amalgamates with the orchestra of the Madrid Conservatory to form the Sociedad de Conciertos, under Joaquín Gaztambide. The Stockholm Conservatory grows out of the Musical Academy. Tchaikovsky begins teaching at the new Moscow Conservatory. The Peabody Conservatory in Baltimore is founded. Baudelaire's 'Richard Wagner et *Tannhäuser* à Paris' is published in the *Revue européenne*. Premières of Smetana's *Prodaná nevesta* (The Bartered Bride) in Prague and Thomas's *Mignon* in Paris. Bruckner writes his Mass No. 2 in E minor. Grieg returns to Norway after a period abroad. Johan Svendsen completes his First Symphony. Rimsky-Korsakov writes the songs 'V tyomnoy rosshche zamolk solovey' (In the Dark Grove the Nightingale is Silent) and 'El' i pal'ma' (The Fir and the Palm).

1867   The Austro-Hungarian 'Dual Monarchy' is established. Garibaldi marches on Rome but is defeated by French and papal troops. The Dominion of Canada is founded. Japanese art is introduced to the West at the Paris Exposition Universelle. Gade founds the Copenhagen Conservatory. The New England Conservatory is founded in Boston. Premières in Paris of Bizet's *La jolie fille de Perth*, Verdi's *Don Carlos*, Gounod's *Roméo et Juliette* and Offenbach's *La grande-duchesse de Gérolstein*. Musorgsky composes *Ivanova noch'na Lïsoy gore* (St John's

Night on the Bare Mountain). Bruckner succeeds Sechter as professor at the Vienna Conservatory. Borodin completes his First Symphony. Balakirev mounts a concert in honour of the delegates to the Pan-Slavic Congress in St Petersburg; the term 'Moguchaya kuchka' (Mighty Handful) is coined by Stasov. Berwald is appointed professor of composition at the Swedish Musical Academy. Lindeman completes his edition of Norwegian folk music. Publication of *Slave Songs of the United States*. Founding of Bilse's Kapelle (named the Berlin Philharmonic Orchestra in 1882). Dubois writes his oratorio *Les sept paroles du Christ*. Publication of the first set of Grieg's *Lyric Pieces*. Hortense Schneider achieves great success in *La grande-duchesse de Gérolstein* at the Paris Exposition. First performance of Paine's Mass in D in Berlin. First performance of Liszt's Hungarian Coronation Mass in Budapest.

1868 Isabella of Spain is driven into exile following uprisings; a constituent assembly of European powers offers the crown to Leopold of Hohenzollern, thereby starting the crisis that leads to the Franco-Prussian War. Founding of the science of Eugenics with the publication of Francis Galton's *Hereditary Genius*. The Berlin Philharmonic is founded. A Philharmonic Society is established in Bucharest. Premières of Wagner's *Die Meistersinger* in Munich, Boito's *Mefistofele* in Milan, and Thomas's *Hamlet*, Charles Lecocq's *Fleur de thé* and Offenbach's *La périchole* in Paris. Bruch writes his G minor Violin Concerto, and Grieg his Piano Concerto. Brahms composes his *German Requiem*. Musorgsky sets Gogol's *Zhenit'ba* (The Marriage). Smetana writes *Dalibor*. George Leybourne, the most acclaimed of the 'swells' in London, is given a contract while at the height of his success with the song 'Champagne Charlie'. First performance of Max Bruch's Symphony No. 1. Publication of Liszt's transcription for piano (two hands) of 'Isoldes Liebestod' from Wagner's *Tristan und Isolde*.

1869 Opening of the Suez Canal. Publication of Matthew Arnold's *Culture and Anarchy*. Opening of the Hofoper on the new Ringstrasse in Vienna, with a performance of Mozart's *Don Giovanni*. Founding of the Rossini Club of Portland, Maine, where women are able to perform to each other in a culture of self-improvement. F. X. Witt founds the Allgemeine Deutscher Cäcilien-Verein at Bamberg, to aid the reform of the practice (as well as the theory) of church music. Opening of the National Theatre in Belgrade. The London Philharmonic Society concerts move from Hanover Square to St James's Hall. Theodore Thomas takes his New York Symphony Orchestra on the first of a series of tours to the Atlantic seaboard and the mid-west. Foundation of the Société Bourgault-Ducoudray to encourage the singing of choral music. Hilarión Eslava publishes a ten-volume anthology of sacred vocal music, *Lira sacro-hispana*. Première of Wagner's *Das Rheingold* in Munich. Balakirev writes his oriental fantasy for piano *Islamey*, and Tchaikovsky the first version of *Romeo and Juliet*. First performance of Brahms's *Alto Rhapsody*, with Pauline Viardot. Joachim Raff composes his Third Symphony, 'Im Walde'. Bruckner composes the graduale *Locus iste*.

1870   Start of the Franco-Prussian War, leading to the defeat of Napoleon III at Sedan. Revolt in Paris is followed by the declaration of the Third Republic. Prussians begin the Siege of Paris. Italians march on Rome and declare it their capital city. Publication of the first Finnish novel, Aleksis Kivi's *Seven Brothers*. Wagner writes the *Siegfried Idyll* and his book *Beethoven*. Official opening of the Vienna Conservatory and the new Grosse Musikvereinssaal. Opening of the National Theatre in Zagreb. Hanslick is appointed as the first *professor ordinarius* in music history and aesthetics at Vienna. Founding of Wislicki's Warsaw Music Society, which performs orchestral and chamber music. Première of Wagner's *Die Walküre* in Munich and Antônio Carlos Gomes's *Il Guarany* in Milan. Delibes writes his ballet *Coppélia*. Musorgsky composes the song cycle *Detskaya* (The Nursery). Rimsky-Korsakov writes the song 'V tsarstvo rozï i vina' (Into the Kingdom of Roses and Wine). Publication of Duparc's song *L'invitation au voyage*, set for the actress Marie Daubrun as a barcarolle. First performance of Bruch's Symphony No. 2.

1871   Wilhelm I of Prussia is declared Emperor of Germany at Versailles. Capitulation of Paris and armistice with Germany. Election of Thiers as President of the Third Republic. Eugène Pottier writes the words of the political chanson the *Internationale*, after the suppression of the Paris Commune (Pierre Degeyter provides music in 1888). The building of the Royal Albert Hall is completed in London. The Société Nationale de Musique is founded in Paris by Saint-Saëns and others. Rimsky-Korsakov is appointed composition teacher at the St Petersburg Conservatory. Founding of the Leeds Philharmonic Society. Charles-Marie Widor succeeds Lefebure-Wély as organist at St Sulpice in Paris, where he remains for sixty-four years. Premières of Verdi's *Aïda* in Cairo and Dvořák's *Král a uhlíř* (King and Charcoal Burner) (rev. 1874 and 1887) in Prague. Mariani conducts the first Italian production of a Wagner opera, *Lohengrin*, in Bologna.

1872   Franck is appointed organ professor at the Paris Conservatoire. The College of Church Music (later Trinity College of Music) is founded in London. Brahms becomes conductor of the Vienna Gesellschafts-konzerte. Founding of the Akademischer Wagner-Verein in Vienna. Opening of the Bösendorfer-Saal, the most popular concert hall in Vienna. Founding of the Finnish National Theatre by Kaarlo Bergbom. John Stainer appointed organist at St Paul's, London. An official report rails against the shamelessness of *café-concert* songwriters in London. Publication of Nietzsche's *Die Geburt der Tragödie aus dem Geiste der Musik*, viewed initially as a work of Wagnerian propaganda. Première in St Petersburg of Dargomïzhsky's *Kamennïy gost'* (The Stone Guest), completed after the composer's death by Cui and Rimsky-Korsakov. Erkel completes his Wagnerian opera *Brankovics György*. Musorgsky begins his opera *Khovanshchina* (–1880, incomplete). Liszt and Wagner are reconciled after their quarrel in the 1860s over their children, and Liszt attends the Bayreuth Festival.

1873   Financial crisis in Vienna, which spreads to other European markets. Fall of Thiers and election of MacMahon as President of France. Founding of a federal republic in Spain following Carlist uprisings. Gottfried Semper designs the Burgtheater in Vienna, to be built by Karl von Hasenauer. The Salle Le Peletier, home of the Paris Opéra, burns down. Spitta begins his study of Bach (–1880). The first Concert National is given in Paris, conducted by Colonne, after whom the series is later named. Founding of the Société de l'Harmonie Sacrée in Paris by Lamoureux. The opening of Alexandra Palace in London. Première of Rimsky-Korsakov's *Pskovityanka* (The Maid of Pskov) (composed in 1868–72) in St Petersburg. First performance, at Weimar, of Liszt's ora-torio *Christus* (completed in 1867).

1874   Restoration of the Spanish monarchy with Alfonso XII. Degas exhibits *The Dancing Class* in the first impressionist exhibition in Paris. Pedro Alarcón Ariza writes *El sombrero de tres picos* (which later inspires a ballet by Falla and an opera by Wolf); Juan Valera writes *Pepita Jiménez* (which inspires an opera by Albéniz). Inauguration of a series of National Concerts in Buenos Aires, promoting local musicians. The Musical

Association (later Royal) founded in London by John Stainer and William Pole. Premières of Francisco Asenjo Barbieri's zarzuela *El barberillo de Lavapiés* in Madrid, Musorgsky's *Boris Godunov* and Tchaikovsky's *Oprichnik* in St Petersburg, Johann Strauss's *Die Fledermaus* in Vienna and Hermann Goetz's *Der Widerspenstigen Zähmung* (composed in 1868–72) in Mannheim. Musorgsky completes the song cycle *Bez solntsa* (Sunless). Lalo writes his *Symphonie espagnole*. Verdi completes his Requiem. Bruckner composes the first version of his Fourth Symphony, the 'Romantic' (completed in 1880).

1875   Opening of the newly designated Théâtre National de l'Opéra at the Palais Garnier; the programme includes extracts from *La juive*, *Les huguenots* and Delibes's ballet *La source*. Founding of the National Hungarian Royal Academy of Music in Budapest (under Liszt and Erkel), the Music School at Harvard University and the Carl Rosa Opera Company. Hans Richter is appointed Kapellmeister at the Hofoper in Vienna. John Knowles Paine becomes professor at Harvard; the department of music he organises becomes a model for others in America. Premières of Karl Goldmark's *Königin von Saba* in Vienna, Dvořák's *Vanda*, 1875 (rev. 1879, 1883) in Prague, and Anton Rubinstein's *Die Maccabäer* in Berlin and *Demon* in St Petersburg. Italian première of Francisco Hargreaves's *La gatta bianca*, the first Argentine opera. Première of Gilbert and Sullivan's *Trial by Jury*, which opens the market for English operetta. Bizet dies shortly after the unsuccessful first première of *Carmen* in Paris. Hans von Bülow conducts the first performance of Tchaikovsky's Piano Concerto No. 1 in Boston. Mahler and Wolf arrive as students at the Vienna Conservatory. First performance of Stanford's oratorio *The Resurrection* in Cambridge; he composes his First Symphony.

1876   John Singer Sargent paints a rehearsal of the Pasdeloup Orchestra at the Cirque d'Hiver in Paris. The Purcell Society begins publication of a complete edition of Purcell's music. Publication of Nietzsche's *Richard Wagner in Bayreuth*. Premières of Ponchielli's *La Gioconda* in Milan and Suppé's *Fatinitza* in Vienna. The first complete performance of Wagner's *Ring* opens the Festspielhaus at Bayreuth. Ibsen's play *Peer Gynt* is given in Christiania (Oslo) with Grieg's incidental music. Brahms completes his First Symphony. Tchaikovsky writes his Variations on a Rococo theme for cello and orchestra. Publication of Widor's first four Organ Symphonies, Op. 13.

1877 Mallarmé writes his eclogue *L'après-midi d'un faune*, which later inspires Debussy's *Prélude*. Thomas Edison designs the phonograph. The Romanian Opera is opened in Bucharest. The government-subsidised Conservatorio Nacional de Música is established in Mexico. A collection of more than thirty early operas under the title *Chefs-d'œuvre classiques de l'opéra français* begins publication in France (–1884). Premières of Saint-Saëns's *Samson et Dalila* in Weimar, Massenet's *Le roi de Lahore* in Paris and Tchaikovsky's ballet *Lebedinoye ozero* (Swan Lake) in Moscow. Fauré composes his Requiem. Goldmark writes his symphonic poem *Ländliche Hochzeit*. The disastrous first performance in Vienna of Bruckner's Symphony No. 3 (recomposed with Josef Schalk in 1888–9). Musorgsky completes his song cycle *Pesni i plyaski smerti* (Songs and Dances of Death) (1875–).

1878 Humbert I succeeds Victor Emanuel II of Italy. Anti-socialist law in Germany drives socialism underground. Romania gains formal independence from the Turks. The Turks are expelled from Bulgaria, Serbia (which had already been ceded a measure of self-government), Bosnia and Herzegovina, and Montenegro. Sarasate organises the first summer festival in Pamplona. Founding of the People's Concert Society in London. Founding of the Frankfurt Hoch Conservatory. The opening of the Steinway Hall in London. August Wilhelm Ambros completes his *Geschichte der Musik* (1862–) which presents music history as cultural history. Première of Gilbert and Sullivan's first collaboration for D'Oyly Carte, *HMS Pinafore*, in London. Brahms writes his Violin Concerto.

1879 Austro-German Dual Alliance is established. The first edition of Grove's *Dictionary of Music and Musicians* begins publication (–1890). Opening of the Central Music Hall in Chicago. Publication of Nietzsche's *Menschliches, Allzumenschliches*, which contains critical aphorisms on 'the artist', referring to Wagner. Premières of Tchaikovsky's *Evgeny Onegin* in Moscow, Suppé's *Boccaccio* in Vienna, Gilbert and Sullivan's *The Pirates of Penzance* in Paignton and Harrigan and Hart's *Mulligan Guards* in New York. The D'Oyly Carte Opera Company is founded in London. Rouget de Lisle's *chant de guerre* 'La Marseillaise' is adopted as the French national anthem. Smetana completes *Má vlast*. Publication of Mel'gunov's first folksong collection. Publication of Fauré's first collection of songs.

1880 Tension between France and Italy in Tunis. Barcelona's first symphonic concert society founded, under Jésus Monasterio. The Internationale Stiftung Mozarteum is established in Salzburg. The examinations of the Associated Board of the Royal Schools of Music in London begin. The Guildhall School of Music founded in London. Rudolph Aronson inaugurates a series of promenade concerts at the Metropolitan Concert Hall in New York. Publication of César Cui's *La musique en Russie*. Première of Catalani's *Elda* in Turin (later revised and performed in 1890 as *Loreley*). First performance of Franck's Piano Quintet in Paris. Borodin writes his short 'musical picture' *V sredney* (On the Steppes of Central Asia), dedicated to Liszt.

1881 Assassination of Tsar Alexander II, followed by the succession of Alexander III and a period of artistic and social retrenchment. Tunis accepts French protectorate. Serbia becomes a protectorate of Austria. Boston Symphony Orchestra founded. Opening of the Savoy Theatre, home of the D'Oyly Carte Company. The inauguration of the Teatro Municipal in Caracas. The New York publisher Harms is established. The Chat Noir cabaret is founded in Montmartre by Rodolphe Salis. Premières of Offenbach's *Les contes d'Hoffmann* and Massenet's *Hérodiade* in Paris, Tchaikovsky's *Orleanskaya deva* (Maid of Orleans) in St Petersburg and Smetana's *Libuše* at the opening of the National Theatre in Prague (the building burns down a few nights later). Brahms's *Academic Festival Overture* (1880) performed in Breslau. Brahms completes his Second Piano Concerto. The singer Lillian Russell achieves her first success in *The Grand Mogul* in New York.

1882 Italy joins the Austro-German alliance, now the Triple Alliance. Britain occupies Egypt and the Sudan. Founding of the Helsinki Music Institute and the Helsinki Orchestral Society. Opening of the Teatro Nacional in Buenos Aires. Founding of the Academia Nacional de Música in Bogotá. Publication of the first edition of Riemann's *Musik-Lexicon*. Premières of Wagner's *Parsifal* at Bayreuth, Rimsky-Korsakov's *Snegurochka* (The Snow Maiden) in St Petersburg, Dvořák's *Dimitrij* in Prague, and Gilbert and Sullivan's *Iolanthe* in London. Glazunov's First Symphony completed. Lalo completes his ballet score *Namouna*. Gounod completes his sacred trilogy *La rédemption*. Parry completes his Symphony No. 1. MacDowell writes his First Piano Concerto. Ciprian Porumbescu composes his *Rapsodia română* and his operetta *Crai nou* (New Moon).

1883   Nietzsche writes *Also sprach Zarathustra*. Royal College of Music
       founded in London (after thirty years of negotiation), under George
       Grove, with Parry, Stanford and Frank Bridge on the staff. Opening of
       the rebuilt National Theatre in Prague. Founding of the Metropolitan
       Opera, New York. The Benedictine monks at Solesmes under Dom
       Joseph Pothier produce their first edition of chant, the *Liber Gradualis*.
       Chabrier writes his orchestral rhapsody *España*. Hugo Wolf begins
       work on a symphonic poem based on Kleist's *Penthesilea* (–1885).
       D'Indy completes *Le chant de la cloche* (1879–), a series of dramatic
       tableaux. Publication of Liszt's third volume of *Années de pèlerinage*
       (composed in 1867–77).

1884   Berlin conference on African affairs provides for free trade in the Congo
       and the abolition of the slave trade. Publication of Joris-Karl
       Huysmans's Symbolist novel *A rebours*, and Verlaine's poem *Art poé-
       tique*, a poetic manifesto for the Symbolist movement. Opening of the
       National Theatre in Brno. Opening of the Royal Hungarian Opera
       House in Budapest. Premières of Fibich's *Nevěsta mesinská* (The Bride
       of Messina) in Prague, Puccini's *Le villi* in Milan, Tchaikovsky's *Mazepa*
       in Moscow, and Massenet's *Manon* and Ernest Reyer's *Sigurd* in
       Brussels. Dvořák conducts his music in England. Grieg writes *Fra
       Holbergs tid* (Holberg Suite). Christian Sinding completes his Piano
       Quintet, Op. 5. Publication of Borodin's String Quartet No. 1 (com-
       posed 1874–9). The first performance of Bruckner's Symphony No. 7
       in Leipzig.

1885   Crisis in Anglo-Russian relations over Afghanistan. The *Revue wag-
       nérienne* is founded in Paris; its contributors include Mallarmé.
       Mitrofan Petrovich Belyayev founds the Russian Symphony Concerts
       in St Petersburg. Founding of the Vierteljahrsschrift für
       Musikwissenschaft by Guido Adler, Philip Spitta and Friedrich
       Chrysander. The New York publisher Witmark is established.
       Premières of Johann Strauss's operetta *Der Zigeunerbaron* in Vienna
       and Massenet's *Le Cid* in Paris. Dvořák's Seventh Symphony com-
       posed for the Philharmonic Society in London. Mahler completes the
       first version of his *Lieder eines fahrenden Gesellen*. Brahms finishes his
       Fourth Symphony. Bach bicentenary concert given by the choral
       society La Concordia in Paris. Richard Strauss begins to establish
       himself as a song composer with *Acht Gedichte aus 'Letzte Blätter' von
       Hermann Gilm*, Op. 10. Publication of Bruant's *chanson réaliste* 'A la

Villette'. Tchaikovsky writes his *Manfred* Symphony. First performance of Dvořák's dramatic cantata *Svatební košile* (The Spectre's Bride). Gounod completes his sacred trilogy, *Mors et vita*, commissioned by the Birmingham Festival.

1886 Nicolau founds and conducts the Orfeó Català. Opening of the National Theatre in Pozsony (Bratislava). Saint-Saëns composes *Le carnaval des animaux* and Symphony No. 3 with organ. Charles Lenepveu writes his opera *Jeanne d'Arc*. First performance of Brahms's Fourth Symphony. D'Indy completes his *Symphonie cévenole* (Symphony on a French Mountaineer's Song) with piano obbligato. Hugo Wolf begins work on an oratorio, *Christnacht* (-1889). Delius begins his studies at the Leipzig Conservatory (-1888).

1887 Anglo-Italian agreement to support the status quo in the Mediterranean supported by Spain. Construction of the Eiffel Tower in Paris. Japan's first music academy, the Tokyo Music School, is opened. Premières of Verdi's *Otello* in Milan, Chabrier's *Le roi malgré lui* in Paris and Gilbert and Sullivan's *Ruddigore* in London. Stainer writes *The Crucifixion*. Debussy visits Bayreuth. César Franck's Violin Sonata (1886) performed by the Société Nationale. Bruckner completes the first version of his Eighth Symphony (recomposed with Schalk in 1889-90).

1888 Wilhelm I of Prussia succeeded by Friedrich III and then by Kaiser Wilhelm II. Toulouse-Lautrec begins to paint the theatres, music halls and cafés of Paris. Founding of the Arts and Crafts movement in Britain to reassert craftsmanship in the face of growing mechanisation. The Neues Deutsches Theater opens in Prague. Opening of the Amsterdam Concertgebouw. Publication of Nietzsche's *Der Fall Wagner*, a vigorous attack on the composer. Lalo completes *Le roi d'Ys*, Mahler his First Symphony and Rimsky-Korsakov *Sheherazade*. Satie writes *Trois gymnopédies*. Giuseppe Martucci conducts the first Italian performance of Wagner's *Tristan und Isolde* in Naples. In America a native variety of operetta is established with Gustave Kerker's *The Pearl of Pekin*. Richard Strauss completes the first version of his tone poem *Macbeth* (rev. 1889-90, 1891). César Franck completes his Symphony in D minor. Publication of Ferrucio Busoni's arrangement of J. S. Bach's Fugue in D major BWV532, the first of what were to be controversial editions and transcriptions of Bach.

1889   Boulanger's attempted *coup d'état* in France is supported by *ancien régime* followers, Catholics and working-class Idealists. Oriental music is heard by Debussy and others at the Paris Exposition Universelle. George Bernard Shaw becomes music critic of *The Star*. Henri Bergson publishes *Essai sur les données immédiates de la conscience*, subordinating the intellect to intuition, an idea welcomed by religious thinkers. Première of Massenet's *Esclarmonde* in Paris. Richard Strauss completes his tone poems *Don Juan* and *Tod und Verklärung*. First Russian performance of Wagner's *Ring* in St Petersburg. Richard Strauss is appointed Kapellmeister at Weimar. Lenepveu writes his *Hymne funèbre et triomphale*, commissioned to inaugurate a monument to Rouen's dead soldiers, and adopted by other towns for similar purposes. Dom André Mocquereau proposes a series of facsimiles of important sources of chant, the *Paléographie musicale*. The two-step is launched, using Sousa's new march, *The Washington Post*. Publication of Wolf's fifty-three Mörike settings and twenty Eichendorff settings. Brahms revises radically his Piano Trio No. 1.

1890   Bismarck is dismissed by Wilhelm II. Ibsen writes *Hedda Gabler*. Widor composes a 'mimed legend' *Jeanne d'Arc*. The Athenaeum School of Music (later the Royal Scottish Academy) is founded. Premières of Mascagni's *Cavalleria rusticana* in Rome, Ernest Reyer's *Salammbô* in Brussels, and Tchaikovsky's *Pikovaya dama* (The Queen of Spades) and ballet *Spyashchaya krasavitsa* (The Sleeping Beauty) in St Petersburg. Acts I and II of Berlioz's *Les troyens* are performed at Karlsruhe as *La prise de Troie*. Première of Borodin's *Knyaz' Igor'* (Prince Igor) in St Petersburg (composed 1869–70, 1874–87, and completed after the composer's death by Rimsky-Korsakov and Glazunov). Franck writes his *Trois chorales* for organ. Sam Jack produces The Creole Show, which includes black women performers and paves the way for the future development of the all-black musical. Busoni writes his *Konzertstück* for piano and orchestra. Publication of Wolf's fifty-one Goethe settings. Debussy composes *Cinq poèmes de Baudelaire*. First performance of Dvořák's Eighth Symphony (1889). Emma Calvé achieves success as Ophelia in Thomas's *Hamlet* at La Scala, Milan.

1891   Triple Alliance of Germany, Austria and Italy renewed for twelve years. Franco-Russian *entente* is established. Trans-Siberian Railway from Moscow to Vladivostok is begun (–1916). The Chicago Symphony Orchestra is founded. Opening of Carnegie Hall in New York. Mahler appointed conductor of the Hamburg Opera. Felipe Pedrell completes his Wagnerian trilogy *Los Pirineos*. Bruckner begins his Ninth Symphony (–1896). Max Bruch begins a twenty-year period of directing composition masterclasses at the Royal Academy of Arts in Berlin. Yvette Guilbert begins singing (and thus popularising) chansons from the Chat Noir cabaret at the Divan Japonais in Paris. Debussy composes *Trois mélodies de Verlaine*. Brahms writes his Clarinet Quintet, Op. 115. First performance of Dvořák's Requiem, at the Birmingham Festival.

1892   The Pan-Slav Conference takes place at Kraków. Founding of the Christiania (Oslo) Conservatory. John Philip Sousa forms his Sousa Band in the USA. F. F. Proctor opens his 23rd Street Theatre, the home of continuous vaudeville. The Internationale Ausstellung für Musik- und Theaterwesen takes place in Vienna, organised by Adler and others. The Slovensko Deželno Gledališče opens in Ljubljana to house the German and Slovene opera companies. Premières of Alberto Franchetti's *Cristoforo Colombo* in Genoa, Massenet's *Werther* in Paris, and Leoncavallo's *Pagliacci* and Catalani's *La Wally* in Milan. Tchaikovsky writes the ballet suite the *Shchelkunchik* (The Nutcracker). First performance of Nielsen's Symphony No. 1 in Copenhagen. Dvořák becomes director of the National Conservatory of Music in New York. Maeterlinck writes *Pelléas et Mélisande*. Sibelius composes *En saga*. Granados begins his *Danzas españolas*. Mahler conducts Wagner's *Ring* at Covent Garden. Charles Harris's hit song 'After the Ball' sells millions of copies in the USA. Publication of Mahler's first volume of *Lieder und Gesänge* (composed *c.* 1880–3).

1893   Opening of the Queen's Hall in London for orchestral concerts. Premières of Verdi's *Falstaff* in Milan and Puccini's *Manon Lescaut* in Turin. Dvořák writes his Ninth Symphony, 'From the New World'. Tchaikovsky dies shortly after completing his Symphony No. 6, the 'Pathétique'. Sibelius composes his *Karelia Suite*. Debussy begins work on *Pelléas et Mélisande* (–1895, orchestrated 1901–2). Richard Strauss conducts the première of Humperdinck's *Hänsel und Gretel* in Weimar. Marie Jaëll's complete Beethoven sonata cycle in six concerts takes place at the Salle Pleyel-Wolff in Paris. Debussy writes his String Quartet.

1894   The Jewish officer Alfred Dreyfus is tried for treason in France and sent to Devil's Island, causing a furore in French politics. Nicholas II succeeds Alexander III in Russia. Publication of Gabriele D'Annunzio's influential modernist novel *Il trionfo della morte*, and Max Nordau's *Dégénerescence*, which blames *fin-de-siècle* decadence on the fatigue of modern life. The Music School at Yale University is founded and Horatio Parker is appointed professor. The *Denkmäler der Tonkunst in Österreich* is founded by Guido Adler. Founding of the Cincinnati Symphony Orchestra by the Ladies' Musical Club, under Helen Herron Taft. Durand begins a complete edition of Rameau. Premières of Massenet's *Thaïs* and (posthumously) Franck's *Hulda* in Paris. Strauss conducts the première of his first opera *Guntram* at Weimar. Debussy completes *Prélude à l'après-midi d'un faune*. Fauré completes his song cycle *La bonne chanson*. Wilhelm Stenhammar composes the first of his six String Quartets. Enrico Caruso makes his debut in Morelli's *L'amico francesco* in Naples.

1895   Lenin organises the St Petersburg League of Struggle. Sigmund Freud publishes *Studien über Hysterie*, the starting-point of modern psycho-analysis. Auguste and Louis Lumière construct the first ciné-camera and projector. Edvard Munch paints *The Scream*, an evocation of emotion which he translates into a lithograph. Melbourne Conservatory founded. Henry Wood inaugurates the Promenade Concerts at the Royal Albert Hall in London. First performance of Mahler's Second Symphony, the 'Resurrection' (rev. 1903). Strauss writes *Till Eulenspiegel*. Percy Grainger enrols at the Hoch Conservatory in Frankfurt. Manns's concert to commemorate the 125th anniversary of Beethoven's birth takes place at Crystal Palace. George Whitefield Chadwick begins his orchestral suite *Symphonic Sketches* (–1904). A new building opens in Zagreb to house the Opera of the Croatian National Theatre.

1896   New evidence for Dreyfus's innocence is suppressed in France. Enrique Morera founds the Catalunya Nova Choir. The Schola Cantorum is founded in Paris by d'Indy and others. Publication of Paul Valéry's *La soirée avec Monsieur Teste*, the model for Debussy's music criticism in *Entretien avec Monsieur Croche* (1901). Edward MacDowell becomes first professor of music at Columbia University. Premières of Puccini's *La bohème* in Turin, Giordano's *Andrea Chenier* in Milan and Chausson's *Le roi Arthus* in Brussels. Albéniz writes his opera *Pepita Jiménez*. Chausson writes his *Poème* for violin and orchestra. Skryabin composes his Piano Concerto. First performances of Richard Strauss's '*Also sprach Zarathustra*' and Mahler's *Lieder eines fahrenden Gesellen*. Ben Harney is the first to make an impact playing ragtime piano in New York, and his 'You've Been a Good Old Wagon' is published. Mahler completes his Third Symphony (rev. 1906).

1897 Anglo-Russian agreement is established to maintain the status quo in the Balkans. Founding of the Vienna Radfahrcapelle, an orchestral society for popular concerts. The Concerts Lamoureux begin in Paris. Chadwick appointed director of the New England Conservatory of Music. Premières of Fibich's *Šárka* in Prague, Rimsky-Korsakov's *Sadko* in Moscow, Alfred Bruneau's *Messidor* in Paris, Francesco Cilea's *L'arlesiana* in Milan and d'Indy's *Fervaal* in Brussels. Sousa writes his march *The Stars and Stripes Forever*. The first publication of a ragtime piece, William Krell's *Mississippi Rag*. Publication of 'On the Banks of the Wabash' by the early Tin Pan Alley songwriter Paul Dresser. Performance of Rachmaninov's First Symphony. Delius settles at Grez-sur-Loing. Mahler becomes director of the Vienna Hofoper (following his baptism as a Catholic). Balakirev writes his First Symphony. Richard Strauss completes his 'fantastic variations' *Don Quixote*. Publication of Aristide Bruant's collection of cabaret acts *Chansons et monologues*.

1898 Emile Zola writes an open letter to the French president on the Dreyfuss affair. The USA declares war on Spain, and takes Cuba, the Philippines and Puerto Rico. Shaw publishes *The Perfect Wagnerite*. Guido Adler is appointed Hanslick's successor as professor of music at Vienna. Tolstoy writes *Chto takoye iskusstvo?* (What is Art?). The English Folk Song Society founded. Premières of Charpentier's *Louise* in Paris, Giordano's *Fedora* in Milan and Caballero's zarzuela *Gigantes y cabezudos* in Madrid. Charles Ives writes his First Symphony. Strauss arrives in Berlin. *Clorindy* (1898) by African-American composer Will Marion Cook is the first all-black musical, featuring the ragtime star Ernest Hogan. Richard Strauss completes his tone poem *Ein Heldenleben*. MacDowell writes his *Sea Pieces* for piano. Ethel Smyth's first opera *Fantasio* is performed in Weimar.

1899 Dreyfus is pardoned by presidential decree. Tsar Nicholas II suppresses liberties in Finland. The International Musical Society is founded. Sibelius writes his First Symphony. Schoenberg composes *Verklärte Nacht*. Ravel writes *Pavanne pour une infante défunte*. First performance of Elgar's *Enigma Variations*. First performance of Richard Strauss's *Ein Heldenleben* in Frankfurt. Debussy completes his *Nocturnes* for orchestra

('Nuages', 'Fêtes', 'Sirènes') and publishes *Chansons de Bilitis*, based on Pierre Louÿs's hoax prose poem (1894). Strauss completes *Drei Gesänge älterer deutscher Dichter*, Op. 43.

1900   Assassination of Humbert I of Italy; he is succeeded by his son Victor Emmanuel III. Freud publishes *Interpretation of Dreams*. Publication of the first edition of *Baker's Biographical Dictionary*. The opening of the Boston Symphony Hall. Premières of Puccini's *Tosca* in Rome, Dvořák's *Rusalka* in Prague, Eduard Caudella's *Petru Rareş* in Bucharest and Zemlinsky's *Es war einmal* in Vienna (conducted by Mahler). Elgar's *The Dream of Gerontius* is performed in Birmingham. Sibelius composes *Finlandia*. Mahler completes his Fourth Symphony (rev. 1901–10).

Institutions

SARAH HIBBERD

Accademia di Santa Cecilia, Rome   Founded in *c.* 1566 as the Congregazione dei Musici de Roma, it was renamed in *c.* 1839. It held meetings to discuss and perform music, and in 1877 became the main conservatory in Italy, the Conservatorio di Musica 'Santa Cecilia'.

Akademie der Künste, Berlin   The first chair of music was created in 1809, and Zelter was appointed to supervise the city's music education. A series of masterclasses in composition was established, in which composers such as Meyerbeer, Bruch and Busoni participated. In 1869 the Hochschule für Musik was founded as part of the Akademie, under the direction of Joachim; from 1872 staff and students gave public recitals and orchestral concerts.

Allgemeiner Deutscher Cäcilienverein, Bamberg   Founded in 1868 by Witt to promote the practical aspect of the reform of German Roman Catholic church music, it was accorded papal ratification in 1870, and became a model for similar organisations in other countries, including Belgium, Poland, Hungary and North America. The Caecilian movement as a whole promoted a historical understanding of the liturgy and focused on medieval chant tradition, thus reinforcing the demarcation between the church and contemporary developments in the arts.

Allgemeine musikalische Zeitung, Leipzig   Founded in 1798 by the publishers Breitkopf & Härtel, it was noted for its breadth of coverage and literary excellence. The division of its contents into essays, biographical information, reviews, descriptions of instruments, news items and miscellaneous became a model for future journals. Its large number of contributors included E. T. A. Hoffmann. Under its first editor, Friedrich Rochlitz (1798–1818), it became recognised internationally as the leading musical journal. However, publication stopped in 1848, largely because it was unable to compete with the *Neue Zeitschrift für Musik*.

Bach-Gesellschaft, Leipzig   Founded by Schumann and others on the centenary of Bach's death (1850), the society intended to publish a complete critical edition of his works, in partnership with Breitkopf & Härtel. The first volume (the first ten cantatas) appeared in 1851. The society enjoyed a reputation for scholarship, despite the variable quality of the editors and the inconsistent approach to sources. The forty-sixth volume was completed in 1900. The society was then dissolved, having completed its work, but it was immediately re-established as the Neue Bach-Gesellschaft, with the aim of popularising the music and promoting discussion.

Bayreuth Festspielhaus   Wagner laid the foundation stone for his theatre outside the town in 1872. Working with the architect Otto Brückwald, he realised his theatrical ideals in a building based on the Classical Greek amphitheatre. The auditorium is on a single raked level, converging on a wide stage. The orchestra is concealed beneath a hood which also serves to blend the orchestral sound with the voices before it is projected back into the auditorium. The *Ring* was performed there in its entirety for the first time in 1876 (three cycles). Six years passed before Wagner could afford another festival, devoted to *Parsifal*, his only work written expressly for the Festspielhaus. His widow Cosima, and then his son Siegfried, took control of the festival after Wagner's death.

Berliner allgemeine musikalische Zeitung   Founded in 1824 by A. B. Marx, Heinrich Dorn and Ludwig Rellstab, it took a leading role in the music journalism of Berlin for the six years of its existence. It was aimed at both 'cultivated music-lovers' and professional artists and connoisseurs. Beethoven and Spontini received particularly wide coverage.

Berlin Philharmonic Orchestra   The orchestra was formed in 1882 by members of Benjamin Bilse's Bilesche Kapelle (established in 1867). Promoted by Hermann Wolf and directed by Franz Wüllner, it was first conducted by Joachim (1884) and Bülow (1887); early guest conductors included Richard Strauss, Tchaikovsky and Grieg. Under Arthur Nikisch (1895) it made international tours and gained a worldwide reputation.

Besední Dům, Brno   The centre of Czech musical life in Brno, it housed the Beseda Brněnská (founded in 1860), whose chorus, with amateur and professional orchestras, performed the major choral works of the Czech and international repertories under such conductors as Janáček and Reissig. Visiting opera troupes also performed there; Jan Pištěk's company gave the Brno première of *Prodaná nevesta* (The Bartered Bride) in 1879.

Birmingham Festival   Established in 1768, it initially performed music chiefly by Handel. Concerts were held triennially from 1784 to 1829, and from 1834. A permanent oratorio chorus was maintained from 1811, supplemented by singers from other cathedral choirs. Its most important period began in 1834, as the grandest festival of its kind, in the new Birmingham Town Hall. Mendelssohn became involved from 1837, directing his own works, including the première of *Elijah* in 1846. Under the direction of Costa (1849–82) more local performers participated, and by 1876 the chorus needed no outside help. From 1873 at least two unfamiliar choral works were performed at each festival; these included Berlioz's *Grande messe des morts* (1888) and Elgar's *The Dream of Gerontius* (1900). Richter took over the direction in 1885.

Boehm, Munich   Theobald Boehm set up a flute factory in 1828. Early in 1832 the first real Boehm flute was made. This 'cone Boehm' had a large tapered bore and was built on a system of 'open holes', controlled by interlinked keys with ring touchpieces. It gradually gained recognition, and was produced in Paris and London (and the same system was adopted by Ward of London and Buffet of Paris). In 1847 Boehm produced an improved design which has remained almost unchanged.

Boosey & Co., London   Established in London in 1816 by Thomas Boosey as foreign music importers, the firm quickly became the English publisher of Hummel, Mercadante and Rossini, and later of Bellini, Donizetti and Verdi. From *c.* 1850 they also manufactured wind instruments and from 1868 brass. During the late nineteenth century their publishing centred on popular and educational music.

Bösendorfer, Vienna   Established in 1828 by Ignaz Bösendorfer, the firm of piano manufactuers received Liszt's approval which brought it international renown. In 1859 Ignaz's son Ludwig took over, and the following year the firm moved to a new factory and patented an improved action. In 1872 Bülow inaugurated the Bösendorfer-Saal, the most popular concert hall in Vienna. It was not until the end of the century that the lighter English action replaced the Viennese.

Boston Symphony Orchestra   The orchestra was founded in 1881 by the banker Henry Lee Higginson who endowed the orchestra to enable it to charge low prices. Like its first conductor, George Henschel (–1884), the majority of the orchestra and many of the successive conductors were of German nationality. The new Symphony Hall, replacing the Music Hall, was opened in 1900.

Breitkopf & Härtel, Leipzig   Established in 1719 by B. C. Breitkopf, the firm was bought in 1796 by G. C. Härtel. His achievements included adopting Alois Senefelder's new lithography process for the printing of music, negotiating with Haydn, Beethoven and Mozart's widow to publish the composers' works, and founding the *Allgemeine musikalische Zeitung*. In 1807 the firm also started manufacturing pianos. Following Härtel's death in 1827, the firm was expanded under the directorship of his sons. The music of a great number of composers was issued, including that of Schubert, Brahms, Chopin, Berlioz, Meyerbeer, Bellini and Lortzing, and a series of complete editions of (mainly) German composers, beginning with Bach, was published. The firm's book division produced many important musicological works.

Broadwood, London   John Broadwood took over the business after the death of his partner, the harpsichord maker Burkat Shudi, in 1773. He made improvements to the design of Zumpe's square piano, upon which the early Broadwood was modelled, then turned to designing grands, increasing dynamic flexibility and volume. From the 1790s until well into the nineteenth century the Broadwood was used by leading musicians. Iron bracing was introduced on the grand in the 1820s to improve tuning stability and to increase tension and power. At its peak in the 1850s, the company was, however, reluctant to embrace new technology, and it fell into decline towards the end of the century.

Carl Rosa Opera Company, Dublin and London   Founded by Karl August
                                    Nicolaus Rose to perform operas in English, it
                                    opened in Dublin and then London in 1875. First
                                    performances in English in the 1890s included
                                    works by Berlioz, Gounod, Verdi and Wagner, and
                                    new British operas were commissioned. Seasons
                                    were given at the King's Theatre (1879–82) and
                                    Drury Lane (1883–90). After Rosa's death in 1889
                                    touring companies were set up and the English
                                    premières of *Hänsel und Gretel* (1894) and *La
                                    bohème* (1897) took place.

Chappell, London   Established in 1810 by J. B. Cramer, Francis
                                    Latour and Samuel Chappell as a firm of music
                                    publishers and concert agents, it also played an
                                    important role in the creation of the Philharmonic
                                    Society (1813). Following Chappell's death in 1834
                                    the firm was taken over by his widow and their
                                    sons; William was noted for his interest in early
                                    music. In the 1840s piano manufacture began, and
                                    the firm's activities expanded greatly in the fields
                                    of popular music and light opera. Under Thomas
                                    Chappell the Monday and Saturday Popular
                                    Concerts were established at St James's Hall in
                                    1858. The firm began an association with Gilbert
                                    and Sullivan in the 1870s.

Classical Chamber Concerts, London   Sterndale Bennett gave this annual
                                    concert series between 1842 and 1856, first at his
                                    own home and then in the Hanover Square
                                    Rooms. The concerts explored the repertory of
                                    chamber music with piano and 'serious' piano
                                    music.

Concert of Ancient Music, London   Founded in 1776 by the Earl of
                                    Sandwich and others, the society gave concerts of
                                    music that was more than twenty years old.
                                    Handel was frequently performed, and Classical
                                    works were gradually included in the repertory
                                    after 1826. However, in the years before its closure

in 1848 it was criticised for not performing still
newer works as they became eligible.

Concerts Musard, Paris   Philippe Musard established the series in 1833 to
give informal promenade concerts, with the
audience moving around freely, eating, drinking
and dancing. The programmes were a mixture of
light classics, from Mozart and Beethoven to
quadrilles, galops and waltzes. The enterprise grew
and was imitated by Louis Jullien, Henri
Valentino, Jules Rivière and others.

Concerts Nationals, Paris Founded in 1873 by Edouard Colonne and the
publisher Hartmann at the Théâtre de l'Odéon, the
concerts (later known as the Concerts Colonne)
benefited from the nationalism that followed the
Franco-Prussian War. Owing to financial
difficulties the following year, however, the two
men dissolved the partnership, and Colonne
formed a new society, the Association Artistique
des Concerts du Châtelet, which rivalled
Pasdeloup's Concerts Populaires. Many first
performances of French works were given, as well
as foreign pieces.

Conservatoire de Paris   Founded in 1795, it grew out of Bernard Sarrette's
Ecole de la Musique de la Garde Nationale which
had been established two years earlier to provide
music for public occasions. Prominent musicians,
including Cherubini, Gossec and Méhul, were
engaged, new textbooks and manuals dealing with
all aspects of the practice of music were
commissioned, and free student tuition was
offered. It was renowned for its high standards,
partly resulting from thorough examinations, and
became the model for conservatories in other
countries.

Copenhagen Musikforening   Founded in 1836, it was the focus of the city's
music until 1931. From 1849 to 1890 it flourished

under the (rather tyrannical) direction of Niels
Gade. A permanent orchestra and choir were
established which gave the first Danish
performance of Bach's *St Matthew Passion* and
Beethoven's Ninth Symphony, as well as the first
performances of Gade's own major works.

Covent Garden Theatre, London   The second Covent Garden theatre
opened in 1809. It had a mixed repertory with a
bias to English-language performance. Henry
Bishop was its musical director in 1811–24, and he
composed and arranged a vast amount of music,
from operas to dramas with interpolated songs.
Under the direction of Alfred Bunn a number of
important productions of German operas were
given in their original language in the 1830s, and
then in 1847 the theatre claimed the title of the
Royal Italian Opera, in rivalry with Her Majesty's.
Frederick Gye took over the management in 1851,
and oversaw the first London performances of
many French grand operas and works by Verdi,
including *Rigoletto* and *Il trovatore*. In 1856 the
theatre burnt down and a new theatre was opened
two years later. Gye's management continued until
1877, during which time the theatre was also the
home of the Royal English Opera (1858–64).
Under Augustus Harris (1887–96) the company
was noted for its superlative performances which
included the debut of Melba and (in 1892) the first
Covent Garden *Ring*, conducted by Mahler.

Croatian National Theatre (Hrvatsko Narodno Kazalište), Zagreb
Established in Zagreb in 1860, it concentrated
initially on spoken drama and, from 1863, operetta;
a permanent opera company was formed in 1870.
Its first director and conductor was Ivan Zajc, also
head of the music school at the Institute of Music
(Glazbeni Zavod). The repertory included
important international works, particularly Italian
operas, often performed soon after their world

premières. The company moved in 1895 to the new
building of the National Theatre.

Crystal Palace, London

The London exhibition hall built in Hyde Park in
1851 was moved to Sydenham the following year,
where it was used for concerts. George Grove did
much to encourage the use of the venue for the
popularisation of music, and its enormous capacity
meant that low admission prices could be charged.
In 1855 August Manns became conductor and
introduced more ambitious programmes; the
orchestra of the Saturday Concerts (1855–1901)
was the first permanent London orchestra. While
Grove promoted the works of Schubert, Manns
favoured Schumann, and the music of Raff,
Brahms, Liszt and Smetana was also performed,
often for the first time in London. Manns also
championed contemporary British music by Parry,
Stanford, Sullivan and others. Crystal Palace
hosted the triennial Handel festivals from 1857.

Deutsches Haus, Brno

German musical life in Brno centred on this hall,
which housed the Brünner Musikverein (founded
in 1862) and the Brünner Schubertbund (founded
in 1879).

Diabelli, Vienna

Established in 1818 by Anton Diabelli with Pietro
Cappi, the firm was continued (following Diabelli's
retirement in 1851), by C. A. Spina, and in 1872 by F.
Schreiber before it merged in 1879 with August
Cranz. It acquired the publications of various extinct
firms, including Weigl, Artaria and Leidesdorf, and
published fashionable opera and dance music as well
more 'serious' works. Schubert in particular was
championed by Diabelli. In 1874 a new catalogue of
works was published, together with a thematic
catalogue of Schubert compiled by Nottebohm.

Dresden Philharmonic Orchestra   Founded *c.* 1870, its early guest
conductors and soloists included Brahms, Dvořák,

Richard Strauss and Tchaikovsky. It gave concerts in the new Gewerbehaussaal, and was the mainstay of musical life in Dresden.

Dresden Hoftheater From 1817 the newly founded German opera at the Hoftheater was conducted by Weber; the repertory consisted mainly of French opéras comiques, but increasingly included German works by Mozart, Beethoven and Weber himself. Marschner and then Reissiger succeeded him as music director, and Wagner conducted premières of *Der fliegende Holländer* (1843) and *Tannhäuser* (1845) as well as performances of Beethoven's symphonies in his short period as conductor. The old court theatre building was replaced in 1841 by the new Königlich Sächsisches Hoftheater. In 1858 regular subscription concerts were introduced by Reissiger. One of the theatre's greatest periods was under Ernst von Schuch (1882–), who gave many new pieces and championed Wagner's later works.

Drury Lane Theatre, London The fourth building of the Theatre Royal opened in 1812. Under Alfred Bunn's direction (from 1831) many new English operas were given, as well as British premières of German and Russian operas. In the mid-1850s, under the management of E. T. Smith, seasons of English and Italian opera were given. When Her Majesty's burnt down in 1867, Mapleson took over Drury Lane and until 1877 it was the home of Her Majesty's Opera. The first performance in England of a Wagner opera took place in 1870 (*Der fliegende Holländer*), and in 1882 a German opera season was given by Hans Richter. From 1883 to 1888 seasons by the Carl Rosa Company took place, and in 1887 a popular Italian season.

Durand, Paris Founded in 1869 by M. A. Durand in partnership with Schoenewerk, the firm was reorganised in

1891 as A. Durand & fils. In 1869 it bought the
Flaxland catalogue of *c.* 1,200 publications (which
included the works of pre-nineteenth-century
composers of various nationalities, piano
reductions of Beethoven's symphonies and many
of Chopin's piano works). To this it added the
collected works of Rameau (1894–, ed. Saint-
Saëns) and others. It also promoted the works of
contemporary French composers including Saint-
Saëns and Debussy.

Empresa de Opera Lírica Nacional, Rio de Janeiro   Established in 1857 by
Emperor Pedro II as the Imperial Academia de
Música e Opera Nacional, it changed its name in
1860 under the direction of the Spanish impresario
José Amat. It sponsored Brazilian opera singers and
the first operas by Brazilians sung in Portuguese,
including two works by Carlos Gomes, *A noite do
castelo* (1861) and *Joana de Flandres* (1863).

Erard, Paris   Founded around 1780 in Paris, the firm of piano
and harp manufacturers opened a London shop in
1792. Major improvements were made to the
instruments, including the double escapement
piano action (1821) and the harp's (now standard)
fork mechanism (1810), which allowed the
construction of a harp that could be played in any
key. Under Pierre Erard the company consolidated
its international reputation, and its pianos were
played by many leading virtuosos. In 1855 the firm
was awarded a gold medal at the Paris Exposition.

Estates Theatre (Stavovské Divadlo), Prague   Founded in 1798 by the
Bohemian Estates (in the Nostitzsches
Nationaltheater), it was a centre for German opera.
Weber was a conductor there from 1813 to 1816 and
presented such works as Beethoven's *Fidelio* (1814),
the première of Spohr's *Faust* (1816) and a number
of French operas. Under Škroup (1827–57) the
repertory included Meyerbeer, Verdi and Wagner.

The Euterpeiad, Boston   America's first true music journal, it was issued by
John Rowe Parker between 1820 and 1823. It
presented news and reviews of Boston musical life
in addition to a serial survey of music history. A
later journal of the same title, published in New
York (1830–31), contained essays on musical style,
biographical sketches and anecdotes as well as
reviews of printed music and concerts.

Frankfurt Hoch Konservatorium   Founded in 1878, it was endowed by the
merchant J. Hoch, who bequeathed his complete
estate to establish it. Directors included Raff
(–1882) and Bernhard Scholz (1883–1908), and
Clara Schumann and Humperdinck were among
its staff. It had an international reputation, and its
students included Percy Grainger and Hans
Pfitzner.

Gazzetta musicale di Milano The first significant general music journal to be
published in Italy (1842–1912), by Ricordi, it gave
special attention to Italian opera and provided
biographical, historical and bibliographical articles
as well as reports on Italian and other musical
centres.

Gesellschaft der Musikfreunde, Vienna   Founded in 1812 to promote music,
the society was also known by the name of its
home from 1870, the Musikverein. Its
conservatory, the Hochschule für Musik und
Darstellende Kunst, founded in 1817, became the
city's principal music school. Its teachers included
Bruckner, and its pupils Mahler and Wolf. Its
Singverein (founded in 1858) gave the premières of
works such as Brahms's *German Requiem* and
Bruckner's *Te Deum* as well as revivals of Bach's
works. Its conductors have included Brahms,
Richter and Furtwängler. The Wiener Concert-
Vereinorchester (later the Wiener Symphoniker)
was established under its auspices in 1900.

Gewandhaus Orchestra, Leipzig   Formed in 1781, it was named after the hall
in Leipzig which opened that year. It had close
connections with church and theatre music.
Mendelssohn was its conductor in 1835–47 and
gave the premières of symphonies by Schumann
and Schubert and his own works, as well as series
of 'historical concerts'. He broadened the
orchestra's repertory, increased players' salaries
and raised performance standards; his deputies
were Niels Gade and Ferdinand Hiller. In the
second half of the century, after Mendelssohn's
death, the programmes tended to be less eclectic.
Carl Reinecke (director 1860–95) avoided newer
music, although Brahms played his First Piano
Concerto with the orchestra in 1859. Guest
conductors included Wagner, Richard Strauss,
Grieg and Tchaikovsky. The orchestra moved to a
new building in 1884.

Hallé Orchestra, Manchester   Charles Hallé established the Hallé Concerts
in the new Free Trade Hall in 1858; he conducted
them (often appearing as piano soloist) for the rest
of his life. A large number of cheap seats were
provided and the programmes were adventurous,
including much contemporary music. Leading
performers of the day were engaged.

Handel and Haydn Society, Boston   America's earliest oratorio society was
founded by Gottlieb Graupner and others in 1815
to cultivate and improve the performance of sacred
music. C. E. Horn was the first conductor.

Händel-Gesellschaft, Leipzig   The society was founded in 1856 by Friedrich
Chrysander and Gottfried Gervinus to publish a
critical edition of Handel's works. Chrysander was
the editor, and following the society's collapse in
1860 he took over the production of the editions
himself, setting up a small printing shop in his
garden. To help fund the project he took on other
editorial work and sold part of his library, but

continuing financial problems meant that he was
unable to complete the edition.

Helsinki Concert Orchestra   Following the success of short-lived orchestras
from 1834, the Theatre Orchestra (1860) and the
new Finnish Theatre Orchestra merged in 1877 as
the Helsinki Concert Orchestra (later reorganised
as the Helsinki City Orchestra). The survival of the
orchestra was due largely to the efforts of Robert
Kajanus, who founded the Helsinki Orchestral
Society in 1882 and an orchestral school three
years later. He championed Finnish music, and
that of Sibelius in particular.

Her Majesty's Theatre, London   The King's Theatre was renamed following
the accession of Queen Victoria in 1837, and
became the main venue for Italian opera in London
in the nineteenth century under John Ebers,
Benjamin Lumley and James Mapleson. It gave
London premières of the operas of Rossini, Bellini,
Donizetti, Verdi, Meyerbeer and Spontini. When
the theatre burnt down in 1867 the company
moved to Drury Lane while the new building was
being constructed. At the end of the century it
hosted some visiting companies, and in 1882 gave
the London première of the *Ring*.

Hofoper, Vienna   The Kärntnertortheater, which housed the court
opera, was leased by the Habsburgs to (usually
Italian) impresarios who favoured Italian
repertory. Following the success of *Fidelio* in 1814,
German operas were occasionally given, including
Weber's *Der Freischütz* in 1821; following its
success the impresario Barbaia commissioned
Euryanthe (1823). In 1854 Karl Eckert was
appointed as the first permanent conductor; he
introduced Wagner's operas to the theatre,
although Italian repertory continued to be
favoured until the end of the century. In 1870 the
Kärntnertortheater was demolished to make way

for the new Ringstrasse. The new opera house, the Kaiserlich-Königliches Hofoperntheater, was inaugurated with a performance of *Don Giovanni* in 1869. Under a series of directors, including Franz Jauner (1875–80) and Wilhelm Jaun (1881–97), productions of Wagner's operas were mounted, as well as a successful performance of *Carmen* in 1875, shortly after its failure in Paris, and the première of Massenet's *Werther* (1892).

La Iberia musical y literaria, Madrid   Founded by M. Soriano Fuertes and edited by J. Espín y Guillén, it was the first significant music journal in Spain. Published between 1842 and 1845, it contained articles on various topics including instrumentation, performers and foreign as well as Spanish music. Its mainly shortlived successors included *La España musical* (published in Barcelona, 1866–74), which notably contained articles on Wagner's operas and Liszt's symphonic poems.

Italian Opera House, New York   Following the success of performances of French and Italian opera by visiting troupes, the city's first Italian Opera House opened in 1833, with the American première of Rossini's *La gazza ladra*. Its backers included Dominick Lynch and Da Ponte. But it had little success, and the house burnt down six years later. Two other short-lived Italian opera companies had some success: Ferdinand Palmo's company (1844–8) and the Astor Place Opera House (1847–52).

Kölner Konservatorium   Established in 1845 as the Rheinische Musikschule by Heinrich Dorn, in 1850 it was expanded to become the conservatory under Ferdinand Hiller (1850–84). He remodelled it on the model of Leipzig, increasing the number of students and attracting excellent teachers, such as Carl Reineke. Franz Wüllner was director for the rest of the century.

Königliche Schauspiele, Berlin   The royal opera and the Nationaltheater merged as the Schauspiele in 1807, but maintained the distinction between their repertories: French and Italian at the former, German at the latter. Premières included Hoffmann's *Undine* (1816), Weber's *Der Freischütz* (1821) and Marschner's *Hans Heiling* (1833), and the works of Méhul, Gluck, Rossini and others were also performed. Music directors included Spontini, Meyerbeer and Botho von Hülson, who gave the Berlin permières of *Tannhäuser* (1856) and *Tristan und Isolde* (1876) and added Offenbach's works to the repertory.

La Fenice, Venice   Opened in 1792 (rebuilt in 1837 following destruction by fire), it became the principal opera house in the city and, until the unification, one of the most important in the peninsula. It gave many important premières (some of them arranged by the impresario Alessandro Lanari), and commissioned and premièred five Verdi operas. Later in the century the national importance of the theatre declined owing to economic troubles and political events and it became essentially a provincial theatre.

La Scala, Milan   Established in 1778, it was the main centre for Italian opera and a leading international opera house, attracting the finest singers. Alessandro Sanquirico's sets (1817–32) had a long-lasting influence on stage design. Verdi was closely associated with the theatre, and the first four and last two of his operas had their premières there. In addition to performances of Italian operas, Wagner's works were eagerly received there under the direction of Franco Faccio.

Leeds Music Festival   The biennial event was established in 1858. Large choral works were commissioned from 1880, when it became a triennial event with Sullivan as conductor. It gained an international reputation through the quality of its chorus and the works presented, which included Dvořák's *St Ludmilla* (1886) and Elgar's *Caractacus* (1898).

Leipzig Conservatory
Established by Mendelssohn in 1843, it engaged prominent teachers including Moscheles, Schumann and Gade as well as members of the Gewandhaus Orchestra. In 1876 it was nominated a royal institution, and in 1887 it moved from its home in the Gewandhaus to more spacious premises. It attracted students from all over the world, particularly from Britain, Scandinavia and the USA.

Liedertafel, Berlin
Established by Zelter in 1809, it was the first male choral society of its kind, and became a model for similar groups throughout Germany. In reaction to the exclusiveness of the society Ludwig Berger and Bernhard Klein formed a new *Liedertafel* in 1819, which included E. T. A. Hoffmann among its members. The tradition of popular choral music in the city was continued with the Berliner Liedertafel (1884) and the Berliner Lehrergesangverein (1886).

Liverpool Philharmonic Orchestra
It was founded in 1840 as the mainly amateur orchestra of the Liverpool Philharmonic Society. It benefited from the presence of musicians in Manchester (playing in the Hallé) and there was friendly rivalry between the two orchestras. Conductors included Alfred Mellon (1865), Max Bruch (1880) and Charles Hallé (1883)

Mariinsky Theatre, St Petersburg
It opened in 1860 and gave the first performances of a series of operas by Russian composers, including Musorgsky's *Boris Godunov* (1874), Rimsky-Korsakov's *Pskovityanka* (The Maid of Pskov) (1873) and Tchaikovsky's *Pikovaya dama* (The Queen of Spades) (1890). Owing to the success of the theatre, the Italian opera company

which had been active in St Petersburg for a
century was disbanded in the early 1880s. The
theatre's fame was further increased by its
excellent ballet company.

Le Ménestrel, Paris   Established in 1833 by the publisher Heugel as a
house journal, it dealt with historical matters as
well as with contemporary musical events, and
provided musical samples for its readers from
1836. It also published for the first time important
works such as Lussy's *Traité de l'expression musicale*.

Metropolitan Opera House, New York   Founded by a number of
millionaires who could not obtain boxes at the
Academy of Music, it opened in 1883 with a
performance of Gounod's *Faust*. In its second
season Leopold Damrosch introduced German
opera into the repertory, and in the seven years
following his death (1885) all Wagner's mature
works, except *Parsifal*, were performed there. In
addition to German repertory, French and Italian
operas were given in German. However, in 1891
the emphasis shifted to French and Italian
works.

Milan Conservatory   Founded in 1807, and partly modelled on the Paris
Conservatoire, it was the most important
conservatory in Italy. Early students were trained
mainly for La Scala. Directors included Francesco
Basili (1827–37), Nicola Vaccai (1837–44) and
Antonio Bazzini (1882–97), and Puccini and
Catalani numbered among its students. In 1901 it
was renamed, after Verdi.

Musical Association, London   Founded in 1874 by John Stainer and others,
it was intended to promote 'the investigation and
discussion of subjects connected with the art,
science and history of music'. In the early years
there was a focus on acoustical and theoretical
aspects of music, although by the 1890s there was

more interest in history and criticism. From 1886 distinguished foreign scholars were invited to become honorary members.

Musical Fund Society, Philadelphia   Founded in 1820, it was probably the oldest charitable musical society in the USA, presenting free concerts, awarding scholarships and sponsoring competitions.

Musical Times, London   Founded in 1844 by J. A. Novello as a continuation of *Mainzer's Musical Times and Singing Circular* (1842–4), it was initially intended to encourage the resurgence in singing being promoted by Mainzer and others. However, it soon developed into a journal covering all aspects of music and musical life.

Musical World, London   First published by Novello and edited by C. Clarke (1836–91), it was England's first comprehensive music journal, partly modelled on its French and German predecessors. It reported on events in Europe and provided historical articles and reviews of concerts and new publications.

National Theatre (Národní Divadlo), Prague   Established in 1881, it grew out of the Provisional Theatre and opened with the première of Smetana's *Libuše*. It was destroyed by fire shortly afterwards, but was rebuilt in 1883. The premières of a number of important Czech works were given, including Dvořák's *Rusalka* in 1901, and the works of Verdi, Wagner and Mozart were frequently performed. Czech opera was also staged at the summer theatres, including the New Town Theatre (Novoměstské Divadlo) and the wooden New Czech Theatre (Nové České Divadlo).

Neue Zeitschrift für Musik, Leipzig   Founded by Schumann (with Friedrich Wieck, Ludwig Schunke and Julius Knorr) in 1834, it was organised along the same lines as the *Allgemeine musikalische Zeitung*. However, its remit was rather different: Schumann's aim was to use the journal as an intellectual forum for the creative artist, to promote the Romantic movement in music. His successor as editor, Franz Brendel (1845–68), used it increasingly to support the New German School, and in 1887 it became the organ of the Allgemeiner Musikverein.

New England Conservatory, Boston Established in 1867 by Eben Tourjée, within ten years it had become the country's largest music school, training more than 14,000 students to meet the growing demand for teachers, organists, soloists and choir directors. Women in particular responded to these opportunities.

New German School This group of musicians associated with Liszt in the mid-1800s included Brendel, Cornelius, von Bülow and Raff. They championed such 'progressive' composers as Berlioz and Wagner both for their advanced harmonic language, and for their interest in music's potential to express literary or pictorial ideas.

New Philharmonic Society, London The society was founded in 1852 to give improved performances of 'great' composers and to introduce contemporary and British music to the public. The founders, under Henry Wylde, aimed to provide an alternative to the (Royal) Philharmonic Society concerts. During the first season Berlioz conducted a performance of part of *Roméo et Juliette* and of Beethoven's Ninth Symphony. In 1856 the concerts moved from Exeter Hall to the smaller Hanover Square Rooms, which resulted in higher seat prices and a more exclusive audience. The Society's activities ceased in 1879, although concerts were continued for three more years by William Ganz.

New York Academy of Music The academy opened in 1854 with a performance of Bellini's *Norma* with Giulia Grisi in

the title role. After the closure of the Astor Place
Opera House in 1852, it was the only theatre in the
city devoted specifically to presenting concerts and
operas; regular opera seasons were given until
1886. It had the largest stage in the world at the
time, and seated 4,600. Max Maretzek was a
frequent lessee and conductor, producing *Rigoletto*
(1855), Meyerbeer's *L'Africaine* (1865) and
Gounod's *Roméo et Juliette* (1867); Mapleson
directed productions in 1878–86.

New York Symphony Orchestra   The orchestra was founded in 1878 by
Leopold Damrosch. Although its concerts were not
as well received critically as those of the
Philharmonic Society, Damrosch's programmes
were often more adventurous, introducing works
by Debussy and Berlioz alongside the more usual
German fare. The orchestra was successful at
raising support from society figures, and performed
at the opening of the Carnegie Hall in 1891.

Le Nouvelliste, St Petersburg   Founded in 1840, from 1844 to 1874 it had a
literary supplement, *Literaturnoye pribavleniye k
'Nuvellistu'*, which was the first attempt at a true
music journal in Russia. It contained mainly
biographical sketches of composers including
Schubert, Chopin, Mendelssohn and Cherubini,
and studies of European and other music.

Opéra, Paris   The principal opera company in Paris, it was
established officially as the Académie de Musique
in 1669 (its name changed frequently over the
centuries, owing to political events). During the
nineteenth century its main homes were the Salle
Le Peletier (1821–73) and the Palais Garnier
(1875–). It gave performances of operas and ballets
and held benefit performances and balls. The late
1820s and early 1830s saw the emergence of
Romantic grand opera, a genre which was typified
above all by the works of Meyerbeer. Louis Véron

(1831–5), the first director to run the theatre as a commercial enterprise (although he retained government support), was responsible for promoting these grand stagings. His successors included Nestor Rocqueplan, Alphonse Royer and Hyacinthe Halanzier. Meyerbeer's works remained an important part of the repertory even after his death, although smaller-scale, literary-inspired works, such as Thomas's *Hamlet* (1868), became increasingly popular.

Opéra-Comique, Paris   Created in 1801 by the merging of the Favart and Feydeau companies, its main homes during the nineteenth century were the Salle Feydeau (1805–29) and the Salle Favart (1840–87, 1898–). It performed opera with spoken dialogue, although by the 1870s occasional works with recitative were given. In the first half of the century a light, often witty tone was established with the works of Boieldieu, Hérold and others; after 1848 more frivolous and sentimental works became popular (notably the works of Adam), alongside the more serious operas of Thomas, Auber and Halévy promoted by the impresario Emil Perrin.

Orphéon, Paris   Established by G. L. B. Wilhem in 1833, it gave its first concert in 1836 with a choir of 300. It grew steadily, and in 1860 it was divided into Right and Left Bank sections. Its conductors included Gounod (1852), Pasdeloup and Bazin (both 1860). By the turn of the century there were more than 2,000 Orphéon societies in France.

Paléographie Musicale, Solesmes   The series was begun in 1889 by Dom André Mocquereau in support of the theories of his teacher Dom Joseph Pothier, who advocated a version of the chant based on the studies of early sources. The purpose of the Paléographie Musicale was to publish a number of important original sources in facsimile, each with an introduction to

the history of the source and a discussion of its
notation.

People's Concert Society, London   Founded by amateurs in 1878 to
popularise 'serious' music in poorer areas of
London, its programmes of orchestral and
chamber music were closely modelled on the
educative and eclectic programmes of the Popular
Concerts at St James's Hall.

Philharmonic Society, London   Founded in 1813 by a group of professional
musicians (including Cramer, Corri and Dance),
the society gave seasons of orchestral concerts
which consisted mainly of music new to London.
It was dependent on aristocratic patronage, and
initially vocal and instrumental solos were
forbidden (until 1816 and 1820 respectively).
During visits to London, Spohr, Mendelssohn and
Moscheles led the orchestra, and a conductor
(Henry Bishop) was appointed for the first time in
1845. Owing to ill-health Bishop resigned the
following year, and was succeeded by Michael
Costa (1846–54). Wagner conducted for one
season before being replaced by Sterndale Bennett,
who engaged spectacular soloists while
maintaining a conservative repertory. Later
conductors included W. G. Cusins, George Mount
and Sullivan.

Philharmonic Symphony Society of New York   The society was founded in
1842, and in its second season gave the American
première of Beethoven's Third Symphony. Initially
members of the orchestra took a turn at
conducting, then one or two conductors assumed
responsibility, notably Theodore Eisfeld,
Theodore Thomas and Anton Seidl. The repertory
reflected the European training of its conductors,
and the emphasis was on the German school.
Thomas in particular championed the works of
Liszt, Wagner, Brahms and Strauss.

Pleyel, Paris	A music shop and publishing firm were established by Ignace Joseph Pleyel in Paris in 1795. During the thirty-nine years of its existence, the firm issued works by Boccherini, Beethoven, Clementi, Haydn and other friends of Pleyel and his son. In 1802 the first miniature scores were issued in a series entitled Bibliothèque Musicale (beginning with symphonies by Haydn). Pleyel employed agents to sell his publications all over France and was in contact with some of the foremost European publishers. In 1807 a piano factory was founded. The firm quickly adopted and improved the best features of the English piano. Ignace's son Camille joined the firm in 1815, and pianists including Friedrich Kalkbrenner, Chopin, Moscheles and Steibelt became closely associated with the company. The firm's success grew through the century; Camille was succeeded by his son-in-law August Wolff, and then by Gustave Lyon.
La Revue musicale, Paris	Founded in 1827 by François-Joseph Fétis, it was the first significant French music journal of the nineteenth century. It amalgamated with Schlesinger's *Gazette musicale de Paris* (1834) in 1835 to form the influential *Revue et Gazette musicale de Paris*, and continued publication until 1880. Its many contributors included Berlioz, Liszt, Joseph d'Ortigue and Wagner.
Ricordi, Milan	Founded in 1808 by Giovanni Ricordi, the firm became publisher to the Milan Conservatory three years later, and won exclusive contracts with La Scala and other theatres in Milan, Venice and Naples. Its catalogue included opera arrangements, method books and guitar pieces and, from the 1830s, vocal scores and performing material (for hire) by the foremost Italian composers. The firm published all but three of Verdi's operas. Giovanni's son Tito, and then his

grandson Giulio (who dealt with Verdi and Puccini), directed the firm through its expansion.

Royal Academy of Music, London   The academy was founded in 1822, with William Crotch as its first principal. It was the first professional music school in England, but was in constant financial straits for its first forty years, and forced to charge high fees to its students.

Royal College of Music, London   It was founded in 1883 and George Grove became its first director, succeeded by Parry. It soon outgrew its original premises, the former National Training School for Music, and in 1894 moved to new buildings in Prince Consort Road.

Royal Hungarian Opera House (Magyar Királyi Operaház) Budapest   The theatre opened in 1884 with its own opera company, formed from the combined forces of the Kassa and Kolozsvár companies which had been performing Hungarian opera (as well as French and Italian repertory) since 1837 at the National Theatre. Its first director, Ferenc Erkel, was succeeded by Hans Richter and Sándor Erkel.

Royal Italian Opera, London   The London theatres and companies that presented seasons of opera in Italian (including translations of French operas) were given this collective title in the nineteenth century. They included Covent Garden, Drury Lane, Her Majesty's Theatre and the Lyceum.

Russian Musical Society, St Petersburg   Founded in 1859 in St Petersburg by Anton Rubinstein, it soon had many branches; Nikolay Rubinstein was its director in Moscow (from 1860). Concert series were arranged, at which new Russian works were given, and in 1860 music classes were instituted. The following year the conservatory was established, with Rubinstein as its director; Tchaikovsky was among the first graduates.

Sacred Harmonic Society, London   Founded in 1832 as an amateur choral
society, it gave the first London performance of
Mendelssohn's *St Paul* (1837), and in 1847 it
performed Handel's *Belshazzar's Feast* and the
revised version of Mendelssohn's *Elijah*, under the
composer's baton. It prospered from 1848 under
Costa's directorship, and finally disbanded in 1888.
Its large collection of music and musical literature
was acquired for the Royal College of Music.

Sacred Music Society, New York   Founded in 1823, it was the first official
choral society in America. It gave a performance of
Messiah (with Mozart's accompaniments) in 1831,
attracting large audiences, and in 1849 it merged
with the Musical Institute to form the New York
Harmonic Society. Their first joint concert was of
Mendelssohn's *Elijah* (1851) in Tripler Hall (with a
capacity of 5,000). The society survived until 1868,
and its conductors included H. C. Timm,
Theodore Eisfeld and James Peck.

St Petersburg Philharmonic Society (Sankt-Peterburgskoye
Filarmonischeskoye Obshchestvo)   Founded in
1802, it survived 100 years, giving more than 200
concerts. It specialised in major choral works by
Handel, Haydn and Cherubini, and arranged for
the première of Beethoven's *Missa solemnis* to take
place in St Petersburg in 1824.

San Carlo, Naples   Built in 1737, it rapidly became the principal
theatre in Naples for opera seria. The new theatre
opened in 1816, under the management of
Domenico Barbaia, who put on several important
Rossini operas (*Mosè*, *Otello*, *La donna del lago*), and
the premières of Donizetti's *Lucia di Lammermoor*
and Verdi's *Attila*.

Schlesinger, Berlin   The firm was established in 1810 by A. M.
Schlesinger, and continued by his son Heinrich
until 1864, when it was sold to Robert Lienau.

Among the most important Prussian firms, its
activities included publishing Weber from 1814,
issuing Beethoven's Opp. 108–12, 132, 135,
sponsoring the *Berliner allgemeine musikalische
Zeitung* and bringing out the first edition of Bach's
St Matthew Passion. Works by Berlioz, Liszt and
Chopin were later added to the catalogue. A. M.
Schlesinger's son Maurice established a firm in
Paris (*c.* 1821–46), specialising in opera (including
first editions of works by Meyerbeer and
Donizetti) and piano music. He also founded the
Gazette musicale de Paris (1834–).

Schola Cantorum, Paris   The society was founded in 1894 by d'Indy,
Charles Bordes and Alexandre Guilmant, and
focused on the revival of old church music. The
institution ran its own music publishing house and
journal, the *Tablettes de la Schola*. Students included
Fauré and Roussel.

Séances Populaires de Musique de Chambre, Paris.   The society was founded
in 1860 by Charles Lamoureux with Colonne,
Adam and Pilet (although the partners changed
several times). New and rarely performed works
were frequently included in the programmes.

Singakademie, Berlin   The society was established in 1791 by C. F. Fasch to
perform primarily eighteenth- and nineteenth-
century choral music; in 1793 it moved into the
Akademie der Künste. It presented a conservative
programme of mainly German works, and was
important in the Bach revival, giving the first
performances after Bach's death of the *St Matthew
Passion* (1829, conducted by Mendelssohn) and the B
minor Mass (1834), among other works. Under its
directors Zelter (1800–32), C. F. Rungenhagen
(1833–51) and Eduard Grell (1853–76) it became one
of the finest vocal groups in Germany. From 1882 it
performed regularly with the Berlin Philharmonic
Orchestra.

Sociedad de Conciertos, Madrid   Founded by Barbieri in 1866, under the leadership of Monasterio (1869–76); the repertory ranged from Haydn and Mozart to Bizet, Rubinstein and Gade. Mariano Vázquez, who directed the concerts from 1877 to 1885, gave the first performance in Madrid of Beethoven's Ninth Symphony in 1882; he also favoured Spanish composers including Rafael Hernando and Felipe Pedrell. At the end of the century the repertory became progressively more international.

Sociedad Euterpe, Barcelona   Founded by Anselmo Clavé in 1857 (it emerged from La Fraternidad, the first Spanish choral society), it spawned many other Sociedades Euterpenses. From 1860 to 1874 Clavé organised annual choral festivals; in the largest of these (1864) fifty-seven societies participated, with more than 2,000 singers and an orchestra of 300.

Société des Jeunes Artistes du Conservatoire, Paris   Founded by Pasdeloup in 1852, the society's aim was to present recognised masterpieces alongside music by young composers. It was influential on French musical life, and continued the work of Habeneck in raising the status of the Viennese Classics and Mendelssohn and Schumann in France.

Société Nationale de Musique, Paris   The society was founded in 1871 by Saint-Saëns and Romain Bussine as a forum for contemporary music. In 1886, however, Saint-Säens and Bussine resigned in protest against the invasion of foreign works; Franck and then d'Indy (1890) succeeded Saint-Saëns as president. Orchestral and chamber music were performed; the society's most significant première was of Debussy's *Prélude à L'après-midi d'un faune* (1894).

Steinway & Sons, New York   Established in 1853 by Heinrich Engelhard Steinway, its success was based initially on overstrung, iron-framed instruments. Steinway's eldest son C. F. Theodor introduced important technological and design innovations, and his younger son William consolidated the firm's commercial position with virtuoso tours and with endorsements from Berlioz, Wagner and Liszt. A Hamburg branch opened in 1880.

Sternscher Gesangverein, Berlin   Established by Julius Stern in 1847, it promoted the music of contemporaries, including Mendelssohn, as well as early music, and was supported by Joachim and Bülow. It gave the first Berlin performances of many of Beethoven's sacred works.

Theater an der Wien   Established in 1801, the theatre also served as a concert hall. The premières of Beethoven's *Fidelio* and several orchestral works, including the Fifth and Sixth Symphonies (1808), took place there. Berlioz conducted four concerts in 1845–6, and Wagner gave three concerts with excerpts from his operas in 1862–3. In the mid-1860s, to solve financial problems, performances of operettas were introduced, including the premières of most of Strauss's operettas.

Teatro Colón, Buenos Aires   Founded in 1857, it opened with a performance of *La traviata*, and concentrated on Italian and French repertory. *Der Freischütz* was performed (in Italian) only in 1864, and *Lohengrin* (also in Italian) in 1883. It was the first theatre in the country to be lit by gas, and enjoyed the most advanced equipment of the day. In the face of mounting competition from the Teatro de la Opera (opened in 1872), it closed in 1888.

Tonkünstlerverein, Dresden   Founded in 1854 by members of the Opera orchestra, led by Moritz Fürstenau, the society aimed to promote and perform chamber music of all periods. Notable artists from outside Dresden also performed at the concerts. From 1856

members were admitted to listen, and the society
eventually became dependent on the support of
the middle classes.

Warsaw Music Society (Warszawskie Towarzystwo Muzyczne)   Founded in
1870 by Moniuszko and M. Kalergis-Muchanov to
perform cantatas and oratorios, the society soon
acquired its own music school (opened in 1884),
library and archives. In 1919 it was renamed, after
Chopin.

Wiener Philharmoniker   Established in 1842, the orchestra was based on
the idea of Lachner's Künstlerverein, and
consisted of professional players from the
Hofoper. Regular seasons were given from 1860. It
performed at the Kärntnertortheater, and from
1870 at the Grosser Musikvereinssaal. One of its
greatest periods was under Hans Richter
(1875–98) who favoured not only the Classical
repertory, but the works of Bruckner, Brahms and
Dvořák; in 1877 he gave the première of Brahms's
Second Symphony. Subsequent conductors
included Mahler and Furtwängler.

Wiener Singakademie   Founded in 1858, it was one of Vienna's principal
choral societies. Brahms was appointed its first
permanent conductor in 1863.

Personalia

SARAH HIBBERD

Adam, Adolphe (1803–56) French composer. He wrote more than eighty stage works, some of which enjoyed lasting success including the opéras comiques *Le chalet* (1834) and *Le postillon de Longjumeau* (1836), and the ballet *Giselle* (1841). He also wrote a large number of arrangements, pot-pourris and songs. His music combines italianate lyricism and grace with a keen sense of drama.

Adler, Guido (1855–1941) Austrian musicologist. He taught music history in Prague (from 1885), organised congresses and was involved in many editions, including the Denkmäler der Tonkunst in Österreich series. In 1898 he succeeded Hanslick at the University of Vienna, where he founded the Musikwissenschaftliches Institut.

Albéniz, Isaac (1860–1909) Spanish composer and pianist. He studied at Brussels Conservatory and with Liszt, Dukas and d'Indy; other important influences were Pedrell, nineteenth-century salon piano music and contemporary French harmony. Most of his works are for piano solo, including the *Suite española* (1886), *Cantos de España* (1896) and *Suite Iberia* (1906–8), although he also wrote a popular opera, *Pepita Jiménez* (1896).

Auber, Daniel-François-Esprit (1782–1871) French composer. The foremost composer of opéras comiques in France, he frequently worked with the librettist Scribe; their creations include *Fra Diavolo* (1830), *Le domino noir*

(1837), *La sirène* (1844) and *Manon Lescaut* (1856),
and in 1828 they created the first grand opera, *La
muette de Portici*. His music, influenced by Rossini,
is characterised by dance-like rhythms, triadic
melodies and adaptations of popular song forms
such as the barcarolle. He was director of the Paris
Conservatoire from 1842 to 1870.

Baillot, Pierre (1771–1842)   French violinist and composer. The last
representative of the Classical Paris violin school,
he founded a professional chamber music series in
1814 and led the Paris Opéra and Chapelle Royale
orchestras in the 1820s. His important treatise
L'art du violon was published in 1834.

Balakirev, Mily Alexeyevich (1837–1910)   Russian composer. He founded
the Free School of Music, and was a mentor for
younger composers including Cui, Musorgsky,
Rimsky-Korsakov and Borodin. From 1862 he
began collecting folktunes in the Caucasus, and
was an advocate of musical nationalism. His works
include the oriental fantasy for piano *Islamey*
(1869), the Symphony in C (1897) and more than
forty songs.

Barbaia, Domenico (1778–1841)   Italian impresario. He managed all the
Neapolitan royal opera houses, the
Kärntnertortheater and Theater an der Wien in
Vienna and La Scala, Milan. He was one of the first
to recognise Rossini's talents, and promoted
Bellini and Donizetti among other composers.

Beethoven, Ludwig van (1770–1827)   German composer. He began as a
successful piano virtuoso and attracted the
patronage of the Viennese aristocracy; his early
publications include piano trios, sonatas and
concertos. In Heiligenstadt in 1802, when he
discovered that he was going deaf, he wrote a
testament to his brothers in which he described his
unhappiness. But he entered a new creative phase,

producing the Symphony No. 3, the *Eroica* (1803), and the first version of his opera *Fidelio* (as *Leonore* 1805, rev. 1806, rev. 1814), in which the influence of French revolutionary music and ideals can be seen. His Violin Concerto (1806), Fifth Piano Concerto, the 'Emperor' (1809), Sixth, Seventh and Eighth Symphonies (1808, 1812, 1812) and more chamber works and piano sonatas followed and his position as the leading composer of the time was confirmed. His later music, including the 'Hammerklavier' Sonata (1818), *Missa Solemnis* (1823), Symphony No. 9 (1824) and String Quartets Opp. 127, 130, 131, 132 (1825-6), considered 'difficult' by his contemporaries, have since come to be viewed as works of remarkable profundity. Instrumental composers of succeeding generations all to a degree either responded to or reacted against his style and achievement.

Bellini, Vincenzo (1801-35) Italian composer. He wrote twelve operas, and with *Il pirata* (1827) began a collaboration with the librettist Felice Romani and the tenor Rubini. His successes include *La sonnambula* and *Norma* (both Milan, 1831). He visited London and then moved to Paris, where he was commissioned to write *I puritani* (1835) for the Opéra. His style is characterised by a close relationship between text and music, long and graceful melodic lines, and cantabile passages in the recitatives.

Berlioz, Hector (1803-69) French composer and critic. An admirer of Beethoven and Gluck, he was also inspired by writers and dramatists, notably Shakespeare (in *Roméo et Juliette*, 1839), Goethe (*La damnation de Faust*, 1846) and Byron (*Harold en Italie*, 1834), as well as by events of his own life – the actress Harriet Smithson (who became his wife in 1833) was a source of inspiration for *Symphonie fantastique* (1830). His pieces frequently combine instrumental and vocal genres, and he was an inspired orchestrator. Frustrated by the lack of recognition for his music in Paris, he was forced to write (wonderfully witty and perceptive) pieces of journalism to support his composing.

Berwald, Franz (1796–1868)   Swedish composer and violinist. His greatest contributions to the repertory are his orchestral works of the 1840s, notably the four symphonies, which exhibit striking harmonic and formal originality, particularly the *Symphonie singulière* (1845). His chamber works show the influence of Mendelssohn.

Bishop, Henry (1786–1855)   English composer. Director of Covent Garden (1811–24) and Drury Lane (1824–), he was also a founder member of the Philharmonic Society. He adapted, arranged and composed music for a great number of theatre pieces including versions of Mozart's and Rossini's operas and countless melodramas; his most ambitious full-length work was the opera *Aladin* (1826). He also wrote many popular songs and glees.

Bizet, Georges (1838–75)   French composer. As a boy he was a brilliant pianist, and showed talent in his early compositions, which included his Symphony in C (1855). Following a period in Italy as a Prix de Rome winner, he concentrated on writing operas. *Les pêcheurs de perles* (1863) and *La jolie fille de Perth* (1867) had only moderate success and *Djamileh* (1872) was a failure; even *Carmen* (1875), in which he developed atmosphere, character depiction and local colour to a new level, was condemned at its première.

Boieldieu, Adrien (1775–1834)   French composer. He was a leading composer of opéras comiques in France, inspired by Grétry and Dalayrac, and in later years also by Rossini. After a period in St Petersburg (1803–11), he produced successes in Paris, notably *La dame blanche* (1825), based on three novels by Walter Scott, which became one of the most popular operas in Europe in the nineteenth century.

Borodin, Alexander (1833–87)   Russian composer. An admirer of Mendelssohn and Schumann, he turned towards Russian nationalism through the acquaintance of Balakirev and others, and became one of the 'Mighty Handful'. His works include the First Symphony (1867), *V sredney* (On the Steppes of Central Asia) (1880) and the opera *Knyaz' Igor'* (Prince Igor) (1869–87), completed and partly orchestrated after his death by Rimsky-Korsakov and Glazunov.

Bourgault-Ducoudray, Louis (1840–1910)   French scholar and composer. His interests included Renaissance polyphony, French folk music, Greek, Russian and oriental music. While he published folksong collections and composed, he had more influence through his lectures and writings advocating broader expressive means for the composer. Debussy was among his pupils.

Brahms, Johannes (1833–97)   German composer. Although well known as a pianist, he had trouble initially in gaining recognition as a composer, in part because of his outspoken opposition to the aesthetic principles of Liszt and the New German School (as illustrated in his D minor Piano Concerto, 1861). In 1863 he was appointed director of the Vienna Singakademie, where he concentrated on historical and modern *a cappella* works, and at the same period met Wagner. He settled permanently in Vienna in 1868. The following year the first complete performance of the *German Requiem* brought him international acclaim, and in the 1870s he wrote a series of masterpieces, including the closely worked First Symphony (1876), which led him to be hailed as

Beethoven's heir, and the Violin Concerto (1878).
In 1881 Hans von Bülow became a valued
colleague and supporter, and in the 1880s he
wrote some inspired chamber works. While
adopting (at least on the surface) conventional
generic and formal models, his technique of
'developing variation', together with phrase and
metrical asymmetries, led Schoenberg to
proclaim him 'Brahms the Progressive'.

Branchu, Alexandrine Caroline (1780–1850)   French soprano. From 1801 to
1826 she was engaged at the Opéra where she
created roles in Cherubini's *Anacréon* (1803) and
Spontini's *La vestale* (1807), and was particularly
successful in the operas of Gluck. She was admired
for her dignified stage presence and fine
declamatory style.

Brendel, Karl Franz (1811–68)   German music historian and critic. He
succeeded Schumann as editor of the *Neue
Zeitschrift für Musik*, and published articles on the
New German School. He wrote an important
history (1852) and taught at the Leipzig
Conservatory.

Bruant, Aristide (1851–1925)   French singer and songwriter. He began as a
chanson writer and performer in *cafés-concerts* in
Paris, but in the 1880s turned increasingly to
cabaret, gaining renown as a critic of social
injustice through his performances at the Chat
Noir in Montmartre. His singing style and lyrics
had a lasting influence on twentieth-century
chanson. Some of his cabaret acts were published
as *Dans la rue: chansons et monologues* (1889–1909).

Bruch, Max (1838–1920)   German composer. He spent time in different parts
of Germany and abroad, and in 1891 was finally
appointed professor at the Berlin Academy. His
secular choral works, such as *Frithjof* (1864), *Das
Lied von der Glocke* (1879) and *Das Feuerkreuz* (1889)

were particularly admired. His tuneful style had affinities with folk music of various countries, and thus stood in sharp contrast to the progressive tendencies of the New German School. Despite the efforts of Pfitzner, only his violin concertos (1868, 1878, 1891) have remained in the standard repertory.

Bruckner, Anton (1824–96)   Austrian composer. During years as a schoolmaster-organist he composed Masses and other sacred works. In 1855 he began counterpoint lessons in Vienna with Sechter, and in the same year was appointed organist at Linz Cathedral. His contact with Wagner's music in 1863 however pointed to new directions, as witnessed in the Masses and First Symphony composed in 1864–8. He travelled to Paris and London as an organ virtuoso and improviser, and back in Vienna concentrated on writing symphonies; however, only No. 7 (1883) enjoyed real success. He was criticised for his Wagnerian leanings, and late in life revised several of his earlier works to meet such criticisms. The epic scale and majestic tone of his symphonies reveal the influences of Beethoven and Schubert as well as of Wagner.

Bülow, Hans von (1830–94)   German conductor and pianist. He became a champion of the New German School, and as the conductor of the Munich Opera gave the premières of *Tristan und Isolde* (1865) and *Die Meistersinger* (1868). He toured as a pianist, performing the première of Tchaikovsky's First Piano Concerto, dedicated to him (1875).

Busoni, Ferrucio (1866–1924)   German-Italian composer and pianist. For much of his life his output consisted mainly of piano and chamber works, including arrangements of Bach (published in seven volumes, 1892–1919). From 1902 he began conducting contemporary music and absorbed broader influences which had

an impact on his own compositions, culminating
with *Doktor Faust* (1924).

Caballero, Manuel Fernández (1835–1906)   Spanish composer. He became
conductor of the Novedades and other theatres in
Madrid and wrote a large number of songs,
choruses and dances. He conducted in Cuba,
Lisbon and South America, and composed almost
200 zarzuelas, including *La viejecita* (1897) and
Gigantes y cabezudos (1898).

Calvé, Emma (1858–1942) French soprano. In the 1890s she was an
international favourite, especially in London and
New York, where her interpretation of Carmen
was considered incomparable. Massenet wrote
Anita (*La navarraise*, 1894) and Fanny (*Sapho*, 1897)
for her. Her voice was remarkable for its steadiness
and rich colour.

Catalani, Angelica (1780–1849)   Italian soprano. She made her debut in
London in 1806, and in 1812 played Susanna in the
first London performance of *Le nozze di Figaro*. She
then sang in Paris, and toured northern Europe.
She had a beautiful and controlled voice, but
apparently lacked dramatic involvement.

Cavaillé-Coll, Aristide (1811–99)   French organ builder. He studied in Paris,
and built his first organ at Notre-Dame de
Lorette (1838). He built some 500 instruments,
including those at Bayeux (1861) and Orléans
Cathedrals (1875). Developing the Classical French
organ, he created the French Romantic instrument
which inspired composers such as Franck and
Messiaen.

Chabrier, Emmanuel (1841–94)   French composer and pianist. He had a
talent for the lyric, the comic and the colourful
which is apparent not only in his operas, such as *Le
roi malgré lui* (1887), but in his orchestral rhapsody
España (1883) and piano pieces including the

Bourrée fantasque (1891), which inspired French composers such as Ravel.

Charpentier, Gustave (1860–1956)   French composer. During his time in Italy, as a winner of the Prix de Rome (1887), he wrote several orchestral pieces, and began work on his opera *Louise* (1900), with its then scandalous theme of women's liberation. It anticipated Puccini's *verismo* works and also recalled elements of Gounod's and Wagner's musical language.

Chausson, Ernest (1855–99)   French composer. Studying with Massenet, he came under the influence of Franck and visited Germany to hear Wagner. He died prematurely in a cycling accident, but his output reflects his growing maturity, from the simplicity of his early songs to a more intense dramatic style in the *Poème de l'amour et de la mer* (1882–93) and the opera *Le roi Arthus* (1886–95), and a more melancholy approach in the *Poème* (1896) for violin and orchestra. From around 1890 his music took a more Classical turn, as he turned towards older Gallic and Italian inspirations including Rameau.

Cherubini, Luigi (1760–1842)   French composer of Italian birth. He taught at the Conservatoire and became its director in 1822. He had success with his opéras comiques, such as *Lodoïska* (1791), *Médée* (1797) and *Les deux journées* (1800); his developments included an emphasis on the orchestra and on the emotions of the protagonists. His tragédies lyriques were less popular, and following his appointment as superintendant of the royal chapel in 1814 he concentrated on church music. His Requiem in C minor (1816) was particularly admired by Beethoven.

Chopin, Fryderyk Francisek (1810–49)   Polish composer. He studied in Warsaw, and achieved public and critical acclaim in concert performances in Vienna and Warsaw in

1829–30. But his despair over the political repression in Poland, together with his musical ambition, led him to move to Paris in 1831. There he quickly established himself as a private teacher and salon performer, and, particularly in the years 1838–47, during his romantic affair with George Sand, enjoyed a productive creative period. These years saw the Sonata in B flat minor (1839) and the Barcarolle (1846) as well as many smaller-scale works. He gave few public concerts, although his playing was much admired. His works are often characterised by a simple texture of accompanied melody, in contrast to the spectacular feats of his contemporaries in Paris, including Liszt. But his harmony was innovatory, and he pushed the accepted conventions of dissonance treatment and key relations into new areas.

Choron, Alexandre (1771–1834)   French writer on music, teacher and composer. A pioneering and influential figure in Parisian musical life, he wrote manuals on thoroughbass and counterpoint and essays on plainsong and church music, published editions of Renaissance and Baroque choral music, collaborated with Fayolle on the *Dictionnaire des musiciens* (1810–11) and was involved in the reorganisation of the *maîtrises* (from 1813). He founded the Institution Royale de Musique Classique et Religieuse (1817–30), which presented popular concerts of early music.

Cinti-Damoreau, Laure (1801–63)   French soprano. Following her debut in 1819 she was engaged at the Théâtre-Italien; in 1826 she arrived at the Opéra where she created the principal roles in Rossini's Paris operas and Auber's *La muette de Portici* (1828), and was admired for her pure tone and stylish ornamentation. She later moved to the Opéra-Comique, and also taught at the Conservatoire, publishing a *Méthode de chant* in 1849.

Clementi, Muzio (1752–1832)   English composer, keyboard player, publisher and piano manufacturer of Italian birth. He travelled widely as a pianist, and in 1798 established a music publishing and piano-making firm whose publications included major works by Beethoven. He wrote a large amount of keyboard and chamber music, and two influential didactic works, *Introduction to the Art of Playing on the Piano Forte* (1801) and the keyboard collection *Gradus ad Parnassum* (1817–26).

Colonne, Edouard (1838–1910)   French violinist and conductor. An orchestral and chamber violinist in the 1860s, in 1873 he founded (with the publisher Hartmann) the orchestral association the Concert National (later known as the Concerts Colonne). His performances of French works, particularly of Berlioz, gained him recognition, and in 1878 he conducted ten concerts at the World Exhibition at the Trocadero. He toured in Europe, directed the Odéon theatre orchestra and became the Opéra's artistic adviser and conductor.

Cornelius, Peter (1824–74)   German composer. Although an admirer of Liszt and the New German School, his songs and operas, including *Der barbier von Bagdad* (1855–58) show his taste for simplicity – and his literary skill. In Vienna he enjoyed productive relationships with Brahms and Tausig, and with Wagner, who summoned him to Munich in 1865 as his private répétiteur and teacher at the Royal School of Music. He wrote poetry and essays defending Wagner and Liszt, and translated vocal works by Berlioz and others.

Costa, Michael (1808–84)   English conductor and composer of Italian birth. He was director and conductor of the Italian opera at the King's Theatre from 1833, and founded the Royal Italian Opera, Covent Garden, in 1845 where he raised the standard of orchestral playing significantly. He also conducted the Philharmonic Society, Sacred Harmonic Society and various festivals.

Cui, César (1835–1918)   Russian composer and critic of French descent. he became friendly with the members of the 'Mighty Handful' and advocated nationalist principles in his writings, which include *La musique en Russie* (1880). His operas reveal the influences of Auber and Meyerbeer, and his piano pieces his fascination with Chopin.

Czerny, Carl (1791–1857)   Austrian piano teacher, composer and pianist. He studied with Beethoven, and was drawn to a career as a teacher rather than as a travelling virtuoso; his students included Liszt and Thalberg. He was also a prolific composer, and wrote studies, exercises and treatises, including the *School of Practical Composition* (1834) and the *Complete Theoretical and Practical Piano School* (1839).

Dargomïzhsky, Alexander Sergeyevich (1813–69)   Russian composer. With Glinka he established a tradition of national opera based on folksong and a concern for dramatic truth; *Rusalka* (1855) and *Kamennïy gost'* (The Stone Guest) (1866–9, completed by Cui and Rimsky-Korsakov in 1870) were influential on later composers including Musorgsky. His orchestral works include folksong fantasies such as *Baba-Yaga* (1862), and his songs range from expressive lyrical romances to powerful dramatic ballads.

David, Félicien (1810–76) French composer. During his travels in the Middle East in the 1830s he found musical inspiration in Egypt, and wrote a number of descriptive pieces on exotic themes, such as the *ode-symphonie Le désert* (1844) and the opéra comique *Lalla-Roukh* (1862), both of which were admired for their lyricism and orchestration. He was influential on later composers including Gounod, Saint-Saëns and Delibes.

Debussy, Claude (1862–1918)   French composer. He studied in Paris, and was influenced by his travels to Rome (1885–7) and Bayreuth (1888, 1889), and by the Javanese music he heard in Paris (1889). Works such as the *Cinq poèmes de Baudelaire* (1889) reveal Wagner's influence. In the G minor String Quartet (1893) he used modality and chromatic symmetries (notably the whole-tone effect) to create a floating harmony which has some analogies with symbolist poets such as Mallarmé (in *Prélude à L'après-midi d'un faune*, 1894) and Maeterlinck (in *Pelleas et Mélisande*, 1893–1902). These works, and others such as the three *Nocturnes* (1899) and *La mer* (1905), introduce a new fluidity of colour and rhythm often associated in later works with 'exotic' imagery (of Spain, the orient, antiquity etc.).

Delibes, Léo (1836–91)   French composer. He began writing operettas in the style of his teacher Adam, then became chorus master at the Théâtre-Lyrique and Opéra. He then produced the ballets *Coppélia* (1870) and *Sylvia* (1876), both appreciated by Tchaikovsky, a serious opera *Jean de Nivelle* (1880), influenced by Meyerbeer, and *Lakmé* (1883), admired for its oriental colour and strong characterisation.

Donizetti, Gaetano (1797–1848)   Italian composer. His first international success, *Anna Bolena* (1830), enabled him to move away from Naples, where he had begun his career, and he had further successes notably with *Lucia di Lammermoor* (1835). He travelled to Paris where *La favorite* and *La fille du régiment* (1840) were well received. He was appointed Kapellmeister to the Austrian court, and had further triumphs with *Maria di Rohan* (Vienna, 1843), *Dom Sébastien* (Paris, 1843) and *Caterina Cornaro* (Naples, 1844).

Building on Rossini's style, he combined his
facility for lyricism with a development of
psychological expression in more than sixty
operas.

Duparc, Henri (1848–1933)   French composer. He studied with Franck and
was influenced by Wagner's use of harmonic
structure and chromaticism, as seen in *Chanson
triste* and *Soupir* (both 1868). However, his poetic
awareness gives a unique emotional intensity to
pieces such as *Le manoir de Rosemonde* (1879). He
destroyed many of his early works, and had a
psychological condition that caused him to give up
composing when he was only thirty-six; he left just
thirteen *mélodies*.

Duprez, Gilbert (1806–96) French tenor. He replaced Nourrit as first tenor at
the Opéra in 1837, and sang in premières of works
by Halévy, Auber and Donizetti, and in Berlioz's
Benvenuto Cellini (1838). His declamation and
smooth *canto spianato* were much admired.

Dvořák, Antonín (1841–1904)   Czech composer. In 1873, after several years
of playing the viola in the Provisional Theatre
orchestra in Prague, under Wagner and Smetana,
he devoted himself to composing. He gained the
attention of Brahms who secured the publisher
Simrock for some of his works in 1878. Foreign
performances of his works became more frequent,
notably of the Slavonic Dances (1878, 1886), the
Sixth Symphony (1880) and the *Stabat mater*
(1877), and he wrote a number of works for
England including *The Spectre's Bride* (1884) and
the Requiem Mass (1890) for the Birmingham
Festival. He travelled to Russia, and in 1892 was
appointed director of the National Conservatory
in New York, where he wrote the Ninth
Symphony (1893) and several chamber works
including the String Quintet in E flat (1893). Back
in Prague his opera *Rusalka* (1901) enjoyed some

success. His works display the various influences of folk musics, Classical composers including Mozart and Beethoven, and Wagner and Brahms

Elgar, Edward (1857–1934)   English composer. He first began to establish a reputation with his choral pieces such as *The Black Knight* (1892) and *Caractacus* (1898), which although written in the English tradition also reveal the influences of German music (notably of Weber, Schumann, Brahms and Wagner). In the *Enigma Variations* (1899) a fully formed original style was established, and taken further in the oratorio *The Dream of Gerontius* (1900); both pieces confirmed his international success. The works that followed similarly combined the qualities of aspiration and nostalgia.

Elsner, Józef Antoni Franciszek (1769–1854)   Polish composer and teacher of German origin. An active member of Warsaw's musical life, he directed the Warsaw Opera (1799–1824), enriching its repertory with his own works, promoted concerts, organised music schools, contributed to the *Allgemeine musikalische Zeitung* and to Polish journals, issued a collection of Polish folksongs and in 1821 became rector of the conservatory where Chopin was among his pupils.

Erkel, Ferenc (1810–93)   Hungarian composer, conductor and pianist. He was conductor at the National Theatre, Pest (1838–74) and for the Philharmonic concerts which he founded, and was appointed director of the new National Hungarian Royal Academy of Music in 1875. His extremely successful opera *Hunyadi László* (1844) combines Italian and Viennese Classical style with Hungarian influences. His other compositions include some early instrumental pieces with Hungarian themes, the popular opera *Bánk bán* (1861), and the Wagnerian *Brankovics György* (1868–72), considered his masterpiece during his lifetime.

Falcon, Cornélie (1814–97)   French soprano. Her most notable roles
included Rachel in Halévy's *La juive* (1835) and
Valentine in Meyerbeer's *Les Huguenots* (1836), and
her repertory also included the heroines of
Rossini's four French operas. She was admired for
her acting ability and dramatic voice, and together
with Nourrit raised the Paris Opéra to
unprecedented popularity. However, owing to
overwork, she lost her voice prematurely and was
forced to retire at the age of twenty-six.

Fauré, Gabriel (1845–1924)   French composer and teacher. He trained at the
Ecole Niedermeyer, coming under the influence of
Saint-Saëns and his circle while working as a
church musician and giving lessons. In 1896 he
was appointed chief organist at the Madeleine and
composition teacher at the Conservatoire. He
wrote six important song cycles, notably *La bonne
chanson* (1894) and three collections of songs, much
chamber music, including the Piano Quintet No. 1
(1895), and some larger-scale pieces including the
Requiem (1877).

Fétis, François-Joseph (1784–1871)   Belgian critic and composer. He studied
at the Paris Conservatoire, and wrote a number of
comic operas and instrumental works. In 1827 he
founded the influential *Revue musicale*, and in 1833
was appointed the first director of the Brussels
Conservatory. He organised series of historical
concerts in Paris and Brussels in the 1830s, wrote a
large amount of music criticism and produced
several books of music history, including the
seminal *Biographie universelle des musiciens*
(1835–44).

Fibich, Zdeněk (1850–1900)   Czech composer. He travelled in Europe,
before returning in 1875 to Prague where he
worked at the Provisional Theatre and then at the
Russian Orthodox Church as choirmaster. From
1881 he worked only as a composer and private

teacher. His solid German training is evident in his three complete symphonies (1883–98), which also reveal his melodic gifts. He also wrote some evocative tone poems and concert overtures such as *Komenský* (1892). Among his many piano works is the set of 376 *Moods, Impressions and Reminiscences* (1892–99) inspired by his love affair with the writer Anežka Shulzová. His operas include *Nevěsta mesinská* (The Bride of Messina) (1884), arguably the finest Czech nineteenth-century tragic opera, and the popular *Šárka* (1897). In his last years he destroyed almost all his church music and many of his songs.

Field, John (1782–1837)   Irish composer and pianist. Following a successful continental tour with Clementi in 1802–3 he stayed in Russia where he taught, gave concerts and composed. He was admired for the sensitive style of his playing, as reflected in his seventeen published nocturnes that anticipated in manner and texture Chopin's own pieces in the genre, and influenced Mendelssohn and Liszt. He also wrote rondos, fantasies and variations, and seven piano concertos.

Foster, Stephen (1826–64)   American composer. He wrote hymns, Sunday school songs and some 200 popular songs (1844–64). These are mainly sentimental pieces such as *My Old Kentucky Home* (1853) and *Jeanie with the Light Brown Hair* (1854), but his thirty or so minstrel songs are often strongly rhythmic, in black dialect and with a choral refrain and instrumental interlude; they include *Oh! Susanna* (1848) and *Campdown Races* (1851).

Franck, César (1822–90)   French composer, teacher and organist of Belgian birth. He found his vocation through appointments as an organist in Paris, notably at Ste Clotilde (1858–) and through teaching. His improvisatory skill attracted notice and led to his

first work *Six pièces* (1862); some ten years later he
was appointed organ professor at the
Conservatoire. His larger-scale compositions
include the oratorio *Les béatitudes* (1879) and
several symphonic poems such as *Psyché* (1888),
but his finest works were smaller-scale pieces such
as the Piano Quintet (1879), the *Prélude, choral et
fugue* for piano (1884) and the String Quartet
(1889). His style combines late Romantic
(Wagnerian) harmony with Baroque-influenced
contrapuntal and formal devices.

Gade, Niels (1817–90)   Danish composer. He went to Leipzig as assistant
conductor of the Gewandhaus Orchestra, where he
wrote his Third Symphony (1847) and String Octet
(1848). In Copenhagen he established a permanent
orchestra and choir at the Musical Society, which
gave the premières of his Symphonies Nos. 4–8,
and his large choral works, including *Comala*
(1846). Although German Romantic (especially
Mendelssohnian) style eclipsed the Scandinavian
colouring of his early works, he was influential on
the next generation of Danish composers.

García, Manuel (1775–1832)   Spanish tenor. Already established in Spain, he
made a successful French debut (1808) and visited
Italy (1811–16), where he created roles in several
Rossini operas. He became the principal exponent
of Rossini's music in Paris, London and New York,
and led the first Italian opera company to visit
America in 1825. He also wrote many songs and
operas. His four children all became singers, the
most celebrated were Pauline Viardot, Maria
Malibran and Manuel García.

Glazunov, Alexander Konstantinovich (1865–1936)   Russian composer. He
studied with Rimsky-Korsakov and became a
member of the circle around the patron Belyayev,
who took him to meet Liszt in Weimar. In 1899 he
was appointed to the St Petersburg Conservatory,

which he directed from 1905 until he left Russia in 1928. His compositions include nine symphonies, seven quartets and the ballet *Raymonda* (1897), in which he combined Russian and European musical styles.

Glinka, Mikhail Ivanovich (1804–57)   Russian composer. He first gained recognition with his opera *Zhizn'za tsarya* (A Life for the Tsar) (1836; originally called *Ivan Susanin*), notable for its quasi-Russian melodies, expressive Russian recitative and use of leitmotif. His next opera *Ruslan i Lyudmila* (1842) was less successful, but has strikingly original elements which were to inspire the oriental and 'magic' idioms of later Russian composers. Following periods in Paris and then Spain (1844–7) he wrote the inventive orchestral variations *Kamarinskaya* (1848).

Gottschalk, Louis Moreau (1829–69)   American composer and pianist. He studied in Paris, where the success of his 'Creole' pieces *Bamboula* (1846–48), *La savane* (1847–9) and *La bananier* (1848) earned him fame throughout Europe. He was hailed as the New World's first 'authentic' musical ambassador, and his virtuosity was compared with that of Chopin. He toured in Europe and then in America, and during a period in the Caribbean he wrote some of his finest works, including his First Symphony, 'La nuit des tropiques' (1858–9), and the opera *Escenas campestres* (1860).

Gounod, Charles (1818–93)   French composer. During his time in Italy (1839–42), after winning the Prix de Rome, he was deeply impressed by the sixteenth-century polyphonic music he heard in the Sistine Chapel, and wrote several Masses; the climax of his liturgical work came in 1855 with the *Messe solennelle de Ste Cécile*. After the failure of two operas, he had more success with *Le médecin malgré lui* (1858) and four others: *Philémon et Baucis* (1860), *Faust* (1858), *Mireille* (1864) and *Roméo et*

Juliette (1867). In 1870 he took refuge in England
from the Franco-Prussian War, and became the
first conductor of the Royal Albert Hall Choral
Society (1871), writing many choruses and songs.
He also had success with his oratorios for the
Birmingham Festival.

Grieg, Edvard (1843–1907)   Norwegian composer. As a student at the
Leipzig Conservatory he became familiar with
early Romantic music, notably that of Schumann,
but from the mid-1860s he turned increasingly
towards a national, folk-inspired style. He
promoted Norwegian music through concerts of
his own works, projected a Norwegian Academy of
Music and helped found the Christiania
Musikforening (1871). He also taught, and toured
as a conductor and pianist. His compositions
include a Piano Concerto (1868), incidental music
to *Peer Gynt* (1875), the *Holberg Suite* (1884) and the
Haugtussa song cycle (1895). His style was
essentially lyrical, but he was also a pioneer in the
impressionistic use of harmony and piano sonority,
especially in his late songs.

Guilbert, Yvette (1865–1944)   French *diseuse*. She made her debut in Paris as
an actress in 1877, and in 1890 began a career as a
café singer. She toured Europe and the USA, where
she became noted for her interpretation of French
folksongs.

Habeneck, François-Antoine (1781–1849)   French conductor. As conductor
of the Paris Opéra (1821–46), he premièred many
works including Rossini's *Guillaume Tell*,
Meyerbeer's *Robert le diable* and Berlioz's *Benvenuto
Cellini*. In 1828 he founded the Société des
Concerts du Conservatoire, and introduced
Beethoven's music to Parisian audiences.

Halévy, Fromental (1799–1862)   French composer. His most successful
opera was *La juive* (1835), but his other grand

operas, notably *La reine de Chypre* (1841) and *Charles VI* (1843) were also popular, as were his opéras comiques, such as *L'éclair* (1835). His lyrical style was influenced by Rossini and Auber, and his orchestration and evocation of 'local colour' were much admired by contemporaries. His writings include *Souvenirs et portraits* (1861).

Hallé, Charles (1819–95) English pianist and conductor of German birth. He studied in Darmstadt and Paris, where he performed the complete Beethoven sonata series, and then settled in Manchester. There he reorganised the old Gentlemen's Concerts orchestra, establishing the Hallé Concerts in 1858. He also helped found the (Royal) Manchester College of Music in 1893.

Hanslick, Eduard (1825–1904) German music critic. He wrote his earliest articles for papers in Prague and Vienna, and in 1849–61 was employed as a civil servant, working mainly at the ministry of culture. He published his influential book *Vom Musikalisch-Schönen* (1854) and lectured on musical appreciation at Vienna University. In spite of his Classical aesthetic, he was interested mainly in music of his own time; his anti-Wagnerian stance provoked much controversy.

Heinrich, Anthony Philip (1781–1861) American composer of German-Bohemian birth. He was considered America's first 'professional' composer, and his large output includes many descriptive pieces, including *Pushmataha, a Venerable Chief of a Western Tribe of Indians* (1831). As a violinist he led the first known performances of a Beethoven symphony in America (Lexington, Ky., 1817), and in 1842 he helped establish the New York Philharmonic Society.

Hérold, Ferdinand (1791–1833) French composer. He worked as an accompanist at the Théâtre-Italien, and a singing coach at the Opéra; his first success as a composer came only in 1826 with *Marie*. *Zampa* (1831) and *Le pré aux clercs* (1832) followed, displaying his talent for effective drama, but he died the following year.

Hoffmann, E. T. A. (1776–1822)   German jurist, writer and composer. He worked as a conductor and theatre director, but was more successful as a writer of stories (which influenced Schumann and Wagner in particular), and of essays and criticism for the *Allgemeine musikalische Zeitung* (1809–15) and other journals; these included perceptive reviews of Beethoven's works. In 1816 his magic opera *Undine* had success and was praised by Weber; he also composed several other stage works and a number of sacred and instrumental pieces.

Indy, Vincent d' (1851–1931)   French composer. He studied with Franck, becoming interested in the standards of German symphonism, and in 1894 founded the Schola Cantorum. He favoured logical construction (notably sonata and variation forms) in his own compositions, and was influenced by Wagnerism (in three *Wallenstein* overtures, 1873–81) and folksong (*Symphonie sur un chant montagnard français* for piano and orchestra, 1886). His other works include two more symphonies, three operas (including *Fervaal*, 1897), and sacred and chamber music.

Jaëll, Marie (née Trautmann) (1846–1925)   French pianist. Her teachers included Herz, Saint-Saëns and Franck, and she was also a friend of Liszt; her compositions, mainly songs and piano pieces, combine Romantic influences with an awareness of innovations of the time, and with her husband she made European concert tours promoting contemporary music. She also developed an important piano method based on economy of hand movement (published 1895–1927).

Joachim, Joseph (1831–1907) Austro-Hungarian violinist and composer. As both a conductor and a performer he was a powerful advocate of Brahms's music. From 1868 he taught in Berlin, and the following year established an influential string quartet. His playing was in the French Classical tradition. His compositions include orchestral and chamber works as well as cadenzas and arrangements of pieces by other composers.

Jullien, Louis (1812–60) French conductor and composer. He produced lively entertainments of dance music in Paris (1836–38) and London (1840–58), where he also conducted promenade concerts, and then toured in America and The Netherlands. The popular programmes consisted largely of quadrilles, galops and waltzes, but he also included complete symphonies by Beethoven and Mendelssohn, thereby introducing Classical music to a wide public.

Kiesewetter, Raphael Georg (1773–1850) Austrian scholar. He collected scores and produced books and articles on the Netherlands style, the history of song and Arabic and ancient Greek music, including *Geschichte der europäisch-abendländischen oder unser heutigen Musik* (1834).

Lablache, Luigi (1794–1858) Italian bass. He began his career as a *buffo* in 1812, and after further study and successful performances in Italy and Vienna, he made brilliant debuts in London and Paris in 1830. He created roles in the operas of Donizetti and Bellini, including Giorgio in *I puritani* and the title roles in *Marino Faliero* and *Don Pasquale*, and also took on smaller roles; he was admired for his varied repertory and for his comic genius.

Lalo, Edouard (1823–92) French composer. In the 1850s he was most interested in playing and composing chamber music, but in the 1870s his *Symphonie espagnole* (1874) and Violin and Cello Concertos (1877) attracted attention. His ballet score *Namouna* (1881–2) was popular as a series of orchestral suites, and in 1888 his opera *Le roi d'Ys* achieved success.

Lamoureux, Charles (1834–99)   French conductor and violinist. He formed his own concert-giving chamber groups (1860, 1872), and in 1873–4 mounted large-scale choral performances (including *Messiah*, *St Matthew Passion*, Massenet's *Eve*). In 1881 he founded the Société des Nouveaux-Concerts (from 1897 known as the Concerts Lamoureux), which gave performances noted for their precision and expressiveness. He travelled to Russia and London, and in the late 1880s and the 1890s produced Wagner operas.

Lind, Jenny (1820–87)   Swedish soprano. She left Stockholm in 1844 and performed in Germany, Austria and Britain where her Alice (in Meyerbeer's *Robert le diable*), Amina (Bellini's *La sonnambula*) and Marie (Donizetti's *La fille du régiment*) were particular favourites. Her vocal agility and purity were admired, and she was nicknamed the 'Swedish nightingale'. In 1850 she toured in America, singing only in concert and oratorio performances, and then she settled in England.

Liszt, Franz (1811–86)   Hungarian composer and pianist. Following tours in Europe as a virtuoso pianist he settled for a while in Paris, where he began a stormy relationship with the Countess Marie d'Agoult. He gave many concerts, maintaining his legendary reputation, and composed works such as the *Années de pèlerinage*. He travelled as a performer again in 1839–47, and then took up a conducting post at the Weimar court, where he wrote or revised many of his major works, including the symphonic poems (*Tasso*, 1849; *Héroïde*, 1850), the Transcendental Studies (1851) and the *Faust-Symphonie* (1857); conducted new operas by Wagner, Verdi and Berlioz; and became the figurehead of the New German School. In 1861–9 he lived mainly in Rome, writing religious works. His compositional style was characterised by experimentation with large-scale structures and with thematic transformation, and his later works reveal strikingly advanced chromaticism.

Lobe, Johann Christian (1797–1881)   German writer, composer and flautist. After composing five operas for Weimar, he turned to editing the *Allgemeine musikalische Zeitung* (1846–8). He wrote a number of didactic works and the series *Fliegende Blätter für Musik* (1855–7).

Lortzing, Albert (1801–51)   German composer. He wrote twenty popular operas, including the comic *Die beiden Schützen* (1835), which reveals his inventive vein of sentimental humour. With *Zar und Zimmermann* (1837) he established his formula of number opera with spoken dialogue, and in later works absorbed musical influences from Spohr and Weber, as seen in the advanced chromatic harmony of *Undine* (1845).

L'vov, Alexey Fyodorovich (1798–1870)   Russian composer and violinist. In 1837 he succeeded his father as director of the imperial court chapel in St Petersburg, for which he composed communion hymns and a *Stabat mater* (1851); his other compositions include the national hymn *Bozhe, tsarya khrani* (God Save the Tsar), commissioned by Nicholas I (1833). As a violinist he was praised by Mendelssohn and Schumann.

MacDowell, Edward (1860–1908)   American composer and pianist. He studied the piano in Paris, Wiesbaden and Frankfurt (where he also studied composition with

Raff), and took up his first post at the Darmstadt
Conservatory. Liszt heard his *First Modern Suite*
(1881) and First Piano Concerto (1882) and
strongly encouraged him. He moved to Boston in
1888 to pursue a performing career, and was
increasingly accepted as a leading figure in
American musical life; compositions during these
years included the *Sonata eroica* (1895). In 1896 he
was appointed the first professor of music at
Columbia University, and wrote some of his best
piano music during this time, including *Sea Pieces*
(1898). His style was influenced by Schumann,
Liszt and Grieg, and retained a bright lyricism and
attractive orchestral colour.

Mahler, Gustav (1860–1911)   Bohemian-Austrian composer. He was
appointed music director at Kassel in 1883, where
he composed the song cycle *Lieder eines fahrenden
Gesellen* (1885). He had a succession of
appointments as a conductor at Prague, Leipzig,
where he directed the *Ring* cycle in 1887,
establishing his reputation as an interpretative
artist, Budapest and Hamburg. Despite his heavy
workload and a claustrophobic artistic atmosphere,
he returned to composition, completing the
Second and Third Symphonies (1894, 1896) and
the song cycle *Des Knaben Wunderhorn* (1892–98).
He then turned his attention to the Vienna
Hofoper, and (following his Catholic baptism) was
appointed Kapellmeister in 1897. There he
brought a stagnating opera house to a position of
unrivalled brilliance, surrounded himself with
radical young composers and continued to
compose further symphonies and songs in an idiom
of striking originality. His ironic 'play' on different
levels of musical meaning influenced later
twentieth-century composers.

Malibran, Maria (1808–1911)   Spanish mezzo-soprano. She studied with her
father, the tenor Manuel García, and sang in Paris,

London, and from 1833, Italy. Renowned for the range and flexibility of her voice, she achieved her greatest success in the title roles of Bellini's *Norma* and *La sonnambula*. She died at the height of her career after a riding accident.

Mariani, Angelo (1821–73)   Italian conductor. He had great success conducting Verdi's *I due Foscari* (1846) and *Nabucco* (1847) in Milan, and then worked mainly in Genoa and Bologna, giving Wagner and Verdi performances, notably *Don Carlo* in 1867. He was admired by Meyerbeer, Rossini and Wagner, but became estranged from Verdi in 1869.

Marschner, Heinrich (1795–1861)   German composer. From 1821 he worked as a stage composer and conductor in Dresden, then Leipzig and Hanover. He won early fame with *Der Vampyr* (1827) and *Der Templer und die Jüdin* (1829), and with *Hans Heiling* (1830) was confirmed as the leading German opera composer. He effectively bridged the gap between Weber and Wagner, integrating all elements of theatre and developing leitmotif technique and, with *Hiarne* (1857–8), through-composition. He also wrote other theatre music, songs and chamber music.

Martucci, Giuseppe (1856–1909)   Italian composer, pianist and conductor. He toured as a piano virtuoso, then in 1808 became professor at Naples Conservatory. He conducted German (and sometimes French and English) repertory in Naples and Bologna, and composed instrumental music, including the lyrical *Notturno* Op. 70, No. 1 (1891), and his First (1888–95) and Second (1904) Symphonies.

Marx, Adolf Bernard (1795–1866)   German music theorist and writer. He edited the *Berliner allgemeine musikalische Zeitung* (1824–30), and then became professor at Berlin University; in 1850 he co-founded the Berlin Musikschule (later the Stern Conservatory). His writings include *Die Lehre von der musikalischen Komposition* (1838–47).

Mascagni, Pietro (1863–1945)   Italian composer. His second opera, *Cavalleria rusticana* (1890) earned him international acclaim and established the vogue for *verismo* opera. Later works, including *L'amico Fritz* (1891) and *Iris* (1898) achieved more modest success.

Mason, Lowell (1792–1872)   American educator and composer. He pioneered the introduction of music education in American schools and was a reformer of American church music, directing the Boston Handel and Haydn Society in 1827–32. He produced many hymn tunebooks, instruction manuals and church music collections, and his compositions include hymn arrangements such as *Olivet* ('My faith looks up to thee') and *Bethany* ('Nearer, my God, to thee').

Mayr, Simon (1763–1845)   German composer. He studied with Bertoni in Venice and became established as one of the most important composers in Italy. In 1802 he was appointed *maestro di cappella* in Bergamo, where he organised performances of works by Haydn, Mozart and Beethoven. His own works include the operas *La rosa bianca e la rosa rossa* and *Medea in Corinto* (1813), which both enjoyed international success, as well as much church music, and he was an influential teacher (notably of Donizetti). His style shows the influences of Gluck and late Neapolitan opera composers, as well as an innovative use of orchestration, harmony and form.

Méhul, Etienne-Nicolas (1763–1817)   French composer. He achieved fame at the end of the eighteenth century with his opéras comiques written in the tradition of Grétry and Dalayrac. After 1800 he had fewer successes, although *Joseph* (1807) and the serious opera *Uthal* (1806) were popular, and the latter reveals his innovative approach to orchestration and his pioneering development of the reminiscence motif to suggest psychological currents. In 1793 he joined the Institut National de Musique and began writing (republican) civic pieces, including the *Chant du départ* (1794). He then turned chiefly to instrumental music; the First Symphony (1809) is comparable to Beethoven's Fifth in terms of rhythmic drive and formal and motivic unity.

Mendelssohn, Felix (1809–47)   German composer. He started composing at an early age, and was inspired by the visitors to his parents' salon (including Hegel and A. B. Marx) as well as the poetry of Goethe's and Schlegel's translations of Shakespeare. These influences can be seen in such works as the String Octet (1825) and the overture to *A Midsummer Night's Dream* (1826). In 1829 he conducted a pioneering performance of Bach's *St Matthew Passion* in Berlin. Travels to England, Scotland and Italy inspired new works, including *The Hebrides* Overture (1830) and the Italian Symphony (1833). In Leipzig (1835–45) he conducted the Gewandhaus Orchestra, championing both historical and modern works, and founded the Leipzig Conservatory (1843). His later compositions include the Violin Concerto (1844) and *Elijah* (1846), which he conducted at the Birmingham Festival and in London.

Mercadante, Saverio (1795–1870)   Italian composer. He achieved European success with his opera buffa *Elisa e Claudio* (1821), but *Il giuramento* (1837) is considered his masterpiece with its musico-dramatic integrity. He was appointed director of the Naples Conservatory in 1840, and became increasingly occupied with writing instrumental works and church music. He did continue to write operas, notably *Il reggente* (1843), in which he varied forms and accompaniments, simplified vocal lines and emphasised the drama.

Meyerbeer, Giacomo (1791–1864)   German composer. He initially won more success as a pianist than as a composer, but following a tour in Italy, during which he wrote six operas, including *Il crociato in Egitto* (1824), he gained a reputation rivalling that of Rossini. From 1825 he worked mainly in Paris, where he and the librettist Scribe collaborated on several key grand operas: *Robert le diable* (1831), *Les Huguenots* (1836) and *Le prophète* (1849). He was admired for his sense of historical colour, his innovative and dramatic use of the orchestra and the chorus, and his understanding of the capabilities of his singers.

Moniuszko, Stanislaw (1819–72)   Polish composer. His opera *Halka*, performed first in Vilnius (1848) then in Warsaw (1857), established him as the foremost Polish nationalist opera composer. He became conductor of the Grand Theatre, Warsaw (1859) and taught at the Music Institute (from 1864). The style revealed in his operas is reminiscent of that of Rossini and Auber, but with greater reliance on the chorus and on Polish dance rhythms. His *Songbooks for Home Use* achieved great popularity, and the simple, usually strophic, songs became models for later Polish composers.

Moscheles, Ignaz (1794–1870)   German pianist, conductor and composer of Czech birth. He travelled through Europe as a performer, settling in London in 1825. There he taught at the Royal Academy, established a series of 'historical soirées', wrote salon music and conducted the Philharmonic Society. In 1832 he conducted the London première of Beethoven's *Missa solemnis*, and he also translated Schindler's biography of the composer as *The Life of Beethoven* (1841). In 1846 he was appointed professor at the Leipzig Conservatory. His compositions include piano sonatas that combine Classical balance with a Romantic vitality and drive.

Möser, Karl (1774–1851) German composer and violinist. Following a period in St Petersburg (1807–11), he returned to Berlin as Konzertmeister of the reorganised Hofkapelle. In 1813 he began regular chamber music evenings, which later developed into symphony concerts. He was appointed director of the Hofkapelle in 1825, and by his retirement was effectively Kapellmeister. He conducted several local Beethoven premières, including Symphony No. 9 in 1826, and was influential on violin playing and teaching.

Mosonyi, Mihály (1815–40) Hungarian composer, teacher and writer on music. His early compositions were most obviously influenced by Beethoven, but in the decade before the Hungarian War of Independence he became more interested in writing in a national style. Encouraged by Liszt, he first used Hungarian idioms in his Second Symphony (1846–56), and *Hódolat Kazinczy Ferenc szellemének* (Homage to Kazinczy) (1860) is a stylised Hungarian rhapsody, using the cimbalom. He also campaigned for the new national style in the music journal *Zenészeti lapok*.

Musard, Philippc (1793–1859) French composer and conductor. From about 1830 he conducted at masked balls at the Théâtre des Variétés in Paris, and was invited to direct a series of popular concerts and dances on the Champs-Elysécs. Thc Concerts-Musard became fashionable, taking place at the Salles Valentino and Vivienne, and he directed other masked balls. He had his greatest successes in 1835–6, conducting balls at the Opéra which exploited the new popularity of the galop and of gimmicks such as pistol shots. In 1840 he conducted the promenade concerts at the Drury Lane Theatre in London, and the following year appeared in a similar role at the Lyceum; he continued to be a popular conductor until 1845.

His compositions included many waltzes and quadrilles, often based on opera tunes.

Musorgsky, Modest Petrovich (1839–81)   Russian composer. In 1857 he met Dargomïzhsky and Cui, and through them Balakirev and Stasov, and persuaded Balakirev to give him lessons. His compositions began to be performed publicly, but following the emancipation of the serfs his family lost much of its wealth and he was obliged to work, notably in government posts. He continued to compose, however, completing his first important orchestral work *Ivanova noch'na Lïsoy gore* (St John's Night on the Bare Mountain) (1867), and the original version of *Boris Godunov* (1869), which was not accepted by the Mariinsky Theatre until 1874 (in a revised form). Meanwhile he had begun work on another opera, *Khovanshchina* (1872–80, incomplete), and written the song cycles *Detskaya* (The Nursery) (1870) and *Bez solntsa* (Sunless) (1874), often regarded as the closest music comes to an aesthetic of Realism. Many works were left unfinished at his death, and their editing and posthumous publication (and often their rewriting) was carried out by Rimsky-Korsakov.

Nicolai, Otto (1810–49)   German composer and conductor. He studied with Baini in Rome where he was also organist at the Prussian Embassy chapel (1833–6), but association with the theatre led him to turn to opera composing. He established himself in Trieste and Turin, and was then appointed principal conductor at the Vienna Hofoper (1841–7). He founded the Vienna Philharmonic Concerts in 1848, and in the same year was made opera Kapellmeister in Berlin, where his comic opera *Die lustigen Weiber von Windsor* (1849) was performed. He also wrote church and orchestral music, and partsongs and choruses.

Niedermeyer, Louis (1802–61)   Swiss composer and educator. His operas
had little success, in spite of the influence of his
friend Rossini in getting them performed in Paris
(these included *Stradella*, 1837). Instead he turned
to sacred music, reviving traditional methods of
performing the Catholic liturgy. He reopened
Choron's church music school as the Ecole
Niedermeyer in 1853, and collaborated with
Joseph d'Ortigue in plainsong publications. He
also revived the declining genre of song, preparing
the way for Duparc, Debussy and Fauré.

Nielsen, Carl (1865–1931) Danish composer. He travelled in Europe (1890–1)
before returning to Copenhagen where he played
the violin in the Danish court orchestra. In his
early compositions, from his Brahmsian First
Symphony (1892), he developed an extended tonal
style often involving 'directional tonality', and
showed a gift for sharp musical characterisation in
his first opera, *Saul and David* (1902). He became an
international figure, often going abroad to conduct
his works, and writing in a variety of genres.

Nourrit, Adolphe (1802–39)   French tenor. He was principal tenor at the
Paris Opéra (1826–37), creating such roles as
Masaniello in Auber's *La muette de Portici* (1828)
Arnold in *Guillaume Tell* (1829) and Raoul in *Les
Huguenots* (1836). He was admired for his
intelligence and subtlety of expression and was
appointed professor of singing at the
Conservatoire in 1827. He left for Italy in 1837,
following Gilbert Duprez's arrival at the Opéra,
and committed suicide two years later.

Offenbach, Jacques (1819–80)   French composer of German origin. He
became a theatre conductor in 1850, and finally
had his own works performed in 1855. He was one
of the leading composers of popular music of the
century. His operettas, including *Orphée aux enfers*
(1858), *La belle Hélène* (1864) and *La grande-*

duchesse de Gérolstein (1867), achieved great
success, and his serious opera *Les contes d'Hoffmann*,
completed after his death by Guiraud, dominated
the stage in the 1870s. His works were usually
satires on contemporary themes, in which the
idiom of eighteenth-century comic opera was both
fondly recalled and parodied. Their international
success helped to establish operetta as a genre, as
practised by Strauss, Sullivan and Léhar, which
evolved into the twentieth-century musical.

Paer, Ferdinando (1771–1839)   Italian composer. He made his mark as a
composer of opera semiseria in Parma and then
Vienna (from 1797), Dresden (from 1801) and
Paris (from 1807), where he also directed the
Théâtre-Italien until 1827. A prolific if
conservative composer, with Mayr he dominated
Italian opera in the first decade of the nineteenth
century. His most successful works include *Camilla*
(1799), *Leonora* (1804) and *Agnese di Fitz-Henry*
(1809), in which tragic and comic elements
appeared side by side, and in which he mingled
different aria types and displayed his gifts for
instrumentation.

Paganini, Nicolò (1782–1840)   Italian violinist and composer. Between 1810
and 1828 he travelled throughout Italy, dazzling
audiences and critics with his extraordinary
virtuoso performances. His compositions of the
period include the bravura variations *Le streghe*
(1813). He then performed in Vienna, Germany,
Paris and London, but in 1834 his failing health
forced his return to Italy. His techniques,
including left-hand pizzicato, double-stop
harmonics and 'ricochet' bowings, influenced later
violinists such as Bériot and Vieuxtemps. Equally,
Liszt, Chopin, Schumann and Berlioz took up his
technical challenge in the search for greater
expression.

Pasdeloup, Jules Etienne (1819–87)   French conductor. With some of his former pupils from the Conservatoire he set up the Société des Jeunes Artistes (1852–61), giving premières of symphonies by Gounod, Saint-Saëns and others. Financial troubles led him to establish the Concerts Populaires de Musique Classique (1861), which offered performances of Classical, German Romantic and French symphonic music to wide audiences. Although his popularity began to wane in the 1870s, owing to the popularity of Colonne and Lamoureux, he and his orchestra continued to be an inspiration to French composers.

Pasta, Giuditta (1797–1865)   Italian soprano. She first excelled in Rossini's roles, notably Desdemona, Tancredi and Semiramis, but achieved even greater success in the title roles of Donizetti's *Anna Bolena* (1830) and Bellini's *La sonnambula* (1831) and *Norma* (1831). She was admired for her combination of lyric genius and dramatic power.

Parry, Hubert (1848–1918)   English composer and teacher. He taught at the Royal College from 1883 (succeeding Grove as director in 1894) and became professor at Oxford in 1900 and president of the Royal Musical Association in 1901. He wrote on the subjects of Bach and the history of musical style. Among his compositions the cantatas *Scenes from Prometheus Unbound* (1880), *Blest Pair of Sirens* (1887) and *L'allegro ed il penseroso* (1890) made an impact for their poetry and Wagnerian language. His anthems and songs, including *Jerusalem*, show a similar attention to text and graceful lyricism. He helped to revive English musical life of the time.

Patti, Adelina (1843–1919)   Italian soprano. She came from a family of singers and toured the USA before making her European debut as Amina in Bellini's *La sonnambula* at Covent Garden in 1861. She sang all over Europe, and returned to New York in 1885 where she was engaged by Mapleson for his operatic tour of the USA. Many farewell concerts followed. She was admired for her pure and flexible voice and her acting skills, and she excelled in such roles as Lucia, Violetta and Rosina as well as in the heavier roles of Leonora and Aïda later in her career.

Pedrell, Felipe (1841–1922)   Spanish composer and musicologist. Though devoted originally to composition – he regarded his masterpiece as the Wagnerian trilogy *Los Pirineos* (1890–91) – he worked increasingly as a writer and editor. His publications include the complete works of Victoria, a biographical series on Catalan musicians, a dictionary of Spanish, Portuguese and Latin American musicians and a critical assessment of Spanish popular songs. He contributed greatly to the revival of interest in church music in Spain.

Petrov, Osip Afanas'yevich (1806–78)   Russian bass. His outstanding creations include Glinka's Ivan Susanin and Ruslan, Dargomïzhsky's Miller (*Rusalka*) and Leporello (*The Stone Guest*) and Varlaam in *Boris Godunov*. His voice was admired for its warmth, depth and evenness, and he was a popular character actor. Although he performed in works by Rossini, Meyerbeer and Weber, his voice was apparently of a particularly Russian character which inspired composers.

Ponchielli, Amilcare (1834–86)   Italian composer. An organist and band conductor in the provinces, he repeatedly tried to establish himself as an opera composer, finally winning success with *I promessi sposi* in 1872 and more convincingly with his stylised grand opera, *La Gioconda* (1876) which in parts anticipates *verismo* opera and aspects of late Verdi. He was appointed professor of composition at Milan Conservatory (1880) and he taught Puccini and (briefly) Mascagni. He also wrote a large amount of sacred music.

Puccini, Giacomo (1858–1924)   Italian composer. His first success came with *Le villi* (1884), and Ricordi commissioned a second opera, *Edgar* (1889), which although coolly received confirmed Puccini's relationship with the publishing house. His most successful opera, *Manon Lescaut* (1893), was followed by *La bohème* (1896) and *Tosca* (1900), his first attempt at *verismo*. These, and the operas that followed, combined his melodic gift and harmonic sensibility with striking orchestration and dramatic skill, and he was perceived as Verdi's successor.

Raff, Joachim (1822–82)   German composer and teacher. He worked for Liszt at Weimar (1850–5), and through his encouragement joined the New German School, where he became a friend of Bülow and composed productively. He fused past and present methods, not always successfully, and had a fondness for salon-like music, but his skilfully orchestrated programme symphonies, notably No. 7 'In den Alpen' (1875) and No. 10 'Zur Herbstzeit' (1879) were influential. He was a teacher and administrator at the Hoch Conservatory, Frankfurt, where his pupils included Edward MacDowell.

Reicha, Antoine (1770–1836)   Czech, later French, composer, theorist and teacher. His interest in harmony and composition was encouraged in Vienna by his friendship with Haydn and lessons with Albrechtsberger. He arrived in Paris in 1808, hoping for operatic success, particularly with *Sapho* (1822), but instead he gained fame as a wind quintet composer, and as a theorist and teacher, as evidenced by his popular *Traité de mélodie* (1814) and the success of his students, including Baillot, Habeneck and Rode. In 1818 he was appointed professor at the Conservatoire, where Berlioz, Liszt and Franck numbered among his pupils. He wrote further didactic works, including the *Traité de haute composition musicale* (1824–6).

Rice, 'Daddy' (1808–60)   American minstrel performer. As a travelling actor he introduced into his act the song-and-dance skit *Jim Crow* (1828) and became one of the first blackface negro impersonators to win fame, even outside the USA. He compiled minstrel tunes in extended sketches called 'Ethiopian operas', which were precursors of the full-scale minstrel show.

Richter, Hans (1843–1916)   Austro-Hungarian conductor. He was closely associated with Wagner and Bülow from 1866–7, becoming conductor at the National Theatre in Pest, the Vienna Hofoper (and Philharmonic concerts) and the Gesellschaft der Musikfreunde. In 1876 he conducted the first *Ring* cycle at Bayreuth. From 1877 he appeared regularly in England, directing the Birmingham Festival and conducting the London Symphony Orchestra and the Hallé; he was a great admirer of Elgar, whose first symphony is dedicated to him.

Riemann, Hugo (1849–1919)   German music theorist and writer. An original and creative scholar, he originated the analysis of music on principles of historical style and genre, and thereby discovered forgotten composers and sources. He transcribed, edited and analysed Byzantine manuscripts of the tenth to fifteenth centuries, John Dunstable, the Mannheim symphonists and Johann Schobert. He produced some sixty books, including the *Musik-Lexikon* (1882), seventy compositions and more than 200 other publications, including his seminal theory of functional harmony, counterpoint and phrasing, the *Grosse Kompositionslehre* (1902–15).

Rimsky-Korsakov, Nikolay Andreyevich (1844–1908)   Russian composer. He wrote songs, orchestral works and an opera, *Pskovityanka* (The Maid of Pskov) (1868–72), before becoming professor at the St Petersburg Conservatory in 1871. He taught himself counterpoint and harmony, conducted at

Balakirev's Free School and collected folksongs. He wrote two more operas, and although his composing was interrupted by official duties at the imperial chapel (1883–91), which involved working on the manscripts of Musorgsky and Borodin and advising the publisher Belyayev, he produced such works as the Third Symphony (1886) and *Sheherazade* (1888). Thereafter he concentrated on writing operas, including *Mlada* (1892) and *Sadko* (1898), which are characterised by the musical delineation of the 'real' and 'unreal' in their fairy-tale scenarios.

Rossini, Gioachino (1792–1868)   Italian composer. Following a series of commissions for northern Italian opera houses, he gained international recognition with the serious *Tancredi* and the comic *L'italiana in Algeri* in 1813, and two years later he was appointed director of the Teatro S Carlo in Naples. There he concentrated on serious opera, including *Otello* (1816), but continued to write comic works for other opera houses, producing *Il barbiere di Siviglia* (1816) and *La Cenerentola* (1817) for Rome. In 1822 he married the singer Isbella Colbran, mistress of the impresario Barbaia, and together they travelled to Vienna, London and Paris, where in 1824 he took on the directorship of the Théâtre-Italien, and composed his final operas for that theatre and for the Opéra. In *Guillaume Tell* (1829), one of the earliest French grand operas, he combined his Italian musical language with the demands of French opera, including ballet, ensembles and a new dramatic integration. He left Paris to live in Italy, but returned in 1855 and wrote his witty piano and vocal pieces *Péchés de vieillesse*.

Rubini, Giovanni Battista (1794–1854)   Italian tenor. He achieved acclaim in Rossini roles, but was also successful in the emerging new Romantic style of Bellini's *Il pirata* (1827), *La sonnambula* (1830) and *I puritani* (1835) and Donizetti's *Anna Bolena* (1830). From 1831 he performed mainly with London or Paris casts that included Grisi (from 1836 Pasta), Tamburini and Lablache, and sang at concerts and festivals. He was celebrated for his high range, natural phrasing and forceful expression.

Rubinstein, Anton (1829–94)   Russian pianist, composer and teacher. After a cosmopolitan childhood as a virtuoso he enjoyed huge international success, his playing being compared with that of Liszt. In 1859 he founded the Russian Musical Society, and was an influential, though controversial, figure in Russian musical life. He established the St Petersburg Conservatory in 1862 to combat what he perceived to be the amateurishness of the new nationalist movement in music, and his work in education made its mark on musical standards throughout the country. He was also a prolific composer.

Saint-Saëns, Camille (1835–1921)   French composer, pianist and organist. He won early admiration from Gounod, Rossini, Berlioz and Liszt, who hailed him as the world's greatest organist. He was organist at the Madeleine (1857–75) and a teacher at the Ecole Niedermeyer (1861–5), where Fauré was among his pupils. His other activities included organising concerts of Liszt's symphonic poems, reviving interest in older music, writing on musical, scientific and historical topics and travelling widely; in 1871 he co-founded the Société Nationale de Musique. Meanwhile he continued to perform and to compose prolifically. His style was characterised by Classical proportions and clarity, as in his Sonatas for violin and for cello, his Piano Quartet Op. 41 (1875), the Third 'Organ' Symphony (1886) and Piano Concerto No. 4 (1875). He also wrote descriptive and dramatic works, notably four symphonic poems (including *Danse macabre*, 1874) in a style influenced by Liszt involving thematic transformation, and thirteen operas, including *Samson et Dalila* (1877). From the 1890s he adopted a more severe, 'Classical' style, which influenced Fauré and Ravel.

Sarasate, Pablo (1844–1908) Spanish violinist and composer. From 1859 concert tours made him famous throughout Europe and in North and South America. Beautiful tone and a superb, apparently effortless, technique distinguished his playing. Many composers dedicated works to him, including Bruch, Saint-Saëns, Joachim and Dvořák. His own compositions were chiefly virtuoso violin works, notably *Zigeunerweisen* (1878) and the four books of *Spanische Tänze* (1878–82).

Satie, Erik (1866–1925) French composer. After studying at the Conservatoire, he wrote the triptychs of *Sarabandes* (1887), *Gymnopédies* (1888) and *Gnossiennes* (1890) in which dissonances are not required to resolve in a traditional manner. In the 1890s he began to frequent Montmartre, playing at the Chat Noir and involving himself with fringe Christian sects; he also met Debussy. Only in about 1911 did his music begin to be noticed widely; the ambitious ballets and cantata of his later years were made possible by Cocteau, who in 1915 saw him as the ideal of the anti-Romantic composer.

Sax, Adolphe (1814–94) Belgian wind-instrument maker. He made flutes and clarinets from the early 1830s, moving to Paris in 1842 to set up his own workshop (with Berlioz's help). He worked on improvements and inventions in the families of saxhorns, saxotrombas and saxophones (1846), and also made improvements to the bassoon and the trombone. He created an original system of six independent valves for brass instruments (1852). From 1858 to 1871 he taught the saxophone at the Conservatoire.

Schnorr von Carolsfeld, Ludwig (1836–65)   German tenor. Principal tenor
                    of the Karlsruhe opera (1858), he became famous
                    in Dresden for his Tannhäuser and Lohengrin,
                    eventually creating Tristan in 1865 with his wife
                    Malvina as Isolde. Wagner praised his voice as 'full,
                    soft and gleaming', admiring his dramatic power
                    and intelligence. His early death resulted from the
                    strains and pressures of performance.

Schröder-Devrient, Wilhelmine (1804–60)   German soprano. A singing
                    actress, she brought new powers to opera,
                    impressing audiences everywhere as Beethoven's
                    Leonore, a role she created (1822). Until the late
                    1830s she also excelled as Donna Anna, Euryanthe,
                    Norma and Desdemona, receiving praise from
                    Goethe, Weber, Schumann and the young Wagner,
                    and influencing the course of German Romantic
                    opera.

Schubert, Franz (1797–1828)   Austrian composer. He showed an
                    extraordinary gift as a child, and by 1814 had
                    composed piano pieces and songs, string quartets,
                    his First Symphony and a three-act opera. His
                    output of 1814–15 includes 'Gretchen am
                    Spinnrade' and 'Erlkönig', two more symphonies,
                    three masses and four stage works. He received an
                    appreciative audience and influential contacts at
                    gatherings (later called Schubertiads) of friends
                    who represented the new phenomenon of an
                    educated, musically aware middle class. He wrote
                    more songs, including 'Der Wanderer' and 'Die
                    Forelle', and instrumental pieces such as piano
                    sonatas and the Fifth and Sixth Symphonies, which
                    began to show increased harmonic subtlety.
                    Despite aristocratic patronage and further
                    introductions and new friendships in 1820–1,
                    financial need and serious illness made this a dark
                    period during which he wrote the epic 'Wanderer'
                    Fantasy for piano, the Eighth Symphony and *Die
                    schöne Müllerin*. In 1824 he turned to chamber

works, sketched the 'Great' C major Symphony, and entered a more assured phase, producing *Winterreise* and two piano trios. But he died several months after a large public concert in 1828. He effectively established the German lied as a new art form in the nineteenth century, and his instrumental works found highly original ways of building sonata structures from extended lyrical paragraphs.

Schumann, Robert (1810–56) German composer. In 1830 he moved to Leipzig where, four years later, he founded the *Neue Zeitschrift für Musik* which he wrote for and edited for ten years. His compositions from these years were mainly for the piano, including *Carnaval* (1835), the *Davidsbündlertänze* (1837) and *Kreisleriana* (1838). In 1840, following his marriage to Clara Wieck, he turned to song, writing some of his finest examples of the genre, including *Frauenliebe und -leben* and *Dichterliebe*. The following year he turned to orchestral music, writing his First Symphony; in 1842 he concentrated on chamber music, composing three string quartets; and in 1843 he switched to choral works, setting a part of Goethe's *Faust*. He also took up a teaching post at the new conservatory. During years of depression, he composed little, but in 1847–8 he wrote his opera *Genoveva*. In 1850 he was appointed musical director in Düsseldorf, where he wrote his Cello Concerto and Third 'Rhenish' Symphony. In 1854 his health deteriorated, and he ended his years in an asylum.

Schumann, Clara (née Wieck) (1819–96) German pianist and composer. She won enormous success as a touring piano virtuoso both before and after she married Robert Schumann in 1840. She was praised for her mastery of a progressive repertory (Chopin, Schumann, Brahms) and for her thoughtful interpretations and singing tone. She taught

privately and at the conservatories in Leipzig and
Frankfurt. She stopped composing in 1854, the
year of Robert's collapse, and went on to prepare a
complete edition of his music; she maintained a
close relationship with Brahms to the end of her
life.

Schuppanzigh, Ignaz (1776–1830)   Austrian violinist and composer. The
greatest figure among the original Beethoven quartet
players, notably leader of Count Rasumovsky's
quartet (1808–14), he played in the first performances
of Beethoven's works from the 1790s to 1828. He
also led orchestral concerts at the Augarten and after
a period in St Petersburg (1816–23) became director
of the Viennese court opera.

Scribe, Eugène (1791–1861)   French dramatist and librettist. He was
celebrated for his well-crafted dramas, which
featured contrasting characters, forward-moving
action and an artful engagement of the audience.
His librettos used similar techniques, blended
with Romantic elements of passionate love,
religious or social conflict and a historical setting,
to create a sequence of scenes and tableaux that
built to a huge finale. Although a prolific writer of
opéra-comique librettos and ballet scenarios for
composers such as Boieldieu, Auber, Adam and
Hérold, he is remembered for his contribution to
grand opera, in collaboration with Auber (*La
muette de Portici*) and Meyerbeer (*Robert le diable*,
Les Huguenots). He also worked with Bellini,
Donizetti, Gounod, Offenbach and Verdi.

Sechter, Simon (1788–1867)   Austrian theorist, composer and teacher. He
was a teacher of piano and singing at the
Blindenerziehungsinstitut in Vienna (1810–25)
and a prolific composer, but he became best known
as a music theorist. In 1851 he was appointed
professor of thoroughbass and counterpoint at
Vienna Conservatory. Schubert, Nottebohm,

Thalberg and Bruckner numbered among his pupils. His many theoretical works include the three-volume *Die Grundsätze der musikalischen Komposition* (1853–4).

Sinding, Christian (1856–1941) Norwegian composer. He studied at Leipzig and spent much of his later life in Germany. He was influenced by Wagner and Strauss, though he is more obviously Grieg's heir in his songs, such as 'Sange' (1882), and lyric pieces, including *Frühlingsrauschen* (1896). His larger works include an opera and four symphonies (No. 1, 1890) and three violin concertos.

Škroup, František Jan (1801–62) Bohemian composer and conductor. He devoted his energies to creating a Czech national opera, composing (and singing in) *Dráteník* (The Tinker) (1826), the successful first Czech opera. He later worked as Kapellmeister at the Estates Theatre, Prague (1837–57) and compiled an anthology, *Věnec ze zpěvů vlasteneckých* (A Garland of Patriotic Songs) (6 vols., 1835–9, 1844).

Skryabin, Alexander Nikolayevich (1872–1915) Russian composer. After studying at the Moscow Conservatory, his career as a pianist was managed by Belyayev, who arranged his tours and published his works; at this stage they were almost exclusively for solo piano, and strongly influenced by Chopin (including the First Piano Sonata, 1892). In the late 1890s he began to write for orchestra, notably his Piano Concerto (1896) and First Symphony (1900). He moved to Europe where his style became more intensely personal, and from 1905, under the influence of the ideas of Mme Blavatsky, he became interested in mysticism.

Smart, George (1776–1867) English conductor, organist and singing teacher. His efficiency, thorough knowledge of performing traditions and personal associations

with Haydn, Beethoven, Weber and Mendelssohn
made him one of the most respected music
directors of his day. He conducted the English
premières of Beethoven's Ninth Symphony and
Mendelssohn's *St Paul*, and presided at many
orchestral concerts, provincial festivals and court
musical events.

Smetana, Bedřich (1824–84)   Czech composer. He was obliged to teach to
earn a living, but in 1856 went to Göteborg, where
he was in demand as a pianist and conductor as
well as a teacher. Encouraged by Liszt, he
composed his first symphonic poems. In 1861 he
returned to Prague, where he wanted to play a role
in the reawakening of Czech culture that followed
the Austrian defeat by Napoleon III at Magenta
and Soferino. However it was not until the success
of his first opera, *Branibori v Cechách* (The
Brandenburgers in Bohemia) (1866), that his
prospects there improved. As principal conductor
of the Provisional Theatre (1866–74) he added
forty-two operas to the repertory, including his
own *Dalibor* (1868). In addition to further operas,
he also wrote an orchestral celebration of his
nation, *Má vlast* (1872‑4), and a String Quartet 'Z
mého života' (From my Life) (1876). In 1874 there
appeared the first signs of the syphilis that was to
result in his deafness, and he ended his life in an
asylum. He is usually considered the first major
nationalist composer of Bohemia, drawing on his
country's legends and scenery with freshness and
colour.

Sousa, John Philip (1854–1932)   American composer, conductor and writer.
He played the violin in theatre orchestras before
turning to conducting. In 1892 he formed the
popular Sousa's Band. He had an impact on
American musical tastes and achieved international
fame; the sousaphone, made to his specifications
was named after him. He was best known as a

composer of marches, including *The Washington Post* (1889) and *The Stars and Stripes Forever* (1897), but also wrote band arrangements and vocal music including the operetta *El capitan* (1895).

Spitta, Julius, August Philip (1841–94) German music historian. A lifelong friend of Brahms and a leading figure in later nineteenth-century musical scholarship, he is remembered particularly for his epoch-making study of Bach (1873–80), emphasising historical context. He was a co-founder of the *Vierteljahrsschrift für Musikwissenschaft* (1885) and from 1875 professor at Berlin University.

Spohr, Louis (1784–1859) German composer, violinist and conductor. A chamber musician at the Brunswick court, he soon became a virtuoso violinist and toured throughout Germany. He took up operatic conducting posts in Vienna and Frankfurt, which coincided with bursts of compositional activity; chamber music and the successful operas *Faust* (1813) and *Zemire und Azor* (1819) date from this time. In 1822 he settled as Kapellmeister at Kassel where he had success with *Jessonda* (1823), the oratorio *Die letzten Dinge* (1826) and the Symphony No. 4 (1832). He contributed to the cultivation of interest in Bach and Wagner, and was celebrated in England. His style combined Classical forms with freely expressive elements; his four Clarinet Concertos, String Quartets and Octet and Nonet for wind and strings were particularly acclaimed, and his operas anticipate Wagner in their use of leitmotif and through-composition.

Spontini, Gaspare (1774–1851) Italian composer and conductor. He first gained public attention in Paris under the patronage of Joséphine with the triumphant première of his tragédie lyrique *La vestale* (1807). *Fernand Cortez*, a historical pageant intended to glorify Napoleon, failed in its first version (1809), but won a place in the repertory when revised (1817). In 1820 he moved to Berlin, where as Generalmusikdirektor he came into conflict with Weber, and his complex and grand works were superseded by the operas of Rossini and Meyerbeer. His style essentially introduced new Italian and French elements into the traditional framework of French opera.

Stainer, John (1840–1901) English organist, scholar and composer. He became organist at St Paul's Cathedral (1872–88), reforming the musical service there, and quickly became a pre-eminent scholar, helping to found the Musical Association and making valuable editions of music before Tallis and Palestrina (*Early Bodleian Music*, 1901). His services, hymn tunes and anthems, and his oratorio *The Crucifixion* (1887), were popular during his lifetime.

Stanford, Charles Villiers (1852–1924)   British composer and teacher. He was appointed organist at Trinity College, Cambridge in 1873, and professor in 1887; from 1883 he also taught at the Royal College. His compositions, which reveal the influences of his education in Leipzig and Berlin, include much Anglican cathedral music, ten operas and a quantity of choral music and songs (including the partsong 'The Blue Bird'), as well as symphonies, string quartets and piano and organ music.

Stasov, Vladimir Vasil'yevich (1824–1906)   Russian critic. By 1856 he had become the champion of Balakirev and his circle, coining their nickname the 'Mighty Handful' in 1867. A passionate lover of Russian legend, he played a leading role in the inception of Rimsky-Korsakov's *Sadko*, Musorgsky's *Khovanshchina* and Borodin's *Knyaz' Igor'* (Prince Igor). His writings include biographies of Musorgsky (1881) and Borodin (1889) and an extended essay on recent Russian music (1883).

Steibelt, Daniel (1765–1823)   German composer and pianist. Until 1810 he was based in Paris, with excursions to Germany and London for concert appearances and productions of his operas and ballets. From 1810 he was director of the French Opera at St Petersburg, where he composed stage works and performed his Eighth Piano Concerto (composed in 1820).

Stenhammar, Wilhelm (1871–1927)   Swedish composer, pianist and conductor. His earlier compositions, such as his Piano Concerto No. 1 (1893) and concert overture *Excelsior!* (1896), show the influences of Brahms, Wagner and Liszt. However he began to question Romantic aesthetics, and around the turn of the century he aimed for a more Classical style, based on the study of Beethoven and Renaissance polyphony; he also incorporated Swedish folk material into his music. He held a number of appointments as a conductor, and performed as a piano soloist all over Sweden.

Stoltz, Rosine (1815–1903)   French mezzo-soprano. She made her debut in 1832 in Antwerp and in 1837 was engaged at the Paris Opéra, where she remained for ten years. She created Ascanio in Berlioz's *Benvenuto Cellini* (1838) and Léonore in Donizetti's *La favorite* (1840) as well as a number of Halévy's roles. She was famed for her fine voice and stage presence.

Strauss, Johann (I) (1804–49)   Austrian composer-conductor. A violinist in Josef Lanner's dance orchestra, he formed a band in 1825 which became famous for its open-air concerts with original dance music and paraphrases on the symphonic and operatic music of the day. From 1833 he took the band on tour in Europe. His compositions were characterised by an Austrian folk flavour and rhythmic piquancy; they include waltzes, galops, quadrilles, marches (including the *Radetzky-Marsch*, 1848), polkas and pot-pourris.

Strauss, Johann (II) (1825–99)   Austrian composer-conductor. He directed
his own orchestra (1844–9) in rivalry with that of
his father; in 1849 the two Strauss orchestras
merged. Appointed Vienna's imperial-royal music
director for balls (1863–71), and Austria's best-
known ambassador, he was acclaimed on his tours
in Europe (1856–86) and America (1872). His
waltzes resemble his father's in form, but the
sections are longer and more organic, the melodies
more sweeping and the harmonic and orchestral
details richer and more subtle. His most celebrated
waltzes include *Accellerationen* (1860), *An die
schönen, blauen Donau* (1867) and *Wein, Weib und
Gesang* (1869); and the most notable of his
seventeen operettas are *Die Fledermaus* (1874) and
Der Zigeunerbaron (1885).

Strauss, Richard (1864–1949)   German composer. He began composing at
an early age, writing his First Symphony in 1880,
and in 1885 he succeeded Bülow as principal
conductor at Meiningen. He left the following year
to travel to Italy, where he composed his first
symphonic poem *Aus Italien*; on his return he was
appointed conductor at the Munich Opera (1896).
He achieved international success as a composer in
1888 with his Wagner-influenced tone poem *Don
Juan*, and in 1895–9 wrote futher virtuoso
orchestral pieces, including *Till Eulenspiegel* (1895)
and *Ein Heldenleben* (1898). He then concentrated
more on conducting, but also produced his first
successful opera, *Feuersnot* (1901). Further operas
followed, including *Salome* (1904), *Elektra* (1909)
and *Der Rosenkavalier* (1911). He continued to
conduct, being appointed joint director of the
Vienna Staatsoper in 1919, and he travelled in
Europe and North and South America.

Sullivan, Arthur (1842–1900)   English composer. The success of his
incidental music for *The Tempest* (1861) and other
early concert works led to festival commissions

and conducting posts, which he complemented
with work as organist, teacher and song and hymn-
tune writer; from 1866 he also started writing
comic operas. In part following the success of *Trial
by Jury* (1875), a collaboration with W. S. Gilbert,
Richard D'Oyly Carte set up a company to
perform their works; with *HMS Pinafore* (1878) the
collaborators became an institution. Their works,
including *The Mikado* (1885) and *The Gondoliers*
(1889), were from 1881 performed at the Savoy
Theatre. Sullivan's eclectic musical style and
inventive melodies complemented Gilbert's witty
verses and satirical subjects.

Suppé, Franz von (1819–95)   Austrian composer and conductor of Belgian
descent. He became Kapellmeister of various
theatres in Vienna and wrote a number of stage
scores, including incidental music, operettas,
opera parodies and operas. The most popular
included the operettas *Flotte Bursche* (1863) and
Boccaccio (1879), admired for their fluent and light
style.

Svendsen, Johan (1840–1911)   Norwegian composer and conductor. He
studied at the Leipzig Conservatory and his early
works include the First Symphony (1865–6,
considered strongly national by Grieg) and the
String Quintet (1867), which were well received.
After periods in Paris and Bayreuth he conducted
the Christiania Music Society concerts (1872–7)
and composed his most notable works, including
the fantasy *Romeo og Julie* (1876), four *Norwegian
Rhapsodies* (1876) and the Romance for violin and
orchestra (1881). From 1883 he was conductor at
the Royal Opera in Copenhagen. He contributed
to the culmination of national Romanticism in
Norway – his two symphonies are the earliest by a
Norwegian to have won an audience in Norway –
though his style was more generally marked by the
use of large Classical forms.

Tamburini, Antonio (1800–76)   Italian baritone. In Paris and London he was
a successful interpreter of Mozart, Rossini, Bellini
and Donizetti, creating the parts of Ernesto in
Bellini's *Il pirata* (1827) and Sir Richard Forth in *I
puritani* (1835). His popularity in London is
attested by the 'Tamburini riots' of 1840.

Tchaikovsky, Pyotr Il'yich (1840–93)   Russian composer. Following studies
with Anton Rubinstein, he went to Moscow in
1866, where he was appointed professor at the
conservatory, and where he came into contact with
Rimsky-Korsakov and his group of young
nationalists. He won acclaim for his Second
Symphony (1872), which incorporates Ukrainian
folktunes, and his First Piano Concerto (1875),
dedicated to Bülow. Following a disastrous and
short-lived marriage in 1877, he wrote the Fourth
Symphony (1878) and *Evgeny Onegin* (1879), two of
his finest works. During a creative trough,
troubled by his homosexuality, he resigned from
the conservatory, and spent some time abroad. In
1884 he wrote his *Manfred Symphony*, and
continued to travel and to conduct. The years
1890–92 saw the composition of two ballets,
Spyashchaya krasavitsa (The Sleeping Beauty) and
Shchelkunchik (The Nutcracker) and the opera
Pikovaya dama (The Queen of Spades). In 1891 he
visited America, conducting at the opening night
of what was to become Carnegie Hall. Following
recognition in France and England, his Sixth
Symphony, the 'Pathétique' (1893), was premièred
in St Petersburg, nine days before his death.

Thalberg, Sigismondo (1812–71)   German/Austrian pianist and composer.
He began an international career in 1830, and with
Liszt (his rival for a time) was the greatest virtuoso
pianist of the period, admired for his brilliant
technique and for his expressive, singing style. He
mostly played his own music, which included
fantasias and variations on opera arias, studies and

nocturnes. In the 1850s he travelled to Brazil and the USA.

Thibaut, Anton Friedrich Justus (1772–1840)   German legal scholar and amateur musician. While in Jena in 1802–5 he began collecting sacred vocal music and folksongs; with Ett and Klein generously contributing copies of works from several European libraries, the library became one of the largest of its kind in Germany. In 1805 he moved to Heidelberg, where in 1811 he directed a small amateur chorus with which he gave about four concerts annually of works from the sixteenth to eighteenth centuries; as its reputation grew, its private rehearsals were attended by Goethe, Mendelssohn, Schumann and others. His book *Über Reinheit der Tonkunst* (1825) was influential on early Caecilian reforms.

Thomas, Ambroise (1811–96)   French composer. His early operas, in the tradition of Auber, include *Le Caïd* (1849) and *Le songe d'une nuit d'été* (1850). Appointed professor at the Conservatoire in 1856, he won greater acclaim for the operas that followed, notably *Mignon* (1866) and *Hamlet* (1868), which both contain effective vocal characterisation and atmospheric writing. In 1871 he succeeded Auber as director of the Conservatoire; troubled by the influence of Wagner, he showed little sympathy for the work of younger French composers (with the exception of Massenet).

Thomas, Theodore (1835–1905)   American conductor. He began conducting in New York in 1859, directing numerous concerts. He held appointments in Philadelphia and Cincinnati and was conductor of the New York Philharmonic Orchestra in 1877–91; later he worked in Chicago. He did much to popularise European music in America.

Tichatschek, Joseph (1807–86)   Bohemian tenor. Associated chiefly with the Dresden Court Opera (from 1838) he was renowned for the beauty and brilliance of his voice. His repertory included the leading roles in *Idomeneo*, *Die Zauberflöte*, *I Capuleti e i Montecchi* and *La muette de Portici*, but he was also the prototype of the Wagner *Heldentenor*, creating the title roles of *Rienzi* (1842) and *Tannhäuser* (1845).

Verdi, Giuseppe (1813–1901)   Italian composer. His first opera, *Oberto* (1839), enjoyed some success at its première at Milan, but his career took off with *Nabucco* (1842). A stream of commissions followed from other Italian cities and from abroad, resulting in thirteen operas in just eight years, including *Ernani* (1844), *Macbeth* (1847) and *Stiffelio* (1850). His models included late Rossini, Mercadante and Donizetti. His pace of composing then relaxed, and some of his most popular operas date from this period, such as *Rigoletto* (1851), *Il trovatore* (1853) and *La traviatia* (1853). In 1853 he went to Paris where *Les vêpres siciliennes* was premièred with success in 1855. Other popular works followed, including *Don Carlos* (1867) for Paris and *Aïda* (1871) for Cairo. During the next fifteen years he concentrated on revising earlier operas, and produced his *Requiem* (1874) in honour of the poet Manzoni. His last two operas *Otello* (1886) and *Falstaff* (1893) were both hailed as brilliant successes. His reputation was strongly linked to ideas about national identity, an association encouraged by Verdi himself.

Verstovsky, Alexey Nikolayevich (1799–1862)   Russian composer. From 1825 he was an inspector of the Moscow theatres, playing an important role in their management until 1860. He composed solo songs and operas with spoken dialogue, notably *Pan Tvardovsky* (1828), the first Russian Romantic Singspiel, and *Askol'dova mogila* (Askold's Grave) (1835), his only real success, and the first Russian opera performed in the USA.

Viardot, Pauline (1821–1910)   French mezzo-soprano of Spanish origin. The younger daughter of Manuel García, she won immediate success in highly dramatic parts, notably as Fidès in the première of Meyerbeer's *Le prophète* (1849) and in the title role of Berlioz's adaptation of Gluck's *Orfeo* (1859). She was the dedicatee of works by Schumann, Saint-Saëns and Fauré and was close to writers including Turgenev (from 1843 she was a principal channel through which Russian music reached the West). Her own compositions include operas and songs.

Wagner, Richard (1813–83)   German composer. His first completed opera, *Die Feen*, dates from 1833, a time when he was working in the theatre as a chorus-master. Ten years later his reputation was established with the premières of *Rienzi* (1842) and *Der fliegende Holländer* (1843) in Dresden, where he was appointed Kapellmeister to the court. He worked on *Tannhäuser* and *Lohengrin* (first performed in 1845 and 1850 respectively) and made preliminary drafts for the *Ring* and *Die Meistersinger* (first performed in 1876 and 1868), and became involved in the republican movement sweeping Europe in the late 1840s. A warrant for his arrest was issued, and (with Liszt's help) he fled to Zurich where he wrote many of his influential essays, including *Das Kunstwerk der Zukunft* (1849) and *Oper und Drama* (1850–1). During this time he also finalised the libretto for the *Ring* and began its composition, and turned to *Tristan und Isolde* (first performed in 1865), which he hoped would finance the building of his planned new theatre. These years also saw a succession of romantic affairs, culminating with his marriage in 1869 to Cosima von Bülow, following the death of his first wife Minna and the annulment of the Bülows' marriage. Meanwhile Wagner had found a patron in Ludwig II of Bavaria, and in 1872 the foundation stone of his new theatre at Bayreuth was laid; four years later the first Bayreuth festival

opened with the first complete performance of the
Ring. The première of his final drama *Parsifal* took
place in 1882. The influence of his ideas, as well as
his music, was such that a journal was devoted to
him (the *Revue wagnérienne*, 1885–8). Even today he
remains one of the most discussed, and written-
about, composers of all time.

Weber, Carl Maria von (1786–1826)   German composer. Following some
years as a virtuoso pianist, in 1813 he was
appointed director of the Prague opera house,
where he set about reforming the repertory,
placing emphasis on Mozart and contemporary
French opera, rather than Italian. In 1817 he was
appointed Kapellmeister in Dresden, where he
antagonised the court, attempting to develop a
national German opera company. The success of
Der Freischütz in Berlin in 1821 was enormous,
however, and it was performed throughout
Europe. His next operas, *Euryanthe* (1823) and
Oberon (1826), did not meet with the same acclaim,
and he died in London, shortly after conducting
the première of *Oberon*.

Weyse, Christoph Ernst Friedrich (1774–1842)   Danish composer of German
extraction. He became distinguished in
Copenhagen as a pianist and church organist. From
1816 he was a professor at the university, and from
1819 court composer, writing cantatas, Singspiels
and songs. His most important works include the
innovatory *Allegri di bravura* for piano (1796), the
ensembles in his cantatas and the spiritual songs
written to texts by Ingemann (1837–8).

Widor, Charles-Marie (1844–1937)   French organist, composer and teacher.
He was organist at St Sulpice, Paris, for more than
sixty years (1870–1934) and professor of organ at
the Conservatoire, where his pupils included
Vierne, Dupré, Honegger and Milhaud. As a
performer he was admired for his rhythmic

precision and traditional interpretations of Bach. His organ pieces were written to explore the elaborate resources of the grandiose contemporary instruments of Cavaillé-Coll and others. He created the organ symphony in which the organ is a sort of self-contained orchestra; of his ten works in the genre the best known is the Fifth (1880), with its powerful Toccata movement.

Witt, Franz Xaver (1834–88)   German church musician and composer. A leader in the Caecilian movement, he wrote books, articles, music and two journals to spread the idea of German Roman Catholic church music reform. He founded the Allgemeiner Deutscher Cäcilien-Verein at Bamberg (1869) and the Scuola Gregoriana in Rome (1880).

Wolf, Hugo (1860–1903)   Austrian composer. His early songs, dating from 1877–8, established the pattern of cyclic mood swings and creativity that was to characterise his career. For three years he wrote music criticism for the *Wiener Salonblatt* (1884–86), siding with Wagner and against Brahms, while working on *Penthesilea* (1883–5) and the D minor Quartet (1878–84). In the late 1880s he turned to literature for inspiration, notably in the Eichendorff and Mörike settings of 1889 with which he established a reputation to match that of Schubert or Schumann, strengthened by his acclaimed public performances. In 1895 he composed his only completed (but unsuccessful) opera, *Der Corregidor*. Two years later he suffered a mental breakdown which led to his terminal illness.

Zelter, Carl Friedrich (1758–1832)   German composer and teacher. He became a highly influential figure in the musical life of Berlin, notably as director (from 1800) of the Singakademie, where he promoted Bach's music in particular. He established the Liedertafel in 1809 and an institute of church music in 1822, and was also a prominent teacher. His compositions include some 200 lieder, many to texts by Goethe, and sacred and secular choral music; he also wrote letters and essays on music.

Index